Southern Living®

ANNUAL RECIPES
MASTER INDEX

1979-2004

Oxmoor House®

ISBN: 0-8487-3016-X
ISSN: 0272-2003

Printed in the United States of America
First printing 2005

To order additional publications, call 1-800-765-6400.

For more books to enrich your life, visit **oxmoorhouse.com**

Oxmoor House, Inc.
Editor in Chief: Nancy Fitzpatrick Wyatt
Executive Editor: Susan Carlisle Payne
Art Director: Cynthia R. Cooper
Copy Chief: Allison Long Lowery

Southern Living®
Executive Editor: Susan Dosier

Southern Living*® *Annual Recipes Master Index 1979-2004
Editor: Terri Laschober
Copy Editor: Donna Baldone
Designer: Kelly Davis
Director of Production: Phillip Lee
Production Manager: Theresa L. Beste
Production Assistant: Faye Porter Bonner

Contributors
Indexer: Mary Ann Laurens
Editorial Intern: Leighton Batte

INTRODUCTION

Welcome to the all-new edition of the *Southern Living® Annual Recipes Master Index*. This cook's companion helps you instantly locate just the recipe you need from thousands of kitchen-tested recipes. When readers call us for help finding their favorite recipes from past issues of *Southern Living,* we turn to this time-saving index for the answer.

We've cross-referenced every recipe in the *Southern Living® Annual Recipes* collection by the type of dish and by one or more of its main ingredients. The handy step-by-step reference on the following page gives simple instructions on how to find the recipe you want—quickly and easily.

Every *Southern Living* recipe is at your fingertips.

As a bonus, you can also find favorite recipes under the headings of our monthly food columns, past and present. Under "From Our Kitchen," you'll find a handy reference to helpful hints and Test Kitchens secrets. Recipes under the headings "Quick & Easy" and "What's for Supper?" will help you get dinner on the table in a hurry. If you're searching for true regional fare, look no further than "Taste of the South." The name of our light section has changed over time, but you can find recipes from past "On the Light Side," "Cooking Light," and "Living Light" columns now under "Healthy & Light."

Occasionally, you'll find that the same recipe appears in different volumes of *Southern Living® Annual Recipes.* There's a simple reason: A recipe may appear in the magazine edition for one state before it appears in the edition for another state. This index gives all of the page references to those bonus recipes that have appeared in more than one edition of the magazine. It also lists those recipes featured in our *Southern Living® Favorites, Southern Living® Cooking School,* and *Southern Living® Cook-Off* bonus sections.

We hope you'll be pleased with this cumulative index of our recipes. Use it to find the perfect recipe for any occasion in just seconds.

Susan Dosier

Susan Dosier
Executive Editor, *Southern Living*

HOW TO FIND A RECIPE—FAST

Look for the main ingredient in the recipe you want or even the basic type of dish it is

(appetizer, cookie, etc.). You can find it either way in this cross-referenced index.

Use the step-by-step guide below to help you find a recipe in record time.

1. *As you turn through the index, "continued" lines in the upper left corner remind you of the current category.*

2. *Main categories help you cross-reference each recipe by the type of dish and one or more of its main ingredients.*

3. *Boldfaced subcategories help you scan for a recipe through long main categories.*

POTATOES, Stuffed
(continued)

Vegetable-Topped Stuffed Potatoes, **'85** 235
Yogurt-Stuffed Potatoes, **'88** 24
Zesty Stuffed Potatoes, **'94** M46
Tacos, Breakfast, **'91** 316
Tortilla Campesina, **'89** 85
Tortilla Española, **'92** 175
Vinaigrette, Potato-Broccoli, **'85** 84
Wedges, Lemon Potato, **'88** 21
Wedges, Lemony Potato, **'90** M61

PRALINE. *See also* **CANDIES/Pralines.**
Almonds, Praline, **'97** 285
Bananas, Praline, **'84** 313
Brownies, Praline, **'93** 243
Buns, Praline, **'90** 195
Buttercream, Praline, **'95** 243
Cake, Praline, **'81** 162
Cake, Praline Ice Cream, **'80** 84
Cake, Praline Pound, **'82** 88
Cheesecake, Praline, **'83** 270; **'89** 93
Coffee, Praline, **'97** 17
Coffee, Praline-Flavored, **'87** 69
Compote, Warm Praline Fruit, **'85** 260
Cookies, Praline, **'91** 271
Cookies, Praline Shortbread, **'88** 242
Cookies, Praline Thumbprint, **'89** 328
Filling, Praline, **'89** 328
Freeze, Praline, **'89** 60; **'90** 48
Glaze, Apple-Stuffed Tenderloin with
Praline-Mustard, **'97** 216
Glaze, Praline, **'82** 196
Ham, Praline, **'85** 302; **'96** 303
Horns, Praline, **'96** 316
Ice Cream, Praline, **'89** 318
Ice Cream, Pralines and Cream, **'82** 184; **'83** 159
Pastries, Praline, **'89** 318
Pecans, Praline, **'97** 285
Pie, Chocolate-Praline, **'86** 259
Pie, Frosty Pumpkin-Praline, **'91** M234
Pie, Peach Praline, **'89** 136
Pie, Pear-Praline, **'97** 192
Pie, Pumpkin Praline, **'80** 244
Powder, Praline, **'95** 243
Sauce, Bourbon Praline, **'81** 170
Sauce, Chocolate-Praline, **'85** M295
Sauce, Peach-Praline, **'85** 161
Sauce, Praline, **'83** 25; **'84** 143; **'89** 95; **'92** 282;
'93 214; **'94** 206, 312; **'96** 285
Sauce, Praline Ice Cream, **'85** 189
Sauce, Southern Praline Ice Cream, **'86** M227
Toast, Orange Praline, **'79** 36
Torte, Chocolate Praline, **'84** 165
Torte, Lucy's Apricot Praline, **'95** 243

PRETZELS
Brownies, Saucepan Pretzel, **'85** 171
Chocolate-Covered Pretzels, **'82** 295
Dressing, Pretzel, **'86** 280
Frosted Pretzels, **'92** 280
Garlands, Pretzel, **'93** 286
Herb Pretzels with Lower Sodium
Horseradish Mustard, **'86** 325
Homemade Pretzels, **'84** 159; **'91** 185
Popcorn, Pretzel, **'84** 30
Soft Pretzels, **'83** 18
Soft Pretzels, Chewy, **'87** 159
Whole Wheat Pretzels, **'89** 20

PRUNES
Bavarian, Prune, **'86** 223
Bread, Prune-Nut, **'87** 255; **'91** 55
Butter, Prune-Orange, **'92** 49
Cake and Sauce, Prune, **'85** 118
Cake, Prune, **'85** 223
Cake, Spicy Prune, **'79** 136
Chicken with Prunes, Saffron, **'97** 264
Compote, Baked Prune, **'94** 50
Muffins, Miniature Prune, **'85** 223
Muffins, Spicy Prune, **'97** 271
Muffins, Wheat Germ-Prune, **'81** 106
Pork Chops Stuffed with Prunes, **'84** 7
Pork Loin Roast, Prune-Stuffed, **'80** 29
Raspberry Prunes, **'82** 124
Relish, Peppy Prune, **'90** 227
Spiced Prunes, Orange-, **'85** 224
Stuffed Prunes, **'85** 47
Tarts, Brandied Prune, **'85** 223
Tzimmes, **'95** 102

PUDDINGS. *See also* **CUSTARDS, MOUSSES.**
Apple-Nut Pudding with Hot Rum Sauce, **'79** 86
Applesauce-Graham Cracker Pudding, **'81** 34
Banana
Almost Banana Pudding, **'88** 174
Banana Pudding, **'82** 53; **'84** 94; **'85** 255;
'88 16, 32
Basic Banana Pudding, **'81** 59
Creamy Banana Pudding, **'89** M130
Delicious Banana Pudding, **'80** 9
Fudge-Banana Pudding, **'97** 331
Mallow Pudding, Banana-, **'86** 139
No-Bake Banana Pudding, **'91** 172
Old-Fashioned Banana Pudding, **'92** 94
Peanut Butter-Banana Pudding, **'93** 340
Pops, Banana Pudding Parfait, **'96** 180
Surprise Banana Pudding, **'86** 7
Beach, The, **'95** 168
Blackberry Pudding Tarts, **'93** 200
Blueberry-Raspberry Pudding, Russian,
'97 128
Bread
Amish Bread Pudding, **'80** 8

4. *Frequently, we'll direct you to other categories to help you find similar recipes.*

5. *Each recipe title is alphabetized by its most descriptive word. We've boldfaced the year in which it appeared in* Southern Living® Annual Recipes; *its page number follows.*

6. *An "M" precedes the page numbers of all microwave recipes. It refers to recipes cooked totally or partially in the microwave.*

7. *An alphabetical guide word at the bottom of each page helps you quickly locate main reference categories.*

MASTER INDEX

This index lists all recipes by their complete titles under a specific food category and ingredient. The volume is indicated in bold, followed by the page number. Microwave recipe page numbers are preceded by an "M." For information about how to use this index, see facing page.

ALMONDS

Appetizers
Ball, Easy Chut-Nut, '00 280
Cheese, Almond, '88 173
Cheese Ball, Fruit-and-Nut, '91 251
Cheese Ball, Pinecone, '93 288
Chicken Almondette Fingers, '93 12
Chicken Nut Puffs, '81 260
Crostini, Almond-Bacon-Cheese, '94 318
Curried Almonds, '82 297
Dip, Almond Delight, '90 226
Dip with Strawberries, Almond Cream, '92 164
Mix, Jalapeño Nut, '96 27
Nippy Nuts, '93 301
Olives, Almond-Stuffed, '88 95
Pastry Cups, Mushroom-Almond, '88 210
Pesto-Spiced Nuts, '95 173
Quick Party Nuts, '04 197
Rollups, Almond-Ham, '89 284
Spread, Curry-Almond Cheese, '01 238
Spread, Date-Orange-Nut, '02 59
Toasts, Cheddar-Almond, '97 30
Tuna Amandine, '02 165
Braid, Almond, '89 86
Bread, Cocoa-Nut Swirl, '80 257
Bread, Lemon-Almond Tea, '04 209
Bread, Saffron, '96 50
Bread, Tipsy Peach, '02 21
Breakfast Ring, Almond-Vanilla, '04 M249
Butter, Almond-Raisin, '02 258
Caramelized Almonds, '92 303
Coffee Cake, Almond-Blueberry, '85 152
Coffee Cake, Apricot-Almond, '93 26; '04 193
Coffee Cake Twist, Almond, '91 22
Coffee, Chocolate-Almond, '84 54
Coffee Delight, Almond-, '84 115
Coleslaw with Grapes and Almonds, '83 59
Couscous with Raisins, Almonds, and Lemon, '00 295
Cream, Peaches 'n' Almond, '86 229
Danish, Almond, '87 301
Desserts
Apricot-Almond Squares, '95 272
Bake, Apple-Almond, '02 M209
Balls, Coconut-Almond, '84 256
Balls, Toasted Almond Chip, '84 240
Bars, Almond-Chocolate, '83 304
Bars, Swedish Almond, '97 322
Biscotti, Almond, '91 108
Biscotti, Almond-Anise, '93 266

Biscotti, Cocoa-Almond, '96 280
Biscuits, Raspberry-Almond, '93 160
Bonbons, Dark Chocolate, '02 297
Bread, Mandel, '97 220
Bread Pudding with Amaretto Cream Sauce, Layered Almond-Cream Cheese, '03 330
Brickle Treats, Almond, '95 321
Brie, Almond-Raspberry, '94 M89
Brittle, Almond, '03 281
Brownies, Date-and-Almond, '88 217
Butter-Nut Strips, '82 167
Cake, Almond-Butter, '86 107
Cake, Almond-Butter Wedding, '86 106
Cake, Almond Legend, '82 8
Cake, Almond Whipping Cream, '80 295
Cake, Apricot-Almond Upside-Down, '97 204
Cake, Chocolate-Almond, '91 248
Cake, Heaven, '04 193
Cake, Peach-Almond Pound, '89 86
Cake, Peachy Almond-Butter, '90 107
Cake Squares, Almond, '79 111
Cake, Sullivan's Lemon-Almond Pound, '04 278
Cake, Toasted Almond-Butter, '99 315
Cake, White Chocolate-Almond, '03 M287
Cake with Cherry Filling, Chocolate-Almond, '84 225
Candied Nuts, '81 261
Candy, Almond Brittle, '80 255
Cheesecake, Amaretto, '99 273
Cheesecake, Black-and-White, '99 334
Cheesecake, Chocolate-Almond, '93 53
Cheesecake, Coconut-Chocolate-Almond, '98 322
Cheesecake, Island Breeze, '03 144
Chocolate-Almond Dessert, '82 306
Chocolate-Almond Hearts, '03 42
Chocolate Almond Velvet, '81 148
Cinnamon Stars, Swiss, '87 293
Cobbler, Blackberry-Almond, '81 132
Combs, Almond, '84 136
Confections, Almond Cream, '87 198; '90 310
Cookies, Almond, '83 22, 181; '91 51; '92 176; '97 288; '99 49
Cookies, Almond Butter, '79 52
Cookies, Almond Lace, '98 336
Cookies, Almond Spritz, '82 306
Cookies, Amaretti, '02 270
Cookies, Chewy Almond, '02 258
Cookies, Chocolate-Almond, '98 293
Cookies, Chocolate-Almond Surprise, '88 M45

Cookies, Chocolate-Brickle, '99 127
Cookies, Cranberry-Almond, '98 26
Cookies, Double Chocolate Chunk-Almond, '95 178
Cookies, Lemon-Almond, '02 293
Cookies, Light Almond, '83 151
Cookies, Skillet Almond, '97 288
Cookies, Snow, '99 167
Cookies, Swedish Almond, '85 312
Cookies, Texan-Size Almond Crunch, '91 236
Cookies with Ice Cream Balls, Almond Brittle, '96 202
Cream, Almond, '00 27
Cream, Chocolate-Almond, '91 108
Cream, Peach Almond, '82 108
Cream with Fresh Strawberries, Almond, '87 93
Crème Brûlée, Almond, '95 323
Crêpes Gelée Amandine, '83 126
Crescents, Almond, '97 273
Crunch, Almond Butter, '80 301
Crunch, Vanilla Almond, '93 243
Crust, Vanilla Wafer, '98 216
Custard with Raspberries, Almond Crème, '88 174
Drops, Cherry-Almond, '81 20
Drops, Chocolate-Coconut Almond, '87 223
Filling, Almond, '87 301; '96 316
Filling, Almond Cream, '85 320; '91 248
Filling, Ground Almond, '87 14
Filling, Nut, '91 35
Flan, Almond-Orange, '04 241
Float, Nutmeg-Almond, '84 106
Frosting, Almond-Butter, '86 107
Frosting, Almond Buttercream, '97 61; '99 155
Frosting, Chocolate-Almond, '83 241
Frozen Almond Crunch, '94 283
Fudge, Creamy Almond, '95 51
Glaze, Honey-Nut, '87 15
Ice Cream, Almond, '98 221
Ice Cream, Almond-Fudge, '93 205
Ice Cream Balls, Almond, '86 315
Ice Cream Dessert, Rocky Road, '00 332
Ice Cream, No-Cook Chocolate-Almond, '04 179
Ice Cream, Peach-Almond, '89 156
Leaves, Almond Holly, '86 319
Mandelbrot, Rhoda's, '98 243
Marzipan Bees, '98 100
Meringue Fingers, Chocolate-Almond, '84 158
Mocha-Almond Dessert, '80 289; '81 62

ALMONDS, Desserts
(continued)

Mousse, Chocolate-Almond, '93 316
Nutcracker Sweets, '02 293
Pastry, Almond, '85 177; '89 317; '92 30
Pears, Almond-Stuffed, '83 207
Petits Fours, Chocolate-Almond, '93 255; '00 72
Pie Amandine, Chocolate, '83 300
Pie, Apple-Amandine, '89 215
Pie, Cinnamon-Almond-Pecan, '98 89
Pie, Creamy Chocolate-Almond, '85 102
Pie, Toasted Almond, '86 163
Pineapple-Almond Delight, '85 96
Polvorones, '00 123
Praline Sauce, '93 214
Pudding, Chocolate-Almond, '82 142; '88 24
Pudding, Chocolate-Almond Silk, '96 266
Pudding, Mandarin-Almond, '85 M12
Roca, Almond, '86 49
Romanoff, Strawberry-Almond, '98 99
Sauce, Almond-Vanilla Custard, '88 M177
Sauce, Angel Food Cake with Amaretto-Almond, '90 199
Shortbread, Apricot-Almond, '99 29
Snaps, Almond, '92 273
Sorbet, Apricot-Almond, '98 126
Sour Cream-Almond Dessert, '92 120
Spread, Almond Cheese, '87 292
Squares, Cream Cheese-Almond, '85 68
Strudel, Pear, '98 253
Tart, Almond, '89 232
Tart, Almond-Apple, '01 253
Tart, Almond-Pear, '01 253
Tart, Apricot-Almond, '97 99
Tart, Bakewell, '97 110
Tarts, Almond Tea, '85 120
Tarts, Raspberry-Almond, '99 280
Tart with Brandy Sauce, Peach, '98 119
Tassies, Lucky Almond, '91 13
Toffee, '01 218
Toffee, Almond, '04 235
Toffee Crunch, Almond-, '88 285
Topping, Almond, '85 152; '86 200
Topping, Ginger-Almond, '01 215
Torte, Chocolate-Almond, '96 M253; '98 273
Tortoni, Coffee-Almond, '81 30
Truffles, Almond, '83 298
Wafers, Almond-Filled, '88 120
French Toast, Almond, '88 62
French Toast, Amaretto, '98 280
Fruit, Almond-Curried, '83 261
Glazed Almonds, '96 64
Liqueur, Almond-Flavored, '81 287
Main Dishes
Casserole, Chicken-Almond, '94 199
Catfish Amandine, Mandarin, '84 183
Catfish Amandine, Spicy, '89 52
Chicken, Almond, '01 26
Chicken and Vegetables, Almond, '86 21
Chicken, Creamy Almond, '89 281
Chicken in Orange-Almond Sauce, '79 219; '80 13
Chicken, Spicy Almond, '88 150
Fish, Almond Baked, '88 270; '89 203
Fish Amandine, '85 179
Fish Amandine, Fillet of, '80 M54
Flounder Amandine, '89 M196
Orange Lake Amandine, '80 99
Pollo Almendrado, '81 193
Quiche, Almond-Topped Crab, '79 127
Salmon with Almonds and Tomato-Lemon Sauce, '04 23

Trout Amandine, '99 53
Trout Amandine, Classic, '96 202; '01 110
Trout Amandine, Gaston's, '96 232
Muffins, Almond, '90 87
Muffins, Banana-Honey-Nut, '88 62
Muffins, Peachy-Almond, '86 301
Phyllo Nests, Nutty, '87 277
Pilaf, Persian Rice, '02 167
Popcorn, Spicy Nut, '02 287; '03 272
Praline Almonds, '97 285
Rice, Almond, '81 195; '85 M112; '89 100; '91 291
Rice, Almond Wild, '86 50
Rice, Indian, '96 202
Rice, Orphan's, '03 32
Rice with Almonds, Curried, '83 M285
Rolls, Almond Crescent, '90 283
Rolls, Cherry-Almond, '84 M198
Salad, Almond-Citrus, '96 274; '01 42
Salad Amandine, Chicken, '81 37
Salad, Cheesy Fruit-'n'-Nut, '87 56
Salad, Chicken-Almond, '81 133
Salad, Crunchy Tuna-and-Almond, '04 72
Salad, Cucumber-Almond, '86 147
Salad Dressing, Almond, '81 37
Salad, Orange-Almond, '99 107
Salad Oriental, Mandarin, '02 175
Salad, Sesame-Almond, '89 123
Salad Shanghai, Almond-Chicken, '90 160
Sandwiches, Chicken-Almond Pocket, '81 240; '83 69
Sauce, Grilled Snapper with Orange-Almond, '01 158
Sauce, Mandarin-Almond Cream, '84 183
Sauce, Shrimp-and-Almond, '87 282
Seasoned Almonds, '03 101
Slaw, Asian, '99 108
Slaw, Crunchy Cabbage, '02 95
Slaw, Pineapple-Almond, '92 171
Snack Balls, Orange-Almond, '95 214
Snack Mix, Sweet 'n' Savory, '03 199
Soup, Almond, '79 48
Soup, Chicken-Almond Cream, '92 21
Spoons, Dipped Chocolate-Almond, '95 M277
Streusel, Almond-Garlic, '95 159
Stuffing, Apple-Almond, '01 184
Sugared Almonds, '04 105
Sunburst, Almond, '94 245
Sweet-and-Spicy Almonds, '96 274; '01 42
Syrup, Almond, '82 47
Tea, Almond, '85 43; '86 329; '89 212; '97 226; '01 93
Tea, Almond-Lemonade, '86 229; '99 207
Tea, Ginger-Almond, '94 131
Toast Amandine, Baked, '82 47
Vegetables
Asparagus, Almond, '83 86; '02 64
Asparagus Amandine, '03 295
Asparagus with Almond Butter, '84 85
Asparagus with Almond Sauce, '91 117
Broccoli Casserole, Almond-, '88 62
Broccoli in Sherry Sauce, Almond, '02 45
Broccoli with Almonds, Glazed, '80 12
Brussels Sprouts Amandine, '79 213
Cabbage with Almonds, Creamed, '79 4
Cauliflower and Peas with Curried Almonds, '79 221; '80 82
Cauliflower with Almond Sauce, '82 270
Celery Almondine, '85 116
Celery Amandine, Buttered, '82 98
Eggplant with Almonds, '79 179
Green Beans Amandine, '79 276; '82 M20; '97 238
Green Beans with Almonds, '84 253
Green Beans with Almonds, Italian, '81 207

Green Beans with Smoked Almonds, Thyme-Scented, '01 57
Leeks with Brussels Sprouts and Almonds, '00 222
Peas with Almonds, Curried, '88 M294
Potatoes, Almond-Fried, '82 25
Potatoes, Broccoli-and-Almond-Topped, '83 3
Stir-Fry, Almond-Vegetable, '86 222
Wild Rice, Cranberry-Almond, '04 204
AMBROSIA
Ambrosia, '00 325; '04 233
Anytime Ambrosia, '86 182
Baked Ambrosia, '83 303
Bowl, Ambrosia, '80 138; '84 313
Brunch, Ambrosia, '83 57
Cake, Ambrosia, '79 229
Cake, Cranberry-Ambrosia, '01 271
Cake Royale, Ambrosia, '89 335
Carrot-Marshmallow Ambrosia, '80 5
Cheesecake, Ambrosia, '02 296
Chicken Salad Ambrosia, '85 216
Citrus Ambrosia, '82 287
Cookies, Ambrosia, '81 301; '82 110; '86 313
Cranberry Ambrosia, Glazed, '00 269
Cups, Sherbet Ambrosia, '82 159
Custard Sauce Ambrosia, '84 256
Easy Ambrosia, '92 45
Fantastic Ambrosia, '91 277
Filling, Cranberry-Ambrosia, '01 271
Fruit Ambrosia, Fresh, '88 184
Fruit Ambrosia, Mixed, '83 10
Ginger Ale Ambrosia, '99 125
Gingered Ambrosia, '02 245
Grandma's Ambrosia, '90 254
Honey Bee Ambrosia, '83 267
Kitchen Express Ambrosia, '04 233
Layered Ambrosia, '88 304
Mold, Ambrosia, '79 241
Mold, Ambrosia Cream Cheese, '79 249
Old-Fashioned Ambrosia, '80 5
Orange Ambrosia Supreme, '79 37
Pancakes with Orange Syrup, Ambrosia, '89 254
Peach Ambrosia, '83 53
Pie, Ambrosia, '79 284
Pie, Orange Ambrosia, '80 237
Pineapple-Orange Ambrosia, '88 252
Rhubarb Ambrosia, '88 93
Salad, Ambrosia, '83 231; '94 271
Salad, Carrot-Ambrosia, '81 252
Sauce, Hot Ambrosia, '89 335
Sherried Ambrosia, '84 324; '86 317
Sorbet, Ambrosia, '04 317
Spread, Ambrosia, '92 50
Sprinkles, Ambrosia with, '01 250
Tropical Ambrosia, '79 74
ANCHOVIES
Antipasto, Grandpa's, '98 183
Appetizers, Zesty Anchovy, '83 93
Butter, Lemon-Anchovy, '97 307
Mayonnaise, Anchovy, '86 179
Rémoulade, Criolla, '97 227
Salad, Caesar, '99 265; '00 19; '02 269
Salad, Dawn's World-Famous Greek, '98 276
Sauce Niçoise, '96 190
Tapenade, '92 194; '00 135
APPETIZERS. *See also* **CRACKERS, FONDUE, PÂTÉS.**
Almond-Ham Rollups, '89 284
Almonds, Curried, '82 297
Anchovy Appetizers, Zesty, '83 93
Antipasto, Easy, '92 24
Antipasto, Grandpa's, '98 183
Antipasto, Lemon-Vinaigrette Marinated, '04 256
Antipasto Relish, '86 327

Antipasto Squares, '03 292
Apple-Phyllo Rolls, '88 213
Apple Quarters, Honey-Baked, '86 93
Artichoke-and-Shrimp Appetizer, '93 271
Artichoke Appetizer Frittata, '92 58
Artichoke Appetizer, Zesty, '80 146
Artichoke-Caviar Mold, '87 239
Artichoke-Cheese Bottoms, Baked, '94 61
Artichoke Oysters, '96 154
Artichoke-Parmesan Phyllo Bites, '87 54
Artichokes, Marinated, '87 250
Artichokes, Spring, '86 62
Asparagus Croquettes, '85 265
Asparagus, Prosciutto-Wrapped, '91 98
Asparagus Rolls, '79 296; '80 31
Asparagus Rolls, Hot, '93 329
Asparagus Rollups, '79 63; '01 239
Asparagus Roll-Ups, '84 270
Asparagus with Dill Sauce, '97 59
Asparagus with Garlic Cream, '95 83; '00 71
Avocado-Crabmeat Cocktail, Sherried, '87 95
Bacon Appetizers, Hot, '80 248
Bacon, Black Pepper-Brown Sugar, '04 70
Bacon, Brown Sugar, '04 70
Bacon-Chestnut Wraps, '84 M216
Bacon-Jalapeño-Tomato Quesadillas, '95 240
Bacon-Onion Appetizers, '94 290
Bacon Rolls, '84 270; '93 330
Bacon Rollups, '79 34
Bacon Swirls, '89 214; '98 26
Bacon-Wrapped Crackers, '93 280
Bacon-Wrapped Pineapple Chunks, '84 25
Bacon-Wrapped Water Chestnuts, '79 63
Bagel Chips, '91 138
Bagel Chips, Cinnamon-and-Sugar, '91 139
Bagel Chips, Garlic, '91 139
Bagel Chips, Lemon-and-Herb, '91 139
Bagel Chips, Parmesan Cheese, '91 138
Bagel Crisps, '86 278
Basil-Pepper Appetizers, '98 133
Bean Burrito Appetizers, '94 226
Beef on a Stick, '99 336
Beef on a Stick, Marinated, '85 234
Beef Sticks, '93 331
Beef Tenderloin, Holiday, '01 238
Beefy Party Snacks, '80 249
Beets, Blue Cheese-Stuffed, '88 211
Beggar's Purses with Smoked Salmon, '04 244
Biscuits, Cornmeal, '04 257
Biscuits, Miniature Buttermilk, '02 103
Biscuits, Quick Whipping Cream, '03 238
Biscuits with Beef and Horseradish-Chive Cream,
    Blue Cheese, '02 313
Biscuits with Ham, Ranch, '97 59
Biscuits with Olive-Parsley Spread, Cream Cheese-
    and-Olive, '04 238
Black Bean Appetizer, '83 50
Black Bean Cakes with Greens and Apple Dressing,
    '92 216
Black-Eyed Pea Cakes, '01 32
Black-Eyed Pea Pinwheels, '85 300; '86 18
Bread Ring, Braided, '96 322
Breadstick Haystacks, '99 246
Broccoli-Cheese Appetizer, '92 265
Broccoli, Cocktail, '80 192
Broccoli Soup, Mock Cream of, '85 288
Bruschetta. *See also* **APPETIZERS/Canapés, Crostini.**
    Black Truffle Bruschetta, '99 323
    Caper-and-Olive Bruschetta, '00 276
    Prosciutto Bruschetta and Cantaloupe Chutney,
        '00 108
    Red-and-Green Bruschetta, '01 62
    Roasted Pepper-Tomato Bruschetta, '02 213
    Roasted Red Pepper Bruschetta, '00 278

Brussels Sprouts, Marinated, '88 265
Burgers, Saucy Cocktail, '83 217
Burrito Rollups, '90 119
Burritos, Chinese, '87 181
Buzzard's Nests, '93 244
Cakes, Little Bitty, '98 154
Canapés. *See also* **APPETIZERS/Bruschetta,
    Crostini.**
    Bread, Canapé, '89 292
    Bread, Rye Canapé, '89 293
    Bread, Whole Wheat Canapé, '89 293
    Chicken-Cucumber Canapés, '98 154
    Crab Canapés, '93 130
    Crab Canapés, Cheesy, '86 262
    Crab Canapés, Hot, '86 70; '87 239
    Crabmeat Canapés, '88 150
    Cucumber Canapés, '95 88
    Fruit-Topped Canapés, '85 80
    Green Onion Canapés, '84 M216
    Lemon-Cheese, Canapés, '87 93
    Mushroom Canapés, '80 285; '97 23
    Party Canapés, '86 128
    Roasted Garlic Canapés, '96 95
    Salmon Canapés, Smoked, '99 140
    Shrimp-and-Cucumber Canapés, '93 164
    Shrimp Canapés, '84 116
    Swiss Canapés, Hot, '83 259
    Vegetable Canapés, '91 252
Caponata, '87 166
Caponata alla Siciliana, '02 269
Caramel Corn, Oven-Made, '91 233
Caramel Good Stuff, Baked, '80 284
Caraway Wafers, '81 261
Carrots, Dilled Baby, '84 80
Carrots, Dill-Spiced, '87 200
Carrots, Pickled, '93 12
Catfish Appetizer, Layered, '92 209
Cauliflower, Crispy Fried, '80 220
Cauliflower, Dilled, '83 93
Cauliflower, French-Fried, '86 211
Cauliflower, Golden Fried, '82 78
Cauliflower, Pickled, '94 183
Cauliflower with Cheese Sauce, Fried, '87 231
Caviar Crown, '83 78
Caviar, Eggplant, '88 262; '99 217
Caviar, Mexican, '98 135
Caviar Pie, '79 154
Caviar Potatoes, '84 80
Caviar Potatoes, Appetizer, '86 223
Caviar, Texas, '86 218; '99 84; '01 160, 257
Caviar Tomatoes, '91 12
Celery, Creamy Stuffed, '82 102
Celery, Jalapeño Stuffed, '79 70
Celery, Stuffed, '82 98
Celery Trunks, Stuffed, '85 115
Cereal Bites, Buttery, '89 97
Cereal Nibblers, Great, '82 297
Cereal Snack, Toasted, '85 215
Ceviche (Marinated Raw Fish), '80 194
Ceviche, Mexican-Style, '88 115
Cheese. *See also* **APPETIZERS/Dips, Spreads
    and Fillings.**
    Bacon-and-Cheese Melts, '04 324
    Bacon-Cheese Fingers, '00 133
    Bacon Puffs, Cheesy, '02 145
    Bagel Chips, Parmesan Cheese, '91 138
    Bake, Appetizer Cheese, '92 209
    Ball, Apple Cheese, '98 250
    Ball, Blue Cheese, '80 259; '84 221
    Ball, Blue Cheese-Olive, '82 248
    Ball, Bourbon Cheese, '81 57
    Ball, Brandied Blue Cheese, '85 283
    Ball, Carrot-Cheese, '86 325
    Ball, Cheese, '82 161; '91 200

Ball, Cheese and Chutney, '87 247
Ball, Cheese 'n' Beef, '83 230
Ball, Chicken-Cheese, '93 216
Ball, Chicken-Curry Cheese, '85 118
Ball, Cocktail Cheese, '83 174
Ball, Curried Shrimp Cheese, '86 135
Ball, Deviled Pecan, '80 258
Ball, Easy Chut-Nut, '00 280
Ball, Festive Cheese, '79 44; '94 279
Ball, Fruit-and-Nut Cheese, '91 251
Ball, Herbed Cheese, '89 246
Ball, Holiday Cheese, '79 285
Ball, Olive Cheese, '80 258
Ball, Parmesan-Cream Cheese, '89 246
Ball, Party Cheese, '84 258
Ball, Party Pecan Cheese, '81 235
Ball, Peanut Butter-Cheese, '86 136
Ball, Pecan Cheese, '83 127
Ball, Peppered Cheese, '79 100; '94 118
Ball, Pimiento Cheese, '80 258
Ball, Pineapple Cheese, '81 160
Ball, Pineapple-Cheese, '84 26
Ball, Pinecone Cheese, '93 288; '98 265
Ball, Pumpkin Cheese, '02 222
Balls, Bite-Size Cheese, '92 321
Balls, Cheese and Mushroom, '79 63
Ball, Shrimp-Cheese, '85 208
Ball, Smoky Salmon Cheese, '82 247
Balls, Olive-Cheese, '84 206
Balls, Pumpkin Patch Cheese, '99 245
Balls with Sun-Dried Tomatoes, Cheese, '94 317
Ball, Tangy Cheese, '81 263, 287
Bar, Savory Cheese, '91 98
Bars, Bacon-Cheese Toast, '79 36
Bars, Camembert, '86 58
Bear Claws, '81 161
Biscuits, Cheese, '79 296; '80 31
Biscuits, Cheesy Sausage, '80 78
Biscuits, Mixer Cheese, '96 22
Biscuits, Petite Ham and Cheese, '79 193
Biscuits, Tiny Cheese, '80 192
Biscuits with Sun-Dried Tomato Spread and
    Bacon, Cream Cheese-and-Olive, '02 313
Biscuits with Tapenade, Cream Cheese-and-
    Olive, '02 313
Bites, Benne Cheese, '80 121
Bites, Cheese, '93 329
Bites, Cheesy Pecan, '82 248
Bites, Crispy Cheese, '03 179
Bites, Curried Swiss, '85 220
Bites, Lemon-Cheese Party, '95 160
Bites, Parmesan Cheese, '99 221; '00 20;
    '01 123; '02 108
Bites, Starlight Cheese, '95 329
Bit-of-Brie Appetizer, '88 M8
Bonbons, Cheese, '87 93
Box, Cranberry-Cheese, '03 238
Brick, Cheese, '99 170
Brie, Chutney-Bacon, '90 M292
Brie en Croute, Stuffed, '97 162
Brie, Honey-Mustard, '91 252
Brie in Braided Bread Ring, '96 322
Brie in Rye, Raspberry, '93 252
Brie, Kahlúa-Pecan, '92 289
Brie, Parmesan-Coated, '95 286
Brie, Tropical Breeze, '94 M18
Brie, Warmed Cranberry, '01 245
Brie with Brown Sugar and Nuts, '03 282
Brie with Fresh Fruit, Caramel, '90 266
Brie, Wrapped, '92 126
Brie Wrapped in Phyllo, '93 173
Calzones, Surprise, '00 282
Camembert Cremes, '03 248
Caraway Cheese, '89 246

APPETIZERS, Cheese
(continued)

Caraway-Cheese Crisps, '95 284
Cheesecake, Cheddar-Chili, '02 251
Cheesecake, Ham-and-Asparagus, '02 103
Cheesecake, Roasted Vegetable, '99 140
Cheesecake, Salsa, '98 33
Cheesecake, Savory Spinach Appetizer, '02 M207
Cheesecakes, Herbed, '99 182
Cheesecake, Smoked Salmon, '99 92
Cheesecake, Southwest, '04 293
Cheesecake, Spinach-Herb, '99 139
Cheesecake, Taco, '00 56
Cheesecake, Three-Layer, '99 140
Chiles-Rellenos Squares, '91 161
Chutney Appetizer, Fiery Cheese-and-, '04 177
Cookie Snacks, Cheese, '01 231
Cracker Nibbles, Cheese, '84 328
Crackers, Cheddar, '84 236
Crackers, Tomato-Blue Cheese, '02 213
Cream Cheese Appetizer, Baked, '92 58
Cream Cheese Round, Pesto-and-, '90 242
Crème Brûlée, Roquefort-and-Black Pepper, '95 324
Crispies, Cheese-Bacon, '84 270
Crispies, Pecan-Cheese, '87 168
Crisps, Blue Cheese, '98 285; '01 235
Crisps, Parmesan, '01 197
Crisps, Spicy Jack Cheese, '02 135
Croquettes, Hot Cheese, '89 182
Crostini, Almond-Bacon-Cheese, '94 318
Crostini, Cheesy, '03 223
Crostini, Mozzarella, '94 319
Crostini, Roasted Peppers-Feta Cheese, '96 87
Crostini, Swiss-Blue Cheese, '94 318; '96 215
Crostini, Zippy Cheese, '97 90
Cucumber Slices, Cheesy, '84 80
Cups, Cottage Cheese-Spinach, '87 190
Cutouts, Sesame-Cheese, '82 296
Feta Cheesecakes, Little, '86 277
Fiesta Cheesecake, '93 273
Flaming Cheese, '84 187
Fondue, Cheese, '81 40
Fondue, Nacho, '94 332; '95 35
Fondue, Party Cheese, '92 20
Fondue, Pub, '94 332; '95 35
Fondue, Swiss Cheese, '91 48
Fried Cheddar Cheese, '89 182
Fried Cheese Balls, '89 181
Fried Cheese Bites, '82 77
Fried Cheese, Italian-Style, '83 250; '89 182
Garnished Cheese, '91 98
Goat Cheese, Dried Tomato Mock, '97 105
Goat Cheese, Endive with Herbed, '04 244
Goat Cheese, Mock, '97 105
Goat Cheese, Peppered, '94 128
Goat Cheese Rosemary, '89 270
Goat Cheese with Sun-Dried Tomatoes and Rosemary, '93 175
Grapes, Blue Cheese-Pecan, '95 48
Green Chile-Cheddar Cheese with Avocado-Mango Salsa, Smoky, '00 328
Grits, Garlic-Cheese, '97 58
Herb Cheese, Pot-of-, '85 210
Herbed Cheese, '88 152
Herb-Pepper Cheese, '97 90
Horseshoe, Strawberry-Cheese, '00 106
Kebabs, Peppered Cheese, '91 279
Little Bits, '79 196
Loaf, Four-Layer Cheese, '99 222
Log, Black Pepper-Goat Cheese, '98 285

Log, Cheesy Surprise, '82 247
Log, Garlic Cheese, '85 21
Log, Hawaiian Cheese, '89 246
Log, Roquefort Pecan, '89 247
Logs, Black Pepper Cheese, '90 61
Logs, Blue Cheese, '04 53
Logs, Candy Cane-Cheese, '03 298
Logs, East Indian Cheese, '88 173
Logs, Port Wine Cheese, '02 279
Logs, Spicy Monterey Jack Cheese, '02 279
Log, Toasted Pecan Cheese, '86 M288
Marinade, Cheese, '04 238
Marinated Cheese, '90 244; '95 21
Marinated Cheese, Olives, and Peppers, '04 238
Meat-and-Cheese Appetizers, '87 7
Melt, Brie-and-Cranberry Chutney, '98 M318
Mexicali Appetizer, Cheesy, '82 108
Mold, Blue Cheese, '85 210
Mold, Cheese-and-Wine, '84 197
Mold, Cream Cheese-Crabmeat, '90 71
Mold, Garlic-Chive Cheese, '85 210
Mousse, Roquefort, '82 71
Nachos, Smoked, '01 146
Nuggets, Cheesy Ham, '81 290
Olive Appetizers, Cheesy, '85 113
Olive Appetizers, Cheesy-, '87 246
Olive Snack, Open-Faced Cheese-and-, '89 97
Pasta Bites, Pesto-Cheese, '87 251
Pastries, Cream Cheese, '80 250
Pastries, Date-Filled Cheese, '83 259
Pastry, Brie Wrapped in, '80 241
Pastry, Sausage Balls in Cheese, '80 248
Pastry Shells, Miniature Cream Cheese, '87 190
Patty, Lemon-Pepper Cheese, '84 117
Patty Shells, Cream Cheese, '82 249
Peachy Cream Cheese, '92 289
Pepper-Cheese Stacks, '87 80
Peppers, Cheesy Jalapeño, '80 195
Phyllo-Cheese Triangles, '87 246
Phyllo Cheese Triangles, '93 329
Phyllo, Goat Cheese Wrapped in, '99 43
Phyllo Triangles, Cheese-Filled, '83 259
Pie, Cheesy Hors d'Oeuvre, '88 91
Pinwheels, Mexican, '95 21
Pinwheels, Santa's, '91 275
Pita Crisps, Cheesy, '97 45
Potato Skins, Cheesy, '82 78
Puffs, Bavarian Cheese, '80 191
Puffs, Blue Cheese, '04 18
Puffs, Blue Cheese-and-Bacon, '97 98; '01 236
Puffs, Cheese, '79 110; '97 240; '02 69; '03 269; '04 107
Puffs, Cheese-and-Spinach, '87 246
Puffs, Cream Cheese, '84 151
Puffs, Gouda-Shrimp, '79 234
Puffs, Ham-and-Cheese, '86 277
Puffs, Mexican Cheese, '87 8
Puffs, Oregano Cheese, '95 21
Puffs, Surprise Cheese, '79 295; '80 31
Quesadillas, Green Chile, '90 121
Quesadillas, Quick, '02 143
Queso Blanco, '93 322
Queso, Chunky Cheese, '99 279
Quiches, Miniature Bacon-Cheese, '83 93
Quiches, Miniature Cheese, '80 150
Quick Cheese Snack, '89 98
Ring, Cheese, '81 261
Ring, Strawberry-Cheese, '86 14
Roll, Chili-Cheese, '84 114
Roll, Ham-and-Cheese, '79 234
Rollups, Cream Cheese, '98 134
Rollups, Ham-and-Swiss, '85 113
Rollups, Mexican, '98 134
Rollups, Southwestern, '01 135

Round, Brie Appetizer, '82 41
Round, Herbed Cheese, '84 300
Rounds, Cheese, '86 262
Rounds, Parmesan, '85 131
Rounds, Parmesan Party, '82 248
Salami-Cheese Snacks, '88 96
Salsa Parmesan, Broiled, '98 33
Sandwiches, Cheese Tea, '92 276
Sandwiches, Cheshire Claret Cheese-and-Ham Striped Tea, '94 16
Sandwiches, Duck Party, '02 48
Sandwiches, Easter Bunny Party, '02 48
Sandwiches, Easter Egg Party, '02 48
Sandwiches, Flower Party, '02 48
Sandwiches, Nutty Cream Cheese Party, '00 119
Sandwiches, Pimiento Cheese Finger, '99 86
Sesame Cheese Bites, '89 24
Shrimp-and-Cheese Appetizer, '01 134
Soufflé, Blue Cheese, '91 244
Sour Cream Appetizer, Cheesy, '84 51
Southwestern Cheese Appetizer, '01 232
Spinach-Cheese Bites, '94 23
Squares, Cream Cheese-Almond, '85 68
Squares, Cream Cheese-Vegetable, '04 293
Squares, Feta, '02 59
Squares, Green Chile-Cottage Cheese, '86 85
Squares, Jalapeño Cheese, '80 195
Squares, Quick Cheese, '84 191
Sticks, Parmesan, '82 297
Sticks, Parmesan-Bacon, '99 65
Sticks, Parmesan Sesame, '81 39
Sticks, Peppery Cheese, '81 M289
Straws, Brie Cheese, '94 216
Straws, Cheese, '80 150; '82 137; '88 77
Straws, Chili-Cheese, '94 216
Straws, Easy-as-Pie Cheese, '94 216
Straws, Italian Cheese, '94 217
Straws, Parmesan Cheese, '94 216
Straws, Sally's Cheese, '97 121
Tartlets, Cheese, '88 211
Tarts, Blue Cheese Appetizer, '85 300; '86 18
Terrine, Basil-Cheese, '96 322
Terrine, Chevre-and-Avocado, '00 276
Terrine, Italian Cheese, '93 64
Terrine with Tomato-Basil Vinaigrette, Blue Cheese, '99 288
Three-Cheese Appetizer, '80 174
Toasts, Cheddar-Almond, '97 30
Toast Treats, Cheese, '83 100
Torta, Basil-Cheese, '01 100
Torta, Three-Layer Cheese, '04 323
Torte, Pesto, '02 278
Torte, Showstopping Appetizer, '98 319
Torte, Tomato-Cheese, '97 49
Tortillas, Jumpin' Jack, '02 54
Turnovers, Cheesy Sesame Seed, '91 252
Twists, Double Cheese, '85 131
Twists, Parmesan, '99 323
Vegetable Cheesecake, '96 110
Wafers, Blue Cheese-Walnut, '00 56
Wafers, Cheese, '80 151; '95 174; '99 279; '00 164
Wafers, Hope Farm Cheese, '93 282
Wafers, Pam's Cheese, '98 268
Wafers, Pecan-Cheese, '81 119
Wafers, Sage-Pecan Cheese, '93 12
Wafers, Spicy Cheese-Walnut, '03 61
Wedges, Cheesy Party, '84 84
Wonton Chips, Parmesan Cheese, '91 138
Wonton Envelopes, Fried, '95 96
Wontons with Hot Sauce, Cheese, '83 74
Yogurt Cheese Appetizer, '04 217
Cherries, Stuffed, '85 81
Cherry Pepper Appetizers, Fiery Stuffed, '97 269

Chicken. *See also* **APPETIZERS/Dips, Spreads and Fillings.**
Balls, Coconut Curried Chicken, '91 165
Balls, Curried Chicken, '91 98
Bites, Curried Chicken, '85 40
Bites, French-Fried Chicken, '85 160
Bites, Savory Chicken, '92 209
Bites with Sweet-Hot Tomato Chutney, Chicken, '00 309
B'steeya with Chicken, '98 210
Cakes with Avocado Cream, Southwestern Chicken-and-Corn, '97 M311
Deep-Fried Walnut Chicken, '87 175
Drummettes, Down-Home Chicken, '93 157
Drummettes, Ginger-Garlic Appetizer, '93 157
Drummettes, Orange-Pecan Chicken, '93 158
Drummettes, Southwestern Chicken, '93 158
Empanadas, '04 135
Fingers, Chicken Almondette, '93 12
Fingers, Chicken Little, '80 249
Fingers with Come Back Sauce, Fried Chicken, '00 211
Firecrackers, Texas, '95 96; '99 94
Jamaican Jerk Raspberry Chicken, '00 88
Liver and Bacon Roll-Ups, Chicken, '80 200; '81 57
Livers, Garlic Chicken, '96 105
Livers, Party Chicken, '83 242
Liver Turnovers, Chicken, '79 141
Log, Chicken-Pecan, '81 290
Mushroom Appetizers, Chicken-, '88 210
Nuggets, Baked Chicken, '81 149
Nuggets, Chicken-Bacon, '03 292; '04 146
Nuggets, Lemon-Chicken, '87 283
Nuggets Supreme, Chicken, '85 160
Nuggets with Pineapple Sauce, Chicken, '84 236
Puffs, Appetizer Chicken, '85 72
Puffs, Chicken Nut, '81 260
Quesadillas, Spicy Chicken, '95 42
Quesadillas with Chipotle Salsa, Chicken-and-Brie, '99 311
Rollups, Southwestern, '01 135
Salad, Old-Fashioned Chicken, '83 79
Salad Spirals, Southwestern Chicken, '02 58
Sandwiches, Curried Chicken Tea, '97 23
Sesame Chicken, '97 256
Sesame Chicken Appetizers, '89 61
Skewers, Taco-Chicken, '99 119
Sticks, Italian Chicken, '98 25
Sticky Chicken, '97 239
Strips, Sesame Chicken, '98 250
Strips with "Come Back" Dipping Sauce, Miss Mary's Chicken, '96 213
Tarts, Chicken Salad, '84 257
Tarts, Deviled Chicken, '94 14
Tempura Delight, Chicken, '85 66
Terrine, Vegetable-Chicken, '83 224
Wings, Broiled Chicken, '80 149
Wings, Buffalo, '00 203
Wings, Buffalo Hot, '03 184
Wings, Chinese Chicken, '96 111
Wings, Curried Chicken, '96 110
Wings, Grilled Honey Chicken, '96 111
Wings, Honey Chicken, '00 15
Wings, Honey-Glazed Chicken, '91 251
Wings, Hot Buffalo, '87 176
Wings, Maple-Glazed Chicken, '99 110
Wings, Satan's, '87 214
Wings, Sesame-Maple Chicken, '00 57
Wings, Spicy Buffalo, '95 239
Wings, Spicy Oriental-Style, '96 215
Wings, Sweet-and-Hot Citrus, '00 202
Wings, Sweet-and-Sour Chicken, '90 206; '96 110

Wings, Tandoori Chicken, '96 110
Wings, Teriyaki Chicken, '85 300; '86 18
Wings with Spanish Rice, Chicken, '00 202
Wontons with Hoisin Peanut Dipping Sauce, Chicken, '99 14
Wraps, Chicken Lettuce, '02 65
Chile-Sausage Squares, '86 297
Chiles Rellenos, Bite-Size, '87 246
Chiles Rellenos, Roasted, '95 64
Chili in Pastry Cups, '90 68
Chips
Bagel Chips, '91 138
Bagel Chips, Cinnamon-and-Sugar, '91 139
Bagel Chips, Garlic, '91 139
Bagel Chips, Lemon-and-Herb, '91 139
Bagel Chips, Parmesan Cheese, '91 138
Beet Chips, '97 229
Cumin Crisps, '02 205
Homemade Texas Chips with Guacamole Spread, '90 119
Pita Chips, '89 19; '91 138
Pita Chips, Baked, '99 138
Plantain Chips, '95 M203
(Plantain Chips), Tostones de Plátano, '92 158
Sweet Potato Chips, '91 138; '93 332; '95 M203
Sweet Potato Chips with Blue Cheese, '93 290
Tortilla Chips, '91 137
Tortilla Chips, Corn, '91 17
Tortilla Chips, Light, '91 257
Wonton Chips, Baked, '91 138; '99 138
Wonton Chips, Cinnamon-and-Sugar, '91 138
Wonton Chips, Garlic, '91 138
Wonton Chips, Lemon-and-Herb, '91 138
Wonton Chips, Parmesan Cheese, '91 138
Chocolate-Almond Cream, '91 108
Chocolate Bites, Snowy, '90 47
Chocolate Clusters, Triple, '01 242
Chocolate-Dipped Horns, '93 197
Chocolate-Peanut Butter Snacks, '90 226
Chocolate-Sesame Sticks, '91 316
Chutney, Cranberry, '96 275
Chutney Roll, '83 259
Chutney, Texas Cranberry, '04 257
Chutney with Cream Cheese, Cranberry-Amaretto, '87 244
Cinnamon Sticks, '95 244
Cinnamon Wafers, '84 324
Clam Crisps, '80 151
Clam Puffs, '90 60
Clams Casino, '81 125
Clams Oreganata, '85 104
Clams with Cilantro-Black Walnut Pesto, Littleneck, '97 164
Cocktail Puffs, '91 106
Confetti Appetizers, '84 191
Corn Salsa, Spicy, '93 322
Crab. *See also* **APPETIZERS/Dips, Spreads and Fillings.**
Balls, Crabmeat, '88 150
Ball, Spicy Crab, '01 332
Bites, Crabmeat, '97 98
Bites, Crab-Zucchini, '84 M216
Bites, Spicy Crab, '91 165
Broiled Crab Meltaways, '93 287
Cakes and Dijon Sauce, Mini Crab, '03 92
Cakes, Crab, '99 267; '01 245
Cakes, Crab-and-Scallop, '02 165
Cakes, Miniature Crab, '96 306
Cakes with Cress Sauce, Baked Crab, '96 176
Cakes with Maui Sauce, Crab, '99 310
Casserole, Easy Crab, '93 270
Chafing Dish Crabmeat, '89 284
Crisps, Crab, '79 63
Deviled Crab, Devilish, '85 264

Hors d'Oeuvre, Crabmeat, '94 236
Imperial, Crab, '02 103
Mold, Crab, '85 318
Oysters, Crabmeat Stuffed, '94 328
Polenta, Crab, '00 277
Pot Stickers, Hoisin Crab, '96 92
Puffs, Crab, '80 20; '84 269
Puffs, Crabmeat, '99 335
Rémoulade, Crabmeat, '93 280
Salsa with Sesame Wontons, Spicy Crab-and-Ginger, '01 283
Sandwiches, Miniature Crab Cake, '96 306
Snacks, Crab, '83 93
Topping, Crabmeat, '91 64
Crackers, Bone, '01 204
Cranberry-Nut Triangles, '04 273
Crawfish on Eggplant, Soft-Shell, '88 222
Crème Brûlée, Onion, '95 324
Crème Brûlée, Roasted Garlic, '95 324
Crème Brûlées, Savory, '95 324
Crêpes, Basic, '04 245
Crostini. *See also* **APPETIZERS/Bruschetta, Canapés.**
Almond-Bacon-Cheese Crostini, '94 318
Artichoke Crostini, Hot, '94 319
Cheese Crostini, Zippy, '97 90
Cheesy Crostini, '03 223
Christmas Crostini, '94 318
Festive Crostini, '98 183; '99 325
Green Onion Crostini, '96 93
Mexican Crostini, '95 142
Mozzarella Crostini, '94 319
Olive Crostini, '02 205
Parmesan-Artichoke Crostini, '98 285
Pear-and-Gorgonzola Crostini, '02 314
Roasted Peppers-Feta Cheese Crostini, '96 87
Roasted Red Pepper-Feta Crostini, '04 69
Spinach Crostini, '01 283
Spinach-Red Pepper Crostini, '03 34
Swiss-Blue Cheese Crostini, '94 318; '96 215
Tomato-and-Goat Cheese Crostini, '04 168
Tomato Crostini, '99 230
Walnut-Blue Cheese, Crostini with, '01 321
Crunch, Oriental, '96 215
Crunchy Munchies, '94 196
Cucumber Delights, '84 117
Cucumber Fingers, Fried, '86 146
Cucumber Rounds, '88 78
Cucumber Sandwiches, '90 81; '94 14; '97 99
Cucumber Soup with Dill Cream, '00 130
Cucumber Vichyssoise, '94 90
Date-Nut Ball, '92 326
Dates, Apricot-Stuffed, '80 250
Dips. *See also* **APPETIZERS/Caviar, Salsas.**
Almond Cream Dip with Strawberries, '92 164
Almond Delight Dip, '90 226
Antipasto Dip, '93 313
Apple Dip, '93 205; '96 M190
Apricot Dip, '86 178
Artichoke-Chile Dip, '98 234
Artichoke Dip, Baked, '95 239; '03 294
Artichoke Dip, Deluxe, '80 87
Artichoke Dip, Florentine, '96 274
Artichoke Dip, Greek, '97 315
Artichoke Dip in a Bread Basket, '93 13
Artichoke Dip, Italian, '97 315
Artichoke Dip, Mexican, '90 292
Artichoke Dip, Quick, '02 69; '03 270; '04 107
Artichoke Dip, Seasoned Mayonnaise, '80 87
Artichoke-Seafood Dip, Hot, '80 241
Artichoke Seafood Dip, Hot, '85 M212
Avocado Dip, '80 285; '81 57, 306
Avocado Dip, "Bring-Home-the-Bacon," '92 80
Avocado Dip, Zippy, '82 9; '83 69

APPETIZERS, Dips
(continued)

Bacon-and-Tomato Dip, '90 147
Bacon-Cheese Dip, '01 194
Bacon Dip, '82 197
Bacon Dip, Zesty, '92 156
Bacon-Guacamole Dip, '85 25
Basket, Dips and Dippers in a, '83 171
Bean Dip, '89 97
Bean Dip, Barbecue, '03 138
Bean Dip, Hot, '04 323
Bean Dip, Hotshot, '87 195
Bean Dip, Prairie Fire, '80 195
Beau Monde Dip in Rye Bread, Party, '83 127
Beef-and-Pasta Sauce Dip, Creamy, '01 108
Beef-and-Spinach Dip, '99 65
Beef Dip, Chipped, '88 M8
Beef Dip, Hot Cheesy, '80 85
Beef Dip, Spicy Cheese-, '02 58
Black Bean Dip, '95 93
Black-Eyed Pea con Queso, '96 274
Black-Eyed Pea Dip, '81 8; '04 M18
Black-Eyed Pea Dip, Bill D's, '97 M89
Blue Cheese-Bacon Dip, '04 287
Blue Cheese Dip, '80 285; '83 169; '93 313;
    '01 194
Braunschweiger-and-Beer Dip, '85 69
Broccoli Dip, Cheesy, '83 92
Broccoli-Garlic Dip, '82 59
Brown Sugar Dip with Fruit, Buttery, '90 243
Cabbage, Dock Dip in, '86 179
Catfish Dip, Layered, '03 185
Cheddar-Bacon Dip, '89 M119
Cheese-and-Chile Dip, '83 31
Cheese and Crab Dip, Hot, '81 261
Cheese-Bean Dip, '85 208
Cheese-Crab Dip, '91 200
Cheese Dip, Hot, '91 171
Cheese Dip, Meaty, '82 59; '92 160
Cheese Dip, Seaside, '85 284
Cheese Dunk, Deviled, '80 265
Cheese-Garlic Dip, '80 192
Cheese-Herb Dip, '89 20
Chicken Dip, Hot, '80 86
Chickpea-and-Red Pepper Dip, '99 138
Chile-Beef Dip, Hot, '83 218
Chile-Cheese Dip, '87 173
Chile con Queso, '80 194; '81 195
Chile Con Queso, Roasted Poblano, '01 186
Chile con Queso Supreme, '80 265
Chile Dip, Hot, '82 248
Chile Sauce, Hot, '92 156
Chili-and-Black-Eyed Pea Dip, '92 155
Chili-and-Cheese Dip, '89 328
Chili-Cheese Dip, '90 225
Chili Con Queso, '04 69
Chili con Queso Dip, '86 81
Chili Dip, '82 161; '88 218; '89 47; '91 143
Chili Dip, Cheesy, '80 150
Chive-Cheese Dip, '94 62
Christmas Confetti Dip, '92 279
Cilantro Dip, '00 248
Clam Dip, '79 151; '80 265; '01 194
Clam Dip, Hot, '82 59; '89 48
Clam Dip, Zesty, '92 25
Confetti Snack Dip, '79 107
Corn-and-Avocado Dip, Roasted, '91 279
Corn-and-Field Pea Dip, '01 177
Cottage Cheese Sun-Dried Tomato Dip, '93 13
Crab-and-Cheese Dip, Hot, '94 282
Crab Dip, Creamy, '80 M135
Crab Dip, Festive, '92 285

Crab Dip, Hot, '93 269; '97 89
Crab Dip, Oven-Baked, '82 59
Crab Dip, Tangy, '83 5
Crab Dip, Trawler, '93 238
Crabmeat Dip, Hot, '95 154
Cranberry Fruit Dip, '89 60
Cranberry-Horseradish Dip, '85 65
Cream Cheese Dip, Fruited, '88 261
Cream Cheese-Onion Dip, '79 236
Creamy Texas Dip, '94 161
Crudité Dip, '86 105
Crudité Platter with Dip, '84 139
Cucumber-and-Yogurt Dipping Sauce, '02 172
Cucumber Dipping Sauce, '94 47
Cucumber-Yogurt Dip, '99 93
Curried Dip, '81 262
Curry Dip, '80 84; '81 9; '85 132; '86 184;
    '87 25; '99 138
Curry Dip and Vegetable Platter, '89 327
Curry Dip, Creamy, '84 206
Curry-Onion Dip, '93 313
Delight, Dipper's, '98 93
Devil, Dipsy, '00 132
Deviled Dip, '87 25
Dill Dip, '80 265; '93 330
Dill Dip, Refreshing, '99 324
Dilled Garden Dip, '84 324
Dried Beef Dip, '01 90
Dried Beef Dip, Extra-Creamy, '03 240
Egg Dip, Festive, '79 285
Eggplant Dip, '96 275
Feta Dip, Zesty, '04 71
Fiesta Dip, '81 206; '92 263; '96 212; '03 284
Fiesta Dip, Quick, '99 M197
Fish Dip, Smoked, '84 46
Fondue, Beer-and-Cheddar, '03 223
Fondue, Cheese, '81 40
Fondue, Fruitcake, '84 258
Fondue, Nacho, '94 332; '95 35
Fondue, Party Cheese, '92 20
Fondue, Peppermint, '94 332; '95 35
Fondue, Pub, '94 332; '95 35
Fondue, Swiss Cheese, '91 48
Fruit Dip, Coconut-Honey, '84 171
Fruit Dip, Creamy, '84 51
Fruit Dip, Fresh, '80 265; '95 94
Fruit Dip, Ginger, '96 110
Fruit Dip, Heavenly, '81 160
Fruit Dip, Marshmallow, '84 171
Fruit Dip, Quick, '90 110
Fruit Dips, Fun, '01 109
Fruit Dip, Sweet, '89 328
Garbanzo Dip, '93 94
Gazpacho Dip, '95 243
Ginger Dip, '94 12, 19; '99 139
Goblin Dip with Bone Crackers, '01 204
Grand Marnier Dip, '86 142
Green Goddess Dip, '84 159
Guacamole, '79 185; '80 74; '83 179; '91 161;
    '96 170; '03 95
Guacamole, Black Bean, '94 277
Guacamole, Creamy, '79 91; '83 174; '99 119;
    '02 168
Guacamole Dip, '86 4; '95 96
Guacamole Dip, Bacon, '85 25
Guacamole, Easy, '95 94
Guacamole in Shells, '86 74
Guacamole, Margarita, '97 167
Guacamole, Roasted Onion, '00 334
"Guacamole" with Cumin Crisps, Green
    Goddess, '02 205
Guac, Baine's, '98 88
Ham Dip, Creamy, '93 125
Herbal Dip, '86 14

Herb Dip, Creamy, '04 54
Holiday Dip, '83 321; '84 289
Honey-Herb Dip, Creamy, '98 135
Horseradish Dip, Creamy, '94 122
Hummas, '92 155
Hummus, '96 158
Hummus, Black-Eyed Pea, '94 123
Hummus, Creamy Dried Tomato, '95 284
Hummus, Low-Fat, '99 137
Hummus, Quick, '95 93
Hummus, Red Pepper, '00 132; '02 31
Hummus, White Bean, '01 32
Indonesian Dip, '96 190
Kahlúa Dip, '99 139
Leek Dip, Creamy, '86 77
Lime-Dill Dip, '92 65
Lime Dressing, Creamy, '04 46
Marmalade Dip, '99 324
Mexican Appetizer, Chilled, '87 197
Mexican Fiesta Dip, '98 234
Mint Dip with Fresh Fruit, '87 146
Monster Mash Dip, '93 244
Mushroom Dip, Hot, '89 48
Mustard Dip, Sweet-and-Spicy, '96 M274
Nacho Dip, '83 239; '93 M330
Nacho Dip, Layered, '81 261; '03 207
Nacho Dip, Quick, '90 168
Niçoise, Sauce, '96 190
Olive-Relish Dip, '84 205
Onion Dip, '94 21
Onion Dip, Cheesy, '83 145
Onion Dip, Chunky, '84 257
Orange Cream, '90 126
Orange Dip, Creamy, '84 117; '87 247
Orange Dip, Spicy, '85 230
Orange Fruit Dip, '96 190
Orange-Lime Dip, '96 248
Orange Sour Cream Dip, '79 208
Oyster Dip, Smoked, '79 233
Parsley-Dill Dip with Fresh Vegetables, '85 79
Peach Dip, Creole, '80 142
Peachy Dip, '92 179
Peanut Butter Dip, '86 135; '01 109
Peanut Butter-Honey Dip, '85 19
Peanut Butter Lovers' Dip, '93 162
Peas, Passion, '89 17
Pepperoncini-Cream Cheese Dip, '91 252
Pesto Dip, '95 93; '97 226
Pesto-Garbanzo Dip, '03 299
Pico de Gallo, '02 168, 306
Pineapple Dip, Cheesy, '80 249
Pineapple-Ginger Dip, '86 104
Pine Nut-Spinach Dip, '99 138
Pink Lemonade-Lime Dip, '04 133
Pizza Dip, '99 65
Pizza Dip, Quick, '00 M168
Plantain Dip, '92 158
Pumpkin Pie Dip, '01 242
Quick Fiesta Dip, '95 M237
Ranch Dip, Skinny, '93 96
Ranch-Style Dip, '90 138; '92 148
Salsa-Bean Dip, '98 285
Salsa, Chunky, '86 130; '90 206
Salsa Cruda, '87 180; '88 148
Salsa, Fresh Summer, '87 89
Salsa, Greek Vegetable, '98 32
Salsa, Olive, '00 277
Salsa Picante, '84 108; '04 41
Salsa, Quick Party, '03 292; '04 146
Salsa with Cinnamon Crisps, Fruit, '01 108
Sauce, Citrus Dipping, '97 208
Sauce, Hoisin Peanut Dipping, '99 14
Seafood Dip, '79 3
Seafood Dip, Hot Cheesy, '84 221

Seafood Dip, Super, '90 292
Shrimp Dip, '86 84; '88 M261; '98 67; '01 194
Shrimp Dip, Chunky, '96 214
Shrimp Dip, Hot, '87 190
Shrimp Dip, Monterey, '99 M65
Shrimp Dip, Quick, '79 153
Shrimp Dip, Zesty, '80 150
Six-Layer Dip, '81 160
Skinny Dip, Santa Fe, '94 137
Smoked Salmon Dip, Extra-Creamy, '03 240
Sour Cream Dip, '86 278
South-of-the-Border Dip, '81 235
Spinach-Artichoke Dip, '00 26
Spinach-Cheese Dip, Hot, '89 48
Spinach con Queso, Easy, '88 101
Spinach Dip, '80 86; '86 159; '87 25, 214;
    '93 324
Spinach Dip, Cheesy, '82 59
Spinach Dip, Creamy, '88 132
Spinach Dip, Hot, '80 249
Spinach Dip in Cabbage, '82 155
Spinach Dip in Sourdough Round, '98 173
Strawberry Dip, '01 109
Sugar Snap Dip, '88 91
Summer Dip, '94 157
Swiss-Onion Dip, '95 93
Taco Dip, Hot, '93 238
Tarragon Dip, '83 78
Tennessee Sin, '95 218; '96 204
Tequila Dip, '91 166
Thick-and-Creamy Dip, '90 271
Tofu Dip, '86 109
Tomato-Basil Dip, Steamed Asparagus with,
    '00 69
Tomato Pesto Dip with Tortellini, Creamy,
    '00 196
Tostada Dip, '84 206
Tropical Dip for Fruit, '91 252
Tuna-Curry Dip, '84 31
Tuna Dip, Low-Cal, '87 25
Tuna Dip, Tasty, '96 190
Turnip Green Dip, '91 13
Turnip Green Dip with Jalapeño-Corn Muffins,
    Hot, '93 164
Vegetable Dip, '79 52; '82 161; '02 18
Vegetable Dip, Creamy, '82 132; '83 99, 180;
    '03 25
Vegetable Dip, Cucumber-Cheese, '83 128
Vegetable Dip, Fresh, '80 249
Vegetable Dip, Herb, '89 269
Vegetable Dip, Quick Creamy, '00 34
Vegetable Dip, Starburst, '82 248
Vegetable Dip, Tangy, '87 196
Vegetable Dip, Zippy, '84 256
Vegetable Garden Dip, '85 215
Vidalia Onion Dip, Baked, '02 88
Water Chestnut Dip, '80 86; '86 183
Yellow Squash-Zucchini Dip, '89 48
Yogurt Dip, '94 21
Yogurt Dip, Fruited, '84 171
Yogurt Herring Dip, '80 232
Zesty Party Dip, '83 259
Dumplings, Steamed Sesame, '97 208
Eggplant Appetizer, '83 187
Eggplant Appetizer, Grilled, '95 198
Eggplant Caviar, '88 262; '99 217
Eggplant, Cheesy Fried, '90 75
Eggplant, Fried Parmesan, '87 166
Eggplant Sticks, Ned's, '95 309
Egg Rolls, '86 81
Egg Rolls, Chiles Rellenos, '86 296
Egg Rolls, Golden Sausage, '03 284
Eggrolls, Shrimp and Pork, '82 240; '83 18
Egg Rolls, Tex-Mex, '01 328

Egg Rolls, Vegetarian, '86 148
Egg Rolls with Creamy Cilantro Dipping Sauce,
    Tex-Mex, '03 327
Eggs and Ham, Green, '96 90
Eggs, Bacon-Stuffed, '04 290
Eggs, Black-and-Blue, '96 90
Eggs, Deviled Green Goblin, '02 222
Eggs, Double Stuffed Spinach-and-Bacon, '00 M333
Eggs, Marbleized Garlic-Cheese-Stuffed, '96 91
Elephant Ears, Garlic-and-Herb Baby, '00 87
Elephant Ears, Mushroom-and-Brie Petite, '00 87
Elephant Ears, Parmesan-Pepper Baby, '00 87
Elephant Ears Provençale, Baby, '00 87
Elephant Ears, Southwestern Baby, '00 87
Empanadas, '92 156; '04 135
Empanadas, Pork Picadillo, '03 60
Endive Boats, '84 80
Endive with Arugula Tabbouleh Appetizers, '98 67
Endive with Caviar, '93 118
Escargots Provençal, '82 238; '83 156
Eye-of-Round, Burgundy, '90 243
Fast Goodies, '84 206
Fig Bites, Baked, '02 160
Figs with Prosciutto, Walnuts, and Cream, '96 194
Filet Mignon, Cajun Blackened, '95 85
Fish Taco Appetizers, '04 324
Flank Steak, Marinated, '83 258; '88 262
Flank Steak, Red Wine-Marinated, '95 283
Flank Steak Skewers, Lemon, '02 134
Frankfurter Appetizers, Bourbon, '85 207
Franks, Pickled Party, '83 174
Franks, Saucy Appetizer, '84 M12
Franks, Tipsy, '85 52
Frog Legs, Crispy, '80 99
Fruit and Cheese Tray, '83 171
Fruit Bowl, Sparkling Fresh, '80 146
Fruit Cascade, '86 104
Fruit Cup, Appetizer, '86 131
Fruit Kebabs, '86 181
Fruit Kebabs with Coconut Dressing, '87 251
Fruit with Curried Rum Sauce, Tropical, '91 164
Fruit with Dressing, Chilled, '85 222
Fruit with Honey-Sour Cream Dip, Fresh, '90 180
Gingerbread Bites with Orange-Cream Cheese
    Frosting, '04 258
Granola, '93 197
Granola, Fabulous, '92 213
Granola Gorp, '89 59
Granola, Nutty, '90 95
Granola, Pecan-Coconut, '02 70
Green Beans and Carrots, Sweet 'n' Hot, '00 211
Green Onion Teasers, '82 42
Griddle Cakes, Levee Camp, '03 29
Grouper Fingers, '00 167
Guacamole. *See also* **APPETIZERS/Dips,
    Spreads and Fillings.**
    Crisps, Guacamole, '98 173
    Mold, Guacamole, '86 184
    Spread, Guacamole, '90 119
Ham-and-Cheese Balls, Fried, '84 221
Ham Appetillas, '93 63
Ham Balls, '03 299
Ham-Filled Party Puffs, '84 116
Ham-Pineapple Nibbles, '95 283
Ham Rolls, '79 153
Ham Rolls, Party, '85 318
Ham Stack-Ups, '96 109
Ham Tapas, Garlic-, '92 175
Ham Turnovers, Chile-, '88 64
Ham Turnovers, Party, '82 39
Ham Twists, Deviled, '82 86
Hawaiian Dream Boats, '86 151
Hazelnuts, Curried, '93 301
Honey-and-Spice Crunch, '94 290

Horseradish Squares, Baked, '92 24
Hot Browns, Baby, '03 238
Hot Munch, Oriental, '87 8
Jalapeño Peppers, Fried Stuffed, '95 22
Jalapeño Peppers, Stuffed, '96 215
Jalapeños, Fiery Fried Stuffed, '90 118
Jalapeños, Fried, '96 292
Jalapeños, Shrimp-Stuffed, '88 115
Jalapeños, Stuffed, '98 234
Jezebel Sauce, '93 331
June Bugs, '85 11
Lamb Chops, Easy Baked, '02 66
Lamb Chops, Fried, '02 66
Lamb Chops, Glazed, '02 66
Lettuce Folds, Thai, '94 47
Links, Cocktail Smoky, '90 168
Liver, Mock Chopped, '00 281
Lobster-and-Roasted Corn Beignets, '00 51
Lobster Scallion Shooters, '00 197
Mango Chutney Torta, '96 322
Meatballs
    Bacon-Wrapped Meatballs, '79 81
    Baked Meatballs, '02 25
    Bourbon Meatballs, '00 252
    Brandied Meatballs, '83 78
    Burgundy-Bacon Meatballs, '80 283
    Chafing Dish Meatballs, '81 260
    Chestnut Meatballs, '79 110
    Cocktail Meatballs, '79 63, 207
    Flavorful Meatballs, '84 206
    German Meatballs, Crisp, '92 326
    Ham Balls, '86 256
    Ham Balls, Appetizer, '82 39
    Polynesian Meatballs, '80 207
    Quesadillas, Meatball, '00 242
    Saucy Party Meatballs, '80 149
    Sauerkraut Meatballs, '86 257
    Spiced Meatballs, '79 284
    Spicy Holiday Meatballs, '01 238
    Spicy Party Meatballs, '00 242
    Sweet-and-Sour Meatballs, '82 247; '99 325
    Sweet-and-Sour Meatballs, Spicy, '03 186
    Sweet-and-Sour Party Meatballs, '79 233
    Tamale Meatballs, '80 194
    Venison Sausage Balls, '80 42
    Zesty Meatballs, '80 250
Melon Balls, Minted, '87 162
Melon, Berry-Filled, '86 93
Mints, Cream Cheese, '93 79; '00 41
Mints, Party, '81 119
Mints, Special, '99 323
Mirliton Balls, '90 217
Mixes, Snack
    Bunny Trail Mix, '95 101
    Buried Treasure Snack Mix, '04 162
    Cereal Snack Mix, '93 129
    Creole Snack Mix, '91 171
    Crunchy Snack Mix, '93 94
    Dried Fruit Mix, '92 22
    Gorp, Elf, '90 270
    Gorp, Fancy, '89 253
    Granola Snack Mix, '86 229
    Honey-Nut Snack Mix, '02 187
    Jalapeño Nut Mix, '96 27
    Make-Ahead Snack Mix, '04 M92
    Mexicali Snack Mix, '86 230
    Nutty Snack Mix, '92 22
    Party Mix, '87 257; '96 306; '97 108, 322;
        '98 234
    Quick Party Mix, '83 92
    Raisin-Nut Party Mix, '83 60
    Rice Mix, Crunchy, '85 327
    Sea-and-Ski Cocktail Mix, '90 319
    Sherry Snack Mix, '00 329

APPETIZERS, Mixes, Snack
(continued)

    Snack-Attack Party Mix, **'84** 328
    Snack Mix, **'89** 19
    Spicy Party Mix, **'81** M138
    Starry Snack Mix, **'00** 329
    Sweet 'n' Savory Snack Mix, **'03** 199
    Trash Mix, **'01** 204
  Monster Eyes, **'02** 222
  Monster Mouths, **'95** 274
  Moroccan Triangles, Crispy, **'03** 60
  Mousses
    Catfish Mousse, **'92** 327
    Caviar Mousse, **'82** 71; **'83** 258; **'85** 86
    Chicken Mousse, Curried, **'95** 328
    Crabmeat Mousse, **'90** 190; **'91** 244
    Crab Mousse, **'79** 117; **'95** 327
    Ham Mousse Pitas, **'95** 328
    Horseradish Mousse, **'84** 126
    Mustard Mousse, **'84** 127; **'86** 184; **'95** 328
    Oyster Mousse, **'81** 245
    Oyster Mousse, Smoked, **'84** 320; **'99** 162
    Salmon Dill Mousse, **'81** 21
    Salmon Mousse, **'83** 79
    Salmon Mousse, Irresistible, **'79** 284
    Shrimp Mousse, **'87** 196, 251
    Tuna Mousse, **'80** 275
  Munchies, Reindeer, **'91** 276
  Mushrooms. *See also* **APPETIZERS/Canapés.**
    Drunk Mushrooms, **'83** 174
    French-Fried Mushrooms, **'82** 78
    French-Fried Mushrooms with Tartar Sauce, **'86** 233
    Logs, Mushroom, **'84** 206
    Marinated Herb Mushrooms, **'86** 327
    Marinated Mushroom Caps, **'83** 128
    Marinated Mushrooms, **'80** 82, 270; **'86** 135; **'91** 306; **'92** 328
    Marinated Mushrooms, Easy, **'86** 217
    Pastry Cups, Mushroom-Almond, **'88** 210
    Rollups, Mushroom, **'85** 318
    Samurai 'shrooms, **'93** 258
    Sour Cream, Mushrooms in, **'00** 106
    Stems, Mushrooms with, **'86** 258
    Stuffed Mushroom Appetizers, **'88** 210
    Stuffed Mushroom Caps, Crab-, **'84** 160
    Stuffed Mushroom Delight, **'87** 281
    Stuffed Mushrooms, **'79** 212; **'81** 239; **'83** 13, 66, 126, 136; **'93** 172
    Stuffed Mushrooms, Artichoke-, **'01** 239
    Stuffed Mushrooms, Beef-, **'00** 278
    Stuffed Mushrooms, Black Olive-, **'86** 258
    Stuffed Mushrooms, Cheese 'n' Bacon-, **'86** 258
    Stuffed Mushrooms, Crab-, **'81** 190; **'97** 102
    Stuffed Mushrooms, Crawfish-, **'86** 258
    Stuffed Mushrooms, Elegant Cheese-, **'81** 57
    Stuffed Mushrooms, Flavor-, **'85** 288
    Stuffed Mushrooms, Herbed Cheese-, **'96** 171
    Stuffed Mushrooms, Italian Sausage-, **'83** 127
    Stuffed Mushrooms, Parmesan, **'83** 115
    Stuffed Mushrooms, Pâté-, **'85** 118
    Stuffed Mushrooms, Pecan-, **'84** 261
    Stuffed Mushrooms, Pesto-, **'86** 150
    Stuffed Mushrooms, Pistachio-, **'86** 141
    Stuffed Mushrooms, Ricotta-, **'85** 20
    Stuffed Mushrooms, Sausage-, **'80** 248; **'91** 164
    Stuffed Mushrooms, Seasoned, **'84** 206
    Stuffed Mushrooms, Shrimp-, **'80** M135; **'99** 324
    Stuffed Mushrooms, Spinach-, **'86** 81; **'88** 131, M261; **'89** M133
    Stuffed Shiitakes Parmigiana, **'98** 25
    Stuffed with Crab, Mushrooms, **'82** 249

    Stuffed with Ham, Mushrooms, **'97** 237
    Tapas, Majorcan Mushroom, **'95** 159
    Tarts, Hot Sherried Mushroom, **'83** 78
    Tarts, Mushroom, **'88** 161
    Tipsy Mushrooms, **'84** M216
    Turnovers, Hot Mushroom, **'97** 102
    Vegetable Mushroom Caps, **'81** 246
  Nachos
    Barbecue Nachos, Commissary, **'91** 171
    Best-Ever Nachos, **'79** 91
    Chicken Nachos, **'84** 244
    Easy Nachos, **'84** 30
    Make-Ahead Nachos, **'80** M135
    South Texas Nachos, **'93** 321
    Southwestern Nachos, **'96** 170
    Supreme, Nachos, **'81** 306
    Texas Oyster Nachos, **'87** 39
    Tex-Mex Nachos, **'89** 97
    Tuna Nachos, **'95** 127; **'96** 201
    Turkey Nachos, **'90** 118
  Nectarine Cocktail, **'85** 107
  New Potatoes, Ham-Stuffed, **'88** 211
  Nibbles, Party, **'90** 249
  Nuts. *See also* **APPETIZERS/Pecans.**
    Cashews, Caribbean, **'04** 196
    Cashews, Spicy, **'01** 134
    Chesapeake Nuts, **'93** 269
    Curried Nuts, Spicy, **'82** 250
    Deviled Nuts, **'93** 118
    Hot Chili Nuts, **'81** 254
    Nippy Nuts, **'93** 301
    Party Nuts, Chesapeake Bay, **'03** 179
    Peanuts, Hot, **'00** 278
    Peanuts, Sugar-and-Spice, **'04** 197
    Peanuts, Sugared, **'82** 249
    Pesto-Spiced Nuts, **'95** 173
    Pistachios, Spicy, **'04** 197
    Quick Party Nuts, **'04** 197
    Sherry-Orange Nuts, **'86** M289
    Soup Nuts, **'96** 106
    Spiced Nuts, **'84** 257; **'91** M316
    Spicy Nuts, **'82** 161
    Walnuts, Chinese Fried, **'81** 254
  Okra Rellenos, **'97** 156
  Olive Cups, Greek, **'99** 221
  Olive Quiche Appetizers, **'86** 159
  Olives, Balsamic Marinated, **'02** 135
  Olives, Caliente Marinated, **'95** 177
  Olives, Herb-Marinated, **'92** 176
  Olives, Lemon-Garlic, **'94** 118
  Onion Blossom, **'94** 226
  Onion Crescent Crunch Sticks, **'90** 206
  Onions, Rosemary Roasted, **'98** 16
  Onion Toasties, **'97** 225
  Orange-Almond Snack Balls, **'95** 214
  Orange-Berry Appetizer, **'85** 81
  Orange Halves, Broiled, **'85** 288
  Oyster Nachos, Texas, **'87** 39
  Oysters à la Casino, **'80** 296
  Oysters Annapolis, **'89** 195
  Oysters, Barbecued, **'82** 247
  Oysters Bienville, Baked, **'90** 27
  Oysters Buccaneer, **'87** 40
  Oysters Chesapeake, **'92** 254
  Oysters, Creamed, **'92** 254
  Oysters, Fried Bacon-Wrapped, **'02** 103
  Oysters in Patty Shells, **'85** 257
  Oysters Italiano, Baked, **'89** 97
  Pasta Bites, Pesto-Cheese, **'87** 251
  Pears, Pineapple-Honey, **'86** 94
  Pecans
    Barbecued Pecans, **'83** 222
    Christmas Eve Pecans, **'91** 276
    Christmas Pecans, **'03** 300

    Citrusy Pecans, **'03** 292; **'04** 146
    Coffee 'n' Spice Pecans, **'88** 256
    Curried Pecans, **'91** 208
    Hot-and-Spicy Pecans, **'89** 161
    Hot Pepper Pecans, **'85** 4
    Hot Smoky Pecans, **'98** 173
    Mexico Nuts, **'01** 27
    Orange-Glazed Pecans, **'97** 225
    Orange Pecans, **'87** 292
    Party Nuts, Chesapeake Bay, **'03** 179
    Pear-Pecan Appetizers, **'96** 262
    Pepper Pecans, **'87** 137; **'93** 79
    Roasted Bacon Pecans, **'96** 262
    Roasted Pecans, Creole, **'01** 241
    Salted Pecans, Southern, **'80** 285
    Savory Southern Pecans, **'95** 240
    Smoky Pecans, **'01** 168
    Spiced Pecans, **'79** 296; **'80** 31
    Spicy Pecans, **'93** 279
    Sticks, Pecan, **'01** 242
    Sugar and Spice Pecans, **'82** 297
    Sugar-and-Spice Pecans, **'86** 121
    Sweet-and-Spicy Pecans, **'92** 321; **'00** 334; **'01** 20
    Sweet-and-Spicy Texas Pecans, **'02** 306
    Toasted Chili Pecans, **'85** 154
    Toasted Pecans, **'84** 321; **'86** 229; **'03** 300
    Toasted Pecans, Buttery, **'88** 77
  Pepper Feet, **'93** 258
  Pepperoni Pie Hors d'Oeuvres, **'98** 251
  Pepperoni Rolls, Ground-, **'83** 244
  Peppers, Marinated Roasted, **'92** 176
  Peppers, Stuffed Hungarian Yellow Banana, **'00** 132
  Peppers with Balsamic Vinaigrette, Roasted, **'94** 128
  Pesto Rounds, Toasted, **'94** 289
  Pickles, French-Fried, **'82** 77
  Pickles, Fried Dill, **'84** 206
  Pineapple and Strawberries, Skewered, **'84** 251
  Pineapple Delight, Fresh, **'79** 111
  Pineapple Spritz, **'86** 94
  Piroshki, **'92** 84
  Pistachio Twists, **'02** 164
  Pita Bread Triangles, **'88** 211
  Pita Chips, **'89** 19; **'91** 138
  Pita Pizza Snack, **'94** 193
  Pita Wedges, Garlic, **'93** 98
  Pizza Bites, **'95** 244
  Pizza-Burger Snacks, **'84** 30
  Pizza, Ham-and-Pineapple, **'96** 169
  Pizza Horns, **'89** 214
  Pizza, Mexican, **'99** 119
  Pizza Party Snacks, **'86** 262
  Pizza Pumpkins, **'98** 255
  Pizzas, Appetizer, **'89** M118
  Pizzas, Cocktail, **'79** 110
  Pizza Slices, **'84** 269
  Pizza Snacks, **'01** 231
  Pizza Snacks, Tasty Little, **'79** 248
  Pizzas, Pita, **'89** 19
  Pizza Squares, **'87** 168
  Pizzas, Quick Little, **'88** 227
  Pizza Turnovers, Little, **'85** 327
  Pizzettes, Party, **'80** 192
  Plantain Chips, **'95** M203
  (Plantain Chips), Tostones de Plátano, **'92** 158
  Pop Graham Munchies, **'96** 28
  Pork Rounds, Sesame, **'89** 122
  Pork Strips, Marinated, **'92** 219
  Pork Tenderloin on Cornmeal Biscuits, **'04** 257
  Pork Tenderloin with Miniature Buttermilk Biscuits, Honey-Mustard, **'02** 103
  Pork Tenderloin with Mustard Sauce, **'03** 238
  Potato-Pea Soup, **'94** 90
  Potato Shell Appetizers, **'89** M119
  Potato Skins, Baked, **'86** 81

Potato Skin Snack, '91 18
Power Munch, '96 180
Puff Nibbles, '84 191
Puffs, Cajun Hot, '94 277
Pull-Apart Ring, Southwestern, '03 298
Quesadillas, Poblano-and-Corn, '01 333
Quesadilla Torta, '97 325
Quiche, South-of-the-Border, '93 321
Quiche Squares, '84 222
Quiches, Tarragon Cocktail, '84 127
Raisin-Granola Treats, '92 22
Raspberry Party Puffs, '90 170
Ravioli, St. Louis Toasted, '95 117
Ravioli, Sweet, '91 107
Relish Tree, Christmas, '84 257
Reuben Rolls, Snappy, '02 58
Reubens, Golden-Baked Mini, '01 62
Reubens, Party, '90 61
Riblets, Sweet-and-Sour, '85 276
Rice Balls, '81 51
Rice with Spring Vegetables, '96 132
Risotto with Greens, '96 132
Risotto with Shellfish and Peas, '96 131
Roasted Red Pepper Rollups, '98 285
Rolls, Blue Cheese, '00 210
Rolls with Thai Dipping Sauce, Summer, '97 236
Rollups, Mediterranean, '00 277
Rosettes, Savory, '91 107
Rumaki, '80 136
Rumaki, Scallop, '98 M173
Rye Appetizers, Party, '86 262
Salami Rollups, '90 226
Salmon Ball, '80 149; '86 262
Salmon, Drizzled Smoked, '88 91
Salmon Log, '81 22
Salmon Party Log, '98 154
Salmon Party Roll, '83 127
Samosas, '89 266; '96 239
Samurai 'shrooms, '93 258
Sandwiches, Apple Party, '92 234
Sandwiches, Asparagus Spear, '84 165
Sandwiches, Bacon-Olive Party, '04 196
Sandwiches, Bread Basket of, '86 126
Sandwiches, Calla Lily, '91 106
Sandwiches, Chicken-Mandarin Orange Spread,
    '04 259
Sandwiches, Cucumber, '90 81; '94 14; '97 99
Sandwiches, Cucumber-Salmon-Watercress, '03 111
Sandwiches, Curried Tea, '91 314
Sandwiches, Dainty Cucumber, '81 119
Sandwiches, Double-Filled Party, '93 159
Sandwiches, Goat Cheese-Olive, '04 272
Sandwiches, Mini Muffuletta Bacon-Olive Party,
    '04 196
Sandwiches, Olive-Nut Spread, '04 259
Sandwiches, Party Ham, '97 240
Sandwiches, Rolled Olive, '01 241
Sandwiches, Stacking, '86 127
Sandwiches, Tiny Ham-and-Cheese, '99 87
Sandwiches, Turkey Tea, '99 86
Sandwiches, Victoria, '94 16
Sandwiches, Watercress, '90 82
Sandwiches, Watercress-Cucumber, '97 108
Sandwiches with Cranberry-Coriander Conserve,
    Pork Tenderloin, '04 286
Sandwiches with Dill, Cucumber-Salmon, '02 131
Sandwich Wreath, Festive, '86 333
Saté Mixed Grill with Spicy Peanut Sauce, '04 134
Sausage-Apple Balls, '90 85
Sausage-Bacon Rollups, '88 51
Sausage Balls, '98 93
Sausage-Mushroom-Phyllo Bites, '89 284
Sausage Party Ryes, '89 315
Sausage Pinwheels, '80 209; '93 238

Sausage Quesadillas, '90 118
Sausage, Sweet-and-Sour, '88 296
Sausages with Mustard Sauce, Smoked, '81 56
Scallop Appetizer, '86 155
Scallop Appetizers, Flaky, '86 327
Scallops, Bacon-Wrapped, '87 94
Scallops in Vermouth-Cream Sauce, '96 49
Scallops with Orange-Honey Sauce, Bacon-
    Wrapped, '97 236
Seafood Appetizer, Layered, '88 2
Seafood Mold, Chilled, '86 70
Seafood Tartlets, '87 247
Sea Scallops with Tomato Puree, Seared, '97 201
Seeds, Santa Fe, '02 145
Sesame Bites, '88 67
Seviche Cocktail, '83 258
Shortbread, Blue Cheese-Walnut, '03 108
Shortbread, Cajun-Benne Seed, '03 108
Shortbread, Herbed-Feta Cheese, '03 109
Shortbread, Jalapeño-Pecan, '03 108
Shortbread, Pesto, '03 108
Shrimp. *See also* **APPETIZERS/Canapés, Dips,
    Spreads and Fillings.**
    Afterburners, '03 159
    Bacon-Shrimp Bites, '98 234; '99 213
    Bacon, Shrimp 'n', '98 222
    Balls, Curried Shrimp, '94 180
    Barbecue Shrimp, '96 210; '97 58; '00 30
    Bayou, Shrimp, '88 261
    Biscuits, Shrimp-and-Grits, '02 313
    Boiled Shrimp, Spicy, '84 289
    Boiled Shrimp with Cocktail Sauce, '79 151
    Braised Shrimp with Garlic Rémoulade, '98 133
    Bundles with Chive Butter Sauce, Crispy Shrimp,
        '03 91
    Butter on Crostini, Shrimp, '04 259
    Cheese Appetizer, Shrimp-and-, '01 134
    Chilled Shrimp with Rémoulade Sauce, '02 134
    Cocktail, Mexican Shrimp, '00 249
    Cocktail Shrimp, '87 173
    Cocktail, Shrimp, '96 174
    Coconut-Beer Shrimp, '85 230
    Coconut Fried Shrimp, '96 248
    Coconut Shrimp with Mustard Sauce, '02 245
    Croustades, Shrimp, '97 23
    Dilled Shrimp, '88 150
    Dippers, Shrimp, '84 324
    Double-Dip Shrimp, '99 112
    Garlic-and-Rosemary Shrimp, '01 101; '04 52
    Grilled Jerk Shrimp with Creamy Tomatillo
        Sauce, '01 332
    Herbed Jalapeño Cheese, Shrimp with, '87 112
    Kebabs, Appetizer Shrimp, '91 251
    Kebabs, Shrimp, '80 150
    Key West Shrimp, '94 278
    Manale, Shrimp, '86 268
    Marinated Shrimp and Artichokes, '97 89;
        '98 335
    Marinated Shrimp and Cucumber, '91 166
    Marinated Shrimp, Icy, '84 215
    Marinated Shrimp with Capers, '00 279
    Marinated Shrimp, Zesty, '87 173
    Miniquiches, Shrimp, '87 146
    Mold, Shrimp, '87 94
    Mold with Asparagus, Shrimp, '93 214
    Mushrooms, Shrimp-Stuffed, '80 M135; '99 324
    Oven-Fried Shrimp with Marmalade Dip, '99 324
    Pickled Shrimp, '94 182
    Pickle, Shrimp-in-a-, '86 326
    Pineapple Appetizer, Shrimp-, '85 80
    Pizza Wedges, Shrimp, '89 158
    Puffs, Shrimp, '96 211; '98 316
    Rémoulade, Galatoire's Shrimp, '04 103
    Rémoulade, Shrimp, '83 173

Rock Shrimp Conga, '80 2
Rolls with Sweet Soy Sauce, Jumbo Shrimp,
    '03 248
Rounds, Shrimp, '98 167
Salsa Picante with Shrimp, '92 210
Sandwiches, Open-Faced Shrimp-Cornbread,
    '02 141
Sesame Shrimp, '95 92
Sherried Garlic Shrimp, '92 175
Skewers with Vegetable Salsa, Shrimp, '98 32
Smoked Shrimp, Citrus-Marinated, '95 114
Smoked Shrimp, Stove-Top, '01 168
Steamed Shrimp, '03 206
Tangy Shrimp, '04 18
Tartlets, Shrimp, '00 71
Toast, Shrimp, '86 91; '00 109
Tortilla Bites, '95 42
Tostadas, Shrimp-and-Black Bean, '93 204
Tree, Shrimp, '83 320; '84 288; '85 318
Vegetable Appetizer, Shrimp-and-, '97 161
Snackwiches, '88 172
Snow Peas and Dip, Crunchy, '86 62
Snow Peas, Crab-Stuffed, '85 288
Snow Peas, Stuffed, '84 80
Spanakopita, '96 233
Spinach and Artichokes in Puff Pastry, '00 277
Spinach-and-Cheese Pastries, Greek, '96 76
Spinach-Artichoke-Tomato Puffs, '95 284
Spinach-Filled Phyllo Triangles, '84 52
Spinach Madeleine in Chafing Dish, '85 319
Spinach-Mushroom Cheesecake, '92 326
Spinach Puffs, '95 316
Spinach Quichelets, '87 67
Spinach Quiches, '01 241
Spinach Quiches, Miniature, '82 38
Spinach-Ricotta Phyllo Triangles, '88 212
Spinach Rollups, '98 251
Spinach Squares, '88 131
Spinach Strudels, '93 249
Spinach Supreme, Layered, '82 38
Spinach Tarts, '82 249
Spinach Triangles, Phyllo-, '87 53
Spreads and Fillings
    Aloha Spread, '83 93
    Antipasto Spread, '81 25
    Apple-Date Spread, '91 231; '92 67
    Apricot Brie Spread, '86 275
    Apricot-Cream Cheese Spread, '82 161; '87 158
    Artichoke-Cheese Spread, '04 294
    Artichoke-Crab Spread, Hot, '85 81
    Artichoke Hearts with Caviar, '79 142
    Artichoke-Parmesan Spread, '92 95
    Artichoke Spread, Chunky, '89 98
    Artichoke Spread, Hot, '79 110
    Avocado-Cheese Spread, Herbed, '98 335
    Beef Spread, Hot, '83 50; '84 M216
    Beef Spread in Puff Pastry, Chipped, '98 M335
    Beer Cheese, '98 82
    Beer Cheese Spread, '81 160; '94 123
    Beer-Cheese Spread, '85 69
    Black-Eyed Pea Spread, '86 77
    Blue Cheese Spread, '90 215; '95 92; '97 240
    Blue Cheese Spread with Walnuts, Buttery,
        '00 329
    Boursin Cheese Spread, Buttery, '94 301; '96 318
    Boursin Cheese Spread, Garlic, '94 301
    Braunschweiger-Onion Spread, '79 82
    Broccamoli Curry Spread, '88 55
    Caraway Spread, '85 276
    Carrot-Pecan Spread, '96 108
    Carrot Spread, Nutty, '94 123
    Catfish Spread, Best-Ever, '98 60
    Caviar-Artichoke Mound, '91 244
    Caviar-Cream Cheese Spread, '84 256

APPETIZERS, Spreads and Fillings
(continued)

Caviar Spread, Creamy, '92 58
Cheese-and-Orange Filling, '93 159
Cheese-Horseradish Spread, '84 222
Cheese-Olive Spread, '79 82
Cheese, Peppered Pimiento, '01 137
Cheese Spread, '86 135
Cheese Spread, Almond, '87 292
Cheese Spread, Confetti, '84 256
Cheese Spread, Creamy Sweet, '79 264
Cheese Spread, Fresh Basil-, '97 108
Cheese Spread, German, '79 82
Cheese Spread, Hawaiian, '87 158
Cheese Spread, Make-Ahead, '93 324
Cheese Spread, Mexican, '90 119
Cheese Spread, Peppered, '01 123
Cheese Spread, Tipsy, '80 150
Cheese Spread, Zippy, '85 4
Cheesy Beer Spread, '87 196
Chicken-Artichoke-Cheese Spread Gift Box,
    '00 328
Chicken Salad Party Spread, '88 M8
Chicken Salad Spread, Curried, '00 68
Chicken Spread, Festive, '87 158
Chicken Spread, Tasty, '84 193
Chickpea Spread, Creamy, '03 293; '04 146
Chile-Cheese Spread, '02 205
Chili Cheese Spread, '93 242
Chili-Cheese Spread, '99 336
Chive-Mustard Spread, '91 12
Chocolate Chip Cheese Loaves, '91 299
Chutney-Onion Cheese Spread, '01 94
Chutney Spread, Curried, '89 283
Clam Spread, Creamy, '91 274
Coconut-Cranberry Cheese Spread, '92 328
Corn-and-Walnut Spread, '96 26
Corned Beef Spread, '87 196
Crabmeat-Horseradish Spread, '90 292
Crabmeat Spread, '79 81
Crabmeat Spread, Layered, '83 127; '04 69
Crab Soufflé Spread, '85 4
Crab Spread, '93 167
Crab Spread, Baked, '80 86
Crab Spread, Best-Ever, '98 60
Crab Spread, Superb, '81 235
Cranberry Ambrosia-Cream Cheese Spread,
    '00 308
Cream Cheese Filling, '90 170
Cream Cheese Spread, Deviled, '81 235
Cream Cheese Spread, Fruited, '91 306; '93 79
Cream Cheese Spread, Nutty, '89 327
Cream Cheese Spread, Tri-Flavored, '98 134
Cucumber Spread, '79 295; '80 31
Curry-Almond Cheese Spread, '01 238
Curry Spread, '93 159
Date-Orange-Nut Spread, '02 59
Date-Walnut-Cheese Spread, '96 322
Dried Tomato-Cheese Spread, '90 204
Edam-Sherry Spread, '84 257
Egg Mound, Frosted, '79 33
Eggplant-Mushroom Spread, '92 156
Egg, Sour Cream, and Caviar Spread, '85 279
Feta Cheese Spread, '96 265
Fruit and Cheese Spread, '81 245
Fruit-and-Cheese Spread, Nutty, '87 246; '02 164
Fruit Spread, '85 135
Garbanzo Bean Spread, Herbed, '99 160
Garden Spread, '86 135
Garlic Spread, '85 111
Goat Cheese Spread, '02 198
Gouda Cheese Spread, '90 36

Green Onion-Cheese Spread, '92 24
Gruyère-Apple Spread, '81 160
Guacamole Spread, '90 119
Ham and Pimiento Spread, '80 285; '81 56
Ham Spread, Buttery, '95 93; '97 98
Ham Spread, Cold, '82 248
Ham Spread, Country, '87 8
Hearts of Palm Spread, '90 293
Herb-Cheese Spread, '91 124
Herb-Cream Cheese Spread, '83 24
Honey-Nut Spread, '87 157
Horseradish-Chive Cream, '02 313
Horseradish Spread, '90 243
Hummus, '96 158; '03 60
Hummus, Black-Eyed Pea, '03 60
Italian Spread, '85 135
Jalapeño-Cheese Spread, '82 248
Lemon-Raisin Spread, '01 48
Lentil Spread, '99 288
Liver Spread, '89 161
Liver Spread, Sherried, '80 86
Mayonnaise, Tex-Mex, '01 134
Mullet Spread, '94 159
Mushroom Spread, Hot, '81 190
Olive Spread, Creamy, '81 290
Olive Spread, Tomatoes with, '85 114
Oyster Spread, Smoked, '91 64
Party Bread Spread, '82 161
Party Spread, Spicy, '97 240
Peanut Butter Spread, '92 21
Pear-Cream Cheese Spread, '93 80
Pepper Spread, Roasted, '94 123
Pesto Goat Cheese, '03 110
Pesto, Lucinda's Garden, '01 100
Pimiento Cheese, Baked, '04 291
Pimiento Cheese, Hot, '87 173
Potato-Garlic Spread, Creamy, '02 35
Radish Spread, Fresh, '84 166
Raisin Spread, Creamy, '90 36
Roasted Red Bell Pepper Spread, '97 217
Salmon-and-Horseradish Spread, '87 146
Salmon Spread, '81 149
Salmon Spread, Smoked, '84 324; '98 285
Salmon Spread with Capers, Smoked, '98 49
Seafood Spread, '86 M58; '87 146
Seafood Spread, Grandma Reed's, '98 268
Shrimp Spread, '81 306; '85 135; '87 111; '93 205
Shrimp Spread, Chunky, '85 300; '86 18
Shrimp Spread, Curried, '87 158
Shrimp Spread, Tempting, '79 57
Shrimp Spread, Zippy, '90 36
Smoked Fish Spread, '92 305
Smoked Whitefish Spread, '92 58
Sombrero Spread, '87 111
Spinach-Bacon Spread, '92 M310
Spinach Spread, '88 132
Spinach Spread, Savory, '82 180
Sweet 'n' Sour Spread, '86 184
Swiss Cheese Spread, '90 60
Tomato-Cheese Spread, '81 157
Tomato-Cheese Spread, Fiery, '87 196
Tomato-Cheese Torte, '00 72
Tomato Spread, '94 123
Tuna Spread, '91 305
Tuna Spread, Chunky, '89 147
Tuna Tapenade, '95 127; '96 201
Turkey Party Spread, '83 282
Turkey Spread, Curried, '92 16
Vegetable Party Spread, '84 166
Vegetable Sandwich Spread, '85 135
Vegetable Spread, '90 144
Vegetable Spread, Garden, '93 184
Watercress Spread, '88 103
White Bean Spread, '95 279

Spring Rolls, '99 238
Spring Rolls with Sweet Chili Sauce, Shanghai,
    '01 236
Squash Nosh, '90 147
Squash, Spinach-Stuffed, '02 165
Stalks, Splendid, '93 258
Steak-and-Chestnut Appetizers, Marinated, '84 323
Strawberries, Spiked, '97 58
Strawberries, Stuffed, '98 155
Strawberries with Chocolate Cream, '85 81
Strawberries with Lemon Cream, '90 170
Strawberries with Walnuts, Stuffed, '85 122
Sugar Peas with Dip, '86 170
Sugar Plums, '92 281
Sugar Snap Pea Appetizers, '86 115
Swamp Sticks, '95 274
Sweet Potato Chips, '91 138; '93 332; '95 M203
Sweet Potato Chips with Blue Cheese, '93 290
Tabbouleh, '88 211
Taco Appetizer, Layered, '84 206
Taco Teasers, '01 134
Tamale Balls, Tangy, '89 60
Tamales, Miniature, '85 154
Tapas with Spicy Ranch Dip, Tortellini, '98 318
Tapenade, '01 70
Tartlets, Country Ham-and-Asparagus, '98 82
Tartlets, Creamy Citrus, '02 136
Tartlets, Raspberry-Brie, '04 287
Tarts, Party, '95 90
Toasted Appetizers, '94 167
Toast Points, '93 270
Toast Strips, Seasoned, '93 98
Tomato Appetizers, Oven-Baked, '95 172
Tomato Bites, '84 80
Tomatoes, Cucumber-Stuffed Cherry, '88 262
Tomatoes, Honey-Baked, '02 166
Tomatoes Rockefeller, '97 169
Tomatoes, Stuffed Cherry, '84 160; '88 95, 212;
    '92 25
Tomatoes, Tuna-Stuffed Cherry, '89 214
Tomato Soup, Appetizer, '86 258
Tomato Soup, Savory, '94 91
Tomato Tapas, Two-, '00 308
Tortilla Appetizers, Tex-Mex, '86 297
Tortilla Bites with Sesame-Soy Dipping Sauce,
    '02 145
Tortilla Chips, '91 137
Tortilla Chips, Corn, '91 17
Tortilla Chips, Light, '91 257
Tortilla Dippers, Rolled, '86 4
Tortilla Espanola, '92 175
Tortilla Snacks, Pesto, '89 19
Tortilla Snack, Two-Cheese, '90 119
Tostadas, Party, '98 M33
Tostados, Hot Chile Salsa with Homemade, '88 115
Tuna Amandine, '02 165
Tuna Mound, '80 276
Tuna Nachos, '95 127; '96 201
Tuna-Pecan Ball, '87 94
Turkey Appetizers, '91 314
Turkey, Country-Fried Wild, '94 306
Turkey Sausage Turnovers, '95 239
Turkey-Spinach Rollups, '00 178
Turnovers, Meat, '86 326
Vegetable Appetizer, Tarragon, '83 277
Vegetable Juice Appetizer, Hot, '93 324
Vegetable Nachos, '91 17
Vegetable Party Tray, Fresh, '82 122
Vegetable Platter with Creamy Honey-Herb Dip,
    '98 135
Vegetable Rollups, '98 134
Vegetables Italian, Marinated, '90 242
Vegetables, Marinated, '94 183; '96 213
Vegewiches, '99 86

Veggie Bites, '91 171
Veggie Rollup, '01 109
Veggies, Fried, '96 19
Venison Tenderloin Appetizers, '88 249
Watermelon and Prosciutto, '98 164
Wienie Rollups, '02 186
Wings and Ribs, Thai, '97 M225
Wonton Chips, Baked, '91 138; '99 138
Wonton Chips, Cinnamon-and-Sugar, '91 138
Wonton Chips, Garlic, '91 138
Wonton Chips, Lemon-and-Herb, '91 138
Wonton Nibbles, '85 287
Zucchini Bites, Scalloped, '91 165
Zucchini Caviar, '88 212
Zucchini French Fries, '82 78
Zucchini Fries, '90 147
Zucchini Hors d'Oeuvres, '80 151
Zucchini Pizzas, '88 212
Zucchini-Shrimp Appetizers, '89 311
Zucchini with Cocktail Sauce, French Fried,
   '86 146
APPLES
Acorn Squash, Apple-Stuffed, '83 296; '84 285
Bacon, Sweet Apple, '03 305
Baked. *See also* **APPLES/Desserts.**
   à l'Orange, Baked Apples, '90 280
   Apples, Baked, '79 276; '86 40
   Carrot-Apple Bake, '98 232
   Carrot Bake, Apple-, '93 304
   Cheese Bake, Apple-, '92 225
   Easy Baked Apples, '82 22, 238
   Ham and Apples, Baked, '82 M237
   Honey-Baked Apple Quarters, '86 93
   Honey-Baked Apples, '83 234; '84 244
   Honey-Baked Apples and Pear, '97 303
   Imperial Baked Apples, '82 273
   Maple Baked Apples, '85 232
   Mincemeat-Filled Apples, Baked, '80 276
   Orange-Pecan Baked Apples, '85 45
   Orange Sauce, Baked Apples with, '84 314
   Sharpe Baked Apples, '99 83
   Squash and Apple Bake, '79 210
   Stuffed Baked Apples, '89 217
   Sweet Potato-Apple Bake, '83 25; '86 282
Balls, Sausage-Apple, '90 85
Beets and Apples, '80 137; '88 155
Beverages
   Aztec Gold, '99 160
   Berry Sparkler, Apple-, '93 104
   Berry Sparkler, Apple, '94 100
   Cider, Apple, '95 198
   Cider, Apple-Orange, '92 20
   Cider, December, '91 260
   Cider, Holiday, '82 264
   Cider, Hot Apple, '90 21, 225
   Cider, Hot Burgundy, '96 306
   Cider, Hot Mexican, '87 213
   Cider, Hot Molasses, '98 242
   Cider, Hot Mulled, '79 205; '84 323
   Cider, Hot Mulled Apple-Orange, '97 301
   Cider, Hot Spiced, '99 248
   Cider, Hot Spiced Apple, '84 318
   Cider Ice, '83 162
   Cider, Mulled, '91 209; '94 227
   Cider, Mulled Apple, '92 208
   Cider, Mulled Cranberry, '99 278
   Cider Nog, Hot, '98 241
   Cider Nog, Hot Apple, '84 42
   Cider, Red Apple, '80 259
   Cider Sipper, Apple, '02 220
   Cider Sipper, Apricot-Apple, '02 220
   Cider Sour, Bourbon, '98 242
   Cider, Sparkling Apple, '88 276
   Cider, Spirited Apple, '96 214

Cider Tea, '98 241; '99 335
Cooler, Apple, '90 14
Cooler, Minted Apple, '88 169
Hot Apple Pie, '99 321
Juice, Hot Apple, '86 270
Juice, Perky Cinnamon-Apple, '90 22
Juice, Sparkling Apple, '95 141
Julep, Apple, '86 103, 215
Lemonade, Apple, '89 212; '03 169
Limeade, Pink Apple, '89 46
Mint Juleps, Apple, '97 120
Punch, Apple Bobbing, '99 246
Punch, Apple-Tea, '85 82
Punch, Hot Apple, '84 324
Punch, Hot Spiced, '80 250
Punch, Party Apple, '00 271
Shrub, Shenandoah Apple Juice, '79 282
Tea, Cranberry-Apple, '88 169
Tea, Hot Apple-Cinnamon, '87 57
Tea, Iced Apple, '98 84
Tea, Johnny Appleseed, '85 23
Braised Carrots, Apples, and Celery, '96 107
Breads
Apple Bread, '79 205; '80 226
Banana-Apple Bread, '85 250
Biscuit Braid, Apple-Pecan, '02 326
Blue Cheese-Apple Sunburst, '94 245
Buns, Cinnamon-Apple Breakfast, '00 M198
Butter Bread, Apple, '84 49; '86 69
Cheddar-Apple Bread, '96 83
Danish, Deep-Dish Apple, '86 161
Date-Nut Ring, Apple-, '90 212
French Toast, Baked Apple, '03 M283
Loaf, Fresh Apple, '82 206
Loaf, Spiced Apple, '79 215
Muffins, Apple, '83 96; '84 193; '87 23; '99 234
Muffins, Apple-Bran, '85 M89
Muffins, Apple-Carrot, '91 213
Muffins, Apple-Cinnamon Oat Bran, '89 106
Muffins, Fresh Apple, '84 264
Muffins, Pumpkin-Apple, '96 242
Muffins, Spiced Apple, '79 60
Muffins, Spicy Apple-Oat, '86 45
Nut Bread, Apple-, '79 12; '85 281
Nut Bread, Fresh Apple-, '87 256
Pinwheel, Quick Apple, '85 42
Pull-Apart Bread, Apple, '86 330
Swirl Bread, Apple, '85 4
Zucchini-Apple Bread, '87 255
Breakfast Apples, Spiced, '00 193
Breakfast Delight, '93 195
Brussels Sprouts with Apples, '02 243
Burgers, Apple, '86 137
Burgers, Apple-Bacon, '99 202
Butter, Apple, '79 200; '81 217; '92 311
Butter, Half-Hour Apple, '81 203
Butternut Squash, Apple-Stuffed, '81 232
Butter, Oven Apple, '00 237
Butter, Slow Cooker Apple, '97 235
Butter, Spiced Oven Apple, '00 237
Cabbage with Apples and Franks, '87 42
Casserole, Apple-Cheese, '84 287
Casserole, Apple-Egg, '85 44
Casserole, Apple Ham, '79 213
Casserole, Cranberry-Apple, '83 311
Casserole, Squash and Apple, '79 209
Casserole, Sweet Potato-and-Apple, '94 280
Casserole, Sweet Potatoes-and-Apple, '90 228
Chard with Onion and Apple, Sautéed, '98 48
Cheese Delight, Apple-and-, '98 97
Chicken, Apple, '85 57
Chicken Breasts, Apple-Bacon Stuffed, '99 313
Chutney, Apple, '92 309
Chutney, Pear-Apple, '89 141

Chutney, Sweet-'n'-Hot Apple, '96 14
Chutney, Sweet Potato, '99 45
Chutney, Tomato-Apple, '84 180
Cider Sauce, '87 224
Cider Sauce, Cheddar-, '98 242
Cinnamon Apples, Rosy, '87 M37
Coffee Cake, Apple, '81 249; '97 326
Coffee Cake, Apple-Pecan, '84 242
Coffee Cake, Fresh Apple, '92 32
Collards with Apples, '98 250
Conserve, Apple-Cranberry, '82 308
Cooked Apples, '93 338
Cornbread-Sausage-Apple Pie, '87 171
Crêpes, Apple Breakfast, '97 331
Curried Apples, '93 252
Desserts. *See also* **APPLES/Pies and Tarts.**
Bake, Apple-Almond, '02 M209
Bake, Cherry-Apple, '04 29
Bake, Cinnamon-Apple, '04 29
Baked Alaska, Apple, '80 226
Baked Apples, Pecan-and-Dried Fruit, '03 269
Baked Apples with Cookie Crumbs, Orange,
   '95 271
Bars, Apple Butter, '84 153
Betty, Apple Brown, '83 213
Betty, Pineapple-Apple, '85 46
Brandied Apples, '81 248
Brandied Apples and Cream, '82 M237
Brownies, Frosted Apple, '86 216
Bundles, Quick Apple, '04 242
Cake, Apple, '83 312; '84 262
Cake, Apple Cider Pound, '84 10
Cake, Apple Coconut, '80 226
Cake, Apple-Ginger Upside-Down, '94 180
Cake, Apple-Nut, '87 76; '96 268
Cake, Apple-Pecan, '92 167
Cake, Apple Pie, '82 226; '86 301
Cake, Apple Pudding, '01 47
Cake, Apple Slice, '85 93
Cake, Apple Spice, '92 225
Cake, Apple-Walnut, '94 242
Cake, Covered Apple, '89 317
Cake, Dried-Apple, '79 13
Cake, Dried Apple Stack, '85 242
Cake, Fresh Apple-Date, '83 300
Cake, Golden Apple-Oatmeal, '86 301
Cake, Honey-Apple, '99 210
Cake Squares, Apple-Date Dream, '85 10
Cake Squares, Apple-Orange, '84 150
Cake with Cream Cheese Frosting, Chunky
   Apple, '01 185
Candied Red Apples, '81 217
Candy Apple Creations, '94 256
Candy Apples, '84 243; '01 M205
Caramel Apples, '79 220; '89 M231; '03 M216
Caramel Apples, Black-and-White, '03 M216
Caramel Apples, Calypso, '03 M216
Caramel Apples, Old English, '85 231
Caramel-Peanut Apples, '93 M244
Charlotte, Apple, '99 84
Cheesecake, Dieter's Apple, '86 318
Chimichangas, Apple, '95 43
Chocolate Apples on a Stick, '96 255
Cinnamon Apples with Brandied Date Conserve,
   '85 315
Cobbler à la Mode, Apple, '97 16
Cobbler, Apple-Berry, '04 330
Cobbler, Apple Dumpling, '04 29
Cobbler, Apple-Gingerbread, '03 21; '04 219
Cobbler, Apple-Pecan, '84 M198
Cobbler, Apple-Pecan Pie, '04 200
Cobbler, Apple-Vinegar Biscuit, '01 215
Cobbler, Apple Walnut, '79 154
Cobbler, Apple-Walnut, '81 248

APPLES, Desserts
(continued)

Cobbler, Country Apple, **'99** 255
Cobbler, Cranberry-and-Apple, **'84** 306; **'90** 294
Cobbler, Easy Apple, **'83** 174
Cobbler for Two, Apple, **'85** 261
Cobbler, New-Fashioned Apple, **'91** 221
Cobbler, Sweet Potato-Apple, **'04** M232
Cobbler with Cinnamon Biscuits, Cranberry-
    Apple, **'99** 256
Cobbler with Oatmeal Muffin Crust, Caramel
    Apple-Pear, **'04** 201
Compote, Apple-Cranberry, **'04** 237
Compote, Apricot-Apple, **'98** 17
Cookies, Apple Butter Spice, **'79** 291
Cookies, Apple-Filled, **'92** 311
Cookies, Apple-Nut, **'80** 228
Cookies, Apple-Oatmeal, **'85** 215; **'90** 218
Cookies, Fresh Apple, **'84** 36
Cranberry Apple Dessert, **'80** 253
Cranberry Apples, **'99** 246
Crisp, Apple, **'84** 122; **'98** 215
Crisp, Apple-Cheese, **'92** 235
Crisp, Delicious Apple, **'82** 303
Crisp, Granola Apple, **'85** 78
Crisp, Oatmeal Cherry-Apple, **'90** M16
Crisp, Orange-Apple, **'80** 295
Crisp, Tart Apple, **'92** 226
Crumble, Whole Wheat-Apple, **'90** M213
Crunch, Apple-Blueberry, **'02** 128
Crunch, Apple-Cranberry, **'86** 300; **'87** 178
Crunch, Apple-Nut, **'82** M238
Cupcakes, Apple-Nut, **'82** 279
Delight, Apple, **'80** 109
Dumplings, Apple, **'82** 273; **'00** 96
Dumplings, Apple-Cranberry, **'00** 16
Dumplings, Cinnamon Apple, **'97** M330
Dumplings, Old-Fashioned Apple, **'84** 226
Dumplings, Quick Apple, **'01** 185
Dumplings with Maple-Cider Sauce, Apple,
    '95 288
Dumplings with Orange Hard Sauce, Apple,
    '88 224
Dutch Apple Dessert, Creamy, **'91** 19
Enchiladas, Apple, **'99** 63
Filling, Apple-Date, **'83** 301
Filling, Dried Apple, **'85** 242; **'87** 229
Flambé, Hot Apples and Rum, **'92** 88
Flan, Apple, **'81** 309
Foldovers, Apple, **'84** 136
Fritter Rings, Apple, **'88** 44
Fritters, Apple, **'81** 105; **'82** 273; **'85** 14; **'97** 153
Fritters, Apple Holiday, **'86** 314
Fritters with Lemon Sauce, Apple, **'01** 184
Goblins, Apple, **'94** 256
Grahams, Caramel-Apple, **'04** M183
Grahams, Peanut Butter-Apple, **'04** M183
Honey-Baked Apple Dessert, **'90** M213
Ice, Cranberry-Apple, **'82** 290
Kuchen, Apple, **'79** 24
Melting Apples, **'88** 19
Mousse, Cran-Apple, **'93** 255
Napoleon, Giant Apple, **'99** 282
Napoleons, Caramel-Apple, **'01** M313
Pears, Saucy Apples 'n', **'96** 72
Pecan Apples, Taffy, **'99** 247
Pizza, Apple-Pineapple Dessert, **'00** 313
Poached Apples, Spicy, **'90** M141
Pudding, Apple-Raisin Bread, **'88** 175
Pudding, Apple Rice, **'91** 217
Pudding with Hot Rum Sauce, Apple-Nut,
    '79 86

Pudding with Vanilla-Nutmeg Sauce, Pineapple-
    Apple Bread, **'02** 208
Quesadillas, Apple, **'99** 248
Quesadillas, Dessert, **'02** 54
Rings, Apple, **'85** 232
Roasted Apples, Orange-Ginger, **'01** 184
Roll, Apple, **'82** 178
Rolls, Cinnamon-Apple, **'02** 215
Rolls, Luscious Apple, **'88** 225
Rugelach, Apple, **'97** 220
Sauce, Apple Ambrosia, **'89** 95
Sauce, Apple-Cinnamon, **'93** 42
Sauce, Apple Dessert, **'87** M165
Sauce, Spicy Apple Dessert, **'82** 177
Shortcake, Quick Apple, **'93** 42
Shortcakes, Caramel-Apple, **'03** 194
Snack Squares, Apple-Oat, **'00** 332
Sorbet, Cran-Apple Spice, **'93** 153
Squares, Apple, **'92** 311
Squares, Apple-Gingerbread, **'03** 297
Squares, Sour Cream Apple, **'82** 262
Strudel, Apple, **'85** 259; **'89** 267; **'92** 269;
    '97 238
Strudel, Autumn-Apple, **'98** 253
Stuffed Apples, **'99** 247
Sugar-Crusted Apples in Walnut-Phyllo Baskets,
    '93 210
Sundae, Hot Apple Spice, **'92** 239
Sundaes, Spicy Apple Ice Cream, **'86** M195
Topping, Apple-Nut, **'93** 162
Topping, Spicy Apple, **'87** 125
Turnovers, Baked Apple, **'93** 338
Turnovers, Delicious Apple, **'86** 25
Turnovers, Fried Apple, **'81** 161
Turnovers, Orange-Apple, **'99** 294
Turnovers, Puffy Apple, **'87** 276
Waffles with Apples and Caramel, Gingerbread,
    '98 M237
Dip, Apple, **'93** 205; **'96** M190
Dressing, Andouille Sausage, Apple, and Pecan,
    '02 249
Dressing, Apple, **'92** 216
Dressing, Sausage-Apple, **'93** 305; **'94** 296
Dried Apple Side Dish, **'92** 226
Dried Lady Apple Slices, **'95** 263
Fillets, Apple-Carrot Stuffed, **'88** M192
Filling, Apple, **'85** 5; **'96** 53; **'97** 239
French Toast, Apple, **'98** 55
Glazed Apples, **'99** 233
Glazed Apples, Honey-, **'90** 125
Glazed Apples, Orange-, **'82** 51
Golden Apples, **'82** 254
Grilled Ham and Apples, **'96** M303
Honey-Yogurt Apples, **'92** 46
Jelly, Apple, **'82** 149
Jelly, Apple-Mint, **'87** 134
Jelly, Crabapple, **'79** 120; **'81** 217
Jelly, Spiced Apple, **'95** 251
Juice, Nectarines in Apple, **'83** 183
Marmalade, Apple, **'79** 120
Minted Apples, **'99** 231; **'00** 21
Minted Apples, Lamb Chops with, **'00** 20
Minted Apples, Pork Chops with, **'00** 21
Monster Mouths, **'95** 274
Muesli, **'89** 208
Omelet Stack, Apple, **'94** 50
Pancake, Apple-Filled, **'86** 96
Pancakes, Apple, **'01** 24
Pancakes, Apple-Topped, **'93** 339
Pancakes with Caramel Sauce, Baked Apple,
    '04 249
Pancakes with Cider Sauce, Spicy Apple,
    '87 224
Pasta with Apple, Curried, **'02** 68

Pies and Tarts
Almond-Apple Tart, **'01** 253
Amandine Pie, Apple-, **'89** 215
Apple Pie, American, **'91** 197
Applesauce Pie, **'98** 259; **'99** 26; **'01** 213
Apricot-Apple Crumb Tart, **'94** 60
Autumn Apple Pie, **'79** 205
aux Pommes, La Tarte, **'80** 125
Berry-Apple Pie, **'88** 251
Blackberry-Apple Pie, **'87** 130
Bourbon Pie, Apple-, **'95** 302
Brandied Apple Tarts, **'96** 284; **'99** 28
Brandy-Apple Pie, **'86** 301
Brandy Raisin-Apple Pie, **'83** 192
Bumbleberry Pie, **'97** 163
Caramel-Pecan Apple Pie, **'85** 247
Cheese Pastry, Apple Tart with, **'88** 225
Cheese Pie, Apple-, **'85** 284
Cider Pie, Apple, **'84** 227
Cinnamon Crème, Apple Pie with Warm, **'99** 337
Cinnamon Sauce, Apple Pie with Hot, **'88** 210
Cran-Apple Pie, **'92** 304
Cranberry-Apple Holiday Pie, **'81** M269
Cranberry-Apple Pie, **'79** 264
Cranberry-Apple-Raisin Pie, **'98** 270
Cranberry-Apple Tart, **'97** M316
Cranberry Pie, Apple-, **'97** 276; **'99** M269
Cranberry Tart, Rustic Apple-, **'01** M314
Cream Cheese Pie, Apple-, **'81** 247
Cream Cheese Tart, Apple-, **'96** 228
Creamed Apple Tart, **'94** 17
Cream Tart, Apple, **'84** 207
Custard Pie, Apple, **'88** 236
Custard Pie, Warm Apple-Buttermilk, **'99** 98
Deluxe Apple Tart, **'84** 227
Dutch Apple Pie, **'81** 105; **'82** 273
Easy-Crust Apple Pie, **'87** 11
Filling in a Jar, Apple Pie, **'95** 251
Fresh Apple Pie, **'84** 178
Fried Apple Pies, **'81** 217; **'86** 302; **'88** 112, 225;
    '94 61
Fried Pies, Delicious, **'83** 84
Georgie's Apple Pie, **'02** 325
Grandmother's Apple Pie, **'87** 212
Granny Smith Apple Pie, **'01** 143
Grated Apple Pie, **'83** 304
Holiday Apple Pie, **'87** 260
Honey Apple Pie, **'00** 331
Honeyed Apple-Cranberry Fried Pies, **'02** 214
Lemon-Apple Pie, Tart, **'80** 100
Lemon Chess Pie, Apple-, **'86** 220
Maple Pie, Apple-, **'97** 276
Mexican Apple Pie, **'94** 97
Mincemeat Pie, Apple-, **'85** 316
No-Crust Apple Pie, **'88** 204
Old-Fashioned Apple Pie, **'82** M299; **'88** 94
Pear-Apple Pie, Natural, **'88** 226
Pear Pie, Apple-, **'83** 249
Pear Pull-Up Pie, Apple-, **'98** 259
Pecan Tarts, Apple-, **'80** 282
Pineapple Pie, Apple-, **'97** 276
Praline-Apple Pie, **'99** 331
Raisin Brandy Pie, Apple-, **'89** 58
Red Apple Pie, **'79** 282
Upside-Down Apple Tart, **'98** 35
Upside-Down Southern Apple Pie, **'88** 226
Piggy Apple, **'94** 194
Poached Lemon Apples, Chilled, **'86** 182
Pockets, Toasted Cream Cheese-and-Apple, **'01** 200
Pork and Vegetables, Apple Cider, **'97** 210
Pork Chops, An Apple-a-Day, **'01** 35
Pork Chops and Apples, Baked, **'81** 10
Pork Chops, Apple, **'91** 198
Pork Chops, Apple-Crumb Stuffed, **'81** 234; **'82** 26

Pork Chops, Apple-Glazed, **'84** 212; **'87** 35
Pork Chops, Apple-Kraut, **'84** 50
Pork Chops, Apple-Sage Stuffed, **'04** 250
Pork Chops, Apple-Stuffed, **'79** 125
Pork Chops, Cider, **'02** 307; **'03** 271
Pork Chops, Glazed Apple, **'86** 300
Pork Chops, Rosemary, **'98** 329
Pork Chops, Sherry-Apple, **'88** 40
Pork Chops, Spicy Apple, **'87** 230
Pork Chops, Stuffed, **'02** 204
Pork Chops with Apples, Balsamic, **'03** 204
Pork Chops with Apples, Parmesan, **'93** 338
Pork Chops with Cornbread-Apple Stuffing, **'99** 14
Pork Chops with Crabapple Peaches, Broiled, **'81** 83
Pork Chops with Mustard-Glazed Apple and Onion,
　'01 47
Pork Chops with Pecans and Apples, Commune's
　Maple-Glazed, **'04** 102
Pork Cutlets, Apple-Glazed, **'92** 181
Pork Loin with Apples and Mushrooms, Roast,
　'92 218
Pork Tenderloin, Apple-Ginger, **'86** 75
Pork Tenderloin, Apple-Mushroom, **'95** 53
Pork Tenderloin with Apples, Celery, and Potatoes,
　Grilled, **'95** 161
Pot Roast, Spicy Apple, **'83** 7
Praline Sweet Potatoes and Apples, **'03** 260
Quail, Sage-Smoked Champagne, **'97** 164
Quesadillas, Apple Pie 'n' Cheddar, **'03** 61
Quiche, Crustless Sausage-Apple, **'87** 70
Red Cabbage, **'96** 272
Red Cabbage and Apples, **'85** 32
Red Cabbage, Braised, **'01** 193; **'02** 277
Red Cabbage, German-Style, **'98** 279
Relish, Apple, **'96** 323; **'97** 27
Relish, Apple-Celery, **'89** 141
Relish, Apple-Raisin, **'03** 83
Relish, Cran-Apple, **'84** 300
Relish, Cranberry, **'98** 310
Relish, Spicy Apple, **'84** M323
Ribs, Apple Barbecued, **'80** 111
Rice, Apple-Cinnamon, **'86** 249
Rice, Curried, **'04** 21
Rings, Cinnamon Apple, **'82** M237; **'90** 250
Rings, Cinnamon-Apple, **'85** 107
Rings, Fried Apple, **'81** 209
Rings, Honey Apple, **'80** 243
Rolls, Apple-Phyllo, **'88** 213
Salads
　Apple Salad, **'87** 233; **'00** 176
　Apricot Salad, Apple-, **'88** 121
　Aspic, Sunshine Apple, **'81** 73
　Avocado-Apple Salad with Maple-Walnut
　　Vinaigrette, **'04** 45
　Beet, Apple, and Walnut Salad, **'98** 269
　Beet Salad, Apple-, **'91** 237
　Blue Cheese Dressing, Apple Salad with, **'87** 103
　Blue Cheese-Pear-Apple Salad, **'81** 224
　Carrot Salad, Apple-, **'85** 22
　Cheesy Apple Salad, **'86** 301
　Cherry-Apple Salad, **'86** 31
　Chicken-Apple Salad, **'90** 216
　Cider Salad, Apple, **'83** 123
　Coleslaw, Apple, **'89** 315
　Coleslaw, Apple-Bacon, **'04** 181
　Congealed Apple Salad, **'85** 252
　Cranberry-Apple Salad, **'02** 255
　Crunch Salad, Apple, **'84** 232; **'86** 331
　Crunchy Apple Salad, **'80** 138
　Curried Apple-Raisin Salad, **'80** 24
　Double Apple Salad, **'84** 227
　English Pea-and-Apple Salad, **'87** 24
　Fennel-and-Apple Salad, **'00** 321
　Fresh Apple Salad, **'81** 207

Frozen Apple-Cream Salad, **'82** 80
Grapefruit-Apple Salad, **'89** 41
Greens with Apple and Brie Salad, **'93** 241
Greens with Seasoned Almonds and Tangy
　Balsamic Vinaigrette, Mixed, **'03** 101
Ham-and-Apple Salad, **'88** 139
Lemony Apple-Bran Salad, **'86** 223
Mold, Apple Cider Salad, **'85** 54
Mold, Cranberry-Apple, **'89** 277
Nut Salad, Apple-, **'80** 226
Peanut-Apple Salad, **'80** 5
Poppyseed Dressing, Apple Wedges with, **'86** 131
Rudolph's Apple Salad, **'02** 277
Sesame-Apple Toss, **'88** 21
Slaw, Apple-Carrot, **'92** 243
Slaw, Apple-Pineapple, **'79** 241
Slaw, Fresh Apple, **'81** 63
Slaw, Nutty Apple, **'88** 216
Slaw, Red Cabbage-and-Apple, **'87** 31; **'91** 309
Snow Salad, Apple, **'81** 224
Spicy Apple Salad, **'85** 215
Spinach-Apple Salad, **'90** 89; **'92** 13; **'97** 308
Spinach Salad, Apple-, **'97** 14; **'99** 222; **'02** 230
Stuffed Apple Ring Salad, **'91** 198
Stuffed Apple Salad, **'92** 266
Summer Apple Salad, **'80** 149
Sweet Potato-Apple Salad, **'96** 240
Swiss-Apple Salad, **'84** 81
Thai Green Apple Salad, **'99** 111
Triple Apple Salad, **'88** 122
Turkey-Apple Salad, **'88** 123; **'90** 181
Waldorf, Pineapple, **'97** 86
Waldorf Salad, **'89** 278; **'97** 204
Waldorf Salad, Congealed, **'82** 80
Waldorf Salad, Creamy, **'87** 311
Waldorf Salad, Deluxe, **'83** 81
Waldorf Salad, Frozen, **'79** 126; **'82** 145
Waldorf Salad, Jiffy, **'88** 100
Waldorf Salad, New Wave, **'92** 36
Waldorf Salad, Old-Fashioned, **'81** 295
Waldorf Salad, Pineapple, **'92** 97
Waldorf Salad, Southern Classic, **'92** 36
Waldorf Salad, Tropical, **'89** 12
Waldorf Salad, Winter, **'04** 245
Wild Rice-Green Apple Salad, **'92** 90
Zucchini Salad, Apple-and-, **'97** 216
Sandwiches, Apple, **'79** 164; **'80** 130
Sandwiches, Apple Breakfast, **'92** 332
Sandwiches, Apple-Cinnamon Breakfast, **'85** 298
Sandwiches, Apple Party, **'92** 234
Sandwiches, Curried Tuna-Apple, **'00** 247
Sandwiches, Sweet Smoky, **'97** 219
Sauce, Apple Barbecue, **'99** 173
Sauce, Apple-Bourbon, **'99** 142
Sauce, Apple-Horseradish, **'82** 229
Sauce, Apple-Pear, **'97** M272
Sauce, Cranberry-Apple, **'92** 203
Sauce, Double Cranberry-Apple, **'03** 231
Sausage-Apple Kraut Dinner, **'02** 234
Sausage-Apple Pie, Cornbread-, **'87** 171
Sausage Patties, Apples on, **'82** 120
Sauté, Chicken-Apple, **'97** 48
Sautéed Apples, Onions, and Pears over Spinach,
　'94 212
Scalloped Apples, **'84** 70; **'87** 156
Scalloped Sweet Potatoes with Apples, **'00** 253
Scallop, Yam-and-Apple, **'91** 199
Shells, Sweet Potatoes in Apple, **'85** 206
Shrunken Heads (Halloween Decor), **'01** 204
Soup, Chestnut, **'02** 272
Soup, Creamed Butternut-and-Apple, **'88** 228
Soup, Curried Acorn Squash-and-Apple,
　'03 221
Spareribs, Apple-Barbecue, **'90** 160

Spiced Apples, **'93** 123; **'03** 36
Spiced Apple Slices, **'83** 289
Spiced Apples, Skillet, **'83** 234; **'84** 244
Spread, Apple-Date, **'91** 231; **'92** 67
Spread, Feta-and-Apple, **'99** 106
Spread, Gruyère-Apple, **'81** 160
Squash, Apple-and-Pecan-Filled, **'88** 228
Squash, Apple-Stuffed, **'85** 206
Stir-Fry, Apple-Sesame-Chicken, **'92** 226
Stuffed Apples, Peanutty, **'85** 25
Stuffed Apples, Sweet Potato-, **'97** 216; **'00** 232
Stuffing, Apple-Almond, **'01** 184
Stuffing, Apple-Crumb, **'81** 234; **'82** 26; **'83** 39
Stuffing, Apple-Walnut, **'95** 289
Sweet-and-Sour Red Cabbage and Apples, **'00** 62
Sweet Potatoes and Apples, **'97** 249
Sweet Potatoes, Apple-Glazed, **'82** 303
Sweet Potatoes, Apple-Stuffed, **'88** 207
Sweet Potatoes, Cinnamon-Apple, **'95** M23
Sweet Potatoes Stuffed with Apples, **'82** 228
Syrup, Spiced Apple, **'79** 114
Tenderloin with Praline-Mustard Glaze, Apple-
　Stuffed, **'97** 216
Toast, Apple, **'81** 278
Topping, Apple, **'89** 107
Turkey, Apple Brandy, **'03** 230
Turkey, Apple-Rosemary Roasted, **'99** 252
Turkey Breast, Apple-Rosemary, **'99** 253
Veal Chops, Apple, **'87** 220
Vinaigrette, Apple Cider, **'98** 284; **'01** 306
Vinaigrette, Spinach Salad with Apple-Onion,
　'94 276
APPLESAUCE
Applesauce, **'90** 255; **'97** 252; **'00** 256
Bread, Applesauce-Honey Nut, **'87** 300
Bread, Applesauce Nut, **'81** 305
Bread, Applesauce-Pecan, **'90** 66
Bread, Bran-Applesauce, **'84** 229
Butter, Half-Hour Apple, **'81** 203
Cake, Applesauce, **'80** 270; **'96** 67
Cake, Applesauce Carrot, **'81** 202
Cake, Applesauce-Oatmeal, **'92** 119
Cake, Applesauce-Spice, **'83** 42
Cake, Applesauce Spice, **'89** 296
Cake, My Favorite Applesauce, **'87** 263
Cakes, Applesauce Snack, **'88** 215; **'89** 20
Cake Squares, Applesauce, **'86** 8
Cake with Bourbon Frosting, Applesauce,
　'88 236
Cobbler with Bourbon-Pecan Ice Cream, Caramel-
　Applesauce, **'00** 260
Dip, Apple-Berry, **'01** 109
Doughnuts, Applesauce, **'81** 203
Doughnuts, Applesauce Drop, **'90** 70
Dressing, Apple, **'83** 181
Fluff, Applesauce, **'91** 173
Fruitcake, Applesauce, **'83** 258
Gingerbread, Applesauce, **'94** 179
Hot Spiced Applesauce, **'01** 60
Loaf, Brandy Applesauce, **'81** 263
Muffins, Applesauce, **'84** 284; **'91** 141
Muffins, Applesauce Spice, **'88** 236
Muffins, Bite-Size Applesauce, **'82** 104
Oatmeal, Applesauce, **'89** 108
Onion Applesauce, Sweet, **'02** 319
Pancakes, Applesauce, **'79** 114
Pie, Applesauce, **'98** 259; **'99** 26; **'01** 213
Pudding, Applesauce-Graham Cracker, **'81** 34
Ribs, Apple Barbecued, **'80** 111
Salad Dressing, Honey-Applesauce, **'99** 210
Savory Applesauce, **'01** 47
Spicy Applesauce, **'82** 296
Squares, Applesauce-Spice, **'86** 248
Sweet Potatoes, Applesauce, **'91** 292; **'92** 256

APRICOTS
Bake, Sweet Potato-Apricot, '85 206
Beverages
Bellinis, Apricot, '99 145
Cooler, Apricot, '81 100
Cooler, Apricot Mint, '90 165
Cooler, Apricot-Orange-Carrot, '96 108
Coolers, Apricot, '99 29
Fruit Flip, Apricot, '91 18
Nectar, Hot Apricot, '81 265
Nectar, Mulled Apricot, '86 229
Punch, Apricot Spiced, '80 269
Shake, Apricot, '84 115
Sipper, Apricot-Apple Cider, '02 220
Slush, Apricot, '93 205
Slush, Apricot Brandy, '91 278
Slush, Apricot-Citrus, '88 82
Tea, Hot Spiced Apricot, '88 248
Wassail, Pineapple-Apricot, '83 275
Bread, Apricot-Nut, '79 24
Bread, Apricot-Orange, '92 285
Bread, Apricot-Pecan, '97 266
Bread, Pineapple-Apricot, '84 7
Bread, Tangy Apricot, '81 249
Butter, Apricot, '82 308; '99 212
Carrots, Apricot, '84 6
Carrots, Apricot Glazed, '80 89
Carrots, Apricot-Glazed, '98 231; '01 212
Chutney, Cranberry-and-Apricot, '02 286
Coffee Cake, Apricot-Almond, '93 26;
    '04 193
Coffee Cake, Apricot Lattice, '94 48
Crescents, Apricot-Cheese, '99 284
Croissants, Strawberry or Apricot, '96 303
Curried Apricots, '91 315
Dates, Apricot-Stuffed, '80 250
Delight, Apricot, '81 42
Desserts
Almond Squares, Apricot-, '95 272
Baked Apricots, Delicious, '82 10
Balls, Apricot, '79 274
Balls, Crunchy Apricot, '89 307
Bars, Apricot, '81 247
Bars, Apricot-Oatmeal, '86 216; '04 331
Bars, Apricot-Raisin, '87 32
Bars, Layered Apricot, '01 161
Cake, Apricot-Almond Upside-Down,
    '97 204
Cake, Apricot Brandy Pound, '83 267
Cobbler, Peach-Apricot, '99 255
Cobbler with Custard Sauce, Apricot,
    '97 16
Cobble Up, Apricot, '82 138
Compote, Apricot-Apple, '98 17
Cookie Rolls, Apricot, '80 282
Cookies, Apricot, '95 322
Cookies, Frosted Apricot, '81 192
Cream, Peachy-Apricot, '86 163
Crescents, Apricot, '90 181
Divinity, Apricot, '83 297
Filling, Apricot, '83 84; '86 107; '93 316;
    '01 330
Filling, Lemon-Apricot, '90 105
Flan, Apricot, '99 146
Freeze, Apricot, '82 10
Frosting, Apricot, '81 192
Frozen Apricot Fluff, '86 242
Glaze, Apricot, '82 8; '97 60; '98 260
Glaze, Apricot-Kirsch, '87 14
Glaze, Sweet Apricot, '82 304
Ice, Apricot Yogurt, '81 177
Ice Cream, Apricot, '99 146
Kolaches, Apricot, '83 84; '94 291
Mousse, Apricot, '82 72; '91 297

Noodle Kugel, Apricot, '92 251
Pastries, Apricot, '83 297
Pastries, Apricot-Cream Cheese, '03 245
Pie, Apricot Surprise, '88 99
Pie, Dried Fruit, '83 249
Pies, Apricot Cream Fried, '00 212
Pies, Apricot Fried, '86 269
Pies, Dried Apricot Hand, '98 259
Pies, Fried Apricot, '95 215
Pies, Special Apricot, '94 60
Pie, Yogurt-Apricot, '85 132
Pinwheels, Apricot, '87 276
Pudding, Apricot Bread, '85 24
Sauce, Apricot, '82 212
Sauce, Apricot Ice Cream, '91 57
Sauce, Apricot-Walnut Hard, '88 153
Sherbet, Apricot, '81 177; '92 164
Shortbread, Apricot-Almond, '99 29
Sorbet, Apricot-Almond, '98 126
Soufflé, Baked Apricot, '88 267
Tart, Apricot-Almond, '97 99
Tart, Apricot-Apple Crumb, '94 60
Tart, Apricot-Nut, '99 249
Tarts, Apricot, '79 282; '88 281
Tarts, Apricot-Pecan-Brie, '97 236
Tea Cakes, Brandied Apricot, '91 241
Torte, Apricot, '02 220
Torte, Apricot-Filled Chocolate, '90 107
Torte, Apricot Sponge, '90 59
Torte, Lucy's Apricot Praline, '95 243
Tortoni, Apricot-Yogurt, '95 124
Turnovers, Fried Apricot, '86 24
Wonders, Apricot, '93 316
Dip, Apricot, '86 178
Dressing, Apricot, '99 245
Dressing, Honeydew Salad with Apricot Cream,
    '84 191
Dried Apricot Spiders, '96 255
French Toast, Stuffed, '96 52
Glaze, Apricot, '80 280; '82 8; '86 197
Glaze for Ham, Apricot, '85 256
Glaze, Sweet Potatoes with Apricot, '89 331
Granola, '99 212
Granola, Superhero, '98 206
Jam, Golden Apricot, '80 31
Jam, Quick-Cooked Apricot, '99 146
Loaf, Apricot-Cranberry, '79 235
Loaf, Apricot-Nut, '81 8
Loaf, Tasty Apricot-Nut, '82 10
Main Dishes
Brisket, Spicy Apricot, '04 247
Chicken, Apricot, '92 12
Chicken Breasts, Apricot, '88 301
Chicken with Apricot Salsa, '98 126
Chicken with Roasted Potato Thins, Apricot,
    '02 23
Chicken with Tangy Apricot Glaze, '98 275
Cornish Hens, Apricot-Glazed, '80 84; '87 306
Cornish Hens, Apricot-Stuffed, '84 6
Ham and Apricots, '90 53
Ham, Apricot Baked, '84 160
Ham Slice, Apricot-Glazed, '93 252
Lamb Kebabs, Apricot-Grilled, '98 102
Pork Chops, Apricot-Mushroom Stuffed, '95 287
Pork Chops, Apricot-Sauced, '85 22
Pork Chops, Apricot-Stuffed, '86 76; '92 219;
    '03 49
Pork Chops, Curried Apricot, '89 191
Pork Chops, Mustard-Apricot, '89 225
Pork Chops with Apricot Glaze, Stuffed,
    '89 M36
Pork Loin, Apricot-Pecan Stuffed, '94 274
Pork Tenderloin with Apricot Sauce, '99 44
Sausage-Apricot Breakfast Dish, '82 10

Mayonnaise, Apricot, '97 320
Rice Pilaf, Apricot, '99 146
Rolls, Apricot-Orange Sweet, '03 235
Rolls, Cheese-Apricot Sweet, '90 195
Salad, Apple-Apricot, '88 121
Salad, Apricot, '81 251; '83 123
Salad, Apricot-Chicken, '99 163
Salad, Apricot Congealed, '02 256
Salad, Apricot Fruit, '82 132
Salad, Apricot Nectar, '83 218; '87 236
Salad, Creamy Apricot, '85 263
Salad, Frosted Apricot, '80 248
Salad, Spinach-Apricot, '94 63
Salad with Cider Vinaigrette, Harvest, '99 322
Salsa, Apricot, '98 126
Sauce, Apricot, '82 212; '87 172
Sauce, Fresh Cranberry-Apricot, '87 243
Sauce, Holiday Cranberry, '02 M311
Spread, Apricot Brie, '86 275
Spread, Apricot-Cream Cheese, '82 161; '87 158
Sweet Potatoes, Apricot, '82 228
Sweet Potatoes, Apricot-Glazed, '81 295
Syrup, Apricot Fruit, '82 10
Topping, Apricot Flambé, '98 127
Vinaigrette, Apricot, '02 120
ARTICHOKES
Appetizers
Baked Artichoke-Cheese Bottoms, '94 61
Caviar, Artichoke Hearts with, '79 142
Crostini, Hot Artichoke, '94 319
Crostini, Parmesan-Artichoke, '98 285
Dip, Artichoke-Chile, '98 234
Dip, Baked Artichoke, '95 239; '03 294
Dip, Deluxe Artichoke, '80 87
Dip, Florentine Artichoke, '96 274
Dip, Greek Artichoke, '97 315
Dip, Hot Artichoke-Seafood, '80 241
Dip, Hot Artichoke Seafood, '85 M212
Dip in a Bread Basket, Artichoke, '93 13
Dip, Italian Artichoke, '97 315
Dip, Mexican Artichoke, '90 292
Dip, Quick Artichoke, '02 69; '03 270;
    '04 107
Dip, Seasoned Mayonnaise Artichoke, '80 87
Dip, Spinach-Artichoke, '00 26
Frittata, Artichoke Appetizer, '92 58
Marinated Artichoke Hearts, '88 95
Marinated Artichokes, '87 250
Marinated Shrimp and Artichokes, '97 89;
    '98 335
Mold, Artichoke-Caviar, '87 239
Mound, Caviar-Artichoke, '91 244
Mushrooms, Artichoke-Stuffed, '01 239
Oysters, Artichoke, '96 154
Phyllo Bites, Artichoke-Parmesan, '87 54
Puff Pastry, Spinach and Artichokes in, '00 277
Puffs, Spinach-Artichoke-Tomato, '95 284
Shrimp Appetizer, Artichoke-and-, '93 271
Spread, Antipasto, '81 25
Spread, Artichoke-Cheese, '04 294
Spread, Artichoke-Parmesan, '92 95
Spread, Chunky Artichoke, '89 98
Spread Gift Box, Chicken-Artichoke-Cheese,
    '00 328
Spread, Hot Artichoke, '79 110
Spread, Hot Artichoke-Crab, '85 81
Zesty Artichoke Appetizer, '80 146
Artichokes, '92 107
au Gratin, Crab, Shrimp, and Artichoke, '90 240
Bake, Spinach-Artichoke, '95 48
Bake, Tomato-and-Artichoke Heart, '85 81
Beef with Tomatoes and Artichokes, '92 282
Bread, Artichoke, '93 140
Casserole, Alii Artichoke, '93 294

Caserole, Asparagus-Artichoke, **'86** 279
Casserole, Brussels Sprouts-and-Artichoke, **'94** 279
Casserole, Chicken-and-Artichoke, **'96** 133
Casserole, Italian Green Bean-and-Artichoke,
    '85 81
Casserole, Mushroom-Artichoke, **'87** 241
Casserole, Spicy Spinach-Artichoke, **'01** 49
Casserole, Spinach and Artichoke, **'81** 103
Casserole, Spinach-Artichoke, **'88** 252; **'93** 44;
    '00 254; **'01** 49
Chicken and Artichoke Hearts, Baked, **'82** 260
Chicken and Artichokes, **'03** 26
Chicken and Artichokes, Italian, **'95** 68; **'00** 219
Chicken, Artichoke, **'81** 97
Chicken, Dijon, **'99** 21
Chicken Pasta with Artichokes and Capers, **'04** 129
Chicken, Sanibel Island, **'97** 66
Chicken Sauté with Artichokes and Mushrooms,
    '03 57
Chicken with Artichoke Hearts, **'88** 54
Chicken with Artichokes, **'02** 314
Chicken with Artichokes and Mushrooms, **'90** 35
Chicken with Artichokes, Sherried, **'87** 143
Chilled Artichokes with Lemon-Pepper Dressing,
    '87 55
Chowder, Artichoke-Shrimp, **'03** 91
Cooked Artichokes, Whole, **'04** 53
Crabmeat with Artichoke Hearts, Creamed, **'93** 26
Dressing, Artichoke, **'84** 126
Dried Beef with Artichokes, Creamed, **'85** 81
Eggs Sardou, **'92** 93
Flan, Artichoke, **'96** 22
Flatbread, Sicilian Artichoke, **'98** 136
Herb-Mayonnaise Dip, Artichokes with, **'84** 67
Lemon, Artichoke Hearts with, **'90** 98
Linguine, Artichoke and Shrimp, **'95** 210
Marinated Artichoke Hearts, **'95** 66
Marinated Artichokes, **'87** 250; **'88** 41
Marinated Cucumbers and Artichokes, **'82** 111
Marinated Mirlitons, Artichokes, and Peppers,
    '00 246
Pasta with Artichoke Hearts, **'86** 209
Pasta with Catfish and Artichokes, **'90** 123
Pasta with Rosemary, Chicken-Artichoke, **'98** 15
Pie, Artichoke, **'79** 25
Pizza, Grilled, **'97** 190
Pizza with Artichoke and Prosciutto, **'87** 182
Quiche, Artichoke, **'91** 71
Quiche, Shrimp-and-Artichoke, **'03** 196
Quick 'n' Easy Whole Cooked Artichokes,
    '96 M132
Ragoût, Veal-and-Artichoke, **'94** 43
Relish, Jerusalem Artichoke, **'89** 197
Salads
    Artichoke Salad, **'86** 333
    Asparagus-Artichoke Salad, **'85** 162
    Aspic, Tomato-Artichoke, **'84** 320; **'86** 92
    Avocado Acapulco, **'83** 2
    Chicken-Rice Salad, Artichoke-, **'94** 132
    Chicken-Rice Salad, Mediterranean Artichoke-,
        '97 321
    Chicken Salad with Artichokes, **'86** 186
    Couscous Salad, Mediterranean, **'03** 127
    Goat Cheese Salad, Artichoke-, **'98** 118
    Italian House Salad, **'02** 300
    Italian Salad, **'87** 145
    Marinated Artichoke Salad, **'83** 241; **'95** 66
    Marinated Cucumbers and Artichokes, **'82** 111
    Orzo Salad, Artichokes with, **'88** M193
    Pasta Salad, Artichoke-, **'94** 180
    Rice Salad, Artichoke-, **'80** 178; **'81** 41; **'85** 81;
        '01 144
    Rice Salad with Artichoke Hearts, **'80** 232
    Shrimp-and-Artichoke Salad, **'04** 50

Stuffed Tomato Salad, Artichoke-, **'82** 101
Tomato Salad, Artichoke-, **'82** 239
Tortellini Salad, **'02** 186
Zucchini-Artichoke Salad, **'91** 229
Salsa, Artichoke-Tomato, **'96** 182
Sandwich, Beef-and-Artichoke Open-Faced Italian,
    '98 22
Sandwich, Italian Stuffed, **'99** 15
Sauté, Herbed Artichoke, **'96** 133
Shrimp Platter with Béarnaise Sauce, Artichoke and,
    '96 132
Soup, Artichoke, **'89** 269
Soup, Artichoke Cream, **'94** 62
Soup, Chicken, Artichoke, and Mushroom, **'92** 324
Soup, Cream of Artichoke, **'82** 232
Soup, Louisiana Oyster-and-Artichoke, **'92** 81
Soup, Oyster-and-Artichoke, **'97** 21
Spring Artichokes, **'86** 62
Steamed Artichokes, **'81** 59
Strata, Artichoke-Cheese, **'90** 236
Stuffed Artichokes, **'79** 76; **'82** 92; **'91** 117; **'99** 64
Stuffed Artichokes, Ham-Mushroom-, **'95** 228
Stuffed Artichokes, Shrimp-, **'84** 67; **'87** 55
Stuffed Artichokes, Shrimp, **'94** 62
Stuffed with Shrimp and Scallops, Artichokes,
    '84 174
Tomatoes with Curry Sauce, Stuffed, **'97** 170
Tortellini Alfredo with Prosciutto and Artichoke
    Hearts, **'02** 322
Turkey Scaloppine with Angel Hair Pasta, **'02** 44
Veal with Artichoke Hearts, Lemon, **'87** 219
Vinaigrette, Artichokes, **'88** 101
Whole Cooked Artichokes, **'94** 61
ASPARAGUS
Almond Asparagus, **'83** 86; **'02** 64
Almond Butter, Asparagus with, **'84** 85
Almond Sauce, Asparagus with, **'91** 117
Amandine, Asparagus, **'03** 295
Basil Butter, Asparagus with, **'85** 40
Basil Sauce, Asparagus with, **'86** 33
Bean Sprouts, Asparagus and, **'96** 95
Beef with Asparagus, **'90** 100
Bundles, Grilled Chile-Rubbed Rib Eyes with Herb
    Cheese and Asparagus, **'03** 326
Caesar, Asparagus, **'88** 133
Carrots and Asparagus, Sunshine, **'99** 277
Cashew Butter, Asparagus with, **'87** 56
Casseroles
    Artichoke Casserole, Asparagus-, **'86** 279
    Asparagus Casserole, **'98** 310
    Cheesy Asparagus Casserole, **'82** 281; **'83** 32
    Chicken-Asparagus Casserole, **'83** 76; **'84** 71
    Creamy Asparagus Casserole, **'80** 76
    Easy Asparagus Casserole, **'83** 255
    English Pea Casserole, Asparagus-and-, **'86** 324
    Pea Casserole, Asparagus-, **'88** M294
    Peas Casserole, Asparagus and, **'80** 152
    Spaghetti Casserole, Asparagus-, **'80** 77
    Turkey-Asparagus Casserole, **'86** 284
Cheesecake, Ham-and-Asparagus, **'90** 174; **'02** 103
Chicken, Asparagus, and Mushrooms with Penne
    Pasta, **'98** 212
Chicken, Szechuan, **'98** 155
Chilled Asparagus with Garlic Dipping Sauce,
    '98 136
Company Asparagus, **'85** 82
Creamed Asparagus on Toast, **'95** 61
Cream Sauce, Asparagus with, **'90** 291
Croquettes, Asparagus, **'85** 265
Curry Sauce, Asparagus with, **'90** 17
Cutlets, Asparagus, **'80** 147
Delight, Asparagus, **'82** 269
Delight, Ham-Asparagus, **'86** 48
Dill Sauce, Asparagus with, **'97** 59

Dilly Asparagus, **'88** 180
Dressing, Asparagus with Warm Citrus, **'96** M86
Eggs à la Asparagus, Creamed, **'81** 201
en Papillote, Shrimp with Asparagus, **'86** 145
Fettuccine, Ham-and-Asparagus, **'94** 84
Fish-Asparagus Divan, **'87** 128
French-Fried Asparagus, **'79** 66; **'83** 46
Frittata, Bacon-and-Asparagus, **'98** 136
Garlic Cream, Asparagus with, **'95** 83; **'00** 71
Ginger, Asparagus With, **'04** 237
Goat Cheese Sauce, Asparagus with, **'93** 116
Goldenrod, Asparagus, **'79** 66
Grilled Asparagus, **'00** 165
Grilled Portobello Mushrooms and Asparagus,
    '02 122
Guacamole, Mock, **'93** 36
"Guacamole" with Cumin Crisps, Green Goddess,
    '02 205
Ham-Asparagus Dinner, **'80** M10
Ham Rolls, Asparagus, **'91** 117
Holiday Asparagus, **'85** 260
Jeweled Asparagus, **'80** 42
Lemon, Asparagus with, **'98** 103
Lemon Butter, Asparagus in, **'80** M123
Lemon Butter, Asparagus with, **'87** M151; **'98** 168
Lemon-Marinated Asparagus, **'03** 119
Lemon Sauce, Asparagus with, **'86** 62
Lemon-Sesame Asparagus, **'91** 31
Loaf, Asparagus-Pimiento, **'84** 86
Marinated Asparagus, **'81** 108; **'83** 46; **'84** 67, 86;
    '86 92; **'87** 74; **'02** 243
Marinated Asparagus, Easy, **'81** 148
Marinated Asparagus Spears, **'88** 130
Marinated Asparagus with Prosciutto, **'95** 83
Mayonnaise, Asparagus with Hot Wine, **'81** 83
Meringue, Asparagus, **'88** 131
Mornay, Asparagus, **'99** 102
Mushrooms, Asparagus and, **'85** 108
Orange Butter Sauce, Asparagus with, **'85** 43
Orange Sauce, Asparagus with, **'83** 46
Pasta with Asparagus, Tomatoes, and Shrimp,
    Garlicky, **'95** 82
Pasta with Shrimp and Asparagus, Angel Hair,
    '92 100
Pasta With Toasted Pecans, Asparagus, **'04** 90
Pickled Asparagus, **'83** 46; **'04** 161
Pie, Cheesy Asparagus, **'01** 103
Pilaf, Turkey-Asparagus, **'88** 200
Pimientos, Asparagus with, **'98** 286
Pork Arlo, **'87** 229
Prosciutto-Wrapped Asparagus, **'91** 98
Quiche, Asparagus-Tomato, **'88** 198
Quiche, Springtime, **'83** 122
Rarebit, Uptown Welsh, **'87** 279
Rice and Asparagus, **'93** 324
Risotto, Asparagus, **'03** 68
Risotto with Shrimp and Asparagus, **'03** 86
Roasted Asparagus-and-Hazelnut Couscous, **'04** 60
Roasted Asparagus, Simple, **'00** 103
Roasted Asparagus with Red Pepper Sauce, **'98** 322
Roasted Shallot Asparagus, **'02** 64
Rolls, Asparagus, **'79** 296; **'80** 31
Rolls, Chicken-Asparagus, **'86** M211
Rolls, Ham-Asparagus, **'79** 41
Rolls, Hot Asparagus, **'93** 329
Rollups, Asparagus, **'79** 63; **'01** 239
Roll-Ups, Asparagus, **'84** 270
Roulade, Asparagus, **'86** 102
Salads
    Artichoke Salad, Asparagus-, **'85** 162
    Asparagus Salad, **'88** 121; **'94** 67
    Aspic, Asparagus, **'96** 65
    Avocado-Asparagus Salad, **'00** 331
    Blue Crab Salad with Asian Vinaigrette, **'98** 142

ASPARAGUS, Salads
(continued)

Bluegrass Salad, '02 255
Chicken Salad, Asparagus-, '89 83
Chicken Salad with Asparagus, Curried, '81 36
Congealed Asparagus Salad, '83 260
Crab-and-Asparagus Salad, '92 141
Crabmeat-and-Asparagus, Congealed Salad with, '84 86
Cups, Asparagus Salad, '83 47
Easy Asparagus Salad, '88 131
Egg Salad, Asparagus-and-, '86 305
Fresh Asparagus Salad, '01 159
Ginger Asparagus, Chilled, '02 64
Grilled Asparagus Salad with Orange Vinaigrette, '99 102
Grilled Mushroom-Asparagus Salad, '02 122
Horseradish Salad, Asparagus-, '87 80
Lemon-Asparagus Salad, Creamy, '93 116
Marinated Asparagus, '83 46; '84 67, 86; '86 92
Marinated Asparagus and Hearts of Palm, '90 91
Marinated Asparagus Medley, '91 105
Marinated Asparagus Salad, '79 20
Marinated Asparagus with Prosciutto, '95 83
Mold, Asparagus, '80 104
Mold, Asparagus-Cucumber, '85 252
Mousse Salad, Asparagus, '86 252
Mustard Sauce, Chilled Asparagus in, '88 130
New Potato Salad, Asparagus-and-, '86 69
Papaya Salsa, Asparagus Salad with, '97 144
Peas-and-Asparagus Salad, '83 141
Roasted-Beet, and Goat Cheese Salad, Asparagus, '02 96
Roasted Beet, and Goat Cheese Salad, Asparagus, '03 98
Tarragon Marinade, Asparagus with, '83 47
Tart Asparagus Salad, '81 203
Tomato-Asparagus Salad, '92 79
Tomatoes with Herb Vinaigrette, Asparagus and, '99 56
Vinaigrette, Asparagus, '80 77; '90 82, 138; '93 174
Vinaigrette, Asparagus Salad, '88 56
Vinaigrette, Light Asparagus, '82 50
Yogurt Dressing, Asparagus with, '79 66
Sandwiches, Asparagus-and-Ham Melt, '88 M96
Sandwiches, Asparagus Grill, '79 164; '80 130
Sandwiches, Asparagus Spear, '84 165
Sandwiches, Ham-and-Asparagus, '01 307
Sandwiches, Ham-Swiss-and-Asparagus, '01 52
Sandwiches, Turkey-Asparagus, '96 74
Sandwich, Warm Asparagus, '99 102
Sauce, Asparagus White, '80 147
Sauté, Asparagus, '01 275
Sauté, Asparagus-and-Mushroom, '93 115
Sautéed Asparagus, '79 66
Sesame Asparagus, '96 154; '00 282; '02 64
Sesame Asparagus, Chilled, '03 67
Shrimp Mold with Asparagus, '93 214
Soufflé, Asparagus, '79 66; '83 265; '89 89
Soup, Asparagus, '84 67; '98 290; '00 84
Soup, Asparagus-Potato, '85 23
Soup, Cream of Asparagus, '84 111
Soup, Creamy Asparagus, '94 225
Soup, Creamy Asparagus-and-Chicken, '95 82
Sour Cream, Asparagus with, '83 46
Spears, Buttered Asparagus, '97 282
Squares, Asparagus, '79 161; '02 183
Squash Rings, Asparagus in, '87 68
Steamed Asparagus, '92 211
Steamed Asparagus with Tomato-Basil Dip, '00 69; '04 53

Stir-Fried Asparagus, '87 52
Stir-Fry, Asparagus, '95 83
Stir-Fry Beef and Asparagus, '91 124
Stir-Fry, Sweet Onion-Asparagus, '98 135
Supreme, Asparagus, '80 77; '89 245
Supreme, Cauliflower and Asparagus, '79 287; '80 35
Sweet-and-Sour Asparagus, '89 159
Tangy Asparagus, '84 86
Tartlets, Country Ham-and-Asparagus, '98 82
Terrine with Dill Sauce, Asparagus-Seafood, '98 157
Tomatoes, Fresh Asparagus and, '94 162
Tomato Sauce, Asparagus with, '83 46
Toss, Asparagus-Carrot-Squash, '91 45
Toss, Asparagus-Vermicelli, '00 102
Tostadas with Goat Cheese, Asparagus-and-Mushroom, '03 242
Vinaigrette, Asparagus, '80 77; '90 82, 138; '93 174

ASPIC
Apple Aspic, Sunshine, '81 73
Asparagus Aspic, '96 65
Basic Aspic for Garnishing, '84 189
Beet Aspic, '90 123
Blue Cheese Aspic, '96 66
Chicken Salad, Aspic-Topped, '88 88
Coating, White Aspic, '85 151
Cucumber-Curry Dressing, Aspic with, '89 178
Fish Aspic, '84 190
Fish 'n Aspic, '84 190
Gazpacho Aspic, '89 179; '96 65
Grapefruit Aspic, '80 297; '82 112; '83 153
Madeira Aspic, '86 65
Orange-and-Carrot Aspic, '86 199
Rosemary Aspic, Spicy, '99 183
Shrimp-Coleslaw Aspic, '79 88
Shrimp-Cucumber Aspic, '83 108
Sunshine Aspic, '80 103
Three-Layer Aspic, '88 120
Tomato
Artichoke Aspic, Tomato-, '84 320; '86 92
Bloody Mary-Tomato Aspic, '81 77
Chicken in Tomato Aspic, '84 190
Chili Sauce Tomato Aspic, '85 252
Classic Tomato Aspic, '91 229
Crab Aspic, Tomato-, '85 287
Herbed Tomato Aspic, '81 73
Layered Tomato Aspic, '90 99
Light Tomato Aspic, '85 83
Ranch Tomato Aspic, '83 218
Shrimp, Tomato Aspic with, '79 241
Spicy Tomato Aspic, '81 40; '89 288
Tangy Tomato Aspic, '83 124
Two, Aspic for, '83 209
Vegetable Aspic, Cheesy, '81 73
Vegetable Aspic with Horseradish Dressing, Crisp, '87 152

AVOCADOS
Baked Avocado-and-Crabmeat, '84 119
Broiled Crab and Avocado, '79 116
Chicken, Orange-Avocado, '80 38
Cocktail, Sherried Avocado-Crabmeat, '87 95
Crabmeat, Avocado with, '86 119
Cream, Avocado, '92 158
Dagwoods, Chicken-Avocado, '96 200; '99 337
Dip, Avocado, '80 285; '81 57, 306
Dip, "Bring-Home-the-Bacon" Avocado, '92 80
Dip, Gazpacho, '95 243
Dip, Roasted Corn-and-Avocado, '91 279
Dip, Six-Layer, '81 160
Dip, Zippy Avocado, '82 9; '83 69
Dressing, Avocado, '80 15; '92 321; '96 138
Dressing, Avocado Fruit Salad, '82 93
Eggs and Ham, Green, '96 90

Filled Avocados, Shrimp-, '83 2
Frittata, Avocado-and-Black Bean, '02 212
Gazpacho, Tomato-Avocado-Corn, '97 182
Guacamole
Baine's Guac, '98 88
Coleslaw, Guacamole Mexican, '82 302
Creamy Guacamole, '79 91; '83 174; '99 119; '02 168
Crisps, Guacamole, '98 173
Dip, Bacon-Guacamole, '85 25
Dip, Guacamole, '86 4; '95 96
Dressing, Guacamole, '92 64
Easy Guacamole, '95 94; '01 17
Guacamole, '79 185; '80 74; '83 179; '89 226; '90 205; '91 161; '94 116; '96 160, 170; '99 84; '02 118; '03 95
Margarita Guacamole, '97 167
Mold, Guacamole, '86 184
Po'Boys, Guacamole-Topped Ham, '04 170
Roasted Onion Guacamole, '00 334
Salad, Guacamole, '80 14; '87 181
Salad, Guacamole-Tomato, '81 302
Sandwiches, Guacamole, '82 9; '83 68
Shells, Guacamole in, '86 74
Spicy Guacamole, '93 218
Spread, Guacamole, '90 119
Subs, Guacamole, '84 293
Ice, Avocado, '83 179
Kebabs, Chicken-Avocado, '82 9; '83 68
Lasagna, Avocado-Vegetable, '01 310
Mayonnaise, Avocado, '00 335
Mayonnaise, Spicy Salmon Fillets with Avocado, '02 327
Mousse with Shrimp Salad, Avocado, '98 333
Omelet, Yogurt-Avocado, '81 33
Pie, Mexican Cheese, '83 69
Potatoes, Avocado-Topped, '83 3
Relish, Avocado, '87 120
Salads
Acapulco, Avocado, '83 2
Apple Salad with Maple-Walnut Vinaigrette, Avocado-, '04 45
Asparagus Salad, Avocado-, '00 331
Avocado Salad, '81 195; '82 9; '83 69; '92 246; '97 250; '02 99
Bread Salad, Avocado-, '02 210
Chicken-Avocado Salad, '80 139
Chicken-Avocado Salad, Fruited, '82 101
Chicken-Avocado Salad Platter, '83 2
Chicken-Avocado Salad, Tossed, '80 4
Chicken Salad, Avocado-, '87 107
Chicken Salad in Avocados, '85 216
Chicken Salad in Avocados, Fruited, '87 41
Citrus-and-Avocado Salad, '99 26
Citrus-Avocado Salad, '82 265
Citrus Salad, Avocado, '01 133
Congealed Avocado Crunch Salad, '85 26
Congealed Avocado Salad, '84 266
Congealed Avocado Salads, '87 42
Corn-Poblano Salad, Avocado-, '01 320
Crab-Avocado Salad, '81 114
Dude Ranch Salad, '80 15
Endive Salad, Avocado-, '94 88
Fruit Salad, Avocado, '87 41
Fruit Salad with Honey-Yogurt Dressing, Avocado-, '93 172
Garbanzo Salad, Avocado-, '81 33
Grapefruit-Avocado Salad, '83 316; '84 16; '89 41
Grapefruit Salad, Avocado-, '85 26; '93 282
Melon Salad, Avocado-, '82 164
Mexican Salad Supper, '82 9; '83 68
Orange-Avocado Salad, '99 331
Orange Salad, Avocado-, '91 44

Pita, Avocado Salad-Hummus, '02 99
Potato Salad with Avocado, '98 332
Potato Salad with Horseradish Dressing, Avocado-, '96 200
Rice-and-Avocado Salad, '89 146
Romaine Salad, Tangy, '80 155
Shrimp and Avocado Salad, '80 266
Shrimp Salad, Avocado Stuffed with, '82 207
Shrimp Salad on the Half Shell, '86 73
Southwestern Spiral Salad, '98 66
Spanish Avocado Salad, '87 41
Spinach Salad, Green, '79 142
Tomato-Avocado Salad, '86 74
Tomatoes, Avocado-Stuffed, '82 101
Zucchini Salad, Creamy Avocado and, '79 208
Salsa, Avocado, '91 182
Salsa, Avocado-Corn, '94 201; '99 335
Salsa, Avocado-Feta, '96 15
Salsa, Avocado-Mango, '00 328
Salsa, Avocado-Peach, '02 159
Salsa, Fresh Avocado, '02 247
Salsa, Sweet, '98 174
Salsa, Tomato-Avocado, '94 83
Sandwiches, Avocado, Bacon, and Cheese, '87 279
Sandwiches, Avocado-Crabmeat, '83 2
Sandwiches, Avocado Deluxe, '99 72
Sandwich with Tomato, Avocado, and Bacon, Grilled Four-Cheese, '00 199
Sauce, Avocado, '80 198; '83 200
Sauce, Avocado Béarnaise, '01 317
Sauce, Avocado-Lime, '03 90
Sauce, Avocado-Tomatillo, '95 206
Sauce, Chunky Avocado, '03 128
Sauce, Grilled Swordfish with Avocado-Lime, '97 127
Shells, Ceviche in Avocado, '81 33
Sherbet, Avocado, '83 162
Sherbet, Mexican, '79 155
Sorbet, Avocado, '88 117
Soup, Avocado, '88 160
Soup, Avocado-Banana-Yogurt, '80 78
Soup, Chilled Avocado, '81 34; '87 37; '93 108
Soup, Creamy Avocado, '79 107; '01 176
Soup, Creamy Avocado-Mushroom, '85 25
Soup, Sherried Avocado, '84 181
Spread, Herbed Avocado-Cheese, '98 335
Stuffed Avocados, Crab-, '86 73
Stuffed Avocados, Salmon-, '86 74
Stuffed Broiled Avocados, '88 246
Terrine, Chevre-and-Avocado, '00 276
Tomatoes, Crab-and-Avocado Stuffed, '94 141
Topping, Avocado, '93 309; '94 96
Tostadas, Crispy, '83 2
Whip, Avocado, '79 107
Wraps, Thai Chicken-Avocado, '02 206

Bacon

Appetizers

Biscuits with Sun-Dried Tomato Spread and Bacon, Cream Cheese-and-Olive, '02 313
Bites, Bacon-Shrimp, '98 234; '99 213
Blue Cheese-and-Bacon Puffs, '97 98
Brie, Chutney-Bacon, '90 M292
Cheese-Bacon Crispies, '84 270
Chestnut Wraps, Bacon-, '84 M216
Crackers, Bacon-Wrapped, '93 280
Crostini, Almond-Bacon-Cheese, '94 318
Crostini, Green Onion, '96 93
Crostini, Pear-and-Gorgonzola, '02 314
Dip, Bacon, '82 197
Dip, Bacon-and-Tomato, '90 147
Dip, Bacon-Cheese, '01 194
Dip, Bacon-Guacamole, '85 25
Dip, Blue Cheese-Bacon, '04 287
Dip, "Bring-Home-the-Bacon" Avocado, '92 80
Dip, Cheddar-Bacon, '89 M119
Dip, Zesty Bacon, '92 156
Eggs, Bacon-Stuffed, '97 52; '00 70; '04 290
Eggs, Double Stuffed Spinach-and-Bacon, '00 M333
Fingers, Bacon-Cheese, '00 133
Hot Bacon Appetizers, '80 248
Meatballs, Burgundy-Bacon, '80 283
Mushrooms, Cheese 'n' Bacon-Stuffed, '86 258
Onion Appetizers, Bacon-, '94 290
Oysters, Fried Bacon-Wrapped, '02 103
Oysters in Bacon, '83 211
Pineapple Chunks, Bacon-Wrapped, '84 25
Popcorn, Bacon-Cheese, '86 74
Puffs, Blue Cheese-and-Bacon, '01 236
Puffs, Cheesy Bacon, '02 145
Quesadillas, Bacon-Jalapeño-Tomato, '95 240
Quiches, Miniature Bacon-Cheese, '83 93
Rolls, Bacon, '84 270; '93 330
Rollups, Bacon, '79 34
Roll-Ups, Chicken Liver and Bacon, '80 200; '81 57
Rollups, Sausage-Bacon, '88 51
Rumaki, '80 M136
Rumaki, Scallop, '98 M173
Scallops, Bacon-Wrapped, '87 94
Scallops with Orange-Honey Sauce, Bacon-Wrapped, '97 236
Shrimp 'n' Bacon, '98 222
Spread, Bacon-Cheese, '83 241
Sticks, Parmesan-Bacon, '99 65
Swirls, Bacon, '89 214; '98 26
Water Chestnuts, Bacon-Wrapped, '79 63
Apple Bacon, Sweet, '03 305
Bagels, Meal-in-One, '88 159
Bake, Bacon, Zucchini, and Cornbread, '99 123
Bake, Lima-Bacon, '86 9
Banana Peppers, Stuffed, '02 55
Bars, Bacon-Cheese Toast, '79 36
Beans, Barbecue, '02 167
Beans, Frolickers Baked, '03 92
Beans, Lowcountry Baked, '98 332
Beef-and-Bacon Twirls, '91 163
Biscuit Bites, Savory Tomato-Bacon, '03 196
Biscuit Cups, Bacon, '99 214
Biscuits, Bacon-Cheese, '88 84
Biscuits, Potato-Bacon, '94 214
Black Pepper-Brown Sugar Bacon, '04 70
Bread, Bacon-and-Cheese, '83 255
Bread, Bacon-Cheese French, '92 54
Bread, Bacon Monkey, '94 283; '97 154
Breakfast Bake, '85 45
Breakfast Eye-Openers, '82 231
Breakfast, Farmer's, '81 44
Broccoli Bakers, '99 308
Broccoli with Bacon, '92 302
Brown Sugar Bacon, '04 70
Bundles, Bean, '80 246
Burgers, Apple-Bacon, '99 202
Burgers, Cheesy Bacon, '81 29
Butterbeans, Bacon, and Tomatoes, '96 36; '00 184
Butterbeans with Bacon and Green Onions, '96 267
Butternut and Bacon, Skillet, '85 9
Cabbage, Creole, '00 105
Cabbage, Fried, '02 272
Canadian Bacon-and-Brie Quiche, '04 248
Canadian Bacon, Lima Beans with, '83 219; '84 245
Canadian Bacon Squares, Sunrise, '99 103
Canadian-Style Bacon, Glazed, '82 197
Carrots with Bacon and Onion, Glazed, '87 200; '02 283
Casserole, Bacon and Egg, '81 225
Casserole, Bacon-and-Egg, '03 166
Casserole, Campfire, '00 173
Casserole, Cheesy Bacon-and-Ham, '01 256
Casserole, Egg-and-Bacon, '85 248
Casseroles, Hot Brown Pasta, '96 290
Casserole with Creole Sauce, Brunch, '98 98
Cauliflower with Parmesan and Bacon, '96 137
Champignons au Vin, '79 47
Chicken-Bacon Nuggets, '03 292
Chicken Breasts, Apple-Bacon Stuffed, '99 313
Chicken Bundles with Bacon Ribbons, '87 68
Chowder, Fresh Corn and Bacon, '93 203
Chowder, Southern Corn-and-Bacon, '96 166
Coleslaw, Apple-Bacon, '04 181
Coleslaw, Bacon, '83 58
Collard Greens, Esau's, '03 17
Cookies, Breakfast, '97 52
Cookies, Take-Along Breakfast, '84 59
Cornbread, Bacon-Cheddar Hot-Water, '01 29; '02 107; '04 25
Cornbread, Cowboy, '81 188
Cornbread, Loaded, '99 214
Corn, Creamy Fried Confetti, '02 160
Corn, Skillet Creamed, '02 204
Corn with Bacon and Caramelized Onion, '99 94
Cream Cheese, Bacon-Olive, '04 196
Cups, Bacon-Cheese, '02 219
Delight, Bacon-and-Egg, '85 143
Dressing, Green Beans with Bacon, '85 147
Dressing, Hot Bacon, '84 12
Dressing, Jeweled Hot Bacon, '97 196
Dressing, Potatoes with Hot Bacon, '88 M294
Dressing, Sweet Bacon, '93 108
Egg Salad, Bacon-Horseradish, '94 181
Eggs, and Hominy, Bacon, '85 143
Eggs, Bacon Deviled, '86 136
Eggs Benedict, '98 55
Eggs Benedict, Bacon-and-Tomato, '87 195
Eggs Benedict, Traditional, '03 52
Eggs, Brunch, '98 93
Eggs Oso Grande, '98 279
Flank Steak, Bacon-Wrapped, '85 59
Franks, Bacon-Wrapped, '81 202
Frittata, Bacon-and-Asparagus, '98 136
Frittata, Potato-Bacon, '95 269; '98 330
Green Beans, Bacon-Topped, '80 M123
Green Beans, Mushroom-Bacon, '91 291; '92 255
Green Beans, Southern Smothered, '02 55
Green Beans with Bacon and Mushrooms, '92 13
Green Beans with Zucchini, '02 251
Greens and Bacon, Shelly, '96 290
Grits, Nassau, '99 214
Hash Browns, Sweet Potato, '02 248
Hush Puppies, Bacon, '91 201
Kale, Homestyle, '00 91
Kebabs, Scallop-Bacon, '81 111
Lettuce Wedges with Blue Cheese Dressing, Iceberg, '00 217
Linguine Carbonara, '87 108
Meatballs, Bacon-Wrapped, '79 81
Meat Loaf, Sweet Ketchup-and-Bacon-Topped, '03 203
Muffins, Bacon-and-Cheese, '89 205
Muffins, Bacon-Cheese, '96 280
Mushrooms with Bacon, Stir-Fried, '80 123
Nuggets, Chicken-Bacon, '04 146
Okra Pilau, '99 184
Omelet, Open-Faced Bacon-and-Potato, '02 246
Omelet, Spinach, Cheddar, and Bacon, '03 204
Oysters, Bacon-Baked, '86 132
Oysters Rockefeller, '98 222
Pancake, Maple-Bacon Oven, '89 255
Pasta, Bacon, '97 52

BACON
(continued)

Peas and Bacon, Sautéed, '89 331
Peas with Crispy Bacon, Green, '04 60
Pecans, Roasted Bacon, '96 262
Pie, Country Breakfast, '93 M328
Pinto Beans, Mexican, '00 241
Pizza, Breakfast, '97 172; '00 193
Pizza, The King Henry, '95 267
Pork Chops, Stuffed, '02 204
Pork Tenderloin, Peppered Bacon-Wrapped, '02 55
Pork Tenderloin, Spinach-and-Bacon Stuffed, '94 81
Potatoes, Bacon-Stuffed, '86 193
Potatoes, Bacon-Topped Blue Cheese, '79 46
Potatoes, Baked Sweet-and-Savory Mashed, '02 244
Potatoes, Cheesy Bacon-Stuffed, '81 M61
Potatoes, Green Onion-and-Bacon Mashed, '02 110
Potatoes, Phyllo, '02 219
Potatoes, Stuffed, '01 48
Quail, Bacon-Wrapped, '02 238
Quiche, Bacon, '85 60
Quiche Lorraine, '80 M108; '99 M218; '01 88
Quiche Lorraine, Classic, '81 131
Quiche Lorraine, Mushroom-, '86 242
Quiche Lorraine, Peppery, '81 228
Quiche, Spinach-and-Bacon, '00 240
Rice, Bacon-Chive, '83 129
Rice, Bacon Fried, '80 115
Rice, Spicy, '99 214
Rolls, Onion-Bacon, '99 47
Rouladen, '99 242
Rutabaga with Bacon, '83 243
Salad, Bacon-Lettuce-Mozzarella-and-Tomato, '98 209
Salad, Bacon-Mandarin, '02 87
Salad, Bacon-Topped Potato, '85 59
Salad, BLT Chicken, '87 144
Salad, Eight-Layer, '99 107
Salad, Endive, Bacon, and Pecan, '89 12
Salad, Escarole-and-Bacon, '84 85
Salad, Hot Bacon and Black-Eyed, '85 7
Salad, Italian BLT Bread, '03 90
Salad, Layered BLT, '01 96
Salad, Spinach, '03 246
Salad, Spinach and Bacon, '81 143
Salad, Wilted Bacon-and-Lettuce, '85 69
Salad with Bacon, Rice, '79 52
Salad with Sweet Parsley Dressing, Spinach, '02 120
Sandwiches
   Avocado, Bacon, and Cheese Sandwiches, '87 279
   Bagel, Breakfast on a, '94 66
   Beef, Bacon, and Blue Cheese Sandwiches, '96 23
   BLT, Caramelized Onion, '03 90
   BLT Sandwiches, Italian, '02 230
   Breakfast Sandwiches, '82 M123; '89 M230
   Breakfast Sandwiches, BLT, '04 171
   Breakfast Sandwiches, Open-Faced, '92 140
   Cheese, and Tomato Sandwiches, Bacon, '84 14
   Cheesy BLT's, '85 92
   Croissants, BLT, '93 158
   Curried BLT Sandwiches, '93 158
   Empanadas, Bacon 'n' Egg Breakfast, '02 324
   Good-Start Sandwiches, '99 134
   Grilled Bacon, Cheese, and Tomato Sandwiches, '97 170
   Grilled Bacon-Cheese Sandwiches, '83 242
   Grilled Four-Cheese Sandwich with Tomato, Avocado, and Bacon, '00 199
   Hoagies, Bacon, Pimiento, and Cheese, '90 144

Hot Browns, Baby, '00 107
Melts, Bacon-and-Cheese, '04 324
Melts, Tomato-Cheese-Bacon, '99 72
Muffuletta Bacon-Olive Party Sandwiches, Mini, '04 196
Olive Party Sandwiches, Bacon-, '04 196
Open-Faced Cheesy Bacon Sandwiches, '80 78
Open-Faced Sandwiches, Super, '97 52
Pita Pockets, BLT in, '93 158
Poor Boys, Oyster-and-Bacon, '87 40
Stuffed Sandwich, Italian, '99 15
Tomato, Swiss, and Bacon Sandwiches, '04 140
Welsh Rarebit with Tomatoes and Bacon, '92 M159
Wrap, BLT, '04 298
Wrap, Southwest BLT, '03 90
Wraps, Western, '99 194
Sauté, Orange-Watercress, '98 83
Scallops, Maple, '99 176
Scramble, Bacon-and-Eggs, '80 M267
Slaw, German Cabbage, '00 105
Soufflés, Parmesan, '97 280
Soup, Bacon-Beer Cheese, '87 M7
Soup, Bacon, Lettuce, and Tomato, '91 207
Soup, Bacon-Topped Cheese, '80 M224
Soup, Bean and Bacon, '83 26
Soup, Potato-Bacon, '84 M38
Spaghetti, Bacon, '86 213; '87 82
Spaghetti Carbonara, '03 123
Spoonbread, Corn and Bacon, '81 129
Spread, Spinach-Bacon, '92 M310
Squash, Bacon-Flavored, '82 158
Squash, Creole, '01 180
Strata, Tomato-Bacon, '03 100
Supper Supreme, Sunday, '79 76
Sweet Potatoes, Bacon-Stuffed, '86 224
Tart, Tomato-Leek-Bacon, '03 325
Taters, Bacon-Fried, '02 55
Tomatoes, Bacon-and-Egg-Stuffed, '80 162
Tomatoes, Cornbread-Stuffed, '02 213
Tomatoes with Bacon, Saucy Fried, '81 210
Tortellini Carbonara, Creamy, '99 171
Trout Stuffed with Crawfish, Bacon-Wrapped, '99 54
Trout, Sweet Onion-Stuffed, '99 52
Turnovers, Turnip-Bacon, '04 213
Vegetable-Bacon Bowl, Marinated, '79 191
Vegetable Skillet, Summer, '00 138
BAKING POWDER
Single-Acting Baking Powder, '96 142
BANANAS
Alaskas, Banana Split, '87 10
Baked Bananas, '79 103; '96 163
Baked Bananas, Coffee-Kissed, '98 279
Baked Bananas, Honey-, '81 268
Baked Bananas with Orange Sauce, '79 115
Bars, Banana Breakfast, '79 124
Beverages
   Berry Flip, Banana-, '88 215; '89 20
   "Concrete," All Shook Up, '94 114
   Coolers, Banana, '91 308
   Crush, Banana, '80 88; '83 142
   Flip, Banana, '83 303
   Float, Strawberry-Banana, '87 160
   Frostee, Banana, '91 66
   Funky Monkey, '99 161
   Kabana, Banana, '86 316
   Malt, Banana-Chocolate, '89 170
   Milkshake, Banana, '85 47; '90 179
   Milk Shake, Banana-Pineapple, '84 59
   Milk Shake, Chocolate-Banana, '94 113
   Nog, Banana, '82 290
   Orange-Banana Flip, '82 48
   Orange-Banana Whip, '95 244

   Orange Slush, Banana-, '80 48; '81 155
   Pineapple-Banana Slush, '90 14
   Punch, Banana, '99 161; '01 93
   Purple Cow, '98 206
   Shake, Banana, '97 172
   Shake, Double Strawberry-Banana, '01 173
   Shake, Light Double Strawberry-Banana, '01 173
   Shake, Peanut Butter-Banana, '97 172
   Shake, Pineapple-Banana, '85 215
   Shake, Pineapple-Orange-Banana, '97 172
   Shake, Raspberry-and-Banana, '89 183
   Shake, Strawberry-Banana, '89 35; '97 172
   Slush, Banana, '83 56
   Smoothie, Banana, '87 160; '93 95
   Smoothie, Banana-Blueberry, '90 104
   Smoothie, Banana Breakfast, '03 46
   Smoothie, Banana-Peach Buttermilk, '04 22
   Smoothie, Berry-Banana Buttermilk, '00 49
   Smoothie, Honey-Banana, '89 144
   Smoothie, Orange-Banana, '97 173
   Smoothie, Quick Banana-Pineapple, '93 195
   Smoothies, Sunshine, '98 330
   Smoothie, Strawberry-Banana, '81 59
   Smoothie, Tropical, '81 50
   Strawberry Frost, Banana-, '87 199
   Tropical Delight, '89 182
Bisque, Banana-Raspberry, '93 161
Boats, Banana, '82 50; '00 173
Breads
   Apple Bread, Banana-, '85 250
   Banana Bread, '87 72
   Blueberry Bread, Banana-, '81 163
   Butterscotch Bread, Banana, '79 116
   Chocolate Chip-Banana Bread, '90 267
   Chocolate Chip-Banana Loaf, '85 115
   Cranberry-Banana Bread, '80 281; '90 294
   Date-Banana Loaves, Tropical, '95 143
   Easy Banana Bread, '96 97
   Fruity Banana Bread, '95 78
   Hawaiian Loaf, '80 225
   Honey-Banana Bread, '91 68
   Jam Bread, Banana-, '84 73
   Muffins, Banana, '80 88; '84 75
   Muffins, Banana Bran, '83 48
   Muffins, Banana-Chocolate, '94 197
   Muffins, Banana-Honey-Nut, '88 62
   Muffins, Banana-Nut, '93 140
   Muffins, Banana-Oat, '87 188
   Muffins, Banana Oat Bran, '89 106
   Muffins, Banana-Oatmeal, '84 20
   Muffins, Banana-Orange, '84 148
   Muffins, Banana-Poppyseed, '89 205
   Muffins, Banana-Praline, '04 21
   Muffins, Banana-Raisin, '89 218
   Muffins, Banana Surprise, '82 105
   Muffins, Jumbo Banana-Chocolate Chip, '93 339
   Muffins, Oat Bran-Banana, '91 18
   Muffins, Peanut Butter-Banana, '03 195
   Nut Bread, Banana-, '86 8, 70; '01 239; '04 259
   Nut Bread, Hawaiian Banana, '79 235
   Nut-Raisin Bread, Banana-, '81 59
   Oat Tea Loaf, Banana-, '87 256
   Roll, Banana-Nut, '85 112
   Sour Cream-Banana Bread, '79 190
   Wheat Bread, Banana, '81 14
   Whole Wheat Banana Bread, '80 88
   Whole Wheat-Banana Nut Bread, '84 50
   Zucchini Bread, Banana-, '85 326
Breakfast-in-a-Bowl, '89 87
Broiled Bananas with Honey, '84 175
Brownies, Banana-Split, '03 M43
Brownies, Chocolate-Banana, '80 160
Cake, Banana, '84 151
Cake, Banana-Blueberry, '86 247

Cake, Banana-Coconut, '93 154
Cake, Banana-Nut, '92 120
Cake, Banana Pound, '96 60; '98 195
Cake, Bananas Foster Crunch, '93 339
Cake, Banana Split, '99 48
Cake, Banana Waldorf, '85 118
Cake, Chocolate-Banana, '86 138
Cake, Deluxe Light Banana, '84 314
Cake, Hummingbird, '03 315
Cake, Lightened Hummingbird, '01 34
Cake, Marvelous Banana, '79 115
Cake, Peanut Butter-Banana, '80 87
Cake, Triple-Layered Banana, '00 244
Cake with Coconut Custard, Supreme Banana,
    '97 131
Candied Bananas, '83 179
Caramelized Bananas, '99 49
Casserole, Sweet Potato-Banana, '86 276
Cheesecake, Chocolate-Wrapped Banana, '99 M48
Chicken with Black Bean Sauce, Banana, '96 156
Cinnamon Toasty Fruity Delight, '00 193
Coffee Cake, Banana, '81 288
Coffee Cake, Banana Cream, '85 46
Coffee Cake, Banana-Sour Cream, '80 186; '97 231;
    '04 194
Coffee Cakes, Banana-Toffee, '02 M324
Cookies, Banana Oatmeal, '79 217
Crêpes Flambé, Banana, '84 262
Cupcakes, Banana-Chocolate, '02 187
Cupcakes, Banana-Cocoa, '80 130
Cupcakes, Banana Pudding Ice-Cream, '01 173
Curried Bananas, Fillets with Horseradish Sauce
    and, '85 230
Delights, Choco-Peanut, '99 197
Dessert, Banana Cream, '81 180
Dessert in a Nutshell, '96 318
Doughnuts, Banana, '86 137
Dressing, Banana-Poppy Seed, '98 184
Éclairs, Banana-Chocolate, '01 45
Fish, Caribbean Banana, '95 202
Flambé, Banana-Peach, '85 316
Foster, Bananas, '79 18; '83 M114; '86 139; '96 99
Foster, Elegant Bananas, '81 59
Foster for Two, Bananas, '80 115
Foster, Orange-Glazed Bananas, '91 91
Foster, Tropical Bananas, '79 231
Fritters, Banana, '79 213
Frosting, Banana-Nut, '79 115
Glace, Bananas, '96 46
Green Bananas Escabeche (Pickled Green Bananas),
    '92 169
Hawaiian, Bananas, '89 94
Ice Cream, Banana-Coconut, '02 164
Ice Cream, Banana-Graham, '91 56
Ice Cream, Banana-Nut, '00 143
Ice Cream, Banana Split, '80 176
Ice Cream, Straw-Ba-Nut, '80 177
Ice Cream, Strawberry-Banana-Nut, '88 203
Ice Milk, Banana Yogurt, '89 199
Jam, Banana, '82 296
Jam, Rosy Peach-Banana, '80 142
Napoleons, Banana, '00 50
Nutty Bananas, '79 251
Pancakes, Banana, '03 305
Pancakes, Banana-Nut, '98 160
Pancakes, Best, '99 194
Pancakes, Island, '87 225
Pancakes, Wheat Germ-Banana, '79 114
Pancakes with Peanut Butter and Jelly Syrups,
    Banana, '01 24
Pie, Banana Cream, '84 48; '87 207
Pie, Blueberry-Banana, '93 115
Pie, Caramel-Banana, '86 M165
Pie, Chocolate-Banana-Pecan Cream, '94 210

Pie, Creamy Coco-Nana, '00 95
Pie, Hawaiian Banana Cream, '90 105
Pie, Layered Banana Split, '83 189
Pie, Luscious Caramel Banana, '79 115
Pie, Peanut Butter-Banana, '01 315
Pie, Strawberry-Banana Glazed, '81 181
Pie, White Chocolate-Banana Cream, '94 314
Pie with Hot Buttered Rum Sauce, Banana, '88 204
Pizza, Banana Split-Brownie, '96 M164
Pops, Banana, '83 60; '84 44
Pops, Orange-Banana, '82 129
Pops, Yummy Banana, '01 231
Praline Bananas, '84 313
Pudding, Almost Banana, '88 174
Pudding, Banana, '82 53; '84 94; '85 255;
    '88 16, 32; '03 24
Pudding, Banana-Mallow, '86 139
Pudding, Bananas Foster Bread, '04 235
Pudding, Basic Banana, '81 59
Pudding, Best-Ever Banana, '00 332
Pudding, Creamy Banana, '89 M130
Pudding, Delicious Banana, '80 9
Pudding, Fudge-Banana, '97 331
Pudding, Graham Banana, '02 62
Pudding, No-Bake Banana, '91 172; '99 197
Pudding, Old-Fashioned Banana, '92 94
Pudding, Over-the-Moon Banana, '03 140
Pudding Parfait Pops, Banana, '96 180
Pudding, Peanut Butter-Banana, '93 340
Pudding, Sour Cream Banana, '98 90
Pudding, Surprise Banana, '86 7
Pudding with Sugar Biscuits, Banana, '04 72
Regal Bananas, '85 46
Salad, Banana, '87 80
Salad, Banana-Mixed Fruit, '79 270
Salad, Banana Split, '91 58
Salad, Frozen Banana, '82 80, 132
Salad with Celery Seed Dressing, Grapefruit-
    Banana, '91 237
Salsa, Banana, '96 85
Salsa, Banana Rum, '94 97
Salsa, Caribbean, '96 70
Sauce, Banana-Pineapple, '83 48
Sauce, Bananas Foster, '03 94
Sauce, Banana Sundae, '84 275
Sauce, Buttered Rum Pound Cake with Bananas
    Foster, '03 94
Sauce, Strawberry-Banana, '81 41
Sherbet, Banana-Orange, '83 162
Shortcake, Banana-Pecan, '93 43
Slaw, Banana-Nut, '86 250
Sorbet, Banana-Orange, '88 117
Soufflé, Banana Daiquiri, '84 317
Soup, Avocado-Banana-Yogurt, '80 78
Soup, Strawberry-Banana, '86 181
Spiced Bananas with Rum Sauce, '99 247
Splits, Cottage Cheese-Banana, '87 56
Splits, French Toast Banana, '96 M164
Sticky Fingers, '03 M168
Sundae, Breakfast, '98 206
Supreme, Banana-Berry, '81 205
Supreme, Bananas, '84 256
Syrup, Maple-Banana, '03 47
Terrine, Banana Split, '96 164
Topping, Pound Cake with Strawberry-Banana,
    '89 200
Topping, Strawberry-Banana, '87 125
Trifle, Banana Pudding, '98 273
Tropical Bananas, Easy, '00 141
Waffles, Banana-Ginger, '86 96
Waffles, Banana-Oatmeal, '94 206
Waffles, Banana Split, '89 205
BARBECUE. *See also* **GRILLED.**
Bean Dip, Barbecue, '03 138

Beans, Barbecue, '02 167
Beans, Barbecued, '94 248
Beans, Barbecued Green, '86 252
Beans, Barbecued Lima, '82 2
Beans, Barbecued Pork and, '79 100
Beans, Commissary Barbecue, '90 120
Beans, Skillet Barbecued, '93 217
Beef. *See also* **BARBECUE/Ribs.**
Barbecued Beef, '81 18
Beach Barbecue, Trish's, '03 206
Bourbon Barbecue, '88 129
Brisket, Barbecued, '86 154; '88 218
Brisket, Barbecued Beef, '83 11
Brisket, Denton, Texas, Barbecued Beef, '81 55
Brisket, Oven Barbecue, '01 259
Brisket, Smoky Barbecue, '03 160
Brisket with Sauce, Barbecued Beef, '86 153
Burgers, Barbecued, '82 168; '89 164
Chuck Roast Barbecue, '96 71
Corned Beef Sandwiches, Barbecued, '83 130
Cups, Barbecue, '79 129
Flank Steak with Molasses Barbecue Glaze,
    Grilled, '00 59
Four-Hour Barbecue, '00 18
Kebabs, Barbecued Steak, '79 89
Liver, Barbecued, '85 219
Loaves, Individual Barbecued Beef, '95 242
Meatballs, Oven Barbecued, '82 233
Meat Loaf, Barbecued, '80 60; '81 275; '87 216
Pot Roast, Barbecued, '79 17; '83 319
Rib Roast, Barbecued, '86 152
Roast, Barbecue, '98 245
Roast Barbecue, Beef, '79 159
Roast, Barbecued Beef, '82 96; '83 103
Sandwiches, Barbecue Beef, '99 327; '01 136
Sandwiches, Barbecued Beef, '81 25; '82 31;
    '83 34
Sandwiches, Debate Barbecue, '97 234
Saucy Barbecued Beef, '82 156
Slow-Cooker Beef Barbecue, '02 299
Steak, Barbecued Flank, '79 89
Steak, Marinated Barbecued Chuck, '80 156
Steak, Saucy Oven-Barbecued, '83 10
Supper, Barbecue Hobo, '99 108
Tenderloin, Barbecued Beef, '94 26
Bread, Barbecue, '99 105
Cabrito, Barbecued, '86 153
Chicken
Bake, Barbecued Chicken, '81 97
Barbecue Chicken, '86 122
Barbecued Chicken, '82 97, 106; '83 103;
    '85 144; '86 153; '89 167
Braised and Barbecued Chicken, Melt-in-Your-
    Mouth, '03 326
Carambola-Glazed Barbecued Chicken, '92 246
Chili-Barbecued Chicken, '98 170
Cranberry Chicken, Barbecued, '83 178
Fingers, Barbecue-Battered Chicken, '04 139
Foil, Barbecued Chicken in, '04 222
Golden Barbecued Chicken, '83 136
Grilled Barbecued Chicken, '81 154
Honey Barbecue Chicken, '04 197
Legs and Thighs, Barbecued Chicken, '94 94
Lemon Barbecued Chicken, '93 215
Marinated Barbecued Chicken, '79 90
Old South Barbecued Chicken, '82 97; '83 103
Orange Barbecued Chicken, '88 123
Oven-Baked Barbecue Chicken, '03 160
Oven-Barbecued Chicken, Kentucky-Style,
    '96 328
Oven-Barbecued Cranberry Chicken, '93 332
Pizza, Barbecue Chicken, '03 49
Pizza, Quick 'n' Easy Chicken Barbecue, '04 139
Salad, Warm Barbecue Chicken, '99 124

BARBECUE, Chicken
(continued)

Sauce, Chicken with White Barbecue, '89 M84;
'97 322; '01 168
Saucy Barbecued Chicken, '83 11
South-of-the-Border Barbecued Chicken,
'97 311
Sweet-and-Spicy Barbecued Chicken, '01 316
Tangy Barbecued Chicken, '86 186; '98 170
Zesty Barbecued Chicken, '80 M76
Zippy Barbecued Chicken, '83 213
Coleslaw, Barbecue, '97 139
Coleslaw, Best Barbecue, '97 214; '04 100
Corn on the Cob, Barbecued, '81 128
Dressing, Barbecue, '99 124
Dressing, Barbecue Salad, '80 74
Eggplant, Barbecue, '02 180
Fish. *See also* **BARBECUE/Seafood.**
Catfish, Barbecue Baked, '02 51
Catfish, Barbecued, '80 157
Catfish, Lemon Barbecued, '89 202
Fillets, Barbecued Fish, '86 182
Salmon, Barbecued, '81 181
Tacos, Barbecued Fish, '95 339
Tuna, Barbecued, '80 275
Frank Barbecue, Tangy, '79 63
Frankfurters, Barbecued, '83 144
Frankfurters, Oven-Barbecued, '83 11
Franks, Barbecued, '85 192
Lamb, Barbecued, '79 58
Lamb Chops, Barbecued, '79 89
Lamb Shanks, Barbecued, '92 128; '93 113
Meat Loaf Sandwiches, Barbecue, '04 188
Muffins, Barbecue, '96 246
Outdoor Cooking, '82 109
Popcorn, Cheesy Barbecue, '95 239
Pork. *See also* **BARBECUE/Ribs.**
Bannister's Barbecue, '92 166
Barbecued Pork, '80 72
Chops, Barbecue-Battered Pork, '04 139
Chops, Barbecued Pork, '81 10
Chops, Marinated Barbecued Pork, '79 90
Chops, Oven-Barbecued Pork, '81 234; '82 26;
'83 40
Ham Slices, Barbecued, '81 110
Home-Style Barbecue, '88 145
Nachos, Commissary Barbecue, '91 171
Pot Pie with Cheese Grits Crust, Barbecue,
'03 21
Pot Pie with Mashed Potato Crust, Barbecue,
'03 21
Quesadillas, Barbecue, '02 121
Quesadillas, Barbecued Pork, '04 187
Roast, Barbecued Pork, '03 147
Roast, Barbecued Pork Loin, '93 34
Roast Barbecue, Pork, '82 97; '83 104
Roast, Berry Barbecued Pork, '80 288
Sandwiches, Barbecue Pork, '00 23
Sausage, Barbecued, '86 153
Shoulder, Barbecued Pork, '81 111; '82 11
Shoulder, Barbecue Pork, '00 274
Spaghetti, Barbecue, '02 121
Spicy Barbecued Pork, '84 296
Sundae, Barbecue, '02 121
Potatoes, Barbecued, '91 311; '92 26
Potatoes, Barbecue Scalloped, '04 139
Rabbit, Hickory Barbecued, '82 216
Ribs
Apple Barbecued Ribs, '80 111
Apple-Barbecue Spareribs, '90 160
Baby Back Ribs, Barbecued, '97 234
Barbecued Ribs, '80 111; '85 159; '91 205

Barbecued Spareribs, '81 112; '82 12; '86 232;
'95 236
Barbecue Ribs, '99 68
Beef Short Ribs, Barbecued, '83 178
Country-Style Barbecued Ribs, '79 42
Country-Style Ribs, Barbecued, '95 237
Country-Style Spareribs, Barbecued, '80 73
Easy Barbecued Spareribs, '82 97; '83 104
Herbed Barbecued Ribs, '86 185
Oven-Barbecued Pork Ribs, '88 132
Saucy Barbecued Spareribs, '79 14
Short Ribs, Barbecued, '90 148
Slow-Cooker Barbecue Ribs, '03 160
Smoky Barbecued Ribs, '80 111
Southern Barbecued Spareribs, '79 90
Spicy Barbecued Spareribs, '84 93
Tangy Barbecued Ribs, '83 160
Tangy Barbecued Spareribs, '82 106
Rub, All-Purpose Barbecue, '03 130; '04 104
Rub, Barbecue, '03 130; '04 104
Rub, Master Class Barbecue, '98 244
Salad, Barbecue Macaroni, '82 276
Sauces
Apple Barbecue Sauce, '99 173
Bannister's Barbecue Sauce, '92 166
Barbecue Sauce, '84 172; '86 153; '88 218;
'91 16, 205; '93 129; '94 27
Barbecue Sauce, Baked Fish with, '84 92
Basting Sauce, '90 120; '01 106
Basting Sauce, Grill, '00 177
Beef Marinade, Tangy, '86 113
Beer Barbecue Sauce, '84 173
Blender Barbecue Sauce, Ribs with, '90 12
Bourbon Barbecue Sauce, '85 90
Brisket with Barbecue Sauce, Smoked, '85 144
Cider Vinegar Barbecue Sauce, '01 148
Cola Barbecue Sauce, '03 130; '04 104
Crickhollow Barbecue Sauce, '99 200
Dressed-Up Barbecue Sauce, '84 173
Drunken Sauce, '03 33
Eastern-Style Barbecue Sauce, '88 145
Easy Barbecue Sauce, '79 90; '82 178
Green Barbecue Sauce, '02 183
Handcrafted Barbecue Sauce, '98 45
Honey Barbecue Sauce, '04 197
John Wills's Barbecue Sauce, '92 255
Lemon Barbecue Sauce, Herbed, '94 154;
'98 334
Lemony Barbecue Sauce, '88 M177; '95 31
Maple Syrup Barbecue Sauce, '94 154
Mustard Barbecue Sauce, '84 173
Orange Barbecue Sauce, Spareribs with, '83 11
Oven Barbecue Sauce, '82 233
Paprika Barbecue Sauce, '79 90
Peanut Butter Barbecue Sauce, '81 233
Peppery Barbecue Sauce, '00 255
Piquant Barbecue Sauce, '79 159
Savory Barbecue Sauce, '86 153
Smoky Chipotle 'Cue Sauce, '04 87
Special Barbecue Sauce, '82 177
Spicy Southwest Barbecue Sauce, '94 154
Sweet-and-Sour 'Cue Sauce, '04 87
Sweet-and-Sour Marinade, '86 113
Sweet-and-Tangy Barbecue Sauce, '00 119
Sweet Sauce, '90 120; '01 106
Tangy Barbecue Sauce, '97 323; '99 104; '00 230
Teriyaki Marinade, '86 114
Texas Barbecue Sauce, '99 210
Texas Barbecue Sauce, LBJ's, '97 42
The Sauce, '00 177
Thick and Robust Barbecue Sauce, '94 95
Thick and Sweet Barbecue Sauce, '94 95
Thin and Tasty Barbecue Sauce, '94 95
Tomato Barbecue Sauce, Fresh, '84 172

Vinegar Sauce, Peppery, '01 148
Western-Style Barbecue Sauce, '88 145
White Barbecue Sauce, '94 95
White Barbecue Sauce, Chicken with, '89 M84;
'97 322; '01 168
Zippy Barbecue Sauce, '92 166
Seafood. *See also* **BARBECUE/Ribs.**
Oysters, Barbecued, '82 247
Shrimp and Cornbread-Stuffed Peppers,
Barbecued, '97 261
Shrimp, Barbecue, '96 210; '97 58; '00 30
Shrimp, Barbecued, '82 74; '84 93; '90 28
Shrimp, Cajun Barbecued, '87 95
Shrimp, Hickory-Smoked Barbecue, '00 89
Shrimp, New Orleans Barbecue, '02 201
Turkey Barbecue, '90 158
BARLEY
Baked Barley, '91 133
Casserole, Barley, '84 281
Pilaf, Barley-Vegetable, '91 33
Rolls, Wine-Sauced Beef-and-Barley, '87 269
Salad, Barley, '92 212
Salad, Barley-Broccoli, '90 135
Salad, Black Bean-and-Barley, '94 174
Soup, Hearty Bean-and-Barley, '86 304
Soup, Turkey-Barley, '91 312
Stuffing, Cornish Hens with Barley-Mushroom,
'97 242
Vegetables, Barley and, '91 81
BEANS. *See also*/**LENTILS.**
Anasazi Beans with Mushrooms, Stewed, '95 226
Bake, Cheesy Beef-and-Bean, '82 89
Baked
Baked Beans, '01 127, 334
Barbecue Beans, '02 167
Barbecued Beans, '94 248
Barbecued Pork and Beans, '79 100
Barbecue Sundae, '02 121
Beefy Baked Beans, '80 136; '84 149; '85 142
Bourbon Baked Beans, '95 182
Chuckwagon Beans, '81 188
Crowd-Pleasing Baked Beans, '82 127
Easy Baked Beans, '85 141
Favorite Baked Beans, '86 210
Five-Bean Bake, '03 139
Franks, Beans and, '85 142
Franks, Beany Kraut and, '79 64
Franks, Hawaiian Baked Beans and, '80 136
Frolickers Baked Beans, '03 92
Genuine Baked Beans, '83 26
Ham, Baked Beans with, '80 136
Hamburger-Bean Bake, '95 121
Hawaiian-Style Baked Beans, '86 210
Hearty Baked Beans, '01 259
Home-Style Baked Beans, '00 172
K.C. Baked Beans, '98 244; '03 107
Lowcountry Baked Beans, '98 332
Maple Heights Baked Beans, '91 223
Meat Baked Beans, Three-, '86 210
Medley, Baked Bean, '80 100
Mixed Baked Beans, '87 92
Molasses Baked Beans, '82 139; '84 327; '86 20;
'99 105
More Beans, Baked Beans and, '92 173
Old-Fashioned Baked Beans, '84 25
Picnic Baked Beans, '83 143; '85 142
Polynesian Beans-and-Franks, '84 M11
Pork Chops with Baked Beans, '93 18
Quick Baked Beans, '80 136
Quintet, Baked Beans, '93 105; '94 100
Root Beer Baked Beans, '04 212
Rum-Laced Bean Bake, '82 283; '83 72
Slow Cooker Bean Bake, '99 88
Smoked Baked Beans, '79 150

Sorghum Baked Beans, '03 106
Spiced Baked Beans, '85 142
Three-Bean Bake, '81 155; '99 88; '03 106
White Bean Bake, Turnip Greens and, '94 246
Barbecue Beans, Commissary, '90 120
Barbecued Beans, Skillet, '93 217
Beefy Beans, '82 59
Black. *See also*/**BEANS/Salads, Soups.**
Appetizer, Black Bean, '83 50
Black Beans, '93 28
Bow Ties, Black Beans, and Key Limes, '96 291
Broth with Black Beans and Cilantro, Southwestern Scallop, '87 123
Burgers, Black Bean, '98 144
Cakes with Greens and Apple Dressing, Black Bean, '92 216
Cakes with Smoked Salmon Salsa, Corn-and-Black Bean, '96 272
Casserole, Easy Enchilada, '02 143
Casserole of Black Beans, '95 27
Chicken Cobbler, Spicy Tex-Mex, '03 324
Chicken with Black Beans and Oranges, '00 94
Chicken with Black Beans and Salsa, Poached, '87 217
Chili, Black Bean, '02 20
Chili Goes Southwest, Basic, '93 326
Chili Marsala, Black Bean, '95 16
Cuban Black Beans, '88 196; '99 56
Cuban Black Beans, Traditional, '98 21
Dip, Black Bean, '95 93
Egg Rolls, Tex-Mex, '01 328
Egg Rolls with Creamy Cilantro Dipping Sauce, Tex-Mex, '03 327
Frijoles con Cerveza (Beans with Beer), '81 66
Frittata, Avocado-and-Black Bean, '02 212
Garbanzo-Black Bean Medley, '99 236
Guacamole, Black Bean, '94 277
Lasagna, Easy Mexican, '03 22
Lasagna, Spinach-Black Bean, '02 44
Marinated Black Beans, '93 131
Mexicorn, Black Bean, '96 189
Pancakes with Gazpacho Butter, Black Bean, '92 86
Pizza, Fiesta, '00 85
Puree, Spicy Chicken with Black Bean, '97 48
Quesadillas, Chicken-and-Black Bean, '96 288
Quesadillas, Chorizo, Black Bean, and Corn, '00 148
Relish, Black Bean-Tomatillo, '87 121
Relish, Cranberry-Black Bean, '03 243
Rice, Black Beans and, '80 222; '89 178; '91 82; '95 309
Rollups, Southwestern, '01 135
Salsa, Black Bean, '93 155; '94 161; '97 226; '00 122; '03 146, 323; '04 25
Salsa, Black Bean-and-Corn, '94 80
Salsa, Black Bean-Corn, '96 126; '04 322
Salsa, Chunky Black Bean, '03 25
Salsa, Corn-Black Bean, '96 15
Salsa, Hill Country, '97 123
Salsa, Orange-Black Bean, '98 231
Salsa Pork Chops, Black Bean-and-Corn, '01 320
Salsa with Beans and Corn, Southwestern, '96 275
Salsa with Citrus Dressing, Black Bean, '01 60
Sandwiches, Caribbean Seafood, '98 105
Sauce, Banana Chicken with Black Bean, '96 156
Sauce, Black Bean, '93 59; '98 46
Sauce, Spicy Beef Fillets with Black Bean, '97 184
Spaghetti, Black Bean, '92 217
Spaghetti, Salsa, '00 58
Spanish Black Beans, '84 327
Spicy Beef and Black Beans, '99 331

Spicy Black Beans, '04 119
Stew, Baja Pork, '98 283
Strudel, Meatless Mexican, '98 29
Terrine with Fresh Tomato Coulis and Jalapeño Sauce, Black Bean, '93 230
Terrine with Goat Cheese, Black Bean, '87 120
Tony's Black Beans, '96 289
Tostadas, Rice-and-Black Bean, '97 65
Tostadas, Shrimp-and-Black Bean, '93 204
Wraps, Black Bean, '00 211
Wraps, Western, '99 194
Yellow Rice, Black Beans and, '95 126
Yellow Rice, Black Beans with, '82 2
Yellow Rice, Easy Black Beans and, '92 308
Burgers, Spicy Bean, '00 84
Burgers with Adobo Mayonnaise, Bean, '02 202
Burrito Appetizers, Bean, '94 226
Burritos, Chicken, '01 55
Burritos, Meat-and-Bean, '81 194
Butterbeans, '90 166
Butterbeans, Bacon, and Tomatoes, '96 36; '00 184
Butterbeans, Smoky Speckled, '04 167
Butterbeans with Bacon and Green Onions, '96 267
Cabbage Rolls, Southwestern, '97 214
Cannellini Beans, Rosemary, '95 213
Casserole, Bean-and-Cornbread, '92 243
Casserole, Chuck Wagon Bean, '93 198
Casserole, Fajita, '97 96
Casserole, Mexican, '00 280
Casserole, Spicy Mexican Bean, '84 114
Casserole, Three-Bean, '88 56
Cassoulet, '96 328
Cassoulet, Easy Chicken, '00 43; '04 325
Cassoulet, Easy Herb Crust, '01 311
Cassoulet, Vegetarian, '96 329
Chickpea-Chipotle Tostadas, '03 181
Chickpea Spread, Creamy, '03 293; '04 146
Chickpea Stew, Chicken, Kale, and, '98 47
Chili, '98 95
Chili and Beans, Ranch, '79 270; '80 11
Chili Bean Roast, '87 268; '88 102
Chili, Big-Batch, '04 242
Chili, Chilly Night, '99 317
Chili, Easy, '02 299
Chili, Game-Day, '00 238
Chili in a Biscuit Bowl, '98 224
Chili, Mom's, '93 292
Chili, Red Bean, '02 20
Chili, Slow-Cooker Red Bean, '02 20
Chili, Spicy 3-Bean, '03 291
Chili Supper, Hot, '99 279
Chili Surprise, '82 229
Chili, Three-Bean, '00 34
Chili, Turkey-Bean, '88 M213
Chili, White, '91 284
Chili, White Bean, '02 20
Chili, White Christmas, '98 266; '02 260
Chili with Beans, Easy, '92 262
Chili with Beans, Meaty, '85 250
Chimichangas, Baked Spicy Beef, '97 319
Chimichangas, Bean-and-Cheese, '01 16
Creole Beans and Rice, '80 223
Crostini, Mexican, '95 142
Crostini, Roasted Red Pepper-Feta, '04 69
Dinner, Quick Mexican, '98 224
Dip, Barbecue Bean, '03 138
Dip, Bean, '89 97
Dip, Cheese-Bean, '85 208
Dip, Chickpea-and-Red Pepper, '99 138
Dip, Fiesta, '96 212; '03 284
Dip, Garbanzo, '93 94
Dip, Hotshot Bean, '87 195
Dip, Layered Nacho, '81 261; '03 207
Dip, Mexican Fiesta, '98 234

Dip, Prairie Fire Bean, '80 195
Dip, Salsa-Bean, '98 285
Dip, South-of-the-Border, '81 235
Dip with Bone Crackers, Goblin, '01 204
Dogs, Taco, '02 M57
Enchiladas, Three-Bean, '91 133
Farmer's Beans and Rice with Rosemary Biscuits, '99 16
Franks, Jiffy Beans and, '91 M172
Franks 'n' Beans, Stove-Top, '88 201
Garbanzo Bean Spread, Herbed, '99 160
Garbanzo Dinner, Beef-and-, '84 31
Garbanzo Dip, Pesto-, '03 299
Garbanzo Stew, Greek, '02 43
Garbanzo-Vegetable Pitas, '00 58
Gorditas with Turkey Mole, '03 18
Green. *See also*/**BEANS/Salads, Soups.**
Alfredo with Cheese Ravioli, Green Bean, '01 180
Almonds, Green Beans with, '84 253
Amandine, Green Beans, '79 276; '82 M20; '85 156; '97 238
Appalachian Green Beans, '81 215
Asian Green Beans, '01 237
au Gratin, Green Beans, '80 116
Bacon and Mushrooms, Green Beans with, '92 13
Bacon Dressing, Green Beans with, '85 147
Bacon-Topped Green Beans, '80 M123
Baked Green Beans, '91 159
Bake, Green Bean, '99 112
Barbecued Green Beans, '86 252
Basil Beans and Tomatoes, '83 172
Basil, Green Beans with, '82 96
Basil Vinaigrette, Green Beans with, '02 172
Blue Cheese, Green Beans with, '88 57
Bow-Tie Green Beans, '94 320
Buffet Green Beans, '93 325
Bundles, Bean, '80 246; '83 67
Bundles, Green Bean, '83 180; '87 118
Buttered Green Beans, '92 54
Buttery Green Beans, '02 307
Caramelized Onion, Green Beans with, '00 33
Caramelized Onions, Green Beans with, '95 288
Cashews, Green Beans with, '89 202
Casserole, Chicken-Green Bean, '85 296
Casserole, Corn-and-Bean, '90 208
Casserole, Creamy Chicken-Green Bean, '97 158
Casserole, Easy Green Bean, '87 284
Casserole, Green Bean, '79 106; '84 145; '02 197
Casserole, Green Bean-and-Corn, '88 123; '99 36
Casserole, Italian Green Bean-and-Artichoke, '85 81
Celery, Green Beans and Braised, '84 254
Cheese-Topped Green Beans, '79 100
Cheesy Green Beans, '80 157
Chinese Green Beans, '96 330
Creamed Green Beans, French-Style, '88 252
Cumin Green Beans, '82 90
Dilled Carrots and Green Beans, '99 223
Dilled Green Beans, '82 106; '86 157; '88 101; '89 203; '93 279; '96 172; '99 170
Dill Green Beans, '93 136
Dilly Green Beans, '80 116
Excellent, Green Beans, '94 321
French Green Beans, '90 208
French Quarter Green Beans, '80 298; '81 26
Fresh Green Beans, '79 122
Garlic Green Beans, '91 159; '94 273; '00 260; '01 111
Garlic-Herb Butter, Green Beans with, '02 61
Garlic-Tarragon Green Beans, '04 246
Gingered Green Beans, '02 283
Goldenrod Beans, '83 111

BEANS, Green
(continued)

Grape Tomatoes, Green Beans with, '03 231
Gratin, Gourmet Green Bean, '99 M334
Greek Green Beans, '94 165
Green Beans, '80 126; '87 M151; '97 263
Ham and Potatoes, Green Beans with, '01 223
Herbed Green Beans, '83 M147, 177; '88 M190
Herb Green Beans, '89 321
Herbs, Green Beans with, '82 90
Indian-Style Green Beans, '88 265
Italian Green Beans, '85 147; '90 164; '92 183
Italian, Green Beans, '87 10
Italian Green Beans, Sesame, '82 174
Italian Green Beans with Almonds, '81 207
Italian Green Beans with Onion and Basil,
   '03 241
Italiano, Green Bean, '94 248
Italiano, Green Beans, '86 144
Lemon-Dill Butter, Green Beans with, '99 141
Lemon-Dill Green Beans, '01 181
Lemon-Dill Sauce, Potatoes and Green Beans
   with, '01 89
Lemon Green Beans, '89 275
Lemon, Green Beans with, '03 66
Lemon-Pecan Green Beans, '04 285
Lemon-Walnut Green Beans, '93 304
Lemony Green Beans, '85 190; '99 259
Linguine with Green Beans and Walnut Sauce,
   '04 128
Lorraine's Green Beans, '99 319
Marinated Beets, Green Beans, and Carrots,
   '88 162
Marinated Green Beans, '83 145
Marinated Green Beans with Tomatoes, Olives,
   and Feta, '03 163
Marinated Italian Beans, '86 M226
Marinated Vegetables, '81 239
Marjoram, Fresh Green Beans with, '91 159
Mediterranean-Style Green Beans, '79 100
Medley, Green Bean, '85 108
Medley, Peppery Green Bean, '93 181
Minted Green Beans, '84 104
Mushroom-Bacon Green Beans, '91 291; '92 255
Mushrooms and Sage, Green Beans with, '02 314
Mushroom Sauce, Green Beans in Sherried,
   '93 206
Mushrooms, Green Beans with, '82 21; '93 89
Mustard, Green Beans and Tomatoes with, '87 83
New Potatoes, Green Beans with, '87 164
Nutty Green Beans, '88 M187
Oregano, Green Beans with, '97 218
Oriental Green Beans, '88 43
Oriental, Green Beans, '91 158
Parmesan Green Beans, '04 327
Pecans, Green Beans with Buttered, '92 61
Pepper Strips, Green Beans and, '86 170
Pesto Green Beans, '01 181; '03 185
Pickled Beans, Dressed-Up, '86 251
Pimiento, Tangy Green Beans with, '00 170
Pole Beans, Old-Fashioned, '80 100
Potatoes, Down-Home Beans and, '85 254
Potatoes, Green Beans and, '91 221
Potatoes, Snap Beans and, '98 177
Provençal, Green Beans, '81 182; '91 158
Red Peppers and Pearl Onions, Green Beans with
   Roasted, '93 260
Red Potatoes, Green Beans and, '03 158
Risotto, Green Bean, '03 68
Roasted Green Beans, Ginger-, '01 180
Roasted Green Beans, Potatoes, and Fennel,
   '00 322

Roasted Green Beans with Mushrooms, '04 182
Roquefort Cheese and Walnuts, Green Beans
   with, '02 255
Saucy Green Beans, '83 206
Savory Green Beans, '89 70, 235
Seasoned Green Beans, '88 304
Shallots and Red Bell Pepper, Green Beans with,
   '97 251
Shallots, Green Beans with, '00 315; '04 248
Shuck Beans, '81 216
Simple Green Beans, '92 100
Smothered Green Beans, Southern, '02 55
Snap Beans, '86 218
Snap Beans, Simple, '85 148
Snap, or Wax Beans, Green, '85 105
Sour Cream, Green Beans in, '80 116
Sour Cream, Green Beans with, '82 90
Southern-Style Green Beans, '79 283
Spaghettini with Green Beans and Walnut Brown
   Butter, '03 170
Spanish Green Beans, '80 116
Spanish-Style Green Beans, '84 128
Special Green Beans, '90 268
Spicy Green Beans with Purple Onion, '98 286
Squash, Beans, and Tomatoes, '83 148
Steamed Green Beans, Basic, '01 180
Stir-Fried Green Beans, '85 148; '86 305
Sugared Green Beans, '04 223
Surprise, Green Bean, '86 9
Sweet-and-Sour Beans, '87 197
Sweet-and-Sour Green Beans, '79 184; '81 158;
   '82 90; '91 250
Sweet-and-Sour Green Beans and Carrots, '83 6
Sweet-and-Sour Snap Beans, '89 173
Sweet 'n' Hot Green Beans and Carrots, '00 211
Tangy Green Beans, '85 M142; '89 314, 332
Tangy Green Beans with Pimiento, '01 21
Tarragon Dressing, Green Beans with Creamy,
   '93 191
Tarragon, Green Beans, '98 328
Thyme-Scented Green Beans with Smoked
   Almonds, '01 57
Tomatoes, Bean-Stuffed, '84 34
Tomatoes, Green Beans with, '85 137
Tomatoes, Green Beans with Cherry, '86 177
Tomato-Feta Green Beans, '99 59
Tomato Sauce, Green Beans in, '01 84
Tomato Skillet, Bean-and-, '90 316
Vegetable-Herb Trio, '83 172
Vinaigrette, Green Beans, '83 25; '93 120;
   '94 90; '96 177
Vinaigrette, Kentucky Wonder Green Beans,
   '94 158
Walnut Dressing, Green Beans with, '94 279
Zucchini, Green Beans with, '84 128; '02 251
Hot Dogs, Beany, '82 190
Hummas, '92 155
Hummus, '96 158; '02 99
Hummus, Creamy Dried Tomato, '95 284
Hummus, Low-Fat, '99 137
Hummus, Quick, '95 93
Hummus, Red Pepper, '00 132; '02 31
Hummus, White Bean, '01 32
Kidney Bean Casserole, '90 136
Kidney Beans and Rice, Smoky, '03 290
Kidney Beans, Mexican, '90 205
Kielbasa with Beans, Easy Cheesy, '01 28
Lasagna, Mexican, '01 282
Lasagna, Spinach-Bean, '92 96
Legumes, Marinated, '90 197
Lemon-Mint Beans, '88 22
Lima. *See also* **BEANS/Salads, Soups.**
   Baked Lima Beans, '96 217
   Bake, Lima-Bacon, '86 9

Barbecued Lima Beans, '82 2
Beans, Lima, '80 127
Beef-and-Lima Bean Dinner, '84 292
Canadian Bacon, Lima Beans with, '83 219;
   '84 245
Casserole, Ham and Lima, '79 192
Casserole, Lima Bean, '79 189; '83 313; '86 225;
   '87 284; '95 132
Casserole, Lima Bean Garden, '83 218; '84 246
Casserole, Spicy Lima Bean, '79 189
Casserole, Swiss Lima Bean, '80 191
Cheese and Limas in Onion Shells, '81 86
Cheese Limas, Spanish, '86 225
Chilly Lima Beans, '81 206
Combo, Hot Lima and Tomato, '83 219
Creole, Lima Beans, '80 191; '85 137
Deluxe, Lima Beans, '79 289; '80 26
Fresh Lima Beans and Scallions, '82 133
Gratin with Lima Beans and Egg, New Potato,
   '01 71
Marinated Limas, '86 225
Medley, Carrot-Lima-Squash, '80 123
Minted Lima Beans, '98 86
Pâté, Lima Bean-and-Fresh Herb, '04 70
Rancho Lima Beans, '80 191
Savory Lima Beans, '83 219; '84 246
Savory Sauce, Lima Beans and Carrots with,
   '84 196
Sour Cream, Lima Beans in, '79 189; '88 41
Spanish-Style Lima Beans, '83 25
Stew, Brunswick, '97 315
Succotash, '98 177; '02 16
Succotash, Easy, '80 165
Succotash, Garden, '04 160
Succotash, Quick, '97 302
Succotash, Savory, '96 63
Super Lima Beans, '79 189
Supper, Sausage-Bean, '86 52
Mogumbo, '93 32
Nachos, Best-Ever, '79 91
Nachos, Easy, '84 30
Nachos, Make-Ahead, '80 M135
Nachos, Southwestern, '96 170
Navy Beans, Curried, '00 201
Pasta, Beans and, '99 35
Pasta with Beans, '99 236
Pasta with Beans and Greens, '02 202
Pie, Tortilla, '96 135
Pigs in a Blanket, Mexican, '00 199
Pinto
   Beef-and-Bean Supper, '82 2
   Best Pinto Beans, '03 159
   Burgers, Pinto, '98 51
   Burritos, Hot Phyllo, '98 312
   Casserole, Beef, Bean, and Cornbread, '99 215
   Chalupa, Bean, '80 223
   Chalupas, Bean, '83 313
   Chalupas, Pork, '83 160
   Chili, Tex-Mex, '83 26
   Chili, Vegetable, '97 179
   Cow Camp Pinto Beans, '94 28
   Dip, Hot Bean, '04 323
   Enchiladas, Spicy Bean, '88 18
   Frijoles, '02 119
   Frijoles Rancheros, '88 148
   Ham, Pinto Beans with, '97 210
   Lasagna, Texas, '98 52
   Mexican Pinto Beans, '93 69; '94 30; '00 241
   Pie, Pinto Bean, '80 40
   Pinto Beans, '87 303
   Potatoes, Chili-Topped, '98 M289
   Ranch Beans, Laredo, '81 75
   Ranch Beans, Texas, '90 198
   Razorback Beans, '84 328

Refried Beans, '79 185
Rice, South Texas Beans and, '85 252
Salsa, Warm Pinto Bean-and-Bacon, '03 331
Sandwiches, Bean Salad, '81 243
Sausage, Hearty Pintos and, '88 296
Smashed Pinto Beans, '03 129
Souper Pintos, Texas, '98 51
Southwestern Beans, '89 16
Spicy-Hot Beans, '89 17
Spicy Hot Pintos, '83 26
Sweet-Hot Pinto Beans, '86 114
Texas Beans, '97 139
Texas Pinto Beans, '01 65
Trailride Pinto Beans, '85 154
Wraps, Chicken-and-Bean Slaw, '04 163
Pitas, Fajita, '99 239
Pizza, Cheesy Mexican, '00 314
Pizza, Mexican, '99 119
Pizza, Red Pepper Hummus, '01 56
Pole Beans, Home-Cooked, '96 46
Pork Chops, Mexican, '99 108
Pork Loin, Braised Tuscan, '04 202
Pot of Beans, Buzz's, '03 19
Quesadillas, Easy, '98 M205
Quesadilla Torta, '97 325
Ragoût with Cilantro-Cornmeal Dumplings, Bean,
    '97 209
Ranch-Style Beans, '00 43
Red Bean Salsa, '97 227
Red Beans and Couscous, '99 22
Red Beans and Rice, '80 58; '83 89; '84 37; '87 45;
    '90 27; '96 218; '02 35
Red Beans and Rice, Cajun, '83 26
Red Beans and Rice, Delta, '98 146
Red Beans and Rice, Easy, '90 220; '99 M219
Red Beans and Rice, New Orleans, '97 235
Red Beans and Rice, Spicy, '02 56
Refried Beans, '79 185; '96 160
Refried Beans, Easy, '99 57
Ribs and Beans, Spicy-Sweet, '02 299; '03 314
Rice, Caribbean Beans and, '99 121
Rollups, Mediterranean, '00 277
Salads
Black Bean-and-Barley Salad, '94 174
Black Bean and Black-Eyed Pea Salad, '03 54
Black Bean-and-Cheese Salad, '92 217
Black Bean-and-Rice Salad, '00 327
Black Bean Salad, '89 217; '97 196; '98 208;
    '01 198
Black Bean Salad, Caribbean Shrimp-and-,
    '93 143
Cannellini Bean Salad, Tuna-and-, '86 143
Chicken-Black Bean Salad, '99 124
Chickpea Salad, '01 55
Chilled Bean Salad, '80 178
Confetti Bean Salad, '01 198
Cornbread Salad, Dianne's Southwestern, '04 133
Corn Salad, Confetti, '96 168
Cucumber-Bean Salad, '83 81
Dill-Icious Green Beans, '98 53
Fennel-Salad, Bean-and-, '01 198
Five-Bean Salad, Hot, '81 149
Four-Bean Salad, '79 20; '84 82
Full o' Beans Salad, '81 38
Garbanzo Salad, '82 2
Garbanzo Salad, Avocado-, '81 33
Garbanzo Salad, Couscous-and-, '02 65
Garden Medley Salad, '80 122
Green Bean-and-Okra Salad with Feta,
    Marinated, '00 131
Green Bean-and-Tomato Salad, '86 180
Green Bean-Peanut Salad, '86 117
Green Bean-Potato Salad, '83 80; '01 181;
    '04 142

Green Bean-Red Potato Salad, '96 175
Green Bean Salad, '87 90
Green Bean Salad, Cold, '84 106
Green Bean Salad, Crispy, '82 239
Green Bean Salad, German, '92 169
Green Bean Salad, Hot, '86 298; '87 176
Green Bean Salad in Tomatoes, '01 181
Green Bean Salad, Lettuce and, '80 79
Green Bean Salad, Molded, '85 252
Green Bean Salad, Paprika-, '86 191
Green Bean Salad, Pickled, '82 239
Green Bean Salad, Potato-and-, '00 162
Green Bean Salad, Roasted Red Pepper-and-,
    '99 322
Green Bean Salad, Speedy, '84 283
Green Bean Salad, Tomato-and-, '97 162
Green Bean Salad with Feta, '04 169
Green Beans-and-Cheese Salad, '91 159
Green Bean Slaw, '95 108
Green Beans Vinaigrette, '83 25; '93 120; '94 90;
    '96 177
Green Bean, Walnut, and Feta Salad, '96 273;
    '00 321
Hominy-Bean Salad, '88 266
Hot German-Style Bean Salad, '91 314
Kidney Bean-Salami Pasta Toss, '85 165
Layered Salad, '86 35
Layered Salad, Mexican, '02 65
Layered Salad, Tex-Mex, '03 201
Layered Southwestern Salad, '01 97
Lima Bean-Tomato Salad, '85 137
Lima Salad), You Lima My Life (Paprika, '96 159
Marinated Bean-and-Rice Salad, '87 152
Marinated Bean-Pasta Salad, '94 167; '97 328
Marinated Bean Salad, '85 137, 296; '89 314;
    '93 312; '94 167; '98 331
Marinated Bean Salad, Crunchy, '84 197
Marinated Combo Salad, '82 267
Marinated Corn-Bean Salad, '87 9
Meal in a Bowl, '96 138
Mexican Dinner Salad, '98 330
Mexican Salad, '94 202
Mexican Tossed Salad, '81 280
Mexicorn-Bean Salad, '96 184
Mixed Bean Salad, '83 217
Niçoise, Salad, '86 35; '03 35
One-Bean Salad with Lime-Mustard Dressing,
    '00 202
Overnight Fiesta Salad, '83 80
Pinto Salad, '86 169
Pole Bean-Potato Salad, Hot, '79 74
Pork-'n'-Bean Salad, '87 83
Potato-Bean Salad, '82 301
Quick Bean Salad, '89 128
Red Bean Slaw, '79 247
Rice-and-Bean Salad, '85 22
Rice-and-Bean Salad, Zesty, '02 84
Rice Salad, Beans-and-, '91 44
Saucy Bean Salad, '84 18
Sausage Salad, Bean-and-, '91 313
Six-Bean Salad, Colorful, '87 82
Southwest Salad, '81 113; '03 280
Spicy Bean Salad, '96 46
Sprout Salad, Bean, '82 113
Supreme Bean Salad, '91 202
Sweet-and-Sour Bean Salad, '85 198; '86 147
Sweet-and-Sour Beans with Sprouts, '86 32
Sweet-and-Sour Vegetable Salad, '81 25
Sweet Bean Salad, '01 46
Tabbouleh Salad, Southwestern, '01 216
Veggie-Bean Salad, '04 328
Veggie Salad, Sweet-and-Hot Bean-and-, '04 184
Veggies, Marinated, '01 127
White Bean-and-Tuna Salad, '01 35

White Bean-and-Tuna Salad Sandwiches, '02 31
White Bean Salad, Tuna-and-, '98 209
White Bean-Tuna Salad, '98 208
Wild Rice-and-Kidney Bean Salad, '01 175
Salsa, Pork Chops with Black-and-White, '97 200
Salsa, Smoky Three-Bean, '02 202
Sandwiches, Falafel, '96 23
Sauce, Picante-Bean, '96 220
Sauce, Pork-and-Onions with Bean, '85 76
Sausage-and-Bean Dinner, '95 108
Sausage-and-Bean Supper, '02 233
Sausage, Beans, and Rice, Texas, '84 296
Sauté, Vegetarian, '95 69
Shuck Beans, '81 216
Soups
Bacon Soup, Bean and, '83 26
Barley Soup, Hearty Bean-and-, '86 304
Bean-Chicken Soup, '99 283
"Bean Counter" Soup, '92 80
Beanolla Soup, '94 248
Bean Soup, '80 25
Black Bean Soup, '88 30, 266; '89 28; '93 231;
    '98 291; '02 121; '03 219
Black Bean Soup, Carolina, '92 139
Black Bean Soup, Marge Clyde's, '96 29
Cabbage-Bean Soup, '97 301
Capitol Hill Bean Soup, '80 222
Chicken Soup, Fiesta, '04 323
Chicken Soup, Mexican, '00 336; '03 63
Chicken Soup, Witches' Brew, '01 205
Chili Bean Soup, '96 71
Chill-Chaser Soup, '87 282
Drunken Bean Soup, '87 283
Fiesta Chowder, '02 305
French Market Soup, '92 49; '94 317
French Market Soup Mix, '94 317
Green Bean, Mushroom, and Ham Chowder,
    Creamy, '99 M336
Green Bean Soup, Cream of, '84 111
Guadalajara Soup, '88 30
Ham-and-Bean Soup, '84 4
Ham-and-Bean Soup, Spicy, '94 322
Ham Soup, Bean-and-, '04 325
Hominy Soup, Bean-and-, '95 23
Italian Soup, Chunky, '99 20
Leafy Bean Soup, '86 223
Minestra, '97 246
Minestrone, Cheesy, '99 17
Minestrone, Meatball, '00 242
Minestrone Soup, '91 258
Minestrone Soup Mix, '91 258
Mix, Bean Soup, '99 283
Navy Bean Soup, '84 280; '96 19
Navy Bean Soup, Chunky, '83 291
Navy Bean Soup, Savory, '87 282
Pasta Soup, Bean and, '94 220
Polish Sausage Soup, '99 317
Quick Bean Soup, '99 97
Red Bean Soup with Walnuts, '96 243
Refried Bean Soup, '96 136
Sausage-Bean Chowder, '83 20
Sausage-Bean Soup, '85 88
Sausage-Bean Soup, Spicy, '83 229
Sausage, Spinach, and Bean Soup, '99 311
Taco Soup, '99 36
Three-Bean Soup, '89 17
Three-Bean Soup, Spicy, '91 28
Tortellini Soup, '98 68
Tortilla Soup, '04 26
Turkey Soup, Bean-and-, '93 319
Vegetable-Bean Soup, '83 317
White Bean Chowder with Sage Pesto, '97 22
White Bean Soup, '83 229; '90 201
White Bean Soup, Spicy, '94 225

BEANS
(continued)

Spicy Beans with Coconut Milk, '03 175
Stew, Brunswick, '01 148, 219
Stew, Santa Fe Chicken, '97 193
Taco Bake, '97 326
Tacos, Chicken-and-Bean, '93 293
Taco Stacks, Soft, '02 54
Tomatoes, Stuffed, '96 82
Tortas, Grilled Chicken, '01 M187
Tostadas, Chickpea-Chipotle, '01 54
Tostadas, Party, '98 M33
Turkey Strips with Roasted Peppers and Beans, Herbed, '04 282
White Bean Chili, '02 20
White Bean Pot, '86 194
White Bean Puree, Pork Chops with, '96 226
White Bean Puree, Stuffed Chicken Breasts with, '98 270; '02 200
White Bean Ragoût, '96 232
White Bean Relish, '93 229
White Beans, Caesar Salad with, '93 30
White Bean Spread, '93 30; '95 279; '96 122
White Bean Spread with Creamy Cucumber Sauce, '00 178

BEEF. *See also* **BEEF, GROUND; CASSEROLES/Meat; GRILLED/Beef; LIVER; SANDWICHES.**
Appetizers, Meat-and-Cheese, '87 7
Asparagus, Beef with, '90 100
Ball, Cheese 'n' Beef, '83 230
Barbecue, Bourbon, '88 129
Barbecued Beef, Saucy, '82 156
Barbecue, Slow-Cooker Beef, '02 299
Baria, '97 91
Bouilli, '80 58
Bourguignon, Beef, '79 104; '82 288
Bourguignon, Royal Beef, '80 106

Brisket
Apricot Brisket, Spicy, '04 247
au Jus, Baked Brisket, '00 281
Baked Brisket, Polly's, '00 194
Barbecue Brisket, Oven, '01 259
Barbecue Brisket, Smoky, '03 160
Barbecued Beef Brisket, '83 11
Barbecued Beef Brisket, Denton, Texas, '81 55
Barbecued Beef Brisket with Sauce, '86 153
Barbecued Brisket, '86 154; '88 218
Beer, Beef Brisket in, '93 63
Brisket, '96 228; '01 273
GG's Brisket, '97 251
Home-Style Brisket, '87 303
Marinated Brisket, '86 129
Passover Brisket, '95 102
Pot Roast, '00 65
Pot Roast, Beef Brisket, '93 20
Roast, Peppery Brisket, '83 319
Saucy Brisket, '00 83
Smoke-at-Home Brisket, '93 192
Smoked Brisket, '89 168; '01 169
Smoked Brisket, Heavenly, '95 114
Smoked Brisket, Texas-, '98 89
Smoked Brisket with Barbecue Sauce, '85 144
Suzi's Brisket, Aunt, '02 321
Traditional Brisket, '03 188
Vegetables, Beef Brisket with Fall, '02 237
Broccoli, Quick Beef and, '91 123
Broccoli with Chive Gravy, Beef and, '88 214
Burgoo, Five-Meat, '87 3
Burgoo, Kentucky, '88 235; '97 138
Burgoo, Old-Fashioned, '87 3

Burgundy, Beef, '82 259; '83 125, 281; '88 25; '95 69
Burgundy, Simple Beef, '90 234
Burgundy with Pearl Onions, Beef, '81 108
Burritos, Carne Guisada, '95 43
Burritos, Cheesy Beef, '85 193
Burritos, Meat-and-Bean, '81 194
Caldo de Rez (Mexican Beef Stew), '89 276
Carne Guisada, '93 68
Chalupa, Bean, '80 223

Chili
Black Bean Chili Marsala, '95 16
Bodacious Chili, '95 14
Chuck Wagon Chili, '81 282; '82 57
Chunky Chili, '82 M282; '86 3
con Carne, Chili, '82 310; '83 30; '86 2
Cowboy Chili, '86 2
Firestarter Chili, '93 34
Out West Chili, '95 15
Red Chili, '93 108
Red Chili, North Texas, '87 303
South-of-the-Border Chili, '83 283; '91 283
Texas Championship Chili, '81 54
Verde, Chili, '95 14
Zippy Chili, '87 110
Chimichangas (Fried Burritos), '85 244; '86 114
Chimichangas, Oven-Fried Beef, '92 124
Chinese-Style Beef, '87 50
Chipped Beef and Toast, Creamy, '79 180
Chipped Beef Spread in Puff Pastry, '98 M335

Corned Beef
Birming "Ham," '94 229
Brunch Bake, Corned Beef, '82 44
Cabbage au Gratin, Corned Beef and, '83 16
Cabbage, Corned Beef and, '83 104; '93 64; '96 328
Cabbage, Corned Beef Squares and, '82 86
Cabbage, Quick Corned Beef and, '79 54
Dijon Glaze, Corned Beef with, '87 54
Dinner, Corned Beef, '87 54
Hash, Corned Beef, '95 262
Hash, Red Flannel, '79 191
Reuben Buns, '88 298
Reuben Casserole, '90 240
Reuben Casserole, Chicken, '03 69
Reuben Cheesecake, '90 175
Reuben Loaf, '95 338
Reuben Meat Pie, '80 189
Reuben Pizza, '03 69
Reuben Puffs, '98 231
Reuben Rolls, Snappy, '02 58
Reuben Sandwiches, '80 M201
Reuben Sandwiches, Broiled, '81 240
Reuben Sandwiches, Crispy, '85 299
Reuben Sandwiches, Grilled, '81 206
Reuben Sandwiches, Open-Face, '91 199
Reuben Sandwich, Rolled, '99 219
Reubens, Golden-Baked Mini, '01 62
Reubens, Open-Faced Coleslaw, '03 169
Reuben Soup, Cream of, '97 26
Reubens, Oven-Grilled, '97 304
Reubens, Party, '90 61
Reubens, Spicy Coleslaw, '04 63
Reubens, Summer, '00 134
Reuben Strudel, '98 28
Reuben Turnovers, '94 253
Roll, Corned Beef, '85 66
Salad, Corned Beef, '80 104
Salad, Corned Beef-Cauliflower, '83 16
Salad, Corned Beef-Potato, '85 213
Salad, Molded Corned Beef, '82 86
Salad, Potato-Corned Beef, '81 36
Salad, Vegetable-Corned Beef, '80 148
Sandwich, Corned Beef and Cheese, '79 214

Sandwiches, Barbecued Corned Beef, '83 130
Sandwiches, Corned Beef, '83 291; '85 242; '92 23
Sandwiches, Grilled Corned Beef, '87 54
Sandwiches, Meal-in-One, '80 218
Soup, Corned Beef, '83 16
Soup, French Onion-Beef, '87 54
Spread, Corned Beef, '87 196
Creamed Beef and Chicken-Topped Potatoes, '83 210
Creamed Chipped Beef, '92 42
Creamed Dried Beef with Artichokes, '85 81
Cubes in Wine Sauce, Beef, '79 264
Curried Beef Dinner, '83 4
Dip, Chipped Beef, '88 M8
Dip, Dried Beef, '01 90
Dip, Hot Cheesy Beef, '80 85
Dried Beef Dip, Extra-Creamy, '03 240
Elégante, Beef, '80 125
en Daube, Beef, '79 163
Fajitas, Beef, '88 233
Fajitas, Favorite, '86 114
Filet Mignon, Cajun Blackened, '95 85
Filet of Beef, Marinated Stuffed, '99 165
Fillet of Beef with Blue Cheese Sauce, Pan-Roasted, '94 320
Fillet of Beef with Red Pepper Butter, '96 32
Flautas, Rancho Ramillete, '96 M125
Ginger Beef with Bok Choy, '96 99
Goulash, Beef, '83 231
Goulash, Hungarian, '81 227; '92 227
Green Peppers, Beef and, '79 104
Grillades and Grits, '89 47; '93 62
Grilled Beef with Mashed Potatoes and Chipotle Cream, '02 M320
Gumbo, Texas Ranch-Style, '82 226
Gumbo z'Herbes, '94 239
Hash, Beef, '95 24; '99 62
Hash with Cabbage Salad, Austrian, '95 262
Jerky, Beef, '80 269; '81 26

Kebabs
Barbecued Steak Kebabs, '79 89
Beef Kebabs, '85 110
Beef on a Stick, '99 336
Chile-Beef Kebabs, '94 251
Deluxe, Beef Kebabs, '82 182
Hot-and-Spicy Kebabs, '87 193
Liver Kebabs, '80 185
Marinated Beef Kebabs, '82 105; '85 159
Marinated Beef Kebabs with Rice, '84 32
Marinated Beef Kebabs with Vegetables, '99 292
Marinated Beef on a Stick, '85 234
Marinated Sirloin Kebabs, '82 162
Marinated Steak Kebabs, '80 184
Pineapple-Beef Kebabs, '83 212
Saucy Beef Kebabs, '83 109
Shrimp Kebabs, Steak-and-, '80 184
Spicy Grilled Kebabs, '98 158
Spirited Beef Kebabs, '87 142
Steak Kebabs, '82 4; '93 95
Steak on a Stick, '83 109
Steak with Vegetables, Skewered, '81 124
Teriyaki Beef Kebabs, '80 207
Vegetable Kebabs, Beef-and-, '91 148
Vegetables, Beef Kebabs with, '90 148

Liver
Balsamic Vinegar, Beef Liver with, '98 130
Creamy Liver and Noodle Dinner, '80 11
Creole Liver, '96 236
Creole Sauce, Liver in, '87 33
French-Style Liver, '80 10
Gravy, Liver and, '80 10
Herbs, Liver with, '81 277
Kebabs, Liver, '80 185

Patties, Beef Liver, '81 277
Saucy Liver, '81 277
Sauté, Liver, '81 277
Spanish-Style Liver, '80 11
Stroganoff, Liver, '79 54
Sweet-and-Sour Liver, '81 277
Tasty Liver, '83 29
Mango-Beef and Rice, '88 138
Meatballs, Quick Processor, '87 111
Medaillons, Italian Beef, '87 305
Medaillons of Beef with Ancho Chile Sauce, '87 122
Medaillons of Beef with Horseradish Cream, '90 96
Mongolian Beef, '85 2, 75; '01 94
Mushrooms, Beef-Stuffed, '00 278
Oriental, Beef and Cauliflower, '80 220
Oriental Beef and Snow Peas, '79 105
Oriental Beef with Pea Pods, '86 M328
Pastichio, '85 194
Peppered Beef in a Blanket, Bourbon, '00 109
Philly Firecrackers, '01 142
Pies, Carry-Along Beef, '80 224; '81 56
Pie, Sensational Beef, '03 M284
Pie, Shepherd's, '92 168
Pot Pie, Oriental Beef, '92 253
Pot Pies with Yorkshire Pudding Topping, Beef, '93 45

Ribs
Baby Loin Back Ribs, '01 106
Barbecued Beef Short Ribs, '83 178
Barbecued Short Ribs, '90 148
Beans, Spicy Black, '04 119
Braised Short Ribs, '98 44; '01 193
Grilled Ribs, Sweet-and-Sour, '98 331
Hearty Beef Shortribs, '79 14
Supreme, Beef Shortribs, '79 14
Rice, Beef and Cauliflower over, '93 94

Roasts
à la Beer, Beef, '98 64
à la Mode, Beef, '98 122
Barbecue, Beef Roast, '79 159
Barbecued Beef Roast, '82 96; '83 103
Barbecue, Four-Hour, '00 18
Barbecue Roast, '98 245
Barbecue, Trish's Beach, '03 206
Beer-and-Onion Sauce, Roast in, '80 124
Brisket Roast, Peppery, '83 319
Burgundy Gravy, Beef Roast with, '95 263
Burgundy Roast, Beef, '85 291
Burritos, Easy, '04 32
Chili Bean Roast, '87 268; '88 102; '89 68
Chuck Roast Barbecue, '96 71
Chuck Roast, Fruited, '91 289
Chuck Roast in Sauce, '91 47
Chuck Roast, Marinated, '80 59
Chuck Roast, Orange Marinated, '85 179
Chuck Roast, Savory, '00 18
Chuck Roast, Slow Cooker, '98 32
Classic Roast Beef, '03 296
Cola Roast, '81 298
Deli-Style Roast Beef, '93 15
Diablo, Beef, '79 17
Easy Banquet Roast, '99 291
Easy Beef Roast, '89 M65
Easy Oven Roast, '93 64
Eye-of-Round, Burgundy, '90 243
Eye of Round, Grilled Beef, '82 91
Eye of Round Roast, '99 60
Eye-of-Round Roast with Fruited Onion Marmalade, '96 323
Eye of Round Roast with Marmalade, '97 27
Eye-of-Round Roast with Rice Gravy, Seasoned, '89 118

Eye of Round, Slow Cooker Spicy Marinated, '99 291
Eye of Round, Spicy Marinated, '99 291
Eye Round Roast, Mexican, '89 190
Flautas, '00 293
French-Style Beef Roast, '89 32
Grillades and Grits, '88 126
Grilled Marinated Beef Roast, '93 141
Grilled Pepper Roast, '81 110
Herbed Roast, '91 288
Java Roast, '83 319
Marengo, Beef, '82 284; '83 14
Marinated Roast, '85 3
Marinated Roast Beef, '97 14
Marinated Roast, Dijon Wine-, '91 289
Mary's Roast Beef, '01 86
Mix, Mexican Meat, '00 292
New York Strip Roast, Spicy, '93 131
Onion-and-Mushroom Gravy, Roast with, '00 293
Patio Steak, '87 141
Pizza, Taco, '00 293
Potatoes, Stuffed Baked, '00 293
Pot Pie, Beef Roast, '88 296
Pot Roast, '00 65
Pot Roast, All-Seasons, '86 89
Pot Roast and Gravy, '89 234
Pot Roast and Gravy, Country-Style, '94 308
Pot Roast, Aunt Mary's, '04 47
Pot Roast, Autumn Gold, '83 7
Pot Roast, Barbecued, '79 17; '83 319
Pot Roast, Basic, '81 M208
Pot Roast, Bavarian-Style, '79 17
Pot Roast, Beef Brisket, '93 20
Pot Roast, Bloody Mary, '86 47
Pot Roast, Cardamom, '79 12
Pot Roast, Company, '79 162; '88 M14
Pot Roast, Country, '87 216
Pot Roast, Dillicious, '81 187
Pot Roast, Easy Oven, '86 52
Pot Roast, Favorite, '89 118
Pot Roast, Fruited, '90 211
Pot Roast, Gee's Italian, '96 18
Pot Roast, Hawaiian, '81 298
Pot Roast, Indian, '87 215
Pot Roast in Red Sauce, '87 215
Pot Roast in Sour Cream, '89 117
Pot Roast in White Wine Gravy, '81 299
Pot Roast, Italian, '81 299; '87 95; '02 88
Pot Roast, Marinated, '85 21
Pot Roast Medley, Vegetable-, '83 319
Pot Roast, Mexican, '98 64
Pot Roast, Mushroom, '79 17; '96 250
Pot Roast of Beef with Vegetables, '98 65
Pot Roast, Old-Fashioned, '98 64
Pot Roast, Peppered, '87 215
Pot Roast, Perfect, '83 7
Pot Roast, Polynesian, '80 59
Pot Roast, Regal, '79 17
Pot Roast, Root Beer, '04 212
Pot Roast, Spicy Apple, '83 7
Pot Roast, Swedish, '80 59
Pot Roast, Sweet-and-Sour, '83 8; '99 291
Pot Roast with Dumplings, '98 245
Pot Roast with Gravy, '81 298
Pot Roast with Herbed Red Sauce, '88 29
Pot Roast with Mushroom Gravy, '02 90
Pot Roast with Sour Cream Gravy, '79 17
Pot Roast with Spaghetti, '80 59
Pot Roast with Vegetables, '80 59; '81 M208; '00 18
Pot Roast with Vegetables, Marinated, '88 M52
Pot Roast, Zesty, '81 206
Pressure-Cooker Roast, '91 289
Pressure Cooker Roast Beef, '01 86

Prime Rib, Perfect, '96 197
Prime Ribs and Yorkshire Puddings, Mini, '01 283
Prime Rib, Smoked, '97 161; '02 177
Prime Rib with Spicy Horseradish Sauce, '02 235
Pumpernickel Roast, '97 234
Rib-Eye Beef, Spicy, '84 259
Rib-Eye Roast, Marinated, '90 318
Rib-Eye Roast, Peppered, '01 122
Rib Roast, Barbecued, '86 152
Rib Roast, Rosemary, '03 294
Rib Roast, Standing, '80 246; '84 187; '95 28
Rib Roast with Yorkshire Pudding, Standing, '80 252; '98 86
Rump Roast, Easy, '93 217
Sandwiches, French Dip, '97 211
Sandwiches, Grilled Roast Beef-and-Brie, '03 296
Sauerbraten, '98 278
Sauerbraten Beef, Marinated, '93 16
Sauerbraten, Quick, '80 139
Simple Roast, '81 298
Sirloin Roast, Canary, '89 117
Sirloin Tip Roast with Mustard Cream Sauce, Herbed, '88 61
Sirloin Tips, Braised, '98 45
Slices, Roast Beef, '02 246
Slow Cooker Roast Beef, '01 86
Sunday Roast Beef, '99 327
Supreme, Roast Beef, '83 8
Vegetables, Beef and, '01 86
Vegetables, Company Beef and, '88 234
Wellington, Beef, '83 319
Rolls, Stuffed Sherried Beef, '79 105
Rolls, Wine-Sauced Beef-and-Barley, '87 269
Rolls with Mustard-Horseradish Cream, Beef, '02 53
Roll-Ups, Mexican Beef, '90 176
Roll-Ups, Savory Beef and Cheese, '96 235
Rollups with Rice, Royal Beef, '79 105
Roulades, Beef, '83 47; '85 234
Roulades, Roquefort Beef, '88 215
Salads. *See also* **BEEF/Corned Beef.**
Broccoli Salad, Beef-and-, '87 187
Cilantro, Beef Salad with, '97 202
Cucumber-Roast Beef Salad, '89 162
Fajita Salad, Beef, '91 70
Gingered Beef Salad, '88 61
Greek Steak Salad, '92 107
Niçoise, Beef Salad, '99 159
Peking Beef Salad, '88 60
Pepper Steak Salad Cups, '86 206
Roast Beef Salad, '80 223; '81 56; '90 318
Sirloin Salad, Grilled, '94 129
Spicy Beef-Pasta Salad, '01 311
Spicy Beef Salad, '02 174
Steak Salad Niçoise, Grilled, '98 148
Steak Salad with Peach Salsa, '97 183
Stir-Fry Beef Salad, '96 129
Tangy Beef Salad, '87 M218
Vinaigrette Salad, Beef, '95 177
Western-Style Beef Salad, '93 321
Zesty Beef Salad, '79 56
Sandwich, Beef-and-Kraut, '91 167
Sandwiches, Beef and Pork Tenderloin, '80 175
Sandwiches, Beef, Bacon, and Blue Cheese, '96 23
Sandwiches, Beef Salad Pocket, '83 267
Sandwiches, Beef Tenderloin Picnic, '90 91
Sandwiches, Dilly Beef, '98 288
Sandwiches, Dried Beef Pita, '86 160
Sandwiches, Hot Beef, '00 98
Sandwiches, Wake-Up, '84 58
Sandwiches with Yogurt-Cucumber Sauce, London Broil, '01 162

BEEF

(continued)

Sandwich, Roast Beef Hero, '91 167
Sandwich, Saucy Beef Pocket, '80 92
Seasoning Blend, Meat, '88 29
Shredded Beef over Rice Noodles, '85 74
Sirloin, Sweet Skillet, '04 20
Sirloin with Cherry-Merlot Sauce and Gorgonzola,
  Peppered, '02 320
Soup, Beefy Lentil, '87 282
Soup, Beefy Vidalia Onion, '97 212
Soup, Chunky Italian, '99 20
Soup, Hearty Vegetable-Beef, '84 102
Soup, Steak, '99 260
Soup, Tomato-Beef-Wild Rice, '04 42
Soup, Vegetable-Beef, '88 296
Spaghetti, Meaty, '82 19
Spicy Beef and Black Beans, '99 331
Spread, Hot Beef, '83 50; '84 M216
Steaks. See also **BEEF/Kebabs, Salads.**
  American Steakhouse Beef, '93 15
  Appetizers, Marinated Steak-and-Chestnut,
    '84 323
  au Poivre, Steak, '88 232
  Bacon Twirls, Beef-and-, '91 163
  Bake, Asian Noodle Beef, '98 31
  Barbecued Beef, '81 18
  Barbecued Steak, Saucy Oven-, '83 10
  Bean Sprouts, Beef and, '82 281; '83 42
  Benedict for Two, Steaks, '85 295
  Biscuits with Beef and Horseradish-Chive Cream,
    Blue Cheese, '02 313
  Bistecca, '02 170
  Blackened 'n' Peppered Steak, '95 174
  Blue Cheese Steaks, '84 171
  Blue Cheese-Walnut Stuffed Fillets, '95 327
  Blue, Elegant Beef, '97 97
  Bourbon Steak, '90 148
  Braised Steaks, Beer-, '87 96
  Broiled Oriental Steaks, '83 110
  Broiled Steaks, '96 172
  Caramel-Brandy Sauce, Steaks with, '03 56
  Carne Guisada, '94 219
  Carpetbagger Steak, '84 87
  Cheesesteaks, Chimichurri, '04 312
  Chicken-Fried Steak, '92 214; '97 307; '01 47;
    '03 72, 311
  Chicken-Fried Steak and Cream Gravy,
    Threadgill's, '98 62
  Chicken-Fried Steak Fingers with Creole Mustard
    Sauce, '99 142
  Chicken-Fried Steak, Matt's, '97 25
  Chicken-Fried Steaks, '88 110
  Chili, Black Bean, '02 20
  Chuck Steak, Marinated Barbecued, '80 156
  Coconut-Beef Stir-Fry, '97 18
  Continental, Steak, '83 178
  Country-Fried Steak and Cream Gravy, '84 8
  Country-Fried Steak, Cajun-Style, '01 318
  Country-Fried Steak in Paradise, '98 62
  Country-Fried Steak, Mock, '87 163
  Crêpes, Special Steak, '91 24
  Curried Beef Steak, '88 60
  Cutlets, Lemon-Flavored, '79 105
  de Burgo, Steak, '84 117
  Diane Flambé, Steak, '79 103
  Diane, Steak, '82 275; '92 306
  Dianne, Steak, '83 47
  Fajita Casserole, '97 96
  Fajita Crêpes, '94 116
  Fajitas, '84 233
  Fajitas, Beef and Chicken, '02 119

Fajitas, Java, '96 227
Fajitas, Plum Good, '94 115
Fajitas, Slow Cooker, '02 43
Fajitas, Tex-Mex, '01 188
Fajitas with Pico de Gallo, '98 87
Fajitas with Pico de Gallo, Beef, '04 61
Fiery Steak with Pimiento Cheese Salsa,
  '99 331
Filet Mignon, Marinated, '84 171
Filet Mignons with Shiitake Madeira Sauce,
  '95 265
Filet Mignon Tarragon, '94 46
Filet Mignon with Horseradish Gravy, '92 262
Filet Mignon with Mushroom Sauce, '94 250
Filets Mignons, Skillet, '03 258
Filets, Spicy Beef, '00 121
Filets with Green Peppercorn Sauce, Beef
  Tenderloin, '00 309
Filets with Stilton-Portobello Sauce, Beef,
  '00 309
Fillet, Acapulco, '98 174
Fillets au Vin, Beef, '79 137
Fillets with Black Bean Sauce, Spicy Beef,
  '97 184
Fillets with Green Peppercorn Sauce, Beef,
  '02 285
Fillets with Horseradish Sauce and Curried
  Bananas, '85 230
Fillets with Orange Cream, Beef, '97 66
Fillets with Stilton-Portobello Sauce, Beef,
  '02 310
Fillets with Wine Sauce, Beef, '01 317
Fingers, Golden Steak, '85 110
Flank Steak and Dried Tomato-Basil Pesto
  Linguine, '04 101
Flank Steak and Mushrooms, '87 61
Flank Steak-and-Spinach Pinwheels, '95 56
Flank Steak, Bacon-Wrapped, '85 59
Flank Steak, Barbecued, '79 89
Flank Steak, Beer-Marinated, '87 35
Flank Steak, Cheese-Stuffed, '98 182
Flank Steak, East-West, '04 90
Flank Steak, Flavorful, '96 32
Flank Steak, Ginger-Marinated, '89 25
Flank Steak, Grilled, '80 152; '89 168; '91 80;
  '92 166; '03 146
Flank Steak, Grilled Marinated, '97 182
Flank Steak, Herbed, '92 127
Flank Steak, Herb-Marinated, '85 275
Flank Steak in Mexican Marinade, '98 128
Flank Steak, Lemon-Lime, '95 55
Flank Steak, Marinated, '82 162; '83 35, 258;
  '85 86; '88 262; '95 237; '04 118
Flank Steak, Mashed Potato-Stuffed, '01 25
Flank Steak, Mediterranean, '00 145
Flank Steak, Oriental, '83 178
Flank Steak, Peppery Grilled, '99 157
Flank Steak Pinwheels, '87 141
Flank Steak, Red Wine-Marinated, '95 283
Flank Steak, Rosemary Grilled, '03 125
Flank Steak Sandwiches with Apple Barbecue
  Sauce, '99 173
Flank Steaks, Delicious Marinated, '83 110
Flank Steak Skewers, Lemon, '02 134
Flank Steak, Soy-Ginger, '02 90
Flank Steak Sukiyaki, '88 233
Flank Steaks with Mushrooms, '00 121
Flank Steak, Tangy, '86 184
Flank Steak, Tenderized, '82 105
Flank Steak Teriyaki, '81 110
Flank Steak, Texas, '86 185
Flank Steak, Tomato-Stuffed, '97 49
Flank Steak with Apple-Bourbon Sauce and
  Roasted Vegetables, Grilled, '99 142

Flank Steak with Black Bean-and-Corn Salsa,
  Grilled, '94 80
Flank Steak with Chili Butter, '00 177
Flank Steak with Horseradish Sauce, Grilled,
  '02 19
Flank Steak with Molasses Barbecue Glaze,
  Grilled, '00 59
Flank Steak with Noodles, Stuffed, '90 101
Flank Steak with Salsa, Southwest, '03 95
Flank Steak with Sweet Peppers, Grilled, '90 138
Flank Steak with Tomato-Olive Relish, '03 210
French Quarter Steak, '81 17
Garlic-Herb Steaks, '98 169; '99 175
Garlic Steak, '84 8
Ginger, Beef with, '03 64
Greek Pocket Steaks, '81 262
Grillades and Baked Cheese Grits, '94 240
Grilled Black Pepper Steak, '86 184
Grilled Steaks, '96 172
Grilled Steaks, Mesquite-, '85 154
Grilled Steak, Spicy, '97 211
Grilled Steaks with Green Chiles, '85 144
Grilled Steaks with Spicy Herb Sauce, Asian,
  '03 280
Grill, Steak Brunch, '82 44
Ham-and-Mushroom Sauce, Steak with, '83 109
Horseradish Steak, '88 39
Italian Steak, '03 180
Kebabs, Spicy Grilled, '98 158
Kebabs, Steak-and-Shrimp, '00 124
Kebabs, Steak-and-Vegetable, '04 218
Korean Steak, '89 190
Lemon-Butter Steak with Brandy Sauce,
  '85 78
lo Mein, Steak, '90 100
London Broil, Grilled, '92 59
London Broil, Marinated, '87 32
London Broil, Peppercorn, '88 60
London Broil, Teriyaki, '92 282
Marinated Bourbon Steak, '95 91
Marinated Steak, '88 233
Marinated Steak, Mexican, '88 148
Mediterranean Steak, '03 180
Mesquite-Ginger Beef with Fresh Fruit Relish,
  '95 158
Mexican Steak, '84 76
Mushroom Sauce, Steak with, '83 212
Mush, Steak and Gravy with, '81 215
Oriental Beef, '85 20
Pan-Grilled Steaks, '96 172
Parmesan, Steak, '93 41
Parmigiana, Beef, '84 8; '85 234
Pasta and Sesame-Ginger Butter, Steak with,
  '99 142
Pepper-Beef Steak, '85 21
Pepper-Cheese Steaks, Mexican, '97 190
Pepper Cream, Steak in, '94 117
Pepper Steak, '81 273; '85 57; '88 113
Pepper Steak and Rice, '81 17
Pepper Steak and Rice, Skillet, '04 326
Pepper Steak, Chinese, '82 236
Pepper Steak, Cold, '91 208
Pepper Steak, Cracked, '83 109
Pepper Steak, Festive Cajun, '03 23
Pepper Steak, Simple, '01 82
Pepper Stir-Fry Steak, '81 240
Pies, Cornish Meat, '84 23
Pirate Steak, '79 89
Quesadillas with Mango Salsa, Beefy Crab,
  '00 124
Red Wine Marinade, Beef with, '91 46
Rib-Eye Grill, '02 306
Rib Eyes, Grecian Skillet, '96 234
Rib-Eyes, Italian, '98 215

Rib-Eye Steaks, Peppered, '97 46; '00 146;
   '02 110
Rib-Eye Steaks with Roquefort Glaze, '89 310
Rib Eyes with Herb Cheese and Asparagus
   Bundles, Grilled Chile-Rubbed, '03 326
Rib Eyes with Red Pepper-Polenta Fries and Chile
   Corn Jus, '00 196
Ropa Vieja, '93 28; '98 20
Rouladen, '99 242
Round Steak, Braised, '87 35
Round Steak over Rice, Burgundy, '90 M33
Round Steak, Parmesan, '80 106
Round Steak, Red Pepper, '88 214
Round Steak, Savory Stuffed, '81 18
Round Steak, Skillet, '83 29
Round Steak, Tangy, '82 284; '83 14
Round Steak, Tender Grilled, '85 3
Saltillo, Beef (Beef with Tomatillos), '82 219
Sandwich, Beef-and-Artichoke Open-Faced
   Italian, '98 22
Sandwiches, Steak, '96 136
Sandwiches, Steak-and-Onion, '02 126
Sandwiches, Steak Bagel, '96 249
Shish Kebabs, Beef Tenderloin, '00 200
Shrimp, Steak and, '88 123
Sirloin in Vodka Sauce, '03 96
Sirloin, Mustard Marinated, '94 41
Sirloin, Peppery Grilled, '02 212
Sirloin Steak, Secret, '81 110
Sirloin Steaks, Italian, '04 61
Sirloin Steaks with Thyme Pesto, '97 182
Sirloin Supreme, Shrimp and, '81 131
Sirloin with Zesty Corn Salsa, Cilantro-Garlic,
   '02 193
Skillet Steak in Red Wine Sauce, '85 21
Skillet Steak 'n Potatoes, '81 18
Smothered Beef and Onions, '85 293
Smothered Steak, '79 212
Smothered Steak, Onion-, '87 M189
Soup, Steak, '99 260
Stately Steaks, '00 121
Stir-Fried Beef, '84 26
Stir-Fried Steak, Fast-and-Easy, '87 50
Stir-Fry, Beef-and-Carrot, '98 335
Stir-Fry, Beef-and-Vegetable, '87 22; '99 204
Stir-Fry Beef-and-Vegetables, '84 141
Stir-Fry, Curried Beef, '01 162
Stir-Fry, Italian Beef, '99 35
Stir-Fry, Pepper Steak, '89 191
Stir-Fry, Steak-and-Vegetable, '84 8
Strip Steaks, Coffee-Rubbed, '03 282
Stroganoff, Creamy Beef, '02 124
Stuffed Steak, Italian-, '88 232
Stuffed Steak Rolls, '82 135
Stuffed Steaks, Cheese-, '81 17
Sweet-and-Sour Marinated Steaks, '83 110
Swiss Steak Cheese Skillet, '80 106
Swiss Steak, Deviled, '80 107
Swiss Steak, Easy, '00 90
Swiss Steak Monterey, '99 23
Swiss Steak, Oven, '85 234
Swiss Steak, Pizza, '02 36
Swiss Steak, Smothered, '04 321
Swiss Steak Surprise, '81 17
Swiss Steak with Vegetables, '81 273
Tabasco Steak, '95 207
Tacos, Jerk Steak, '01 170
Tartare, Steak, '83 78
Tenderloin Steak, Gingered, '96 154
Tenderloin Steaks with Balsamic Sauce, Beef,
   '98 319
Tenderloin Steaks with Peperonata, Beef, '97 291
Teriyaki Beef Broil, '92 56
Teriyaki, Marinated Steak, '84 50

Thai Beef, Spicy Lemon, '97 320
Thai Lemon Beef, '97 292
Tomatoes and Artichokes, Beef with, '92 282
Vegetables, Beef with Chinese, '81 211
Vegetables, Beef with Oriental, '84 140
Wellingtons, Individual Beef, '82 259
Wellingtons, Mini Beef, '01 252
Wraps, Cheese-Steak, '00 M335
Zippy Steak and Gravy, '90 35

Stews
Beef Stew, '86 51; '90 230; '96 16
Brown Stew, '85 239
Brunswick Stew, Bama, '87 4
Brunswick Stew, Easy, '92 280
Brunswick Stew, Georgian, '92 35
Brunswick Stew, Virginia Ramsey's Favorite,
   '91 16
Burgundy Beef Stew, '88 234
Burgundy Stew with Drop Dumplings, '83 125
Celery Root Stew, Beef-and-, '98 292
Company Beef Stew, '83 85; '97 198
Dumplings, Beef Stew with, '84 3
Dumplings, Beef Stew with Parsley, '81 76;
   '82 13; '85 M246
Emerald Isle Stew, '95 71
Hungarian Beef Stew, '03 35
Hungarian Stew with Noodles, '80 263
Irish Stew, '90 64
Mexican Stew, '82 231
Mexican Stew Olé, '86 296
Onion Stew, Beef-and-, '87 18
Oven Beef Stew, '79 222; '80 64
Quick Beef Stew, '92 71
Red Chili Stew, '95 226
Spicy Beef Stew, '86 228
Sweet-and-Sour Beef and Vegetable Stew, '85 87
Texas Stew, '97 211
Vegetable-Beef Stew, '94 323
Vegetable-Beef Stew, Shortcut, '89 218
White Wine Stew, '82 228
Stir-Fried Beef and Vegetables, '88 301
Stir-Fry Beef and Asparagus, '91 124
Stir-Fry Beef and Broccoli, '79 47
Stir-Fry, Beef-and-Broccoli, '91 46
Stir-Fry Beef and Pea Pods, '80 19
Stir-Fry, Beef-and-Shrimp, '93 32
Stir-Fry, Beef and Snow Pea, '82 98
Stir-Fry Beef and Snow Peas, '83 22
Stir-Fry, Beef-and-Vegetable, '81 211
Stir-Fry Broccoli and Beef, '83 110
Stir-Fry, Chinese Beef, '83 151
Stir-Fry, Hungarian, '93 64
Stir-Fry, Indian, '92 126
Stir-Fry, Lime-Ginger Beef, '92 65
Stir-Fry, Mongolian Beef, '89 25
Stir-Fry, Peanutty Beef, '95 157
Stir-Fry, Teriyaki, '83 110
Stock, Beef, '95 17
Stock, Brown Meat, '90 31
Stroganoff, Beef, '79 163; '81 179; '91 134; '93 18;
   '03 23
Stroganoff, Beef Burgundy, '85 31
Stroganoff, Light Beef, '86 36
Stroganoff, Liver, '79 54
Stroganoff, Quick Beef, '92 20; '99 327
Stroganoff Sandwiches, Steak, '85 110
Stroganoff, Sirloin, '81 297
Stroganoff with Parslied Noodles, Steak, '85 31
Tacos al Carbón, '86 19
Tacos al Carbón, Tailgate, '79 185
Tamales, '80 195
Tempting Twosome, '81 240
Tenderloin, Barbecued Beef, '94 26
Tenderloin Bundles, Peppered Beef, '89 272

Tenderloin, Chutneyed Beef, '94 270
Tenderloin Deluxe, Beef, '85 109
Tenderloin, Easy Beef, '90 268
Tenderloin, Elegant Beef, '88 244
Tenderloin for Two, Beef, '90 295
Tenderloin, Garlic-and-Rosemary Beef, '02 255
Tenderloin, Grilled, '91 166
Tenderloin, Hampton Place Beef, '04 272
Tenderloin, Herb Marinated, '83 109
Tenderloin, Holiday Beef, '01 238
Tenderloin in Wine Sauce, Beef, '02 136
Tenderloin, Lobster-Stuffed Beef, '87 248
Tenderloin, Marinated, '80 146
Tenderloin, Marinated Beef, '81 246; '85 302;
   '93 215; '03 241
Tenderloin, Mustard Greens-Stuffed, '96 324
Tenderloin Picnic Sandwiches, Beef, '90 91
Tenderloin, Spicy Beef, '88 29
Tenderloin, Spicy Marinated Beef, '83 262
Tenderloin, Spinach-Stuffed, '89 311
Tenderloin, Stuffed, '86 323; '88 50
Tenderloin, Stuffed Beef, '00 124
Tenderloin, Stuffed Tuscany, '99 269
Tenderloin with Avocado Béarnaise Sauce, Beef,
   '01 317
Tenderloin with Five-Onion Sauce, Beef, '98 272
Tenderloin with Henry Bain Sauce, Beef, '00 107;
   '01 20; '04 52
Tenderloin with Horseradish Cream Sauce, Pepper-
   Seared Beef, '01 280
Tenderloin with Mushroom Sauce, Beef, '88 3
Tenderloin with Mushrooms, Beef, '87 115
Tenderloin with Mushroom-Sherry Sauce, Beef,
   '87 306
Tenderloin with Pan-Roasted Pears, Beef, '02 197
Tenderloin with Peppercorns, Beef, '91 246
Tips and Noodles, Beef, '86 293
Tips on Rice, Beef, '85 87
Tournedos Diables, '87 60
Tournedos Mouton, '83 262
Turnovers, Roast Beef, '88 273; '89 180
Tzimmes, Sweet Potato-Beef, '92 234
Tzimmes with Brisket, Mixed Fruit, '93 114
Vegetables in a Noodle Ring, Beef and, '85 285
Vegetables, Savory Beef and, '79 163
Wellington, Beef, '93 288

BEEF, GROUND
Acorn Squash, Stuffed, '83 15
Appetizer, Cheesy Mexicali, '82 108
Barbecue Cups, '79 129
Bean Bake, Cheesy Beef-and-, '82 89
Bean Medley, Baked, '80 100
Beans, Beefy, '82 59
Beans, Beefy Baked, '80 136; '84 149; '85 142
Beans, Rancho Lima, '80 191
Beans, Three-Meat Baked, '86 210
Brunswick Stew, Breeden Liles's, '91 14
Burger Boat, '95 70
Burgoo, Harry Young's, '87 3
Burritos, Chinese, '87 181
Burritos, Fiesta, '86 114
Cabbage-and-Beef Rolls, Easy, '88 49
Cabbage, Italian Stuffed, '84 294
Cabbage Leaves, Stuffed, '00 270
Cabbage Rolls, '83 104
Cabbage Rolls, Beef Stuffed, '81 87; '82 7
Cabbage Rolls, Fried, '95 270
Cabbage Rolls, Hungarian, '94 47
Cabbage Rolls, Spicy, '84 2
Cabbage Rolls, Stuffed, '84 217
Cabbage Rollups, Beef-and-, '80 63
Cabbage, Stuffed, '84 282
Calzones, Beef-and-Pepperoni, '03 202
Calzones, Easy, '99 133

BEEF, GROUND
(continued)

Calzones, Ground Beef, '97 95
Calzones with Italian Tomato Sauce, '03 202
Casseroles. *See also* **BEEF, GROUND/Lasagna.**
　Bean, and Cornbread Casserole, Beef, '99 215
　Bean Bake, Hamburger-, '95 121
　Bean Bake, Three-, '03 106
　Beef Casserole, '01 199
　Biscuit Casserole, Beef-and-, '83 75
　Cabbage Beef Bake, Zesty, '80 300
　Cavatini, '94 214
　Cheese, and Noodle Casserole, Beef, '99 58
　Cheeseburger Casserole, '95 255
　Cheesy Ground Beef Casserole, '79 44
　Cheesy Mexican Casserole, '82 224
　Chiles Rellenos Casserole, '98 48
　Chili-Rice Casserole, '79 54
　Cornbread Casserole, '81 91
　Cornbread Skillet Casserole, '83 243; '84 101
　County Fair Casserole, '79 130
　Creamy Ground Beef Casserole, '81 142
　Crusty Beef Casserole, '82 88
　Easy Beef Casserole, '86 M58; '00 208
　El Dorado Casserole, '81 140
　Enchilada Casserole, '87 287
　Enchilada Casserole, Firecracker, '80 260
　Enchilada Casserole, Sour Cream, '82 113
　Enchiladas, American, '81 170
　Enchiladas, Chili and, '00 55
　Enchiladas, Enticing, '99 57
　Enchiladas, Quicker, '96 103
　Enchiladas, Sour Cream, '87 37
　Enchiladas, Weeknight, '93 63
　Five-Layer Meal, '81 140
　Grits Italiano, '92 43
　Hamburger Casserole, '95 210
　Hamburger-Corn Bake, '99 58
　Italian Cabbage Casserole, '87 42
　Italian Casserole, '80 81
　Italian Casserole, Light, '03 198
　Lasagna, Egg-Noodle, '04 219
　Lasagna, Ground Sirloin, '03 143
　Layered Beef Casserole, '82 M203
　Layered Grecian Bake, '82 119
　Linguine with Meat Sauce, Baked, '01 41
　Linguine with Meat Sauce Casserole, '03 22
　Lombardi, Beef, '03 214
　Macaroni Bake, Beef-, '94 255
　Macaroni-Cheese-Beef Casserole, '95 125
　Macaroni Combo, Beef-, '79 194
　Manicotti, Ground Beef-and-Tomato, '03 257
　Manicotti, Meaty Stuffed, '00 19
　Matador Mania, '86 19
　Mexican Casserole, '92 M22; '00 280
　Mexican Casserole, Cabin, '97 95
　Mexican Casserole, Microwave, '90 M231
　Mexi Casserole, '83 M87
　Moussaka, '97 94
　Moussaka Casserole, '79 179
　Noodle Bake, Hamburger-, '81 140
　Noodles Casserole, Beef-and-, '84 72
　Pasta Bake, Layered, '04 326
　Pasta Italiano, '01 41
　Pastitsio, '87 12; '88 11; '99 167
　Pizza Bake, Upside-Down, '98 224
　Pizza Casserole, '88 273; '89 181
　Pizza Casserole, Microwave, '89 M248
　Pizza Casserole, Quick, '83 266
　Potato Casserole, Beefy, '03 218
　Rotini, Baked, '01 185
　Sausage Casserole, Ground Beef and, '80 260

　Seashell-Provolone Casserole, '80 189
　Shells, Spinach-Stuffed, '99 64
　Sour Cream-Noodle Bake, '79 55
　Spaghetti and Beef Casserole, '79 129
　Spaghetti-and-Spinach Casserole, '02 199
　Spaghetti, Casserole, '95 132
　Spinach and Beef Casserole, '79 192
　Spinach-Beef-Macaroni Casserole, '83 313
　Stroganoff Casserole, '98 48
　Taco Bake, '97 326
　Taco Beef-Noodle Bake, '81 141
　Taco Casserole, '80 33
　Taco Squares, Deep-Dish, '91 88
　Tamale, Mozzarella, '95 70
　Tortilla Bake, Texas, '94 285
　Vegetable Casserole, Beefy, '79 248
　Vegetable Chow Mein Casserole, Beef-and-,
　　'83 313
　Zucchini-Beef Bake, '86 146
Chiles Rellenos Egg Rolls, '86 296
Chili
　Basic Chili, '82 M11; '93 326
　Basic Chili Embellished, '93 327
　Basic Chili Goes Southwest, '93 326
　Bean Chili, Spicy 3-, '03 291
　Bean Chili, Three-, '00 34
　Before-and-After Burner, Roy's, '89 316
　Big-Batch Chili, '04 242
　Biscuit Bowl, Chili in a, '98 224
　Cheese-Topped Chili, '82 M11
　Cheesy Chili, '82 310
　Chili, '87 17; '89 143; '93 89; '98 95
　Chilly Night Chili, '99 317
　Choo-Choo Chili, '89 316
　Cincinnati Chili, '96 18
　Cincinnati-Style Chili, '00 34
　Company Chili, '82 311; '83 30
　con Carne, Beef and Sausage Chili, '83 284
　con Carne, Chili, '84 72
　Con Carne, Chili, '03 19
　con Carne, Favorite Chili, '86 293
　con Carne, Quick-and-Easy Chili, '86 2
　Dip, Chili, '89 47
　Double-Meat Chili, '79 269; '80 12
　Easy Chili, '82 310; '83 30; '02 299
　Easy Texas Chili, '90 201
　Five-Ingredient Chili, '95 212
　Friday Night Chili, '86 228
　Game-Day Chili, '00 238
　Greek Chili, '95 16
　Hominy Bake, Chili, '81 282; '82 58
　Hot Dog Chili, '04 199
　Hot Texas Chili, '80 222; '81 77
　Hotto Lotto Chili, '89 316
　I-Cious, Chili-, '89 315
　"In-the-Redd Chili over "Rolling-in-Dough"
　　Biscuits, '92 80
　Kielbasa Chili, Hearty, '91 28
　Lolly's Pop Chili, '89 316
　Lunchtime Chili, '81 230
　Meaty Chili, '81 282; '82 58
　Meaty Chili with Beans, '85 250
　Mexican Chili, '89 18
　Noodles, Chili with, '81 282; '82 57
　Now, Thatsa Chili, '95 16
　Pastry Cups, Chili in, '90 68
　Potato Chili, Savory, '83 284
　Potatoes, Chili-Topped, '83 3; '98 M289
　Quick-and-Easy Chili, '92 20
　Quick and Simple Chili, '81 282; '82 58
　Quick Chili, '83 283
　Ranch Chili and Beans, '79 270; '80 11
　Red Bean Chili, '02 20
　Red Bean Chili, Slow-Cooker, '02 20

　Rice, Chili with, '82 M11
　Roundup Chili, '79 269; '80 12
　Sauce, Chili Meat, '83 4
　Sausage-Beef Chili, '86 232
　Sausage Chili, Beefy, '82 M11
　Simple Chili, '79 269; '80 11
　Slow Cooker Cincinnati-Style Chili, '00 34
　Speedy Chili, '92 66
　Spiced Chili, Hot, '83 214
　Spicy Chili, Old-Fashioned, '79 269; '80 11
　Supper, Hot Chili, '99 279
　Texas-Style Chili, '82 311; '83 30
　Tex-Mex Chili, '83 26
　Tree-Hunt Chili, '87 292
Chimichangas, Baked Spicy Beef, '97 319
Chimichangas, Traditional Spicy Beef, '97 319
Cornbread, Beefy Jalapeño, '82 142
Cornbread, Cheesy Beef, '81 242
Cornbread Tamale Bake, '79 163
Crêpes, Italian, '90 157
Crêpes, Sherried Beef, '85 M29
Crêpes, Southwestern Cornbread, '98 42
Curried Beef and Rice, '88 164
Dinner, Beef-and-Garbanzo, '84 31
Dinner, Beef-and-Lima Bean, '84 292
Dinner, Beef-Cabbage, '81 179
Dinner, Beefy Sausage, '80 M9
Dinner, Black-Eyed Pea Skillet, '86 6
Dinner, Fiesta, '85 110
Dinner, Ground Beef Skillet, '82 60
Dinner, Mexican Beef-and-Rice, '88 199
Dip, Beef-and-Spinach, '99 65
Dip, Creamy Beef-and-Pasta Sauce, '01 108
Dip, Hot Chile-Beef, '83 218
Dip, Meaty Cheese, '82 59; '92 160
Dip, Quick Nacho, '90 168
Dip, Spicy Cheese-Beef, '02 58
Dip, Tostada, '84 206
Dumplings, Steamed Sesame, '97 208
Eggplant, Baked Stuffed, '81 133
Eggplant, Beefy Stuffed, '81 204
Eggplant, Cheesy Stuffed, '79 188
Empanadas, '92 156
Enchiladas. *See also* **BEEF, GROUND/Casseroles.**
　Green Chile Enchiladas, '02 188
　Hot and Saucy Enchiladas, '81 141; '82 6
　Skillet Enchiladas, '82 89
Fiesta, '87 180
Filet Mignon, Mock, '80 81
Filet Mignon Patties, Mock, '82 M68
Fillets, Poor Boy, '82 106
Filling, Beef, '80 81
Filling, Blue-Corn Crêpes with Beef, '97 197
Flips, Pea, '80 7
Gumbo, Carolina, '95 70
Gumbo, Ground Beef, '87 283
Gumbo Joes, '88 158
Hamburgers
　Apple-Bacon Burgers, '99 202
　Apple Burgers, '86 137
　au Poivre Blanc, Burgers, '87 186
　Bacon Burgers, Cheesy, '81 29
　Barbecued Burgers, '82 168; '89 164
　Beefburger on Buns, '84 71
　Beerburgers, '79 129
　Big Juicy Burgers, Barbara's, '03 M138; '04 M178
　Blue Cheese Burgers, '89 M66
　Brie-Mushroom Burgers, '95 128
　Burgundy Burgers, '80 156
　Caramelized Onions, Beef Burgers with, '98 143
　Cheeseburger Biscuits, '79 194
　Cheeseburger Loaves, '86 19
　Cheese Burgers, Beef-and-, '96 139
　Cheeseburgers, Fried Green Tomato, '94 138

Cheeseburgers, Inside Out, '99 202
Cheeseburgers, Mini-, '97 203
Cheesy Beef Burgers, '83 217
Chili Burgers, Open-Face, '81 24; '82 31; '83 33
Cocktail Burgers, Saucy, '83 217
Cracked Pepper Patties, '89 M131
Deluxe, Burgers, '84 125
Dill Pickle Rémoulade, Beef Burgers with,
    '04 310
Favorite Burgers, '89 165
Garden Herb Burgers, '01 136
Glorified Hamburgers, '81 73
Grilled Hamburgers, '93 198
Grilled Hamburgers, Flavorful, '81 110
Grilled Hamburgers, Spicy, '98 158
Gyro Burgers with Tahini Sauce, '03 183
Hawaiian, Beefburgers, '86 137
Italian Burgers, '00 326
Jalapeño-Stuffed Burgers with Roasted Bell
    Pepper Ketchup, '97 318
Marmalade-Glazed Beef Patties, '01 136
Mexicali Beef Patties, '86 137
Mexicali, Hamburgers, '93 217
Mushroom Burgers, '89 164
Nutty Burgers, '87 185
Old-Fashioned Hamburgers, '79 149
Oven Burgers, '83 130
Party Burgers, '83 164; '84 39
Patties, Deviled-Beef, '87 22
Patties, Hamburger, '82 M172
Pepper Burgers with Caramelized Onions, '00 218
Pineapple Burgers, '82 169
Pizza Burger, '87 185
Pizza Burgers, '80 M201; '81 73
Pizza Burgers, All-American, '92 148
Pizza Burgers, Easy, '82 190
Sauce, Hamburgers with Tomato, '81 73
Saucy Burgers, '80 93
Saucy Hamburgers, Quick, '82 60
Sausage Burgers, '83 212
Seasoned Burgers, '85 158
Seasoned Hamburgers, '84 230
Seasoned Stuffed Burgers, '86 136
Sour Cream Burgers, Grilled, '87 287
Spinach Burgers, '00 26
Spirals, Burger, '94 139
Sprouts, Burgers with, '89 164
Steak, Hamburger, '99 45
Steak-House Burgers, '87 186
Steaks, Company Hamburger, '82 169
Steaks, Smothered Hamburger, '00 289
Steaks with Mustard Sauce, Hamburger, '84 230
Stuffed Border Burgers, '04 127
Stuffed Burgers, '85 159
Stuffed Hamburger Steaks, Mushroom-,
    '99 202
Stuffed Southwestern-Style Burgers, '99 201
Superburgers, '79 89
Super Hamburgers, '79 129
Super Supper Burgers, '82 110
Surprise Burgers, '82 169
Sweet-and-Savory Burgers, '03 163
Sweet-and-Sour Burgers, '90 128
Taco Burgers, '98 224
Tahiti Burgers, '85 179
Teriyaki Burgers, '81 72
Teriyaki, Hamburgers, '89 309; '99 332
Teriyaki Hamburgers, '94 138
Tortilla Burgers, '94 138
Triple-Layer Burgers, '89 165
Vegetable Burgers, '89 164
Vegetable Burgers, Beef-and-, '84 125
Vegetable Burgers, Beefy, '98 143
Venison Burgers, '87 304

Italian-Style Meat and Potatoes, '03 97
Kheema, Indian, '81 226
Kielbasa, '92 242
Lasagna
    Beefy Lasagna, '80 81
    Bun, Lasagna in a, '90 176
    Cheesy Lasagna, '82 224; '88 299
    Cups, Lasagna, '04 293
    Easy Lasagna, '92 M197; '93 M24
    Ellie's Lasagna, '02 186
    Extra-Easy Lasagna, '00 326
    Lasagna, '82 119; '83 M6; '98 95
    Light Lasagna, '95 212
    Mexican Lasagna, '89 63; '01 282
    Microwave Lasagna, '96 M225
    Noodles Lasagna, Lots of, '91 M127
    Quick Lasagna, '84 220
    Quick 'n Easy Lasagna, '80 M10
    Simple Lasagna, '81 188
    South-of-the-Border Lasagna, '84 31
    Spinach Lasagna, Cheesy, '83 204
    Supreme, Lasagna, '92 198; '93 24
    Two, Lasagna for, '81 91
    Vintage Lasagna, '79 194
    White Lasagna, Gourmet, '96 225
Log, Stuffed Beef, '79 71
Macaroni, Cheeseburger, '02 119
Macaroni, Easy Beef and, '02 188
Macaroni, Ground Beef and, '85 218
Macaroni, Skillet Beef and, '82 130
Madras, Beef, '87 284
Manicotti, Quick, '79 6
Manicotti, Saucy Stuffed, '83 288
Manicotti, Special, '88 50
Meatballs
    Bacon-Wrapped Meatballs, '79 81
    Baked Meatballs, '02 25
    Barbecued Meatballs, Oven, '82 233
    Brandied Meatballs, '83 78
    Burgundy-Bacon Meatballs, '80 283
    Chafing Dish Meatballs, '81 260
    Charleston Press Club Meatballs, '93 129
    Chestnut Meatballs, '79 110
    Chinese Meatballs, '83 116; '87 194
    Cocktail Meatballs, '79 63, 207
    Creole, Meatball-Okra, '83 156
    Creole, Meatballs, '82 233
    Espanol, Meatballs, '82 110
    Flavorful Meatballs, '84 206
    Golden Nugget Meatballs, '82 233
    Gravy, Meatballs in, '79 136
    Hawaiian Meatballs, '85 86
    Hawaiian Meatballs, Tangy, '79 129
    Heidelberg, Beef Balls, '83 164; '84 39
    Horseradish Dressing, Meatballs and Vegetables
        with, '91 32
    Kebabs, Meatball, '95 192
    Marmalade-Glazed Meatballs, '01 136
    Meatballs, '89 237
    Paprikash with Rice, Meatballs, '85 31
    Pineapple and Peppers, Meatballs with,
        '90 145
    Pizza Meatballs, '85 86
    Polynesian Meatballs, '80 207
    Red Delicious Meatballs, '85 85
    Red Sauce and Meatballs, '04 17
    Royal Meatballs, '87 268; '88 102; '89 67
    Sandwiches, Open-Faced Meatball, '99 239
    Sandwich, Giant Meatball, '92 196
    Saucy Meatballs, '85 68; '90 122
    Saucy Party Meatballs, '80 149
    Sauerbraten Meatballs, '85 85
    Soup, Mexican Meatball, '98 315
    Spaghetti-and-Herb Meatballs, '84 75

    Spaghetti with Meatballs, '81 38
    Spiced Meatballs, '79 284
    Spicy Holiday Meatballs, '01 238
    Spicy Meatballs and Sausage, '79 163
    Stew, Meatball, '79 198
    Stroganoff, Meatball, '81 297; '02 50
    Stroganoff, Mushroom-Meatball, '85 85
    Swedish Meatballs, '80 80; '86 256
    Sweet-and-Sour Meatballs, '82 233; '86 240;
        '99 325
    Sweet-and-Sour Party Meatballs, '79 233
    Tamale Balls, Tangy, '89 60
    Tamale Meatballs, '80 194
    Zesty Meatballs, '80 250
Meat Loaf
    Alabama Meat Loaf, '04 188
    All-American Meat Loaf, '92 341; '93 46
    Barbecued Beef Loaves, Individual, '95 242
    Barbecued Meat Loaf, '80 60; '81 275; '84 50;
        '87 216
    Basic Meat Loaf, '88 M14
    Blue Cheese Meat Loaf Roll, '93 247
    Cheeseburger Loaf, '81 236, 276
    Cheeseburger Meat Loaf, '03 204
    Cheesy Meat Roll, '82 136
    Chili Meat Loaf, '81 275
    Corny Meat Loaf, '86 68
    Crunchy Meat Loaf Oriental, '79 212
    Curried Meat Loaf, '86 43
    Easy Meat Loaf, '88 M214; '95 125; '97 24
    Elegant Meat Loaf, '89 243
    Family-Style Meat Loaf, '93 18
    Fennel Meat Loaf, '88 46
    French Market Meat Loaf, '02 33
    German Meat Loaf, '87 216
    Glazed Beef Loaf, '86 19
    Gonzales Meat Loaf, '04 206
    Hurry-Up Meat Loaf, '82 21
    Hurry-Up Meat Loaves, '88 15
    Individual Meat Loaves, '81 279; '82 24; '83 154;
        '92 229; '00 214
    Italian Meat Loaf, '79 187
    Ketchup-and-Bacon-Topped Meat Loaf, Sweet,
        '03 203
    Meat Loaf, '81 170; '89 109
    Mexicali Meat Loaf, '81 275
    Mexican Meat Loaf, '87 217
    Mexican Meat Loaves, Mini-, '02 90
    Mini Alabama Meat Loaves, '04 188
    Miniature Meat Loaves, '85 24
    Moist-and-Saucy Meat Loaf, '99 270
    Mozzarella-Layered Meat Loaf, '79 71
    My-Ami's Meat Loaf, '94 229
    Oriental Meat Loaf, '81 M122; '83 M194
    Parsleyed Meat Loaf, '83 35
    Parsley Meat Loaf, '87 22
    Pineapple Loaves, Individual, '81 M121
    Pizza Meat Loaf, Cheesy, '81 M121
    Roll, Meat Loaf, '79 129
    Sandwich, Meat Loaf, '01 210
    Saucy Meat Loaves, '79 186
    Savory Meat Loaf, '87 216
    Southwestern Meat Loaf, '93 248
    Southwestern Roll with Cilantro Hollandaise
        Sauce, '99 16
    Spaghetti Sauce, Meat Loaves with, '03 204
    Special Meat Loaf, '89 70
    Spicy Meat Loaf, '79 71
    Spinach Meat Loaf, '96 131
    Sprout Meat Loaf, '85 51
    Stuffed Beef Log, '79 71
    Stuffed Meat Loaf, '79 187
    Stuffed Meat Loaf, Rolled, '80 80
    Summer Meat Loaf, '01 162

BEEF, GROUND, Meat Loaf
(continued)

    Sun-Dried Tomatoes and Herbs, Meat Loaf with, '92 192
    Supreme, Meat Loaf, '92 33
    Swedish Meat Loaf, '81 M121
    Sweet 'n' Saucy Meat Loaf, '01 210
    Tasty Meat Loaf, '83 213
    Teriyaki Loaves, Mini, '98 224
    Teriyaki Meat Loaf, '98 224; '03 172
    Teriyaki Meat Loaf, Mini-, '90 69
    Tex-Mex Meat Loaf for Two, '90 234
    Tomato Gravy, Meat Loaf with, '00 330
    Tomato Sauce, Meat Loaf with Chunky, '95 264
    Triple Meat Loaf, '79 186
    Vegetable Loaf, Beef-, '79 164
    Vegetable Meat Loaf, '85 M29
    Wellington, Meat Loaf, '79 186; '87 284
    Wrap, Meat Loaf in a, '89 122
Mexican Dinner, Quick, '98 224
Mexican Stack-Up, '95 69
Mexicorn Main Dish, '96 189
Mix, Ground Beef, '84 71
Mix, Ground Meat, '89 143
Moussaka, '87 166; '90 68
Moussaka, Corn, '87 190
Muffins, Barbecue, '96 246
Mushrooms, Stuffed, '83 13
Noodle Dinner, Beefy, '81 179
Noodles, Easy Beef and, '83 288
Omelet, Beefy Vegetable, '83 188
Omelet con Carne, Tex-Mex, '81 209
Pasta, Easy Skillet Beef 'n', '02 63
Patties, Foo Yong, '80 223
Peppers, Beefed-Up, '82 186
Peppers, Beef-Stuffed, '84 154; '85 146; '91 M127
Peppers, Beefy Stuffed Green, '81 86
Peppers for Two, Stuffed, '80 84
Peppers, Mexican Green, '80 65
Peppers, Stuffed, '81 239; '83 66
Peppers, Stuffed Green, '03 62
Peppers Stuffed with Beef, '84 72
Picadillo II, '93 72
Picadillo, Lettuce-Wrapped, '03 193
Picadillo (Spanish Hash), '91 87
Picadillo (Spicy Beef over Rice), '80 193; '84 118; '85 57
Picadillo Tarts, '91 279
Pies
    Broccoli-Beef Pie, '83 196
    Burrito Pie, Mexican, '87 287
    Cheese-Beef Pie, '85 33
    Cheeseburger Pie, '89 121
    Cheeseburger Pie, Jack-O'-Lantern, '00 234
    Continental Meat Pie, '95 256; '96 75
    Cornbread Pie, Beef-and-Onion, '01 298
    Corn Burger Pie, '83 156
    Country Pie, '83 155
    Enchilada Pie, '83 155
    Fried Beef Pies, '96 108
    Hamburger Pie, '81 92; '84 13
    Hamburger Pie, Deep-Dish, '00 334
    Italian Meat Pie, '01 297
    Mexicali Meat Pie, '81 194
    Natchitoches Meat Pies, '84 21; '91 241
    Old-Fashioned Meat Pie, '82 110
    Potato Pie, Meat-and-, '84 23
    Savory Beef Pies, '01 230
    Shepherd Pie, '83 116
    Shepherd's Pie, '00 55
    Sombrero Pie, '81 140
    Spaghetti Pie, '81 32

    Spaghetti Pie, Weeknight, '95 312
    Taco Pie, '88 256
    Taco Pie, Crescent, '80 80
    Taco Pie, Double-Crust, '88 272; '89 180
    Taco Pies, Individual, '82 M282
    Vegetable-Beef Pies, '80 286
Pintos, Texas Souper, '98 51
Pitas, Curried Beef, '85 220
Pizza, Best Ever Homemade, '80 233
Pizza-Burger Snacks, '84 30
Pizza, Cheeseburger, '97 318
Pizza, Cheesy Ground Beef, '03 62
Pizza Cups, '81 215
Pizza, Double Cheesy Beef-and-Sausage, '86 77
Pizza Horns, '89 214
Pizza, Quick Hamburger, '85 243
Pizzas, Five-Ring, '96 180
Pizza Supreme, '81 214
Pizza, Taco, '98 176
Pizza, Tostada, '81 16; '82 13
Pizza, Upside-Down, '91 185
Potatoes, Taco-Topped, '93 M18
Quiche, Green Chile, '83 31
Ravioli, Homemade, '87 230
Rice, Arabic, '94 200
Rice, Dirty, '03 147
Rice, Picadillo, '98 237
Rice, Spanish, '81 51
Rice, Spiced Beef and, '84 285
Rice, Spicy Beef and, '83 231
Rolls, Italian Meat, '86 137
Rolls, Spicy Beef, '85 110
Roulades, Beef, '80 80
Salad, Beef-and-Lime Rice, '03 172
Salad, Beefy Taco, '03 128
Salad Cups, Taco, '85 M29
Salad, Dude Ranch, '80 15
Salad in a Shell, Mexican, '86 4
Salad, Mexican, '81 36
Salad, Mexican Chef, '85 84; '92 64
Salad, Mexican Dinner, '98 330
Salad, Mexican Olive, '85 84
Salad, Mexi-Pea, '81 7
Salad, Party Taco, '97 19
Salad, Spicy Chili, '86 71
Salad, Spicy Taco, '87 287
Salad Supper, Mexican, '82 9; '83 68
Salad, Taco, '79 56; '83 145; '84 221; '85 84; '90 20
Salisbury Steak Deluxe, '81 170
Salisbury Steak with Mushroom Gravy, '03 202
Sandwiches, Barbecue Beef, '01 136
Sandwiches, Barbecued Beef, '81 25; '82 31; '83 34
Sandwiches, Bavarian Pita, '83 31
Sandwiches, Beef-Eater, '86 72
Sandwiches, Hearty Pocket, '80 93
Sandwiches, Hot Pita, '83 217; '87 M6
Sandwiches, Open-Face Pizza, '82 3
Sauce, Italian, '90 67
Sauce, Italian Meat, '83 193; '01 160
Sauce, Szechuan Noodles with Spicy Beef, '97 95
Sausage, Summer, '99 85
Shells, Cheesy Beef-Stuffed, '83 217
Shells, Mexican Stuffed, '91 87
Skillet, Hamburger-Rice, '00 236
Skillet, Vegetable-Beef, '86 172
Slice, French Beef, '79 125
Sloppy Joe Cups, '98 204
Sloppy Joe Dogs, '85 192
Sloppy Joe Pocket Sandwiches, '81 200
Sloppy Joes, '81 279; '82 24; '83 153; '89 143; '91 172; '02 188
Sloppy Joes, Easy, '82 31, 278; '83 34
Sloppy Joes, Pocket, '85 M328
Sloppy Joe Squares, '97 95

Sloppy Joes, Simple, '82 130
Sloppy Joes, Super, '83 130
Snacks, Beefy Party, '80 249
Soup, Beef-and-Barley Vegetable, '89 31
Soup, Beefy Black-Eyed, '85 6
Soup, Beefy Vegetable, '79 113; '84 M38
Soup, Cheeseburger, '04 298
Soup, Chunky Italian, '99 20
Soup, Hamburger, '80 263
Soup, Italian-Style Beef-and-Pepperoni, '00 316
Soup, Mexican Meatball, '98 315
Soup, Quick Beefy Vegetable, '80 25
Soup, Quick Italian Beef and Vegetable, '96 235
Soup, Spicy Vegetable-Beef, '88 11
Soup, Taco, '94 225; '99 36
Soup, Tamale, '95 213
Soup, Vegetable-Beef, '99 219
Soup, Vegetable-Burger, '82 6
Spaghetti. *See also* **BEEF, GROUND/Casseroles, Meatballs, Pies.**
    All-in-One Spaghetti, '98 295
    Black-Eyed Pea Spaghetti, '81 7
    Easy Spaghetti, '83 M317; '84 72; '92 66
    Italian Spaghetti, Real, '81 233
    Marzetti's Spaghetti, '99 85
    Meaty Spaghetti, '82 19
    Mushrooms, Spicy Spaghetti with, '85 2
    One-Pot Spaghetti, '00 58
    Pepperoni Spaghetti, Quick, '88 40
    Pizzazz, Spaghetti with, '80 85
    Sauce, Beer Spaghetti, '85 13
    Sauce for 4, Easy Spaghetti Meat, '92 244
    Sauce for Spaghetti, Meat, '00 256
    Sauce for 25, Easy Spaghetti Meat, '92 245
    Sauce, Herbed Spaghetti, '85 13
    Sauce, Quick Spaghetti and Meat, '94 64
    Sauce, Sicilian Spaghetti, '03 62
    Sauce, Spaghetti with Meat, '02 188
    Sauce, Thick Spaghetti, '84 118
    Thick-and-Spicy Spaghetti, '83 287
    Zucchini Spaghetti, '83 160
Squash, Beef-Stuffed, '83 134
Steak, Matt's Chicken-Fried, '97 25
Steak, Spanish, '80 80
Stew, Camp, '02 42
Stew, Campeche Bay Rib-Tickling, '89 317
Stew, Hamburger Oven, '84 4
Stew, Mixed Vegetable, '84 13
Stew, Quick Beef, '86 302
Sticks, Beef, '93 331
Stroganoff, Easy Hamburger, '79 208
Stroganoff, Ground Beef, '84 71
Stroganoff, Hamburger, '82 108, 110
Stroganoff, Quickie, '81 200
Stromboli, '87 283
Supper, Beef-and-Bean, '82 2
Supper, Beef-and-Eggplant, '84 291
Supper, Beef-and-Vegetable, '03 219
Supper, Oriental Beef, '79 192
Supper, Quick Skillet, '84 69
Supreme, Beef, '83 196
Taco Joes, '91 167
Tacoritos, '90 133
Taco Rolls, Chinese, '95 339
Tacos, '80 196
Tacos, Basic, '83 199
Tacos, Corn Chip, '81 67
Tacos, Easy, '96 159
Tacos, Easy Skillet, '04 180
Tacos, Jiffy, '83 M318
Tacos, Microwave, '88 M213
Tacos, Soft Beef, '91 88
Tacos Wrapidos, '03 172

Taco Tassies, '95 339
Taco Teasers, '01 134
Texas Straw Hat, '85 293
Torta Mexican Style, '89 122
Tostada Compuestas, '81 194
Tostadas, Crispy, '83 2
Tostadas, Super, '83 199
Turnovers, Meat, '86 326
Wontons, Tex-Mex, '87 196
Zucchini, Beef-Stuffed, '86 M139

BEETS
Apples, Beets and, '80 137; '88 155
Asparagus, Roasted-Beet, and Goat Cheese Salad,
    '02 96
Aspic, Beet, '90 123
Borscht, Crawfish, '92 84
Borscht, Ruby Red, '83 176
Cake, Chocolate Beet, '80 40
Cake with Almond Topping, Beet, '86 200
Chilled Beets and Cauliflower, '80 137
Chips, Beet, '97 229
Creamy Beets, '80 136
Deviled Beets, '84 217; '86 252
Eggs, Marbleized Garlic-Cheese-Stuffed, '96 91
Fritters, Beet, '96 36
Fruited Beets, '97 28
Glazed Beets, Ginger-Marmalade, '93 35
Glazed Beets, Orange-, '81 167; '85 289; '86 187;
    '99 24
Glazed Beets, Strawberry-, '83 234
Glazed Fresh Beets, '81 167
Glazed Orange Beets, '02 138
Greens, Beets 'n', '95 179
Harvard Beets, '83 M195
Ivy League Beets, '84 122
Marinated Beets, Green Beans, and Carrots,
    '88 162
Orange Beets, '91 219
Orange Beets, Spicy, '94 280
Orange-Ginger Beets, '80 137
Pickled Beets, '79 276; '81 216; '87 163; '97 229;
    '02 138
Pickled Beets, Easy, '80 137
Pickles, Beet, '81 210
Pineapple, Beets with, '79 249; '82 204
Relish, Beet, '84 179
Relish, Colorful Beet, '85 136
Relish, Horseradish, '01 60
Rice Ring with Beets, '79 225
Salad, Apple-Beet, '91 237
Salad, Asparagus, Roasted Beet, and Goat Cheese,
    '03 98
Salad, Beet, Apple, and Walnut, '98 269
Salad, Beet-Nut, '79 74
Salad, Fresh Beet, '02 236
Salad, Marinated Beet, '83 216
Salad Mold, Beet, '82 267
Salad, Orange-and-Beet, '88 43
Salad, Pickled Beet, '83 234
Salad, Red-and-Green, '90 55
Salad, Tangy Beet, '86 199
Salad with Orange Vinaigrette, Roasted Beet-and-
    Sugared Walnut, '97 229
Slaw, "Think Pink," '94 247
Soup, Potato-Beet, '88 156
Sour Cream Dressing, Beets with, '88 M295
Spiced Beets, '79 22
Spread, Beet-and-Pecan Sandwich, '99 274
Stuffed Beets, '88 155
Stuffed Beets, Blue Cheese-, '88 211
Stuffed Beets, Potato-, '83 234
Sweet-and-Sour Beets, '81 167; '82 22; '89 314
Vinaigrette, Beet, '97 229
Winter Beets, '02 283

BEVERAGES. *See also* **COFFEE, EGGNOG, TEA.**
  Alcoholic
Almond-Flavored Liqueur, '81 287
Amaretto, '90 272
Amaretto Breeze, '83 172
Amaretto Slush, '90 322; '95 90
Apricot Brandy Slush, '91 278
Apricot Slush, '93 205
Aztec Gold, '99 160
Banana Flip, '83 303
Banana Kabana, '86 316
Batida, Citrus, '02 274
Bay Bloodies, '93 268
Bellini, '01 89
Bellinis, '88 77
Bellinis, Apricot, '99 145
Bellinis, Frosted, '97 122
Bellinis, Mint, '02 136
Bloody Mary, '80 221
Bloody Mary Bowl, '99 268
Bloody Mary, Easy, '84 115
Bloody Marys, '79 33, 38; '80 51; '04 68
Bloody Marys, Eye-Opener, '82 48
Bloody Marys, Overnight, '81 270
Bloody Marys, Pitcher, '81 198
Bloody Marys, Spicy, '87 173; '90 207
Blueberry Cordial, '95 142
Blue Woo-Woo, '94 226
Bole, '97 245
Bourbon Blizzard, '92 287
Bourbon, Hot Buttered, '97 17
Bourbon Slush, '84 58
Bourbon Slush, Summertime, '81 101
Brandy Alexander, '92 283
Brandy Cream, '84 312; '00 271
Brandy Slush, '89 110
Brandy Velvet, '89 170
Burgundy Bowl, Sparkling, '83 276
Champagne Delight, '83 304
Champagne Fruit Slush, '90 322
Champagne Shooters, '02 280
Champagne with Orange Juice, '91 71
Chimayo Cocktails, '02 118
Chocolate, Flaming Brandied, '80 M290
Chocolate, Hot Laced Marshmallow, '93 53
Christmas Blossom, '99 321
Cider, Cinnamon Winter, '95 337
Cider, December, '91 260
Cider, Hot Burgundy, '96 306
Cider, Hot Mexican, '87 213
Cider, Hot Mulled, '84 323
Cider Nog, Hot, '98 241
Cider, Red Apple, '80 259
Cider Sour, Bourbon, '98 242
Cider, Spirited Apple, '96 214
Clam Diggers, '91 63
Cocktails, Sea Breeze, '97 161
Coconut Frost, Pink, '79 174; '80 128
Coconut-Pineapple Drink, '83 172
Cranapple Glogg, Hot, '90 22
Cranapple Wine, '90 272
Cranberry Cooler, '86 229; '01 93
Cranberry-Rum Slush, '84 259
Cranberry-Vodka Refresher, '91 210
Cranberry Wine Cup, '85 23
Cricket, '89 289
Cruising Drink, '00 167
Daiquiris, Cranberry, '81 245
Daiquiris, Creamy Strawberry, '91 66
Daiquiris, Freezer Lime, '79 141
Daiquiris, Mint, '89 157
Daiquiris, Peach, '90 322
Daiquiris, Strawberry, '90 125; '98 99
Daiquiri, Strawberry, '81 156

Daiquiritas, '82 160
Daiquiri, Watermelon, '95 143; '98 165; '04 172
Dessert, After Dinner-Drink, '82 100
Dessert Drink, Creamy, '86 131
Dessert Drink, Simply Super, '83 303
Frosty Sours, '81 156
Fruit 'ritas, '94 157
Funky Monkey, '99 161
Fuzz Buzz, '82 160
Game-Cocktails, '93 214
Gin Cooler, Sparkling, '90 272
Ginger Beer, '84 159
Golden Dream, '82 100
Grapefruit Drink, '95 238
Hot Apple Pie, '99 321
Hot Chocolate Deluxe, '90 272; '00 33
Hot Chocolate, Tennessee, '96 214
Kahlúa Beverage Sipper, '99 27
Kahlúa Hummer, '91 176
Kahlúa Smoothie, '87 242
Kahlúa Velvet Frosty, '82 244
King Alfonso, '80 259
Lemonade, Claret, '93 72
Lemonade, Hot Buttered, '88 208
Lemonade, Loaded, '01 93
Lemon Cooler, '82 48
Limeade, Pineapple, '01 235
Limeade, Rio Grande, '01 186
Lime Fizz, '81 172
Liqueur Sampler, Miniature, '95 332
Magnolia Blossoms, '87 72
Magnolias, '82 196
Margarita Granita, '02 49
Margaritas, '92 210; '93 273
Margaritas, Blue, '02 143
Margaritas, Frances's, '02 118
Margaritas, Frosted, '84 115
Margaritas, Frosty, '83 172
Margaritas, Lemon-Lime, '94 227
Margaritas, Mango, '96 126
Margaritas, Merry, '04 275
Margaritas, Orange-Lime, '97 140
Margaritas, Pitcher, '83 175
Margaritas Supreme, Frozen, '80 160
Margaritas, Tangy, '01 93
Margaritas, Tart, '85 153
Margarita, Strawberry, '04 107
Margaritas, Watermelon, '02 185
Martini, Individual Chocolate, '02 88
Martini, Mint Julep, '04 106
Martinis, Chocolate, '02 88
Melon Ball Cooler, '86 131
Mimosa, '04 106
Mimosa Hawaiian, '85 44
Mimosas, '86 91
Minted Delight, '87 107
Mint Julep, '97 120; '02 49
Mint Julep, Classic, '03 129
Mint Juleps, '81 155; '82 41; '85 40; '90 81; '04 94
Mint Juleps, Apple, '97 120
Mix, Bloody Mary, '89 110
Mix, Hot Wine, '81 287
Mix, Mulled Wine Spice, '85 266
Mocha Chocolate Fluff, '89 170
Mocha Deluxe Hot Drink, '82 289
Mocha Polka, '89 171
Mocha, Spirited Hot, '91 M260
Mojito, A Ritzy, '03 171
New Orleans, Mr. Funk of, '95 57
Oklahoma Sunrise, '87 67
Old-Fashioneds, '86 270
Old-Fashioned Slush, '93 340
Orange Blossom Flips, '80 51
Orange Brandy Smash, '99 30

BEVERAGES, Alcoholic
(continued)

Orange-Champagne Cocktail, '79 39
Orange Liqueur, '81 287
Orange Milk Shake, '84 166
Orange Thing, '04 290
Peach Frosty, '81 156
Peach Petals, '90 104
Peach Smash, '88 161
Peppermint Flip, Hot, '86 329
Peppermint Patti, The Peabody, '99 321
Pimm's Cup, '96 214
Piña Coladas, '95 203; '96 127
Piña Coladas, Frosty, '83 176
Piña Coladas, Luscious, '81 134
Piña Colada Slush, '95 90
Pineapple-Strawberry Slush, '94 227
Pink Palace, '93 293
Pirate's Painkiller, '99 161
Plum Slush, '84 139
Punch, Amaretto, '91 277
Punch, Anytime Wine, '79 232
Punch, Autumn Harvest, '96 277
Punch, Berry-Colada, '96 277
Punch, Bloody Mary, '04 106
Punch, Bourbon, '92 208
Punch, Bourbon-Citrus, '94 227
Punch, Bourbon-Tea, '87 57
Punch, Brandy Milk, '85 44; '88 83
Punch, Brandy Slush, '87 72
Punch, Caribbean, '95 173
Punch, Champagne, '85 153, 257; '86 101; '96 277; '98 310; '99 30; '03 118, 141
Punch, Champagne Blossom, '81 50; '99 290
Punch, Chatham Artillery, '80 121
Punch, Chilly Coffee, '01 64
Punch, Citrus-Wine, '98 197
Punch, Cranapple-Vodka, '87 72
Punch, Cranberry, '85 90
Punch, Cranberry Percolator, '88 248
Punch, Cranberry-Wine, '01 242
Punch, Extra-Kick, '91 209
Punch, Festive, '94 289
Punch, Frozen Margarita, '95 91
Punch, Fruit, '83 52; '02 162
Punch, Fruit Juice-and-Vodka, '96 214
Punch, Fruit Juicy Rum, '91 175
Punch, Gin, '80 160
Punch, Golden Gin, '79 233
Punch, Golden Spiked, '79 285
Punch, Health-Kick, '80 174
Punch, Hot Cranberry, '84 41
Punch, Hot Molasses-Milk, '86 329
Punch, Hot Pineapple, '82 264
Punch, Hot Spiced Rum, '96 214
Punch, Hot Wine, '85 265
Punch, Hurricane, '00 61
Punch, Irish Coffee-Eggnog, '95 314
Punch, Jefferson County, '86 267
Punch, Lemonade-Bourbon, '95 287
Punch, Lemon Champagne, '94 176
Punch, Lime, '84 58
Punch, Milk, '79 38; '02 298
Punch, Mixed Fruit, '95 239
Punch, Mulled Wine, '95 337
Punch, New Orleans Milk, '81 50
Punch, Orange-Lime, '82 160
Punch, Party, '81 265
Punch, Perky Rum, '85 116
Punch, Pimms, '92 167
Punch, Piña Colada, '89 212
Punch, Pineapple, '79 174; '80 128

Punch, Pineapple-Gin, '95 140
Punch, Pink, '96 190
Punch, Poinsettia, '02 251
Punch, Raspberry-Rose, '87 242
Punch, Red Velvet, '89 289
Punch, Refreshing Champagne, '84 259
Punch, Rum, '85 265
Punch, Southern Fruit, '95 238
Punch, Sparkling Champagne, '84 58
Punch, Sparkling Holiday, '81 290
Punch, Spiced Rum, '86 179
Punch, Spiked Tea, '86 101
Punch, Spirited Fruit, '81 100
Punch, Stormy Petrel Rum Thunder, '93 269
Punch, Strawberry Champagne, '90 315
Punch, Streetcar Champagne, '88 82
Punch, Tropical Fruit, '83 176
Punch, Vodka, '85 265
Punch, Wedding, '86 107
Punch, Whiskey, '90 64; '91 175
Punch, Whiskey Sour, '91 209
Punch, Wine, '93 331
Punch, Yacht Club Milk, '89 86
Raspberry Kir, '86 183
Red Roosters, '87 147
Red Ruby, '92 209
Rum, Hot Buttered, '80 259; '82 244; '88 247; '96 213
Rum Slush, Easy, '79 174; '80 129
Sangría, '79 186; '81 67, 196; '82 121; '86 214; '98 178; '00 122
Sangría, Cranberry, '95 238
Sangría, Easy Citrus, '80 218
Sangría, Easy Frozen, '92 208
Sangría, Garden, '01 100
Sangría, Grapefruit, '89 92
Sangría, Orange, '81 237
Sangría, Pineapple, '91 176
Sangría, Punchy, '80 160
Sangría, Quick, '81 156
Sangría Slush, White, '90 322
Sangría, Spanish, '83 81
Sangría, Teaberry, '87 147
Sangría, Texas White, '02 86
Sangría, Three-Fruit, '89 212
Sangría, White, '83 180; '94 289
Sazerac, '04 106
Screwdrivers, '79 33
Sea Mist, '93 167
Sherry Sour, '87 74
Sipper, Creamy Coconut, '02 298
Sipper, Sunshine, '86 179
Slush, Lemon-Rum, '00 271; '04 240
Slush, Mexican, '83 176
Slush, Strawberry, '02 185
Slush with a Punch, '90 322
Spritzer, Cranberry, '91 66; '92 265
Spritzer, Fruit, '01 174
Spritzer, Lemon-Mint, '99 175
Spritzer, Pineapple-Grapefruit, '04 143
Spritzers, Bellini, '90 110
Spritzers, Citrus, '91 231; '92 67
Spritzers, Cranberry, '89 213
Spritzers, Grapefruit-White Wine, '96 56; '01 319
Spritzers, Spiced, '86 229
Spritzers, Wine, '81 94
Strawberry-Banana Smoothie, '81 59
Strawberry Mimosa, Sparkling, '88 169
Strawberry Slush, '98 178
Strawberry Sparkler, '99 49
Sunny Morning, '93 295
Sunrise, Bourbon, '01 326
Sunrise, St. Pete, '94 227
Swamp Breeze, '01 146

Syllabub, '81 265; '84 319
Syrup, Bourbon, '03 233
Tangerine Sparkler, '98 54
Tart Caribbean Cooler, '81 134
Tea Juleps, '99 90
Tequila Slush, '83 176
Tequila Sunrise, '83 175
Toddy, Molasses Rum, '91 36
Tomato Bouillon, New Year's, '94 24
Tomato-Orange Juice Cocktail, '83 169
Tomato Sipper, Peppy, '94 227
Vanilla Cream, '97 272
Vodka, Frozen Pink, '89 170
Vodka-Orange Slush, '89 92
Vodka Slush, '88 82
Wassail, '83 311
Wassail, Bourbon, '86 270
Wassail, Four-Fruit, '90 22
Whiskey Sour, '04 107
Whiskey Sours, '03 258
Whiskey Sours, Frozen, '93 176
Whiskey Sours, Frozen Orange-, '92 67
Whiskey Sour Slushies, '04 106
Whiskey Sours, Slushy, '03 258
Whisky Sour Slush, '86 183
Whispers, '86 317
Wine, Christmas Dreams in, '91 260
Wine Cocktail, Citrus, '99 93
Wine Cooler, '82 41
Wine Cooler, Fruited, '86 176
Wine, Hot Mulled, '83 251
Wine, Hot Spiced, '84 41; '03 210
Wine, Mulled, '03 233
Wine Tasting, '95 332
Wine Welcomer, '81 100
Yellow Birds, '90 103
Apple-Berry Sparkler, '93 104
Apple Berry Sparkler, '94 100
Apple Cooler, '90 14
Apple Cooler, Minted, '88 169
Apple Juice, Hot, '86 270
Apple Juice, Perky Cinnamon-, '90 22
Apple Juice Shrub, Shenandoah, '79 282
Apple Juice, Sparkling, '95 141
Apple Julep, '86 103, 215
Apricot Bellinis, '99 145
Apricot-Citrus Slush, '88 82
Apricot Cooler, '81 100
Apricot Coolers, '99 29
Apricot Fruit Flip, '91 18
Apricot Mint Cooler, '90 165
Apricot Nectar, Hot, '81 265
Apricot Nectar, Mulled, '86 229
Apricot-Orange-Carrot Cooler, '96 108
Aztec Gold, '99 160
Banana-Berry Flip, '88 215; '89 20
Banana-Chocolate Malt, '89 170
Banana Coolers, '91 308
Banana Crush, '80 88; '83 142
Banana Frostee, '91 66
Banana Nog, '82 290
Banana-Orange Slush, '80 48; '81 155
Banana Slush, '83 56
Banana-Strawberry Frost, '87 199
Berry Shrub, '95 29
Blackberry Breeze, '98 179
Black Russian, Mock, '92 322
Bloodless Mary, '80 146
Breakfast Drink, Yummy, '01 133
Breakfast Eye-Opener, '87 199
Brew, Beach, '91 177
Brew, Holiday, '90 272
Brew, Quilter's, '85 43
Brew, Witch's, '93 244

Bullshots, **'86** 91
Cantaloupe-Lime Refresher, **'01** 332
Carambola-Yogurt Calypso, **'90** 169
Caribbean Cooler, **'95** 203
Carrot Cooler, **'89** 35
Champagne, Mock Pink, **'89** 46
Champions' Cooler, **'96** M181
Chiller, Royal Cup, **'98** 218
Chocolate Malt, **'86** 183
Chocolate, Mexican-Style, **'81** 187
Chocolate Milk, French, **'79** 38
Chocolate Sipper, **'88** 83
Cider, Apple, **'95** 198
Cider, Apple-Orange, **'92** 20
Cider, Cherry, **'94** 288
Cider, Holiday, **'82** 264
Cider, Hot Apple, **'90** 21, 225
Cider, Hot Molasses, **'98** 242
Cider, Hot Mulled, **'79** 205
Cider, Hot Mulled Apple-Orange, **'97** 301
Cider, Hot Spiced, **'82** 290; **'99** 248
Cider, Hot Spiced Apple, **'84** 318
Cider, Hot Spicy, **'84** 265
Cider, Mulled, **'91** 209; **'94** 227
Cider, Mulled Apple, **'92** 208
Cider Nog, Hot, **'98** 241
Cider Nog, Hot Apple, **'84** 42
Cider Sipper, Apple, **'02** 220
Cider Sipper, Apricot-Apple, **'02** 220
Cider, Sparkling Apple, **'88** 276
Cider, Spiced Apple, **'85** 256
Cider, Spiced Cranberry, **'84** 261; **'98** 278
Cider, Warm Citrus, **'01** 46
Citrus Blush, **'98** 197
Citrus Cooler, **'82** 160; **'93** 105
Citrus Float, **'89** 171
Citrus Slush, **'93** 198
Cocoa, Mocha, **'83** 318
Coco-Berry Calypso, **'89** 171
Coffee Soda, **'97** 272
Cooler, Caribbean, **'98** 333
Cooler, Speedy Spring, **'02** 58
Cooler, Spring, **'86** 214
Cranberry Cocktail, Hot, **'89** 310
Cranberry Drink, Mulled, **'92** 12; **'03** 36
Cranberry Frappé, **'82** 263
Cranberry Juice, Sparkling, **'88** 275
Cranberry-Orange Soda, **'79** 148
Cranberry-Raspberry Drink, **'97** 154
Cranberry Shimmer, **'98** 168
Cubes, Berry-Good, **'95** 201
Cubes, Cranberry, **'95** 201
Cubes, Florida, **'95** 201
Cubes, Lemonade, **'95** 201
Cubes, Lemon-Mint, **'95** 201
Currant Warmer, **'00** 271
Fizz, Berry Blue, **'03** M164
Float, Classic Cola, **'04** 107
Float, Frosty Fruit, **'87** 159
Float, Nutmeg-Almond, **'84** 106
Float, Pineapple Sherbet, **'79** 148
Float, Root Beer, **'04** 211
Floats, Maple-Coffee, **'86** 195
Float, Sparkling Cranberry, **'86** 195
Float, Strawberry-Banana, **'87** 160
Frappé, Hootenanny, **'89** 110
Fruit Beverage, Blender, **'83** 318
Fruit Cooler, Four-, **'86** 101
Fruit Coolers, **'98** 197
Fruit Drink, Three-, **'79** 38; **'80** 50; **'87** 199
Fruit Drink, Tropical, **'85** 43
Fruit Juice Cooler, **'92** 67
Fruit Juicy, Breakfast, **'86** 176
Fruit Refresher, **'91** 203

Fruit Refresher, Four-, **'79** 174; **'80** 129
Fruit Slush, **'96** 157
Fruit Slush, Refreshing, **'82** 35
Fruit Slushy, **'80** 146
Fruit Whisper, Tropical, **'89** 212
Funshine Fizz, **'91** 66
Ginger Beer, **'01** 292
Ginger-Mint Cooler, **'89** 92
Grapefruit Cooler, **'88** 81
Grapefruit Drink, **'90** 84; **'95** 238
Grapefruit-Orange Refresher, **'82** 174
Grapefruit Refresher, **'88** 85
Grape Juice, Mulled, **'90** 21
Grape Juice, Spiced White, **'92** 320
Grape-Lime Cooler, **'94** 227
Hawaiian Crush, **'91** 66
Hot Chocolate, **'94** 290; **'04** 209
Hot Chocolate, Cherry Cordial, **'02** 220
Hot Chocolate, Creole, **'80** M290
Hot Chocolate, Favorite, **'83** 55
Hot Chocolate, French, **'86** 328
Hot Chocolate, Mexican, **'98** 313; **'04** 210, 299
Hot Chocolate, Old-Fashioned, **'85** 23
Hot Chocolate, Special, **'82** 5
Hot Chocolate, Spiced, **'80** 50
Hot Chocolate, Spicy, **'85** 278
Hot Chocolate, Sugar-and-Spice, **'95** 34
Hot Cocoa, Fudgy, **'00** 235
Hot Cocoa, Quick, **'82** 5
Ice Bowl, **'83** 152
Ice Cream Ginger Fizz, **'83** 303
Ice Cubes, Lemonade, **'02** 48
Ice Mold, Strawberry, **'91** 278
Ice Ring, **'95** 140; **'03** 141
Ice Ring, Easy, **'03** 141
Ice Ring, Strawberry, **'94** 176
Jogger's Sunrise, **'93** 213
Kid's Cooler, **'90** 95
Kiwi-Peach Slushy, **'00** 201
Kona Luscious, **'84** 54
Lemonade, Apple, **'89** 212; **'03** 169
Lemonade, Berry Delicious, **'93** 205
Lemonade, Blackberry, **'99** 130; **'03** 89
Lemonade, Blueberry, **'98** 179
Lemonade by the Glass, **'96** 161
Lemonade, Cayenne, **'03** 169
Lemonade, Cherry-Berry, **'03** 89
Lemonade Concentrate, **'89** 110
Lemonade Cooler, Watermelon-, **'04** 172
Lemonade, Dazzling, **'97** 99
Lemonade, Fresh, **'00** 139
Lemonade, Fresh Squeezed, **'81** 172
Lemonade, Fresh-Squeezed, **'99** 220
Lemonade, Front Porch, **'90** 156
Lemonade, Homemade, **'01** 143
Lemonade, Hot Buttered, **'94** 18
Lemonade, Pineapple, **'93** 194
Lemonade, Raspberry, **'03** 89
Lemonade Slush, Pink, **'80** 151
Lemonade, Strawberry, **'80** 160
Lemonade, Sunny Spring, **'00** 70
Lemonade, Sweet-Tart, **'96** 161; **'02** 160
Lemonade, Watermelon, **'98** 165
Lemonade with Frozen Tea Cubes, **'85** 161
Lemon Frappé, **'92** 44
Lemon Slush, **'00** 271
Lemon Velvet, **'90** 15
Limeade, **'01** 143
Limeade, Fresh, **'00** 139
Limeade, Pineapple, **'01** 235
Limeade, Pink Apple, **'89** 46
Lime Cooler, **'87** 160
Lime Fizz, Frosty, **'90** 104
Malt, Chocolate-Yogurt, **'01** 173

Malt Special, **'85** 198
Mango Frappé, **'86** 216
Margaritas, Mock, **'88** 209; **'99** 120
Melon Julep, Rainbow, **'80** 183
Milk Shakes. *See* **BEVERAGES/Shakes.**
Milk, Santa Claus, **'92** 281
Mint Juleps, Apple, **'97** 120
Mix, Beetle Cider, **'82** 308
Mix, Bloody Mary, **'89** 110
Mix, Cappuccino, **'90** 87
Mix, Deluxe Hot Chocolate, **'80** M290
Mix, Hot Chocolate, **'04** 209
Mix, Hot Cocoa, **'81** 287
Mix, Hot Mocha-Cocoa, **'82** 296
Mix, Hot Spiced Cider, **'84** 42
Mix, Instant Cocoa, **'86** 332
Mix, Mexican Mocha Spice, **'00** 334
Mix, Minted Hot Cocoa, **'91** 316
Mix, Mocha-Flavored Hot Cocoa,
  '91 316
Mix, Spiced Cider, **'03** 289
Mix, Spiced Mocha, **'01** 64
Mix, Spicy-Hot Chocolate, **'85** 278
Mocha Espresso, Italian, **'82** 254
Mocha Frosty, **'92** 44
Mocha, Hot, **'84** 60
Mocha Latte Beverage, **'03** 46
Mocha Melt, Spiced, **'01** 240
Mocha, Mexican, **'93** M341
Mocha, Quick Viennese, **'79** 232
Mocha, Swiss-Style, **'82** 253
Mocha Warmer, **'97** 272
Nicely Iced, **'03** 164
Orange-Banana Flip, **'82** 48
Orange-Banana Whip, **'95** 244
Orange Blush, **'80** 51
Orange-Cranberry Cocktail, **'01** 103
Orange Frosty, **'86** 101
Orange Jubilee, **'03** 305
Orange Juicy, **'90** 178
Orange-Lemon Mist, **'79** 288; **'80** 35
Orange Pick-Me-Up, **'80** 232
Orange-Pineapple Drink, **'89** 35
Orange Slush, **'82** 49
Patio Blush, **'92** 43; **'99** 93
Peach Cooler, **'85** 198
Peaches 'n' Almond Cream, **'86** 229
Peach Frost, **'89** 155
Peach Frosty, **'83** 318
Peach Pick-Me-Up, **'89** 183
Peach Refresher, **'86** 103
Peanut Butter Cooler, **'84** 115
Piña Colada, Mock, **'92** 322
Piña Colada, Parson's, **'89** 46
Pineapple-Banana Slush, **'90** 14
Pineapple Cooler, **'90** 207
Pineapple Drink, Hot Buttered, **'91** 260
Pineapple Nectar, Hot, **'90** 21
Pineapple Slush, **'88** 82
Pineapple Soda, **'90** 179
Pineapple Sparkle, Spiced, **'92** 322
Pineapple-Yogurt Whirl, **'91** 132
Pink Soda, Blushing, **'90** 104
Punch. *See* **BEVERAGES/Alcoholic.**
  Apple Bobbing Punch, **'99** 246
  Apple Punch, Hot, **'84** 324
  Apple Punch, Party, **'00** 271
  Apple-Tea Punch, **'85** 82
  Apricot Spiced Punch, **'80** 269
  Autumn Punch, **'88** 209
  Banana Punch, **'99** 161; **'01** 93
  Berry-Colada Punch, **'96** 277
  Berry Punch, **'92** 67
  Brew-Ha-Ha Punch, **'98** 255

BEVERAGES, Punch
(continued)

Brunch Punch, '04 281
Bubbling Jade Punch, '79 174; '80 129
Bunch, Punch for a, '95 90
Cantaloupe Punch, '81 147; '00 140
Caribbean Punch, '95 173
Champagne Punch, '99 30
Children's Punch, '85 322
Christmas Eve Punch, '86 314
Christmas Punch, '84 259; '89 330
Cider Punch, Hot, '95 238
Cider Punch, Spiced, '84 258
Citrus Party Punch, '83 141; '92 289
Citrus Punch, '85 319; '93 99
Citrus Punch, Budget, '82 121
Citrus Punch, Fresh, '85 154
Citrus Punch, Party, '84 117
Citrus Punch, Sparkling, '95 337
Cola Punch, '91 144
Cottontail Punch, '02 48
Cranapple Punch, '83 142
Cranberry-Cherry Punch, '91 176
Cranberry-Cinnamon Punch, '86 270
Cranberry-Pineapple Punch, '00 284
Cranberry Punch, '83 275; '99 290
Cranberry Punch, Holiday, '85 265
Cranberry Punch, Hot, '80 288; '84 319; '85 265
Cranberry Punch, Sparkling, '85 277; '95 101
Cranberry Punch, Spiced, '89 290
Cranberry Punch, Tart, '83 318
Cran-Grape-Tea Punch, '92 209
Emerald Sea Punch, '04 163
False-Kick Punch, '82 121
Frozen Punch Ring, '83 152
Fruited Ice-Cube Punch, '98 197
Fruit Juice Punch, '96 214
Fruit Punch, '01 106
Fruit Punch, Can-Can, '94 122
Fruit Punch, Florida, '92 247
Fruit Punch, Fresh, '98 155
Fruit Punch, Golden, '80 299; '83 56; '96 278
Fruit Punch, Holiday, '79 232
Fruit Punch, Holiday Hot, '92 286
Fruit Punch, Hot, '83 33
Fruit Punch, Mixed, '90 207; '95 239
Fruit Punch, Party, '82 137
Fruit Punch, Passion, '90 169
Fruit Punch, Slushy, '98 92
Fruit Punch, Southern Fresh, '99 70
Fruit Punch, Spiced, '88 2
Fruit Punch, Summertime, '80 160
Fruit Punch, Tropical, '80 51; '90 169
Fruit Slush Punch, '91 278
Fruit Sparkle, '99 289
Fruity Witches' Brew, '95 273
Ginger Ale-Nectar Punch, '92 171
Goblin Punch, '88 228
Golden Punch, '85 207
Grape Punch, Sparkling, '82 48
Happy New Year Punch, '98 26
Holiday Punch, '87 252
Hot Cider Punch, '03 233
Hot Spiced Punch, '96 214
Irish Coffee-Eggnog Punch, '95 314
Lemonade Punch, Sparkling, '88 276
Lemon Balm Punch, '80 42
Lime-Pineapple Punch, '83 142
Lime Punch, Calypso Presbyterian Church
    Women's, '95 141
Lime Punch, Foamy, '82 264
Lime Slush Punch, '90 273

Margarita Punch, '98 88
Merry Christmas Punch, '79 285
Mocha Punch, '84 58, 166; '86 270; '95 141
Mock Champagne Punch, '93 340
Morning Punch, '88 82
Nectar Punch, '93 283
Nog Punch, Creamy, '01 240
Orange Blossom Punch, '83 142
Orange-Mint Punch, '82 121
Orange Punch, Refreshing, '81 39
Orange Sherbet Party Punch, '83 142
Orange Soda Punch, '87 214
Parsonage Punch, '79 148
Party Punch, '91 106, 278
Party Punch in a Pail, '94 289
Party Punch, Special, '81 119
Peppermint-Eggnog Punch, '90 273
Peppermint Punch, Cupid's Creamy, '04 253
Percolator Punch, '91 306
Percolator Punch, Hot, '81 288
Pineapple-Citrus Punch, '96 134
Pineapple Fruit Punch, '02 49
Pineapple-Mint Punch, '88 209
Pineapple-Orange Punch, '85 236
Pineapple Punch, '79 174
Pineapple Punch, Frosty, '91 66
Pineapple Punch, Spiced, '83 33; '92 66
Pineapple Sherbet Punch, '95 141
Pink Lady Punch, '81 100
Polka Dot Punch, '95 178
Ponche de Piña, '84 58
Raspberry Sherbet Punch, '95 141
Raspberry Sparkle Punch, '84 57
Sherbet Punch, Double, '79 232
Spiced Punch, Hot, '80 250
Strawberry-Lemonade Punch, '85 116; '91 175
Strawberry Punch, '90 273
Strawberry Punch, Creamy, '86 195
Sunset Punch, '96 278
Tangy Punch, '83 142
Tea Party Punch, '87 147
Tea Punch, '90 143, 207
Tea Punch, Citrus-, '85 116
Tea Punch, Mint, '04 63
Tea Punch, Minted, '00 164
Traders' Punch, '87 94
Tropical Punch, '90 207
Vegetable Punch, Hot, '93 12
Watermelon Punch, '89 204; '92 190; '00 140
White Grape Punch, '90 15
White Grape Punch, Spiced, '96 170
Purple Cow, '98 206
Raspberry Cooler, '89 171
Raspberry Fizz, Rosy, '90 179
Raspberry Shrub, Red, '97 132
Refresher, Peach Yogurt, '03 166
Rice-and-Cinnamon Cooler, '00 139
Sangría, Mock Tea, '99 336
Sangría, Southern, '88 170
Sangría, Virgin, '89 46
Scarlet Sipper, '90 198
Scuppernong Juice, '98 221
Shakes
    Apricot Shake, '84 115
    Banana Milkshake, '85 47; '90 179
    Banana-Pineapple Milk Shake, '84 59
    Banana Shake, '97 172
    Berry Blue Shake, '01 200
    Berry Milk Shake, Double-, '00 81
    Chocolate-Banana Milk Shake, '94 113
    Chocolate Mint Shake, '89 170
    "Concrete," Abaco Mocha, '94 114
    "Concrete," All Shook Up, '94 114
    "Concrete," Cardinal Sin, '94 113

"Concrete," Foxtreat, '94 113
Cranberry Shake, '83 171
Date Shake, '92 44
Fruit Shake, Frosty, '87 23
Fruit Shake, Tangy, '95 129
Fruit Yogurt Shake, Three-, '01 173
Get-Up-and-Go Shake, '00 179
Mocha Milkshake, '89 35
Mocha-Mint Shake, '02 297
Orange Milk Shake, '84 166
Orange Shake, Peachy, '81 156
Papaya Shake, '90 169
PBJ Shake, '93 292
Peach Melba Shake, '02 158
Peach Melba Sundae Shake, '93 134
Peanut Butter-Banana Shake, '97 172
Peanut Butter Milkshakes, '85 198
Peanut Butter Shake, '82 48
Pep Shake, '79 38
Pineapple-Banana Shake, '85 215
Pineapple-Buttermilk Shake, '01 173
Pineapple-Buttermilk Shake, Light, '01 173
Pineapple Milkshake, '87 199
Pineapple Milk Shake, '94 113
Pineapple-Orange-Banana Shake, '97 172
Raisin Shake, Amazin', '86 195
Raspberry-and-Banana Shake, '89 183
Raspberry Milk Shakes, '95 238
Strawberry-Banana Shake, '89 35; '97 172
Strawberry-Banana Shake, Double, '01 173
Strawberry-Banana Shake, Light Double, '01 173
Strawberry-Cheesecake Shake, '92 44
Strawberry Milk Shake, '94 113
Strawberry Milkshake, Fresh, '82 113
Strawberry-Orange Breakfast Shake, '87 186
Strawberry-Pear Shake, '92 139
Strawberry-Pineapple Shake, '84 166
Strawberry Shake, '97 172
Strawberry Shake, Double, '00 179
Strawberry-Yogurt Shake, '87 199
Summer Shake, '82 161
Sunshine Shake, '79 53
Tropical Shake, '87 200; '93 212; '00 179; '04 21
Sipper by the Glass, Fresh Mint-Citrus, '03 89
Sipper, Fresh Mint-Citrus, '03 89
Slush, Peach, '04 141
Slush, Santa's, '90 271
Slush, Strawberry-Lemonade, '03 169
Slush, Strawberry Tea, '04 63
Slushy, Fruit Parfait, '02 185
Smoothies
Banana-Blueberry Smoothie, '90 104
Banana Breakfast Smoothie, '03 46
Banana-Peach Buttermilk Smoothie, '04 22
Banana-Pineapple Smoothie, Quick, '93 195
Banana Smoothie, '87 160; '93 95
Berry-Banana Buttermilk Smoothie, '00 49
Berry Smoothie, Four-, '97 173
Blackberry Smoothies, '04 141
Chocoholic Smoothie, '97 173
Chocolate-Mint Smoothie, '84 166
Citrus Smoothie, '98 17; '99 196
Cranberry Smoothie, '86 183; '91 307
Fruit Smoothie, '89 87
Fruit Smoothie, Two-, '89 182
Honey-Banana Smoothie, '89 144
Honey-Yogurt Smoothie, '97 326
Honey-Yogurt Smoothie, Fruited, '88 231; '89 23
Kahlúa Smoothie, '87 242
Mango-Orange Smoothie, '86 216
Mango Smoothie, '03 122
Orange-Banana Smoothie, '97 173
Peachy-Pineapple Smoothie, '97 173
Pineapple Smoothie, '97 172

Pineapple Smoothie, Easy, '00 199
Strawberry-Banana Smoothie, '81 59
Strawberry-Peach Smoothie, '89 182
Strawberry Smoothie, '86 183; '97 173
Sunrise Smoothie, '93 139
Sunshine Smoothies, '98 330
Tropical Smoothie, '81 50; '90 169
Yogurt-Fruit Smoothie, '03 25
Soda, Homemade Orange, '03 141
Southern Breeze, '02 185
Sparkler, Cherry, '00 329
Spiced Brew, Hot, '91 36
Spices, Barclay House Mulling, '86 289
Spritzers. *See also* **BEVERAGES/Alcoholic.**
Fruit Spritzer, '01 174
Kiwi-Lemonade Spritzer, '03 89
Lemon-Mint Spritzer, '99 175
Raspberry Spritzers, '99 207
Strawberry-Kiwi-Lemonade Spritzer, '03 89
Strawberry Spritzer, '90 14; '97 272
Strawberry Cooler, '83 56; '84 51
Strawberry Coolers, '92 67
Strawberry-Mint Cooler, '84 57
Strawberry-Orange Slush, '83 172
Strawberry Refresher, Frozen, '93 213
Strawberry Slurp, '81 96
Strawberry Soda, '84 115
Strawberry Soda, Old-Fashioned, '79 49
Strawberry Sparkler, '99 49
Sunshine Fizz, '92 44
Syllabub, Plantation, '79 233
Syrup, Berry, '96 161
Syrup, Ginger, '96 161
Syrup, Mint, '90 89; '96 161; '97 120
Syrup, Mint Simple, '03 129
Syrup, Orange, '96 161
Syrup, Simple, '99 161
Syrup, Sugar, '96 161; '03 224
Tahitian Flower, '87 159
Toddy, Jolly, '86 229
Toddy, Tasty, '88 82
Tofruitti Breakfast Drink, '88 26
Tomato Bouillon, '83 8
Tomato-Clam Cocktail, '87 252
Tomato Cocktail, '83 M203
Tomato Juice Cocktail, '79 212; '83 230; '90 12
Tomato Juice Cocktail, Zesty, '83 289
Tomato Juice, Homemade, '81 50
Tomato Juice, Spicy, '85 189
Tomato Refresher, '83 318
Tomato Sipper, Peppy, '94 227
Tomato Sipper, Spicy, '86 229
Tomato Warm-Up, Spicy, '95 328
Tropical Cooler, '84 120
Tropical Delight, '89 182
Tropical Ice, '79 174; '80 129
Tropical Refresher, '85 198; '96 157
Vanilla Cream, '97 272
Vanilla Frosty, French, '79 148
Vegetable Cocktail, Fresh, '82 165
Vegetable Juice Delight, '84 58
Virgin Mary, Spicy, '92 323
Wassail, '84 259, 318; '88 248; '90 273; '97 240; '99 268
Wassail, Christmas, '93 295
Wassail, Cranberry, '88 289
Wassail, Golden, '96 278
Wassail, Holiday, '89 289; '91 260
Wassail, Pineapple, '01 240
Wassail, Pineapple-Apricot, '83 275
Wassail, Winter, '03 295
Watermelon-Berry Slush, '90 137
Watermelon-Strawberry Cooler, '98 178
Zippy Red Eye, '91 209

BISCUITS
Angel Biscuits, '80 49; '90 28; '93 270
Angel Biscuits, Ham-Filled, '80 159
Anise Biscuits with Balsamic Strawberries, '02 170
Bacon Biscuit Cups, '99 214
Baking Powder Biscuits, '82 195; '89 144
Basic Buttery Biscuits, '04 280
Basil Biscuits, '93 160
Beaten Biscuits, '86 54
Benne Seed Biscuits, '79 38
Biscuits, '92 31
Blueberry Biscuits, '00 286
Blueberry Buttermilk Biscuits, '89 210
Blue Cheese-and-Ham Cornmeal Biscuits, '98 136
Bowl, Chili in a Biscuit, '98 224
Bowls, Biscuit, '03 222
Bowls, Chicken Pot Pie in Biscuit, '03 222
Bowls, Creamed Chicken in Biscuit, '03 222
Bran Biscuits, '85 228
Bread, Biscuit, '84 284
Bread, Brown Sugar Biscuit, '02 M224
Buttermilk Biscuits, '83 208; '85 255, 321; '99 32; '03 24
Buttermilk Biscuits, Basic, '94 214; '00 48
Buttermilk Biscuits, Deluxe, '82 130
Buttermilk Biscuits, Favorite, '81 191
Buttermilk Biscuits, Fluffy, '84 102
Buttermilk Biscuits, Old-Fashioned, '80 77
Buttermilk Biscuits, Quick, '83 311; '88 15; '92 269; '03 314
Buttermilk Biscuits with Virginia Ham, '96 142
Buttermilk-Raisin Biscuits, '92 338
Caramel Dessert Biscuits, '95 36
Casserole, Beef-and-Biscuit, '83 75
Casserole, Biscuit-Topped Tuna, '79 113
Cheese
Angel Biscuits, Cheese, '89 211
Bacon-Cheese Biscuits, '88 84
Beer-and-Cheese Biscuits, '94 215
Blue Cheese Biscuits, '88 83
Blue Cheese Biscuits with Beef and Horseradish-Chive Cream, '02 313
Butter Cheese Dips, '80 46
Cheddar Biscuits, Easy, '01 103
Cheese Biscuits, '79 296; '80 31; '81 288; '83 253; '85 32; '87 78
Cheeseburger Biscuits, '79 194
Chipotle Butter, Cheese Biscuits with, '01 234
Chive Biscuits, Cheese-, '94 324
Cream Cheese-and-Olive Biscuits with Olive-Parsley Spread, '04 238
Cream Cheese-and-Olive Biscuits with Sun-Dried Tomato Spread and Bacon, '02 313
Cream Cheese-and-Olive Biscuits with Tapenade, '02 313
Easy Cheese Biscuits, '81 99
Garlic Biscuits, Cheese-, '02 260
Garlic Biscuits, Cheese, '03 185
Ham and Cheese Biscuits, Petite, '79 193
Ham-and-Swiss Cheese Biscuits, '04 209
Hot Cheesy Biscuits, '80 186
Lightnin' Cheese Biscuits, '90 283
Mixer Cheese Biscuits, '96 22
Onion Biscuits, Cheesy, '95 98; '01 330
Pepper-Cheese Biscuit Fingers, '88 283
Refrigerator Biscuits, '96 17
Roquefort Biscuits, Herbed, '84 95
Rosemary Biscuits, '99 17
Sausage Biscuits, Cheesy, '80 78
Tiny Cheese Biscuits, '80 192
Chicken in a Biscuit, '79 263
Cinnamon Biscuits, Cranberry-Apple Cobbler with, '99 256

Cinnamon-Pecan Biscuits with Cinnamon Butter, '01 309
Cinnamon-Raisin Breakfast Biscuits, '93 159
Cloud Biscuits, '87 15
Coconut Biscuits, Yummy, '95 99
Cornmeal Biscuits, '85 228; '95 98; '04 257
Cornmeal-Jalapeño Biscuits, '94 214
Country Ham Biscuits, '94 215
Country Ham, Biscuits with, '90 93
Cranberry-Orange-Glazed Biscuits, '04 280
Daisy Biscuits, '90 86
Dressing, Cornbread-Biscuit, '79 296
Dumplings and Chicken, Biscuit, '99 326
Easy-Bake Biscuits, '96 157
Elf Biscuits, '99 309
Elgin Biscuits, '93 281
Elsie's Biscuits, '97 129
Feather Biscuits, '80 78
Feather Light Biscuits, '80 246
Flaky Biscuits, '84 228
Grapefruit Juice Biscuits, '83 10
Green Chile Biscuits, '04 233
Green Elf Biscuits and Ham, '02 277
Ham and Biscuits, Southern, '91 12
Ham Biscuits, '99 233
Ham 'n' Angel Biscuits, Kentucky, '90 83
Heart Biscuits, Country Ham in, '86 105
Heart Biscuits with Sausage, Angel, '87 156
Hearty Biscuits, '83 121
Herb Biscuits, Easy, '90 283
Herbed Biscuit Ring, '95 161
Herbed Biscuits, '85 228; '93 67
Homemade Biscuits, '04 209
Honey Angel Biscuits, '95 138; '03 111
Hot Biscuits, '86 269
Hot Browns, Biscuit, '02 94
Lemon Drop Biscuits, '97 332
Light Biscuits, '89 53
Marmalade Biscuits, Carolina, '85 42
Marmalade Biscuit Squares, '79 193
Mile-High Biscuits, '85 41
Miniature Buttermilk Biscuits, '02 103
Muffins, Biscuit, '98 136
Nannie's Biscuits, '82 156
Nutty Tea Biscuits, '89 210
Oatmeal Biscuits, '89 108
Omelet Biscuits, Deluxe, '98 101
One-Step Biscuits, '82 173
Orange Biscuits, '88 85
Orange Puffs, Upside-Down, '83 57
Pandy's Biscuits, '99 277
Parker House-Style Biscuits, '79 162
Pecan Biscuits, Peppered Pork with, '01 33
Pepperoni Biscuits, '84 95
Potato-Bacon Biscuits, '94 214
Processor Biscuits, Easy, '84 218
Pudding, Biscuit, '79 86; '93 51
Pudding, Chocolate Biscuit Bread, '94 215
Pull-Apart Biscuits, Surprise, '95 46
Quick Biscuits, '89 30
Raised Biscuits, Southern, '82 94
Raisin Biscuits, Glazed, '89 210
Ranch Biscuits with Ham, '97 59
Raspberry-Almond Biscuits, '93 160
Rise-and-Shine Biscuits, '89 211
"Rolling-in-Dough" Biscuits, '92 80
Rosemary Biscuits, '95 91; '99 17
Rye Biscuits, '84 96
Sausage and Biscuits, Southern, '82 43
Sausage, Best Biscuits with, '99 103
Sausage Biscuit Bites, '84 95
Sausage Gravy, Biscuits and, '92 270; '94 20
Shrimp-and-Grits Biscuits, '02 313

BISCUITS
(continued)

Snowflake Biscuits, '90 158
Sour Cream Biscuits, '79 128; '04 209
Sour Cream Biscuits, Soft-as-a-Cloud, '86 138
Sourdough Biscuits, '82 201
Southern Biscuits, Old, '02 218
Spicy Kickin' Biscuits, '03 207
Spoon Biscuits, Mexican Fiesta, '95 161
Sugar Biscuits, '03 85; '04 72
Sweetened Biscuits, '80 42
Sweet Little Biscuits, '85 305
Sweet Potato Angel Biscuits, '93 312; '01 42
Sweet Potato Biscuits, '80 287; '84 140; '89 210;
    '98 222; '00 232; '01 250
Taco Biscuit Bites, '91 89
Three-Step Biscuits, '98 97
Tomato-Bacon Biscuit Bites, Savory, '03 196
Tomato Biscuits, '86 72
Tomato Biscuits, Fresh, '04 138
Tomato-Eggplant Biscuit Cakes, '95 170
Tomato-Herb Biscuits, '94 215
Topping, Biscuit, '86 157, 265
Up-and-Down Biscuits, '88 263
Velvet Cream Biscuits, '92 303
Wheat Bran Biscuits, '81 49
Wheat Germ Biscuits, '86 261
Wheat Quick Biscuits, '85 278
Whipping Cream Biscuits, '80 77
Whipping Cream Biscuits, Quick, '02 27; '03 238
Whole Wheat Biscuits, '83 18; '84 60, 268; '85 227;
    '88 83; '91 222
Yeast Biscuits, '87 71, 301
Yeast Biscuits, Refrigerator, '85 48
BISQUE. *See* **SOUPS/Bisques.**
BLACKBERRIES
Bars, Blackberry, '87 130
Bars, Blackberry-Filled, '79 124
Bars, Blackberry Jam, '82 M185
Berry Shrub, '95 29
Breeze, Blackberry, '98 179
Butter, Blackberry, '97 306; '03 27
Cake, Blackberry-Raspberry Truffle, '03 245
Cake, Blackberry Upside-Down, '01 314
Cake, Fresh Blackberry, '81 132
Cake, Tennessee Jam, '04 55
Cake, Triple-Layer Tennessee Jam, '04 55
Chantilly, Blackberries, '99 130
Cobbler, Blackberry, '82 139; '83 175; '99 131;
    '02 17
Cobbler, Blackberry-Almond, '81 132
Cobbler, Deep-Dish Blackberry, '80 186
Cobbler, Deluxe Blackberry, '81 132
Cobbler, Juicy Blackberry, '89 137
Cobbler, New-Fashioned Blackberry, '87 164
Cobbler, Southern Blackberry, '81 132
Crème Brûlée, Berry, '95 323
Crisp, Lemon-Blackberry, '98 171
Custard, Blackberry, '99 132
Dumplings, Blackberries and, '86 196
Dumplings, Blackberry, '97 253
Flan, Blackberry, '79 182
Gazpacho, Berry, '97 181
Jam, Berry Refrigerator, '89 139
Jam, Blackberry, '82 149; '89 138; '99 M131
Jam, Freezer Blackberry, '84 M181
Jelly, Blackberry, '82 149
Lemonade, Blackberry, '99 130; '03 89
Napoleons, Berry, '94 120
Parfait, Blackberries-and-Cream, '87 129
Pie, Berry-Apple, '88 251
Pie, Blackberry, '84 141; '86 152

Pie, Blackberry-Apple, '87 130
Pie, Blackberry Cream, '81 132
Pie, Creamy Blackberry, '88 179
Pie, Fresh Blackberry, '03 164
Pie, Peach-and-Blackberry, '89 136
Roll, Blackberry, '82 178
Sandwiches, Smoked Turkey, Mozzarella, and
    Blackberry, '99 220
Sauce, Berry, '94 130
Sauce, Blackberry, '86 152; '94 232
Sauce, Ducklings with Blackberry, '82 251
Sauce, Grilled Quail with Red Wine-Blackberry,
    '98 319
Sauce, Pork Medaillons with Blackberry, '02 136
Sherbet, 1-2-3 Blackberry, '99 130; '00 21
Sherbet, Three-Ingredient Blackberry, '01 105
Smoothies, Blackberry, '04 141
Sorbet, Blackberry-Lemon, '02 85
Supremes, Blackberry, '99 179
Syrup, Blackberry, '99 131
Tamales, Blackberry Dessert, '94 190
Tart, Cherry and Blackberry, '83 225
Tart, Pick-a-Berry, '91 118
Tarts, Berry Good Lemon, '91 119
Tarts, Blackberry Pudding, '93 200; '00 147
Tea, Blackberry Iced, '04 158
Vinaigrette, Blackberry-Basil, '04 97
BLUEBERRIES
à la Frederick, Blueberries, '93 123
Appetizer, Orange-Berry, '85 81
Basket, Summer Berry, '84 158
Berry Tartlets, Fresh, '91 98
Bordeaux, Beauberries, '98 18
Breads
    Banana-Blueberry Bread, '81 163
    Biscuits, Blueberry, '00 286
    Biscuits, Blueberry Buttermilk, '89 210
    Buns, Deluxe Blueberry, '81 164
    Hot Blueberry Bread, '81 164
    Lemon Bread, Blueberry-, '85 190
    Muffin Batter, Blueberry, '04 200
    Muffins, Blueberry, '80 143; '91 140, 203;
        '99 234; '04 200, 209
    Muffins, Blueberry-Bran, '89 23
    Muffins, Blueberry Buttermilk, '80 16
    Muffins, Blueberry-Cinnamon, '02 177
    Muffins, Blueberry-Cream Cheese, '86 14
    Muffins, Blueberry Ice Cream, '82 143
    Muffins, Blueberry-Lemon, '79 7
    Muffins, Blueberry-Oat, '92 119
    Muffins, Blueberry Oat Bran, '89 106
    Muffins, Blueberry-Oatmeal, '87 24
    Muffins, Blueberry Streusel, '80 46
    Muffins, Blueberry-Streusel, '96 146; '01 131
    Muffins, Blueberry Sweet, '00 210
    Muffins, Easy Blueberry, '81 197
    Muffins, Golden Blueberry, '79 235
    Muffins, Lemon-Blueberry, '03 26
    Muffins, Old-Fashioned Blueberry, '86 161
    Muffins, Speedy Blueberry, '95 135
    Muffins with Streusel Topping, Blueberry,
        '88 129
    Oatmeal Bread, Blueberry-, '83 139
    Orange Bread, Blueberry-, '87 140; '02 21
    Orange Nut Bread Blueberry-, '84 141
    Pinwheels, Blueberry, '82 205
    Tea Bread, Blueberry, '96 146
Buckle, Blueberry, '85 30
Buckle Blueberry, Huckle-, '86 151
Cake, Banana-Blueberry, '86 247
Cake, Blueberry Brunch, '83 183
Cake, Blueberry-Sour Cream, '90 140
Cake, Blueberry Streusel, '92 144
Cheesecake, Blueberries 'n' Cream, '87 140

Cheesecake, Blueberry, '00 153; '03 182
Cheesecake, Blueberry Chiffon, '87 76
Cheesecake, Reduced-fat Blueberry, '00 153
Chutney, Blueberry, '95 190; '00 154
Cobbler, Blueberry, '83 175
Cobbler, Blueberry-Pecan, '00 154; '03 106
Cobbler, Blueberry Pinwheel, '87 140
Cobbler, Blueberry Upside-Down, '96 146
Cobbler, Cran-Blueberry, '04 28
Cobbler, Easy Blueberry, '83 183
Cobbler, Fresh Blueberry, '80 144
Cobbler, No-Dough Blueberry-Peach, '86 177
Cobbler, Peachy Blueberry, '80 143
Cobbler, Warm Blueberry, '98 153
Coffee Cake, Almond-Blueberry, '85 152
Coffee Cake, Blueberry, '82 206; '85 326; '88 263
Coffee Cake, Blueberry Streusel, '88 154
Coffee Cake, Fresh Blueberry, '81 164
Coffee Cake, Sour Cream-Blueberry, '00 154
Cointreau, Blueberries and, '82 100
Compote, Berry-Peach, '82 133
Compote, Peach-Berry, '89 112
Conserve, Blueberry, '82 149
Cordial, Blueberry, '95 142
Cream, Lemon-Blueberry, '92 153
Crisp, Blueberry, '84 177
Crumble, Blueberry, '81 84
Crunch, Apple-Blueberry, '02 128
Crunch, Blueberry, '96 146
Crunch, Fresh Blueberry, '82 143
Cupcakes, Lemon-Blueberry Ice-Cream, '01 172
Delight, Blueberry, '96 17
Dessert, Easy Blueberry, '89 M130
Dessert, Peach-Blueberry, '92 184
Dessert Squares, Chocolate-Blueberry, '87 299
Dream, Blueberry, '88 94
Fritters, Blueberry, '85 152
Gazpacho, Berry, '97 181
Glaze, Blueberry, '83 143
Ice Cream, Blueberry, '88 203
Ice Cream, Blueberry-Peach, '00 153
Jam, Blueberry, '79 120; '85 130
Jam, Blueberry Refrigerator, '89 139
Jam, Green Tomato-Blueberry, '01 140
Kuchen, Blueberry, '80 143
Lemonade, Blueberry, '98 179
Lemon Curd with Berries, '90 102
Marmalade, Blueberry, '96 145
Marmalade, Spicy Blueberry-Citrus, '03 135
Napoleons, Blueberry, '96 147
Napoleons, Blueberry-Lemon, '94 122
Pancake, Brunch Popover, '96 28
Pancakes, Blueberry, '85 152; '89 138
Pancakes, Blueberry Buttermilk, '79 114
Pancakes, Blue Cornmeal-Blueberry, '94 115
Pancakes, Lemon-Blueberry, '04 148
Pancakes, Sour Cream Blueberry, '81 164
Pie, Blueberry-Banana, '93 115
Pie, Blueberry Cream, '84 142
Pie, Blueberry-Cream Cheese, '88 154
Pie, Blueberry-Peach, '94 158
Pie, Blueberry-Sour Cream, '83 183
Pie, Bumbleberry, '97 163
Pie, Chilled Blueberry, '89 136
Pie, Fresh Blueberry, '83 183; '85 152
Pie, Fresh Blueberry Cream, '80 144
Pie, Fresh Blueberry Streusel, '89 137
Pie, Old-Fashioned Blueberry, '89 136
Pie, Red, White, and Blueberry, '98 162
Pie, Spicy Blueberry, '96 147
Pizza, Blueberry, '96 147
Pudding, Blueberry Bread, '88 154; '03 119
Pudding, Russian Blueberry-Raspberry, '97 128
Puree, Grapefruit with Pear-Berry, '89 213

Quick Blueberry Slump, '91 20
Raspberry Custard Sauce, Fresh Berries with,
     '88 163
Salad, Chicken-Blueberry, '02 177
Salad, Layered Berry, '79 173
Salad, Melon-Berry, '90 180
Salad, Watercress, '97 249
Sauce, Berry, '94 130; '95 103
Sauce, Blueberry, '80 144; '86 248; '88 155;
     '89 M130; '94 122; '95 135
Sauce, Blueberry-Lemon, '01 117
Sauce, Cinnamon-Blueberry, '86 11
Sauce, Melon Wedges with Berry, '86 178
Sauce, Peach-Berry, '87 M165
Sauce, Peach-Blueberry, '81 170
Sauce, Peach-Blueberry Pancake, '82 177
Shake, Berry Blue, '01 200
Sherbet, Blueberry, '04 283
Shortcake, Warm Blueberry-Nectarine, '97 205
Smoothie, Banana-Blueberry, '90 104
Smoothie, Banana Breakfast, '03 46
Smoothie, Four-Berry, '97 173
Snow, Berries on, '82 227
Sorbet, Blueberry-Kirsch, '83 120
Squares, Blueberry-Amaretto, '83 220
Tart, Pick-a-Berry, '91 118
Tarts, Berry Good Lemon, '91 119
Topping, Blueberry, '87 125
Trifle, Lemon-Blueberry, '88 210
Vinaigrette, Blueberry, '00 154
Yum Yum, Blueberry, '98 91
BOK CHOY
Beef with Bok Choy, Ginger, '96 99
Greens, Super-Charged, '01 211
Pork on Mixed Greens, Hot Sesame, '97 19
Salad, Bok Choy, '01 129
Salad, Ramen Noodle, '97 18
Stir-Fried Bok Choy, '97 105
Stir-Fry, Bok Choy-Broccoli, '84 2
BOYSENBERRIES
Cobbler, Boysenberry, '82 133
Compote, Berry-Peach, '82 133
Cream Mold, Peachy Berry, '83 130
Cream Supreme, Boysenberries and, '82 133
Crisp, Berry, '83 130
Pie, Boysenberry, '82 133
BRAN
Biscuits, Bran, '85 228
Biscuits, Wheat Bran, '81 49
Bread, Bran-Applesauce, '84 229
Bread, Honey-Oat, '93 232
Bread, Wheat-and-Oat Bran, '92 102
Bread, Whole Wheat Bran, '79 58
Chocolate-Bran Raisin Jumbos, '91 142
Crêpes, Bran, '83 70; '86 44
Cupcakes, Carrot-Bran, '82 16
Eggplant, Ratatouille-Bran Stuffed, '86 44
Muesli, Bran-and-Fruit, '91 134
Muffins
All-Bran Oat Bran Muffins, '91 134
Apple-Bran Muffins, '85 M89
Apple-Cinnamon Oat Bran Muffins, '89 106
Banana Bran Muffins, '83 48
Banana Oat Bran Muffins, '89 106
Big Batch Moist Bran Muffins, '95 214
Blueberry-Bran Muffins, '89 23
Blueberry Oat Bran Muffins, '89 106
Bran Muffins, '84 53
Buttermilk Muffins, Bran-, '85 7
Cranberry Oat Bran Muffins, '89 107
Easy Bran Muffins, '83 55
Ever-Ready Bran Muffins, '81 106
Freezer Bran Muffins, '91 141
Fruit-and-Bran Muffins, '04 22

High-Fiber Muffins, '85 250
Honey Bran Muffins, '88 171
Honey-Bran Muffins, '89 250
Made of Bran Muffins, '86 103
Maple-Bran Muffins, '90 66
Oat Bran-Banana Muffins, '91 18
Oat Bran Muffins, '89 106
Oatmeal Bran Muffins, '81 236
Oatmeal-Bran Muffins, '91 83
Quick Bran Muffins, '86 85
Raisin Oat Bran Muffins, '89 106
Refrigerator Bran Muffins, '79 6
Sour Cream-Bran Muffins, '87 98
Spiced Bran Muffins, '84 229
Two, Bran Muffins for, '84 211
Whole Wheat Bran Muffins, '88 M274
Pancakes with Cinnamon Syrup, Bran, '91 315
Rolls, Bran, '85 145
Rolls, Bran Yeast, '87 116
Salad, Lemony Apple-Bran, '86 223
Waffles, Oat Bran, '92 139
BREADS. *See also* **APPETIZERS/Crostini;**
     BISCUITS; CAKES/Coffee Cakes;
     CORNBREADS; CRACKERS; CRÊPES;
     CROUTONS; FRENCH TOAST;
     MUFFINS; PANCAKES; PIES, PUFFS,
     AND PASTRIES/Pastries; ROLLS AND
     BUNS; WAFFLES.
Apple Bread, '79 205; '80 226
Apple Butter Bread, '84 49; '86 69
Apple Loaf, Fresh, '82 206
Apple Loaf, Spiced, '79 215
Apple-Nut Bread, '79 12; '85 281
Apple-Nut Bread, Fresh, '87 256
Applesauce-Honey Nut Bread, '87 300
Applesauce Loaf, Brandy, '81 263
Applesauce Nut Bread, '81 305
Applesauce-Pecan Bread, '90 66
Apple Toast, '81 278
Apricot Bread, Tangy, '81 249
Apricot-Cranberry Loaf, '79 235
Apricot-Nut Bread, '79 24
Apricot-Nut Loaf, '81 8
Apricot-Nut Loaf, Tasty, '82 10
Apricot-Orange Bread, '92 285
Apricot-Pecan Bread, '97 266
Artichoke Bread, '93 140
Asparagus Squares, '79 161
Bacon-and-Cheese Bread, '83 255
Bacon-Cheese Cups, '02 219
Bacon-Cheese Toast Bars, '79 36
Banana-Apple Bread, '85 250
Banana-Blueberry Bread, '81 163
Banana Bread, '87 72
Banana Bread, Easy, '96 97
Banana Bread, Fruity, '95 78
Banana Bread, Sour Cream-, '79 190
Banana Bread, Whole Wheat, '80 88
Banana Butterscotch Bread, '79 116
Banana-Jam Bread, '84 73
Banana-Nut Bread, '86 8, 70; '01 239; '04 259
Banana Nut Bread, Hawaiian, '79 235
Banana Nut Bread, Whole Wheat-, '84 50
Banana-Nut-Raisin Bread, '81 59
Banana-Nut Roll, '85 112
Banana-Oat Tea Loaf, '87 256
Banana Wheat Bread, '81 14
Banana-Zucchini Bread, '85 326
Barbecue Bread, '99 105
Basket, Bread Dough, '04 64
Batter Bread, Soft, '84 253
Batter, Primary, '89 192
Beer Bread, '00 238
Beer Bread, Easy, '79 213; '84 160

Beer Bread, Sweet, '03 207
Biscuit Bread, '84 284
Black-Eyed Pea Bread, '02 224
Blueberry Bread, Hot, '81 164
Blueberry-Lemon Bread, '85 190
Blueberry-Oatmeal Bread, '83 139
Blueberry-Orange Bread, '87 140; '02 21
Blueberry-Orange Nut Bread, '84 141
Blueberry Tea Bread, '96 146
Blue Cheese-Apple Sunburst, '94 245
Blue Cheese Bread, '03 54
Bourbon-Pecan Bread, '93 308; '96 27
Bowls, Toasted Bread, '98 30
Bowl, Veggie Bread, '01 132
Braided Bread Ring, '96 322
Bran-Applesauce Bread, '84 229
Breadstick Haystacks, '99 246
Breadsticks, Easy, '04 298
Breadsticks, Italian Herb, '04 35
Breadsticks, Quick, '00 317
Breakfast Bread, Crunchy, '93 327
Breakfast Bread, Easy, '83 289
Brie Bread, '87 143
Brie Cheese Bake, '87 117
Brown Bread, '84 242; '88 63
Brown Bread, Eighteenth-Century, '79 72
Brown Bread, Steamed Buttermilk, '86 261
Brown Sugar Biscuit Bread, '02 M224
Bruschetta and Cantaloupe Chutney, Prosciutto,
     '00 108
Bruschetta, Black Truffle, '99 323
Bruschetta, Red-and-Green, '01 62
Bruschetta, Roasted Red Pepper, '00 278
Buschetta, Caper-and-Olive, '00 276
Buttermilk-Cheese Loaf, '91 52
Butternut-Raisin Bread, '79 25
Butternut Spice Loaf, '92 235
Calas, Easy, '92 89
Calas, Quick, '96 64
Carrot Bread, '89 143
Carrot Bread, Tasty, '84 328
Carrot-Nut Loaf, '83 117
Carrot-Pineapple Bread, '82 210
Carrot Puffs, '87 200
Carrot-Walnut Bread, '88 284
Cheddar-Apple Bread, '96 83
Cheddar Cheese Loaf, '00 317
Cheddar Cheese-Pepper Bread, '98 25
Cheddar-Chive Beer Bread, '03 207
Cheddar-Nut Bread, '85 41; '03 42
Cheese Bread, '82 174
Cheese Bread, Dilly, '83 5
Cheese Bread, Easy, '82 74; '86 17
Cheese Bread, Peppery, '04 295
Cheese Bread, Quick, '83 9
Cheese Breadsticks, Italian, '95 126
Cheese Delights, Toasted, '79 37
Cheese-Herb Bread, '85 283
Cheese Loaf, '87 92; '90 93
Cheese Loaves, Little, '86 213
Cheese-Olive Bread, Spicy, '84 150
Cheese Puffs, '03 269
Cheese Puffs, Bavarian, '80 191
Cheesy Twists, '84 284
Cheesy Witches' Brooms, '01 205
Cherry Nut Bread, '81 306; '82 36
Cherry Nut Bread, Maraschino,
     '79 234
Cherry-Nut Bread, Quick, '85 55
Chocolate Chip-Banana Bread, '90 267
Chocolate Date-Nut Bread, '81 284
Chocolate-Zucchini Bread, '93 308
Cinnamon Loaves, '99 260
Cinnamon Loaves, Miniature, '99 260

BREADS
(continued)

Cinnamon Logs, '98 325
Cinnamon Puffs, '81 209
Cinnamon Sticks, '95 244
Cinnamon Toast, Buttery Skillet, '79 36
Citrus-Nut Bread, '83 294
Coconut Bread, '83 140
Cracklin' Cakes, Grannie's, '98 252
Cranberry-Banana Bread, '80 281; '90 294
Cranberry Bread, '79 242
Cranberry Fruit-Nut Bread, '79 275
Cranberry-Orange Bread, '87 244
Cranberry-Orange Nut Bread, '80 288
Crescent Twists, Pecan, '99 47
Crostini with Walnut-Blue Cheese, '01 321
Damper, '97 22
Date-Banana Loaves, Tropical, '95 143
Date-Nut Bread, '85 306
Date-Nut Loaf, '85 10
Date-Walnut Loaf, Blue Ribbon, '80 15
Easy Bread, '87 168
Egg Bread, '95 121
Eggnog Bread, '83 294
Feta Cheese-Spinach Roll, '91 22
Flatbread, Mexican, '80 197
Flatbread, Quick, '00 119
Flatbread, Sicilian Artichoke, '98 136
Focaccia, Basil Pesto, '00 195
Focaccia, Easy Herb, '02 201
Focaccia, Fast Rosemary-Dried Tomato, '98 53
Focaccia, Herb, '97 31
Focaccia, Mustard-and-Onion, '90 321; '92 97
Focaccia, Rosemary-Red Pepper, '01 307
Focaccia with Roasted Pepper Vinaigrette, Stuffed,
   '00 134; '04 142
Fou-Fou, '96 325
French Baguettes, Rosemary, '97 165
French Bread, Bacon-Cheese, '92 54
French Bread Bowls, '95 58
French Bread, Cheesy, '88 172; '95 218; '96 205;
   '97 325
French Bread, Chive-Garlic, '89 29
French Bread, Herbed, '82 174; '93 283; '99 47
French Bread, Herb-Seasoned, '83 198
French Bread, Hot Garlic, '81 83
French Bread, Lemony, '97 147
French Bread, Onion-Cheese, '89 29
French Bread, Tangy, '98 166
French Loaf, Herbed, '87 243
Frozen Roll Dough, '03 224
Fruit-Nut Bread, Kahlúa, '79 235
Fruit-Nut Twists, '82 253
Fry Bread, '84 140; '85 155
Fry Bread, Indian, '81 56
Garlic Bread, '82 19; '89 282; '91 204; '95 218;
   '96 204; '04 288
Garlic Bread, Buttery, '02 25, 110
Garlic Bread, Cheesy, '84 150
Garlic Bread, Dilly, '95 218; '96 205
Garlic Bread, Quick, '90 283
Garlic Breadsticks, '79 70
Garlic-Stuffed Bread, Cheesy, '95 176
Gingerbread, Gingery, '96 100
Gingerbread Loaf, '82 14
Gingerbread, Mocha, '81 207; '82 14
Gingerbread, Molasses, '88 203
Gingerbread, Old English, '79 265
Gingerbread, Old-Fashioned, '81 157, 207; '82 14;
   '91 240
Gingerbread, Refrigerator, '80 52
Gingerbread, Spicy, '84 263

Gingerbread Squares, '84 16
Gingerbread Squares, Apple-, '03 297
Gingerbread, Very Moist, '86 261
Gingerbread with Key Lime Curd, Kahlúa, '96 126
Gorditas with Turkey Mole, '03 18
Greek Bread, '89 200
Greek Sunburst, '94 245
Grilled Bread, '00 88
Ham-and-Cheese Bread, '86 213
Hawaiian Loaf, '80 225
Herb-and-Cheese Pull Aparts, '87 143
Herb Bread, '86 17
Herb Loaf, Toasted, '84 150
Herbs-and-Cheese Bread, '93 56
Herb Sticks, '83 252
Herb-Vegetable-Cheese Bread, '88 172
Hobo Bread, '86 86
Honey-Banana Bread, '91 68
Irish Bread, '02 67
Irish Soda Bread, '90 214; '95 71
Italian Bread, Easy, '03 48
Jam-and-Cheese Loaf, '89 246
Koulourakia, '90 193
Lahvosh Cracker Bread Bowls, '95 58
Lemon-Almond Tea Bread, '04 209
Lemon Bread, '79 275; '87 256
Lemon-Cream Tea Loaf, '84 50
Lemon-Nut Bread, '79 24
Lemon-Pecan Bread, '83 54
Lemon Tea Bread, '92 268; '93 183; '04 209
Mandel Bread, '97 220
Mandelbread, Chocolate Chip, '00 282
Mango Bread, '96 205
Marbled Loaves with Orange Glaze, '99 293
Mayonnaise Bread, '89 29
Mix, Quick Bread, '81 90; '86 8
Molasses-Nut Bread, '84 24
Monkey Bread, Bacon, '94 283; '97 154
Monkey Bread Bites, '04 333
Monkey Bread, Cheese-Filled, '91 21
Monkey Bread, Quick, '81 306; '82 36
Mustard Bread, '01 146
Mustard-Rye Ovals, '84 149
Nautical Knots, '93 168
Nut Bread, '04 281
Oatmeal Bread, '81 236, 300
Oatmeal Raisin Bread, '81 14
Onion Bread, Easy, '81 162
Onion-Cheese Bread, '79 180; '81 8
Onion-Cheese Supper Bread, '83 112
Onion-Herb Bread, Toasted, '83 266
Onion-Parmesan Bread, '84 284
Orange, Baba au, '86 138
Orange-Cranberry Bread, '85 266
Orange-Cream Cheese Bread, '82 210
Orange-Nut Bread, '82 75
Orange Nut Loaf, '80 226
Orange-Pecan Bread, '79 148
Orange-Pecan Bread, Glazed, '81 250
Orange-Pecan Loaves, '79 215
Orange Praline Toast, '79 36
Orange Puffs, Upside-Down, '83 57
Orange-Pumpkin Bread, '87 300
Orange Tea Bread, '79 234
Pane Cunsado (Fixed Bread), '95 218
Pane Cunsado (Sicilian for "Fixed Bread"), '96 205
Papaya Bread, '88 138
Parmesan Cheese Bread, '99 61
Parmesan-Garlic Breadsticks, '99 46
Parmesan Herb Bread, '82 235; '83 41
Parmesan-Pepper Toasts, '98 242
Parmesan Puffs, '98 235
Parmesan Rounds, '79 170
Parmesan Sesame Sticks, '81 39

Parmesan Twists, '83 239; '99 323
Parmesan-Wine Bread, '97 31
Peach Bread, '82 170
Peach Bread, Georgia, '79 161
Peach Bread, Tipsy, '02 21
Peanut Bread, '87 184
Peanut Butter Bread, '88 64; '99 111
Pear Bread, '80 218
Pecan-Cornmeal Rounds, '95 99
Pepper Bread, '85 156
Persimmon Bread, '80 228
Persimmon Date-Nut Bread, '82 218
Pig-in-a-Blanket Bread, '99 134
Pineapple-Apricot Bread, '84 7
Pineapple Bread, '83 139
Pineapple Breakfast Puffs, '98 326
Pineapple-Carrot Bread, '79 106
Pineapple-Nut Bread, '79 215
Pineapple-Pecan Loaf Bread, '87 256
Pita Bread Salad, '95 86
Pita Triangles, Cheesy, '93 70
Pizza Sticks, '98 255
Pizza Sunburst, '94 245
Popovers
   Blender Popovers, Perfect, '79 53
   Cheddar Cheese Popovers, '85 41
   Cheddar Popovers, '00 64
   Cheese Popover Puffs, '85 6
   Cinnamon Popovers, '90 66
   Good Old Southern Popovers, '79 138
   Herbed Popovers, '00 64
   Jumbo Popovers, '83 225
   Muffin Tin Popovers, '79 138
   Parmesan Popovers, '90 66; '00 64
   Pecan Popovers, '01 206
   Pecan Popovers, Giant, '83 208
   Pimiento Popovers, '79 138
   Popovers, '94 43; '00 64
   Ring, Cheesy Popover, '80 45
   Seasoned Popovers, '86 86
   Two, Popovers for, '81 304
   Whole Wheat Popovers, '90 66
   Yorkshire Popovers, '00 65
Poppy-Onion Loaf, '04 35
Poppy Seed Bread, '83 140
Poppy Seed Bread, Orange-, '04 300
Poppy Seed Loaf, Quick, '82 75
Poppy Seed-Swiss Cheese Bread, '91 52
Potato Bites, Mashed, '98 249
Prune-Nut Bread, '87 255; '91 55
Puddings
   Almond-Cream Cheese Bread Pudding with
      Amaretto Cream Sauce, Layered, '03 330
   Amish Bread Pudding, '80 8
   Apple-Raisin Bread Pudding, '88 175
   Apricot Bread Pudding, '85 24
   Bananas Foster Bread Pudding, '04 235
   Blueberry Bread Pudding, '88 154; '03 119
   Blueberry-Lemon Sauce, Bread Pudding with,
      '01 117
   Bread Pudding, '89 M130; '90 219
   Buttermilk Bread Pudding with Butter-Rum
      Sauce, '95 134
   Cheesy Bread Pudding, '83 68
   Chocolate Bread Pudding, '80 8
   Chocolate Bread Pudding with Custard Sauce,
      '03 244
   Chocolate Bread Pudding with Whiskey Sauce,
      '99 277
   Cinnamon-Raisin Bread Pudding, '01 315
   Cinnamon Toast Pudding with Caramel Sauce,
      '96 284
   Cranberry-Raisin Bread Pudding, Stuffed
      Pumpkin with, '02 231

Croissant Bread Pudding, '03 66
Custard Sauce, Bread Pudding with, '97 313
Durfee's Bread Pudding, '96 48
Fig-Walnut Pudding, '03 244
French Bread Pudding, '85 231
Lemon Bread Pudding, Old-Fashioned, '88 95
Mushroom Bread Pudding, '99 58
Old-Fashioned Bread Pudding, '83 213; '88 175;
   '00 105; '01 223
Old-Fashioned Bread Pudding with Bourbon
   Custard Sauce, '95 271
Old-Fashioned Bread Pudding with Rum Sauce,
   '88 32
Peachy Bread Pudding, '88 175
Piña Colada Bread Pudding, '98 34
Pineapple-Apple Bread Pudding with Vanilla-
   Nutmeg Sauce, '02 208
Plum Bread Pudding, Refrigerator, '97 177
Pumpkin Bread Pudding, '98 240
Raisin Bread Pudding, '94 215
Raisin Bread Pudding with Bourbon Sauce,
   '98 336
Rosemary-Tasso Bread Pudding, '00 104
Sauce, Bread Pudding, '04 235
Soufflé, Creole Bread Pudding, '92 87
Spiced Bread Pudding, '93 52
Sweet Potato Bread Pudding, '94 241
Sweet Roll Pudding, '96 283
Tennessee Bread Pudding with Bourbon Sauce,
   '93 51
Vanilla Sauce, Bread Pudding with, '97 M15
Whiskey Sauce, Bread Pudding with, '80 58;
   '90 230; '92 93
White Chocolate Bread Pudding, '00 M104
Pull-Apart Ring, Southwestern, '03 298
Pull-Apart Ring, Veggie Southwestern, '03 299
Pull-Away Bread, '98 137
Pull-Away Bread, Cinnamon, '98 137
Pumpkin Bread, '81 8
Pumpkin Bread, Brother Boniface's, '98 26
Pumpkin Bread, Harvest, '90 M215
Pumpkin Bread, Holiday, '03 281
Pumpkin Bread, Moist, '80 245
Pumpkin Bread, Spiced, '91 233
Pumpkin Bread with Cream Cheese and Preserves,
   '84 264
Pumpkin-Coconut Bread, '87 255
Pumpkin Loaf, Harvest, '85 232
Pumpkin-Nut Bread, '83 294
Pumpkin-Oatmeal Loaf, '81 49
Pumpkin-Pecan Bread, '87 221; '02 224
Raisin-Cranberry Bread, '81 305; '82 36
Roasted Garlic-Rosemary Bread, '04 16
Rollups, Pizza Bread, '04 M35
Saffron Tea Bread, '85 26
Salad, Avocado-Bread, '02 210
Salad, Italian BLT Bread, '03 90
Salad, Italian Bread, '99 259; '03 54
Sally Lunn, Quick, '87 16
Salt-Rising Bread, '79 145
Santa Gertrudis Pan de Campo, '94 27
Sausage-Onion Squares, '83 112
Scones
   Breakfast Scones, '88 231; '89 22
   Cheddar Cheese Scones, Golden, '99 82
   Cherry-and-Cream Scones, '99 49
   Cranberry-Nut Yeast Scones, Merry, '99 274
   Cranberry-Orange Scones, '97 45
   Cranberry Scones, '95 283
   Cream Scones, '97 44
   Cream Scones, Classic, '02 41
   Currant Scones, '84 117; '92 332
   Drop Scones, '00 239
   Drop Scones, Breakfast, '88 83

Hazelnut Scones, '94 16
   Lemon-Poppy Seed Scones, '97 44
   Lemon-Raisin Scones, '87 69
   Mocha-Pecan Scones, '97 45
   Orange-Pecan Scones, '94 215; '01 72
   Orange Scones with Orange Butter, Double-,
     '97 44
   Pizza Scones, '03 207
   Scottish Scones, '97 44
Seasoned Breadsticks, '81 84; '96 46
Sesame Bread Twists, '84 283
Sesame-Cheddar Sticks, '81 150
Sesame-Cheese Breadsticks, '97 31
Sesame Sticks, '83 9
Sesame Wheat Crisps, '81 106
Shrimp Toast, '86 91
Sourdough Dill Bread, '89 192
Sourdough Starter, '89 192
Sourdough Wedges, '90 199
Spinach Bread, '83 121; '87 144
Spoonbreads
   Barbara Sue's Spoonbread, '99 83
   Cheddar Spoonbread, '82 196
   Cheese Spoonbread, '86 261
   Chorizo, Spoonbread with Simple, '04 207
   Corn and Bacon Spoonbread, '81 129
   Corn-Cheese Spoonbread, '88 9
   Corn Spoonbread, '97 301
   Dressing, Southwestern-Style Spoonbread,
     '94 273
   Garlic Spoonbread, '79 269; '80 14
   Golden Spoonbread, '83 286; '84 17
   Grits Spoonbread, '79 38
   Grits with Savory Mushroom Sauce, Spoonbread,
     '96 236
   Memmie's Spoonbread, '95 27; '04 57
   Old Virginia Spoonbread, '84 102
   Spoonbread, '80 43; '81 138; '90 200; '95 156; '04 58
Squash Bread, '79 210
Squash Bread, Spicy, '83 121
Stars, Bread, '93 286
Starter Food, '94 324; '95 77
Sticks, Crispy, '03 211
Stollen, '86 291
Strawberry Bread, '81 250; '83 140; '84 49
Strawberry Jam Bread, '79 216
Strawberry-Nut Bread, '79 24
Tacos, Navajo, '84 246
Tennessee Sin, '95 218; '96 204
Three-C Bread, '81 284
Toast, Basil Pesto, '01 17
Toast Points, '93 270
Toast Points, Parmesan, '00 316
Toasts, Crispy Parmesan, '01 307
Toasts, Tomato-Basil, '01 254
Toast Strips, Seasoned, '93 98
Tomato-Cheese Bread, '98 172; '99 M157
Tomato-Cheese Bread, Herbed, '88 143
Tortillas, Flour, '81 303
Tortillas, Never-Fail Flour, '80 198
Vegetable Bread, Breakaway, '82 74
Wampus Bread, '81 305
Wheat Loaf, Nutty, '90 65
Whole Wheat Cardamom Bread, '86 223
Whole Wheat Coffee Can Bread, Molasses, '85 111
Whole Wheat Date-Nut Bread, '04 208
Whole Wheat Nut Bread, '04 208
Whole Wheat Orange Bread, '85 5
Whole Wheat Quick Bread, '82 65; '00 49
Whole Wheat Raisin-Nut Bread, '04 208
Wine-Date Nut Bread, '82 253
Yeast
   Almond Braid, '89 86
   Almond Danish, '87 301

Anillos, '02 82
Anise-Orange Bread, '83 295
Apple Danish, Deep-Dish, '86 161
Apple-Date-Nut Ring, '90 212
Apple-Pecan Biscuit Braid, '02 326
Apple Pull-Apart Bread, '86 330
Apple Swirl Bread, '85 4
Armenian Thin Bread, '94 108
Austrian Sweet Bread, '83 294
Austrian Twists, '80 45
Bagels, '89 266
Bagels, Whole Wheat, '84 20
Baguettes, '85 70
Baguettes and Rolls, '98 168
Beer Bread, Best-Ever, '82 129
Beer Bread, Hearty, '87 226; '88 133
Beignets, '84 56; '01 59
Beignets, French Market, '92 88; '93 219;
   '94 319; '95 80
Beignets, Lobster-and-Roasted Corn, '00 51
Binning Bread, '80 68
Bowls, Irish Tater Bread, '96 111
Bowls, Italian Bread, '98 292
Braided Bread, '88 76
Braided Loaf, '82 17
Braids, Festive, '87 297
Braids, Holiday, '83 295
Braid, Sweet Yeast, '90 46
Break-Away Bread, '86 56
Brioche, '81 122; '89 90
Brioche Chicken Curry, '88 124
Brioche Loaves, Vienna, '87 300
Brioche, Morrison House, '96 53
Brown Bread, Light-, '84 268
Bubble Bread, '81 107
Bunny Bread, Glazed, '92 102
Butter-Egg Bread, '85 269
Butterhorns, '84 267
Buttermilk-Oatmeal Bread, '97 212
Cake Bread, Golden, '84 269
Canapé Bread, '89 292
Caramel Bread, '82 75
Caramel-Orange Coffee Ring, '80 45
Caraway Breadsticks, '89 239
Caraway Puffs, '82 174
Caraway Seed Bread, Dark, '80 256
Challah, '92 62
Cheddar Cheese Bread, '84 268
Cheese Bread, '83 208; '87 11
Cheese Bread, Crusty, '86 233
Cheese-Caraway Batter Bread, '85 33
Cheese Crescents, '82 18
Cheese-Herb Bread, '84 M144
Cheese Loaf, Jalapeño-, '84 76
Cheese-Wine Bread, '87 254
Chocolate Loaf Bread, '88 M188
Chocolate Pinwheel Loaf, '80 256
Christmas Bread, '87 296; '88 288
Christmas Bread, Norwegian, '79 234
Christmas Wreath, '80 280
Cinnamon Loaf, '82 18; '85 55
Cinnamon-Nut Bubble Bread, '80 22
Cinnamon-Oat Bread, '90 135
Cinnamon Raisin Bread, '80 22
Cinnamon Swirl Loaf, '79 23
Cinnamon Twists, '83 53
Cocoa-Nut Swirl Bread, '80 257
Coffee Ring, Filled, '82 18
Coffee Ring, Sugarplum, '83 M37
Cornmeal Yeast Bread, '89 54
Cottage Cheese-Dill Bread, '83 154
Country Ham Bread with Herb Butter, '99 18
Cracker Bread, Sesame, '87 2
Cream Cheese Braids, '82 243; '97 287

BREADS, Yeast
(continued)

Cream Cheese Loaves, Processor, '85 48
Crescents, Festive, '80 281
Croissants, '83 54; '84 188; '96 303
Croissants, Chocolate-Filled, '96 303
Croissants, Cinnamon-Sugar, '96 303
Croissants, Flaky Butter, '85 42
Croissants, Strawberry or Apricot, '96 303
Crust Bread, Country, '80 225
Cuernitos, '02 82
Dill-Oat Bread, '91 95
Dough, Basic Yeast, '88 74
Easter Bread, Golden, '91 54
Easter Egg Bread, '84 94; '96 88
Easy Yeast Bread, '79 147
Egg Bread, Braided, '03 M234
Egg Bread, County Fair, '87 68
Elephant Ears, '84 18
Empanadas, '02 82
English Muffin Bread, '95 M79
English Muffin Loaf, '82 96
English Muffin Loaves, '85 42
Figure-8 Bread, '79 171
Flatbread, '98 106
Flat Bread, Italian-Style, '82 235; '83 41
Flatbread, Parmesan-Onion, '98 65
Focaccia, Dried Tomato, '94 65
Focaccia, Herbed, '04 208
Focaccia, Onion, '93 77
Focaccia, Roquefort-and-Onion, '98 54
Focaccia, Rosemary, '95 190
Focaccia with Rosemary, '96 84
French Bread, '79 158; '87 227; '89 54; '96 191
French Bread, Easy, '88 299
French Bread, Glazed, '88 75
French Bread, Herbed, '85 222; '86 166
French Bread, Mom's, '98 281
French Bread, New Orleans, '80 212
French Bread, Whole Wheat, '88 63
French Loaves, Crusty, '85 37
French Onion Bread, '91 90
French Pistou Bread, Crusty, '97 68
Fruit-and-Cheese Braid, '86 214
Gingerbread Men, Yeast, '92 312
Golden Bread, '90 47
Gouda Bread, '91 52
Grittibanz (Swiss Bread Figure), '93 265
Ham Bread with Herb Butter, Country, '86 255
Heartland Loaves, '89 287
Herb Bread, '84 268
Herb Bread, No-Knead, '81 217
Herb-Cheese Bread, '85 70
Herbed Bread, '89 34
Herb Loaf, Butterflake, '86 261
Herb-Sour Cream Bread, '85 268
Herman Food, '82 200
Holiday Wreath, '81 284
Honey-Cinnamon Swirl Bread, '88 287
Honey-Curry Bread, '89 250
Honey Graham Bread, '99 211
Honey-Granola Bread, '86 56
Honey Loaves, Hint o', '81 104
Honey-Oat Bread, '89 107; '93 232; '98 27
Honey Oatmeal Bread, '80 60
Honey Puffs, '96 153
Honey Twist, '79 80
Honey-Walnut Swirl, '80 21
Honey Wheat Bread, '85 18, 268
Honey-Wheat Bread, '91 223
Italian Bread, '82 297; '04 208
Knots, Two-Seed Bread, '02 292

Kolecz (Polish Bread), '80 29
Kulich, '01 87
Lightbread, Coffee Can, '79 59
Light Yeast Bread, '81 299
Loaf Bread, Hospitality, '86 299
Loaf Bread, Old-Fashioned, '88 75
Loaves, Sweet-Filled Yeast, '90 46
Mandelkrantz, '92 32
Marble Loaf, '80 230
Monkey Bread, '82 243; '95 174
Monkey Bread, Easy, '90 214
Multi-Grain Bread, '86 236
Oat Bread, Caraway-Raisin, '86 44
Oatmeal Bread, '81 300; '92 212; '97 130
Oatmeal Bread, Round, '84 20
Oatmeal-Molasses Bread, '97 194
Oatmeal Pan Bread, Herbed, '97 243
Oatmeal-Raisin Bread, '83 59
Oat-Molasses Bread, '82 139
Old-Fashioned Yeast Bread, '79 284
Olive Bread, '93 78
Olive-Dill Casserole Bread, '92 16
Onion-Dill Bread, Easy, '85 5
Onion-Herb Bread, '90 165
Onion-Poppy Seed Twist, '97 242
Onion-Rye Bread, '99 55
Onion Twist Loaves, '84 300
Pandoro, '93 267
Panettone, '93 266
Parmesan Bread, '92 19; '93 231; '00 54
Party Bread, '86 218
Peanut Butter Bread, '86 171
Peanut Lover's Bread, '93 211
Pimiento-Cheese Bread, '85 223; '86 166
Pitas, Puffy, '97 69
Pizza Batter Bread, '85 56
Pizza Crust, '04 208
Pizza Dough, '04 58
Pocket Bread, '79 58
Poppy Seed Loaf, '83 254
Portuguese Round Bread, '83 295
Potato Bread, '85 56
Potato Bread, Old-Fashioned, '86 57
Potato Lightbread, '80 225
Potato Loaves, '86 162
Pull-Apart Yeast Bread, '94 132
Pumpernickel Boule, Walnut-Raisin, '02 259
Pumpernickel Bread, '02 259
Pumpernickel Bread, Sour-Rye, '02 259
Raisin Batter Bread, Salt-Free, '86 33
Raisin Bread, Curried Chicken Salad on, '85 96
Raisin Bread, Homemade, '87 300
Raisin Bread, Round, '89 230
Raisin-Whole Wheat Bread, '93 77
Refrigerator Bread, No-Knead, '83 155
Roasted Red Bell Pepper Bread, '95 241
Rounds, Individual Bread, '83 159
Rye Bread, '84 21
Rye Bread, Swedish Orange-, '85 111
Rye Canapé Bread, '89 293
Rye Loaves, Swedish, '97 68
Rye Sandwich Bread, '82 65
Saffron Bread, '96 50
Sally Lunn, '81 157; '88 163; '94 233
Sally Lunn Bread, '03 27
Sandwiches, Stacking, '86 127
Savarin, Holiday, '80 280
Scones, Merry Cranberry-Nut Yeast, '99 274
Sesame-Wheat Breadsticks, '93 114
Soft Breadsticks, '83 115
Sopaipillas, '80 197
Sour Cream Bread, '79 59
Sour Cream-Cheese Bread, '85 33
Sourdough Bread, '82 201

Sourdough Bread Dough, Potato, '94 324; '95 77
Sourdough Bread, Potato, '94 325; '95 77
Sourdough Starter, Herman, '82 200
Sourdough Starter, Potato, '94 324; '95 77
Sour Starter, '02 259
"Sponge," '93 267
Squares, Yeast Bread, '83 155
Starter Food, '94 324
Sugar Plum Bread, '80 256
Sweet Bread Wreath, Glazed, '90 192
Sweet Christmas Loaf, '84 278
Swiss Cheese Bread, '79 60
Swiss Cheese Loaves, Mini, '95 80
Techniques of Breadmaking, '82 17
Trinity Feast Bread, '82 92; '83 83
Walnut Bread, '93 77
Wheat-and-Oat Bran Bread, '92 102
Wheat Bread, Buttermilk, '86 236
Wheat Bread, Pull-Apart Maple, '85 222; '86 166
White Bread, '79 275
White Bread, Cardamom, '82 236; '83 41
White Bread, Old-Fashioned, '81 285
White Bread, Special, '86 57
Whole Wheat Bran Bread, '79 58
Whole Wheat Bread, '83 17
Whole Wheat Bread, Anchorage Country Store,
   '00 272
Whole Wheat Bread and Rolls, Hearty, '79 92
Whole Wheat Bread, Anise-, '93 36
Whole Wheat Bread, Quick, '92 25
Whole Wheat Breadsticks, '84 228
Whole Wheat Canapé Bread, '89 293
Whole Wheat Honey Bread, '82 65; '83 106
Whole Wheat-Oatmeal Bread, '87 85
Whole Wheat-Rye Bread, '83 M37
Whole Wheat-White Bread, '82 130
Wreaths, Holiday Coffee Cake, '00 307
Yogurt Bread, '97 130
Yellow Squash Bread, '84 140
Zucchini-Apple Bread, '87 255
Zucchini Bread, '85 111; '86 93
Zucchini Bread, Spiced, '79 161; '86 162
Zucchini Bread, Spicy, '81 305; '82 36
Zucchini-Carrot Bread, '83 190
Zucchini-Honey Bread, '89 143
Zucchini Loaves, '96 130

BROCCOLI
Almond Broccoli in Sherry Sauce, '02 45
Appetizer, Broccoli-Cheese, '92 265
au Gratin, Broccoli, '82 M20
Bacon, Broccoli with, '92 302
Bake, Broccoli, '81 246; '89 279
Bakers, Broccoli, '99 308
Beef and Broccoli, Quick, '91 123
Beef and Broccoli with Chive Gravy, '88 214
Burritos, Broccoli, '83 200
Carnival Broccoli, '81 2
Casseroles
   Almond-Broccoli Casserole, '88 62
   au Gratin, Broccoli-and-Eggs, '85 289
   au Gratin, Broccoli-Ham, '90 239
   Bake, Broccoli, '89 279
   Blue Cheese Casserole, Broccoli-, '85 260
   Breakfast Casserole, Broccoli-Cheese, '99 233
   Broccoli Casserole, '87 284; '88 M146, 265
   Cheese Casserole, Broccoli-, '82 269; '84 9;
      '94 132
   Cheesy Broccoli Bake, '83 255
   Cheesy Broccoli Casserole, '84 293; '92 342;
      '95 M191
   Cheesy Italian Broccoli Bake, '83 5
   Chicken, Broccoli, and Cauliflower Casserole,
      '00 337
   Chicken-Broccoli Casserole, '79 48; '91 315

Chicken Casserole, Broccoli-, '82 33
Company Broccoli Bake, '83 279
Corn Casserole, Broccoli-, '83 313
Crabmeat-Broccoli Casserole, '84 232
Divan Casserole, Chicken, '82 M203
Divan, Chicken, '80 10; '87 M218
Divan, Creamy Turkey, '90 M34
Divan, Curried Chicken, '80 83
Divan, Easy Chicken, '94 310
Divan, Gourmet Chicken, '82 83
Divan, Overnight Chicken, '83 198
Divan Quiche, Chicken, '88 M125
Divan, Quick Turkey, '89 178
Divan, Sherried Chicken, '80 38
Divan, Turkey, '82 268
Easy Broccoli Casserole, '03 M49
Egg Casserole, Broccoli-and-, '86 324
English Walnut Broccoli, '89 68
Garden Surprise, '83 112
Gratin, Broccoli-and-Cauliflower, '01 43
Ham and Broccoli Casserole, '81 133
Ham and Broccoli Strata, '80 261
Ham-Broccoli Casserole, Quick, '82 40
Italian Broccoli Casserole, '82 6, 280; '83 32
Macaroni and Cheese, Broccoli, '02 36
Onion Deluxe, Broccoli-, '81 75
Pimiento Cheese Sauce, Broccoli with, '02 291
Potato-Broccoli-Cheese Bake, '80 114
Rice Casserole, Broccoli-, '81 101
Sausage and Broccoli Casserole, '80 33
Squash Casserole, Broccoli-and-, '01 175
Strata, Turkey-Cheddar-Broccoli, '03 100
Stuffing, Broccoli with, '95 341
Supreme, Broccoli, '85 68; '02 312
Swiss Cheese Casserole, Broccoli-, '83 322;
    '85 M211
Tuna-Broccoli Casserole, Tangy, '83 75
Turkey-and-Broccoli Casserole, '86 332
Winter Broccoli Casserole, '94 280
Cheese Sauce, Broccoli with, '82 107
Chicken with Broccoli, Spicy Ginger-and-Orange,
    '02 309
Chinese Broccoli, '85 M12
Chowder, Broccoli, '79 16
Chowder, Swiss-Broccoli, '80 73
Cocktail Broccoli, '80 192
Crêpes, Royal Brunch, '81 44
Cups, Broccoli, '00 53
Dip, Broccoli-Garlic, '82 59
Dip, Cheesy Broccoli, '83 92
Dip, Santa Fe Skinny, '94 137
Eggs, Broccoli and Creamed, '83 84
Elegant, Broccoli, '81 267
Fettuccine, Broccoli-Parmesan, '93 55
Fettuccine with Broccoli, '90 97
Filling, Broccoli, '81 44
French Sauce, Broccoli with, '81 295
Frittata, Broccoli-Cheese, '81 243
Frittata, Ham-and-Broccoli, '98 101
Fritters, Broccoli-Cauliflower, '02 45
Fritters, Cheesy Broccoli, '79 53
Garlic Broccoli, '93 35; '95 54; '99 46
Glazed Broccoli with Almonds, '80 12
Herbed Broccoli, '88 101
Herbed Broccoli, Lemony, '02 45
Hollandaise Sauce, Broccoli with, '79 244, 276
Hollandaise Sauce, Broccoli with Mock, '82 272
Horseradish Sauce, Broccoli with, '81 2; '83 206;
    '84 33
Horseradish Sauce, Carrots and Broccoli with,
    '91 246
Italian-Style Broccoli, '88 41
Italienne, Broccoli, '82 300
Jade-Green Broccoli, '80 12

Lemon Broccoli, '88 119; '95 53
Lemon-Broccoli Goldenrod, '84 M89
Lemon Cream, Broccoli with, '89 245
Lemon Dressing, Chilled Broccoli with, '88 270
Lemon Sauce and Pecans, Broccoli with, '86 71
Lemon Sauce, Broccoli with, '91 292; '92 256
Linguine, Broccoli, '98 30
Linguine, Chicken-Broccoli, '98 30
Lo Mein Noodles and Broccoli, '97 18
Mac 'n' Cheese, Broccoli, '00 53
Marinated Broccoli, '80 79; '81 40; '85 207;
    '86 157; '88 255
Marinated Fresh Broccoli, '81 M139
Medley, Buttery Broccoli, '03 259
Medley, Cauliflower-Broccoli, '81 69
Muffins, Broccoli-Chicken, '96 27
Muffins, Broccoli Cornbread, '03 81
Olive-Butter Sauce, Broccoli with, '83 118
Omelet, Broccoli-Mushroom, '85 45
Onions, Broccoli-Stuffed, '84 154
Orange Broccoli, Easy, '85 267
Orange Sauce, Broccoli with, '80 243; '04 285
Parmesan, Broccoli, '97 302
Parsnips with Horseradish, Broccoli and, '02 235
Pasta, Broccoli, '84 176
Pasta, Chicken-and-Broccoli, '87 286
Pasta with Broccoli and Sausage, '87 109; '97 266
Pasta with Peppers and Broccoli, '91 69
Pickled Broccoli, '81 308
Pie, Broccoli-and-Turkey Pasta, '88 269
Pie, Broccoli-Beef, '83 196
Pie, Broccoli-Cheese, '84 235
Pimiento Broccoli, '86 268
Pizza, Broccoli Supreme, '02 312
Polonaise, Broccoli, '86 55
Potatoes and Broccoli, Creamy, '92 61
Potatoes, Breakfast-Stuffed, '00 179
Potatoes, Broccoli-and-Almond-Topped, '83 3
Potatoes, Broccoli-Shrimp Stuffed, '92 M228
Potatoes, Broccoli-Topped Baked, '86 17
Potatoes, Cheddar, Broccoli, and Ham Stuffed,
    '04 26
Potatoes, Stuffed Mashed, '98 328
Pot Pie, Ham-Broccoli, '03 83
Puff, Broccoli, '81 94; '82 95
Quiche, Broccoli-Rice, '81 228
Quiche, Easy Broccoli, '82 34
Quiche, Italian Broccoli, '85 45
Quick-and-Easy Broccoli, '86 55
Rice, Holiday Broccoli with, '87 252
Risotto with Parmesan, Broccoli, '99 120
Roasted Broccoli and Cauliflower, '01 132
Rolls, Broccoli-Cheddar, '91 21
Rolls, Ham-and-Broccoli, '86 212; '87 82
Salads
    Barley-Broccoli Salad, '90 135
    Beef-and-Broccoli Salad, '87 187
    Broccoli Salad, '82 24; '85 249; '90 292; '95 95;
        '99 84; '00 213; '01 58
    Carrot-Broccoli Salad, '99 26
    Cauliflower, and Carrot Salad, Broccoli, '04 140
    Cauliflower-Broccoli Crunch, '88 216
    Cauliflower-Broccoli Salad, '79 20
    Cauliflower-Broccoli Toss, '82 54
    Cauliflower Salad, Broccoli-, '92 97; '00 90
    Cauliflower Salad, Broccoli and, '81 280
    Cauliflower Salad, Broccoli 'n', '90 32
    Cauliflower Salad, Creamy Broccoli and, '81 23
    Cauliflower Toss, Crunchy Broccoli, '83 25
    Chicken Salad, Broccoli-, '90 129; '00 53
    Congealed Broccoli Salad, '84 124
    Corn Salad, Broccoli-, '87 24
    Creamy Broccoli Salad, '79 143
    Crunchy Broccoli Salad, '83 39

Curried Broccoli Salad, '86 225
Fresh Broccoli Salad, '82 34; '87 103
Grape Salad, Broccoli-, '01 163
Mandarin Salad, Broccoli-, '93 325
Marinated Broccoli, '80 79
Marinated Broccoli Salad, '83 240
Marinated Broccoli, Tangy, '80 284
Medley, Broccoli, '81 206
Orange Salad, Broccoli-, '94 281
Pasta Salad, Broccoli-Cauliflower, '88 269
Pasta Salad, Broccoli-Cheese-, '96 184
Peanut Salad, Broccoli-, '92 35
Pepperoni-and-Broccoli Salad, '83 216
Potato Salad, Hot Broccoli-, '85 23
Raisin Salad, Classic Broccoli-, '02 24
Raisin Salad, Creamy Broccoli-, '92 106
Ramen Noodle Salad, '02 24
Red Pepper Salad, Broccoli and, '83 224
Red, White, and Green Salad, '90 18
Slaw, Broccoli, '01 49
Slaw, Sweet Broccoli, '96 20; '98 332
Slaw, Zesty Broccoli, '93 246
Supreme, Broccoli Salad, '83 260
Toss, Broccoli, '86 294
Toss, Crunchy Romaine, '00 30
Toss, Italian Cauliflower-Broccoli, '88 269
Warm Broccoli Salad, '92 35
Sauce, Broccoli, '91 85
Sauté, Broccoli and Walnut, '95 52
Sautéed Broccoli, '79 246
Savory Broccoli, '79 268; '80 14
Sesame Broccoli, '84 69; '85 8; '03 67
Sesame, Broccoli with, '80 13
Sesame Seeds, Broccoli with, '82 34; '02 45
Shrimp Sauce, Broccoli and Cauliflower with,
    '84 248
Soufflé, Broccoli, '81 24
Soufflé, Golden Broccoli, '84 283
Soufflés, Broccoli, '96 218
Soup, Broccoli, '86 161, M194; '87 288
Soup, Broccoli-and-Chicken, '90 202
Soup, Broccoli-Swiss, '86 6
Soup, Cheese-and-Broccoli, '89 276
Soup, Cheesy-Broccoli, '86 258
Soup, Creamed Broccoli, '85 24
Soup, Cream of Broccoli, '79 130; '80 188, M225;
    '82 314; '83 66; '86 259
Soup, Cream-of-Broccoli, '88 56
Soup, Creamy Broccoli, '81 75; '82 13; '83 99;
    '91 307
Soup, Easy Broccoli, '81 307
Soup, Fresh Broccoli, '91 86
Soup, Hot Broccoli, '81 235; '83 44
Soup, Light Cream of Broccoli, '93 17
Soup, Mock Cream of Broccoli, '85 288
Sour Cream Sauce, Broccoli with, '87 127
Spears, Saucy Broccoli, '84 35
Spears, Zesty Broccoli, '79 152
Spread, Broccamoli Curry, '88 55
Stack-Ups, Jiffy Tomato, '80 161
Steamed Broccoli, '80 122
Steamed Broccoli, Lemon Pepper, '02 215
Steamed Broccoli with Tangy Chive Sauce, '83 101
Stew, Oyster-Broccoli, '89 242
Stir-Fried Broccoli, '83 227; '00 99
Stir-Fry Beef and Broccoli, '79 47
Stir-Fry, Beef-and-Broccoli, '91 46
Stir-Fry, Bok Choy-Broccoli, '84 2
Stir-Fry Broccoli, '80 19
Stir-Fry Broccoli and Beef, '83 110
Stir-Fry, Chicken-Broccoli, '82 33
Stir-Fry, Turkey-Broccoli, '91 62
Stroganoff, Chicken-and-Broccoli, '89 M248
Sunshine Sauce, Broccoli with, '84 248

BROCCOLI
(continued)

Supreme, Broccoli, '82 34; '85 68
Supreme, Broccoli-Carrot, '89 331
Supreme, Creamy Broccoli, '82 287
Tomatoes, Broccoli-Stuffed, '83 136; '93 216
Vinaigrette, Potato-Broccoli, '85 84
White Wine, Broccoli with, '80 12
Wine Sauce, Broccoli with, '84 187
Ziti with Sausage and Broccoli, '95 340

BROWNIES. *See also* **COOKIES/Bars and Squares.**
Alaskas, Brownie, '83 299
Amaretto Brownies, '86 246
Amaretto-Walnut Brownies, '99 311; '04 142
Angel Fluff Brownies, '99 221
Apple Brownies, Frosted, '86 216
Banana-Split Brownies, '03 M43
Basic Brownies, '97 M34
Birthday Party Brownie Cakes, '00 199
Biscuit Mix Brownies, '94 M51
Blonde Brownies, Nutty, '81 64
Blonde Brownies with Chocolate Chunks, '91 271
Broadway Brownie Bars, '97 M35
Buttermilk Brownies, '85 249
Buttermilk Cake Brownies, '87 198
Butterscotch Brownies, '85 248
Butterscotch-Chocolate Brownies, '03 47
Cake, Brownie-Carrot, '92 120
Candy Bar Brownies, '92 204; '01 63
Caramel-Pecan Filled Brownies, '03 M43
Cheesecake Brownies, '85 249
Chocolate-Banana Brownies, '80 160
Chocolate Brownies, '02 M207
Chocolate Brownies, Chunky, '04 248
Chocolate Brownies, Double-, '01 63; '04 100
Chocolate Brownies, Double, '04 M220
Chocolate Brownies with Caramel Frosting, Double,
   '04 M220
Chocolate Chip Brownies, '81 162
Chocolate Chip-Peanut Butter Brownies, '84 73
Chocolate-Coconut Brownies, '97 35
Chocolate-Glazed Brownies, '01 143
Chocolate Ice Cream Brownies, '89 124
Chocolate-Kahlúa Brownies, '93 99
Chocolate-Marshmallow Brownies, '01 246
Chocolate-Mint Brownies, '85 M294; '88 80
Chocolate-Mint Brownies, Southern, '93 216
Chocolate-Nut Brownies, '81 129
Chocolate-Peanut Butter Chip Brownies, '91 306
Chocolate-Pecan Brownies, '81 64
Chocolate-Peppermint Brownies, '88 262
Chocolate Tea Brownies, '83 79
Chocolate-Walnut Brownies, '89 325
Choco-Mallow Brownies, '87 198; '90 309
Cinnamon Brownie Bars, '81 230
Cocoa Brownies, Nutty, '81 64
Coconut-Pecan-Frosted Brownies, '97 99
Cookies, Brownie Chip, '90 320
Cookies, Brownie Waffle, '86 245
Cream Cheese Brownies, '04 M330
Cream Cheese Brownies à la Mode, Magnolias,
   '97 M178
Cream Cheese Brownies, Magnolia, '01 M63
Cream Cheese Swirl Brownies, '79 51
Crème de Menthe Brownies, '83 244
Crunch-Crust Brownies, '87 198
Dark Chocolate Brownies, '00 M211
Date-and-Almond Brownies, '88 217
Deluxe, Brownies, '03 330
Derby Brownies, Special, '90 94
Easy Brownies, '83 245
Elephant Stomp Brownies, '03 43

Favorite Brownies, '86 158
Frosted Brownies, '97 M87
Fudge Brownies, Nutty, '80 M171
Fudge Cake Brownies, '03 223
German Cream Cheese Brownies, '80 269
Glaze, Brownie, '02 M252
Gooey Brownies, '97 133
Heavenly Hash Brownies, '83 245
Honey Brownies, Heavenly, '79 83
Layered Brownies, '02 M252
Macadamia-Fudge Designer Brownies, '94 51
Marshmallow Brownies, Chewy, '83 306
Mint Dessert, Brownie-, '82 227
Mint Julep Brownies, '93 165
Mississippi Mud Brownies, '89 M25
Mississippi Mud Dessert Brownies, '01 M314
Mix, Blond Brownie, '01 247
Mix, Brownie, '82 6
Mocha Brownies, '87 93
Mocha Frosting, Brownies with, '94 292
Mother's Brownies, '93 239
Muffins, Fudge Brownie, '95 M50
No-Bake Brownies, '94 330
Oat Brownies, '89 59
Oatmeal Brownies, '87 199
Oat 'n' Crunch Brownies, '91 233
Passover Brownies, '98 M104
Passover, Brownies for, '99 56
Peanut Butter Brownies, '87 199
Peanut Butter Brownies, Frosted, '92 272; '00 M155
Pistachio-Mint Brownies, '94 50
Pizza, Banana Split-Brownie, '96 M164
Praline Brownies, '93 243
Pretzel Brownies, Saucepan, '85 171
Quick and Easy Brownies, '82 6
Quick Brownies, '87 M302
Raspberry Brownies, '92 274; '97 M35
Rich Brownies, '95 84
Rocky Road Brownies, '86 320
Sundaes, Cream Cheese Brownie, '03 223
Trifle, Brownie, '03 85
Trifle, Peanut Butter-Brownie, '03 200
Triple Decker Brownies, '92 319
Walnut-Cream Cheese Brownies, '84 240
White Chocolate Brownies, '89 169; '97 36

BRUSSELS SPROUTS
Amandine, Brussels Sprouts, '79 213
Apples, Brussels Sprouts with, '02 243
Beer, Brussels Sprouts in, '85 69
Brussels Sprouts, '89 278
Caramelized Onion-and-Pecan Brussels Sprouts,
   '99 254
Carrots and Brussels Sprouts, '82 300
Cashews, Brussels Sprouts with, '81 2
Casserole, Brussels Sprouts-and-Artichoke, '94 279
Casserole of Brussels Sprouts, '86 294
Celery, Brussels Sprouts and, '79 21
Cheese Sauce, Brussels Sprouts with, '79 246
Citrus Brussels Sprouts, Calico, '85 303
Creamed Brussels Sprouts and Celery, '83 322
Creamy Brussels Sprouts, '79 212
Deviled Brussels Sprouts, '84 248
Dijon, Brussels Sprouts, '96 91
Dilled Brussels Sprouts, '88 180
Fried Brussels Sprouts, '81 308
Glazed Brussels Sprouts and Baby Carrots, '97 302
Glorified Brussels Sprouts, '86 282
Leeks with Brussels Sprouts and Almonds, '00 222
Lemon Sauce, Brussels Sprouts in, '82 269
Lemon Sprouts, '85 288
Lemony Brussels Sprouts with Celery, '85 25
Marinated Brussels Sprouts, '88 265; '96 252;
   '97 29
Medley, Brussels Sprouts, '79 212; '85 267

Mustard Sauce, Brussels Sprouts in, '87 253;
   '90 228
Onion Sauce, Brussels Sprouts in, '81 308
Orange Brussels Sprouts, '84 34
Orange Sauce, Brussels Sprouts in, '86 55
Pierre, Brussels Sprouts, '84 248
Polonaise, Brussels Sprouts, '85 79
Rice, Brussels Sprouts and, '79 288; '80 26
Salad, Brussels Sprouts, '87 233
Salad, Cauliflower-Brussels Sprouts, '83 240
Sautéed Brussels Sprouts with Parmesan Soufflés,
   '97 280
Sesame Brussels Sprouts, '86 55
Shallots and Mustard, Brussels Sprouts with,
   '85 258
Spicy Brussels Sprouts, '02 307
Stir-Fry, Brussels Sprouts, '81 308
Tangy Brussels Sprouts, '88 40
Tarragon Brussels Sprouts, '83 291
Wine Butter, Brussels Sprouts in, '86 327

BULGUR
Burgers with Cucumber Sauce, Lamb, '98 102
Lentils, Tex-Mex, '99 288
Salad, Cracked Wheat-Fruit, '96 240
Salad with Citrus and Mint, Wheat, '99 163
Tabbouleh, '93 70; '99 175
Tabbouleh Pitas, '98 105
Tabbouleh Salad, '92 212; '94 174; '01 57
(Tabbouleh Salad), Boot Scoot Tabbouli, '96 159
Wild Rice Bulgur, '91 83

BUNS. *See* **ROLLS AND BUNS.**
BURRITOS
Bean Burrito Appetizers, '94 226
Beef Burritos, Cheesy, '85 193
Breakfast Burritos, '84 57; '90 192; '97 172;
   '99 103
Broccoli Burritos, '83 200
Brunch Burritos, '91 77
Burritos, '80 196
Carne Guisada Burritos, '95 43
Chicken Burritos, '01 55
Chimichangas (Fried Burritos), '81 196; '85 244;
   '86 114
Chinese Burritos, '87 181
Easy Burritos, '04 32
Egg Burritos, Tex-Mex, '95 34
Fiesta Burritos, '86 114
Lentil Burritos, '99 287
Meat-and-Bean Burritos, '81 194
Monterey Burritos, '84 292
Phyllo Burritos, Hot, '98 312
Pie, Mexican Burrito, '87 287
Pork Burritos with Pico de Gallo, '97 140
Potato-and-Egg Burritos, '02 72
Rollups, Burrito, '90 119
Vegetable Burritos, '80 197; '90 134; '92 138
Vegetable Burritos with Avocado Sauce, '83 200
Vegetarian Burritos, '93 319
Veggie Burritos, Tony's, '96 289

BUTTER
Acorn Squash-and-Bourbon Butter, '94 266
Almond-Raisin Butter, '02 258
Ancho Chile Butter, '99 93
Apple Butter, '79 200; '81 217; '92 311
Apple Butter, Half-Hour, '81 203
Apple Butter, Oven, '00 237
Apple Butter, Slow Cooker, '97 235
Apple Butter, Spiced Oven, '00 237
Apricot Butter, '82 308; '99 212
Balls, Butter, '82 189; '89 90
Basil Butter, '87 171; '99 274
Basil Butter, Asparagus with, '85 40
Basil-Garlic Butter, '03 208
Beehive Butter, '00 68

Beurre Blanc, '01 281
Blackberry Butter, '97 306; '03 27
Blue Cheese Butter, '97 306
Bourbon Butter, '97 306
Cashew Butter, Asparagus with, '87 56
Cheese Butter, '84 114
Chervil Butter, '83 129
Chervil Butter, Swordfish Steak with, '91 147
Chili Butter, '82 219; '97 306; '00 177
Chipotle Butter, '01 234
Chipotle Pepper Butter, '97 307
Chive-Mustard Butter, '98 156
Cilantro Butter, '98 182
Cilantro-Lime Butter, '98 156; '01 24; '02 109
Cinnamon Butter, '92 319; '01 M309
Cinnamon-Honey Butter, '89 281
Citrus Butter, '97 307
Clarified Butter, '81 59
Clarifying Butter, '82 189
Cranberry Butter, '97 307
Curls, Butter, '82 51, 189; '89 90
Flavored Butters, '97 306
Frosting, Browned Butter, '97 247
Garlic-Basil Butter, '98 156
Garlic Butter, '83 193; '84 108; '95 89; '00 90
Garlic-Chive Butter, Corn on the Cob with, '01 331
Garlic-Herb Butter, Green Beans with, '02 61
Garlic-Lemon Butter, '04 54
Gazpacho Butter, '92 86
Ginger Butter, '91 26
Green Peppercorn Butter, '88 60; '90 117
Herb Butter, '86 128, 255, 261, 306; '96 309;
  '97 306; '99 19
Herb Butter, Cauliflower with, '81 2
Herb Butter, Corn-on-the-Cob with, '84 160
Herbed Caper Butter, '94 62
Herbed Unsalted Butter, '82 67
Herb-Garlic Butter, '96 173
Herb-Pesto Butter, '04 255
Honey Butter, '93 309; '94 206; '95 139; '97 307;
  '03 111
Honey-Lemon Butter, '04 231
Honey-Orange Butter, '79 36; '85 19
Horseradish-Chive Butter, '86 277
Horseradish-Parsley Butter, '98 156
Jalapeño Butter, '97 306
Jalapeño-Chili Butter, '98 156
Jalapeño-Lime Butter, Grilled Corn with, '01 158;
  '04 178
Jalapeño-Pecan-Mustard Butter, '03 205
Lemon-Anchovy Butter, '97 307
Lemon Butter, '95 32; '96 124; '02 141
Lemon Butter, Asparagus with, '87 M151; '98 168
Lemon-Dill Butter, Green Beans with, '99 141
Lemon Pepper Butter, '97 307
Lemon-Thyme-Pecan Butter, Catfish Pecan with,
  '04 68
Lime Butter, Chicken with, '84 68
Maple-Flavored Butter, Whipped, '79 36
Marjoram Butter, Zesty, '00 145
Mediterranean Butter, '97 307
Molds, Butter, '89 90
Nectarine Butter, '79 175
Olive Butter, '91 295
Onion Butter, '86 253
Onion Butter, Sweet, '93 124
Orange Butter, '81 8, 42; '90 323; '92 319; '94 115;
  '97 44
Orange-Pecan Butter, '84 75; '97 15
Peach Butter, '82 308
Peach Butter, Golden, '91 178
Pear Butter, '85 130
Pear Butter, Spiced, '80 218
Pecan Butter, '97 307

Pesto Butter, '97 307
Plum Butter, '88 152
Prune-Orange Butter, '92 49
Radish-and-Chive Butter, '01 101
Radish Butter, '01 101
Raisin Butter, '81 272
Red Pepper Butter, Fillet of Beef with, '96 32
Roasted-Garlic Beurre Blanc, '03 324
Roasted Garlic Butter, '97 46
Roasted Red Bell Pepper Butter, '95 242
Sage Butter, '96 269
Sauce, Brown Butter, '91 65
Sauce, Butter-Rum, '95 134
Sauce, Chive Butter, '03 91
Sauce, Cinnamon-Butter, '00 254
Sauce, Garlic Buerre Blanc, '88 222
Sauce, Garlic-Butter, '95 327
Sauce, Garlic-Ginger Butter, '94 89
Sauce, Honey-Butter, '98 45
Sauce, Lemon-Butter, '99 198
Sauce, New Potatoes with Lemon-Butter, '00 103
Sauce, Pecan-Butter, '91 65
Sauce, Red Wine-Butter, '96 173
Sauce, Strawberry-Butter, '96 87
Sauce, White Butter, '92 107
Seafood Butter, '97 306
Sesame Butter, '97 307
Sesame-Ginger Butter, '99 142
Shrimp Butter, '92 91
Southwestern Butter, '92 320; '01 194
Spread, Cranberry-Butter, '99 86
Spread, Garlic-Butter, '96 199
Spread, Honey Mustard-Butter, '99 86
Strawberry Butter, '79 36; '81 286; '91 71;
  '99 44, 234
Sweet Potato Butter, '95 M290
Thyme-Lemon Butter, '96 121
Tomato Butter, '86 128
Tomato-Curry-Orange Butter, '93 159
Walnut Brown Butter, Spaghettini with Green Beans
  and, '03 170

BUTTERSCOTCH
Bars, Butterscotch, '82 209; '83 297
Bars, Chocolate-Butterscotch, '81 197
Bread, Banana Butterscotch, '79 116
Brownies, Butterscotch, '85 248
Brownies, Butterscotch-Chocolate, '03 47
Cake, Butterscotch, '91 270
Cake, Butterscotch-Pecan Pound, '92 153
Cheesecake, Butterscotch, '86 188
Cookies, Butterscotch, '87 58
Cookies, Butterscotch-Pecan, '84 36
Drops, Butterscotch, '01 33
Fantastic, Butterscotch, '83 76
Filling, Butterscotch, '91 271; '02 323
Fudge, Butterscotch-Peanut, '98 M282
Fudge, Butterscotch Rum, '88 256
Fudge, Four Chips, '92 318
Fudge Scotch Ring, '79 273
Mousse, Butterscotch, '93 254
Pie, Butterscotch, '97 212
Pie, Butterscotch Cream, '84 48; '87 207
Pie, Butterscotch Meringue, '83 158
Pinwheels, Butterscotch, '90 49
Pralines, Butterscotch, '81 253
Sauce, Butterscotch-Pecan, '82 212
Sticky Buns, Christmas Morning, '97 245
Trail Mix, Bunny, '95 101

C

ABBAGE. *See also* **SAUERKRAUT, SLAWS.**
Apples and Franks, Cabbage with, '87 42
au Gratin, Cabbage, '83 279

Bake, Zesty Cabbage Beef, '80 300
Beef-Cabbage Dinner, '81 179
Bubbling Cabbage, '84 2
Caraway Cabbage, '85 32, 289
Caraway, Cabbage with, '93 181
Casserole, Cabbage, '97 88
Casserole, Cheesy Cabbage, '79 4
Casserole, Creamy Cabbage, '80 63
Casserole, Italian Cabbage, '87 42
Casserole, Savory Cabbage, '82 168
Chop Suey, Cabbage, '81 101
Chow-Chow, '82 196
Chowchow, '87 150
Chowder, Hearty Cabbage, '80 25
Colcannon, '90 64
Corned Beef and Cabbage, '83 104; '93 64;
  '96 328
Corned Beef and Cabbage au Gratin, '83 16
Corned Beef and Cabbage, Quick, '79 54
Corned Beef Squares and Cabbage, '82 86
Country-Style Cabbage, '81 271
Creamed Cabbage, '01 49
Creamed Cabbage with Almonds, '79 4
Creole Cabbage, '87 189; '00 105
Duck Breast, Tender, '97 215
Dumplings, Steamed Sesame, '97 208
Egg Rolls, Scrumptious, '96 101
Frankfurter-Cabbage Skillet, '80 166
Fried Cabbage, '02 272
Garlic, Cabbage with, '04 62
Hot Cabbage Creole, '87 42
Kielbasa and Cabbage, '85 67; '89 M196
Kielbasa, Cabbage, '87 42
Lemon-Butter Cabbage, '88 156
Medley, Cabbage, '80 64; '83 104
Medley, Cabbage-Onion-Sweet Pepper, '96 252;
  '97 28
Orange Juice, Cabbage Cooked in, '97 129
Pasta with Cabbage and Cheese Sauce, '00 105
Peppers, Carrot-and-Cabbage Stuffed, '99 63
Piccalilli, Kentucky, '81 216
Pork Chops, Chinese, '97 320
Quick Cooked Cabbage, '95 270
Red Cabbage, '96 272
Red Cabbage and Apples, '85 32
Red Cabbage and Apples, Sweet-and-Sour, '00 62
Red Cabbage and Pears, Braised, '01 298
Red Cabbage, Braised, '95 343; '99 243; '01 193;
  '02 277
Red Cabbage, Cooked, '97 28
Red Cabbage, German, '94 254
Red Cabbage, German-Style, '84 2; '98 279
Red Cabbage, Pickled, '81 271
Red Cabbage, Sweet-Sour, '79 5
Red Cabbage with Pineapple, '97 215
Relish, Cabbage, '83 260
Relish, Spanish Cabbage, '95 270
Reuben Strudel, '98 28
Rolls, Beef Stuffed Cabbage, '81 87; '82 7
Rolls, Cabbage, '83 104
Rolls, Crunchy Cabbage-Rice, '85 32
Rolls, Easy Cabbage-and-Beef, '88 49
Rolls, Fried Cabbage, '95 270
Rolls, Hot-and-Spicy Cabbage, '84 249
Rolls, Hungarian Cabbage, '94 47
Rolls, Southwestern Cabbage, '97 214
Rolls, Spicy Cabbage, '84 2
Rolls, Stuffed Cabbage, '84 217; '88 18; '92 251
Rolls, Vegetarian Cabbage, '91 86
Rollups, Beef-and-Cabbage, '80 63
Salad, Austrian Hash with Cabbage, '95 262
Salad, Cabbage, '87 120, 233
Salad, Cabbage and Fruit, '79 286
Salad, Chinese Cabbage, '81 271

CABBAGE
(continued)

Salad, Chinese Green, '88 48
Salad, Garden Cabbage, '81 210
Salad, Nutty Cabbage, '87 42
Salad, Overnight Cabbage, '79 83
Salad, Red Cabbage Citrus, '94 72
Salad, Tangy Cabbage, '82 55
Salad, Turkish, '96 137
Salad, Wilted Cabbage, '94 281
Salad, Winter Cabbage, '98 284
Salad with Cabbage Wraps, Spicy Chicken, '04 62
Salad with Dijon Vinaigrette, '03 237
Salad with Honey-Dijon Vinaigrette, Rice-Cabbage, '04 321
Salad with Pecan Vinaigrette, Ranch House, '00 162
Salad, Zesty Shredded, '04 324
Sausage and Cabbage, Skillet, '01 28
Sausage, Cabbage with Polish, '83 104
Sausage-Sauced Cabbage, '81 271
Sausage Surprise, '83 245; '84 42
Scalloped Cabbage, '82 269; '01 43
Scalloped Cabbage, Cheese, '81 87; '82 7
Shrimp and Cabbage, Asian, '00 105
Skillet Cabbage, '89 314; '90 229
Skillet, Cabbage-and-Tomato, '86 110
Skillet, Rutabaga-Cabbage, '99 285
Soup, Cabbage, '83 291
Soup, Cabbage-Bean, '97 301
Soup, Sweet-and-Sour Cabbage, '89 314
Spinach Dip in Cabbage, '82 155
Stir-Fried Cabbage, '81 75, 271; '85 109
Stir-Fry, Cabbage, '04 62
Stir-Fry, Spicy Cabbage, '04 62
Stuffed Cabbage, '84 282
Stuffed Cabbage, Italian, '84 294
Stuffed Cabbage Leaves, '00 270
Supper, Cabbage, '89 314
Supreme, Cabbage, '79 4; '83 206
Sweet-and-Sour Cabbage, '86 295; '87 189
Tex-Mex Cabbage, '80 63
Tomatoes, Cabbage and, '83 104
Tomatoes, Tasty Cabbage and, '86 72
Wedges, Saucy Cabbage, '83 86
Wedges, Smothered Cabbage, '81 87; '82 7
Wilted Cabbage, '80 64; '88 229

CAKES. *See also* **BREADS, CHEESECAKES.**
Acorn Squash Cake, '96 216
Almond-Butter Cake, '86 107
Almond-Butter Cake, Peachy, '90 107
Almond-Butter Cake, Toasted, '99 315
Almond-Butter Wedding Cake, '86 106
Almond Legend Cake, '82 8
Almond Whipping Cream Cake, '80 295
Amaretto Cake, Easy, '85 79
Ambrosia Cake, '79 229
Ambrosia Cake Royale, '89 335

Angel Food
Amaretto-Almond Sauce, Angel Food Cake with, '90 199
Blue Ribbon Angel Food Cake, '01 35
Cappuccino Mousse Cake, '99 154
Chocolate Angel Cake, '88 128
Chocolate Angel Food Cake, '87 21; '90 111; '91 55
Chocolate Angel Food Cake with Custard Sauce, '88 259
Coconut Angel Cake, Spiked, '85 279
Deluxe Angel Food Cake, '86 121
Ice Cream Angel Cake, '83 23
Ice-Cream Angel Dessert, Triple Mint, '93 86
Lemon Angel Cake, '80 147; '97 163

Orange Angel Food Cake, '96 246
Orange-Coconut Angel Food Cake, '94 294
Pineapple-Orange Sauce, Angel Cake with, '84 14
Surprise, Angel Cake, '93 86
Trifle, Pineapple Angel Food, '93 86
White Chocolate Mousse Cake, Strawberry-Studded, '99 154
Apple-Blueberry Crunch, '02 128
Apple Cake, '83 312; '84 262
Apple Cake, Dried-, '79 13
Apple Cake with Cream Cheese Frosting, Chunky, '01 185
Apple-Date Cake, Fresh, '83 300
Apple-Ginger Upside-Down Cake, '94 180
Apple-Nut Cake, '87 76; '96 268
Apple-Oatmeal Cake, Golden, '86 301
Apple-Pecan Cake, '92 167
Apple Pie Cake, '86 301
Apple Pudding Cake, '01 47
Applesauce Cake, '80 270; '96 67
Applesauce Cake, My Favorite, '87 263
Applesauce Cake with Bourbon Frosting, '88 236
Applesauce Carrot Cake, '81 202
Applesauce-Oatmeal Cake, '92 119
Applesauce Snack Cakes, '88 215; '89 20
Applesauce-Spice Cake, '83 42
Applesauce Spice Cake, '89 296
Apple Shortcake, Quick, '93 42
Apple Slice Cake, '85 93
Apple Spice Cake, '92 225
Apple Stack Cake, Dried, '85 242
Apple-Walnut Cake, '94 242
Apricot-Almond Upside-Down Cake, '97 204
Banana-Blueberry Cake, '86 247
Banana Cake, '84 151
Banana Cake, Deluxe Light, '84 314
Banana Cake, Marvelous, '79 115
Banana Cake, Triple-Layered, '00 244
Banana Cake with Coconut Custard, Supreme, '97 131
Banana-Coconut Cake, '93 154
Banana-Nut Cake, '92 120
Banana-Pecan Shortcake, '93 43
Bananas Foster Crunch Cake, '93 339
Banana Split Cake, '99 48
Banana Waldorf Cake, '85 118

Bars and Squares
Almond Cake Squares, '79 111
Angel Squares, Mocha, '98 61
Apple-Date Dream Cake Squares, '85 10
Apple-Gingerbread Squares, '03 297
Apple-Orange Cake Squares, '84 150
Applesauce Cake Squares, '86 8
Applesauce-Spice Squares, '86 248
Buttermilk Fudge Squares, '99 99
Carrot-Lemon Squares, Golden, '80 40
Carrot Snack Cake, Easy, '82 235
Carrot Squares, '79 256
Cherry Cheesecake Bars, '97 330
Cinnamon Cake Squares, '87 222
Cream Cheese Cake Squares, '84 321
Crumb Cake, Calico, '87 261
Gingerbread, Gingery, '96 100
Gingerbread Squares, '84 16
Ginger Cake, '87 222
Honey Cake Squares, '89 250
Honey-Oatmeal Cake, '87 222
Jam Squares, '81 M289
Orange Cake Squares, '81 34
Orange-Pumpkin Cake Squares, '83 242
Pecan Squares, Easy, '81 230
Pumpkin Cake Bars, '80 245
Rhubarb Squares, '92 129

Strawberry Shortcake Squares, '85 122; '86 124
Zucchini-Carrot Cake, '93 20
Beerquick Sugar Cake, '96 112
Beet Cake with Almond Topping, '86 200
Birdhouse Cake, '93 284
Birthday Cake, Clowning Around, '94 52
Blackberry Cake, Fresh, '81 132
Blackberry Flan, '79 182
Black Walnut Cake, '80 253; '84 316; '90 308
Blueberry-Sour Cream Cake, '90 140
Blueberry Streusel Cake, '92 144
Boston Cream Pie, '83 220
Bourbon Cake, '98 277
Bourbon-Pecan Cake, '84 25
Brown Mountain Cake, '84 39
Brown Sugar Meringue Cake, '81 70
Brown Sugar Snack Cake, '98 195
Bûche de Noël, '84 304; '87 241
Bûche de Noël Cake, '82 262
Bunny Cake, '94 98
Butter Brickle Cake, '85 118
Butter Brickle Loaf Cakes, '98 137
Butter Cake, Old-Fashioned, '97 60
Butter Cake, Ooey-Gooey, '00 86
Buttermilk Layer Cake, '00 48
Butter Pecan Cake, '80 229
Butter Pecan Cake, Caramel-Filled, '88 278
Butterscotch Cake, '91 270
Cajun Cake, '87 138
Candy Bar Cake, '92 204; '98 90
Candy Bar Cake, Heavenly, '04 211
Caramel Cake, '89 55; '90 307
Caramel Layer Cake, Creamy, '81 71
Carolina Dream Cake, '88 278

Carrot
Applesauce Carrot Cake, '81 202
Best Carrot Cake, '97 230
Blue Ribbon Carrot Cake, '81 70
Brownie Carrot Cake, '92 120
Carrot Cake, '79 45; '82 137; '84 315; '98 275
Cheater's Carrot Cake, '96 20
Coconut-Carrot Cake, Fresh, '80 299
Coconut-Pecan Carrot Cake, '84 322
Easy Carrot Cake, '83 215
Easy Carrot Snack Cake, '82 235
Frosted Carrot Cake, '92 19
Fruited Carrot Cake, Spicy, '85 117
German Carrot-Hazelnut Cake, '97 230
Madeira Syrup and Vanilla Ice Cream, Carrot Cakes with, '98 247
Miniature Carrot Cakes, '90 94
Old-Fashioned Carrot Cake, '83 M232; '97 330
Old-Fashioned Carrot Sheet Cake, '97 330
Old-South Carrot Cake, '80 120
Pecan-Carrot Cake, '99 223
Pound Cake, Carrot, '87 41
Praline-Filled Carrot Cake, '03 332
Pudding Cake, Carrot, '83 24
Quick-and-Easy Carrot Cake, '84 150
Raisin Cake, Carrot-, '01 58
Sheet Cake, Best Carrot, '03 55
Shortcut Carrot Cake, '02 83
Spiced Carrot Cake, '87 296
Zucchini-Carrot Cake, '93 20
Chart, Cake Failure, '81 72
Cherry Bourbon Cake, '82 287
Cherry Cake, '79 165
Cherry Cake, Dried, '97 33
Cherry Cake, Quick, '81 238
Cherry-Pineapple Dump Cake, '02 128
Cherry Upside-Down Cake, '82 56

Chocolate. *See also* **CAKES/Angel Food, Pound, Tortes.**
Almond Cake, Chocolate-, '91 248
Almond Cake with Cherry Filling, Chocolate-, '84 225
Banana Cake, Chocolate-, '86 138
Banana Loaf, Chocolate Chip-, '85 115
Basket Cake, Chocolate-Strawberry, '98 100
Batter, Chocolate Velvet Cake, '03 M286
Beet Cake, Chocolate, '80 40
Birthday Cake, Fishin'-for-Fun, '93 194
Blackberry-Raspberry Truffle Cake, '03 245
Black Forest Cake, '81 126; '92 174
Black Forest Cake, Six-Layer, '85 125
Black Forest Cherry Cake, '83 302
Black Forest Crisp, '02 128
Black Forest Dump Cake, '85 13
Black Forest Pudding Cake, '02 210
Bourbon-Pecan Cake, Chocolate-, '03 287
Breakfast Cake, Chocolate-Swirl, '04 M41
Brownie Baked Alaska, '80 66
Brownie Delight, Chocolate, '87 224
Buttercream Cake, Chocolate, '90 108
Buttermilk Cake, Chocolate-, '00 48
Buttermilk Chocolate Cake, '79 13
Buttermilk Fudge Squares, '99 99
Cameo Cake, '94 58
Candy Cake, Chocolate, '81 238
Candy Corn Chocolate Cakes, '00 235
Caramel-Nut Cake, Chocolate-, '83 23
Carrot Cake, Brownie, '92 120
Cherry Cake, Choco-, '96 229
Cherry Cake, Chocolate-, '84 200; '86 239
Cherry Fudge Cake, '98 214
Chiffon Cake with Coffee Buttercream, Chocolate, '95 277
Chocolate Cake, '97 283
Cinnamon Cake, Chocolate-, '93 154
Cocoa Crown Cake, '90 107
Coconut Cake, Chocolate-, '83 23
Coconut-Fudge Cake, '99 206
Cola Cake, '81 238
Cola Cake, Quick, '00 120
Cola Cake, Quick Chocolate, '95 56
Cookies-and-Cream Cake, '92 163
Custard Cake, Chocolate, '88 175
Decadence, Chocolate, '03 319
Decadent Chocolate Cake, '86 142
Easy Chocolate Cake, '80 140
Easy Perfect Chocolate Cake, '99 307
Eclair Cake, Chocolate, '03 206
Extra-Rich Chocolate Cake, '99 271
Father's Day Cake, '92 134
Frosting, Chocolate Cake with Double, '86 314
Fudge Cake, '94 M293; '98 110; '99 176
Fudge Cake, Best, '83 301
Fudge Cake, Brown Sugar, '86 316
Fudge Cake, Chocolate, '80 279
Fudge Cake, Coconut-, '99 206
Fudge Cake for Two, '81 205
Fudge Cake, Hot, '99 105
Fudge Cake, One-Foot-in-the-Fire, '90 252
Fudge Frosting, Chocolate Cake with, '89 56
German Chocolate Cake, '81 296; '83 M233
German Chocolate Chip Cake, '86 247
German Chocolate Sheet Cake, '03 147
German Chocolate Snack Cake, '02 128
Grandma's Chocolate Cake, '94 133
Heart, Chocolate-Amaretto, '98 56
Italian Cake, Chocolate, '02 256
Kahlúa Cake, Chocolate, '91 298
Kahlúa Chocolate Cake, '81 303
Layers, Chocolate Cake, '96 229
Loaf Cakes, Chocolate Chip, '98 137
Macadamia-Fudge Cake, '01 278
Marbled Cake, Cocoa, '82 265
Marshmallow Cake, No-Egg Chocolate, '87 M97
Mayonnaise Cake, Chocolate, '83 99
Milk Chocolate Bar Cake, '00 86
Mint Cake, Chocolate-, '03 286
Mississippi Mud Cake, '03 288; '04 136
Mocha Cake, '02 87
Mocha Cake, Belgian, '84 316
Mocha Cake, Double, '84 311
Mocha Chiffon Cake, Delta, '00 286
Mocha-Chocolate Cake, Dark, '84 311
Mousse Cake, Chocolate, '87 264; '98 270; '03 320
Nut Cake, Rich Chocolate-, '86 8
Pastry Cake, Chocolate, '91 196
Peanut Butter Cake, Chocolate-, '84 240
Peanut Butter Cake, Fudgy, '85 91
Peanut Butter-Fudge Cake, '96 254; '01 59
Peanut Butter Mousse Cake, Chocolate-, '98 71
Peanut Cluster Cake, Chocolate-, '87 184
Perfect Chocolate Cake, '82 244; '90 307; '03 318
Praline Cake, Chocolate-, '01 235
Praline Pecan Cake, Chocolate-, '03 288
Pudding Cake, Hot Fudge, '88 255
Pudding, Chocolate Cake, '81 99
Pudding, Hot Fudge Sundae Cake, '88 167
Pumpkin, Chocolate, '96 254
Queen's Chocolate Cake, '89 271
Raspberry Cake, Chocolate-, '92 173; '01 M319
Raspberry-Fudge Cake, '97 34
Rich Chocolate Cake, '89 43
Rocky Road Cake, '81 178
Roll, Chocolate, '04 85
Roll, Chocolate Cream, '85 317
Roll, Chocolate-Frosted Ice Cream, '84 200
Roll, Chocolate-Mocha Cream, '84 304
Roll, Chocolate Mousse, '83 290; '88 280
Roll, Chocolate-Orange, '87 21
Roll, Make-Ahead Chocolate-Mint Cake, '95 220
Rolls, Chocolate Cake, '94 312
Root Beer Float Cake, '04 211
Roulade, Kahlúa-and-Cream, '97 199
Royal, Chocolate Cake, '86 239
Rum Cake, Chocolate, '79 67
Sachertorte, '84 253
Sachertorte, Shortcut, '99 M243
Sheet Cake, Texas, '03 19
Shortbread Fudge Cake, '03 M331
Shortcake, Chocolate-Raspberry, '95 99
Snack Cake, Black Widow, '93 245
Snack Cake, Frosted Chocolate, '90 194
Sour Cream Cake, Chocolate-, '87 222
Sour Cream Cake, Chocolate Chip-, '85 115
Sour Cream Chocolate Cake, '79 282
Spice Potato Cake, Chocolate-, '96 111
Strawberry Shortcake, Chocolate-, '89 216
Swiss Chocolate Chip Cake, '87 85
Texas Cake, '01 59
Tic-Tac-Toe Cake, '94 52
Tiered Cameo Cake, '94 125
Toffee Cake, Chocolate-, '89 335
Tree Cakes, Miniature Chocolate Truffle, '97 M285
Triangle Cake, Chocolate, '85 126
Truffle Angel Cake, Chocolate, '97 283
Truffle Cake, Chocolate, '89 43
Truffle Cake, Rudolph's Chocolate, '04 M253
Turtle Cake, '03 287
Velvet Cake with Coconut-Pecan Frosting, Chocolate, '03 289
Velvet Cake with Cream Cheese-Butter Pecan Frosting, Chocolate, '03 288
Velvet Cake with Vanilla Buttercream Frosting, Chocolate, '03 287
Wedding Cake, Cameo, '94 124
Wedding Cake, Double Chocolate, '91 100
Whipped Cream Cake, Chocolate-Mint, '90 265
White Chocolate-Almond Cake, '03 M287
White Chocolate-Cherry Cake, '88 268
White Chocolate Mousse Cake, '89 160
White Chocolate Mousse Cake, Strawberry-Studded, '99 154
White Chocolate-Raspberry Cake, '98 323
Yule Log, '79 281; '82 289
Zucchini Cake, Chocolate, '85 156
Zucchini Cake, Chocolate-, '02 181
Chocolate-Raspberry Cake, '01 M319
Cinderella Fantasy Cake, '98 70
Cinnamon Crumb Cake, '85 290
Cinnamon Streusel Cake, '84 151
Cinnamon Swirl Cake, '01 255
Coca-Cola Cake, '02 181
Coconut
Anniversary Cake, '00 117
Apple Coconut Cake, '80 226
Cake, Coconut, '92 120
Carrot Cake, Coconut-Pecan, '84 322
Carrot Cake, Fresh Coconut-, '80 299
Chocolate-Coconut Cake, '83 23
Christmas Coconut Cake, '82 262
Coconut Cake, '03 278
Cream Cake, Coconut, '81 179; '91 269
Creamy Coconut Cake, '84 43
Four-Layer Coconut Cake, '00 117
Fresh Coconut Cake, '80 289; '82 52; '85 281
Fudge Cake, Coconut-, '99 206
Hibiscus-Nectar Cake, '96 248
Holiday Coconut Cake, '90 308
Layer Cake, Coconut-Pineapple, '80 140
Layer Cake, Stately Coconut, '81 70
Lemon Cake, Coconut-, '95 319
Lemon-Coconut Cream Cake, '81 179
Lemon-Coconut Sheet Cake, '85 117
MaMa's Coconut Cake, '97 71
Party Cake, Gathering of Stars, '00 307
Piña Colada Cake, '99 117
Pineapple Cake, Coconut-, '89 56
Pineapple Cake, Nanny's Famous Coconut-, '97 277
Pineapple Cake Roll, Coconut-, '84 304
Pineapple-Coconut Cake, '00 86
Regal Coconut Cake, '83 299
Rum-Orange Coconut Cake, '88 224
Sheet Cake, Coconut, '04 136
Spice Cake, Coconut-, '84 255; '87 296
Star Cake, Twinkling, '00 306
Toasted Coconut Cake, '86 60
Unforgettable Coconut Cake, '90 104; '01 330
White Chocolate-Coconut Cake, '87 263
Coffee Cakes
Almond-Blueberry Coffee Cake, '85 152
Almond Coffee Cake Twist, '91 22
Almond Sunburst, '94 245
Almond-Vanilla Breakfast Ring, '04 M249
Apple Coffee Cake, '81 249; '97 326
Apple Coffee Cake, Fresh, '92 32
Apple Loaf, Spiced, '79 215
Apple-Pecan Coffee Cake, '84 242
Apricot-Almond Coffee Cake, '93 26; '04 193
Apricot Lattice Coffee Cake, '94 48
Banana Coffee Cake, '81 288
Banana Cream Coffee Cake, '85 46
Banana-Sour Cream Coffee Cake, '80 186; '97 231; '04 194
Banana-Toffee Coffee Cakes, '02 M324
Blueberry Brunch Cake, '83 183

CAKES, Coffee Cakes
(continued)

Blueberry Coffee Cake, '82 206; '85 326; '88 263
Blueberry Coffee Cake, Fresh, '81 164
Blueberry Streusel Coffee Cake, '88 154
Braid Coffee Cake, Daisy, '82 197
Breakfast Pullapart, '81 278
Butterflake Coffee Ring, '79 216
Buttermilk Coffee Cake, '89 50
Buttermilk Crumb Cake, '79 72
Caramel Bread, '82 75
Caramel Breakfast Rolls, '79 193
Caramel-Orange Coffee Ring, '80 45
Caramel Ring, Easy, '85 M89
Cardamom Coffee Cake, '83 246; '84 17
Cheesecake Coffee Cake, Deep-Dish, '90 50
Cherry Blossom Coffee Cake, '80 21
Cherry Coffee Cake, '94 49
Chocolate-Chip Coffee Cake, '79 249
Chocolate Chip Coffee Cake, '83 231; '97 232;
   '04 194
Chocolate Coffee Cake, Triple-, '04 M299
Chocolate-Cream Cheese Coffee Cake, '03 288
Christmas-Tree Coffee Cakes, '87 298
Christmas Wreath, '80 280
Cinnamon-Buttermilk Coffee Cake, '80 45
Cinnamon-Cherry Coffee Cake, '98 330
Cinnamon Coffee Cake, '83 M203
Cinnamon Crisps, '81 113
Cinnamon-Nut Bubble Bread, '80 22
Cinnamon-Pecan Coffee Cake, '87 69
Cinnamon-Raisin Coffee Cake, '93 180
Cinnamon Twist Coffee Cake, '84 322
Cinnamon Upside-Down Coffee Cake, '85 256
Coffee Cake, '94 167
Cora's Coffee Cake, '91 186
Cowboy Coffee Cake, '95 84
Cranberry-Coconut Coffee Cake, '93 332
Cranberry Coffee Cake, '81 14; '90 159
Cranberry Crunch Coffee Cake, '97 231
Cranberry-Nut Coffee Cake, '81 250
Cranberry-Orange Coffee Cake, '82 283
Cream Cheese Coffee Cake, '86 290
Crescent Coffee Cake, '81 229
Danish Coffee Ring, '80 20
Fig Coffee Cake, Easy, '80 116
Heaven Cake, '04 193
Holiday Coffee Cake, '84 284
Holiday Wreath, '81 284
Honey Twist, '79 80
Lemon Coffee Cake, Lightly, '81 14
Macadamia Ring Coffee Cake, '85 326
Maple-Nut Coffee Twist, '86 290
Marbled Coffee Cake, '86 9
Mix, Quick, '94 167
Muffins, Coffee Cake, '79 7
Oatmeal-Coconut Coffee Cake, '83 312
Orange Breakfast Ring, '81 229
Orange Butter Coffee Cake, '89 229
Orange Coffee Cake, '85 M88
Orange Coffee Cake, Nutty, '95 160
Orange Marmalade Swirl Coffee Cake, '81 107
Orange-Pecan Coffee Cake, '86 86
Overnight Coffee Cake, '80 52; '92 213
Peach Flip, '79 217
Pecan-Topped Coffee Cake, '81 41
Pineapple-Coconut Coffee Cake, '94 49; '03 198
Plum Preserves Coffee Cake, '02 211
Raisin Coffee Cake, Spicy, '88 63
Raspberry-Cheese Coffee Cake, '97 231
Raspberry Coffee Cake, '83 112
Raspberry Tea Cake, '91 271

Ring, Coffee Cake, '85 M89
Savarin, Holiday, '80 280
Snack Cake, Coffee, '86 247
Sour Cream-Blueberry Coffee Cake, '00 154
Sour Cream Coffee Cake, '81 270; '93 154;
   '03 126; '04 333
Sour Cream-Walnut Coffee Cake, '79 209
Special Coffee Cake, Mama Cle's, '94 287
Strawberry Coffee Cake, '85 46
St. Timothy's Coffee Cake, '91 54
Sugar Cake, Moravian, '87 228
Sugar Cake, Polish, '89 267
Sugarplum Coffee Ring, '79 235; '83 M37
Sweet Roll Dough, '79 80
Tropical Coffee Cake, '80 232; '90 323
Walnut Coffee Cake, '93 124
Whole Wheat Coffee Cake, Crunchy-Topped,
   '79 93
Cola Cake, '81 238; '00 120
Cola Cake, Quick, '00 120
Compromise Cake, The, '90 253
Cranberry-Ambrosia Cake, '01 271
Cranberry Upside-Down Cake, '87 8
Cream Cheese Cake, Regal, '80 140
Cream Cheese Loaf Cake, '84 151
Crème de Menthe Cake, '81 178
Crêpe Cake, Southern Custard, '99 166
Cupcakes
Angel Cakes with Almond Sugar, Mixed-Berry,
   '02 175
Apple-Nut Cupcakes, '82 279
A Tisket, a Tasket, '92 15
Banana-Chocolate Cupcakes, '02 187
Banana-Cocoa Cupcakes, '80 130
Birthday Balloon Cakes, '92 15
Black Bottom Cups, '82 279
Brownie Cupcakes, '82 280
Brown Sugar-Frosted Cupcakes, '01 201
Candy Bar Cupcakes, Heavenly, '04 210
Carrot-Bran Cupcakes, '82 16
Choco Cupcakes, '03 200
Chocolate-Chip Chewies, '01 320
Chocolate Chip Cupcakes, '97 108
Chocolate Chip Cupcakes, Marble, '81 239
Chocolate-Cream Cheese Cupcakes, '03 169
Chocolate Cupcakes, '92 14
Chocolate Cupcakes, Chewy, '01 334
Chocolate-Peppermint Candy Cupcakes,
   '03 M287
Chocolate Surprise Cupcakes, '85 91
Cinnamon-Chocolate Cupcakes, '81 M139
Confetti Cupcakes, New Year's, '92 15
Cream Cheese Party Cupcakes, '82 279
Date Cupcakes, '84 7
Graveyard Grumblings, '92 15
Happy Day Cupcakes, '80 129
Hot Fudge Sundae Cakes, '00 333
Ice-Cream Cone Cakes, Fourth-of-July, '92 15
Ice-Cream Cupcakes, Banana Pudding, '01 173
Ice-Cream Cupcakes, Chocolate-Brickle,
   '01 M172
Ice-Cream Cupcakes, Lemon-Blueberry, '01 172
Ice-Cream Cupcakes, Mint-Chocolate Chip,
   '01 172
Lemonade Cupcakes, '04 163
Lemon Moist Cupcakes, '82 112; '83 153
Mocha Cupcakes, '85 250
Orange Cupcakes, '97 32
Piglets, '98 203
Pumpkin Cupcakes, '85 121
Red Velvet Cupcakes, '03 94
Self-Filled Cupcakes, '80 129
Surprises, Cupcake, '01 299
Sweetheart Cupcakes, '92 15

Tannenbaum Temptations, '92 14
Turkey Talk, '92 15
Vanilla Cupcakes, '92 14
Vanilla Cupcakes, Golden, '85 121
Yellow Cupcakes, Easy, '83 241
Daffodil Cake, '84 161
Date Nut Cake, '79 176; '80 5
Date-Nut Cake Roll, '89 94
Decorating Techniques, Cake, '83 72, 240; '84 224
Divinity Cake, '01 270
Dump Cake, Tropical, '02 128
Easter Egg Cake, '94 98
Easter Rabbit Cake, '94 99
Éclair Cake, '93 42
Fig Cake, '79 32; '99 314; '02 166
Fig Preserve Cake, '79 140; '84 316
Fig Preserves Cake, '89 335
Friendship Cake, '82 250
Fruit-and-Cereal Brunch Cake, '88 263
Fruit-and-Nut Cake, Stately, '84 226
Fruitcakes
Applesauce Fruitcake, '83 258
Aronowitz Fruitcake, '86 285
Black Cake (A Kwanzaa Fruitcake), '01 292
Bourbon Fruitcake, '85 315
Brandy Fruitcake, '82 261
Burgundy Fruitcake, '85 292
Cake Mix Fruit Cake, '95 248
Chocolate Fruitcakes, '95 250
Classic Fruitcake, '91 258
Favorite Fruitcake, Family, '88 284
Fondue, Fruitcake, '84 258
Grandmother's Fruitcake, '95 248
Japanese Fruitcake, '83 268; '90 252
Jeweled Fruitcake, '88 260
Jill's Fruitcake, '95 249
Kentucky Fruitcake, '86 266
Layered Fruitcake, '87 265
Lemon Fruitcake, '83 258
Light Fruitcake, '90 309
Loaf, Fruitcake, '96 286
Mom's Fruitcake, '85 321
No-Bake Fruitcake, '95 249
Old-South Fruitcake, '79 289
Regal Fruitcake, '83 257
Sherry-Nut Fruitcake, '84 266; '00 299
Spice Cake, Fruit and, '87 M97
White Fruitcake, '80 280; '85 316; '00 299;
   '03 248
Zucchini Fruitcake, '88 284
Funnel Cakes, '83 250
Funnel Cakes, Nutty, '91 233
Gift Box Cake, '96 319
Gingerbread, '01 313
Gingerbread, Applesauce, '94 179
Gingerbread Cake Roll, '89 214
Gingerbread Mix, '92 312
Gingerbread, No-Molasses, '92 313
Gingerbread, Old English, '79 265
Gingerbread, Old-Fashioned, '91 240
Gingerbread, Refrigerator, '80 52
Gingerbread, Spicy, '84 263
Gingerbread with Caramel Sauce, Pumpkin, '93 235
Gingerbread with Key Lime Curd, Kahlúa, '96 126
Ginger Cake with Candied Cream, Spiced, '04 300
Ginger-Pear Upside-Down Cake, '97 205
Ginger Shortcakes, '94 179
Graham Cracker Cake, '79 13
Grapefruit Cake, Fresh, '89 308
Holiday Cake, Favorite, '81 264
Honey-Apple Cake, '99 210
Honey Bun Cake, '91 214
Honey Cake, '92 250
Honey Cake, Southern, '89 251

Hummingbird Cake, '82 244; '90 305; '03 315
Hummingbird Cake, Lightened, '01 34
Ice Cream Cake, '86 321; '89 71
Ice Cream Cake for Grown-Ups, '88 M192
Ice Cream Cake, Fruity, '87 110
Ice Cream Yule Log, '83 253
Irish Cream Cake, '02 323
Italian Cream Cake, '96 262
Italian Cream Cake, Fresh Orange, '02 294
Italian Cream Cake, Quick, '99 307
Jam Cake, Spicy, '89 236
Jellyroll, Easy, '82 176
Jellyroll Layer Cake, '85 125
Jellyroll, Spiced, '82 176
Journey Cakes, '04 99
Journey Cakes, Rosemary-Garlic, '04 99
Journey Cakes, Tomato, Parmesan, and Kalamata
    Olive, '04 99
Key Lime Cake, '91 214
King Cake, '90 20; '00 61
Lady Baltimore Cake, '90 45
Lane Cake, '80 121; '83 269; '96 144
Lane Cake, Holiday, '99 306
Lane Cake, Nanny's, '89 55
Lemon Cake, Easy, '83 24
Lemon Cake, Glazed, '86 70
Lemon Cake, Luscious, '93 81
Lemon Cake Pudding, '92 96; '98 35
Lemon Cake Roll, '89 312
Lemon Cake Roll, Elegant, '80 70
Lemon-Cheese Cake, Tart, '88 7; '03 317
Lemon Gold Cake, '83 301
Lemon Layer Cake, Luscious, '86 61
Lemon Layer Cake, Old-Fashioned, '85 191
Lemon Meringue Cake, '89 296; '99 118
Lemon-Pineapple Cake, '86 60, 239
Lemon-Poppy Seed Cake, '93 154
Lemon Pudding Cake, '83 106
Lemon-Raspberry Cake, '91 247
Lemon Roll, Snow-Capped, '79 68
Lemon Sponge Cups, '83 10
Light Cake, Basic, '90 107
Lime Cakes, Creamy, '04 89
Lime Icebox Pie Cake, '03 104
Lime Layer Loaf, '85 96
Little Bitty Cakes, '98 154
Little Cakes, Spring's, '01 M91
Lord Baltimore Cake, '90 45
Mandarin-Rum Cake, '84 150
Mango Cake, '83 150
Maple Nut Cake, '96 17
Maraschino Nut Cake, '83 268
Mincemeat Spice Cake, '79 246
Molasses Snack Cake, '86 20
Moravian Sugar Cake, '95 304
Neapolitan Cake, '88 168
Nutmeg Feather Cake, '81 238
Nutty Cakes, '89 50
Oatmeal Cake, '01 58
Oatmeal Cake, Dutch, '83 95
Orange Blossom Cake, '96 162
Orange Butter Cake, '95 46
Orange Cake, '86 61; '95 320
Orange Cake, Fresh, '83 300
Orange Cake, Mandarin, '83 24
Orange Cake, Williamsburg, '81 120; '82 23
Orange Chiffon Cake, '91 56
Orange Chiffon Cake, Fresh, '88 179
Orange Chiffon Cake with Orange Icebox Pie
    Filling, '03 105
Orange-Cranberry Cake, '85 314
Orange Cream Cake, '99 118
Orange-Date Cake, '94 60
Orange Date-Nut Cake, '01 285

Orange-Lemon Cake, General Robert E. Lee, '88 92
Orange Liqueur Cake, '87 84
Orange Marmalade Cake, '85 53
Orange Meringue Cake, '86 336; '87 84
Orange-Nut Butter Cake, '80 254
Orange Nut Cake, '80 70
Orange-Pecan Crunch Cake, '83 10
Orange Rum Cake, '79 2
Orange-Slice Cake, '81 264
Orange Streusel Cake, '88 10
Peach Cake, Fresh, '85 178
Peaches and Cream Cake, '80 142
Peaches-and-Cream Cake, '96 118
Peach Shortcakes, Spicy, '89 154
Peach Upside-Down Cake, '87 8
Peachy Picnic Cake, '79 178
Peanut Butter-and-Jelly Cake, '85 34
Peanut Butter-Banana Cake, '80 87
Peanut Butter Cake, '79 51; '83 M233
Peanut Butter Swirl Cake, '86 109
Peanutty Layer Cake, Super, '83 222
Pear Cake, Caramel-Glazed, '02 196
Pear Cakes with Praline Sauce, '96 284
Pear Cake with Caramel Drizzle, '86 247
Pear Preserve Cake, '85 52
Pear Preserves Cake, '00 139
Pecan Cake, '97 256
Pecan Cake, Kentucky, '84 263
Pecan Cake with Praline Glaze, '82 196
Pecan-Carrot Cake, '99 223
Pecan-Cornmeal Rounds, '95 99
Pecan Pie Cake, '98 254; '03 316
Pecan Roulade, '87 183
Peppermint Cake, Red Velvet, '98 308
Peppermint Candy Cake, '89 254
Persimmon Cake, '79 205
Petit Fours, Simple, '92 277
Petits Fours, '79 117; '96 282
Petits Fours, Chocolate-Almond, '93 255; '00 72
Petits Fours, From-the-Heart, '03 110
Petits Fours, Teatime, '85 119
Pig Pickin' Cake, '04 112
Pineapple Cake, Heavenly, '83 303
Pineapple-Cherry Dump Cake, '04 91
Pineapple-Coconut Cake, '00 86
Pineapple-Pecan Upside-Down Cake, '84 25
Pineapple Right-Side-Up Snack Cake, '99 28
Pineapple Upside-Down Cake, '80 102; '88 10
Pineapple Upside-Down Cake, Express, '03 65
Pineapple Upside-Down Cake, Fresh, '97 204
Pineapple Upside-Down Cake Roll, '96 162
Pineapple Upside-Down Cake, Skillet, '85 242;
    '03 65
Pineapple Upside-Down Cake, Spiced, '02 214
Pineapple Upside-Down Cake, Stacked, '86 239
Plum Cake, '97 177
Popcorn-Gumdrop Cake, '87 262
Poppy Seed Cake, '92 174; '95 63
Poppy Seed Cake, Lemon-, '93 154
Poppy Seed Cake, Plantation, '79 13
Poppy Seed Loaf Cake, '81 63
Poppy Seed Loaf, Quick, '82 75
Pound
    Apple Cider Pound Cake, '84 10
    Apricot Brandy Pound Cake, '83 267
    Aztec Pound Cake, '96 61
    Banana Pound Cake, '96 60; '98 195
    Batter, Pound Cake, '04 84
    Black Pepper Pound Cake, '96 61
    Black Walnut Pound Cake, '92 16
    Bourbon-Pecan Pound Cake, '91 270
    Brandied Pound Cake, '89 292
    Brown Sugar Pound Cake, '82 135;
        '04 278

Brown Sugar Pound Cake with Creamy Holiday
    Glaze, '03 281
Brown Sugar-Rum Pound Cake, '96 60
Buttered Rum Pound Cake with Bananas Foster
    Sauce, '03 94
Buttermilk Pound Cake, '79 285; '85 255; '99 98
Buttermilk Pound Cake, Old-Fashioned, '82 52;
    '88 16
Buttermilk Pound Cake, Spiced, '84 73
Butter-Nut Pound Cake, '86 235
Butternut Pound Cake with Caramel Sauce,
    Betty's, '95 308
Butterscotch-Pecan Pound Cake, '92 153
Caramel Frosting, Pound Cake with, '87 39
Caramel Pound Cake, '98 194
Carrot Pound Cake, '87 41
Cheesy Pound Cake, '96 62
Cherry Pound Cake, Cute-as-a-Button, '95 139
Chocolate Chip Pound Cake, '86 178; '93 105;
    '94 100
Chocolate Marble Pound Cake, '88 16
Chocolate-Orange Pound Cake, '89 94
Chocolate Pound Cake, '82 88; '84 10; '89 325;
    '94 288; '98 336
Chocolate Pound Cake with Frosting, '90 284
Chocolate Pound Cake with Fudge Frosting,
    '87 296
Chocolate-Sour Cream Pound Cake, '83 239;
    '92 153
Chocolate-Swirled Pound Cake, '97 329
Chocolate Velvet "Pound" Cake, '03 286
Coconut-Cream Cheese Pound Cake, '85 297;
    '90 305
Coconut Cream Pound Cake, '84 10
Coconut Pound Cake, '82 87; '91 224
Cream Cheese-Bourbon-Pecan Pound Cake,
    '04 280
Cream Cheese-Coconut-Pecan Pound Cake,
    '04 280
Cream Cheese Pound Cake, '81 290; '86 287; '95
    304; '01 244; '03 312
Cream Cheese Pound Cake, Crusty, '89 124
Cream Cheese Pound Cake with Strawberries and
    Cream, '02 104
Croutons, Cinnamon Pound Cake, '93 161
Daiquiri Pound Cake, '93 83
Eggnog-Pecan Pound Cake, '95 313
Eggnog Pound Cake, '90 253
Favorite Pound Cake, '81 132; '92 171
Five-Flavor Pound Cake, '87 264
Four-Flavor Pound Cake, '91 136
French Toast, Pound Cake, '04 33
Fruited Pound Cake, '81 265
Gentleman's Pound Cake, '00 287
German Chocolate Pound Cake, '97 M254
Ginger Pound Cake, '02 97; '03 99
Ginger Pound Cake with Glazed Cranberry
    Ambrosia, '00 269
Glazed Pound Cake, '89 207
Golden Pound Cake, '90 284
I Remember Pound Cake, '86 180
Irish Cream-and-Coffee Pound Cake, '92 287
Lemon-Almond Pound Cake, Sullivan's,
    '04 278
Lemon Curd Pound Cake, '04 278
Lemon Geranium Pound Cake, '01 131
Lemon Pound Cake, '82 88; '03 94
Lemon Pound Cake with Mint Berries and Cream,
    '99 183
Lemon-Sour Cream Pound Cake, '87 38
Lemon Sour Cream Pound Cake, '01 117
Lemony Pound Cake, '96 60
Loaf, Noel Pound Cake, '04 279
Loaf, Pound Cake, '85 306

CAKES, Pound
(continued)

Loaf, Pretty and Pink Pound Cake, '96 60
Mahogany Pound Cake, '89 207
Marbled Pecan Pound Cake, '93 313
Marble Pound Cake, '95 29
Milk Chocolate Pound Cake, '90 306
Million Dollar Pound Cake, '90 306; '02 239;
     '03 270
Mini Pound Cakes, '86 148
Mocha Marble Pound Cake, '99 23
Old-Fashioned Pound Cake, '80 279; '82 88;
     '93 120
Orange-Pecan Pound Cake, '93 13
Orange-Pecan-Spice Pound Cake, '02 295
Orange Pound Cake, '87 84, 221; '92 69
Pastel Cake, '97 173
Peach-Almond Pound Cake, '89 86
Pecan Pound Cake, '01 253
Pineapple Pound Cake, '79 148
Pound Cake, '92 94
Praline Pound Cake, '82 88
Problems to Avoid Chart, '84 319
Pumpkin Pound Cake, '92 235
Rose-Geranium Pound Cake, Mrs. Willoughby's,
     '84 318
Rum Pound Cake, Buttered, '83 220
Sandwich, Grilled Pound Cake Dessert, '94 171
S'mores, Grilled Pound Cake, '98 179
Sour Cream-Orange Pecan Pound Cake, '89 207
Sour Cream Pound Cake, '89 56; '92 153
Sour Cream Pound Cake, Cinnamon-Topped,
     '82 43
Sour Cream Pound Cake, Elegant, '83 79
Sour Cream Pound Cake with Raspberry Sauce,
     '99 259
Southern Pound Cake, Smoothest, '93 237
Stick, Colorful Cakes on a, '04 84
Strawberry-Banana Topping, Pound Cake with,
     '89 200
Sweet Potato Pound Cake, '83 85
Teapot Cake, '04 83
Tea Pound Cake, '99 90
Two-Step Pound Cake, '00 36
Whipping Cream Pound Cake, '90 284
White Chocolate Pound Cake, '91 101
Wine Jelly, Pound Cake with, '98 125
Yogurt Pound Cake, '84 10
Praline Cake, '81 162
Praline Cream Cake, '01 272
Praline Ice Cream Cake, '80 84
Prune Cake, '85 223
Prune Cake and Sauce, '85 118
Prune Cake, Spicy, '79 136
Pudding Cake, Danish, '91 269
Pudding Cake, Saucy, '98 196
Pudding Cake with Blueberry Sauce, Buttermilk-
     Lemon, '95 135
Pumpkin Cake, '81 272; '93 303; '98 241
Pumpkin Cake with Little Ghosts, '03 212
Pumpkin Date Cake, '79 251
Pumpkin Kahlúa Cake, '86 292
Pumpkin Layer Cake, '80 245
Pumpkin Roll, '79 206; '91 297; '04 297
Queen Bee Cake, '81 237
Raisin Layer Cake, Spicy, '79 230
Red Velvet Cake, '93 318; '96 282; '01 244
Rhubarb Upside-Down Cake, '00 87
Root Beer Float Cake, '99 196
Satin Ribbon Cake, '92 68
Sauerkraut Cake, '94 254
Savarin, '79 171

Shortcakes
Blueberry-Nectarine Shortcake, Warm, '97 205
Caramel-Apple Shortcakes, '03 194
Chicken Shortcakes, Cheesy, '95 98
Chocolate-Raspberry Shortcake, '95 99
Cinnamon-Crunch Shortcakes, '03 194
Cinnamon-Crunch Shortcakes with Fruit
     Compote, '03 194
Ginger-Pear Shortcakes, '03 194
Orange Shortcake, Fresh, '80 100
Orange-Strawberry Shortcake, '95 100
Round Shortcakes, '02 105
Shortcut, Shortcake, '02 105
Strawberry-Brown Sugar Shortcake, '00 82
Strawberry Crispy Shortcakes, '93 42
Strawberry Pinwheel Shortcake, '89 112
Strawberry Shortcake, '81 96; '83 122; '92 184;
     '94 162
Strawberry Shortcake, A Favorite, '88 136
Strawberry Shortcake, Elegant, '88 37
Strawberry Shortcake Jubilee, '88 209
Strawberry Shortcake Shells, '88 196
Strawberry Shortcakes, Party-Perfect, '02 105
Strawberry Shortcakes with Mint Cream, '97 144
Sorghum Cake, '85 239
Sorghum Tea Cakes, '85 239
Sour Cream Cake Layers, '01 270
Spice Cake, '81 162
Spice Cake, Buttermilk, '81 211
Spice Cake, Dark, '82 314; '83 43
Spice Cake, Old South, '84 263
Spice Cake, Sugar 'n, '84 226
Spice Cake with Caramel Frosting, '82 314; '83 42
Spice Cake with Chocolate-Coffee Frosting, '88 268
Spice Cake with Cream Cheese Frosting, Harvest,
     '02 209
Spice Cake, Yule Log, '85 314
Spice Layer Cake with Coffee Frosting, '94 86
Sponge
Burnt Sugar Sponge Cake with Berry Sauce,
     '95 103
Chocolaty Sponge Cake, '86 60
Coffee Sponge Cake, '83 229; '91 55
Coffee Sponge Cake, Two-Day, '86 75
Daffodil Sponge Cake, '79 175; '80 6; '84 315
Passover Sponge Cake, '90 106
Strawberries 'n Cream Sponge Cake Roll, '81 95
Yellow Sponge Cake, '80 250
Squash Cake, '86 200
Stack Cake, Favorite, '87 228
Stack Cake, Old-Fashioned, '81 216
Strawberry Cake, Layered, '00 82
Strawberry Cake Roll, '79 49; '83 129; '84 305;
     '85 172
Strawberry Cake, Triple-Decker, '04 55
Strawberry Cream Cake, '86 61
Strawberry Crunch Cake, '79 288; '80 35
Strawberry Delight Cake, '85 30
Strawberry Ice Cream Roll, '84 105
Strawberry-Lemon Sheet Cake, '04 137
Strawberry Meringue Cake, '86 240
Strawberry Roll, '82 120
Strawberry Roll, Heavenly, '82 176
Strawberry Yogurt Layer Cake, '94 85
Sweet Potato Cake, '79 207; '89 295
Sweet Potato Cakes, '01 105
Sweet Potato Cake with Citrus Filling, '02 221
Sweet Potato Cake with Coconut Filling and
     Caramel Frosting, '03 329
Sweet Potato Loaf Cake, '81 224
Sweet Potato Log Roll, '82 227
Sweet Potato Surprise Cake, '80 287
Tea Cake, Lemon, '82 169
Tea Cakes and Fresh Strawberries, Telia's, '98 110

Teddy Bear Cakes, '92 278
Tennessee Jam Cake, '04 55
Tennessee Jam Cake, Triple-Layer, '04 55
Tilden Cake with Cherry-Wine Sauce, '97 132
Tipsy Squire, '85 41
Tortes
Almond Torte, Chocolate-, '96 M253
Amaretto Torte, '82 303
Apricot Praline Torte, Lucy's, '95 243
Apricot Sponge Torte, '90 59
Apricot Torte, '02 220
Black Forest Torte, '88 209
Black Forrest Cherry Torte, '88 178
Blitz Torte, '01 65
Bourbon-Chocolate Torte, '98 M84
Caramel-Sweet Potato Torte, '96 312
Carob-Pecan Torte, '85 218
Chocolate-Almond Torte, '98 273
Chocolate Mint Torte, '94 86
Chocolate-Pecan Torte, '89 42
Chocolate Praline Torte, '84 165
Chocolate-Strawberry Ice Cream Torte, '79 7
Chocolate Torte, Apricot-Filled, '90 107
Chocolate Torte, Double-, '79 67
Chocolate Torte Royale, '82 263
Chocolate Torte, Triple, '96 58
Chocolate Torte with Firewater Cream, '00 161
Chocolate-Vanilla Holiday Torte, '01 252
Chocolate Velvet Torte, '86 316
Graham Cracker-Nut Torte, '97 275; '98 35
Hazelnut Torte, '91 248
Lemon Meringue Torte with Raspberry Sauce,
     '93 82
Mocha Brownie Torte, '85 102
Mocha-Pecan Torte, '86 26
Mocha Torte, '99 66
Mocha Velvet Torte, '92 318
Passover Linzer Torte, '90 106
Pecan Torte, Ground, '04 273
Pecan Torte, Heavenly, '81 266
Praline-Pumpkin Torte, '01 285
Spring Torte, '91 57
Strawberry Meringue Torte, '88 136
Sugar Cookie Torte, '79 68
Toffee Meringue Torte, '87 118
White Chocolate Mousse Torte, '99 154
Twelfth Night Cake, '93 337
Upside-Down Cake, Blackberry, '01 314
Upside Down Cake, Quick, '90 219
Upside-Down Sunburst Cake, '87 9
Vanilla Chiffon Cake, '79 266
Walnut Cream Roll, '84 192
Wedding Cake, Rose Garden, '97 60
Whipped Cream Cake, '96 96
White Cake Batter, Basic, '99 117
White Cake, Buttermilk, '86 235
White Cake with Strawberries and Chocolate Glaze,
     '87 76
White Cake with Strawberry Frosting, Rich, '89 184
Winter Squash-Spice Bundt Cake, '99 248
Yogurt-Lemon-Nut Cake, '89 169
Zucchini Cake, '79 24
Zucchini-Pineapple Cake, '95 160
Zuppa Inglese, '85 229
CANDIES
Almond Brittle, '03 281
Almond Brittle Candy, '80 255
Almond Butter Crunch, '80 301
Almond Roca, '86 49
Almond-Toffee Crunch, '88 285
Apples, Candied Red, '81 217
Apples, Candy, '84 243
Apricot Balls, '79 274
Balls, Buckeye, '00 M280; '01 M322

Balls, No-Cook Candy, '85 14
Bourbon Balls, '81 254; '83 315; '90 83; '02 30
Bourbon Balls, Chocolate, '84 298
Bow, Candy, '99 M306
Box, White Candy, '97 M54
Brandy Balls, '86 319
Brittle, Cooktop, '02 223
Brittle, Microwave Pecan, '97 M245
Brittle with Crushed Peanuts, '87 184
Buckeyes, '85 321
Butter Creams, '80 302
Buttermilk Candy, '80 302
Candy Cane Swizzle Sticks, '02 298
Caramel Corn Candy, '84 243
Caramel Good Stuff, Baked, '80 284
Caramel O's, '99 M196
Caramel-Peanut Squares, '85 247
Caramels, Chocolate-Dipped, '02 30
Caramels, Coconut-Macadamia, '98 305
Caramels, Soft-and-Chewy, '03 297
Cherries, Cordial, '02 30
Cherry-Pistachio Bark, '00 M41
Chocolate-Almond Hearts, '03 42
Chocolate Bonbons, Dark, '02 297
Chocolate Brittle, '83 315
Chocolate Brittle, Quick, '82 114
Chocolate Caramels, '91 35
Chocolate-Coconut Almond Drops, '87 223
Chocolate-Covered Cherries, '81 286; '84 298;
   '97 M55
Chocolate-Covered Pecan Fritters, '79 205
Chocolate-Covered Pretzels, '82 295
Chocolate Drops, '84 111
Chocolate Greeting Card, '83 40
Chocolate-Lemon Creams, '98 M235
Chocolate-Marshmallow Squares, '92 M50
Chocolate-Nut Log Candy, '86 335
Chocolate Nut Teasers, '91 35
Chocolate-Peanut Butter Balls, '80 87
Chocolate-Peanut Butter Bites, '92 M317
Chocolate-Peanut Butter Drops, '92 322
Chocolate-Peanut Clusters, '81 16
Chocolate Peanutty Swirls, '94 M330
Chocolate Rudolph Reindeer, '04 M254
Chocolate Rum Balls, '80 302
Chocolate-Rum Balls, '88 285
Chocolates, Liqueur Cream-Filled, '87 258
Chocolate Spiders, '85 236
Chocolates, Spirited, '86 278
Chocolate, Tempered, '91 35
Chocolate Velvets, '84 298
Coconut-Almond Balls, '84 256
Coconut-Black Walnut Bonbons, '82 307
Coconut Candy, '79 272; '80 250
Coconut Joys, '98 282
Coconut Joys, Chocolate-Covered, '98 M282
Coffee Buttons, '99 66
Cola Candy, '02 298
Corn Brittle, Crunchy, '85 208
Cracker Candy, '02 30
Crème de Cacao Balls, '86 266
Crème de Menthe Chocolates, '91 36
Crystal Candy, '84 299
Date Candy, '89 308
Date Loaf Candy, '80 302
Date Logs, '79 274
Divinity, Apricot, '83 297
Divinity Candy, '01 271
Divinity Candy with Sugared Maraschino Cherries,
   '01 271
Divinity, Cherry, '97 316
Divinity, Christmas, '81 286
Divinity Ghosts, '95 273
Divinity, Lemon, '97 316

Divinity, Mrs. Floyd's, '00 315
Divinity, Peanut, '85 233; '87 M278
Divinity, Pink, '86 49
Divinity, Strawberry, '91 272
Easter Egg Kaleidoscopes, '02 48
Frosting, Chocolate Candy, '81 238
Fruit Balls, '82 296; '84 299
Fudge. See FUDGE.
Kentucky Colonels, '79 273
Lollipops, Colorful Molded, '81 218
Marzipan, '83 306
Millionaires, '79 M262; '97 M55
Millionaires, Texas, '00 291
Mints, Butter, '03 300
Mints, Cream Cheese, '93 79; '00 41
Mints, Dinner, '88 66
Mints, Easy Holiday, '84 299
Mints, Party, '79 273; '81 119
Mints, Special, '99 323
Mint Twists, '86 106
Molded Candies, '84 40
Nests, Robin's Egg, '02 M48
Nut Clusters, '81 254
Nuts, Candied, '81 261
Orange Balls, '94 331
Orange-Nut Balls, '02 297
Orange Peel, Candied, '81 286
Peanut Brittle, '79 M263; '80 87; '84 298; '92 240
Peanut Brittle, Classic, '02 M223
Peanut Brittle, Golden, '83 223
Peanut Brittle, Never-Fail, '79 273
Peanut Brittle, Orange, '80 302
Peanut Brittle, Popcorn, '02 M223
Peanut Butter Candy, '93 166
Peanut Butter-Chocolate Balls, '80 269
Peanut Butter-Chocolate Candy Squares, '82 56
Peanut Butter Creams, '79 273
Peanut Butter Easter Eggs, '87 86
Peanut Butter Temptations, '84 29
Peanut Butter Yummies, '83 223
Peanut Clusters, '87 184; '92 288; '98 M282
Peanutty Clusters, '83 143
Pecan Brittle, '91 272; '02 M223
Pecan Clusters, '81 266; '98 305
Pecan Clusters, Roasted, '85 233; '90 310; '03 315
Pecan Clusters, Toasted, '00 M14
Pecan-Coconut Clusters, '86 M251
Pecan Rolls, '79 285
Pecans, Brown Sugar, '81 266
Pecans, Glazed, '81 254
Pecans, Honeycomb, '84 300
Pecans, Orange, '84 299
Pecans, Spiced, '79 296; '81 286
Pecans, Spicy, '81 289
Pecans, Sugar-and-Honey, '86 319
Penuche, Coffee, '98 305
Peppermint Patties, '86 278
Potato Candy, '79 273
Pralines
   After-the-Dance Pralines, '03 251
   Basic Pralines, '92 313; '93 50
   Bourbon Pralines, '92 313; '93 51
   Buttermilk Pralines, '99 99; '00 49
   Butterscotch Pralines, '81 253
   Café au Lait Pralines, '92 313; '93 51
   Chocolate-Mint Pralines, '92 313; '93 51
   Chocolate-Peanut Butter Pralines, '92 313; '93 51
   Chocolate Pralines, '92 313; '93 51
   Cinnamon Pralines, '97 317
   Coffee Pralines, Plantation, '86 241
   Creamy Pralines, '80 198; '92 289
   Dark Praline Clusters, '86 313
   Dark Pralines, '83 52
   Hot Spicy Pralines, '92 313; '93 51

   Maple-Pecan Pralines, '83 222
   Mocha Pralines, '92 313; '93 51
   New Orleans-Style Pralines, '86 335
   Old-Fashioned Pralines, '89 318
   Orange Pralines, '92 313; '93 51
   Peanut Butter Pralines, '92 313; '93 51
   Pecan Pralines, Original, '81 11
   Pralines, '79 272; '86 M288; '89 60; '90 48;
      '99 295; '01 90, 201
   Southern Pralines, '79 M263
   Spicy Praline Delights, '84 299
   Texas-Size Pralines, '79 186
   Vanilla Pralines, '92 313; '93 51
Quemada (Burnt-Sugar Candy), '87 38
Raisin Candy, Mixed, '84 111
Raspberry Cream Chocolates, '91 36
Red Rock Candy, '92 240
Rocky Road, '84 298
Rocky Road-Peanut Butter Candy Cups, '04 M330
Rum Balls, '93 314
Strawberries, Christmas, '94 331
Sugared Rabbits, '04 94
Taffy, Old-Fashioned, '80 302
Toffee, '01 218
Toffee, Almond, '04 235
Toffee, Bourbon-Pecan, '04 235
Toffee, English, '79 273
Toffee, Hawaiian, '04 235
Toffee, Microwave, '92 M317
Toffee, Microwave Peanut, '04 M234
Toffee, Mildred's, '04 235
Toffee, Nutty, '79 M263
Toffee, Pecan, '00 42
Truffles
   Almond Truffles, '83 298
   Amaretto Dessert Truffles, '86 319
   Bittersweet Truffles, '94 330
   Chocolate-Cherry Cordial Truffles, '99 127
   Chocolate-Kahlúa Truffles, '92 285
   Chocolate Marble Truffles, '97 284
   Chocolate-Praline Truffles, '97 284
   Chocolate Truffles, '85 114; '89 43; '91 108
   Hazelnut-Chocolate Truffles, '03 243
   Hazelnut Truffles, '97 M54
   Orange-Pecan Truffles, '95 92
   Raspberry-Fudge Truffles, '00 M41
   White Chocolate-Praline Truffles, '97 284
   White Chocolate Truffles, '87 45
   Yule Street Truffles, '90 242
Turtle Candies, '93 M41
White Chocolate-Peanut Butter Crunch, '02 M296
White Chocolate Salties, '92 50
White Chocolate Surprises, '91 36
CANNING AND PRESERVING
Apple Rings, Cinnamon, '85 107
Asparagus, Pickled, '83 46
Beets, Pickled, '81 216
Berries (except Strawberries), '80 128
Black-Eyed, Field, and Crowder Peas, '80 126
Cantaloupe, Pickled, '99 171
Carrot Marmalemon, '96 107
Catsup, Homemade, '85 188
Catsup, Spicy Tomato, '83 182
Chiles Medley, Fiery Pickled, '01 333
Chili Sauce, '81 175
Chili Sauce, Chunky, '85 188
Chow-Chow, '82 196
Chowchow, '00 158
Chutney, Pear, '98 243
Confit, Roasted Shallot-Garlic, '94 303
Corn, Cold-Pack, '81 216
Corn, Cream-Style, '80 127; '85 106
Corn, Whole Kernel, '85 106
Cranberry Conserve, '83 279

CANNING AND PRESERVING
(continued)

Fruit Juices, '85 107
Fruit, Unsweetened Mixed, '83 182
Grapes, Spiced, '98 220
Green Beans, '80 126
Green Bean Salad, Pickled, '82 239
Green Beans, Appalachian, '81 215
Green Beans, Dill, '93 136
Green Beans, Dilled, '99 170
Green, Snap, or Wax Beans, '85 105
Green Tomatoes, Pickled, '99 143
Lemons, Fresh Preserved, '00 17
Lima Beans, '80 127
Mincemeat, Homemade, '79 245
Nectarines in Apple Juice, '83 183
Okra, '80 127
Okra, Pickled, '98 177
Oranges, Brandied Cranberry, '98 309
Peaches, '80 128
Peaches and Pears, '85 106
Peaches, Honey-Sweet, '85 107
Pear Mincemeat, '79 196
Piccalilli, Kentucky, '81 216
Plums, Brandied, '97 176
Pomegranate Syrup, '96 241
Relish, Green Tomato, '98 124
Sauerkraut, Homemade, '81 216
Squash Pickles, '97 119
Squash, Summer, '80 127; '85 105
Succotash, '85 106
Sugar Snap Peas, Pickled, '01 112
Tomatoes, '80 128; '85 106
Tomatoes, Canned Flavored, '95 217
Tomatoes, Stewed, '83 182
Tomatoes with Okra, '85 106
Tomato Juice, Spicy, '85 189
Tomato Puree, Seasoned, '83 182
Vegetable Soup, '80 128; '85 106
Vegetables, Pickled Confetti, '00 133
CANTALOUPE. *See* **MELONS.**
CARAMEL
Apples, Black-and-White Caramel, '03 M216
Apples, Calypso Caramel, '03 M216
Apples, Caramel, '79 220; '89 M231; '03 M216
Apples, Caramel-Peanut, '93 M244
Apples, Old English Caramel, '85 231
Baked Caramel Good Stuff, '80 284
Bars, Cranberry-Caramel, '98 277
Bars, Gooey Turtle, '96 M189
Bars, Oatmeal-Caramel, '85 247
Bars, Turtle, '00 334
Bars, Yummy, '92 171
Biscuits, Caramel Dessert, '95 36
Bombe, Caramel-Toffee, '93 214; '00 112
Bread, Caramel, '82 75
Brie with Fresh Fruit, Caramel, '90 266
Brownies, Caramel-Pecan Filled, '03 M43
Buns, Caramel Sticky, '00 52
Buns, Overnight Caramel Sticky, '00 52
Cake, Caramel, '89 55; '90 307
Cake, Caramel-Filled Butter Pecan, '88 278
Cake, Caramel-Glazed Pear, '02 196
Cake, Caramel Pound, '98 194
Cake, Chocolate-Caramel-Nut, '83 23
Cake, Creamy Caramel Layer, '81 71
Cake, Turtle, '03 287
Cheesecake, Chocolate-Caramel-Pecan,
'91 197
Cheesecake, Peach-Caramel, '02 M158
Chocolate Caramels, '91 35
Chocolate-Dipped Caramels, '02 30

Cobbler, Peach-Caramel, '86 300; '87 178
Cobbler with Bourbon-Pecan Ice Cream, Caramel-
Applesauce, '00 260
Cobbler with Oatmeal Muffin Crust, Caramel Apple-
Pear, '04 201
Coconut-Macadamia Caramels, '98 305
Cookies, Caramel-Filled Chocolate, '92 319;
'02 53
Cookies, Peanut Butter-Toffee Turtle, '02 M325
Corn, Baked Caramel, '81 218
Corn Candy, Caramel, '84 243
Corn, Caramel, '88 64
Corn, Crispy Caramel, '04 112
Corn, Nutty Caramel, '92 317
Corn, Oven-Made Caramel, '91 233
Crème d'Ange, '83 91
Crunch, Caramel, '95 165
Custard, Caramel, '01 237
Dessert, Coconut-Caramel, '92 44
Dessert, Turtle, '04 127
Dip, Apple, '96 M190
Drizzle, Caramel, '86 247
Filling, Caramel, '88 278; '03 287
Filling, Caramel Whipped Cream, '96 312
Flans, Caramel-Crowned, '90 227
Flan with Caramel, Baked, '92 231
Fondue, Caramel, '94 331; '95 35
French Toast, Caramel-Pecan, '03 328
French Toast, Caramel-Soaked, '03 307
Frosting, Caramel, '81 278, M289; '82 314; '83 43;
'84 39, 263; '86 239; '87 265; '89 55, 236;
'90 307; '98 195; '00 52; '03 329
Frosting, Creamy Caramel, '81 71
Frosting, Double Chocolate Brownies with Caramel,
'04 M220
Frosting, Easy Caramel, '87 39
Frosting, Favorite Caramel, '83 106
Frosting, Quick Caramel, '04 55
Fudge, Caramel, '91 273
Glaze, Caramel, '98 195; '02 196
Grahams, Caramel-Apple, '04 M183
Helado, Caramel-Vanilla (Caramel-Vanilla Ice
Cream), '81 67
Ice Cream Dessert, Caramel, '95 36
Ice Cream, No-Cook Turtle, '04 M179
Ice Cream, Pecan-Caramel Crunch, '02 322
Millionaires, '79 M262; '97 M55
Millionaires, Texas, '00 291
Napoleons, Caramel-Apple, '01 M313
O's, Caramel, '99 M196
Peaches, Caramel, '93 134
Pecan Triangles, Caramel-, '99 281
Pie, Burnt Caramel, '82 53
Pie, Caramel, '96 72
Pie, Caramel-Banana, '86 M165
Pie, Caramel Ice Cream, '82 181
Pie, Caramel Meringue, '97 109
Pie, Caramel-Nut Crunch, '94 244
Pie, Caramel-Peanut, '86 259
Pie, Caramel-Pecan, '88 282
Pie, Caramel-Pecan Apple, '85 247
Pie, Cracked Caramel-Pumpkin, '99 254
Pie, Luscious Caramel Banana, '79 115
Pie, Maverick Lunar, '98 111
Pies, Coconut-Caramel, '87 260
Popcorn, Caramel, '79 219; '86 M212
Popcorn, Caramel Crunch, '96 255
Popcorn Clusters, Caramel-Nut, '00 M223
Popcorn, Crispy Caramel, '85 247
Ring, Caramel-Orange Coffee, '80 45
Ring, Easy Caramel, '85 M89
Rolls, Caramel Breakfast, '79 193
Rolls, Caramel-Nut, '86 312
Rolls, Easy Caramel, '90 195

Sauce, Caramel, '79 79; '91 56, 180; '93 210, 235,
296; '94 234; '95 308; '96 284, 310; '97 178;
'00 52, 256; '01 313; '03 194; '04 249
Sauce, Caramel-Raisin, '88 127
Sauce, Easy Caramel, '87 38
Sauce, Pears with Orange-Caramel, '95 281
Sauce, Steaks with Caramel-Brandy, '03 56
Sauce, The Best Ever Caramel, '03 216
Sauce, Toffee-Fudge, '89 95
Sauce, White Caramel, '92 195; '99 28
Shortcakes, Caramel-Apple, '03 194
Soft-and-Chewy Caramels, '03 297
Squares, Caramel-Peanut, '85 247
Squares, Chocolate-Caramel Layer, '79 83
Sticky Buns, Easy Caramel-Chocolate, '95 36
Surprise, Caramel, '88 202
Syrup, Caramel, '82 43
Syrup, Citrus Compote with Caramel, '98 313
Tart, Caramel Turtle Truffle, '93 M131
Tarts, Caramel, '82 43
Tarts, Tiny Caramel, '99 179
Torte, Caramel-Sweet Potato, '96 312
Torte, Peanut Butter Turtle, '04 316
Torte, X-Treme Chocolate Double Nut Caramel
Ladyfinger, '04 M315
Waffles with Apples and Caramel, Gingerbread,
'98 M237
CARROTS
Aloha Carrots, '85 261
Ambrosia, Carrot-Marshmallow, '80 5
Apricot Carrots, '84 6
Asparagus, Sunshine Carrots and, '99 277
Aspic, Orange-and-Carrot, '86 199
Baby Carrots, Balsamic, '02 43
Baby Carrots, Zucchini with, '88 24
Bake, Apple-Carrot, '93 304
Bake, Carrot-Apple, '98 232
Bake, Creamy Carrot, '85 67
Ball, Carrot-Cheese, '86 325
Balls, Carrot, '79 178
Beef à la Mode, '98 122
Bourbon Carrots, '03 295
Bourbonnaise, Baby Carrots, '85 89
Braised Carrots and Celery, '86 327
Braised Carrots, Apples, and Celery, '96 107
Braised Red Cabbage, '99 243
Brandied Carrots, '87 253
Brandy Sauce, Carrots in, '83 86
Breads
Carrot Bread, '89 143
Cornbread, Carrot, '80 89; '81 163
Muffins, Apple-Carrot, '91 213
Muffins, Carrot-and-Raisin, '87 24
Muffins, Carrot-Date-Nut, '86 262
Muffins, Carrot-Pineapple, '81 6
Muffins, Carrot-Wheat, '88 9
Muffins, Carrot-Zucchini, '01 200
Muffins, Morning Glory, '93 327
Pineapple Bread, Carrot-, '82 210
Pineapple-Carrot Bread, '79 106
Tasty Carrot Bread, '84 328
Three-C Bread, '81 284
Walnut Bread, Carrot-, '88 284
Zucchini-Carrot Bread, '83 190
Brisket, Aunt Suzi's, '02 321
Brussels Sprouts, Carrots and, '82 300
Buttered Carrots and Celery, '89 44
Cakes. *See* **CARROTS/Desserts.**
Caprice, Carrots, '84 6
Cardamom Carrots, '89 271
Casserole, Carrot, '86 279; '87 285
Casserole, Carrot and Zucchini, '83 256
Casserole, Carrot-Pecan, '93 44; '98 231; '02 282
Casserole, Cauliflower-and-Carrot, '83 280

Casserole, Scrumptious Carrot, '84 328
Casserole, Squash-Carrot, '81 157
Casserole, Zucchini-Carrot, '99 61
Celeriac and Carrots, '91 219
Chicken, Sweet-and-Sour, '97 325
Chowchow, Carrot, '93 218
Classy Carrots, '94 36
Coleslaw, Best Barbecue, '97 214
Coleslaw, Memphis-Style, '98 104
Combo, Carrot, '79 45
Cooler, Apricot-Orange-Carrot, '96 108
Cooler, Carrot, '89 35
Curried Carrots and Pineapple, '90 228
Desserts
  Cake, Applesauce Carrot, '81 202
  Cake, Best Carrot, '97 230
  Cake, Best Carrot Sheet, '03 55
  Cake, Blue Ribbon Carrot, '81 70
  Cake, Brownie Carrot, '92 120
  Cake, Carrot, '79 45; '82 137; '84 315; '98 275
  Cake, Carrot Pound, '87 41
  Cake, Carrot Pudding, '83 24
  Cake, Carrot-Raisin, '01 58
  Cake, Cheater's Carrot, '96 20
  Cake, Coconut-Pecan Carrot, '84 322
  Cake, Easy Carrot, '83 215
  Cake, Easy Carrot Snack, '82 235
  Cake, Fresh Coconut-Carrot, '80 299
  Cake, Frosted Carrot, '92 19
  Cake, German Carrot-Hazelnut, '97 230
  Cake, Old-Fashioned Carrot, '83 M232; '97 330
  Cake, Old-Fashioned Carrot Sheet, '97 330
  Cake, Old-South Carrot, '80 120
  Cake, Pecan-Carrot, '99 223
  Cake, Praline-Filled Carrot, '03 332
  Cake, Quick-and-Easy Carrot, '84 150
  Cake, Shortcut Carrot, '02 83
  Cakes, Miniature Carrot, '90 94
  Cake, Spiced Carrot, '87 296
  Cake, Spicy Fruited Carrot, '85 117
  Cakes with Madeira Syrup and Vanilla Ice Cream, Carrot, '98 247
  Cake with Candied Cream, Spiced Ginger, '04 300
  Cake, Zucchini-Carrot, '93 20
  Cookies, Carrot, '82 137
  Cookies, Carrot-Orange, '83 149
  Cookies, Frosted Carrot, '81 7
  Cupcakes, Carrot-Bran, '82 16
  Loaf, Carrot-Nut, '83 117
  Pie, Carrot, '83 117
  Pie, Carrot Custard, '79 45
  Pie, Carrot Ice Cream, '86 200
  Squares, Carrot, '79 256
  Squares, Golden Carrot-Lemon, '80 40
Deviled Carrots, '83 322
Dilled Baby Carrots, '84 80; '92 145
Dilled Carrots, '85 24; '90 17
Dilled Carrots and Green Beans, '99 223
Dill-Spiced Carrots, '87 200
Dilly Carrots, '85 85
Fillets, Apple-Carrot Stuffed, '88 M192
Fried Carrot Balls, '82 16
Fried Carrots, Crispy, '94 36
Garden Surprise, '83 112
Ginger Carrots, '83 9; '85 139
Gingered Carrots, '85 95; '92 302
Glazed
  Apricot Glazed Carrots, '80 89
  Apricot-Glazed Carrots, '98 231; '01 212
  Baby Carrots, Glazed, '91 291; '92 256
  Baby Carrots, Mint-Glazed, '89 102
  Bacon and Onion, Glazed Carrots with, '87 200; '02 283

Brown Sugar-Glazed Carrots, '99 24
Brussels Sprouts and Baby Carrots, Glazed, '97 302
Candied Carrots, '82 269; '83 225
Ginger Carrots, '83 9
Ginger-Cinnamon Carrots, '93 168
Gingered Carrots, '85 95
Ginger-Glazed Carrots, '87 68
Glazed Carrots, '81 304; '83 117; '85 258; '88 304; '89 106, 235
Golden Carrots, '85 267
Grapes, Glazed Carrots with, '82 287
Harvard Carrots, '83 117
Honey-Glazed Carrots, '80 115; '84 121; '85 18; '92 229; '99 63
Honey-Kissed Carrots, '84 122
Horseradish Glaze, Carrots with, '85 66
Lemon-Glazed Carrots, '84 16
Light Glazed Carrots, '92 227
Mint-Glazed Carrots and Peas, '90 291
Onions, Glazed Carrots and, '83 25; '87 128
Orange-Glazed Carrots, '79 12; '81 M165; '90 M98
Orange-Raisin Carrots, '80 24
Parsnips, Glazed Carrots and, '02 129
Peach-Glazed Carrots, '90 13
Pepper Jelly-Glazed Carrots, '02 291
Pineapple Carrots, '83 198
Rutabaga, Lemon-Glazed Carrots and, '97 46
Spice-Glazed Carrots, '83 M58
Sunshine Carrots, '82 16
Hash Browns, Carrot, '96 107
Herbed Carrots and Onions, '87 31
Honey, Carrots with, '02 59
Horseradish Sauce, Carrots and Broccoli with, '91 246
Julienne Carrots, How to Prepare, '84 120
Julienne Carrots, Sautéed, '82 91
Julienne Carrots with Walnuts, '84 188
Julienne, Tarragon Carrots, '84 329
Julienne, Turnips and Carrots, '86 295
Julienne Zucchini and Carrots, '90 14
Lemon-Carrot Bundles, '91 80
Lemon Carrots, '82 300; '83 111
Madeira, Carrots, '80 125; '83 281
Marinated Beets, Green Beans, and Carrots, '88 162
Marinated Carrots, '86 108, 111; '91 103
Marinated Carrots, Creamy, '87 200
Marinated Carrots, Crispy, '81 7
Marinated Carrots, Crunchy, '02 197
Marinated Carrot Strips, '88 176
Marmalade, Carrot-Citrus, '81 148
Marmalade, Carrot-Orange, '03 134
Marmalemon, Carrot, '96 107
Marsala, Carrots, '83 56
Mash, Rutabaga-Carrot, '02 275
Medley, Carrot-and-Leek, '88 102
Medley, Carrot-Lima-Squash, '80 123
Medley, Parsnip-Carrot, '96 36
Minted Carrots, '81 101
Minted Carrots, Saucy, '82 252
Orange Carrots and Turnips, Sunset, '94 213
Orange Carrots, Julienned, '04 297
Orange-Fennel Carrots, '92 133
Orange Sauce, Carrots in, '82 107
Orange-Spiced Carrots, '88 18
Orangy Carrot Strips, '89 312
Parsleyed Turnips and Carrots, '79 253
Patties, Carrot, '80 89
Pecans, Carrots and Celery with, '84 254
Peppers, Carrot-and-Cabbage Stuffed, '99 63
Pickled Carrots, '93 12
Pie, Cauliflower-Carrot, '82 191
Polynesian, Carrots, '79 45

Pudding, Carrot-Potato, '94 279
Puff, Carrot, '84 328; '89 89
Puffs, Carrot, '87 200
Puree, Carrot-and-Sweet Potato, '94 56
Puree, Carrot-Sweet Potato, '92 90; '00 M32; '02 M285
Relish, Carrot, '03 67
Ring, Festive Carrot, '82 16
Ring, Rice-Carrot, '79 246
Roasted Carrots, '92 340
Roasted Celery Root, Carrots, and Onions, '98 293
Roasted Potatoes, Carrots, and Leeks, '94 276
Rosemary Carrots, '91 219
Salad, Apple-Carrot, '85 22
Salad, Broccoli, Cauliflower, and Carrot, '04 140
Salad, Carrot, '82 137
Salad, Carrot-Ambrosia, '81 252
Salad, Carrot-and-Dill, '02 129; '03 99
Salad, Carrot-and-Zucchini, '83 240
Salad, Carrot-Broccoli, '99 26
Salad, Carrot-Caraway, '89 105
Salad, Carrot-Pineapple, '91 83
Salad, Carrot-Raisin, '83 117; '84 174; '87 10
Salad, Carrot-Tangerine, '83 316; '84 16
Salad, Creamy Carrot-Nut, '86 331
Salad, Favorite Carrot, '80 33
Salad, Fruity Carrot-and-Seed, '86 223
Salad, Harvest Carrot, '89 128
Salad, Honey-Sweet Carrot, '89 161
Salad, Lime-Carrot, '92 65
Salad, Orange-Carrot, '80 89; '84 325
Salad, Shredded Carrot, '80 178
Salad, Simple Carrot, '82 101; '84 152
Salad, Sunny Day, '96 90
Salad, Sunshine Carrot, '82 132
Salad, Sweet-and-Sour Carrot, '98 211
Salad, Turkey-Carrot, '86 283
Salad, Turnip-and-Carrot, '91 212
Salad with Orange-Nutmeg Dressing, Carrot-Raisin, '97 305; '98 19
Saucy Carrots, '87 41
Sauté, Carrot-Turnip, '93 241
Sautéed Zucchini and Carrots, '92 62, 99
Savory Sauce, Lima Beans and Carrots with, '84 196
Scalloped Carrots, '81 6; '96 107; '02 129; '03 99
Scalloped Carrots-and-Celery, '84 M112
Scalloped Carrots, Cheese, '94 36
Slaw, Apple-Carrot, '92 243
Slaw, Shredded Celery Root-and-Carrot, '98 293
Soufflé, Carrot, '79 73; '98 231; '99 25; '01 84, 284
Soufflé, Carrots, '83 265
Soufflés, Carrot, '96 309
Soup, Carrot, '80 88; '89 146; '98 123
Soup, Carrot-and-Leek, '02 260
Soup, Carrot Cream, '90 210
Soup, Carrot-Leek, '86 34
Soup, Carrot-Orange, '79 172
Soup, Cheesy Carrot, '81 262
Soup, Chilled Carrot-Mint, '90 M168
Soup, Cream of Carrot, '81 307; '88 46; '91 69
Soup, Cream of Carrot-and-Tomato, '94 176
Soup, Creamy Carrot, '92 218
Soup, Curried Carrot, '82 157
Soup, Gingered Carrot-and-Parsnip, '03 221
Soup, Potato-Carrot, '88 297
Soup, Savory Carrot, '84 107
Soup with Parslied Croutons, Carrot-and-Butternut Squash, '97 217
Special Carrots, '81 108; '84 6
Spiced Carrots Polynesian, '88 85
Spread, Carrot-Pecan, '96 108
Spread, Feta-and-Apple, '99 106
Spread, Nutty Carrot, '94 123

CARROTS

(continued)

Squash, Stuffed, '98 177
Steamed Carrots, Lemon-Dill, '93 180
Sticks, Carrot, '89 106
Stir-Fry, Beef-and-Carrot, '98 335
Stir-Fry, Turnip-and-Carrot, '96 36
Stuffed Carrots, '86 324; '87 40
Sugar Snaps and Carrots, Creamed, '93 139
Sunshine Carrots, '82 16; '83 25
Supreme, Broccoli-Carrot, '89 331
Swamp Sticks, '95 274
Sweet-and-Sour Carrots, '82 137
Sweet-and-Sour Green Beans and Carrots, '83 6
Sweet 'n' Hot Green Beans and Carrots, '00 211
Tarragon Carrots, '83 173
Tipsy Carrots, '87 40
Toss, Asparagus-Carrot-Squash, '91 45
Toss, Carrot-Fruit, '82 235
Tropical Carrots, '84 34
Veal and Carrots, Company, '85 22
Veal and Carrots in Wine Sauce, '81 31; '86 M139
White Wine, Carrots in, '81 109
Wine Sauce, Carrots in, '80 88
Zesty Carrots, '84 5
Zucchini and Carrots, Buttered, '83 252
Zucchini, Carrots and, '84 262

CASSEROLES. *See also* **LASAGNA.**

Apple-Cheese Casserole, '84 287
Barley, Baked, '91 133
Barley Casserole, '84 281

Bean

Baked Bean Medley, '80 100
Baked Beans, Hawaiian-Style, '86 210
Baked Beans, Maple Heights, '91 223
Baked Beans Quintet, '94 100
Baked Beans, Three-Meat, '86 210
Baked Beans with Ham, '80 136
Beef-and-Bean Bake, Cheesy, '82 89
Beef, Bean, and Cornbread Casserole, '99 215
Black Beans, Casserole of, '95 27
Chuck Wagon Bean Casserole, '93 198
Cornbread Casserole, Bean-and-, '92 243
Five-Bean Bake, '03 139
Green Bean and Artichoke Casserole, Italian,
  '85 81
Green Bean-and-Corn Casserole, '88 123; '99 36
Green Bean Casserole, '79 106; '84 145; '02 197
Green Bean Casserole, Easy, '87 284
Green Bean Italiano, '94 248
Green Bean Salad, Hot, '86 298
Green Beans au Gratin, '80 116
Green Beans, Baked, '91 159
Green Beans, French Quarter, '80 298; '81 26
Green Beans, Herbed, '83 M147
Green Beans in Sour Cream, '80 116
Green Beans, Italian, '85 147
Green Beans Italian, '87 10
Green Bean Surprise, '86 9
Green Beans with Sour Cream, '82 90
Kidney Bean Casserole, '90 136
Lentils with Cheese, Baked, '84 113
Lima-Bacon Bake, '86 9
Lima Bean Casserole, '79 189; '83 313; '86 225;
  '87 284; '95 132
Lima Bean Casserole, Spicy, '79 189
Lima Bean Casserole, Swiss, '80 191
Lima Bean Garden Casserole, '83 218; '84 246
Lima Beans Deluxe, '79 289; '80 26
Lima Beans, Savory, '83 219; '84 246
Lima Beans, Super, '79 189
Lima Beans with Canadian Bacon, '83 219; '84 245

Lima Casserole, Ham and, '79 192
Limas, Spanish Cheese, '86 225
Mexican Bean Casserole, Spicy, '84 114
Three-Bean Bake, '81 155; '03 106
Three-Bean Casserole, '88 56
White Bean Bake, Turnip Greens and, '94 246

Breakfast and Brunch

Apple-Egg Casserole, '85 44
Bacon and Egg Casserole, '81 225
Bacon-and-Egg Casserole, '03 166
Bacon-and-Eggs Scramble, '80 M267
Bacon-and-Ham Casserole, Cheesy, '01 256
Breakfast Casserole, '91 285; '99 273;
  '01 130, 243
Breakfast, Mexican, '00 194
Brie-and-Sausage Breakfast Casserole, '00 284;
  '03 36
Broccoli-Cheese Breakfast Casserole, '99 233
Brunch Casserole, '82 124
Bunch, Brunch for a, '88 57
Campfire Casserole, '00 173
Cheese-and-Egg Casserole, '99 268
Cheese Blintz Casserole, '92 251
Cheesy Breakfast Casserole, '85 247
Cheesy Brunch Casserole, Easy, '92 91
Chile-Hominy Casserole, '81 29
Chile 'n' Cheese Breakfast Casserole, '88 57
Christmas Morning Strata, '95 282
Corned Beef Brunch Bake, '82 44
Cornmeal Puff, '82 42
Cranberry-Apple Casserole, '83 311
Creole Sauce, Brunch Casserole with, '98 98
Egg-and-Bacon Casserole, '85 248
Egg-and-Cheese Casserole, '84 293
Egg-and-Cheese Puff, '85 45
Egg Casserole, '83 311; '98 98
Egg Casserole, Brunch, '86 329
Egg Casserole, Cheesy, '81 244; '86 15
Egg Casserole, Saucy Scrambled, '89 213
Egg Casserole, Scrambled, '80 51; '86 241
Egg Casserole, Sunday, '95 100
Egg-Mushroom Casserole, '83 49
Eggs Bel-Mar, '90 92
Eggs, Brunch, '98 93
Eggs, Bruncheon, '83 83
Eggs, Chile, '88 80
Eggs, Creole, '82 42
Eggs, Layered, '96 97
Egg Soufflé Casserole, '83 55
Enchiladas, Breakfast, '04 281
English Muffin Breakfast Strata, '03 100
Fruit Bake, Hot, '81 270
Grits, Baked Cheese-and-Garlic, '83 292
Grits, Baked Garlic-and-Herb, '01 326
Grits Bake, Santa Fe, '00 123
Grits Casserole, Cheesy, '81 270
Grits Casserole, Garlic, '81 47
Grits, Chili-Cheese, '01 86
Grits, Garlic, '00 194
Grits, Garlic-Cheese, '86 180; '99 270; '00 215
Grits, Jalapeño-Cheese, '00 239; '01 328
Grits, Mexican Cheese, '02 34
Grits, Orange, '81 47
Grits-Sausage Casserole, '84 75; '86 241
Grits, Swiss-and-Cheddar Baked, '91 71
Ham and Egg Casserole, Breakfast, '79 253
Hash Brown Breakfast Casserole, '03 306
Hash Brown Cheese Bake, '82 50
Hash Brown-Ham-Cheese Bake, '97 323
Hash Brown Potato Casserole, '81 40
Hominy, Gold Coast, '83 52
Huevos Rancheros, '82 197
Italian Brunch Casserole, '03 29
Mexican Breakfast, '00 194

Potato Breakfast Casserole, '80 52
Sausage-and-Egg Casserole, '94 284
Sausage Breakfast Casserole, '81 270
Sausage Brunch, Italian, '88 57
Sausage Casserole, Hawaiian, '85 42
Sausage Casserole, Swiss, '80 209
Sausage-Cheese Bake, '88 58
Sausage, Country Grits and, '83 54
Sausage Egg Bake, '81 225
Sausage-Egg Bake, Smoked, '85 248
Sausage-Egg Casserole, '86 M12
Sausage-Ham Breakfast Casserole, '01 54;
  '04 332
Sausage-Hash Brown Breakfast Casserole,
  '03 218
Sausage-Mushroom Breakfast Casserole, '86 95
Sausage-Spud Bake, Sunday Night Spicy Cheesy,
  '03 331
Sausage Strata, '83 243
Southwestern Brunch Casserole, '03 197
Broccoli-Ham au Gratin, '90 239
Brown Rice Casserole, '87 118
Cajun Casserole, Ragin', '02 199
Cannelloni, '92 17
Cheese Bake, Continental, '81 89
Cheese Casserole, Feather-Light, '79 84
Cheese Casserole, Four, '92 170
Chile-Cheese Casserole, '82 90
Chiles Rellenos Casserole, '79 84; '92 18
Chili Casserole, '90 176
Chili-Rice Casserole, '79 54
Chili-Tamale Pie, '83 68
Cornbread-Chili Strata, '03 100
Egg and Rice Bake, '83 119
Eggplant-and-Oyster Louisiane, '95 196
Eggplant-Sausage-Pasta Casserole, Freezer, '95 197
Enchilada Casserole, '87 287
Enchilada Casserole, Easy, '02 143
Enchilada Casserole, Green, '79 76
Franks, Mexican, '93 78
Fruit Casserole, Sherried, '80 284
Fruit, Gingered Baked, '81 232
Grits, Garlicky Ham-and-Spinach, '94 177
Grits Italiano, '92 43
Grits with Green Chiles, Cheese, '95 208
Hominy-and-Corn Casserole, '97 291
Hominy Casserole, Cheesy, '83 170
Hominy Casserole), Four-Part Hominy (Cheesy,
  '96 158
Hominy-Chili Casserole, '86 255
Hominy, Hot Cheese, '84 77
Hominy, Jalapeño, '82 51
Hominy with Chiles and Cheese, '86 78
Italian Casserole, '90 238
Kale, Scalloped, '86 224
Lentils-and-Rice Casserole, '93 301
Mac and Texas Cheeses with Roasted Chiles,
  '04 207
Macaroni and Blue Cheese, '93 248
Macaroni and Cheese, '00 273
Macaroni-and-Cheese Bake, '01 41
Macaroni and Cheese, Baked, '00 271; '02 26;
  '03 184
Macaroni and Cheese, Caramelized Onion, '04 231
Macaroni and Cheese, Creamy, '93 249; '02 26
Macaroni and Cheese, Divine, '99 314
Macaroni and Cheese, Eleanor's, '97 253
Macaroni and Cheese, Golden, '04 24
Macaroni and Cheese, Italian, '04 327
Macaroni and Cheese, Old-Fashioned, '92 215
Macaroni and Cheese, Quick-and-Easy, '00 15
Macaroni and Cheese, Souper, '00 92
Macaroni and Cheese, Spicy Tomato, '03 68
Macaroni and Cheese, Tex-Mex, '00 92

Macaroni and Cheese, Thick-and-Rich, '84 329
Macaroni Bake, Jack-in-the-, '93 249
Macaroni Casserole, '84 220; '87 154
Macaroni, Extra Cheesy, '00 92
Macaroni, Glorious, '84 76
Macaroni, Gorgonzola, '97 28
Macaroni, Mexican, '96 73
Macaroni Mousse, '96 73
Macaroni-Mushroom Bake, '97 96
Macaroni-Mushroom Bake, Cheesy, '81 243
Macaroni, Three-Cheese, '00 M92
Macaroni with Blue Cheese and Walnuts, '02 M208
Manicotti, Make-Ahead, '98 68
Meat. *See also* **CASSEROLES/Pork.**
Beef-and-Bean Bake, Cheesy, '82 89
Beef-and-Biscuit Casserole, '83 75
Beef-and-Noodles Casserole, '84 72
Beef-and-Vegetable Chow Mein Casserole, '83 313
Beef Bake, Zesty Cabbage, '80 300
Beef Bake, Zucchini, '86 146
Beef, Bean, and Cornbread Casserole, '99 215
Beef Casserole, '01 199
Beef Casserole, Crusty, '82 88
Beef Casserole, Easy, '00 208
Beef Casserole, Macaroni-Cheese-, '95 125
Beef Casserole, Spinach and, '79 192
Beef, Cheese, and Noodle Casserole, '99 58
Beef Lombardi, '03 214
Beef-Macaroni Bake, '94 255
Beef-Macaroni Combo, '79 194
Beef-Noodle Bake, Taco, '81 141
Beef Supreme, '83 196
Beefy Sausage Dinner, '80 M9
Beefy Vegetable Casserole, '79 248
Cavatini, '94 214
Cheeseburger Casserole, '95 255
Cheesy Mexican Casserole, '82 224
Chiles Rellenos Casserole, '79 84; '84 31, 234;
    '92 18; '98 48
Chili and Enchiladas, '00 55
Chili Casserole, Ultimate, '99 239
Chili Hominy Bake, '81 282; '82 58
Chili Manicotti, '99 239
Cornbread Casserole, '81 91
Cornbread Skillet Casserole, '83 243; '84 101
Cornbread Tamale Bake, '79 163
Corned Beef and Cabbage au Gratin, '83 16
County Fair Casserole, '79 130
El Dorado Casserole, '81 140
Enchilada Casserole, Firecracker, '80 260
Enchilada Casserole, Sour Cream, '82 113
Fajita Casserole, '97 96
Five-Layer Meal, '81 140
Frankaroni Potluck Dish, '88 201
Franks 'n' Beans, Stove-Top, '88 201
Ground Beef and Sausage Casserole, '80 260
Ground Beef-and-Tomato Manicotti, '03 257
Ground Beef Casserole, Cheesy, '79 44
Ground Beef Casserole, Creamy, '81 142
Hamburger-Bean Bake, '95 121
Hamburger Casserole, '95 210
Hamburger-Corn Bake, '99 58
Hamburger-Noodle Bake, '81 140
Hamburger Pie, '81 92
Hot Doggie Casserole, '88 200
Italian Casserole, '80 81
Italian Casserole, Light, '03 198
Italian-Style Meat and Potatoes, '03 97
Layered Grecian Bake, '82 119
Linguine with Meat Sauce, Baked, '01 41
Linguine with Meat Sauce Casserole, '03 22
Manicotti, Meaty Stuffed, '00 19
Matador Mania, '86 19
Mexican Casserole, '00 280

Mexican Casserole, Cabin, '97 95
Moussaka, '87 166; '90 68; '97 94
Moussaka Casserole, '79 179
Moussaka, Corn, '87 190
Pasta Florentine, Layered, '00 56
Pastichio, '85 194
Pastitsio, '87 12; '88 11; '99 167
Pizza Bake, Upside-Down, '98 224
Pizza Casserole, '88 273; '89 181
Pizza Casserole, Quick, '83 266
Rotini, Baked, '01 185
Sausage-Ham Breakfast Casserole, '04 332
Shells, Spinach-Stuffed, '99 64
Sloppy Joe Squares, '97 95
Sour Cream-Noodle Bake, '79 55
Spaghetti and Beef Casserole, '79 129
Spaghetti Casserole, '84 241
Spaghetti, Casserole, '95 132
Spinach and Beef Casserole, '79 192
Spinach-Beef-Macaroni Casserole, '83 313
Stroganoff Casserole, '98 48
Swiss Steak, Pizza, '02 36
Taco Bake, '97 326
Taco Beef-Noodle Bake, '81 141
Taco Casserole, '80 33
Taco Squares, Deep-Dish, '91 88
Tamale, Mozzarella, '95 70
Tortilla Bake, Texas, '94 285
Veal and Wild Rice Casserole, '79 180
Veal Cutlet Casserole, '79 109
Venison-Vegetable Bake, '87 304
Ziti, Baked, '94 65
Microwave
Asparagus-Pea Casserole, '88 M294
Beans-and-Franks, Polynesian, '84 M11
Beef Casserole, Easy, '86 M58
Beef Casserole, Layered, '82 M203
Beefy Sausage Dinner, '80 M9
Broccoli Casserole, '88 M146
Broccoli-Swiss Cheese Casserole, '85 M211
Carrots-and-Celery, Scalloped, '84 M112
Chicken Divan, '80 M10
Chicken Divan Casserole, '82 M203
Chicken Mexicana, '91 M127
Chicken Tetrazzini, Cheesy, '83 M87
Green Beans, Herbed, '83 M147
Ham-and-Potato Casserole, '83 M87
Ham-Asparagus Dinner, '80 M10
Ham Roll Casserole, '91 M127
Macaroni-Ham Casserole, '81 M177
Macaroni with Blue Cheese and Walnuts, '02 M208
Mexican Casserole, '92 M22
Mexican Casserole, Microwave, '90 M231
Mexi Casserole, '83 M87
Okra and Tomatoes, Fresh, '81 M165
Onion-Potato Bake, '83 M195
Pineapple, Scalloped, '84 M323
Pizza Casserole, Microwave, '89 M248
Pork Casserole, Cheesy, '81 M74
Potato Casserole, Creamy, '84 M113
Potatoes, Parmesan, '90 M62
Sausage and Rice Casserole, Oriental, '82 M123
Sausage Casserole, Easy, '87 M189
Sausage-Egg Casserole, '86 M12
Sausage Jambalaya Casserole, '82 M203
Spinach Delight, '84 M144
Squash Bake, Cheddar-, '84 M113
Squash Casserole, Cheesy, '82 M21
Squash Casserole, Jiffy, '81 M144
Squash Medley, Fresh, '81 M165
Tuna Casserole, Easy, '82 M203
Turkey Casserole, Crunchy, '89 M282
Zucchini-Egg Casserole, '84 M113
Zucchini, Italian, '83 M147

Mostaccioli Casserole, '04 316
Noodle Casserole, Sweet, '02 238
Orzo, Mozzarella-and-Olive, '97 249
Paella Casserole, '95 254
Pasta Bake, Cheesy, '02 161
Pasta Bake, Layered, '04 326
Pasta Casseroles, Hot Brown, '96 290
Pasta Italiano, '01 41
Pasta Shells Florentine, '00 326
Pineapple Bake, '79 251; '96 84
Pineapple, Baked, '84 287
Pineapple, Scalloped, '79 106
Pork
Bacon-and-Ham Casserole, Cheesy, '01 256
Casserole, Pork, '83 116
Chop Casserole, Peppered Pork, '81 235; '82 25;
    '83 39
Chop Casserole, Pork, '94 255
Chops and Potato Scallop, Pork, '82 114
Chops Italiano, Pork, '80 72
Chop-Vegetable Casserole, Pork, '90 208
Fiesta Pork Bake, '79 265
Frankfurter Casserole, Layered, '79 64
Franks, Family-Style, '79 54
Ham and Broccoli Casserole, '81 133
Ham and Broccoli Strata, '80 261
Ham-and-Cheese Casserole, '87 78
Ham-and-Cheese Layered Casserole, '98 160
Ham and Lima Casserole, '79 192
Ham and Noodle Casserole, '80 300
Ham-and-Potato Casserole, '96 103
Ham-and-Potato Casserole, Cheesy, '84 326
Ham-and-Rice Casserole, '84 75
Ham-and-Swiss Casserole, Savory, '01 308
Ham and Turkey Bake, Layered, '79 252
Ham Bake, Harvest, '79 210
Ham-Broccoli Casserole, Quick, '82 40
Ham Casserole, '96 302; '98 314
Ham Casserole, Apple, '79 213
Ham Casserole, Creamy, '03 83
Ham Casserole, Golden, '82 119
Ham Casserole, Macaroni-, '83 283
Ham Casseroles, Creamy, '01 55
Ham Casserole, Vegetable-and-, '84 91
Ham Medley, Creamy, '84 90
Ham Pie, Golden, '87 78
Ham-Rice-Tomato Bake, '87 78
Ham Strata, '95 308
Ham Strata, Baked, '83 283
Ham Tetrazzini, '84 241; '03 174
Pizza Casserole, Upside-Down, '03 284
Salami-Corn Casserole, '80 209
Sausage and Broccoli Casserole, '80 33
Sausage and Noodle Casserole, '82 123
Sausage-and-Noodle Casserole, '95 255
Sausage-and-Rice Bake, Creole, '88 58
Sausage and Rice Casserole, Oriental, '82 M123
Sausage-and-Tomato Manicotti, Cheesy,
    '03 257
Sausage and Wild Rice Casserole, '83 196
Sausage Bake, Eggplant, '85 221
Sausage Bake, Hominy-, '88 51
Sausage-Bean Supper, '86 52
Sausage Casserole, '81 112; '82 12
Sausage Casserole, Cheesy, '82 124
Sausage Casserole, Country, '79 192
Sausage Casserole, Crunchy, '81 288
Sausage Casserole, Easy, '87 M189
Sausage Casserole, Eggplant-, '84 215
Sausage Casserole, Ground Beef and, '80 260
Sausage Casserole, Skillet, '99 123
Sausage-Chile Rellenos Casserole, '88 52
Sausage-Egg Casserole, '86 M12
Sausage Grits, '86 92

CASSEROLES, Pork
(continued)

Sausage Jambalaya Casserole, **'82** M203
Sausage-Lasagna Rollups, **'80** 236
Sausage-Noodle Bake, **'81** 92
Sausage-Potato Casserole, **'86** 217
Sausage-Rice Casserole, **'82** 50; **'83** 75
Sausages, Baked Zucchini and, **'80** 300
Sausage-Stuffed Shells, **'96** 102
Sausage, Wild Rice and, **'86** 268
Sausage-Wild Rice Casserole, **'84** 250
Sausage Wild Rice Casserole, Turkey-and-,
   '03 239
Spaghetti Bake, Pork, **'81** 11
Spaghetti Casserole, Low-Fat, **'99** 215
Strata, Christmas Morning, **'95** 282
Supper Supreme, Sunday, **'79** 76
Vegetable-Pork Combo, **'85** 113
Poultry
Chicken à la Russell, **'95** 175
Chicken-Almond Casserole, **'94** 199
Chicken-and-Artichoke Casserole, **'96** 133
Chicken and Artichokes, **'03** 26
Chicken-and-Cheese Enchiladas, Baked, **'03** 332
Chicken-and-Chiles Casserole, **'93** 107
Chicken-and-Dressing Casserole, **'81** 263
Chicken and Dressing, Santa Fe, **'03** 48
Chicken and Green Noodle Casserole, **'80** 32
Chicken and Grits, **'95** 263
Chicken-and-Pasta Casserole, **'97** 192
Chicken and Rice, **'95** 54
Chicken and Rice Casserole, **'80** 260
Chicken-and-Rice Casserole, Creamy, **'02** 309
Chicken-and-Rice Casserole, Crispy, **'03** 203
Chicken-and-Rice Casseroles, **'01** 52
Chicken-and-Shrimp Florentine, **'89** 64
Chicken-and-Spinach Enchiladas, **'91** 222
Chicken and Wild Rice, **'79** 248
Chicken-and-Wild Rice Casserole, **'97** 192;
   '00 257
Chicken-and-Wild Rice Casserole, Leslie's
   Favorite, **'00** 209; **'03** 107
Chicken-Asparagus Casserole, **'83** 76; **'84** 71
Chicken Bake, Company, **'80** 301
Chicken Bake, Spicy, **'85** 251
Chicken Bake with Sweet Bacon Dressing,
   Vegetable-, **'93** 108
Chicken, Broccoli, and Cauliflower Casserole,
   '00 337
Chicken-Broccoli Casserole, **'79** 48; **'91** 315
Chicken-Brown Rice Bake, **'91** 314
Chicken Cannelloni with Roasted Red Bell
   Pepper Sauce, **'02** 287
Chicken Casserole, **'96** 103, 302
Chicken Casserole, Broccoli-, **'82** 33
Chicken Casserole, Cheesy, **'85** 34
Chicken Casserole, Chow Mein, **'96** 276
Chicken Casserole D'Iberville, **'04** 182
Chicken Casserole, Hearty Tex-Mex Squash-,
   '99 312; **'03** 107
Chicken Casserole, Jalapeño, **'02** 50
Chicken Casserole, King Ranch, **'00** 280
Chicken Casserole, Light King Ranch, **'04** 57
Chicken Casserole, Macaroni and, **'80** 260
Chicken Casserole, Make-Ahead, **'84** 241
Chicken Casserole, Mexi-, **'93** 69; **'94** 30
Chicken Casserole, Mexican, **'82** 143
Chicken Casserole, Oyster-and-, **'99** 320
Chicken Casserole, Pesto-, **'94** 231
Chicken Casserole, Quick, **'81** 91
Chicken Casserole, Rice-and-, **'87** 154
Chicken Casserole, Simply Good, **'95** 255

Chicken Casserole, Sunday, **'83** 290
Chicken Casserole, Swiss, **'90** 67
Chicken Casserole, Unforgettable, **'04** 294
Chicken Cassoulet, Easy, **'00** 43; **'04** 325
Chicken, Cheesy Mexican, **'01** 199
Chicken Chili Bake, **'93** 302
Chicken Chimichangas, **'93** 68
Chicken Dinner, Hot-and-Spicy, **'94** M94
Chicken Divan, **'80** M10
Chicken Divan Casserole, **'82** M203
Chicken Divan, Curried, **'80** 83
Chicken Divan, Easy, **'94** 310
Chicken Divan, Gourmet, **'82** 83
Chicken Divan, Overnight, **'83** 198
Chicken Divan, Sherried, **'80** 38
Chicken-Eggplant Parmigiana, **'82** 212
Chicken Enchiladas, **'80** 301; **'00** 45; **'03** 214
Chicken Enchiladas, Creamy, **'97** 250; **'01** M94
Chicken Enchiladas, Easy, **'82** 89
Chicken Enchiladas, Three-Cheese, **'99** 330
Chicken Florentine, **'93** 107
Chicken, Fontina-Baked, **'90** 64
Chicken, French Herbed, **'86** 89
Chicken, Garlic-Spinach, **'92** 56
Chicken-Green Bean Casserole, **'85** 296
Chicken-Green Bean Casserole, Creamy, **'97** 158
Chicken, King Ranch, **'95** 193; **'99** 330; **'03** 313
Chicken Lasagna Bake, **'95** 55
Chicken, Lemony Pecan, **'96** 82
Chicken Linguine, **'01** 128
Chicken-Macaroni Casserole, **'85** 219
Chicken Mexicana, **'91** M127
Chicken-Noodle Casserole, **'94** 286
Chicken Noodle Casserole, **'01** 308
Chicken, Orzo, and Spinach Casserole, **'02** 124
Chicken Parmesan, **'04** 42
Chicken Parmigiana, **'80** 190
Chicken Parmigiana, Zesty, **'00** 19
Chicken, Poppy Seed, **'99** 195
Chicken Reuben Casserole, **'03** 69
Chicken-Rice Casserole, **'86** 52; **'99** 215
Chicken-Rice Casserole, Creamy, **'99** 21
Chicken Salad, Baked, **'86** 297
Chicken Sausage and Shiitake Mushrooms,
   Cheese Grits with, **'03** 254
Chicken, Scarborough, **'80** 38
Chicken Skillet Casserole, Spaghetti Squash and,
   '94 134
Chicken-Sour Cream Enchiladas, **'04** 274
Chicken-Spaghetti Casserole, **'84** 15
Chicken Spaghetti, Spicy, **'02** 327
Chicken, Spicy Mexican, **'82** 89
Chicken-Squash Casserole, **'95** 121
Chicken, Stuffed Alfredo, **'04** 56
Chicken Superb Casserole, **'89** 83
Chicken Supreme Casserole, **'84** 219
Chicken Supreme, Hot, **'81** 76
Chicken, Swiss, **'95** 54
Chicken Tetrazzini, **'79** 268; **'80** M75; **'99** 61;
   '00 45; **'02** 171; **'04** 221
Chicken Tetrazzini, Cheesy, **'83** M87
Chicken Thighs, Swiss, **'94** 282
Chicken Tortilla Bake, **'82** 89
Chicken Tortilla Casserole, **'81** 166
Chicken-Wild Rice Casserole, **'84** 241; **'85** 65
Chicken-Wild Rice Supreme, **'79** 77
Chicken with Spinach Fettuccine, Creamy Basil,
   '97 328
Cornish Hens-and-Rice Casserole, **'92** 267
Crêpes Divan, Elegant, **'81** 91
Day-After-the-Holiday Casserole, **'96** 276
Duck and Wild Rice Casserole, **'79** 224
King Ranch Casserole, **'02** 210
Leftovers Casserole, Holiday, **'04** 232

Pollo, Chilaquiles con (Tortillas with Chicken),
   '81 66
Rice Casserole, Mexican, **'83** 31
Shells, Southwestern Stuffed, **'99** 238
Southwestern Casserole, **'99** 216
Turkey-and-Broccoli Casserole, **'86** 332
Turkey-and-Sausage Wild Rice Casserole,
   '03 239
Turkey-and-Shrimp Florentine Casserole, **'92** 122
Turkey-Asparagus Casserole, **'86** 284
Turkey Bake, Layered Ham and, **'79** 252
Turkey Casserole, **'84** 327; **'96** 302
Turkey Casserole, Crunchy, **'89** M282
Turkey Casserole, Golden, **'80** 271
Turkey Casserole, Stuffed, **'88** 246
Turkey-Cheddar-Broccoli Strata, **'03** 100
Turkey Florentine, **'88** 264
Turkey Noodle Bake, **'93** 243
Turkey-Noodle-Poppyseed Casserole, **'90** 239
Turkey-Olive Casserole, **'87** 268
Turkey Parmigiana, **'87** 193
Turkey Salad Bake, **'79** 253
Turkey Salad, Hot, **'86** 297
Turkey-Spinach Casserole, **'84** 71
Turkey-Swiss Casserole, **'86** 283
Turkey Tetrazzini, **'00** 318
Turkey Tetrazzini, Herbed, **'86** 47
Turkey Tetrazzini, Smoked, **'02** 286
Wraps, Southwestern, **'99** 238
Provolone Casserole, Seashell-, **'80** 189
Quiche Casserole, **'95** 33
Ravioli, Mediterranean, **'93** 301
Reuben Casserole, **'90** 240
Rice-and-Cheese con Chiles, **'89** 99
Rice and Green Chiles, **'83** 152
Rice au Gratin Supreme, **'86** 78
Rice, Baked, **'94** 270
Rice, Baked Spicy, **'96** 125
Rice Bake, Green, **'79** 43
Rice Casserole, **'87** 45
Rice Casserole, Chili-, **'79** 54
Rice Casserole, Colorful, **'82** 199
Rice Casserole, Green, **'95** 181
Rice Casserole, Jalapeño, **'81** 66
Rice Casserole, Spanish, **'79** 192
Rice Chantilly, **'86** 82
Rice, Easy Mushroom, **'89** 286
Rice, Fiesta, **'84** 76
Rice, Hot Pepper, **'92** 310
Rice Mélange, **'87** 240
Rice, Mexican, **'85** 147
Rice Pilaf, **'86** 82
Rice, Savannah Red, **'95** 27
Rice, Spanish, **'81** 51; **'90** 183
Rice, Spicy, **'85** 256
Rotini Romano, **'87** 193
Seafood
Crab-and-Mushroom Casserole, **'89** 96
Crab-and-Shrimp Casserole, **'84** 71
Crab and Spinach Casserole, Creamy, **'80** 3
Crab Bake, Quick, **'87** 192
Crab Casserole, **'79** 228
Crab Casserole, Deviled, **'91** 238; **'92** 27
Crab Casserole, Easy, **'93** 270
Crab, Dressed, **'82** 276
Crab-Egg Casserole, **'80** 260
Crab Imperial, **'79** 82, 116
Crab Imperial, Elegant, **'83** 245
Crabmeat-Broccoli Casserole, **'84** 232
Crabmeat Imperial, **'82** 311
Crabmeat with Artichoke Hearts, Creamed,
   '93 26
Crab Puff, **'79** 116
Crab, Shrimp, and Artichoke au Gratin, **'90** 240

Crawfish Lasagna, '91 89
Crawfish Pasta Casserole, '97 106
Fish and Potato Bake, Herbed, '79 287; '80 34
Fish Casserole, Green Chile-and-, '84 32
Miss Hannah's Casserole, '92 236
Oyster-and-Chicken Casserole, '99 320
Oyster-and-Corn Bake, '83 34; '84 44
Oyster-and-Spinach Casserole, '83 34; '84 44
Oyster-and-Wild Rice Casserole, '83 34; '84 44
Oyster Casserole, '79 228
Oyster Casserole, Wild Rice-, '86 256
Oysters Johnny Reb, '82 42
Oysters, Scalloped, '79 225; '84 213; '86 132;
   '95 318; '99 321
Parmesan, Savannah Seafood, '99 312
Salmon Casserole, '81 22
Salmon Florentine, '83 43
Scallop Casserole, '79 228
Seafood Casserole, '87 109; '89 63
Shrimp-and-Chicken Casserole, '91 102
Shrimp-and-Grits Casserole, Cheesy, '03 28
Shrimp-and-Noodle Casserole, '90 240
Shrimp and Rice Casserole, '79 228
Shrimp-and-Rice Casserole, '94 328
Shrimp-and-Scallops Casserole, Creamy, '01 256
Shrimp au Gratin, '85 79
Shrimp Casserole, '85 240
Shrimp Casserole, Chayotes and, '80 230
Shrimp Casserole, Spicy, '96 62
Shrimp-Crab Puff, '79 57
Shrimp Delight, '79 192
Shrimp Enchiladas, '01 104
Shrimp Fettuccine, '96 210
Shrimp Florentine Casserole, Turkey-and-,
   '92 122
Shrimp Manicotti, '97 96
Tuna and Peas in Wine Sauce, Baked, '83 196
Tuna-Broccoli Casserole, Tangy, '83 75
Tuna Casserole, '82 119; '96 103
Tuna Casserole, Biscuit-Topped, '79 113
Tuna Casserole, Easy, '83 255
Tuna Casserole, Nippy, '84 241
Tuna Casserole with Cheese Swirls, '88 256
Tuna Chopsticks, '94 255
Tuna-Macaroni Treat, '82 131
Tuna-Noodle Casserole, Fabulous, '02 63
Tuna Vegetable Casserole, '81 135
Shells and Cheese, Creamy, '01 216
Shells, Southwestern Stuffed, '93 234
Spaghetti-and-Spinach Casserole, '02 199
Spaghetti, Casserole, '95 132
Tamale Casserole, Quick, '94 255
Vegetable. *See also* CASSEROLES/Bean.
Artichoke Casserole, Alii, '93 294
Asparagus-and-English Pea Casserole, '86 324
Asparagus and Peas Casserole, '80 152
Asparagus-Artichoke Casserole, '86 279
Asparagus Casserole, '98 310
Asparagus Casserole, Cheesy, '82 281; '83 32
Asparagus Casserole, Creamy, '80 76
Asparagus Casserole, Easy, '83 255
Asparagus Delight, '82 269
Asparagus, Holiday, '85 260
Asparagus-Pea Casserole, '88 M294
Asparagus-Pimiento Loaf, '84 86
Asparagus-Spaghetti Casserole, '80 77
Asparagus Supreme, '89 245
Beets, Fruited, '97 28
Black-Eyed Peas with Rice, '83 12
Broccoli-and-Cauliflower Gratin, '01 43
Broccoli-and-Egg Casserole, '86 324
Broccoli-and-Eggs au Gratin, '85 289
Broccoli-and-Squash Casserole, '01 175
Broccoli Bake, '81 246; '89 279

Broccoli Bake, Cheesy, '83 255
Broccoli Bake, Cheesy Italian, '83 5
Broccoli Bake, Company, '83 279
Broccoli-Blue Cheese Casserole, '85 260
Broccoli Casserole, '87 284; '88 M146, 265
Broccoli Casserole, Almond-, '88 62
Broccoli Casserole, Cheesy, '84 293; '92 342;
   '95 M191
Broccoli Casserole, Easy, '03 M49
Broccoli Casserole, Italian, '82 6, 280; '83 32
Broccoli Casserole, Winter, '94 280
Broccoli-Cheese Casserole, '82 269; '84 9;
   '94 132
Broccoli-Corn Casserole, '83 313
Broccoli Elegant, '81 267
Broccoli, English Walnut, '89 68
Broccoli Macaroni and Cheese, '02 36
Broccoli-Onion Deluxe, '81 75
Broccoli Puff, '82 95
Broccoli-Rice Casserole, '81 101
Broccoli Supreme, '82 34; '85 68; '02 312
Broccoli-Swiss Cheese Casserole, '83 322;
   '85 M211
Broccoli with Lemon Cream, '89 245
Broccoli with Pimiento Cheese Sauce, '02 291
Broccoli with Rice, Holiday, '87 252
Broccoli with Stuffing, '95 341
Brussels Sprouts-and-Artichoke Casserole,
   '94 279
Brussels Sprouts, Casserole of, '86 294
Butternut Casserole, '83 280
Butternut Casserole, Sweet, '83 256
Butternut Squash Casserole, '79 210; '96 216;
   '01 293
Butternut Squash Puff, '85 205
Cabbage au Gratin, '83 279
Cabbage, Caraway, '85 32, 289
Cabbage Casserole, '97 88
Cabbage Casserole, Cheesy, '79 4
Cabbage Casserole, Creamy, '80 63
Cabbage Casserole, Italian, '87 42
Cabbage Casserole, Savory, '82 168
Cabbage, Cheese Scalloped, '81 87; '82 7
Cabbage, Scalloped, '82 269; '01 43
Cabbage Wedges, Smothered, '81 87; '82 7
Cabbage with Apples and Franks, '87 42
Calabaza Mexicano (Mexican Squash), '81 196
Carrot and Zucchini Casserole, '83 256
Carrot-Apple Bake, '98 232
Carrot Bake, Creamy, '85 67
Carrot Casserole, '86 279; '87 285
Carrot Casserole, Scrumptious, '84 328
Carrot-Pecan Casserole, '93 44; '98 231; '02 282
Carrot Puff, '84 328
Carrots, Scalloped, '81 6; '96 107; '02 129;
   '03 99
Carrots, Zesty, '84 5
Cashew Casserole, '95 166
Cauliflower and Asparagus Supreme, '79 287;
   '80 35
Cauliflower-and-Carrot Casserole, '83 280
Cauliflower and Peas with Curried Almonds,
   '80 82
Cauliflower au Gratin, '99 59
Cauliflower Bake, '95 342
Cauliflower Bake, Curried, '01 49
Cauliflower Casserole, '86 10, 279
Cauliflower Casserole, Easy, '82 204
Cauliflower Casserole, Festive, '87 232
Cauliflower Casserole, Herbed, '79 221
Cauliflower, Cheddar, '99 318
Cauliflower, Curried, '91 315
Cauliflower Italiano, Cheesy, '82 300
Cauliflower, Main-Dish, '79 221; '80 83

Cauliflower Medley, '80 220
Cauliflower 'n' Chiles Casserole, '87 285
Cauliflower-Pea Casserole, '85 260
Cauliflower Scallop, '88 270
Cauliflower, Spanish-Style, '79 21
Cauliflower Surprise, Crunchy, '99 318
Celery and Cheese Casserole, '79 178
Celery au Gratin, '83 38
Celery, Baked, '82 98
Celery Casserole, '80 246; '96 92
Celery Casserole, Creamy, '82 98; '83 255
Celery, Creamed, '79 247
Celery, Exotic, '83 280
Celery Oriental, '83 206; '85 116
Celery, Saucy, '83 39
Chayote-Cheese Bake, '80 230
Cheesy Vegetable Casserole, '81 103
Chilaquiles, '82 220
Chipotle Manicotti, Creamy, '03 96
Collards Casserole, Parmesan-, '95 233
Corn-and-Bean Casserole, '90 208
Corn and Cheese Casserole, '81 128
Corn-and-Green Chile Casserole, '89 68
Corn and Tomato Casserole, '81 127
Corn-and-Tomato Casserole, '84 145
Corn Bake, Cheesy, '98 244
Corn, Baked Jack, '97 86
Corn, Baked Scalloped, '85 290
Corn Casserole, '79 247; '89 126; '93 141
Corn Casserole, Chili-, '88 266
Corn Casserole, Fresh, '80 165
Corn Casserole, Jalapeño-, '83 256
Corn, Creamy Baked, '90 60; '02 234
Corn, Elegant Scalloped, '86 268
Corn Pudding, '86 192
Corn-Rice Casserole, '01 46
Corn, Scalloped, '80 164; '81 128; '86 111;
   '88 218
Corn with Sour Cream, Baked, '86 170
Corn-Zucchini Bake, '79 178
Creamy Vegetable Casserole, '98 96
Curry Casserole, Vegetable-, '91 286; '92 27
Eggplant and Noodle Casserole, '82 230
Eggplant and Squash, '83 187
Eggplant-and-Tomato Casserole, '83 187
Eggplant and Zucchini, Italian-Style, '79 289;
   '80 26
Eggplant Bake, '80 82
Eggplant Cakes, '95 196
Eggplant Casserole, '81 205; '84 217; '93 44;
   '94 214
Eggplant Casserole, Easy, '80 202
Eggplant Casserole, Elegant, '82 168
Eggplant Casserole, Flavorful, '79 92
Eggplant Casserole, Spicy Hot, '93 92
Eggplant Casserole, Super, '80 202
Eggplant Chiles Rellenos, '91 86
Eggplant Creole, '86 110
Eggplant Crêpes with Marinara Sauce, Mini,
   '99 266
Eggplant, Heavenly, '93 293
Eggplant, Italian, '84 216
Eggplant Italiano, '91 212
Eggplant, Lebanese, '81 24
Eggplant, Mexican, '83 187
Eggplant Parmesan, '83 186; '84 215; '92 18;
   '95 84; '01 53
Eggplant Parmesan with Feta, '03 174
Eggplant Parmigiana, '81 19; '95 197;
   '01 310
Eggplant, Rolled Stuffed, '80 63
Eggplant, Scalloped, '91 223
Eggplant, Spinach-and-Basil Stuffed, '02 147
Eggplant-Spinach Casserole, '99 217

CASSEROLES, Vegetable
(continued)

Eggplant Supreme, '79 188; '86 170
English Pea Casserole, Cheesy, '83 216
English Pea Casserole, Quick Fresh, '84 145
English Pea-Pimiento Casserole, '83 207
Étouffée, Okra, '98 207
Fennel, Creamy Pan-Braised, '02 43
Fresh Vegetable Casserole, '82 225
Garden Casserole, '82 168; '88 122
Garden Medley, '98 236
Garden Surprise, '83 112
Green-and-Gold Scallop, '81 159
Greens Dinner Bake, Grits 'n, '84 281
Green Vegetable Medley, '79 287; '80 34
Hash Brown Casserole, Cheesy, '03 218
Hash Brown Casserole, Creamy, '03 193
Hash Brown Cheese Bake, '82 50
Hash Brown-Cheese Bake, '97 323
Hominy, Mexican, '91 133, 162
Hominy Olé, '01 17
Hubbard Squash, Tart, '80 214
Lasagna Casserole, Vegetable, '92 198; '93 25
Layered Vegetable Casserole, '91 286; '92 27
Lentils with Cheese, Baked, '84 113
Mac-and-Cheese, Veggie, '01 111
Macaroni Primavera, '96 73
Medley, Baked Vegetable, '81 75
Medley Bake, Vegetable, '81 268
Medley, Vegetable-Cheese, '99 M287
Mexican Vegetarian Casserole, '96 276
Mixed Vegetable Casserole, '83 208, 256; '86 327
Mixed-Vegetable Casserole, '87 154
Mixed Vegetables, Scalloped, '83 5
Mushroom-Artichoke Casserole, '87 241
Mushroom Bake, Windsor, '88 132
Mushroom Casserole, '95 211; '96 47
Mushroom-Cheese Casserole, '83 216
Mushroom Deluxe Casserole, '96 20
Mushroom-Macaroni Casserole, '95 180
Mushrooms Supreme, '84 214
New Potatoes, Cheesy, '85 156
New Potatoes, Cheesy Jalapeño, '01 89
New Potato Gratin, Creamy, '01 M320
Noodle Casserole, Vegetable, '91 30
Okra Casserole, '79 160
Okra-Tomato Bake, '80 298; '81 26
Onion Bake, Four, '93 304
Onion Casserole, Cheesy, '79 101
Onion Casserole, French, '95 26
Onion Casserole, Sweet, '00 103
Onions, Baked Sweet, '91 79
Pea Casserole, Curry, '87 154
Pea Casserole, Reunion, '87 11
Pea Casserole Supreme, '82 281; '83 32
Peas and Rice, '88 97
Peas, Cajun, '88 3
Peas, Chinese-Style Baked, '86 305
Peas, Mexi-, '88 3
Peas, Party, '79 102
Peas, Sweet-and-Sour, '88 3
Potato-and-Rutabaga Gratin, '96 237
Potato Bake, '83 209
Potato Bake, Creamy, '82 201
Potato Bake, Smoky Mashed, '00 214; '01 21
Potato Bake, Swirled Mashed-, '02 98
Potato Bake, Thyme-, '96 121
Potato-Broccoli-Cheese Bake, '80 114
Potato-Butternut Squash-and-Gruyère Gratin, '01 43
Potato Casserole, '87 190; '99 274
Potato Casserole, Beefy, '03 218

Potato Casserole, Cheesy, '80 244; '83 53; '92 229
Potato Casserole, Easy, '80 114
Potato Casserole, Fluffy, '80 268
Potato Casserole, Hash Brown, '81 40
Potato Casserole, Holiday, '92 302
Potato Casserole, Irish, '81 263
Potato Casserole, Mashed, '85 296; '99 223
Potato Casserole, Mushroom-, '84 5
Potato Casserole, Pepper Jack-, '03 218
Potato Casserole, Peppery, '95 182
Potato Casserole, Processor, '86 159
Potato Casserole, Saucy, '81 276
Potato Casserole, Three-Cheese Mashed, '03 72
Potato Casserole with Caramelized Onions, '03 231
Potato-Cheese Casserole, '79 101
Potato-Egg Casserole, Cheesy, '84 5
Potato-Eggplant Casserole, '87 166
Potatoes and Eggs au Gratin, '79 107
Potatoes and Onions, Cheesy, '00 275
Potatoes and Turnips, Scalloped, '85 235
Potatoes-and-Zucchini au Gratin, '84 5
Potatoes au Gratin, '02 197
Potatoes au Gratin, Shredded, '89 69
Potatoes, Baked Sweet-and-Savory Mashed, '02 244
Potatoes, Barbecue Scalloped, '04 139
Potatoes, Buffet, '98 92
Potatoes, Caramelized Onion-and-Gorgonzola Mashed, '01 256
Potatoes, Cheesy Scalloped, '83 82
Potatoes, Christmas, '88 252
Potatoes, Cottage, '89 69
Potatoes, Cream Cheese Mashed, '02 35
Potatoes, Double Cheddar Cheese, '00 331
Potatoes, Double-Cheese, '86 6
Potatoes, Easy Oven-Baked, '82 202
Potatoes, Escalloped, '01 239
Potatoes, Fix-Ahead Mashed, '89 70
Potatoes, Fluffy, '84 296; '85 196
Potatoes for Company, Saucy, '82 202
Potatoes, Garlic, '84 296; '85 196
Potatoes Gourmet, '80 114
Potatoes, Gruyère, '83 193
Potatoes, Hot Deviled, '84 296; '85 196
Potatoes, Italian-Style, '89 69
Potatoes, Jalapeño, '84 39
Potatoes, Jazzy Mashed, '87 192
Potatoes, Lemon and Nutmeg, '80 36
Potatoes, Light Scalloped, '89 311
Potatoes Lorraine, '87 190
Potatoes, Mexican-Style, '91 78
Potatoes, Missy, '85 259
Potatoes Moussaka, '93 44
Potatoes, Mushroom Scalloped, '87 191
Potatoes, Olive, '80 114
Potatoes, Out-of-This-World Scalloped, '04 296
Potatoes, Parmesan, '82 270; '90 M62
Potatoes, Party Scalloped, '87 191
Potatoes, Rosemary's, '98 53
Potatoes, Russian, '03 255
Potatoes, Scalloped, '82 300; '83 211; '92 48
Potatoes, Sour Cream, '84 39
Potatoes, Special Scalloped, '88 162
Potatoes, Three-Cheese Mashed, '00 112
Potatoes, Two-Cheese, '80 114
Potatoes, Wayside Scalloped, '79 283
Potatoes, Winter Herb Garden Scalloped, '99 289
Potatoes with Feta Cheese, '84 295; '85 196
Potatoes with Ham Bits, Creamy, '87 191
Potatoes with Sweet Marjoram and Parmesan Cheese, Scalloped, '91 246
Potato Gratin, Smoky, '00 233

Potato-Horseradish Gratin with Caramelized Onions, '99 314
Potato-Tomato Bake, '86 17
Potato-Tomato Casserole, Saucy, '79 46
Potato Tuna Bake, Shoestring, '82 211
Pumpkin, Baked, '82 217
Spinach and Artichoke Casserole, '81 103
Spinach-and-Celery Casserole, '84 294
Spinach and Egg Casserole, '82 270
Spinach-Artichoke Bake, '95 48
Spinach-Artichoke Casserole, '88 252; '93 44; '00 254; '01 49
Spinach-Artichoke Casserole, Spicy, '01 49
Spinach Bake, Creamy, '89 68
Spinach, Baked Macaroni with, '99 244
Spinach Casserole, '79 265; '91 31; '99 271
Spinach Casserole, Cheesy, '81 263
Spinach Casserole, Cottage Cheese-and-, '84 77
Spinach Casserole, Creamy, '86 111
Spinach-Cheese Bake, '88 10
Spinach-Cheese Casserole, '83 216; '89 64
Spinach-Cheese Puff, '84 96
Spinach, Cheesy Topped, '84 85
Spinach, Company, '89 280
Spinach, Creamy Lemon, '82 302
Spinach Fantastic, '93 173
Spinach-Gorgonzola Custards, Savory, '99 313
Spinach, Gourmet Baked, '82 180
Spinach Parmesan, '93 72
Spinach-Parmesan Casserole, '82 281; '83 32
Spinach Rice, '85 146
Spinach Shells, '97 50
Spinach Supreme, '84 77
Spinach Surprise, '82 42
Spinach with Cheese, Scalloped, '79 8
Squares, Checkerboard Vegetable, '96 178
Squash, Amarillo, '99 M218
Squash and Apple Casserole, '79 209
Squash-and-Corn Casserole, Easy, '03 69
Squash and Egg Casserole, '80 146
Squash and Tomato Bake, '95 180
Squash, Bacon-Flavored, '82 158
Squash Bake, '82 107
Squash Bake, Cheddar-, '84 128
Squash Bake, Cheesy, '80 183
Squash-Carrot Casserole, '81 157
Squash Casserole, '87 163; '89 159; '90 161; '92 342; '96 247, 252; '97 29; '04 126
Squash Casserole, Baked, '83 149
Squash Casserole, Blender, '81 212
Squash Casserole, Calico, '90 290
Squash Casserole, Cheesy, '79 123
Squash Casserole, Company, '81 183
Squash Casserole, Creamy Rice and, '95 26
Squash Casserole, Crunchy, '84 293
Squash Casserole, Fresh, '82 204
Squash Casserole, Jiffy, '81 M144
Squash Casserole, Summer, '81 102, 184
Squash Casserole, Two-, '79 101
Squash Casserole, Two-Cheese, '04 126
Squash Casserole, Yellow, '79 179; '85 135; '88 166
Squash Casserole, Zippy, '80 183
Squash, Country Club, '88 M16
Squash, Greek-Style, '91 285; '92 26
Squash, Mexican, '83 31
Squash Nicholas, '94 236
Squash, Posh, '81 159
Squash, Savory, '99 111
Squash, South-of-the-Border, '89 148; '96 178; '00 137
Strata, Vegetable-Cheese, '98 98
Summer Vegetable Gratin, '03 159
Sweet Potato-and-Apple Casserole, '94 280

Sweet Potato-Apple Bake, '83 25
Sweet Potato-Apricot Bake, '85 206
Sweet Potato Bake, '80 287
Sweet Potato Bake, Holiday, '90 291
Sweet Potato-Banana Casserole, '86 276
Sweet Potato Casserole, '79 289; '80 26; '85 256;
    '89 279; '02 309; '03 M24
Sweet Potato Casserole, Bell's, '04 271
Sweet Potato Casserole, Glazed, '90 250
Sweet Potato Cassserole, Pear-, '86 280
Sweet Potato Delight, '86 335
Sweet Potato-Eggnog Casserole, '95 291
Sweet Potatoes-and-Apple Casserole, '90 228
Sweet Potatoes-and-Berries Casserole, '84 231
Sweet Potatoes, Bourbon, '86 324; '87 280
Sweet Potatoes, Candied, '86 111; '88 207
Sweet Potatoes, Mashed, '98 269
Sweet Potatoes, Orange-Spice Mashed, '02 34
Sweet Potatoes, Praline-Topped, '98 96
Sweet Potatoes Royale, '91 250
Sweet Potatoes with Sherry and Walnuts, '86 286
Sweet Potato-Rum Casserole, '84 231
Sweet Potato Supreme, '94 196
Sweet Potato Surprise, '81 267
Swiss Vegetable Medley, '95 26
Tomato-and-Artichoke Heart Bake, '85 81
Tomato-Bacon Strata, '03 100
Tomato Casserole, Scalloped, '88 144
Tomato Casserole, Stuffed Fried Green, '04 145
Tomatoes, Herbed, '81 102
Tomatoes, Italian-Sauced Green, '85 214
Tomatoes, Scalloped, '84 142
Torta, Mexican, '88 149
Turnip Casserole, '83 242; '84 229; '04 213
Turnip Casserole, Baked, '82 274
Turnip Puff, Whipped, '00 254
Turnips au Gratin, '84 229
Turnips, Scalloped, '79 254
Vegetarian Casserole, '96 302
Veggies Casserole, '88 123
Vidalia Deep Dish, '89 120
Vidalia Onions, Cheesy Baked, '01 145
Vidalia Onion Soufflé, '04 167
Wine Sauce Casserole, Vegetables in, '95 133
Winter Root Vegetable Casserole, '98 265
Yam-and-Apple Scallop, '91 199
Yams, Brandied, '94 273
Zucchini, and Cornbread Bake, Bacon, '99 123
Zucchini and Tomato Bake, '82 158
Zucchini-and-Tomato Casserole, '88 265
Zucchini, Baked, '83 209
Zucchini-Carrot Casserole, '99 61
Zucchini Casserole, '79 157; '87 154
Zucchini Casserole, Cheese-Egg-, '84 114
Zucchini Casserole, Cheesy, '82 168; '84 145
Zucchini Casserole, Italian, '85 59
Zucchini-Jack Casserole, '85 296
Zucchini-Rice Casserole Italiano, '89 146
Zucchini with Pasta, Stuffed, '97 101
Wild Rice Casserole, '82 199; '895 176

CAULIFLOWER

Almond Sauce, Cauliflower with, '82 270
au Gratin, Cauliflower, '82 204; '99 59
Bake, Cauliflower, '95 342
Bake, Curried Cauliflower, '01 49
Baked Swiss Cauliflower, '79 100
Beef and Cauliflower Oriental, '80 220
Beef and Cauliflower over Rice, '93 94
Beets and Cauliflower, Chilled, '80 137
Browned Butter, Cauliflower in, '02 45
Casserole, Cauliflower, '86 10, 279
Casserole, Cauliflower-and-Carrot, '83 280
Casserole, Cauliflower 'n' Chiles, '87 285
Casserole, Cauliflower-Pea, '85 260

Casserole, Chicken, Broccoli, and Cauliflower,
    '00 337
Casserole, Easy Cauliflower, '82 204
Casserole, Festive Cauliflower, '87 232
Casserole, Herbed Cauliflower, '79 221
Cheddar Cauliflower, '99 318
Cheese-Frosted Cauliflower, '85 68
Cheese Sauce, Cauliflower with, '81 101
Cheesy Cauliflower Italiano, '82 300
Crunchy Cauliflower Surprise, '99 318
Curried Cauliflower, '91 315
Dilled Cauliflower, '83 93
Festive Cauliflower, '84 34
French-Fried Cauliflower, '86 211
French-Fried Cauliflower au Gratin, '79 221; '80 82
Fried Cauliflower, '83 5; '84 248; '90 18
Fried Cauliflower, Crispy, '80 220
Fried Cauliflower, Golden, '82 78
Fried Cauliflower, Oven-, '99 318
Fried Cauliflower with Cheese Sauce, '87 231
Fritters, Broccoli-Cauliflower, '02 45
Fritters, Cauliflower-Cheddar, '98 25
Frosted Cauliflower, '97 105
Garden Surprise, '83 112
Goldenrod, Cauliflower, '79 21
Gratin, Broccoli-and-Cauliflower, '01 43
Gratin, Cauliflower with Chinese Mustard, '94 45
Herb Butter, Cauliflower with, '81 2
Italian-Style Cauliflower, '92 36
Lemon Cauliflower, Easy, '83 322
Main-Dish Cauliflower, '79 221; '80 83
Medley, Cauliflower, '80 220
Medley, Cauliflower-Broccoli, '81 69
Medley, Cauliflower-Snow Pea, '87 305
Oriental Cauliflower, '81 75
Peas and Cauliflower, '82 288
Peas with Curried Almonds, Cauliflower and,
    '79 221; '80 82
Pickled Cauliflower, '94 183
Pie, Cauliflower-Carrot, '82 191
Pimiento Sauce, Cauliflower with, '87 232
Quiche, Cauliflower, '83 86
Roasted Broccoli and Cauliflower, '01 132
Salads
    Broccoli and Cauliflower Salad, '81 280
    Broccoli and Cauliflower Salad, Creamy, '81 23
    Broccoli and Cauliflower Toss, Crunchy, '83 25
    Broccoli, Cauliflower, and Carrot Salad, '04 140
    Broccoli-Cauliflower Pasta Salad, '88 269
    Broccoli-Cauliflower Salad, '92 97; '00 90
    Broccoli Crunch, Cauliflower-, '88 216
    Broccoli 'n' Cauliflower Salad, '90 32
    Broccoli Salad, Cauliflower-, '79 20
    Broccoli Toss, Cauliflower-, '82 54
    Broccoli Toss, Italian Cauliflower-, '88 269
    Brussels Sprouts Salad, Cauliflower-, '83 240
    Cauliflower Salad, '79 221; '80 83; '81 225;
        '84 291; '85 240, 279; '92 36
    Celery-and-Cauliflower Salad, '83 39
    Corned Beef-Cauliflower Salad, '83 16
    Creamy Cauliflower Salad, '82 102; '04 36
    Crunchy Cauliflower Salad, '80 4; '82 75
    English Pea Salad, Cauliflower-, '95 66
    Green Salad, Crunchy, '89 321
    Layered Cauliflower Salad, '83 240
    Lemon Salad, Cauliflower-, '81 23
    Marinated Cauliflower Salad, '82 303; '84 232
    Olive Toss, Cauliflower-, '85 198; '86 147
    Orange-Cauliflower Salad, '82 266
    Parmesan and Bacon, Cauliflower with, '96 137
    Pea Salad, Cauliflower-, '87 231
    Pea Salad, Savory Cauliflower and, '81 280
    Red, White, and Green Salad, '90 18
    Slaw, Cauliflower, '92 167

Sweet-and-Sour Cauliflower Salad, '81 2
Vegetable Salad, Cauliflower-, '85 158
Sauté, Cauliflower, '94 67
Scallop, Cauliflower, '88 270
Shrimp Sauce, Broccoli and Cauliflower with,
    '84 248
Soufflé, Cauliflower, '82 76; '89 279; '90 17
Soup, Cauliflower, '90 211; '99 318
Soup, Cauliflower and Caraway, '82 264
Soup, Cream of Cauliflower, '87 M7; '88 12;
    '96 277
Soup, Cream of Cauliflower and Watercress,
    '83 126
Soup, Creamy Cauliflower, '82 76
Soup, Fresh Cauliflower, '84 279
Spanish-Style Cauliflower, '79 21
Supreme, Cauliflower and Asparagus, '79 287;
    '80 35
Toss, Cauliflower, '85 289

CAVIAR

Artichoke Hearts with Caviar, '79 142
Crown, Caviar, '83 78
Eggplant Caviar, '88 262; '99 217
Eggplant Caviar with Tapenade, '92 194
Eggs, Black-and-Blue, '96 90
Endive with Caviar, '93 118
Homemade Cowboy Caviar, '94 64
Mexican Caviar, '98 135
Mold, Artichoke-Caviar, '87 239
Mound, Caviar-Artichoke, '91 244
Mousse, Caviar, '82 71; '83 258; '85 86; '92 83
Pie, Caviar, '79 154
Potato Blini with Sour Cream and Caviar, '01 274
Potatoes, Appetizer Caviar, '86 223
Potatoes, Caviar, '84 80
Spread, Caviar-Cream Cheese, '84 256
Spread, Creamy Caviar, '92 58
Spread, Egg, Sour Cream, and Caviar, '85 279
Texas Caviar, '86 218; '99 84; '01 160, 257
Tomatoes, Caviar, '91 12
Zucchini Caviar, '88 212

CELERY

Almondine, Celery, '85 116
Amandine, Buttered Celery, '82 98
Ants on a Float, '91 177
au Gratin, Celery, '83 38
Baked Celery, '82 98
Braised Carrots and Celery, '86 327
Braised Carrots, Apples, and Celery, '96 107
Braised Celery, Green Beans and, '84 254
Brussels Sprouts and Celery, '79 21
Brussels Sprouts with Celery, Lemony,
    '85 25
Buttered Carrots and Celery, '89 44
Carrots and Celery with Pecans, '84 254
Casserole, Celery, '80 246; '96 92
Casserole, Celery and Cheese, '79 178
Casserole, Creamy Celery, '82 98; '83 255
Casserole, Spinach-and-Celery, '84 294
Chicken-and-Celery Skillet, '88 6
Coleslaw, Cumin-Celery-Scented, '02 51
Creamed Brussels Sprouts and Celery, '83 322
Creamed Celery, '79 247
Croutons, Celery, '79 16
Curried Corn and Celery, '86 192
Dressing, Celery-Honey, '80 42
Dressing, Watermelon Salad with Celery-Nut,
    '80 182
Exotic Celery, '83 280
Olives Scaciati, '99 266
Orange Sauce, Celery in, '79 70
Oriental, Celery, '83 206; '85 116
Peas and Celery, '93 289
Peas and Celery, Deluxe, '81 267

CELERY

(continued)

Pork Tenderloin with Apples, Celery, and Potatoes, Grilled, **'95** 161
Potatoes, Whipped Celery, **'94** 305; **'99** 45; **'01** 212
Potato Puffs, Celeried, **'89** 279
Relish, Apple-Celery, **'89** 141
Rice, Holiday, **'98** 289
Rice, Island, **'98** 276
Salad, Celery, **'79** 70
Salad, Celery-and-Cauliflower, **'83** 39
Salad, Chicken-Celery, **'81** 187
Salad, Overnight Alfalfa-Celery, **'82** 97
Salad, Pear-and-Celery, **'87** 56
Salad, Pineapple-Celery, **'85** 95
Sauce, Baked Fillets in Lemon-Celery, **'84** 91
Saucy Celery, **'83** 39
Scalloped Carrots-and-Celery, **'84** M112
Snow Peas with Celery, Skillet, **'84** 123
Soup, Burnet-Celery, **'84** 107
Soup, Celery-and-Potato, **'84** 279
Soup, Cream of Celery, **'79** 71; **'90** 210
Soup, Light Cream-of-Celery, **'82** 279
Soup, Tomato-Celery, **'83** M58
Splendid Stalks, **'93** 258
Stuffed Celery, **'82** 98; **'86** 324
Stuffed Celery, Creamy, **'82** 102
Stuffed Celery, Jalapeño, **'79** 70
Stuffed Celery, Nutty, **'03** 184
Stuffed Celery Trunks, **'85** 115
Toss, Celery-Parmesan, **'84** 34

CELERY ROOT

Carrots, Celeriac and, **'91** 219
Mashed Potatoes, Celery Root, **'98** 293
Roasted Celery Root, Carrots, and Onions, **'98** 293
Slaw, Shredded Celery Root-and-Carrot, **'98** 293
Stew, Beef-and-Celery Root, **'98** 292

CHAYOTES

Bake, Chayote-Cheese, **'80** 230
Casserole, Chayotes and Shrimp, **'80** 230
Fried Chayotes, **'80** 230
Mirliton-Corn Chowder, **'00** 246
Mirlitons, Artichokes, and Peppers, Marinated, **'00** 246
Mirlitons, Stuffed, **'97** 263; **'00** 246
Mirliton Stew, **'02** 57
Pickles, Chayote Squash, **'89** 197
Sautéed Chayote Squash with Cilantro, **'95** 227
Stuffed Chayote, **'92** 247

CHEESE. *See also* **APPETIZERS/Cheese; CHEESECAKES.**

Almond Cheese, **'88** 173
Apple-Cheese Bake, **'92** 225
Bake, Brie Cheese, **'87** 117
Bake, Chicken, Ham, and Cheese, **'87** 217
Baked Brie, Walnut-, **'93** 241
Bake, Pineapple-Cheese, **'79** 106
Bake, Spinach-Ricotta, **'88** 97
Batter, Cheese Grits Crust, **'03** 21
Beef and Black Beans, Spicy, **'99** 331
Beef Blue, Elegant, **'97** 97
Beef 'n' Pasta, Easy Skillet, **'02** 63
Beef Parmigiana, **'85** 234
Beef Roulades, Roquefort, **'88** 215
Blintzes, Cheese, **'82** 146; **'83** 71; **'92** 84
Blue Cheese, Creamy, **'88** 173

Breads

Apple Bread, Cheddar-, **'96** 83
Bacon-and-Cheese Bread, **'83** 255
Bacon-Cheese Toast Bars, **'79** 36
Batter Bread, Cheese-Caraway, **'85** 33
Biscuit Cups, Bacon, **'99** 214

Biscuit Fingers, Pepper-Cheese, **'88** 283
Biscuits, Bacon-Cheese, **'88** 84
Biscuits, Beer-and-Cheese, **'94** 215
Biscuits, Blue Cheese, **'88** 83
Biscuits, Blue Cheese-and-Ham Cornmeal, **'98** 136
Biscuits, Cheese, **'81** 288; **'83** 253; **'85** 32; **'87** 78
Biscuits, Cheese Angel, **'89** 211
Biscuits, Cheeseburger, **'79** 194
Biscuits, Cheese-Chive, **'94** 324
Biscuits, Cheese-Garlic, **'02** 260
Biscuits, Cheese Garlic, **'03** 185
Biscuits, Cheesy Onion, **'95** 98; **'01** 330
Biscuits, Deluxe Omelet, **'98** 101
Biscuits, Easy Cheddar, **'01** 103
Biscuits, Easy Cheese, **'81** 99
Biscuits, Ham-and-Swiss Cheese, **'04** 209
Biscuits, Herbed Roquefort, **'84** 95
Biscuits, Hot Cheesy, **'80** 186
Biscuits, Lightnin' Cheese, **'90** 283
Biscuits, Mexican Fiesta Spoon, **'95** 161
Biscuits, Mixer Cheese, **'96** 22
Biscuits, Petite Ham and Cheese, **'79** 193
Biscuits, Refrigerator, **'96** 17
Biscuits, Rosemary, **'99** 17
Biscuits, Spicy Kickin', **'03** 207
Biscuits, Surprise Pull-Apart, **'95** 46
Biscuits, Tiny Cheese, **'80** 192
Biscuits with Beef and Horseradish-Chive Cream, Blue Cheese, **'02** 313
Biscuits with Chipotle Butter, Cheese, **'01** 234
Biscuits with Olive-Parsley Spread, Cream Cheese-and-Olive, **'04** 238
Biscuits with Sun-Dried Tomato Spread and Bacon, Cream Cheese-and-Olive, **'02** 313
Biscuits with Tapenade, Cream Cheese-and-Olive, **'02** 313
Black-Eyed Pea Bread, **'02** 224
Blue Cheese-Apple Sunburst, **'94** 245
Blue Cheese Bread, **'03** 54
Bobolis, Easy Cheesy, **'92** 278
Bowls, Toasted Bread, **'98** 30
Breadsticks, Italian Cheese, **'95** 126
Breadsticks, Italian Herb, **'04** 35
Breadsticks, Parmesan-Garlic, **'99** 46
Breadsticks, Sesame-Cheese, **'97** 31
Brie Bread, **'87** 143
Buns, Cheesy Onion, **'85** 5
Buns, Hurry-Up Cheese, **'81** 300
Buns, Onion-Cheese, **'88** 218
Butter Cheese Dips, **'80** 46
Buttermilk-Cheese Loaf, **'91** 52
Cheddar Cheese Bread, **'84** 268
Cheddar Cheese Loaf, **'00** 317
Cheddar Cheese-Pepper Bread, **'98** 25
Cheddar-Chive Beer Bread, **'03** 207
Cheddar-Nut Bread, **'85** 41
Cheese Bread, **'82** 174; **'83** 208; **'87** 11
Cinnamon Logs, **'98** 325
Cornbread, Bacon-Cheddar Hot-Water, **'01** 29; **'02** 107; **'04** 25
Cornbread, Cheddar, **'83** 285; **'84** 17
Cornbread, Cheddar-Jalapeño, **'85** 3
Cornbread, Cheesy Beef, **'81** 242
Cornbread, Chile-Cheese, **'87** 171
Cornbread, Cottage Cheese, **'80** 90
Cornbread, Jalapeño, **'98** 178
Cornbread, Loaded, **'99** 214
Cornbread, Southwestern Hot-Water, **'01** 29; **'02** 107; **'04** 25
Cornbread, Sweet Onion, **'98** 252
Cornbread, Swiss Cheese, **'79** 60
Cornbread, Vicksburg, **'96** 35
Corn Sticks, Pimiento-Cheese, **'03** 20

Cottage Cheese-Dill Bread, **'83** 154
Cream Cheese Braids, **'82** 243; **'97** 287
Cream Cheese Loaves, Processor, **'85** 48
Cream Cheese Pinches, **'87** 85
Crescents, Apricot-Cheese, **'99** 284
Crescents, Cheese, **'82** 18
Croissants, Cream Cheese, **'92** 159
Crusty Cheese Bread, **'86** 233
Cups, Bacon-Cheese, **'02** 219
Danish, Cheese, **'97** 31
Danish, Cream Cheese, **'98** 325
Dilly Cheese Bread, **'83** 5
Easy Cheese Bread, **'82** 74; **'86** 17
Elephant Ears, Mushroom-and-Brie Petite, **'00** 87
Elephant Ears, Parmesan-Pepper Baby, **'00** 87
English Cheese Muffins, **'02** 41
Flatbread, Parmesan-Onion, **'98** 65
Flatbread, Quick, **'00** 119
Flatbread, Sicilian Artichoke, **'98** 136
Focaccia, Roquefort-and-Onion, **'98** 54
French Bread, Bacon-Cheese, **'92** 54
French Bread, Cheesy, **'88** 172; **'95** 218; **'96** 205; **'97** 325
French Bread, Herbed, **'99** 47
French Bread, Onion-Cheese, **'89** 29
French Bread, Tangy, **'98** 166
French Toast au Fromage, **'88** 288
French Toast, Cottage-Topped, **'85** 49
French Toast, Stuffed, **'96** 52; **'98** 55, 313; **'02** 105
French Toast, Three Cheese Stuffed, **'93** 122
French Toast with Strawberry Sauce, Make-Ahead, **'02** 131
Fruit-and-Cheese Braid, **'86** 214
Garlic Bread, Cheesy, **'84** 150
Garlic-Stuffed Bread, Cheesy, **'95** 176
Gouda Bread, **'91** 52
Grilled Bread, **'00** 88
Ham-and-Cheese Bread, **'86** 213
Herb-and-Cheese Pull Aparts, **'87** 143
Herb Bread, Cheese-, **'84** M144; **'85** 283
Herb-Cheese Bread, **'85** 70
Herbs-and-Cheese Bread, **'93** 56
Herb-Vegetable-Cheese Bread, **'88** 172
Jalapeño-Cheese Loaf, **'84** 76
Jam-and-Cheese Loaf, **'89** 246
Lemon-Cream Tea Loaf, **'84** 50
Little Cheese Loaves, **'86** 213
Loaf, Cheese, **'90** 93
Mashed Potato Bites, **'98** 249
Monkey Bread, Cheese-Filled, **'91** 21
Muffin Mix, Cheese-and-Pepper, **'89** 330
Muffins, Bacon-and-Cheese, **'89** 205
Muffins, Bacon-Cheese, **'96** 280
Muffins, Blueberry-Cream Cheese, **'86** 14
Muffins, Breakfast, **'04** 209
Muffins, Broccoli Cornbread, **'03** 81
Muffins, Buttery Herb-Cheese, **'03** 232
Muffins, Caraway-Cheese, **'91** 213
Muffins, Cheddar, **'89** 15
Muffins, Cheddar-Raisin, **'91** 51
Muffins, Cheese, **'96** 54; **'97** 287
Muffins, Cheese-and-Pepper, **'84** 139
Muffins, Cheesy Cornbread, **'88** M275
Muffins, Cheesy Sausage, **'92** 252; **'93** 144
Muffins, Chive-and-Cheese, **'04** 332
Muffins, Dilly Cheese, **'95** 245; **'96** 55
Muffins, Green Onion-and-Cream Cheese, **'01** 289
Muffins, Ham-and-Cheddar, **'03** 81
Muffins, Ham-and-Cheese, **'92** 252; **'93** 144
Muffins, Ham-and-Swiss, **'03** 81
Muffins, Marvelous Cheese, **'83** 96
Muffins, Parmesan Cheese, **'04** 209

Muffins, Parmesan Corn, '01 255
Muffins, Pepper-Cheese, '96 280
Muffins, Peppered Cheddar, '99 234
Muffins, Reduced-Fat Ham-and-Cheddar, '03 81
Muffins, Sausage-and-Cheese, '03 81
Muffins, Sausage-Cheese, '86 213
Muffins, Sesame-Cheese, '86 16; '03 81
Muffins, Southwestern Corn, '02 212
Nut Bread, Cheddar-, '03 42
Olive Bread, Spicy Cheese-, '84 150
Onion-Cheese Bread, '79 180; '81 8
Onion-Cheese Supper Bread, '83 112
Onion-Parmesan Bread, '84 284
Orange-Cream Cheese Bread, '82 210
Pane Cunsado (Fixed Bread), '95 218
Pane Cunsado (Sicilian for "Fixed Bread"),
   '96 205
Parmesan Bread, '92 19; '93 231; '00 54
Parmesan Cheese Bread, '99 61
Parmesan Herb Bread, '82 235; '83 41
Parmesan Puffs, '98 235
Parmesan Sesame Sticks, '81 39
Parmesan Twists, '83 239; '99 323
Peppery Cheese Bread, '04 295
Pig-in-a-Blanket Bread, '99 134
Pimiento-Cheese Bread, '85 223; '86 166
Pita Triangles, Cheesy, '93 70
Pizza Bread Rollups, '04 M35
Pizza Crust Wedges, Toasted, '03 280
Popover Puffs, Cheese, '85 6
Popover Ring, Cheesy, '80 45
Popovers, Cheddar, '00 64
Popovers, Cheddar Cheese, '85 41
Popovers, Parmesan, '90 66; '00 64
Poppy Seed-Swiss Cheese Bread, '91 52
Pull-Apart Ring, Southwestern, '03 298
Pull-Apart Ring, Veggie Southwestern, '03 299
Pull-Away Bread, '98 137
Quick Cheese Bread, '83 9
Roll, Feta Cheese-Spinach, '91 22
Rolls, Beer-Parmesan, '03 259
Rolls, Broccoli-Cheddar, '91 21
Rolls, Cheese, '80 286
Rolls, Cheese-Apricot Sweet, '90 195
Rolls, Cottage Cheese, '81 78
Rolls, Cream Cheese-Filled Cinnamon, '02 327
Rolls, Crunchy, '97 160
Rolls, Ham-and-Cheese, '82 3
Rolls, Italian Parker House, '99 47
Rolls, Parmesan, '79 181
Rolls, Romano Sesame, '87 144
Rolls, Whole Wheat, '96 50
Scones, Golden Cheddar Cheese, '99 82
Scones, Pizza, '03 207
Sour Cream-Cheese Bread, '85 33
Spinach Bread, '87 144
Spoonbread, Cheddar, '82 196
Spoonbread, Cheese, '86 261
Spoonbread, Corn-Cheese, '88 9
Sticks, Crispy, '03 211
Sticks, Sesame-Cheddar, '81 150
Swiss Cheese Bread, '79 60
Swiss Cheese Bread, Poppy Seed-, '91 52
Swiss Cheese Loaves, Mini, '95 80
Tennessee Sin, '96 204
Toasted Cheese Delights, '79 37
Toast Points, Parmesan, '00 316
Toasts, Crispy Parmesan, '01 307
Toasts, Parmesan-Pepper, '98 242
Tomato-Cheese Bread, '98 172; '99 M157
Tomato-Cheese Bread, Herbed, '88 143
Triangles, Savory, '02 54
Twists, Cheesy, '84 284
Wine Bread, Cheese-, '87 254

Wine Bread, Parmesan-, '97 31
Witches' Brooms, Cheesy, '01 205
Bugs in a Rug, '95 178
Burgers, Beef-and-Cheese, '96 139
Burgers, Blue Cheese, '89 M66
Burgers, Brie-Mushroom, '95 128
Burgers, Cheesy Bacon, '81 29
Burgers, Cheesy Beef, '83 217
Burgers, Spinach-Feta, '99 135
Burgers, Stuffed Southwestern-Style, '99 201
Burritos, Breakfast, '90 192; '97 172
Burritos, Cheesy Beef, '85 193
Burritos, Easy, '04 32
Burritos, Lentil, '99 287
Butter, Cheese, '84 114
Calzones, Spinach-and-Cheese, '95 310
Canadian Bacon Squares, Sunrise, '99 103
Casseroles
   Apple-Cheese Casserole, '84 287
   Asparagus Casserole, Cheesy, '82 281; '83 32
   Bacon-and-Ham Casserole, Cheesy, '01 256
   Beef-and-Bean Bake, Cheesy, '82 89
   Beef Casserole, '01 199
   Beef, Cheese, and Noodle Casserole, '99 58
   Beef Lombardi, '03 214
   Blintz Casserole, Cheese, '92 251
   Breakfast Casserole, '91 285; '99 273;
      '01 130, 243
   Breakfast Casserole, Brie-and-Sausage, '03 36
   Breakfast Casserole, Cheesy, '85 247
   Breakfast, Mexican, '00 194
   Breakfast Strata, English Muffin, '03 100
   Brie-and-Sausage Breakfast Casserole, '00 284
   Broccoli-and-Squash Casserole, '01 175
   Broccoli Bake, Cheesy, '83 255
   Broccoli-Blue Cheese Casserole, '85 260
   Broccoli Casserole, Cheesy, '84 293; '92 342;
      '95 M191
   Broccoli-Cheese Breakfast Casserole, '99 233
   Broccoli-Cheese Casserole, '82 269; '84 9;
      '94 132
   Broccoli-Ham au Gratin, '90 239
   Broccoli Supreme, '02 312
   Broccoli-Swiss Cheese Casserole, '83 322;
      '85 M211
   Broccoli with Pimiento Cheese Sauce, '02 291
   Brunch Casserole, '82 124
   Brunch Casserole, Easy Cheesy, '92 91
   Brunch Casserole, Italian, '03 29
   Brunch Casserole, Southwestern, '03 197
   Brunch Casserole with Creole Sauce, '98 98
   Brunch for a Bunch, '88 57
   Cabbage au Gratin, '83 279
   Cabbage Casserole, Cheesy, '79 4
   Campfire Casserole, '00 173
   Caramelized Onion Macaroni and Cheese,
      '04 231
   Carrots, Cheese Scalloped, '94 36
   Carrots, Scalloped, '02 129; '03 99
   Cauliflower Surprise, Crunchy, '99 318
   Celery and Cheese Casserole, '79 178
   Celery au Gratin, '83 38
   Chayote-Cheese Bake, '80 230
   Cheeseburger Casserole, '95 255
   Chicken and Dressing, Santa Fe, '03 48
   Chicken-and-Wild Rice Casserole, Leslie's
      Favorite, '03 107
   Chicken Cannelloni with Roasted Red Bell
      Pepper Sauce, '02 287
   Chicken Casserole, Cheesy, '85 34
   Chicken Casserole, Jalapeño, '02 50
   Chicken Casserole, King Ranch, '00 280
   Chicken Casserole, Swiss, '90 67
   Chicken, Cheesy Mexican, '01 199

Chicken Enchiladas, '03 214
Chicken Enchiladas, Creamy, '97 250
Chicken Enchiladas, Quicker, '97 312
Chicken, Fontina-Baked, '90 64
Chicken, King Ranch, '99 330; '03 313
Chicken Parmesan, '04 42
Chicken, Poppy Seed, '99 195
Chicken Salad, Hot, '98 290
Chicken, Swiss, '95 54
Chicken Tetrazzini, '02 171
Chicken Tetrazzini, Cheesy, '83 M87
Chicken Thighs, Swiss, '94 282
Chilaquiles, '82 220
Chile-Cheese Casserole, '82 90
Chile 'n' Cheese Breakfast Casserole, '88 57
Chiles Rellenos Casserole, '79 84; '84 31, 234;
   '92 18; '98 48
Chili Casserole, Ultimate, '99 239
Collards Casserole, Parmesan-, '95 233
Continental Cheese Bake, '81 89
Corn and Cheese Casserole, '81 128
Corn Bake, Cheesy, '98 244
Corn, Baked Jack, '97 86
Cornbread-Chili Strata, '03 100
Corned Beef and Cabbage au Gratin, '83 16
Corn-Rice Casserole, '01 46
Crab, Shrimp, and Artichoke au Gratin, '90 240
Egg-and-Cheese Casserole, '84 293
Egg Casserole, '98 98
Egg Casserole, Cheese-and-, '99 268
Egg Casserole, Cheesy, '81 244; '86 15
Eggplant Crêpes with Marinara Sauce, Mini,
   '99 266
Eggplant Parmesan, '83 186; '84 215; '86 53;
   '95 84; '01 53
Eggplant Parmesan with Feta, '03 174
Eggplant Parmigiana, '81 19; '01 310
Eggplant, Spinach-and-Basil Stuffed, '02 147
Eggplant-Spinach Casserole, '99 217
Eggs, Brunch, '98 93
Enchilada Casserole, Easy, '02 143
Enchiladas, Baked Chicken-and-Cheese, '03 332
Enchiladas, Chicken, '00 45
Enchiladas, Chicken-Cheese, '02 236
Enchiladas, Quicker, '96 103
Enchiladas, Three-Cheese Chicken, '99 330
Enchiladas Verde, Chicken, '00 M240
English Pea Casserole, Cheesy, '83 216
Feather-Light Cheese Casserole, '79 84
Florentine Bake, Cheesy, '95 131
Four Cheese Casserole, '92 170
Garden Medley, '98 236
Green Bean Bake, '99 112
Green Bean Gratin, Gourmet, '99 M334
Grits, Baked Cheese, '80 49, 99; '83 311; '85 41;
   '01 289
Grits, Baked Cheese-and-Garlic, '83 292;
   '84 78
Grits, Baked Garlic-and-Herb, '01 326
Grits Bake, Santa Fe, '00 123
Grits Casserole, Cheesy, '81 270
Grits, Cheese, '86 242
Grits, Chile-Blue Cheese, '04 240
Grits, Chili-Cheese, '01 86
Grits, Garlic-Cheese, '80 47; '81 197; '86 180;
   '00 215
Grits, Jalapeño-Cheese, '00 239; '01 328
Grits, Mexican Cheese, '02 34
Grits, Swiss-and-Cheddar Baked, '91 71
Grits with Chicken Sausage and Shiitake
   Mushrooms, Cheese, '03 254
Ground Beef Casserole, Cheesy, '79 44
Ham-and-Cheese Casserole, '87 78
Ham-and-Cheese Layered Casserole, '98 160

Ham-and-Swiss Casserole, Savory, '01 308
Ham Casserole, Creamy, '03 83
Ham Casseroles, Creamy, '01 55
Ham Tetrazzini, '03 174
Hash Brown Casserole, Cheesy, '03 218
Hash Brown Casserole, Creamy, '03 193
Hash Brown-Cheese Bake, '97 323
Hash Brown-Ham-Cheese Bake, '97 323
Hominy Casserole, Cheesy, '83 170
Hominy Casserole), Four-Part Hominy (Cheesy,
    '96 158
Hominy Olé, '01 17
Hominy with Chiles and Cheese, '86 78
Italian Casserole, Light, '03 198
King Ranch Casserole, '02 210
Lasagna, '98 95
Lasagna, Cheesy, '82 224; '88 299
Lasagna, Cheesy Spinach, '80 32; '83 204;
    '01 196
Lasagna, Cheesy Vegetable, '79 84
Lasagna, Crabmeat, '96 290
Lasagna, Easy Mexican, '03 22
Lasagna, Ellie's, '02 186
Lasagna, Extra-Easy, '00 326
Lasagna, Gourmet White, '96 225
Lasagna, Ground Sirloin, '03 143
Lasagna, Italian Sausage, '96 225
Lasagna Maria, '90 191
Lasagna, Meatball, '00 243; '03 142
Lasagna, Mexican, '98 283
Lasagna, Roasted Vegetable-Meat, '99 M332
Lasagna, Saucy Cheese-Vegetable, '01 306
Lasagna, Southwestern Chicken, '03 173
Lasagna, Spinach-Black Bean, '02 44
Lasagna, Texas, '98 52
Lasagna, Vegetable, '99 97
Leftovers Casserole, Holiday, '04 232
Lentils and Rice, Spanish-Style, '03 201
Lentils with Cheese, Baked, '84 113
Lima Bean Casserole, Swiss, '80 191
Limas, Spanish Cheese, '86 225
Linguine with Meat Sauce, Baked, '01 41
Linguine with Meat Sauce Casserole, '03 22
Mac-and-Cheese, Veggie, '01 111
Mac and Texas Cheeses with Roasted Chiles,
    '04 207
Macaroni and Blue Cheese, '93 248; '94 44
Macaroni and Cheese, '83 M7; '88 M147, M190;
    '90 30; '00 273
Macaroni-and-Cheese Bake, '01 41
Macaroni and Cheese, Baked, '82 199; '00 271;
    '02 26; '03 184
Macaroni and Cheese, Broccoli, '02 36
Macaroni and Cheese, Creamy, '93 249; '94 45;
    '02 26
Macaroni-and-Cheese Deluxe, '79 84
Macaroni and Cheese Deluxe, '80 236
Macaroni and Cheese, Divine, '99 314
Macaroni and Cheese, Eleanor's, '97 253
Macaroni and Cheese, Golden, '04 24
Macaroni and Cheese, Italian, '04 327
Macaroni and Cheese, Old-Fashioned, '92 215
Macaroni and Cheese, Quick-and-Easy, '00 15
Macaroni and Cheese, Souper, '00 92
Macaroni and Cheese, Tasty, '83 288
Macaroni and Cheese, Tex-Mex, '00 92
Macaroni and Cheese, Thick-and-Rich, '84 329
Macaroni-and-Cheese with Wine, '86 78
Macaroni Bake, Jack-in-the-, '93 249; '94 45
Macaroni, Cheese, and Tomatoes, '95 213

Macaroni-Cheese-Beef Casserole, '95 125
Macaroni, Double Cheese, '82 224
Macaroni, Extra Cheesy, '00 92
Macaroni, Gorgonzola, '97 28
Macaroni, Mexican, '96 73
Macaroni Mousse, '96 73
Macaroni-Mushroom Bake, Cheesy, '81 243
Macaroni Primavera, '96 73
Macaroni, Three-Cheese, '00 M92
Macaroni with Blue Cheese and Walnuts,
    '02 M208
Macaroni with Spinach, Baked, '99 244
Manicotti, Cheesy, '83 216
Manicotti, Cheesy Sausage-and-Tomato, '03 257
Manicotti, Creamy Chipotle, '03 96
Manicotti, Ground Beef-and-Tomato, '03 257
Manicotti, Make-Ahead, '98 68
Manicotti, Meaty Stuffed, '00 19
Manicotti, Special, '88 50
Manicotti, Stuffed, '83 M6
Mashed Potato Casserole, Three-Cheese, '03 72
Meat and Potatoes, Italian-Style, '03 97
Mexican Casserole, Cabin, '97 95
Mexican Casserole, Cheesy, '82 224
Mexican Casserole, Microwave, '90 M231
Mushroom-Cheese Casserole, '83 216
Mushroom Deluxe Casserole, '96 20
Mushrooms au Gratin, '81 108
New Potato Gratin, Creamy, '01 M320
Onion Casserole, Cheesy, '79 101
Onions, Cheesy Baked Vidalia, '01 145
Orzo, Mozzarella-and-Olive, '97 249
Parmigiana, Eggplant, '95 197
Pasta Bake, Cheesy, '02 161
Pasta Bake, Layered, '04 326
Pasta Shells Florentine, '00 326
Pepper Jack-Potato Casserole, '03 218
Pineapple Bake, '96 84
Pineapple-Cheese Bake, '79 106
Pizza Bake, Upside-Down, '98 224
Pizza Casserole, Upside-Down, '03 284
Pork Casserole, Cheesy, '81 M74
Pork Parmigiana, Easy, '94 57
Potato Bake, Smoky Mashed, '01 21
Potato-Butternut Squash-and-Gruyère Gratin,
    '01 43
Potato Casserole, Beefy, '03 218
Potato Casserole, Cheesy, '80 244; '83 53;
    '92 229
Potato Casserole, Mashed, '99 223
Potato-Cheese Casserole, '79 101
Potato-Cheese Dream, '91 307
Potato-Egg Casserole, Cheesy, '84 5
Potatoes and Eggs au Gratin, '79 107
Potatoes and Onions, Cheesy, '00 275
Potatoes au Gratin, '02 197
Potatoes au Gratin, Shredded, '89 69
Potatoes, Baked Sweet-and-Savory Mashed,
    '02 244
Potatoes, Barbecue Scalloped, '04 139
Potatoes, Buffet, '98 92
Potatoes, Caramelized Onion-and-Gorgonzola
    Mashed, '01 256
Potatoes, Cheesy Scalloped, '83 82
Potatoes, Cottage, '89 69
Potatoes, Cream Cheese Mashed, '02 35
Potatoes, Double Cheddar Cheese, '00 331
Potatoes, Double-Cheese, '86 6
Potatoes, Escalloped, '01 239
Potatoes Gourmet, '80 114
Potatoes, Gruyère, '83 193
Potatoes, Mushroom Scalloped, '87 191
Potatoes, Out-of-This-World Scalloped, '04 296
Potatoes, Rosemary's, '98 53

Potatoes, Russian, '03 255
Potatoes, Scalloped, '83 211
Potatoes, Special Scalloped, '88 162
Potatoes, Three-Cheese Mashed, '00 112
Potatoes, Winter Herb Garden Scalloped, '99 289
Reuben Casserole, '90 240
Rice-and-Cheese con Chiles, '89 99
Rice au Gratin, '83 129
Rice au Gratin Supreme, '86 78
Rice, Cheese-Parslied, '89 99
Rice Strata, Cheese-, '81 176
Rotini, Baked, '01 185
Sausage Brunch, Italian, '88 57
Sausage Casserole, Cheesy, '82 124
Sausage Casserole, Swiss, '80 209
Sausage-Cheese Bake, '88 58
Sausage-Chile Rellenos Casserole, '88 52
Sausage-Spud Bake, Sunday Night Spicy Cheesy,
    '03 331
Seafood Parmesan, Savannah, '99 312
Seashell-Provolone Casserole, '80 189
Shells and Cheese, Creamy, '01 216
Shrimp-and-Grits Casserole, Cheesy, '03 28
Shrimp-and-Scallops Casserole, Creamy, '01 256
Shrimp Enchiladas, '01 104
Spaghetti-and-Spinach Casserole, '02 199
Spinach Casserole, '99 271
Spinach Casserole, Cheesy, '81 263
Spinach Casserole, Cottage Cheese-and-, '84 77
Spinach-Cheese Bake, '88 10
Spinach-Cheese Casserole, '83 216; '89 64
Spinach-Gorgonzola Custards, Savory, '99 313
Spinach-Parmesan Casserole, '82 281; '83 32
Spinach Ring au Fromage, '79 8
Spinach Shells, '97 50
Squash-and-Corn Casserole, Easy, '03 69
Squash Bake, Cheddar-, '84 M113, 128
Squash Casserole, Cheesy, '79 123; '82 M21
Squash Casserole, Two-Cheese, '04 126
Squash-Chicken Casserole, Hearty Tex-Mex,
    '03 107
Squash, Savory, '99 111
Squash, South-of-the-Border, '96 178; '00 137
Strata, Vegetable-Cheese, '98 98
Stroganoff Casserole, '98 48
Tamale, Mozzarella, '95 70
Tomato-and-Okra Bake, '03 158
Tomato Macaroni and Cheese, Spicy, '03 68
Tuna Casserole with Cheese Swirls, '88 256
Turkey-Cheddar-Broccoli Strata, '03 100
Turkey Parmigiana, '87 193
Turkey-Swiss Casserole, '86 283
Turkey Tetrazzini, '03 257
Turnip Casserole, '04 213
Vegetable Casserole, Cheesy, '81 103
Vegetable-Cheese Medley, '99 M287
Vegetable Medley, Swiss, '95 26
Vegetable Squares, Checkerboard, '96 178
Wraps, Southwestern, '99 238
Zucchini Casserole, Cheese-Egg-, '84 114
Zucchini Casserole, Cheesy, '82 168; '84 145
Zucchini-Jack Casserole, '85 296
Catfish Parmesan, '79 184; '86 210; '99 91
Catfish, Parmesan, '92 309
Cheeseburgers, Inside Out, '99 202
Cheeseburgers, Mini-, '97 203
Chicken Alouette, '91 295
Chicken, Baked Parmesan, '83 320
Chicken Breasts, Celebrity, '95 60
Chicken Breasts, Cream Cheese, '90 234
Chicken Breasts Gruyère, '80 189
Chicken Breasts over Angel Hair, Goat Cheese-
    Stuffed, '97 144
Chicken Breasts Romano, '79 218

Chicken Breasts Saltimbocca, '98 19
Chicken Breasts with White Bean Puree, Stuffed,
    '02 200
Chicken Bundles, Southwestern, '02 215
Chicken Caprese with Tomato-Basil Cream, '99 240
Chicken, Cheesy Mexican, '02 91
Chicken Cobbler, Spicy Tex-Mex, '03 324
Chicken Cordon Bleu, '81 304; '82 83; '86 37
Chicken, Crispy Parmesan, '80 M76
Chicken Fiesta, Breast-of-, '88 151
Chicken in Phyllo, Cheese-Stuffed, '01 251
Chicken in Phyllo, Cheesy, '02 308
Chicken Macaroni and Cheese, Spicy, '02 63
Chicken Monterey, '82 275
Chicken-Mozzarella Melt, Italian, '95 153
Chicken, Oven-Fried, '99 212
Chicken, Oven-Fried Parmesan, '81 97; '82 148
Chicken Packets, '96 104
Chicken Parmesan, '83 184; '95 210; '00 219
Chicken Parmesan, Baked, '83 137
Chicken Penne, Cheesy, '00 289
Chicken Penne, Spicy Cheesy, '00 289
Chicken Presents, Holiday, '01 251
Chicken Provolone, '93 323
Chicken Rollups, Cheesy, '82 44
Chicken, Roquefort, '89 320
Chicken, Seasoned, '99 316
Chicken Shortcakes, Cheesy, '95 98
Chicken Skillet, Cheesy, '80 115
Chicken, Stuffed Alfredo, '04 56
Chiles Rellenos, '88 116; '89 226
Chiles Rellenos, Roasted, '95 64
Chiles Rellenos with Walnut Cream Sauce, Havarti-
    and-Corn-Stuffed, '93 M275
Chili-Cheese Dogs, '81 M176
Chili, Cheese-Topped, '82 M11
Chili, Cheesy, '82 310
Chimichangas, Baked Spicy Beef, '97 319
Chimichangas, Bean-and-Cheese, '01 16
Chimichangas, Chicken, '98 95
Chunky Cream Cheese, '85 306
Chutney with Cream Cheese, Cranberry-Amaretto,
    '87 244
Coffee Cake, Chocolate-Cream Cheese, '03 288
Coffee Cake, Cream Cheese, '86 290
Coffee Cake, Deep-Dish Cheesecake, '90 50
Coffee Cake, Raspberry-Cheese, '97 231
con Queso, Chile, '97 25
Cookie Snacks, Cheese, '01 231
Corn on the Cob, Parmesan, '88 M187
Cottage Cheese, Italian, '01 124
Country Ham Puff, Cheesy, '90 88
Couscous with Peas and Feta, '01 158
Crab Bake, Quick, '87 192
Crabmeat au Gratin, '86 154
Crackers, Hot Nut, '90 206
Crackers, Taco-Cheese Animal, '94 197
Cream Puffs with Chicken Salad, Cheesy, '86 260
Cream-Style Cheese, '85 209
Crème Brûlée, Roquefort-and-Black Pepper, '95 324
Crêpe Cups, Florentine, '89 44
Crêpes, Cheese and Mushroom, '81 88
Crêpes, Cheesy Sausage, '82 240; '83 71
Crêpes con Queso, '96 48
Crêpes, Goat Cheese-Filled Cornbread, '98 43
Crêpes, Mushroom-Cheese, '87 289; '88 135
Crêpes, Sausage-Filled, '98 266; '99 25
Crêpes, Spinach-Ricotta, '81 52
Crispies, Pecan-Cheese, '87 168
Crisps, Blue Cheese, '96 106
Crisps, Peppered Cheese, '98 107
Crostini, Feta-Tomato, '92 159
Croutons, Goat Cheese-and-Chive, '01 312
Croutons, Prosciutto, '99 89

Crust, Cheese, '80 286; '86 264
Crust, Cheesy Crumb, '88 86
Crust, Chicken Pot Pie with Cheese, '86 264
Crust, Parmesan, '94 304
Crust, Parmesan Pizza, '93 58

Desserts
Almond-Raspberry Brie, '94 M89
Apple-and-Cheese Delight, '98 97
Bites, Starlight Cheese, '95 329
Blackberry Supremes, '99 179
Blintzes, Cheese, '82 146
Blueberry Yum Yum, '98 91
Bread Pudding with Amaretto Cream Sauce,
    Layered Almond-Cream Cheese, '03 330
Brownie Bars, Broadway, '97 M35
Brownies à la Mode, Magnolias Cream Cheese,
    '97 M178
Brownies, Cream Cheese, '04 M330
Brownies, Cream Cheese Swirl, '79 51
Brownies, German Cream Cheese, '80 269
Brownies, Magnolia Cream Cheese, '01 M63
Brownies, Walnut-Cream Cheese, '84 240
Cake, Cheesy Pound, '96 62
Cake, Coconut-Cream Cheese Pound, '85 297;
    '90 305
Cake, Cream Cheese-Bourbon-Pecan Pound,
    '04 280
Cake, Cream Cheese-Coconut-Pecan Pound,
    '04 280
Cake, Cream Cheese Loaf, '84 151
Cake, Cream Cheese Pound, '81 290; '86 287;
    '95 304; '01 244; '03 312
Cake, Crusty Cream Cheese Pound, '89 124
Cake, Ooey-Gooey Butter, '00 86
Cake, Poppy Seed, '95 63
Cake, Regal Cream Cheese, '80 140
Cake Squares, Cream Cheese, '84 321
Cake, Tart Lemon-Cheese, '88 7
Cake, Twinkling Star, '00 306
Cake with Strawberries and Cream, Cream
    Cheese Pound, '02 104
Cake with Wine Jelly, Pound, '98 125
Cannoli, '91 20
Chocolate-Cheese Cups, '91 142
Chocolate Heaven, '98 323
Cobbler, Country Apple, '99 255
Cobbler, Double-Cherry Cheesecake, '03 21
Cookies, Breakfast, '97 52
Cookies, Cream Cheese, '80 282; '02 229;
    '03 131
Cookies, Cream Cheese-Chocolate Chip, '02 229;
    '03 131
Cottage Cheese Dessert, Creamy, '87 191
Cream Cheese Eggs, '99 118
Cream Cheese Frills, '79 291
Cream, Molded French, '99 72
Crisp, Apple-Cheese, '92 235
Cupcakes, Chocolate-Cream Cheese, '03 169
Cupcakes, Cream Cheese Party, '82 279
Cupcakes, Lemonade, '04 163
Cupcake Surprises, '01 299
Custard, Goat Cheese, '96 285
Date-Cream Cheese Rollups, '83 298
Date Dessert Cheese, Nutty, '87 299
Dip, Citrus-Cream Cheese, '03 93
Dip, Orange-Flavored Cream Cheese, '03 93
Dip, Orange Marmalade-Cream Cheese, '03 93
Dip, Strawberries with Fluffy Cream Cheese,
    '03 93
Éclairs, Mini Tiramisù, '03 M41
Filling, Cream Cheese, '04 273
Filling, Mascarpone, '02 146
Flan, Cream Cheese, '03 328
Frosting, Cherry-Nut Cream Cheese, '96 249

Frosting, Chocolate-Cream Cheese, '02 256
Frosting, Cinnamon-Cream Cheese, '03 332
Frosting, Citrus Cream Cheese, '99 223
Frosting, Coconut Cream Cheese, '86 60
Frosting, Coconut-Cream Cheese, '04 137
Frosting, Cream Cheese, '79 45; '80 140, 253,
    299; '82 135, 244; '83 105, 215, M233;
    '84 201, 255, 315, 316; '85 118, 121; '86 217,
    337; '87 58; '90 305, 308; '92 120; '93 20;
    '94 254; '95 139; '96 282; '97 230, 277, 330;
    '98 275; '99 307, 315; '01 34, 185, 244, 271;
    '02 83, 209, 323; '03 55, 315
Frosting, Cream Cheese-Butter Pecan, '03 288
Frosting, Deluxe Cream Cheese, '80 120
Frosting, Fluffy Cream Cheese, '80 245
Frosting, Lemon-Cream Cheese, '81 157
Frosting, Nutty Cream Cheese, '85 117; '96 263
Frosting, Orange Cream, '82 14
Frosting, Orange-Cream Cheese, '81 70; '82 16;
    '92 19; '04 258
Frosting, Pecan-Cream Cheese, '02 294
Frosting, Peppermint Cream Cheese, '98 308
Frosting, Pineapple-Cream Cheese, '95 160
Frosting, White Chocolate-Cream Cheese, '94 58;
    '98 323
Frosting, White Chocolate-Cream Cheese Tiered
    Cake, '94 125
Fruit, Cheese, and Nuts, '93 324
Fruited Cream Cheese, '85 306
Fruit with Cheese, Luscious Fresh, '79 153
Fudge, Cream Cheese, '84 111
Ginger Cheese, '92 163
Glaze, Cream Cheese, '84 150; '94 242
Icing, Chunky Cherry, '03 94
Jamwiches, Sweetheart, '03 M41
Kuchen, Cheese, '86 84
Lemon-Cream Cheese Dessert, '84 95
Loaves, Chocolate Chip Cheese, '91 299; '92 264
Mints, Butter, '03 300
Mints, Cream Cheese, '93 79; '00 41
Molds, Heavenly Dessert Cheese, '85 209
Noodle Casserole, Sweet, '02 238
Pastries, Apricot-Cream Cheese, '03 245
Pastries, Cream Cheese, '80 250
Pastries, German, '86 78
Pastry, Apple Tart with Cheese, '88 225
Pastry, Cheddar, '86 206
Pastry, Cheddar Cheese, '80 219; '82 194
Pastry, Cream Cheese, '86 78; '89 136;
    '96 228, 264
Pastry Mini Shells, Cream Cheese, '99 180
Pastry Shell, Cheese, '85 284
Pastry Shells, Cream Cheese, '86 13
Patty Shells, Cream Cheese, '81 266
Pear-Blue Cheese Gratin, '93 328
Pears Blue, '99 246
Pie, Apple-Cheese, '85 284
Pie, Apple-Cream Cheese, '81 247
Pie, Black-and-White Fudge, '99 249
Pie, Blueberry-Cream Cheese, '88 154
Pie, Cheddar-Pear, '02 197
Pie, Chocolate-Cream Cheese, '80 69
Pie, Chocolate Cream Cheese, '92 240
Pie, Coconut Cream, '02 92; '03 106
Pie, Cottage Cheese, '82 85
Pie, Fruited Cheese, '92 228
Pie, Lemon-Blueberry Cream, '02 92
Pie, Lemon Cheese, '81 136; '82 146
Pie, Lemon-Cottage Cheese, '79 44
Pie, Lemon Cottage Cheese, '81 143
Pie, Mystery Pecan, '02 249
Pie, Tiramisù Toffee Trifle, '04 195
Pie with Berry Glaze, Mascarpone Cream,
    '00 312

CHEESE, Desserts
(continued)

Pie, Yogurt-Cheese, '82 121
Pizza Dolce (Italian Sweet Pies), '00 283
Quad, Chocolate, '02 272
Quesadillas, Apple, '99 248
Quesadillas, Apple Pie 'n' Cheddar, '03 61
Quesadillas, Dessert, '02 54
Soufflé, Blintz, '88 155
Soufflé, Cream Cheese, '88 11
Spread, Chocolate Cheese, '87 292
Spread, Orange Cheese, '87 292
Squares, Lemony Cream Cheese, '82 159
Strawberry Cheese Delight, '79 50
Strawberry-Cream Cheese Dessert, '83 123
Strudel, Fig, '98 253
Sundaes, Cream Cheese Brownie, '03 223
Tart, Apple-Cream Cheese, '96 228
Tart, Cream Cheese-Peach, '99 169
Tart, Pine Nut, '97 86
Tarts, Cranberry-Cream Cheese, '80 154
Tarts, Cream Cheese, '84 74; '90 312
Tarts, Lemon-Cheese, '79 2
Tart, Strawberry-Mascarpone, '02 146
Tiramisù, '91 21; '94 295; '98 280; '00 288;
    '02 285
Tiramisù, Easy, '00 167
Torte, Chocolate-Vanilla Holiday, '01 252
Trifle, Brownie, '03 85
Truffles, Raspberry-Fudge, '00 M41
Devonshire Cream, Mock, '99 275
Dogs, Taco, '02 M57
Dressing, Blue Cheese, '79 69; '82 166; '86 233;
    '90 286; '97 98; '98 248; '99 244; '00 217
Dressing, Blue Cheese-Buttermilk, '01 112
Dressing, Blue Cheese Salad, '82 94
Dressing, Cheese Fluff, '91 256
Dressing, Cheesy Barbecue Salad, '92 255
Dressing, Creamy, '95 66
Dressing, Creamy Blue Cheese, '81 150; '91 307
Dressing, Creamy Blue Cheese Salad, '86 123
Dressing, Creamy Roquefort, '84 12
Dressing, Garden Salad with Tomato-Cream Cheese,
    '79 173
Dressing, Low-Fat Blue Cheese, '00 337
Dressing, Oregano-Feta, '01 57
Dressing, Parmesan, '86 192; '97 326; '01 96, 101
Dressing, Romano, '80 174
Dressing, Roquefort, '79 85; '80 74; '93 128
Dressing, Special Blue Cheese, '80 74
Dressing, Spinach Salad with Zesty Blue Cheese,
    '02 121
Dressing, Tangy Blue Cheese, '87 81
Dressing, Thick Roquefort Cheese, '97 63
Dressing, Zesty Blue Cheese, '79 104
Dumplings, Chicken Ragoût with Cheddar, '94 44
Dumplings, Goat Cheese, '99 70
Egg Medley, Cheddary, '81 M176
Eggs and Cheese, '95 165
Eggs Benedict, Southwest, '03 53
Eggs, Black-and-Blue, '96 90
Eggs, Blue Cheese Stuffed, '93 87
Eggs, Cheddar, '94 M141
Eggs, Cheese-Chive Scrambled, '95 34
Eggs, Chile-Cheese Deviled, '93 87
Eggs, Cottage, '85 44
Eggs, Cottage Cheese Scrambled, '81 142
Eggs, Cottage-Scrambled, '80 49
Eggs, Cream Cheese Scrambled, '81 287
Eggs, Marbleized Garlic-Cheese-Stuffed, '96 91
Empanadas, Easy Turkey, '96 63
Enchiladas, Cheese, '81 194; '85 154; '95 311

Enchiladas, Cheesy Sour Cream, '79 25
Enchiladas, Enticing, '99 57
Enchiladas, Healthy Chicken, '02 19
Enchiladas, Meatless, '93 106
Enchiladas, Saucy Cheese, '84 220
Enchiladas, Vegetable-Cheese, '94 42
Fajitas, Chicken, '99 158
Fettuccine, Broccoli-Parmesan, '93 55
Fettuccine, Crab, '98 142
Fettuccine, Creamy, '96 136
Fig Flowers, '96 195
Fillets, Blue Cheese-Walnut Stuffed, '95 327
Fillets, Parmesan, '86 M112
Fillings
Blintz Filling, '92 84
Cheese Filling, '89 91
Chocolate-Cheese Filling, '90 47
Cinnamon-Cheese Filling, '90 46
Cream Cheese Filling, '90 170; '97 287
Four Cheese Filling, '97 171
Lemon-Cheese Filling, '79 68; '88 7
Orange-Cheese Filling, '90 47
Orange Filling, Cheese-and-, '93 159
Ricotta Filling, '80 58
Spinach and Feta Filling, '97 171
Spinach-Ricotta Filling, '81 53
Firecrackers, Roquefort, '97 19
Flank Steak, Cheese-Stuffed, '98 182
Flautas, Rancho Ramillete, '96 M125
Flounder au Fromage, Baked, '86 234
Flounder, Cheesy Broiled, '84 69
Fondue, Beer-and-Cheddar, '03 223
Fondue, Nacho, '94 332
Fondue, Pub, '94 332
Fondue, Warm Goat Cheese, '96 234
Fowl, Fancy, '81 76
French Toast, Ham-and-Cheese Oven, '97 172
French Toast, Stuffed, '00 193
Fried Brie, Walnut-, '86 244
Fries, Parmesan Oven, '98 235
Frittata, Bacon-and-Asparagus, '98 136
Frittata, Broccoli-Cheese, '81 243
Frittata, Potato-Bacon, '98 330
Fritters, Cauliflower-Cheddar, '98 25
Fritters, Cheese-Stuffed Potato, '96 153
Fritters, Cheesy Zucchini, '88 44
Frosting. *See* **CHEESE/Desserts.**
Gnocchi à la Narciso, '97 246
Gnocchi with Olive Oil, Tomato, and Parmesan,
    '04 47
Goat Cheese and Greens, '90 54
Gratin with Lima Beans and Egg, New Potato,
    '01 71
Grits and Cheese, '00 327
Grits, Baked Cheese, '94 240
Grits, Cheese, '90 102
Grits, Creamy, '96 24
Grits, Garlic, '03 211
Grits, Garlic-and-Herb Cheese, '95 122
Grits, Garlic-Cheese, '88 126; '89 47; '97 58;
    '99 270
Grits, Good Morning, '87 156
Grits, Grillades and Baked Cheese, '94 240
Grits, Gruyère Cheese, '81 47
Grits, Hot Tomato, '01 131
Grits, Jalapeño Cheese, '85 43
Grits, Margaret's Creamy, '99 18; '00 21
Grits, Parmesan Cheese, '02 233
Grits, Quick Cheese, '83 M203; '96 97
Grits, Quick Double-Cheese, '03 167
Grits, Saga Blue-Chile, '98 202
Grits, Sausage-Cheese, '90 238
Grits, Sliced Cheese, '84 75
Grits, Smoked Gouda, '02 319; '04 173

Grits Squares, Chili-Cheese, '01 86
Grits, Tomato, '03 199
Grits with Black Bean Salsa, Sautéed Smoked
    Gouda Cheese, '03 323
Grits with Green Chiles, Cheese, '95 208
Grouper, Heavenly Broiled, '99 91
Ham-and-Cheese Bundles, '93 63
Ham-and-Cheese Flips, '92 46
Ham and Eggs Mornay, '02 130
Ham and Eggs on Toast with Cheese Sauce, '81 43
Ham-Cheese Chips, '82 34
Ham Dinner, Cheesy, '84 90
Ham, Frosted, '89 71
Ham Towers, Cheesy, '82 M77
Herb Cheese and Asparagus Bundles, Grilled Chile-
    Rubbed Rib Eyes with, '03 326
Hominy, Hot Cheese, '84 77
Hot Dog Deluxe, '97 140
Huevos con Queso, '00 123
Hush Puppies, Cheesy Mexican, '91 201
Kebabs, Swiss-Ham, '81 124
Kielbasa with Beans, Easy Cheesy, '01 28
Lamb Meat Loaf with Feta Cheese, '97 24
Little Bits, '79 196
Loaf, Cheese, '87 92
Loaf, Cheeseburger, '81 236, 276
Loaf, Pepperoni and Cheese, '82 32
Loaves, Sausage-Cheese, '88 235
Macaroni and Cheese, Chicken, '02 63
Macaroni, Cheeseburger, '02 119
Marinated Cheese, '90 244
Mayonnaise, Parmesan, '86 79
Meatballs, Golden Nugget, '82 233
Meatballs, Mock, '81 243
Meat Loaf, Cheeseburger, '03 204
Meat Loaf, Gonzales, '04 206
Meat Loaf, Mozzarella-Layered, '79 71
Meat Loaf Roll, Blue Cheese, '93 247
Monster Eyes, '02 222
Nachos, Southwestern, '96 170
Nachos, Tuna, '96 201
Noodles and Mushrooms, Cheesy, '79 84
Noodles, Blue Cheese, '98 290
Noodles, Cheesy Parmesan, '83 M7
Noodles, Ham and Swiss on, '87 108
Noodles, Parmesan, '83 118
Omelet, Cheddar-Vegetable, '83 205
Omelet, Cheesy Picante, '86 95
Omelet, Cheesy Vegetable, '85 49
Omelet, Dill-Cheese-Ham, '95 33
Omelet, Farmer's Oven-Baked, '03 204
Omelet, Golden Cheese-Shiitake, '95 265
Omelet, Ham and Cheese, '79 262; '80 123
Omelet, Ham-and-Cheese, '02 246
Omelet, Herbed Cheese, '93 47
Omelet, Open-Faced Bacon-and-Potato, '02 246
Omelet, Puffed Cheese, '89 227
Omelets, George's, '80 68
Omelet, Shrimp-and-Cheddar, '84 57
Omelet, Shrimp-and-Cheese, '94 31
Omelet, Spinach, Cheddar, and Bacon, '03 204
Omelet, Spinach-Cheese, '83 119
Omelet, Swiss Oven, '80 189
Omelet, Zippy Cheese, '87 287
Orange Cream Cheese, '91 177
Pancakes, Cottage Cheese, '79 115
Pancakes, Cream Cheese, '97 70
Pancakes, Featherweight, '99 43
Pancakes with Goat Cheese, Sweet Potato, '96 271
Parmesan Crisps, '01 197; '03 142
Parmesan Toasts, '96 66
Pasta and Lentils, Cheesy, '99 287
Pasta, Basil-Cheese, '96 136
Pasta, Easy Taco, '03 124

Pasta, Garlic Shrimp-and-Goat Cheese, '00 174
Pasta, Mamma Mia, '95 25
Pasta Primavera, Peppery, '02 161
Pasta Stuffed with Five Cheeses, '88 197
Pasta with Parmesan, Creamy, '98 233
Pastries, Greek Spinach-and-Cheese, '96 76
Pastry, Cheese, '88 56
Pastry, Cream Cheese, '82 39; '86 78; '89 136
Pastry Shells, Miniature Cream Cheese, '87 190
Pastry Tart Shells, Cheese, '85 216
Pâté, Cream Cheese, '80 154
Pâté, Liver-Cheese, '85 276
Patty Shells, Cream Cheese, '81 266; '82 249
Pears, Cheese-Filled, '81 268
Pears Stuffed with Cheese, '82 290
Penne with Spinach and Feta, '03 170
Penne with Spinach and Feta, '04 328
Peppers, Macaroni-and-Cheese-Stuffed, '80 65
Peppers with Chicken and Corn, Stuffed, '02 147
Perch, Parmesan-Crusted, '93 91
Pesto, Basil, '03 208
Pesto, Garden, '04 186
Pesto, Homemade, '01 22
Pesto, Ruth's, '96 170
Pie, Breakfast, '86 242
Pie, Broccoli-Cheese, '84 235
Pie, Cheese-Beef, '85 33
Pie, Cheesy Mexican Chicken, '82 142
Pie, Green Chile-Cheese, '84 234
Pie, Ham-and-Cheese, '95 256; '96 75
Pie, Italian Meat, '01 297
Pie, Jack-O'-Lantern Cheeseburger, '00 234
Pie, Mexican Cheese, '82 9; '83 69
Pie, Mincemeat-Cheese, '80 253
Pie, Onion-Cheese, '88 86
Pie, Quick and Cheesy Corn, '82 191
Pie, Savory Summer, '03 182
Pie, Tortilla, '85 M211
Pie, Tumbleweed, '98 205
Pie, Turkey-Cheese, '88 264
Pie, Zucchini-Ham-Cheese, '80 272
Pigs in a Blanket, Mexican, '00 199
Pineapple Gratin, '93 328
Pinwheels, Pepperoni, '96 247
Pizza, Breakfast, '88 288; '97 172
Pizza, Broccoli Supreme, '02 312
Pizza, Cheese-and-Mushroom, '83 226
Pizza, Cheeseburger, '97 318
Pizza, Cheesy Mexican, '00 314
Pizza, Chicken Parmesan, '00 134
Pizza, Double Cheesy Beef-and-Sausage, '86 77
Pizza, Fresh Mozzarella and Basil, '04 58
Pizza, Greek Eggplant, Tomato, and Feta, '01 312
Pizza, Gruyère-Chicken, '87 182
Pizza, Maca-, '99 195
Pizza, Nutty Pesto, '97 267
Pizza, Peppers-and-Cheese, '03 235
Pizza Pie, Meaty, '03 145
Pizza, Portobello, '03 175
Pizza, Portobello-Pine Nut, '99 216
Pizza, Quick 3-Cheese, '00 94
Pizza, Reuben, '03 69
Pizzas, Chicken-and-Three-Cheese French Bread,
     '96 94
Pizza, Seafood Alfredo, '03 236
Pizzas, Eggplant, '98 183
Pizzas, Five-Ring, '96 180
Pizza, Southwestern, '03 146
Pizza Squares, Easy, '02 61
Poblanos with Mango Salsa, Crab-and-Goat Cheese,
     '04 59
Polenta and Green Chiles, Stuffed Red Peppers with
     Cheesy, '04 169
Polenta Squares, Skillet, '94 22

Polenta Triangles, '98 181
Polenta with Cheese and Okra, Baked, '99 232
Popcorn, Bacon-Cheese, '86 74
Popcorn, Basil, Garlic, and Parmesan, '00 223
Popcorn, Cheese, '98 205
Popcorn, Cheesy Barbecue, '95 239
Popcorn, Chili, '00 M223
Popcorn, Sesame-Cheese, '79 220
Pork Chops, Cheese-Stuffed, '84 81
Pork Chops, Garlic-Parmesan, '02 61
Pork Chops Italian, '98 334
Pork Chops, Stuffed, '02 204
Pork Chops with Apples, Parmesan, '93 338
Pork Chops with Ripieno, '97 245
Pork Scaloppine, '04 221
Pork Tenderloin, Southern-Style Stuffed, '99 45
Pork Tenderloin with Blue Cheese, '86 76
Potatoes with Ham, Scalloped, '02 42
Pot Pie, Ham-Broccoli, '03 83
Preserves, Cream Cheese and Peach, '84 264
Pudding, Baked Cheese, '86 78
Pudding, Cheesy Bread, '83 68
Pudding, Corn-Cheese, '80 244
Puff, Egg-and-Cheese, '85 45
Puff, Macaroni and Cheese, '79 5
Puffs, Bavarian Cheese, '80 191
Puffs, Turkey-Cheese, '87 301
Quesadillas, Breakfast Sausage, '04 183
Quesadillas, Easy, '98 M205
Quesadillas, Greek, '03 61
Quesadillas, Quick, '89 87
Quesadillas, Sausage, '90 118
Quesadillas, Western, '97 65
Quesadillas with Chipotle Salsa, Chicken-and-Brie,
     '99 311
Quesadillas with Shrimp and Brie, '94 173
Quiches
  Bacon-Cheese Quiches, Miniature, '83 93
  Benedict Quiche, '80 M107
  Blue Cheese Quiche, '84 52
  Canadian Bacon-and-Brie Quiche, '04 248
  Cheddar-Leek Quiche, '88 198
  Chicken-Olive-Cheddar Quiche, '03 58
  Chiles Rellenos Quiche, '02 321
  Crabmeat-Parmesan Quiche, '03 59
  Cream Cheese Quiche, '96 203
  Eggless Quiche, '87 220
  Green Onion Quiche, Cheesy, '83 194;
     '84 42
  Ham-and-Cheese Quiches, Individual, '98 24
  Ham-Cheese Quiche, '79 26
  Ham Quiche, Cheesy, '79 127
  Individual Quiches, '98 101
  Jalapeño Quiche, Cheesy, '84 31
  Lorraine, Perfect Quiche, '79 127
  Lorraine, Quiche, '79 40; '80 M108; '99 M218;
     '01 88
  Miniature Cheese Quiches, '80 150
  Mushroom-Spinach-Swiss Quiche, '03 59
  Sausage-Cheddar Quiche, '79 26
  Sausage Quiche, Spicy, '80 M108
  Shrimp-and-Artichoke Quiche, '03 196
  South-of-the-Border Quiche, '93 321
  Spinach Quiche, Cheesy, '81 228
  Spinach Quiches, Triple-Cheese, '00 220
  Squares, Cheesy Hot Quiche, '79 124
  Swiss Alpine Quiche, '90 18
  Swiss-Zucchini Quiche, '82 49
  Tasty Quiche, '82 264
  Tomato Florentine Quiche, '04 332
  Vegetable Quiche, Cheese-, '81 228
  Vegetable Quiche, Light, '97 332
  Veggie Sausage Quiche, Crustless, '03 175
  Zucchini Quiche, Cheesy, '83 312

Ragù with Tortellini, Wild Mushroom, '04 220
Ramekins, Three-Cheese, '79 26
Rarebit, Cheese, '86 78
Rarebit, Tangy Welsh, '88 159
Rarebit, Uptown Welsh, '87 279
Raspberry Brie in Rye, '93 252
Ravioli, Green Bean Alfredo with Cheese, '01 180
Refried Beans, Easy, '99 57
Rice, Chili-Cheesy, '79 43
Risotto, Asparagus, '03 68
Risotto, Crawfish, '99 120
Risotto, Green Bean, '03 68
Risotto, Onion, '03 98
Risotto, Roasted Garlic-and-Cheese, '04 283
Risotto with Parmesan, Broccoli, '99 120
Risotto with Saffron, Pistachio, '98 272
Roll, Cheesy Meat, '82 136
Rolls, Ham-and-Cheese Lettuce, '89 217
Rollups, Pizza, '99 197
Rounds, Parmesan, '79 170
Rounds, Turkey-Mozzarella, '82 3
Salads
  Apple Salad, Cheesy, '86 301
  Apple Salad, Swiss-, '84 81
  Artichoke-Goat Cheese Salad, '98 118
  Asparagus, Roasted-Beet, and Goat Cheese Salad,
     '02 96
  Asparagus, Roasted Beet, and Goat Cheese Salad,
     '03 98
  Aspic, Blue Cheese, '96 66
  Aspic, Cheesy Vegetable, '81 73
  Baby Blue Salad, '01 20; '03 178
  Baby Lettuces with Vidalia Onion Vinaigrette,
     Salad of, '99 168
  Bacon-Lettuce-Mozzarella-and-Tomato Salad,
     '98 209
  Baked Goat Cheese Salad, '96 26
  Banana Splits, Cottage Cheese-, '87 56
  Black Bean-and-Cheese Salad, '92 217
  BLT Bread Salad, Italian, '03 90
  Blue Cheese Chicken Salad, '94 81
  Blue Cheese Salad, '88 48
  Blue Cheese Salad with Spicy Pecans, '02 300
  Blue Cheese Tossed Salad, '84 195
  Bluegrass Salad, '02 255
  Bread Salad, Italian, '03 54
  Broccoli-Cheese-Pasta Salad, '96 184
  Cantaloupe-Cheese Salad, '88 184
  Cauliflower with Parmesan and Bacon, '96 137
  Chicken Salad, Greek, '98 329
  Chicken Salad, Parmesan-, '98 234
  Chicken Salad with Blue Cheese, '97 97
  Citrus-Blue Cheese Salad, '92 220
  Coleslaw, Blue Cheese, '89 13; '95 270
  Coleslaw, Cottage, '80 64
  Cottage Cheese Salad, Different, '85 328; '86 22
  Cottage Cheese Salad, Out-of-This-World, '79 44
  Couscous Salad with Fennel and Goat Cheese,
     Israeli, '00 312
  Cranberry-Cheese Ribbon Salad, '79 241
  Cranberry Congealed Salad Parfaits, Frosted,
     '02 292
  Crunchy-Creamy Salad, '88 100
  Freeze Salad, Party, '82 145
  Fruit-'n'-Nut Salad, Cheesy, '87 56
  Fruit Salad, Cottage Cheese-and-, '86 16
  Garden Salad, Italian, '99 203
  Goat Cheese and Black-Eyed Pea Salad,
     Fearrington House, '95 60
  Green Bean Salad with Feta, '04 169
  Green Beans-and-Cheese Salad, '91 159
  Green Bean, Walnut, and Feta Salad, '96 273;
     '00 321
  Greens with Parmesan Walnuts, Mixed, '95 301

CHEESE, Salads
(continued)

Ham-and-Cheese Salad, '88 138
Ham-Pecan-Blue Cheese Pasta Salad, '90 62
Harvest Salad with Cider Vinaigrette, '99 322
Italian House Salad, '02 300
Layered Salad, Cheesy, '81 37
Layered Salad, Old-Fashioned, '01 96
Leaf Lettuce Salad with Sweet-and-Sour
    Dressing, Red, '03 28
Lemon-Cheese Salad, '85 240
Lettuce, Cheesy Stuffed, '79 175
Lettuce Salad, Blue Cheese-Stuffed, '94 202
Lime-Cheese Salad, Frosted, '79 286
Macaroni and Cheese Salad, '97 203
Macaroni-Cheese Salad, Dilled, '86 208
Marinated Tomato and Brie Salad, '95 95
Mexican Salad, '81 36
Mold, Ambrosia Cream Cheese, '79 249
Mold, Cheesy Lemon, '79 241
Mold, Creamy Tuna-Cheese, '81 135
Molds, Snowcap Cheese, '79 242
Mozzarella-Tomato Basil Salad, Fresh, '02 110
Mushroom Salad, Quick Cheesy-, '89 128
Orange-Cottage Cheese Salad, '79 44
Pasta Salad, Greek, '02 139
Pasta Salad, Smoked Mozzarella, '03 126
Pear-Apple Salad, Blue Cheese-, '81 224
Pear-Swiss Cheese Salad, '91 237
Pea Salad, '98 274
Pea Salad, Cheddar-, '84 82
Pepper Toss, Parmesan, '93 208
"Pig in the Garden" Salad, '92 255
Pine Nut, Rice, and Feta Salad, '96 26; '98 331
Potato Cobb Salad, '03 140
Potato Salad, Blue Cheese-, '91 208
Potato Salad, Cottage Cheese-, '79 147, 285
Potato Salad, Hot Parmesan, '79 78
Potato Salad, Warm Goat Cheese and, '96 234
Ribbon Salad, Christmas, '02 257
Romaine Salad with Raspberry Dressing, '03 28
Roquefort Salad, Creamy, '79 73
Spinach-Blue Cheese Salad, '82 166
Spinach Salad with the Blues, '95 66
Suzie or Steven Salad, '98 204
Tomato-Basil-Mozzarella Salad, '95 171
Tomato-Basil Salad, Fresh Mozzarella-, '93 131
Tomatoes, Cottage Cheese Salad in, '86 208
Tomato-Feta Salad, '81 246; '91 168
Tomato-Gruyère-Basil Salad, '99 172
Tomato-Mozzarella Salad, '89 220
Tomato Salad, Cottage-, '85 163
Tortellini Pasta Salad, Cheese, '02 139
Tuna Salad, Cheese-Sauced, '87 M124
Tuna Salad, Swiss, '86 186
Vegetable Congealed Salad, Cheesy-, '86 199
Vinaigrette with Greens, '98 184
Walnut Salad, Gorgonzola-, '96 170
Warm Cheese Salad, '97 246
Warm Goat Cheese Salad, '01 179
Watercress-Orange Salad with Blue Cheese,
    '04 45
Watercress Salad, '97 249
Ziti-Cheddar Salad, '85 165
Salmon Patties, Cheesy, '89 99
Salsa, Avocado-Feta, '96 15
Salsa, Fiery Steak with Pimiento Cheese, '99 331
Sandwiches
Avocado, Bacon, and Cheese Sandwiches, '87 279
Bacon, Cheese, and Tomato Sandwiches, '84 14
Bacon-Cheese Sandwiches, Grilled, '83 242
Bacon, Pimiento, and Cheese Hoagies, '90 144

Bacon Sandwiches, Open-Faced Cheesy, '80 78
Bagel Sandwiches, Mozzarella-Pepper, '98 145
Bat Sandwiches, '00 234
Beef and Cheese Roll-Ups, Savory, '96 235
Beef, Bacon, and Blue Cheese Sandwiches,
    '96 23
Black Bean Wraps, '00 211
BLT's, Cheesy, '85 92
Breakfast Sandwiches, '80 52
Breakfast Sandwiches, Cheesy, '90 140
Brown Bread-Cream Cheese Sandwiches, '87 M6
Buns, Snack, '87 279
Burgers, Chicken-Cheese, '04 56
Calzones, Ground Beef, '97 95
Calzones with Italian Tomato Sauce, '03 202
Calzones with Pasta Sauce, '01 54
Cheesesteaks, Chimichurri, '04 312
Chicken-and-Cheese Sandwiches, Toasted,
    '85 242
Chicken 'n' Cheese Sandwiches, Grilled, '99 240
Chicken Parmigiana Sandwich, '94 65
Chicken Salad Melts, Open-Faced Cheesy,
    '00 134
Chicken Sandwiches, Cheesy, '82 190
Chicken Sandwiches, Gouda Lover's, '99 195
Christmas Tree Sandwiches, '92 279
Corned Beef and Cheese Sandwich, '79 214
Crab-and-Cheese Sandwiches, Hot, '87 279
Eggplant Parmesan Sandwiches, '03 213
Eggplant Sandwiches, '99 240
Eggplant, Tomato, and Feta Sandwiches, '98 106
Egg Sandwiches, Open-Faced Cheesy, '86 67
Feta Salad Sandwich, Tuscan, '99 289
Focaccia Sandwiches, '98 53
Fruit-and-Cheese Breakfast Sandwiches, '89 M21
Gingered Tea Sandwiches, '84 116
Good-Start Sandwiches, '99 134
Grilled Bacon, Cheese, and Tomato Sandwiches,
    '97 170
Grilled Cheese, '97 328
Grilled Cheese Meat Loaf Sandwiches, '04 188
Grilled Cheese Sandwiches, '82 M172; '94 167
Grilled Cheese Sandwich, Mexican, '92 63
Grilled Cheeses, Mexican, '97 170
Grilled Chili con Queso Sandwiches, '96 139
Grilled Four-Cheese Sandwich with Tomato,
    Avocado, and Bacon, '00 199
Grilled Roast Beef-and-Brie Sandwiches, '03 296
Grilled Sandwiches, Tasty, '84 30
Grilled Spinach Fondue Sandwiches, '99 337
Grills, Double Cheese, '97 170
Grills, Triple Cheese, '97 170
Ham-and-Cheese Pita Pockets, '90 271
Ham-and-Cheese Pita Sandwiches, '87 202;
    '88 44
Ham-and-Cheese Sandwiches, '01 299
Ham-and-Cheese Sandwiches, Hot, '85 299
Ham-and-Cheese Sandwiches, Tiny, '99 87
Ham-and-Cheese Sandwich Round, '94 326
Ham-and-Cheese Sandwich, Tex-Mex, '86 4
Ham and Swiss in the Pocket, '83 31
Ham-and-Swiss Sandwiches, '98 287
Ham-and-Swiss Sandwiches, Tangy, '85 164
Ham-and-Turkey Specials, Cheesy, '84 14
Ham 'n' Cheese Chicken Sandwich, '95 153
Ham Sandwiches, Creamy Blue Cheese-, '87 279
Ham-Swiss-and-Asparagus Sandwiches, '01 52
Herbed Cheese Sandwiches with Artichoke-
    Tomato Salsa, '96 182
Hot Browns, '98 287
Hot Browns, Baby, '00 107
Hot Browns, Biscuit, '02 94
Hot Browns, Kentucky, '02 94
Hot Browns, Southwestern, '02 94

Hot Browns with Fried Cheese Grits, '02 94
Hot Cheddar Cheese Sandwiches, '97 179
Hot French Cheese Sandwiches, '82 3
Lasagna in a Bun, '90 176
Leafy Cheese Sandwiches, '90 56
Meatball Sandwiches, '04 170
Melts, Bacon-and-Cheese, '04 324
Monte Cristo Sandwiches, '97 319
Monte Cristo Sandwiches, Open-Faced, '01 171
Muffin, Stuffin', '99 193
Muffuletta Loaf, '97 86
Muffulettas, '98 184
"Muffy" Sandwich, Fertitta's, '94 34
Open-Faced Mexican Sandwiches, '98 230
Open-Faced Sandwiches, Super, '97 52
Parmesan-Turkey-Ranch Rollups, '01 177
Party Sandwiches, Duck, '02 48
Party Sandwiches, Easter Bunny, '02 48
Party Sandwiches, Easter Egg, '02 48
Party Sandwiches, Flower, '02 48
Peanut-Cheese-Raisin Sandwiches, '88 140
Philly Firecrackers, '01 142
Pimiento Cheese Finger Sandwiches, '99 86
Pimiento Cheese Sandwiches, '82 278
Pita, Stuffed, '89 87
Pockets, Toasted Cream Cheese-and-Apple,
    '01 200
Quesadillas, Quick Fiesta, '02 246
Reuben Melts, Southern, '03 69
Reubens, Open-Faced Coleslaw, '03 169
Roast Beef Slices, '02 246
Rollup, Hot Ham-and-Cheese, '01 217
Sausage-Cheese Muffin Sandwiches, '92 M212
Sebastian, The, '94 184
Shrimp-Cheese Sandwiches, '85 242
Smoked Turkey, Mozzarella, and Blackberry
    Sandwiches, '99 220
Steak Wraps, Cheese-, '00 M335
Stuffed Sandwich, Deli, '98 287
Sub, Chicken, '98 287
Tea Sandwiches, Cheese, '92 276
Tomato-Cheese-Bacon Melts, '99 72
Tomato, Swiss, and Bacon Sandwiches, '04 140
Tortilla Stack-Ups, '92 196
Tuna Cheesies, '82 191
Tuna Melt, Southwestern, '96 201
Turkey-Cheese Dogs, '97 203
Turkey Schoolwich Sandwiches, '00 198
Welsh Rarebit, '00 239
Wrapidos, Tacos, '03 172
Wraps, Western, '99 194
Yummy Sandwiches, '81 229
Sauces
Blue Cheese Sauce, '90 142; '94 320
Blue Cheese Sauce, Fettuccine with, '98 247
Cheddar Cheese Sauce, '91 286
Cheese Sauce, '79 M156; '81 43, 44, 225;
    '82 M123; '83 49, 138, 188; '84 57; '85 92;
    '86 241; '88 78, 272; '89 181, 229; '90 235;
    '93 48; '02 94; '04 281
Cider Sauce, Cheddar-, '98 242
Cilantro Dipping Sauce, Creamy, '03 327
Cottage Cheese Sauce, '87 232
Cream Sauce, Cheesy, '82 79
Devonshire Sauce, Processor, '86 337
Dipping Sauce, Olive Oil-Balsamic, '04 46
Easy Cheese Sauce, '79 22
Garlic-Cheese Sauce, '84 M70
Guilt-Free Cheese Sauce, '93 M95
Lemon-Cheese Sauce, '91 24
Lemony Cheese Sauce, '84 183
Monterey Jack Sauce, '84 293
Mornay Sauce, '80 120; '81 90; '89 195
Mushroom-Cheese Sauce, '83 190; '86 48

Parmesan Cheese Sauce, '79 165; '80 162;
  '85 143
Parmesan Sauce, '92 17
Parmesan-Sour Cream Sauce, Baked Fish with,
  '01 209
Pesto Sauce, Walnut-Parmesan, '97 104
Pimiento Cheese Sauce, '02 291
Rich Cheese Sauce, '81 89
Roquefort Sauce, '89 321
Seafood Cheese Sauce, '89 240
Swiss Cheese Sauce, '79 35; '87 289; '88 135;
  '03 52
Swiss Sauce, '83 M195
Swiss Sauce, Creamy, '80 M53
Topper, Vegetable-Cheese Potato, '86 6
Vegetable-Cheese Sauce, '85 M152
Vegetable Sauce, Cheesy, '92 M134
Walnut-Parmesan Pesto Sauce, '96 251
Wine-Cheese Sauce, '00 310
Sausage, Grilled Pork, Cheddar, and Jalapeño,
  '98 311
Scallops, Baked Gruyère, '92 57
Scallops, Chip and Cheese, '80 301
Scallops Mornay, '80 164
Schnitzel, Swiss, '80 189
Shake, Strawberry-Cheesecake, '92 44
Shell, Rice-Cheese, '82 49
Shells, Cheesy Beef-Stuffed, '83 217
Shells, Cream Cheese, '79 2
Shortcakes, Cheesy Chicken, '95 98
Shrimp and Grits, Garlic, '03 246
Shrimp and Pasta with Two Cheeses, '98 49
Shrimp au Gratin, '85 79
Shrimp Palermo, '04 241
Shrimp, Parmesan-Stuffed, '85 103
Shrimp Tartlets, '00 71
Shrimp with Feta Cheese, '00 221
Sirloin with Cherry-Merlot Sauce and Gorgonzola,
  Peppered, '02 320
Smoked Cheddar, Easy, '01 168
Soufflés. *See also* **CHEESE/Desserts.**
  Blue Cheese Soufflé, '91 244
  Cheddar Cheese Soufflé, '98 24
  Cheese Soufflé, '79 72, 261; '94 116
  Chile-Cheese Soufflés, '96 219
  Corn-and-Cheese Soufflé, '88 122
  Cups, Hot Soufflé, '85 284
  Egg Cheese Soufflé, Three-, '87 234
  Grits Soufflé, Garlic-Cheese, '99 18
  Individual Frozen Soufflés, '80 52
  Individual Soufflés, '80 190
  Italian Pizzola Soufflé, '98 232
  Mexican Pizzola Soufflé, '98 232
  Parmesan Soufflés, '97 280
  Rice-Cheese Soufflé, '79 270
  Rolled Cheese Soufflé, '89 13
  Spinach Soufflé, Cheese-and-, '98 235
  Spinach Soufflé, Cheesy, '81 53
  Three-Cheese Soufflés, '96 219
  Two, Cheese Soufflé for, '81 226
Soups
  Anytime Soup, Cheesy, '81 307; '82 314; '83 66
  Bacon-Beer Cheese Soup, '87 M7
  Bacon-Topped Cheese Soup, '80 M224
  Beer-Cheese Soup, '84 246
  Bell Pepper-Cheese Chowder, '95 240
  Blue Satin Soup, '98 248
  Broccoli Soup, Cheese-and-, '89 276
  Broccoli Soup, Cheesy-, '86 258
  Broccoli-Swiss Soup, '86 6
  Carrot Soup, Cheesy, '81 262
  Cauliflower Soup, '99 318
  Cheddar Cheese Chowder, '97 30
  Cheddar Chowder, Hearty, '79 16

Cheddar-Potato Soup, '03 M283
Chicken Chowder, Cheesy, '92 21
Chicken-Corn Soup, Cheesy, '97 158
Chicken Noodle Soup, Creamy, '99 20
Chicken Soup, Fiesta, '04 323
Chunky Cheese Soup, '98 31
Cilantro Soup, Cream of, '00 249
Corn and Cheese Chowder, '80 228
Cream Cheese Soup, Austrian, '98 M85
Cream of Cheese Soup, '83 99
Cream with Greens Soup, '94 277
Favorite Cheese Soup, Uncle Ed's, '94 228
Gazebo Cheese Soup, '90 158
Gazpacho, Shrimp-Cream Cheese, '94 137
Golden Cheese Chowder, '80 73
Ham-and-Cheese Chowder, '89 15
Ham 'n Cheese Chowder, '79 199
Hearty Cheese Soup, '84 4
Herbed Cheese Soup, '96 219
Hot Brown, Soup, '00 318
Hot Cheese Chowder, '89 16
Macaroni and Cheese Soup, '95 264
Mexican Cheese Soup, '97 268
Minestrone, Cheesy, '99 17
Monterey Jack Cheese Soup, '81 112; '85 M211
Onion-Cheese Soup, '87 81
Onion Soup, Double-Cheese, '85 227
Onion Soup, Double Cheese-Topped, '79 49
Oyster-Cheese Soup, '84 213
Pimiento "Mac and Cheese" Soup, '97 M325
Potato-and-Wild Rice Soup, Cheesy, '89 16
Potato Soup, Baked, '03 29
Reuben Soup, Cream of, '97 26
Rice Soup, Wildest, '01 66
Roquefort Vichyssoise, Velvety, '83 223
Shrimp-Cheese Soup, '01 145
Swiss-Broccoli Chowder, '80 73
Tomato Soup with Parmesan Cheese, Cream of,
  '86 161
Tortilla Soup, '99 310
Vegetable-Cheese Soup, '89 15
Vegetable-Cheese Soup, Creamy, '81 244
Vegetable Cheese Soup, Creamy, '83 230
Vegetable Chowder, Cheese-, '02 305
Vegetable Chowder, Cheesy, '80 25; '83 20;
  '00 272; '01 18
Vegetable Soup, Cheesy, '80 73; '97 241
Velvet Soup, Cheese, '80 74; '92 193
Yukon Gold-Cheese Chowder, '03 296
Zucchini Soup, Cold, '99 164
Spaghetti, Chicken, '98 329
Spaghetti, Marzetti's, '99 85
Spaghetti, Three-Cheese, '83 105
Spanakopita, '86 58; '96 233
Spiders, Dried Apricot, '96 255
Spreads
  Almond Cheese Spread, '87 292
  Aloha Spread, '83 93
  Apricot Brie Spread, '86 275
  Apricot-Cream Cheese Spread, '82 161; '87 158
  Artichoke-Parmesan Spread, '92 95
  Bacon-Cheese Spread, '83 241
  Bacon-Olive Cream Cheese, '04 196
  Basil-Cheese Spread, Fresh, '97 108
  Beer Cheese Spread, '81 160; '85 69
  Beer Spread, Cheesy, '87 196
  Blue Cheese Spread, '90 215; '95 79, 92; '97 240
  Boursin Cheese Spread, Buttery, '94 301; '96 318
  Boursin Cheese Spread, Garlic, '94 301
  Butter, Blue Cheese, '97 306
  Caviar-Cream Cheese Spread, '84 256
  Cheddar-Swiss Spread, '99 106
  Cheese Spread, '96 122; '99 24
  Chile-Cheese Spread, '86 297

Chili Cheese Spread, '93 242
Chili-Cheese Spread, '99 336
Chocolate Cheese Spread, '87 292
Chutney-Onion Cheese Spread, '01 94
Coconut-Cranberry Cheese Spread, '92 328
Confetti Cheese Spread, '84 256
Cottage Cheese Spread, '87 107
Cottage-Egg Salad Spread, '82 146
Cream Cheese-and-Olive Pimiento Cheese,
  '01 169; '03 315
Cream Cheese-Olive Spread, '82 35
Cream Cheese Spread, Deviled, '81 235
Cream Cheese Spread, Fruited, '91 306; '93 79
Cream Cheese Spread, Peachy, '90 M215
Cream Cheese Spread, Pear-, '93 80
Cucumber and Cream Cheese Spread, '82 140
Date-Walnut-Cheese Spread, '96 322
Edam-Sherry Spread, '84 257
Feta-and-Apple Spread, '99 106
Feta Cheese Spread, '96 265
Feta Spread, Herbed, '00 135
Four-Cheese Spread, '99 106
Fruit and Cheese Spread, '81 245
Fruit-and-Cheese Spread, Nutty, '87 246
Garlic-and-Dill Feta Cheese Spread, '04 238
Garlic Pimiento Cheese Spread, '79 58
German Cheese Spread, '79 82
Gouda Cheese Spread, '90 36
Green Onion-Cheese Spread, '92 24
Gruyère-Apple Spread, '81 160
Ham and Pimiento Spread, '80 285
Hawaiian Cheese Spread, '87 158
Herb-Cream Cheese Spread, '83 24
Herbed Avocado-Cheese Spread, '98 335
Herbed Cheese Spread, '87 247
Herbed Goat Cheese, '01 310
Horseradish Spread, '02 53; '03 139
Horseradish Spread, Cheese-, '84 222
Jalapeño-Cheese Spread, '82 248
Jalapeño Pimiento Cheese, '03 315
Make-Ahead Cheese Spread, '93 324
Mexican Cheese Spread, '90 119
Olive Spread, Cheese-, '79 82
Orange Cheese Spread, '87 292
Parmesan-Spinach Spread, '93 55
Party Spread, Spicy, '97 240
Pecan Pimiento Cheese, '03 315
Pesto-Goat Cheese Spread, '03 208
Pimiento and Three Cheeses, '86 296
Pimiento Cheese, '01 169; '03 139, 315
Pimiento Cheese, Chile-, '04 325
Pimiento Cheese, Chunky, '86 295; '88 91
Pimiento Cheese, Creamy, '86 296
Pimiento Cheese, Fabulous, '98 315
Pimiento Cheese, Green Chile-, '01 61
Pimiento Cheese, Incredible, '96 22
Pimiento Cheese, Jalapeño, '98 315; '01 169
Pimiento Cheese, Pecan, '01 169
Pimiento Cheese, Peppered, '01 137
Pimiento Cheese Spread, '82 35; '83 93; '86 127;
  '99 106, 276
Pimiento Cheese Spread, Creamy, '92 159
Pimiento Cheese Spread, Low-Calorie,
  '85 215
Pimiento Cheese, West Texas, '84 9
Pimiento Cheese, White Cheddar, '99 106
Pineapple-Cheese Spread, '86 126; '91 167
Pineapple-Cream Cheese Spread, '82 35
Rosemary Cheese with Fig Preserves, '02 256
Sandwich Spread, Benedictine, '80 299
Swiss Cheese Spread, '90 60
Tomato-Cheddar Spread, '01 321
Tomato-Cheese Spread, '81 157
Tomato-Cheese Spread, Fiery, '87 196

CHEESE, Spreads
(continued)

    Tropical Cheese Spread, '95 46
    Vegetable Sandwich Spread, '83 174
    Waldorf Cheese Spread, '88 173
    Zesty Cheese Spread, '82 140
    Zippy Cheese Spread, '85 4
Steak Cheese Skillet, Swiss, '80 106
Steak Parmesan, '93 41
Steak, Parmesan Round, '80 106
Steaks, Blue Cheese, '84 171
Steaks, Cheese-Stuffed, '81 17
Steaks, Mexican Pepper-Cheese, '97 190
Strata, Artichoke-Cheese, '90 236
Strata, Tomato-Cheese, '81 209
Stromboli, '88 272; '89 181
Strudel, Chicken-Goat Cheese, '98 28
Strudel, Meatless Mexican, '98 29
Strudel, Reuben, '98 28
Stuffing, Catfish with Cream Cheese, '89 52
Supper Supreme, Sunday, '79 76
Sweet Potato Chips with Blue Cheese, '93 290
Tacos, Easy Skillet, '04 180
Taco Stacks, Soft, '02 54
Tart, Dried Tomato-Cheese, '90 203
Tart, Ham-and-Cheese, '92 332
Tart, Herb-Cheese, '87 98
Tart, Leek-Goat Cheese, '04 109
Tart Milan, '87 70
Tart Shells, Cheese, '88 88
Tart, Southwestern, '04 109
Tarts, Sausage 'n' Cheese, '88 51
Tart, Tomato-Basil, '98 132
Tart, Tomato-Pesto, '00 195
Tenderloin, Stuffed Tuscany, '99 269
Terrine, Italian Cheese, '93 64
Terrine with Goat Cheese, Black Bean, '87 120
Terrine with Tomato-Basil Vinaigrette, Blue Cheese,
    '99 288
Tomato, Basil, and Cheese, '95 165
Topping, Blue Cheese Burger, '93 218
Topping, Breadcrumb, '02 233
Topping, Cheese, '86 233
Topping, Yogurt-Cheese, '88 55
Tortellini, Creamy, '99 171
Tortellini with Rosemary-Parmesan Sauce, '92 284
Tortillas, Cheesy, '81 62
Tortilla Snack, Two-Cheese, '90 119
Tortilla Stack, Cheesy Chicken-, '86 3
Toss, Ham and Cheese, '79 55
Tostadas, Quick Chicken, '99 159
Trout Florentine, Cheesy, '85 53
Turkey Cutlets, Parmesan, '01 81
Turkey Parmesan, '82 268
Turnovers, Sausage-Cheese, '88 231; '89 22
Twists, Cheese, '92 125
Veal Parmigiana, '81 227
Vegetables
    Artichoke-Cheese Bottoms, Baked, '94 61
    Artichokes, Stuffed, '99 64
    Asparagus-and-Mushroom Tostadas with Goat
        Cheese, '03 242
    Asparagus Mornay, '99 102
    Asparagus on Toast, Creamed, '95 61
    Asparagus Pie, Cheesy, '01 103
    Asparagus Squares, '02 183
    Asparagus with Goat Cheese Sauce, '93 116
    Banana Peppers, Stuffed, '02 55
    Broccoli-and-Eggs au Gratin, '85 289
    Broccoli au Gratin, '82 M20
    Broccoli Bakers, '99 308
    Broccoli Cups, '00 53

Broccoli Fritters, Cheesy, '79 53
Broccoli Mac 'n' Cheese, '00 53
Broccoli Parmesan, '97 302
Broccoli with Cheese Sauce, '82 107
Brussels Sprouts with Cheese Sauce, '79 246
Cabbage, Cheese Scalloped, '81 87; '82 7
Cabbage Rolls, Southwestern, '97 214
Cauliflower au Gratin, '82 204; '99 59
Cauliflower au Gratin, French-Fried, '79 221;
    '80 82
Cauliflower, Baked Swiss, '79 100
Cauliflower, Cheddar, '99 318
Cauliflower, Cheese-Frosted, '85 68
Cauliflower, Frosted, '97 105
Cauliflower Italiano, Cheesy, '82 300
Cauliflower with Cheese Sauce, '81 101
Celery, Nutty Stuffed, '03 184
Cherry Tomatoes, Cheesy, '83 135
Chiles Rellenos, Cheese, '96 24
Chiles Rellenos (Stuffed Chiles), '82 220;
    '83 150
Corn-and-Swiss Cheese Bake, '92 133
Corn, Creamy Fried Confetti, '02 160
Corn, Grilled Parmesan, '82 127
Eggplant, Cheesy Fried, '90 75
Eggplant, Cheesy Stuffed, '79 188; '82 208
Eggplant, Fried Parmesan, '87 166
Eggplant Parmesan, '82 230; '92 18
Eggplant, Parmesan Fried, '79 189
Eggplant Parmesan, No-Fry, '92 172
Eggplant, Scalloped, '91 223
Fries, Cheesy Oven, '91 187
Green Beans au Gratin, '80 116
Green Beans, Cheese-Topped, '79 100
Green Beans, Cheesy, '80 157
Green Beans, Parmesan, '04 327
Green Beans, Tomato-Feta, '99 59
Green Beans with Blue Cheese, '88 57
Green Beans with Roquefort Cheese and Walnuts,
    '02 255
Hash Brown Cheese Bake, '82 50
Hash Browns, Smothered-Covered, '02 248
Jalapeño Cheese Pie, '96 292
Jalapeños, Hot Stuffed, '99 123
Lentils with Cheese, Baked, '84 113
Limas in Onion Shells, Cheese and, '81 86
Loaf, Pureed Vegetable-Cheese, '85 297
Mushrooms, Herbed Cheese-Stuffed, '96 171
Mushrooms, Parmesan Stuffed, '83 115
Mushrooms, Ricotta-Stuffed, '85 20
New Potatoes, Cheesy, '85 156
New Potatoes, Cheesy Jalapeño, '01 89
New Potatoes, Crispy Roasted, '98 166
Okra with Cheese, '80 185
Onion Bake, Cheese, '82 32
Onion Bake, Romano, '90 98
Onions, Cheese-Stuffed, '90 34
Onions, Parmesan, '93 170
Onions, Sherried Cheese, '82 32
Parmesan Vegetables, '97 147
Pie, Savory Summer, '99 159
Pie, Summer Garden, '02 182
Potato-and-Blue Cheese Pastries, '03 258
Potato Boats, Southwestern, '96 33
Potato Bowls, Mashed, '97 199
Potato-Broccoli-Cheese Bake, '80 114
Potato-Cheese Puff, '95 269
Potato Croquettes, Baked, '97 30
Potato Croquettes, Parmesan, '84 210
Potatoes, Accordion, '98 69
Potatoes Alfredo, '89 204
Potatoes-and-Zucchini au Gratin, '84 5
Potatoes au Gratin, '93 90, 217
Potatoes, Bacon-Topped Blue Cheese, '79 46

Potatoes, Basil-Cheese, '90 M316
Potatoes, Blue Cheese, '98 247; '04 214
Potatoes, Blue Cheese Mashed, '92 330
Potatoes, Blue Cheese Stuffed, '81 276; '92 M228
Potatoes, Blue Cheese-Stuffed, '89 69
Potatoes, Breakfast-Stuffed, '00 179
Potatoes, Cheddar, Broccoli, and Ham Stuffed,
    '04 26
Potatoes, Cheesy, '82 211
Potatoes, Cheesy Bacon-Stuffed, '81 61
Potatoes, Cheesy Caraway, '86 17
Potatoes, Cheesy Chive, '79 46
Potatoes, Cheesy Chive-Stuffed, '91 128
Potatoes, Cheesy Crab-Stuffed, '86 17
Potatoes, Cheesy Frank-Topped, '83 3
Potatoes, Cheesy Mashed, '02 98
Potatoes, Cheesy Scalloped, '96 33
Potatoes, Cheesy Stuffed, '02 175
Potatoes, Chicken-Cheese Stuffed, '86 55
Potatoes, Chili-Cheese, '90 M62
Potatoes, Chive-Cream Cheese Mashed, '92 330
Potatoes, Crab-Stuffed, '99 307
Potatoes, Cream Cheese Mashed, '97 14
Potatoes, Creamy Cheese, '88 M146
Potatoes, Creamy Cheese-and-Chive, '99 308
Potatoes, Creamy Chive-and-Gorgonzola Stuffed,
    '99 308
Potatoes, Feta Cheese, '04 214
Potatoes, Feta Mashed, '92 330
Potatoes, Garlic-Gruyère Mashed, '98 322
Potatoes, Golden, '96 139
Potatoes, Harvest Mashed, '98 248
Potatoes, Horseradish Mashed, '98 69
Potatoes, Italian Mashed, '03 M135
Potatoes, Loaded Garlic Smashed, '01 325
Potatoes, Parmesan, '82 270; '90 M62; '92 M341;
    '93 M46
Potatoes, Parmesan-Cream, '97 54
Potatoes, Parmesan-Paprika, '99 169
Potatoes, Roasted Garlic-Parmesan Mashed,
    '97 263; '00 146
Potatoes Roquefort, '79 211
Potatoes, Stuffed, '01 48; '02 283
Potatoes, Stuffed Mashed, '98 328
Potatoes, Two-Cheese, '80 114
Potatoes with Cheese Sauce, Baked, '83 239
Potatoes with Cheese Sauce, Stuffed, '87 192
Potatoes with Feta Cheese, '84 295; '85 196
Potatoes with Sweet Marjoram and Parmesan
    Cheese, Scalloped, '91 246
Potato Fans, Parmesan-, '88 M190
Potato Gratin, Dual, '93 328
Potato Skins, Cheese, '84 M239
Potato Soufflé, Cheesy, '89 332
Potato Wedges, Parmesan, '95 181
Rice au Gratin, '83 129
Rutabaga au Gratin, '79 254
Spinach-Cheese Puff, '84 96
Spinach, Cheesy Topped, '84 85
Spinach, Creamed, '96 252
Spinach, Easy Italian, '02 235
Spinach-Gorgonzola Custards, Savory, '02 284
Spinach Parmesan, '93 72
Spinach Pie Parma, '96 203
Spinach Pie with Muenster Crust, '95 48
Spinach, Savory Parmesan, '85 68
Spinach with Cheese, Scalloped, '79 8
Spinach with Feta, Lemon, '85 190
Spuds, Mushroom-Swiss, '96 M238
Squash and Tomato Bake, '95 180
Squash Bake, Cheesy, '80 183
Squash Boats, Parmesan-Stuffed, '79 156
Squash, Cheesy Stuffed, '82 134
Squash, Greek-Style, '92 26

Squash Pie, Italian, '02 183
Squash Soufflé, Cheesy, '82 146
Stalks, Splendid, '93 258
Sugar Snap Peas and Goat Cheese, '01 112
Summer Vegetables, Cheesy, '94 119
Sweet Potato Blues, Stacked, '95 290
Sweet Potato Hash Browns, Cheesy, '02 248
Swiss Chard Bundles, '94 48
Tomato Cheese Puffs, '81 48
Tomatoes, Baked Cheddar, '85 43
Tomatoes, Broiled Parmesan, '04 322
Tomatoes, Cheese Herbed-Topped, '86 108
Tomatoes, Cheese-Stuffed, '91 69
Tomatoes, Cheese-Topped, '81 160
Tomatoes, Cheesy Grilled, '79 150
Tomatoes, Cheesy Puff-Top, '86 187
Tomatoes, Cheesy Stuffed, '80 161
Tomatoes, Chile-Cheese Stuffed, '94 141
Tomatoes, Greek, '98 173
Tomatoes, Parmesan, '80 161
Tomatoes, Parmesan-Stuffed, '92 182
Tomatoes, Provençal, '98 267
Tomatoes, Romano Broiled, '80 42
Tomatoes, Spinach-Feta Stuffed, '04 285
Tomatoes with Cheese Sauce over Toast, '88 159
Tomato-Feta Green Beans, '99 59
Tomato Stacks, Fried Green, '02 184
Tomato Tart, '03 158
Tomato Tart, Herbed, '96 94
Tomato with Fresh Mozzarella, Sautéed, '00 163
Turnip au Gratin, '79 289
Turnips au Gratin, '88 229; '89 244
Turnips in Cheese Sauce, '84 229
Vidalia Onions, Baked, '00 102
Yellow Squash with Cheese Sauce, Stuffed,
    '80 162
Zucchini and Tomato au Gratin, '82 208
Zucchini Fries, Parmesan-, '95 129
Zucchini, Ham and Cheese Stuffed, '79 157
Zucchini Parmesan, '81 108; '82 103
Zucchini, Parmesan, '81 234
Zucchini Pie, Cheesy, '82 103
Zucchini, Southwestern Stuffed, '03 M127
Zucchini with Feta, Greek Grilled, '95 190
Vermicelli, Shrimp and Feta Cheese on, '87 108
Vinaigrette, Blue Cheese, '90 55, 280
Vinaigrette, Garlic-Blue Cheese, '92 57
Wafers, Cheese, '95 174; '00 164
Wafers, Hope Farm Cheese, '93 282
Wafers, Italian, '87 36
Wafers, Sage-Pecan Cheese, '93 12
Walnut-Baked Brie, '93 241
Yogurt Cheese, '04 217

CHEESECAKES
Amaretto Cheesecake, '81 150; '99 273
Amaretto Cheesecakes, No-Bake, '00 205
Amaretto-Irish Cream Cheesecake, '90 266
Ambrosia Cheesecake, '02 296
Apple Cheesecake, Dieter's, '86 318
Banana Cheesecake, Chocolate-Wrapped, '99 M48
Bars, Cherry Cheesecake, '97 330
Bavarian Cheesecake, '97 55
Black-and-White Cheesecake, '99 334
Black Forest Cheesecake, '84 74; '89 93; '94 21;
    '97 330
Blueberries 'n' Cream Cheesecake, '87 140
Blueberry Cheesecake, '00 153; '03 182
Blueberry Cheesecake, Reduced-fat, '00 153
Blueberry Chiffon Cheesecake, '87 76
Brownies, Cheesecake, '85 249
Brown Sugar-and-Spice Cheesecake, '89 93
Butter Pecan Cheesecake, '86 61
Butterscotch Cheesecake, '86 188
Candy Bar Cheesecake, '85 298; '86 120

Cherry Cheesecake, '79 50
Cherry-Topped Cheesecake, '80 23
Chocolate-Almond Cheesecake, '93 53
Chocolate-Amaretto Cheesecake, '85 M294; '93 97
Chocolate-Caramel-Pecan Cheesecake, '91 197
Chocolate Cheesecake, '81 16; '82 305
Chocolate Cheesecake, Rich, '84 74; '85 38
Chocolate Cheesecakes, Tiny, '92 288
Chocolate Cheesecake with Whipped Cream
    Frosting, '89 42
Chocolate Chip Cheesecake, '85 114
Chocolate Cookie Cheesecake, '91 298
Chocolate-Glazed Triple-Layer Cheesecake,
    '86 315; '90 310
Chocolate Marble Cheesecake, '89 93
Chocolate-Mint Baked Alaska Cheesecake, '94 142
Chocolate-Mint Cheesecake, '91 104
Chocolate-Raspberry Truffle Cheesecake, '91 270
Chocolate Swirl Cheesecake, '84 295; '85 26
Coconut-Chocolate-Almond Cheesecake, '98 322
Coffee Cake, Deep-Dish Cheesecake, '90 50
Cottage Cheese Cheesecake, '80 24
Cream Cheesecake, Rich, '83 270
Crème de Menthe Cheesecake, '82 263; '89 93
Daiquiri Chiffon Cheesecake, '88 66
Deluxe Cheesecake, '80 23
Fruit-Glazed Cheesecake, '80 24; '90 162
Fudge Cheesecake, '98 M213
Fudge-Filled Cheesecake, Warm, '98 34; '03 320
German Chocolate Cheesecake, '87 265; '00 245
Glazed Cheesecake, '83 142
Grasshopper Cheesecake, '80 191
Individual Cheesecakes, So Easy, '85 30
Island Breeze Cheesecake, '03 144
Kahlúa Cheesecake, Heavenly, '83 48
Key Lime Cheesecake with Strawberry-Butter
    Sauce, '96 87
Key Lime Cheesecake with Strawberry Sauce,
    '03 55
Lemon Cheesecake, '86 194; '91 308; '92 24
Lemon Cheesecake, Luscious, '90 M196
Lemon Cheesecakes with Raspberry Sauce, Mini,
    '02 123
Lemon Cheesecake with Orange-Pineapple Glaze,
    '81 60
Lemon Delight Cheesecake, '95 219
Light-and-Easy Cheesecake, '88 55
Lime Cheesecake with Raspberry Sauce, '00 204
Make-Ahead Cheesecake Pie, '81 233
Marbled Cheesecake, '87 261
Marble Mint Cheesecake, '84 152
Margarita Cheesecake, '92 211; '94 142
Mile-High Cheesecake, '86 334
Mincemeat Cheesecake, Holiday, '00 319
Miniature Cheesecakes, '82 305; '90 170
Mint Cheesecake Bites, '99 282
Mocha Cheesecake, '98 278
Mocha-Chocolate Cheesecake, '88 258
Mocha Swirl Cheesecake, '87 262
New York-Style Cheesecake, '00 205
Orange Cheesecake, '81 84; '85 38
Parfaits, Sugar-Free Peachy Cheesecake, '02 326
Passover Cheesecake, '91 53; '04 86
Passover Cheesecake, Lemony, '02 51
Peach-Caramel Cheesecake, '02 M158
Peaches 'n' Cream Cheesecake, '88 137
Peanut Butter Cheesecake, '94 142
Pear-Berry Cheesecake, '82 M141
Pear-Glazed Cheesecake, '79 67
Pecan Cheesecake, '85 38
Pecan Pie Cheesecake, '02 318; '03 316
Pecan Praline Cheesecake, '03 269
Peppermint Cheesecake, Frozen, '94 143
Petite Cheesecakes, Holiday, '86 321

Phyllo Cheesecakes, Little, '87 275
Piña Colada Cheesecake, '92 70
Piña Colada Cheesecake, Festive, '01 286
Pineapple Cheesecake, '81 32
Pineapple Cheesecake, Ultimate, '85 38
Praline Cheesecake, '83 270; '89 93
Praline-Crusted Cheesecake, '99 295
Pumpkin Cheesecake, '80 254; '85 280; '96 268
Raspberry-Lemon Sauce, Cheesecake with, '96 30
Raspberry Sauce, Cheesecake with, '87 116
Raspberry Sauce, Frozen Cheesecake with, '84 73
Red Velvet Cheesecake, '04 292
Ricotta Cheesecake, Italian, '95 303
Savory
    Cheddar-Chili Cheesecake, '02 251
    Chicken Cheesecake, Curried, '90 174
    Chicken Cheesecakes, Pesto-, '00 118
    Chicken-Chile Cheesecake, '92 42
    Feta Cheesecakes, Little, '86 277
    Fiesta Cheesecake, '93 273
    Ham-and-Asparagus Cheesecake, '90 174; '02 103
    Herbed Cheesecakes, '99 182
    Reuben Cheesecake, '90 175
    Salsa Cheesecake, '98 33
    Shrimp-and-Gruyère Cheesecake, '92 57
    Smoked Salmon Cheesecake, '99 92
    Southwest Cheesecake, '04 293
    Spinach Appetizer Cheesecake, Savory, '02 M207
    Spinach-Herb Cheesecake, '99 139
    Spinach-Mushroom Cheesecake, '92 326
    Spinach Pesto Cheesecake, '90 175
    Sun-Dried Tomato Cheesecake, '03 118
    Taco Cheesecake, '00 56
    Three-Layer Cheesecake, '99 140
    Vegetable Cheesecake, '96 110
    Vegetable Cheesecake, Layered, '91 62; '92 51
    Vegetable Cheesecake, Roasted, '99 140
Shake, Strawberry-Cheesecake, '92 44
Sour Cream Cheesecake, '86 320
Squares, Cheesecake, '84 151
Strawberry Cheesecake, '02 176, 209
Strawberry Cheesecake, Almost, '86 32
Strawberry-Lemon Cheesecake, '04 237
Sweet Potato Cheesecake, '80 287; '96 312
Tarts, Cream Cheese, '84 74
Three-Layer Cheesecake, '99 140
Tofu Cheesecake, Tropical, '00 204
Ultimate Cheesecake, '98 260
Vanilla Cheesecake, Creamy, '89 93
White Chocolate Cheesecake, '87 44; '88 267;
    '94 180
Yam Cheesecake, '81 224
CHERRIES
à la Mode, Cherries, '88 202
Bake, Cherry-Apple, '04 29
Bark, Cherry-Pistachio, '00 M41
Bars, Cherry Cheesecake, '97 330
Bars, Delightful Cherry, '86 217
Black Forest Crisp, '02 128
Bread, Cherry Nut, '81 306; '82 36
Bread, Maraschino Cherry Nut, '79 234
Bread, Quick Cherry-Nut, '85 55
Cake, Black Forest Cherry, '83 302
Cake, Black Forest Pudding, '02 210
Cake, Cherry, '79 165
Cake, Cherry Bourbon, '82 287
Cake, Cherry Fudge, '98 214
Cake, Cherry-Pineapple Dump, '02 128
Cake, Cherry Upside-Down, '82 56
Cake, Choco-Cherry, '96 229
Cake, Chocolate-Cherry, '84 200; '86 239
Cake, Cute-as-a-Button Cherry Pound, '95 139
Cake, Dried Cherry, '97 33
Cake, Maraschino Nut, '83 268

CHERRIES
(continued)

Cake, Pineapple-Cherry Dump, '04 91
Cake, Quick Cherry, '81 238
Cake, Upside-Down Sunburst, '87 9
Cake, White Chocolate-Cherry, '88 268
Cheesecake, Black Forest, '89 93; '94 21; '97 330
Cheesecake, Cherry, '79 50
Cheesecake, Cherry-Topped, '80 23
Chocolate-Covered Cherries, '81 286; '84 298; '97 M55
Chocolates, Cherry, '95 321
Chutney, Glazed Ham with Cherry-Peach, '97 315
Cider, Cherry, '94 288
Cloud, Cherry-Berry on a, '79 94
Cobbler, Berry-Cherry, '83 270
Cobbler, Cherry, '82 91, 139; '99 156
Cobbler, Colossal Cherry, '89 137
Cobbler, Double-Cherry Cheesecake, '03 21
Cobbler, Fresh Cherry, '84 178
Cobbler, Raspberry-Cherry, '93 230
Cobbler, Too-Easy Cherry, '04 28
Coffee Cake, Cherry, '94 49
Coffee Cake, Cherry Blossom, '80 21
Coffee Cake, Cinnamon-Cherry, '98 330
Compote, Cherry, '83 139
Compote, Watermelon-Cherry, '90 180
"Concrete," Cardinal Sin, '94 113
Cookies, Cherry Bonbon, '93 52
Cookies, Cherry Pecan, '82 136
Cookies, Chocolate-Cherry, '85 324
Cookies, Chocolate-Covered Cherry, '99 280
Cookies, Christmas Cherry, '88 282
Cookies, Coconut-Cherry, '79 292
Cookies, Frosted Chocolate-Cherry, '89 294
Cookies, Neapolitan, '00 290
Cordial Cherries, '02 30
Cordial Hot Chocolate, Cherry, '02 220
Cream, Maraschino Russian, '79 231
Crêpes, Cherry, '91 67
Crêpes Flambé, Cherry, '79 18
Crisp, Cherry, '91 20
Crisp, Oatmeal Cherry-Apple, '90 M16
Crowns, Cherry, '92 275
Dessert, Cherry Cordial, '84 312
Dessert, Holiday Cherry, '80 255
Divinity Candy with Sugared Maraschino Cherries, '01 271
Divinity, Cherry, '97 316
Dried Cherry-Walnut Sweet Rolls, '03 235
Drops, Cherry-Almond, '81 20
Filling, Cherry, '83 302; '84 225; '88 178
Frosting, Cherry, '86 217
Frosting, Cherry-Nut Cream Cheese, '96 249
Frosting, Chocolate-Cherry, '89 294
Fudge, Cherry Nut, '83 315
Glaze, Cherry, '83 143; '93 52; '98 260
Ice Cream, Black Forest, '88 203
Ice Cream, Cherry, '84 184; '99 156
Ice Cream, Cherry-Nut, '86 129
Ice Cream, Cherry-Pecan, '88 203
Icing, Chunky Cherry, '03 94
Jubilee, Cherries, '79 18; '83 139
Jubilee, Quick Cherries, '82 M100
Jubilite, Cherries, '86 317
Kirsch, Melon Balls and Cherries in, '91 91
Muffins, Cherry, '82 105
Muffins, Cherry-Nut, '90 87
Muffins, Dried Cherry, '94 59
Nuggets, Cherry Nut, '81 286
Pies
Berry Pie, Cherry-, '92 316

Coconut Crumb Cherry Pie, '92 30
Cranberry-Cherry Pie, Tart, '87 299
Cream Pie with Almond Pastry, Cherry, '92 30
Dried Cherry-and-Pear Fried Pies, '00 213
Easy Cherry Pie, '82 M299
Filling, Dried Cherry Fried Pie, '96 109
Fresh Cherry Pie, '88 178
Lemony Cherry Pie, '92 30
No-Bake Cherry Confetti Pie, '93 114
Pecan Pie, Cherry-, '92 30
Prize-Winning Cherry Pie, '82 57
Red Cherry Pie, '83 192
Scrumptious Cherry Pie, '83 250
Pork Roast, Cherry-Glazed, '91 84
Pound Cake Loaf, Noel, '04 279
Punch, Cranberry-Cherry, '91 176
Relish, Cherry-Honey, '97 32
Rolls, Cherry-Almond, '84 M198
Sabayon, Cherries, '88 178
Salads
Apple Salad, Cherry-, '86 31
Best Cherry Salad, '82 302
Bing Cherry-and-Cranberry Salad, '04 297
Bing Cherry-Grapefruit Salad, '00 285
Bing Cherry Salad, '01 46
Cola Salad, Cherry, '80 104
Cola Salad, Cherry-, '91 224; '95 94
Congealed Cherry Salad, '89 278
Festive Cherry Salad, '84 265
Fresh Cherry Salad, '83 120
Frozen Black Cherry Salad, '89 163
Frozen Cherry Salad, '79 126
Frozen Cherry Salad, Delicious, '81 252
Fruit Salad, Cherry, '87 236
Honey-Lime Dressing, Cherry Salad with, '83 139
Orange Salad, Cherry-, '79 74; '82 56
Port Wine-Cherry Salad, '86 11
Ribbon Salad, Christmas, '02 257
Sherry Dressing, Cherry Salad with, '79 165
Sweet Cherry Salad, '89 326
Wine Salad, Elegant Cherry-, '82 56
Salsa, Cherry, '99 156
Sauce and Gorgonzola, Peppered Sirloin with Cherry-Merlot, '02 320
Sauce, Cherry, '79 91; '83 276; '84 91; '91 67
Sauce, Cherry-Wine, '95 285; '97 132
Sauce, Chocolate-Cherry, '85 189
Sauce, Chocolate Cherry, '87 M165
Sauce, Elegant Cherry, '79 M156
Sauce, Ham Balls with Spiced Cherry, '81 112; '82 12
Sauce, Maraschino-Orange, '96 164
Sauce, Pork Fillets with Dark Cherry, '04 221
Sauce, Roast Ducklings with Cherry, '86 312
Sauce, Roast Pork with Spiced Cherry, '89 324
Sauce, Royal Cherry, '85 224; '86 83
Sauce, Smoked Pork Chops with Jalapeño-Cherry, '01 208
Sauce, Spicy Cherry, '83 244
Scones, Cherry-and-Cream, '99 49
Sherried Cherries, '93 289
Slump, Cherry, '83 139
Snow, Berries on, '82 227
Sorbet, Cherry, '03 171
Sparkler, Cherry, '00 329
Spread, Cherry, '93 309
Squares, Cherry, '97 273
Squares, Surprise Cherry, '82 57
Stuffed Cherries, '85 81
Sugared Maraschino Cherries and Mint Sprigs, '01 271
Syrup, Cherry-Lemonade, '86 214

Tart, Cherry and Blackberry, '83 225
Tart, Chocolate-Cherry, '97 33
Tarts, Cheery Cherry, '80 238
Topping, Cherry-Pineapple, '87 126
Torte, Black Forest Cherry, '88 178
Truffles, Chocolate-Cherry Cordial, '99 127
CHICKEN
Acapulco, Chicken, '84 32
à la King, Chicken, '79 218; '83 137; '87 197; '94 41
à la King, Easy Chicken, '93 14
Alfredo, Chicken Fettuccine, '00 57
Almond Chicken, '01 26
Almond Chicken and Vegetables, '86 21
Almond Chicken, Creamy, '89 281
Almond Chicken, Spicy, '88 150
à l'Orange, Chicken, '84 277
Alouette, Chicken, '91 295
Andalusia, Chicken, '87 103
Appetizers, Chicken-Mushroom, '88 210
Appetizers, Sesame Chicken, '89 61
Apple Chicken, '85 57
Apricot Chicken, '92 12
Apricot Chicken Breasts, '88 301
Apricot Chicken with Roasted Potato Thins, '02 23
Apricot Glaze, Chicken with Tangy, '98 275
Ariosto, Shrimp and Chicken, '79 31
Arroz con Pollo, '01 279
Artichoke Chicken, '81 97
Artichoke Hearts, Chicken with, '88 54
Artichokes and Mushrooms, Chicken with, '90 35
Artichokes, Chicken with, '02 314
Artichokes, Italian Chicken and, '95 68
Bag, Chicken in a, '86 M57; '87 23
Bake, Chicken, Ham, and Cheese, '87 217
Bake, Chicken-Italian Dressing, '91 199
Bake, Chicken-Tomato, '83 35
Bake, Crispy Chicken, '83 115
Baked Breast of Chicken with Marinated Bermuda Onions, '92 194
Baked Chicken and Artichoke Hearts, '82 260
Baked Chicken and Dressing, '79 296
Baked Chicken, Breaded, '81 76
Baked Chicken Breasts, Basic, '04 215
Baked Chicken Breasts, Sherried, '79 83
Baked Chicken Breasts, Wine-, '83 177
Baked Chicken, Buttermilk, '00 48; '01 212
Baked Chicken, Citrus Herb, '85 303
Baked Chicken, Fancy, '79 85
Baked Chicken, Fruity, '01 48
Baked Chicken, Herb-, '82 229
Baked Chicken in Wine, '81 109
Baked Chicken, Italian, '82 84
Baked Chicken, Marmalade, '99 286
Baked Chicken Parmesan, '83 137
Baked Chicken, Tomato-, '81 281; '82 30
Baked Chicken with Tarragon Sauce, '94 126
Baked Chicken with Wine-Soaked Vegetables, '84 277
Baked Hen with Cranberry Pan Gravy, '94 308
Baked Honey Chicken, '99 110
Baked in Wine, Chicken, '97 128
Baked Italian Chicken, '83 184
Baked Lemon Chicken, '85 190
Baked Mustard Chicken, '87 10
Baked Parmesan Chicken, '83 320
Bake, Herb Chicken, '82 186
Bake, Individual Chicken, '90 279
Bake, Mushroom-Chicken, '89 147
Bake, Parslied Chicken, '90 65
Bake, Pineapple Chicken, '82 120
Bake, Saucy Chicken, '84 220
Bake, Savory Chicken, '98 31
Bake, Seasoned Chicken, '94 278

Ball, Chicken-Cheese, '93 216
Ball, Chicken-Curry Cheese, '85 118
Balls, Coconut Curried Chicken, '91 165
Balls, Curried Chicken, '91 98
Banana Chicken with Black Bean Sauce, '96 156
Barbecued
  Bake, Barbecued Chicken, '81 97
  Braised and Barbecued Chicken, Melt-in-Your-
    Mouth, '03 326
  Chicken, Barbecue, '86 122
  Chicken, Barbecued, '82 97, 106; '83 103;
    '85 144; '86 153; '89 167
  Chili-Barbecued Chicken, '98 170
  Cranberry Chicken, Barbecued, '83 178
  Fingers, Barbecue-Battered Chicken, '04 139
  Foil, Barbecued Chicken in, '04 222
  Glazed Barbecue Chicken, Carambola-, '92 246
  Golden Barbecued Chicken, '83 136
  Grilled Barbecued Chicken, '81 154
  Honey Barbecue Chicken, '04 197
  Legs and Thighs, Barbecued Chicken, '94 94
  Lemon Barbecued Chicken, '93 215
  Marinated Barbecued Chicken, '79 90
  Old South Barbecued Chicken, '82 97; '83 103
  Orange Barbecued Chicken, '88 123
  Oven-Baked Barbecue Chicken, '03 160
  Oven-Barbecued Chicken, Kentucky-Style,
    '96 328
  Oven-Barbecued Cranberry Chicken, '93 332
  Pizza, Barbecue Chicken, '03 49
  Saucy Barbecued Chicken, '83 11
  South-of-the-Border Barbecued Chicken, '97 311
  Sweet-and-Spicy Barbecued Chicken, '01 316
  Tangy Barbecued Chicken, '86 186; '98 170
  White Barbecue Sauce, Chicken with, '89 M84;
    '97 322
  Zesty Barbecued Chicken, '80 M76
  Zippy Barbecued Chicken, '83 213
Basil Chicken, '87 171
Beer-Can Chicken, '04 118
Beer-Can Chicken, Basic, '03 130; '04 104
Beer-Smothered Chicken, '01 107
Bengalese Chicken, '79 12
Benne Seed Chicken, '01 107
Bird's-Nest Chicken, '88 152
Birds of Paradise, '82 224
Biscuit, Chicken in a, '79 263; '80 30
Bites, Curried Chicken, '85 40
Bites, Savory Chicken, '92 209
Bites with Sweet-Hot Tomato Chutney, Chicken,
  '00 309
Black Bean Puree, Spicy Chicken with, '97 48
Black Beans and Oranges, Chicken with, '00 94
Boiled Chicken Breasts, '04 215
Bourbon Chicken with Gravy, '94 252
Bourbon-Laced Tipsy Chicken with Peaches,
  '97 136
Bourbon-Purple Onion Relish, Chicken with,
  '95 253
Braised Bourbon Chicken, '86 51
Braised Chicken Breast in Lemon Cream Sauce,
  '94 184
Brandado, Chicken, '84 195
Breaded Chicken Breasts, '89 M196
Breast of Chicken, Herbed, '79 100
Breasts, Celebrity Chicken, '95 60
Breasts Diane, Chicken, '99 213
Breasts, Greek Chicken, '95 170; '98 19
Breasts, Island Chicken, '84 68
Breasts Lombardy, Chicken, '82 242
Breasts, Salsa-Topped Chicken, '94 144
Breasts Saltimbocca, Chicken, '98 19
Breasts, Saucy Chicken, '83 184; '87 167
Breasts with Herb Butter, Chicken, '89 120

Breasts with Orange-Ginger Sauce, Chicken, '97 47
Breasts with Sage Orzo, Chicken, '98 169
Brioche Chicken Curry, '88 124
Broiled Chicken Breast Tarragon, '89 310
Broiled Chicken, Island, '84 288
Broth, Easy Microwave Chicken, '90 M167
B'steeya with Chicken, '98 210
Buffalo Chicken Twice-Baked Potatoes, '04 184
Bundles, Cheesy Chicken-and-Ham, '84 261
Bundles, Chicken-Mushroom, '80 157
Bundles, San Antonio-Style Chicken, '85 251
Bundles, Southwestern Chicken, '02 215
Bundles with Bacon Ribbons, Chicken, '87 68
Burgers, Open-Faced Chicken-Onion, '94 139
Burgoo, Five-Meat, '87 3
Burgoo, Harry Young's, '87 3
Burgoo, Kentucky, '97 138
Burgoo, Old-Fashioned, '87 3
Buttermilk-Pecan Chicken, '89 166; '97 252
Cacciatore, Chicken, '99 213
Cacciatore, Hearty Chicken, '02 269
Cajun Chicken over Rice, '87 268; '88 102; '89 67
Cakes with Avocado Cream, Southwestern Chicken-
  and-Corn, '97 M311
Canapés, Chicken-Cucumber, '98 154
Caprese with Tomato-Basil Cream, Chicken,
  '99 240
Caramelized Chicken with Cranberry Conserve,
  '98 320
Cashew Chicken, '79 255; '80 8; '83 21; '01 188
Cashew, Chicken, '88 38
Cashews, Chicken with, '79 207
Casseroles
  à la Russell, Chicken, '95 175
  Almond Casserole, Chicken-, '94 199
  Artichoke Casserole, Chicken-and-, '96 133
  Artichokes, Chicken and, '03 26
  Asparagus Casserole, Chicken-, '83 76; '84 71
  Basil Chicken with Spinach Fettuccine, Creamy,
    '97 328
  Breast-of-Chicken Fiesta, '88 151
  Breasts, Creamy Baked Chicken, '83 24
  Broccoli, and Cauliflower Casserole, Chicken,
    '00 337
  Broccoli Casserole, Chicken-, '79 48; '91 315
  Broccoli-Chicken Casserole, '82 33
  Brown Rice Bake, Chicken-, '91 314
  Cacciatore, Chicken, '80 39; '83 118; '84 9;
    '86 42
  Cacciatore, Quick Chicken-and-Rice, '88 38
  Cannelloni with Roasted Red Bell Pepper Sauce,
    Chicken, '02 287
  Cassoulet, Easy Chicken, '00 43; '04 325
  Cheesy Chicken Casserole, '85 34
  Chicken Casserole, '96 103, 302
  Chilaquiles con Pollo (Tortillas with Chicken),
    '81 66
  Chile Chicken with Salsa, Baked, '88 147
  Chiles Casserole, Chicken-and-, '93 107
  Chili Bake, Chicken, '93 302
  Chimichangas, Chicken, '93 68; '94 30
  Chow Mein Chicken Casserole, '96 276
  Company Chicken Bake, '80 301
  Countryside Chicken Bake, '88 39
  D'Iberville, Chicken Casserole, '04 182
  Dilly Chicken, '90 65
  Divan Casserole, Chicken, '82 M203
  Divan, Chicken, '80 M10; '87 M218
  Divan, Curried Chicken, '80 83
  Divan, Easy Chicken, '94 310
  Divan, Elegant Crêpes, '81 91
  Divan, Gourmet Chicken, '82 83
  Divan, Overnight Chicken, '83 198
  Divan, Sherried Chicken, '80 38

Dressing Casserole, Chicken-and-, '81 263
Dressing, Santa Fe Chicken and, '03 48
Enchilada Casserole, Easy, '02 143
Enchiladas, Baked Chicken-and-Cheese, '03 332
Enchiladas, Chicken, '80 301; '86 296; '90 121;
  '00 45; '03 214
Enchiladas, Chicken-and-Spinach, '91 222
Enchiladas, Chicken-Cheese, '02 236
Enchiladas, Chicken-Sour Cream, '04 274
Enchiladas, Creamy Chicken, '97 250; '01 M94
Enchiladas, Easy Chicken, '82 89; '86 231
Enchiladas, Quicker Chicken, '97 312
Enchiladas, Three-Cheese Chicken, '99 330
Enchiladas Verde, Chicken, '00 M240
Enchiladas with Tomatillo Sauce, Chicken,
  '95 206
Florentine, Chicken, '93 107
Florentine, Chicken-and-Shrimp, '89 64
Fontina-Baked Chicken, '90 64
Garlic-Spinach Chicken, '92 56
Good Chicken Casserole, Simply, '95 255
Green Bean Casserole, Chicken-, '85 296
Green Bean Casserole, Creamy Chicken-, '97 158
Grits, Chicken and, '95 263
Grits with Chicken Sausage and Shiitake
  Mushrooms, Cheese, '03 254
Herbed Chicken, French, '86 89
Hot-and-Spicy Chicken Dinner, '94 M94
Jalapeño Chicken Casserole, '02 50
King Ranch Casserole, '02 210
King Ranch Chicken, '95 193; '99 330; '03 313
King Ranch Chicken Casserole, '00 280
King Ranch Chicken Casserole, Light, '04 57
Lasagna Bake, Chicken, '95 55
Lasagna, Chicken, '87 M302; '88 90; '92 197;
  '93 25; '96 16
Lasagna, Creamy Ham-and-Chicken, '95 88
Lasagna, Easy Mexican, '03 22
Lasagna Florentine, Chicken, '95 158; '02 232
Lasagna, Green Chile-Chicken, '00 338
Lasagna, Heavenly Chicken, '00 310
Lasagna, Southwestern Chicken, '03 173
Linguine, Chicken, '01 128
Macaroni-and-Cheese Bake, '01 41
Macaroni and Chicken Casserole, '80 260
Macaroni Casserole, Chicken-, '85 219
Make-Ahead Chicken Casserole, '84 241
Manicotti, Creamy Chicken, '85 60
Mexicana, Chicken, '91 M127
Mexican Chicken Casserole, '82 143
Mexican Chicken, Cheesy, '01 199
Mexican Chicken, Spicy, '82 89
Mexi-Chicken Casserole, '93 69; '94 30
Noodle Casserole, Chicken-, '94 286
Noodle Casserole, Chicken, '01 308
Noodle Casserole, Chicken and Green, '80 32
Orzo, and Spinach Casserole, Chicken, '02 124
Oyster-and-Chicken Casserole, '99 320
Paella Casserole, '95 254
Parmesan, Chicken, '04 42
Parmigiana, Chicken, '80 190
Parmigiana, Chicken-Eggplant, '82 212
Parmigiana, Zesty Chicken, '00 19
Pasta Casserole, Chicken-and-, '97 192
Pecan Chicken, Lemony, '96 82
Pesto-Chicken Casserole, '94 231
Poppy Seed Chicken, '99 195
Quick Chicken Casserole, '81 91
Reuben Casserole, Chicken, '03 69
Rice-and-Chicken Casserole, '87 154
Rice Casserole, Chicken-, '86 52; '99 215
Rice Casserole, Chicken and, '80 260
Rice Casserole, Creamy Chicken-, '99 21
Rice Casserole, Creamy Chicken-and-, '02 309

CHICKEN, Casseroles
(continued)

Rice Casserole, Crispy Chicken-and-, **'03** 203
Rice Casseroles, Chicken-and-, **'01** 52
Rice, Chicken and, **'95** 54
Salad, Baked Chicken, **'86** 297; **'87** 176
Scarborough Chicken, **'80** 38
Shrimp-and-Chicken Casserole, **'91** 102
Southwestern Casserole, **'99** 216
Spaghetti Casserole, Chicken-, **'84** 15
Spaghetti, Spicy Chicken, **'02** 327
Spaghetti Squash and Chicken Skillet Casserole, **'94** 134
Spicy Chicken Bake, **'85** 251
Squash Casserole, Chicken-, **'95** 121
Squash-Chicken Casserole, Hearty Tex-Mex, **'99** 312; **'03** 107
Sunday Chicken Casserole, **'83** 290
Superb Casserole, Chicken, **'89** 83
Supreme Casserole, Chicken, **'84** 219
Supreme, Hot Chicken, **'81** 76
Swiss Chicken, **'95** 54
Swiss Chicken Casserole, **'90** 67
Swiss Chicken Thighs, **'94** 282
Tangy Chicken, **'85** 251
Tetrazzini, Cheesy Chicken, **'83** M87
Tetrazzini, Chicken, **'79** 268; **'80** M75; **'83** 288; **'99** 61; **'00** 45; **'02** 171; **'04** 221
Tortilla Bake, Chicken, **'82** 89
Tortilla Casserole, Chicken, **'81** 166
Unforgettable Chicken Casserole, **'04** 294
Vegetable-Chicken Bake with Sweet Bacon Dressing, **'93** 108
Wild Rice Casserole, Chicken-, **'84** 241; **'85** 65
Wild Rice Casserole, Chicken-and-, **'97** 192; **'00** 257
Wild Rice Casserole, Leslie's Favorite Chicken-and-, **'00** 209; **'03** 107
Wild Rice, Chicken and, **'79** 248
Wild Rice Supreme, Chicken-, **'79** 77
Cassoulet, **'96** 328
Celery Skillet, Chicken-and-, **'88** 6
Chafing Dish Chicken, **'82** 284
Chalupas, Chicken, **'79** 185
Chalupas, Chicken-Olive, **'81** 227
Champagne Chicken, **'85** 251
Champagne Sauce, Chicken Breasts with, **'86** 49
Charcoal Broiled Chicken, **'79** 90
Charlemagne, Chicken, **'86** 293
Cheesecake, Chicken-Chile, **'92** 42
Cheesecake, Curried Chicken, **'90** 174
Cheesecakes, Pesto-Chicken, **'00** 118
Chili, White, **'91** 284
Chili, White Bean, **'02** 20
Chili, White Christmas, **'98** 266; **'02** 260
Chili, White Lightning Texas, **'92** 321
Chimichangas, Chicken, **'98** 95
Chimichangas, Oven-Fried Chicken, **'90** 175
Chinese, Chicken, **'94** 33
Chinese Chicken and Vegetables, **'81** 212
Chinese Chicken, Lazy Day, **'81** 3
Chinese-Style Chicken Dinner, **'89** 247
Chinese-Style Dinner, **'84** 26
Chop Suey, Chicken, **'81** 227
Chowder, Cheesy Chicken, **'92** 21
Chowder, Chicken, **'83** 20
Chowder, Creamy Chicken-Vegetable, **'92** 20
Chowder, Curried Chicken-and-Corn, **'92** 21
Chowder, Mexican Chicken-Corn, **'01** 18
Chow Mein, Chicken, **'90** 68; **'98** 283
Chutney Chicken, **'86** 249
Cobbler, Spicy Tex-Mex Chicken, **'03** 324

Cobbler with Caramelized Onions, Chicken, **'00** 44
Coconut Chicken, **'98** 20
Coconut Chicken with Fresh Fruit, **'93** 294
Coconut Milk, Chicken in, **'97** 202
Cola-Can Chicken, **'03** 130; **'04** 104
Company Chicken, **'80** 39; **'83** 125
Continental, Chicken, **'82** 274
Cordon Bleu, Chicken, **'81** 304; **'82** 83; **'86** 37; **'93** 126
Cordon Bleu, Company Chicken, **'82** 274
Cordon Bleu, Easy Chicken, **'02** 175
Cordon Bleu in Mushroom Sauce, Chicken, **'86** 198
Cordon Bleu, Pasta, **'97** 327
Corn Flake Chicken, **'91** 172
Country Captain Chicken, **'94** 252
Country Poulet, **'86** 292
Couscous, Chicken with, **'97** 325
Crabmeat Stuffing, Chicken Breasts with, **'85** 302
Cracked Wheat, "Fried," **'89** 31
Cream Cheese Chicken Breasts, **'90** 234
Creamed Chicken, **'82** 49, 284; **'83** 14
Creamed Chicken and Vegetables, **'91** 90
Creamed Chicken, Company, **'82** 84
Creamed Chicken in a Shell, **'79** 138
Creamed Chicken in Biscuit Bowls, **'03** 222
Creamed Chicken in Patty Shells, **'86** 123
Creamed Chicken over Confetti Rice Squares, **'81** 282; **'82** 31
Creamed Chicken over Cornbread, **'86** 231
Creamed Chicken Toppers, **'99** 240
Creamed Ham and Chicken, **'81** M74
Creole, Chicken, **'86** 231; **'89** 33; **'90** 146
Creole Chicken, **'94** 93; **'95** 261
Creole Chicken and Rice, **'92** 262
Crêpes, Chicken, **'80** 39
Crêpes, Chicken-Vegetable, **'83** 70
Crêpes, Creamy Chicken, **'81** 200
Crêpes Divan, Elegant, **'81** 91
Crispy Chicken, **'84** 152; **'01** 246
Croissants, Chutney-Chicken, **'92** 22
Croquettes and Mushroom Sauce, Chicken, **'91** 220
Croquettes, Chicken, **'81** 133
Croquettes, Crispy Chicken, **'88** 206
Crunchy Chicken, Janet's, **'96** 22
Curried Chicken, **'86** 43
Curried Chicken, Quick, **'89** 219; **'99** 92
Curried Chicken, Regal, **'84** 110
Curry, Chicken, **'84** 110; **'85** 220; **'86** 21; **'89** 219
Curry, Indian-Style Chicken, **'97** 119
Curry, Turban Chicken, **'94** 266
Cutlets with Lemon, Chicken, **'85** 8
Dante's Chicken, **'88** 25
Delicacy, Chicken, **'99** M23
Deviled Chicken, Zesty, **'90** 232
Dijon Chicken, **'81** 156; **'99** 21
Dijon, Chicken, **'04** 196
Dijon Chicken with Pasta, **'90** 318
Dijon-Herb Chicken, **'89** 120
Dilled Chicken Paprika, **'86** 41
Dinner, Chicken-Mushroom, **'81** 3
Dinner, Chicken Peach, **'79** 77
Dinner, Curried Chicken Skillet, **'95** 47
Dinner, Healthful Chicken, **'83** 232
Dip, Hot Chicken, **'80** 86
Dixie Manor, Chicken à la, **'85** 3
Dressing, Chicken and, **'99** 42
Dressing, Chicken and Rice, **'79** 288
Dressing, Chicken Cornbread, **'90** 159
Dressing, Tipsy Chicken and, **'88** 151
Drummettes. *See also* **CHICKEN/Wings.**
Down-Home Chicken Drummettes, **'93** 157
Fried Chicken Drummettes with Horseradish Sauce, **'88** 207
Ginger-Garlic Appetizer Drummettes, **'93** 157

Orange-Pecan Chicken Drummettes, **'93** 158
Southwestern Chicken Drummettes, **'93** 158
Drumsticks, Breaded Chicken, **'99** 110
Drumsticks, Cajun-Style, **'87** 159
Drumsticks, Tangy, **'97** 120
Dumplings and Chicken, Biscuit, **'99** 326
Dumplings, Chicken and, **'97** 208; **'00** 111; **'01** 231; **'03** 25
Dumplings, Chicken and Potato, **'99** 326
Dumplings, Chicken and Tortilla, **'99** 327
Dumplings, Country Chicken and, **'85** 254
Dumplings, Easy Chicken and, **'86** 21
Dumplings, Old-Fashioned Chicken and, **'79** 55; **'83** 228; **'93** 302
Dumplings, Quick Chicken and, **'95** 125; **'02** 16
Dumplings with Herbed Broth, Chicken and, **'95** 338
Dumplings with Vegetables, Chicken and, **'85** M56
Easy Chicken, **'89** M129
Egg Bread, Chicken on, **'95** 120
Eggs, Chicken-Stuffed, **'98** 102
Empanadas, **'92** 156
Enchiladas, Chicken, **'04** 96
Enchiladas, Chicken-Chile, **'97** 313
Enchiladas, Creamy, **'93** 174
Enchiladas, Healthy Chicken, **'02** 19
Enchiladas Terrificas, **'84** 32
Enchiladas Verde, Chicken, **'93** 274
Enchiladas with Spicy Sauce, Chicken, **'84** 76
Enchiladas with Tomatillo Sauce, Chicken, **'94** 231
English Muffin Delight, **'82** 45
en Papillote, Chicken and Vegetables, **'86** 145
Fajita Fettuccine, **'94** 84
Fajitas, Beef and Chicken, **'02** 119
Fajitas, Chicken, **'88** 231; **'89** 100; **'90** 204; **'99** 158
Fajita Spuds, Chicken, **'96** 238
Fajita Spuds with Black Bean Salsa, Chicken, **'04** 25
Fancy Fowl, **'81** 76; **'82** 13
Fennel and Mushrooms, Chicken with, **'97** 93
Fennel, Chicken with, **'00** 322
Fettuccine, Cajun Chicken, **'96** 198
Fettuccine, Chicken and Dried Tomatoes over, **'98** 233
Fettuccine, Chicken-and-Tomatoes over, **'90** 204
Fettuccine, Chicken-Pecan, **'86** 52
Fettuccine, Ranch House, **'03** 123
Fiesta Chicken, Spicy, **'84** 234
Filling, Chicken, **'81** 200
Filling, Chicken Divan, **'81** 91
Filling, Chicken-Olive, **'81** 227
Filling, Crêpe, **'96** 48
Filling, Curried Chicken, **'88** 125
Filling Luau, Chicken, **'79** 81
Fingers, Buttermilk-Pecan Chicken, **'93** 165
Fingers, Chicken Little, **'80** 249
Fingers, Herb-Baked Chicken, **'86** 249
Fingers, No-Fry-Pan Chicken, **'91** 120
Fingers, Spicy Chicken, **'91** 162
Fingers with Honey-Horseradish Dip, Chicken, **'02** 308
Firecrackers, Texas, **'95** 96; **'99** 94
Flautas, **'83** 199
Flautas with Guacamole, Chicken, **'89** 226
Florentine with Mushroom Sauce, Chicken, **'87** 250
Foil, Chicken in, **'91** 134; **'94** 93
Foil Supper, Chicken Olé, **'04** 222
Foil-Wrapped Chicken, **'99** 108
Fricassee, White Chicken, **'98** 122
Fried
Beaumont Fried Chicken, **'88** 92
Best Ever Sunday Chicken, **'89** 234
Best Fried Chicken, Our, **'97** 311
Bites, French-Fried Chicken, **'85** 160
Buttermilk Fried Chicken, Company, **'86** 177
Cajun Fried Chicken, **'01** 334

Cakes with Creole Sauce, Chicken, '02 32, 284
Cakes with Rémoulade Sauce, Chicken, '00 44
Cheese-Stuffed Chicken Thighs, Fried, '88 206
Cream Gravy, Fried Chicken with, '85 241
Crispy Fried Chicken Breasts, '80 155
Crunchies, Tex-Mex Chicken, '03 328
Curried Fried Chicken, '85 160
Delicious Fried Chicken, '86 156
Dixie Fried Chicken, '88 14
Drummettes with Horseradish Sauce, Fried
    Chicken, '88 207
Drumsticks, Buttermilk, '87 175
Edna's Fried Chicken, '99 126
Finger Chicken, '96 89
Fingers, Chicken Almondette, '93 12
Fingers with Come Back Sauce, Fried Chicken,
    '00 211
Fritters with Lime-Cayenne Mayonnaise,
    Chicken-and-Mashed Potato, '04 121
Garlic-Flavored Fried Chicken, '79 147
Garlic Fried Chicken, '82 148
Gravy, Fried Chicken, '95 235
Herbed Fried Chicken, '87 91
Herb-Seasoned Fried Chicken, '80 8
Kudzu Fried Chicken, '95 198
Lemon-Fried Chicken, '79 77
Lemon Fried Chicken, '82 275
Mama's Fried Chicken, '02 180
Mandarin Chicken, Crispy, '86 119
Mexican Fried Chicken, '81 166; '87 176
Mom's Fried Chicken, '01 163
Mushroom Sauce, Chicken with, '04 255
Nuggets, Golden Chicken, '80 159
Nuggets, Lemon-Chicken, '87 283
Oven-Fried Chicken, '84 118; '93 90; '95 236;
    '99 212
Oven-Fried Chicken, Buttermilk, '03 213
Oven-Fried Chicken, Crisp, '94 220
Oven-Fried Chicken, Crunchy, '87 163
Oven-Fried Chicken, Crusty, '79 77
Oven-Fried Chicken Cutlets, '04 81
Oven-Fried Chicken, Golden-Brown, '86 21
Oven-Fried Chicken Legs, Jalapeño, '94 94
Oven-Fried Chicken, Nutty, '85 160
Oven-Fried Chicken, Southern, '86 37
Oven-Fried Chicken, Spicy, '97 307
Oven-Fried Chicken with Honey-Butter Sauce,
    '85 18
Oven-Fried Parmesan Chicken, '81 97; '82 148
Oven-Fried Pecan Chicken, '84 288
Oven-Fried Sesame Chicken, '79 77
Pan-Fried Chicken, Virginia, '96 142
Peppery Chicken Fried Chicken, '04 57
Picnic Fried Chicken, '01 125
Poppers, Chicken, '01 321
Sesame Chicken, '82 148
Southern Fried Chicken Breasts, '98 20
Southern Fried Chicken, Our Best, '95 235;
    '00 142; '02 106; '03 178, 310
Special Fried Chicken, '88 220
Spicy Country-Fried Chicken, '82 148
Spicy Fried Chicken, '83 5; '88 129; '94 162
Spinach-Stuffed Chicken Breasts, Fried, '88 206
Stuffed Chicken with Roasted Red Pepper-and-
    Vidalia Onion Gravy, Southern-Fried, '03 322
Sunday Dinner Fried Chicken, '88 110
Super Fried Chicken, '82 148
Sweet 'n' Sour Chicken, '04 311
Timely Fried Chicken, '98 274
Traditional Fried Chicken, '82 148
Walnut Chicken, Deep-Fried, '87 175
Wings, Hot Buffalo, '87 176
Fried Rice, Chicken-Cashew, '99 171
Fruited Chicken en Crème, '83 264

Garden, Chicken-in-a-, '80 18
Garlic Chicken, Forty-Cloves-of-, '95 261
Garlic Chicken, Moroccan, '99 15
Garlic Sauce, Chicken with, '00 270
Ginger-and-Orange Chicken with Broccoli, Spicy,
    '02 309
Ginger Chicken and Cashews, '85 M11
Ginger-Nut Chicken, '90 M33
Glazed Chicken and Pears, '99 21
Glazed Chicken, Fruit-, '80 211
Glazed Chicken, Wine-, '03 26
Glazed Roasted Chicken, '03 217
Gold Nugget Chicken, '95 120
Gravy, Chicken, '99 34
Gravy, Chicken Smothered in, '99 41
Greek Lemon Chicken, '90 65
Green Onions, Chicken with Grilled, '01 94
Grilled Bahamian Chicken with Cha-Cha Salsa,
    '97 160
Grilled Basil Chicken, '93 201
Grilled Chicken, '89 200; '92 170; '94 167
Grilled Chicken and Onions, Grits with, '99 17
Grilled Chicken and Vegetables, '99 200
Grilled Chicken Breasts, '84 172; '04 214
Grilled Chicken Breasts with Fig-and-Melon
    Compote, '00 163
Grilled Chicken Breasts with Lemon-Yogurt
    Coleslaw, '98 148
Grilled Chicken, Creole, '04 289
Grilled Chicken, Garlic-, '87 180
Grilled Chicken, Garlic-and-Wine, '00 136
Grilled Chicken, Honey-Glazed, '99 213
Grilled Chicken, Honey-Lime, '96 189; '98 332
Grilled Chicken, Lemon-Herb, '95 87
Grilled Chicken, Lime-, '02 142; '04 320
Grilled Chicken, Smoky, '85 160
Grilled Chicken Tortas, '01 M187
Grilled Chicken with Basting Sauce, '01 146
Grilled Chicken with Cha-Cha Salsa, '98 333
Grilled Chicken with Creamy Sauce, '01 318
Grilled Chicken with Dill Sauce, '88 162
Grilled Chicken with Spicy Soba Noodles, '00 93
Grilled Chicken with Sweet Soy Slaw and Dipping
    Sauce, '04 123
Grilled Chicken with Tabbouleh Salad, '91 70
Grilled Chicken with Vegetables Vinaigrette, '91 26
Grilled Cumin Chicken, '87 142
Grilled Ginger-Glazed Chicken, '98 166
Grilled Ginger-Orange Chicken, '91 26
Grilled Herbed Chicken Quarters, '96 171
Grilled Jalapeño Chicken, '93 213
Grilled Lime-Jalapeño Chicken, '91 87
Grilled Margarita-Marinated Chicken, '97 167
Grilled Southwestern Chicken with Pineapple Salsa,
    '04 196
Grilled Tarragon-Dijon Thighs, '97 120
Grilled Teriyaki Chicken, '92 59
Grilled Yogurt-Lemon Chicken, '81 111
Gruyère, Chicken Breasts, '80 189
Gumbo, Chicken, '79 199; '90 26
Gumbo, Chicken-Andouille, '98 14
Gumbo, Chicken and Oyster, '81 198
Gumbo, Chicken-and-Sausage, '89 275; '90 256;
    '94 20; '00 221; '01 324; '03 313; '04 213
Gumbo, Chicken-Ham-Seafood, '81 6
Gumbo, Chicken-Sausage, '04 288
Gumbo, Combo, '81 198
Gumbo, Easy Chicken, '83 156
Gumbo, Old-Style Shrimp, '98 97
Gumbo, The Gullah House, '92 237
Gumbo, Wild Game, '91 290
Gumbo with Smoked Sausage, Chicken, '81 199
Gumbo Ya Ya, '87 210
Hawaiian Chicken, '82 274

Hawaiian, Chicken, '84 88
Herb Chicken, Smoky, '95 116
Herbed Chicken-and-Rice Bake, '02 215
Herbed Chicken, Sunny, '86 156
Herbed Chicken, Tangy, '87 M302
Herbs and Vegetables, Chicken with Fresh, '02 91
Herb-Seasoned Chicken Breasts, '93 M325
Holiday Chicken Presents, '01 251
Honey Chicken, '82 55; '88 67
Honey-Curry Chicken, '87 36
Honey-Pecan Chicken, '03 147
Honey Sauce, Chicken in, '89 82
Honolulu Chicken, '85 52
Imperial Chicken, '81 238; '98 91
Italian Chicken, '86 122; '91 206
Italian Chicken and Artichokes, '00 219
Italian Chicken Cutlets, '89 82
Italian Chicken-Mozzarella Melt, '95 153
Jalapeño, Easy Chicken, '92 310
Jamaican Jerk Raspberry Chicken, '00 88
Jambalaya, '90 26
Jambalaya, Chicken-and-Sausage, '88 200; '91 216;
    '01 278; '02 36; '03 201
Jambalaya, 1-2-3, '97 301
Jambalaya, Red Rice, '91 18
Jambalaya, Smoky Cajun, '96 62
Jambalaya with Shrimp, Chicken-and-Ham, '04 99
Jerk Chicken, Jamaican, '96 120; '99 121
Kebabs, Chicken, '87 141; '03 180
Kebabs, Chicken-Avocado, '82 9; '83 68
Kebabs, Chicken-Pineapple, '00 200
Kebabs, Chicken-Vegetable, '03 95
Kebabs, Good-and-Easy Chicken, '85 87
Kebabs, Hawaiian, '85 157
Kebabs, Marinated Chicken, '84 M144
Kebabs, Oriental Chicken, '95 193
Kebabs, Pineapple-Chicken, '86 M328
Kebabs, Sesame Chicken, '82 165
Kebabs, Soy-Chicken, '86 156
Kebabs Supreme, Chicken, '81 124
Kiev, Chicken, '80 39
Kiev, Cranberry Chicken, '87 250
Kiev, Oven-Baked Chicken, '86 37
Kiev, Oven Chicken, '82 83
King Ranch Chicken, '94 26
la France, Chicken, '86 248
Lemonade Chicken, '82 163
Lemon and Wine, Chicken in, '83 281
Lemon-Basil Chicken, '02 91
Lemon Chicken, '81 M138; '86 173; '96 49
Lemon Chicken and Vegetables, '88 118
Lemon Chicken Breasts, '89 18
Lemon Chicken, Sweet, '79 218
Lemon-Chicken, Sweet, '84 69
Lemon-Dill Chicken, '93 19
Lemon-Dill Chicken Sauté, '91 186
Lemon-Frosted Chicken, '88 170
Lemon-Garlic Chicken, '89 M132; '90 35
Lemon-Herb Chicken, '85 127; '00 90
Lemon Marinade, Chicken in, '98 128
Lemon-Pepper Chicken, '89 104
Lemon-Rosemary Chicken, '94 201
Lemon-Spinach Chicken, '97 104
Limeade Chicken, '01 257
Lime Butter, Chicken with, '84 68
Lime Chicken with Grilled Pineapple, '04 88
Lime-Roasted Chicken Breasts, '97 100
Linguine, Chicken-Broccoli, '98 30
Livers
    Bits and Livers, Chicken, '84 222
    Chopped Chicken Livers, Grandma Rose's,
        '96 105
    en Brochette, Chicken Livers, '84 222
    Fried Chicken Livers, '96 105

CHICKEN, Livers
(continued)

Garlic Chicken Livers, '96 105
Italian Sauce, Chicken Livers in, '83 117
Kebabs, Rumaki, '82 182
Mushrooms, Chicken Livers with, '81 133
Omelet, Chicken Liver, '82 44
Orange Sauce, Chicken Livers in, '82 218
Party Chicken Livers, '83 242
Pâté, Chicken Liver, '79 153; '81 235; '83 108;
 '84 205; '88 M132
Pâté Maison, '84 222
Potatoes, Chicken Livers and, '82 218
Rice, Chicken Livers with, '80 200; '81 58;
 '84 292
Rice Dish, Chicken Livers and, '82 218
Risotto, Chicken Livers, '82 218
Roll-Ups, Chicken Liver and Bacon, '80 200;
 '81 57
Rumaki, '80 M136
Sautéed Chicken Livers, '80 200; '81 57
Scrumptious Chicken Livers, '84 230
Spread, Sherried Liver, '80 86
Stroganoff, Chicken Livers, '80 200; '81 57
Supreme, Chicken Livers, '81 298
Turnovers, Chicken Liver, '79 141
Wine Sauce, Chicken Livers in, '81 104
Wine Sauce, Chicken Livers with Marsala, '81 76
Log, Chicken-Pecan, '81 290
Luzianne, Poulet, '86 197
Macadamia-Mango Chicken, '02 162
Macaroni and Cheese, Chicken, '02 63
Macaroni and Cheese, Spicy Chicken, '02 63
Madrid, Chicken, '97 326
Maple-Balsamic Chicken, '04 195
Marbella, Chicken, '04 34
Marengo, Chicken, '92 70
Marinade, Zesty Chicken, '03 180
Marinara, Chicken, '86 77
Marinated Breast of Chicken, '87 123
Marinated Chicken, '87 61
Marinated Chicken, Balsamic, '98 130
Marinated Chicken Breasts, '90 54
Marinated Chicken Quarters, '02 142
Marinated Chicken Strips and Vegetables, '90 110
Marsala, Chicken, '83 137; '89 237
Meatballs, White Spaghetti and, '03 34
Medaillons in Pepper Pesto, Chicken-Rice, '90 97
Mediterranean Chicken, '91 27; '94 72
Mediterranean, Chicken, '01 17
Medley, Creamy Ham-and-Chicken, '92 272
Mexican Chicken, '80 124
Mexican Chicken, Cheesy, '02 91
Milano, Chicken, '84 220
Minted Chicken, '81 102
Mole, Chicken, '81 193
Mole Sauce, Chicken with, '93 34
Monterey, Chicken, '82 275
Mornay Sauce, Chicken Breasts in, '81 273
Moroccan Chicken, '00 309
Mousse, Curried Chicken, '95 328
Muffins, Broccoli-Chicken, '96 27
Muffins, Chicken-and-Green Chile, '03 81
Murphy, Chicken, '89 82
Mushroom Sauce, Chicken with, '99 22
Mushrooms, Chicken-Stuffed, '80 162
Mustard Chicken, '80 222; '86 293; '93 239
Mustard Cream Sauce, Chicken in, '92 181
Nachos, Chicken, '84 244
Nuggets, Baked Chicken, '81 149; '89 18
Nuggets, Chicken-Bacon, '03 292; '04 146
Nuggets, Golden Chicken, '80 159; '81 237

Nuggets, Lemon-Chicken, '86 337
Nuggets Supreme, Chicken, '85 160
Nuggets with Pineapple Sauce, Chicken, '84 236
Olives, Chicken with Green, '03 87
Omelet, Indian, '99 92
Onion-Crusted Chicken, '88 40
Onions, Down-Home Chicken and, '02 271
Orange-Almond Sauce, Chicken in, '79 219; '80 13
Orange-Avocado Chicken, '80 38
Orange Chicken, '83 278; '86 M140
Orange Chicken Breasts with Parslied Rice, '87 242
Orange Chicken, Skillet-Seared, '96 68
Orange, Lime, and Ginger Sauce, Chicken with,
 '92 123
Orange Sauce, Chicken Breasts with, '79 77
Orange Sauce, Chicken in, '83 8
Orange Sauce, Skillet Chicken in, '94 252
Oregano Chicken, '95 84
Oriental Chicken, '80 40, 208; '82 131
Oriental, Chicken, '01 36
Oriental Chicken with Peanuts, '82 236
Oriental Chicken with Pineapple, '86 42
Packets, Chicken, '96 104
Paella, '97 328
Paella, Chicken-Pork-Shrimp, '82 245
Paella, Chicken-Seafood, '88 68
Paella, Shortcut, '01 309
Paella, Shrimp-and-Chicken, '94 168
Paella, Spanish, '85 26
Paella Valenciana, '82 246
Paprika Chicken, '95 125
Parchment, Chicken and Leeks in, '97 290
Parmesan, Chicken, '83 184; '95 210; '00 219
Parmesan Chicken, Crispy, '80 M76
Pasquale, Chicken, '83 67
Pasta and Chicken, Taste-of-Texas, '92 78
Pasta and Garden Vegetables, '87 192
Pasta, Chicken-and-Broccoli, '87 286
Pasta, Chicken-and-Pepper, '03 199
Pasta, Chicken Caesar, '97 87
Pasta, Chicken Picante, '01 164
Pasta, Mediterranean Chicken and, '03 63
Pasta Platter, Cold, '88 42
Pasta Primavera, Chicken-, '91 72
Pasta, Quick Chicken and, '93 14
Pasta, Spicy Chicken, '02 125
Pasta with Artichokes and Capers, Chicken, '04 129
Pasta with Rosemary, Chicken-Artichoke, '98 15
Pastry, Chicken in, '86 122
Pâté, Curried Chicken, '00 106
Pâté, Vegetable-Chicken, '86 66
Peach Sauce, Chicken with, '98 334
Peachy Chicken, '90 212
Peanut Butter-Marmalade Chicken, '81 282; '82 30
Pecan Chicken, '90 54; '99 332
Pecan-Rice Dressing, Chicken with, '85 M57
Pecan-Sausage Stuffing, Chicken Breasts with,
 '94 212
Penne, Cheesy Chicken, '00 289
Penne Pasta, Chicken, Asparagus, and Mushrooms
 with, '98 212
Penne, Spicy Cheesy Chicken, '00 289
Pepper-Sage Chicken, '96 237
Peppers, Chicken Breasts with Curried, '90 227
Peppers, Curried Chicken-Stuffed, '87 19
Peppers, Devilish Chicken, '80 65
Peppers with Chicken and Corn, Stuffed, '02 147
Pesto Chicken and Pasta, '89 M132
Pesto Chicken with Basil Cream, '89 158
Phyllo, Cheese-Stuffed Chicken in, '01 251
Phyllo, Cheesy Chicken in, '02 308
Phyllo, Chicken in, '87 286
Phyllo Pastry, Chicken Breasts in, '91 105
Piccata, Chicken, '83 35; '84 230

Piccata, Herbed Chicken, '88 28
Pie, Biscuit-Topped Chicken, '86 157, 264
Pie, Brunswick Stew-Cornbread, '02 121
Pie, Cheesy Mexican Chicken, '82 142
Pie, Chicken, '81 281; '82 31
Pie, Chicken-and-Egg Pot, '00 98
Pie, Chicken Dumpling, '95 245; '96 55; '00 336
Pie, Chicken Pot, '81 210; '82 114; '84 21; '94 21;
 '95 54, 256; '96 75; '01 282; '03 247
Pie, Chicken-Vegetable Pot, '81 281; '82 30
Pie, Deluxe Chicken, '88 298
Pie, Double-Crust Chicken, '87 111
Pie, Double-Crust Chicken Pot, '90 220
Pie, Easy Chicken Pot, '83 156; '89 218
Pie, Egg-Stra Special Chicken, '86 264
Pie Filling, Pot, '03 247
Pie, Greek Chicken Phyllo, '92 328
Pie in Biscuit Bowls, Chicken Pot, '03 222
Pie, Montezuma Tortilla, '83 199
Pie, Nana's Chicken, '90 25
Pie, Old-Fashioned Chicken Pot, '92 271
Pie, Savory Southern Chicken, '90 24
Pie, Thick 'n' Crusty Chicken Pot, '87 267; '88 102;
 '89 67
Pie with Cheese Crust, Chicken Pot, '86 264
Pilaf, Chicken, '82 246
Pilaf, Chicken-Vegetable, '97 51
Pilau, Chicken, '99 184
Pilau, Chicken-and-Smoked Sausage, '04 204
Piña Colada Chicken, '86 21
Pineapple Chicken, '83 M194; '85 3
Pineapple, Chicken and, '81 281; '82 30
Pineapple Chicken, Oriental, '84 288
Pineapple, Oriental Chicken with, '86 42
Piquant Chicken, '86 76
Piquant, Chicken, '94 19
Pita, Oriental Chicken, '89 216
Pita, Peppery Chicken in, '93 62
Pitas, Acadian Stuffed, '90 177
Pizza, Broccoli Supreme, '02 312
Pizza, Chicken, '94 218
Pizza, Chicken-and-Purple Onion, '97 47
Pizza, Chicken Fajita, '03 235
Pizza, Chicken Parmesan, '00 134
Pizza, Gruyère-Chicken, '87 182
Pizza, Mexican Chicken, '97 321
Pizza, Quick 'n' Easy Chicken Barbecue, '04 139
Pizzas, Chicken-and-Three-Cheese French Bread,
 '96 94
Pizza, Southwest Deluxe, '95 268
Pizza, Southwestern, '03 146
Pizza with Mango Pico de Gallo, Fajita Chicken,
 '04 318
Plum Sauce, Chicken with, '82 236
Poached Chicken and Vegetables, Ginger-, '98 229
Poached Chicken Breast in Wine, '91 184
Poached Chicken Breasts, Wine-, '85 58
Poached Chicken Breast with Turned Vegetables and
 Chive Sauce, '94 309
Poached Chicken, Whole, '98 229
Poached Chicken with Black Beans and Salsa,
 '87 217
Poached Chicken with Creamy Mustard Sauce,
 Champagne-, '94 24
Poblano Chicken, Creamy, '98 42
Polenta, Chicken with, '02 87
Pollo Almendrado (Chicken in Almond Sauce),
 '81 193
Pollo con Calabacita (Mexican Chicken with
 Zucchini), '82 219
Pollo en Mole de Cacahuate (Chicken with Peanut
 Mole Sauce), '80 194
Pollo en Pipián, Mexican, '88 31
Poppy Seed Chicken, '94 108

Potatoes, Chicken-Cheese Stuffed, '86 55
Potatoes, Creamed Beef and Chicken-Topped,
    '83 210
Potatoes, Gumbo, '95 22
Potatoes, Sweet-and-Sour-Topped, '83 4
Pot, Chicken in a, '81 3
Pretzel-Crusted Chicken, '94 252
Princess Chicken, '86 122
Provolone, Chicken, '93 323
Puffs, Appetizer Chicken, '85 72
Puffs, Chicken Nut, '81 260
Quesadillas, Chicken-and-Black Bean, '96 288
Quesadillas, Grilled Chicken, '04 36
Quesadillas, Sesame-Ginger Chicken, '00 147
Quesadillas, Spicy Chicken, '95 42
Quesadillas with Chipotle Salsa, Chicken-and-Brie,
    '99 311
Quiche, Chicken Divan, '88 M125
Quiche, Chicken-Olive-Cheddar, '03 58
Quiche, Chicken-Pecan, '91 206
Quiche Noël, '82 310
Quick, Chicken, '90 117
Ragoût with Cheddar Dumplings, Chicken, '94 44
Raspberry Chicken, '97 66
Rice and Chicken, Salsa, '99 109
Rice, Chicken Caruso and, '89 177
Rice, Chicken with Curried, '98 127
Rice, Island Chicken and, '04 165
Rice, Moorish Chicken with, '98 127
Rice, One-Dish Chicken and, '01 279
Rice Pilaf, Chicken Breasts with Fruited, '92 307
Rice, Shortcut Chicken and, '90 220
Rice, Spicy Chicken and, '88 200
Risotto, Smoked Chicken-and-Roasted Shallot,
    '00 30
Roast Chicken, '93 14
Roast Chicken and Brown Rice, '83 268
Roast Chicken and Vegetables, '81 3
Roast Chicken with Pineapple-Mustard Glaze,
    '89 83
Roast Chicken with Rice, '95 261
Roasted Chicken and Potatoes, '98 289
Roasted Chicken, Chipotle, '03 44
Roasted Chicken, Glazed, '00 14; '01 327
Roasted Chicken, Herb-, '87 155; '00 330
Roasted Chicken, Hot Oven-, '98 108
Roasted Chicken, Jan's, '01 224
Roasted Chicken, Lemon-, '95 24
Roasted Chicken, Lemon-Garlic, '98 108
Roasted Chicken, Lemon-Thyme, '03 44
Roasted Chicken, Peanut-, '01 107
Roasted Chicken, Rice-Stuffed, '88 38
Roasted Chicken, Savory, '98 21
Roasted Chicken, Slow-, '98 108
Roasted Chicken with Lemon, Garlic, and
    Rosemary, '97 61
Roasted Chicken with Poblano Vinaigrette and Corn
    Pudding, '99 71
Roasted Chicken with Vegetables, '98 108
Roasted Chicken with Wild Rice, Orange-Glazed,
    '02 85
Roasted Citrus Chicken, Clay Oven-, '98 108
Roasted Stuffed Chicken, '98 109
Rockefeller Chicken, '79 219
Rolls à la Swiss, Chicken-and-Ham, '92 42
Rolls, Chicken-Asparagus, '86 M211
Rolls, Crispy Chicken, '84 288
Rolls Elégante, Chicken, '80 210
Rolls, Hearts of Palm Chicken, '89 201
Rolls, Hearty Salad, '81 206
Rolls Jubilee, Chicken, '87 118
Rolls, Mexican Chicken, '93 242
Rolls, Pesto-Stuffed Chicken, '93 82
Rolls, Southwestern Cabbage, '97 214

Rollups, Cheesy Chicken, '82 44
Rollups, Chicken, '85 179; '88 38
Rollups, Chicken and Spinach, '80 90; '82 M68
Rollups, Imperial Chicken, '80 217
Rollups in Gravy, Chicken, '83 184
Rollups, Sunshine Chicken, '85 251
Romano, Chicken alla, '83 M58
Romano, Chicken Breasts, '79 218
Romanoff, Chicken, '84 292
Roquefort Chicken, '89 320
Rosemary Chicken, Pinot Noir Risotto with, '97 214
Rotelle, Chicken and Tomato with, '87 108
Saffron Chicken with Prunes, '97 264
Salads
    Almond-Chicken Salad Shanghai, '90 160
    Almond Salad, Chicken-, '81 133
    Aloha Chicken Salad, '80 297
    Amandine, Chicken Salad, '81 37
    Ambrosia, Chicken Salad, '85 216
    Apple Salad, Chicken-, '90 216
    Apricot-Chicken Salad, '99 163
    Apricot Salsa, Chicken with, '98 126
    Artichoke-Chicken-Rice Salad, '94 132
    Artichoke-Chicken-Rice Salad, Mediterranean,
        '97 321
    Artichokes, Chicken Salad with, '86 186
    Asian Chicken Salad, '99 124
    Asparagus-Chicken Salad, '89 83
    Aspic-Topped Chicken Salad, '88 88
    Autumn Chicken Salad, '01 312
    Avocado-Chicken Salad, '87 107
    Avocado Salad, Chicken-, '80 139
    Avocado Salad, Fruited Chicken-, '82 101
    Avocado Salad Platter, Chicken-, '83 2
    Avocado Salad, Tossed Chicken-, '80 4
    Avocados, Chicken Salad in, '85 216
    Baked Chicken Salad, '86 297; '87 176
    Barbecue Chicken Salad, Warm, '99 124
    Basil-Chicken-Vegetable Salad, '92 162
    Black-and-Blue Salad, '00 337
    Black Bean Salad, Chicken-, '99 124
    Black-Eyed Pea Salad, Chicken-and-, '97 305
    BLT Chicken Salad, '87 144
    Blueberry Salad, Chicken-, '02 177
    Blue Cheese Chicken Salad, '94 81
    Blue Cheese, Chicken Salad with, '97 97
    Broccoli-Chicken Salad, '90 129; '00 53
    Buffalo Tenders Salad, '03 184
    Caesar Salad, Chicken, '96 26
    Celery Salad, Chicken-, '81 187
    Chef's Salad, '98 209
    Chicken Salad, '86 232, 261; '96 67
    Chop Suey Salad, '81 37
    Chutney-Chicken Salad, '87 74
    Chutney Salad, Chicken, '82 108
    Cobb Salad, Southern-Style, '01 112
    Coconut-Chicken Salad, Curried Poached Pears
        with, '97 93
    Coleslaw, Chicken, '84 2
    Cream Puff Bowl, Chicken Salad in, '86 232
    Crisp Salad, Crunchy, '95 28
    Crunchy Chicken Salad, '86 157, 207
    Curried Chicken-and-Orange Salad, '87 144
    Curried Chicken-Rice Salad, '92 190
    Curried Chicken Salad, '79 219; '84 66; '85 96;
        '86 131; '89 176
    Curried Chicken Salad, Royal, '96 200
    Curried Chicken Salad with Asparagus, '81 36
    Dilled Chicken Salad, '91 212
    Exotic Luncheon Salad, '83 210
    Fancy Chicken Salad, '79 55
    Filling, Chicken Salad, '87 106
    Fried Chicken Ginger Salad, '93 290
    Fried Chicken Salad, Fiesta, '03 120

Fruit, Chicken Salad with, '82 171
Fruit-Chicken Salad with Blueberry Vinaigrette,
    Summer, '00 154
Fruited Chicken Salad, '84 25, 290; '88 88;
    '90 318
Fruited Chicken Salad in Avocados, '87 41
Fruit Salad, Chicken-, '82 79; '90 234
Fruit Salad, Chicken-and-, '01 178
Fruity Chicken Salad, '83 157
Gazpacho-Chicken Salad, '00 203
Grapes, Chicken Salad with, '86 117
Greek Chicken Salad, '97 92; '98 329
Green Salad with Chicken, Mixed, '80 54
Grilled Asian Chicken Salad, '96 158
Grilled Chicken-and-Fruit Salad, '96 155
Grilled Chicken on Greens, '99 201
Grilled Chicken-Rice Salad, '98 148
Grilled Chicken Salad, Moroccan, '95 231
Grilled Chicken Salad with Raspberry Dressing,
    '95 202
Hoisin Chicken-and-Pasta Salad, '99 125
Honey Chicken Salad, '04 51
Horseradish Salad, Chicken-, '02 235
Hot Chicken Salad, '81 201; '83 196; '98 290
Hot Chicken Salad, Country Club-Style, '86 10
Hot Chicken Salad, Crunchy, '80 138
Hot Chicken Salad Pinwheel, '80 139
Italian, Chicken Salad, '89 18
Layered Chicken Salad, '89 162
Lemon-Chicken Salad, Lively, '00 16
Macadamia Chicken Salad, '80 138
Macaroni-Chicken Salad, '85 296; '86 302
Macaroni-Chicken Salad, Dilled, '92 142
Mama Hudson's Chicken Salad, '93 238
Mandarin Chicken, Carousel, '79 88
Mango, Chicken Salad with, '86 215
Marinated Chicken-Grape Salad, '85 74
Marinated Chicken-Raspberry Salad, '93 190
Marinated Chicken Strips and Vegetables, '00 54
Melts, Open-Faced Cheesy Chicken Salad,
    '00 134
Mexican Chicken Salad, '85 84; '88 272
Minted Chicken Salad, '92 104
Mold, Chicken-Cucumber, '80 175
Mold, Chicken Salad, '83 80; '84 163
Nectarine Chicken Salad, '79 175
Noodle Chicken Salad, '03 143
Noodle Salad, Chicken, '95 25
Old-Fashioned Chicken Salad, '83 79
Oriental Chicken Salad, '85 216; '88 271; '91 43;
    '96 92
Oriental, Chicken Salad, '90 146
Overnight Salad, '97 305; '98 18
Parmesan-Chicken Salad, '98 234
Pasta, Chicken-and-Bow Tie, '01 164
Pasta-Chicken Salad, Tarragon, '87 155
Pasta Salad, Bayou, '00 203
Pasta Salad, Chicken, '88 89
Pasta Salad, Grilled Chicken-, '94 64
Pasta Salad, Zesty Chicken-, '02 186
Peachy Chicken Salad, '97 193
Peanut-Chicken Salad, Sweet, '03 54
Pea Salad, Chicken-, '83 218
Persian Chicken Salad, '81 12
Pineapple-Chicken Salad Pie, '80 138
Pineapple-Nut Chicken Salad, '83 80
Pocket, Chicken Salad in a, '88 139
Polynesian Chicken Salad, '88 272
Poulet Rémoulade, '87 144
Rice Salad, Chicken-, '81 203; '97 93
Rice Salad, Chicken-and-, '97 92
Rice Salad, Hot Chicken-and-, '83 22
Rice Salad, Nutty Chicken-, '83 157
Ring, Chicken Salad, '90 123

CHICKEN, Salads
(continued)

Ring Salad, Chicken Jewel, '83 282
Roasted Chicken Salad, '93 14
Roasted Red Pepper Salad, Chicken and, '03 291
Rolls, Hearty Salad, '81 206
Sandwiches, Asian Chicken Salad, '98 223
Sandwiches, Chicken-Salad Finger, '85 119
Sandwiches, Grilled Chicken Salad, '00 164
Sandwiches, Hot Chicken Salad, '96 74
Sherried Chicken-and-Grape Salad, '01 61
South Sea Island Chicken Salad, '97 88
Southwestern Chicken Salad, '88 88
Southwestern Chicken Salad Spirals, '02 58
Spaghetti Salad, Chicken-, '90 146
Spaghetti Salad, Chicken-and-Veggie, '04 129
Special Chicken Salad, '85 82; '87 183; '88 M193
Spicy Chicken Salad with Cabbage Wraps, '04 62
Spicy Chicken Salad with Veggies, '04 177
Spinach-Strawberry Salad, Chicken-, '97 92
Spinach Tossed Salad, Chicken-and-, '83 157
Spread, Chicken Salad Party, '88 M8
Spread, Curried Chicken Salad, '00 68
Stack-Up Salad, Chicken, '83 80
Strawberry-Chicken Salad, '04 50
Summer Chicken Salad, '83 145
Summery Chicken Salad, '95 138
Super Chicken Salad, '82 174
Supreme, Chicken Salad, '79 107, 152; '89 176
Taco Chicken Salad, Ranch, '97 315
Taco Salad, Chicken, '94 M136
Tahitian Chicken Salad, '84 120
Tarragon Chicken Salad, '90 199
Tarts, Chicken Salad, '84 257
Thai Chicken Salad, '95 177
Tortellini Salad, Chicken, '87 288
Tortilla Salads, Mexican Chicken, '95 129
Tropical Chicken Boats for Two, '82 186
Tropical Chicken Salad, '85 216; '96 127
Tropical Spinach Salad with Grilled Chicken, '04 51
Twist, Chicken Salad with a, '84 221
Vegetable-Chicken Salad, '91 287
Vegetable-Chicken Vinaigrette Salad, '86 135
Vegetable Patch Chicken Salad, '04 92
Walnut-Chicken Salad, '89 14; '96 243
Walnut Salad, Sunburst Chicken-and-, '93 91
Wild Rice-and-Chicken Salad, '02 52
Wild Rice-Chicken Salad, '83 146; '99 55; '01 72
Wild Rice Salad, '01 247
Wraps, Lemon-Basil Chicken Salad, '00 216
Saltimbocca alla Romana, Chicken, '80 212
San Antonio-Style Chicken, '81 166
Sandwiches
Asian Chicken Salad Sandwiches, '98 223
Bagel Sandwiches, Chicken-Benedict, '96 250
Baked Chicken Sandwiches, '79 164; '80 130; '84 165
Broiled Chicken Sandwiches with Fresh Salsa, '00 59
Burgers, Chicken-Cheese, '04 56
Burritos, Chicken, '01 55
Cheesy Chicken Sandwiches, '82 190
Club Sandwiches, Chicken, '86 160
Crispy Chicken Sandwich, '81 114
Curried Chicken Tea Sandwiches, '97 23
Dagwoods, Chicken-Avocado, '96 200; '99 337
Finger Sandwiches, Chicken-Salad, '85 119
Focaccia with Roasted Pepper Vinaigrette, Stuffed, '00 134
Focaccia with Roasted Pepper Vinaigrette, Stuffed, '04 142

Gouda Lover's Chicken Sandwiches, '99 195
Grilled Chicken-and-Pesto Clubs, '01 22
Grilled Chicken 'n' Cheese Sandwiches, '99 240
Grilled Chicken Salad Sandwiches, '00 164
Ham 'n' Cheese Chicken Sandwich, '95 153
Hot Brown Sandwiches, '80 202
Hot Chicken Salad Sandwiches, '96 74
Hot Chicken Sandwiches, '83 291
Jamaican Chicken Sandwich, '95 153
Jerk Chicken Sandwich, '98 333
Mandarin Orange Spread Sandwiches, Chicken-, '04 259
Marinated Chicken in a Sandwich, '86 185
Marinated Chicken Sandwiches, '86 M45
Open-Faced Sandwiches, Summer, '99 201
Panini, Chicken Florentine, '02 236
Parmigiana Sandwich, Chicken, '94 65
Pita, Fajita in a, '90 177
Pita Pockets, Chicken-Spinach, '01 66
Pita Sandwiches, Mango-Chicken, '03 123
Pitas, Fajita, '99 239
Pocket, Chicken Salad in a, '88 139
Pocket Sandwiches, Chicken-Almond, '81 240; '83 69
Pockets, Oriental Stuffed, '79 14
Puffed Chicken Sandwiches, '82 35
Southwestern Chicken Sandwiches, '96 23
Sub, Chicken, '98 287
Toasted Chicken-and-Cheese Sandwiches, '85 242
Wraps, Chicken-and-Bean Slaw, '04 163
Wraps, Chicken-Cranberry, '01 34
Wraps, Chicken Lettuce, '02 65
Wraps, Southwestern, '99 238
Wraps, Thai Chicken-Avocado, '02 206
Sanibel Island Chicken, '97 66
Saté, Chicken, '99 134
Sauce, Chicken Curry, '90 117
Sauce, Creamy Chicken, '81 91
Sauce, Curry, '95 18
Sauce, Fettuccine with Chicken-and-Creamy Herb, '01 257
Saucy Chick-Wiches, '81 25; '82 31; '83 34
Sausage with Fennel, Chicken, '98 312
Sauté, Chicken-Apple, '97 48
Sautéed Chicken Breasts, '87 36
Sauté, Savory Chicken, '88 254; '89 120
Sauté, Sherry-Chicken, '87 218
Sauté, Sweet Pepper-Chicken, '89 104
Sauté with Artichokes and Mushrooms, Chicken, '03 57
Scallopini with Lemon Sauce, Chicken, '86 156
Scallopini with Peppers, Chicken, '85 78
Scaloppine in Lemon Sauce, Chicken, '00 166
Scaloppine with Linguine Alfredo, Chicken, '04 96
Scotch Cream, Chicken in, '88 42
Seared Chicken, Zesty, '01 82
Seasoned Browned Chicken, '85 25
Seasoned Chicken, '99 316
Seasoned Chicken, Crunchy, '87 217
Seasoning Blend, Poultry, '88 28
Sesame Chicken, '85 252; '86 122; '97 256; '98 20
Sesame Chicken, Hawaiian, '81 106
Sesame Chicken Strips, '98 250
Sesame Chicken with Noodles, '88 M125
Sesame-Crusted Chicken with Pineapple Salsa, '96 226
Sesame-Dijon Chicken, '98 96
Sesame-Ginger Chicken, '00 219
Shells, Southwestern Stuffed, '99 238
Sherried Chicken, '79 214
Sherried Chicken with Artichokes, '87 143
Sherry Chicken with Rice, '81 97
Shortcakes, Cheesy Chicken, '95 98

Sicilian Chicken, '97 142
Skewers, Taco-Chicken, '99 119
Skewers with Peanut Sauce, Chicken, '02 173
Skewers with Peanut Sauce, Chicken, '04 324
Skillet, Cheesy Chicken, '80 115
Skillet Chicken, '81 180
Skillet Chicken Dinner, '86 249; '89 247
Skillet Chicken, Spicy, '94 220
Skillet Company Chicken, '82 60
Skillet, Confetti Chicken, '97 327
Skillet Dinner, Antipasto, '97 327
Skillet Dinner, Chicken-and-Rice, '98 127
Skillet Supper, Chicken-and-Sausage, '03 49
Smothered Chicken with Lemon Mashed Potatoes, '04 180
Snow Peas, Chicken with, '83 187
Soufflé, Chicken-Chestnut, '79 107
Soups
Artichoke, and Mushroom Soup, Chicken, '92 324
Asparagus-and-Chicken Soup, Creamy, '95 82
Bean-Chicken Soup, '99 283
Bisque, Curried Chicken, '00 144
Broccoli-and-Chicken Soup, '90 202
Chicken Soup, '81 98
Chowder, Chicken-and-Roasted Vegetable, '97 21
Chowder, Chicken Corn, '02 305
Chowder, Chicken-Vegetable, '04 326
Chowder, Fiesta, '02 305
Chowder Sauterne, Chicken, '84 235
Chunky Chicken-Noodle Soup, '88 12
Corn Soup, Cheesy Chicken-, '97 158
Country Chicken-and-Buttermilk Soup, '02 144
Cream of Chicken Soup, '85 243
Cream Soup, Chicken-Almond, '92 21
Curried Chicken Soup, '86 34
Enchilada Soup, Chicken, '86 22
Fiesta Chicken Soup, '04 323
French Soup Maigre, '98 125
Ham, and Oyster Soup, Chicken, '79 198
Homemade Chicken Soup, '82 34
Lime Soup, '88 31
Mexican Chicken Soup, '84 234; '00 336; '03 63
Noodle Soup, Chicken, '80 264; '95 45; '98 30
Noodle Soup, Creamy Chicken, '99 20
Pepper-and-Chicken Soup, Roasted, '90 58
Quick Chicken Soup, '86 M72
Rice Soup, Chicken-and-, '88 236
Sopa de Lima, '79 211
Spicy Chicken Soup, '97 268
Stock, Chicken, '95 18
Stock, Light Poultry, '90 31
Tortilla Soup, '98 291; '99 310; '00 98, 110; '04 26
Tortilla Soup, Supereasy, '00 199
Vegetable Soup, Chicken-, '88 18; '99 60
Vegetable Soup, Spicy Chicken-, '02 168
Wild Rice Soup, Chicken-and-, '04 26
Wild Rice Soup, Creamy Chicken-and-, '98 M334
Witches' Brew Chicken Soup, '01 205
Southwestern Chicken, '03 180
Soy and Wine, Chicken in, '84 26
Soy-Garlic Chicken, '98 128
Spaghetti, Chicken, '83 105; '87 221; '98 329
Spaghetti, Chicken-Vegetable, '92 281; '98 296
Spanish Chicken, '98 183
Special Occasion Chicken, '91 206
Spiced Chicken, Crunchy, '85 M57
Spiced Fruited Chicken with Almond Rice, '81 195
Spicy Chicken Dish, '87 267; '88 103; '89 66
Spicy Chicken 'n' Dumplings, Quick-and-, '03 325
Spinach Fettuccine, Easy Chicken with, '88 89
Spinach Noodles, Chicken and, '82 19

Spread, Festive Chicken, '87 158
Spread Gift Box, Chicken-Artichoke-Cheese,
    '00 328
Spread, Low-Fat Chicken, '82 290
Spread, Tasty Chicken, '84 193
Spring Rolls, '99 238
Steamed Dinner, Easy, '83 M314
Stews
    Brunswick Chicken Stew, '87 4
    Brunswick Stew, '80 264; '97 138, 315;
        '01 148, 219; '03 29
    Brunswick Stew, Bama, '87 4
    Brunswick Stew, Breeden Liles's, '91 14
    Brunswick Stew, Chicken, '97 234
    Brunswick Stew, Dan Dickerson's, '91 16
    Brunswick Stew, Gay Neale's, '91 17
    Brunswick Stew, Georgian, '92 35
    Brunswick Stew, Jeff Daniel's, '91 16
    Brunswick Stew, Sonny Frye's, '87 4
    Brunswick Stew, Van Doyle's Family-Size, '91 14
    Brunswick Stew, Virginian, '92 34
    Brunswick Stew, Virginia Ramsey's Favorite,
        '91 16
    Camp Stew, '02 42
    Chicken Stew, '97 26
    Chili-Chicken Stew, '90 319
    Dumplings, Chicken Stew and, '84 4
    Greek-Style Chicken Stew, '03 219
    Kale, and Chickpea Stew, Chicken, '98 47
    Santa Fe Chicken Stew, '97 193
    Speedy Chicken Stew, '03 42
    Strader Stew, '89 28
    Zesty Chicken Stew, '02 127
Sticks, Italian Chicken, '98 25
Sticky Chicken, '97 239
Stir-Fry
    à l'Orange, Stir-Fry Chicken, '83 82
    Apple-Sesame-Chicken Stir-Fry, '92 226
    Broccoli Stir-Fry, Chicken-, '82 33
    Chinese Chicken Stir-Fry, '90 100
    Curry, Stir-Fried Chicken, '87 51
    Easy Chicken Stir-Fry, '91 124
    Herb-Chicken Stir-Fry, '89 177
    Hurry-Up Chicken Stir-Fry, '91 124
    Mexican Stir-Fry, '92 126
    Orange-Chicken Stir-Fry, '84 68
    Orange-Chicken Stir-Fry, Kyoto, '87 96
    Pineapple-Chicken Stir-Fry, '89 176
    Shiitake-Chicken Stir-Fry, '89 61
    Snow Pea Stir-Fry, Chicken and, '95 157
    Sweet-and-Sour Chicken Stir-Fry, '98 204
    Thai Chicken Stir-Fry, '00 23
    Vegetables Stir-Fry Chicken-and-, '86 68
    Vegetables Stir-Fry Chicken and, '86 249
    Vegetables, Stir-Fry Chicken with, '96 128
    Vegetable Stir-Fry, Chicken-, '83 151;
        '84 13, 141; '01 175
    Vegetable Stir-Fry, Chicken, '00 245
    Vegetable Stir-Fry, Chicken and, '82 237
    Vegetable Stir-Fry, Chicken-and-, '96 19
    Vegetables with Chicken Stir-Fry, '84 195
    Zesty Stir-Fried Chicken, '83 82
    Zucchini Stir-Fry, Chicken-, '84 50
Stock, Light Poultry, '90 31
Strips, Nutty Chicken, '99 111
Strips with "Come Back" Dipping Sauce, Miss
    Mary's Chicken, '96 213
Strips with Honey Sauce, Chicken, '03 27
Strips, Zippy Chicken, '84 205
Stroganoff, Chicken, '99 41
Stroganoff, Chicken-and-Broccoli, '89 M248
Stroganoff, Strolling-Through-the-Holidays,
    '01 282
Strudel, Chicken-Goat Cheese, '98 28

Strudel with White Wine Gravy, Chicken-Herb,
    '04 318
Stuffed Alfredo Chicken, '04 56
Stuffed Chicken Breasts, '82 36; '85 291; '88 50;
    '89 274
Stuffed Chicken Breasts, Apple-Bacon, '99 313
Stuffed Chicken Breasts, Hawaiian, '99 64
Stuffed Chicken Breasts over Angel Hair, Goat
    Cheese-, '97 144
Stuffed Chicken Breasts, Peach-, '79 177
Stuffed Chicken Breasts Sardou, '87 269
Stuffed Chicken Breasts, Walnut-, '85 293
Stuffed Chicken Breasts with Sweet-and-Sour
    Tomato Sauce, '01 120
Stuffed Chicken Breasts with White Bean Puree,
    '98 270; '02 200
Stuffed Chicken Breasts with White Grape Sauce,
    '80 38
Stuffed Chicken, Crab-, '84 101
Stuffed Chicken, Creamy Tomato-, '04 16
Stuffed Chicken in Puff Pastry, Spinach-, '92 125
Stuffed Chicken, Rice-, '81 4
Stuffed Chicken Rolls, Spinach-, '86 248
Stuffed Chicken Thighs, '82 84
Stuffed Chicken, Vegetable-, '89 M65
Stuffed Chicken, Wild Rice-, '79 219
Stuffed Chicken with Sautéed Peppers and
    Mushrooms, Herb-, '91 26
Stuffed Chicken with Tomato-Basil Pasta, Basil-,
    '94 M204
Sunday Chicken, '95 228
Sunshiny Chicken, '81 309
Supremes de Volaille à Blanc (Chicken Breasts in
    Cream Sauce), '82 83
Sweet-and-Sour Chicken, '79 106; '83 184; '84 218;
    '86 217, 240; '90 161; '91 202; '97 325
Sweet-and-Sour Chicken and Rice, '03 97
Sweet-and-Sour Chicken Nuggets, '90 168
Sweet-and-Sour Chicken Wings, '90 206
Sweet-and-Sour Lemon Chicken, '84 93
Sweet-and-Sour Shrimp and Chicken, '87 267;
    '88 103; '89 66
Szechuan Chicken, '83 85; '98 155
Szechuan Chicken with Angel Hair Pasta, '97 91
Szechwan Chicken with Cashews, '81 212
Tacos, Chicken-and-Bean, '93 293
Tacos, Pizza-Flavored Chicken, '95 340
Taco Stacks, Soft, '02 54
Tahitian Chicken, '84 68
Tamales, Chicken, '88 151
Tandoori Chicken, '03 165
Tangy Chicken, '85 251; '86 292; '87 35
Tarragon Chicken, '86 231
Tarts, Deviled Chicken, '94 14
Tempura Delight, Chicken, '85 66
Tenders, Buffalo, '03 184
Tenders, Lemon Chicken, '03 184
Teriyaki, Chicken, '80 M76
Teriyaki Chicken, '91 163
Terrine, Chicken-Vegetable, '84 131
Terrine, Cold Chicken-Leek, '92 145
Terrine Ring, Chicken, '84 132
Terrine, Vegetable-Chicken, '83 224
Thighs, Herb-Roasted Chicken, '02 127
Thighs, Honey-Pecan Chicken, '02 127
Thighs, Sweet Glazed Chicken, '04 202
Tomato Aspic, Chicken in, '84 190
Tomatoes and Sausage, Chicken with, '97 266
Tortilla Stack, Cheesy Chicken-, '86 3
Toss, Quick Chicken, '87 M124
Tostadas, Chicken, '93 204; '95 122
Tostadas, Quick Chicken, '99 159
Undercover Chicken, '97 64
Valencia, Chicken-and-Rice, '85 113

Vegetable Platter, Chicken-and-, '88 M52
Vegetables, Chicken and, '88 165
Vegetables, Jim's Chicken and, '99 237
Vegetables with Ginger-Soy Sauce, Chicken and,
    '91 32
Vermicelli, Chicken, '01 237
Vermouth, Chicken and Vegetables, '87 M37
Véronique, Chicken, '84 260; '85 302
Waffles, Southern Chicken-Pecan, '82 231
Walnut Chicken, '85 126
Walnut Chicken and Vegetables, '85 194
Walnut Chicken, Crispy, '90 89
Wellington, Chicken Breasts, '84 22
White Barbecue Sauce, Chicken with, '01 168
White Wine, Chicken in, '81 97
Wild Rice, Chicken and, '01 279
Wild Rice, Chicken-Fried, '89 24; '91 132
Wild Rice, Elegant Chicken with, '80 M76
Wine Sauce, Chicken and Mushrooms in, '81 109
Wine Sauce, Chicken in, '80 8
Wings. *See also* **CHICKEN/Drummettes.**
    Broiled Chicken Wings, '80 149
    Buffalo Hot Wings, '03 184
    Buffalo Wings, '00 203
    Buffalo Wings, Spicy, '95 239
    Chinese Chicken Wings, '96 111
    Chipotle Chicken Wings, Sweet-and-Spicy,
        '04 176
    Curried Chicken Wings, '96 110
    Honey Chicken Wings, '00 15
    Honey Chicken Wings, Grilled, '96 111
    Honey-Glazed Chicken Wings, '91 251
    Hot 'n' Spicy Chicken Wings, '04 132
    Maple-Glazed Chicken Wings, '99 110
    Oriental-Style Wings, Spicy, '96 215
    Satan's Wings, '87 214
    Sesame-Maple Chicken Wings, '00 57
    Spanish Rice, Chicken Wings with, '00 202
    Sweet-and-Hot Citrus Wings, '00 202
    Sweet-and-Sour Chicken Wings, '96 110
    Tandoori Chicken Wings, '96 110
    Teriyaki Chicken Wings, '85 300; '86 18
Wontons, Chicken, '92 284
Wontons with Hoisin Peanut Dipping Sauce,
    Chicken, '99 14
Yogurt Chicken, Savory, '91 238; '92 28
Yogurt-Sesame Chicken, '90 216
CHILI
Bake, Chili Hominy, '81 282; '82 58
Basic Chili, '82 M11; '93 326
Basic Chili Embellished, '93 327
Basic Chili Goes Southwest, '93 326
Bean Chili, Spicy 3-, '03 291
Bean Chili, Three-, '00 34
Before-and-After Burner, Roy's, '89 316
Big-Batch Chili, '04 242
Biscuit Bowl, Chili in a, '98 224
Black Bean Chili, '02 20
Black Bean Chili Marsala, '95 16
Bodacious Chili, '95 14
Burgers, Open-Face Chili, '82 31; '83 33
Casserole, Chili, '90 176
Casserole, Chili-Rice, '79 54
Casserole, Hominy-Chili, '86 255
Casserole, Ultimate Chili, '99 239
Cheese-Topped Chili, '82 M11
Cheesy Chili, '82 310
Chili, '87 17; '93 89; '98 95
Chilly Night Chili, '99 317
Choo-Choo Chili, '89 316
Chuck Wagon Chili, '81 282; '82 57
Chunky Chili, '82 M282; '86 3
Cincinnati Chili, '96 18
Cincinnati-Style Chili, '00 34

CHILI

(continued)

Company Chili, **'82** 311; **'83** 30
con Carne, Beef and Sausage Chili, **'83** 284
con Carne, Chili, **'82** 310; **'83** 30; **'84** 72; **'86** 2; **'03** 19
con Carne, Favorite Chili, **'86** 293
con Carne, Quick-and-Easy Chili, **'86** 2
Cowboy Chili, **'86** 2
Dip, Cheesy Chili, **'80** 150
Dip, Chili, **'82** 161; **'88** 218; **'89** 47; **'91** 143
Dip, Chili-and-Cheese, **'89** 328
Dog, Dinglewood Pharmacy's Scrambled, **'95** 118
Dogs, Chili-Cheese, **'81** M176
Double-Meat Chili, **'79** 269; **'80** 12
Easy Chili, **'82** 310; **'83** 30; **'02** 299
Easy Chili with Beans, **'92** 262
Easy Texas Chili, **'90** 201
Eggplant Chili, **'85** 88
Enchiladas, Chili and, **'00** 55
Firestarter Chili, **'93** 34
Five-Ingredient Chili, **'95** 212
Friday Night Chili, **'86** 228
Game-Day Chili, **'00** 238
Greek Chili, **'95** 16
Hot Dog Chili, **'04** 199
Hot Spiced Chili, **'83** 214
Hotto Lotto Chili, **'89** 316
I-Cious, Chili-, **'89** 315
"In-the-Red" Chili over "Rolling-in-Dough" Biscuits, **'92** 80
Kielbasa Chili, Hearty, **'91** 28
Lolly's Pop Chili, **'89** 316
Lunchtime Chili, **'81** 230
Manicotti, Chili, **'89** 247; **'99** 239
Meat Loaf, Chili, **'81** 275
Meaty Chili, **'81** 282; **'82** 58
Meaty Chili with Beans, **'85** 250
Mexican Chili, **'89** 18
Microwave Chili, **'91** M232
Mom's Chili, **'93** 292
Noodles, Chili with, **'81** 282; **'82** 57
Now, Thatsa Chili, **'95** 16
Out West Chili, **'95** 15
Pastry Cups, Chili in, **'90** 68
Pie, Chili-Tamale, **'82** 9; **'83** 68
Potato Chili, Savory, **'83** 284
Potatoes, Chili-Topped, **'83** 3; **'98** M289
Potatoes, South-of-the-Border Stuffed, **'86** 54
Quick-and-Easy Chili, **'92** 20
Quick and Simple Chili, **'81** 282; **'82** 58
Quick Chili, **'83** 283
Ranch Chili and Beans, **'79** 270; **'80** 11
Red Bean Chili, **'02** 20
Red Bean Chili, Slow-Cooker, **'02** 20
Red Chili, **'93** 108
Red Chili, North Texas, **'87** 303
Rice, Chili with, **'82** M11
Roundup Chili, **'79** 269; **'80** 12
Salad, Chili-Corn Chip Stack-Up, **'04** 242
Salad, Spicy Chili, **'86** 71
Sauce, Chili, **'81** 175; **'94** 287
Sauce, Chili Meat, **'83** 4
Sauce, Chunky Chili, **'85** 188
Sauce, Spicy Chili, **'87** 127
Sausage-Beef Chili, **'86** 232
Sausage Chili, Beefy, **'82** M11
Simple Chili, **'79** 269; **'80** 11
Slow Cooker Cincinnati-Style Chili, **'00** 34
Soup, Chili Bean, **'96** 71
Soup, Chili Vegetable, **'94** 120
South-of-the-Border Chili, **'83** 283; **'91** 283

Southwestern Chili, **'91** 284
Spaghetti, Herbed Chili-, **'84** 222
Speedy Chili, **'92** 66
Spicy Chili, Old-Fashioned, **'79** 269; **'80** 11
Stew, Red Chili, **'95** 226
Strata, Cornbread-Chili, **'03** 100
Supper, Hot Chili, **'99** 279
Surprise, Chili, **'82** 229
Texas Championship Chili, **'81** 54
Texas Chili, Hot, **'80** 222; **'81** 77
Texas-Style Chili, **'82** 311; **'83** 30
Tex-Mex Chili, **'83** 26
Topping, Chili, **'84** 246; **'94** 22
Tree-Hunt Chili, **'87** 292
Turkey-Bean Chili, **'88** M213
Vegetable Chili, **'91** 28; **'97** 179
Vegetarian Chili, **'84** 280, 327; **'91** 284
Veggies Chili, Full-of-, **'00** 294
Venison Chili, **'82** 216; **'86** 3; **'87** 304
Venison Chili, Hot, **'91** 283
Verde, Chili, **'95** 14
White Bean Chili, **'02** 20
White Chili, **'91** 284
White Christmas Chili, **'98** 266; **'02** 260
White Lightning Texas Chili, **'92** 321
Zippy Chili, **'87** 110

CHOCOLATE. *See also* **BROWNIES, COOKIES, FUDGE.**

Apples, Black-and-White Caramel, **'03** M216
Apples, Candy, **'01** M205
Apples on a Stick, Chocolate, **'96** 255
Bags, Chocolate-Raspberry, **'95** 97
Banana Pops, **'84** 44

Bars and Cookies

Almond Chip Balls, Toasted, **'84** 240
Almond-Chocolate Bars, **'83** 304
Almond Cookies, Chocolate-, **'98** 293
Almond Cream Confections, **'87** 198; **'90** 310
Almond Surprise Cookies, Chocolate-, **'88** M45
Biscotti, Chocolate Chip-Cinnamon, **'96** 281
Biscotti, Chocolate-Hazelnut, **'95** 80
Biscotti Cioccolata, **'93** 268
Biscotti, Cocoa-Almond, **'96** 280
Blond Nut Squares, **'82** 156
Bonbons, Chocolate-Filled, **'89** 162
Bran Raisin Jumbos, Chocolate-, **'91** 142
Brazil Squares, **'82** 306
Brickle Cookies, Chocolate-, **'99** 127
Butter Cookies, Chocolate-Tipped, **'84** 258; **'90** 312
Butter Pecan Turtle Bars, **'90** 70
Butterscotch Bars, Chocolate-, **'81** 197
By-Cracky Bars, **'84** 212
Cake Mix Cookies, **'97** 133
Candy Wrap Cookies, **'04** 139
Cappuccino Cookies, Chocolate, **'01** 315
Caramel-Filled Chocolate Cookies, **'92** 319; **'02** 53
Caramel Layer Squares, Chocolate-, **'79** 83
Cereal Bars, Chewy Chocolate, **'97** 317
Cherry Chocolates, **'95** 321
Cherry Cookies, Chocolate-, **'85** 324
Cherry Cookies, Chocolate-Covered, **'99** 280
Chess Squares, Chocolate, **'92** 45
Chewies, Chocolate, **'93** 216
Chewies, Double Chocolate, **'00** 333
Chewies, Easy Chocolate, **'93** 296; **'94** 234
Chewy Chocolate Chip Squares, **'91** 175
Chewy Chocolate Cookies, **'80** 208; **'97** 166
Chip Bars, Chocolate, **'81** 130
Chip Cookies, **'84** 120
Chip Cookies, Chocolate, **'86** 245; **'90** 193; **'00** 276
Chip Cookies, Chocolate-Chocolate, **'82** 35

Chip Cookies, Mom Ford's Chocolate, **'94** 287
Chippers, Chocolate, **'92** 206
Chips Cookies, Loaded-with-, **'87** 223
Chip Squares, Chocolate, **'83** 170; **'89** 143
Chubbies, Chocolate, **'01** 144
Cinnamon Bars, Chocolate, **'82** 209
Cocoa Drop Cookies, **'80** 217
Cocoa Kiss Cookies, **'85** 171
Coconut Robin's Nests, **'98** M111
Coconut Squares, Chocolate-, **'90** 70
Coconut Swirls, **'97** 274
Coffee Kisses, Chocolate-Dipped, **'96** 313
Congo Squares, **'96** 94
Cream Cheese-Chocolate Chip Cookies, **'02** 229; **'03** 131
Crème de Menthe Bars, Chocolate-, **'86** 245
Crème de Menthe Bites, Chocolate, **'88** 285
Crème de Menthe Squares, **'93** 256
Crispies, Chocolate-Peanut, **'93** 80
Crispy Cookies, Chocolate, **'85** 115
Crumble Bars, Choco-, **'79** 292
Crunch Cookies, Chocolate, **'91** 316
Crunchies, Chocolate, **'92** 50
Cupcake Cookies, **'04** 273
Dainties, Choco-Nut, **'04** M124
Date-Nut Chocolate Chip Cookies, Rich, **'92** 207
Deluxe Chocolate Chip Cookies, **'79** 216
Devil Doggies, **'84** 37
Different Chocolate Chip Cookies, **'83** 114
Double Chip Cookies, **'81** 301
Double Chocolate Chip Cookies, **'79** 217
Double Chocolate Chunk-Almond Cookies, **'95** 178
Double Chocolate Chunk-Peanut Cookies, **'04** 125
Double-Chocolate Cookies, **'95** 272
Doubly-Good Chocolate Cookies, **'82** M185
Dream Bars, Chocolate, **'79** 256; **'82** 298
Drop Cookies, Chocolate, **'84** 36
Easy Cookies, **'00** 133
Fibber McGee Cookies, **'95** 72
Flying Brooms, **'98** 255
Forget 'em Cookies, **'83** 256
Frosted Chocolate-Cherry Cookies, **'89** 294
Fudge Bars, **'86** 93
Fudge Bars, Yummy, **'87** 158
Fudge-Pecan Chewies, Alabama, **'95** 143
Fudge Puddles, **'94** 292
German Chocolate Chess Squares, **'94** 51
Giant Chocolate Chip Cookies, **'84** 119
Gingerbread Cookies, Chocolate-, **'94** 293
Graham Cracker Layered Cookies, Chocolate, **'98** 94
Jumbo Chocolate Chip Cookies, **'82** 110
Keyboard Cookies, **'94** M330
Kiss Cookies, Chocolate, **'03** 298
Kissy Cookies, **'93** 331
Light Chocolate Chip Cookies, **'86** 46
Log Cookies, Chocolate-Tipped, **'87** 294
Lollapalooza, **'94** 194
Macaroon Cookies, Chocolate, **'88** 217
Macaroons, Chocolate, **'83** 300; **'87** 57
Macaroons, White Chocolate Tropical, **'00** M166
Magic Cookie Bars, **'02** 253
Meltaways, Chocolate, **'81** 302
Melt-Aways, Chocolate Chip, **'84** 118
Meringue-Chocolate Chip Bars, **'84** 118
Meringue Cookies, Heavenly Chocolate-Chip, **'01** 218
Meringue Kiss Cookies, **'86** 121
Mint Chip Cookies, Chocolate-, **'86** 245
Mint Cookies, Chocolate-, **'92** 206
Mint Snaps, Chocolate-, **'83** 103; **'84** 96
Monster Cookies, **'84** 36

Neapolitan Cookies, '00 290
Nugget Cookies, '79 291
Nut Chews, Chocolate-, '81 92
Nut Freezer Cookies, Chocolate-, '88 217
Nutty Choco Snacks, '83 305
Nutty Oatmeal-Chocolate Chip Cookies,
    '82 M185
Oatmeal Bars, Chocolate-Topped, '86 110
Oatmeal-Chocolate Chippers, '90 218
Oatmeal-Chocolate Chunk Cookies, Nutty, '01 19
Oatmeal-Chocolate Morsel Cookies, '95 46
Oatmeal Cookies, Chocolate-, '80 105
Oatmeal Cookies, Chocolate Chip-, '84 119
Oatmeal Cookies, Double-Chip, '03 200
Oatmeal-Peanut Butter Chocolate Chip Cookies,
    '92 207
Oatmeal-Toffee Lizzies, Crispy, '95 136
Olympic Medal Cookies, '96 180
Orange-Chocolate Cookies, '83 113
Orange Cookies, Chocolate-Dipped, '04 299
Orange Delights, Chocolate-, '93 52
Peanut Bars, Chocolate-, '03 195
Peanut Blossom Cookies, '95 245; '96 55;
    '97 324
Peanut Butter and Chocolate Chunk Cookies,
    '94 169
Peanut Butter-and-Fudge Bars, '80 M172
Peanut Butter Bars, '84 243
Peanut Butter-Chocolate Chip Cookies, Freezer,
    '86 230
Peanut Butter-Chocolate Kiss Cookies, '86 49
Peanut Butter-Chocolate Treats, Crispy, '02 287;
    '03 271
Peanut Butter Cones, Chocolate-, '85 14
Peanut Butter Cookies, Chocolate-, '85 90
Peanut Butter Cookies, Chocolate Chip-, '99 68
Peanut Butter Cups, Chocolate-, '85 14; '97 134
Peanut Butter Fingers, '79 256
Peanut Butter-Kiss Cookies, '03 42
Peanut Butter Squares, Chocolate Chip-, '84 118
Peanut Chip Cookies, Choco-, '92 318
Peanut Cookies, Chocolate-, '83 223
Peanut Cookies, Chocolate Chunk-, '04 125
Peppermint Cookies, Chocolate-Chocolate Chip-,
    '97 289
Peppermint Squares, Chocolate-, '81 119
Pinwheel Cookies, '93 316
Pinwheel Cookies, Chocolate, '86 245
Pinwheels, '95 321
Pixies, Chocolate, '00 M155
Pizza Cookies, Candy Shop, '02 299
Polka Dots, '95 272
Praline-Chocolate Chip Cookies, Crispy, '02 229;
    '03 131
Praline-Chocolate Fudge Bars, Chewy, '04 M330
Pudding Cookies, Chocolate Chip-, '93 21
Pumpkin-Chocolate Chip Cookies, '93 235
Raisin Oatmeal Cookies, Chocolate-, '95 136
Rudolph Cookies, '99 M309
Sachertorte Cookies, '00 155
Sandwich Cookies, Chocolate, '81 192
Sandwich Cookies, Choco-Nut, '84 200
Sandwiches, Chocolate Cookie Ice Cream,
    '87 147
Scotch Bars, Chewy, '98 M291
Seashells, Chocolate, '91 178
Shortbread Cookies, Chocolate, '99 147
Shortbread, Marble-Topped Hazelnut, '99 M29
Shortbread, Mocha-Chocolate, '04 173
Shortbread, Peanut-Toffee, '04 329
Shortbread Squares, Mocha-Chocolate, '02 176
Shortbread Wafers, Cocoa, '88 243
Snack Bars, Chocolate, '04 124
Snappers, Jumbo Chocolate, '81 218

Snowball Cookies, Chocolate, '82 295
Snowballs, Chocolate, '03 273
Snowcaps, Smoky Mountain, '00 288
Snowflake Cookies, Chocolate, '89 329
Spice Cookies, Lemon-Iced Chocolate, '97 123
Sugar-Coated Chocolate Cookies, '92 274
Sugar Cookies, Double-Chocolate, '92 206
Super Chocolate Chunk Cookies, '88 217
Supreme Cookies, Chocolate-Chip, '01 218
Surprise Bonbon Cookies, '88 119
Surprise Cookies, Choco, '80 60
Teasers, Chocolate, '87 44
Toffee Cookie Bites, '03 M273
Toffee Treats, '89 330
Turtle Bars, '00 334
Turtle Bars, Gooey, '96 M189
Wedding Cookies, Chocolate, '04 275
White Chocolate Chip-Oatmeal Cookies, '99 127;
    '04 43
White Chocolate Cookies, Chunky Macadamia
    Nut, '92 207
White Chocolate-Macadamia Nut Cookies,
    '94 315
White Chocolate-Orange Dream Cookies,
    '98 294
Whoopie Pies, '86 246
Witches' Hats, '98 256
Yummy Bars, '92 171
Zucchini Cookies, Spicy, '97 273
Baskets with Berry Cream, Chocolate, '92 118
Beverages
Brandied Chocolate, Flaming, '80 M290
Café au Lait, German Chocolate, '92 264
Café Colombian Royal, '80 M290
Café Mexicano, '92 208
Café Mocha Latte, '01 64
Cappuccino, Chocolate Castle, '84 53
Cocoa Mix, Instant, '86 332
Coffee, Chocolate, '82 43; '97 17
Coffee, Chocolate-Almond, '84 54
Coffee, Chocolate Iced, '01 166
Coffee, Cocoa-, '83 55
Coffee, Fireside, '03 M298
Coffee, Mexican, '83 175, 275; '88 247; '91 78;
    '93 310; '94 97
"Concrete," Abaco Mocha, '94 114
"Concrete," Cardinal Sin, '94 113
"Concrete," Foxtreat, '94 113
Hot Chocolate, '94 290; '04 209
Hot Chocolate, Cherry Cordial, '02 220
Hot Chocolate, Creole, '80 M290
Hot Chocolate Deluxe, '90 272; '00 33
Hot Chocolate, Favorite, '83 55
Hot Chocolate, French, '86 328
Hot Chocolate, Mexican, '98 313;
    '04 210, 299
Hot Chocolate Mix, '04 209
Hot Chocolate Mix, Deluxe, '80 M290
Hot Chocolate Mix, Spicy, '85 278
Hot Chocolate Nog, '02 297
Hot Chocolate, Old-Fashioned, '85 23
Hot Chocolate, Special, '82 5
Hot Chocolate, Spiced, '80 50
Hot Chocolate, Spicy, '85 278
Hot Chocolate, Sugar-and-Spice, '95 34
Hot Chocolate, Tennessee, '96 214
Hot Cocoa, Fudgy, '00 235
Hot Cocoa Mix, '81 287
Hot Cocoa Mix, Minted, '91 316
Hot Cocoa Mix, Mocha-Flavored, '91 316
Hot Cocoa, Quick, '82 5
King Alfonso, '80 259
Malt, Banana-Chocolate, '89 170
Malt, Chocolate, '86 183

Malt, Chocolate-Yogurt, '01 173
Marshmallow Chocolate, Hot Laced, '93 53
Martini, Individual Chocolate, '02 88
Martinis, Chocolate, '02 88
Mexican-Style Chocolate, '81 187
Milk, French Chocolate, '79 38
Mocha Blend, '95 276
Mocha Cappuccino, '02 M220
Mocha Chocolate Fluff, '89 170
Mocha Cocoa, '83 318
Mocha-Cocoa Mix, Hot, '82 296
Mocha Coffee, '85 M329
Mocha Cream, Café, '84 54
Mocha Deluxe Hot Drink, '82 289
Mocha Espresso, Italian, '82 254
Mocha Frosty, '92 44
Mocha, Hot, '84 60
Mocha Latte, Spiced, '04 333
Mocha Melt, Spiced, '01 240
Mocha, Mexican, '93 M341
Mocha Mix, Spiced, '01 64
Mocha Polka, '89 171
Mocha Punch, '84 58, 166; '95 141
Mocha, Quick Viennese, '79 232
Mocha Spice Mix, Mexican, '00 334
Mocha, Spirited Hot, '91 M260
Mocha Warmer, '97 272
Peppermint Patti, The Peabody, '99 321
Shake, Chocolate-Banana Milk, '94 113
Shake, Chocolate Mint, '89 170
Shake, Mocha-Mint, '02 297
Sipper, Chocolate, '88 83
Smoothie, Chocoholic, '97 173
Smoothie, Chocolate-Mint, '84 166
White Chocolate Latte, '04 210
Bites, Snowy Chocolate, '90 47
Black-Bottom Goodies, '89 251
Bombe, Double-Chocolate, '97 282
Bread, Chocolate Chip-Banana, '90 267
Bread, Chocolate Date-Nut, '81 284
Bread, Chocolate Loaf, '88 M188
Bread, Chocolate-Zucchini, '93 308
Bread, Cocoa-Nut Swirl, '80 257
Brickle Squares, Chocolate, '94 290
Buns, Chocolate-Cinnamon, '85 5
Buns, Chocolate Sticky, '81 300; '82 124
Cakes and Tortes
Almond Cake, Chocolate-, '91 248
Almond Cake with Cherry Filling, Chocolate-,
    '84 225
Almond Torte, Chocolate-, '96 M253; '98 273
Amaretto Heart, Chocolate-, '98 56
Angel Cake, Chocolate, '88 128
Angel Cake, Chocolate Truffle, '97 283
Angel Food Cake, Chocolate, '87 21; '90 111;
    '91 55
Angel Food Cake with Custard Sauce, Chocolate,
    '88 259
Angel Squares, Mocha, '98 61
Apricot-Filled Chocolate Torte, '90 107
Banana Cake, Chocolate-, '86 138
Banana Loaf, Chocolate Chip-, '85 115
Banana-Toffee Coffee Cakes, '02 M324
Basket Cake, Chocolate-Strawberry, '98 100
Batter, Chocolate Velvet Cake, '03 M286
Beet Cake, Chocolate, '80 40
Birthday Balloon Cakes, '92 15
Birthday Cake, Fishin'-for-Fun, '93 194
Black Forest Cake, '81 126; '92 174
Black Forest Pudding Cake, '02 210
Black Forest Torte, '88 209
Bourbon-Chocolate Torte, '98 M84
Bourbon-Pecan Cake, Chocolate-, '03 287
Breakfast Cake, Chocolate-Swirl, '04 M41

CHOCOLATE, Cakes and Tortes
(continued)

Brownie Cakes, Birthday Party, '00 199
Brownie Delight, Chocolate, '87 224
Brown Mountain Cake, '84 39
Bûche de Noël, '84 304; '87 241
Bûche de Noël Cake, '82 262
Buttercream Cake, Chocolate, '90 108
Buttermilk Cake, Chocolate-, '00 48
Buttermilk Chocolate Cake, '79 13
Buttermilk Fudge Squares, '99 99
Candy Cake, Chocolate, '81 238
Candy Corn Chocolate Cakes, '00 235
Caramel-Nut Cake, Chocolate-, '83 23
Carrot Cake, Brownie, '92 120
Cheesecake Bites, Mint, '99 282
Cheesecake, Black-and-White, '99 334
Cheesecake, Black Forest, '84 74; '89 93; '94 21;
   '97 330
Cheesecake, Candy Bar, '86 120
Cheesecake, Chocolate, '81 16; '82 305
Cheesecake, Chocolate-Almond, '93 53
Cheesecake, Chocolate-Amaretto, '85 M294;
   '93 97
Cheesecake, Chocolate-Caramel-Pecan, '91 197
Cheesecake, Chocolate Chip, '85 114
Cheesecake, Chocolate Cookie, '91 298
Cheesecake, Chocolate-Glazed Triple-Layer,
   '86 315; '90 310
Cheesecake, Chocolate Marble, '89 93
Cheesecake, Chocolate-Mint, '91 104
Cheesecake, Chocolate-Mint Baked Alaska,
   '94 142
Cheesecake, Chocolate-Raspberry Truffle,
   '91 270
Cheesecake, Chocolate Swirl, '84 295; '85 26
Cheesecake, Chocolate-Wrapped Banana,
   '99 M48
Cheesecake, Coconut-Chocolate-Almond,
   '98 322
Cheesecake, Fudge, '98 M213
Cheesecake, German Chocolate, '87 265; '00 245
Cheesecake, Marbled, '87 261
Cheesecake, Marble Mint, '84 152
Cheesecake, Mocha, '98 278
Cheesecake, Mocha-Chocolate, '88 258
Cheesecake, Mocha Swirl, '87 262
Cheesecake, Rich Chocolate, '84 74; '85 38
Cheesecakes, Tiny Chocolate, '92 288
Cheesecake, Warm Fudge-Filled, '98 34; '03 320
Cheesecake, White Chocolate, '87 44; '88 267;
   '94 180
Cheesecake with Whipped Cream Frosting,
   Chocolate, '89 42
Cherry Cake, Choco-, '96 229
Cherry Cake, Chocolate-, '84 200; '86 239
Cherry Fudge Cake, '98 214
Chewies, Chocolate-Chip, '01 320
Chiffon Cake with Coffee Buttercream,
   Chocolate, '95 277
Chocolate Cake, '97 283
Cinnamon Cake, Chocolate-, '93 154
Cocoa Crown Cake, '90 107
Coconut Cake, Chocolate-, '83 23
Coconut Cake, White Chocolate-, '87 263
Coconut-Fudge Cake, '99 206
Coffee Cake, Chocolate-Chip, '79 249
Coffee Cake, Chocolate Chip, '83 231; '97 232;
   '04 194
Coffee Cake, Chocolate-Cream Cheese, '03 288
Coffee Cake, Triple-Chocolate, '04 M299
Cola Cake, Quick, '00 120

Cola Cake, Quick Chocolate, '95 56
Crumb Cake, Calico, '87 261
Cupcakes, Banana-Chocolate, '02 187
Cupcakes, Banana-Cocoa, '80 130
Cupcakes, Brownie, '82 280
Cupcakes, Chewy Chocolate, '01 334
Cupcakes, Choco, '03 200
Cupcakes, Chocolate, '92 14
Cupcakes, Chocolate-Brickle Ice-Cream,
   '01 M172
Cupcakes, Chocolate Chip, '97 108
Cupcakes, Chocolate-Cream Cheese, '03 169
Cupcakes, Chocolate-Peppermint Candy,
   '03 M287
Cupcakes, Chocolate Surprise, '85 91
Cupcakes, Cinnamon-Chocolate, '81 M139
Cupcakes, Marble Chocolate Chip, '81 239
Cupcakes, Mint-Chocolate Chip Ice-Cream,
   '01 172
Cupcakes, Mocha, '85 250
Cupcakes, Self-Filled, '80 129
Cupcake Surprises, '01 299
Cups, Black Bottom, '82 279
Custard Cake, Chocolate, '88 175
Decadence, Chocolate, '03 319
Decadent Chocolate Cake, '86 142
Double-Chocolate Torte, '79 67
Easy Chocolate Cake, '80 140
Easy Perfect Chocolate Cake, '99 307
Éclair Cake, Chocolate, '03 206
Extra-Rich Chocolate Cake, '99 271
Father's Day Cake, '92 134
Firewater Cream, Chocolate Torte with, '00 161
Frosting, Chocolate Cake with Double, '86 314
Fruitcakes, Chocolate, '95 250
Fudge Cake, '94 M293; '98 110; '99 176
Fudge Cake, Best, '83 301
Fudge Cake, Brown Sugar, '86 316
Fudge Cake, Chocolate, '80 19
Fudge Cake, Coconut-, '99 206
Fudge Cake for Two, '81 205
Fudge Cake, Hot, '99 105
Fudge Cake, One-Foot-in-the-Fire, '90 252
Fudge Cake, Shortbread, '03 M331
Fudge Frosting, Chocolate Cake with, '89 56
Fudge Sundae Cakes, Hot, '00 333
German Chocolate Cake, '81 296; '83 M233
German Chocolate Chip Cake, '86 247
German Chocolate Sheet Cake, '03 147
German Chocolate Snack Cake, '02 128
Grandma's Chocolate Cake, '94 133
Graveyard Grumblings, '92 15
Holiday Torte, Chocolate-Vanilla, '01 252
Ice-Cream Torte, Toffee-Coffee, '04 234
Italian Cake, Chocolate, '02 256
Kahlúa Cake, Chocolate, '91 298
Kahlúa Chocolate Cake, '81 303
Layers, Chocolate Cake, '96 229
Loaf Cakes, Chocolate Chip, '98 137
Macadamia-Fudge Cake, '01 278
Marbled Cake, Cocoa, '82 265
Marshmallow Cake, No-Egg Chocolate, '87 M97
Mayonnaise Cake, Chocolate, '83 99
Milk Chocolate Bar Cake, '00 86
Mint Cake, Chocolate-, '03 286
Mint Torte, Chocolate, '94 86
Mississippi Mud Cake, '03 288; '04 136
Mocha Brownie Torte, '85 102
Mocha Cake, Belgian, '84 316
Mocha Cake, Double, '84 311
Mocha Chiffon Cake, Delta, '00 286
Mocha-Chocolate Cake, Dark, '84 311
Mocha Cream Roll, Chocolate-, '84 304
Mocha-Pecan Torte, '86 26

Mocha Torte, '99 66
Mocha Velvet Torte, '92 318
Mousse Cake, Chocolate, '87 264; '98 270;
   '03 320
Mousse Cake, Chocolate-Peanut Butter, '98 71
Mousse Cake, Strawberry-Studded White
   Chocolate, '99 154
Mousse Cake, White Chocolate, '89 160
Mousse Roll, Chocolate, '88 280
Mousse Torte, White Chocolate, '99 154
Nut Cake, Rich Chocolate-, '86 8
Pastry Cake, Chocolate, '91 196
Peanut Butter Cake, Chocolate-, '84 240
Peanut Butter Cake, Fudgy, '85 91
Peanut Butter-Fudge Cake, '96 254; '01 59
Peanut Butter Turtle Torte, '04 316
Peanut Cluster Cake, Chocolate-, '87 184
Pecan Torte, Chocolate-, '89 42
Perfect Chocolate Cake, '82 244; '90 307;
   '03 318
Petits Fours, Chocolate-Almond, '93 255; '00 72
Piglets, '98 203
Pound Cake, Chocolate, '82 88; '84 10; '89 325;
   '94 288; '98 336
Pound Cake, Chocolate Chip, '86 178; '93 105;
   '94 100
Pound Cake, Chocolate Marble, '88 16
Pound Cake, Chocolate-Orange, '89 94
Pound Cake, Chocolate-Sour Cream, '83 239;
   '92 153
Pound Cake, Chocolate-Swirled, '97 329
"Pound" Cake, Chocolate Velvet, '03 286
Pound Cake, German Chocolate, '97 M254
Pound Cake, Mahogany, '89 207
Pound Cake, Marble, '95 29
Pound Cake, Marbled Pecan, '93 313
Pound Cake, Milk Chocolate, '90 306
Pound Cake, White Chocolate, '91 101
Pound Cake with Frosting, Chocolate, '90 284
Pound Cake with Fudge Frosting, Chocolate,
   '87 296
Praline Cake, Chocolate-, '01 235
Praline Pecan Cake, Chocolate-, '03 288
Praline Torte, Chocolate, '84 165
Pudding Cake, Hot Fudge, '88 255
Pudding Cake, Warm Chocolate, '92 324
Pudding, Chocolate Cake, '81 99
Pumpkin Cake with Little Ghosts, '03 212
Pumpkin, Chocolate, '96 254
Queen's Chocolate Cake, '89 271
Raspberry Cake, Chocolate-, '92 173; '01 M319
Raspberry-Fudge Cake, '97 34
Rich Chocolate Cake, '89 43
Rocky Road Cake, '81 178
Roll, Chocolate, '04 85
Roll, Chocolate Cream, '85 317
Roll, Chocolate-Frosted Ice Cream, '84 200
Roll, Chocolate Mousse, '83 290
Roll, Chocolate-Orange, '87 21
Roll, Make-Ahead Chocolate-Mint Cake, '95 220
Rolls, Chocolate Cake, '94 312
Root Beer Float Cake, '04 211
Roulade, Kahlúa-and-Cream, '97 199
Roulage, Chocolate-Cranberry, '94 313
Roulage, Chocolate-Orange, '94 314
Roulage, Mint-Chocolate, '94 314
Royal, Chocolate Cake, '86 239
Royale, Chocolate Torte, '82 263
Rum Cake, Chocolate, '79 67
Sachertorte, '84 253
Sachertorte, Shortcut, '99 M243
Sheet Cake, Texas, '03 19
Shortcake, Chocolate-Raspberry, '95 99
Shortcake, Chocolate-Strawberry, '89 216

Snack Cake, Black Widow, **'93** 245
Snack Cake, Frosted Chocolate, **'90** 194
Sour Cream Cake, Chocolate-, **'87** 222
Sour Cream Cake, Chocolate Chip-, **'85** 115
Sour Cream Chocolate Cake, **'79** 282
Spice Potato Cake, Chocolate-, **'96** 111
Sponge Cake, Chocolaty, **'86** 60
Strawberry Ice Cream Torte, Chocolate-, **'79** 7
Sugar Cookie Torte, **'79** 68
Swiss Chocolate Chip Cake, **'87** 85
Tannenbaum Temptations, **'92** 14
Texas Cake, **'01** 59
Toffee Cake, Chocolate-, **'89** 335
Tree Cakes, Miniature Chocolate Truffle,
    '97 M285
Triangle Cake, Chocolate, **'85** 126
Triple Chocolate Torte, **'96** 58
Truffle Cake, Chocolate, **'89** 43
Truffle Cake, Rudolph's Chocolate, **'04** M253
Turkey Talk, **'92** 15
Turtle Cake, **'03** 287
Velvet Cake with Coconut-Pecan Frosting,
    Chocolate, **'03** 289
Velvet Cake with Cream Cheese-Butter Pecan
    Frosting, Chocolate, **'03** 288
Velvet Cake with Vanilla Buttercream Frosting,
    Chocolate, **'03** 287
Velvet Torte, Chocolate, **'86** 316
Wedding Cake, Double Chocolate, **'91** 100
Whipped Cream Cake, Chocolate-Mint, **'90** 265
White Chocolate-Almond Cake, **'03** M287
White Chocolate-Cherry Cake, **'88** 268
White Chocolate Mousse Cake, **'89** 160
White Chocolate Mousse Cake, Strawberry-
    Studded, **'99** 154
White Chocolate Mousse Torte, **'99** 154
White Chocolate-Raspberry Cake, **'98** 323
X-Treme Chocolate Double Nut Caramel
    Ladyfinger Torte, **'04** M315
Yule Log, **'79** 281; **'82** 289
Zucchini Cake, Chocolate-, **'85** 156; **'02** 181
Candies
Almond Hearts, Chocolate-, **'03** 42
Almond Roca, **'86** 49
Balls, Buckeye, **'00** M280; **'01** M322
Bourbon Balls, **'83** 315; **'90** 83; **'02** 30
Bourbon Balls, Chocolate, **'84** 298
Brittle, Chocolate, **'83** 315
Brittle, Quick Chocolate, **'82** 114
Butter Creams, **'80** 302
Candy Cane Swizzle Sticks, **'02** 298
Caramels, Chocolate, **'91** 35
Caramels, Chocolate-Dipped, **'02** 30
Cherries, Chocolate-Covered, **'81** 286; **'84** 298;
    '97 M55
Cherries, Cordial, **'02** 30
Chunks of Snow, **'02** 298
Clusters, Triple Chocolate, **'01** 242
Coconut Almond Drops, Chocolate-, **'87** 223
Coconut Joys, **'98** 282
Coconut Joys, Chocolate-Covered, **'98** M282
Coffee Buttons, **'99** 66
Cracker Candy, **'02** 30
Cream-Filled Chocolates, Liqueur, **'87** 258
Creams, Chocolate-Lemon, **'98** M235
Crème de Cacao Balls, **'86** 266
Crème de Menthe Chocolates, **'91** 36
Crunch, White Chocolate-Peanut Butter,
    '02 M296
Dark Chocolate Bonbons, **'02** 297
Drops, Chocolate, **'84** 111
Fudge, **'86** 266
Fudge Balls, Strawberry, **'93** 80
Fudge Bites, Peanut-, **'91** M231; **'92** M68

Fudge, Cherry Nut, **'83** 315
Fudge, Chocolate, **'82** 20
Fudge, Chocolate-Peanut Butter, **'87** 257; **'90** 311
Fudge, Coffee-Chip, **'86** 74
Fudge, Cream Cheese, **'84** 111
Fudge, Creamy, **'81** 218
Fudge, Creamy Almond, **'95** 51
Fudge, Creamy Dark, **'82** 295
Fudge, Creamy Mocha, **'95** 51
Fudge, Creamy Pecan, **'84** 321
Fudge, Diamond, **'92** 193
Fudge, Dinner Mint, **'88** 285
Fudge, Double-Good, **'79** M263; **'95** M50
Fudge, Double Good, **'87** M278
Fudge, Double Peanut, **'85** 91
Fudge, Fast, **'79** 274
Fudge, Five Pounds of Chocolate, **'95** 51
Fudge, Four Chips, **'92** 318
Fudge, Holiday Mocha, **'84** 298
Fudge, Mama's, **'03** 279
Fudge, Marbled Peanut Butter, **'88** 65
Fudge, Microwave Chocolate, **'92** M50; **'02** M31
Fudge, Mint, **'95** 50
Fudge, Orange-Walnut, **'92** 288
Fudge, Peanut Butter, **'89** 307
Fudge-Peanut Butter Chewies, **'98** 215
Fudge, Pistachio, **'83** 298
Fudge, Quick-and-Easy, **'88** M190
Fudge, Quick Nut, **'83** 316
Fudge Scotch Ring, **'79** 273
Fudge Squares, Chocolate-Peanut Butter,
    '97 M54
Fudge, White Chocolate, **'92** 317; **'95** 51
Fudge, White Chocolate-Coffee, **'94** 232
Greeting Card, Chocolate, **'83** 40
Kentucky Colonels, **'79** 273
Marshmallow Squares, Chocolate-, **'92** M50
Millionaires, **'79** M262; **'97** M55
Millionaires, Texas, **'00** 291
Mints, Dinner, **'88** 66
Molded Candies, **'84** 40
Nut Clusters, **'81** 254
Nut Log Candy, Chocolate-, **'86** 335
Nut Teasers, Chocolate, **'91** 35
Peanut Brittle, Chocolate-Dipped, **'02** M223
Peanut Butter Balls, Chocolate-, **'80** 87
Peanut Butter Bites, Chocolate-, **'92** M317
Peanut Butter-Chocolate Balls, **'80** 269
Peanut Butter-Chocolate Candy Squares, **'82** 56
Peanut Butter Creams, **'79** 273
Peanut Butter Drops, Chocolate-, **'92** 322
Peanut Clusters, **'92** 288; **'98** M282
Peanut Clusters, Chocolate-, **'81** 16
Peanutty Clusters, **'83** 143
Peanutty Swirls, Chocolate, **'94** M330
Pecan Clusters, **'98** 305
Pecan Clusters, Roasted, **'90** 310
Pecan Clusters, Toasted, **'00** M14
Pecan Fritters, Chocolate-Covered, **'79** 205
Pralines, Chocolate, **'92** 313; **'93** 51
Pralines, Chocolate-Mint, **'92** 313; **'93** 51
Pralines, Chocolate-Peanut Butter, **'92** 313;
    '93 51
Pralines, Mocha, **'92** 313; **'93** 51
Pretzels, Chocolate-Covered, **'82** 295
Raspberry Cream Chocolates, **'91** 36
Rocky Road, **'84** 298
Rum Balls, Chocolate, **'80** 302
Rum Balls, Chocolate-, **'88** 285
Spiders, Chocolate, **'85** 236
Spirited Chocolates, **'86** 278
Tempered Chocolate, **'91** 35
Tiger Butter, **'86** 48
Toffee, **'01** 218

Toffee, English, **'79** 273
Toffee, Microwave, **'92** M317
Toffee, Nutty, **'79** M263
Truffles, Almond, **'83** 298
Truffles, Amaretto Dessert, **'86** 319
Truffles, Bittersweet, **'94** 330
Truffles, Chocolate, **'85** 114; **'89** 43; **'91** 108
Truffles, Chocolate-Cherry Cordial, **'99** 127
Truffles, Chocolate-Kahlúa, **'92** 285
Truffles, Chocolate Marble, **'97** 284
Truffles, Chocolate-Praline, **'97** 284
Truffles, Hazelnut, **'97** M54
Truffles, Hazelnut-Chocolate, **'03** 243
Truffles, Orange-Pecan, **'95** 92
Truffles, Raspberry-Fudge, **'00** M41
Truffles, White Chocolate, **'87** 45
Truffles, White Chocolate-Praline, **'97** 284
Truffles, Yule Street, **'90** 242
Turtle Candies, **'93** M41
Velvets, Chocolate, **'84** 298
White Chocolate Salties, **'92** 50
White Chocolate Surprises, **'91** 36
Cannoli, **'80** 58
Charlotte Russe, Chocolate, **'87** 74
Charlottes, Mocha, **'02** 171
Cheese Cups, Chocolate-, **'91** 142
Cinnamon-Chocolate Cream, **'94** 199
Cocoa to Chocolate Equivalents, **'84** 200
Combo, Strawberry-Chocolate, **'85** 96
Cones, Chocolate-Coffee, **'96** M316
Cracker Bites, Miniature Peanut Butter, **'02** 298
Cream, Chocolate-Almond, **'91** 108
Cream, Heavenly Chocolate, **'88** 128
Cream, Strawberries with Chocolate, **'85** 81
Crème Brûlée, Black-and-White, **'98** 267; **'02** 62
Crème Brûlée, Chocolate, **'95** 323
Crème Brûlée, White Chocolate-Macadamia Nut,
    '95 323
Crêpes, Chocolate, **'86** 164
Crêpes, Chocolate Chantilly, **'82** 183
Crêpes, Chocolate Dessert, **'84** 84; **'85** 262
Crêpes, Chocolate Dream, **'86** 164
Crêpes, Chocolate-Orange, **'85** 263
Crêpes, Fruit-Filled Chocolate, **'89** 325
Crescents, Chocolate, **'03** 283
Croissants, Chocolate-Filled, **'96** 303
Crust, Chocolate, **'87** 264; **'90** M15; **'03** 320
Crust, Chocolate-Coconut, **'87** 261
Crust, Chocolate Crumb, **'87** 261
Crust, Chocolate-Macadamia Crumb, **'96** 254
Crust, Chocolate Wafer, **'89** 42, 93
Cups, Chocolate, **'80** 207
Cups, Chocolate Crinkle, **'93** 270
Cups, Chocolate Lace, **'87** 133
Cups, Chocolate-Mint, **'80** 71
Cups, Chocolate-Walnut, **'85** 213
Cups, Miniature Chocolate, **'87** 132
Custard, Chocolate, **'88** 258
Custard, Chocolate-Topped Amaretto, **'87** M37
Date-Nut Delight, Chocolate, **'88** 168
Decadence, Chocolate, **'89** 183
Delights, Choco-Peanut, **'99** 197
Dessert, Chilled Chocolate, **'83** 177
Dessert, Chocolate-Almond, **'82** 306
Dessert, Chocolate-Coffee Frozen, **'85** 172
Dessert, Chocolate Dream, **'83** 198
Dessert, Chocolate Ladyfinger, **'86** 162
Dessert, Chocolate-Mint, **'82** 100
Dessert, Chocolate-Rum, **'81** 247
Dessert, Chocolate Truffle, **'88** 281
Dessert, Choco-Maple Frozen, **'86** 300; **'87** 178
Dessert, Cool Chocolate-Mint, **'80** 109
Dessert, Easy Chocolate, **'79** 75
Dessert, Frozen Chocolate, **'83** 76

CHOCOLATE
(continued)

Dessert, Fudge-Peanut Ice Cream, '88 167
Dessert, Hello Dolly, '95 168
Dessert, Layered Ice Cream, '83 189
Dessert, Nutty Fudgy Frozen, '94 28
Dessert, Peanut-Chocolate, '80 86
Dessert Squares, Chocolate-Blueberry, '87 299
Dessert, Triple Cream, '94 244
Dessert with Kahlúa Cream, Fudge, '91 197
Dip, Chocolate, '92 50
Doughnuts, Chocolate, '83 95
Doughnuts, Chocolate-Covered, '84 55
Doughnuts, Chocolate-Glazed Potato, '85 6
Dream Drops, '99 328
Éclairs, Banana-Chocolate, '01 45
Éclairs , Chocolate, '96 191
Éclairs , Peanut Butter-Chocolate, '01 45
Flan, Layered, '89 45
Fondue, Brandied Chocolate, '93 162
Fondue, Chocolate, '91 142
Fondue, Dessert, '89 281
Fondue, White Chocolate, '92 287
Frostings, Fillings, and Toppings
  Almond Frosting, Chocolate-, '83 241
  Buttercream, Chocolate, '84 156
  Buttercream Frosting, Chocolate, '96 229;
    '98 M100
  Butter Frosting, Chocolate, '89 271
  Buttermilk Frosting, Chocolate-, '99 99
  Candy Frosting, Chocolate, '81 238
  Cheese Filling, Chocolate-, '90 47
  Cherry Frosting, Chocolate-, '89 294
  Chocolate Filling, '96 316; '03 200
  Chocolate Frosting, '80 M171; '81 265; '82 262;
    '83 79, 99, M233, 253; '84 200; '85 323;
    '86 8, 93, 138, 239, 314; '87 M97, 198, 199,
    293; '89 M25; '90 194, 252, 265, 284, 309;
    '91 248; '92 319; '93 239; '94 133;
    '96 253, 254; '97 M87, 254; '99 271; '04 136
  Chocolate Icing, '03 19
  Cocoa Frosting, '86 60; '96 253, 254
  Coconut Chocolate Frosting, '79 13
  Coffee Buttercream Filling, Chocolate-,
    '00 M287
  Coffee Frosting, Chocolate-, '84 36; '88 269
  Cola Frosting, '00 120
  Cola Frosting, Chocolate-, '95 56
  Cranberry Filling, Nutty, '00 M306
  Cream Cheese Frosting, Chocolate-, '02 256
  Cream, Chocolate, '94 57
  Creamy Chocolate Frosting, '85 314; '86 316;
    '87 241; '99 307
  Creamy Chocolate Glaze, '82 88
  Fluffy Chocolate Frosting, '86 336; '87 58
  Fudge Filling, '94 292
  Fudge Frosting, '81 303; '87 296; '89 56; '94 51;
    '01 59
  Fudge Frosting, Chocolate, '83 105; '00 287
  Fudge Frosting, Quick, '81 278
  Ganache, Chocolate, '93 255; '97 282; '00 M72;
    '01 M235; '03 M286
  Ganache Cream, '92 318
  Ganache, Simple Chocolate, '03 M212
  Ganache, White Chocolate, '01 253
  Glaze, Brownie, '02 M252
  Glaze, Chocolate, '81 119; '83 220; '84 10, 55,
    253; '85 6; '86 315, 316; '89 325; '90 310;
    '91 M296; '93 52; '97 M35, 231; '99 206;
    '01 M45, M126
  Glaze, Creamy Chocolate, '98 90
  Glaze, French Chocolate, '98 M57

Glaze, White Cake with Strawberries and
    Chocolate, '87 76
Glaze, White Chocolate, '01 M45
Gravy, Chocolate, '99 35, 88
Honey Chocolate Frosting, '79 83
Honey Glaze, Chocolate-, '82 306
Hot Fudge Ice Cream Topping, '98 317
Hot Fudge Ice-Cream Topping, '02 109
Kahlúa Frosting, Chocolate, '91 298
Macadamia-Fudge Topping, '01 278
Marshmallow Frosting, Chocolate-, '83 245;
    '04 210
Marzipan Bees, '98 100
Midnight Filling, Chocolate, '96 120
Mint Chocolate Frosting, '99 M176
Mocha Butter Cream Frosting, '79 281
Mocha-Buttercream Frosting, '86 26
Mocha Cream, '94 47
Mocha Cream Filling, '84 305
Mocha Frosting, '83 301; '84 316; '87 224;
    '94 292; '97 35
Mocha Frosting, Creamy, '82 289; '84 311;
    '91 248
Mocha Ganache, '04 M260
Nut Frosting, Chocolate, '80 140
Peanut Butter Frosting, Chocolate-, '84 240;
    '87 222; '00 120
Peanut Butter-Fudge Frosting, '87 184
Peanut Topping, Chocolate-, '79 222
Perfect Chocolate Frosting, '90 307; '03 319
Praline Fudge Icing, '04 331
Rich Chocolate Filling, '79 68
Rich Chocolate Frosting, '84 304
Root Beer Frosting, '04 211
Rum Frosting, Chocolate, '79 67
Satiny Chocolate Frosting, '85 126; '89 43
Truffle Filling, Chocolate, '87 69; '04 M253
Velvet Frosting, '02 297
Whipped Cream Frosting, '89 43
White Chocolate Buttercream Frosting, '97 M284
White Chocolate-Cream Cheese Frosting, '94 58;
    '98 323
White Chocolate-Cream Cheese Tiered Cake
    Frosting, '94 125
White Chocolate Filling, '89 160
White Chocolate Frosting, '88 280; '91 101;
    '97 M111; '00 306
Garnishes, Chocolate, '85 16
Garnishes, Lacy Chocolate, '89 43
Gâteau Panache, '83 269
Granola with Chocolate Morsels, '86 69
Grapefruit, Chocolate-Topped, '89 88
Hearts, Crispy Chocolate, '03 M41
Horns, Chocolate-Dipped, '93 197
Ice Cream, Almond-Fudge, '93 205
Ice Cream Balls, Easy, '84 106
Ice Cream Balls, Nutty, '89 72
Ice Cream, Chocolate, '80 176; '86 129
Ice Cream, Chocolate Chunk-Peanut Butter, '85 297;
    '86 120
Ice Cream, Chocolate Cookie, '95 245
Ice Cream, Chocolate-Covered Peanut, '88 203
Ice Cream, Double-Chocolate, '88 203
Ice Cream, Mexican Chocolate, '91 162
Ice Cream, Mint-Chocolate Chip, '88 202
Ice Cream, Mocha, '88 202; '97 M145
Ice Cream, No-Cook Chocolate, '04 179
Ice Cream, No-Cook Chocolate-Almond, '04 179
Ice Cream, Orange Pekoe-Chocolate, '99 90
Ice Cream Party Squares, '91 214
Ice Cream Sandwiches, Chocolate, '89 72
Ice-Cream Sandwiches, Chocolate, '04 329
Ice Cream Squares, Mint-Chocolate Chip, '94 245
Kahlúa Delight, '83 67

Leaves, Chocolate, '88 281; '89 42; '98 270
Loaf, Chocolate Pinwheel, '80 256
Loaves, Chocolate Chip Cheese, '91 299; '92 264
Log, Chocolate Cream, '94 220
Lollipops, Harvest Moon, '02 M223
Mandelbread, Chocolate Chip, '00 282
Meringue Acorns, '93 284
Meringue Fingers, Chocolate-Almond, '84 158
Mexican Fiesta Confection, '82 223
Mint Freeze, Chocolate, '88 167
Mississippi Mud, '96 253
Mocha Alaska Dessert, '84 191
Mocha Chiffon, '86 75
Mocha Delight, Frozen, '96 179
Mocha Dessert, Frozen, '84 311
Mocha Freeze, Royal, '84 53
Mocha Squares, Frozen, '81 187
Molletes, Chocolate, '02 83
Mousse. *See also* **CHOCOLATE/Cakes and
    Tortes, Pies and Tarts.**
  Almond Mousse, Chocolate-, '93 316
  Amaretto-Chocolate Mousse, '86 50
  Amaretto-Chocolate Mousse, Elegant, '86 337
  au Grand Marnier, Chocolate Mousse, '91 296
  Baked Alaska, Chocolate Mousse, '85 195
  Blender Chocolate Mousse, '82 71
  Blender-Quick Chocolate Mousse, '80 269
  Brandy-Chocolate Mousse, '85 102
  Chocolate Mousse, '88 280; '97 282; '02 M277
  Creamy Chocolate Mousse, '87 133
  Honeyed Chocolate Mousse, '87 223
  Kid-Pleasin' Chocolate Mousse, '90 271
  Loaf with Raspberry Puree, Chocolate Mousse,
    '97 34
  Orange Liqueur, Chocolate Mousse with, '02 315
  Orange Mousse, Chocolate-, '81 16, 205
  Parfait, Chocolate Mousse, '94 90
  Parfaits, Chocolate-Peanut Butter Mousse, '98 71
  Present, Chocolate Mousse, '99 281
  Quick Chocolate Mousse, '85 87
  Rum Mousse, Chocolate, '86 189
  Truffle Mousse with Raspberry Sauce, Chocolate,
    '95 327
  White Chocolate Mousse, '91 247; '93 315;
    '97 282; '98 M57,
  White Chocolate Mousse, Quick, '99 155
Muffins, Banana-Chocolate, '94 197
Muffins, Chocolate Chip, '90 87
Muffins, Fudge Brownie, '95 M50
Muffins, Jumbo Banana-Chocolate Chip, '93 339
Muffins, Peanut Butter-Chocolate Chip, '94 167
Napoleons, Coffee, '95 276
Napoleons, Peanut Butter-and-Chocolate, '94 121
Parfait, Bodacious Peanut, '95 167
Parfaits, Chocolate-Crème de Menthe, '85 161
Parfaits, Chocolate-Mint, '90 M15
Parfaits, Chocolate-Peanut Butter Mousse, '98 71
Parfaits, Chocolate-Peppermint, '88 65
Parfaits, Hooray, '96 229
Parfaits, Mocha-Mallow, '80 219
Parfaits, Speedy, '83 76
Parfait, White Chocolate-Raspberry Swirl, '93 315
Party Mix, White Chocolate, '03 M289
Pastries, Chocolate-Chestnut, '02 M273
Pies and Tarts
  Almond Pie, Creamy Chocolate-, '85 102
  Amandine, Chocolate Pie, '83 300
  Amaretto Heavenly Tarts, Chocolate-, '88 4
  Amaretto Mousse Pie, Chocolate-, '80 180;
    '81 30
  Banana-Pecan Cream Pie, Chocolate-, '94 210
  Bavarian Pie, Chocolate, '89 326
  Berry Pie, Heavenly Chocolate-, '85 102
  Best-Ever Chocolate Pie, '88 M45

Black Bottom Mocha-Cream Tart, '92 304
Black Bottom Pie, '82 53
Black-Bottom Pie, '98 161
Bluegrass Chocolate Tarts, '90 84
Bourbon-Chocolate-Pecan Tarts, '96 264
Bourbon Pie, Chocolate, '88 99
Brownie-Mint Pie, '97 303
Brownie Pie, Crustless, '82 33
Brownie Pie, Frozen Chocolate, '96 57
Caramel Turtle Truffle Tart, '93 M131
Cherry Tart, Chocolate-, '97 33
Chess Pie, Chocolate, '81 161; '86 220; '92 13
Chess Pie, Chocolate-Pecan, '00 60; '02 107
Chess Tarts, Chocolate, '92 214
Chilled Chocolate Pie, '88 99
Chip Pie, Chocolate, '85 114
Coffee Tart, '99 67
Cream Cheese Pie, Chocolate-, '80 69
Cream Cheese Pie, Chocolate, '92 240
Cream Pie, Chocolate, '83 192; '84 49; '87 208;
   '94 208
Creamy Chocolate Pie, '85 298; '86 119
Custard Tart, Chocolate, '99 27
Double Chocolate Pie, '82 M282
Easy Chocolate Pie, '83 158
Fox Hunter's Pie, '97 109
French Silk Pie, '80 247
French Silk Tarts, '79 236
Frozen Chocolate-Macadamia Nut Pie, '96 254
Frozen Chocolate Pie, '80 154
Frozen Chocolate Pie with Pecan Crust, '89 291;
   '98 180
Fudge Pie, '87 168; '89 252; '01 129
Fudge Pie, Black-and-White, '99 249
Fudge Pie, Chocolate, '98 336
Fudge Pie, Sweetheart, '86 316; '90 313; '03 319
Fudge Truffle-Pecan Tart, '99 315; '02 208
Fudgy Chocolate Malt-Peppermint Pie, '00 313
German Chocolate Pie, '93 129
Heaven, Chocolate, '98 323
Heavenly Chocolate Pie, '87 260
Ice Cream Pie, Chocolate-, '87 224
Ice Cream Pie, Chocolate, '91 56
Ice Cream Pie, Chocolate-Mint, '81 144
Ice Cream Pie, Chocolate-Peanut Butter, '98 244
Ice Cream Sundae Pie, '94 244
Kahlúa Pie, '83 191
Kentucky Derby Tarts, '79 102
Meringue Pie, Chocolate, '80 238; '82 206;
   '83 158; '92 216
Meringue Pie, Chocolate-Filled, '86 121
Microwave Chocolate Pie, '90 M15
Midnight Delights, '95 278
Mint Chocolate Mousse Tarts, '03 283
Mocha Crunch Pie, Chocolate-, '81 136
Mocha Meringue Pie, '80 242
Mocha Pie, '94 168
Mousse Pie, Chocolate, '81 136
Mousse Pie, Chocolate-Amaretto, '80 180; '81 30
Mud Pie, Decadent, '89 252
Mud Pie, Mississippi, '89 26
Mud Pie, Tipsy, '80 255; '97 251
Party Tarts, '95 90
Peanut Butter Cup Pie, Fudgy, '04 211
Peanut Butter Pie, Chocolate-, '85 91
Peanut Butter Swirl Pie, Chocolate-, '87 262
Peanut Butter Tarts, Chocolate-, '92 277
Pecan Chess Pie, Chocolate-, '93 251
Pecan Pie, Bourbon-Chocolate, '98 258
Pecan Pie, Choco-, '82 86
Pecan Pie, Chocolate, '80 237; '83 12; '90 184
Pecan Pie, Chocolate-, '91 272; '02 176
Pecan Tart with Caramel Sauce, Chocolate-,
   '93 296; '94 234

Pizza Dolce (Italian Sweet Pies), '00 283
Praline Pie, Chocolate-, '86 259
Silk Pie, Chocolate, '88 67
Strawberry-Chocolate Truffle Pie, '89 112
Tin Roof Pie, '85 91
Turtle Pecan Pie, '93 250
Whipped Cream Pie, Chocolate, '79 124
White Chocolate-Banana Cream Pie, '94 314
White Chocolate Chess Tart, '95 303
Pineapple with Raspberry Sauce, Chocolate-
   Drizzled, '90 57
Pizza, Chocolate, '91 298
Plunge, Chocolate, '94 332; '95 35
Popcorn, Delicious Chocolate, '00 223
Pots de Chocolat, Petits, '82 272
Pots de Crème, '81 15; '84 M145
Pots de Crème au Chocolate, '93 53
Pots de Crème, Chocolate, '93 296; '94 234
Pots de Crème for Two, '89 275
Pots de Crème, Mocha, '88 M45
Pots de Crème, Rum-Flavored, '85 102
Pots de Crème with Orange Meringues, Chocolate,
   '95 318
Present, Chocolate Mousse, '99 281
Pudding, Brownie, '79 265; '80 295
Pudding, Chocolate, '02 323
Pudding, Chocolate-Almond, '82 142; '88 24
Pudding, Chocolate-Almond Silk, '96 266
Pudding, Chocolate Biscuit Bread, '94 215
Pudding, Chocolate Bread, '80 8
Pudding, Chocolate Cookie, '03 183
Pudding, Chocolate-Peanut Butter Cookie, '03 183
Pudding, Creamy Chocolate, '83 106
Pudding, Fudge-Banana, '97 331
Pudding, Fudgy Chocolate, '96 285
Pudding, Hot Fudge, '81 208
Pudding, Hot Fudge Sundae Cake, '88 167
Pudding, Mocha-Chocolate Cookie, '03 183
Pudding, Rich Black-and-White, '01 111
Pudding, White Chocolate Bread, '00 M104
Pudding with Custard Sauce, Chocolate Bread,
   '03 244
Pudding with Lemon Meringue, Chocolate, '88 258
Pudding with Whiskey Sauce, Chocolate Bread,
   '99 277
Quad, Chocolate, '02 272
Reindeer Food, Magic, '99 M309
Roulage, '90 266
Roulage, Chocolate-Mocha, '80 216
Roulage, Frozen Chocolate, '90 56
Roulage, White Chocolate, '92 230
Sack, Large Chocolate, '93 314
Sack, Small Chocolate, '93 314
Sauces
   Amaretto-Chocolate Sauce, '92 154
   Bittersweet Chocolate Sauce, '92 319
   Cherry Sauce, Chocolate-, '85 189
   Cherry Sauce, Chocolate, '87 M165
   Chocolate Sauce, '83 189; '84 208, 313; '86 322;
      '90 57; '91 56, 57; '93 276; '94 121;
      '97 178, 331
   Cinnamon-Fudge Sauce, '85 141
   Classic Chocolate Sauce, '85 207
   Creamy Chocolate Sauce, '88 M177
   Dark Chocolate Sauce, '93 296; '94 234, 283;
      '96 310; '98 336
   Dark Chocolate Sauce, Poached Pears with,
      '90 M141
   Double Chocolate Sauce, '83 79
   Easy Chocolate Sauce, '92 148
   Fudge Sauce, '91 174
   Heavenly Chocolate Sauce, '79 79; '82 167
   Honey-Chocolate Sauce, '89 251
   Hot Fudge Sauce, '82 181, 295; '84 143; '97 255

   Hot Fudge Sauce, Easy, '84 69; '94 194
   Hot Fudge Sauce, Heavenly, '00 256
   Hot Fudge Sauce, Pecan Pie with, '01 306
   Hot Fudge Sauce, Quick, '82 212
   Kahlúa Chocolate Sauce, '85 155
   Mint Sauce, Chocolate-, '93 86; '94 314; '98 217
   Mint Sauce, Quick Chocolate, '86 M58
   Mocha Sauce, '98 57
   Orange Sauce, Chocolate-, '86 165; '94 314
   Peanut Butter Sauce, Chocolate-, '79 91, M156
   Peppermint Sauce, Chocolate-, '94 205
   Praline Sauce, Chocolate-, '85 M295
   Semisweet Chocolate Sauce, '00 104
   Supreme, Chocolate Sauce, '85 189
   Toffee-Fudge Sauce, '89 95
   White Chocolate Sauce, '92 164; '96 310;
      '00 104
Scones, Mocha-Pecan, '97 45
Shavings, Chocolate Hearts and, '86 26
Shell, Chocolate-Coconut Pie, '82 210; '83 100
Shell, Chocolate Pastry, '87 262
Shell, Chocolate Tart, '99 315; '02 208
Shells with Kahlúa Cream, Chocolate, '88 195
S'mores, Grilled Pound Cake, '98 179
S'mores, Indoor, '01 33
Snacks, Chocolate-Peanut Butter, '90 226
Snowballs, Chocolate Mint, '04 M211
Sorbet, Chocolate, '97 111
Soufflé au Chocolat Cointreau, '94 56
Soufflé, Chocolate, '84 317; '94 46
Soufflé, Chocolate Mint, '81 16
Soufflé, Light Chocolate, '83 278
Soufflé with White Chocolate Mousse, Chocolate,
   '98 57
Soup, Mexican Chocolate, '96 277
Spoons, Dipped Chocolate-Almond, '95 M277
Spread, Chocolate Cheese, '87 292
Stars, White Chocolate, '00 M307
Sticks, Chocolate-Sesame, '91 316
Sticky Buns, Easy Caramel-Chocolate, '95 36
Strawberries, Chocolate-Dipped, '98 M100
Strawberries Dipped in White Chocolate, '90 83
Sundae Dessert, Hot Fudge, '84 313; '86 322
Sundaes, Chocolate Mint, '03 M120
Sundaes, Cocoa-Kahlúa, '83 M58
Sundaes, Cream Cheese Brownie, '03 223
Supreme, Chocolate, '84 94
Tacos, Dessert, '97 141
That's Incredible, '02 322
Torte, Frozen Viennese, '93 171
Trees, Holiday, '02 298
Trifle, Brownie, '03 85
Trifle, Chocolate, '88 258; '93 326
Trifle, Peanut Butter-Brownie, '03 200
Velvet, Chocolate Almond, '81 148
Waffles, Fudge, '94 205
Waffles with Strawberry Cream, Chocolate, '88 153
Whip, Chocolate, '89 326
White Chocolate Ribbons and Bow, '01 253
Yogurt, Mocha Sauce with Chocolate, '92 243
Zuppa Inglese, '99 M267
CHOP SUEY
Cabbage Chop Suey, '81 101
Chicken Chop Suey, '81 227
Salad, Chop Suey, '81 37
CHOWDERS. *See also* **GUMBOS, SOUPS.**
Artichoke-Shrimp Chowder, '03 91
Bell Pepper-Cheese Chowder, '95 240
Bluefish Chowder, '84 282
Broccoli Chowder, '79 16
Cabbage Chowder, Hearty, '80 25
Cheddar Cheese Chowder, '97 30
Cheddar Chowder, Hearty, '79 16
Cheese Chowder, Golden, '80 73

CHOWDERS
(continued)

Cheese Chowder, Hot, '89 16
Cheese-Vegetable Chowder, '02 305
Chicken-and-Corn Chowder, Curried, '92 21
Chicken-and-Roasted Vegetable Chowder, '97 21
Chicken Chowder, '83 20
Chicken Chowder, Cheesy, '92 21
Chicken Chowder Sauterne, '84 235
Chicken Corn Chowder, '02 305
Chicken-Corn Chowder, Mexican, '01 18
Chicken-Vegetable Chowder, '04 326
Chicken-Vegetable Chowder, Creamy, '92 20
Clam-and-Sausage Chowder, '94 104
Clam Chowder, '79 182; '81 32; '85 9; '86 36;
    '89 95; '90 202
Clam Chowder, New England, '86 M72; '98 289
Clam Chowder, Ocracoke, '79 31
Clam Chowder, Shopping Day, '02 305
Clam Chowder, Tomato-, '84 251
Corn and Bacon Chowder, Fresh, '93 203
Corn-and-Bacon Chowder, Southern, '96 166
Corn and Cheese Chowder, '80 228
Corn-and-Poblano Chowder, '03 193
Corn Chowder, '81 128; '83 20; '84 M38; '85 10;
    '90 202; '91 132; '97 241; '98 31
Corn Chowder, Delicious, '82 279
Fiesta Chowder, '02 305
Fish Chowder, '79 152; '84 M38
Fish Chowder, Basque, '86 36
Fish Chowder, Chunky, '92 331
Fish Chowder, Creamy, '79 16
Fish Chowder, Tasty, '80 188
Green Bean, Mushroom, and Ham Chowder,
    Creamy, '99 M336
Greens Chowder, Mixed, '97 262
Ham-and-Cheese Chowder, '89 15
Ham and Corn Chowder, '79 16
Ham-and-Corn Chowder, '82 40
Ham Chowder, Creamy, '88 M53
Ham 'n Cheese Chowder, '79 199
Harvest Chowder, '83 317
Mirliton-Corn Chowder, '00 246
Mushroom Chowder, '79 16
Mushroom-Potato Chowder, '92 331
Okra Chowder, Quick, '80 185
Oyster Chowder, '83 229
Oyster-Corn Chowder, '83 211
Potato Chowder with Green Chiles, '00 329
Potato Chowder with Ham, '99 141
Potato-Corn Chowder, '94 66
Potato-Vegetable Chowder, '98 335
Pumpkin-Corn Chowder, '97 219
Red Snapper Chowder, '85 217
Salmon Chowder, '97 125
Sausage-Bean Chowder, '83 20
Seafood Chowder, '85 9; '92 122
Seafood Chowder, Curried, '94 103
Seafood Chowder, So-Quick, '01 18
Seafood Chowder, Southern, '83 20
Shrimp and Corn Chowder, '79 199
Shrimp Chowder, '89 218
Shrimp Chowder, Quick, '04 27
Sweet Potato Chowder, Asian, '97 213
Swiss-Broccoli Chowder, '80 73
Turkey Chowder, '85 10; '91 312
Turkey-Corn Chowder, '81 98; '96 279
Vegetable Chowder, Cheesy, '80 25; '83 20; '00 272;
    '01 18
Vegetable Chowder, Easy, '97 304
Vegetable Chowder, Hearty, '88 56
Vegetable Chowder, Oven-Roasted, '95 229

White Bean Chowder with Sage Pesto, '97 22
Yukon Gold-Cheese Chowder, '03 296
CHOW MEIN
Beef-and-Vegetable Chow Mein Casserole, '83 313
Chicken Casserole, Chow Mein, '96 276
Chicken Chow Mein, '90 68
Noodles, Chow Mein over Crispy, '85 286
Pork Chow Mein, '80 208; '90 101
Shrimp Chow Mein, '82 30
CHRISTMAS
Beverages
Blossom, Christmas, '99 321
Milk, Santa Claus, '92 281
Punch, Christmas, '84 259; '89 330
Punch, Christmas Eve, '86 314
Punch, Cupid's Creamy Peppermint, '04 253
Punch, Merry Christmas, '79 285
Tea, Christmas Fruit, '83 275; '01 240
Wassail, Christmas, '93 295
Bread, Christmas, '87 296; '88 288
Bread, Norwegian Christmas, '79 234
Bread Stars, '93 286
Buns, Christmas Morning Sticky, '97 245
Cake, Christmas Coconut, '82 262
Cake Loaf, Noel Pound, '04 279
Cake, Rudolph's Chocolate Truffle, '04 M253
Cake, Twinkling Star, '00 306
Candy Canes and Wreaths, Braided, '92 276
Cheese Logs, Candy Cane-, '03 298
Chicken Presents, Holiday, '01 251
Chili, White Christmas, '98 266; '02 260
Chocolate Rudolph Reindeer, '04 M254
Cinnamon Ornaments, '85 284
Coeur à la Crème, Christmas, '86 278
Coffee Cakes, Christmas-Tree, '87 298
Cookies
Calendar, Cookie Advent, '85 325
Candy Canes and Wreaths, Braided,
    '92 276
Cards, Christmas Cookie, '84 302
Cherry Cookies, Christmas, '88 282
Date Cookies, Christmas, '88 287
Eggnog Christmas Cookies, '79 255
Elf Biscuits, '99 309
Elf Cookie, '80 279, 303
Fruit Squares, Christmas, '88 282
Gingerbread Bowl, Christmas, '93 266
Gingerbread Cookies, '80 278
Gingerbread Men, '99 294
Gingerbread Snowflake Cookies, '98 324
Gingerbread Votives, '98 309
Granny's Christmas Cookies, '02 278
Jammies, Christmas, '95 322
Lizzies, Christmas, '87 257
Moravian Christmas Cookies, '91 282
Mrs. Claus Cookie, '80 279, 303
Nutcracker Cookies, '97 286
Painted Cookies, '86 322
Pfeffernuesse, '01 65
Reindeer Cookies, Jolly, '91 273
Rudolph Cookie, '80 279, 303
Rudolph Cookies, '99 M309
Santa Claus Cookie, '80 278, 303
Santa Cookies, Easy, '95 321
Santa's Whiskers, '85 323
Sleigh Cookie, '80 279, 303
Spiced Christmas Cookies, '87 294
Spritz Cookies, Christmas, '96 314
Strawberries, Christmas, '87 293
Sugarplum Fairy Wands, '97 M286
Sugarplum Sticks, '95 321
Swedish Christmas Cookies, '79 290
Tea Cakes, Victorian Christmas, '02 253
Tree Cookies, Christmas, '93 286

Trees, Christmas, '89 294
Votives, Edible, '98 309
Wreaths, Christmas, '97 288
Corn, Christmas, '93 325
Cottage, Quick-Fix Christmas, '91 280
Cottage, Sugarplum, '88 309
Cranberry Hearts, '93 286
Crostini, Christmas, '94 318
Custard, Boiled Christmas, '95 329
Dessert, White Christmas, '82 261
Dip, Christmas Confetti, '92 279
Divinity, Christmas, '81 286
Doughnuts, Snowy, '93 286
Grittibanz (Swiss Bread Figure), '93 265
Hotcakes, Christmas Tree, '03 305
Icing, Royal, '98 324
Jam, Christmas, '88 288
Jam, Christmas Brunch, '81 286
Jelly, Christmas Freezer, '86 M288
Ketchup, Christmas, '97 254
Loaf, Sweet Christmas, '84 278
Muffins, Dasher's Dill Mini-, '04 252
Munchies, Reindeer, '91 276
Nuggets, Golden North Pole, '99 M309
Orange Baskets, '93 286
Ornaments, Edible, '94 316
Paints, Powdered Sugar, '97 286
Pandoro, '93 267
Panettone, '93 266
Peanut Butter Elf Bites, '91 275
Pecans, Christmas, '03 300
Pecans, Christmas Eve, '91 276
Pie, White Christmas, '88 281; '93 289
Pinecones, Peanut Butter-Suet, '93 286
Pinwheels, Santa's, '91 275
Potatoes, Christmas, '88 252
Potpourri, Christmas, '94 317
Pretzel Garlands, '93 286
Pudding with Brandy Sauce, Baked Christmas,
    '88 279
Reindeer Food, Magic, '99 M309
Reindeer Nibbles, '92 280
Relish Tree, Christmas, '84 257
Salad, Christmas, '88 249
Salad, Christmas Ribbon, '02 257
Salad, Christmas Snow, '82 266
Salad, Cranberry Christmas, '79 243
Salad, Eggnog Christmas, '86 281
Salmon with Caribbean Fruit Salsa, Blitzen's Baked,
    '04 252
Sandwiches, Christmas Tree, '92 279
Sandwich Wreath, Festive, '86 333
Santa's Hat, '92 279
Santa's Whiskers, '85 323
Scent, Christmas, '84 325
Snowman, Marshmallow, '96 311
Spices, Barclay House Mulling, '86 289
Strata, Christmas Morning, '95 282
Strawberries, Christmas, '87 293; '94 331
Sugarplum Fairy Wands, '97 M286
Sugar Plums, '92 281
Tannenbaum Temptations, '92 14
Wine, Christmas Dreams in, '91 260
Wreath, Christmas, '80 280
Wreath, Della Robbia Fruit, '87 294
Wreaths, Braided Candy Canes and, '92 276
CHUTNEYS. *See also* **PESTOS, RELISHES,
    SALSAS, SAUCES, TOPPINGS.**
Apple Chutney, '92 309
Apple Chutney, Sweet-'n'-Hot, '96 14
Blueberry Chutney, '95 190; '00 154
Cantaloupe Chutney, '00 108
Cantaloupe Chutney, Fresh, '97 148
Cherry-Peach Chutney, Glazed Ham with, '97 315

Commander's Chutney, '87 245
Cranberry-Amaretto Chutney with Cream Cheese,
    '87 244
Cranberry-and-Apricot Chutney, '02 286
Cranberry Chutney, '80 243; '83 260; '84 265;
    '96 275; '98 276, 318
Cranberry Chutney, Texas, '04 257
Cranberry-Ginger Chutney, '00 253
Cranberry-Orange Chutney, '79 292
Cranberry-Pear Chutney, Hot-and-Spicy, '00 255
Dressing, Chutney, '00 53
Dressing, Warm Chutney, '02 242
Fruit Chutney, Autumn, '88 M230
Fruit Chutney, Fall, '97 218
Green Tomato-Cranberry Chutney, '00 140
Kiwifruit-Onion Chutney, '93 125
Mango Chutney, '89 141; '96 182; '03 123
Mango Chutney, Blue-Ribbon, '96 206
Orange-Cranberry Chutney, '86 266
Peach Chutney, '84 179; '96 207
Pear-Apple Chutney, '89 141
Pear Chutney, '95 251; '98 243
Pear Chutney, Sunny, '01 281
Pepper Chutney, Jeweled, '94 316
Plum Chutney, '84 179
Rhubarb Chutney, '87 245
Roll, Chutney, '83 259
Rosy Chutney, '80 120
Sauce, Chutney-Mustard, '89 242
Sweet Potato Chutney, '99 45
Tomato-Apple Chutney, '84 180
Tomato Chutney, '99 143

CLAMS

Backyard Clambake, '81 92
Bisque, Clam, '86 228
Casino, Clams, '81 125
Casino, Maryland Clams, '89 196
Chase, Clams, '79 85
Chowder, Clam, '79 182; '81 32; '85 9; '86 36;
    '89 95; '90 202
Chowder, Clam-and-Sausage, '94 104
Chowder, New England Clam, '86 M72;
    '98 289
Chowder, Ocracoke Clam, '79 31
Chowder, Shopping Day Clam, '02 305
Chowder, Tomato-Clam, '84 251
Cocktail, Tomato-Clam, '87 252
Crisps, Clam, '80 151
Dip, Clam, '79 151; '80 265; '01 194
Dip, Hot Clam, '82 59; '89 48
Dip, Zesty Clam, '92 25
Fritters, Clam, '79 151; '86 71
Linguine, Clam, '95 212
Linguine, Quick Clam, '90 233
Littleneck Clams with Cilantro-Black Walnut Pesto,
    '97 164
Oreganata, Clams, '85 104
Pizza, Baby Clam, '87 182
Puffs, Clam, '90 60
Quiche, Clam, '83 215
Sauce, Linguine in Clam, '81 83
Sauce, Linguine with Clam, '84 124; '88 90;
    '89 178
Sauce, Pasta with Clam, '84 291
Sauce, Pasta with Pesto-Clam, '98 17
Sauce, Tricolor Pasta with Clam, '93 272
Sauce, Vermicelli and Sprouts with Red Clam,
    '86 143
Sauce, Vermicelli with Clam, '85 295
Sauce with Linguine, Clam, '84 9
Shells, Baked Clam, '87 94
Soup, Clam Florentine, '85 23
Spread, Creamy Clam, '91 274
Steamed Clams Chesapeake, '89 196

COBBLERS. *See* **PIES, PUFFS, AND
    PASTRIES/Cobblers, Crisps, and
    Crumbles.**

COCONUT

Ambrosia Sorbet, '04 317
Apples, Calypso Caramel, '03 M216
Balls, Coconut-Almond, '84 256
Balls, Orange-Nut, '02 297
Bars and Cookies
    Brownies, Chocolate-Coconut, '97 35
    Brownies, Coconut-Pecan-Frosted, '97 99
    Cherry Cookies, Coconut-, '79 292
    Chocolate Macaroon Cookies, '88 217
    Clear-the-Cupboard Cookies, '99 278; '02 176
    Crinkle Sunflower Cookies, '83 149
    Crisp Coconut Cookies, '89 162
    English Cherubs, '83 257
    Golden Bars, '84 255
    Graham Cracker Layered Cookies, '98 94
    Graham Cracker Layered Cookies, Chocolate,
        '98 94
    Granola Bars, Coconut, '85 202
    Hawaiian Bars, '84 153
    Kisses, Coconut, '90 106
    Lace Cookies, Crunchy, '01 294
    Lemon-Coconut Cookies, '02 293
    Macadamia Cookies, Coconut-, '98 294
    Macaroon Cookies, '03 282
    Macaroons, Chewy Peanut Butter, '95 214
    Macaroons, Chocolate, '83 300
    Macaroons, Coconut, '79 52
    Macaroons, Soft Coconut, '02 229; '03 131
    Macaroons, White Chocolate Tropical, '00 M166
    Magic Cookie Bars, '02 253
    Mix, Blond Brownie, '01 247
    Neapolitan Cookies, '00 290
    No-Bake Bars, Creamy, '97 166
    Oatmeal-Coconut Cookies, '80 218
    Oatmeal-Coconut Crispies, '01 19
    Oatmeal Cookies, Crispy Coconut-, '93 80
    Peanut Butter-Coconut Cookies, '83 113
    Robin's Nests, Coconut, '98 M111
    Shortbread, Coconut, '02 224
    Shortbread Cookies, Coconut, '93 316
    Squares, Chocolate-Coconut, '90 70
    Swirls, Coconut, '97 274
    Toasted Coconut Cookies, '02 245
Biscuits, Yummy Coconut, '95 99
Bonbons, Coconut-Black Walnut, '82 307
Bread, Coconut, '83 140
Bread, Pumpkin-Coconut, '87 255
Broth with Noodles, Thai Coconut, '98 295
Cakes
    Angel Cake, Spiked Coconut, '85 279
    Anniversary Cake, '00 117
    Apple Coconut Cake, '80 226
    Banana-Coconut Cake, '93 154
    Banana Split Cake, '99 48
    Black Forest Crisp, '02 128
    Brown Sugar Snack Cake, '98 195
    Carrot Cake, Fresh Coconut-, '80 299
    Carrot Cake, Shortcut, '02 83
    Cheesecake, Ambrosia, '02 296
    Cheesecake, Coconut-Chocolate-Almond,
        '98 322
    Cheesecake, Festive Piña Colada, '01 286
    Cheesecake, Tropical Tofu, '00 204
    Chocolate-Coconut Cake, '83 23
    Christmas Coconut Cake, '82 262
    Coconut Cake, '92 120; '03 278
    Coffee Cake, Cranberry-Coconut, '93 332
    Coffee Cake, Oatmeal-Coconut, '83 312
    Coffee Cake, Pineapple-Coconut, '94 49; '03 198
    Cream Cake, Coconut, '81 179; '91 269

Creamy Coconut Cake, '84 43
    Four-Layer Coconut Cake, '00 117
    Fresh Coconut Cake, '80 289; '82 52; '85 281
    Fudge Cake, Coconut-, '99 206
    Hibiscus-Nectar Cake, '96 248
    Holiday Coconut Cake, '90 308
    Italian Cake, Chocolate, '02 256
    Italian Cream Cake, '96 262
    Italian Cream Cake, Fresh Orange, '02 294
    Italian Cream Cake, Quick, '99 307
    Layer Cake, Stately Coconut, '81 70
    Lemon Cake, Coconut-, '95 319
    Lemon-Coconut Cream Cake, '81 179
    Lemon-Coconut Sheet Cake, '85 117
    MaMa's Coconut Cake, '97 71
    Orange-Coconut Angel Food Cake, '94 294
    Party Cake, Gathering of Stars, '00 307
    Piña Colada Cake, '99 117
    Pineapple Cake, Coconut-, '89 56
    Pineapple Cake, Nanny's Famous Coconut-,
        '97 277
    Pineapple-Coconut Cake, '00 86
    Pineapple Layer Cake, Coconut-, '80 140
    Pound Cake, Coconut, '82 87; '91 224
    Pound Cake, Coconut Cream, '84 10
    Pound Cake, Coconut-Cream Cheese, '85 297;
        '90 305
    Pound Cake, Cream Cheese-Coconut-Pecan,
        '04 280
    Regal Coconut Cake, '83 299
    Roll, Coconut-Pineapple Cake, '84 304
    Rum-Orange Coconut Cake, '88 224
    Sheet Cake, Coconut, '04 136
    Spice Cake, Coconut-, '84 255; '87 296
    Star Cake, Twinkling, '00 306
    Toasted Coconut Cake, '86 60
    Unforgettable Coconut Cake, '90 104; '01 330
    White Chocolate-Coconut Cake, '87 263
Calypso, Coco-Berry, '89 171
Candy, Coconut, '79 272; '80 250
Caramels, Coconut-Macadamia, '98 305
Chicken Balls, Coconut Curried, '91 165
Chicken, Coconut, '98 20
Chicken with Fresh Fruit, Coconut, '93 294
Cloud, Coconut, '80 70
Clusters, Pecan-Coconut, '86 M251
Coffee, Coconut, '97 17
Cookies. *See* **COCONUT/Bars and Cookies.**
Cream, Coconut, '00 27
Cream, Orange-Coconut, '84 24
Cream, Red Curry-Coconut, '00 197
Crème Brûlée, Piña Colada, '04 246
Crisp, Tropical Pineapple, '02 232
Crust, Chocolate-Coconut, '87 261
Crust, Coconut, '89 160
Custard, Coco Loco, '02 89
Custard, Coconut, '86 109; '97 131
Custard, Coconut Cream, '03 85
Dessert, Chilled Coconut, '83 116
Dessert, Coconut-Caramel, '92 44
Dessert in a Nutshell, '96 318
Dessert, Macaroon-Sherbet Frozen, '79 212
Dip, Coconut-Honey Fruit, '84 171
Dressing, Coconut, '87 251
Dressing, Coconut-Orange, '97 93
Dressing, Orange-Coconut, '80 158
Dressing, Tangy Coconut-Fruit, '84 171
Drink, Coconut-Pineapple, '83 172
Drops, Chocolate-Coconut Almond, '87 223
Filling, Coconut, '81 265; '00 117; '03 329
Filling, Coconut Cream, '84 200
Filling, Piña Colada, '99 117
Filling, Sour Cream-Coconut, '92 120
Frosting, Coconut, '82 262; '91 269

COCONUT
(continued)

Frosting, Coconut Chocolate, '79 13
Frosting, Coconut Cream Cheese, '86 60
Frosting, Coconut-Cream Cheese, '04 137
Frosting, Coconut Milk, '00 117
Frosting, Coconut-Pecan, '81 296; '83 M233; '84 43, 322; '97 99; '03 289
Frosting, Creamy Coconut, '80 287
Frosting, Lemon-Coconut, '90 253
Frosting, Nutty Coconut, '86 8
Frost, Pink Coconut, '79 174; '80 128
Fruit Bowl, Coconut, '83 111
Granola, '99 212
Granola, Pecan-Coconut, '02 70
Ice Cream, Banana-Coconut, '02 164
Ice Cream, Coconut, '98 180
Ice Cream, Coconut Fried, '85 141
Ice Cream, Fresh Coconut, '79 166
Ice Cream, No-Cook Coconut, '04 179
Ice Cream, Simple Coconut, '02 232
Ice Cream, Toasted Coconut, '00 143
Ice Cream with Sweet Heat Salsa and Cinnamon Crisps, South Seas, '04 315
Icing, Chunky Cherry, '03 94
Joys, Chocolate-Covered Coconut, '98 M282
Joys, Coconut, '98 282
Macaroon Charlotte, '81 296
Macaroon-Stuffed Peaches, '79 178
Milk, Chicken in Coconut, '97 202
Mousse, Coconut-Pineapple, '94 198
Muffins, Coconut, '95 214
Muffins, Coconut-Molasses, '82 210
Nests, Strawberry Coconut, '88 136
Nog, Coconut, '83 275
Pears, Spicy Coconut, '83 207
Pecan Coils, Coconut-, '90 196
Pies
  Blender Coconut Pie, '84 236
  Butter Coconut Pie, '01 244
  Buttermilk-Coconut Pie, '94 246
  Buttermilk Pie, Rancher's, '04 208
  Caramel Pies, Coconut-, '87 260
  Cherry Pie, Coconut Crumb, '92 30
  Chess Pie, Coconut, '86 220; '00 60; '02 107
  Coconut Pie, '93 115
  Cream Pie, Coconut, '80 238; '81 136; '82 85; '84 49; '87 207; '89 236; '90 312; '98 161; '02 92; '03 106
  Cream Pie, Fresh Coconut, '80 289
  Cream Pie, Surprise Coconut, '92 43
  Creamy Coco-Nana Pie, '00 95
  Crunch Pie, Coconut, '90 105
  Custard Pie, Coconut, '82 33
  French Coconut Pie, '90 162
  Macadamia Nut Pie, Coconut-, '97 110
  Macaroon Pie, Coconut, '88 204
  Magic Coconut Pie, '79 53
  Mock Coconut Pie, '86 200
  Orange Chess Pie, Coconut-, '89 169
  Orange-Coconut Cream Pie, '94 208
  Orange-Coconut Pie, '90 90
  Pecan Chess Pie, Coconut-, '81 248
  Pecan Pie, Coconut, '81 161
  Pineapple-Coconut Chess Pie, '92 214
  Pineapple Pie, Coconut-, '84 256
  Quick Coconut Pie, '83 115
  Shell, Chocolate-Coconut Pie, '82 210; '83 100
  Toasted Coconut Pie, '90 105
Pirate's Painkiller, '99 161
Pudding, Piña Colada Bread, '98 34
Puffs, Coconut, '87 277

Relish, Pineapple-Coconut, '96 323; '97 27
Rice, Coconut, '00 201
Rice, Polynesian Pork Tenderloin with Orange-Curry Sauce and Coconut, '04 309
Salad, Cantaloupe Colada, '97 148
Salad, Chunky Fruit-and-Coconut, '84 24
Salad, Curried Poached Pears with Coconut-Chicken, '97 93
Salsa, Tropical, '01 60
Sauce, Coconut, '98 34
Sauce, Coconut-Orange, '85 189
Sauce, Creamy Light Coconut, '82 177
Shrimp, Coconut, '00 175
Shrimp, Coconut-Beer, '85 230; '89 23
Shrimp, Coconut Fried, '96 248
Shrimp Martinis with Napa Cabbage Slaw, '02 280
Shrimp with Mustard Sauce, Coconut, '02 245
Shrimp with Orange Dipping Sauce, Coconut-Pecan, '03 212
Sipper, Creamy Coconut, '02 298
Soufflé, Coconut, '79 73; '85 212
Spread, Coconut-Cranberry Cheese, '92 328
Spread, Coconut-Pineapple, '93 309
Stir-Fry, Coconut-Beef, '97 18
Sundae, Tropical, '04 179
Sweet Potatoes, Coconut-Broiled, '84 231
Sweet Potatoes, Coconut-Orange, '84 252
Sweet Potatoes, Coconut-Stuffed, '82 204
Tartlets, Zamaani's Nutty Yam, '02 21
Tarts, Coconut-Pecan Cookie, '04 305
Tarts with Macadamia Nut Crusts, Coconut Cream, '97 62
Toffee, Hawaiian, '04 235
Topping, Coconut-Pecan, '04 41
Torte, Blitz, '01 65
Trifle, Tropical Rum, '03 85
Tropical Snow, '86 34

COFFEE
Beverages
  After-Dinner Coffee, '81 262
  After-Dinner Coffee, Spiced, '02 270
  Almond-Coffee Delight, '84 115
  Blends, Coffee, '95 276
  Bourbon-Barrel Coffee, '03 233
  Brandied Coffee, '81 244
  Brandy Coffee, '97 17
  Cappuccino, Café, '82 253
  Cappuccino, Chocolate Castle, '84 53
  Cappuccino Coffee Dessert, '92 264
  Cappuccino Cooler, Low-Fat, '01 166
  Cappuccino, Flaming, '79 293
  Cappuccino, Iced, '99 333
  Cappuccino Sipper, '99 29
  Chiller, Royal Cup, '98 218
  Chocolate-Almond Coffee, '84 54
  Chocolate Coffee, '82 43; '97 17
  Cocoa-Coffee, '83 55
  Coconut Coffee, '97 17
  Colombian Royal, Café, '80 M290
  Colonial Coffee, '89 290
  Concentrate, Coffee, '04 68
  "Concrete," Abaco Mocha, '94 114
  Cream, Café, '82 312
  Cream, Icy Rum Coffee, '83 172
  Creamy Coffee, '81 244
  Dessert Drink, Simply Super, '83 303
  Dessert, Light Coffee, '88 260
  Diablo, Café, '80 259
  Espresso, Amaretto, '92 263
  Fireside Coffee, '03 M298
  Floats, Maple-Coffee, '86 195
  Freeze, Amaretto-Coffee, '99 161
  Frosted Coffee, '81 244
  Frozen Coffee Cooler, '02 163

German Chocolate Café au Lait, '92 264
Hazelnut-Coffee Ice, '94 233
Holiday Coffee, '90 273
Hot Buttered Bourbon, '97 17
Iced Coffee, '04 68
Iced Coffee, Chocolate, '01 166
Irish Coffee, Creamy, '79 232
Irish Coffee, Flaming, '79 293
Irish Coffee Nog, '84 258; '93 340
Irish Cream Nog, '82 312
Kahlúa Beverage Sipper, '99 27
Kahlúa Delight, Make-Ahead, '84 M89
Kona Luscious, '84 54
Liqueur, Coffee-Flavored, '86 266
Maple Coffee, '97 17; '01 130
Mexican Coffee, '83 175, 275; '88 247; '91 78; '93 310; '94 97
Mexicano, Café, '92 208
Mix, Cappucino, '90 87
Mix, Fireside Coffee, '87 241
Mix, Hot Mocha-Cocoa, '82 296
Mix, Mocha-Flavored Hot Cocoa, '91 316
Mix, Spiced Mocha, '01 64
Mocha Blend, '95 276
Mocha Cappuccino, '02 M220
Mocha Chocolate Fluff, '89 170
Mocha Cocoa, '83 318
Mocha Coffee, '85 M329
Mocha Cream, Café, '84 54
Mocha Deluxe Hot Drink, '82 289
Mocha Espresso, Italian, '82 254
Mocha Frosty, '92 44
Mocha, Hot, '84 60
Mocha Latte Beverage, '03 46
Mocha Latte, Café, '01 64
Mocha Latte, Spiced, '04 333
Mocha Melt, Spiced, '01 240
Mocha, Mexican, '93 M341
Mocha Milkshake, '89 35
Mocha-Mint Shake, '02 297
Mocha Polka, '89 171
Mocha, Quick Viennese, '79 232
Mocha, Spirited Hot, '91 M260
Mocha, Swiss-Style, '82 253
Mocha Warmer, '97 272
Nog, Brandied Coffee, '86 329
Orange Blend, '95 276
Orange Coffee, '96 313
Orange Coffee, Viennese, '84 54
Pontalba, Café, '92 83
Praline Coffee, '97 17; '01 291
Praline-Flavored Coffee, '87 69
Punch, Chilly Coffee, '01 64
Punch, Coffee, '80 50; '83 275; '88 83
Punch, Coffee-and-Cream, '85 116
Punch, Coffee-Eggnog, '86 281
Punch, Coffee Eggnog, '92 264
Punch, Creamy Coffee, '81 50
Punch, Eggnog-Coffee, '02 297
Punch, "Eye-Opener" Coffee, '92 80
Punch, Irish Coffee-Eggnog, '95 314
Punch, Mocha, '84 58, 166; '86 270; '95 141
Punch, Rich-and-Creamy Coffee, '82 121
Punch, Vanilla-Nut Coffee, '03 282
Refresher, Velvet Coffee, '79 149
Royal, Café, '80 259
Shake, Peach-Coffee Milk, '84 284
Slush, Café Latte, '01 64
Soda, Coffee, '97 272
Spiced Brew, Hot, '91 36
Spiced Coffee, Special, '84 284
Spiced-Up Coffee, '89 92
Turkish-Style Coffee, '02 257
Vienna Blend, '95 276

Viennese, Café, '82 254
White Chocolate Latte, '04 210
Buttercream, Coffee, '95 277
Buttons, Coffee, '99 66
Cake, Cappuccino Mousse, '99 154
Cake, Coffee Sponge, '83 229; '91 55
Cake, Extra-Rich Chocolate, '99 271
Cake, Two-Day Coffee Sponge, '86 75
Chill, Coffee-and-Cream, '99 126
Cones, Chocolate-Coffee, '96 M316
Cookies, Chocolate Cappuccino, '01 315
Cookies, Java Shortbread, '94 233
Cream, Coffee, '00 27
Cream Puffs, Java, '81 187
Crème Brûlée, Coffee, '95 323
Crêpes, Coffee Ice Cream, '84 85
Dessert, Chocolate-Coffee Frozen, '85 172
Dip, Kahlúa, '99 139
Fajitas, Java, '96 227
Filling, Chocolate-Coffee Buttercream, '00 M287
Filling, Chocolate Midnight, '96 120
Filling, Coffee, '96 316
Frosting, Chocolate-Coffee, '84 36; '88 269
Frosting, Coffee, '94 86
Frosting, Coffee Buttercream, '99 155
Fudge, Coffee-Chip, '86 74
Fudge, White Chocolate-Coffee, '94 232
Granita, Coffee-Kahlúa, '88 118
Ice Cream, Coffee, '88 202
Ice Cream Crunch, Coffee, '82 182
Kisses, Chocolate-Dipped Coffee, '96 313
Mallow, Coffee, '80 109
Meringues with Butterscotch Mousse, Coffee,
  '93 254
Mocha. *See also* **COFFEE/Beverages.**
  Angel Squares, Mocha, '98 61
  Blend, Mocha, '95 276
  Brownies, Mocha, '87 93
  Buttercream, Mocha, '89 42
  Cake, Belgian Mocha, '84 316
  Cake, Dark Mocha-Chocolate, '84 311
  Cake, Delta Mocha Chiffon, '00 286
  Cake, Double Mocha, '84 311
  Cake, Mocha, '02 87
  Cake, Mocha Marble Pound, '99 23
  Charlottes, Mocha, '02 171
  Cheesecake, Mocha, '98 278
  Cheesecake, Mocha-Chocolate, '88 258
  Cheesecake, Mocha Swirl, '87 262
  Chiffon, Mocha, '86 75
  "Concrete," Abaco Mocha, '94 114
  Cupcakes, Mocha, '85 250
  Dessert, Frozen Mocha, '84 311
  Dessert, Mocha Alaska, '84 191
  Dessert, Mocha-Almond, '80 289; '81 62
  Éclairs, Mocha, '01 45
  Filling, Mocha, '80 55; '82 262
  Filling, Mocha Cream, '81 187; '84 305
  Freeze, Royal Mocha, '84 53
  Frosting, Creamy Mocha, '82 289; '84 311;
    '91 248
  Frosting, Mocha, '83 301; '84 316; '87 224;
    '94 292; '97 35; '99 66
  Frosting, Mocha Butter Cream, '79 281
  Frosting, Mocha-Buttercream, '86 26
  Frozen Mocha Delight, '96 179
  Frozen Mocha Squares, '81 187
  Fudge, Creamy Mocha, '95 51
  Ganache, Mocha, '04 M260
  Gingerbread, Mocha, '81 207; '82 14
  Ice Cream, Mocha, '88 202; '97 M145
  Mix, Mexican Mocha Spice, '00 334
  Parfaits, Mocha-Mallow, '80 219
  Pie, Chocolate-Mocha Crunch, '81 136

Pie, Mocha, '94 168
Pie, Mocha Meringue, '80 242; '88 163
Pie, Mocha Pecan Mud, '00 245
Pots de Crème, Mocha, '88 M45
Pralines, Mocha, '92 313; '93 51
Pudding, Mocha-Chocolate Cookie, '03 183
Pudding, Pecan-Mocha, '89 M130
Roll, Chocolate Mocha Cream, '84 304
Roulage, Chocolate-Mocha, '80 216
Sauce, Mocha, '98 57
Sauce with Chocolate Yogurt Mocha, '92 243
Scones, Mocha-Pecan, '97 45
Shortbread, Mocha-Chocolate, '04 173
Shortbread Squares, Mocha-Chocolate, '02 176
Syrup, Mocha Latte, '03 46
Tart, Black Bottom Mocha-Cream, '92 304
Torte, Mocha, '99 66
Torte, Mocha Brownie, '85 102
Torte, Mocha Mousse, '04 260
Torte, Mocha Velvet, '92 318
Mousse, Coffee, '84 126
Mousse, Coffee-Nut, '86 319
Mousse Present, Chocolate, '99 281
Mousse, Quick-as-a-Wink, '84 311
Napoleons, Coffee, '95 276
Nuggets, Coffee, '95 278
Parfaits, Coffee Crunch, '82 159
Pastry Cream, Coffee, '01 45
Pecans, Coffee 'n' Spice, '88 256
Penuche, Coffee, '98 305
Pie, Coffee, '96 148
Pie, Coffee Cream, '94 209
Pie, Coffee Ice Cream, '79 231
Pie, Coffee Pecan, '82 74
Pie, Decadent Mud, '89 252
Pie, Tipsy Mud, '97 251
Pie, Tiramisù Toffee Trifle, '00 312; '04 195
Pralines, Café au Lait, '92 313; '93 51
Pralines, Plantation Coffee, '86 241
Pudding, French Vanilla Latte, '03 M282
Slush, Caffè Latte, '02 209
Steaks, Coffee-Rubbed Strip, '03 282
Syrup, Coffee, '01 64
Tart, Coffee, '99 67
Tiramisù, '98 280; '00 288; '02 285
Tiramisù, Easy, '00 167
Tiramisù Éclairs, Mini, '03 M41
Torte, Toffee-Coffee Ice-Cream, '04 234
Tortoni, Coffee-Almond, '81 30
Tortoni, Creamy Coffee, '88 268
Wafers, Kahlúa, '99 147
COFFEE CAKES. *See* **CAKES/Coffee Cakes.**
COLESLAW. *See* **SLAWS.**
COLLARD GREENS. *See* **GREENS.**
COOKIES. *See also* **BROWNIES.**
  Almond-Anise Biscotti, '93 266
  Almond Biscotti, '91 108
  Almond Brittle Cookies with Ice Cream Balls,
    '96 202
  Almond Butter Cookies, '79 52
  Almond Chip Balls, Toasted, '84 240
  Almond Cookies, '83 22, 181; '91 51; '92 176
  Almond Cookies, Chewy, '02 258
  Almond Cookies, Light, '83 151
  Almond Cookies, Skillet, '97 288
  Almond Cookies, Swedish, '85 312
  Almond Snaps, '92 273
  Almond Spritz Cookies, '82 306
  Apple-Filled Cookies, '92 311
  Apricot Cookies, '95 322
  Bars and Squares
    Almond Bars, Swedish, '97 322
    Almond Brickle Treats, '95 321
    Almond Cake Squares, '79 111

Almond-Chocolate Bars, '83 304
Almond Cream Confections, '87 198; '90 310
Apple Butter Bars, '84 153
Apple Kuchen, '79 24
Apple-Oat Snack Squares, '00 332
Apricot-Almond Squares, '95 272
Apricot Bars, '81 247
Apricot Bars, Layered, '01 161
Apricot-Oatmeal Bars, '86 216
Apricot-Raisin Bars, '87 32
Banana Breakfast Bars, '79 124
Blackberry Bars, '87 130
Blackberry-Filled Bars, '79 124
Blackberry Jam Bars, '82 M185
Blondie Swirls, '85 248
Blond Nut Squares, '82 156
Brazil Squares, '82 306
Butter Pecan Pie Squares, '81 262
Butter Pecan Turtle Bars, '90 70
Butterscotch Bars, '82 209; '83 297
By-Cracky Bars, '84 212
Caramel-Pecan Triangles, '99 281
Carrot-Lemon Squares, Golden, '80 40
Carrot Squares, '79 256
Cherry Bars, Delightful, '86 217
Cherry Squares, '97 273
Cherry Squares, Surprise, '82 57
Choco-Crumble Bars, '79 292
Chocolate-Butterscotch Bars, '81 197
Chocolate-Caramel Layer Squares, '79 83
Chocolate Cereal Bars, Chewy, '97 317
Chocolate Chess Squares, '92 45
Chocolate Chip Bars, '81 130
Chocolate Chip-Peanut Butter Squares, '84 118
Chocolate Chip Squares, '83 170; '89 143
Chocolate Chip Squares, Chewy, '91 175
Chocolate Cinnamon Bars, '82 209
Chocolate-Coconut Squares, '90 70
Chocolate-Crème de Menthe Bars, '86 245
Chocolate Crème de Menthe Bites, '88 285
Chocolate Dream Bars, '79 256; '82 298
Chocolate-Peanut Bars, '03 195
Chocolate-Peanut Crispies, '93 80
Chocolate-Peppermint Squares, '81 119
Cinnamon Chews, '84 110
Cinnamon Sand Bars, '91 178
Coconut Granola Bars, '85 202
Coffee Bars, Frosted, '79 256
Congo Squares, '96 94
Cranberry-Caramel Bars, '98 277
Cranberry-Cinnamon Granola Bars, '03 26
Crème de Menthe Squares, '93 256
Date Bars, '84 313; '95 322
Date Bars, No-Bake, '79 256
Date Bars, Nutty, '84 153
Date Bars, Walnut-, '03 272
Date-Nut Bars, '80 166
Date-Oat Bars, '80 M172
English Cherubs, '83 257
Fudge Bars, '86 93
Fudge Bars, Yummy, '87 158
German Chocolate Chess Squares, '94 51
Golden Bars, '84 255
Graham Cracker Layered Cookies, '98 94
Graham Cracker Layered Cookies, Chocolate,
  '98 94
Granola Bars, '83 305; '95 214
Granola Bars, Fruit and Nut, '81 49
Granola Bars, No-Bake, '97 220
Hawaiian Bars, '84 153
Honey Cake Squares, '89 250
Jam-It Bars, '87 159
Jam Squares, '81 M289
Janhagel Cookies, '86 195

COOKIES, Bars and Squares
(continued)

Key Lime Bars with Macadamia Crust, **'99** 282
Layer Squares, Novelty, **'90** 70
Lemon Bars Deluxe, **'79** 35
Lemon Bars, Luscious, **'01** 161
Lemon Bars, Tangy, **'86** 217
Lemon-Pecan Squares, **'89** 124
Lemon Squares, **'81** 197; **'97** 329
Lemon Yogurt Wheat Bars, **'79** 93
Lime Squares, **'79** 2
Magic Cookie Bars, **'02** 253
Marmalade Biscuit Squares, **'79** 193
Meringue-Chocolate Chip Bars, **'84** 118
Mincemeat-Spice Bars, **'88** 231; **'89** 22
Mystery Bars, **'93** 239
Nutmeg Logs, Frosted, **'85** 324
Nutty Choco Snacks, **'83** 305
Oatmeal Bars, Chocolate-Topped, **'86** 110
Oatmeal-Caramel Bars, **'85** 247
Oatmeal-Date Bars, Layered, **'85** 10
Peanut Bars, **'89** 307
Peanut Bars, Chewy, **'80** M172
Peanut Butter-and-Fudge Bars, **'80** M172
Peanut Butter Bars, **'84** 243; **'93** 166
Peanut Butter-Chocolate Treats, Crispy, **'02** 287;
    '03 271
Peanut Butter Fingers, **'79** 256
Peanut Butter Frosts, **'84** 153
Peanut Butter-Jam Bars, **'94** 291
Peanut Butter Logs, No-Bake, **'84** 211
Peanut Butter 'n' Jelly Bars, **'83** 305
Peanut Butter Squares, **'83** 116
Peanut Squares, Crispy, **'01** M161
Pecan Bars, **'82** 209
Pecan Bars, Gooey, **'94** 133
Pecan Squares, **'79** 205; **'90** 69; **'98** 336; **'04** 271
Pecan Squares, Easy, **'81** 230
Pecan Squares, Twice-Baked, **'79** 291
Pecan Sticks, **'01** 242
Praline-Chocolate Fudge Bars, Chewy, **'04** M330
Pumpkin Bars, **'80** 40
Pumpkin Nut Bars, **'82** 217
Raisin Bars, **'94** 228
Raspberry Bars, **'82** 209; **'84** 212
Rhubarb Squares, **'91** 146
Rhubarb Squares, Rosy, **'79** 111
Scotch Bars, Chewy, **'98** M291
Shortbread, **'85** 266
Shortbread, Butter-Mint, **'99** 28
Shortbread, Orange, **'91** 272
Shortbread Squares, Mocha-Chocolate, **'02** 176
Snack Bars, Chocolate, **'04** 124
Strawberry Bars, **'81** 301
Sushi Bars, **'00** 50
Sushi Bars, Confetti, **'00** 50
Toffee Treats, **'89** 330
Tropical Bars, **'80** 284
Turtle Bars, **'00** 334
Turtle Bars, Gooey, **'96** 189
Walnut-Date Bars, **'02** 287
Wheat Germ Squares, Spicy, **'80** 44
Yummy Bars, **'92** 171
Zucchini Bars, **'85** 77
Benne Seed Wafers, **'96** 315
Bird's Nest Cookies, **'93** 284
Biscochos, Betty's, **'00** 325
Biscotti, Anise, **'96** 282
Biscotti, Chocolate Chip-Cinnamon, **'96** 281
Biscotti Cioccolata, **'93** 268
Biscotti, Cocoa-Almond, **'96** 280
Biscotti, Fruitcake, **'96** 281

Biscotti, Orange-Pecan, **'01** 207
Black-Eyed Susans, **'00** 291
Bonbon Cookies, Surprise, **'88** 119
Bourbon Balls, **'81** 254
Bourbon Balls, Chocolate, **'84** 298
Bourbon Dunkers, Crunchy, **'85** 90
Brutti Ma Buoni (Ugly but Good), **'93** 267
Butter Cookies, **'85** 322
Butter Cookies, Chocolate-Tipped, **'84** 258; **'90** 312
Butter Cookies, Holiday, **'92** 317
Butter Cookies, Lemon, **'01** 90
Butter Cookies, Lemon-Basil, **'01** 117
Butter Cookies, Melt-Away, **'81** 20
Butter-Nut Strips, **'82** 167
Butter Pecan Cookies, **'82** 139
Cake Mix Cookies, **'97** 133
Candy Wrap Cookies, **'04** 139
Cats' Tongues, **'96** 145
Cheesecake Cookies, Chewy, **'82** 109
Cherry Bonbon Cookies, **'93** 52
Cherry Crowns, **'92** 275
Cherry Nut Nuggets, **'81** 286
Chocolate-Almond Cookies, **'98** 293
Chocolate-Cherry Cookies, Frosted, **'89** 294
Chocolate Chewies, Easy, **'93** 296; **'94** 234
Chocolate Chip Cookies, **'84** 120; **'86** 245; **'90** 193;
    '00 276
Chocolate Chip Cookies, Giant, **'84** 119
Chocolate Chip Melt-Aways, **'84** 118
Chocolate-Chip Supreme Cookies, **'01** 218
Chocolate Chunk-Peanut Cookies, **'04** 125
Chocolate Chunk-Peanut Cookies, Double, **'04** 125
Chocolate Cookies, Caramel-Filled, **'92** 319; **'02** 53
Chocolate Cookies, Chewy, **'97** 166
Chocolate Cookies, Sugar-Coated, **'92** 274
Chocolate-Covered Cherry Cookies, **'99** 280
Chocolate Crunch Cookies, **'91** 316
Chocolate-Filled Bonbons, **'89** 162
Chocolate Kiss Cookies, **'03** 298
Chocolate-Mint Snaps, **'83** 103; **'84** 96
Chocolate-Peanut Butter Cones, **'85** 14
Chocolate-Peanut Butter Cookies, **'85** 90
Chocolate-Peanut Butter Cups, **'85** 14
Chocolate Pixies, **'00** M155
Chocolate Seashells, **'91** 178
Chocolate Snappers, Jumbo, **'81** 218
Chocolate Snowflake Cookies, **'89** 329
Chocolate Spice Cookies, Lemon-Iced, **'97** 123
Chocolate-Tipped Log Cookies, **'87** 294
Chocolate Wedding Cookies, **'04** 275
Choco-Nut Dainties, **'04** M124
Choco-Nut Sandwich Cookies, **'84** 200
Christmas
    Calendar, Cookie Advent, **'85** 325
    Candy Canes and Wreaths, Braided, **'92** 276
    Cards, Christmas Cookie, **'84** 302
    Cherry Cookies, Christmas, **'88** 282
    Date Cookies, Christmas, **'88** 287
    Eggnog Christmas Cookies, **'79** 255
    Elf Biscuits, **'99** 309
    Elf Cookie, **'80** 279, 303
    Fruit Squares, Christmas, **'88** 282
    Gingerbread Bowl, Christmas, **'93** 266
    Gingerbread Cookies, **'80** 278
    Gingerbread Men, **'99** 294
    Gingerbread Snowflake Cookies, **'98** 324
    Gingerbread Votives, **'98** 309
    Granny's Christmas Cookies, **'02** 278
    Jammies, Christmas, **'95** 322
    Lizzies, Christmas, **'87** 257
    Moravian Christmas Cookies, **'91** 282
    Mrs. Claus Cookie, **'80** 279, 303
    Nutcracker Cookies, **'97** 286
    Nutcracker Sweets, **'02** 293

    Painted Cookies, **'86** 322
    Pfeffernüesse, **'01** 65
    Reindeer Cookies, Jolly, **'91** 273
    Rudolph Cookie, **'80** 279, 303
    Rudolph Cookies, **'99** M309
    Santa Claus Cookie, **'80** 278, 303
    Santa Cookies, Easy, **'95** 321
    Santa's Whiskers, **'85** 323
    Sleigh Cookie, **'80** 279, 303
    Spiced Christmas Cookies, **'87** 294
    Spritz Cookies, Christmas, **'96** 314
    Strawberries, Christmas, **'87** 293
    Sugarplum Fairy Wands, **'97** M286
    Sugarplum Sticks, **'95** 321
    Swedish Christmas Cookies, **'79** 290
    Swedish Holiday Cookies, **'01** 296
    Tree Cookies, Christmas, **'93** 286
    Trees, Christmas, **'89** 294
    Votives, Edible, **'98** 309
    Wreaths, Christmas, **'97** 288
Cinnamon Balls, **'79** 23
Cinnamon Sticks, Italian, **'93** 204
Cinnamon Wafers, **'81** 192
Cocoa Kiss Cookies, **'85** 171
Coconut Cookies, Crisp, **'89** 162
Coconut-Oatmeal Cookies, Crispy, **'93** 80
Coconut Swirls, **'97** 274
Coffee Kisses, Chocolate-Dipped, **'96** 313
Cream, Cookies and, **'96** 179
Cupcake Cookies, **'04** 273
Curled Cookies, French, **'87** 16
Date Balls, **'01** 90
Drop
    Almond Cookies, **'97** 288; **'99** 49
    Almond Lace Cookies, **'98** 336
    Amaretti Cookies, **'02** 270
    Ambrosia Cookies, **'81** 301; **'82** 110; **'86** 313
    Apple Butter Spice Cookies, **'79** 291
    Apple Cookies, Fresh, **'84** 36
    Apple-Nut Cookies, **'80** 228
    Apple Oatmeal Cookies, **'85** 215
    Apple-Oatmeal Cookies, **'90** 218
    Apricot Cookies, Frosted, **'81** 192
    Banana Oatmeal Cookies, **'79** 217
    Benne Seed Cookies, **'84** 318
    Breakfast Cookies, **'97** 52
    Breakfast Cookies, Take-Along, **'84** 59
    Brownie Chip Cookies, **'90** 320
    Butterscotch Cookies, **'87** 58
    Butterscotch-Pecan Cookies, **'84** 36
    Candy Bit Cookies, **'81** 192
    Carrot Cookies, **'82** 137
    Carrot Cookies, Frosted, **'81** 7
    Carrot-Orange Cookies, **'83** 149
    Cashew Crunch Cookies, **'92** 17
    Cherry-Almond Drops, **'81** 20
    Chip Cookies, Double, **'81** 301
    Chips Cookies, Loaded-with-, **'87** 223
    Chocolate-Bran Raisin Jumbos, **'91** 142
    Chocolate-Brickle Cookies, **'99** 127
    Chocolate Cappuccino Cookies, **'01** 315
    Chocolate Chewies, **'93** 216
    Chocolate Chewies, Double, **'00** 333
    Chocolate Chip Cookies, **'84** 120; **'86** 245;
        '90 193
    Chocolate Chip Cookies, Deluxe, **'79** 216
    Chocolate Chip Cookies, Different, **'83** 114
    Chocolate Chip Cookies, Double, **'79** 217
    Chocolate Chip Cookies, Giant, **'84** 119
    Chocolate Chip Cookies, Jumbo, **'82** 110
    Chocolate Chip Cookies, Light, **'86** 46
    Chocolate Chip Cookies, Mom Ford's, **'94** 287
    Chocolate Chip Cookies, Nutty Oatmeal-,
        '82 M185

Chocolate Chip-Oatmeal Cookies, '84 119
Chocolate Chip-Peanut Butter Cookies, '99 68
Chocolate Chippers, '92 206
Chocolate Chip-Pudding Cookies, '93 21
Chocolate-Chocolate Chip Cookies, '82 35
Chocolate-Chocolate Chip-Peppermint Cookies,
   '97 289
Chocolate Chubbies, '01 144
Chocolate Chunk-Almond Cookies, Double,
   '95 178
Chocolate Chunk Cookies, Super, '88 217
Chocolate Cookies, Double-, '95 272
Chocolate Cookies, Doubly-Good, '82 M185
Chocolate Crispy Cookies, '85 115
Chocolate Drop Cookies, '84 36
Chocolate Macaroon Cookies, '88 217
Chocolate Macaroons, '83 300; '87 57
Chocolate-Mint Chip Cookies, '86 245
Chocolate-Mint Cookies, '92 206
Chocolate-Nut Chews, '81 92
Chocolate-Oatmeal Cookies, '80 105
Chocolate-Orange Delights, '93 52
Chocolate-Peanut Butter Cups, '97 134
Chocolate-Peanut Cookies, '83 223
Chocolate-Raisin Oatmeal Cookies, '95 136
Chocolate Sandwich Cookies, '81 192
Choco-Peanut Chip Cookies, '92 318
Clear-the-Cupboard Cookies, '99 278; '02 176
Cocoa Drop Cookies, '80 217
Coconut-Cherry Cookies, '79 292
Coconut Cookies, Toasted, '02 245
Coconut Kisses, '90 106
Coconut-Macadamia Cookies, '98 294
Coconut Macaroons, '79 52
Coconut Robin's Nests, '98 M111
Cranberry-Almond Cookies, '98 26
Cream Cheese-Chocolate Chip Cookies, '02 229;
   '03 131
Cream Cheese Cookies, '80 282; '02 229;
   '03 131
Date-Nut Chocolate Chip Cookies, Rich, '92 207
Devil Doggies, '84 37
Easy Cookies, '00 133
English Rocks, '01 295
Fibber McGee Cookies, '95 72
Forget 'em Cookies, '83 256
Fruitcake Cookies, '79 291; '86 320; '88 286;
   '96 314; '98 294
Fruitcake Cookies, Holiday, '81 301
Fruitcake Drop Cookies, '92 275
Fruit Cookies, Bourbon, '86 334
Fruit Cookies, Spicy Holiday, '83 298
Fruit Drops, Candied, '89 329
Fudge-Pecan Chewies, Alabama, '95 143
Gumdrop Cookies, '79 292
Jack-o'-Lantern Cookies, '87 214
Lace Cookies, '86 8
Lemonade Cookies, '79 51
Lemon Yummies, '81 301
Macadamia Nut White Chocolate Cookies,
   Chunky, '92 207
Macaroons, Soft Coconut, '02 229; '03 131
Macaroons, White Chocolate Tropical, '00 M166
Melting Moments, '85 191
Meringue Kiss Cookies, '86 121
Meringue Surprise Cookies, '86 320
Mincemeat Drop Cookies, '79 246
Molasses Cookies, Chewy, '87 257
Molasses Cookies, Crispy-Chewy, '90 218
Monster Cookies, '84 36
Nugget Cookies, '79 291
Oatmeal-Chocolate Chippers, '90 218
Oatmeal-Chocolate Chunk Cookies, Nutty, '01 19
Oatmeal-Chocolate Morsel Cookies, '95 46

Oatmeal-Coconut Crispies, '01 19
Oatmeal Cookies, '92 82; '99 280
Oatmeal Cookies, Cake Mix, '96 247
Oatmeal Cookies, Cinnamon, '84 72
Oatmeal Cookies, Crunchy, '85 202
Oatmeal Cookies, Double-Chip, '03 200
Oatmeal Cookies, Easy, '80 105
Oatmeal Cookies, Nutty, '81 130
Oatmeal Cookies, Old-Fashioned, '80 106;
   '85 250
Oatmeal Cookies, Orange-Glazed, '80 60
Oatmeal Cookies, Peanutty, '80 106; '83 95
Oatmeal Cookies, Pudding-, '98 215
Oatmeal Cookies, Spicy, '81 197; '01 19
Oatmeal Cookies, Toasted, '92 273; '95 136
Oatmeal-Date Cookies, '82 109
Oatmeal Krispies, '85 115
Oatmeal-Peanut Butter Chocolate Chip Cookies,
   '92 207
Oatmeal-Peanut Butter Cookies, '85 171
Oatmeal-Raisin Cookies, '87 221; '93 127
Oatmeal-Raisin Cookies, Frosted, '79 290
Oatmeal-Spice Cookies, Giant, '80 105; '03 59
Oatmeal Sunshine Cookies, '89 59
Oatmeal-Toffee Cookies, '04 234
Oats-and-Peanut Cookies, '89 60
Olympic Medal Cookies, '96 180
Orange-Chocolate Cookies, '83 113
Orange Cookies, Frosted, '83 114
Orange Crinkles, '95 272
Orange Crispies, Grandmom Lucy's, '02 253
Orange Slice Cookies, '98 324
Peanut Butter Cookies, No-Bake, '94 197
Peanut Butter Macaroons, Chewy, '95 214
Peanut Butter-Oatmeal Cookies, '81 218
Peanut Butter-Toffee Turtle Cookies, '02 M325
Peanut Cookies, Salted, '87 92
Pecan Crispies, '99 337
Pecan Lace Shells, '97 167
Pecan Sandies, Basil-, '97 166
Persimmon Cookies, '96 242
Persimmon-Raisin Cookies, '85 232
Pfeffernüesse, '01 65
Pineapple Cookies, '79 216
Polka Dots, '95 272
Potato Chip Cookies, '86 93
Praline-Chocolate Chip Cookies, Crispy, '02 229;
   '03 131
Praline Cookies, '91 271
Praline Cookies, Crispy, '02 229; '03 131
Pumpkin-Chocolate Chip Cookies, '93 235
Pumpkin Drop Cookies, '79 206
Pumpkin-Walnut Cookies, Frosted, '82 217
Rainy Day Cookies, '94 168
Raisin Cookies, Alltime Favorite, '80 24
Raisin-Granola Treats, '92 22
Red, White, and Blue Cookies, Chewy, '03 163
Snowcaps, Smoky Mountain, '00 288
Sour Cream Cookies, Southern, '83 113
Sour Cream-Nutmeg Cookies, '85 171
Sugar Biscuits, '04 72
Sugar Cookies, Nutmeg, '79 136
Sugar Cookies, Stir-and-Drop, '92 174
Sunflower Cookies, Crinkle, '83 149
Tea Cakes, Dropped, '90 156
Toffee Crunch Cookies, '93 80
Walnut Spice Kisses, '89 295
White Chocolate Chip-Oatmeal Cookies, '99 127;
   '04 43
White Chocolate-Macadamia Nut Cookies,
   '94 315
White Chocolate-Orange Dream Cookies,
   '98 294
Zucchini Cookies, Spicy, '97 273

Easter Basket and Eggs, '95 101
Eggnog Logs, '92 274
Finikia, '96 21
Flying Brooms, '98 255
Ginger Cookies, '85 306; '96 314
Ginger Crinkles, '83 149
Ginger-Oatmeal Sorghum Cookies, '00 230; '02 230
Gingersnaps, '79 146; '91 299; '92 264
Gingersnaps, Best-Ever, '79 208
Hamburger Cookies, '00 171
Hazelnut Bonbons, Crisp, '97 274
Hazelnut Cookies, '84 111
Hazelnut Crinkle Cookies, '98 294
Hazelnut-Lemon Logs, '84 117
Heavenly Delights, '85 324
Jumbles, Mrs. Jemison's, '97 133
Keyboard Cookies, '94 M330
Kissy Cookies, '93 331
Lace Cookies, Crunchy, '01 294
Lace Cookies, Florentine, '88 120
Lemon Cookies, '03 298
Lemon Cookies, Sunshine, '86 69
Lemon Crinkle Cookies, '81 287
Lemon Crisps, '95 272
Lemon Thumbprint Cookies, '03 298
Lemon Zephers, '81 172
Lollipop Cookies, '94 196
Macadamia-Oat Snowballs, '92 274
Madeleines, Snow-Capped, '85 120
Mailing Cookies, Tips on, '83 305
Mandel Bread, '97 220; '99 57
Mandelbrot, Rhoda's, '98 243
Meringue Cookies, '98 71
Meringue Cookies, Vanilla, '01 197
Miracle Cookies, '83 149
Mix, Quick, '94 167
Molasses Crinkles, '92 276
Nutcracker Sweets, '02 293
Oat Cookies, Crispy, '88 203; '90 311
Oatmeal Cookies, Special, '81 236
Orange Fingers, '87 57
Peanut Blossom Cookies, '95 245; '96 55; '97 324
Peanut Butter and Chocolate Chunk Cookies,
   '94 169
Peanut Butter-Chocolate Kiss Cookies, '86 49
Peanut Butter-Cinnamon Cookies, '84 30
Peanut Butter Cookies, '82 56
Peanut Butter Cookies, Double-Chip, '89 169
Peanut Butter Cookies, Easy, '92 272
Peanut Butter Cookies, Quick, '86 109; '02 229;
   '03 131
Peanut Butter Cup Cookies, '03 298
Peanut Butter-Kiss Cookies, '03 42
Peanut Butter-Oatmeal Cookies, '84 72
Peanut Butter Temptations, '84 29
Peanut-Date Balls, '81 92
Peanut Truffle Cookies, '93 212
Pecan-Butter Cookies, '83 113
Pecan Crescent Cookies, '85 324
Pecan Crescents, '04 284
Pecan Pie Cookies, '92 289; '00 290
Pecan Sticks, Crispy, '00 258
Peppermint Candy Cookies, '88 286
Peppermint Crescents, '03 273
Peppermint Sandwich Cookies, '92 277
Peppermint Wreaths, Melt-Away, '85 324
Pizza Cookies, Candy Shop, '02 299
Pizzelles, '83 298
Pumpkin Cookies, Peppy, '89 253
Refrigerator
   Almond Crescents, '97 273
   Almond Crunch Cookies, Texan-Size, '91 236
   Apple Rugelach, '97 220
   Apricot Kolaches, '83 84

COOKIES, Refrigerator
(continued)

Berliner Kranse, '96 311
Biscotti, Chocolate-Hazelnut, '95 80
Biscotti, Light, '91 310
Brown Sugar-Pecan Cookies, '91 236
Brown Sugar Wafers, '96 213
Buckin' Bronco Cookies, '90 95
Butter Cookie Dough, Basic, '95 320
Butter Cookies, '00 288
Butter Cookies, Valentine, '81 20
Cardamom Cookies, '79 12
Cheese Wafers, '00 164
Cheese Wafers, Hope Farm, '93 282
Cherry Chocolates, '95 321
Cherry Pecan Cookies, '82 136
Chocolate-Almond Surprise Cookies, '88 M45
Chocolate-Cherry Cookies, '85 324
Chocolate-Gingerbread Cookies, '94 293
Chocolate Meltaways, '81 302
Chocolate-Nut Freezer Cookies, '88 217
Chocolate Pinwheel Cookies, '86 245
Chocolate Snowball Cookies, '82 295
Chocolate Teasers, '87 44
Choco Surprise Cookies, '80 60
Cinnamon Chip Icebox Cookies, '01 308
Coffee Nuggets, '95 278
Cran-bear-y Bread Cookies, '02 254
Crème de Menthe Cookies, '86 230
Crescents, '85 321
Date-Cream Cheese Rollups, '83 298
Date Moons, '01 295
Date Nut Roll, '79 249
Date Pinwheel Cookies, '02 93
Fruit Rugelach, '97 220
Fudge Puddles, '94 292
Ghosts on a Stick, '00 M235
Gingerbirds, '93 283
Gingerbread Boys, '02 252
Gingerbread Men, '84 299
Gingerbread Men, Miniature, '84 318
Ginger Icebox Cookies, '93 205
Gingersnaps, Raisin, '85 324
Hat Cookies, '01 91
Holiday Garland Cookies, '83 299
Holiday Riches, '83 257
Jack-o'-Lantern Cookies, '95 273
Lemon-Almond Cookies, '02 293
Lemon-Coconut Cookies, '02 293
Lemon Ice Box Cookies, '02 293
Lemon-Pecan Cookies, '02 293
Lemon-Poppy Seed Cookies, '02 293
Lemon Thyme Cookies, '96 124
Linzer Cookies, '02 293
Lollipop Cookies, '95 322
Macaroon Cookies, '03 282
Memory Book Cookies, '92 45
Molasses Cookies, '86 20
Neapolitan Cookies, '00 290
Oatmeal Cookies, Crispy, '89 328
Oatmeal-Date Sandwich Cookies, '83 257
Oatmeal-Toffee Lizzies, Crispy, '95 136
Orange Cookies, Chocolate-Dipped, '04 299
Orange Crispies, '84 205
Orange Refrigerator Cookies, '86 230
Orange-Slice Cookies, '89 294
Peanut Butter-Chocolate Chip Cookies, Freezer,
    '86 230
Peanut Butter-Coconut Cookies, '83 113
Peanut Butter Cookie Ice Cream Sandwiches,
    '93 199
Peanut Butter Cookies, '87 58

Peanut Butter Crisps, '79 50
Peanut Butter Slice-and-Bakes, '82 M185
Peanut Butter Snaps, '81 237
Pecan-Cheese Wafers, '81 119
Pecan Crescent Cookies, '97 274
Pecan Crisps, Sugar, '86 230
Peppermint Rounds, '94 19
Pfeffernusse, German, '98 293
Pinwheel Cookies, '93 316
Raisin-Oatmeal Cookies, '01 19
Raspberry Sandwich Cookies, '82 306
Ravioli, Sweet, '91 107
Ribbon Cookies, '87 293
Sandwich Cookies, Grandmother's, '82 306
Sesame-Cheese Cutouts, '82 296
Shortbread, Brown Sugar, '98 278
Shortbread, Cinnamon, '98 202
Shortbread Cookie Crumbs, '83 298
Shortbread Cookies, '87 58
Shortbread Cookies, Angel, '97 M285
Shortbread Cookies, Crispy, '83 113
Shortbread, Rum-Currant, '98 277
Shortbreads, Pecan-Cornmeal, '04 230
Snowball Surprises, '93 315
Sour Cream Cookies, Dutch, '83 149
Spice Cookies, '03 307
Spice Cookies, Slice-of-, '79 290
Spice-Molasses Cookies, '89 289
Spooky Eyes, '95 273
Spring Bonnet Cookies, '97 111
Springerle, '81 251
Sugar Cookies, Crisp, '84 243
Sugar Cookies, Golden, '88 286
Sugar Cookies, Molasses, '80 270
Sugar Cookies, Pastel, '99 179
Sugar Cookies, Red-, '81 21
Sugar Cookies, Symbol, '91 282
Sugar Cookies, Valentine, '82 20
Sugar 'n Spice Cookies, '81 21
Swedish Cookies, '82 306
Swedish Holiday Cookies, '01 296
Tea Cakes, '02 161
Tea Cakes, Old-Fashioned, '91 72; '99 319
Tea Cakes, Victorian Christmas, '02 253
Tea Cookies, '83 170
Vanilla Crescents, '82 307
Vanilla Slice-and-Bake Cookies, '85 171
Wafers, Italian, '87 36
Walnut Cookies, '81 301; '97 275; '98 35
Watermelon Cookies, '92 179
Rolled
Almond-Filled Wafers, '88 120
Almond Holly Leaves, '86 319
A-Pees, '97 133
Apricot Cookie Rolls, '80 282
Apricot Kolaches, '94 291
Apricot Wonders, '93 316
Bears, Red-Bellied, '92 277
Biscochitos, '92 230
Chocolate Cookies, Chewy, '80 208
Cinnamon Cookies, GrandLady's, '00 323
Cinnamon Stars, Swiss, '87 293
Cranberry-Walnut Swirls, '00 290
Cream Cheese Frills, '79 291
Crème de Menthe Cookies, '80 282
Cutout Cookies, Frosted, '85 236
Cutout Cookies, Old-Fashioned, '92 273
Date-Filled Cookies, '91 95
Fruit Cookies, Rolled, '80 15
Fruit-Nut Twists, '82 253
Gingerbread Animal Cookies, '86 70
Gingerbread Cookies, '80 278; '92 343
Gingerbread Man Cookies, '88 227
Gingerbread Men, '85 259; '99 294; '00 297

Gingerbread Men Cookies, '85 319
Gingerbread People, '92 312
Gingerbread Snowflake Cookies, '98 324
Ginger Cookies, Swedish, '85 323
Grandmother's Cookies, '85 319
Ice Box Filled Cookies, '79 112
Lemon Pecan Dainties, '80 208
Lemony Cutout Cookies, '85 323
Maple Sandwich Cookies, '85 322
Mincemeat Cookies, '79 51
Mincemeat Sweetheart Cookies, '87 293
Oat Crispies, '83 96
Oatmeal-Coconut Cookies, '80 218
Oatmeal Cookies, Date-Filled, '86 314
Oatmeal Cookies, Slice-and-Bake, '80 105
Oatmeal Nut Crispies, '80 208
Orange-Pecan Cookies, '88 119
Ornaments, Edible, '94 316
Peanut Butter Cookies, Double, '80 209
Peanuttiest Cookies, Crisp, '88 65
Pear Mincemeat Cookies, '84 264
Pecan Cookies, Easy, '80 208
Peppermint Cookies, '95 322
Pinwheels, '95 321
Polvorones, '00 123
Pueblo Indian Cookies, '95 228
Pumpkin Cookies, Great, '91 234
Raspberry Swirl Cookies, '90 111
Rugelach, '92 252
Sand Tarts, '00 323
Scones, Currant, '84 117
Sherry Snaps, '87 94
Shortbread, Apricot-Almond, '99 29
Shortbread Cookies, '99 147
Shortbread Cookies, Butter Pecan, '80 282
Shortbread Cookies, Chocolate, '99 147
Shortbread Cookies, Coconut, '93 316
Shortbread, Easy Roll-Out, '81 21
Shortbread, Raspberry, '99 29
Shortbread Sugarplums, Pecan-, '83 298
Snowflake Cookies, '92 278
Snow Flurries, '92 275
Strawberry Cookie Tarts, '89 112
Sugar Cookies, '94 271
Sugar Cookies, Crescent, '87 294
Sugar Cookies, Molasses, '80 270
Sugar Cookies, Moravian, '85 321
Sugar Cookies, Old-Fashioned, '86 313
Sugar Cookies, Orange, '89 329
Sugar Cookies, Rolled, '79 291
Sweetheart Cookies, '93 53
Tea Cake Hat Cookies, '04 84
Tea Cakes, '02 161
Tea Cakes, Back-Home, '90 156
Teacakes, Currant, '80 88
Tea Cakes, Decorative, '90 156
Tea Cakes, Grandma's, '90 156
Teacakes, Old-Fashioned, '84 43
Tea Cakes, Sorghum, '85 239
Wafers, Kahlúa, '99 147
Sachertorte Cookies, '00 155
Sandwich Cookies, Viennese, '87 293
Sesame Cookies, Italian, '85 311
Shortbread, '85 266
Shortbread, Brown Sugar, '93 331
Shortbread, Coconut, '02 224
Shortbread Cookie, Old-Fashioned, '88 242
Shortbread Cookies, Java, '94 233
Shortbread Cookies, Praline, '88 242
Shortbread Cookies, Spiced, '88 242
Shortbread Madeleines, Orange, '88 242
Shortbread, Marble-Topped Hazelnut, '99 M29
Shortbread, Peanut Butter, '95 321
Shortbread, Peanut-Toffee, '04 329

Shortbread, Raspberry, '02 33
Shortbread, Scottish, '94 242; '95 34
Shortbread Wafers, Cocoa, '88 243
Snickerdoodles, '04 223
Snowballs, Chocolate, '03 273
Snow Cookies, '99 167
Spice Cookies, '87 M278
Spice Thins, '95 322
Spider Cookies, '93 M166
Spooky Ghosts, '98 M256
Spritz Cookies, '04 284
Spritz Cookies, Butter, '91 175
Spritz Hearts, '91 107
Sugar Cookies, '97 288; '03 298
Sugar Cookies, Cinnamon, '84 73
Sugar Cookies, Double-Chocolate, '92 206
Sugar Cookies, Holiday, '04 331
Sugar Cookies, Molasses, '82 140
Sugar Cookies, Sour Cream, '79 51
Sugar Cookies, Winning, '97 108
Swedish Heirloom Cookies, '81 129; '90 311
Tea Cakes, Brandied Apricot, '91 241
Tea Cakes, Mexican, '81 196
Tea Cakes, Royal Raspberry, '02 253
Thumbprint Cookies, Childhood, '85 323
Thumbprint Cookies, Praline, '89 328
Toffee Cookie Bites, '03 M273
Turkey Treats, '93 256
Turtle Cookies, Snappin', '85 323
Waffle Cookies, Brownie, '86 245
Walnut Cookies, Simply, '91 236
Wedding Cookies, '82 M185; '00 332
Whoopie Pies, '86 246
Witches' Hats, '98 256
CORN
Bacon and Caramelized Onion, Corn with, '99 94
Bake, Corn-and-Swiss Cheese, '92 133
Baked Corn, Creamy, '90 60
Balls, Zesty Corn Dressing, '82 307
Beignets, Lobster-and-Roasted Corn, '00 51
Boil, Monroe County Corn, '96 167
Cabbage Rolls, Southwestern, '97 214
Cakes with Avocado Cream, Southwestern Chicken-
    and-Corn, '97 M311
Cakes with Smoked Salmon Salsa, Corn-and-Black
    Bean, '96 272
Casseroles
    Baked Corn, Creamy, '02 234
    Baked Jack Corn, '97 86
    Bean Casserole, Corn-and-, '90 208
    Broccoli-Corn Casserole, '83 313
    Cheese Casserole, Corn and, '81 128
    Cheesy Corn Bake, '98 244
    Chili-Corn Casserole, '88 266
    Corn Casserole, '79 247; '89 126; '93 141
    Creamy Corn, '79 213; '90 207
    Escalloped Corn, '79 251
    Fresh Corn Casserole, '80 165
    Green Bean-and-Corn Casserole, '88 123; '99 36
    Green Chile Casserole, Corn-and-, '89 68
    Hamburger-Corn Bake, '99 58
    Hominy-and-Corn Casserole, '97 291
    Jalapeño-Corn Casserole, '83 256
    Moussaka, Corn, '87 190
    Oyster-and-Corn Bake, '83 34; '84 44
    Rice Casserole, Corn-, '01 46
    Salami-Corn Casserole, '80 209
    Scalloped Corn, '80 164; '81 128; '86 111;
        '88 218
    Scalloped Corn, Baked, '85 290
    Scalloped Corn, Elegant, '86 268
    Scalloped Corn for Two, '82 208
    Sour Cream, Baked Corn with, '86 170
    Squash-and-Corn Casserole, Easy, '03 69

Tomato Casserole, Corn and, '81 127
Tomato Casserole, Corn-and-, '84 145
Zucchini Bake, Corn-, '79 178
Chiles Rellenos with Walnut Cream Sauce, Havarti-
    and-Corn-Stuffed, '93 M275
Chili, White Bean, '02 20
Christmas Corn, '93 325
Cob
    Baked Corn on the Cob, Seasoned, '82 134
    Barbecued Corn on the Cob, '81 128
    Basil Corn on the Cob, Fresh, '00 M170
    Chili Corn on the Cob, '03 M185
    Corn on the Cob, '79 122
    Foil-Baked Corn on the Cob, '81 128
    Foiled Corn on the Cob, '80 165
    Garlic-Chive Butter, Corn on the Cob with,
        '01 331
    Grill, Corn on the, '94 161; '97 191
    Grilled Corn in the Style of Oaxaca, '04 134
    Grilled Corn-on-the-Cob, '90 166
    Grilled Corn with Jalapeño-Lime Butter, '01 158;
        '04 178
    Grilled Corn with Maple Vinaigrette, '98 171
    Grilled Parmesan Corn, '82 127
    Herb Butter, Corn-on-the-Cob with, '84 160
    Herb Butter Sauce, Corn with, '79 150
    Hickory-Smoked Corn, '85 145
    Lemony Corn on the Cob, '89 200
    Mexican Corn on the Cob, '96 167
    Microwaved Corn on the Cob, '80 M122
    Parmesan Corn on the Cob, '88 M187
    Parslied Corn, '90 155
    Roasted Red Pepper Corn, '91 122
    Spicy Corn-on-the-Cob, '84 149
    Spicy Corn on the Cob, '87 M151
Cold-Pack Corn, '81 216
Combo, Field Peas, Okra, and Corn, '01 214
Combo, Zucchini-Corn, '86 218
Cornbread, Sour Cream, '96 17
Creamed Corn, '97 136; '02 16
Creamed Corn, Freezer-Fresh, '96 46
Creamed Corn, Skillet, '02 204
Creamed Corn, Southern-Style, '81 M165; '92 201
Creamed Fresh Corn, '82 158
Cream-Style Corn, '80 127; '85 106
Creamy Corn, '79 213; '90 207
Creole Corn, '81 128
Creole, Corn-and-Okra, '89 127
Creole, Okra-Corn, '83 157
Crêpes, Blue-Corn, '97 197
Crêpes with Beef Filling, Blue-Corn, '97 197
Curried Corn and Celery, '86 192
Curried Corn and Sweet Red Peppers, '95 47
Custard, Fresh Corn, '89 127
Deviled Corn, '86 192
Dinner, Corn-and-Ham Skillet, '83 190
Dip, Corn-and-Field Pea, '01 177
Dip, Quick Fiesta, '99 M197
Dip, Roasted Corn-and-Avocado, '91 279
Dressing, Corny Cornbread, '99 258
Flan, Corn, '98 246; '99 25
Flan, Corn-Chive, '94 172
Fresh Corn, Seasoned, '83 M147
Fried Confetti Corn, Creamy, '02 160
Fried Corn, '89 127; '94 158
Fried Corn, Buttermilk, '96 167; '00 184
Fried Corn, Skillet, '83 190
Frittata, Corn-and-Squash, '89 144
Frittata, Skillet Corn, '87 90
Fritters, Corn, '86 192; '94 22; '98 207
Fritters, Corn-and-Crab, '97 227
Fritters, Corn-Jalapeño, '96 153
Fritters, Golden Corn, '80 165; '81 128
Fritters, Skillet-Fried Corn, '85 14

Grilled Corn and Squash, '02 122
Hush Puppies, Corn Soufflé, '98 M328
Hush Puppies with Corn, '83 286; '84 17
Indian Corn, '96 287
Jus, Chile Corn, '00 197
Limping Susan, '90 155
Macque Choux (Smothered Corn), '94 236
Maque Choux, Cajun Corn, '01 284
Meat Loaf, Corny, '86 68
Medley, Corn-and-Okra, '99 203
Medley, Okra-Corn-Tomato, '81 159
Medley, Peas-and-Corn, '85 138
Medley, Skillet Corn, '86 192
Medley, Summer Garden, '84 158
Medley, Zucchini-and-Corn, '80 298; '81 25
Mexican Corn, '80 157, 165
Mexican Corn, Spicy, '93 90
Mexi-Corn, '82 M21
Mexicorn, '96 189
Mexicorn, Black Bean, '96 189
Mexicorn Main Dish, '96 189
Muffins, Corn, '98 313
Muffins, Corn-Oat, '89 108
Muffins, Southwestern Corn, '02 212
Muffins, Sunny Corn, '96 166
Muffins, Tex-Mex Corn, '92 253; '93 144
Okra and Corn in Cream, '79 160
Okra, Corn, and Peppers, '87 M151
Okra, Corn, and Tomatoes, '95 203
Pancakes, Corn, '93 43
Peppers, Corn-Stuffed, '84 104
Peppers, Ham-and-Corn Stuffed, '81 87
Peppers with Chicken and Corn, Stuffed, '02 147
Pie, Quick and Cheesy Corn, '82 191
Pies, Maque Choux, '02 182
Pie with Fresh Tomato Salsa, Buttercrust Corn,
    '95 181
Poblanos, Corn-Stuffed, '97 269
Pork Chops, Mexican, '99 108
Pork Chops, Southwestern, '98 131
Posole, '95 226
Pudding, Baked Corn, '83 314
Pudding, Corn, '79 276; '81 128; '86 192; '90 219;
    '98 124; '99 71, 270
Pudding, Corn-Cheese, '80 244
Pudding, Creamy Corn, '81 267
Pudding, Dashiell Corn, '98 274
Pudding, Easy Corn, '83 280
Pudding, Fresh Corn, '80 157, 165; '89 172
Pudding, Green Tomato-Tomatillo-Corn, '04 103
Pudding, Southwestern Corn, '01 165; '03 178
Pudding, Tee's Corn, '95 318; '01 165; '03 178
Puppies, Corn, '97 140
Quesadillas, Chorizo, Black Bean, and Corn,
    '00 148
Quesadillas, Poblano-and-Corn, '01 333
Quesadilla Torta, '97 325
Quiche, Jalapeño-Corn, '85 122
Quick Corn Fix-Up, '81 M4
Relish, Corn, '81 129, 175; '83 189; '84 107;
    '85 136; '87 120, 245; '92 241
Relish Dogs, Corn, '85 192
Relish, Easy Corn, '83 260
Relish, Quick Corn, '90 13
Relish, Summer Corn, '89 127
Relish, Sweet Corn, '93 119
Relish, Sweet White Corn-and-Tomato, '00 130
Relish, Virginia Corn, '79 283
Rice with Corn, Tex-Mex, '03 129
Salads
    Avocado-Corn-Poblano Salad, '01 320
    Bean Salad, Mexicorn-, '96 184
    Broccoli-Corn Salad, '87 24
    Chilled Corn Salad, '79 20

CORN, Salads
(continued)

Colorful Corn Salad, '00 139
Confetti Corn Salad, '96 168
Corn Salad, '80 247; '81 139; '85 236; '91 27;
'95 214; '02 234
Festive Corn Salad, '92 263
Fresh Corn Salad, '91 126; '94 162
Garden Medley Salad, '80 122
Marinated Corn-Bean Salad, '87 9
Marinated Corn Salad, '89 126
Pea Salad, Corn-and-, '90 181
Roasted Corn Salad, '97 196
Shoepeg Corn Salad, '81 23
Shuck Salad, Corn-in-the-, '93 236
Slaw, Corn and Cabbage, '79 135
Tabbouleh Salad, Southwestern, '01 216
Tangy Corn Salad, '88 176
Tasty Corn Salad, '84 289
Wheat Berry-and-Roasted Corn Salad, '94 175
Wild Rice-and-Corn Salad, '98 288
Zucchini-Corn Marinated Salad, '98 236
Salsa, Avocado-Corn, '94 201; '99 335
Salsa, Black Bean-and-Corn, '94 80
Salsa, Black Bean-Corn, '96 126; '04 322
Salsa, Corn, '00 164
Salsa, Corn-Black Bean, '96 15
Salsa, Grilled Corn, '99 162
Salsa, Mexi-Corn, '91 182
Salsa Pork Chops, Black Bean-and-Corn, '01 320
Salsa, Spicy Corn, '93 322
Salsa, Sweet Corn, '95 156
Salsa with Black Beans and Corn, Southwestern,
'96 275
Salsa, Yellowfin Tuna with Corn, Pepper, and
Tomato, '94 164
Salsa, Zesty Corn, '02 193
Sauce, Fresh Corn, '98 43
Sauté, Corn, '80 165
Sautéed Corn and Okra, '84 158
Sauté, Spicy Okra-Tomato-Corn, '04 327
Skillet, Zucchini-and-Corn, '01 137
Smoked Corn, '01 169
Soufflé, Corn-and-Cheese, '88 122
Soufflés, Zucchini-Corn, '97 203
Soufflé, Zucchini-and-Corn, '83 265
Soups
Bisque, Crab-and-Corn, '87 137
Bourbon Soup, Corn-and-, '92 194
Chicken-Corn Soup, Cheesy, '97 158
Chowder, Chicken Corn, '02 305
Chowder, Corn, '81 128; '83 20; '84 M38;
'85 10; '90 202; '91 132; '97 241; '98 31
Chowder, Corn and Cheese, '80 228
Chowder, Corn-and-Poblano, '03 193
Chowder, Curried Chicken-and-Corn, '92 21
Chowder, Delicious Corn, '82 279
Chowder, Fresh Corn and Bacon, '93 203
Chowder, Ham and Corn, '79 16
Chowder, Ham-and-Corn, '82 40
Chowder, Mexican Chicken-Corn, '01 18
Chowder, Mirliton-Corn, '00 246
Chowder, Oyster-Corn, '83 211
Chowder, Potato-Corn, '94 66
Chowder, Pumpkin-Corn, '97 219
Chowder, Shrimp and Corn, '79 199
Chowder, Southern Corn-and-Bacon, '96 166
Chowder, Turkey-Corn, '81 98; '96 279
Corn Soup, '80 56; '85 243; '87 156
Crab Soup, Fresh Corn-and-, '92 183
Cream of Corn Soup, '90 210
Favorite Corn Soup, '85 155

Gazpacho, Tomato-Avocado-Corn, '97 182
Grilled Corn Soup, '87 121
Pimiento-Corn Soup, '89 126
Pumpkin-Corn Soup with Ginger-Lime Cream,
'95 227
Shrimp-and-Corn Soup, '84 88
Sweet Corn Soup with Crab, '02 159
Sweet Corn Soup with Shiitakes and Shrimp,
'99 168
Tortilla Soup, '98 291
Spoonbread, Corn, '97 301
Spoonbread, Corn and Bacon, '81 129
Spoonbread, Corn-Cheese, '88 9
Spread, Corn-and-Walnut, '96 26
Stew, Frogmore, '00 174, 336
Succotash, '02 16
Succotash, Easy, '80 165
Succotash, Garden, '04 160
Succotash, Savory, '96 63
Timbales, Corn-and-Zucchini, '92 100
Tomatoes-and-Corn, Creole-Style, '84 142
Tomatoes, Corn-Stuffed, '82 270
Tomatoes, Stuffed, '96 82
Tomatoes with Corn, Baked, '80 161
Vinaigrette, Okra-Corn-and-Tomato, '90 173
Waffles, Corn, '01 24
Waffles, Corn-Chile, '94 206
Waffles with Cilantro-Lime Butter, Corn,
'02 109
Whole Kernel Corn, '85 106
Zucchini and Corn, '86 177
Zucchini and Corn, Dilled, '83 173
Zucchini, Corn and, '83 190
CORNBREADS. *See also* **HUSH PUPPIES.**
Bake, Bacon, Zucchini, and Cornbread, '99 123
Bake, Cornbread Tamale, '79 163
Basic Cornbread, '99 257; '02 141
Batter, Cornbread Crust, '03 20
Beef Cornbread, Cheesy, '81 242
Biscuits, Cornmeal-Jalapeño, '94 214
Bites, Corn Dog, '85 245
Black-Eyed Pea Cornbread, '98 44
Black-Eyed Pea Cornbread, One-Dish, '03 215
Bowls, Cornbread, '95 58
Buttermilk Cornbread, '79 34; '82 70; '99 235
Carrot Cornbread, '80 89; '81 163
Casserole, Bean-and-Cornbread, '92 243
Casserole, Beef, Bean, and Cornbread, '99 215
Casserole, Cornbread, '81 91
Casserole, Cornbread Skillet, '83 243; '84 101
Cheddar Cornbread, '83 285; '84 17
Cheddar-Jalapeño Cornbread, '85 3
Chicken over Cornbread, Creamed, '86 231
Chile-Cheese Cornbread, '87 171
Chile Cornbread, '86 254
Confetti Cornbread, '94 170
Cornbread, '80 272; '86 231; '87 197; '92 324;
'93 122; '01 234
Cornish Hens, Cranberry-Cornbread Stuffed,
'95 325
Cottage Cheese Cornbread, '80 90
Cowboy Cornbread, '81 188
Cracklin' Cornbread, '92 216
Cracklin' Cornbread, Grannie's, '98 252
Cracklin' Cornbread, Southern, '80 119
Crackling Cornbread, '85 200
Crackling Cowboy Cornbread, '82 114
Crêpes, Cornbread, '98 42
Crêpes, Goat Cheese-Filled Cornbread, '98 43
Crêpes, Southwestern Cornbread, '98 42
Crispy Cornbread, '92 340
Croutons, Cornbread, '93 192
Croutons, Honeyed Cornbread, '94 106
Crust, Turkey and Peppers in Cornbread, '95 312

Crusty Cornbread, '85 255
Dieter's Cornbread, '87 164
Dressings
Biscuit Dressing, Cornbread-, '79 296
Cakes, Southwestern Cornbread Dressing,
'01 233
Chicken and Dressing, '99 42
Chicken Cornbread Dressing, '90 159
Cornbread Dressing, '86 286; '88 254; '92 267;
'98 269; '00 259; '02 249; '03 231
Corny Cornbread Dressing, '99 258
Crawfish-Cornbread Dressing, '99 257
Fruited Cornbread Dressing, '80 262
Green Chile-Cornbread Dressing, '93 306;
'94 296
Herb-Seasoned Cornbread Dressing, '83 315
Kentucky Cornbread Dressing, '86 281
Light Cornbread Dressing, '92 324
Louise's Cornbread Dressing, '03 251
Nannie's Cornbread Dressing, '95 306
Old-Fashioned Cornbread Dressing, '84 321
Oyster-Cornbread Dressing, Ma E's Traditional,
'96 35
Quail and Dressing, '99 42
Quail Stuffed with Cornbread Dressing, '93 280
Roast Turkey and Cornbread Dressing, '89 324
Sage-Cornbread Dressing, '84 283
Sage Dressing, Cornbread-, '80 262
Sausage, and Pecan Dressing, Cornbread, '99 257
Sausage-Cornbread Dressing, '95 289
Sausage-Cornbread Dressing, Turkey with,
'83 287
Sausage Dressing, Cornbread-, '82 307; '85 280
Sausage Dressing, Cornbread-and-, '83 213
Savory Cornbread Dressing, '88 303
Spoonbread Dressing, Southwestern-Style,
'94 273
Sweet Cornbread Dressing, '97 303
Texas Cornbread Dressing, '82 243
Dumpling Dough, Cornbread Dressing, '03 239
Easy Cornbread, '94 158
Fresh Cornbread, '80 165
Green Chile Cornbread, '82 134
Herbed Cornbread, '90 214
Hoecake, Hot Water, '81 56
Hoecakes, Green Onion, '88 112
Honey Cornbread, '83 286; '84 17
Hot Water Cornbread, '88 92
Hot-Water Cornbread, '01 29; '02 107; '03 112;
'04 25
Hot-Water Cornbread, Bacon-Cheddar, '01 29;
'02 107; '04 25
Hot-Water Cornbread, Baked, '01 29; '02 107;
'04 25
Hot-Water Cornbread, Country Ham, '01 29;
'02 107; '04 25
Hot-Water Cornbread, Southwestern, '01 29;
'02 107; '04 25
Jalapeño Cornbread, '85 200; '94 78; '98 178
Jalapeño Cornbread, Beefy, '82 142
Jalapeño Pepper Bread, '83 121
Lacy Corncakes, '81 242
Lightbread, Corn, '81 137
Light Bread, Corn, '00 270
Light Cornbread, Old Southern, '81 242
Loaded Cornbread, '99 214
Loaf, Cornbread, '85 200
Menfolks' Cornbread, '82 156
Mexican Cornbread, '80 198; '81 137; '84 140, 242;
'93 182; '01 247
Mexican Cornbread, Hot, '83 286; '84 17
Mexican Cornbread, Quick, '81 242
Mexican Flatbread, '80 197
Mex-Tex Cornbread, Lynda's, '01 273

Muffins
  Angel Cornbread Muffins, Heavenly, '98 43
  Blue Corn Muffins, '89 145; '92 52; '94 114
  Broccoli Cornbread Muffins, '03 81
  Cheesy Cornbread Muffins, '88 M275
  Cornmeal Muffins, '80 90; '88 92; '96 248
  Corn Muffins, '82 M282; '84 16
  Corn-Oat Muffins, '89 166
  Four-Grain Muffins, '80 46
  Jalapeño-Corn Muffins, '93 164
  Miniature Cornmeal Muffins, '93 119
  Parmesan Corn Muffins, '01 255
  Quick Corn Muffins, '88 15
  Sage-Corn Muffins, '83 207
  Sour Cream Corn Muffins, '95 176
  Southern Cornbread Muffins, '85 201
  Spicy Cornbread Muffins, '90 59
  Sunny Corn Muffins, '96 166
  Tex-Mex Corn Muffins, '93 144
  Tomato Corn Muffins, '81 137
  Yeast Muffins, Cornmeal, '92 49
Mush, '81 215
Old-Fashioned Cornbread, '81 242
Onion Cornbread, '88 283
Onion Cornbread, Sweet, '98 252
Onion-Topped Cornbread, '84 153
Oysters Casino on Cornbread, '79 34
Paprika Cornbread, '90 213
Pastry, Cornmeal, '81 140
Pecan Cornbread, '94 169; '98 252
Picante Cornbread, '94 169
Pie, Beef-and-Onion Cornbread, '01 298
Pie, Brunswick Stew-Cornbread, '02 121
Pie, Cornbread-Sausage-Apple, '87 171
Pie, Cornbread-Tamale, '92 123
Pie, Sausage-and-Cornbread, '90 25
Puff, Cornmeal, '82 42
Quick-and-Easy Cornbread, '83 9
Quick Cornsticks, '81 192
Salad, Cornbread, '87 172
Salad, Dianne's Southwestern Cornbread, '04 133
Salad, Layered Cornbread-and-Turkey, '02 141
Salad, Mexican Cornbread, '95 210
Sandwiches, Open-Faced Shrimp-Cornbread, '02 141
Seasoned Cornbread, '90 320
Serrano Chile Blue Cornbread, '94 114
Skillet Cornbread, '81 31; '84 102; '85 200; '90 13; '97 137; '00 22; '01 291; '03 112
Soufflé Cornbread, '96 34
Sour Cream Cornbread, '81 137; '96 17
Southern Cornbread, '79 123; '81 56; '83 12
Southern Corncakes, '88 166
Spinach Cornbread, '95 49
Spoonbread, '81 138
Spoonbread, Cheddar, '82 196
Spoonbread, Golden, '83 286; '84 17
Spoonbread, Old Virginia, '84 102
Spoonbread, Ozark, '85 202
Spoon Cornbread, '98 252
Sticks
  Angel Corn Sticks, '84 20
  Blue Ribbon Corn Sticks, '84 102
  Buttermilk Corn Sticks, '80 120; '01 319
  Cornbread Sticks, '87 15
  Corn Sticks, '79 275; '89 54; '90 214; '00 43
  Favorite Corn Sticks, '85 202
  Firecracker Corn Sticks, '85 241
  Garlic-Thyme Corn Sticks, '93 242
  Golden Cornbread Sticks, '94 213
  Old-Fashioned Corn Sticks, '90 232
  Pimiento-Cheese Corn Sticks, '03 20
  Quick Corn Sticks, '88 15
  Savory Corn Sticks, '93 33
  Southern Corn Sticks, '81 242
Strata, Cornbread-Chili, '03 100
Stuffed Cornish Hens, Cranberry-Cornbread-, '95 325
Stuffed Peppers, Barbecued Shrimp and Cornbread-, '97 261
Stuffing, Cornbread, '94 305
Stuffing, Pork Chops with Cornbread-Apple, '99 14
Stuffing, Spicy Pecan-Cornbread, '01 207
Super-Moist Cornbread, '02 260
Supper, Cornbread-Vegetable, '97 319
Supreme, Cornbread, '93 67
Swiss Cheese Cornbread, '79 60
Toasted Cornbread, '82 174
Tomatoes, Cornbread-Stuffed, '97 169; '02 213
Topping, Cornbread, '01 215, 298
Ultimate Cornbread, '80 90
Vicksburg Cornbread, '96 35
Waffles, Cornbread, '79 265; '91 90; '98 42; '03 205
Waffles, Cornmeal, '85 201
Wampus Bread, '81 305; '82 36
CORNISH HENS
  à l'Orange, Cornish Hens, '95 325
  Barley-Mushroom Stuffing, Cornish Hens with, '97 242
  Brandied Cornish Hens, '81 259
  Brown Rice, Cornish Hens with, '82 275
  Buttered Cornish Hens, Brandy-, '79 292; '80 32
  Cajun-Fried Cornish Hens, '95 326
  Casserole, Cornish Hens-and-Rice, '92 267
  Chutney-Mustard Glaze, Game Hens with, '93 66
  Company Cornish Hens, '83 263
  Cranberry Cornish Hens, '86 303
  Cranberry-Orange Sauce, Cornish Hens with, '86 119
  Cranberry Sauce, Cornish Hens with, '79 180
  Elegant Cornish Hens, '80 227; '81 52
  Flambé, Cornish Hens, '80 227; '81 52
  Fruited Stuffing, Cornish Hens with, '90 191
  Glazed Cornish Hens, Apricot-, '80 84; '87 306
  Glazed Cornish Hens, Asian, '00 111
  Glazed Cornish Hens, Jelly-, '89 193; '93 251
  Glazed Cornish Hens, Orange-, '83 267; '99 293; '00 292
  Glazed Stuffed Cornish Hens, Orange-, '84 M89
  Grilled Cornish Hens, '88 243; '92 59
  Grilled Cornish Hens, Asian, '99 41
  Grilled Cornish Hens, Orange-Glazed, '86 250
  Grilled Cornish Hens with Tropical Fruit, '97 310
  Herbed Cornish Hens, '82 271
  Marinated Cornish Hens, Sherry-, '91 148
  Mesquite-Smoked Cornish Hens, '92 144
  Orange-Ginger Hens with Cranberry Salsa, '98 321
  Orange Glaze, Cornish Hens with, '79 244
  Pecan-Cornbread Stuffing, Cornish Hens with Spicy, '01 206
  Port and Sour Cream, Cornish Hens in, '86 323
  Roast Cornish Hens, '86 89
  Roasted Cornish Hens, Herb-, '88 29
  Roasted Cornish Hens, Lemon, '82 260
  Roasted Cornish Hens with Vegetables, Tarragon, '94 79
  Roasted Rock Cornish Hens, '82 66
  Smoked Cornish Hens, '86 142, 154; '88 168
  Stuffed Cornish Hens, '85 261
  Stuffed Cornish Hens, Apricot-, '84 6
  Stuffed Cornish Hens, Cranberry-Cornbread, '95 325
  Stuffed Cornish Hens, Rice-, '82 302
  Tarragon, Cornish Hens, '95 326
  Tarragon, Cornish Hens with, '83 143
  Teriyaki Cornish Hens, '86 198
  Texas-Style Game Hens, '87 61
  Vermouth, Cornish Hens in, '86 33
  Wild Rice Stuffing, Cornish Hens with, '79 222; '80 64; '82 136
COUSCOUS
  Chicken, Moroccan Garlic, '99 15
  Chicken with Couscous, '97 325
  Currants, Pine Nuts, and Pork, Couscous with, '00 295
  Fruit, Couscous with Mixed, '95 232
  Lemon Couscous, '96 154; '00 99; '02 237
  Orange-Ginger Couscous, '00 295
  Peas and Feta, Couscous with, '01 158
  Raisins, Almonds, and Lemon, Couscous with, '00 295
  Red Beans and Couscous, '99 22
  Roasted Asparagus-and-Hazelnut Couscous, '04 60
  Salad, Basil-and-Tomato Couscous, '94 175
  Salad, Couscous-and-Garbanzo, '02 65
  Salad, Curried Couscous, '91 44
  Salad, Mediterranean Couscous, '03 127
  Salad, Shrimp-and-Couscous, '96 157
  Salad with Dried Tomato Vinaigrette, Couscous, '96 244
  Salad with Fennel and Goat Cheese, Israeli Couscous, '00 312
  Shrimp, Hot Red Curry, '02 125
  Spinach-and-Onion Couscous, '98 23
  Tabbouleh Couscous, '96 251; '97 103; '02 200
  Tabbouleh Salad, '91 70
  Vegetables and Couscous, '96 136
  Vegetables with Couscous, Curried, '04 328
CRAB
  Appetizers
    Balls, Crabmeat, '88 150
    Ball, Spicy Crab, '01 332
    Bites, Crabmeat, '97 98
    Bites, Crab-Zucchini, '84 M216
    Bites, Spicy Crab, '91 165
    Broiled Crab Meltaways, '93 287
    Cakes and Dijon Sauce, Mini Crab, '03 92
    Cakes, Crab, '01 245
    Cakes, Crab-and-Scallop, '02 165
    Cakes, Miniature Crab, '96 306
    Cakes with Cress Sauce, Baked Crab, '96 176
    Cakes with Jalapeño Tartar Sauce, Chesapeake Bay Crab, '96 69
    Cakes with Maui Sauce, Crab, '99 310
    Canapés, Cheesy Crab, '86 262
    Canapés, Crab, '93 130
    Canapés, Crabmeat, '88 150
    Canapés, Hot Crab, '86 70; '87 239
    Chafing Dish Crabmeat, '89 284
    Cherry Tomatoes, Crab-Stuffed, '82 289; '88 78
    Cocktail Puffs, '91 106
    Cocktail, Sherried Avocado-Crabmeat, '87 95
    Deviled Crab, Devilish, '85 264
    Dip, Cheese-Crab, '91 200
    Dip, Creamy Crab, '80 M135
    Dip, Festive Crab, '92 285
    Dip, Hot Cheese and Crab, '81 261
    Dip, Hot Crab, '93 269; '97 89
    Dip, Hot Crab-and-Cheese, '94 282
    Dip, Hot Crabmeat, '95 154
    Dip, Oven-Baked Crab, '82 59
    Dip, Tangy Crab, '83 5
    Dip, Trawler Crab, '93 238
    Hors d'Oeuvre, Crabmeat, '94 236
    Imperial, Crab, '02 103
    Mold, Crab, '85 318
    Mousse, Crab, '79 117; '95 327
    Mousse, Crabmeat, '90 190; '91 244; '94 159
    Mushroom Caps, Crab-Stuffed, '84 160
    Mushrooms, Crab-Stuffed, '81 190; '97 102
    Mushrooms Stuffed with Crab, '82 249

CRAB, Appetizers
(continued)

Oysters, Crabmeat Stuffed, '94 328
Pâté, Crab, '79 233
Pot Stickers, Hoisin Crab, '96 92
Puffs, Crab, '80 20; '84 269
Puffs, Crabmeat, '99 335
Salsa with Sesame Wontons, Spicy Crab-and-
    Ginger, '01 283
Sandwiches, Miniature Crab Cake, '96 306
Snacks, Crab, '83 93
Snow Peas, Crab-Stuffed, '85 288
Spread, Baked Crab, '80 86
Spread, Best-Ever Crab, '98 60
Spread, Crab, '93 167
Spread, Crabmeat-Horseradish, '90 292
Spread, Crab Soufflé, '85 4
Spread, Hot Artichoke-Crab, '85 81
Spread, Layered Crabmeat, '83 127; '04 69
Spread, Superb Crab, '81 235
Topping, Crabmeat, '91 64
au Gratin, Crabmeat, '86 154
au Gratin, Crab, Shrimp, and Artichoke, '90 240
Baked Avocado-and-Crabmeat, '84 119
Bake, Easy Crab, '95 209
Bake, Quick Crab, '87 192
Benedict, Crab, '92 63
Benedict, Lion, '93 121
Blue Crabs, Festive, '85 103
Blue Crabs, Spicy Steamed, '84 162
Blue Crabs, Steamed, '89 195; '02 141
Bow Ties with Crab and Vegetables, '98 233
Broiled Crab and Avocado, '79 116
Brunch Scramble, Crabmeat, '95 32
Burgers, Crab, '00 58
Burgers, Potato-Crusted Crab, '94 139
Cakes, Baltimore Crab, '92 117
Cakes, Chesapeake Bay Crab, '89 194; '95 155
Cakes, Country Crab, '95 20
Cakes, Crab, '81 125; '90 71; '91 122; '98 140, 222;
    '99 267
Cakes, Crispy Fried Crab, '80 119
Cakes, Down-East Crab, '79 151
Cakes, Faidley's Crab, '01 97
Cakes, Gulf Coast Crab, '94 71
Cakes, Mock Crab, '95 159
Cakes Our Way, Crab, '01 145
Cakes, Victoria Crab, '92 195
Cakes, Virginia Jumbo Lump Crab, '97 180
Cakes with Collard Greens and Roasted-Garlic
    Beurre Blanc, Down-South Crab, '03 324
Cakes with Sweet White Corn-and-Tomato Relish,
    Crab, '00 130
Cakes with Tomato Cream, Crab, '94 70
Casserole, Crab, '79 228
Casserole, Crab-and-Mushroom, '89 96
Casserole, Crab-and-Shrimp, '84 71
Casserole, Crab-Egg, '80 260
Casserole, Crabmeat-Broccoli, '84 232
Casserole, Creamy Crab and Spinach, '80 3
Casserole, Deviled Crab, '91 238; '92 27
Casserole, Easy Crab, '93 270
Chicken, Crab-Stuffed, '84 101
Cornbread, Crab with Chile, '86 254
Creamed Crabmeat with Artichoke Hearts, '93 26
Crêpes, Crab, '79 165
Crêpes, Sautéed Crab, '84 84
Crisps, Crab, '79 63
Delight, Crab-and-Egg, '84 261
Deviled Crab, '85 104; '92 117
Dressed Crab, '82 276
Dressing, Crabmeat-and-Oyster, '02 243

Eggs New Orleans, Crabmeat and, '82 45
Eggs, Shrimp and Crab Scrambled, '79 261
Eggs Stuffed with Crabmeat, '04 18
Étouffée, Crab-and-Shrimp, '89 96
Fettuccine, Crab, '98 142
Filling, Crab, '89 13
Flounder, Crab-Stuffed, '80 120
Fresh Crab, Preparing, '82 127
Fried Soft-Shell Crabs, '95 154
Fritters, Corn-and-Crab, '97 227
Fritters, Crab, '98 142
Gravy, Tomato-and-Crabmeat Cream, '04 165
Gumbo, Shrimp-Crab, '03 111
Hash with Three-Pepper Hollandaise, Lump Crab,
    '96 52
Imperial, Crab, '79 82, 116; '89 194; '95 155;
    '96 148
Imperial, Crabmeat, '82 311; '83 72
Imperial, Easy Crab, '93 128
Imperial, Elegant Crab, '83 245
Imperial, Pineapple-Crab, '84 M286
Imperial, Speedy Crabmeat, '90 M112
Karen, Crabmeat, '93 49
Lasagna, Crabmeat, '96 290
Lasagna, Crabmeat-and-Spinach, '04 292
Lobster Tails, Crab-Stuffed, '95 326
Marinière, Mashed Potatoes with Crab, '99 165
Melts, Open-Faced Crab, '01 171
Meunière, Soft-Shell Crab, '80 57
Mold, Cream Cheese-Crabmeat, '90 71
Mushrooms on Toast Points, Crabmeat and,
    '82 M91
Oysters and Crabmeat, Creamy, '83 211
Poblanos with Mango Salsa, Crab-and-Goat Cheese,
    '04 59
Polenta, Crab, '00 277
Potatoes, Cheesy Crab-Stuffed, '86 17
Potatoes, Crabmeat-Topped, '83 3; '95 22
Potatoes, Crab-Stuffed, '91 311; '92 26; '99 307
Puff, Crab, '79 116
Puff, Shrimp-Crab, '79 57
Quesadillas with Mango Salsa, Beefy Crab, '00 124
Quiche, Almond-Topped Crab, '79 127
Quiche, Crab, '82 M122, 243
Quiche, Crabmeat-Parmesan, '03 59
Quiche, Quick Crab, '84 96
Quiche, Sherried Crab, '83 180
Quiche, Simple Crab, '85 207
Ravigote, Crabmeat, '82 250; '92 329
Redfish with Shrimp and Crab, Coastal Bend,
    '01 281
Relish, Crabmeat, '99 198
Salads
    Asparagus Salad, Crab-and-, '92 141
    Avocado Salad, Crab-, '81 114
    Avocados, Crab-Stuffed, '86 73
    Avocado with Crabmeat, '86 119
    Blue Crab Salad with Asian Vinaigrette, '98 142
    Cakes with Greens and Dijon Dressing, Crab,
        '96 176
    Caribbean Crabmeat Salad with Creamy
        Gingered Dressing, '97 263
    Chesapeake Crab Salad, '89 195
    Congealed Salad with Crabmeat-and-Asparagus,
        '84 86
    Crabmeat Salad, '91 169
    Cucumber-and-Crab Salad, '98 208
    Delightful Crab Salad, '87 145
    Louis, Crab, '95 94
    Luncheon Salad, Crab, '00 17
    Luncheon Salad, Crabmeat, '82 207
    Macaroni-Crabmeat Salad, '81 153
    Marinated Crab-and-Endive Salad, '93 22
    Rémoulade, Crabmeat, '93 280

    Shrimp Pasta Salad, Crabmeat-, '86 208
    Tomato Salad, Crab-Stuffed, '80 148
    Wild Rice Salad, Crab-, '86 207
    Wild Rice Salad, Crab and, '79 116
Sandwiches, Avocado-Crabmeat, '83 2
Sandwiches, Crab Cake, '02 60
Sandwiches, Crabmeat, '84 285
Sandwiches, Deluxe Crabmeat, '81 M74
Sandwiches, Hot Crab-and-Cheese, '87 279
Sandwiches, Mango-Crab Salad, '99 72
Sandwiches, Open-Face Crab Tomato, '81 29
Sandwiches, Open-Faced Crab, '87 106
Sandwiches, Puffy Crab, '83 291
Sauce Piquante, Crab and Shrimp, '83 92
Sauce, Quick Crab Marinara, '85 M151
Sauce, Stone Crab Mustard, '80 3
Sauce, Tangy Stone Crab, '80 3
Sautéed Crabmeat, Roussos, '84 88
Shrimp Bundles, Crab-Stuffed, '81 176
Shrimp, Crab-Stuffed, '84 259
Soft-Shell Crabs, Chesapeake, '89 194
Soft-Shell Crabs, Fried Stuffed, '98 140
Soups
    Beaufort Crab Soup, '92 238
    Bisque, Crab, '88 251
    Bisque, Crab-and-Corn, '87 137
    Bisque, Crab-and-Leek, '94 104
    Bisque, Crab-and-Spinach, '97 241
    Bisque, Stone Crab, '96 86
    Chowder, Maryland Crab, '97 23
    Corn-and-Crab Soup, Fresh, '92 183
    Corn Soup with Crab, Sweet, '02 159
    Crabmeat Soup, '84 123
    Cream of Crab Soup, '88 302
    Cream of Crab Soup, Steamboat's, '81 127
    Creamy Crab Soup, '80 M224
    Elegant Crab Soup, '80 188
    Gazpacho, Crab, '97 181
    Gumbo, Crab and Shrimp, '81 200
    Gumbo, Shrimp-Crab, '98 15
    Gumbo with Whole Crabs, Seafood, '85 2
    Old-Fashioned Crab Soup, '90 71
    Plantation Crab Soup, '92 237
    Quick Crab Soup, '84 279
    She-Crab Soup, '03 137
    She-Crab Soup with Marigold, '79 32
Spread, Crabmeat, '79 81
Stroganoff, Crab, '79 116
Strudel, Crab-and-Mushroom, '98 28
Stuffed Soft-Shell Crabs, '83 91
Stuffed Soft-Shell Crabs, Steamboat's, '81 127
Stuffing, Chicken Breasts with Crabmeat, '85 302
Stuffing, Crabmeat, '94 68
Stuffing, Tropical Orange Roughy with Crab,
    '99 122
Supreme, Crab, '79 181
Tomatoes, Crab-and-Avocado Stuffed, '94 141
Tostadas, Crab, '93 203
Veal with Crabmeat, New Orleans, '86 94
CRACKERS
Bacon-Wrapped Crackers, '93 280
Bisque Crackers, Easy, '83 252
Blue Cheese Crisps, '96 106
Bone Crackers, '01 204
Bread, Sesame Cracker, '87 2
Cheddar Crackers, '84 236
Cheese Cracker Nibbles, '84 328
Cheese Crisps, Peppered, '98 107
Cranberry Crackers, '99 258
Critter Crackers, '93 193
Dessert Crackers, '87 3
Fennel-Rye Crackers, '87 2
Florida Crackers, '86 179
Hot Nut Crackers, '90 206

Hush Puppies, Cracker, '80 99
Oatmeal-Wheat Germ Crackers, '84 236
Olive-Rye Snack Crackers, '84 191
Pie, Cracker, '79 113
Snack Crackers, '00 133
Snackers, Cracker, '86 229; '93 197
Soup Nuts, '96 106
Tortilla-Lime Crackers, '99 17
Vegetable Crackers, '96 105

CRANBERRIES
Acorn Squash, Cranberry-Filled, '81 M231
Ambrosia, Glazed Cranberry, '00 269
Beverages
  Apple-Berry Sparkler, '93 104
  Apple Berry Sparkler, '94 100
  Beach Brew, '91 177
  Cabernet Cranberries, '00 327
  Cider, Mulled Cranberry, '99 278
  Cider, Spiced Cranberry, '84 261; '98 278
  Cobbler, Cran-Blueberry, '04 28
  Cocktail, Orange-Cranberry, '01 103
  Cocktails, Sea Breeze, '97 161
  Cooler, Cranberry, '86 229; '01 93
  Cooler, Cranberry Tea, '01 322
  Cubes, Cranberry, '95 201
  Daiquiris, Cranberry, '81 245
  Fizz, Cranberry-Ginger, '99 93
  Float, Sparkling Cranberry, '86 195
  Frappé, Cranberry, '82 263
  Juice, Sparkling Cranberry, '88 275
  Lemonade, Spiced Cranberry, '87 292
  Mulled Cranberry Drink, '92 12; '03 36
  New Orleans, Mr. Funk of, '95 57
  Punch, Cranberry, '83 275; '85 90; '99 290
  Punch, Cranberry-Cherry, '91 176
  Punch, Cranberry-Cinnamon, '86 270
  Punch, Cranberry Percolator, '88 248
  Punch, Cranberry-Pineapple, '00 284
  Punch, Cranberry-Wine, '01 242
  Punch, Cran-Grape-Tea, '92 209
  Punch, Holiday Cranberry, '85 265
  Punch, Hot Cranberry, '80 288; '84 41, 319;
    '85 265
  Punch, Hot Spiced, '80 250
  Punch, Pink Lady, '81 100
  Punch, Sparkling Cranberry, '85 277; '95 101
  Punch, Spiced Cranberry, '89 290
  Punch, Tart Cranberry, '83 318
  Raspberry Drink, Cranberry-, '97 154
  Red Roosters, '87 147
  Refresher, Cranberry-Vodka, '91 210
  Sangría, Cranberry, '95 238
  Shake, Cranberry, '83 171
  Shimmer, Cranberry, '98 168
  Slush, Cranberry-Rum, '84 259
  Smoothie, Cranberry, '86 183; '91 307
  Soda, Cranberry-Orange, '79 148
  Spritzer, Cranberry, '91 66; '92 265
  Spritzers, Cranberry, '89 213
  Tea, Cranberry, '94 131; '97 121, 160; '04 63
  Tea, Cranberry-Apple, '88 169
  Tea, Holiday Cranberry, '03 233
  Tea, Mulled Cranberry, '01 240
  Tea, Pink Sangría, '95 200
  Wassail, Cranberry, '88 289
  Wine Cup, Cranberry, '85 23
Biscuits, Cranberry-Orange-Glazed, '04 280
Brandied Cranberries, '86 269; '95 306
Bread, Cranberry, '79 242
Bread, Cranberry-Banana, '80 281; '90 294
Bread, Cranberry Fruit-Nut, '79 275
Bread, Cranberry-Orange, '87 244
Bread, Cranberry-Orange Nut, '80 288
Bread, Orange-Cranberry, '85 266

Bread, Raisin-Cranberry, '81 305; '82 36
Brie, Warmed Cranberry, '01 245
Butter, Cranberry, '97 307
Casserole, Cranberry-Apple, '83 311
Casserole, Sweet Potatoes-and-Berries, '84 231
Cheese Box, Cranberry-, '03 238
Chicken, Barbecued Cranberry, '83 178
Chicken Kiev, Cranberry, '87 250
Chicken, Oven-Barbecued Cranberry, '93 332
Chunks of Snow, '02 298
Chutney, Cranberry, '80 243; '83 260; '84 265;
    '96 275; '98 276, 318
Chutney, Cranberry-and-Apricot, '02 286
Chutney, Cranberry-Ginger, '00 253
Chutney, Cranberry-Orange, '79 292
Chutney, Green Tomato-Cranberry, '00 140
Chutney, Hot-and-Spicy Cranberry-Pear, '00 255
Chutney Melt, Brie-and-Cranberry, '98 M318
Chutney, Orange-Cranberry, '86 266
Chutney, Texas Cranberry, '04 257
Chutney with Cream Cheese, Cranberry-Amaretto,
    '87 244
Cocktail, Hot Cranberry, '89 310
Coffee Cake, Cranberry, '81 14; '90 159
Coffee Cake, Cranberry-Coconut, '93 332
Coffee Cake, Cranberry Crunch, '97 231
Coffee Cake, Cranberry-Nut, '81 250
Coffee Cake, Cranberry-Orange, '82 283
Compote, Pear-Cranberry, '02 196
Conserve, Apple-Cranberry, '82 308
Conserve, Caramelized Chicken with Cranberry,
    '98 320
Conserve, Cranberry, '79 243; '83 279; '85 266;
    '03 278
Conserve, Cranberry-Coriander, '04 287
Cornish Hens, Cranberry, '86 303
Cornish Hens, Cranberry-Cornbread Stuffed,
    '95 325
Crackers, Cranberry, '99 258
Cream, Cranberry, '90 66
Croissant, Turkey-Cranberry, '96 320
Desserts
  Apple Dessert, Cranberry, '80 253
  Apples, Cranberry, '99 246
  Bake, Hot Cranberry, '91 250
  Bars, Cranberry-Caramel, '98 277
  Bars, Cranberry-Cinnamon Granola, '03 26
  Bread Pudding, Stuffed Pumpkin with Cranberry-
    Raisin, '02 231
  Cake, Cranberry-Ambrosia, '01 271
  Cake, Cranberry Upside-Down, '87 8
  Cake, Orange-Cranberry, '85 314
  Cloud, Cranberry, '90 287
  Cobbler, Cranberry, '81 275
  Cobbler, Cranberry-and-Apple, '84 306; '90 294
  Cobbler, Cranberry-Peach, '92 322
  Cobbler, Cran-Blueberry, '04 28
  Cobbler, Easy Cranberry, '86 260
  Cobbler Roll, Cranberry, '80 288; '81 248
  Cobbler with Cinnamon Biscuits, Cranberry-
    Apple, '99 256
  Compote, Apple-Cranberry, '04 237
  Compote, Berry, '81 275
  Compote, Cranberry, '97 264
  Cookies, Cran-bear-y Bread, '02 254
  Cookies, Cranberry-Almond, '98 26
  Crêpes, Cranberry, '85 262
  Crisp, Cranberry-Pear, '83 207; '97 16
  Crunch, Apple-Cranberry, '86 300; '87 178
  Crusts, Cranberry-Pecan, '02 198
  Dumplings, Apple-Cranberry, '00 16
  Filling, Cranberry-Ambrosia, '01 271
  Filling, Cranberry-Pecan, '04 305
  Filling, Nutty Cranberry, '00 M306

Glaze, Cranberry, '84 306
Ice, Cranberry-Apple, '82 290
Ice, Tangy Cranberry, '87 305
Ice, Tart Cranberry-Orange, '86 317
Jubilee, Cranberries, '85 312; '90 293
Jubilee, Tasty Cranberry, '84 305; '85 189
Mousse, Cran-Apple, '93 255
Orange Surprise, Cran-, '94 143
Pie, Apple-Cranberry, '97 276; '99 M269
Pie, Autumn Apple, '79 205
Pie, Berry-Apple, '88 251
Pie, Cran-Apple, '92 304
Pie, Cranberry-Apple, '79 264
Pie, Cranberry-Apple Holiday, '81 M269
Pie, Cranberry-Apple-Raisin, '98 270
Pie, Cranberry-Pecan, '92 316
Pie, Cranberry-Raisin, '80 283; '85 316
Pie, Cranberry Streusel, '98 258
Pie, Cran-Raspberry, '87 244
Pie, Festive Cranberry Freezer, '84 306
Pie, Frosty Cranberry, '79 249
Pie, Nutty Cranberry, '82 M298
Pie, Peach-Cranberry, '83 249
Pies, Honeyed Apple-Cranberry Fried, '02 214
Pie, Tart Cranberry-Cherry, '87 299
Pie, Walnut-Cranberry, '87 259
Pizzas, Cranberry Dessert, '96 320
Pockets, Cranberry, '96 320
Pudding, Cranberry, '84 306
Roulage, Chocolate-Cranberry, '94 313
Rugalach, Cranberry-Pecan, '04 305
Sherbet, Cranberry, '88 280
Sorbet, Cranberry, '82 251
Sorbet, Cranberry Juice, '85 259
Soufflé, Cranberry-Topped Holiday, '84 306
Supreme, Cranberry, '85 280
Surprise Dessert, Cranberry, '79 242
Swirls, Cranberry-Walnut, '00 290
Tart, Cranberry-Apple, '97 M316
Tart, Cranberry-Nut, '84 305
Tartlets, Fresh Cranberry, '87 244
Tart, Rustic Apple-Cranberry, '01 M314
Tarts, Cranberry-Cream Cheese, '80 154
Tarts, Cranberry Holiday, '83 279
Tarts, Cran-Raspberry Meringue, '92 286
Dip, Cranberry Fruit, '89 60
Dip, Cranberry-Horseradish, '85 65
Dipper's Delight, '98 93
Dressing, Cranberry-Orange, '91 287
Dressing, Orange Salad with Honey-Berry, '89 250
Frosted Cranberries, '82 280
Fruit Bake, Cranberry-Mustard, '90 287
Glaze, Chili-Cranberry, '98 320
Glaze, Cranberry, '84 306; '86 171; '88 244
Glaze, Cranberry-Honey, '89 273
Gravy, Baked Hen with Cranberry Pan, '94 308
Ham, Cranberry Broiled, '88 301
Ham, Cranberry Glazed, '81 274
Ham, Cranberry-Orange Glazed, '81 295
Hearts, Cranberry, '93 286
Jam, Christmas, '88 288
Jam, Christmas Brunch, '81 286
Jelly, Cranberry-Wine, '81 290
Ketchup, Christmas, '97 254
Lamb, Cranberry Leg of, '90 52
Loaf, Apricot-Cranberry, '79 235
Loaf, Cranberry-Ham, '82 M77
Mexican Cranberries, '94 273
Muffins, Cranberry, '81 249
Muffins, Cranberry Oat Bran, '89 107
Muffins, Cranberry-Orange, '04 209
Muffins, Cranberry-Pecan, '84 269
Muffins, Cranberry Streusel Cake, '88 M274
Muffins, Miniature Cranberry, '90 294

CRANBERRIES
(continued)

Orange Delight, Cranberry-, '90 168
Oranges, Brandied Cranberry, '98 309
Popcorn, Trick or Treat, '03 210
Pork Chops, Cranberry, '80 288; '90 53
Pork Chops, Orange-Cranberry, '86 335; '87 84
Pork, Cranberry, '90 293
Pork Loin, Cranberry-Glazed, '04 251
Pork Roast, Berry Barbecued, '80 288
Relish, Cran-Apple, '84 300
Relish, Cranberry, '81 275; '83 144; '85 258, 264;
   '86 283; '87 245; '91 257; '92 341; '95 318;
   '98 310; '02 276
Relish, Cranberry-Black Bean, '03 243
Relish, Cranberry-Nut, '86 275
Relish, Cranberry-Orange, '81 M289; '88 254;
   '99 15
Relish, Cranberry-Pear, '85 232
Relish, Frozen Cranberry, '95 302
Relish, Holiday Cranberry, '88 304
Relish, Lemony Cranberry, '79 243
Relish, Old-Fashioned Cranberry, '82 297
Relish, Tipsy Cranberry, '92 M310
Ring, Cranberry, '90 291
Rolls, Cranberry, '00 244
Rolls, Cranberry-Pineapple, '86 275
Salads
   Apple Salad, Cranberry-, '02 255
   Bing Cherry-and-Cranberry Salad, '04 297
   Cheese Ribbon Salad, Cranberry-, '79 241
   Christmas Salad, Cranberry, '79 243
   Congealed Cranberry Salad, '90 124
   Congealed Salad, Cranberry, '91 296; '02 292
   Congealed Salad, Lemon-Cranberry, '87 311
   Congealed Salad Parfaits, Frosted Cranberry,
      '02 292
   Cranberry Salad, '88 250; '99 290
   Cup, Berry Grapefruit, '79 242
   Festive Cranberry Salad, '81 264, 296
   Frosted Cranberry Salad, '90 288
   Frozen Cranberry-Pineapple Salad, '91 237
   Green Salad, Cranberry-Topped, '87 311
   Holiday Cranberry Salad, '82 266, 288; '95 301
   Holiday Jewel Salad, '81 252
   Holiday Salad, Cranberry, '89 277
   Jellied Cranberry Salad, '83 279; '85 281
   Layered Cranberry Salad, '84 322; '86 325
   Mold, Cranberry, '79 250
   Mold, Cranberry-Apple, '89 277
   Mold, Cranberry Gelatin, '92 271
   Oriental, Cranberry, '79 126
   Pear-and-Cranberry Wild Rice Salad, '03 199
   Ring, Cranberry Salad, '80 247
   Ring, Spicy Peach-Cranberry, '85 264
   Spinach-and-Cranberry Salad with Warm
      Chutney Dressing, '02 242
   Strawberry-Jícama Salad, Cranberry-, '02 300
   Tart Cranberry Salad, '79 286
   Whipped Cream Salad, Cranberry-, '83 261
   Wild Rice-and-Cranberry Salad, '99 272
Sauces
   Apple Sauce, Cranberry-, '92 203
   Apricot Sauce, Fresh Cranberry-, '87 243
   Baked Cranberry Sauce, '88 257
   Cranberry Sauce, '86 278; '88 280; '92 269
   Double Cranberry-Apple Sauce, '03 231
   Dried Cranberry Sauce, Pork Medaillons with
      Port Wine and, '95 330
   Fresh Cranberry Sauce, '79 283; '84 275;
      '04 271
   Holiday Cranberry Sauce, '02 M311

Jalapeño-Cranberry Sauce, '92 310
Jezebel Sauce, Cranberry, '03 250
Juice Sauce, Cranberry, '85 224; '86 83
Orange Sauce, Cornish Hens with Cranberry-,
   '86 119
Raisin Sauce, Baked Ham with Cranberry-,
   '88 244
Salsa, Cranberry, '98 321; '99 316; '00 269;
   '01 254
Salsa, Cranberry-Citrus, '97 290
Salsa, Cranberry-Jalapeño, '01 234
Salsa, Grilled Turkey Breast with Cranberry,
   '95 252
Salsa with Sweet Potato Chips, Cranberry,
   '93 332
Spiced Cranberry Sauce, '96 267
Tart Cranberry Sauce, '83 261
Wine Sauce, Cranberry, '83 276
Scones, Cranberry, '95 283
Scones, Cranberry-Orange, '97 45
Scones, Merry Cranberry-Nut Yeast, '99 274
Spiced Cranberries, '82 254, 287
Spread, Coconut-Cranberry Cheese, '92 328
Spread, Cranberry Ambrosia-Cream Cheese,
   '00 308
Spread, Cranberry-Butter, '99 86
Stuffing, Cranberry, '04 246
Stuffing, Cranberry-Orange-Pecan, '01 249
Stuffing, Cranberry-Pecan, '96 309
Stuffing, Crown Roast of Pork with Cranberry-
   Sausage, '88 49
Sugared Cranberries, '04 279
Triangles, Cranberry-Nut, '04 273
Turkey Loaf, Cranberry-Glazed, '86 171
Vinaigrette, Cranberry, '98 321
Vinegar, Cranberry, '91 288
Wild Rice, Cranberry-Almond, '04 204
Wild Rice, Cranberry-Pear, '83 279
Wraps, Chicken-Cranberry, '01 34
CRAWFISH
   Boil, Crawfish, '01 95
   Borscht, Crawfish, '92 84
   Cakes with Cilantro-Lime Cream, Crawfish, '98 129
   Casserole, Crawfish Pasta, '97 106
   Delicacy, Crawfish, '99 M23
   Dressing, Crawfish-Cornbread, '99 257
   Dressing, Louisiana Crawfish, '90 103
   Dressing, Pecan, Rice, and Crawfish, '00 252
   Étouffée, Crawfish, '83 91; '86 156; '90 103;
      '94 239; '02 85
   Fettuccine, Crawfish, '96 98
   Fettuccine, Crawfish and Tasso, '96 290
   Lasagna, Crawfish, '91 89
   Mushrooms, Crawfish-Stuffed, '86 258
   Pasta, Creamy Crawfish, '03 277
   Risotto, Crawfish, '99 120
   Salad, Dilled Crawfish, '83 126
   Soft-Shell Crawfish on Eggplant, '88 222
   Spaghetti, Crawfish, '85 104
   Stroganoff, Crawfish, '91 89
   Trout Stuffed with Crawfish, Bacon-Wrapped,
      '99 54
CRÈME BRÛLÉE. *See* **CUSTARDS.**
CRÈME FRAÎCHE
   Crème Fraîche, '85 39; '91 99; '01 275; '02 312
   Sauce, Crème Fraîche, '79 281; '93 135
CRÊPES
   Apple Breakfast Crêpes, '97 331
   Basic Crêpes, '84 83; '86 38; '04 245
   Beef Crêpes, Sherried, '85 M29
   Beef Roulades, '80 80
   Beggar's Purses with Smoked Salmon, '04 244
   Blintzes, Cheese, '92 84
   Blue-Corn Crêpes, '97 197

Blue-Corn Crêpes with Beef Filling, '97 197
Bran Crêpes, '83 70; '86 44
Breakfast Crêpes, Country-Style, '79 22
Brunch Crêpes, Nutritious, '80 44
Brunch Crêpes, Royal, '81 44
Cannelloni Crêpes, '86 143
Cheese and Mushroom Crêpes, '81 88
Cheese Blintzes, '82 146; '83 71
Cheesy Party Wedges, '84 84
Chicken Crêpes, '80 39
Chicken Crêpes, Creamy, '81 200
Chicken-Vegetable Crêpes, '83 70
con Queso, Crêpes, '96 48
Coquilles St. Jacques Crêpes, '83 13
Cornbread Crêpes, '98 42
Cornbread Crêpes, Goat Cheese-Filled, '98 43
Cornbread Crêpes, Southwestern, '98 42
Cornmeal Sombreros, '93 277
Crab Crêpes, '79 165
Crab Crêpes, Sautéed, '84 84
Crêpes, '82 38, 46, 146, 240; '83 13, 71, 122, 127,
   205, 282; '84 186; '86 216; '87 126; '88 295;
   '89 44; '90 157; '91 24; '92 41, 88; '93 123;
   '94 116; '96 191; '97 332; '98 266; '99 25,
   166; '00 310
Cups, Florentine Crêpe, '89 44
Desserts
   Amandine, Crêpes Gelée, '83 126
   Amaretto-and-Orange Crêpes, '86 260
   Banana Crêpes Flambé, '84 262
   Basic Dessert Crêpes, '82 183; '85 262; '86 275
   Cheese Blintzes, '82 146
   Cherry Crêpes, '91 67
   Cherry Crêpes Flambé, '79 18
   Chocolate Chantilly Crêpes, '82 183
   Chocolate Crêpes, '86 164
   Chocolate Crêpes, Fruit-Filled, '89 325
   Chocolate Dessert Crêpes, '84 84; '85 262
   Chocolate Dream Crêpes, '86 164
   Chocolate-Orange Crêpes, '85 263
   Coffee Ice Cream Crêpes, '84 85
   Cranberry Crêpes, '85 262
   Dessert Crêpes, '84 84; '86 260; '87 290; '88 134
   Dixie Dessert Crêpes, '79 222
   Fruit Crêpes, Tropical, '87 77
   Fruit Filling, Crêpes with, '81 96
   Lemon Crêpes with Fruit Filling, '82 46
   Low-Calorie Crêpes, '87 77
   Mango-Pineapple Crêpes, '86 216
   Orange Dream Crêpes, '82 183
   Peach Crêpes, '82 184
   Peach Crêpes, Fresh, '84 186
   Plain Crêpes, '83 70
   Processor Crêpes, Basic, '87 289; '88 135
   Raspberry Crêpes, '87 126
   Raspberry Crêpes with Yogurt Filling, Fresh,
      '93 123
   Spicy Dessert Crêpes, '84 262
   Strawberry Dessert Crêpes, '83 122
   Strawberry Ice Cream Crêpes, '87 290; '88 135
   Suzette, Raspberry Crêpes, '84 84
   Suzettes, Light Crêpes, '83 71
   Tropical Crêpes, '86 275
   Whole Wheat Crêpes, '83 70
Divan, Elegant Crêpes, '81 91
Eggplant Crêpes with Marinara Sauce, Mini,
   '99 266
Entrée Crêpes, '79 264
Fajita Crêpes, '94 116
Filling, Crêpe, '96 48
Florentine Crêpe Pie, '79 34
Florentine, Crêpes, '80 190
Ham-and-Egg Crêpes, '83 204
Ham-and-Egg Crêpes with Mushroom Sauce, '82 46

Italian Crêpes, '90 157
Light Crêpes, '86 143
Mushroom-Cheese Crêpes, '87 289; '88 135
Plain Crêpes, '83 70
Processor Crêpes, Basic, '87 289; '88 135
Sausage Crêpes, '88 295
Sausage Crêpes, Cheesy, '82 240; '83 71
Sausage-Filled Crêpes, '79 39; '98 266; '99 25
Shellfish Crêpes in Wine-Cheese Sauce, '00 310
Spinach-Ricotta Crêpes, '81 52
Steak Crêpes, Special, '91 24
Turkey Crêpes, '92 41
Turkey Crêpes, Elegant, '83 282
Virginia Crêpes, '79 264
Whole Wheat Crêpes, '80 44; '83 70
Zucchini Crêpes, '79 157
CRISPS. *See* **PIES, PUFFS, AND PASTRIES/**
Cobblers, Crisps, and Crumbles.
CROUTONS
Bagel Croutons, '93 192
Bourbon Croutons, '93 234
Bread Croutons, Hawaiian, '94 107
Bread, Quick Crouton, '90 138
Celery Croutons, '79 16
Cheese Grits Croutons and Vidalia Onion-Balsamic
Vinaigrette, Southern Spinach Salad with,
'04 316
Cinnamon Pound Cake Croutons, '93 161
Cornbread Croutons, '93 192
Cornbread Croutons, Honeyed, '94 106
Creole Croutons, '02 121
Crispy Italian Croutons, '84 126
Crostini, '92 56
Croutes, Croutons and, '93 30
Croutons, '86 M288
Curried Croutons, '00 322
Dilled Croutons, '93 161
Egg Roll Fan, Sesame, '94 107
Fried Okra Croutons, Salad Greens and Veggies
with, '96 178
Garlic Croutons, '92 71
Garlic-Flavored Croutons, '86 47
Goat Cheese-and-Chive Croutons, '01 312
Herb Croutons, '81 150
Microwave Croutons, '86 M227
Parslied Croutons, Carrot-and-Butternut Squash
Soup with, '97 217
Pita Croutons, '93 192; '96 64; '98 329
Prosciutto Croutons, '99 89
Pumpernickel Croutons, '94 62
Seasoned Croutons, '96 326
Spiced Croutons, '00 317
Sweet Croutons, '00 296
Tortilla Triangles, '94 107
Vegetable-Flavored Croutons, '84 148
CRUMBLES. *See* **PIES, PUFFS, AND**
PASTRIES/Cobblers, Crisps, and
Crumbles.
CUCUMBERS
Bisque, Shrimp-Cucumber, '79 172
Canapés, Chicken-Cucumber, '98 154
Canapés, Cucumber, '95 88
Canapés, Shrimp-and-Cucumber, '93 164
Chips, Cucumber, '85 176
Cool Cucumbers, '84 152
Creamy Cucumbers, '92 62
Delights, Cucumber, '84 117
Dills, Lazy Wife, '87 149
Dip, Cucumber-Cheese Vegetable, '83 128
Dip, Cucumber-Yogurt, '99 93
Dip, Refreshing Dill, '99 324
Dressing, Benedictine, '98 83
Dressing, Creamy Cucumber Salad, '82 79
Dressing, Cucumber, '80 74; '90 144

Dressing, Cucumber-Curry, '89 179
Dressing, Cucumber-Mint, '87 153
Dressing, Cucumber-Radish, '00 99
Dressing, Tomato, Onion, and Cucumber in Italian,
'81 83
Fried Cucumber Fingers, '86 146
Gazpacho, '00 118; '02 130
Gazpacho Blanco, '01 177
Gazpacho, Pineapple, '01 85
Gazpacho-Stuffed Endive, '95 287
Gazpacho, White, '97 181
Lemony Cucumbers, '89 102
Marinated Cucumbers and Artichokes, '82 111
Marinated Cucumbers and Squash, '86 146
Marinated Shrimp and Cucumber, '91 166
Pasta, Asian Cucumbers and, '96 177
Pepper Combo, Cucumber-and-, '88 176
Pickled Cucumber Rounds, Easy, '90 143
Pickled Onion and Cucumber, '02 126
Pickles, Cucumber Sandwich, '81 174
Pickles, Dill, '81 174
Pickles, Freezer Cucumber, '99 87
Pickles, Hot-and-Sweet Freezer, '04 160
Pickles, Lime, '96 206
Pickles, Mixed, '81 174
Pickles, Peppery Texas, '04 M161
Pickles, Quick Sweet, '87 149
Pickles, Sour Cucumber, '85 176
Pickles, Sweet Icicle, '85 176
Pico de Gallo, '98 174
Red Snapper Rolls, Cucumber-Stuffed, '83 176
Relish, Cucumber, '85 176; '96 23
Rounds, Cucumber, '88 78
Salads
Almond Salad, Cucumber-, '86 147
Asian Greens, Cucumber, '98 66
Aspic, Shrimp-Cucumber, '83 108
Bean Salad, Cucumber-, '83 81
Congealed Salad, Pineapple-Cucumber, '83 118
Cool Cucumber Salad, '03 165
Cooler, Simple Cucumber, '86 147
Crab Salad, Cucumber-and-, '98 208
Creamy Cucumber Salad, '86 147; '92 97;
'01 56; '02 258
Dilled Cucumber and Tomato Salad, '81 153
Dilled Cucumber on Tomatoes, '84 142
Dilled Cucumber Salad, '82 229; '92 72; '93 65
Grapefruit-Cucumber Salad, '80 100
Marinated Cucumber Salad, '82 111
Marinated Cucumber-Tomato Salad, '02 167
Marinated Tomato-and-Cucumber Salad, '92 216
Mold, Asparagus-Cucumber, '85 252
Mold, Chicken-Cucumber, '80 175
Mold, Creamy Cucumber, '84 164
Mold, Cucumber Salad, '82 111; '83 81, 253
Mold, Lemon-Cucumber, '87 90
Mousse, Cucumber, '79 11; '88 121
Mousse with Dill Sauce, Cucumber, '95 216
Pineapple Salad, Cucumber-, '84 124
Potato Salad with Cucumbers and Tomatoes,
'03 92
Roast Beef Salad, Cucumber-, '89 162
Roasted Red Bell Pepper Dressing, Cucumber
Salad with, '03 28
Scallions, Cukes and, '91 168
Slaw, Creamy Cucumber, '89 49
Sour Cream, Cucumbers in, '79 52; '80 178
Tomato-and-Cucumber Summer Salad, '93 141
Tomato-Cucumber-Onion Salad, '81 239
Tomato-Cucumber Salad, '86 218; '92 199
Tomato-Cucumber Salad with Yogurt-Herb
Dressing, '92 96
Tomato Salad, Cucumber-, '90 144
Tomato Salad, Cucumber-and-, '01 127

Tuna Boats, Cucumber, '83 136
Vinaigrette Oriental, Cucumber-, '85 198;
'86 147
Winter Fruit-and-Cucumber Salad, '02 274
Yogurt-Cucumber Salad, '82 122
Yogurt Salad, Cucumber-, '87 33
Salsa, Cucumber, '95 131
Salsa, Cucumber-Dill, '95 107
Salsa, Cucumber-Radish, '01 187
Salsa, Radish-Cucumber, '04 119
Sandwiches, Cucumber, '88 159; '90 81; '94 14;
'97 99; '00 208
Sandwiches, Cucumber Pinwheel, '85 120
Sandwiches, Cucumber-Salmon-Watercress, '03 111
Sandwiches, Dainty Cucumber, '81 119
Sandwiches, Watercress-Cucumber, '97 108
Sandwiches with Dill, Cucumber-Salmon, '02 131
Sauce, Cucumber, '82 111; '84 M286; '92 41
Sauce, Cucumber-and-Yogurt Dipping, '02 172
Sauce, Cucumber Cream, '92 33
Sauce, Cucumber-Dill, '86 5; '91 62; '92 51
Sauce, Cucumber Dipping, '94 47
Sauce, Cucumber-Yogurt, '03 44
Sauce, Lamb Burgers with Cucumber, '98 102
Sauce, Lemony Cucumber, '89 245
Sauce, London Broil Sandwiches with Yogurt-
Cucumber, '01 162
Sauce, Tomato-Cucumber, '98 45
Sauce, Tuna Steaks with Cucumber, '97 180
Sauce, Tzatziki, '04 108
Sauce, White Bean Spread with Creamy Cucumber,
'00 178
Sauce, Yogurt-Cucumber, '04 216
Sesame Cucumbers, '85 85
Sherbet, Jalapeño-Mint, '98 202
Slices, Cheesy Cucumber, '84 80
Slices, Fresh Cucumber, '86 177
Soup, Chilled Cucumber, '79 144
Soup, Chilled Cucumber-Buttermilk, '95 134
Soup, Cold Cucumber, '79 130; '81 130
Soup, Cold Minted Cucumber, '86 34
Soup, Cold Potato-Cucumber, '88 160
Soup, Cream of Cucumber, '81 98
Soup, Creamy Cucumber, '80 171
Soup, Cucumber-Dill, '01 176
Soup, Cucumber-Yogurt, '82 157; '83 205
Soup, Dilled Cucumber, '90 M167
Soup with Dill Cream, Cucumber, '00 130
Sour Cream, Cucumber and Onion in, '81 69
Sour Cream, Cucumbers and, '93 203
Sour Cream, Cucumbers in, '99 243
Spread, Cucumber, '79 295; '80 31; '93 158
Spread, Cucumber and Cream Cheese, '82 140
Spread, Cucumber-Yogurt, '00 135
Spread, Shrimp-Cucumber, '79 81
Stuffed Cucumbers, '81 237
Tartlets, Smoked Salmon and Cucumber, '95 216
Tomatoes, Cucumber-Stuffed Cherry, '88 262
Topping, Lamb Pockets with Dilled Cucumber,
'87 104
Vichyssoise, Cucumber, '94 90
Vichyssoise with Mint Cream, Cucumber, '98 246
CUPCAKES. *See* **CAKES/Cupcakes.**
CURRY
Almonds, Cauliflower and Peas with Curried,
'79 221
Appetizers
Almonds, Curried, '82 297
Bites, Curried Swiss, '85 220
Cheese Ball, Chicken-Curry, '85 118
Cheese Ball, Curried Shrimp, '86 135
Chicken Balls, Coconut Curried, '91 165
Chicken Balls, Curried, '91 98
Chicken Bites, Curried, '85 40

CURRY, Appetizers
(continued)

　　Chicken Tea Sandwiches, Curried, **'97** 23
　　Dip and Vegetable Platter, Curry, **'89** 327
　　Dip, Curried, **'81** 262
　　Dip, Curry, **'80** 84; **'81** 9; **'85** 132; **'86** 184;
　　　　'87 25; **'99** 138
　　Dip, Curry-Onion, **'93** 313
　　Dip, Tuna-Curry, **'84** 31
　　Hazelnuts, Curried, **'93** 301
　　Nuts, Spicy Curried, **'82** 250
　　Pecans, Curried, **'91** 208
　　Popcorn Mix, Curried, **'86** 326
　　Sandwiches, Curried Tea, **'91** 314
　　Sauce, Curry, **'94** 54
　　Shrimp Balls, Curried, **'94** 180
　　Spread, Broccamoli Curry, **'88** 55
　　Spread, Curried Chutney, **'89** 283
　　Spread, Curried Shrimp, **'87** 158
　　Spread, Curry-Almond Cheese, **'01** 238
　Apples, Curried, **'93** 252
　Apricots, Curried, **'91** 315
　Bananas, Fillets with Horseradish Sauce and
　　　Curried, **'85** 230
　Beef and Rice, Curried, **'88** 164
　Beef Dinner, Curried, **'83** 4
　Beef Pitas, Curried, **'85** 220
　Beef Steak, Curried, **'88** 60
　Beef Stir-Fry, Curried, **'01** 162
　Bisque, Curried Butternut-Shrimp, **'01** 248
　Bread, Honey-Curry, **'89** 250
　Butter, Tomato-Curry-Orange, **'93** 159
　Carrots and Pineapple, Curried, **'90** 228
　Casserole, Curry Pea, **'87** 154
　Casserole, Vegetable-Curry, **'91** 286; **'92** 27
　Cauliflower Bake, Curried, **'01** 49
　Cauliflower, Curried, **'91** 315
　Chicken. *See also* **CURRY/Appetizers, Salads.**
　　Bisque, Curried Chicken, **'00** 144
　　Brioche, Chicken Curry, **'88** 124
　　Cheesecake, Curried Chicken, **'90** 174
　　Chowder, Curried Chicken-and-Corn, **'92** 21
　　Country Captain Chicken, **'94** 252
　　Curried Chicken, **'86** 43
　　Curry, Chicken, **'84** 110; **'85** 220; **'86** 21;
　　　　'89 219
　　Divan, Curried Chicken, **'80** 83
　　Filling, Curried Chicken, **'88** 125
　　Fried Chicken, Curried, **'85** 160
　　Honey-Curry Chicken, **'87** 36
　　Indian-Style Chicken Curry, **'97** 119
　　Mousse, Curried Chicken, **'95** 328
　　Pâté, Curried Chicken, **'00** 106
　　Peppers, Chicken Breasts with Curried, **'90** 227
　　Peppers, Curried Chicken-Stuffed, **'87** 19
　　Quick Curried Chicken, **'89** 219; **'99** 92
　　Regal Curried Chicken, **'84** 110
　　Sauce, Chicken Curry, **'90** 117
　　Skillet Dinner, Curried Chicken, **'95** 47
　　Soup, Curried Chicken, **'86** 34
　　Stir-Fried Chicken Curry, **'87** 51
　　Turban Chicken Curry, **'94** 266
　　Wings, Curried Chicken, **'96** 110
　Chops, Pineapple-Curry Glazed, **'82** 106
　Chowder, Curried Seafood, **'94** 103
　Corn and Celery, Curried, **'86** 192
　Corn and Sweet Red Peppers, Curried, **'95** 47
　Cream, Red Curry-Coconut, **'00** 197
　Croutons, Curried, **'00** 322
　Dressing, Cucumber-Curry, **'89** 179
　Dressing, Curried, **'84** 115; **'00** 217
　Dressing, Curry, **'80** 242; **'82** 78; **'97** 63

Eggs, Curried Deviled, **'93** 87
Eggs, Saucy Shrimp-Curried, **'84** 143
Fish, Curried Baked, **'87** 5
Fish, Curry-Baked, **'91** 196
Fruit, Almond-Curried, **'83** 261
Fruit Bake, Curried, **'87** 241
Fruit, Baked Curried, **'03** 247
Fruit, Hot Curried, **'79** 225; **'81** 264; **'84** 287;
　　'95 72
Fruit Medley, Curried, **'95** 329
Ham and Peaches, Curried, **'82** 60
Ham Steak, Curried, **'82** 120
Ham with Rice, Curried, **'80** 111
Hurry Curry, **'79** 103
Kheema, Indian, **'81** 226
Lamb Curry, Creamy, **'04** 202
Lamb Curry with Rice, **'80** 83; **'81** 10
Lamb with Cucumber-Yogurt Sauce, Curried Leg of,
　　'03 44
Lamb with Rice Mold, Curried, **'85** 36
Mayonnaise, Curry, **'95** 66
Meat Loaf, Curried, **'86** 43
Mushrooms, Curried, **'84** 214
Navy Beans, Curried, **'00** 201
Nuts, Spicy Curried, **'82** 250
Onions, Curried, **'90** 34
Pasta with Apple, Curried, **'02** 68
Peas with Almonds, Curried, **'88** M294
Pecans, Curried, **'91** 208
Pineapple, Curried, **'03** 201
Pork Chops, Curried Apricot, **'89** 191
Pork Tenderloin, Curried, **'86** 76
Rice and Shrimp, Curried, **'83** 231
Rice, Chicken with Curried, **'98** 127
Rice, Curried, **'90** 183; **'97** 51; **'98** 237; **'04** 21
Rice, Curry-Spiced, **'86** M226
Rice Mix, Fruited Curry-, **'86** 326
Rice Mold, Curried, **'85** 36
Rice, Quick Curried, **'86** 81
Rice with Almonds, Curried, **'83** M285
Rice with Curry, Raisin, **'85** 83
Rice with Pineapple, Curried, **'79** 142
Salad Dressing, Curry, **'96** 326
Salads
　Apple-Raisin Salad, Curried, **'80** 24
　Broccoli Salad, Curried, **'86** 225
　Chicken-and-Orange Salad, Curried, **'87** 144
　Chicken-Rice Salad, Curried, **'92** 190
　Chicken Salad, Curried, **'79** 219; **'84** 66; **'85** 96;
　　'86 131; **'89** 176
　Chicken Salad, Royal Curried, **'96** 200
　Chicken Salad Spread, Curried, **'00** 68
　Chicken Salad with Asparagus, Curried, **'81** 36
　Coleslaw, Curried, **'85** 139
　Coleslaw, Curried Pineapple, **'88** 172
　Couscous Salad, Curried, **'91** 44
　Gift, Curried Salad, **'96** 326
　Indian Curry Salad, Hot, **'83** 23
　Melon and Shrimp Curry Salad, **'97** 129
　Pears with Coconut-Chicken Salad, Curried
　　Poached, **'97** 93
　Potato Salad, Curried, **'99** 137
　Rice Salad, Curried, **'80** 84; **'85** 147, 220;
　　'96 240
　Rice Salad, Curry, **'89** 146
　Shrimp Salad, Aloha, **'95** 46
　Shrimp Salad, Curried, **'00** 217
　Spinach Salad, Curry, **'80** 242
　Tuna Salad, Curried, **'86** 208
　Tuna Salad with Grapes, Curried, **'87** 201
　Turkey Salad, Chutney Curried, **'98** 314
　Turkey Salad, Curried, **'88** 140
Sandwiches, Curried BLT, **'93** 158
Sauce, Asparagus with Curry, **'90** 17

Sauce, Curried Rum, **'91** 164
Sauce, Curried Sour Cream, **'90** 174
Sauce, Curry, **'79** 156; **'83** 138; **'84** M71; **'95** 18;
　　'97 170; **'99** 92
Sauce, Curry-Mustard, **'96** 249
Sauce, Halibut with Orange-Curry, **'87** 91
Sauce, Pineapple-Curry, **'79** 252
Sauce, Turkey Slices with Curried Cream, **'91** 60
Seasoning Salt, Gourmet, **'97** 254
Shrimp, Curried, **'84** 110
Shrimp Curry, **'99** 91
Shrimp Curry, Creamy, **'90** 145
Shrimp, Curry-Ginger, **'00** 316
Shrimp Curry, Polynesian, **'89** 23
Shrimp Curry, Sour Cream, **'80** 83
Shrimp Curry, Sour Cream and, **'81** 10
Shrimp, Hot Red Curry, **'02** 125
Shrimp Malai Curry, **'84** 110
Shrimp, Quick Curried, **'84** M198
Snapper, Honey-Curried, **'85** 181
Soup, Cold Curried Pea, **'91** 120
Soup, Cream of Curried Peanut, **'02** 242
Soup, Curried, **'81** 130
Soup, Curried Acorn Squash-and-Apple, **'03** 221
Soup, Curried Carrot, **'82** 157
Soup, Curried Chicken, **'86** 34
Soup, Curried Mushroom, **'84** M89
Soup, Curried Pumpkin, **'96** 242
Soup, Curried Turkey, **'86** 332
Spread, Curried Chicken Salad, **'00** 68
Spread, Curried Shrimp, **'87** 158
Spread, Curried Turkey, **'92** 16
Spread, Curry, **'93** 159
Stir-Fry, Indian, **'92** 126
Tomatoes, Curried Green, **'93** 138
Topping, Curry Salad, **'96** 326
Tuna-Apple Sandwiches, Curried, **'00** 247
Tuna Melts, Curried, **'95** 46
Turkey Pie, Crumb-Crust Curried, **'86** 265
Vegetable Curry, **'99** 91; **'04** 217
Vegetables, Curried, **'89** 219
Vegetables with Couscous, Curried, **'04** 328
Vegetables with Curry, Stir-Fried, **'87** 51
Vinaigrette, Ginger-Curry, **'97** 146
Vinaigrette, Warm Curry, **'93** 107
CUSTARDS. *See also* **MOUSSES, PUDDINGS.**
Acorn Squash, Custard-Filled, **'86** 334
Almond Crème Custard with Raspberries, **'88** 174
Amaretto Custard, Chocolate-Topped, **'87** M37
Amaretto Custard, Range-Top, **'87** 77
Amaretto Custard with Raspberries, **'86** 152
Ambrosia, Custard Sauce, **'84** 256
Baked Custard, **'80** 219
Baked Custard, Creamy, **'86** 7
Baked Custard, Easy, **'85** 52
Baked Vanilla Custard, **'82** 129
Blackberry Custard, **'99** 132
Boiled Christmas Custard, **'95** 329
Boiled Custard, Favorite, **'81** 181
Boiled Custard, Perfect, **'81** 34
Cake, Chocolate Custard, **'88** 175
Cake, Southern Custard Crêpe, **'99** 166
Caramel Custard, **'01** 237
Chocolate Custard, **'88** 258
Citrus Custard with Fresh Fruit, **'93** 70
Coco Loco Custard, **'02** 89
Coconut Cream Custard, **'03** 85
Coconut Custard, **'86** 109; **'97** 131
Corn Custard, Fresh, **'89** 127
Crema, **'80** 175
Crème Brûlée, Almond, **'95** 323
Crème Brûlée, Basic, **'95** 323
Crème Brûlée, Berry, **'95** 323
Crème Brûlée, Black-and-White, **'98** 267; **'02** 62

Crème Brûlée, Chocolate, '95 323
Crème Brûlée, Coffee, '95 323
Crème Brûlée, Double Raspberry, '95 323
Crème Brûlée, Ginger, '95 323
Crème Brûlée, Onion, '95 324
Crème Brûlée, Orange, '95 323
Crème Brûlée, Peppermint, '95 323
Crème Brûlée, Piña Colada, '04 246
Crème Brûlée, Roasted Garlic, '95 324
Crème Brûlée, Roquefort-and-Black Pepper,
    '95 324
Crème Brûlées, Savory, '95 324
Crème Brûlée, Sweet Potato, '02 275
Crème Brûlée, White Chocolate-Macadamia Nut,
    '95 323
Crème Patissière, '84 207
Easy Custard with Nutmeg, '90 316
Filling, Creamy Custard, '81 180
Filling, Custard, '82 52, 298; '85 281
Filling, Egg Custard, '87 14
Flans
    Almendra, Flan, '80 199
    Almond-Orange Flan, '04 241
    Apricot Flan, '99 146
    Baked Flan with Caramel, '92 231
    Blackberry Flan, '79 182
    Caramel-Crowned Flans, '90 227
    Corn-Chive Flan, '94 172
    Corn Flan, '98 246; '99 25
    Cream Cheese Flan, '03 328
    de Leche (Flan with Milk), Flan, '92 169
    de Queso, Flan, '95 303
    Flaming Flan, '85 313
    Flan, '88 247
    Individual Flans, '85 52
    Layered Flan, '89 45
    Luscious Flan, '90 56
    Orange Flan, '84 95
    Pineapple Flan, '01 85
    Pumpkin Flan, '82 217
    Spanish Flan, '85 51, 311
    Sweet Potato Flan, '95 291
Goat Cheese Custard, '96 285
Ice Cream, Vanilla Custard, '96 145; '00 143
Lemon-Buttermilk Custards, '89 49
Lemon Custard in Meringue Cups, '80 295; '81 172
Mexican Custard, Light, '88 149
Napoleon Cream, '84 138
Orange Custard Pudding, '88 174
Peach Custard Dessert, Fresh, '86 162
Pears in Custard, Poached, '88 20
Pie, Apple Custard, '88 236
Pie, Carrot Custard, '79 45
Pie, Coconut Custard, '82 33
Pie, Custard Pecan, '87 184
Pie, Old-Fashioned Egg Custard, '82 261
Pie, Perfect Custard, '82 92
Pie, Quick 'n' Easy Custard, '96 28
Pie, Strawberry Custard, '00 81
Pie, Warm Apple-Buttermilk Custard, '99 98
Preserves, Custard, '98 126
Pumpkin Custard, '88 279
Rice Custard, Baked, '92 308
Sauce, Bourbon Custard, '95 271
Sauce, Buttermilk Custard, '96 183
Sauce, Custard, '85 41; '88 154, 251, 259; '89 291;
    '97 16, 313; '03 244, 318
Sauce, Fresh Berries with Raspberry Custard,
    '88 163
Sauce, Vanilla Custard, '99 27
Spinach-Gorgonzola Custards, Savory, '99 313;
    '02 284
Stirred Custard, '92 45; '99 126
Stirred Custard, Old-Fashioned, '85 52

Stirred Custard over Fruit, '84 83
Stirred Custard, Sherried Gel with, '99 126
Tart, Chocolate Custard, '99 27
Tocino del Cielo, '93 29
Trifle Custard, '03 84
Vanilla Cream, '83 M115
Vanilla Custard, '99 27
Vanilla Custard, Pecan Pie with Chilled, '00 331

Dates
Ball, Date-Nut, '92 326
Bars and Cookies
    Balls, Date, '01 90
    Balls, Date-Nut, '85 10
    Balls, Peanut-Date, '81 92
    Brownies, Date-and-Almond, '88 217
    Chocolate Chip Cookies, Rich Date-Nut, '92 207
    Christmas Date Cookies, '88 287
    Cranberry-Caramel Bars, '98 277
    Date Bars, '84 313; '95 322
    Filled Cookies, Date-, '91 95
    Fruit Cookies, Rolled, '80 15
    Moons, Date, '01 295
    No-Bake Date Bars, '79 256
    Nut Bars, Date-, '80 166
    Nutty Date Bars, '84 153
    Oat Bars, Date-, '80 M172
    Oatmeal-Date Bars, Layered, '85 10
    Oatmeal-Date Cookies, '82 109
    Oatmeal-Date Sandwich Cookies, '83 257
    Pinwheel Cookies, Date, '02 93
    Squares, Date, '90 49
    Walnut-Date Bars, '02 287; '03 272
Breads
    Apple-Date-Nut Ring, '90 212
    Banana Loaves, Tropical Date-, '95 143
    Chocolate Date-Nut Bread, '81 284
    Muffins, Carrot-Date-Nut, '86 262
    Muffins, Date, '79 142
    Muffins, Date-Nut, '84 75; '99 234
    Muffins, Miniature Date, '02 171
    Muffins, Orange-Date, '92 119; '97 243
    Muffins, Surprise Date, '79 216
    Nut Bread, Date-, '85 306
    Nut Loaf, Date-, '85 10
    Persimmon Date-Nut Bread, '82 218
    Walnut Loaf, Blue Ribbon Date-, '80 15
    Whole Wheat Date-Nut Bread, '04 208
    Wine-Date Nut Bread, '82 253
Cake, Bourbon, '98 277
Cake, Date Nut, '79 176; '80 5
Cake, Fresh Apple-Date, '83 300
Cake, Orange-Date, '94 60
Cake, Orange Date-Nut, '01 285
Cake, Pumpkin Date, '79 251
Cake, Queen Bee, '81 237
Cake Roll, Date-Nut, '89 94
Cake Squares, Apple-Date Dream, '85 10
Candy, Date, '89 308
Candy, Date Loaf, '80 302
Cheese, Nutty Date Dessert, '87 299
Chocolate Date-Nut Delight, '88 168
Conserve, Brandied Date, '85 315
Cupcakes, Date, '84 7
Dessert Squares, Date, '89 255
Dressing, Date, '87 57
Filling, Apple-Date, '83 301
Filling, Date, '80 15; '83 257; '86 314
Filling, Date Cream, '81 303
French Toast, Stuffed, '02 105
June Bugs, '85 11
Logs, Date, '79 274
Muffins, Date, '00 239

Pastries, Date-Filled Cheese, '83 259
Pie, Date-Pecan, '80 15
Pie, Dried Fruit, '83 249
Pudding, Steamed Date, '79 86
Relish, Lemon-Date, '96 271
Rice), Basted Dates and Basted Rice (Date-Nut,
    '96 158
Roll, Date Nut, '79 249
Rollups, Date-Cream Cheese, '83 298
Salad, Festive Fruit, '80 16
Sandwich, Date-Nut Lettuce, '94 202
Sauce, Date-Nut Sundae, '82 167
Spread, Apple-Date, '91 231; '92 67
Spread, Breakfast Date, '84 7
Spread, Date-Orange-Nut, '02 59
Spread, Date-Walnut, '87 292
Spread, Date-Walnut-Cheese, '96 322
Stuffed Date Drops, '97 247
Stuffed Dates, Apricot-, '80 250
DESSERT OF THE MONTH
Bananas, Caramelized, '99 49
Beverage Sipper, Kahlúa, '99 27
Bombe, Double-Chocolate, '97 282
Brownies à la Mode, Magnolias Cream Cheese,
    '97 M178
Cake, Banana Split, '99 48
Cake, Best Carrot, '97 230
Cake, Buttermilk Pound, '99 98
Cake, Chocolate-Peanut Butter Mousse, '98 71
Cake, German Carrot-Hazelnut, '97 230
Cake, Mama's Coconut, '97 71
Cake, Nanny's Famous Coconut-Pineapple, '97 277
Cake, Pastel, '97 173
Cake, Pecan-Carrot, '99 223
Cake with Coconut Custard, Supreme Banana,
    '97 131
Cake with Wine Jelly, Pound, '98 125
Candied Rose Petals, '98 57
Caramels, Coconut-Macadamia, '98 305
Cheesecake, Bavarian, '97 55
Cheesecake, Chocolate-Wrapped Banana, '99 M48
Cheesecake, Praline-Crusted, '99 295
Cheesecake, Warm Fudge-Filled, '98 34
Cobbler à la Mode, Apple, '97 16
Cobbler with Custard Sauce, Apricot, '97 16
Coffee Buttons, '99 66
Cookies, Chocolate-Brickle, '99 127
Cookies, Chocolate Shortbread, '99 147
Cookies, Gingerbread Snowflake, '98 324
Cookies, Orange Slice, '98 324
Cookies, Shortbread, '99 147
Cookies, White Chocolate Chip-Oatmeal, '99 127
Cream, Spanish, '99 27
Crisp, Cranberry-Pear, '97 16
Crust, Gingersnap, '98 161
Crust, Peanut-Graham, '99 49
Crust, Vanilla Wafer, '98 216
Custard, Coconut, '97 131
Custard, Vanilla, '99 27
Filling, Pineapple, '97 277
Frosting, Amaretto Buttercream, '98 57
Frosting, Chocolate-Buttermilk, '99 99
Frosting, Citrus Cream Cheese, '99 223
Frosting, Cream Cheese, '97 230, 277
Frosting, Mocha, '99 66
Frosting, Seven-Minute, '97 71
Ganache, Chocolate, '97 282
Glaze, Buttermilk, '97 230; '99 98
Glaze, Chocolate, '97 231
Glaze, Pineapple, '97 55
Heart, Chocolate-Amaretto, '98 56
Ice Cream, Mocha, '97 M145
Ice Cream, Rum-Raisin, '97 145
Ice Cream Sandwiches, '99 147

Icing, Royal, '98 324
Jelly, Wine, '98 125
Meringue, '97 109
Mousse, Chocolate, '97 282
Mousse Parfaits, Chocolate-Peanut Butter, '98 71
Mousse, White Chocolate, '97 282; '98 M57, M111
Pecan Clusters, '98 305
Penuche, Coffee, '98 305
Pie, Black-and-White Fudge, '99 249
Pie, Black-Bottom, '98 161
Pie, Caramel Meringue, '97 109
Pie, Coconut Cream, '98 161
Pie, Coconut-Macadamia Nut, '97 110
Pie, Fox Hunter's, '97 109
Pie, Georgia Peach-and-Praline, '98 196
Pie, Lemony Ice Cream, '99 207
Pie, Maverick Lunar, '98 111
Pie, Peach Melba, '98 216
Pie, Pear Streusel, '97 109
Pie, Raspberry Baked Alaska, '98 216
Pie, Red, White, and Blueberry, '98 162
Pie, Triple Mint Ice Cream, '98 217
Pie, Warm Apple-Buttermilk Custard, '99 98
Pralines, '99 295
Pralines, Buttermilk, '99 99
Preserves, Custard, '98 126
Pudding, Lemon Cake, '98 35
Pudding, Piña Colada Bread, '98 34
Sauce, Caramel, '97 178
Sauce, Chocolate, '97 178
Sauce, Chocolate-Mint, '98 217
Sauce, Coconut, '98 34
Sauce, Custard, '97 16
Sauce, Mocha, '98 57
Sauce, Raspberry, '98 216
Sauce, Vanilla Custard, '99 27
Sherbet, Buttermilk, '99 99
Shortcake, Warm Blueberry-Nectarine, '97 205
Soufflé with White Chocolate Mousse, Chocolate,
    '98 57
Soup, Fresh Fruit, '98 196
Spritzers, Raspberry, '99 207
Squares, Buttermilk Fudge, '99 99
Strudel, Autumn-Apple, '98 253
Strudel, Fig, '98 253
Strudel, Pear, '98 253
Tart, Apricot-Nut, '99 249
Tart, Bakewell, '97 110
Tart, Chocolate Custard, '99 27
Tart, Coffee, '99 67
Tart, Golden Peach Meringue, '98 197
Tart, Upside-Down Apple, '98 35
Tea, Almond-Lemonade, '99 207
Torte, Mocha, '99 66
Truffles, Chocolate-Cherry Cordial, '99 127
Wafers, Kahlúa, '99 147
Waffles with Apples and Caramel, Gingerbread,
    '98 M237
DESSERTS. *See also* **AMBROSIA; BROWNIES;**
    CAKES; CHEESECAKES; COOKIES;
    CUSTARDS; ICE CREAMS;
    MERINGUES; MOUSSES; PIES,
    PUFFS, AND PASTRIES; PUDDINGS;
    SHERBETS; SOUFFLÉS/Dessert.
Alaska, Peachy Melba, '88 266
Alaskas, Brownie, '83 299
Almond Dessert, Sour Cream-, '92 120
Amaretto Cream Tortoni, '85 161
Apple
    Bake, Apple-Almond, '02 M209

Baked Alaska, Apple, '80 226
Baked Apples and Pear, Honey-, '97 303
Baked Apples, Imperial, '82 273
Baked Apples, Orange-Pecan, '85 45
Baked Apples, Pecan-and-Dried Fruit, '03 269
Baked Apples with Orange Sauce, '84 314
Baked Mincemeat-Filled Apples, '80 276
Brandied Apples, '81 248
Brandied Apples and Cream, '82 M237
Brown Betty, Apple, '83 213
Caramel Apples, Old English, '85 231
Charlotte, Apple, '99 84
Cheese Crisp, Apple-, '92 235
Cinnamon Apples with Brandied Date Conserve,
    '85 315
Compote, Apple-Cranberry, '04 237
Compote, Apricot-Apple, '98 17
Cooked Apples, '93 338
Cranberry Apple Dessert, '80 253
Cranberry Apples, '99 246
Cranberry Crunch, Apple-, '86 300; '87 178
Crisp, Delicious Apple, '82 303
Crisp, Granola Apple, '85 78
Crumble, Whole Wheat-Apple, '90 M213
Delight, Apple, '80 109
Dumplings, Apple, '82 273; '00 96
Dumplings, Quick Apple, '01 185
Dumplings with Orange Hard Sauce, Apple,
    '88 224
Dutch Apple Dessert, Creamy, '91 19
Enchiladas, Apple, '99 63
Flambé, Hot Apples and Rum, '92 88
Flan, Apple, '81 309
Fritters, Apple, '82 273
Fritters with Lemon Sauce, Apple, '01 184
Golden Apples, '82 254
Honey-Baked Apple Dessert, '90 M213
Kuchen, Apple, '79 24
Melting Apples, '88 19
Nut Crunch, Apple-, '82 M238
Oatmeal Cherry-Apple Crisp, '90 M16
Orange-Apple Crisp, '80 295
Pecan Apples, Taffy, '99 247
Pizza, Apple-Pineapple Dessert, '00 313
Poached Lemon Apples, Chilled, '86 182
Quesadillas, Apple Pie 'n' Cheddar, '03 61
Rings, Apple, '85 232
Rings, Cinnamon Apple, '82 M237
Roasted Apples, Orange-Ginger, '01 184
Saucy Apples 'n' Pears, '96 72
Sour Cream Apple Squares, '82 262
Sundae, Hot Apple Spice, '92 239
Apricot-Apple Compote, '98 17
Apricot Cream, Peachy-, '86 163
Avocado Whip, '79 107
Baklava, '96 20
Banana
    Alaska, Banana Split, '87 10
    Baked Bananas, '96 163
    Baked Bananas, Coffee-Kissed, '98 279
    Baked Bananas with Orange Sauce, '79 115
    Berry Supreme, Banana-, '81 205
    Boats, Banana, '00 173
    Candied Bananas, '83 179
    Caramelized Bananas, '99 49
    Cream Dessert, Banana, '81 180
    Flambé, Banana-Peach, '85 316
    Flip, Banana, '83 303
    Foster, Bananas, '79 18; '83 M114; '86 139;
        '88 20; '96 99
    Foster, Elegant Bananas, '81 59
    Foster for Two, Bananas, '80 115
    Foster, Tropical Bananas, '79 231
    Glacé, Bananas, '96 46

Pie, Layered Banana Split, '83 189
Pops, Banana, '83 60; '84 44
Pops, Orange-Banana, '82 129
Praline Bananas, '84 313
Regal Bananas, '85 46
Soufflé, Banana Daiquiri, '84 317
Spiced Bananas with Rum Sauce, '99 247
Splits, French Toast Banana, '96 M164
Supreme, Bananas, '84 256
Tropical Bananas, Easy, '00 141
Bavarian Cream with Fresh Fruit, '88 137
Bavarian Cream with Raspberry Sauce, '91 180
Bavarian Dessert, Light, '86 6
Berried Treasure, '89 124
Berries on Snow, '82 227
Berries with Raspberry Custard Sauce, Fresh,
    '88 163
Berry Basket, Summer, '84 158
Berry Compote, '81 275
Berry Grapefruit Cup, '79 242
Beverages. *See also* **BEVERAGES.**
    Berry Smoothie, Four-, '97 173
    Brandy Alexander, '92 283
    Brandy Float, Blazing, '85 314
    Cappuccino Coffee Dessert, '92 264
    Champagne Delight, '83 304
    Chocoholic Smoothie, '97 173
    Coconut Sipper, Creamy, '02 298
    Creamy Dessert Drink, '86 131
    Golden Dream, '82 100
    Grape Juice-Fruit Refresher, '86 182
    Ice Cream Ginger Fizz, '83 303
    Nog, Hot Chocolate, '02 297
    Orange-Banana Smoothie, '97 173
    Pineapple Smoothie, '97 172
    Pineapple Smoothie, Peachy-, '97 173
    Punch, Eggnog-Coffee, '02 297
    Punch, Milk, '02 298
    Shake, Mocha-Mint, '02 297
    Strawberry Smoothie, '97 173
    Super Dessert Drink, Simply, '83 303
Birds' Nests, '04 84
Birds' Nests, Peanut-Butter, '04 84
Biscotti, Light, '91 310
Biscuits, Elf, '99 309
Biscuits, Sugar, '03 85
Biscuits, Sweet Little, '85 305
Biscuits with Balsamic Strawberries, Anise, '02 170
Blackberries and Dumplings, '86 196
Blackberries Chantilly, '99 130
Blackberry Dessert Tamales, '94 190
Blackberry Flan, '79 182
Blueberries and Cointreau, '82 100
Blueberry-Amaretto Squares, '83 220
Blueberry Crumble, '81 84
Blueberry Crunch, '96 146
Blueberry Crunch, Fresh, '82 143
Blueberry Delight, '96 17
Blueberry Dessert, Easy, '89 M130
Blueberry Dream, '88 94
Blueberry Pizza, '96 147
Blueberry Yum Yum, '98 91
Boysenberries and Cream Supreme, '82 133
Bread, Fry, '85 155
Brie, Almond-Raspberry, '94 M89
Brownie Ice Cream Sandwich Shells, '88 195
Brûlé, Petit, '93 219
Buñuelos, '80 199
Buñuelos, King-Size, '86 5
Butter-Nut Strips, '82 167
Butterscotch Drops, '01 33
Butterscotch Fantastic, '83 76
Cakes, Funnel, '83 250
Cakes, Spanish Wind, '84 157

Cannoli, '80 58; '91 20
Cantaloupe Compote, '81 147
Cantaloupe Cream Delight, '82 179
Cantaloupe Delight, '89 204
Caramel Dessert Biscuits, '95 36
Caramel Fondue, '94 331; '95 35
Caramel Surprise, '88 202
Champagne Shooters, '02 280
Charlotte, Macaroon, '81 296
Charlotte, Peach, '79 68
Charlotte, Pineapple, '90 288
Charlotte Russe, '80 71; '82 M142; '90 288
Charlotte Russe, Chocolate, '87 74
Charlotte Russe, Fresh Lemon, '80 13
Charlotte Russe, Lemon, '84 192
Charlotte Russe, Wine Jelly and, '82 305
Charlotte Russe with Strawberry Sauce, '92 85
Charlottes, Mocha, '02 171
Cheese Blintzes, '82 146; '83 71
Cheese Kuchen, '86 84
Cheese Molds, Heavenly Dessert, '85 209
Cheese, Nutty Date Dessert, '87 299
Cheese Squares, Lemony Cream, '82 159
Cherries à la Mode, '88 202
Cherries Jubilee, '79 18; '83 139
Cherries Jubilee, Quick, '82 M100
Cherries Jubilite, '86 317
Cherries Sabayon, '88 178
Cherries, Sherried, '93 289
Cherry-Berry on a Cloud, '79 94
Cherry Compote, '83 139
Cherry Dessert, Holiday, '80 255
Chocolate. See also DESSERTS/Frozen, Sauces.
    Almond Dessert, Chocolate-, '82 306
    Almond Meringue Fingers, Chocolate-, '84 158
    Bags, Chocolate-Raspberry, '95 97
    Baskets with Berry Cream, Chocolate, '92 118
    Black-Bottom Goodies, '89 251
    Bombe, Double-Chocolate, '97 282
    Brickle Squares, Chocolate, '94 290
    Brownie-Mint Dessert, '82 227
    Buttercream, Chocolate, '84 156
    Charlotte Russe, Chocolate, '87 74
    Chilled Chocolate Dessert, '83 177
    Cinnamon-Chocolate Cream, '94 199
    Coffee Mallow, '80 109
    Cones, Chocolate-Coffee, '96 M316
    Cream, Heavenly Chocolate, '88 128
    Crêpes, Chocolate Dream, '86 164
    Crêpes, Fruit-Filled Chocolate, '89 325
    Cups, Chocolate, '80 207
    Cups, Chocolate Crinkle, '93 270
    Cups, Chocolate Lace, '87 133
    Cups, Chocolate-Mint, '80 71
    Cups, Miniature Chocolate, '87 132
    Date-Nut Delight, Chocolate, '88 168
    Decadence, Chocolate, '89 183
    Dip, Chocolate, '92 50
    Dream Dessert, Chocolate, '83 198
    Easy Chocolate Dessert, '79 75
    Fondue, Dessert, '89 281
    Fondue, White Chocolate, '92 287
    Fudge Dessert with Kahlúa Cream, '91 197
    Hearts, Crispy Chocolate, '03 M41
    Hello Dolly Dessert, '95 168
    Ladyfinger Dessert, Chocolate, '86 162
    Loaves, Chocolate Chip Cheese, '91 299; '92 264
    Log, Chocolate Cream, '94 220
    Midnight Delights, '95 278
    Mint Dessert, Chocolate-, '82 100
    Mint Dessert, Cool Chocolate-, '80 109
    Mississippi Mud, '96 253
    Peanut-Chocolate Dessert, '80 86
    Pizza, Chocolate, '91 298

Plunge, Chocolate, '94 332; '95 35
Pots de Chocolat, Petits, '82 272
Pots de Crème, '81 15; '84 M145
Pots de Crème au Chocolate, '93 53
Pots de Crème, Chocolate, '93 296; '94 234
Pots de Crème for Two, '89 275
Pots de Crème, Mocha, '88 M45
Pots de Crème, Rum-Flavored, '85 102
Pots de Crème with Orange Meringues,
    Chocolate, '95 318
Quad, Chocolate, '02 272
Roll, Chocolate Cream, '85 317
Roll, Chocolate Mousse, '83 290
Roulage, '90 266
Roulage, Chocolate-Cranberry, '94 313
Roulage, Chocolate-Mocha, '80 216
Roulage, Chocolate-Orange, '94 314
Roulage, Mint-Chocolate, '94 314
Roulage, White Chocolate, '92 230
Rum Dessert, Chocolate-, '81 247
Sack, Large Chocolate, '93 314
Sack, Small Chocolate, '93 314
Shells with Kahlúa Cream, Chocolate, '88 195
Squares, Chocolate-Blueberry Dessert, '87 299
Strawberry-Chocolate Combo, '85 96
Sundae Dessert, Hot Fudge, '84 313
Supreme, Chocolate, '84 94
Trifle, Chocolate, '88 258; '93 326
Truffle Dessert, Chocolate, '88 281
Turtle Bars, Gooey, '96 M189
Waffles with Strawberry Cream, Chocolate,
    '88 153
Cinnamon Crisps, '93 106
Coconut Cloud, '80 70
Coconut Dessert, Chilled, '83 116
Coeur à la Crème, Christmas, '86 278
Coffee-Almond Tortoni, '81 30
Coffee-and-Cream Chill, '99 126
Cookies and Cream, '96 179
Corn, Indian, '96 287
Cottage Cheese Dessert, Creamy, '87 191
Crackers, Dessert, '87 3
Cranberries, Brandied, '86 269
Cranberries Jubilee, '85 312; '90 293
Cranberry Apple Dessert, '80 253
Cranberry Bake, Hot, '91 250
Cranberry Compote, '97 264
Cranberry Dessert Pizzas, '96 320
Cranberry Jubilee, Tasty, '84 305
Cranberry-Pear Crisp, '97 16
Cranberry Pockets, '96 320
Cranberry Supreme, '85 280
Cranberry Surprise Dessert, '79 242
Cream, Bavarian, '86 M165
Cream Cheese, Chunky, '85 306
Cream Cheese Eggs, '99 118
Cream Cheese, Fruited, '85 306
Cream Cheese Squares, Lemony, '82 159
Cream, Molded French, '85 311; '99 72
Cream Puffs, Captivating, '81 180
Cream Puffs, Java, '81 187
Cream Puffs, Strawberry, '81 95
Cream Puffs, Tutti-Frutti, '79 231
Cream Puff Tree, '96 310
Cream, Spanish, '99 27
Crème Celeste, '88 94
Crème d'Ange, '83 91
Crème Patissiere, '84 207
Crêpes, Basic Dessert, '82 157; '86 275
Crêpes, Dessert, '86 260; '87 290; '88 134
Crêpes, Dixie Dessert, '79 222
Crêpes Flambé, Cherry, '79 18
Crêpes, Strawberry Dessert, '83 122
Crêpes Suzettes, Light, '83 71

Date Dessert Squares, '89 255
Date-Nut Balls, '85 10
De-Light-Ful Dessert, '95 220
Dip, Citrus-Cream Cheese, '03 93
Dip, Orange-Flavored Cream Cheese, '03 93
Dip, Orange Marmalade-Cream Cheese, '03 93
Dip, Pink Lemonade-Lime, '04 133
Doughnuts, Orange Spiced, '79 136
Dough, Peanut Butter Fun, '00 171
Dumplings, Apple, '00 96
Éclair Cake, '93 42
Éclairs, Miniature Orange, '95 92
Éclairs, Mini Tiramisù, '03 M41
Éclairs, Minted Miniature, '88 66
Éclairs, Pistachio-Cream, '91 296
Éclairs with Pecan Sauce, '83 219
Eggnog Dessert, '95 314
Figs, Sugar-Crusted, '96 195
Flan. See CUSTARDS.
Frozen
    After Dinner-Drink Dessert, '82 100
    Almond Crunch, Frozen, '94 283
    Amaretto Chantilly, '89 14
    Amaretto Freeze, '82 182
    Amber Bombe, '80 255
    Applesauce Fluff, '91 173
    Apricot Fluff, Frozen, '86 242
    Apricot Freeze, '82 10
    Baked Alaska, '84 105; '85 295
    Baked Alaska, Apple, '80 226
    Baked Alaska, Brownie, '80 66
    Baked Alaska, Chocolate Mousse, '85 195
    Banana Pops, Yummy, '01 231
    Banana Pudding Parfait Pops, '96 180
    Banana Split Alaskas, '87 10
    Banana Split Pie, Layered, '83 189
    Banana Split Terrine, '96 164
    Bars, Creamy No-Bake, '97 166
    Bombe, Caramel-Toffee, '00 112
    Bombe, Ice Cream, '90 269
    Bombe with Raspberry Sauce, Creamy, '89 322
    Caffe Latte Slush, '02 209
    Cantaloupe Cream, Frozen, '82 159
    Cantaloupe Whip, '89 198
    Caramel-Toffee Bombe, '93 214
    Cassata, '01 125
    Charlotte, Spumoni, '90 193
    Cherry Cordial Dessert, '84 312
    Chocolate Almond Velvet, '81 148
    Chocolate-Coffee Frozen Dessert, '85 172
    Chocolate Dessert, Frozen, '83 76
    Chocolate Mint Freeze, '88 167
    Chocolate Roulage, Frozen, '90 56
    Chocolate-Walnut Cups, '85 213
    Chocolate Whip, '89 326
    Choco-Maple Frozen Dessert, '86 300; '87 178
    Cinnamon Ice Cream Sombreros, '93 276
    Citrus Cup, Snowball, '79 2
    Coconut-Caramel Dessert, '92 44
    Coffee Dessert, Light, '88 260
    Coffee Ice Cream Crunch, '82 182
    Coffee Tortoni, Creamy, '88 268
    Cookies 'n' Cream Dessert, Gold-Dusted,
        '94 271
    Cream, Betty's Holiday, '95 303
    Cream Dessert, Triple, '94 244
    Elegant Ending, '86 145
    Frappé, Hawaiian, '81 178
    Fruit Cream Freeze, '82 144
    Fruit Cups, Frozen, '93 197
    Fruit Freeze, Holiday, '88 283
    Fruit Ice, Mixed, '88 85
    Fudge-Peanut Ice Cream Dessert, '88 167
    Fudgy Frozen Dessert, Nutty, '94 28

DESSERTS, Frozen
(continued)

Grand Marnier Cream, '84 312
Grapefruit Freeze, '93 242; '00 241
Grasshopper Freeze, Creamy, '81 180
Ice-Cream Angel Dessert, Triple Mint, '93 86
Ice Cream Balls, Cinnamon-Chip, '00 198
Ice Cream Bombe, '82 305
Ice Cream Delight, '80 69
Ice Cream Dessert, Caramel, '95 36
Ice Cream Dessert, Decadent, '91 56
Ice Cream Dessert, Layered, '83 189;
  '84 94, 105; '86 163
Ice Cream Dessert, Mint, '88 66
Ice Cream Dessert, Rocky Road, '00 332
Ice Cream Dessert, Toffee, '87 110
Ice Cream Party Squares, '91 214
Ice Cream Pumpkin, '96 255
Ice Cream Sandwiches, Chocolate Cookie,
  '87 147
Ice Cream-Toffee Dessert, '00 176; '03 182
Ice-Cream Torte, Toffee-Coffee, '04 234
Ice Cream Treats, Crunchy, '86 300; '87 178
Ice, Hazelnut-Coffee, '94 233
Ice, Lemon, '01 330
Ice, Mimosa, '94 24
Lemon-Chiffon Frozen Yogurt, '85 54
Lemon Cream, Frozen, '83 118
Lime-Mint Refresher, '82 144
Lime Whip, '89 199
Little Bits, '79 196
Macaroon-Sherbet Frozen Dessert, '79 212
Mint Patty Alaska, '80 219
Mocha Alaska Dessert, '84 191
Mocha Delight, Frozen, '96 179
Mocha Dessert, Frozen, '84 311
Mocha Freeze, Royal, '84 53
Mocha Squares, Frozen, '81 187
Orange Alaska, '83 177
Orange Dessert, Frozen, '92 44
Oranges Grand Marnier, '92 82
Ozark Pudding, Frozen, '88 127
Peach Freeze, Creamy, '82 144
Peach Torte, Frozen, '93 135
Peanut Butter Delight, Frozen, '88 137
Pineapple Delight, Fresh, '79 111
Pineapple-Orange Bars, '82 129
Pops, Banana, '83 60; '84 44
Pops, Berry, '99 133
Pops, Cherry-Berry Lemonade, '03 89
Pops, Deep Blue Sea, '94 143
Pops, Fruit, '87 168
Pops, Hawaiian Orange-Pineapple, '94 143
Pops, Kiwi Margarita, '99 133
Pops, Orange-Banana, '82 129
Pops, Orange Float, '99 132
Pops, Peach, '04 141
Pops, Pineapple-Yogurt, '91 173
Pops, Purple People Eater, '99 132
Pops, Sangría, '99 133
Pops, Strawberry, '04 141
Pops, Strawberry-Cinnamon, '99 132
Pops, Strawberry-Orange, '03 179
Popsicles, Smoothie Strawberry, '82 112
Praline Freeze, '89 60
Pumpkin Dessert, Frozen, '88 167
Rainbow Delight, Frozen, '84 105
Raspberry Dessert, Frozen, '84 192
Raspberry Fluff, '89 198
Sherbet Ambrosia Cups, '82 159
Sherbet Dessert, Layered, '87 109
Strawberry Cups, Frozen, '91 173
Strawberry Delight, Frozen, '82 112, 174
Strawberry Freeze, '04 141
Strawberry Frost, '82 24; '83 154
Strawberry Puff, '82 5
Strawberry Whip, '89 198
Texas Tornadoes for Grown-Ups, '94 143
Toffee Dessert, Ice Cream-, '04 82
Torte, Frozen Viennese, '93 171
Tortoni, Apricot-Yogurt, '95 124
Turtle Dessert, '04 127
Vanilla Almond Crunch, '93 243
Vanilla Frozen Yogurt, '87 125
Vanilla Soufflé, Frozen, '79 230; '82 173
Watermelon Frost, '86 196
Watermelon, Looks-Like, '03 179

Fruit
Amaretto Crème on Fresh Fruit, '93 176
Bake, Nutty Fruit, '83 127
Beauberries Bordeaux, '98 18
Bowl, Fresh Fruit, '89 137
Caribbean Fruit Dessert, '84 314
Cheese, and Nuts, Fruit, '93 324
Cheese, Luscious Fresh Fruit with, '79 153
Chilled Fruit with Dressing, '85 222
Combo, Fresh Fruit, '86 178
Compote, Baked Fruit, '80 276; '84 314
Compote, Baked Mustard Fruit, '85 47
Compote, Champagne Fruit, '81 309; '82 124
Compote, Chilled Fruit, '83 123
Compote, Citrus, '98 17
Compote, Dried Fruit, '98 18
Compote, Fresh Fruit, '79 162; '82 197, 272;
  '84 82; '94 190
Compote, Fruit, '86 330
Compote, Gingered Fruit, '88 184
Compote, Hot Fruit, '81 203; '83 53
Compote, Jicama-Fruit, '92 49
Compote, Mixed Fruit, '93 123
Compote, Warm Praline Fruit, '85 260
Compote, Wine Fruit, '81 272
Compote with Caramel Syrup, Fruit, '98 313
Crisp, Fruit, '94 168
Cup, Fruit, '81 141; '91 202
Cup with Rum, Fruit, '83 55
Curried Fruit, Hot, '95 72
Dumplings, Delicious Fruit, '97 210
Flame, Sherried Fruit, '85 313
Flaming Fruit Dessert, '83 302
Fondue, Fruitcake, '84 258
Gazpacho, Tropical, '95 204
Gingered Fruit, '83 151
Glazed Fruit, '85 83
Hot Fruit Delight, '83 281
Island Fruit Chill, '98 180
Kebabs with Mint Marinade, '82 157
Lemon Curd, Fresh Fruit with, '88 21
Marinated with Kirsch, Mixed Fruit, '03 86
Medley, Chinese Fruit, '83 22
Medley, Fancy Fruit, '84 82
Medley, Fresh Fruit, '81 141
Medley, Frosty Fruit, '82 226
Medley of Fruit, Tropical, '86 53
Meringue Shells, Fruited, '87 32
Mint-Balsamic Tea, Fresh Fruit with, '95 232
Orange, Fruit Dessert, '84 314
Planter's Punch Dessert, '95 175
Rainbow Fruit Dessert, '85 108
Soup, Fresh Fruit, '79 172
Soup, Fresh Fruit, '98 196
Spiced Fruit Delight, '82 229
Spiced Fruit Dessert, '82 50
Tequila, Fruit in, '82 223
Trifle, Tropical, '95 204
Turnovers, Fruit, '79 150

Gâteau Panache, '83 269
Gel with Stirred Custard, Sherried, '99 126
Glacé, Sabayon, '89 306
Grahams, Caramel-Apple, '04 M183
Grahams, Peanut Butter-Apple, '04 M183
Grahams, Praline, '92 239
Honeydew-Berry Dessert, '83 120
Honeydew Melon with Grapes, '91 91
Ice-Cream Dessert, Toffee, '97 134
Jelly, Rosy Wine, '85 306
Jelly, Wine, '98 125
Kahlúa Cream, '87 134
Kahlúa Delight, '83 67
Kahlúa Delight, Make-Ahead, '84 M89
Kahlúa Velvet Dessert, '85 M294
Kiwi and Cream in Meringue Cups, '81 279
Kiwi-and-Orange Dessert, '93 295
Kiwi-Berry Pizza, '86 198
Kiwifruit Pizza, '89 306
Kiwi Jubilee, '83 120
Kugel, Apricot Noodle, '92 251
Kugel, Sweet, '90 254
Lemon Angel Rolls with Raspberry Sauce, '94 294
Lemon-Cream Cheese Dessert, '84 95
Lemon Cups, Baked, '87 128
Lemon Curd, '89 334; '04 259, 279
Lemon Curd with Berries, '90 102
Lemon Delight, '82 227
Lemon Dessert, Layered, '88 134
Lemon Solid, '93 279
Little Nothings, '79 135
Lollapalooza, '94 194
Lollipops, Harvest Moon, '02 M223
Madeleines, '88 79
Mango Dessert Tamales, '94 190
Mango Pan Dowdy, '83 150
Maple Nut Dessert, '81 84
Maraschino Russian Cream, '79 231
Margarita Tacos, '97 167
Maverick Lunar Pie, '98 111
Melon Ball Compote, '85 157
Melon Balls and Cherries in Kirsch, '91 91
Melon Balls in Watermelon Sauce, '79 177
Melon-Mint Julep, '86 196
Melons in Mint Sauce, '85 164
Melon Wedges with Berry Sauce, '86 178
Meringue Baskets with Fresh Fruit and Ice Cream,
  '98 179
Meringue Cream Cups, Lemon, '84 23
Meringue Flowers, '84 156
Meringue, Piping, '84 156
Meringues, Baked Pear, '85 232
Meringues, Strawberry, '84 188
Mocha-Almond Dessert, '80 289; '81 62
Mocha Chiffon, '86 75
Nectarines Royale, '85 132
Noodle Casserole, Sweet, '02 238
Nuggets, Golden North Pole, '99 M309
Oatmeal Cherry-Apple Crisp, '90 M16
Omelet, Puffy Dessert, '00 35
Orange. *See also* **DESSERTS/Frozen, Sauces.**
  Baked Apples, Orange-Pecan, '85 45
  Baked Orange Elegance, '80 13
  Baskets, Orange, '81 308
  Champagne Oranges, '93 83
  Chiffon Dessert, Orange, '93 295
  Cream Dessert, Orange, '80 254; '84 165
  Cream, Orange, '81 12
  Cream, Orange Chantilly, '84 156
  Cream, Orange-Coconut, '84 24
  Crisp, Orange-Apple, '80 295
  Curd, Fresh Orange, '02 294
  Delight, Pumpkin-Orange, '86 321
  Dip, Creamy Orange, '84 117

Doughnuts, Orange Spiced, '79 136
Éclairs, Miniature Orange, '95 92
Flambé, Dessert Orange, '85 313
Frosted Oranges, '83 270
Fruit Dessert Orange, '84 314
Grand Marnier, Oranges, '92 82
Kiwi-and-Orange Dessert, '93 295
Molded Dessert, Orange, '83 302
Parfaits, Chilled Orange, '80 219
Parfaits, Orange Cream, '94 198
Pears Flambé, Orange-Poached, '85 313
Poached Oranges, Wine-, '84 M323
Rice Cream with Mandarin Oranges, '85 317
Sections with Chocolate and Raspberry Sauce,
    Orange, '97 33
Slices, Burgundy-Spiced Orange, '93 294
Soufflé, Chilled Orange, '84 317; '86 189
Soufflé, Frozen Orange, '79 211
Soufflé, Orange Dessert, '83 206
Strawberries with Brandied Orange Juice,
    '82 160
Tapioca Crème, Orange-, '82 M283
Tapioca Fluff, Orange, '87 31
Pancakes, Dessert Ginger, '88 153
Pancakes, Luau Dessert, '88 154
Parfaits
    Blackberries-and-Cream Parfait, '87 129
    Cheesecake Parfaits, Sugar-Free Peachy, '02 326
    Chocolate-Crème de Menthe Parfaits, '85 161
    Chocolate-Mint Parfaits, '90 M15
    Chocolate Mousse Parfait, '94 90
    Chocolate-Peanut Butter Mousse Parfaits, '98 71
    Chocolate-Peppermint Parfaits, '88 65
    Coffee Crunch Parfaits, '82 159
    Eggnog Bavarian Parfait, '79 255
    Family, Parfait, '94 130
    Hooray Parfaits, '96 229
    Kiwi Parfait, '86 199; '87 55
    Lime Parfaits, '80 153
    Mocha-Mallow Parfaits, '80 219
    Orange Cream Parfaits, '94 198
    Orange Parfaits, Chilled, '80 219
    Peach Parfait, '82 166
    Peanut Butter Parfaits, Crunchy, '79 176; '80 6
    Peppermint Parfait, '93 315
    Pineapple Parfait, '84 83
    Speedy Parfaits, '83 76
    Strawberry-Lemon Parfaits, '84 198
    Strawberry Meringue Parfaits, '02 62
    Strawberry Parfait, '79 99
    Strawberry Parfaits, Frosty, '85 213
    Strawberry Parfait, Surprise, '86 151
    Strawberry-Yogurt Parfait, Crunchy, '79 124
    Surf-and-Sand Parfaits, '93 169
    Tropical Trilogy Parfait, '92 247
    White Chocolate-Raspberry Swirl Parfait,
        '93 315
Pavlova, '92 101
Peach. *See also* **DESSERTS/Frozen, Sauces.**
    Baked Peaches, '92 179
    Blueberry Dessert, Peach-, '92 184
    Brandy Peaches, '85 275
    Caramel Peaches, '93 134
    Cardinale, Peach, '89 155
    Champagne, Peaches, '79 146
    Charlotte, Peach, '79 68
    Compote, Berry-Peach, '82 133
    Compote, Peach-Berry, '89 112
    Cream, Bavarian Peach, '82 171
    Cream, Peach Almond, '82 108
    Cream, Peaches and, '95 196
    Cream, Peachy-Apricot, '86 163
    Crisp, Gingered Peach, '97 303
    Crisp, Peach, '92 13

Custard Dessert, Fresh Peach, '86 162
Dumplings, Peach, '85 177
Foster, Peaches, '86 240
Ginger Peaches with Rum, '84 M323
Gingersnap Peaches, '85 M329
Honeyed Peaches 'n' Cream, '93 134
Layered Peach Dessert, '95 196
Marinated Peaches, '91 91
Melba, Peach, '81 83; '83 M114
Melt-Away Dessert, Peachy, '87 298
Oven-Baked Peaches with Ginger, '82 170
Parfait, Peach, '82 166
Quick Peach Dessert, '85 178
Sherbet Cooler, Peachy, '91 187
Spiced Peach Dessert, '83 9
Spiced Peaches with Nutty Dumplings, '87 164
Split, Peach, '85 277
Strawberry Sauce, Peaches with, '85 8
Stuffed Peaches, Macaroon-, '79 178
Stuffed Peach Halves, '86 196
Sundaes Flambé, Peach, '81 88
Trifle, Peach, '92 179
Wine Sauce, Peaches in, '79 184
Peanut Butter Dessert, '92 164
Peanut-Buttery Dessert, Crunchy, '92 204
Pear. *See also* **DESSERTS/Sauces.**
    Amaretto Pears with Meringue, '90 M58
    Baked Apples and Pear, Honey-, '97 303
    Baked in Molasses-Port Sauce, Pears, '97 195
    Baked Pears à la Mode, '95 129
    Baked Pears Elegant, '91 48
    Belle Helene, Pears, '86 164
    Blue, Pears, '99 246
    Coconut Pears, Spicy, '83 207
    Crème Chantilly, Holiday Pears with, '91 297
    Crème de Menthe Pears, '94 50
    Crisp, Cranberry-Pear, '97 16
    Crisp, Raspberry-Pear, '89 109
    Dumplings, Pear, '97 210
    Flaming Pears, '84 313
    Gratin, Pear-Blue Cheese, '93 328
    Maple-Sugared Pears, '81 232
    Meringues, Baked Pear, '85 232
    Orange-Caramel Sauce, Pears with, '95 281
    Poached in Red Wine, Pears, '83 302
    Poached Pear Fans with Raspberry-Orange
        Sauce, '88 22
    Poached Pears, Champagne-, '01 289
    Poached Pears Flambé, Orange-, '85 313
    Poached Pears in Custard, '88 20
    Poached Pears in Wine, '82 194
    Poached Pears, Lemon, '82 74
    Poached Pears, Vanilla, '90 57
    Poached Pears with Berry Sauce, Wine-, '86 144
    Poached Pears with Dark Chocolate Sauce,
        '90 M141
    Poached Pears with Honey-Yogurt Sauce, '92 306
    Poached Pears with Raspberry Sauce, '84 213;
        '87 69; '88 223
    Poached Pears with White Caramel Sauce, '99 28
    Red Wine, Pears in, '82 254
    Sautéed Pears, '03 195
    Stewed Pears, '98 280
    Stuffed Pears, Almond-, '83 207
    Sundaes, Quick Pear, '86 71
Pecans, Sugared, '82 167
Peppermint Bavarian, '80 153
Peppermint Fondue, '94 332
Peppermint Wafer Dessert, '79 176; '80 7
Pineapple-Almond Delight, '85 96
Pineapple Boats with Rum Sauce, '97 192
Pineapple Dessert Chimichangas, '86 4
Pineapple Filling, '97 277
Pineapple, Meringue-Topped, '84 178

Pineapple 'n' Cream, '88 202
Pineapple, Scalloped, '79 106; '82 254
Pineapple Skewers with Rum Sauce, Grilled,
    '04 247
Pineapple, Stuffed, '00 160
Pineapple with Natillas Sauce, Baked, '83 179
Pineapple with Raspberry Sauce, Chocolate-
    Drizzled, '90 57
Pizza Dessert, Rocky Road, '99 196
Pizzelles, '83 298
Plum Crunch, Layered, '86 174
Plums in Port Wine, '97 176
Port Wine Jelly with Whipped Cream, '84 254
Pots de Crème, Easy, '93 281
Praline Horns, '96 316
Profiteroles, '84 208
Prune Bavarian, '86 223
Prunes in Merlot, '98 18
Pumpkin Chiffon, '82 216; '86 283; '88 260
Pumpkin Chiffon Dessert, '88 128
Pumpkin Flan, '97 219
Pumpkin Mold, '82 311
Pumpkin-Orange Delight, '86 321
Pumpkin Swirl, Easy, '93 234
Quesadillas, Dessert, '02 54
Raspberry Dream, '83 108
Raspberry-Jellyroll Dessert, '85 95
Raspberry Jellyrolls, '93 M255
Raspberry-Pear Crisp, '89 109
Raspberry Prunes, '82 124
Raspberry-Strawberry Bavarian, '89 15
Reindeer Food, Magic, '99 M309
Rhubarb Crisp, '91 146; '92 130
Rhubarb-Strawberry Bavarian, '86 140
Rhubarb Whip, '79 112
Rice Cream with Mandarin Oranges, '85 317
Roulage, Toffee-Pecan, '94 312
Rum Balls, '93 314
Sabayon, '93 272
Sabayon, Champagne, '00 288
Santa's Hat, '92 279
Sauces
    Almond-Vanilla Custard Sauce, '88 M177
    Amaretto-Chocolate Sauce, '92 154
    Amaretto-Cinnamon Sauce, '93 171
    Amaretto Cream Sauce, '03 330
    Amaretto-Strawberry Sauce, '87 M165
    Ambrosia Sauce, Hot, '89 335
    Apple Ambrosia Sauce, '89 95
    Apple-Cinnamon Sauce, '93 42
    Apple Dessert Sauce, '87 M165
    Apple Dessert Sauce, Spicy, '82 177
    Apple Topping, Spicy, '87 125
    Apricot Ice Cream Sauce, '91 57
    Apricot Sauce, '82 212
    Apricot-Walnut Hard Sauce, '88 153
    Banana-Pineapple Sauce, '83 48
    Bananas Foster Sauce, '03 94
    Banana Sundae Sauce, '84 275
    Berry Mimosa Sauce, '90 315
    Berry Sauce, '87 290; '88 135; '94 130; '95 103
    Bittersweet Chocolate Sauce, '92 319
    Blackberry Sauce, '86 152; '94 232
    Blueberry-Lemon Sauce, '01 117
    Blueberry Sauce, '88 155; '89 M130; '94 122;
        '95 135
    Blueberry Topping, '87 125
    Bourbon Cream Sauce, '98 84
    Bourbon Praline Sauce, '81 170
    Bourbon Sauce, '93 51; '98 336; '01 223; '03 66
    Brandied Hard Sauce, '80 264; '83 250; '85 313
    Brandy-Butter Sauce, '79 230
    Brandy-Macadamia Sauce, '82 311
    Brandy Sauce, '88 279; '98 119

DESSERTS, Sauces
(continued)

Bread Pudding Sauce, '04 235
Brown Sugar Sauce, '90 314
Buttered Rum Sauce, '83 249
Buttered Rum Sauce, Hot, '88 204
Buttermilk Custard Sauce, '96 183
Buttermilk Sauce, '95 183
Butter Pecan Sauce, '91 174
Butter-Rum Sauce, '95 134
Butterscotch-Pecan Sauce, '82 212
Caramel-Raisin Sauce, '88 127
Caramel Sauce, '79 79; '91 56, 180; '93 210,
   235, 296; '94 234; '95 308; '96 284, 310;
   '97 178; '00 52, 256; '01 313; '03 194
Caramel Sauce, Easy, '87 38
Caramel Sauce, The Best Ever, '03 216
Caramel Sauce, White, '92 195
Cherry-Pineapple Topping, '87 126
Cherry Sauce, '79 91
Cherry Sauce, Elegant, '79 M156
Cherry-Wine Sauce, '97 132
Chocolate and Raspberry Sauce, Orange Sections
   with, '97 33
Chocolate-Cherry Sauce, '85 189
Chocolate Cherry Sauce, '87 M165
Chocolate-Mint Sauce, '93 86; '94 314; '98 217
Chocolate Mint Sauce, Quick, '86 M58
Chocolate-Orange Sauce, '86 165; '94 314
Chocolate-Peanut Butter Sauce, '79 91, M156
Chocolate-Peppermint Sauce, '94 205
Chocolate-Praline Sauce, '85 M295
Chocolate Sauce, '83 189; '84 208, 313; '86 322;
   '90 57; '91 56, 57; '93 276; '94 121;
   '97 178, 331
Chocolate Sauce, Classic, '85 207
Chocolate Sauce, Creamy, '88 M177
Chocolate Sauce, Dark, '93 296; '94 234, 283;
   '96 310; '98 336
Chocolate Sauce, Double, '83 79
Chocolate Sauce, Easy, '92 148
Chocolate Sauce, Heavenly, '79 79; '82 167
Chocolate Sauce, Semisweet, '00 104
Chocolate Sauce Supreme, '85 189
Cinnamon-Blueberry Sauce, '86 11
Cinnamon-Butter Sauce, '00 254
Cinnamon-Fudge Sauce, '85 141
Cinnamon Sauce, Apple Pie with Hot, '88 210
Coconut-Orange Sauce, '85 189
Coconut Sauce, '98 34
Coconut Sauce, Creamy Light, '82 177
Cranberry Jubilee, Tasty, '85 189
Cranberry Sauce, '86 278; '88 280
Crème Anglaise, '92 164
Crème Fraîche Sauce, '79 281; '93 135
Custard Sauce, '85 41; '88 154, 251, 259;
   '89 291; '97 16, 313; '03 244, 318
Date-Nut Sundae Sauce, '82 167
Fig Sauce, '79 140
Fruit Dessert Sauce, Hot, '87 299
Fruit Puree, '94 190
Fruit Sauce, Golden, '89 281
Fruit Sauce, Quick, '82 212
Fudge Sauce, '91 174
Fudge Sauce, Easy Hot, '84 69; '94 194
Fudge Sauce, Heavenly Hot, '00 256
Fudge Sauce, Hot, '82 181, 295; '84 143; '97 255
Fudge Sauce, Quick Hot, '82 212
Golden Sauce, '88 267
Hard Sauce, '80 265; '82 14
Hard Sauce, Special, '86 318
Honey-Chocolate Sauce, '89 251

Honey-Orange Sauce, '85 108
Honeyscotch Sundae Sauce, '82 167
Honey-Yogurt Sauce, '92 307
Kahlúa Chocolate Sauce, '85 155
Lemon Cream Sauce, '93 200
Lemon Dessert Sauce, '87 M165
Lemon Sauce, '84 258, 306; '85 77, 190;
   '91 240; '96 283; '01 184; '04 98
Lemon Sauce, Tart, '85 191
Lemon Sauce, Zesty, '97 318
Lemon-Vanilla Sauce, '02 231
Mandarin Dressing, '89 137
Mandarin Orange Sauce, '89 204
Mango Sauce, '83 120
Marshmallow Sauce, '91 91
Melba Sauce, '87 77
Mint Sauce, '96 127
Mint Sauce, Party, '82 212
Mocha Sauce, '98 57
Orange Dessert Sauce, '86 337; '87 58
Orange Hard Sauce, '88 225
Orange Sauce, Fresh, '85 209
Peach-Berry Sauce, '87 M165
Peach-Blueberry Pancake Sauce, '82 177
Peach Blueberry Sauce, '81 170
Peach-Praline Sauce, '85 161
Peach Sauce, '84 144
Peach Sauce, Creamy, '85 189
Peach Sauce, Fresh, '87 167
Peanut Butter Ice Cream Sauce, '84 30
Peanut Butter Sauce, '03 289
Peanut Dessert Sauce, '86 M251
Pear Sauce, '92 164
Pecan Sauce, '83 219
Piña Colada Topping, Chunky, '87 125
Pineapple Ice Cream Sauce, '81 M289
Pineapple-Rhubarb Sauce, '88 94
Pineapple-Rum Sauce, '84 275
Plum Sauce, Fresh, '94 129
Praline Ice Cream Sauce, '85 189
Praline Ice Cream Sauce, Southern, '86 M227
Praline Sauce, '83 25; '84 143; '89 95; '92 282;
   '93 214; '94 206, 312; '96 285
Raspberry-Amaretto Sauce, '88 130
Raspberry-Lemon Sauce, Cheesecake with,
   '96 30
Raspberry-Orange Sauce, '88 22; '92 154
Raspberry-Peach Topping, '87 126
Raspberry Sauce, '82 289; '83 108; '84 73, 213;
   '87 69, 117, 183; '88 267; '89 183, 322;
   '91 96, 180, 270; '92 130; '93 82, 99, 315;
   '94 295; '95 327; '96 183, 310; '98 157, 216;
   '99 167, 259; '02 123; '03 319; '04 33
Raspberry Sauce, Crimson, '79 91; '85 30
Raspberry Sauce Dessert, '80 147
Raspberry Sauce Flambé, '84 142
Raspberry Sauce, Fresh, '93 120
Rhubarb Sauce, Chilled, '88 94
Rum-Butter Sauce, '86 301
Rum-Fruit Sauce, '84 312
Rum-Raisin Sauce, '84 7; '94 295
Rum Sauce, '88 32; '94 241; '03 244
Rum Sauce, Brown Sugar-, '85 231
Rum Sauce, Hot, '79 86
Rum Sundae Sauce, '93 162
Sherry Sauce, '84 109
Spicy Sauce, '93 52
Strawberries Arnaud Sauce, '93 50
Strawberry-Banana Topping, '87 125
Strawberry-Butter Sauce, '96 87
Strawberry-Orange Sauce, '96 95
Strawberry-Peach Sauce, '92 154
Strawberry Sauce, '84 144; '87 93, 198; '92 85;
   '94 121; '03 55

Strawberry Sauce, Brandied, '88 196
Strawberry Sauce, Fresh, '82 177
Strawberry Sauce, Old-Fashioned, '94 130
Strawberry Sauce, Peaches with, '85 8
Strawberry Sauce with Crunchy Topping, '81 170
Strawberry Sauce with Dumplings, '84 314
Taffy Dessert Sauce, '86 20
Tea-Berry Sauce, '94 130; '99 334
Toffee-Fudge Sauce, '89 95
Toffee Sauce, '94 72
Vanilla Crème Sauce, '94 243; '96 155
Vanilla Custard Sauce, '99 27
Vanilla-Nutmeg Sauce, '02 208
Vanilla Sauce, '97 M15
Watermelon Sauce, Melon Balls in, '79 177
Whiskey Sauce, '90 230; '92 87, 93; '99 277
White Caramel Sauce, '99 28
White Chocolate Sauce, '92 164; '96 310;
   '00 104
Savarin, '79 171
Sherbet-Cantaloupe Surprise, '91 105
S'mores, Indoor, '01 33
Sopaipillas, '80 197; '88 112; '91 78
Sopaipillas, Pineapple, '83 179
Soufflés
Banana Daiquiri Soufflé, '84 317
Brandy Alexander Soufflé, '82 173; '83 M114
Chocolate-Mint Soufflé, '81 16
Chocolate Soufflé, Light, '83 278
Chocolate Soufflé with White Chocolate Mousse,
   '98 57
Coconut Soufflé, '85 212
Daiquiri Soufflé, Elegant, '80 69
Devonshire Soufflé, Chilled, '88 279
Gingerbread Soufflés with Lemon Cream,
   '04 300
Grand Marnier Soufflé, '79 281
Grand Marnier Soufflés, '03 318
Grasshopper Soufflé, '81 248; '86 188
Kahlúa Soufflé, '82 173
Lemon-Lime Soufflé, Cold, '84 24
Lemon Soufflé, '82 170
Lemon Soufflé, Tart, '85 82
Orange Dessert Soufflé, '83 206
Orange Soufflé, Chilled, '84 317; '86 189
Orange Soufflé, Frozen, '79 211
Pineapple Dessert Soufflé, '80 153
Raspberry Soufflé, '86 188
Raspberry-Topped Soufflé, '85 317
Vanilla Soufflé, Frozen, '79 230; '82 173
Vanilla Soufflés with Vanilla Crème Sauce,
   '96 155
Soup, Sherry-Berry Dessert, '91 180
Spumoni and Berries, '91 204
Sticky Fingers, '03 M168
Strawberry. *See also* **DESSERTS/Frozen,
   Parfaits, Sauces.**
Almond Cream with Fresh Strawberries, '87 93
Arnaud, Strawberries, '93 50
Balsamic Strawberries, '02 170
Banana-Berry Supreme, '81 205
Bavarian, Raspberry-Strawberry, '89 15
Bavarian, Rhubarb-Strawberry, '86 140
Best-Dressed Berries, '96 317
Brandied Orange Juice, Strawberries with,
   '82 160
Carousel, Strawberry, '91 247
Cheese Delight, Strawberry, '79 50
Cherry-Berry on a Cloud, '79 94
Chilled Strawberry Dessert, '84 164
Chocolate Combo, Strawberry-, '85 96
Coconut Nests, Strawberry, '88 136
Compote, Peach-Berry, '89 112
Cream Cheese Dessert, Strawberry-, '83 123

Cream in Vanilla Lace Cups, Strawberry, '98 93
Cream Puffs, Strawberry, '81 95
Cream, Strawberries and, '82 100
Cream, Strawberries 'n', '90 30
Cream, Strawberries with Strawberry, '84 108
Crêpes, Strawberry Dessert, '83 122
Deep-Fried Strawberries, '84 109
Delight, Strawberry, '81 85
Dipped Strawberries, '94 17
Dip, Strawberries with Brown Sugar-and-Sour
    Cream, '03 93
Dip, Strawberries with Fluffy Cream Cheese,
    '03 93
Dip, Strawberries with Mint Yogurt, '03 93
Dip, Strawberries with Vanilla Pudding, '03 93
French Cream, Strawberries with, '83 191
Frost, Strawberry, '81 279; '82 24; '83 154
Glazed Strawberry Dessert, '84 33
Honeydew-Berry Dessert, '83 120
Jamaica, Strawberries, '85 161; '93 239
Juliet, Strawberries, '84 82
Lemon Dessert, Strawberry-, '86 162
Marsala, Strawberries, '88 171
Meringues, Strawberry, '84 188
Napoleons, Strawberry, '81 126
Pizza, Kiwi-Berry, '86 198
Pizza, Strawberry, '79 94
Raspberry Custard Sauce, Fresh Berries with,
    '88 163
Rock Cream with Strawberries, Old-Fashioned,
    '90 125
Romanoff, Strawberries, '84 108; '88 95; '91 126
Romanoff, Strawberry-Almond, '98 99
Ruby Strawberries, '82 100
Sabayon, Strawberries, '79 94
Shortcake Squares, Strawberry, '85 122
Soup, Sherry-Berry Dessert, '91 180
Spumoni and Berries, '91 204
Strawberry Dessert, '83 123
Stuffed Strawberries with Walnuts, '85 122; '86 124
Summer Strawberry Dessert, '92 143
Sweet-and-Sour Strawberry Dessert, '92 54
Swirl, Strawberry, '84 108
Trifle, Easy Strawberry, '88 201
Yogurt Delight, Strawberry, '85 77
Yogurt Dessert, Strawberry-, '90 295
Zabaglione, Strawberries, '81 95

Sundaes
Apple Spice Sundae, Hot, '92 239
Berry Sundaes, Very, '03 126
Brownie Sundaes, Cream Cheese, '03 223
Cantaloupe Sundae, '89 166
Chocolate Mint Sundaes, '03 M120
Cocoa-Kahlúa Sundaes, '83 M58
Hot Fudge Sundae Dessert, '86 322
Mauna Loa Sundaes, '80 126
Peach Sundaes Flambé, '81 88
Pear Sundaes, Quick, '86 71
Strawberry Sundaes, Hot, '81 M5
Sushi, Crisp Rice Cereal, '00 50
Syrup, Madeira, '98 247
Tacos, Dessert, '97 141
Tea Cakes and Fresh Strawberries, Telia's, '98 110
That's Incredible, '02 322
Tiramisù, '91 21; '94 295; '98 280; '00 288; '02 285
Tiramisù, Easy, '00 167
Toffee Dessert, English, '88 136
Torte, Mocha Mousse, '04 260
Torte, Peanut Butter Turtle, '04 316
Torte, X-Treme Chocolate Double Nut Caramel
    Ladyfinger, '04 M315
Tortilla Baskets, '94 97
Tortilla Triangles with Fruit Salsa, Sweet, '02 54
Trees, Holiday, '02 298

Trifles
Angel Food Trifle, '91 184
Banana Pudding Trifle, '98 273
Brownie Trifle, '03 85
English Trifle, '93 289
Individual Trifles, Easy, '92 239
Island Trifle, '92 238
Jumbleberry Trifle, '03 84
Lemon-Blueberry Trifle, '88 210
Lemon Trifle, All Seasons, '95 219
Olde English Trifle, '95 331
Peach Trifle, Georgia, '04 169
Peanut Butter-Brownie Trifle, '03 200
Pineapple Angel Food Trifle, '93 86
Raspberry Trifle, '88 259
Raspberry Trifles, Individual, '99 112
Rum Trifle, '86 322
Savannah Trifle, '80 121
Strawberry-Sugar Biscuit Trifle, '03 84
Strawberry Trifle, Easy, '88 201
Toffee Trifle, '94 168
Tropical Rum Trifle, '03 85
Tropical Snow, '86 34
Vacherin Moka, '80 55
Vanilla Cream, '83 M115
Vanilla Lace Cups, '98 M93
Vanilla Sherry Dessert, Glorified, '81 85
Waffles, Banana Split, '89 205
Waffles with Apples and Caramel, Gingerbread,
    '98 M237
Waffles with Mandarin Orange Sauce, Dessert
    Pumpkin, '89 204
Waffle, Whole Wheat Dessert, '79 92
White Christmas Dessert, '82 261
Wine Jelly, Rosy, '85 306
Yule Log, '79 281; '82 289
Zabaglione with Fruit, Champagne Vanilla,
    '00 31
Zuppa Inglese, '99 M267

DOUGHNUTS
Applesauce Doughnuts, '81 203
Applesauce Drop Doughnuts, '90 70
Banana Doughnuts, '86 137
Beignets, '84 56
Cake Doughnuts, Quick, '82 226
Chocolate-Covered Doughnuts, '84 55
Chocolate Doughnuts, '83 95
Cinnamon Puffs, '81 209; '01 126
Dutch Doughnuts, '81 50
Fry Bread, '84 140
Glazed Doughnuts, '83 94
Hanukkah Doughnuts with Strawberry Preserves,
    '01 M275
Jelly-Filled Doughnuts, '84 55
Orange Spiced Doughnuts, '79 136
Pineapple Drop Doughnuts, '83 95
Potato Doughnuts, Chocolate-Glazed, '85 6
Potato Doughnuts, Old-Fashioned, '84 56
Puffs, Doughnut, '86 85
Puffs, Wheat Quick Doughnut, '85 278
Pumpkin Doughnut Drops, '90 323
Quick Doughnuts and Doughnut Holes, '01 126
Raised Doughnuts, '01 126
Snowy Doughnuts, '93 286
Spice Doughnuts, '84 56
Sufganiyot (Jelly-Filled Doughnuts), '90 255
Whole Wheat Doughnuts, '84 56

DOVE. *See* **GAME.**
DRESSINGS. *See also* **SALAD DRESSINGS,
    STUFFINGS.**
Andouille Sausage, Apple, and Pecan Dressing,
    '02 249
Cajun Dressing, '82 307
Chicken and Dressing, Baked, '79 296

Cornbread
Biscuit Dressing, Cornbread-, '79 296
Cakes, Southwestern Cornbread Dressing,
    '01 233
Chicken and Dressing, '99 42
Chicken Cornbread Dressing, '90 159
Cornbread Dressing, '86 286; '88 254; '92 267;
    '98 269; '00 259; '02 249; '03 231
Corny Cornbread Dressing, '99 258
Crawfish-Cornbread Dressing, '99 257
Fruited Cornbread Dressing, '80 262
Green Chile-Cornbread Dressing, '93 306;
    '94 296
Herb-Seasoned Cornbread Dressing, '83 315
Kentucky Cornbread Dressing, '86 281
Light Cornbread Dressing, '92 324
Louise's Cornbread Dressing, '03 251
Nannie's Cornbread Dressing, '95 306
Old-Fashioned Cornbread Dressing, '84 321
Oyster-Cornbread Dressing, Ma E's Traditional,
    '96 35
Quail and Dressing, '99 42
Quail Stuffed with Cornbread Dressing, '93 280
Sage-Cornbread Dressing, '84 283
Sage Dressing, Cornbread-, '80 262
Sausage, and Pecan Dressing, Cornbread, '99 257
Sausage-Cornbread Dressing, '95 289
Sausage-Cornbread Dressing, Turkey with,
    '83 287
Sausage Dressing, Cornbread-, '82 307; '85 280
Sausage Dressing, Cornbread-and-, '83 213
Savory Cornbread Dressing, '88 303
Squash Dressing, '01 160
Sweet Cornbread Dressing, '97 303
Texas Cornbread Dressing, '82 243
Turkey and Cornbread Dressing, Roast, '89 324
Corn Dressing Balls, Zesty, '82 307
Crabmeat-and-Oyster Dressing, '02 243
Crawfish Dressing, Louisiana, '90 103
Creole Dressing, '95 289
Eggplant Dressing, '90 236
Fruit-and-Pecan Dressing, '84 252
Fruit Dressing, Baked, '87 253
Giblet Dressing, '91 255
Grandmother's Dressing, '91 254
Green Onion Dressing, '96 17
Grits Dressing, '93 306; '94 296
Oyster Bread Dressing, '82 251
Oyster Dressing, '79 250
Peanut Dressing, Roast Turkey with, '79 283
Pecan, Rice, and Crawfish Dressing, '00 252
Pecan-Rice Dressing, Chicken with, '85 M57
Pecan-Sage Dressing, '80 262
Pretzel Dressing, '86 280
Rice Dressing, '91 217; '01 222
Rice Dressing, Chicken and, '79 288
Rice Dressing, Mexican, '87 253
Rice Dressing, Roast Turkey with, '82 286
Rice Dressing, Southern, '99 256
Roasted Garlic Dressing, '99 269
Sausage-Apple Dressing, '93 305; '94 296
Sausage Dressing, '86 280
Sausage Dressing, Harvest, '88 254
Seasoned Dressing, Stuffed Turkey Breast with,
    '83 320; '84 128
Spoonbread Dressing, Southwestern-Style, '94 273
Squash Dressing, '83 315; '86 280; '95 290
Squash Dressing, Turkey with, '87 248
Turkey and Dressing, Easy, '79 296
Turkey-and-Dressing Pie, '84 326
Turkey Dressing, '85 298
Turkey Dressing, Fruited, '99 257
Whole Wheat-Mushroom Dressing, '84 283
Zucchini Dressing, '86 282

DUCK. *See* **GAME.**
DUMPLINGS
Apple Dumpling Cobbler, '04 29
Apple Dumplings, '82 273; '00 96
Apple Dumplings, Cinnamon, '97 M330
Apple Dumplings, Old-Fashioned, '84 226
Apple Dumplings, Quick, '01 185
Apple Dumplings with Maple-Cider Sauce, '95 288
Apple Dumplings with Orange Hard Sauce, '88 224
Beef Stew with Dumplings, '84 3
Biscuit Dumplings and Chicken, '99 326
Blackberries and Dumplings, '86 196
Blackberry Dumplings, '97 253
Cheddar Dumplings, Chicken Ragoût with, '94 44
Chicken and Dumplings, '97 208; '00 111; '01 231;
     '03 25
Chicken and Dumplings, Country, '85 254
Chicken and Dumplings, Easy, '86 21
Chicken and Dumplings, Old-Fashioned, '79 55;
     '83 228; '93 302
Chicken and Dumplings, Quick, '95 125; '02 16
Chicken and Dumplings with Herbed Broth, '95 338
Chicken and Dumplings with Vegetables, '85 M56
Chicken Dumpling Pie, '96 55
Chicken 'n' Dumplings, Quick-and-Spicy, '03 325
Chicken Stew and Dumplings, '84 4
Cilantro-Cornmeal Dumplings, Bean Ragoût with,
     '97 209
Cornbread Dressing Dumpling Dough, '03 239
Cornbread Dressing Dumplings, Turkey Soup with,
     '03 239
Cornmeal Dumplings, Turnip Greens with, '82 211
Drop Dumplings, Burgundy Stew with, '83 125
Fruit Dumplings, Delicious, '97 210
Gnocchi à la Narciso, '97 246
Gnocchi with Olive Oil, Tomato, and Parmesan,
     '04 47
Goat Cheese Dumplings, '99 70
Green Peas and Dumplings, '80 102
Old-Fashioned Dumplings, '81 191
Parsley Dumplings, Beef Stew with, '81 76; '82 13;
     '85 M246
Peach Dumplings, '80 143; '85 177; '96 172
Pear Dumplings, '97 210
Pie, Chicken Dumpling, '00 336
Pork Dumplings, Make-Ahead, '03 64
Potato Dumplings, Chicken and, '99 326
Potato Dumplings, Venison Stew with, '87 304
Pot Roast with Dumplings, '98 245
Sesame Dumplings, Steamed, '97 208
Shrimp with Dumplings, Stewed, '79 31
Spinach and Dumplings, '00 85
Strawberry Sauce with Dumplings, '84 314
Tomato Dumplings, '88 144; '97 209
Tortilla Dumplings, Chicken and, '99 327

EGGNOG
Beverages
Blender Eggnog, '93 341
Breakfast Nog, Speedy, '82 47
Christmas Eggnog, '87 242
Cider Nog, Hot, '98 241
Cider Nog, Hot Apple, '84 42
Coconut Nog, '83 275
Coffee Nog, Brandied, '86 329
Cooked Custard Eggnog, '91 305
Creamy Eggnog, '80 259; '83 303; '85 300
Creamy Eggnog, Aunt Kat's, '01 287
Easy Eggnog, '91 305
Edenton Eggnog, '84 251
Eggnog, '83 318
Egg Nog, '00 274
Holiday Brew, '81 265

Holiday Eggnog Deluxe, '79 232
Hot Chocolate Nog, '02 297
Irish Coffee Nog, '84 258; '93 340
Irish Cream Nog, '82 312
Mock Eggnog with Orange and Nutmeg,
     '92 323
Orange Spiced Nog, '82 48
Punch, Coffee-Eggnog, '86 281
Punch, Coffee Eggnog, '92 264
Punch, Creamy Nog, '01 240
Punch, Eggnog-Coffee, '02 297
Punch, Holiday Eggnog, '86 281
Punch, Irish Coffee-Eggnog, '95 314
Punch, Peppermint-Eggnog, '90 273
Sparkling Eggnog, '79 232
Thick and Creamy Eggnog, '80 261
Bread, Eggnog, '83 294
Cake, Eggnog-Pecan Pound, '95 313
Cake, Eggnog Pound, '90 253
Casserole, Sweet Potato-Eggnog, '95 291
Cookies, Eggnog Christmas, '79 255
Dessert, Eggnog, '95 314
French Toast, Eggnog, '95 313
Parfait, Eggnog Bavarian, '79 255
Pie, Eggnog, '80 254; '83 205; '86 317; '87 295
Pie, Eggnog Chiffon, '86 281
Pie, Fluffy Eggnog, '81 M269
Salad, Eggnog Christmas, '86 281
Tarts, Creamy Eggnog, '79 255
EGGPLANT
Almonds, Eggplant with, '79 179
Appetizer, Eggplant, '83 187
Appetizer, Grilled Eggplant, '95 198
Balsamic-Flavored Eggplant, '95 342
Barbecue Eggplant, '02 180
Biscuit Cakes, Tomato-Eggplant, '95 170
Cakes, Eggplant, '95 196
Caponata, '87 166; '98 50
Caponata alla Siciliana, '02 269
Caponata, Sicilian-Style, '01 124
Casseroles
Bake, Eggplant, '80 82
Cakes, Eggplant, '95 196
Chiles Rellenos, Eggplant, '91 86
Creole Eggplant, '86 110
Crêpes with Marinara Sauce, Mini Eggplant,
     '99 266
Easy Eggplant Casserole, '80 202
Eggplant Casserole, '81 205; '84 217; '93 44;
     '94 214
Elegant Eggplant Casserole, '82 168
Flavorful Eggplant Casserole, '79 92
Frittata, Fresh Vegetable, '93 140
Heavenly Eggplant, '93 293
Italian Eggplant, '84 216
Italian-Style Eggplant and Zucchini, '79 289;
     '80 26
Lebanese Eggplant, '81 24
Mexican Eggplant, '83 187
Moussaka, '87 166; '90 68; '97 94
Moussaka Casserole, '79 179
Moussaka, Potatoes, '93 44
Noodle Casserole, Eggplant and, '82 230
Oyster Louisiane, Eggplant-and-, '95 196
Parmesan, Eggplant, '82 230; '83 186; '84 215;
     '86 53; '92 18; '95 84; '01 53
Parmesan, No-Fry Eggplant, '92 172
Parmesan with Feta, Eggplant, '03 174
Parmigiana, Chicken-Eggplant, '82 212
Parmigiana, Eggplant, '81 19; '82 186; '95 197;
     '01 310
Potato-Eggplant Casserole, '87 166
Sausage Bake, Eggplant-, '85 221
Sausage Casserole, Eggplant-, '84 215

Sausage-Pasta Casserole, Freezer Eggplant-,
     '95 197
Scalloped Eggplant, '91 223
Spanish Eggplant, '79 21
Spicy Hot Eggplant Casserole, '93 92
Spinach Casserole, Eggplant-, '99 217
Stuffed Eggplant, Spinach-and-Basil, '02 147
Super Eggplant Casserole, '80 202
Supreme, Eggplant, '79 188; '86 170
Tomato Casserole, Eggplant-and-, '83 187
Caviar, Eggplant, '88 262; '99 217
Caviar, Homemade Cowboy, '94 64
Caviar with Tapenade, Eggplant, '92 194
Crawfish on Eggplant, Soft-Shell, '88 222
Creole, Eggplant, '82 107; '83 86; '86 110
Dip, Eggplant, '96 275
Dressing, Eggplant, '90 236
Easy Eggplant, '87 M151
French-Fried Eggplant, '81 204
Fried Eggplant, '79 178; '83 187; '88 111; '03 158
Fried Eggplant, Cheesy, '90 75
Fried Eggplant, Oven-, '91 187
Fried Eggplant, Parmesan, '79 189
Fried Parmesan Eggplant, '87 166
Fritters, Eggplant, '91 211
Georgian Eggplant with Walnuts, '01 87
Gravy, Roast Duck with Sweet Potato-Eggplant,
     '83 90
Grilled Eggplant, '80 202; '89 174
Grilled Eggplant, Sage-, '96 269
Italiano, Eggplant, '91 212
Italian Style, Eggplant, '01 111
Jackstraw Eggplant, '82 230
Julienne, Eggplant, '85 221
Main Dish, Sausage-Eggplant, '80 211
Medley, Eggplant-Shrimp, '79 188
Mexicano, Eggplant à la, '82 229
Parmigiana, Eggplant, '01 310
Patties, Eggplant, '83 186
Pizza, Eggplant, '85 221
Pizza, Greek Eggplant, Tomato, and Feta, '01 312
Pizzas, Eggplant, '98 183
Provençal, Eggplant, '92 82
Ratatouille, Eggplant-Zucchini, '81 205
Relish, Eggplant, '95 342
Salad, Eggplant, '90 99
Sandwiches, Baked Eggplant, '82 230
Sandwiches, Eggplant, '99 240
Sandwiches, Eggplant Parmesan, '03 213
Sandwiches, Eggplant, Tomato, and Feta, '98 106
Sandwiches, Open-Face Eggplant, '95 124
Sautéed Eggplant and Zucchini, '82 96
Sauté, Eggplant, '96 135
Slices, Quick Eggplant, '90 75
Soup, Eggplant Supper, '85 221
Soup, Herbed Eggplant, '90 173
Spaghetti Squash with Sesame Eggplant, '92 252
Spicy Eggplant, '99 217
Spicy Oriental Eggplant, '96 130
Spread, Eggplant, '86 278
Spread, Eggplant-Mushroom, '92 156
Squash, Eggplant and, '83 187
Stacks, Eggplant, '91 211
Sticks, Ned's Eggplant, '95 309
Stuffed
à la Creole, Eggplant, '96 177
Baked Stuffed Eggplant, '81 133
Beefy Stuffed Eggplant, '81 204
Cheesy Stuffed Eggplant, '79 188; '82 208
Creole Stuffed Eggplant, '82 230
Eggplant, Stuffed, '80 158
Ham-Stuffed Eggplant, '80 162
Italian-Stuffed Eggplant, '90 74
Mushroom-Stuffed Eggplant, '83 136

Ratatouille-Bran Stuffed Eggplant, '86 44
Ratatouille-Stuffed Eggplant, '83 187
Rolled Stuffed Eggplant, '80 63
Sausage Stuffed Eggplant, '81 204
Sausage-Stuffed Eggplant, '91 211
Seafood Stuffed Eggplant, '79 187
Shrimp-Stuffed Eggplant, '92 99
Supper, Beef-and-Eggplant, '84 291
Tophats, Eggplant, '79 188
Vinaigrette, Italian Eggplant, '03 125
Zaalouk, Eggplant, '98 210

EGGS. *See also* **QUICHES, SOUFFLÉS.**
Armadillo Eggs, '97 270
Baked Egg Crisps, '83 57
Baked Eggs Florentine, '86 M12
Baked Eggs in Spinach Nests, '82 70
Baked in Mushroom Sauce, Eggs, '93 47
Bake, Egg and Rice, '83 119
Bedeviled Eggs, '86 67
Benedict, Bacon-and-Tomato Eggs, '87 195
Benedict, Country Ham Eggs, '03 52
Benedict, Easy Eggs, '80 M268
Benedict, Eggs, '79 40, 254; '85 49; '98 55
Benedict, Light Eggs, '93 M68
Benedict, Lion, '93 121
Benedict, Shrimp-and-Grits Eggs, '03 53
Benedict, Southwest Eggs, '03 53
Benedict, Traditional Eggs, '03 52
Benedict with Cheese Sauce, Eggs, '81 225
Brandied Cream Sauce, Eggs in, '82 70
Bread, Butter-Egg, '85 269
Bread, County Fair Egg, '87 68
Bread, Easter Egg, '84 94; '96 88
Breakfast Eye-Openers, '82 231
Breakfast, Farmer's, '81 44
Breakfast, Mexican, '00 194
Brunch Eggs, '85 44
Brunch, Texas, '82 70
Bunwiches, '80 92
Burritos, Brunch, '91 77
Burritos, Potato-and-Egg, '02 72
Burritos, Tex-Mex Egg, '95 34
Casseroles
   Apple-Egg Casserole, '85 44
   Bacon and Egg Casserole, '81 225
   Bacon-and-Egg Casserole, '03 166
   Bacon-and-Ham Casserole, Cheesy, '01 256
   Bacon Casserole, Egg-and-, '85 248
   Bel-Mar, Eggs, '90 92
   Breakfast Bake, '85 45
   Breakfast Casserole, '01 130, 243
   Broccoli-and-Egg Casserole, '86 324
   Broccoli-and-Eggs au Gratin, '85 289
   Brunch Casserole, Southwestern, '03 197
   Brunch Casserole with Creole Sauce, '98 98
   Brunch Egg Casserole, '86 329
   Brunch Eggs, '98 93
   Bruncheon Eggs, '83 83
   Campfire Casserole, '00 173
   Cheese-and-Egg Casserole, '99 268
   Cheese Casserole, Egg-and-, '84 293
   Cheese-Egg-Zucchini Casserole, '84 114
   Cheesy Egg Casserole, '81 244; '86 15
   Chile Eggs, '88 80
   Crab-Egg Casserole, '80 260
   Creole Eggs, '82 42
   Egg Casserole, '83 311; '98 98
   Frittata, Fresh Vegetable, '93 140
   Ham and Egg Casserole, Breakfast, '79 253
   Layered Eggs, '96 97
   Mushroom Casserole, Egg-, '83 49
   Potato-Egg Casserole, Cheesy, '84 5
   Potatoes and Eggs au Gratin, '79 107
   Sausage-and-Egg Casserole, '94 284

Sausage Breakfast Casserole, '81 270
Sausage Egg Bake, '81 225
Sausage-Egg Bake, Smoked, '85 248
Sausage-Egg Casserole, '86 M12
Scrambled Egg Casserole, '80 51; '86 241
Scrambled Egg Casserole, Saucy, '89 213
Soufflé Casserole, Egg, '83 55
Spinach and Egg Casserole, '82 270
Squash and Egg Casserole, '80 146
Strata, Cheese-Rice, '81 176
Strata, English Muffin Breakfast, '03 100
Strata, Sausage, '84 101
Strata, Tomato-Bacon, '03 100
Strata, Tomato-Cheese, '81 209
Strata, Turkey-Cheddar-Broccoli, '03 100
Sunday Egg Casserole, '95 100
Zucchini-Egg Casserole, '84 M113
Cheddar Eggs, '94 M141
Cheese, Eggs and, '95 165
Cottage Eggs, '85 44
Crabmeat and Eggs New Orleans, '82 45
Creamed Eggs à la Asparagus, '81 201
Creamed Eggs, Broccoli and, '83 84
Creamed Eggs in Patty Shells, '80 M267
Creamed Eggs in Toast Cups, '83 83
Creole, Eggs, '92 86
Creole, Skillet Eggs, '85 143
Crêpes, Ham-and-Egg, '83 204
Crêpes with Mushroom Sauce, Ham-and-Egg,
   '82 46
Croissant Eggwiches, '91 160
Croquettes, Tuna-Egg, '80 275
Delight, Bacon-and-Egg, '85 143
Delight, Crab-and-Egg, '84 261
Delight, Mushroom-Egg, '83 14
Deviled Eggs. *See* **EGGS/Stuffed.**
Dip, Festive Egg, '79 285
Dressing, Egg, '86 79
Eagle Nest Egg, '99 194
Featherbed Eggs, '93 122
Florentine, Eggs, '79 39; '83 56
Florentine-Style Eggs, '82 38
Foo Yong, Egg, '80 19; '86 232
Foo Yong Noodles, Egg, '98 233
Foo Yong Patties, '80 223
Foo Yong, Shrimp Egg, '83 22
Frittata, Avocado-and-Black Bean, '02 212
Frittata, Bacon-and-Asparagus, '98 136
Frittata, Bell Pepper, '96 204
Frittata, Broccoli-Cheese, '81 243
Frittata, Corn-and-Squash, '89 144
Frittata, Firecracker Pasta, '94 230
Frittata, Ham-and-Broccoli, '98 101
Frittata, Potato, '89 145
Frittata, Potato-Bacon, '95 269; '98 330
Frittata, Spinach, '81 53
Frittata, Vegetable, '92 48; '93 183
Garden District Eggs, '04 66
Ham and Eggs à la Swiss, '88 158
Ham and Eggs, Creamed, '82 40
Ham and Eggs, Creamy, '87 286
Ham and Eggs on Toast with Cheese Sauce, '81 43
Ham and Eggs, Savory, '82 231
Hard-Cooked Eggs (garnish), '82 280
Hash Brown Skillet Breakfast, '82 5
Herb Sauce, Eggs in, '88 80
Hominy, Bacon, Eggs, and, '85 143
Huevos con Queso, '00 123
Huevos Rancheros, '82 197; '91 77; '02 72
Medley, Cheddary Egg, '81 M176
Mexicana, Eggs, '82 146
Mornay, Ham and Eggs, '02 130
Mound, Frosted Egg, '79 33
Muffin, Stuffin', '99 193

Mushroom Eggs, Sherried, '83 49
Mushrooms and Eggs in Patty Shells, '85 143;
   '88 197
Mushrooms and Eggs, Saucy, '79 138
Nests, Fluffy Egg, '79 128
Omelets
   Apple Omelet Stack, '94 50
   Bacon-and-Potato Omelet, Open-Faced, '02 246
   Baked Omelets, '94 50
   Biscuits, Deluxe Omelet, '98 101
   Broccoli-Mushroom Omelet, '85 45
   Cheese Omelet, Herbed, '93 47
   Cheese Omelet, Puffed, '89 227
   Cheese Omelet, Zippy, '87 287
   Cheese-Shiitake Omelet, Golden, '95 265
   Cheesy Picante Omelet, '86 95
   Chicken Liver Omelet, '82 44
   Country Omelets, '91 128
   Creole Sauce, Omelets with, '89 228
   Dessert Omelet, Puffy, '00 35
   Dill-Cheese-Ham Omelet, '95 33
   Fines Herbes, Omelette aux, '92 82
   Fluffy Omelet, '84 56
   George's Omelets, '80 68
   Ham and Cheese Omelet, '79 262; '80 123
   Ham-and-Cheese Omelet, '02 246
   Indian Omelet, '99 92
   Italian Omelet, '92 47
   Mexican Omelet, '79 128; '81 225
   Mexican Omelet, Easy, '88 114
   Mushroom Omelet, Rolled, '82 70
   Mushroom Sauce, Puffy Omelets with, '85 40
   Ole Omelet, '87 M124
   Ole, Omelet, '94 31
   Oven-Baked Omelet, Farmer's, '03 204
   Oyster Omelets, Smoked, '84 96
   Potato Omelet, Family-Size, '94 31
   Potato-Sprout Omelet, '79 128
   Primavera, Omelet, '87 71
   Rising Sun Omelet, '82 281; '83 42
   Rolled Omelet, '89 228
   Sandwich, Omelet, '86 95
   Sausage Filling, Omelet with, '81 43
   Sausage Omelet, Puffy, '80 M268
   Shrimp-and-Cheddar Omelet, '84 57
   Shrimp-and-Cheese Omelet, '94 31
   Shrimp-and-Vegetable Oven Omelet, '99 286
   Sour Cream-Ham Omelet, '79 261
   Spanish Omelet, '81 201; '83 243; '84 101;
      '00 35
   Spanish Omelet with Fresh Avocado Salsa,
      '02 247
   Spanish-Style Omelets, '83 188
   Spinach, Cheddar, and Bacon Omelet, '03 204
   Spinach-Cheese Omelet, '83 119
   Strawberry-Sour Cream Omelet, '89 229
   Sunrise Omelet, '83 289
   Swiss Oven Omelet, '80 189
   Tarragon Omelet, '89 144
   Tex-Mex Omelet con Carne, '81 209
   Vegetable Omelet, Beefy, '83 188
   Vegetable Omelet, Cheddar-, '83 205
   Vegetable Omelet, Cheesy, '85 49
   Vegetable Omelet, Fresh, '84 211
   Vegetable Omelet, Golden, '82 M123
   Vegetable Omelet, Puffy, '83 188
   Vegetable-Pasta Oven Omelet, '99 286
   Vegetarian Omelet, '84 114
   Veggie Omelet, Creamy, '02 248
   White Wine Omelet, '79 103
   Yogurt-Avocado Omelet, '81 33
   Zucchini Omelet, '81 99
Oso Grande, Eggs, '98 279
Paint, Egg Yolk, '86 322

EGGS

(continued)

Peanut Butter Easter Eggs, '87 86
Pickled Eggs, Beet, '84 287
Pickled Eggs, Rosy, '86 68
Pickled Eggs, Spiced, '84 288
Pie, Country Breakfast, '93 M328
Pie, Egg Custard, '99 82
Pie, Egg-Stra Special Chicken, '86 264
Pie, Old-Fashioned Egg Custard, '82 261
Pillows, Egg, '92 332
Pizza, Breakfast, '85 44
Pizza, Ham-and-Eggs Crescent, '93 47
Poached Eggs, '92 87, 93; '93 121; '03 53
Poached Eggs, Basic, '82 58
Poached Eggs, Easy, '03 70
Poached Eggs, French-Style, '82 58
Poached Eggs, Microwave, '02 M131
Potatoes with Eggs and Meat, '91 311; '92 25
Potato Nests, Mashed, '94 141
Pot Pie, Chicken-and-Egg, '00 98
Puff, Egg-and-Cheese, '85 45
Rancheros, Easy Eggs, '88 81
Rice, Egg Fried, '79 252; '80 19
Roll-Ups, Spicy Egg, '90 140
Roulade with Mushroom Filling, Egg, '88 84
Salads
    Asparagus-and-Egg Salad, '86 305
    Bacon-Horseradish Egg Salad, '94 181
    Club, Shrimp-Egg Salad, '02 203
    Club, Sweet-Pickle Egg Salad, '02 203
    Deviled Egg Salad, '83 124
    Ham-and-Egg Potato Salad, '86 84
    Ham 'n Egg Salad, '81 36
    Rice Salad, Egg-, '84 18; '86 169
    Sandwiches, Egg Salad, '03 179
    Sandwiches, Egg Salad Club, '02 203
    Shrimp-and-Egg Salad Sandwiches, '94 182
    Shrimp-Egg Salad, Tossed, '80 4
    Smoked Salmon-and-Egg Salad, '02 203
    Spread, Cottage-Egg Salad, '82 146
    Spread, Egg Salad, '86 127
    Tacos, Mexican Egg Salad, '94 181
    Tuna-Egg Salad, '81 135
    Vegetable and Egg Salad, Green, '79 191
    Yolkless Egg Salad, '94 181
Sandwiches, BLT Breakfast, '04 171
Sandwiches, Breakfast, '82 M123; '89 M230
Sandwiches, Confetti, '79 236
Sandwiches, Eggsclusive, '79 164; '80 130
Sandwiches, Eggs-Tra Special, '81 240; '83 69
Sandwiches, Open-Faced Cheesy Egg, '86 67
Sandwiches, Open-Face Egg, '83 292; '84 78;
    '86 160
Sandwiches, Saucy Egg, '91 160
Sardou, Eggs, '92 93
Saucy Eggs, '83 84
Saucy Eggs on Toast, '81 209
Sauté, Vegetable-Egg, '96 204
Scotch Eggs, '79 261; '83 289; '98 101
Scrambled
    Bacon-and-Eggs Scramble, '80 M267
    Buttermilk Scrambled Eggs, '79 72
    Casserole, Saucy Scrambled Egg, '89 213
    Casserole, Scrambled Egg, '80 51; '86 241
    Cheese-Chive Scrambled Eggs, '95 34
    Cottage Cheese Scrambled Eggs, '81 142
    Cottage-Scrambled Eggs, '80 49
    Country Eggs, '86 330
    Country-Style Scrambled Eggs, '79 22
    Crabmeat Brunch Scramble, '95 32
    Cream Cheese Scrambled Eggs, '81 287

    Creamy Scrambled Eggs, '90 82
    Empanadas, Bacon 'n' Egg Breakfast, '02 324
    Enchiladas, Scrambled Egg, '97 153
    Home-Style Scrambled Eggs, '84 66
    Mexican-Style Scrambled Eggs, '85 50
    Migas, '87 180; '94 26; '98 312
    Onion Scrambled Eggs, Creamy, '83 M203
    Shrimp and Crab Scrambled Eggs, '79 261
    Sonora, Eggs, '80 196
    Spanish Scrambled Eggs, '83 49; '84 60
    Special Scrambled Eggs, '81 103
    Supreme, Scrambled Eggs, '79 39
    Tostadas, Scrambled Egg, '86 95
    Veggie Scramble, '01 288
    Wild Rice, Scrambled Eggs with, '80 42
Soufflés, Little Egg, '83 57
Soufflé, Three-Egg Cheese, '87 234
Soup, Egg Drop, '83 21; '86 16
Soup, Egg-Drop, '85 M12
Soup, Egg Flower, '81 307; '82 313; '83 65
Soup, Egg-Lemon, '96 88
Soup, Lemon-Egg Drop, '93 81
Soup, Spinach Egg Drop, '03 65
Spread, Cottage-Egg Salad, '82 146
Spread, Egg Salad, '86 127
Spread, Egg, Sour Cream, and Caviar, '85 279
Spread, Ham-and-Egg, '79 59
Spread, Vegetable-Egg, '87 106
Stuffed
    Bacon-Stuffed Eggs, '97 52; '00 70; '04 290
    Black-and-Blue Eggs, '96 90
    Blue Cheese Stuffed Eggs, '93 87
    Chicken-Stuffed Eggs, '98 102
    Crabmeat, Eggs Stuffed with, '04 18
    Creamed Eggs, '86 67
    Creamy Stuffed Eggs, '84 143
    Crunchy Stuffed Eggs, '86 67
    Deluxe, Eggs, '82 79
    Deviled Eggs, '86 176; '94 161; '01 299
    Deviled Eggs, Bacon, '86 136
    Deviled Eggs, Basic, '03 88
    Deviled Eggs, Best, '80 159
    Deviled Eggs, Chile-Cheese, '93 87
    Deviled Eggs, Creamed, '82 79
    Deviled Eggs, Curried, '93 87
    Deviled Eggs, Easy, '82 127
    Deviled Eggs, Mexican, '04 93
    Deviled Eggs, Nippy, '80 217
    Deviled Eggs, Pimiento-, '84 143
    Deviled Eggs, Saucy, '82 80
    Deviled Eggs Surprise, '79 83
    Deviled Eggs, Sweet, '93 88
    Deviled Eggs, Tex-Mex, '97 247
    Deviled Eggs with Smoked Oysters, '84 161
    Deviled Eggs, Zesty, '84 205
    Deviled Green Goblin Eggs, '02 222
    Devil's Island Eggs, '82 79
    Double-Stuffed Eggs, '00 70
    Eggs, Stuffed, '80 155; '88 95
    Garlic-Cheese-Stuffed Eggs, Marbleized, '96 91
    Green Eggs and Ham, '96 90
    Ham Devils, '93 88
    Herb-Sour Cream Stuffed Eggs, '93 87
    Mustard Eggs, Spicy, '84 143
    Pecan-Stuffed Deviled Eggs, '04 93
    Pecan-Stuffed Eggs, '80 78
    Shrimp-Curried Eggs, Saucy, '84 143
    Shrimp-Stuffed Eggs, '00 70
    Spicy-Sweet Deviled Eggs, '04 198
    Spinach-and-Bacon Eggs, Double Stuffed,
      '00 M333
    Stuffed Eggs, Easy, '93 87
    Tomato Slices, Stuffed Eggs-and-, '84 152
    Tuna-Stuffed Eggs, '83 83

Substitute, Homemade Egg, '92 47
Sunny-Side-Up Eggs, '79 38
Tacos, Breakfast, '80 43
Tamales, Breakfast, '00 122
Tomatoes, Bacon-and-Egg-Stuffed, '80 162
Tortilla, Potato, '00 85
Tortillas, Chorizo and Egg, '81 193
Tortillas, Egg-and-Sausage, '83 246; '84 42
Tulsa Eggs, '87 95
ENCHILADAS
American Enchiladas, '81 170
Apple Enchiladas, '99 63
Bean Enchiladas, Spicy, '88 18
Bean Enchiladas, Three-, '91 133
Breakfast Enchiladas, '04 281
Casserole, Easy Enchilada, '02 143
Casserole, Enchilada, '87 287
Casserole, Firecracker Enchilada, '80 260
Casserole, Green Enchilada, '79 76
Casserole, Sour Cream Enchilada, '82 113
Cheese Enchiladas, '81 194; '85 154; '95 311
Cheese Enchiladas, Saucy, '84 220
Chicken-and-Cheese Enchiladas, Baked, '03 332
Chicken-and-Spinach Enchiladas, '91 222
Chicken-Cheese Enchiladas, '02 236
Chicken-Chile Enchiladas, '97 313
Chicken Enchiladas, '80 301; '86 296; '90 121;
    '00 45; '03 214; '04 96
Chicken Enchiladas, Creamy, '97 250; '01 M94
Chicken Enchiladas, Easy, '82 89; '86 231
Chicken Enchiladas, Healthy, '02 19
Chicken Enchiladas, Quicker, '97 312
Chicken Enchiladas, Three-Cheese, '99 330
Chicken Enchiladas Verde, '93 274; '00 M240
Chicken Enchiladas with Spicy Sauce, '84 76
Chicken Enchiladas with Tomatillo Sauce, '94 231;
    '95 206
Chicken-Sour Cream Enchiladas, '04 274
Chili and Enchiladas, '00 55
Creamy Enchiladas, '93 174
Dove Enchiladas, '85 270
Duck Enchiladas with Red Pepper-Sour Cream,
    Smoked, '87 121
Egg Enchiladas, Scrambled, '97 153
Enticing Enchiladas, '99 57
Green Chile Enchiladas, '02 188
Green Chile-Sour Cream Enchiladas, '84 234
Hot and Saucy Enchiladas, '81 141; '82 6
Meatless Enchiladas, '93 106
New Mexican Flat Enchiladas, '85 244
Pie, Enchilada, '83 155
Poblano-Shrimp Enchiladas, '00 311
Pork Enchiladas, '97 M94
Quicker Enchiladas, '96 103
Sauce, Enchilada, '81 194
Sauce, Red Chile Enchilada, '85 245
Shrimp Enchiladas, '01 104
Shrimp Enchiladas in Tomatillo Sauce, '95 310
Skillet Enchiladas, '82 89
Soup, Chicken Enchilada, '86 22
Soup, Shrimp Enchilada, '94 103
Sour Cream Enchiladas, '83 200; '87 37
Sour Cream Enchiladas, Cheesy, '79 25
Spinach Enchiladas, '83 60; '84 14
Terrificas, Enchiladas, '84 32
Weeknight Enchiladas, '93 63
ESCARGOTS
Provençal, Escargots, '82 238; '83 156
ESCAROLE. *See* **GREENS.**

FAJITAS
Beef and Chicken Fajitas, '02 119
Beef Fajitas, '88 233

Beef Fajita Salad, '91 70
Beef Fajitas with Pico de Gallo, '04 61
Casserole, Fajita, '97 96
Chicken Fajita Pizza, '03 235
Chicken Fajitas, '88 231; '89 100; '90 204; '99 158
Chicken Fajita Spuds, '96 238
Chicken Fajita Spuds with Black Bean Salsa, '04 25
Crêpes, Fajita, '94 116
Fajitas, '84 233
Favorite Fajitas, '86 114
Fettuccine, Fajita, '94 84
Java Fajitas, '96 227
Pico de Gallo, Fajitas with, '98 87
Pita, Fajita in a, '90 177
Pitas, Fajita, '99 239
Plum Good Fajitas, '94 115
Slow Cooker Fajitas, '02 43
Tex-Mex Fajitas, '01 188
Turkey Fajitas, '01 108

FETTUCCINE
Alfredo, Fettuccine, '80 236; '86 158
Blue Cheese Noodles, '98 290
Blue Cheese Sauce, Fettuccine with, '98 247
Broccoli and Sausage, Pasta with, '97 266
Broccoli, Fettuccine with, '90 97
Broccoli-Parmesan Fettuccine, '93 55
Chicken-and-Creamy Herb Sauce, Fettuccine with, '01 257
Chicken and Dried Tomatoes over Fettuccine, '98 233
Chicken and Pasta, Pesto, '89 M132
Chicken-and-Tomatoes over Fettuccine, '90 204
Chicken-Artichoke Pasta with Rosemary, '98 15
Chicken Fettuccine Alfredo, '00 57
Chicken Fettuccine, Cajun, '96 198
Chicken Pasta with Artichokes and Capers, '04 129
Chicken-Pecan Fettuccine, '86 52
Chicken with Pasta, Dijon, '90 318
Cordon Bleu, Pasta, '97 327
Crab Fettuccine, '98 142
Crawfish and Tasso Fettuccine, '96 290
Crawfish Fettuccine, '96 98
Creamy Fettuccine, '92 283; '96 136
Eggplant Sauté, '96 135
Fajita Fettuccine, '94 84
Greens, Pasta with, '95 211
Ham-and-Asparagus Fettuccine, '94 84
Parsley, Fettuccine with, '83 115
Peas and Pasta, '93 139
Pepper Pasta, '89 321
Poppy Seeds, Fettuccine with, '91 48
Portobello-Alfredo Sauce, Fettuccine with, '04 135
Primavera, Fettuccine, '89 238; '94 85
Primavera, Fettuccini, '04 64
Prosciutto, Party Pasta with, '94 176
Ranch House Fettuccine, '03 123
Salmon Fettuccine, '90 123
Scallop-Mushroom Fettuccine, '96 198
Seafood Pasta, Herbed, '04 255
Shrimp-and-Creamy Herb Sauce, Fettuccine with, '01 257
Shrimp and Tomatoes, Fettuccine with, '96 198
Shrimp Elégante, '83 48
Shrimp Fettuccine, '94 84; '96 210
Shrimp-Herb Fettuccine, '01 308
Shrimp-Tomato Pasta, '98 172
Shrimp with Dried Tomato Pesto, Fettuccine and, '94 249
Shrimp with Fettuccine, Dilled, '99 141
Spinach Alfredo Fettuccine, '01 164
Spinach Fettuccine, '82 179
Spinach, Fettuccine and, '88 90
Spinach Fettuccine, Creamy Basil Chicken with, '97 328
Spinach Fettuccine, Easy Chicken with, '88 89
Spinach Fettuccine, Fresh, '83 60
Spinach Fettuccine with Mustard Greens, '94 247
Spinach Sauce, Fettuccine with, '84 329
Supreme, Fettuccine, '83 288; '86 333
Tetrazzini, Smoked Turkey, '02 286
Thai-Style Noodles with Peanut Basil Sauce, '98 133
Tomato-Olive Pasta Toss, '86 209
Vegetable Fettuccine, '83 312
Vegetables, Fettuccine and, '97 178
Vegetables, Noodles with Spring, '02 125

FIGS
Baked Fig Bites, '02 160
Cake, Fig, '79 32; '99 314; '02 166
Cake, Fig Preserve, '79 140; '84 316
Cake, Fig Preserves, '89 335
Cobbler, Cajun Fig, '94 196
Cobbler, Fig, '79 140
Cobbler, Fig-and-Raspberry, '02 160
Cobbler, Super Fig, '86 206
Coffee Cake, Easy Fig, '80 116
Compote, Grilled Chicken Breasts with Fig-and-Melon, '00 163
Flowers, Fig, '96 195
Ice Cream, Fig, '87 139
Ice Cream, No-Cook Fig-Mint, '04 179
Jam, Fig, '86 206
Marinated Grilled Figs, '96 194
Muffins, Fig, '86 206
Pickled Figs, '79 140
Pies with Fruit Salsa, Lone Star Fried, '97 124
Pork Loin, Fig-Balsamic Roasted, '03 45
Preserves, Fig, '79 140; '82 150; '89 140; '96 195; '00 175
Preserves, Quick Strawberry-Fig, '96 194
Preserves, Rosemary Cheese with Fig, '02 256
Prosciutto, Walnuts, and Cream, Figs with, '96 194
Pudding, Fig-Walnut, '03 244
Sauce, Fig, '79 140
Snacks, Sliced Fig, '86 206
Strudel, Fig, '98 253
Sugar-Crusted Figs, '96 195

FILLINGS
Savory
Baria, '97 91
Beef Filling, '80 81
Broccoli Filling, '81 44
Chicken Divan Filling, '81 91
Chicken Filling, '81 200
Chicken Filling, Curried, '88 125
Chicken Filling Luau, '79 81
Chicken-Olive Filling, '81 227
Chicken Salad Filling, '87 106
Crab Filling, '89 13
Crêpe Filling, '96 48
Four Cheese Filling, '97 171
Green Tomato Pie Filling, '01 141
Mushroom Filling, '81 89; '88 84
Omelet Filling, Greek, '80 68
Omelet Filling, Spanish, '80 68
Peanut Filling, '93 211
Pesto, '89 158
Pot Pie Filling, '03 247
Shrimp and Dill Filling, '97 171
Shrimp Filling, '89 320
Shrimp Salad Filling, '87 106
Spinach and Feta Filling, '97 171
Spinach Filling, '95 316
Spinach-Mushroom Filling, '80 215
Spinach-Ricotta Filling, '81 53
Sweet
Almond Cream Filling, '85 320; '91 248
Almond Filling, '87 301; '96 316

Almond Filling, Ground, '87 14
Amaretto Filling, '87 241
Apple-Date Filling, '83 301
Apple Filling, '85 5; '96 53; '97 239
Apple Filling, Dried, '85 242; '87 229
Apricot Filling, '83 84; '86 107; '93 316; '01 330
Blintz Filling, '92 84
Butterscotch Filling, '91 271; '02 323
Caramel Filling, '88 278; '03 287
Caramel Whipped Cream Filling, '96 312
Chantilly Crème, '80 280
Cheese-and-Orange Filling, '93 159
Cheese Filling, '89 91
Cherry Filling, '83 302; '84 225; '88 178
Cherry Fried Pie Filling, Dried, '96 109
Chocolate Buttercream, '84 156
Chocolate-Cheese Filling, '90 47
Chocolate-Coffee Buttercream Filling, '00 M287
Chocolate Filling, '96 316; '03 200
Chocolate Filling, Rich, '79 68
Chocolate Midnight Filling, '96 120
Chocolate Truffle Filling, '87 69; '04 M253
Cinnamon-Cheese Filling, '90 46
Cinnamon Roll Filling, '03 247
Citrus Filling, '02 221
Coconut Cream Filling, '84 200
Coconut Filling, '81 265; '00 117; '03 329
Coffee Filling, '96 316
Coffee Pastry Cream, '01 45
Cran-Apple Mousse, '93 255
Cranberry-Ambrosia Filling, '01 271
Cranberry Filling, Nutty, '00 M306
Cranberry-Pecan Filling, '04 305
Cream Cheese Filling, '90 170; '97 287; '04 273
Cream Filling, '83 220; '84 37; '87 198; '90 311
Crème Fraîche, '91 99
Custard Filling, '82 52, 298; '85 281
Custard Filling, Creamy, '81 180
Custard Filling, Egg, '87 14
Date Cream Filling, '81 303
Date Filling, '80 15; '83 257; '86 314
Fluffy Filling, '81 192; '86 246
Fluffy White Filling, '90 252
Fruit Filling, '94 245
Fruit Filling, Nutty, '99 306
Fruit Fried Pie Filling, Mixed, '96 109
Fruit-Nut Filling, '80 289
Fudge Filling, '94 292
Grand Marnier Pastry Cream, '01 45
Honey Filling, '88 287
Honey-Walnut Filling, '80 21
Lane Cake Filling, '89 55; '96 144
Lemon-Apricot Filling, '90 105
Lemon-Cheese Filling, '79 68; '88 7; '03 317
Lemon Cream, '91 119
Lemon Cream Filling, '84 23; '87 14
Lemon Filling, '81 172; '84 137; '85 191; '86 235; '87 293; '89 312; '90 308; '94 122; '95 319; '97 255; '99 118
Lemon Filling, Creamy, '80 70
Lemon Icebox Pie Filling, '03 104
Lemon-Orange Filling, '81 71
Lime Icebox Pie Filling, '03 104
Mascarpone Filling, '02 146
Mint-Cream Filling, '96 229
Mocha Cream Filling, '81 187; '84 305
Mocha Filling, '80 55; '82 262
Napoleon Cream, '84 138
Nut-and-Fruit Filling, '84 263
Nut Filling, '91 35
Orange-Cheese Filling, '90 47
Orange Cream Filling, '99 118
Orange Curd Filling, '96 120
Orange Curd, Fresh, '02 294

FILLINGS, Sweet
(continued)

 Orange Filling, '79 229; '86 336; '87 84;
  '88 224; '89 287; '96 316
 Orange Icebox Pie Filling, '03 104
 Orange-Pineapple Fried Pie Filling, '96 109
 Pastry Cream, Luscious, '82 304
 Peach Filling, '89 154; '90 107; '96 119
 Peach Pie Filling, Fresh, '95 195
 Peanut Butter Filling, '96 229
 Peanut Butter Pastry Cream, '01 45
 Pecan Filling, '04 305
 Pecan Pie Filling, '98 254; '03 316
 Peppermint Filling, '81 119; '89 254
 Piña Colada Filling, '99 117
 Pineapple Filling, '80 140; '83 179; '84 153;
  '89 57; '97 277
 Praline Buttercream, '95 243
 Praline Cream Filling, '03 332
 Praline Filling, '89 328
 Raisin Filling, '90 86
 Raspberry Filling, '90 111
 Ricotta Filling, '80 58
 Sour Cream-Coconut Filling, '92 120
 Strawberry-Lemon Filling, '04 137
 Vanilla Pastry Cream, '01 45
 Whipped Cream Filling, '90 265, 307; '99 307;
  '03 319
 White Chocolate Cream Filling, '92 230
 White Chocolate Filling, '89 160

FISH. *See also* **CLAMS, CRAB, CRAWFISH,**
  LOBSTER, OYSTERS, SALMON,
  SCALLOPS, SEAFOOD, SHRIMP, TUNA.
Amandine, Fillet of Fish, '80 M54
Amberjack Sandwiches, Grilled, '91 195
Asparagus Divan, Fish-, '87 128
Baked
 Almond Baked Fish, '88 270; '89 203
 Barbecue Sauce, Baked Fish with, '84 92
 Creamy Baked Fillets, '84 91
 Crunchy Baked Fish Fillets, '85 217
 Fast Fish Bake, '85 218
 Herbed Fish and Potato Bake, '79 287; '80 34
 Lemon-Celery Sauce, Baked Fillets in, '84 91
 Saucy Fish Bake, '79 75
 Southern Baked Fish, '82 73
Beer-Batter Fish, '85 68
Bluefish Chowder, '84 282
Broiled Fish Fillets Piquante, '84 91
Broiled Herb Fish Fillets, '79 99
Cakes, Fish, '85 54
Catfish
 Amandine, Mandarin Catfish, '84 183
 Amandine, Spicy Catfish, '89 52
 Appetizer, Layered Catfish, '92 209
 Baked Catfish, '94 67
 Baked Catfish, Barbecue, '02 51
 Baked Catfish, Cajun-, '02 218
 Barbecued Catfish, '80 157
 Barbecued Catfish, Lemon, '88 271; '89 202
 Battered Catfish and Chips, '02 140
 Blackened Catfish, '97 82
 Breaded Catfish with Creole Sauce, '90 28
 Breaded Herbed Fish Fillets, '91 121
 Broiled Manchac, Catfish, Middendorf's, '84 183
 Cakes, Catfish, '94 70
 Cakes, Creole Catfish, '97 82
 Caribbean Catfish with Spicy Island Sweet
  Potatoes, '04 310
 Cream Cheese Stuffing, Catfish with, '89 52
 Crispy Catfish, '03 101
 Crunchy Catfish, '02 256

Dip, Layered Catfish, '03 185
Eldorado de Colorado, Catfish, '84 183
Fingers, Crackermeal Catfish, '89 53
Fingers with Curried Rice, Crunchy Catfish,
 '04 20
Fried Catfish, '82 135; '83 169; '00 172; '04 100
Fried Catfish, Classic, '97 82; '01 135
Fried Catfish, Crisp, '82 242
Fried Catfish, Crisp-, '88 110
Fried Catfish, Delta-Style, '04 121
Fried Catfish, Front Porch, '96 233
Fried Catfish, Front-Porch, '02 166
Fried Catfish, Golden, '80 99
Fried Catfish, Jack's, '04 164
"Fried" Catfish with Lemon Cream, Spicy,
 '03 212
Fried Lemon-Rosemary Catfish, '02 319
Fry, Burk's Farm-Raised Catfish, '95 158
Fry, Catfish, '84 184
Grilled Catfish Cajun-Style, '90 129
Grilled Catfish over Mixed Greens, '04 326
Grilled Catfish with Red Salsa, '90 172
Grilled Catfish with Relish, '92 54
Grilled Fish with Heather Sauce, Catfish Inn's,
 '84 182
Gumbo, Catfish, '90 278; '91 216
Jack's Catfish, '99 32
Kiev-Style, Catfish, '84 184
Lafitte, Catfish, '97 83
Lime-Orange Catfish, '02 22
Louisiana, Catfish, '93 291
Meunière, Catfish, '80 57
Microwave Catfish, '89 M52
Mousse, Catfish, '92 327
Nuggets with Spicy Tartar Sauce, Hushpuppy-
 Battered Catfish, '04 313
Oven-Baked Catfish with Tartar Sauce, '01 316
Oven-Fried Catfish, '95 106; '99 174
Oven-Fried Catfish, Southern, '87 163
Parmesan, Catfish, '79 184; '86 210; '99 91
Parmesan Catfish, '92 309
Pasta with Catfish and Artichokes, '90 123
Pecan, Catfish, '85 53
Pecan Catfish, '98 329
Pecan Catfish with Lemon Sauce, '03 185
Pecan with Lemon-Thyme-Pecan Butter, Catfish,
 '04 68
Pilaf, Catfish, '94 171
Potato-Crusted Catfish and Chips, '02 140
Potato-Crusted Catfish with Warm Pinto Bean-
 and-Bacon Salsa, '03 331
Ranchero Catfish, '04 322
Sandwiches, Fried Catfish, '02 60
Sesame, Catfish, '81 106
Smoked Catfish, '84 47
South by Southwest Catfish with Guacamole
 Aïoli, '04 314
Southern-Fried Catfish and Chips, '02 140
Spicy Catfish, '01 209
Spicy Catfish with Vegetables and Basil Cream,
 '03 56
Spicy-Seasoned Catfish, '89 M66
Spread, Best-Ever Catfish, '98 60
Stew, Cajun-Style Catfish, '88 12
Stir, Catfish, '84 184
Stuffed Catfish, Crown Room's Shrimp-, '84 182
Stuffed Catfish, Soufflé-, '84 183
Taco Appetizers, Fish, '04 324
Tacos, Baja-Style Fried Catfish, '04 311
Ceviche in Avocado Shells, '81 33
Ceviche (Marinated Raw Fish), '80 194; '82 220
Ceviche, Mexican-Style, '88 115
Chart, Fat and Lean Fish, '85 180
Chowder, Chunky Fish, '92 331

Chowder, Creamy Fish, '79 16
Chowder, Fish, '79 152; '84 M38
Chowder, Tasty Fish, '80 188
Corned Fish, '79 32
Dinner, Jollof Rice, '91 230; '92 325
Dip, Smoked Fish, '84 46
en Papillote, Fish with Snow Peas, '86 144
Fillet of Fish a l'Orange, '89 180
Fillets, Lemon-Coated, '80 M53
Florentine, Fish, '86 35
Florentine in Parchment, Fish, '87 22
Flounder
 Amandine, Flounder, '89 M196
 Ambassador, Flounder, '86 234
 Aspic, Fish 'n, '84 190
 Baked Flounder, '79 31; '90 316
 Baked Flounder au Fromage, '86 234
 Baked Flounder Supreme, '79 75
 Broiled Flounder, '88 28; '89 310
 Broiled Flounder, Cheesy, '84 69
 Broiled Flounder, Pesto, '86 150
 Broil, Flounder-Grapefruit, '85 53
 Caesar's Fish, '90 76
 Casserole, Green Chile-and-Fish, '84 32
 Chowder, Basque Fish, '86 36
 Creole Flounder with Lemon Couscous, '00 99
 Creole-Style Flounder, '85 180
 Crunchy Flounder, Quick, '90 76
 Crust, Fish in a, '84 294
 Delight, Fish, '86 M212
 Dijon, Flounder, '85 95
 Fried Fish, '79 151
 Fried Fish, Crispy, '84 92
 Fried Flounder, Crispy, '84 93
 Fried Flounder, Seasoned, '79 214
 Grilled Flounder Fillets, '83 213
 Hollandaise-Shrimp Sauce, Flounder with,
  '86 234
 Italian Fish, '88 270; '89 203
 Monterey, Fish, '84 293
 Nicole, Flounder, '85 217
 Oven-Fried Fish Fillets, '79 75
 Papillote, Ocean, '84 M287
 Poached Fish with Greek Sauce, '91 M183
 Rolls, Vegetable-Filled Fish, '86 M251
 Rollups, Shrimp-Stuffed, '82 234
 Royal Flounder Fillets, '91 128
 Sesame Flounder, '89 33
 Shrimp Sauce, Flounder Fillets in, '83 227
 Stuffed Flounder, Crab-, '80 120; '81 176
 Stuffed Flounder Fillets, '86 234
 Stuffed Flounder, Grand Lagoon, '94 68
 Stuffed Flounder Rolls, Vegetable-, '87 6
 Stuffed Flounder Rolls with Citrus Sauce,
  '85 180
 Stuffed with Shrimp, Flounder, '88 51
 Thermidor, Flounder, '85 190
 Vegetable Medley, Flounder-, '85 217
 Wine Sauce, Fillet of Flounder in, '80 179; '81 30
 Wrap, Fish in a, '97 64
Fresh Fish, Preparing, '82 127
Fried Fish, Golden, '82 134
Fried Fish, Sephardic-Style, '00 324
Fried Fish, Southern, '92 168
Grecian Seafood, '97 314
Greek Fish with Vegetable Sauce, '82 72
Grilled Fish and Vegetables, '89 179
Grilled Fish, Easy, '91 194
Grilled Fish with Caribbean Salsa, Montego Bay,
 '96 70
Grill Fish, How to Charcoal-, '84 48
Grouper
 Baked Fish, '98 122
 Baked Grouper, Creamy, '85 292

Batter-Fried Grouper Sandwiches, '96 197
Breaded Grouper Fillets, '89 M36
Broiled Grouper, Heavenly, '99 91
Creole Fish, '87 M79
Fingers, Grouper, '00 167
Gourmet Fish, '86 71
Grilled Grouper, '86 185
Grilled Herbed Grouper, '99 178
Grilled Marinated Grouper, '90 166
Guadalajara Grouper, '98 17
Herb-Coated Fish, '86 M112
Hot Spicy Grouper, '94 78
Macadamia, Grouper, '85 127
Marinated Grouper, Garlic-Basil, '94 160
Pan-Fried Fish Fillets, '91 196
Pan-Fried Grouper with Vanilla Wine Sauce,
    '94 241
Parmesan Fillets, '86 M112
Pesto Grouper with Orzo, '97 321
Sauté, Shrimp-and-Grouper, '87 91
Spectacular, Grouper, '84 163
Steamed Fish and Vegetables, '91 32
Stuffed Fillets, Apple-Carrot, '88 M192
Tarragon Fillets, Easy, '00 14
Vegetables, Grouper with Confetti, '88 M189
Vegetables, Grouper with Sautéed, '90 M233
Gumbo, Easy Fish, '81 6
Haddock, Baked, '80 179; '81 30
Haddock Fillets in White Wine, '90 76
Haddock Fillets with Zucchini Stuffing, '88 M191
Haddock Italiano, '81 M4
Halibut, Chinese-Style Fried, '80 179; '81 30
Halibut Steaks Italiano, '88 M191
Halibut Steak, Wine-Herb, '94 171
Halibut with Champagne Sauce, Baked, '90 29
Halibut with Cider, '79 182
Halibut with Orange-Curry Sauce, '87 91
Halibut with Swiss Sauce, '83 M195
Hash, Smoked Fish, '92 306
Heroes, Neptune, '84 281
Herring Dip, Yogurt, '80 232
Italian Fish, Easy, '86 M112
Kebabs, Fish, '98 223
Mackerel Creole, '80 126
Mackerel, Lemon-Baked, '79 182
Mackerel, Rosemary-Garlic, '92 200
Mackerel, Smoked Salmon or, '84 46
Mahimahi in Grape Sauce, '91 218
Mahi Mahi, Macadamia, '88 164
Mahimahi, Middle Eastern, '96 92
Mahi-Mahi with Lemon Mayonnaise, '99 178
Marinated Beer-Battered Fish, '86 180
Mix, Fish Herb, '98 51
Monkfish, Greek-Style, '87 M79
Mullet, Festive, '79 75
Mullet, Smoked, '84 47
Mullet Spread, '94 159
Orange Roughy
    Asian-Inspired Orange Roughy, '99 122
    Baked Fish with Parmesan-Sour Cream Sauce,
        '01 209
    Basil-Orange Roughy with Vegetables, '92 98
    Caper Sauce, Fish in, '95 209
    Caribbean Fish, '99 109
    Curried Baked Fish, '87 5
    Curry-Baked Fish, '91 196
    Dijon, Orange Roughy, '99 122
    Fillets, Crispy Baked, '99 90
    Fillets, Quick Fish, '96 196
    Fillets Tomatillo, '94 135
    Fillets with Herb Sauce, Orange Roughy, '91 29
    Kiwi Orange Roughy, '87 193
    Mustard Fish, Spicy, '99 90
    Oven-Fried Fish, '91 172; '94 172

Oven-Fried Fish, Mexi-Style, '90 76
Pan-Fried Roughy with Tomato-Basil Salsa,
    '99 123
Pecan Roughy with Brown Butter Sauce, '91 64
Pesto-Crusted Orange Roughy, '96 156
Sour Cream, Fish with, '89 180
Spinach Pesto, Orange Roughy with, '88 M192
Steamed Orange Roughy with Herbs, '95 189
Stew, Fish-and-Vegetable, '87 220
Stir-Fry, Orange Roughy, '98 50
Stir-Fry, Orange Roughy-and-Vegetable, '91 50
Tropical Orange Roughy with Crab Stuffing,
    '99 122
Vegetable-Topped Orange Roughy, '93 67
Perch Fillets, Buttery Baked, '81 134
Perch, Parmesan-Crusted, '93 91
Poached Fish in Creamy Swiss Sauce, '80 M53
Po'boys, Zesty Fish, '03 120
Pollock with Summer Squash Relish, '92 200
Potatoes, Fish-Stuffed, '92 306
Potato Platter, Fish-and-, '89 M248
Redfish Court Bouillon, '83 290; '84 93
Redfish with Shrimp and Crab, Coastal Bend,
    '01 281
Salad, Smoked Fish-Potato, '84 233
Salad, Smoky Seafood, '84 46
Sautéed Seafood Platter, '83 89
Scamp, Tangy Broiled, '87 5
Sea Bass, Hong Kong-Style, '96 196
Seasoning Blend, Fish-and-Seafood, '88 28
Seviche Cocktail, '83 258
Shad Roe with Lemon-Butter Sauce, Baked, '84 252
Shark, Marinated, '79 151
Skillet Fish Dinner, '88 199
Skillet Fish, Spicy, '03 165
Smoked Fish, '92 305
Smoked Fish Log, '85 144
Snapper
    Baked Snapper à l'Orange, '85 181
    Baked Snapper and Stuffing, '82 72
    Baked Snapper with Tarragon Stuffing, '82 136
    Blackened Red Snapper, '90 27
    Captain's Spicy One, '81 125
    Caribbean Banana Fish, '95 202
    Caribbean Snapper, '87 5
    Chowder, Red Snapper, '85 217
    Company Red Snapper, '82 72
    Destin, Snapper, '88 222
    Dill, Snapper with, '84 190
    Fingers with Banana Salsa, Snapper, '96 85
    Glazed Snapper with Rosemary, '98 51
    Grilled Snapper with Orange-Almond Sauce,
        '01 158
    Gumbo, Savannah Snapper, '94 105
    Honey-Curried Snapper, '85 181
    Horseradish-Crusted Red Snapper, '96 227
    Huachinango à la Veracruzana (Veracruz-Style
        Red Snapper), '80 193
    Lemon Sauce, Red Snapper with, '01 83
    Louisiane, Red Snapper, '85 217
    Orangy Snapper, '88 23
    Oven-Fried Snapper, '90 75
    Pecan-Crusted Snapper with Crabmeat Relish,
        Lemony, '99 198
    Peppered Snapper with Creamy Dill Sauce,
        '94 42
    Poached Fish with Vegetables, '89 332; '90 18
    Poached Red Snapper, '85 127
    Poached Snapper, '83 101
    Provençal, Snapper, '91 M170
    Rome, Fillet of Snapper, '80 57
    Southwestern Snapper, '91 195
    Spanish-Style Fillets, '86 M112
    Spicy Snapper, '89 179

Stuffed Red Snapper Rolls, Cucumber-, '83 176
Stuffed Red Snapper with Lime, '83 246
Stuffed Snapper, '87 138
Vegetables, Yellowtail Snapper with Julienne,
    '93 31
Veracruz, Red Snapper, '88 149; '92 142
Wine Sauce, Red Snapper in, '85 138
Sole Divan, '87 21
Sole Fillets, Herbed, '82 21
Sole Fillets in Wine Sauce, '81 109
Sole in Papillote, '82 22
Sole Provençal, Fillet of, '85 78
Sole Royale, '89 104
Sole, Saucy, '82 M68
Sole Véronique, '85 181
Sole with Cucumber Sauce, '84 M286
Soup with Garlic Mayonnaise, Rich Fish, '92 56
Spread, Smoked Fish, '92 305
Steaks, Soy Fish, '86 M112
Stock, Fish, '95 19; '00 65
Stock, Homemade Fish, '92 237
Surprise, Fish, '84 231
Sweet-and-Sour Fish, '80 M54
Swordfish, Foil-Baked, '87 5
Swordfish, Mediterranean, '02 237
Swordfish Salad, '00 18
Swordfish-Shiitake Skewers, '97 168
Swordfish, Skewered, '86 256
Swordfish Steaks, Orange-Ginger Marinated,
    '93 271
Swordfish Steak with Chervil Butter, '91 147
Swordfish Stir-Fry, '96 128
Swordfish with Caper Sauce, Grilled, '95 230
Swordfish with Cashew-and-Cracked Pepper Crust,
    '96 196
Tacos, Barbecued Fish, '95 339
Trout
    Amandine, Classic Trout, '96 202; '01 110
    Amandine, Fish, '85 179
    Amandine, Gaston's Trout, '96 232
    Amandine, Orange Lake, '80 99
    Amandine, Trout, '99 53
    Baked Fish Fillets, Creamy, '85 217
    Baked Trout, '95 106
    Cakes with Lemon-Butter Sauce, Mountain
        Trout, '92 337
    Cornmeal-Crusted Trout, '99 52
    Delmonico, Trout, '80 57
    Fillets with Capers, Trout, '95 252
    Florentine, Cheesy Trout, '85 53
    Grilled Rainbow Trout with Mushroom Stuffing,
        '97 162
    Grilled Trout, '95 106
    Grilled Trout with Ginger and Soy Sauce, '85 228
    Laurie, Trout, '88 270; '89 202
    Pecan-Crusted Trout with Orange Sauce,
        '98 M82
    Poached Trout, '95 106
    Salad with Black Pepper Vinaigrette, Trout-and-
        Tomato, '98 284
    Smoked Trout, '84 47
    Spread, Smoked Trout, '84 47
    Stuffed Rainbow Trout, '93 121
    Stuffed Trout, Sweet Onion-, '99 52
    Stuffed with Crawfish, Bacon-Wrapped Trout,
        '99 54
    Sunshine Trout, '84 M286
    Tomato Sauce, Fish in, '85 75
    Wine Sauce, Trout in, '80 180; '81 31
Two, Fish for, '92 60
Vegetable Dinner, Fish-and-, '91 196
Vegetables, Cheesy Fish and, '94 254
Veracruz Fish with Shrimp, '86 130
Whitefish Spread, Smoked, '92 58

FLAN. *See* **CUSTARDS/Flans.**
FOKTY. *See* **FROM OUR KITCHEN.**
FONDUE
  Beer-and-Cheddar Fondue, '03 223
  Caramel Fondue, '94 332; '95 35
  Cheese Fondue, '81 40
  Cheese Fondue, Party, '92 20
  Chocolate Fondue, '91 142
  Chocolate Fondue, Brandied, '93 162
  Chocolate Plunge, '94 332; '95 35
  Dessert Fondue, '89 281
  Fruitcake Fondue, '84 258
  Goat Cheese Fondue, Warm, '96 234
  Nacho Fondue, '94 332; '95 35
  Peppermint Fondue, '94 332; '95 35
  Pub Fondue, '94 332; '95 35
  Spinach Fondue Sandwiches, Grilled, '99 337
  Swiss Cheese Fondue, '91 48
  White Chocolate Fondue, '92 287
FRANKFURTERS
  Appetizer Franks, Saucy, '84 M12
  Appetizers, Bourbon Frankfurter, '85 207
  Bacon-Wrapped Franks, '81 202
  Barbecued Frankfurters, '83 144; '84 M12
  Barbecued Frankfurters, Oven-, '83 11
  Barbecued Franks, '85 192
  Barbecue, Tangy Frank, '79 63
  Beans and Franks, '85 142
  Beans and Franks, Hawaiian Baked, '80 136
  Beans and Franks, Jiffy, '91 M172
  Beans-and-Franks, Polynesian, '84 M11
  Beans, Stove-Top Franks 'n', '88 201
  Beany Hot Dogs, '82 190
  Cabbage with Apples and Franks, '87 42
  Casserole, Hot Doggie, '88 200
  Casserole, Layered Frankfurter, '79 64
  Chafing Dish Franks, '83 143
  Chili-Cheese Dogs, '81 M176
  Chili, Hot Dog, '04 199
  Corn Dog Bites, '85 245; '93 79
  Corn Dogs and Taters, '02 57
  Corn Dogs, Favorite, '83 144
  Corn Puppies, '97 140
  Corn Relish Dogs, '85 192
  Crusty Franks, '80 166
  Delicious, Hot Dogs, '81 202
  Deluxe, Hot Dog, '97 140
  Family-Style Franks, '79 54
  Fried Hot Dogs, '02 56
  Grilled Stuffed Franks, '82 163
  Hash Browns, Franks and, '80 166
  Hawaiian Franks, '81 202
  Jubilee, Hot Dog, '81 113
  Kraut and Franks, Beany, '79 64
  Marrow's Famous Dogs, '04 198
  Mexicali Hot Dogs, '82 131
  Mexican Franks, '93 78
  Pickled Party Franks, '83 174
  Pigs in a Blanket, '95 178
  Pigs in a Blanket, Mexican, '00 199
  Pigs on a Roll, Three Little, '98 203
  Pizza Dogs, Grilled, '97 139
  Pizzas, Hot Dog, '93 78
  Potatoes, Cheesy Frank-Topped, '83 3
  Potatoes, Frank-Filled, '84 M11
  Potluck Dish, Frankaroni, '88 201
  Rollups, Wienie, '02 186
  Sandwiches, Frankfurter, '84 M11
  Sauce, Hot Diggity Dog, '93 198
  Saucy Franks, '88 201
  Scrambled Dog, Dinglewood Pharmacy's, '95 118
  Skillet Dinner, Frankfurter, '80 166
  Skillet, Frankfurter-Cabbage, '80 166
  Skillet, Hot Dog and Spaghetti, '83 144

  Sloppy Joe Dogs, '85 192
  Soup, Split Pea and Frankfurter, '79 64
  Spanish Frankfurters, '80 166
  Spicy Frankfurters, '81 202
  Stuffed Franks and Potatoes, '81 202
  Supper, Hot Dog, '93 78
  Taco Dogs, '02 M57
  Tipsy Franks, '85 52
  Wiener Worms, '02 223
FRENCH TOAST
  Almond French Toast, '88 62
  Amandine, Baked Toast, '82 47
  Amaretto French Toast, '98 280
  Apple French Toast, '98 55
  au Fromage, French Toast, '88 288
  Baked Apple French Toast, '03 M283
  Banana Splits, French Toast, '96 M164
  Caramel-Pecan French Toast, '03 328
  Caramel-Soaked French Toast, '03 307
  Caribbean French Toast, '92 46
  Cinnamon French Toast, '84 211
  Cinnamon Toasty Fruity Delight, '00 193
  Cottage-Topped French Toast, '85 49
  Easy French Toast, '82 M172
  Eggnog French Toast, '95 313
  English Muffin French Toast, '00 179
  Grand Marnier Fruit Sauce, French Toast with, '90 93
  Ham-and-Cheese Oven French Toast, '97 172
  Macadamia French Toast, '86 96
  Macadamia Nut French Toast, '95 282
  Make-Ahead French Toast with Strawberry Sauce,
    '02 131
  Orange Butter, French Toast with, '81 42
  Orange French Toast, '83 292; '84 78; '86 329
  Orange Sauce, French Toast with, '82 47
  Oven-Baked French Toast, '82 47; '90 192
  Oven-Baked French Toast, Easy, '93 195
  Overnight French Toast, '89 227
  Overnight French Toast Deluxe, '79 216
  Pain Perdu, '04 67
  Pain-Perdu Po-Boy, '93 291
  Painted French Toast, '98 206
  Peach-Filled French Toast, '98 160
  Peachy French Toast, '98 56
  Peanut Butter and Jelly French Toast, '00 198
  Peanut Butter French Toast, '93 166
  Potato-Crusted Texas Toast, '94 142
  Pound Cake French Toast, '04 33
  Praline French Toast, '98 55
  Sandwiches, Strawberry-French Toast, '91 160
  Slender French Toast, '86 103
  Stuffed French Toast, '96 52; '98 55, 313; '00 193;
    '02 105
  Stuffed French Toast, Orange-, '98 54
  Stuffed French Toast, Three Cheese, '93 122
  Waffled French Toast, '82 47
FRITTERS
  Apple Fritter Rings, '88 44
  Apple Fritters, '81 105; '82 273; '85 14; '97 153
  Apple Fritters with Lemon Sauce, '01 184
  Apple Holiday Fritters, '86 314
  Banana Fritters, '79 213
  Beet Fritters, '96 36
  Blueberry Fritters, '85 152
  Broccoli-Cauliflower Fritters, '02 45
  Broccoli Fritters, Cheesy, '79 53
  Buñuelos, '93 29
  Cauliflower-Cheddar Fritters, '98 25
  Chicken-and-Mashed Potato Fritters with Lime-
    Cayenne Mayonnaise, '04 121
  Clam Fritters, '79 151; '86 71
  Corn-and-Crab Fritters, '97 227
  Corn Fritters, '86 192; '94 22; '98 207
  Corn Fritters, Golden, '80 165; '81 128

  Corn Fritters, Skillet-Fried, '85 14
  Corn-Jalapeño Fritters, '96 153
  Crab Fritters, '98 142
  Eggplant Fritters, '91 211
  Ham Fritters, '82 39
  Ham Fritters with Creamy Sauce, '81 105
  Honey Puffs, '96 153
  Leek-and-Potato Fritters, '00 324
  Okra, Fritter-Fried, '86 218
  Okra Fritters, '79 160; '98 159
  Orange Fritters, Puffy, '81 169
  Oyster Fritters, '79 31; '97 20
  Pear Fritters, Ol' Timey, '86 51
  Pecan Fritters, Chocolate-Covered, '79 205
  Pineapple Fritters, '88 112; '00 238
  Potato Fritters, Cheese-Stuffed, '96 153
  Potato-Ham Fritters, '98 249
  Shrimp Fritters, '00 238
  Squash Fritters, '89 68
  Squash-Jalapeño Fritters, '98 249
  Sweet Potato Fritters, '88 44
  Sweet Potato Fritters, Golden, '79 9
  Zucchini Fritters, '81 163
  Zucchini Fritters, Cheesy, '88 44
FROG LEGS
  Crispy Frog Legs, '80 99
  Fried Frog Legs, '88 110
FROM OUR KITCHEN (FOK)
  Alcohol, substituting in recipes, '92 314; '99 148;
    '00 66; '01 138
  Almond brickle chips, '02 28
    substitute for, '02 28
  Almonds, salted, '00 330
  Aluminum foil, '02 100, 216
  Apples, '84 227, 228
    adding to meat loaf, '98 138
    amounts to buy, '84 228
    preventing browning after cutting, '84 228
    selecting for cooking, '84 227, 228
    selecting for eating, '84 227, 228
    storing, '84 228; '01 202
  Appliances, kitchen. *See* **FOK/Dishwasher, Food**
    processor, Freezer, Kitchen, Microwave
    oven, Ovens, Refrigerator, Slow cooker.
  Arrowroot, as a thickening agent, '83 147
  Artichokes, '00 66, '03 30
    discoloration of, '03 30
  Asparagus, '01 118
    pickled, '04 174
    selecting, '01 118
    storing, '01 118
  Avocados, '03 132
    preserving color of, '03 132
    removing the seed from, '03 132
    softening, '96 76
    storing, '03 132
  Bacon
    cooking, '00 330; '01 335
    freezing, '02 28
  Baking soda, as ice melter, '98 36
  Barbecue, '94 155. *See also* **FOK/Grilling.**
    bottled sauces, '00 180
    chicken, '94 155
    recipe, Barbecue Ribs, '99 68
    tongs, using to reach things, '97 206
  Basil
    fresh, '03 208
    recipes for purees, '03 208
  Bay leaves, removing from soups, '95 314; '96 51
  Beans, canned, '01 98
    baked, '01 166
  Beans, dried, '88 4; '99 250
    amount of folate in, '99 250
    baked, '01 166

buying, '88 4
cooking, '88 4; '99 100
soaking, '88 4; '03 30
storing, '88 4
Beans, green, steaming, '03 132
Beef, '83 38; '92 65, 66; '94 140; '04 130
barbacoa, '02 148
bresaola, '02 148
browning, '83 38; '02 132
buying, '83 38; '90 276; '92 65; '04 130
churrascos, '02 148
cooking methods, '83 38
fat content of, '92 65, 66; '94 140;
'04 130
freezing, '02 178
freezing cooked, '02 28
handling properly, '87 208; '94 140; '96 76;
'01 335
making gravy from pan drippings, '83 38
marinating, '02 46
removing fat from browned, '02 132
selecting (chart), '02 100
stir-frying, '01 335
storing, '94 140
tenderizing, '83 38
Beers
selecting, '99 250; '00 250
tasting, '99 250; '00 250
types of, '99 250; '00 250
Berries. *See also* **FOK/Blueberries.**
selecting, '99 148
storing, '99 148
Beverages, '83 191; '90 276, 277; '97 174; '98 218.
See also **FOK/Alcohol, Beers, Buttermilk,
Coffee, Eggnog, Ice, Tea, Water, Wines.**
chilling quickly, '96 21
determining amounts to buy for entertaining,
'90 276, 277
as food preservative, '02 70
freezing, '92 314
garnishing, '97 56
glasses, '97 184
ice cubes of tea and fruit juice, '01 260
ice molds, '86 331
limeade, '03 224
placement of in basic table setting, '90 182
placement of when entertaining, '90 277
recipe, Chocolate Iced Coffee, '01 166
recipe, Low-Fat Cappuccino Cooler, '01 166
recipe, Mint Juleps, '04 94
recipe, Royal Cup Chiller, '98 218
substituting for alcohol in recipes, '92 314;
'99 148; '00 66
sugar syrup, recipe, '03 224
Biscuits, '89 211, 212; '92 52. *See also*
FOK/Breads, Rolls, Yeast.
baking, '89 211, 212
cutting dough, '89 211; '95 30; '97 36
freezing, '89 212
kneading, '92 52
making dough for, '89 211; '92 52
reheating, '89 212
removing burned bottoms from, '96 51
storing leftovers, '89 212
using food processor to make, '89 211, 212;
'96 256
Blueberries, '04 148
buying, '04 148
freezing, '01 166; '03 148; '04 148
freezing before adding to batter, '98 138
serving amounts, '00 156
storing, '00 156; '01 166; '03 148
washing, '00 156; '04 148
Bouillon cubes, '00 100

Breads, '82 198; '84 92; '89 268; '92 52, 102, 314;
'93 183. *See also* **FOK/Biscuits, Muffins,
Rolls, Yeast.**
commercial products, '03 148
cutting, '91 144, 145
doubling recipes, '91 22
freezing, '89 268; '90 315; '91 95; '92 102
as gifts, '91 95
metal dough scraper, '90 126; '92 52
microwave oven, '89 268
in pudding, '00 128
purchasing, '03 148
quick breads, '84 92; '89 268; '04 224
recipe, Bread Dough Basket, '04 64
recipe, Icebox Rolls, '04 130
refrigerated products, '01 202
rising procedures, '87 12; '89 268; '98 72
selecting fresh, '01 202
serving warm, '01 260
substituting oat flour, '00 28
testing for doneness, '84 92; '92 314
yeast breads, '84 92; '87 12; '89 268; '92 314
yeast rolls, '83 323
Broccoli, '84 249
cutting, '93 132
preparing, '84 249
selecting, '84 249
Broths. *See* **FOK/Soups.**
Brussels sprouts, '84 249
preparing, '84 249
selecting, '84 249
Butter, '82 189; '95 314; '99 296; '00 300
availability of, '82 189
balls, how to make, '82 189
clarifying, '82 189; '97 232
curls, how to make, '82 189
fat content of, '82 189; '00 300
softening, '00 300
storing, '82 189; '00 300
substituting for in baked goods, '90 314; '97 134
Buttermilk
adding to bottled salad dressings, '00 66
freezing, '92 314; '97 72
powdered, '00 66
substitutes for, '00 66
Butterscotch, '98 238
Cactus (Nopales), '94 29
cooking, '94 29
selecting, '94 29
storing, '94 29
Cakes, '89 57, 58; '91 144, 200, 201;
'92 154, 155, 314; '94 59; '00 128. *See also*
FOK/Fruitcakes.
assembling Twinkling Star Cake, '00 330
baking techniques, '89 57; '98 218
cheesecakes, cutting, '96 140
cheesecakes, disguising cracks in, '96 112
cheesecakes, eliminating cracks in, '91 300
cooling, '92 155; '96 208; '99 128, 328
cutting, '91 144; '92 314; '95 30
decorating, '94 59; '99 328
dry ingredients, '87 12; '92 155
freezing, '89 58; '90 314, 315; '99 328; '02 316
frosting, '89 57, 58; '02 316
as gifts, '02 316
greasing pans, '92 314
jellyroll cakes, '92 314
mixing procedures, '89 57; '92 154, 155; '99 328
pan sizes, '92 154, 314; '96 332; '00 128
personalized cakepans, '04 148
pound cakes '84 92, 319 (baking tips chart);
'92 154, 155; '00 206; '03 102
repairing disasters, '96 21
server, '02 316

as snacks, '91 200, 201
storing, '89 57, 58; '92 155; '99 328; '01 300
substituting flours, '92 155
testing for doneness, '84 92; '92 155;
'96 112, 332
Campsite cooking, '86 172
cleaning up, '86 172
making lists, '86 172
packing, '86 172
planning, '86 172
Candy
crushing hard, '96 21, 76; '02 28
as dessert topping, '02 194
recipe, Sugared Rabbits, '04 94
using leftover in baking, '01 220
Canning fruits and vegetables, '84 180;
'89 141, 142; '93 136, 137; '99 180. *See also*
FOK/Paraffin.
and altitude, '03 148
boiling water bath, '84 180; '89 141, 142;
'91 300; '93 136, 137; '03 148
equipment, '93 137; '97 278; '99 180; '00 156;
'03 148
packing, '84 180; '89 141, 142; '03 148
safety, '84 180; '89 141, 142; '91 300; '93 137;
'03 148
steam pressure method of, '84 180; '89 141, 142
sterilizing equipment, '03 148
Caramel, '98 238; '00 66
Casseroles
doubling recipes, '91 22, 23, 96; '01 335
freezing, '90 314; '91 96; '96 112; '03 274
preventing spoilage of, '87 208
using oats in, '00 28
Cast-iron cookware, '93 33; '99 50; '04 48
caring for, '93 33; '99 50
cleaning, '99 50
seasoning, '93 33; '99 50
Cauliflower, '84 249
cutting, '93 132
maintaining color of during cooking, '01 118
preparing, '84 249; '99 100
selecting, '84 249
Celery, chopping, '01 202
Centerpieces, '90 205; '97 232; '01 335
Easter, '04 94
entrée as, '04 276
Cereal, hot, adding oat bran to, '00 28
Champagne. *See* **FOKTY/Wines.**
Cheese, '82 109
browning, '01 50
buying, '85 210; '90 276
cheese straws, '02 216
cooking with, '85 210; '87 12; '01 98
freezing, '82 109; '85 211; '02 28
fresh mozzarella, '04 174
grating, '00 224
handling properly, '87 208
melting, '01 50
preshredded combinations, '01 138
rinds of, '01 138
serving, '85 210, 211; '02 240; '04 276
shredding, '95 31 (illustration)
as snacks, '91 200, 201
storing, '85 210
waxed coverings of, '01 138
Cheesecakes. *See* **FOKTY/Cakes.**
Chicken, '87 12; '88 39; '94 155, 253
barbecuing, '94 155
boning, '88 39
cooking, '87 12; '88 39; '95 246; '97 112
cutting up, '94 253
handling properly, '87 208; '99 128; '03 50
marinating, '02 46

microwaving, '88 39
packaging of, '88 39; '02 148
pounder, '04 204
preparing for stir-frying, '91 160; '01 335
recipe, Chicken-and-Smoked Sausage Pilau,
  '04 204
Children in the kitchen, '91 92; '92 102, 207
gadgets for, '00 206
Chili, types of, '03 30
China, '88 301
removing marks from, '88 301
storing, '88 301
washing, '88 301
Chinese cooking, '85 76
equipment, '85 76
garnishing, '85 76
preparing food for, '85 76
Chocolate, '86 246, 247; '92 314; '93 317; '00 224
dipping, '86 330, 331; '04 94
garnishing with, '86 247; '93 317; '94 59;
  '96 230, 256
illustrations for chocolate sacks, '93 317
kinds of, '86 246, 247
measuring, '01 118
melting, '92 314; '93 317; '96 21, 332; '02 46
storing, '01 220; '02 46
substitutions, '86 246, 247; '00 156
using to line pie shells, '97 36
white chocolate, '86 246, 247; '94 59
Cholesterol, '90 72
and food labels, '90 72
Cleaning up. *See* **FOK/Recipe preparation.**
Clothing for "chefs," '97 278
Club soda, using to remove stains, '96 304
Coconut, '98 238
Coffee
accessories, '04 30
beverages, '98 218
freezing excess, '98 306
recipe, Chocolate Iced Coffee, '01 166
recipe, Low-Fat Cappuccino Cooler, '01 166
using spices in to enhance flavor of, '00 224
Commercial food products
baking mix, '03 132
breads, '03 148
frozen roll dough, '03 224
jalapeño jelly, '03 186
olive oil, '03 102
pickles and pickle relish, '03 102
seasoning blend, '03 132
vinegars, '03 102
Computer, index online, '01 300
Cookbooks, '02 148, 240
creating keepsake, '03 274
making notations in, '96 160
Cookies, '91 234; '92 207, 208; '95 30
baking, '92 208; '98 326; '02 216
cooling, '92 208; '96 208; '98 326
crushing, '95 30
equipment, '92 208; '00 100, 330
freezing, '90 314; '92 207, 208; '02 216, 316
freezing dough, '97 112
as gifts, '91 95
mixing procedures, '92 207
recipe, Chocolate Chip-Peanut Butter Cookies,
  '99 68
shaped cookie cutters, '97 56
slicing dough, '96 140, 230; '97 112
storing, '92 208; '01 300
testing for doneness, '84 92

uneven baking, '00 330
using dough as piecrust, '01 335
using oats in dough, '00 28
Cooking directions, basic, '87 12, 208. *See also*
  **FOK/Handling food properly, Recipe
  preparation.**
chicken, '87 12
shrimp, '87 12
Cooking oils, '98 112; '01 50, 118
best for frying, '02 216
checking for freshness, '02 216
flavored, '01 50
reusing, '02 216
storing used, '02 216
varieties of, '98 112; '02 216
Cooking spray. *See* **FOKTY/Vegetable cooking
  spray.**
Cooking torch, '01 50, 118
Cookware, '85 329; '86 227; '90 50; '93 33, 183,
  220; '03 70. *See also* **FOK/Cast-iron
  cookware, Kitchen.**
broken, '02 46
caring for, '85 329; '93 33, 183
keeping metal handles cool, '97 184
for microwave, '86 227
selecting, '85 329; '86 227; '93 220;
  '01 220
Corn, '04 64
buttering on the cob, '03 186
cutting from the cob, '96 192
grating, '02 178
removing silks, '98 198
Cornbread, '87 16; '02 28
cornmeal, '87 16
ingredients in, '87 16
making cornbread, '87 16
Cornmeal, '87 16
making cornbread, '87 16
understanding the label, '87 16
Cornstarch, '83 146, 147
adding to hot mixture, '01 335
as a thickening agent, '83 146, 147
Couscous, '01 50
Crab, cracking, '95 156
Crackers, '02 28
Cranberries, '04 30
buying, '92 314
enhancing canned sauce, '99 296
freezing, '92 314; '02 28; '04 30
frosted cranberries (garnish), '82 280
Crystal, '88 300, 301
removing discolorations and stains, '88 300, 301
repairing chips, '88 300
storing, '88 300
washing, '88 300, 301
Custards
preparing and storing properly (chart), '87 208
testing for doneness, '84 92
thickening, '83 147
Cutting boards, '87 208; '98 138, 198
acrylic, '87 208
cleaning, '87 208; '99 224
food safety, '87 208; '02 28
wooden, '87 208
Desserts. *See also* **FOK/Butterscotch, Cakes,
  Candy, Caramel, Cookies, Custards, Fruits,
  Garnishes, Meringue, Piecrust, Puddings,
  Soufflés, Tarts.**
gelatin molds, '99 100
glazing pastries, '01 50
sauces, '01 335
topping, '02 194
using ready-made products, '97 174
using toasted oats as topping, '00 28

Dishwasher, '87 130
freshening interior, '02 194
Dressing/Stuffing
preparing ahead, '01 260
Drying foods, '93 23
cherry tomatoes, '93 23
equipment, '93 23
safety, '93 23
uses for, '93 23
Eggnog, freezing, '92 314
Eggplant
cooking, '01 166
peeling, '01 166
types of, '01 166
Eggs, '83 147, 214; '89 26. *See also*
  FOK/Meringue.
cooking methods, '83 214; '98 112
cooking omelets, '00 46
eggshell vases and candy dishes, '04 94
handling properly, '87 208 (chart)
pasteurized egg substitute, '89 26
poached, recipe, '03 70
preventing curdling, '82 198; '83 147
separating, '01 335
using oat bran in, '00 28
using raw egg whites, '91 300
using raw egg yolks, '89 26
yolks, thick and lemon colored, '83 214
Entertaining, '84 122, 123; '88 276;
  '90 182, 276, 277; '91 300; '94 17, 18;
  '02 316; '03 274
accumulating supplies for, '02 148
beverage glasses, '97 184
cleaning up, '02 46
decorating, '02 194
determining amounts of food to buy, '90 276
  (chart)
determining traffic flow, '84 122, 123; '86 191;
  '90 276, 277
during the holidays, '03 274
making preparations for, '84 122; '86 191;
  '94 17, 18; '96 21; '97 154; '02 148
outdoors, '86 191; '96 230; '03 148, 176
presenting food, '84 122; '88 276; '97 56, 174;
  '98 112; '01 260; '02 194; '04 276
"referral coffee," '97 154
seafood server, '03 224
selecting menus for, '84 122; '86 191; '88 276;
  '90 276; '97 308; '02 178
serving food safely, '91 300; '96 230
setting up a bar for, '90 277
sharing recipes, '97 72
table setting, '90 182 (illustration), 276; '96 192;
  '97 184; '01 335
tailgating, '96 230
Equivalents of ingredients, '91 22, 23
Etiquette, '90 225
basic manners at the table, '90 225; '96 208
tipping in restaurants, '96 140
Fat, dietary, '82 189; '90 72; '91 200, 201;
  '92 65, 66; '93 207
in beef, '92 65, 66
in butter, '82 189; '90 314
eliminating in snacks, '91 200, 201
and food labels, '90 72; '92 65; '93 207
in margarine, '82 189; '90 314
removing excess from foods, '00 300
storing, '82 189
Fish, '84 48; '87 79, 80; '90 130; '94 105, 106. *See
  also* **FOK/Seafood, Shellfish, Shrimp,
  Surimi.**
boning, '96 256
buying, '84 48; '87 79, 80; '90 130; '94 106;
  '97 112; '99 68; '01 220

cooking, '87 80; '01 220

deep frying, '98 238

eliminating odors on hands, '82 109

fat fish, '87 79

freezing, '87 80; '02 28

grilling, '84 48; '92 52

handling properly, '87 208

lean fish, '87 79

market forms of, '87 79; '01 220; '02 194

selecting, '02 194

selecting fish for grilling, '84 48; '90 130

storing, '87 80; '90 130; '94 105, 106; '97 112; '01 220

substituting, '90 130

thawing, '87 80; '90 130

transporting fresh, '94 105, 106

Flour, '82 197, 198; '04 224

all purpose, '82 197, 198; '87 12; '99 224; '04 224

bread, '99 224; '04 224

cake flour, '82 197, 198; '87 12; '04 224

cracked wheat, '82 197, 198

measuring, '00 180

oat flour, '00 28

self rising, '99 224; '04 224

sifting, '82 197, 198; '87 12

Southern flours, '04 224

storing, '82 197, 198; '00 180

types of, '82 197,198; '96 256; '99 224; '04 224

whole wheat, '99 224

Flowers, '94 59; '96 304

crystallizing edible, '94 59; '99 100

edible, '96 304

keeping fresh, '99 100

toxic, '96 304

Food processor, '82 109; '86 13

chopping nuts, '92 314; '95 208

easy cleanup, '01 50

Food safety. See **FOK/Handling food properly.**

Freezer, '83 14, 15; '86 50, 51; '87 112, 208; '93 83, 84; '02 28

amount of food to store in, '87 112

casseroles in, '87 112

checking temperature of, '01 166

cleaning, '84 11; '87 112

cleaning out, '01 30

constant freezer temperature, '86 50; '99 50

defrosting, '87 112; '99 50

foods that don't freeze well, '01 98

foods that freeze well, '86 50; '87 112; '90 314, 315; '01 98; '02 28; '03 186, 274

fruits in, '87 112

labeling foods in, '84 11; '86 51; '87 112; '00 100; '03 186

leftovers, freezing safely, '87 112; '96 140, 160; '99 50; '02 28

organizing foods in, '87 112; '02 28

and power loss, '83 14, 15; '93 83, 84

preventing sogginess of particular foods to be frozen, '87 112

refreezing foods, '83 15; '93 83, 84; '99 50

reheating frozen foods, '87 112

sausage, '87 238

storage times, '03 186

storing nuts in, '01 50

vegetables in, '87 112

wraps and containers for freezing foods, '86 50, 51; '87 112; '02 28; '03 274

Fruitcakes, '83 285; '86 331; '95 343

purchasing candied fruit for, '92 314

shortcut for, '99 224

storing, '83 285; '86 331

Fruits, '83 94; '85 233; '89 141, 142; '92 248, 249, 250; '01 30. See also **FOK/Apples, Avocados, Berries, Blueberries, Coconut, Cranberries, Garnishes, Grapefruit, Kiwifruit, Lemons, Mangoes, Melons, Oranges, Peaches, Pears, Persimmons, Raspberries, Strawberries, Tangerines, Tomatillos.**

candied, '02 28

canning, '84 180; '89 141, 142

in centerpieces, '90 205

as "containers" for food, '97 174

cooking with, '97 36

dressing for fruit salad, '97 134

exotic fruits, '92 248, 249, 250; '02 240

fall fruits, '85 233

freezing, '87 112

grating citrus peel, '95 314; '96 140; '98 138; '00 28

health benefits of, '00 46

nutritive values of, '92 248, 249, 250

preparing, '92 248, 249, 250; '97 134; '02 178

preserving cut, '02 70, 178

pureeing, '01 335

selecting, '84 186, 187; '92 248, 249, 250

as snacks, '91 200, 201

storing, '83 94; '92 248, 249, 250; '01 98, 166, 300; '02 132, 148; '03 176

using yogurt instead of puree, '97 206

winter fruits, '04 30

Frying foods, '84 211; '88 112, 113; '01 118. See also **FOK/Lard.**

cooking fat to use, '88 113

equipment, '88 113

safety, '90 22

techniques, '88 113

Gardening, '98 112

Garlic, '93 182; '00 100

baker, '94 332

conversions of bottled for fresh, '99 50

freezing, '01 335

press, '94 332; '97 134

storing, '03 70

tool for peeling easily, '97 154

Garnishes, '82 138, 280; '89 100; '90 108; '93 317; '94 59; '96 230, 256; '04 276. See also **FOK/Flowers.**

butter curls, '82 189

candy holly leaves, '99 328

chocolate, '86 247; '94 59; '96 230, 256

chocolate leaves, '96 230

chocolate sacks, '93 317

containers as garnishes, '97 174

curling garnishes, '89 100

eggs, hard-cooked, '82 280

fruit garnishes, '82 280; '96 230; '97 36

illustrations, '89 100; '90 108; '93 317

making ahead, '89 100

pastry garnishes, '96 230; '04 276

piped garnishes, '82 280; '86 330; '90 108

soup garnish, '96 160

sugar, lemon, '97 56

sugar, powdered, '96 51

utensils for creating, '89 100; '90 108

vegetable garnishes, '82 280; '89 100, 243; '95 343

whipped cream, '86 330

Gelatin, '83 124, 125; '91 300

chilling, '83 124; '86 13

molds, determining size of, '82 313

molds, substituting, '99 100

softening, '91 300

unmolding, '83 124, 125; '86 330

using fresh fruits and vegetables in, '91 300

Gifts of food, '86 289; '91 95, 96; '95 343; '96 112; '02 132

assembling, '02 178

containers for, '86 289; '91 95, 96; '98 36; '00 224

freezing, '91 95, 96; '95 343

gift baskets, '02 178

mailing, '86 289; '95 343

mail orders from favorite restaurants, '97 308

safety of, '02 132

storing, '91 95, 96; '02 132

wrapping, '86 289; '95 343

Gifts, nonfood, '97 134; '98 326; '00 330; '01 300

coupons, '02 316

gift certificates, '97 308

Gingerroot, '94 29

cooking with, '92 314; '94 29; '01 335

freezing, '98 138

grating, '98 138

selecting, '94 29

in stir-frying, '92 314

storing, '92 314; '98 138

Glasses, cleaning stemmed, '02 46

Gloves, disposable, '96 76; '03 50

Granita, '00 156

Grapefruit, '01 30

sectioning, '04 48

Grating

citrus rind, '95 314; '96 140; '98 138

corn, fresh, '02 178

Gravies, '83 38; '86 330

serving and storing properly, '87 208 (chart)

thickening, '00 28

Greens

arugula, '03 224

cleaning, '96 304; '97 206; '03 30

radicchio, '97 232

Grilling, '82 109; '83 191; '84 48; '86 172; '88 145, 146; '92 202; '93 103, 104; '00 128. See also **FOK/Smoking (cooking method).**

avoiding flare-ups, '88 145; '92 202; '99 148, 180

basting, '82 109; '88 146; '93 103

charcoal, '82 109; '93 103, 104; '00 128

cleanup, '93 104

cooking times, '95 194 (chart)

direct/indirect cooking methods, '88 145; '93 103, 104; '95 194; '97 206; '99 148

equipment, '82 109; '88 146; '92 52; '93 103; '95 274; '99 148; '02 132

flavoring with wood chips, '88 145; '93 103; '00 128

kebabs, '88 146; '93 103; '99 180; '00 128

safety, '99 148; '02 132

temperature of fire, '82 109; '88 145, 146; '95 195

thermometer, '93 103, 104; '95 195; '99 148

Grits

eliminating lumps in, '97 154; '00 224

storing, '00 224

Grocery shopping, '84 11; '91 187, 188; '00 206

best time for, '84 11

comparative shopping, '91 188

determining best values, '91 188 (chart)

making lists for, '82 312; '83 248; '84 11; '00 206; '01 98

planning menus, '82 312; '83 284; '84 11

saving time and money, '91 187, 188; '00 206

stocking up, '91 188

transporting cold and frozen items, '00 206; '01 118

using coupons, '91 188

Ham, '89 333, 334; '90 276

cooking in microwave oven, '89 333, 334

determining amount to buy for entertaining, '90 276

FROM OUR KITCHEN (FOK), Ham
  (continued)

  freezing, '89 334
  preparing, '89 333, 334
  reducing saltiness during cooking, '97 134
  selecting, '89 333
  storing, '89 334
**Handling food properly, '87 208; '89 26; '91 300;
  '92 202; '93 23, 83, 84; '96 76, 230; '99 224;
  '01 330.** *See also* **FOK/Beef, Canning,
  Chicken, Eggs, Fish, Turkey.**
  chart, '87 208
  egg whites, raw, '91 300
  egg yolks, raw, '89 26
  holiday hot lines, '97 278; '98 306
  irradiating foods, '02 100
  transporting food, '01 220
  when entertaining, '91 300; '96 230
  when grilling, '99 148
Herbs, '85 58; '89 121; '99 208. *See also*
  FOK/Seasonings, Spices.
  amounts to use, '89 121; '95 30
  chart '89 121
  cooking with, '85 58
  as decoration, '01 118
  drying, '85 58; '98 198
  freezing, '85 58
  gathering fresh, '85 58; '89 121
  mint, '02 132
  rosemary, '00 28
  sage, '01 260
  storing, '85 58; '89 121; '98 198; '00 206;
  '03 176
  substituting, '01 118
  substituting fresh for salt, '99 208
  types of, '99 208
  using fresh, '00 206; '02 132
Holiday
  baking, '98 326
  entertaining, '03 274
  hot lines, '97 278; '98 306; '01 300; '03 274
Honey, '02 100
Ice
  dry ice, '82 14, 15
  freezing beverages as ice cubes, '01 260
  molds, '86 331
Ice cream, '82 171; '86 215; '00 156
  adding fresh fruit to homemade, '82 171
  fat content of, '00 156
  homemade, '82 171; '03 176
  varieties of, '86 215
Ingredients, uncommon, '97 232; '02 28
Jams and jellies
  commercial, '03 186
  jars for, '03 148
  storing, '02 132
**Kitchen, '83 191; '84 10, 11, 148, 149; '90 22, 50;
  '93 220; '94 332**
  aluminum foil cooking bags, '99 68
  appliances, '87 130
  baking pans, '98 138; '99 128; '00 128, 250; '02 46
  baking stone, '99 68; '02 46
  basic equipment, '90 50; '93 220; '94 332;
  '97 56, 308; '98 138; '00 128, 224; '02 46
  cleaning, '02 148
  cookware, '85 329; '90 50; '93 220; '96 160;
  '98 326; '03 70
  countertops, '84 148, 149
  fire extinguisher for, '99 50
  gadgets, '86 13; '90 126; '94 332; '95 343;
  '97 154; '98 36, 218; '00 28, 206, 224;
  '01 50, 118, 138, 300; '02 194, 316

  keeping cool in summer, '83 191
  knives, '91 144, 145
  organizing, '84 10, 11
  safety in, '84 37; '90 22; '96 256
  shears, '91 160; '92 52
  toolbox, '96 21
Kiwifruit, peeling, '95 31 (illustration)
Knives, '84 11; '91 144, 145; '01 260
  buying, '91 144, 145; '03 50
  sharpening, '91 144, 145
  storing, '84 11; '03 50
  using properly, '86 13; '91 144, 145
  varieties of, '91 144, 145 (illustration); '03 50
Labels, food, '90 72; '92 65; '93 207; '94 140
  chart, '90 72
  margarine or "spread" labels, '97 134
  sample label, '93 207
  "sell by" date, '99 128
  understanding, '90 72; '93 207
Lamb, '88 59; '02 70
  buying, '88 59; '01 98
  cooking, '88 59; '95 105 (chart); '01 98
  seasoning, '95 105
  selecting, '88 59; '01 98
  storing, '88 59; '95 105 (chart); '01 98
Lard, '96 160
Lasagna noodles, no-cook, '00 180
Lavosh, '00 66
**Leftovers, '82 313; '87 112, 208; '92 314;
  '95 30, 274; '96 230**
  bread slices, '82 313
  buns, '82 313
  freezing, '87 112, 208; '92 314; '01 30; '02 28
  of ham, '01 30
  of jams and jellies, '97 232
  storing, '01 30, 166; '02 178
  of turkey, '01 30
  using, '02 178
Lemons
  using for routine kitchen cleanup, '96 51
  using juice as a substitute in recipes, '00 66
Lettuce, '86 80; '95 67
  coring, '86 80
  mâche, '04 30
  selecting, '86 80
  storing, '86 80
  types of, '86 80 (illustration)
  yields, '86 80
Limes, '01 98
List making, '82 312; '83 284; '84 11, 122; '86 172
  and grocery shopping, '88 165; '91 188
  and meal planning, '82 312; '83 284; '84 11;
  '91 188
  telephone numbers for emergencies, '84 37
Low-fat, low-calorie foods
  substituting fresh herbs for salt, '99 208
  using frozen juice concentrate as a sweetener,
  '99 208
  using lemon or lime juice, '99 208
Lunch, packing for kids, '00 224
Mailing food, '86 289
Mangoes, '94 192
Manners. *See* **FOK/Etiquette.**
Margarine, '82 189
  availability of, '82 189
  colored, '02 70
  diet margarine, '82 189
  fat content of, '82 189; '90 314
  storing, '82 189
  substituting in baked goods, '90 314; '97 137
Marinating, '88 165; '95 30
  containers to use, '87 208; '02 100
  vinaigrette, '04 204
Masa harina, '94 192

Mayonnaise
  recipe, Homemade Mayonnaise, '99 180
**Meal planning, '82 312, 313; '83 191, 284;
  '84 122, 123; '86 13; '88 165, 276; '99 30.**
  See also **FOK/Campsite cooking, Snacks.**
  advance planning, '82 312, 313; '86 172
  for a crowd, '82 313; '86 191
  family dinners, '03 30
  for holidays, '83 284
  making lists, '82 312; '83 284; '84 11, 122;
  '86 172
  party menus, '82 313; '84 122, 123; '86 191;
  '88 276
  for specific recipes in 2001, '01 67
Measuring, '85 192, 193; '86 13; '98 36; '04 224
  butter, '85 192, 193
  determining cup measurement of dish, '85 193;
  '96 332
  dry measuring utensils, '85 192, 193, '00 224;
  '04 224
  how to measure accurately, '85 192, 193
  liquid measuring utensils, '85 192, 193
  salt, '01 138
  seasonings, '03 176
  sifting ingredients for, '82 197, 198;
  '85 192, 193; '87 12
  solid shortening, '85 192, 193
Meat loaf, '02 46
  additives, '98 138
Meats, '89 191, 192; '91 300; '92 202; '99 224.
  See also **FOK/Beef, Pork.**
  alternatives to, '02 148
  garnishing, '97 56
  handling properly, '87 208; '99 224; '03 50
  meat-cure mix, '91 300
  pounder, '04 204
  serving safely, '87 208; '91 300; '03 102
  standing time, '89 192
  suggested cooking temperatures, '89 191, 192;
  '92 202
  tenderizer, '02 316
  using a meat thermometer, '89 191, 192; '92 202
Melons, '88 183
  cantaloupe, '88 183
  enhancing flavor of, '00 206
  honeydew, '88 183
  selecting, '88 183
  storing, '88 183
  watermelon, '88 183; '96 192; '98 198
Meringue, '83 214
  baking, '83 214
  browning, '01 50
  equipment, '83 214
  humidity, effects of, '83 214
  making, '83 214
  powder, '92 314; '04 94
  preventing weeping, '83 214; '95 246; '02 194
  recipe, Dream Drops, '99 328
**Microwave oven, '83 191; '84 211; '86 113, 227;
  '87 130; '92 176; '99 296; '02 288**
  cleaning, '87 130; '99 128
  cookware for, '86 227
  drying herbs in, '98 198
  features, '86 113
  melting chocolate in, '02 46
  recipe, Microwave Fudge, '91 92
  removing odors from, '99 30
  roasting peppers in, '92 176
  safety when using, '91 92; '00 28
  sizes, '86 113
  steaming vegetables in, '99 296; '02 70
  using to clean microwave cookware, '98 256
  variations of, '86 113
  wattage, '86 113

Milk, as cooling agent to burning taste buds, **'01** 138
Mirlitons, **'00** 250; **'01** 260
Muffins, preparing ahead, **'97** 174
Mushrooms
dried, **'01** 202
as garnish, **'82** 280
portobello, **'03** 176
preparing, **'00** 180; **'01** 202; **'03** 176 (recipe)
serving, **'02** 194
shiitake, **'97** 232
slicing, **'98** 198
storing, **'92** 314; **'01** 202
varieties of, **'01** 202
Noodles
cooking, **'00** 100
rinsing, **'00** 100
Nopales. *See* **FOK/Cactus.**
Nutrition, '90 72; **'91** 200, 201; **'92** 65
food labels, **'90** 72; **'92** 65
snacks, **'91** 200, 201
Nuts
storing, **'02** 132
storing in freezer, **'01** 50
toasting frozen, **'01** 50
Oats
types of, **'00** 28; **'03** 30
uses for, **'00** 28
Okra
cooking, **'01** 166
types of, **'01** 166
Oils. *See* **FOK/Cooking oils, Olive oils, Sesame oil, Vegetable oil, Walnut oil.**
Olive oils, '89 175; **'98** 112; **'01** 50
commercial, **'03** 102
flavored, **'89** 175
selecting, **'89** 175
storing, **'89** 175
using to store garlic, **'03** 70
varieties of, **'89** 175; **'98** 112
Onions, '88 87; **'95** 30; **'98** 36
caramelizing, **'98** 72
chopping, **'92** 314; **'95** 246; **'97** 134
cooking with, **'88** 87
eliminating odor on hands, **'82** 109; **'94** 332; **'96** 51
extracting onion juice, **'88** 87
grating, **'92** 314; **'95** 30; **'97** 134; **'01** 335
OSO Onions, **'04** 30
paste, **'98** 218
recipe, Caramelized Onions, **'04** 30
selecting, **'88** 87
substituting for shallots in recipes, **'00** 100
using in salads, **'96** 192
varieties of, **'88** 87 (illustrations)
Oranges
types of, **'99** 250; **'01** 30
using in recipes, **'99** 250
Outdoor cooking. *See* **FOK/Campsite cooking, Grilling, Smoking (cooking method).**
Ovens, '83 191; **'84** 211; **'86** 113; **'87** 130
checking oven temperature, **'96** 230; **'01** 98
cleaning, **'87** 130; **'01** 335
convection, **'86** 113
conventional, **'86** 113
microwave, **'83** 191; **'84** 211; **'86** 113, 227; **'87** 130; **'92** 176
preheating, **'86** 13
racks, cleaning, **'01** 260
Pancakes, '04 148
adding fruit to batter, **'04** 148
batter, **'04** 148
cooking, **'04** 148
as dessert, **'02** 70
recipe, Lemon-Blueberry Pancakes, **'04** 148

Pan sizes, **'96** 332; **'97** 112 (chart); **'00** 128; **'01** 98
Paraffin, '89 244
as a seal in canning, **'84** 180; **'89** 142; **'91** 300
Parchment paper, **'99** 250
Parsley, keeping fresh, **'98** 72
Pastas, '87 177; **'96** 208
basic categories, **'87** 177
cooking, **'87** 177; **'95** 30
measuring, **'87** 177
recipe, Fettuccine Primavera, **'04** 64
reheating, **'87** 177; **'95** 31
salads, **'02** 240
storing, **'87** 177; **'03** 186
substituting, **'87** 177
Pastry. *See* **FOK/Piecrust.**
Peaches
kinds of, **'02** 178
overripe fruit, uses for, **'97** 174
selecting, **'02** 178
Peanut butter, '96 256
storing, **'01** 202
Peanuts, '83 228, 229
boiling, **'83** 228
chopping, **'83** 229
roasting, **'83** 228
Pears, '85 233
cooking, **'85** 233; **'00** 250
peeling, **'85** 233
ripening, **'85** 233; **'02** 216
selecting, **'85** 233
storing, **'02** 216
types of, **'02** 216
Peas, black-eyed
recipe, Marinated Black-Eyed Peas, **'01** 30
recipe, Pickled Black-Eyed Peas, **'01** 30
Peas, dried, '88 4
buying, **'88** 4
cooking, **'88** 4; **'00** 180
soaking, **'88** 4
storing, **'88** 4
Pecans, '83 228, 229; **'94** 59
chopping, **'83** 229; **'95** 208
as garnish, **'94** 59
toasting, **'83** 228
Pepper, ground, cayenne, or red, '98 58
pepper mill, **'02** 316
Peppers, '85 4; **'92** 176; **'94** 29; **'95** 208
cooking stuffed, **'01** 118
dried chiles, **'01** 202
freezing, **'85** 4; **'02** 132
as garnish, **'82** 280; **'89** 100
removing skins of, **'85** 4; **'02** 132
roasting, **'92** 176; **'02** 132
selecting, **'94** 29; **'01** 202
storing, **'94** 29
substituting, **'85** 4
types of, **'85** 4; **'98** 218; **'01** 166, 202
working with hot peppers, **'85** 4; **'94** 29; **'95** 208; **'01** 202
Persimmons, '85 233; **'00** 250
freezing, **'85** 233; **'00** 250
preparing, **'85** 233
selecting, **'85** 233; **'00** 250
types of, **'00** 250
Pesto
paste, **'98** 218
storing, **'00** 206
using, **'02** 316
using as a spread, **'00** 206
Pickles, '87 150
pickling vegetables, **'87** 150
relishes, **'03** 102
spoilage, **'87** 150

Picnic
storage containers for, **'03** 176
supplies, **'03** 176
Piecrust, '82 234; 235; **'92** 52, 314; **'94** 210; **'95** 246; **'96** 76
crumb crust, **'99** 250
equipment, **'82** 234; **'94** 332; **'95** 208
finishing, **'82** 234; **'98** 36
flavor variations of, **'97** 72; **'00** 330; **'01** 335
glazing, **'82** 235
lining with melted chocolate, **'97** 36
mixing, **'82** 234; **'92** 52; **'95** 246
phyllo dough, leftover, **'02** 178
preventing overbrowning, **'92** 314; **'95** 30
preventing sogginess, **'86** 330; **'91** 300; **'92** 314
puff pastry, **'97** 56
recipe, Water-Whipped Baked Pastry Shell, **'95** 246
rolling, **'82** 234; **'92** 314
using cookie dough as, **'01** 335
variations of, **'82** 234, 235
Pineapple
adding to pancakes, **'02** 70
juice as food preservative, **'02** 178
Planning meals. *See* **FOK/Meal planning.**
Plastic containers, storing, **'99** 250
Poaching, '85 127
eggs, **'85** 127
equipment, **'85** 127
fish, **'85** 127
fruits, **'85** 127
liquid to use, **'85** 127
Pomegranate seeds, '00 250
freezing, **'00** 250
using, **'00** 250
Popcorn, '00 224
restoring moisture to dry kernels, **'00** 224
Pork. *See also* **FOK/Ham.**
carnitas, **'02** 148
cooking, **'95** 246
nutritional value, **'98** 198
recipe, Barbecue Ribs, **'99** 68
Potatoes, '84 210, 211. *See also* **FOK/Sweet Potatoes.**
adding to soups and stews, **'02** 46
Easter Egg Potatoes, **'04** 94
frozen prepared, **'02** 46
instant, **'02** 46
methods of mashing, **'97** 278
preparing, **'84** 210, 211; **'97** 206; **'99** 100; **'00** 206; **'01** 335
selecting, **'84** 210, 211; **'98** 256
storing, **'84** 211; **'98** 256; **'03** 70
using to absorb too much pepper or salt in cooking, **'96** 76
Poultry. *See* **FOK/Chicken, Turkey.**
Pound cakes. *See* **FOK/Cakes.**
Pressure cooker, using to cook peas, **'00** 180
Puddings, '86 330; **'96** 256. *See also* **FOK/Custards.**
bread, **'00** 128
preventing "skin" from forming, **'86** 330
Pumpkins, '85 233
as jack-o'-lanterns, **'97** 232
preparing for cooking, **'85** 233
selecting, **'85** 233
as a side dish, **'01** 220
storing, **'85** 233
substituting canned for fresh, **'98** 256
using pumpkin shell as serving container, **'98** 256
Raisins
chopping, **'02** 316
freezing, **'02** 316
selecting, **'02** 316

FROM OUR KITCHEN (FOK), Raisins
(continued)

storing, '**02** 316
using in recipes, '**02** 316
Raspberries
making sauce, '**92** 314
morsels, '**02** 28
Recipe preparation, '86 13; '**91** 22, 23; '**93** 235;
'**96** 76; '**99** 30; '**01** 98. *See also* **FOK/**
Cooking directions, Handling food properly,
Substitutions.
baking techniques, '**89** 57; '**98** 218; '**02** 100
cleaning up, '**86** 13; '**95** 31 (illustration);
'**98** 198, 256; '**99** 100, 128, 224; '**00** 66, 206,
330; '**01** 50, 166, 300; '**02** 216, 316
cutting recipes for smaller yields, '**97** 184;
'**02** 194
determining solutions to problems, '**93** 235;
'**96** 21, 76
doubling recipes, '**91** 22, 23; '**92** 66; '**95** 30;
'**01** 335; '**02** 194; '**03** 274
enhancing recipes, '**00** 156; '**02** 148
equipment, '**86** 13; '**96** 160, 208; '**98** 218;
'**01** 260; '**02** 100, 240; '**03** 274
following instructions in *Southern Living Annual*
Recipes, '**02** 240
freezing berries, '**98** 138
frying, '**02** 216
greasing bakeware, '**98** 238; '**01** 335
measuring, '**86** 13; '**95** 274; '**02** 100
mistakes in, '**01** 50
parchment paper, '**99** 250
planning menus, '**86** 13; '**02** 178
preparing ingredients, '**86** 13; '**95** 30, 31
(illustration), 208; '**00** 156, 206; '**02** 288
presentation, '**99** 128, 148; '**02** 194
securing wooden spoons on cook pots, '**00** 300
shortcuts in, '**96** 256
tasting along the way, '**98** 138
trying new recipes, '**01** 202
tubes of paste: onion, pesto, tomato, '**98** 218
utensils, '**86** 13; '**01** 98
Recipes
creating handmade cookbooks, '**03** 274
enlarging copies of, '**01** 260
organizing, '**98** 198; '**03** 274
prize-winning tips, '**04** 48
recording, '**02** 316
Recycling, '92 28; '**02** 148
items to be recycled, '**92** 28
packaging of products, '**92** 28
setting up home recycling center, '**92** 28
the three Rs, '**92** 28
Refrigerator, '83 94; '**87** 130; '**01** 98
canned foods (opened), '**83** 94
checking temperature of, '**01** 166
cleaning, '**84** 11; '**87** 130; '**01** 166
cleaning out, '**00** 300
dairy products, '**83** 94
food storage chart, '**83** 94
meats, '**83** 94
Relishes, '03 102
Rhubarb, freezing, '01 118
Rice, '87 46
cooking, '**95** 30; '**98** 238; '**01** 335; '**02** 216
flavoring, '**87** 46; '**01** 335
mixes, '**04** 204
preparing, '**87** 46
ready-to-eat, '**04** 204
recipe, Cranberry-Almond Wild Rice, '**04** 204
recipe, Pecan Rice, '**04** 204
recipe, Saffron Rice Pilaf, '**04** 204

reheating, '**87** 46
storing, '**87** 46
types of, '**87** 46; '**99** 208; '**01** 220
Rolls, '83 323. *See also* **FOK/Biscuits, Breads,**
Yeast.
frozen roll dough, '**03** 224
glazing, '**83** 323
removing burned bottoms from, '**96** 51
variations of, '**83** 323
yeast, '**83** 323
Rosemary, '00 28
Roux, '87 211, 212
color of, '**87** 211, 212
cooking temperature, '**87** 211
cooking times, '**87** 211
ingredient amounts, '**87** 211
microwave roux, '**87** 211, 212
oven roux, '**87** 211
reducing fat in roux, '**87** 212
utensils to use, '**87** 212
Safety, '84 37, 180; '**90** 22; '**91** 92, 300. *See also*
FOK/Handling food properly.
canning fruits and vegetables, '**84** 180; '**91** 300
extinguishing a range-top fire, '**99** 50
first aid for burns, '**90** 22; '**99** 50
in the kitchen, '**84** 37; '**90** 22; '**96** 256; '**99** 50
preventing burns in the kitchen, '**84** 37; '**90** 22
when serving food, '**91** 300
when using the microwave, '**91** 92; '**00** 28
Salad dressings, '97 184
adding flavor to bottled dressings, '**00** 66
recipe, Fresh Lemon Vinaigrette, '**04** 30
recipe, Grandpa Jim's Salad Dressing, '**01** 182
recipe, Sugar-and-Vinegar Dressing, '**04** 174
Salads, '82 313; '**91** 300
congealed, '**82** 313; '**91** 300
equipment, '**94** 332
using toasted oats as topping, '**00** 28
washing salad greens, '**97** 36
Salsa
using leftover for soup, '**00** 206
using as a marinade, '**02** 46
Salt
as cleaning agent on dishes, '**01** 335
measuring, '**01** 138
types of, '**01** 138
using on boil overs in oven, '**01** 335
Sandwiches
on the road, '**02** 194
storing finger sandwiches, '**01** 335
Sauces, '83 146, 147; '**92** 314; '**94** 274; '**95** 30
chilling quickly, '**86** 13
reduction sauces, '**94** 274; '**96** 332
thickening, '**83** 146, 147; '**00** 28
Sausage, '87 238
classifications of, '**87** 238
freezing, '**87** 238; '**02** 28
meat-cure mix, '**91** 300
mock, '**00** 330
Scallops, '99 180
amounts to buy, '**99** 180
cooking, '**99** 180
selecting, '**99** 180
types of, '**99** 180
Seafood, '90 130; '**01** 220. *See also* **FOK/Crab,**
Fish, Scallops, Shellfish, Shrimp, Surimi.
Seasonings, '92 121, 344; '**93** 182; '**96** 304. *See*
also **FOK/Herbs, Oils, Spices.**
bouquet garni, '**03** 30
frozen seasoning blend, '**03** 132
Greek seasoning, '**03** 132
how to use, '**03** 176
measuring, '**03** 176
in recipes, '**91** 22

recipes for seasoning blends, '**92** 121
storing, '**82** 198; '**84** 11; '**92** 121; '**98** 36; '**03** 208
substitutions, '**92** 344; '**01** 118; '**03** 132
Secrets from the *Southern Living* Test Kitchens,
'**02** 240
Sesame oil, '**01** 118
Shelf life, '83 65
of canned foods, '**83** 65
chart, '**83** 65
of packaged mixes, '**83** 65
of staples, '**83** 65
Shellfish, '94 105, 106
buying, '**94** 106
cooking, '**01** 220
storing, '**01** 220
transporting fresh, '**94** 105, 106
Sherbet, '**00** 156
Shopping. *See* **FOK/Grocery shopping.**
Shrimp, '87 12; '**94** 105, 106; '**00** 180
amounts to buy, 00 180
cooking, '**87** 12; '**00** 180
deveining, '**92** 52; '**01** 138
freezing, '**00** 224
grilling, '**92** 52
recipe, Grandpa Jim's Shrimp Sauce, '**01** 182
recipe, Shrimp Cocktail Sauce, '**01** 182
recipe, Shrimp Sauce, '**01** 182
selecting, '**94** 106
serving, '**03** 224
storing, '**00** 180
transporting fresh, '**94** 105
Sifting, '82 197, 198; '**85** 192, 193; '**87** 12
flour, '**82** 197, 198; '**87** 12
powdered sugar, '**85** 192; '**87** 12
Silver, '88 300
avoiding spotting and pitting, '**88** 300
buying sterling, '**02** 178
cleaning, '**88** 300
removing tarnish from, '**88** 300
serving spoons, '**99** 296
storing, '**88** 300
Slow cookers, using to serve food, '**03** 224
Smoking (cooking method), '95 116
adding the food, '**95** 116
cleaning the smoker, '**95** 117
filling the water pan, '**95** 116
maintaining the temperature, '**95** 116
soaking the wood, '**95** 116
starting the fire, '**95** 116
Snacks, '91 200, 201; '**01** 118
health bars, '**02** 100
nutritious, '**91** 200, 201
planning, '**91** 200, 201
recipes for, '**91** 200, 201
on the road, '**02** 194
Sodium, '90 72
content of in surimi, '**90** 130
and food labels, '**90** 72
Sorbet, '00 156
homemade, '**03** 176
Soufflés, '84 92
testing for doneness, '**84** 92
Soups, '89 30; '**95** 274; '**96** 160; '**00** 206. *See also*
FOK/Stews.
as appetizers, '**98** 112; '**00** 206
bouillons, '**00** 250
broths, '**89** 30; '**98** 138; '**00** 100; '**01** 98
dashi, '**00** 100
freezing, '**89** 30
as gifts, '**91** 95
presentation, '**98** 112
pureeing, '**99** 250
recipe, '**03** 274
reheating, '**89** 30

removing bay leaf, '95 314
stocks, '89 30; '95 30
storing, '89 30
Sour cream, as cooling condiment to spicy foods,
 '01 202
Spaghetti sauce, substituting vegetable juice for
 tomato sauce, '98 256
Spices, '87 297; '99 180. *See also* **FOK/Herbs,
 Seasonings.**
 amounts to use, '87 297; '99 208
 buying, '87 297; '98 58
 checking for freshness, '84 11; '87 297; '98 58
 grinding your own, '87 297; '98 58
 soothing burning taste buds, '01 138
 sprinkle opening, '99 180
 storing, '82 198; '84 11; '87 297; '98 58
 substituting, '87 297; '01 118
 toasting, '98 58
 using to enhance coffee, '00 224
 whole spices, '87 297; '98 58
Spinach
 eliminating excess moisture from, '02 240
 freezing, '02 132
 nutritional value of, '02 132, 240
 using frozen, '02 240
Squash, winter, '88 229, 230; '00 250
 cooking, '88 229, 230
 determining amount to buy, '88 229
 selecting, '88 229, 230
 storing, '88 229, 230
 types of, '88 229, 230
Stains, removing, '96 304; '99 100; '02 194
Stews, baking in oven, '98 256
Stir frying, '95 30; '01 335
Stocks. *See* **FOK/Soups.**
Storage containers
 for jams, jellies, and preserves, '03 148
 for picnics, '03 176
Strawberries, '82 109
 buying, '82 109
 freezing, '01 118
 as garnish, '82 138
 preparing, '99 100
Substitutions, '92 344; '96 208; '98 256; '00 100
 alcohol, '92 314; '99 148; '00 66; '01 138
 emergency substitutions, '92 344 (chart); '00 66;
  '01 220
 flour, '99 224
 herbs and spices, '01 118
 lemon juice, '99 100
 light ingredients, '00 100
 using tofu as a substitution, '99 128
 vinegar, '99 100; '00 66
Sugar, '85 19
 making colored sugar, '86 331
 making lemon sugar, '97 56
 measuring, '85 19; '87 12
 preventing brown sugar from drying out, '85 19
 sifting powdered sugar, '85 192; '87 12
 softening brown, '98 198
 substitutions, '85 19
 types of, '85 19
Surimi, '90 130
Sweet potatoes, '88 208; '00 250. *See also*
 FOK/Potatoes.
 cooking, '88 208; '00 250; '01 220
 handling, '88 208
 selecting, '88 208
 storing, '88 208; '00 250
 substituting canned for fresh, '88 208
 yams, '88 208
Syrups, commercial, '04 130
Table setting, '90 182, 225
 centerpieces, '90 205; '98 72; '01 335

for formal entertaining, '90 182
 illustration, '90 182
Tahini (sesame seed paste), '96 304
 storing, '01 202
Tamales, '94 192. *See also* **FOK/Masa harina.**
 making tamale dough, '94 192
Tangerines, types of, '01 30
Tapioca, as a thickening agent, '83 147
Tarts, '95 274
Tea, '85 120, 121
 brewing, '85 120,121
 storing, '85 121
 types of, '85 120, 121
Templates for holiday gift box cake, '03 308
Thawing food, '83 14, 15; '86 330; '87 208; '88 165
 turkey, '83 284; '86 330
Thermometers, '89 191, 192; '92 202; '98 306
 deep-fat frying, '84 37
 instant-read, '89 191, 192; '92 202, 314; '93 104;
  '03 102
 meat, '89 191, 192; '92 202
 storing, '89 192; '92 202
 testing for accuracy, '89 192; '92 202; '96 230
Thickening agents, '83 146, 147. *See also*
 **FOK/Arrowroot, Cornstarch, Eggs, Oats,
 Tapioca.**
Tofu, '99 128
Tomatillos, about, '97 232
Tomatoes, '85 181, 182; '93 23; '95 30
 drying cherry tomatoes, '93 23
 enhancing flavor of, '01 335
 freezing leftover paste, '96 160
 frying, '01 118
 as garnish, '82 280; '89 100
 paste, '98 218
 peeling large amount of, '82 138; '85 181, 182
 recipe, Marinated Dried Cherry Tomatoes, '93 23
 ripening, '85 181
 seeding, '85 182
 selecting, '85 181
 slicing, '85 181, 182
 storing, '85 181; '00 206
 stuffing, '85 182
Topping, toasted oats, '00 28
Tortillas, '95 44; '00 224; '03 132
 equipment, '95 44
 how to cook, '95 44
 how to shape, '95 44
 recipe, Flour Tortillas, '95 44
 reheating, '95 44
 storing, '95 44
 using for quesadillas, '00 156
 using leftover, '01 202; '03 132
 as wraps, '03 132
Transporting food, '01 220
 for road trips, '02 194
Turkey, '83 284, 285; '93 306, 307
 carving, '93 306, 307
 chart, '83 285
 cooking, '83 284, 285; '86 330; '98 306; '02 288
 cuts of, '01 260
 deep-frying, '00 300
 determining amounts to buy for entertaining,
  '90 276; '99 296
 handling properly, '87 208
 leftovers, storing, '83 285; '98 306; '02 288
 recipe, Benny Sauce Marinated Turkey, '98 306
 roasting, '02 288
 selecting fresh or frozen, '99 296; '02 288
 stuffing, '83 284; '98 306
 thawing, '83 284; '86 330; '98 306; '99 296;
  '00 300; '02 288
 trussing, '02 288
Turnips, '01 220

U.S. Department of Agriculture (USDA), '89 142;
 '90 72; '92 65, 202; '93 83; '02 100
Vegetable cooking spray, '92 208; '98 138
 cleanup, easy, '82 198, 314; '84 48; '92 314;
  '93 104; '95 31; '01 50
Vegetable oil, '82 189; '84 211; '88 112, 113;
 '98 112
 deep-fat frying thermometer, '84 37; '88 113
 preventing fire, '84 37; '88 112, 113
Vegetables, '82 138; '83 94; '84 180, 211, 249;
 '86 140, 141; '89 243, 244; '92 344; '93 132;
 '94 29, 92; '95 30. *See also* **FOK/Broccoli,
 Brussels sprouts, Canning, Cauliflower,
 Celery, Corn, Garnishes, Greens, Lettuce,
 Mirlitons, Mushrooms, Onions, Peas,
 Peppers, Potatoes, Pumpkins, Rhubarb,
 Squash, Sweet potatoes, Tomatoes, Turnips.**
 basic cooking methods, '82 138; '84 249;
  '94 29, 92 (chart)
 blackening to remove skins, '01 50
 broths, '00 100
 canning, '84 180; '93 136, 137
 as centerpiece, '01 335
 as "containers" for food, '97 174
 cutting, '86 13; '92 52; '93 132; '94 29; '96 21;
  '98 72; '01 202, 260
 determining amounts to buy for entertaining,
  '90 276
 enhancing flavor of steamed, '01 30
 exotic, '01 166
 freezing, '87 112; '01 260, 335
 grilling, '83 191; '92 52; '95 274; '97 56
 growing your own, '98 112
 health benefits of, '00 46
 julienning, '02 316
 microwaving, '82 138; '83 191; '99 296
 "perking up," '01 335
 pre-packaged, '02 70
 preparing, '86 140, 141; '89 243, 244; '98 238;
  '99 100
 seasoning, '94 92 (chart)
 selecting, '84 249; '86 140, 141; '89 243, 244;
  '94 29
 steaming, '99 296; '01 30; '02 70
 stir-frying, '82 138; '83 191
 storing, '83 94; '84 211; '86 140, 141; '89 243,
  244; '94 29; '96 208; '01 98; '02 132; '03 176
 substitutions, '92 344
 winter vegetables, '84 249; '88 229; '01 30
Vinegar
 flavored, '03 102
 as a stain remover, '99 100
 as a substitute in recipes, '99 100; '00 66
 using to enhance flavors, '99 100; '01 30
Walnut oil, '01 118
Water, adding flavor to bottled or tap water, '96 21
Web sites, watermelon, '98 198
Whipping cream, '97 72
 stabilizer, '02 216
White chocolate. *See* **FOK/Chocolate.**
Wines, '85 292, 293; '98 162; '99 30, 328
 adding fresh ginger to, '01 335
 amounts to buy for entertaining, '99 328
 champagne, '85 293; '96 21; '98 306; '99 328
 chilling, '99 328
 cooking with, '00 46; '01 335; '02 132
 freezing, '00 46; '02 132
 mirin, '00 100
 removing the cork, '99 328
 selecting, '85 292; '99 30, 68, 100, 128, 224,
  328; '00 46; '01 300
 selecting in restaurants, '96 140
 serving, '85 292, 293; '99 328; '00 46
 storing, '85 292

FROM OUR KITCHEN (FOK), Wines
(continued)

substituting for in recipes, '00 46
sugar content of, '99 328
Wok cooking, '85 76
equipment, '85 76
preparing food for, '85 76
Yams. *See* **FOK/Sweet potatoes.**
Yeast, '89 268; '04 224. *See also* **FOK/Biscuits, Breads, Rolls.**
kinds of, '89 268
proofing, '01 50
using leftover, '99 50; '01 335
Yogurt
drinkable, '02 194
frozen, '00 156
instead of fruit puree, '97 206
as a substitute for buttermilk in recipes, '00 66
FROSTINGS. *See also* **FILLINGS, GLAZES, TOPPINGS.**
Almond Buttercream Frosting, '97 61; '99 155
Almond-Butter Frosting, '86 107
Amaretto Buttercream Frosting, '98 57
Amaretto Frosting, '86 246
Apricot Frosting, '81 192
Banana-Nut Frosting, '79 115
Boiled Frosting, '90 45; '92 14; '93 318
Bourbon Buttercream Frosting, '03 286
Bourbon Frosting, '88 236
Brandy Cream Frosting, '86 239
Browned Butter Frosting, '97 247
Brown Sugar Frosting, '79 13; '87 296; '91 236; '01 201
Brown Sugar Meringue Frosting, '81 70
Buttercream Frosting, '85 322; '92 230; '93 53, 285; '96 96; '98 155; '00 235, 244; '03 200
Butter Cream Frosting, '88 279
Buttercream Frosting, White, '93 337
Buttercream Icing, '83 73
Buttercream, Spiced, '84 226
Butter Frosting, '80 129
Butter Frosting, Browned, '86 248
Butter Frosting, Williamsburg, '81 120; '82 23
Buttermilk Frosting, '85 249
Butter Pecan Frosting, '80 229
Butter Whip Frosting, '96 119
Caramel Frosting, '81 278, M289; '82 314; '83 43; '84 39, 263; '86 239; '87 265; '89 55, 236; '90 307; '98 195; '00 52; '03 329
Caramel Frosting, Creamy, '81 71
Caramel Frosting, Easy, '87 39
Caramel Frosting, Favorite, '83 106
Caramel Frosting, Quick, '04 55
Carob Frosting, '85 218
Carolina Dream Frosting, '88 278
Cheese Spread, Tropical, '95 46
Cherry Frosting, '86 217
Cherry Icing, Chunky, '03 94
Cherry-Nut Cream Cheese Frosting, '96 249
Chocolate
Almond Frosting, Chocolate-, '83 241
Buttercream Frosting, Chocolate, '96 229; '98 M100
Butter Frosting, Chocolate, '89 271
Buttermilk Frosting, Chocolate-, '99 99
Candy Frosting, Chocolate, '81 238
Cherry Frosting, Chocolate-, '89 294
Chocolate Frosting, '80 M171; '81 265; '82 262; '83 79, 99, M233, 253; '84 200; '85 323; '86 8, 93, 138, 239, 314; '87 M97, 198, 199, 293; '89 M25; '90 194, 252, 265, 284, 309; '91 248; '92 319; '93 239; '94 133; '96 253, 254; '97 M87, 254; '99 271; '04 136

Chocolate Icing, '03 19
Coca-Cola Frosting, '02 181
Cocoa Frosting, '86 60
Coconut Chocolate Frosting, '79 13
Coffee Frosting, Chocolate-, '84 36; '88 269
Cola Frosting, '81 238; '00 120
Cola Frosting, Chocolate-, '95 56
Cream Cheese Frosting, Chocolate-, '02 256
Creamy Chocolate Frosting, '85 314; '86 316; '87 241; '99 307
Fluffy Chocolate Frosting, '86 336; '87 58
Fudge Frosting, '81 303; '87 296; '89 56; '94 51; '01 59
Fudge Frosting, Chocolate, '83 105; '00 287
Fudge Frosting, Quick, '81 278
Ganache, Chocolate, '93 255; '01 M235
Honey Chocolate Frosting, '79 83
Kahlúa Frosting, Chocolate, '91 298
Marshmallow Frosting, Chocolate-, '83 245; '04 210
Mint Chocolate Frosting, '99 M176
Mocha Buttercream, '89 42
Mocha Butter Cream Frosting, '79 281
Mocha-Buttercream Frosting, '86 26
Mocha Frosting, '83 301; '84 316; '87 224; '94 292; '97 35; '99 66
Mocha Frosting, Creamy, '82 289; '84 311; '91 248
Nut Frosting, Chocolate, '80 140
Peanut Butter Frosting, Chocolate-, '84 240; '87 222; '00 120
Peanut Butter-Fudge Frosting, '87 184
Perfect Chocolate Frosting, '90 307; '03 319
Rich Chocolate Frosting, '84 304
Root Beer Frosting, '04 211
Rum Frosting, Chocolate, '79 67
Satiny Chocolate Frosting, '85 126; '89 43
Velvet Frosting, '02 297
White Chocolate Buttercream Frosting, '97 M284
White Chocolate-Cream Cheese Frosting, '94 58; '98 323
White Chocolate-Cream Cheese Tiered Cake Frosting, '94 125
White Chocolate Frosting, '88 280; '91 101; '97 111; '00 306
White Chocolate Ganache, '01 253
Cinnamon-Cream Cheese Frosting, '03 332
Cinnamon-Cream Frosting, '84 311
Cinnamon Frosting, Buttery, '81 M139
Cinnamon Roll Icing, '03 247
Coconut Cream Cheese Frosting, '86 60
Coconut-Cream Cheese Frosting, '04 137
Coconut Frosting, '82 262; '91 269
Coconut Frosting, Creamy, '80 287
Coconut Frosting, Nutty, '86 8
Coconut Milk Frosting, '00 117
Coconut-Pecan Frosting, '81 296; '83 M233; '84 43, 322; '97 99; '03 289
Coffee Buttercream, '95 277
Coffee Buttercream Frosting, '99 155
Coffee Frosting, '94 86
Cola Frosting, '81 238; '02 298
Colored Frostings, '90 21; '00 61
Cream Cheese-Butter Pecan Frosting, '03 288
Cream Cheese Frosting, '79 45; '80 140, 253, 299; '82 135, 244; '83 105, 215, M233; '84 201, 255, 315, 316; '85 118, 121; '86 217, 337; '87 58; '90 305, 308; '92 120; '93 20; '94 254; '95 139; '96 282; '97 230, 277, 330; '98 275; '99 307, 315; '01 34, 185, 244, 271; '02 83, 209, 323; '03 55, 315
Cream Cheese Frosting, Deluxe, '80 120
Cream Cheese Frosting, Fluffy, '80 245
Cream Cheese Frosting, Nutty, '85 117; '96 263

Creamy Frosting, '04 83
Crème Chantilly, '87 9; '91 297
Crème de Menthe Frosting, '86 245; '93 256; '97 35
Decorating Techniques, Cake, '83 72, 240
Decorator Frosting, '82 20, 307; '83 106; '87 86; '91 282; '93 285; '01 91
Decorator Frosting, Creamy, '79 117
Decorator Frosting, Green, '93 286
Decorator Frosting, Yellow, '93 283
Divinity Frosting, '79 229; '01 270
Fluffy Frosting, '79 246; '86 235; '88 268; '89 254; '90 308
Fluffy White Frosting, '90 105; '95 319; '01 330
Fondant, Faux, '98 M154
Fondant, Rolled, '92 69
Fondant Teapot Spout, Handle, Daisies, and Butterflies, '04 83
Ganache Cream, '92 318
Grapefruit Frosting, '89 308
Heavenly Frosting, '80 140
Lemon
Buttercream Frosting, Lemon, '83 301; '86 61; '91 247; '03 105
Butter Cream Frosting, Lemon-, '85 117
Coconut Frosting, Lemon-, '90 253
Cream Cheese Frosting, Lemon-, '81 157
Creamy Lemon Frosting, '79 93
Lemon Frosting, '85 191; '86 217; '93 81
Orange-Lemon Frosting, '88 92
White Frosting, Lemony, '88 7; '03 317
Lime Buttercream Frosting, '03 105
Maple Frosting, '82 217; '85 322; '96 17
Meringue Frosting, '86 336; '87 84; '99 118
Meringue Frosting, Italian, '98 70
Mint Cream Frosting, '93 216
Mint Frosting, '88 80
Never Fail Frosting, '86 314
Orange
Buttercream Frosting, Orange, '80 70; '99 117; '03 105
Butter Frosting, Orange, '83 300
Cream Cheese Frosting, Citrus, '99 223
Cream Cheese Frosting, Orange, '81 70; '82 16; '92 19
Cream Frosting, Orange, '81 207; '82 14
Creamy Orange Frosting, '83 24, 241
Lemon Frosting, Orange-, '88 92
Orange Frosting, '81 7; '86 61; '88 119
Orange-Cream Cheese Frosting, '04 258
Panocha Frosting, '89 296
Peanut Butter Frosting, '83 223; '84 153; '85 34
Peanut Butter Swirl Frosting, '86 109
Peanut Frosting, Creamy, '80 87
Pecan-Cream Cheese Frosting, '02 294
Pecan Frosting, '86 86
Peppermint Birthday Cake Frosting, Pink, '92 269
Peppermint Cream Cheese Frosting, '98 308
Peppermint Frosting, Quick, '98 308
Pineapple-Cream Cheese Frosting, '95 160
Piping Icing, '92 69
Piping Icing, Tips for, '84 302
Powdered Sugar Frosting, '96 319
Praline Frosting, '01 235
Praline Fudge Icing, '04 331
Quick Pour Frosting, '85 119
Royal Icing, '80 278; '81 21; '83 73; '84 303; '85 323; '87 295; '88 309; '91 281; '98 324; '02 49
Rum Buttercream Frosting, '99 117
Rum Cream, '88 154, 224
Sea Foam Frosting, '81 211; '91 271
Seven-Minute Double Boiler Frosting, '81 278
Seven-Minute Frosting, '80 289; '83 299, 301; '87 296; '89 55, 57; '94 98, 99; '97 71

Snow Peak Frosting, '82 53; '85 281
Spiced Cream, '89 215
Strawberry Buttercream Frosting, '04 55
Strawberry Frosting, '89 184
Toffee Frosting, English, '85 125
Vanilla Buttercream Frosting, '92 239; '94 99;
    '96 229; '97 111; '99 117; '03 286
Vanilla Frosting, '84 36; '85 236; '92 14, 274
Vanilla-Rum Frosting, '85 324
Whipped Cream Frosting, '83 229; '85 125;
    '87 263; '89 43; '93 86; '96 229; '03 105
White Chocolate-Cream Cheese Frosting, '94 58
White Frosting, '83 268
White Frosting, Fluffy, '81 278
White Frosting, Luscious, '81 71
FRUIT. *See also* **specific types.**
Acorn Squash, Fruited, '85 235
Acorn Squash, Fruit-Stuffed, '81 295
Appetizers
    Bowl, Sparkling Fresh Fruit, '80 146
    Brie, Tropical Breeze, '94 M18
    Brown Sugar Dip with Fruit, Buttery, '90 243
    Canapés, Fruit-Topped, '85 80
    Cascade, Fruit, '86 104
    Cheese Ball, Fruit-and-Nut, '91 251
    Cup, Appetizer Fruit, '86 131
    Curried Rum Sauce, Tropical Fruit with, '91 164
    Dip, Ginger Fruit, '96 110
    Dip, Orange Fruit, '96 190
    Dips, Fun Fruit, '01 109
    Fresh Fruit, Mint Dip with, '87 146
    Fresh Fruit with Lemon Sauce, '82 290
    Kebabs with Coconut Dressing, Fruit, '87 251
    Mix, Trash, '01 204
    Picks, Fruit on, '80 159
    Soup, Cold Fresh Fruit, '87 157
    Soup, Swedish Fruit, '82 313; '83 65
    Spread, Fruit and Cheese, '81 245
    Spread, Fruited Cream Cheese, '91 306
    Spread, Nutty Fruit-and-Cheese, '87 246; '02 164
Bake, Cranberry-Mustard Fruit, '90 287
Baked Curried Fruit, '03 247
Baked Fruit, Gingered, '81 232
Baked Fruit, Ginger-Orange, '93 313
Baked Spiced Fruit, '89 305
Bake, Hot Fruit, '81 270
Bake, Mustard Fruit, '90 291
Bake, Nutty Fruit, '83 127
Bars, Fruit and Nut Granola, '81 49
Beets, Fruited, '97 28
Beverages
    Apricot Fruit Flip, '91 18
    Batida, Citrus, '02 274
    Blender Fruit Beverage, '83 318
    Breakfast Drink, Yummy, '01 133
    Breakfast Fruit Juicy, '86 176
    Brew, Fruity Witches', '95 273
    Brunch Punch, '04 281
    Champagne Fruit Slush, '90 322
    Champions' Cooler, '96 M181
    Cider, Warm Citrus, '01 46
    Citrus Blush, '98 197
    Cocktails, Sea Breeze, '97 161
    Cooler, Four-Fruit, '86 101
    Cooler, Fruited Wine, '86 176
    Cooler, Fruit Juice, '92 67
    Coolers, Fruit, '98 197
    Cooler, Speedy Spring, '02 58
    Float, Frosty Fruit, '87 159
    Four-Fruit Refresher, '79 174
    Frappé, Hootenanny, '89 110
    Honey-Yogurt Smoothie, Fruited, '88 231; '89 23
    Ice Ring, '03 141
    Ice Ring, Easy, '03 141
    Ice Tropical, '79 174
    Lemonade, Cherry-Berry, '03 89
    Patio Blush, '99 93
    Punch, Autumn Harvest, '96 277
    Punch, Can-Can Fruit, '94 122
    Punch, Caribbean, '95 173
    Punch, Champagne, '03 141
    Punch, Citrus-Wine, '98 197
    Punch, Cottontail, '02 48
    Punch, Emerald Sea, '04 163
    Punch, Florida Fruit, '92 247
    Punch for a Bunch, '95 90
    Punch, Fresh Fruit, '98 155
    Punch, Fruit, '83 52; '01 106; '02 162
    Punch, Fruited Ice-Cube, '98 197
    Punch, Fruit Juice, '96 214
    Punch, Fruit Juice-and-Vodka, '96 214
    Punch, Fruit Juicy Rum, '91 175
    Punch, Fruit Slush, '91 278
    Punch, Golden Fruit, '80 299; '83 56; '96 278
    Punch, Happy New Year, '98 26
    Punch, Holiday Fruit, '79 232
    Punch, Holiday Hot Fruit, '92 286
    Punch, Hot Cider, '03 233
    Punch, Hot Fruit, '83 33
    Punch, Hot Spiced, '96 214
    Punch, Hot Spiced Rum, '96 214
    Punch, Hurricane, '00 61
    Punch, Margarita, '98 88
    Punch, Mixed Fruit, '90 207; '95 239
    Punch, Party Fruit, '82 137
    Punch, Passion Fruit, '90 169
    Punch, Pineapple Fruit, '02 49
    Punch, Poinsettia, '02 251
    Punch, Polka Dot, '95 178
    Punch, Slushy Fruit, '98 92
    Punch, Southern Fresh Fruit, '99 70
    Punch, Southern Fruit, '95 238
    Punch, Spiced Fruit, '88 2
    Punch, Spirited Fruit, '81 100
    Punch, Summertime Fruit, '80 160
    Punch, Sunset, '96 278
    Punch, Tropical Fruit, '81 51; '83 176; '90 169
    Refresher, Fruit, '91 203
    'ritas, Fruit, '94 157
    Sangría, '00 122
    Sangría, Garden, '01 100
    Sangría, Mock Tea, '99 336
    Sangría, Texas White, '02 86
    Sangría, Three-Fruit, '89 212
    Shake, Frosty Fruit, '87 23
    Shake, Tangy Fruit, '95 129
    Shake, Three-Fruit Yogurt, '01 173
    Shake, Tropical, '93 212; '04 21
    Sipper by the Glass, Fresh Mint-Citrus, '03 89
    Sipper, Fresh Mint-Citrus, '03 89
    Slush, Fruit, '96 157
    Slushy, Fruit, '80 146
    Slushy, Fruit Parfait, '02 185
    Smoothie, Citrus, '98 17
    Smoothie, Fruit, '89 87
    Smoothie, Two-Fruit, '89 182
    Smoothie, Yogurt-Fruit, '03 25
    Sparkle, Fruit, '99 289
    Sparkle, Tangerine, '98 54
    Spritzer, Fruit, '01 174
    Tea, Christmas Fruit, '83 275; '01 240
    Tea, Citrus Iced, '00 139
    Tea Cooler, Fruited, '94 131
    Tea, Fruit-and-Mint Iced, '98 84
    Tea, Fruited Mint, '88 79; '91 81
    Tea, Fruity Mint, '04 143
    Tea, Hot Russian, '97 274
    Tea, Hot Spiced Fruit, '87 242
    Tea, Refreshing Fruit, '97 122
    Tea-Ser, Tropical, '95 200
    Tea, Spiced Iced, '97 121
    Three-Fruit Drink, '79 38; '80 50; '87 199
    Tropical Fruit Drink, '85 43
    Tropical Fruit Whisper, '89 212
    Tropical Refresher, '96 157
    Wassail, '97 240; '99 268
    Wassail, Golden, '96 278
    Wassail, Winter, '03 295
    Whiskey Sours, '03 258
    Whiskey Sour Slushies, '04 106
    Whiskey Sours, Slushy, '03 258
Boats, Honeydew Fruit, '81 147
Bowl, White Grape Juice Fruit, '00 160
Braid, Fruit-and-Cheese, '86 214
Brandied Fruit, Hot, '80 48
Bread, Cranberry Fruit-Nut, '79 275
Bread, Fruity Banana, '95 78
Bread, Kahlúa Fruit-Nut, '79 235
Canning and Preserving
    Apple Rings, Cinnamon, '85 107
    Berries (except Strawberries), '80 128
    Conserve, Dried Fruit, '82 308
    Dehydration Chart, Fruit and Vegetable, '84 147
    Freezing Chart, Fruit, '85 187
    Jam, Tri-Berry Lemon, '98 214
    Juices, Fruit, '85 107
    Mixed Fruit, Unsweetened, '83 182
    Peaches, '80 128
    Peaches and Pears, '85 106
    Peaches, Honey-Sweet, '85 107
    Preserves, Fruity, '98 214
    Syrup, Fruit, '86 176
Chafing Dish Fruit, '89 305
Cheesecake, Island Breeze, '03 144
Chilled Fruit with Dressing, '85 222
Chutney, Autumn Fruit, '88 M230
Chutney, Fall Fruit, '97 218
Compotes
    Amaretto-Hot Fruit Compote, '90 250
    Baked Fruit Compote, '80 276; '84 314; '87 228
    Baked Mustard Fruit Compote, '85 47
    Beauberries Bordeaux, '98 18
    Brandied Fruit Compote, '96 286
    Champagne Fruit Compote, '81 309; '82 124
    Chilled Fruit Compote, '83 123
    Citrus Compote, '98 17
    Citrus Compote with Caramel Syrup, '98 313
    Dried Fruit Compote, '98 18
    Festive Fruit Compote, '94 279
    Fresh Fruit Compote, '79 162; '82 197, 272;
        '84 82; '94 190
    Fruit Compote, '86 330
    Gingered Fruit Compote, '88 184
    Hot Fruit Compote, '81 203; '83 53; '86 324;
        '90 124; '03 307
    Jícama-Fruit Compote, '92 49
    Mixed Fruit Compote, '93 123
    Praline Fruit Compote, Warm, '85 260
    Pudding Compote, Fresh Fruit, '86 151
    Raspberry Puree, Fruit Compote with, '88 81
    Shortcakes with Fruit Compote, Cinnamon-
        Crunch, '03 194
    Wine Fruit Compote, '81 272
Couscous with Mixed Fruit, '95 232
Cup, Mixed Fruit, '94 60
Cup, Tipsy Fruit, '81 268
Curried Fruit, Almond-, '83 261
Curried Fruit Bake, '87 241
Curried Fruit, Hot, '79 225; '81 264; '84 287; '95 72
Delight, Fruit, '86 131
Delight, Hot Fruit, '83 281
Delight, Winter Fruit, '80 243

FRUIT
(continued)

Desserts. *See also* **FRUIT/Fruitcakes.**
Amaretto Crème on Fresh Fruit, '93 176
Angel Cakes with Almond Sugar, Mixed-Berry, '02 175
Balls, Fruit, '82 296; '84 299
Bavarian Cream with Fresh Fruit, '88 137
Biscotti, Fruitcake, '96 281
Brandied Fruit Starter, '82 249
Bread Pudding, Old-Fashioned, '01 223
Brie with Fresh Fruit, Caramel, '90 266
Briwatts with Fruit, '98 211
Cake, Fruit-and-Cereal Brunch, '88 263
Cake, Fruit and Spice, '87 M97
Cake, Fruited Pound, '81 265
Cake, Fruity Ice Cream, '87 110
Cake, Holiday Lane, '99 306
Cake, Southern Custard Crêpe, '99 166
Cake, Spicy Fruited Carrot, '85 117
Cake, Stately Fruit-and-Nut, '84 226
Caribbean Fruit Dessert, '84 314
Cassata, '01 125
Cheese, and Nuts, Fruit, '93 324
Cheesecake, Fruit-Glazed, '80 24; '90 162
Cobbler, Apple-Berry, '04 330
Cobbler, Fruit, '99 33
Cobbler, Mixed-Berry, '02 214
Cobbler, Quick Fruit, '91 20
Cobbler, Three-Berry, '04 29
Cobbler, Too-Easy Berry, '04 28
Cookies, Bourbon Fruit, '86 334
Cookies, Fruitcake, '79 291; '86 320; '88 286; '96 314; '98 294
Cookies, Fruitcake Drop, '92 275
Cookies, Holiday Fruitcake, '81 301
Cookies, Rolled Fruit, '80 15
Cookies, Spicy Holiday Fruit, '83 298
Cream Cheese, Fruited, '85 306
Cream Freeze, Fruit, '82 144
Cream Puffs, Tutti-Frutti, '79 231
Crêpes, Fruit-Filled Chocolate, '89 325
Crêpes, Tropical, '86 275
Crêpes, Tropical Fruit, '87 77
Crisp, Fruit, '94 168
Cup, Fruit, '81 141
Cup, Snowball Citrus, '79 2
Cup, Vanilla Fruit, '80 183
Curried Fruit, Hot, '95 72
Custard over Fruit, Stirred, '84 83
Custard with Fresh Fruit, Citrus, '93 70
Drops, Candied Fruit, '89 329
Dumplings, Delicious Fruit, '97 210
Elegant Fruit, '91 91
English Rocks, '01 295
Filling, Crêpes with Fruit, '81 96
Filling, Fruit, '94 245
Filling, Fruit-Nut, '80 289
Filling, Lemon Crêpes with Fruit, '82 46
Filling, Mixed Fruit Fried Pie, '96 109
Filling, Nutty Fruit, '99 306
Filling, Tutti-Frutti, '79 231
Flaming Fruit Dessert, '83 302
Freeze, Holiday Fruit, '88 283
Fresh Fruit with Cheese, Luscious, '79 153
Frozen Fruit Cream, '94 129
Frozen Fruit Cups, '93 197
Glaze, Berry, '00 312
Glazed Fruit, '85 83
Ice Cream, Tutti-Frutti, '86 129
Ice, Fruit, '86 176
Ice, Mixed Fruit, '81 178; '88 85

Ice, Three-Fruit, '02 51
Ice, Tropical, '99 105
Island Fruit Chill, '98 180
Kebabs, Fruit, '86 181
Kebabs with Mint Marinade, Fruit, '82 157
Lemon Curd, Fresh Fruit with, '88 21
Marinated Fruit Bowl, '80 297
Marinated with Kirsch, Mixed Fruit, '03 86
Meringue Baskets with Fresh Fruit and Ice Cream, '98 179
Meringue Shells, Fruit-Filled, '86 151
Meringues, Tropical, '98 71
Parfait, Tropical Trilogy, '92 247
Pie, Bumbleberry, '97 163
Pie, Crispy-Crust Fruit, '88 68
Pie, Fruitcake, '80 237
Pie, Fruited Cheese, '92 228
Pie, Fruit-Topped Vanilla Cream, '84 49
Pie, Japanese Fruit, '80 238
Pies, Baked Fruit, '84 7
Pizza, Peanut Butter-Fruit, '94 60
Planter's Punch Dessert, '95 175
Pops, Cherry-Berry Lemonade, '03 89
Pops, Fruit, '87 168
Pudding, Fruited Rice, '86 95
Pudding, Summer, '98 217; '04 159
Puff, Giant Fruit, '85 72
Puff Pastry Baskets, Tropical, '93 177
Puree, Fruit, '94 190
Rainbow Fruit Dessert, '85 108
Refresher, Grape Juice-Fruit, '86 182
Ribbons, Sugared Fruit, '02 295
Rugelach, Fruit, '97 220
Rumtopf, '95 142
Sabayon, Champagne, '00 288
Sauce, Fruit, '81 177
Sauce, Golden Fruit, '89 281
Sauce, Hot Fruit Dessert, '87 299
Sauce, Quick Fruit, '82 212
Sauce, Rum-Fruit, '84 312
Shells, Fruited Meringue, '87 32
Sherbet, Freezer Fruit, '86 334
Sherbet, Frozen Fruit, '79 155
Sherbet, Fruit Punch, '86 129
Sherbet, Instant Fruit, '85 158
Sherried Fruit Flame, '85 313
Slush, Refreshing Fruit, '82 35
Sorbet, Tropical, '97 110
Soup Dessert, Fruit, '79 172
Soup, Fresh Fruit, '98 196
Spiced Fruit Dessert, '82 50
Squares, Christmas Fruit, '88 282
Strudels, Dried Fruit, '01 48
Sugarplum Sticks, '95 321
Sundaes, Very Berry, '03 126
Tart, Fancy Fruit, '82 128; '91 119
Tart, Fresh Fruit, '84 178; '90 58
Tart, King Cake Fruit, '96 57
Tartlets, Fresh Fruit, '93 96
Tart, Open-Face Fruit, '84 207
Tart, Rainbow Fruit, '82 304
Tarts, Bowl-Me-Over Fresh Fruit, '93 200
Tequila, Fruit in, '82 223
Topping, Fruity Dessert, '82 167
Trifle, Jumbleberry, '03 84
Trifle, Olde English, '95 331
Trifle, Tropical Rum, '03 85
Turnovers, Fruit, '79 150
Winter Fruit with Custard Sauce, '88 251
Zabaglione with Fruit, Champagne Vanilla, '00 31
Dips
Citrus-Cream Cheese Dip, '03 93
Coconut-Honey Fruit Dip, '84 171

Cranberry Fruit Dip, '89 60
Cream Cheese Dip, Fruited, '88 261
Fresh Fruit Dip, '80 265; '95 94
Ginger Fruit Dip, '96 110
Heavenly Fruit Dip, '81 160
Honey-Sour Cream Dip, Fresh Fruit with, '90 180
Marshmallow Fruit Dip, '84 171
Orange Fruit Dip, '96 190
Quick Fruit Dip, '90 110
Sweet Fruit Dip, '89 328
Tropical Dip for Fruit, '91 252
Yogurt Dip, Fruited, '84 171
Dressings. *See also* **FRUIT/Salads, Stuffings.**
Avocado Fruit Salad Dressing, '82 93
Baked Fruit Dressing, '87 253
Coconut-Fruit Dressing, Tangy, '84 171
Cornbread Dressing, Fruited, '80 262
Fluffy Fruit Dressing, '79 69
Fresh Fruit Dressing, '87 134
Lime-Honey Fruit Salad Dressing, '87 81
Marmalade-Fruit Dressing, '84 171
Nutty Fruit Dressing, '88 68
Pecan Dressing, Fruit-and-, '84 252
Salad Dressing for Fruit, '86 40
Salad, Dressing for Fruit, '87 81
Salad Dressing, Fruit, '79 69; '93 184
Turkey Dressing, Fruited, '99 257
Whipped Cream Fruit Dressing, '79 270
Dried Fruit Baked Apples, Pecan-and-, '03 269
Fresh Fruit Combo, '86 178
Fresh Fruit with Lemon-Yogurt Dressing, '93 17
Fruitcakes
Applesauce Fruitcake, '83 258
Aronowitz Fruitcake, '86 285
Black Cake (A Kwanzaa Fruitcake), '01 292
Bourbon Fruitcake, '85 315
Brandy Fruitcake, '82 261
Burgundy Fruitcake, '85 292
Cake Mix Fruit Cake, '95 248
Chocolate Fruitcakes, '95 250
Classic Fruitcake, '91 258
Favorite Fruitcake, Family, '88 284
Fondue, Fruitcake, '84 258
Grandmother's Fruitcake, '95 248
Japanese Fruitcake, '83 268; '90 252
Jeweled Fruitcake, '88 260
Jill's Fruitcake, '95 249
Kentucky Fruitcake, '86 266
Layered Fruitcake, '87 265
Lemon Fruitcake, '83 258
Light Fruitcake, '90 309
Loaf, Fruitcake, '96 286
Mom's Fruitcake, '85 321
No-Bake Fruitcake, '95 249
Old-South Fruitcake, '79 289
Regal Fruitcake, '83 257
Sherry-Nut Fruitcake, '84 266; '00 299
White Fruitcake, '80 280; '85 316; '00 299; '03 248
Zucchini Fruitcake, '88 284
Garnishes, '82 280; '85 339
Gazpacho, Berry, '97 181
Gazpacho, Citrus, '96 70
Gingered Fruit, '83 151
Granola, Fruity, '84 148
Granola, Mixed Fruit, '01 290
Grilled Fruit with Honey Yogurt, '95 87
Hawaiian Fruit Dish, '82 112
Hot Fruit Delight, '83 281
Kebabs, Fruit, '86 181; '89 85
Kebabs, Fruity Mermaid, '91 177
Kebabs, Grilled Fruit, '97 147
Kebabs, Winter Fruit, '89 34

Main Dishes
  Brisket, Mixed Fruit Tzimmes with, '93 114
  Chicken Breasts with Fruited Rice Pilaf, '92 307
  Chicken en Crème, Fruited, '83 264
  Chicken, Fruit-Glazed, '80 211
  Chicken, Fruity Baked, '01 48
  Chicken with Almond Rice, Spiced Fruited,
    '81 195
  Chicken with Fresh Fruit, Coconut, '93 294
  Chuck Roast, Fruited, '91 289
  Cornish Hens with Fruited Stuffing, '90 191
  Cornish Hens with Tropical Fruit, Grilled,
    '97 310
  Goose, Fruit- and Pecan-Stuffed, '83 268
  Goose, Fruited Stuffed Wild, '88 248
  Goose, Fruit Stuffed, '83 320
  Ham Slice, Fruited, '83 M317
  Poblanos Stuffed with Pork and Fruit, '97 269
  Pork Chops, Fruited, '87 194
  Pork Chops, Fruited Stuffed, '86 197
  Pork Chops, Fruit-Stuffed, '82 136
  Pork Chops, Fruit-Topped, '94 41
  Pork Chops with Rice, Fruit-Glazed, '82 73
  Pork Loin, Fruitcake-Stuffed, '95 250
  Pork Loin, Roast, '01 222
  Pork Medaillons with Fresh Fruit, '97 104
  Pork Pilaf, Fruited, '82 246
  Pork Tenderloins, Fruit-Stuffed, '87 270
  Pork Tenderloin with Fruit Stuffing and Shiitake
    Sauce, '97 218
  Pot Roast, Fruited, '90 211
  Salad, Main Dish Fruit, '83 119
  Shrimp with Louis Sauce, Citrus-Marinated,
    '03 66
  Spareribs, Fruit-Stuffed, '79 14
  Turkey-and-Fruit Kebabs, '88 140
  Turkey Breast, Citrus-Rosemary, '02 270
Marinade, Citrus, '04 51
Marinade, Fruit with Lime, '98 92
Marinated Fruit, '91 67
Marinated Fruit, Minted, '92 138
Marmalade, Citrus, '97 32
Marmalade, Delicious Fruit, '81 285
Marmalade, Fruited Onion, '96 323; '97 27
Marmalade, Spicy Blueberry-Citrus, '03 135
Medleys
  Baked Fruit Medley, '81 297
  Chilled Fruit Medley, '84 60
  Chinese Fruit Medley, '83 22
  Cup Medley, Fruit, '85 47
  Curried Fruit Medley, '95 329
  Fancy Fruit Medley, '84 82
  Fresh Fruit Medley, '81 141
  Frosty Fruit Medley, '82 226
  Fruit Medley, '89 235
  Midsummer Fruit Medley, '88 182
  Minted Fruit Medley, '80 182
  Tropical Medley of Fruit, '86 53
Mélange, Fruit, '88 M295
Mélange, Melon, '84 139
Mint-Balsamic Tea, Fresh Fruit with, '95 232
Mix, Dried Fruit, '92 22; '96 286
Mixed Fruit Grand, '02 212
Mix, Trash, '01 204
Muesli, Bran-and-Fruit, '91 134
Muesli, Homestyle, '91 315
Muffins, Fruit-and-Bran, '04 22
Muffins, Fruited Wheat, '79 93
Nuggets, Dried Fruit, '86 326
Oatmeal, Fruited, '88 19
Pick, Fruit-on-a-, '90 179
Preserving. *See* **FRUIT/Canning and Preserving.**
Relish, Fresh Fruit, '95 158
Rhapsody, Fruit, '80 158

Rice, Far East Fruited, '81 175
Rice Mix, Fruited, '90 267; '97 317
Rice Mix, Fruited Curry-, '86 326
Rice Pilaf, Fruit-and-Vegetable, '84 196
Rice Pilaf, Fruited, '04 271
Rice, Sweet Jamaican, '96 71
Salads
  Almond-Citrus Salad, '96 274; '01 42
  Apricot Fruit Salad, '82 132
  Avocado Citrus Salad, '01 133
  Avocado Fruit Salad, '87 41
  Avocado-Fruit Salad with Honey-Yogurt
    Dressing, '93 172
  Baby Blue Salad, '01 20; '03 178
  Banana-Mixed Fruit Salad, '79 270
  Berry-Citrus Twist, '95 100
  Blackberry-Basil Vinaigrette, Fruit Salad with,
    '04 97
  Bowl, Fresh Fruit, '89 137
  Cabbage and Fruit Salad, '79 286
  Cantaloupe, Fruit-Filled, '83 120
  Carrot-and-Seed Salad, Fruity, '86 223
  Carrot-Fruit Toss, '82 235
  Chef Salad, Fruited, '85 222
  Chef's Fruit Salad, '86 35
  Cherry Fruit Salad, '87 236
  Chicken-and-Fruit Salad, '01 178
  Chicken-and-Fruit Salad, Grilled, '96 155
  Chicken-Avocado Salad, Fruited, '82 101
  Chicken-Fruit Salad, '82 79
  Chicken Fruit Salad, '90 234
  Chicken Salad, Autumn, '01 312
  Chicken Salad, Fruited, '84 25, 290; '88 88;
    '90 318
  Chicken Salad, Fruity, '83 157
  Chicken Salad in Avocados, Fruited, '87 41
  Chicken Salad, Summery, '95 138
  Chicken Salad, Sweet Peanut-, '03 54
  Chicken Salad, Tropical, '96 127
  Chicken Salad with Fruit, '82 171
  Citrus-and-Avocado Salad, '99 26
  Citrus and Greens with Orange-Ginger Dressing,
    '96 240
  Citrus-Cilantro Dressing, Fruit Salad with,
    '93 310; '94 97; '00 160
  Citrus Dressing, Fruit Salad with, '88 6
  Citrus Salad with Sweet-and-Sour Dressing,
    '01 104
  Citrus-Strawberry Salad, '04 249
  Coconut Fruit Bowl, '83 111
  Coconut Salad, Chunky Fruit-and-, '84 24
  Coleslaw, Fruited, '83 209; '85 139
  Coleslaw, Three-Fruit, '86 250
  Colorful Fruit Bowl, '91 58
  Colorful Fruit Salad, '82 113
  Congealed Fresh Fruit, Jeweled, '95 89
  Cottage Cheese-and-Fruit Salad, '86 16
  Cottage-Fruit Split, '86 169
  Cracked Wheat-Fruit Salad, '96 240
  Cream Dressing, Fruit Salad with, '89 277
  Creamy Fruit Salad, '84 265; '04 333
  Creamy Holiday Fruit Salad, '90 251
  Cup, Fruit, '81 141; '91 202
  Cup, Mixed Fruit, '87 233; '94 60
  Cups, Honeydew Fruit, '82 179
  Cups, Royal Fruit, '81 146
  Cup with Mint Dressing, Fresh Fruit, '80 183
  Curried Fruit Salad, '85 107
  Date Dressing, Fruit Salad with, '87 57
  Dressed-Up Fruit, '82 5
  Easy Fruit Salad, '80 221
  Easy Patio Fruit Salad, '88 184
  Fall Salad with Ginger Dressing, '82 194
  Favorite Fruit Salad, '99 220

Festive Fruit Salad, '80 16
Freeze, Fruity Lemon, '82 145
Fresh Fruit Salad, '82 165; '97 122
Fresh Fruit Salad with Celery-Honey Dressing,
  '80 42
Fresh Fruit Salad with Celery Seed Dressing,
  '00 68
Fresh Fruit Salad with Orange-Ginger Syrup,
  '03 167
Fresh Fruit Salad with Poppy Seed Dressing,
  '91 168
Fresh Fruit with Lime Sauce, '02 68
Frisky Fruit Salad, '85 46
Frozen Fruit Salad, '83 110; '97 158; '00 160
Frozen Fruit Salad, Dreamy, '79 126
Frozen Fruit Salad, Luscious, '81 204
Frozen Fruit Salad, Summertime, '89 111
Frozen Salad Christmas Wreath, '79 241
Fruit Salad, '83 209; '89 277; '03 42
Gingered Fruit Salad, '95 95
Glazed Fruit Salad, '83 48; '84 290
Green-and-Gold Salad with Fresh Citrus Ranch
  Dressing, '04 91
Green Fruit Salad with Honey-Lime Dressing,
  '93 71
Ham Salad, Fruited, '81 36, 146
Harvest Salad with Cider Vinaigrette, '99 322
Heavenly Salad, '81 252
Holiday Fruit Salad, '87 236
Honeydew Fruit Bowl, '84 186
Honey Dressing, Fruit Salad with, '87 129
Honey Fruit Salad, '80 276
Honey-Lemon Dressing, Fruit Salad with, '93 21
Honey-Pecan Dressing, Fruit Salad with, '03 28
Hurry-Up Fruit Salad, '87 236
Jícama-Fruit Salad, '86 83
Jícama Salad, Fruit-, '00 203
Layered Fruit Salad, '84 290; '89 277; '91 58
Lemonade Fruit Salad, '84 24
Lettuce and Fruit Salad with Poppy Seed
  Dressing, '80 152
Main Dish Fruit Salad, '83 119
Marinated Fruit Deluxe, '81 146
Melange Delight, Fruit, '81 302
Melon-Citrus Mingle, '79 177
Minted Fruit Toss, '99 160
Mint-Gin Fruit Salad, '92 92
Mint Sauce, Fruit Salad with, '88 M96
Mixed Fruit with Sour Cream Sauce, '02 169
Mold, Sherried Fruit, '90 124
Multi-Fruit Salad, '93 184
Nut Salad, Cheesy Fruit-'n'-, '87 56
Old-Fashioned Fruit Salad, '82 80
Orange Cream, Fresh Fruit Salad with, '90 126
Orange Fruit Cup, '91 277
Oriental Dressing, Fruit Salad with, '91 277
Pasta Salad, Fruited, '92 108
Peachy Fruit Salad, '89 206
Persimmon Fruit Salad, '79 206
Pineapple Cream Dressing, Fruit Cups with,
  '83 81
Pineapple Dressing, Fruit Salad with, '85 207
Pineapple-Fruit Salad, Icy, '87 9
Pita, Fresh Fruit Salad, '02 99
Platter, Fresh Fruit Salad, '92 213
Platter, Fruit Salad, '83 261
Poppy Seed Dressing, Fruit Salad with, '88 78
Potato Salad, Fruity, '85 214
Quick-and-Easy Fruit Salad, '81 99
Raspberry Fruit Mounds, '79 35
Refreshing Fruit Salad, '85 92
Rum, Fruit Cup with, '83 55
Sangría Fruit Cups, '89 34
Shrimp Salad, Fruited, '86 156

FRUIT, Salads
(continued)

Sour Cream Fruit Salad, '80 138
Sparkling Fruit Salad, '82 266
Spiced Autumn Fruit Salad, '87 228
Spiced Fruit Salad, '98 54
Spring Mix Salad, Fruity, '04 105
Springtime Fruit Salad, '81 96
Summer Fruit-Chicken Salad with Blueberry
    Vinaigrette, '00 154
Summer Fruit Salad, '82 164; '92 171
Summer Fruit Salad with Blueberry Vinaigrette,
    '00 154
Summer Salad, Favorite, '80 158
Sunny Fruit Salad, '91 58
Sweet-and-Sour Fruit Salad, '80 13; '84 125
Sweet Potato Fruit Salad, '00 325
Tossed Fruit Salad, '92 106
Tropical Fruit Salad, '89 306; '02 163
Tropical Fruit Salad with Fresh Mint Dressing,
    '84 126
Turkey-Fruit Salad, '79 56
Turkey Fruit Salad, '83 233; '84 244
Turkey Salad, Fruit-and-, '89 176
Turkey Salad, Fruit-and-Spice, '94 325
Turkey Salad, Fruitful, '84 197
Twenty-Four-Hour Fruit Salad, '96 279
Watermelon Fruit Basket, '84 161
Wheat Salad with Citrus and Mint, '99 163
Winter Fruit-and-Cucumber Salad, '02 274
Winter Fruit Cup, '02 22
Winter Fruit Salad, '80 248; '82 23
Winter Fruit with Poppy Seed Dressing, '95 317
Wreath, Della Robbia Fruit, '87 294
Yogurt Fruit Salad, '81 114; '96 247
Yogurt-Granola Fruit Medley, '91 58
Salsa and Cinnamon Crisps, South Seas Ice Cream
    with Sweet Heat, '04 315
Salsa, Caribbean Fruit, '04 252
Salsa, Cranberry-Citrus, '97 290
Salsa, Fresh Citrus, '03 291
Salsa, Fruit, '97 124; '02 54; '04 168
Salsa, Grilled Shrimp with Citrus, '97 141
Salsa, Key Lime Pie with Minted Tropical, '99 333
Salsa, Spicy Summer, '03 186
Salsa, Tropical, '01 60
Salsa with Cinnamon Crisps, Fruit, '01 108
Sandwiches, Fruit-and-Cheese Breakfast, '89 M21
Sandwiches, Glazed Breakfast Fruit, '93 178
Sauce, Citrus Dipping, '97 208
Sauce for Fruit, Tangy, '90 161
Sauce, Grand Marnier Fruit, '90 93
Sauce, Grilled Shrimp with Tropical Fruit, '01 195
Sherried Fruit Casserole, '80 284
Sherried Fruit Mélange, '80 158
Snack Mix, Fruity, '03 47
Soup, Chilled Fresh Fruit, '88 160
Soup, Dried Fruit, '79 23
Soup, Fiesta Citrus, '01 176
Soup, Fruit, '87 98
Soup, Yogurt Fruit, '86 176
Spiced Fruit, '79 23
Spiced Fruit, Cold, '90 269
Spiced Fruit Delight, '82 229
Spiced Fruit, Warm, '86 39
Spiced Mixed Fruit, '01 88
Spiced Winter Fruit, '83 262
Spicy Fruit and Veggies with Lime, '04 141
Spicy Tropical Fruit, '04 166
Spread, Fruit, '85 135
Spread, Fruited Cream Cheese, '91 306; '93 79
Spread, Sugarless Fruit, '84 60

Strudel, Fruit Basket, '87 276
Stuffing Mix, Fruited, '89 331
Summer Fruit Fantasy, '91 178
Sundae, Breakfast, '98 206
Syrup, Apricot Fruit, '82 10
Terrine with Raspberry Sauce, Fruit, '98 157
Topping, Fruit, '81 42; '87 225; '89 50;
    '03 145
Tropical Fruit Fluff, '88 68
Tropical Fruit Tray, '93 72
Twists, Fruit-Nut, '82 253
White Wine, Fruit in, '81 48
Wontons, Fruit-Filled, '85 287
Wreath, Tex-Mex, '96 241
FUDGE
Almond Fudge, Creamy, '95 51
Buttermilk Fudge, '95 52; '97 317
Butterscotch-Peanut Fudge, '98 M282
Butterscotch Rum Fudge, '88 256
Caramel Fudge, '91 273
Cherry Nut Fudge, '83 315
Chocolate Fudge, '82 20
Chocolate Fudge, Five Pounds of, '95 51
Chocolate-Peanut Butter Fudge, '87 257; '90 311
Chocolate-Peanut Butter Fudge Squares, '97 M54
Chunks of Snow, '02 298
Coffee-Chip Fudge, '86 74
Cream Cheese Fudge, '84 111
Creamy Dark Fudge, '82 295
Creamy Fudge, '81 218
Diamond Fudge, '92 193
Double-Good Fudge, '79 M263
Double Good Fudge, '87 M278
Double-Good Fudge, '95 M50
Fast Fudge, '79 274
Four Chips Fudge, '92 318
Fudge, '86 266
Mama's Fudge, '03 279
Microwave Chocolate Fudge, '92 M50; '02 M31
Microwave Fudge, '91 M92
Mint Fudge, '95 50
Mint Fudge, Dinner, '88 285
Mocha Fudge, Creamy, '95 51
Mocha Fudge, Holiday, '84 298
Nut Fudge, Quick, '83 316
Nutty White Fudge, '81 253
Orange-Walnut Fudge, '92 288
Peanut Butter Chewies, Fudge-, '98 215
Peanut Butter Fudge, '80 302; '89 307; '95 51;
    '02 296
Peanut Butter Fudge, Creamy, '92 240
Peanut Butter Fudge, Marbled, '88 65
Peanut-Fudge Bites, '91 M231; '92 M68
Peanut Fudge, Double, '85 91
Pecan Fudge, Creamy, '84 321
Penuche, '79 272
Pistachio Fudge, '83 298
Quick-and-Easy Fudge, '88 M190
Scotch Ring, Fudge, '79 273
Sour Cream Fudge, '95 52
Strawberry Fudge Balls, '93 80
Tiger Butter, '86 48
White Chocolate-Coffee Fudge, '94 232
White Chocolate Fudge, '92 317; '95 51

Game

Birds in Wine Marinade, Game, '94 306
Chili, Double-Meat, '79 269; '80 12
Dove and Sausage Gumbo, '81 199
Dove au Vin, '95 309
Dove Enchiladas, '85 270
Doves, Pan-Roasted, '87 240
Doves, Sherried, '91 290

Duck and Duckling
Baked Duck, Sherried, '79 224
Blackberry Sauce, Ducklings with, '82 251
Breasts, Blackened Duck, '93 259
Breasts, Charcoaled Marinated Duck, '79 226
Breasts, Smoked Duck, '87 121
Breasts with Raspberry Sauce, Duck, '87 240
Breast, Tender Duck, '97 215
Casserole, Duck and Wild Rice, '79 224
Enchiladas with Red Pepper-Sour Cream,
    Smoked Duck, '87 121
Foxfire Duck, '89 241
Grilled Duck with Orange Sauce, '94 305
Gumbo, Duck, Oyster, and Sausage, '79 226
Holiday Duckling, '80 251
Kebabs with Almond Rice, Grilled Duck, '91 291
Mallard, Prairie Wings, '83 252
Muscovy Duck with Parsnip Mash, Honey-
    Orange-Glazed, '97 262
Orange Duck, Chafing Dish, '79 226
Orange Gravy, Duck with, '81 259
Pâté, Duck, '79 226
Pâté, Duck Liver, '79 227
Roast Ducklings with Cherry Sauce, '86 312
Roast Duckling with Orange Sauce, '81 125
Roast Duckling with Tangerine Stuffing, '90 16
Roast Duckling with Wine Jelly, '88 243
Roast Duck with Sweet Potato-Eggplant Gravy,
    '83 90
Roast Long Island Duckling, '84 87
Wild Duck, Buffet, '86 268
Wild Duck with Orange Gravy, Roast, '89 323
Wild Duck with Pecan Stuffing, '85 269
Goose, Fruit- and Pecan-Stuffed, '83 268
Goose, Fruited Stuffed Wild, '88 248
Goose, Fruit-Stuffed, '83 320
Goose with Currant Sauce, Wild, '87 240
Gumbo, Wild Game, '91 290
Gumbo Ya Ya, '87 210
Pepper Feet, '93 258
Pheasant, Gin-Marinated, '02 250
Pheasant Muscatel, '85 269
Pheasants with Port Wine Sauce, '84 252
Pot Pie with Parmesan Crust, Game, '94 304
Quail
Bacon-Wrapped Quail, '02 238
Baked Quail with Cornbread Stuffing, '94 305
Baked Quail with Mushroom Gravy, '89 273
Baked Quail with Mushrooms, '81 259
Breasts, Southern Quail, '85 270
Currant Jelly Sauce, Quail with, '86 94
Dressing, Quail and, '99 42
Étouffée, Roasted Quail, '96 34
Foxfire Quail, '89 240
Fried Quail, '82 45
Fried Quail, Seasoned, '88 220
Fried Quail with Onion Gravy, '82 214
Glazed Quail with White Bean Ragout, Maple-,
    '96 232
Gravy, Georgia Quail with, '87 240
Gravy, Quail Smothered in, '99 41
Grilled Breakfast Quail, '88 220
Grilled Quail, '92 90
Grilled Quail, Asian, '99 41
Grilled Quail with Red Wine-Blackberry Sauce,
    '98 319
Hatcreek Quail, '89 270
J.W. Quail, '89 240
Magnificent Quail, '82 214
Marinated Quail, '80 221
Marinated Quail, Chipotle-, '04 240
Mushrooms, Quail with, '85 138
Orange Sauce in Potato Baskets, Quail with,
    '86 193

Pan-Roasted Chipotle-Marinated Quail, '98 201
Red Plum Sauce, Quail with, '80 48
Roasted Quail with Cranberry-Orange-Pecan
    Stuffing, '01 249
Smoked Champagne Quail, Sage-, '97 164
Smoked Quail, '93 236
Stroganoff, Quail, '99 41
Stuffed Quail, Hawkeye-, '89 241
Stuffed with Cornbread Dressing, Quail, '93 280
Superb, Quail, '81 303
Rabbit, Hickory Barbecued, '82 216
Rabbit, Santa Fe Spanish, '94 307
Squab, Baked Stuffed, '82 260
Turkey, Country-Fried Wild, '94 306
Venison
    Bake, Venison-Vegetable, '87 304
    Burgers, Venison, '87 304
    Chili, Hot Venison, '91 283
    Chili, Venison, '82 216; '86 3; '87 304
    Chutney-Mustard Sauce, Bostick Venison with,
        '89 242
    Country-Fried Venison, '81 233
    Kebabs, Venison, '82 215; '88 249
    Loin, Mushroom-Crusted Venison, '94 302
    Roast, Grilled Venison, '93 278
    Roast, Lillie Bell's Venison, '89 242
    Roast, Venison, '82 226
    Roast with Red Wine Gravy, Venison, '85 270
    Sauce, Venison Reduction, '94 303
    Sausage Balls, Venison, '80 42
    Soup, Venison, '82 216
    Steak, Country-Fried Venison, '83 262
    Steaks, Country-Style Venison, '82 215
    Steaks, Grilled Venison, '82 215
    Stew, Hunter's, '85 270
    Stew, Venison, '86 294
    Stew, Venison Sausage, '87 238
    Stew with Potato Dumplings, Venison, '87 304
    Stock, Venison, '94 302
    Tenderloin Appetizers, Venison, '88 249
    Tomatoes, Venison and, '85 270
GARLIC
Aioli, Mint, '01 71
Asparagus, Marinated, '02 243
Beans, Buzz's Pot of, '03 19
Beans, Molasses Baked, '99 105
Beans, Spicy Black, '04 119
Beef Brisket with Fall Vegetables, '02 237
Beef Tenderloin, Garlic-and-Rosemary, '02 255
Beef Tenderloin, Hampton Place, '04 272
Black Beans, Cuban, '99 56
Bread, Barbecue, '99 105
Bread, Buttery Garlic, '02 25, 110
Broccoli, Garlic, '99 46
Bruschetta, Black Truffle, '99 323
Burgers, Spinach-Feta, '99 135
Butter, Garlic, '83 193; '84 108; '95 89; '00 90
Butter, Garlic-Basil, '98 156
Butter, Green Beans with Garlic-Herb, '02 61
Butter, Herb-Pesto, '04 255
Butter, Roasted Garlic, '97 46
Cabbage with Garlic, '04 62
Canapés, Roasted Garlic, '96 95
Casserole, Savory Ham-and-Swiss, '01 308
Cauliflower in Browned Butter, '02 45
Cheesesteaks, Chimichurri, '04 312
Chicken and Potatoes, Roasted, '98 289
Chicken Breasts, Greek, '98 19
Chicken, Forty-Cloves-of-Garlic, '95 261
Chicken, Garlic-and-Wine Grilled, '00 136
Chicken, Garlic-Spinach, '92 56
Chicken, Glazed Roasted, '00 14; '03 217
Chicken, Herb-Roasted, '00 330
Chicken, Jan's Roasted, '01 224

Chicken, Lemon-Garlic, '90 35
Chicken Marbella, '04 34
Chicken Mediterranean, '01 17
Chicken, Soy-Garlic, '98 128
Chicken with Green Olives, '03 87
Chicken with Lemon Mashed Potatoes, Smothered,
    '04 180
Chili, Black Bean, '02 20
Chili Con Carne, '03 19
Chili, Game-Day, '00 238
Chili, Spicy 3-Bean, '03 291
Collard Greens, Esau's, '03 17
Confit, Roasted Shallot-Garlic, '94 303
Crawfish Boil, '01 95
Cream, Red Curry-Coconut, '00 197
Crème Brûlée, Roasted Garlic, '95 324
Crisps, Garlic, '99 60
Crostini, Roasted Red Pepper-Feta, '04 69
Croutons, Garlic, '92 71
Dip, Zesty Feta, '04 71
Dressing, Basil-and-Garlic, '94 55
Dressing, Fresh Tomato, '00 182
Dressing, Garlic-Ginger Vinaigrette, '92 195
Dressing, Lime-Peanut, '01 26
Dressing, Purple Parrot Sensation, '04 289
Dressing, Rice, '01 222
Dressing, Southern Rice, '99 256
Eggplant Vinaigrette, Italian, '03 125
Eggplant with Walnuts, Georgian, '01 87
Eggs, Garden District, '04 66
Elephant Ears, Garlic-and-Herb Baby, '00 87
Étouffée, Crawfish, '02 85
Flatbread, Quick, '00 119
Frijoles, '02 119
Fritters, Shrimp, '00 238
Garbanzo-Black Bean Medley, '99 236
Gazpacho, Classic Tomato, '99 172
Gnocchi with Olive Oil, Tomato, and Parmesan,
    '04 47
Green Beans, Garlic, '91 159; '00 260; '01 111
Green Beans with Mushrooms, Roasted, '04 182
Green Beans with Pimiento, Tangy, '01 21
Greens with Raspberry Vinaigrette, Gourmet,
    '00 163
Grits, Baked Cheese-and-Garlic, '83 292; '84 78
Grits Casserole, Garlic, '81 47
Grits, Garlic-and-Herb Cheese, '95 122
Grits, Garlic Cheese, '80 47; '81 197
Grits, Garlic-Cheese, '86 180; '88 126; '89 47;
    '97 58; '99 270
Grits, Garlicky Ham-and-Spinach, '94 177
Grits Soufflé, Garlic-Cheese, '99 18
Guacamole, '02 118
Gumbo, Chicken-and-Sausage, '01 324
Gumbo, Green Tomato, '04 314
Hamburgers Teriyaki, '99 332
Ham, Pineapple-Glazed, '03 82
Hash Browns, Rosemary-Garlic, '02 248
Hoppin' John, Esau's, '03 17
Hummus, '02 99
Jelly, Garlic, '99 283
Jelly, Garlic Pepper, '99 221
Journey Cakes, Rosemary-Garlic, '04 99
Kale with Tomatoes, Spicy, '99 243
Lamb Chops, Glazed, '02 66
Lamb Chops with Chipotle and Cilantro Oils,
    Grilled, '02 96; '03 98
Lamb Chops with Mint Aioli, '01 70
Lamb Chops with Minted Apples, '99 230; '00 20
Lamb Extraordinaire, '99 242
Lamb, Mint-Crusted Rack of, '98 118
Lamb, Roast Leg of, '00 275
Lamb Shanks, Braised, '00 62
Leeks, Creamed, '00 222

Leg of Lamb, Garlic-and-Herb Stuffed, '99 241
Leg of Lamb, Roast, '99 242
Leg of Lamb with Port, Roasted, '02 258
Linguine, Grilled Pepper-Pesto, '04 136
Marinade, Basic, '02 19
Marinade, Garlic-Basil, '94 160
Marinade, Italian, '03 180
Marinade, Southwestern, '00 177
Marinade, Zesty Chicken, '03 180
Mayonnaise, Garlic, '92 56
Mayonnaise, Garlic-Dill, '00 324
Mayonnaise, Roasted Garlic, '97 47
Meatballs, Red Sauce and, '04 17
Meat Loaf, Gonzales, '04 206
Mirlitons, Stuffed, '00 246
Mushrooms, Garlic and, '95 165
Mussels Marinara, '00 283
Oil, Roasted Garlic, '96 122
Olives, Citrus Party, '03 124
Olives Scaciati, '99 266
Panzanella, '00 62
Pasta, Creamy Crawfish, '03 277
Pasta, Tomato-Garlic, '94 177
Pasta with Marinara Sauce, Garlic, '92 78
Peanuts, Hot, '00 278
Penne with Pancetta, '00 51
Pesto, '00 118
Pesto, Basil, '03 208
Pesto, Cilantro, '00 148
Pesto, Dried Tomato, '01 62
Pesto, Garlic, '84 108
Pesto, Homemade, '01 22
Pesto, Lucinda's Garden, '01 100
Pesto, Roasted Garlic-Basil, '98 145
Pesto, Roasted Garlic-Rosemary, '97 46
Pickles, Peppery Texas, '04 M161
Pizza Squares, Easy, '02 61
Pork Chops, Garlic-Parmesan, '02 61
Pork Chops, Grilled Asian, '03 271
Pork, Garlic-Orange Roast, '03 277
Pork Loin, Garlic-Honey Marinated, '99 334
Pork Roast, Festive, '01 276
Pork, Slow-Roasted, '02 274
Pork, Smoked, '99 81; '03 121
Pork Tenderloin, Asian, '02 33
Pork Tenderloin, Bourbon-Marinated, '04 168
Pork Tenderloin, Grilled, '02 187
Pork Tenderloin, Honey-Garlic, '01 16
Pork Tenderloins, Honey-Garlic, '01 318
Pork with Garlic, Sweet, '04 17
Potato Bake, Smoky Mashed, '00 214
Potatoes, Creamy Lemon-Poppy Seed Mashed,
    '03 294
Potatoes, Garlic Mashed, '92 330; '97 308; '02 281
Potatoes, Garlic-Parsley, '90 290
Potatoes, Garlic-Roasted, '95 87
Potatoes, Leek Mashed, '02 98; '03 293
Potatoes, Loaded Garlic Smashed, '01 325
Potatoes, Roasted Garlic Mashed, '95 288
Potatoes, Roasted Garlic-Parmesan Mashed,
    '97 263; '00 146
Pot Roast, '00 65
Pot Roast, Italian, '02 88
Prime Rib, Smoked, '02 177
Puree, Roasted Garlic, '92 55
Quail, Chipotle-Marinated, '04 240
Red Beans and Rice, Spicy, '02 56
Rémoulade, Braised Shrimp with Garlic, '98 133
Risotto, Crawfish, '99 120
Roasted Garlic, '94 177; '96 304
Roasted Garlic-and-Cheese Risotto, '04 283
Roasted-Garlic Beurre Blanc, '03 324
Roasted Garlic Bulbs, '97 46
Roasted Garlic Dressing, '99 269

GARLIC

(continued)

Roasted Garlic, Herbed, '94 177
Roasted Garlic-Rosemary Bread, '04 16
Roast, Peppered Rib-Eye, '01 122
Roast, Roasted Lime-Cilantro Eye of Round, '04 88
Roast, Rosemary Rib, '03 294
Rollups, Mediterranean, '00 277
Salad, Caesar, '00 19
Salad Dressing, Creamy Garlic, '03 211
Salad, Lemon-Basil Potato, '01 178
Salad, Peanut-Noodle, '02 163
Salsa, Fiery, '01 174
Salsa, Zesty Santa Fe, '03 198
Saté Mixed Grill with Spicy Peanut Sauce, '04 134
Sauce, Brisket Mopping, '03 188
Sauce, Chilled Asparagus with Garlic Dipping,
   '98 136
Sauce, Come Back, '00 211
Sauce, Crescent City Grill Creole, '04 289
Sauce, Garlic, '92 56
Sauce, Garlic Beurre Blanc, '88 222
Sauce, Lemon-Butter, '99 198
Sauce, Parsley-Garlic, '83 138; '84 M76
Sauce, Pasta, '01 53
Sauce, Red Pepper-Garlic, '98 140
Sauce, Red Wine Garlic, '94 250
Sauce, Rémoulade, '04 66
Sauce, Roasted Garlic, '95 268; '98 176
Sauce, Roasted Garlic-Tomato, '97 46
Sauce, The, '00 177; '03 312
Scampi, Speedy, '02 161
Shrimp, Barbecue, '00 30
Shrimp Cocktail, Mexican, '00 249
Shrimp, Daufuskie, '00 174
Shrimp di Santo, '99 265
Shrimp, Garlic-and-Rosemary, '01 101; '04 52
Shrimp, Grilled Garlic, '99 178
Shrimp, New Orleans Barbecue, '02 201
Shrimp Scampi, '00 283
Shrimp Stir-Fry, '01 258
Shrimp with Fettuccine, Dilled, '99 141
Shrimp with Smoky Sweet Sauce, Mexican-Grilled,
   '03 32
Soup, Butternut Squash-Lime, '03 236
Soup, Golden Garlic-and-Potato, '04 214
Soup, Roasted Garlic-and-Basil Tomato, '01 17
Soup, Spanish Fiesta, '01 66
Soup, Tortilla, '99 310
Soup with Goat Cheese-and-Chive Croutons,
   Caramelized Onion, '01 312
Spinach Pie, '00 26
Spread, Creamy Potato-Garlic, '02 35
Spread, Cucumber-Yogurt, '00 135
Spread, Tri-Flavored Cream Cheese, '98 134
Steak, Garlic, '84 8
Steaks, Garlic-Herb, '98 169; '99 175
Steaks, Italian Sirloin, '04 61
Sugar Snap Peas, Pickled, '01 112
Tapenade, '00 135
Taquitos with Pork Picadillo, '04 206
Tart, Tomato, '03 158
Tenderloins, Honey-Grilled, '00 126
Torta, Goat Cheese, '04 186
Turkey, Rosemary Roasted, '99 312
Turkey Scaloppine, '04 321
Vegetable Curry, '04 217
Vegetable Medley, Herbed, '99 46; '00 138
Vegetable Medley, Root, '03 260
Vegetables, Bill's Roasted, '00 276
Vegetables with Fresh Sage, Roasted, '00 125
Vermicelli with Chunky Vegetable Sauce, '04 180

Vinaigrette, Dijon, '03 237
Vinaigrette, Garlic, '95 65; '03 142
Vinaigrette, Garlic-Blue Cheese, '92 57
Vinaigrette, Roasted Garlic, '97 47
Vinaigrette, Warm Garlic, '00 324
Vinegar, Shallot-Tarragon-Garlic, '93 191
Wings, Sweet-and-Hot Citrus, '00 202

GARNISHES

Boxwood Garland, '02 295

Butter

   Balls, Butter, '82 189; '89 90
   Curls, Butter, '82 51, 189; '89 90
   Molds, Butter, '89 90
Candy Bow, '99 M306
Candy Box, White, '97 M54

Chocolate

   Cups, Chocolate, '80 207
   Cups, Chocolate Crinkle, '93 270
   Cups, Miniature Chocolate, '87 132
   Curls, Chocolate, '85 338
   Hearts and Shavings, Chocolate, '86 26
   Lacy Chocolate Garnishes, '89 43
   Leaves, Chocolate, '88 281; '89 42; '98 270
   Ribbons and Bow, White Chocolate, '01 253
   Sack, Large Chocolate, '93 314
   Sack, Small Chocolate, '93 314
   Stars, White Chocolate, '00 M307
Eggs, Hard-Cooked, '82 280

Flowers

   Candied Flowers and Raspberries, '98 155
   Pansies, Candied, '96 118
   Rose Petals and Mint Leaves, Candied, '99 155
   Rose Petals, Candied, '98 57
   Roses and Leaves, Crystallized, '97 61
Fondant Teapot Spout, Handle, Daisies, and
   Butterflies, '04 83

Fruit

   Cherries and Mint Sprigs, Sugared Maraschino,
      '01 271
   Citrus Cups, '85 339
   Citrus Cups, Notched, '82 280
   Cranberries, Frosted, '82 280; '85 339
   Cranberries, Sugared, '04 279
   Grapes, Frosted, '82 51; '85 339
   Lemon Peel, Candied, '94 199
   Lemon Roses, '82 280; '85 338
   Lemon Slices, Fluted, '82 51
   Orange Rind, Candied, '96 162; '97 32
   Orange Rose, '85 338
   Orange Zest, Candied, '95 320
   Ribbons, Sugared Fruit, '02 295
   Tangerine Segments, Glazed, '02 295
   Vegetable and Fruit Garnishes, '82 280
Ghosts, Little, '03 M212
Guide, Garnishing, '82 138
Holiday Trees, '98 308
Holly Leaves, '99 M306
Marzipan Bees, '98 100
Pastry Garnish, '98 254; '03 317
Pastry Strips, Decorated, '02 M296
Pecans, Spiced, '03 332
Piped Garnishes, '82 280
Rosemary, Sugared, '04 M279

Vegetable

   Broccoli Bouquet, '87 115
   Carrot Curls, '85 338
   Carrot Flowers, '85 338
   Celery Fans, '85 339
   Fruit Garnishes, Vegetable and, '82 280
   Green Onion Fans, '85 339
   Green Pepper Cups, '85 339
   Mushrooms, Aztec, '82 51
   Mushrooms, Fluted, '82 280; '85 338
   Onion Mum, '85 339

   Onion Mums, '96 318
   Onion Rose, '87 114
   Radish Rose, '85 339
   Squash Buttercup, '87 114
   Tomato Cups, '85 339
   Tomato Flower, Marinated Pasta in, '87 115
   Tomato Rose, '82 51; '85 338
   Zucchini Fan, '87 114

GIFTS

Bars, Chewy Chocolate Cereal, '97 317
Biscuits with Olive-Parsley Spread, Cream Cheese-
   and-Olive, '04 238
Brownie Mix, Blond, '01 247
Cake, Gift Box, '96 319
Candy Cane Swizzle Sticks, '02 298
Candy, Cola, '02 298
Cheese Marinade, '04 238
Cookies, Candy Shop Pizza, '02 299
Cookies, Skillet Almond, '97 288
Cracker Bites, Miniature Peanut Butter, '02 298
Cream Cheese Braids, '97 287
Divinity, Cherry, '97 316
Divinity, Lemon, '97 316
Extract, Vanilla, '97 288
Filling, Cream Cheese, '97 287
Frosting, Cola, '02 298
Fudge, Buttermilk, '97 317
Gadgets, Off-the-Wall, '95 332
Gifts That Measure Up, '95 332
Glaze, '99 284
Glaze, Powdered Sugar, '97 287
Hot Handlers, '95 332
Jambalaya Mix, '98 317
Jelly, Garlic, '99 283
Marinated Cheese, Olives, and Peppers, '04 238
Miniature Liqueur Sampler, '95 332
Muffins, Cheese, '97 287
Mustard, Easy Sweet-Tangy, '01 247
Pralines, Cinnamon, '97 317
Rice Mix, Fruited, '97 317
Rice Mix, Seasoned, '01 248
Rolls, Cinnamon, '99 M284
Salad Gift, Asian, '96 327
Salad Gift, Caesar, '96 326
Salad Gift, Curried, '96 326
Sauce, Peach Rib, '01 248
Sauce, Zesty Lemon, '97 318
Snow, Chunks of, '02 298
Soup Mix, Bean, '99 283
Spice Mix, Tex-Mex, '01 247
Spread, Garlic-and-Dill Feta Cheese, '04 238
Topping, Hot Fudge Ice Cream, '98 317
Topping, Maple-Pecan Ice Cream, '98 317
Trees, Holiday, '02 298
Wine Tasting, '95 332
Wreaths, Christmas, '97 288

GLAZES. *See also* **FILLINGS, FROSTINGS,
   TOPPINGS.**

Apricot Glaze, '80 280; '82 8; '86 197; '97 60;
   '98 260
Apricot Glaze for Ham, '85 256
Apricot Glaze, Sweet, '82 304
Apricot-Kirsch Glaze, '87 14
Berry Glaze, '83 225; '00 312
Blueberry Glaze, '83 143
Brandy Glaze, Powdered Sugar-, '86 291
Brownie Glaze, '02 M252
Brown Sugar Glaze, '83 312; '96 268
Buttered Rum Glaze, '03 94
Buttermilk Glaze, '79 140; '81 70; '84 316; '97 230;
   '99 98; '02 166; '03 55
Caramel Glaze, '85 320; '98 195; '02 196
Cherry Glaze, '83 143; '93 52; '98 260
Chili-Cranberry Glaze, '98 320

Chocolate Glaze, **'81** 119; **'83** 220; **'84** 10, 55, 253;
  '85 6; **'86** 315, 316; **'89** 325; **'90** 310;
  '91 M296; **'93** 52; **'97** M35, 231; **'99** 206;
  '01 M45, M126
Chocolate Glaze, Creamy, **'82** 88; **'98** 90
Chocolate Glaze, French, **'98** M57
Chocolate-Honey Glaze, **'82** 306
Cinnamon Glaze, **'88** 83
Citrus Glaze, **'82** 128; **'89** 205
Cranberry Glaze, **'84** 306; **'86** 171; **'88** 244
Cranberry-Honey Glaze, **'89** 273
Cream Cheese Glaze, **'84** 150; **'94** 242
Currant Jelly Glaze, **'00** 82
Daiquiri Glaze, **'93** 83
Dijon Glaze, **'87** 54
Drizzle Glaze, **'87** 94
Drizzling Icing, **'91** 35
Holiday Glaze, Creamy, **'03** 281
Honey Glaze, **'88** 287
Honey-Nut Glaze, **'87** 15
Irish Cream Glaze, **'92** 287
Kahlúa Glaze, **'86** 292
Lemon Glaze, **'79** 285; **'86** 194; **'87** 41; **'92** 269;
  '93 154, 183; **'97** 123, 332; **'01** 117
Orange-Bourbon Glaze, **'03** 249
Orange Butter Glaze, **'90** 194
Orange Glaze, **'79** 2; **'80** 257; **'81** 34, 107; **'82** 75,
  206; **'83** 33, 114, 140, 267; **'84** 161; **'86** 298;
  '92 263; **'95** 320; **'99** 293; **'03** 35, 281, 307
Orange Glaze, Nutty, **'80** 45
Orange-Pineapple Glaze, **'81** 60
Paint, Egg Yolk, **'86** 322
Pineapple Glaze, **'83** 143; **'85** 38; **'97** 55
Powdered Sugar Glaze, **'79** 24; **'82** 92, 283;
  '83 83, 295; **'85** 55; **'90** 95; **'97** 287; **'04** 279
Praline Glaze, **'82** 196
Raspberry Glaze, **'00** 88
Root Beer Glaze, **'99** 196
Rum Glaze, Buttered, **'83** 220
Scuppernong-Orange Glaze, **'98** 220
Snowy Glaze, **'82** 295
Strawberry Glaze, **'80** 35; **'83** 142
Sugar Glaze, **'86** 161; **'90** 47; **'01** 89
Teriyaki Glaze, **'94** 82
Topping Glaze, **'87** 69
Vanilla Glaze, **'85** M89; **'89** 211; **'04** M84
White Chocolate Glaze, **'01** M45
GOOSE. *See* **GAME.**
GRANOLA
Apple Crisp, Granola, **'85** 78
Bars, Coconut Granola, **'85** 202
Bars, Cranberry-Cinnamon Granola, **'03** 26
Bars, Fruit and Nut Granola, **'81** 49
Bars, Granola, **'83** 305; **'95** 214
Bars, No-Bake Granola, **'97** 220
Bread, Honey-Granola, **'86** 56
Chocolate Morsels, Granola with, **'86** 69
Crunchy Granola, **'81** 218; **'84** 144
Easy Granola, **'81** 49
Fabulous Granola, **'92** 213
Fruit Medley, Yogurt-Granola, **'91** 58
Fruity Granola, **'84** 148
Gorp, Granola, **'89** 59
Granola, **'79** 190; **'93** 197; **'99** 212
Healthful Granola, **'97** 204
Homemade Granola, **'84** 58
Mix, Bunny Trail, **'95** 101
Mixed Fruit Granola, **'01** 290
Mix, Granola, **'94** 168
Mix, Granola Snack, **'86** 229
Muffins, Granola, **'95** 78
Nutty Granola, **'90** 95
Orange Granola, Sunny, **'84** 212
Pancakes, Granola-Squash, **'94** 267

Peanut Butter Granola, **'82** 296
Peanut Granola, Crunchy, **'90** 48
Pecan-Coconut Granola, **'02** 70
Raisin-Granola Treats, **'92** 22
Reindeer Nibbles, **'92** 280
Salad, Rudolph's Apple, **'02** 277
Sunshine Granola, **'79** 37
Superhero Granola, **'98** M206
Toasty Granola, **'79** 37
Whole Wheat Granola, **'82** 167
GRAPEFRUIT
Beverages
Cocktails, Sea Breeze, **'97** 161
Cooler, Grapefruit, **'88** 81
Drink, Grapefruit, **'90** 84; **'95** 238
Freeze, Grapefruit, **'93** 242
Refresher, Grapefruit, **'88** 85
Refresher, Grapefruit-Orange, **'82** 174
Sangría, Grapefruit, **'89** 92
Spritzer, Pineapple-Grapefruit, **'04** 143
Spritzers, Grapefruit-White Wine, **'96** 56; **'01** 319
Tea, Grapefruit, **'92** 67
Three-Fruit Drink, **'80** 50
Biscuits, Grapefruit Juice, **'83** 10
Broiled Grapefruit, **'85** 7; **'96** 55
Broiled Grapefruit, Holiday, **'88** 251
Broiled Grapefruit, Sherried, **'80** 50
Broil, Flounder-Grapefruit, **'85** 53
Cake, Fresh Grapefruit, **'89** 308
Chocolate-Topped Grapefruit, **'89** 88
Compote, Spicy Grapefruit-Berry, **'91** 19
Cup, Berry Grapefruit, **'79** 242
Delight, Winter Fruit, **'80** 243
Dressing, Grapefruit French, **'80** 101
Dressing, Grapefruit Salad, **'84** 262
Freeze, Grapefruit, **'00** 241
Frosting, Grapefruit, **'89** 308
Ice, Grapefruit, **'91** 122
Ice, Pink Grapefruit, **'85** 304
Marmalade, Combination Citrus, **'80** 50
Marmalade, Grapefruit, **'82** 308
Minted Grapefruit, **'88** 81
Pear-Berry Puree, Grapefruit with, **'89** 213
Pie, Grapefruit Chess, **'01** 23
Pie, Grapefruit Meringue, **'96** 56
Salads
Apple Salad, Grapefruit-, **'89** 41
Aspic, Grapefruit, **'80** 297; **'82** 112; **'83** 153
Avocado-Grapefruit Salad, **'85** 26; **'93** 282
Avocado Salad, Grapefruit-, **'83** 316; **'84** 16;
  '89 41
Banana Salad with Celery Seed Dressing,
  Grapefruit-, **'91** 237
Bing Cherry-Grapefruit Salad, **'00** 285
Combo Salad, Grapefruit, **'80** 50
Congealed Grapefruit Salad, **'84** 325; **'85** 279
Congealed Salad, Grapefruit, **'83** 190
Cucumber Salad, Grapefruit-, **'80** 100
Grapefruit Salad, **'83** 124; **'84** 325; **'88** 122
Greens and Grapefruit Salad, **'95** 301
Orange-Grapefruit Salad, **'93** 294
Orange Salad, Grapefruit-, **'91** 276
Shrimp Salad, Grapefruit-and-, **'88** 5
Winter Salad, Grapefruit, **'84** 24
Sorbet, Grapefruit, **'03** 171
Sorbet, Grapefruit-Mint, **'93** 153
Sorbet, Pink Grapefruit and Tarragon, **'95** 163
Spiced Pink Grapefruit, **'96** 55
Supreme, Grapefruit, **'80** 50
Tart, Grapefruit, **'04** 43
GRAPES
Beverages
Cooler, Grape-Lime, **'94** 227
Juice, Scuppernong, **'98** 221

Mulled Grape Juice, **'90** 21
Punch, Sparkling Grape, **'82** 48
Punch, Spiced White Grape, **'96** 170
Punch, White Grape, **'90** 15
Tea, White Grape Iced, **'98** 84
Tea, White Grape Juice, **'87** 57
Blue Cheese-Pecan Grapes, **'95** 48
Caribbean Grapes, **'95** 48
Carrots with Grapes, Glazed, **'82** 287
Chicken Véronique, **'84** 260; **'85** 302
Desserts
Beauberries Bordeaux, **'98** 18
Cobbler, Muscadine, **'98** 221
Granita, Grape, **'88** 118
Ice Cream, Scuppernong, **'88** 216
Ice, Grape, **'83** 162
Ice, Muscadine, **'82** 202
Pie, Grape, **'85** 212
Pie, Grape Juice, **'79** 123
Pie, Muscadine, **'82** 202
Pie, Scuppernong, **'88** 216
Pops, Purple People Eater, **'99** 132
Refresher, Grape Juice-Fruit, **'86** 182
Tart, Green Grape, **'87** 77
Tarts, Scuppernong Pudding, **'98** 221
Frosted Grapes, **'82** 51; **'85** 339
Glaze, Scuppernong-Orange, **'98** 220
Green Grapes Supreme, **'88** 81
Ham Véronique, **'85** 90
Honeydew Melon with Grapes, **'91** 91
Honeyed Grapes, **'95** 47
Jelly, Grape, **'89** 140
Jelly, Grape-Burgundy Freezer, **'85** 130
Jelly, Quick Grape, **'89** M156
Jelly, Scuppernong, **'98** 220
Jelly, Thyme-Grape, **'89** 193
Jelly, Wild Muscadine, **'79** 32
Marmalade, Muscadine, **'98** 220
Mold, Double Grape-Cantaloupe, **'79** 173
Pork Loin, Scuppernong-Orange Glazed, **'98** 220
Salad, Broccoli-Grape, **'01** 163
Salad, Chicken, **'96** 67
Salad, Marinated Chicken-Grape, **'85** 74
Salad Mold, Grape, **'83** 120
Salad, Sherried Chicken-and-Grape, **'01** 61
Salad Véronique, Macaroni, **'85** 164
Salad with Grapes, Chicken, **'86** 117
Salad with Grapes, Curried Tuna, **'87** 201
Sauce, Muscadine, **'04** 231
Sauce, Pears in Muscadine, **'88** 216
Sauce, White Grape, **'80** 38
Scallops Véronique, **'83** 144
Slaw, Grape-Poppy Seed, **'86** 225
Sole Véronique, **'85** 181
Spiced Grapes, **'98** 220
Wild Rice with Grapes, **'95** 48
GRAVIES. *See also* **SAUCES.**
Black-Eyed Pea Gravy, **'87** 12
Burgundy Gravy, Beef Roast with, **'95** 263
Chicken Gravy, **'99** 34
Chive Gravy, Beef and Broccoli with, **'88** 214
Chocolate Gravy, **'99** 35, 88
Cranberry Pan Gravy, Baked Hen with, **'94** 308
Cream Gravy, **'88** 15; **'97** 25; **'03** 68
Cream Gravy, Country-Fried Steak with, **'84** 8
Cream Gravy, Fried Chicken with, **'85** 241
Cream Gravy, Fried Pork Chops with, **'03** 24
Currant Gravy, **'83** 276
Dill-Cream Gravy, Pork Chops with, **'84** 81
Fried Chicken Gravy, **'95** 235
Fried Ripe Tomatoes with Gravy, **'82** 180
Giblet Gravy, **'79** 283; **'88** 253; **'03** 256
Giblet Gravy, Roast Turkey and, **'94** 308
Gravy, **'88** 303

GRAVIES
(continued)

Ham with Gravy, Virginia, '86 15
Horseradish Gravy, Filet Mignon with, '92 262
Meat Gravy, '03 68
Milk Gravy, Buttermilk-Marinade Turkey with
  Peppery, '98 311
Mushroom Gravy, '99 34
Mushroom Gravy, Baked Quail with, '89 273
Mushroom Gravy, Pot Roast with, '02 90
Mushroom Gravy, Salisbury Steak with, '03 202
Onion-and-Mushroom Gravy, Roast with, '00 293
Onion Gravy, Fried Quail with, '82 214
Onion Gravy, Pork Chops in, '99 222
Orange Gravy, '81 259; '89 323
Pork Chops and Gravy, '96 71
Red-Eye Gravy, Country Ham with, '79 37; '99 34
Redeye Gravy, Country Ham with, '86 254; '98 271;
  '00 216
Red-Eye Gravy, Ham and, '88 221
Red Wine Gravy, Venison Roast with, '85 270
Roasted Red Pepper-and-Vidalia Onion Gravy,
  '03 323
Sage Gravy, '96 269
Sausage Gravy, '92 271; '94 20; '97 243; '03 67
Sawmill Gravy, '03 67
Shallot Gravy, '02 239
Sour Cream Gravy, '92 301
Sour Cream Gravy, Pot Roast with, '79 17
Southwestern Gravy, '99 34
Sweet Potato-Eggplant Gravy, Roast Duck with,
  '83 90
Tasso Gravy, '92 236; '96 270
Tomato-and-Crabmeat Cream Gravy, '04 165
Tomato Gravy, '93 18; '99 35; '00 216, 330;
  '02 17, 33
Tomato Gravy, Spicy, '95 172
Turkey Gravy, '91 255; '94 306
Turkey with Gravy, Old-Fashioned Roasted, '04 270
White Wine Gravy, '89 322
White Wine Gravy, Chicken-Herb Strudel with,
  '04 318
White Wine Gravy, Pot Roast in, '81 299

GREENS
Bacon, Shelly Greens and, '96 290
Bake, Grits 'n Greens Dinner, '84 281
Beets 'n' Greens, '95 179
Chowder, Mixed Greens, '97 262
Collard Green Risotto and Pot Liquor, '01 121
Collard Greens, '95 233; '96 272; '03 324
Collard Greens, Esau's, '03 17
Collard Greens, Nana's, '03 278
Collard Greens, Seasoned, '82 211
Collard Greens Soup, '00 293
Collard 'n' Black-Eyed Pea Stew, '04 24
Collards, '79 32
Collards and Sausage, Pasta with, '94 230
Collards Casserole, Parmesan-, '95 233
Collards, Country-Style, '03 252
Collards, Risotto with, '96 203
Collards, Southern-Style, '82 107
Collard Stew, '02 17
Collards, Uptown, '92 23
Collards with Apples, '98 250
Edna's Greens, '96 144; '00 184
Escarole-and-Bacon Salad, '84 85
Escarole, Easy Cooked, '84 85
Green and Gold, '00 91
Grits and Greens, '95 233
Gumbo z'Herbes, '94 239
Kale, Homestyle, '00 91
Kale, Pasta with Sausage and, '03 279

Kale, Scalloped, '86 224
Kale Soup, Creamy, '96 203
Kale, Sweet-and-Sour, '80 298
Kale with Salsa, Southwest, '94 246
Kale with Tomato and Onion, '92 244
Kale with Tomatoes, Spicy, '99 243
Mustard Greens and Potatoes, '86 224
Mustard Green Soup, Cream of, '93 280
Mustard Greens, Spinach Fettuccine with, '94 247
Mustard Greens-Stuffed Tenderloin, '96 324
Pasta with Beans and Greens, '02 202
Pasta with Greens, '95 211; '96 47
Pasta with Greens, Creamy, '00 91
Pork Tenderloin, Southern-Style Stuffed, '99 45
Pot Pie with Cornbread Crust, Ham-and-Greens,
  '03 20
Risotto with Greens, '96 132
Salad with Warm Pecan Dressing, Mess o' Greens,
  '98 250
Sauce, Cress, '96 176
Stewed Tomatoes and Greens, '95 234
Stir-Fried Greens, '94 33; '97 270
Super-Charged Greens, '01 211
Turnip-and-Carrot Salad, '91 212
Turnip-and-Collard Greens, '92 215
Turnip Green Dip, '91 13
Turnip Green Dip with Jalapeño-Corn Muffins, Hot,
  '93 164
Turnip Greens, '90 13, 232; '95 306
Turnip Greens and Ham Hock, Southern, '80 119
Turnip Greens and Ham Hocks, Southern, '03 220
Turnip Greens and White Bean Bake, '94 246
Turnip Greens, Fresh, '92 339
Turnip Greens, Old-Fashioned, '85 255
Turnip Greens, Saucy, '83 12
Turnip Greens, Simple, '01 211; '02 106
Turnip Greens Stew, '02 17; '04 24
Turnip Greens, Suppertime, '04 34
Turnip Greens with Cornmeal Dumplings, '82 211
Turnip Greens with Turnips, '84 230; '01 211
Watercress-and-Mushroom Salad, '88 104
Watercress Mousse, '88 104
Watercress Soup, '88 104
Watercress Soup, Cream of, '96 66
Watercress Spread, '88 103

GRILLED. *See also* **BARBECUE.**
Beef
Brisket, Smoked, '01 169
Burgers, All-American Pizza, '92 148
Burgers, Barbara's Big Juicy, '03 M138;
  '04 M178
Burgers, Beefy Vegetable, '98 143
Burgers, Burgundy, '80 156
Burgers, Favorite, '89 165
Burgers, Grilled Sour Cream, '87 287
Burgers, Italian, '00 326
Burgers, Mushroom, '89 164
Burgers, Nutty, '87 185
Burgers, Party, '83 164; '84 39
Burger Spirals, '94 139
Burgers, Sausage, '83 212
Burgers, Seasoned, '85 158
Burgers, Spinach, '00 26
Burgers, Steak-House, '87 186
Burgers, Stuffed, '85 159
Burgers, Stuffed Border, '04 127
Burgers, Sweet-and-Savory, '03 163
Burgers, Sweet-and-Sour, '90 128
Burgers, Tortilla, '94 138
Burgers, Triple-Layer, '89 165
Burgers with Caramelized Onions, Beef,
  '98 143
Burgers with Caramelized Onions, Pepper,
  '00 218

Burgers with Roasted Bell Pepper Ketchup,
  Jalapeño-Stuffed, '97 318
Burgers with Sprouts, '89 164
Burgers with Tahini Sauce, Gyro, '03 183
Cheeseburgers, Fried Green Tomato, '94 138
Cheesesteaks, Chimichurri, '04 312
Eye of Round, Grilled Beef, '82 91
Fajita Salad, Beef, '91 70
Fajitas, Beef and Chicken, '02 119
Fajitas, Favorite, '86 114
Fajitas, Java, '96 227
Fajitas, Plum Good, '94 115
Fajitas with Pico de Gallo, '98 87
Filet Mignon, Marinated, '84 171
Fillet, Acapulco, '98 174
Fillets with Orange Cream, Beef, '97 66
Flank Steak and Mushrooms, '87 61
Flank Steak, Cheese-Stuffed, '98 182
Flank Steak, East-West, '04 90
Flank Steak, Flavorful, '96 32
Flank Steak, Ginger-Marinated, '89 25
Flank Steak, Grilled, '80 152; '89 168; '91 80;
  '92 166; '03 146
Flank Steak, Grilled Marinated, '97 182
Flank Steak in Mexican Marinade, '98 128
Flank Steak, Lemon-Lime, '95 55
Flank Steak, Marinated, '82 162; '83 35; '85 86;
  '95 237; '04 118
Flank Steak, Mediterranean, '00 145
Flank Steak, Oriental, '83 178
Flank Steak, Peppery Grilled, '99 157
Flank Steak Pinwheels, '87 141
Flank Steak, Rosemary Grilled, '03 125
Flank Steak Sandwiches with Apple Barbecue
  Sauce, '99 173
Flank Steaks, Delicious Marinated, '83 110
Flank Steak Skewers, Lemon, '02 134
Flank Steak, Soy-Ginger, '02 90
Flank Steaks with Mushrooms, '00 121
Flank Steak, Tangy, '86 184
Flank Steak, Tenderized, '82 105
Flank Steak Teriyaki, '81 110
Flank Steak, Texas, '86 185
Flank Steak with Apple-Bourbon Sauce and
  Roasted Vegetables, Grilled, '99 142
Flank Steak with Black Bean-and-Corn Salsa,
  Grilled, '94 80
Flank Steak with Chili Butter, '00 177
Flank Steak with Horseradish Sauce, Grilled,
  '02 19
Flank Steak with Molasses Barbecue Glaze,
  Grilled, '00 59
Flank Steak with Salsa, Southwest, '03 95
Flank Steak with Sweet Peppers, Grilled, '90 138
Grilled Steaks, '96 172
Hamburgers, Flavorful Grilled, '81 110
Hamburgers, Grilled, '93 198
Hamburgers, Old-Fashioned, '79 149
Hamburgers, Spicy Grilled, '98 158
Hamburgers, Teriyaki, '94 138
Hamburgers Teriyaki, '99 332
Kebabs, Beef, '85 110
Kebabs, Beef-and-Vegetable, '91 148
Kebabs Deluxe, Beef, '82 182
Kebabs, Marinated Beef, '82 105; '85 159
Kebabs, Marinated Steak, '80 184
Kebabs, Meatball, '95 192
Kebabs, Pineapple-Beef, '83 212
Kebabs, Saucy Beef, '83 109
Kebabs, Spicy Grilled, '98 158
Kebabs, Spirited Beef, '87 142
Kebabs, Steak, '93 95
Kebabs, Steak-and-Shrimp, '80 184; '00 124
Kebabs, Teriyaki Beef, '80 207

Kebabs with Rice, Marinated Beef, '84 32
Kebabs with Vegetables, Beef, '90 148
Kebabs with Vegetables, Marinated Beef, '99 292
London Broil Sandwiches with Yogurt-Cucumber
  Sauce, '01 162
London Broil, Teriyaki, '92 282
Marinated Beef on a Stick, '85 234
Mashed Potatoes and Chipotle Cream, Grilled
  Beef with, '02 M320
Medaillons of Beef with Horseradish Cream,
  '90 96
Pigs on a Roll, Three Little, '98 203
Pizza, Taco, '98 176
Poor Boy Fillets, '82 106
Prime Rib, Smoked, '97 161; '02 177
Red Wine Marinade, Beef with, '91 46
Rib-Eye Grill, '02 306
Rib-Eyes, Italian, '98 215
Rib-Eye Steaks, Peppered, '97 46; '00 146;
  '02 110
Rib Eyes with Herb Cheese and Asparagus
  Bundles, Grilled Chile-Rubbed, '03 326
Rib Eyes with Red Pepper-Polenta Fries and Chile
  Corn Jus, '00 196
Ribs, Baby Loin Back, '01 106
Ribs, Sweet-and-Sour Grilled, '98 331
Roast, Grilled Marinated Beef, '93 141
Roast, Grilled Pepper, '81 110
Round Steak, Tender Grilled, '85 3
Salad, Beef Vinaigrette, '95 177
Salad, Spicy Beef, '02 174
Sirloin Kebabs, Marinated, '82 162
Sirloin, Peppery Grilled, '02 212
Sirloin Salad, Grilled, '94 129
Sirloin Steak, Secret, '81 110
Sirloin Steaks, Italian, '04 61
Sirloin Steaks with Thyme Pesto, '97 182
Sirloin with Zesty Corn Salsa, Cilantro-Garlic,
  '02 193
Steak-and-Onion Sandwiches, '02 126
Steak-and-Vegetable Kebabs, '04 218
Steak, Bourbon, '90 148
Steak Continental, '83 178
Steak, Curried Beef, '88 60
Steak, Grilled Black Pepper, '86 184
Steakhouse Beef, American, '93 15
Steak, Italian, '03 180
Steak, Marinated Bourbon, '95 91
Steak, Mediterranean, '03 180
Steak, Mesquite-Grilled, '85 154
Steak on a Stick, '83 109
Steak, Patio, '87 141
Steak, Pirate, '79 89
Steak Salad Niçoise, Grilled, '98 148
Steaks, Blue Cheese, '84 171
Steaks, Garlic-Herb, '99 175
Steaks, Mexican Pepper-Cheese, '97 190
Steak, Spicy Grilled, '97 211
Steaks, Stately, '00 121
Steaks, Sweet-and-Sour Marinated, '83 110
Steaks with Green Chiles, Grilled, '85 144
Steaks with Spicy Herb Sauce, Asian Grilled,
  '03 280
Steak, Tabasco, '95 207
Steak with Ham-and-Mushroom Sauce, '83 109
Steak with Mushroom Sauce, '83 212
Steak with Pimiento Cheese Salsa, Fiery, '99 331
Steak with Vegetables, Skewered, '81 124
Superburgers, '79 89
Tacos al Carbon, '86 19
Tacos al Carbon, Tailgate, '79 185
Tacos, Jerk Steak, '01 170
Tenderloin, Grilled, '91 166
Tenderloin, Herb Marinated, '83 109

Tenderloin, Marinated Beef, '93 215
Tenderloin Shish Kebabs, Beef, '00 200
Tenderloin with Mushrooms, Beef, '87 115
Tomatoes and Artichokes, Beef with, '92 282
Tournedos Diables, '87 60
Bratwurst, Grilled, '94 253; '01 159
Bread, Barbecue, '99 105
Bread, Greek, '89 200
Bread, Grilled, '00 88
Bread, Lemony French, '97 147
Burgers, Pizza, '89 165
Cantaloupe Wedges, Grilled, '87 162
Cheddar, Easy Smoked, '01 168
Chicken
  Bahamian Chicken with Cha-Cha Salsa, Grilled,
    '97 160
  Barbecued Chicken, Grilled, '81 154
  Basil Chicken, Grilled, '93 201
  Basil-Stuffed Chicken with Tomato-Basil Pasta,
    '94 204
  Basting Sauce, Grilled Chicken with, '01 146
  Beer-Can Chicken, '04 118
  Beer-Can Chicken, Basic, '03 130; '04 104
  Breast of Chicken, Marinated, '87 123
  Breasts, Grilled Chicken, '84 172; '04 214
  Breasts, Marinated Chicken, '90 54
  Breasts with Fig-and-Melon Compote, Grilled,
    Chicken, '00 163
  Breasts with Lemon-Yogurt Coleslaw, Grilled
    Chicken, '98 148
  Bundles with Bacon Ribbons, Chicken, '87 168
  Burgers, Open-Faced Chicken-Onion, '94 139
  Charcoal Broiled Chicken, '79 90
  Clubs, Grilled Chicken-and-Pesto, '01 22
  Cola-Can Chicken, '03 130; '04 104
  Creamy Sauce, Grilled Chicken with, '01 318
  Creole Grilled Chicken, '04 289
  Cumin Chicken, Grilled, '87 142
  Dill Sauce, Grilled Chicken with, '88 162
  Fajitas, Beef and Chicken, '02 119
  Fajitas, Chicken, '99 158
  Foil-Wrapped Chicken, '99 108
  Garlic-and-Wine Grilled Chicken, '00 136
  Garlic-Grilled Chicken, '87 180
  Ginger-Glazed Chicken, Grilled, '98 166
  Ginger-Orange Chicken, Grilled, '91 26
  Green Onions, Chicken with Grilled, '01 94
  Greens, Grilled Chicken on, '99 201
  Grilled Chicken, '89 200; '92 170
  Grits with Grilled Chicken and Onions, '99 17
  Herbed Chicken Quarters, Grilled, '96 171
  Honey-Glazed Grilled Chicken, '99 213
  Honey-Lime Grilled Chicken, '96 189; '98 332
  Jalapeño Chicken, Grilled, '93 213
  Jamaican Jerk Chicken, '96 120; '99 121
  Jamaican Jerk Raspberry Chicken, '00 88
  Kebabs, Chicken, '87 141; '03 180
  Kebabs, Chicken-Pineapple, '00 200
  Kebabs, Chicken-Vegetable, '03 95
  Kebabs, Hawaiian, '85 157
  Kebabs, Oriental Chicken, '95 193
  Kebabs, Rumaki, '82 182
  Kebabs, Sesame Chicken, '92 165
  Kebabs, Soy-Chicken, '86 156
  Kebabs Supreme, Chicken, '81 124
  Lemonade Chicken, '82 163
  Lemon-Herb Grilled Chicken, '95 87
  Lemon-Mustard Chicken, '99 109
  Lime Chicken with Grilled Pineapple, '04 88
  Lime-Grilled Chicken, '02 142; '04 320
  Lime-Jalapeño Chicken, Grilled, '91 87
  Macadamia-Mango Chicken, '02 162
  Margarita-Marinated Chicken, Grilled, '97 167
  Marinated Chicken, '87 61

  Marinated Chicken Quarters, '02 142
  Mushroom Bundles, Chicken-, '80 157
  Orange, Lime, and Ginger Sauce, Chicken with,
    '92 123
  Pesto Chicken with Basil Cream, '89 158
  Polenta, Chicken with, '02 87
  Provolone, Chicken, '93 323
  Quesadillas, Grilled Chicken, '04 36
  Salad, Chicken-and-Fruit, '01 178
  Salad, Chicken-Blueberry, '02 177
  Salad, Grilled Asian Chicken, '96 158
  Salad, Grilled Chicken-and-Fruit, '96 155
  Salad, Grilled Chicken-Pasta, '94 64
  Salad, Grilled Chicken-Rice, '98 148
  Salad, Moroccan Grilled Chicken, '95 231
  Salad, Strawberry-Chicken, '04 50
  Salad, Thai Chicken, '95 177
  Salad with Grilled Chicken, Tropical Spinach,
    '04 51
  Salad with Mango Chutney, Grilled Chicken,
    '96 182
  Salad with Raspberry Dressing, Grilled Chicken,
    '95 202
  Salsa, Grilled Chicken with Cha-Cha, '98 333
  Sandwiches, Chicken-Benedict Bagel, '96 250
  Sandwiches, Grilled Chicken Salad, '00 164
  Sandwiches, Open-Faced Mexican, '98 230
  Sandwiches, Summer Open-Faced, '99 201
  Sandwich, Ham 'n' Cheese Chicken, '95 153
  Sandwich Jamaican Chicken, '95 153
  Sandwich, Jerk Chicken, '98 333
  Sandwich, Marinated Chicken in a, '86 185
  Saté, Chicken, '99 134
  Sausage with Fennel, Chicken, '98 312
  Sesame-Ginger Chicken, '00 219
  Skewers with Peanut Sauce, Chicken, '02 173;
    '04 324
  Slaw and Dipping Sauce, Grilled Chicken with
    Sweet Soy, '04 123
  Smoky Grilled Chicken, '85 160
  Soba Noodles, Grilled Chicken with Spicy, '00 93
  South-of-the-Border Barbecued Chicken, '97 311
  Southwestern Chicken, '03 180
  Southwestern Chicken with Pineapple Salsa,
    Grilled, '04 196
  Soy-Garlic Chicken, '98 128
  Tabbouleh Salad, Grilled Chicken with, '91 70
  Tarragon-Dijon Thighs, Grilled, '97 120
  Teriyaki Chicken, '91 163
  Teriyaki Chicken, Grilled, '92 59
  Tomatillo Salsa, Grilled Chicken with, '02 123
  Tortas, Grilled Chicken, '01 M187
  Vegetables, Grilled Chicken and, '99 200
  Vegetables Vinaigrette, Grilled Chicken and,
    '91 26
  White Barbecue Sauce, Chicken with, '97 322;
    '01 168
  Wings, Grilled Honey Chicken, '96 111
  Wings, Hot 'n' Spicy Chicken, '04 132
  Wings, Maple-Glazed Chicken, '99 110
  Yogurt-Lemon Chicken, Grilled, '81 111
Cornish Hens, Asian Grilled, '99 41
Cornish Hens, Grilled, '88 243; '92 59
Cornish Hens, Jelly-Glazed, '93 251
Cornish Hens, Orange-Glazed Grilled, '86 250
Cornish Hens, Sherry-Marinated, '91 148
Cornish Hens with Tropical Fruit, Grilled, '97 310
Crostini, Tomato-and-Goat Cheese, '04 168
Dogs, Marrow's Famous, '04 198
Duck Breasts, Charcoal Marinated, '79 226
Duck Kebabs with Almond Rice, Grilled, '91 291
Duck with Orange Sauce, Grilled, '94 305
Duck with Parsnip Mash, Honey-Orange-Glazed
  Muscovy, '97 262

GRILLED
(continued)

Fennel and Radicchio with Orange Vinaigrette,
  Grilled, '95 253
Figs, Marinated Grilled, '96 194
Fish. *See also* **GRILLED/Seafood.**
  Amberjack Sandwiches, Grilled, '91 195
  Caribbean Fish, '99 109
  Catfish Cajun-Style, Grilled, '90 129
  Catfish, Lime-Orange, '02 22
  Catfish over Mixed Greens, Grilled, '04 326
  Catfish with Red Salsa, Grilled, '90 172
  Catfish with Relish, Grilled, '92 54
  Easy Grilled Fish, '91 194
  Fillets Tomatillo, '94 135
  Flounder Fillets, Grilled, '83 213
  Grouper, Garlic-Basil Marinated, '94 160
  Grouper, Grilled, '86 185
  Grouper, Grilled Herbed, '99 178
  Grouper, Grilled Marinated, '90 166
  Grouper, Hot Spicy, '94 78
  Heather Sauce, Catfish Inn's Grilled Fish with,
    '84 182
  Kebabs, Fish, '98 223
  Mahi-Mahi with Lemon Mayonnaise, '99 178
  Montego Bay Grilled Fish with Caribbean Salsa,
    '96 70
  Rainbow Trout with Mushroom Stuffing, Grilled,
    '97 162
  Salmon Fillets, Fresh Herb-Rubbed, '03 207
  Salmon Fillets with Sweet Corn Relish, '93 119
  Salmon, Orange-Basil, '97 165
  Salmon Quesadilla with Cucumber Salsa, Grilled,
    '95 131
  Salmon Steaks, Grilled, '94 278
  Salmon Steaks, Grilled Herbed, '93 176
  Salmon Steaks, Mint-Marinated, '96 175
  Salmon Steaks with Lemon-Mustard Sauce,
    '97 124
  Salmon Steaks with Tarragon Butter, '87 155
  Salmon Steaks with Tarragon Sauce, Grilled,
    '97 42
  Salmon with Mustard-Molasses Glaze, Grilled,
    '01 209
  Salmon with Sweet Soy Slaw and Dipping Sauce,
    Grilled, '04 123
  Salmon with Tangy Dill Sauce, Grilled, '04 320
  Snapper with Orange-Almond Sauce, Grilled,
    '01 158
  Swordfish Salad, '00 18
  Swordfish-Shiitake Skewers, '97 168
  Swordfish, Skewered, '86 256
  Swordfish Steaks, Orange-Ginger Marinated,
    '93 271
  Swordfish Steak with Chervil Butter, '91 147
  Swordfish with Avocado-Lime Sauce, Grilled,
    '97 127
  Swordfish with Caper Sauce, Grilled, '95 230
  Trout, Grilled, '95 106
  Tuna, Grilled Florida, '93 128
  Tuna, Inland Grilled, '96 197
  Tuna Sandwiches, Grilled-, '02 173
  Tuna Steaks, Grilled, '90 129
  Tuna Steaks on Mixed Greens with Lemon-Basil
    Vinaigrette, Seared, '94 205
  Tuna Steaks with Cucumber Sauce, '97 180
  Tuna with Poblano Salsa, Grilled, '91 135
  Tuna with Sautéed Vegetables, '98 222
  Yellowfin Tuna with Corn, Pepper, and Tomato
    Salsa, '94 164
Franks, Grilled Stuffed, '82 163
Fruit Kebabs, Grilled, '97 147

Fruit with Honey Yogurt, Grilled, '95 87
Game Hens, Texas-Style, '87 61
Grits, Grilled Andouille, '04 165
Grits, Hot Grilled, '97 191
Ham. *See* **GRILLED/Pork.**
Lamb
  Burgers, Mesquite-Grilled Lamb, '88 59
  Chops, Grilled Lamb, '91 163
  Chops, Joan's Rosemary Lamb, '97 42
  Chops, Peppercorn-Crusted Lamb, '92 142
  Chops, Rosemary Grilled Lamb, '03 125
  Chops, Smart and Saucy Rosemary-Cherry
    Lamb, '02 193
  Chops, Teriyaki Lamb, '87 60
  Chops with Chipotle and Cilantro Oils, Grilled
    Lamb, '02 96; '03 98
  Chops with Rosemary Sauce and Wild Rice-
    Fennel Pilaf, Grilled Lamb, '97 127
  Chops with Shrimp, Lamb, '88 58
  Kebabs, Apricot-Grilled Lamb, '98 102
  Kebabs, Lamb, '85 159; '95 192; '00 220;
    '03 136
  Kebabs, Lamb Shish, '93 70
  Kebabs, Overnight Shish, '81 124
  Kebabs, Rosemary Marinated Lamb, '93 203
  Kebabs, Saucy Lamb, '89 167
  Kebabs, Savory Lamb, '80 184
  Kebabs, Shish, '82 182
  Kebabs Teriyaki, Shish, '85 37
  Leg of Lamb, Greek-Style, '93 170
  Leg of Lamb, Grilled, '96 88; '98 103
  Mango Salsa, Grilled Lamb with, '95 104
  Patties, Grilled Lamb, '02 167
  Rosemary-Skewered Lamb, '97 190
  Sandwiches, Lamb, '97 107
  Steaks with Béarnaise Sauce, Lamb, '85 37
  Sweet Pepper Relish, Grilled Lamb with, '95 104
Liver Kebabs, '80 185
Melon Salad with Orange-Raspberry Vinaigrette,
  Grilled, '95 144
Nachos, Smoked, '01 146
Peaches, Grilled Balsamic-Glazed, '02 159
Pecans, Smoky, '01 168
Pie, Pear-Praline, '97 192
Pineapple Boats with Rum Sauce, '97 192
Pineapple Skewers with Rum Sauce, Grilled, '04 247
Pineapple with Vanilla-Cinnamon Ice Cream,
  Grilled, '00 127; '01 195
Pizza Dogs, Grilled, '97 139
Pizza, Grilled, '97 190
Pizzas, Grilled, '93 178; '98 176
Polenta, Grilled, '00 126
Polenta with Black Bean Salsa, Grilled, '93 155
Pork
  Burgers, Hearty Sauced Pork, '84 125
  Burgers, Sausage, '83 212
  Chops, Apricot-Stuffed Pork, '92 219
  Chops, Country Pride Pork, '79 159
  Chops, Glazed Pork, '86 185
  Chops, Grilled Asian Pork, '02 307; '03 271
  Chops, Grilled Pork, '88 113; '98 246
  Chops, Hawaiian Grilled Pork, '85 159
  Chops, Herbed Pork, '97 147
  Chops, Honey-Glazed, '97 200
  Chops, Lemon-Herb Pork, '84 81
  Chops, Marinated Grilled Pork, '81 110
  Chops, Mexican Pork, '99 108
  Chops on Smoked Gouda Grits, Grilled Maple
    Chipotle Pork, '04 172
  Chops, Pineapple-Curry Glazed, '82 106
  Chops, Rosemary Pork, '98 329
  Chops with Ancho Cream Sauce, Boneless Pork,
    '95 205
  Chops with Black-and-White Salsa, Pork, '97 200

Chops with Garlic Mashed Potatoes, Grilled Pork,
  '02 281
Chops with Jalapeño-Cherry Sauce, Smoked
  Pork, '01 208
Chops with Tangy Barbecue Sauce, Pork, '99 104
Glazed Pork Chops, Bourbon-, '04 44
Ham and Apples, Grilled, '96 M303
Ham, Easy Grilled, '92 134
Ham, Golden Grilled, '79 90
Ham, Hickory-Grilled, '92 81
Ham Kebabs, Honey, '80 156
Ham Kebabs, Swiss-, '81 124
Ham 'n' Cheese Chicken Sandwich, '95 153
Ham Slice, Apricot-Glazed, '93 252
Honey-and-Herb Grilled Pork, '90 148
Jalapeño Grilled Pork, '99 160
Kebabs, Margarita Pork, '98 M223
Kebabs, Pineapple-Pork, '99 144
Kebabs, Spicy Pork, '82 182
Kebabs with Sesame Seeds, Pork, '00 337
Loin, Grandma Ruth's Grilled Pork, '96 250
Loin, Honey-Grilled Pork, '92 219
Loin, Marinated Pork, '01 331
Loin, Minted Pork, '99 96
Maple-Glazed Pork Chops with Pecans and
  Apples, Commune's, '04 102
Medaillons, Grilled Pork, '93 229
Medaillons with Blackberry Sauce, Pork, '02 136
Ribs, Adams', '95 236; '00 177; '03 312
Ribs, Baby Back, '04 86
Ribs, Chipotle Grilled Pork, '01 319
Ribs, Jamaican Jerk Raspberry, '00 88
Ribs, Lemon Grilled, '81 154
Ribs McCoy, '04 132
Ribs, Smoky, '84 172
Ribs, Smoky Chipotle Baby Back, '04 87
Ribs with Plum Sauce, Crispy, '98 182
Roast, Company Pork, '99 276
Roast, Grilled Pork, '97 323
Salad, Grilled Pork Cosmopolitan, '04 123
Salsa, Grilled Pork with, '90 128
Sausage, Grilled Pork, Cheddar, and Jalapeño,
  '98 311
Sausage Pasta, Three Pepper-, '02 122
Sesame Pork, '01 177
Smoked Pork, '01 233; '03 121
Smoked Pork Shoulder, '01 147
Spareribs, Baked and Grilled, '97 211
Spareribs, Grilled Maple, '99 136
Spareribs, Honey-Glazed, '82 163
Spareribs in Plum Sauce, '99 136
Spareribs, Peach-Glazed, '86 14
Spareribs, Spicy, '89 168
Steaks, Glazed Pork, '83 178
Superburgers, '79 89
Tacos with Cucumber-Radish Salsa, Adobo
  Grilled Pork, '01 186
Tenderloin, Coriander-Pepper Pork, '99 145
Tenderloin, Garlic Grilled Pork, '90 172
Tenderloin, Grilled Marinated Pork, '91 199
Tenderloin, Grilled Pork, '91 163; '94 88; '02 187
Tenderloin, Honey-Garlic Pork, '01 16
Tenderloin, Marinated Pork, '84 175
Tenderloin, Molasses-Grilled Pork, '96 265
Tenderloins, Grilled Pork, '88 98; '94 158
Tenderloins, Honey-Grilled, '92 199; '00 126
Tenderloin, Spicy Grilled Pork, '04 96
Tenderloins with Rosemary Pesto, Grilled Pork,
  '01 174
Tenderloins with Rosemary Pesto, Grilled Pork,
  '04 82
Tenderloin Towers, Pork, '86 75
Tenderloin, Tropical Spinach Salad with Grilled
  Pork, '04 51

Tenderloin with Apples, Celery, and Potatoes, Grilled Pork, '95 161

Tenderloin with Brown Sauce, Grilled Pork, '89 32

Tenderloin with Gingered Jezebel Sauce, Grilled Pork, '04 138

Tenderloin with Lime and Chipotle, Sweet Pork, '04 184

Tenderloin with Molasses Sauce, Grilled Pork, '97 193

Tenderloin with Mustard Sauce, Pork, '99 145; '03 238

Tenderloin with Onion-Balsamic Sauce, Pork, '99 44

Tenderloin with Orange-Curry Sauce and Coconut Rice, Polynesian Pork, '04 309

Tenderloin with Orange Marmalade, Grilled Pork, '03 181

Tenderloin with Parmesan-Pepper Toasts, Herbed Pork, '98 242

Tenderloin with Red Wine Sauce, Molasses Pork, '02 290

Tenderloin with Sauce Caribe, Jamaican Pork, '02 320

Tenderloin with Yogurt and Lime, Grilled Pork, '04 216

Tenders, Skewered Pork, '00 200

Quail, Asian Grilled, '99 41

Quail, Grilled, '92 90

Quail, Grilled Breakfast, '88 220

Quail, Marinated, '80 221

Quail, Sage-Smoked Champagne, '97 164

Quail with Red Wine-Blackberry Sauce, Grilled, '98 319

Sandwiches, Grilled Garden, '98 315

Saté Mixed Grill with Spicy Peanut Sauce, '04 134

Seafood. *See also* **GRILLED/Fish.**

Brochette, Seafood, '87 96

Oriental Marinade, Seafood in, '98 128

Oysters Mornay, Grilled, '89 195

Oysters Supreme, Smoky, '87 60

Po'Boy, Grilled Seafood, '96 244

Scallop-Bacon Kebabs, '81 111

Scallop Kebabs, Grilled, '83 101

Scallop Kebabs, Sea, '82 162

Scallops, Grilled Sweet-and-Sour, '01 92

Scallops, Marinated Grilled, '84 171

Scallops Tostada, Grilled, '87 120

Scallops with Cilantro-Lime Vinaigrette, Grilled Orange, '94 77

Shrimp and Cornbread-Stuffed Peppers, Barbecued, '97 261

Shrimp-and-Scallop Kebabs, Grilled, '92 210

Shrimp and Vegetables, Grilled Parsleyed, '04 256

Shrimp, Grilled, '85 103

Shrimp, Grilled Garlic, '99 178

Shrimp, Grilled Margarita-Marinated, '97 167

Shrimp, Grilled Marinated, '87 173

Shrimp, Grilled Sweet-and-Sour, '97 100

Shrimp, Grilled Zucchini-Wrapped, '98 200

Shrimp Gyros with Herbed Yogurt Spread, Grilled-, '02 M169

Shrimp Kebabs, Marinated, '85 158

Shrimp Kebabs, Steak-and-, '80 184; '00 124

Shrimp, Marinated and Grilled, '87 141

Shrimp, Orange, and Watermelon Salad with Peppered Peanuts in a Zesty Citrus Dressing, Grilled, '04 308

Shrimp Skewers with Vegetable Salsa, '98 32, 223

Shrimp, Stove-Top Smoked, '01 168

Shrimp, Tropical Spinach Salad with Grilled, '04 51

Shrimp with Citrus Salsa, Grilled, '97 141

Shrimp with Creamy Tomatillo Sauce, Grilled Jerk, '01 332

Shrimp with Smoky Sweet Sauce, Mexican-Grilled, '03 32

Shrimp with Tropical Fruit Sauce, Grilled, '01 195

S'mores, Grilled Pound Cake, '98 179

Tortilla Bites, '95 42

Turkey-and-Fruit Kebabs, '88 140

Turkey Breast, Citrus-Marinated, '94 272

Turkey Breast, Smoky, '89 323

Turkey Breast, Spicy-Sweet Smoked, '03 250

Turkey Breast with Cranberry Salsa, Grilled, '95 252

Turkey Burgers, Grilled, '91 61

Turkey Drumsticks, Grilled, '89 168

Turkey, Seasoned Smoked, '97 85

Turkey Steaks, Grilled Marinated, '93 170

Turkey Tenderloins, Lime-Buttered, '92 127

Vegetables

Acorn Squash with Rosemary, Grilled, '96 266

à la Grill, Vegetables, '88 130

Asparagus, Grilled, '00 165

Asparagus Salad with Orange Vinaigrette, Grilled, '99 102; '01 110

Barbecue Hobo Supper, '99 108

Burgers, Vegetable, '89 164

Cilantro Butter, Grilled Vegetables with, '98 182

Corn and Squash, Grilled, '02 122

Corn-and-Squash Quesadillas, Grilled, '02 123

Corn, Grilled Parmesan, '82 127

Corn in the Style of Oaxaca, Grilled, '04 134

Corn-on-the-Cob, Grilled, '90 166

Corn on the Cob, Lemony, '89 200

Corn on the Cob, Mexican, '96 167

Corn on the Cob with Garlic-Chive Butter, '01 331

Corn on the Grill, '94 161; '97 191

Corn Salsa, Grilled, '99 162

Corn Salsa, Zesty, '02 193

Corn, Smoked, '01 169

Corn Soup, Grilled, '87 121

Corn with Herb Butter Sauce, '79 150

Corn with Jalapeño-Lime Butter, Grilled, '01 158; '04 178

Corn with Maple Vinaigrette, Grilled, '98 171

Eggplant Appetizer, Grilled, '95 198

Eggplant, Balsamic-Flavored, '95 342

Eggplant, Grilled, '80 202

Eggplant, Sage-Grilled, '96 269

Eggplant Vinaigrette, Italian, '03 125

Gazpacho, Grilled Vegetable, '97 181

Gazpacho, Southwestern Grilled, '00 84

Grilled Vegetables, '84 172; '92 124; '96 123, 173

Herbs, Grilled Vegetables with, '00 220

Italian-Style Grilled Vegetables, '92 143

Kebabs, Beef-and-Vegetable, '91 148

Kebabs, Easy Vegetable, '02 142

Kebabs, Fresh Vegetable, '92 101

Kebabs, Grilled Vegetable, '93 170

Kebabs, Tangy Marinated Vegetable, '88 142

Kebabs, Vegetable, '87 116; '01 132

Marinated Grilled Vegetables, '95 162; '00 126

Marinated Vegetables, Grilled, '00 137; '04 133

Medley, Grilled Vegetable, '98 158

Mushroom-Asparagus Salad, Grilled, '02 122

Mushroom Burgers, '97 101; '99 135

Okra and Tomatoes, Grilled, '98 124

Onion Flowers with Pecans, Grilled, '96 217

Onion Salad, Grilled, '99 96

Onions, Grilled Stuffed, '95 180

Onions, Smoky Sweet, '97 191

Parmesan Vegetables, '97 147

Pasta, Grilled Vegetable, '97 142

Pepper Grill, Three-, '02 122

Pepper Kebabs, Pretty, '90 166

Pepper-Pesto Linguine, Grilled, '04 136

Peppers, Marinated Roasted, '97 123

Pepper Tacos, Grilled, '95 340

Pizza, Grilled Vegetable, '98 176

Pizzas, Grilled Vegetable, '97 323

Poblano Chile con Queso, Roasted, '01 186

Portabello Mushrooms, Grilled, '95 123

Portobello Burger, Grilled, '98 331

Portobello Burgers with Avocado Mayonnaise, '00 335

Portobello Mushroom Burgers, '01 144

Portobello Mushrooms and Asparagus, Grilled, '02 122

Portobello Pizza Burgers, Grilled, '00 89

Portobello Pizzas, Grilled, '00 89

Potatoes, Grilled Herb, '84 172

Potatoes, Grilled Irish, '97 53

Potatoes, Italian Grilled, '98 171

Potatoes, Smoked Baked, '97 25

Red Onions, Grilled, '03 139

Romaine Salad with Buttermilk-Chive Dressing, Grilled, '04 105

Salad, Avocado-Corn-Poblano, '01 320

Salad, Grilled Marinated Vegetable, '01 143

Salad, Grilled Vegetable, '94 203; '00 146

Sandwiches, Grilled Vegetable, '01 310

Sandwiches, Open-Faced Summer, '01 171

Shiitakes, Grilled, '95 265

Skewers, Grilled Vegetable, '94 160

Squash and Onion, Grilled, '79 150

Squash-and-Pepper Kebabs, Summery, '95 193

Squash and Tomatoes, Grilled Summer, '99 144

Squash Fans, Grilled, '97 118

Squash, Marinated Grilled, '02 110

Sweet Potatoes, Grilled, '93 213

Tomatillo Salsa, '02 123

Tomato, Bell Pepper, and Portobello Salad, Grilled, '98 211

Tomatoes, Cheesy Grilled, '79 150

Tomatoes, Grilled, '85 158; '99 173; '04 178

Tomatoes with Basil Vinaigrette, Grilled, '97 168

Yellow Squash and Tomatoes, Grilled, '00 102

Zucchini Fans, Grilled, '89 200

Zucchini with Feta, Greek Grilled, '95 190

Venison Kebabs, '82 215; '88 249

Venison Roast, Grilled, '93 278

Venison Steaks, Grilled, '82 215

Wiener Worms, '02 223

GRITS

Bake, Grits 'n Greens Dinner, '84 281

Biscuits, Shrimp-and-Grits, '02 313

Cakes, Southwestern Grits, '93 61

Casserole, Garlic Grits, '81 47

Casserole, Grits-Sausage, '84 75; '86 241

Cheese

Baked Cheese-and-Garlic Grits, '83 292; '84 78

Baked Cheese Grits, '80 49, 99; '83 311; '85 41; '94 240; '01 289

Baked Cheese Grits, Grillades and, '94 240

Baked Grits, Swiss-and-Cheddar, '91 71

Bake, Santa Fe Grits, '00 123

Casserole, Cheesy Grits, '81 270

Casserole, Cheesy Shrimp-and-Grits, '03 28

Cheese Grits, '86 242; '90 102

Chicken Sausage and Shiitake Mushrooms, Cheese Grits with, '03 254

Chile-Blue Cheese Grits, '04 240

Chili-Cheese Grits, '01 86

Creamy Grits, '96 24

Creamy Grits, Margaret's, '99 18; '00 21

GRITS, Cheese
(continued)

    Croutons and Vidalia Onion-Balsamic
      Vinaigrette, Southern Spinach Salad with
      Cheese Grits, **'04** 316
    Crust Batter, Cheese Grits, **'03** 21
    Double-Cheese Grits, Quick, **'03** 167
    Fried Cheese Grits, Hot Browns with, **'02** 94
    Garlic-and-Herb Cheese Grits, **'95** 122
    Garlic-and-Herb Grits, Baked, **'01** 326
    Garlic Cheese Grits, **'80** 47; **'81** 197
    Garlic-Cheese Grits, **'86** 180; **'88** 126; **'89** 47;
      '97 58; **'99** 270; **'00** 215
    Garlic Grits, **'00** 194; **'03** 211
    Green Chiles, Cheese Grits with, **'95** 208
    Grilled Grits, Hot, **'97** 191
    Grits and Cheese, **'00** 327
    Gruyère Cheese Grits, **'81** 47
    Jalapeño Cheese Grits, **'85** 43
    Jalapeño-Cheese Grits, **'00** 239; **'01** 328
    Mexican Cheese Grits, **'02** 34
    Parmesan Cheese Grits, **'02** 233
    Quick Cheese Grits, **'83** M203; **'96** 97
    Saga Blue-Chile Grits, **'98** 202
    Sausage-Cheese Grits, **'90** 238
    Sautéed Smoked Gouda Cheese Grits with Black
      Bean Salsa, **'03** 323
    Sliced Cheese Grits, **'84** 75
    Smoked Gouda Grits, **'02** 319; **'04** 173
    Soufflé, Garlic-Cheese Grits, **'99** 18
    Squares, Chili-Cheese Grits, **'01** 86
Chicken and Grits, **'95** 263
Chicken and Onions, Grits with Grilled, **'99** 17
Chiles Rellenos, Southern-Style, **'96** 24
Country Grits and Sausage, **'83** 54
Creamy Grits, **'92** 237, 238; **'93** 60; **'00** 215
Dressing, Grits, **'93** 306; **'94** 296
Eggs Benedict, Shrimp-and-Grits, **'03** 53
Eggs Creole, **'92** 86
Fried Grits, **'83** 292; **'84** 78
Garlic Shrimp and Grits, **'03** 246
Good Morning Grits, **'87** 156
Greens, Grits and, **'95** 233
Grillades and Grits, **'88** 126; **'89** 47; **'93** 62
Grilled Andouille Grits, **'04** 165
Ham-and-Spinach Grits, Garlicky, **'94** 177
Italiano, Grits, **'92** 43
Nassau Grits, **'81** 47; **'99** 214
Orange Grits, **'81** 47
Pan-Fried Grits, **'93** 62
Patties, Grits, **'83** 52
Pie, Crustless Grits-and-Ham, **'86** 103
Pie, Grits Fiesta, **'92** 43
Pie, Pineapple-Grits, **'96** 236
Pudding, Grits, **'96** 28
Quiche, Ham-and-Grits Crustless, **'94** 89
Risotto, Redneck, **'98** 107
Salad, Stacked Grits-Spinach, **'98** 66
Sausage Grits, **'86** 92
Sausage, Grits with, **'99** 233
Scrambled Grits, **'80** 48
Shrimp and Grits, **'01** 258
Shrimp and Grits, Crook's Corner, **'04** 102
Shrimp and Grits, Garlic-Chili, **'00** 23
Shrimp and Grits, Spicy, **'04** 176
Shrimp-Manchego-Chorizo Grits with Red Bean
    Salsa, **'97** 227
Shrimp Stew and Grits, **'80** 118
Shrimp Stew over Grits, **'88** 126; **'89** 47
Soufflé, Grits, **'80** 30
Soufflé, Mexican Grits, **'79** 55
Spoonbread, Grits, **'79** 38

Spoonbread Grits with Savory Mushroom Sauce,
    '96 236
Stackable Grits, **'02** 204
Stuffing, Grits, **'96** 270
Tarts, Shrimp 'n' Grits, **'03** 254
Timbales, Chives-Grits, **'90** 172
Timbales, Grits, **'88** 223
Tomato Grits, **'03** 199
Tomato Grits, Hot, **'95** 171; **'01** 131
Wedges, Southwestern Grits, **'04** 332
GUACAMOLE. *See* **APPETIZERS/Dips,**
    Guacamole.
GUMBOS. *See also* **CHOWDERS, JAMBALAYAS,**
    SOUPS, STEWS.
Carolina Gumbo, **'95** 70
Chicken
    Andouille Gumbo, Chicken-, **'98** 14
    Chicken Gumbo, **'79** 199; **'90** 26
    Easy Chicken Gumbo, **'83** 156
    Gullah House Gumbo, The, **'92** 237
    Ham-Seafood Gumbo, Chicken-, **'81** 6
    Oyster Gumbo, Chicken and, **'81** 198
    Sausage Gumbo, Chicken-, **'04** 288
    Sausage Gumbo, Chicken-and-, **'89** 275; **'90** 256;
      '94 20; **'00** 221; **'01** 324; **'03** 313; **'04** 213
    Smoked Sausage, Chicken Gumbo with, **'81** 199
    Ya Ya, Gumbo, **'87** 210
Dove and Sausage Gumbo, **'81** 199
Duck, Oyster, and Sausage Gumbo, **'79** 226
Fish
    Catfish Gumbo, **'90** 278; **'91** 216
    Easy Fish Gumbo, **'81** 6
    Snapper Gumbo, Savannah, **'94** 105
Green Tomato Gumbo, **'04** 314
Ground Beef Gumbo, **'87** 283
Gumbo, **'01** 160
Mogumbo, **'93** 32
Okra Gumbo, **'86** 210; **'91** 206; **'01** 165
Okra Gumbo, Deep South, **'79** 48
Okra Gumbo Freezer Mix, **'86** 210; **'01** 165
Seafood
    Cajun Seafood Gumbo, **'94** 238
    Champion Seafood Gumbo, **'86** 293
    Chicken-Ham-Seafood Gumbo, **'81** 6
    Combo Gumbo, **'81** 198
    Crab and Shrimp Gumbo, **'81** 200
    Crabs, Seafood Gumbo with Whole, **'85** 2
    Creole Gumbo, **'86** 228
    Creole Gumbo, Quick, **'82** 87
    Creole Seafood Gumbo, **'82** 278
    Ham and Seafood Gumbo, **'81** 199
    Okra Gumbo, Light Seafood-, **'86** 155
    Oyster Gumbo, Chicken and, **'81** 198
    Seafood Gumbo, **'79** 198, 286; **'80** 34; **'81** 5;
      '83 90; **'84** 87, 92; **'87** 210; **'90** 154; **'96** 98
    Shrimp-Crab Gumbo, **'98** 15; **'03** 111
    Shrimp Gumbo, **'81** 199
    Shrimp Gumbo, Old-Style, **'98** 97
    Shrimp Gumbo, Quick, **'86** 71
    Southern Gumbo, **'82** 242
    Spicy Seafood Gumbo, **'91** 207
Texas Ranch-Style Gumbo, **'82** 226
Turkey Gumbo, **'82** 268; **'85** 258
Wild Game Gumbo, **'91** 290
z'Herbes, Gumbo, **'94** 239

HAM. *See also* **PORK.**
Acorn Squash, Ham-Stuffed, **'81** 239; **'83** 66
Appetizers
    Appetillas, Ham, **'93** 63
    Balls, Appetizer Ham, **'82** 39
    Balls, Fried Ham-and-Cheese, **'84** 221
    Balls, Ham, **'86** 256; **'03** 299

    Balls with Spiced Cherry Sauce, Ham, **'81** 112;
      '82 12
    Biscuits, Country Ham in Heart, **'86** 105
    Biscuits, Cured Ham and, **'85** 320
    Biscuits, Kentucky Ham 'n' Angel, **'90** 83
    Biscuits, Petite Ham and Cheese, **'79** 193
    Biscuits, Southern Ham and, **'91** 12
    Biscuits with Country Ham, **'90** 93
    Biscuits with Ham, Ranch, **'97** 59
    Cheesecake, Cheddar-Chili, **'02** 251
    Cheesecake, Ham-and-Asparagus, **'02** 103
    Chips, Ham-Cheese, **'82** 34
    Deviled Ham Twists, **'82** 86
    Dip, Creamy Ham, **'93** 125
    Eggs and Ham, Green, **'96** 90
    Fig Bites, Baked, **'02** 160
    Meat-and-Cheese Appetizers, **'87** 7
    Mousse Pitas, Ham, **'95** 328
    Mushrooms Stuffed with Ham, **'97** 237
    New Potatoes, Ham-Stuffed, **'88** 211
    Nuggets, Cheesy Ham, **'81** 290
    Pâté, Ham, **'85** 279
    Pineapple Nibbles, Ham-, **'95** 283
    Prosciutto Bruschetta and Cantaloupe Chutney,
      '00 108
    Prosciutto, Walnuts, and Cream, Figs with,
      '96 194
    Prosciutto, Watermelon and, **'98** 164
    Prosciutto-Wrapped Asparagus, **'91** 98
    Puffs, Ham-and-Cheese, **'86** 277
    Puffs, Ham-Filled Party, **'84** 116
    Roll, Ham-and-Cheese, **'79** 234
    Rolls, Ham, **'79** 153
    Rollups, Almond-Ham, **'89** 284
    Rollups, Asparagus, **'01** 239
    Rollups, Ham-and-Swiss, **'85** 113
    Sandwiches, Party Ham, **'97** 240
    Sandwiches, Tiny Ham-and-Cheese, **'99** 87
    Spread, Buttery Ham, **'95** 93; **'97** 98
    Spread, Cold Ham, **'82** 248
    Spread, Country Ham, **'87** 8
    Spread, Ham, **'86** 126
    Spread, Ham and Pimiento, **'80** 285; **'81** 56
    Stack-Ups, Ham, **'96** 109
    Tapas, Garlic-Ham, **'92** 175
    Tennessee Ham, **'95** 263
    Tennessee Sin, **'95** 218; **'96** 204
    Turnovers, Chile-Ham, **'88** 64
    Turnovers, Party Ham, **'82** 39
Apricots, Ham and, **'90** 53
Artichokes, Ham-Mushroom-Stuffed, **'95** 228
Baked
    Apricot Baked Ham, **'84** 160
    Bourbon Glaze, Baked Ham with, **'98** M271;
      '01 M42
    Burgundy Ham, Baked, **'94** 326
    Cranberry-Raisin Sauce, Baked Ham with,
      '88 244
    Festive Baked Ham, **'83** 263
    Maple-Raisin Sauce, Baked Ham with, **'83** 215
    Marinated Baked Ham, **'86** 94; **'88** 133
    Michelle's Baked Ham, **'03** 16
    Orange-Honey Glaze, Baked Ham with, **'90** 53
    Orange Sauce, Baked Ham with, **'86** 294
    Pineapple-Baked Ham, **'86** 48
    Plum Ham, **'80** 110
    Royale, Ham, **'84** 260
    Slice, Baked Ham, **'83** 12
Balls, Ham, **'84** 91; **'86** 256
Barbecued Ham Slices, **'81** 110
Birming "Ham," **'94** 229
Biscuits, Blue Cheese-and-Ham Cornmeal, **'98** 136
Biscuits, Ham, **'99** 233
Biscuits, Ham-and-Swiss Cheese, **'04** 209

Biscuits, Ham-Filled Angel, '80 159
Biscuits, Surprise Pull-Apart, '95 46
Black-Eyed Peas and Ham, Quick, '00 336
Black-Eyed Peas, Cajun, '96 218
Black-Eyed Peas, Hearty, '02 107
Black-Eyed Peas with Ham Hocks, '79 122
Bread, Ham-and-Cheese, '86 213
Broiled Ham, Cranberry, '88 301
Brunch Egg Nests, '03 246
Bundles, Ham-and-Cheese, '93 63
Burritos, Breakfast, '97 172
Butterbeans, Smoky Speckled, '04 167
Cakes, Hawaiian Ham, '79 252
Casseroles
Apple Ham Casserole, '79 213
Apples, Baked Ham and, '82 M237
Asparagus Dinner, Ham-, '80 M10
Asparagus Ham Rolls, '91 117
au Gratin, Broccoli-Ham, '90 239
Bacon-and-Ham Casserole, Cheesy, '01 256
Beans with Ham, Baked, '80 136
Breakfast Casserole, '91 285
Breakfast Casserole, Sausage-Ham, '01 54
Broccoli Casserole, Ham and, '81 133
Broccoli Casserole, Quick Ham-, '82 40
Brunch Casserole, Southwestern, '03 197
Cheese Casserole, Ham-and-, '87 78
Cheese Layered Casserole, Ham-and-, '98 160
Chicken, Ham, and Cheese Bake, '87 217
Creamy Ham Casserole, '03 83
Creamy Ham Casseroles, '01 55
Creamy Ham Medley, '84 90
Egg Casserole, '98 98
Egg Casserole, Breakfast Ham and, '79 253
Golden Ham Casserole, '82 119
Ham Casserole, '96 302; '98 314
Harvest Ham Bake, '79 210
Hash Brown-Ham-Cheese Bake, '97 323
Lasagna, Creamy Ham-and-Chicken, '95 88
Lima Casserole, Ham and, '79 192
Macaroni-Ham Casserole, '81 M177; '83 283
Noodle Casserole, Ham and, '80 300
Pasta Casseroles, Hot Brown, '96 290
Potato Casserole, Cheesy Ham-and-, '84 326
Potato Casserole, Ham-and-, '83 M87; '96 103
Potatoes with Ham Bits, Creamy, '87 191
Potato-Pineapple Bake, Ham-, '93 302
Quiche Casserole, '95 32
Rice Casserole, Ham-and-, '84 75
Rice-Stuffed Ham Rolls, '83 190
Rice-Tomato Bake, Ham-, '87 78
Roll Casserole, Ham, '91 M127
Sausage-Ham Breakfast Casserole, '04 332
Spaghetti, Ham-and-Turkey, '95 19
Spinach-and-Ham Rollups, '86 84
Spinach-Ham Rolls, '88 78
Spinach Roll-Ups, Ham and, '81 143
Strata, Baked Ham, '83 283
Strata, Ham, '95 308
Strata, Ham and Broccoli, '80 261
Swiss Casserole, Savory Ham-and-, '01 308
Tetrazzini, Ham, '82 M77; '84 241; '03 174
Turkey Bake, Layered Ham and, '79 252
Vegetable-and-Ham Casserole, '84 91
Cheesecake, Ham-and-Asparagus, '90 174
Cheesy Ham Dinner, '84 90
Cheesy Ham Towers, '82 M77
Chicken-and-Ham Bundles, Cheesy, '84 261
Chicken Breasts Saltimbocca, '98 19
Chicken Medley, Creamy Ham-and-, '92 272
Chowder, Creamy Green Bean, Mushroom, and
    Ham, '99 336
Chowder, Creamy Ham, '88 M53
Chowder, Ham-and-Cheese, '89 15

Chowder, Ham and Corn, '79 16
Chowder, Ham-and-Corn, '82 40
Chowder, Ham 'n Cheese, '79 199
Chowder with Ham, Potato, '99 141
Citrus-and-Spice Ham, '88 40
Collard Greens, '03 324
Collard Greens, Esau's, '03 17
Cordon Bleu, Chicken, '81 304; '82 83; '93 126
Cordon Bleu, Company Chicken, '82 274
Cordon Bleu, Easy Chicken, '02 175
Cordon Bleu, Veal, '87 219
Country Ham
Biscuits, Country Ham, '94 215
Biscuits, Country Ham in Heart, '86 105
Biscuits with Country Ham, '90 93
Bread with Herb Butter, Country Ham, '86 255;
    '99 18
Brown Sugar Coating, Country Ham with, '90 88
Chips, Country Ham, '92 338
Cider-Baked Country Ham, '82 195
Cider, Country Ham in Apple, '80 251
Cornbread, Country Ham Hot-Water, '01 29;
    '02 107; '04 25
Cornbread, Crab with Chile, '86 254
Country Ham, '99 19; '00 298
Eggs Benedict, Country Ham, '03 52
Grits Stuffing, Country Ham with, '96 270
Kentucky Hot Brown, '86 254
Kentucky Jack, '86 254
Oven-Braised Country Ham, '90 87
Oysters and Ham, Edwards', '86 253
Puff, Cheesy Country Ham, '90 88
Quiche, Country Ham, '87 287
Raisin Sauce, Country Ham with, '99 19
Red-Eye Gravy, Country Ham with, '79 37;
    '99 34
Redeye Gravy, Country Ham with, '86 254;
    '98 271; '00 216
Roasted Country Ham, Edwards', '86 253
Sauce, Country Ham, '90 117; '96 24
Shrimp with Country Ham and Capers, Sautéed,
    '04 241
Sotterley Plantation Country Ham, '93 270
Stuffed Country Ham, '90 317
Stuffed Country Ham, Maryland, '88 49
Swirls, Veal-and-Smithfield Ham, '86 253
Tartlets, Country Ham-and-Asparagus, '98 82
Virginia Ham, Buttermilk Biscuits with, '96 142
Virginia Ham with Gravy, '86 15
Wine, Country Ham in, '81 260
Creamed Ham and Chicken, '81 M74
Creamed Ham and Eggs, '82 40
Creamy Ham Towers, '79 138
Crêpes, Ham-and-Egg, '83 204
Crêpes with Mushroom Sauce, Ham-and-Egg,
    '82 46
Croquettes, Ham, '82 119
Curried Ham and Peaches, '82 60
Curried Ham Steak, '82 120
Curried Ham with Rice, '80 111
Deviled Delight, '83 130
Devils, Ham, '93 88
Eggplant, Ham-Stuffed, '80 162
Egg Rolls, Chinese, '96 101
Eggs, Creamy Ham and, '87 286
Eggs on Toast with Cheese Sauce, Ham and, '81 43
Eggs, Savory Ham and, '82 231
Enchiladas, Scrambled Egg, '97 153
Fettuccine, Ham-and-Asparagus, '94 84
Flips, Ham-and-Cheese, '92 46
French Toast, Ham-and-Cheese Oven, '97 172
French Toast, Stuffed, '00 193
Fried Rice, Ham, '04 125
Frittata, Ham-and-Broccoli, '98 101

Fritters, Ham, '82 39
Fritters, Potato-Ham, '98 249
Fritters with Creamy Sauce, Ham, '81 105
Frosted Ham, '89 71
Glazed
Apricot-Glazed Ham Slice, '93 252
Baked Glazed Ham, '01 52
Bourbon Glaze, Baked Ham with, '98 M271;
    '01 M42
Bourbon-Glazed Ham, '04 296
Brown Sugar Glaze, Smithfield Ham with,
    '86 253
Cherry-Peach Chutney, Glazed Ham with,
    '97 315
Cranberry Glazed Ham, '81 274
Cranberry-Honey Glaze, Baked Ham with,
    '89 273
Cranberry-Orange Glazed Ham, '81 295
Currant-Glazed Ham, '91 249
Fruited Ham Slice, '83 M317
Honey-Glazed Ham Slice, '81 104
Honey-Orange Glazed Ham, '83 320
Marmalade-Glazed Ham, '89 M196
Molasses-Coffee Glazed Ham, '03 119
Molasses-Glazed Ham, '84 24
Orange-Glazed Ham, '89 324
Orange-Glazed Ham, Sweet, '02 286
Orange-Honey Glaze, Baked Ham with, '90 53
Peachy Glazed Ham, '96 189
Pineapple-Glazed Ham, '01 288; '03 82
Praline-Mustard Glazed Ham, '01 306
Steak, Glazed Ham, '91 13
Strawberry-Glazed Ham, '91 84
Stuffed Ham, Glazed, '84 321
Sunshine-Glazed Ham, '84 252
Sweet-and-Sour Glazed Ham, '88 M15
Sweet-Sour Glazed Ham, '83 311
Green Beans with Ham and Potatoes, '01 223
Green Peppers, Ham-Stuffed, '80 65
Griddle Cakes, Ham, '89 255
Grilled Ham and Apples, '96 M303
Grilled Ham, Easy, '92 134
Grilled Ham, Golden, '79 90
Grilled Ham, Hickory-, '92 81
Grits, Garlicky Ham-and-Spinach, '94 177
Gumbo, Chicken-Ham-Seafood, '81 6
Gumbo, Combo, '81 198
Gumbo, Ham and Seafood, '81 199
Hash Brown Bake, '95 281
Hopping John with Ham, '81 7
Jambalaya, '04 288
Jambalaya, Creole, '87 210; '03 83
Jambalaya de Covington, '87 211
Jambalaya with Shrimp, Chicken-and-Ham, '04 99
Kebabs, Honey Ham, '80 156
Kebabs, Swiss-Ham, '81 124
Loaves
Chili-Sauced Ham Ring, '81 M122
Country Ham Loaves, '86 255
Cranberry-Ham Loaf, '82 M77
Glazed Ham Loaf, '79 187; '90 212
Ham Loaf, '79 180; '80 272
Ham Loaves, '90 235
Hawaiian Ham Loaf, '79 71
Pineapple Upside-Down Ham Loaf, '79 253
Ring, Ham, '84 91
Saucy Ham Loaf, '86 M328
Spicy Ham Loaf, '80 110
Supreme Ham Loaf, '79 242
Upside-Down Ham Loaf, '82 40
Mirlitons, Shrimp-and-Ham Stuffed, '03 251
Mirlitons, Stuffed, '00 246
Mornay, Ham and Eggs, '02 130
Muffins, Ham-and-Cheddar, '03 81

HAM
(continued)

Muffins, Ham-and-Cheese, '92 252; '93 144
Muffins, Ham-and-Swiss, '03 81
Muffins, Reduced-Fat Ham-and-Cheddar, '03 81
Noodles, Ham and Swiss on, '87 108
Omelet, Dill-Cheese-Ham, '95 33
Omelet, Ham and Cheese, '79 262; '80 123
Omelet, Ham-and-Cheese, '02 246
Omelet, Rolled, '89 228
Omelet, Sour Cream-Ham, '79 261
Omelets with Creole Sauce, '89 228
Pancakes, Potato-Ham, '96 138
Pancetta, Penne with, '00 51
Patties, Ham, '81 99
Patties, Ham-Sprout, '85 51
Patties, Pineapple-Ham, '80 110
Patties, Spicy Ham, '90 235
Peach Holiday Ham, '04 251
Peas and Ham, Southern, '85 138
Peas and Pasta, '99 68
Peppers, Ham-and-Corn Stuffed, '81 87
Peppers with Rice and Ham, Stuffed, '82 131
Pie, Crustless Grits-and-Ham, '86 103
Pie, Golden Ham, '87 78
Pie, Ham-and-Cheese, '95 256; '96 75
Pie, Ham Pot, '90 25
Pie, Omelet, '00 M35
Pie, Spaghetti-Ham, '93 19
Pie with Cheese Crust, Ham, '80 286
Pie with Cornbread Crust, Ham-and-Greens Pot,
    '03 20
Pie, Zucchini-Ham-Cheese, '80 272
Pineapple-Flavored Ham, '87 160
Pinto Beans with Ham, '97 210
Pinwheels, Ham, '90 235
Pizza, Greek, '03 145
Pizza, Ham-and-Eggs Crescent, '93 47
Pizza, Ham-and-Pineapple, '96 169
Pizzas, Muffuletta, '00 M335
Pizza, Southern Classic, '95 268
Po-Boy, Pain-Perdu, '93 291
Potatoes, Cheddar, Broccoli, and Ham Stuffed,
    '04 26
Potatoes, Ham Stuffed, '79 210
Potatoes, Ham-Stuffed Baked, '02 52
Potatoes, Jalapeño-Ham Stuffed, '81 M61
Potatoes, Stuffed Mashed, '98 328
Potatoes with Ham, Herbed, '00 318
Pot Pie, Ham-Broccoli, '03 83
Praline Ham, '85 302; '96 303
Prosciutto and Artichoke Hearts, Tortellini Alfredo
    with, '02 322
Prosciutto Croutons, '99 89
Prosciutto, Party Pasta with, '94 176
Prosciutto, Pizza with Artichoke and, '87 182
Quiches
    Cheese Quiche, Ham-, '79 26
    Cheese Quiches, Individual Ham-and-, '98 24
    Cheesy Ham Quiche, '79 127
    Crustless Ham Quiche, '84 235
    Grits Crustless Quiche, Ham-and-, '94 89
    Ham Quiche, '80 110
    Jalapeño Quiche, Cheesy, '84 31
    Mushroom Quiche, Ham-and-, '81 11
    Vegetable Quiche, Ham-and-, '84 326
Raisin Ham, '80 124
Raisin Sauce, Ham with, '82 M76
Red-Eye Gravy, Ham and, '88 221
Red Rice and Ham, '00 289
Rice, Charleston, '97 310
Rice, Fried, '00 273

Rice, Orphan's, '03 32
Rice, Savannah Red, '80 119
Roast of Ham, Brandied, '98 320
Roast, Peachy Ham, '86 118
Rolls à la Swiss, Chicken-and-Ham, '92 42
Rolls, Ham-and-Broccoli, '86 212; '87 82
Rolls, Ham-and-Cheese, '82 3
Rolls, Ham-and-Cheese Lettuce, '89 217
Rolls, Ham-Asparagus, '79 41
Salads
    Apple Salad, Ham-and-, '88 139
    Asparagus with Prosciutto, Marinated, '95 83
    Baked Ham Salad, Crunchy, '83 23
    Boats, Salad, '80 93
    Bread Salad, Italian, '03 54
    Cheese Salad, Ham-and-, '88 138
    Cheese Toss, Ham and, '79 55
    Coleslaw, Ham, '84 195
    Congealed Ham Salad, '81 36
    Egg Salad, Ham 'n, '81 36
    Fruited Ham Salad, '81 36, 146
    Hearty Ham Salad, '82 40
    Italian Ham Salad, Spicy, '85 74
    Macaroni-Ham Salad, '85 218
    Macaroni Salad, Ham and, '79 220
    Mandarin Ham-and-Rice Salad, '87 145
    Noodle Salad, Ham-, '85 249
    Pasta Salad, Ham-and-, '90 128
    Pasta Salad, Ham-and-Pea, '00 217
    Pasta Salad, Ham-Dijon, '92 191
    Pasta Salad, Ham-Pecan-Blue Cheese, '90 62
    Pasta Salad with Ham, '92 108
    Pilaf Mold, Ham, '86 222
    Potato Salad, Ham and, '80 272
    Potato Salad, Ham-and-, '95 94
    Potato Salad, Ham-and-Egg, '86 84
    Prosciutto Salad, Melon-and-, '92 191
    Rice Salad, Colorful Ham-and-, '90 319
    Rice Toss, Ham-, '82 40
    Rolls, Hearty Salad, '81 206
    Spread, Ham Salad, '87 92
    Sweet Potato Salad, Hawaiian Ham-, '82 232
    Tropical Ham Salad, '89 175
    Watermelon-Prosciutto Salad, '04 171
Sandwiches. *See also* **HAM/Appetizers.**
    Asparagus-and-Ham Melt Sandwiches, '88 M96
    Asparagus Delight, Ham-, '86 48
    Asparagus Sandwiches, Ham-and-, '01 307
    Baked Ham Sandwiches, '81 29
    Biscuits and Ham, Green Elf, '02 277
    Blue Cheese-Ham Sandwiches, Creamy, '87 279
    Cheese-and-Ham Striped Tea Sandwiches,
        Cheshire Claret, '94 16
    Cheese Chicken Sandwich, Ham 'n', '95 153
    Cheese Sandwiches, Ham-and-, '01 299
    Cheese Sandwiches, Hot Ham-and-, '85 299
    Cheese Sandwich Round, Ham-and-, '94 326
    Cheese Sandwich, Tex-Mex Ham-and-, '86 4
    Club Sandwiches, Double-Decker, '91 231;
        '92 68
    Club Sandwich, Italian, '01 22
    Croissant Sandwiches, '89 161
    Eggs à la Swiss, Ham and, '88 158
    Focaccia Sandwiches, '98 53
    French Market Sandwiches, '98 230
    Giant Ham-and-Pepper Sandwich, '96 74
    Hamwiches, '96 246
    Hideaways, Ham, '81 29
    Holiday Ham Sandwiches, '02 286
    Hot Browns, '98 287
    Hot Ham Sandwiches, '79 214
    Hot Rods, Ham, '86 136
    Meal-in-One Sandwiches, '80 218
    Monte Cristo Sandwiches, '83 134; '97 319

Monte Cristo Sandwiches, Open-Faced, '01 171
    Muffin, Stuffin', '99 193
    Muffuletta, '04 27
    Muffuletta, Doodles, '94 35
    Muffulettas, '98 184
    Open-Faced Sandwiches, '79 214
    Open-Face Ham Sandwiches, '82 40; '85 8
    Panhandle Sandwiches, '01 56
    Pineapple-Ham Sandwich Loaf, '91 167
    Pineapple Slaw Sandwiches, Ham-and-, '96 199
    Pita Pockets, Ham-and-Cheese, '90 271
    Pita Sandwiches, Denver, '86 M12
    Pita Sandwiches, Ham-and-Cheese, '87 202;
        '88 44
    Pita, Stuffed, '89 87
    Po'Boys, Guacamole-Topped Ham, '04 170
    Pocket, Ham and Swiss in the, '83 31
    Quesadillas, Quick Fiesta, '02 246
    Reuben Melts, Southern, '03 69
    Rollup, Hot Ham-and-Cheese, '01 217
    Rollups, Creamy Pineapple-and-Ham, '04 163
    Rollups, Pizza, '99 197
    Salad Sandwich, Tangy Ham, '80 272
    Sebastian, The, '94 184
    Stroganoff on Cheesy Onion Biscuits, Ham,
        '95 98
    Stuffed Sandwich, Deli, '98 287
    Swiss-and-Asparagus Sandwiches, Ham-, '01 52
    Swiss Sandwiches, Ham-and-, '98 287
    Swiss Sandwiches, Tangy Ham-and-, '85 164
    Torta, Mediterranean, '98 23
    Turkey and Ham Pine-Berry Sandwiches, '00 59
    Turkey Specials, Cheesy Ham-and-, '84 14
    Virginia Ham Sandwiches, '80 155
    Wraps, Club, '01 23
    Yummy Sandwiches, '81 229
Sauce, Steak with Ham-and-Mushroom, '83 109
Scalloped Potatoes with Ham, '02 42
Skillet Dinner, Corn-and-Ham, '83 190
Skillet Dinner, Ham, '85 179
Skillet Ham-and-Vegetables, '84 90
Skillet, Ham-Noodle, '87 78
Skillet, Ham Spaghetti, '83 283
Slice with Cinnamon Apple Rings, Holiday Ham,
    '90 250
Smoked Ham, '86 92
Soufflé, Virginia Ham Breakfast, '93 121
Soufflé with Cucumber Sauce, Ham, '92 41
Soup, Bean-and-Ham, '04 325
Soup, Chicken, Ham, and Oyster, '79 198
Soup, Creamy Kale, '96 203
Soup, Ham-and-Bean, '84 4
Soup, Hearty Ham, '82 4
Soup, Hot Brown, '00 318
Soup, New Year's Day, '00 25
Soup, Pot Liquor, '98 273
Soup, Spicy Ham-and-Bean, '94 322
Spread, Deviled Ham, '79 81
Spread, Ham-and-Egg, '79 59
Spread, Ham Salad, '87 92
Spread, Hawaiian Ham, '87 106
Spread, Horseradish-Ham, '91 167
Stew, Blakely Brunswick, '87 4
Stew, Collard, '02 17
Stew, Collard 'n' Black-Eyed Pea, '04 24
Stew, Ham-and-Black-Eyed Pea, '93 20
Stew, Quick Okra, '97 88
Stew, Turnip Greens, '02 17; '04 24
Stir-Fry, Easy Ham, '86 332
Stir-Fry, Ham and Zucchini, '79 47
Stroganoff, Ham, '82 40
Stromboli, '88 272; '89 181
Stuffed Ham, '86 323
Succotash, Savory, '96 63

Superburgers, '79 89
Supper, Top-of-Stove, '86 332
Tart, Ham-and-Cheese, '92 332
Tart Milan, '87 70
Tart, Supreme Ham, '84 22
Tasso Hollandaise, '04 67
Tennessee Ham, '95 263
Turnip Greens and Ham Hock, Southern, '80 119
Turnip Greens and Ham Hocks, Southern, '03 220
Véronique, Ham, '85 90
Waffles, Ham, '80 44
Zucchini, Ham and Cheese Stuffed, '79 157
HEALTHY & LIGHT
Andouille, '92 242
  Appetizers
    Ambrosia, Sherried, '84 324
    Apple-Phyllo Rolls, '88 213
    Artichokes, Marinated, '87 250
    Artichokes with Herb-Mayonnaise Dip, '84 67
    Beets, Blue Cheese-Stuffed, '88 211
    Buzzard's Nests, '93 244
    Carrot-Cheese Ball, '86 325
    Cheese Tartlets, '88 211
    Cherry Tomatoes, Crab-Stuffed, '82 289
    Cherry Tomatoes, Stuffed, '88 212
    Chicken-Mushroom Appetizers, '88 210
    Chicken Wontons, '92 284
    Chiles Medley, Fiery Pickled, '01 333
    Chips, Bagel, '91 138
    Chips, Baked Pita, '99 138
    Chips, Baked Wonton, '91 138; '99 138
    Chips, Cinnamon-and-Sugar Bagel, '91 139
    Chips, Cinnamon-and-Sugar Wonton, '91 138
    Chips, Corn Tortilla, '91 17
    Chips, Garlic Bagel, '91 139
    Chips, Garlic Wonton, '91 138
    Chips, Lemon-and-Herb Bagel, '91 139
    Chips, Lemon-and-Herb Wonton, '91 138
    Chips, Light Tortilla, '90 278; '91 257
    Chips, Parmesan Cheese Bagel, '91 138
    Chips, Parmesan Cheese Wonton, '91 138
    Chips, Pita, '89 19; '91 138
    Chips, Plantain, '95 M203
    Chips, Sweet Potato, '91 138; '95 M203
    Chips, Tortilla, '91 137
    Crab Ball, Spicy, '01 332
    Crab Cakes with Jalapeño Tartar Sauce,
      Chesapeake Bay, '96 69
    Crackers, Cranberry, '99 258
    Crostini, Festive, '99 324
    Crostini, Spinach-Red Pepper, '03 34
    Crudité Platter with Dip, '84 139
    Dip, Apple-Berry, '01 109
    Dip, Cheese-Herb, '89 20
    Dip, Chickpea-and-Red Pepper, '99 138
    Dip, Cilantro, '00 248
    Dip, Creamy Beef-and-Pasta Sauce, '01 108
    Dip, Creamy Ham, '93 125
    Dip, Curry, '87 25; '99 138
    Dip, Deviled, '87 25
    Dip, Dilled Garden, '84 324
    Dip, Festive Crab, '92 285
    Dip, Garbanzo, '93 94
    Dip, Ginger, '99 139
    Dip, Kahlúa, '99 139
    Dip, Low-Cal Tuna, '87 25
    Dip, Marmalade, '99 324
    Dip, Monster Mash, '93 244
    Dip, Peanut Butter, '01 109
    Dip, Pine Nut-Spinach, '99 138
    Dip, Quick Fruit, '90 110
    Dip, Ranch-Style, '90 138
    Dip, Refreshing Dill, '99 324
    Dip, Santa Fe Skinny, '94 137

Dips, Fun Fruit, '01 109
Dip, Skinny Ranch, '93 96
Dip, Spinach, '87 25
Dip, Strawberry, '01 109
Dip, Tofu, '86 109
Dip, Vegetable Garden, '85 215
Dumplings, Make-Ahead Pork, '03 64
Eggplant Appetizer, Grilled, '95 198
Empanadas, '04 135
Fruit Kebabs with Coconut Dressing, '87 251
Fruit with Lemon Sauce, Fresh, '82 290
Goat Cheese Wrapped in Phyllo, '99 43
Hummus, '96 158
Hummus, Low-Fat, '99 137
Meatballs, Sweet-and-Sour, '99 325
Mix, Crunchy Snack, '93 94
Mix, Snack, '89 19
Mousse, Shrimp, '87 251
Mushroom-Almond Pastry Cups, '88 210
Mushroom Appetizers, Stuffed, '88 210
Mushrooms, Shrimp-Stuffed, '99 324
Mushrooms, Spinach-Stuffed, '89 M133
Nectarine Cocktail, '85 107
New Potatoes, Ham-Stuffed, '88 211
Nuts, Mexico, '01 27
Orange Halves, Broiled, '85 288
Oysters Bienville, Baked, '90 27
Oysters Italiano, Baked, '89 97
Pasta Bites, Pesto-Cheese, '87 251
Pâté, Black-Eyed Pea, '93 97
Pâté, Lentil, '92 285
Pâté, Mock, '87 251
Pears Stuffed with Cheese, '82 290
Pita Bread Triangles, '88 211
Pita Wedges, Garlic, '93 98
Pizzas, Pita, '89 19
Poblanos with Mango Salsa, Crab-and-Goat
  Cheese, '04 59
Popcorn, Chili, '91 17
Popcorn Mix, Curried, '86 326
Popcorn with Pizzazz, '93 245
Potato Skin Snack, '91 18
Pretzels, Whole Wheat, '89 20
Quesadillas, Green Chile, '90 121
Quesadillas, Poblano-and-Corn, '01 333
Salsa, Chunky Black-Eyed Pea, '01 333
Salsa with Cinnamon Crisps, Fruit, '01 108
Saté Mixed Grill with Spicy Peanut Sauce,
  '04 134
Scallop Appetizer, '86 155
Shrimp Cocktail, Mexican, '00 249
Shrimp Dippers, '84 324
Shrimp with Creamy Tomatillo Sauce, Grilled
  Jerk, '01 332
Shrimp with Marmalade Dip, Oven-Fried, '99 324
Snow Peas, Crab-Stuffed, '85 288
Spinach-Ricotta Phyllo Triangles, '88 212
Spread, Artichoke-Parmesan, '92 95
Spread, Broccamoli Curry, '88 55
Spread, Creamy Potato-Garlic, '02 35
Spread, Feta Cheese, '96 265
Spread, Low-Fat Chicken, '82 290
Spread, Roasted Red Bell Pepper, '97 217
Spread, Smoked Salmon, '84 324
Steak-and-Chestnut Appetizers, Marinated,
  '84 323
Tabbouleh, '88 211
Tortilla Snacks, Pesto, '89 19
Vegetable Appetizer, Tarragon, '83 277
Vegetable Nachos, '91 17
Yogurt Cheese Appetizer, '04 217
Zucchini Caviar, '88 212
Zucchini Pizzas, '88 212
Zucchini-Shrimp Appetizers, '89 311

Apple-Cheese Bake, '92 225
Apples, Baked, '86 40
Apple Side Dish, Dried, '92 226
Apples, Stuffed Baked, '89 217
Apples with Orange Sauce, Baked, '84 314
Barley, Baked, '91 133
Beans, Molasses Baked, '99 105
Beans, Ranch-Style, '00 43
Beans, Smashed Pinto, '03 129
Beverages
  Apple Cooler, '90 14
  Apple Julep, '86 103
  Apricot Fruit Flip, '91 18
  Apricot Mint Cooler, '90 165
  Banana Coolers, '91 308
  Banana Nog, '82 290
  Banana Smoothie, '93 95
  Bellini Spritzers, '90 110
  Black Russian, Mock, '92 322
  Bourbon Blizzard, '92 287
  Breakfast Drink, Yummy, '01 133
  Brew, Witch's, '93 244
  Cantaloupe-Lime Refresher, '01 332
  Caribbean Cooler, '95 203
  Carrot Cooler, '89 35
  Cider, Hot Spiced, '82 290; '99 248
  Cocoa, Mocha, '83 318
  Cranberry Cocktail, Hot, '89 310
  Cranberry Smoothie, '91 307
  Eggnog, '83 318
  Eggnog with Orange and Nutmeg, Mock, '92 323
  Fruit Beverage, Blender, '83 318
  Fruit Refresher, '91 203
  Fruit Slush, '96 157
  Fruit Smoothie, '89 87
  Grapefruit Refresher, '88 85
  Hot Chocolate, Mexican, '98 313
  Kiwi-Peach Slushy, '00 201
  Lemon Velvet, '90 15
  Milkshake, Mocha, '89 35
  Mocha, Hot, '84 60
  Orange Juicy, '90 178
  Orange-Pineapple Drink, '89 35
  Orange Slush, '82 49
  Peach Cooler, '86 6
  Peach Frosty, '83 318
  Peach Refresher, '86 103
  Piña Colada, Mock, '92 322
  Piña Coladas, '95 203
  Pineapple-Banana Slush, '90 14
  Pineapple Sparkle, Spiced, '92 322
  Pineapple-Yogurt Whirl, '91 132
  Punch, Apple-Tea, '85 82
  Punch, Citrus, '93 99
  Punch, Holiday, '87 252
  Punch, Holiday Hot Fruit, '92 286
  Punch, Hot Apple, '84 324
  Punch, Tart Cranberry, '83 318
  Punch, White Grape, '90 15
  Scarlet Sipper, '90 198
  Shake, Double Strawberry, '00 179
  Shake, Frosty Fruit, '87 23
  Shake, Get-Up-and-Go, '00 179
  Shake, Strawberry-Banana, '89 35
  Shake, Strawberry-Orange Breakfast, '87 186
  Shake, Strawberry-Pear, '92 139
  Shake, Tropical, '00 179
  Strawberry Cooler, '83 56
  Strawberry Spritzer, '90 14
  Tea Mix, Spiced, '86 32
  Tea Mix, Sugar-Free Spiced, '91 258
  Tofruitti Breakfast Drink, '88 26
  Tomato-Clam Cocktail, '87 252
  Tomato Refresher, '83 318

HEALTHY & LIGHT, Beverages
(continued)

Tropical Refresher, '96 157
Vegetable Cocktail, Fresh, '82 165
Virgin Mary, Spicy, '92 323
Watermelon-Berry Slush, '90 137
Breads
Apricot-Orange Bread, '92 285
Apricot-Pecan Bread, '97 266
Banana Bread, '87 72
Banana Bread, Fruity, '95 78
Barbecue Bread, '99 105
Biscuits and Sausage Gravy, '94 20
Biscuits, Angel, '90 28
Biscuits, Buttermilk, '03 24
Biscuits, Cheese-Chive, '94 324
Biscuits, Easy-Bake, '96 157
Biscuits, Herbed, '93 67
Biscuits, Light, '89 53
Biscuits, Oatmeal, '89 108
Biscuits, Orange, '88 85
Biscuits, Whole Wheat, '84 60; '91 222
Biscuits, Yeast, '87 71
Bowls, Italian Bread, '98 292
Breadsticks, Quick, '00 317
Caraway Breadsticks, '89 239
Cinnamon-Oat Bread, '90 135
Cornbread, '92 324
Cornbread, Dieter's, '87 164
Cornbread, Jalapeño, '94 78
Cornbread, Mexican, '93 182
Cornbread Supreme, '93 67
Cornmeal Yeast Bread, '89 54
Corn Sticks, '89 54; '00 43
Cranberry-Banana Bread, '90 294
Crouton Bread, Quick, '90 138
English Muffin Bread, '95 M79
Flatbread, '98 106
Focaccia, Rosemary, '95 190
French Bread, '89 54
French Pistou Bread, Crusty, '97 68
French Toast, Cottage-Topped, '85 49
French Toast, English Muffin, '00 179
French Toast, Slender, '86 103
Garlic Bread, '82 19; '91 204
Herbed Bread, '89 34
Honey-Oat Bread, '89 107
Hush Puppies, Baked, '89 53; '95 108
Loaf, Cheddar Cheese, '00 317
Muffins, All-Bran Oat Bran, '91 134
Muffins, Apple, '84 193
Muffins, Applesauce, '91 141
Muffins, Banana-Oat, '87 188
Muffins, Banana-Raisin, '89 218
Muffins, Blueberry, '91 140, 203
Muffins, Blueberry-Cinnamon, '02 177
Muffins, Bran-Buttermilk, '85 7
Muffins, Corn, '98 313
Muffins, Cornmeal, '91 19
Muffins, Cornmeal Yeast, '92 49
Muffins, Corn-Oat, '89 108
Muffins, Freezer Bran, '91 141
Muffins, Granola, '95 78
Muffins, Green Onion-and-Cream Cheese,
'01 289
Muffins, Honey Bran, '88 171
Muffins Made of Bran, '86 103
Muffins, Miniature Cranberry, '90 294
Muffins, Oat Bran, '89 106
Muffins, Oat Bran-Banana, '91 18
Muffins, Oatmeal-Bran, '91 83
Muffins, Orange-Oatmeal, '00 24

Muffins, Parmesan Corn, '01 255
Muffins, Spicy Apple-Oat, '86 45
Muffins, Spicy Cornbread, '90 59
Muffins, Yogurt, '88 55
Oat Bread, Caraway-Raisin, '86 44
Oatmeal-Molasses Bread, '97 194
Onion-Herb Bread, '90 165
Pitas, Puffy, '97 69
Pizza Dough, '04 58
Pumpkin-Pecan Bread, '87 221
Roasted Garlic-Rosemary Bread, '04 16
Rolls, Dinner, '89 312
Rolls, Honey Wheat, '83 278
Rolls, Old-Fashioned Cinnamon, '92 226
Rolls, Parsley-Garlic, '93 319
Rolls, Vegetable Salad, '82 278
Rolls, Whole Wheat, '90 111
Rolls, Yogurt Crescent, '91 123
Rye Loaves, Swedish, '97 68
Sourdough Wedges, '90 199
Spoonbread, '90 200
Swiss Cheese Loaves, Mini, '95 80
Toast Points, Parmesan, '00 316
Toasts, Parmesan-Pepper, '98 242
Toasts, Tomato-Basil, '01 254
Toast Strips, Seasoned, '93 98
Whole Wheat Cardamom Bread, '86 223
Breakfast-in-a-Bowl, '89 87
Burritos, Hot Phyllo, '98 312
Cheese, Yogurt, '04 217
Chorizo, '92 241
Chutney, Blueberry, '95 190
Chutney, Fall Fruit, '97 218
Chutney, Green Tomato-Cranberry, '00 140
Chutney, Mango, '96 182
Chutney, Peach, '96 207
Chutney, Pear, '98 243
Couscous, Lemon, '02 237
Couscous with Mixed Fruit, '95 232
Crab Cakes, Country, '95 20
Cream, Lemon, '03 213
Crêpes, Basic, '86 38
Crêpes, Bran, '83 70; '86 44
Crêpes, Ham-and-Egg, '83 204
Crêpes, Light, '86 143
Crêpes, Low-Calorie, '87 77
Crêpes, Plain, '83 70
Crêpes, Whole Wheat, '83 70
Crisps, Parmesan, '01 197
Croutons, Bagel, '93 192
Croutons, Cornbread, '93 192
Croutons, Garlic, '92 71
Croutons, Pita, '93 192
Croutons, Spiced, '00 317
Crust, Whole Wheat, '94 78
Desserts
Alaska, Orange, '83 177
Alaska, Peachy Melba, '88 266
Ambrosia, Baked, '83 303
Ambrosia, Layered, '88 304
Apple Crisp, Tart, '92 226
Apples a l'Orange, Baked, '90 280
Applesauce Fluff, '91 173
Apples, Caramel-Peanut, '93 M244
Apples, Melting, '88 19
Bananas, Easy Tropical, '00 141
Bananas Foster, '88 20; '96 99
Bananas with Honey, Broiled, '84 175
Bananas with Rum Sauce, Spiced, '99 247
Bars, Apricot-Raisin, '87 32
Bars, Pineapple-Orange, '82 129
Bavarian Dessert, Light, '86 6
Berries, Best-Dressed, '96 317
Biscotti, Chocolate-Hazelnut, '95 80

Biscotti, Light, '91 310
Blackberries and Dumplings, '86 196
Blintzes, Cheese, '83 71
Blueberry Crisp, '84 177
Brownies, Chocolate-Kahlúa, '93 99
Brownies, Chocolate-Walnut, '89 325
Cake, Apple-Nut, '87 76
Cake, Apple Spice, '92 225
Cake, Banana-Coconut, '93 154
Cake, Black Widow Snack, '93 245
Cake, Blueberry Streusel, '92 144
Cake, Blue Ribbon Angel Food, '01 35
Cake, Chocolate Angel Food, '87 21; '90 111
Cake, Chocolate-Cinnamon, '93 154
Cake, Chocolate Custard, '88 175
Cake, Chocolate Pound, '89 325
Cake, Cinderella Fantasy, '98 70
Cake, Cinnamon Swirl, '01 255
Cake, Deluxe Light Banana, '84 314
Cake, Four-Flavor Pound, '91 136
Cake, Frosted Carrot, '92 19
Cake, German Chocolate Sheet, '03 147
Cake, Heavenly Pineapple, '83 303
Cake, Lemon-Poppy Seed, '93 154
Cake, Lightened Hummingbird, '01 34
Cake, Mocha Marble Pound, '99 23
Cake, Orange Angel Food, '96 246
Cake, Orange-Coconut Angel Food, '94 294
Cake, Orange Pound, '87 221
Cake, Pound, '92 94
Cake, Pumpkin, '93 303
Cake, Red Velvet, '93 318
Cake Roll, Lemon, '89 312
Cake Roll, Make-Ahead Chocolate-Mint, '95 220
Cakes, Creamy Lime, '04 89
Cake, Strawberry Yogurt Layer, '94 85
Cake, Warm Chocolate Pudding, '92 324
Cake, Winter Squash-Spice Bundt, '99 248
Cake with Amaretto-Almond Sauce, Angel Food,
'90 199
Cake with Coffee Frosting, Spice Layer, '94 86
Cake with Custard Sauce, Chocolate Angel Food,
'88 259
Cake with Pineapple-Orange Sauce, Angel,
'84 14
Cake with Raspberry Sauce, Sour Cream Pound,
'99 259
Cake with Strawberries and Chocolate Glaze,
White, '87 76
Cantaloupe Whip, '89 198
Cheesecake, Almost Strawberry, '86 32
Cheesecake, Black Forest, '94 21
Cheesecake, Blueberry Chiffon, '87 76
Cheesecake, Chocolate-Amaretto, '93 97
Cheesecake, Dieter's Apple, '86 318
Cheesecake, Fudge, '98 M213
Cheesecake, Lemon, '91 308
Cheesecake, Lemon Delight, '95 219
Cheesecake, Light-and-Easy, '88 55
Cheesecake, Strawberry-Lemon, '04 237
Cheesecakes with Raspberry Sauce, Mini Lemon,
'02 123
Cheesecake with Raspberry-Lemon Sauce, '96 30
Cherries Jubilite, '86 317
Chocolate-Bran Raisin Jumbos, '91 142
Chocolate-Cheese Cups, '91 142
Chocolate-Coffee Cones, '96 M316
Chocolate Cream Log, '94 220
Chocolate Cream Roll, '85 317
Chocolate Fondue, '91 142
Chocolate Glaze, '89 325
Chocolate-Orange Roll, '87 21
Chocolate Whip, '89 326
Chocolat, Petits Pots de, '82 272

Cobbler, Cranberry-and-Apple, '90 294
Cobbler, Fresh Cherry, '84 178
Cobbler, New-Fashioned Apple, '91 221
Cobbler, New-Fashioned Blackberry, '87 164
Cobbler, Peach, '84 178
Cobbler, Raspberry-Cherry, '93 230
Coffee Cake, Sour Cream, '93 154
Coffee Dessert, Light, '88 260
Compote, Apple-Cranberry, '04 237
Compote, Baked Fruit, '84 314
Compote, Fresh Fruit, '82 272; '84 82
Compote, Jicama-Fruit, '92 49
Compote, Melon Ball, '85 157
Compote, Spicy Grapefruit-Berry, '91 19
Compote with Caramel Syrup, Citrus, '98 313
Cookies, Almond, '91 51
Cookies, Apple-Oatmeal, '85 215
Cookies, Light Almond, '83 151
Cookies, Light Chocolate Chip, '86 46
Cookies, Meringue, '98 71
Cookies, Oatmeal-Raisin, '87 221; '93 127
Cookies, Sunshine Lemon, '86 69
Cookies, Vanilla Meringue, '01 197
Cranberries Jubilee, '90 293
Cream Puffs, Strawberry-Lemon, '87 75
Crêpes, Fruit-Filled Chocolate, '89 325
Crêpes Suzettes, Light, '83 71
Crêpes, Tropical Fruit, '87 77
Crust, Gingersnap, '90 296
Crust, Graham Cracker, '86 32; '88 55; '91 308
Crust, Lattice, '90 294
Custard, Baked Rice, '92 308
Custard, Baked Vanilla, '82 129
Custard, Coconut, '86 109
Custard, Light Mexican, '88 149
Custard over Fruit, Stirred, '84 83
Custard, Range-Top Amaretto, '87 77
Custard with Raspberries, Almond Crème,
  '88 174
De-Light-Ful Dessert, '95 220
Filling, Almond, '96 316
Filling, Chocolate, '96 316
Filling, Coffee, '96 316
Filling, Lemon, '89 312
Filling, Orange, '96 316
Flambé, Banana-Peach, '85 316
Flan, Luscious, '90 56
Flan, Pumpkin, '97 219
Frosting, Boiled, '93 318
Frosting, Coffee, '94 86
Frosting, Cream Cheese, '01 34
Frosting, Italian Meringue, '98 70
Frosting, Orange-Cream Cheese, '92 19
Fruitcake, Classic, '91 258
Fruitcake, Jeweled, '88 260
Fruit Cup, '91 202
Fruit Dessert, Caribbean, '84 314
Fruit Dessert, Flaming, '83 302
Fruit Dessert Orange, '84 314
Fruit Dessert, Rainbow, '85 108
Fruit Dessert, Spiced, '82 50
Fruit, Gingered, '83 151
Fruit, Glazed, '85 83
Fruit Medley, Fancy, '84 82
Fruit with Lemon Curd, Fresh, '88 21
Fruit with Mint-Balsamic Tea, Fresh, '95 232
Glaze, Lemon, '93 154
Glaze, Orange, '03 35
Honeydew-Berry Dessert, '83 120
Ice, Cranberry-Apple, '82 290
Ice-Cream Freeze, Two-Layered, '01 197
Ice Cream, Vanilla-Cinnamon, '00 127
Ice, Grapefruit, '91 122
Ice, Kiwi, '84 315

Ice Milk, Banana Yogurt, '89 199
Ice Milk, Fresh Strawberry, '92 94
Ice, Mixed Fruit, '88 85
Ice, Peach-Yogurt, '84 83
Ice, Pink Grapefruit, '85 304
Ice, Strawberry, '84 175; '85 108
Ice, Strawberry-Orange, '86 196
Ice, Tangy Cranberry, '87 305
Ice, Tart Cranberry-Orange, '86 317
Ice, Tropical, '99 105
Ice, Watermelon, '91 173
Kiwi Jubilee, '83 120
Lemon Angel Rolls with Raspberry Sauce,
  '94 294
Lemon Curd with Berries, '90 102
Lime Strips, Candied, '94 137
Lime Whip, '89 199
Mandelbrot, Rhoda's, '98 243
Melon Melange, '84 139
Melon-Mint Julep, '86 196
Meringue Mixture, Basic, '98 70
Meringue Mushrooms, '96 317
Meringue Shells, Fruited, '87 32
Meringues, Peach Melba, '87 76
Meringues, Tropical, '98 71
Meringues with Buttermilk Custard Sauce, Peach
  Melba, '96 183
Mocha Sauce with Chocolate Yogurt, '92 243
Mousse, Coffee-Nut, '86 319
Mousse, Peach, '85 54
Mousse, Strawberry-Lemon, '82 128
Orange-Mallow Cream, '94 295
Orange Molded Dessert, '83 302
Oranges and Pineapple, Glazed, '86 318
Parfait, Peach, '82 166
Parfait, Pineapple, '84 83
Pastry, Light, '92 95
Peach-Blueberry Dessert, '92 184
Peach Dessert, Spiced, '83 9
Peaches with Honey-Lime Whip, '85 108
Peaches with Nutty Dumplings, Spiced, '87 164
Peaches with Strawberry Sauce, '85 8
Peach Halves, Stuffed, '86 196
Pear Fans with Raspberry-Orange Sauce,
  Poached, '88 22
Pears Baked in Molasses-Port Sauce, '97 195
Pears in Custard, Poached, '88 20
Pears in Orange Sauce, Poached, '82 19
Pears Poached in Red Wine, '83 302
Pears, Vanilla Poached, '90 57
Pears with Berry Sauce, Wine-Poached, '86 144
Pears with Honey-Yogurt Sauce, Poached, '92 306
Pears with Meringue, Amaretto, '90 M58
Pie, Buttermilk, '92 95
Pie, Chocolate Bavarian, '89 326
Pie, Eggnog, '83 205
Pie, Fresh Apple, '84 178
Pie, Frozen Chocolate Brownie, '96 57
Pie, Fruited Cheese, '92 228
Pie, New-Fashioned Pumpkin, '90 296
Pie, Orange Cream, '03 35
Pineapple, Meringue-Topped, '84 178
Pineapple with Raspberry Sauce, Chocolate-
  Drizzled, '90 57
Pineapple with Vanilla-Cinnamon Ice Cream,
  Grilled, '00 127
Plum Slush, '84 139
Pops, Orange-Banana, '82 129
Pops, Pineapple-Yogurt, '91 173
Praline Horns, '96 316
Prune Bavarian, '86 223
Pudding, Almost Banana, '88 174
Pudding, Apple-Raisin Bread, '88 175
Pudding, Banana, '03 24

Pudding, Chocolate-Almond, '88 24
Pudding, Chocolate-Almond Silk, '96 266
Pudding, Layered Lemon, '82 128
Pudding, Lemon Cake, '92 96
Pudding, Lemon Fluff, '85 304
Pudding, Light Plum, '86 318
Pudding, Old-Fashioned Banana, '92 94
Pudding, Old-Fashioned Bread, '88 175
Pudding, Orange Custard, '88 174
Pudding, Peachy Bread, '88 175
Pudding, Raisin-Pumpkin, '84 315
Pudding, Russian Blueberry-Raspberry, '97 128
Pudding with Whiskey Sauce, Bread, '90 230
Pumpkin Chiffon, '86 283; '88 260
Quesadillas, Apple, '99 248
Raspberry Fluff, '89 198
Raspberry-Pear Crisp, '89 109
Rice Cream with Mandarin Oranges, '85 317
Rice Custard, Baked, '92 308
Roulage, Frozen Chocolate, '90 56
Salsa with Cinnamon Crisps, Fruit, '01 108
Sauce, Buttermilk Custard, '96 183
Sauce, Chocolate, '90 57
Sauce, Creamy Light Coconut, '82 177
Sauce, Custard, '88 259
Sauce, Golden, '88 267
Sauce, Honey-Orange, '85 108
Sauce, Honey-Yogurt, '92 307
Sauce, Mango, '83 120
Sauce, Melba, '87 77
Sauce, Pineapple-Orange, '84 14
Sauce, Raspberry, '88 267; '93 99; '94 295;
  '96 183; '99 259; '02 123
Sauce, Raspberry-Orange, '88 22
Sauce, Rum-Raisin, '94 295
Sauce, Special Hard, '86 318
Sauce, Spicy Apple Dessert, '82 177
Sauce, Whiskey, '90 230
Sherbet, Blueberry, '04 283
Sherbet, Easy Pineapple, '92 199
Sherbet, Fresh Mint, '88 23
Sherbet, Instant Fruit, '85 158
Sherbet, Lemon, '91 309
Sherbet, Nectarine, '89 199
Sherbet, Peach, '90 179
Sherbet, Pineapple, '84 83; '89 199
Sherbet, Watermelon, '92 124
Shortcake, Strawberry, '92 184
Sorbet, Blackberry-Lemon, '02 85
Sorbet, Blueberry-Kirsch, '83 120
Sorbet, Fresh Orange, '92 143
Sorbet, Mango, '86 196
Sorbet, Pink Grapefruit and Tarragon, '95 163
Sorbet, Strawberry-Champagne, '95 20
Soufflé, Baked Apricot, '88 267
Soufflé, Light Chocolate, '83 278
Soufflé, Orange Dessert, '83 206
Soufflé, Raspberry-Topped, '85 317
Soufflé, Tart Lemon, '85 82
Spumoni and Berries, '91 204
Strawberries Juliet, '84 82
Strawberries Marsala, '88 171
Strawberries 'n' Cream, '90 30
Strawberry Cups, Frozen, '91 173
Strawberry Dessert, Glazed, '84 33
Strawberry Dessert, Summer, '92 143
Strawberry Puff, '82 5
Strawberry Whip, '89 198
Strawberry-Yogurt Dessert, '90 295
Tapioca Fluff, Orange, '87 31
Tart, Fancy Fruit, '82 128
Tart, Fresh Fruit, '84 178; '90 58
Tart, Green Grape, '87 77
Tart, Kiwifruit-Peach, '88 20

Tartlets, Fresh Fruit, '93 96
Tart, Pear, '92 72
Tarts, Cran-Raspberry Meringue, '92 286
Tart Shell, '87 77; '88 20
Tarts, Orange, '96 317
Tiramisù, '94 295; '02 285
Topping, Blueberry, '87 125
Topping, Cherry-Pineapple, '87 126
Topping, Chunky Piña Colada, '87 125
Topping, Raspberry, '85 317
Topping, Raspberry-Peach, '87 126
Topping, Reduced-Calorie Whipped, '85 55
Topping, Spicy Apple, '87 125
Topping, Strawberry, '86 32
Topping, Strawberry-Banana, '87 125
Torte, Apricot Sponge, '90 59
Torte, Chocolate Mint, '94 86
Torte, Triple Chocolate, '96 58
Tortoni, Apricot-Yogurt, '95 124
Trifle, All Seasons Lemon, '95 219
Trifle, Angel Food, '91 184
Trifle, Olde English, '95 331
Trifle, Raspberry, '88 259
Trifle, Tropical, '95 204
Truffles, Chocolate-Kahlúa, '92 285
Wafers, Cinnamon, '84 324
Watermelon Frost, '86 196
Yogurt, Frozen Fresh Peach, '90 139
Yogurt, Lemon-Chiffon Frozen, '85 54
Yogurt, Vanilla Frozen, '87 125
Di-Calcium Phosphate Solution, '89 138
Dressing, Creamy Lime, '04 46
Dressing, Light Cornbread, '92 324
Dressing, Savory Cornbread, '88 303
Eggs and Omelets
Benedict, Eggs, '85 49
Benedict, Light Eggs, '93 M68
Florentine, Eggs, '83 56
Garden Omelet, '99 174
Italian Omelet, '92 47
Primavera, Omelet, '87 71
Roulade with Mushroom Filling, Egg, '88 84
Scrambled Eggs, Mexican-Style, '85 50
Scrambled Eggs, Spanish, '84 60
Substitute, Homemade Egg, '92 47
Vegetable Omelet, Cheddar-, '83 205
Vegetable Omelet, Cheesy, '85 49
Enchiladas, Three-Bean, '91 133
Fettuccine and Spinach, '88 90
Fettuccine Primavera, '89 238
Filling, Chicken Salad, '87 106
Filling, Mushroom, '88 84
Filling, Shrimp Salad, '87 106
Fruit Kebabs, Winter, '89 34
Fruit Medley, Chilled, '84 60
Fruit, Minted Marinated, '92 138
Fruit Nuggets, Dried, '86 326
Fruit-on-a-Pick, '90 179
Fruit, Warm Spiced, '86 39
Fruit with Lemon-Yogurt Dressing, Fresh, '93 17
Glaze, Cranberry-Honey, '89 273
Glaze, Teriyaki, '94 82
Gnocchi with Olive Oil, Tomato, and Parmesan, '04 47
Granola, Mixed Fruit, '01 290
Grapefruit, Broiled, '85 7
Grits, Baked Cheese, '01 289
Grits, Cheese, '90 102
Grits, Garlic-and-Herb Cheese, '95 122
Guacamole, Mock, '93 36

Ham-and-Cheese Lettuce Rolls, '89 217
Jam, Berry Refrigerator, '89 139
Jam, Blackberry, '89 138
Jam, Blueberry Refrigerator, '89 139
Jam, Plum Refrigerator, '89 139
Jam, Strawberry, '89 138
Jelly, Crabapple, '89 139
Jelly, Grape, '89 140
Kielbasa, '92 242
Lentils, Bean Pot, '01 35
Lentils, Tangy Marinated, '00 94
Linguine with Garlic and Lemon, '88 91
Linguine with Green Beans and Walnut Sauce, '04 128
Linguine with Red Pepper Sauce, '93 127
Low Sodium
Applesauce, Spicy, '82 296
Asparagus with Basil Sauce, '86 33
Beef and Rice, Spicy, '83 231
Beef Burgundy, '83 281
Beef Goulash, '83 231
Beef Roast, French-Style, '89 32
Biscuits, Flaky, '84 228
Bread, Bran-Applesauce, '84 229
Bread, Salt-Free Raisin Batter, '86 33
Breadsticks, Whole Wheat, '84 228
Brussels Sprouts, Calico Citrus, '85 303
Butter, Herbed Unsalted, '82 67
Carrots Madeira, '83 281
Catsup, Spicy Tomato, '83 182
Cereal Snack, Toasted, '85 215
Chicken à l'Orange, '84 277
Chicken-and-Vegetables, Stir-Fry, '86 68
Chicken, Citrus-Herb Baked, '85 303
Chicken, Creole, '89 33
Chicken Dinner, Healthful, '83 232
Chicken, Herb-Baked, '82 229
Chicken in Lemon and Wine, '83 281
Chicken Piccata, '83 35
Chicken-Tomato Bake, '83 35
Chicken with Wine-Soaked Vegetables, Baked, '84 277
Chili Surprise, '82 229
Cookies, Sunshine Lemon, '86 69
Cornish Hens in Vermouth, '86 33
Cornish Hens, Roasted Rock, '82 66
Dressing, Basil, '88 24
Dressing, Lemon-Herb Salad, '82 67
Dressing, Orange-Yogurt, '85 304
Fish, Curried Baked, '87 5
Flank Steak, Marinated, '83 35
Flounder Rolls, Vegetable-Stuffed, '87 6
Flounder, Sesame, '89 33
Fruit Delight, Hot, '83 281
Fruit Delight, Spiced, '82 229
Fruit, Unsweetened Mixed, '83 182
Green Beans, Minted, '84 104
Ice, Pink Grapefruit, '85 304
Jam, Banana, '82 296
Jam, Freezer Peach, '83 182
Lamb Chops, Dijon, '84 277
Lamb Chops, Orange, '83 35
Linguine with Seafood Sauce, '83 232
Meat Loaf, Corny, '86 68
Meat Loaf, Parsleyed, '83 35
Mocha-Cocoa Mix, Hot, '82 296
Mousse, Orange, '86 69
Muffins, Honey-Oatmeal, '84 229
Muffins, Spiced Bran, '84 229
Mustard, Lower Sodium Horseradish, '86 325
Nectarines in Apple Juice, '83 183
Onions, Glazed, '84 104
Pastry Shell, Sesame, '82 67
Peppers, Corn Stuffed, '84 104

Pie, Nutty Pumpkin, '82 67
Pork, Roast Loin of, '84 276
Pork Tenderloin with Brown Sauce, Grilled, '89 32
Potato Bake, Chive-, '82 229
Potatoes, Yogurt-Stuffed, '88 24
Pretzels with Lower Sodium Horseradish Mustard, Herb, '86 325
Pudding, Chocolate-Almond, '88 24
Pudding, Lemon Fluff, '85 304
Ratatouille, '84 105
Rice and Shrimp, Curried, '83 231
Rice, Calico Brown, '86 33
Rolls, Low-Sodium Refrigerator, '82 67
Rolls, Low-Sodium Yeast, '84 228
Salad, Asparagus-and-New Potato, '86 69
Salad, Citrus Green, '85 304
Salad, Dilled Cucumber, '82 229
Salad Mold, Golden Citrus, '85 303
Salad, Mushroom-and-Pepper, '86 68
Salad, Sesame-Citrus Green, '86 33
Salmon, Poached, '83 35
Salmon Steaks, Marinated, '87 6
Sauce, Apple-Horseradish, '82 229
Sauce, Brown, '89 32
Sauce, Green Herb, '83 36
Sauce, Seafood, '83 36
Scallops, Sherried, '83 281
Scampi, Orange, '85 303
Scamp, Tangy Broiled, '87 5
Seasoning Blend, '82 296
Shake, Pineapple-Banana, '85 215
Shrimp Kebabs, Marinated, '84 276
Shrimp, Special Boiled, '83 36
Snapper, Caribbean, '87 5
Snapper, Orangy, '88 23
Soup, Chunky Chicken-Noodle, '88 12
Soup, Chunky Mushroom, '88 12
Soup, Cream of Cauliflower, '88 12
Soup, Spicy Vegetable-Beef, '88 11
Squash Sauté, '82 67
Squash, Vegetable-Stuffed, '84 104
Stew, Cajun-Style Catfish, '88 12
Stew, White Wine, '82 228
Stuffing, Low-Sodium, '82 66
Swordfish, Foil-Baked, '87 5
Tomatoes, Stewed, '83 182
Tomato Puree, Seasoned, '83 182
Tropical Snow, '86 34
Veal, Savory, '83 281
Veal Spaghetti, '84 276
Vegetable Stir-Fry, '84 104
Waffles, Whole Wheat, '84 228
Zucchini, Herbed, '84 104
Zucchini with Baby Carrots, '88 24
Macaroni and Cheese, Baked, '82 199
Macaroni with Pesto, Whole Wheat, '89 238
Main Dishes
Asparagus Roulade, '86 102
Beans and Rice, Red, '90 27
Beans and Rice, Smoky Kidney, '03 290
Beans with Coconut Milk, Spicy, '03 175
Beef, American Steakhouse, '93 15
Beef-and-Barley Rolls, Wine-Sauced, '87 269
Beef and Cauliflower over Rice, '93 94
Beef-and-Rice Dinner, Mexican, '88 199
Beef and Vegetables, Company, '88 234
Beef-and-Vegetable Stir-Fry, '87 22; '99 204
Beef, Bean, and Cornbread Casserole, '99 215
Beef Burgundy, '88 25
Beef Chimichangas, Oven-Fried, '92 124
Beef, Chinese-Style, '87 50
Beef Fajitas, '88 233
Beef Fillets with Black Bean Sauce, Spicy, '97 184

Beef Fillets with Green Peppercorn Sauce, '02 285
Beef Hash, '95 24
Beef Kebabs, Chile-, '94 251
Beef Kebabs, Spirited, '87 142
Beef Kebabs with Rice, Marinated, '84 32
Beef, Marinated Sauerbraten, '93 16
Beef Medaillons, Italian, '87 305
Beef Patties, Deviled-, '87 22
Beef Stir-Fry, Chinese, '83 151
Beef Stroganoff, '91 134
Beef Stroganoff, Light, '86 36
Beef Tenderloin Bundles, Peppered, '89 272
Beef Tenderloin for Two, '90 295
Beef Tenderloin Steaks with Peperonata, '97 291
Beef with Asparagus, '90 100
Beef with Ginger, '03 64
Black Beans and Rice, '91 82
Black Beans and Yellow Rice, Easy, '92 308
Burgers, Barbecued, '89 164
Burgers, Beefy Vegetable, '98 143
Burgers, Black Bean, '98 144
Burgers, Favorite, '89 165
Burgers, Lentil, '95 123
Burgers, Mushroom, '89 164; '97 101
Burgers, Pizza, '89 165
Burgers, Salmon, '98 144
Burgers, Seasoned, '85 158
Burgers, Triple-Layer, '89 165
Burgers, Vegetable, '89 164
Burgers, Walnut, '89 163
Burgers with Caramelized Onions, Beef, '98 143
Burgers with Sprouts, '89 164
Burgers with Tahini Sauce, Gyro, '03 183
Burritos, Cheesy Beef, '85 193
Burritos, Tony's Veggie, '96 289
Burritos, Vegetable, '90 134; '92 138
Cabbage Rolls, Stuffed, '88 18
Cannelloni, '92 17
Carne Guisada, '94 219
Casserole, Bean-and-Cornbread, '92 243
Casserole, Breakfast, '91 285
Casserole, Chicken, Orzo, and Spinach, '02 124
Casserole, Chiles Rellenos, '92 18
Casserole, Crab-and-Mushroom, '89 96
Casserole, Creamy Chicken-and-Rice, '02 309
Casserole, Freezer Eggplant-Sausage-Pasta, '95 197
Casserole, Low-Fat Spaghetti, '99 215
Casserole, Southwestern, '99 216
Casserole, Turkey-and-Shrimp Florentine, '92 122
Catfish, Baked, '94 67
Catfish, Lime-Orange, '02 22
Catfish, Oven-Fried, '95 106; '99 174
Catfish, Parmesan, '92 309
Catfish, Southern Oven-Fried, '87 163
Catfish with Creole Sauce, Breaded, '90 28
Catfish with Lemon Cream, Spicy "Fried," '03 212
Chicken à la King, '94 41
Chicken, Almond, '01 26
Chicken and Dumplings, '03 25
Chicken and Dumplings, Old-Fashioned, '93 302
Chicken and Leeks in Parchment, '97 290
Chicken and Rice, Spicy, '88 200
Chicken and Rice, Sweet-and-Sour, '03 97
Chicken and Spinach Noodles, '82 19
Chicken and Vegetables, Ginger-Poached, '98 229
Chicken and Vegetables, Stir-Fry, '86 249
Chicken and Vegetables, Walnut, '85 194
Chicken and Vegetables with Ginger-Soy Sauce, '91 32
Chicken-Apple Sauté, '97 48

Chicken, Asparagus, and Mushrooms with Penne Pasta, '98 212
Chicken, Baked Honey, '99 110
Chicken Bake, Individual, '90 279
Chicken Breast in Wine, Poached, '91 184
Chicken Breasts, Hawaiian Stuffed, '99 64
Chicken Breasts, Lime-Roasted, '97 100
Chicken Breasts Sardou, Stuffed, '87 269
Chicken Breasts, Wine-Baked, '83 177
Chicken Breasts with Fruited Rice Pilaf, '92 307
Chicken Breasts with Orange-Ginger Sauce, '97 47
Chicken, Buttermilk Oven-Fried, '03 213
Chicken Cacciatore, '86 42
Chicken Cakes with Creole Sauce, '02 284
Chicken Chili Bake, '93 302
Chicken, Chutney, '86 249
Chicken Cordon Bleu, '86 37; '93 126
Chicken, Creamed, '82 49
Chicken, Creamy Tomato-Stuffed, '04 16
Chicken Croquettes and Mushroom Sauce, '91 220
Chicken, Crunchy Oven-Fried, '87 163
Chicken, Curried, '86 43
Chicken Curry, Stir-Fried, '87 51
Chicken Cutlets with Lemon, '85 8
Chicken, Dante's, '88 25
Chicken Dinner, Skillet, '86 249
Chicken Drumsticks, Breaded, '99 110
Chicken Enchiladas, '90 121
Chicken Fingers, Herb-Baked, '86 249
Chicken Fingers, No-Fry-Pan, '91 120
Chicken Fingers with Honey-Horseradish Dip, '02 308
Chicken-Fried Wild Rice, '91 132
Chicken Gumbo, '90 26
Chicken, Honey-Pecan, '03 147
Chicken in a Bag, '87 23
Chicken in Foil, '91 134
Chicken in Orange Sauce, '83 8
Chicken in Phyllo, Cheesy, '02 308
Chicken Kebabs, Sesame, '82 165
Chicken Kiev, Oven-Baked, '86 37
Chicken la France, '86 248
Chicken Lasagna, '88 90
Chicken-Leek Terrine, Cold, '92 145
Chicken, Lemon-Frosted, '88 170
Chicken, Lemon-Mustard, '99 109
Chicken, Lemon-Roasted, '95 24
Chicken Marengo, '92 70
Chicken Marsala, '89 237
Chicken, Orange, '83 278
Chicken, Oven-Fried, '93 90
Chicken Paprika, Dilled, '86 41
Chicken Pasta with Artichokes and Capers, '04 129
Chicken, Pineapple, '83 M194
Chicken Pot Pie, '94 21
Chicken-Rice Casserole, '99 215
Chicken Rolls, Spinach-Stuffed, '86 248
Chicken, Salsa Rice and, '99 109
Chicken, Savory Roasted, '98 21
Chicken, Sicilian, '97 142
Chicken, Southern Oven-Fried, '86 37
Chicken Spaghetti, '87 221
Chicken Stir-Fry, Apple-Sesame-, '92 226
Chicken Stir-Fry, Chinese, '90 100
Chicken Strips and Vegetables, Marinated, '90 110
Chicken, Sweet-and-Sour, '91 202
Chicken Thighs, Sweet Glazed, '04 202
Chicken Twice-Baked Potatoes, Buffalo, '04 184
Chicken Tostadas, '95 122
Chicken-Vegetable Stir-Fry, '83 151; '84 13

Chicken, Whole Poached, '98 229
Chicken Wings, Maple-Glazed, '99 110
Chicken with Artichoke Hearts, '88 54
Chicken with Artichokes, Sherried, '87 143
Chicken with Black Bean Puree, Spicy, '97 48
Chicken with Black Beans and Oranges, '00 94
Chicken with Broccoli, Spicy Ginger-and-Orange, '02 309
Chicken with Grilled Pineapple, Lime, '04 88
Chicken with Mole Sauce, '93 34
Chicken with Mushroom Sauce, '99 22
Chicken with Orange, Lime, and Ginger Sauce, '92 123
Chicken with Pineapple, Oriental, '86 42
Chicken with Pineapple Salsa, Sesame-Crusted, '96 226
Chicken with Prunes, Saffron, '97 264
Chicken with Roasted Potato Thins, Apricot, '02 23
Chicken with Salsa, Baked Chile, '88 147
Chicken with Spinach Fettuccine, Easy, '88 89
Chicken with Tabbouleh Salad, Grilled, '91 70
Chicken with Tomato-Basil Pasta, Basil-Stuffed, '94 M204
Chicken with Vegetables, Stir-Fry, '96 128
Chicken with Wild Rice, Orange-Glazed Roasted, '02 85
Chiles Rellenos, Light, '93 156
Chiles Rellenos with Tomatillo Sauce, Roasted, '94 203
Chile Verde, Light, '88 148
Chili, '93 89
Chili, Firestarter, '93 34
Chili, Hot Venison, '91 283
Chili, South-of-the-Border, '91 283
Chili, Southwestern, '91 284
Chili, Vegetarian, '91 284
Chili, White, '91 284
Cornbread-Tamale Pie, '92 123
Cornish Hens, Herbed, '82 271
Cornish Hens, Mesquite-Smoked, '92 144
Cornish Hens, Orange-Glazed Grilled, '86 250
Cornish Hens with Vegetables, Tarragon Roasted, '94 79
Crab-and-Shrimp Étouffée, '89 96
Crab Burgers, '00 58
Crab Cakes, '91 122
Crabmeat au Gratin, '86 154
Cracked Wheat, "Fried,", '89 31
Crawfish Étouffée, '86 156
Crawfish Fettuccine, '96 98
Crêpes, Cannelloni, '86 143
Crêpes, Chicken-Vegetable, '83 70
Eggplant Parmesan, '92 18
Eggplant Parmesan with Feta, '03 174
Enchiladas, Spicy Bean, '88 18
Fajita Fettuccine, '94 84
Fajita in a Pita, '90 177
Fajitas, Java, '96 227
Fajitas, Turkey, '01 108
Fettuccine and Shrimp with Dried Tomato Pesto, '94 249
Fettuccine, Ham-and-Asparagus, '94 84
Fettuccine Primavera, '94 85
Fettuccine, Shrimp, '94 84
Filet Mignon with Mushroom Sauce, '94 250
Fillets, Apple-Carrot Stuffed, '88 M192
Fillets Tomatillo, '94 135
Fish and Vegetables, Steamed, '91 32
Fish, Caribbean Banana, '95 202
Fish Dinner, Skillet, '88 199
Fish Fillets, Breaded Herbed, '91 121
Fish Florentine, '86 35
Fish Florentine in Parchment, '87 22

HEALTHY & LIGHT, Main Dishes
(continued)

Fish with Greek Sauce, Poached, '91 M183
Flank Steak, Grilled, '03 146
Flank Steak, Grilled Marinated, '97 182
Flank Steak Sukiyaki, '88 233
Flank Steak with Black Bean-and-Corn Salsa, Grilled, '94 80
Flank Steak with Molasses Barbecue Glaze, Grilled, '00 59
Flank Steak with Noodles, Stuffed, '90 101
Flank Steak with Sweet Peppers, Grilled, '90 138
Flounder, Creole-Style, '85 180
Flounder Rolls with Citrus Sauce, Stuffed, '85 180
Frijoles Rancheros, '88 148
Frittata, Vegetable, '92 48
Game Hens with Chutney-Mustard Glaze, '93 66
Goulash, Hungarian, '92 227
Grits-and-Ham Pie, Crustless, '86 103
Grouper, Grilled Marinated, '90 166
Grouper, Hot Spicy, '94 78
Haddock Fillets with Zucchini Stuffing, '88 M191
Halibut Steaks Italiano, '88 M191
Halibut with Champagne Sauce, Baked, '90 29
Halibut with Swiss Sauce, '83 M195
Hamburger Pie, '84 13
Ham, Pineapple-Glazed, '01 288
Ham-Potato-Pineapple Bake, '93 302
Ham with Cranberry-Honey Glaze, Baked, '89 273
Hopping John with Grilled Pork Medaillons, '93 229
Jambalaya, '90 26
Jambalaya, Black-Eyed Pea, '92 70
Jambalaya, Chicken-and-Sausage, '88 200
Jambalaya, Red Rice, '91 18
Kebabs, Hawaiian, '85 157
Lamb Chops, Broiled, '85 22
Lamb Chops, Joan's Rosemary, '97 42
Lamb Chops, Peppercorn-Crusted, '92 142
Lamb Chops, Smart and Saucy Rosemary-Cherry, '02 193
Lamb Chops with Herbs, '90 164
Lamb Chops with Rosemary Sauce and Wild Rice-Fennel Pilaf, Grilled, '97 127
Lamb Curry, Creamy, '04 202
Lamb with Five Spices, Stewed, '92 72
Lasagna, Cheesy Spinach, '83 204; '01 196
Lasagna, Creamy Ham-and-Chicken, '95 88
Lasagna in a Bun, '90 176
Lasagna, Lean, '86 37
Lasagna, Light, '95 212
Lasagna, Spinach-Bean, '92 96
Lasagna, Vegetable, '84 201; '99 97
Lasagna with Cream Sauce, Polenta, '03 237
Lasagna, Won Ton Spinach, '04 129
Lasagna, Zucchini, '85 194
Lentil-and-Rice Supper, '84 202
Lentils-and-Rice Casserole, '93 301
Linguine with Clam Sauce, '88 90
Liver, Creole, '86 108
Liver in Creole Sauce, '87 33
Lobster Tails with Spiced Orange Sauce, '86 155
London Broil, Marinated, '87 32
Mackerel, Rosemary-Garlic, '92 200
Manicotti, Creamy Chipotle, '03 96
Manicotti, Spinach, '82 199
Meat and Potatoes, Italian-Style, '03 97
Meatballs and Vegetables with Horseradish Dressing, '91 32
Meatballs, Red Sauce and, '04 17

Meat Loaf, '89 109
Meat Loaf, Curried, '86 43
Meat Loaf, Oriental, '83 M194
Meat Loaf, Parsley, '87 22
Meat Loaf, Summer, '01 162
Meat Loaves, Individual, '00 214
Migas, '98 312
Orange Roughy-and-Vegetable Stir-Fry, '91 50
Orange Roughy, Pesto-Crusted, '96 156
Orange Roughy, Vegetable-Topped, '93 67
Orange Roughy with Herbs, Steamed, '95 189
Orange Roughy with Spinach Pesto, '88 M192
Pasta, Creamy Turkey-Basil, '89 216
Pasta, Mamma Mia, '95 25
Pasta Primavera, Almost, '86 38
Pasta Salad, Main-Dish, '82 199
Pasta, Vegetable Stir-Fry, '96 29
Pasta Verde, '84 201
Pasta with Beans and Greens, '02 202
Pasta with Fennel, '98 46
Pasta with Peanut Sauce, '95 252
Pastichio, '85 194
Peppers Stuffed with Shrimp-and-Orzo Salad, '91 203
Perch, Parmesan-Crusted, '93 91
Picadillo, Lettuce-Wrapped, '03 193
Pie, Italian Meat, '89 109
Pizza, Breakfast, '90 178
Pizza, Chicken-and-Purple Onion, '97 47
Pizza, Fresh Mozzarella and Basil, '04 58
Pizza, Garden, '89 108
Pizza, Portobello, '03 175
Pizza, Quick 3-Cheese, '00 94
Pizzas, Veggie, '99 97
Pizzas, Veggie Sausage, '00 294
Pizza, Turkey-Vegetable, '90 139
Pizza, Vegetable, '94 218
Pizza, Veggie, '94 78
Pizza, Whole Wheat, '84 33
Polenta with Black Bean Salsa, Grilled, '93 155
Pollock with Summer Squash Relish, '92 200
Pork-and-Noodles Skillet Dinner, '88 199
Pork, Cajun Pecan, '01 27
Pork, Chinese Roast, '91 308
Pork Chop Dinner, '88 25
Pork Chops, An Apple-a-Day, '01 35
Pork Chops, Apricot-Sauced, '85 22
Pork Chops, Creole-Style, '91 49
Pork Chops, Fruit-Topped, '94 41
Pork Chops, Honey-Lime, '91 33
Pork Chops in Gravy, '91 137
Pork Chops with Cream Gravy, Fried, '03 24
Pork Chops with Tangy Barbecue Sauce, '99 104
Pork Chops with Warm Pineapple Salsa, '02 144
Pork Chops with White Bean Puree, '96 226
Pork Chow Mein, '90 101
Pork, Cranberry, '90 293
Pork Loin, Braised Tuscan, '04 202
Pork Loin Roast, Barbecued, '93 34
Pork Medaillons, Grilled, '93 229
Pork Medaillons with Port Wine and Dried Cranberry Sauce, '95 330
Pork, Oven-Roasted Vegetables and, '99 259
Pork Roast, Barbecued, '03 147
Pork Roast, Orange-Glazed, '04 M236
Pork Roast, Oven-Barbecued, '91 50
Pork Roast, Stuffed Crown, '89 272
Pork, Stir-Fried, '87 51
Pork, Sweet-and-Sour, '85 34, 194
Pork Tacos with Pineapple Salsa, '03 128
Pork Tenderloin, Apple-Mushroom, '95 53
Pork Tenderloin, Honey-Mustard, '95 52
Pork Tenderloin, Marinated, '84 175
Pork Tenderloin, Molasses-Grilled, '96 265

Pork Tenderloin, Sesame, '95 53
Pork Tenderloins, Fruit-Stuffed, '87 270
Pork Tenderloin, Spinach-and-Bacon Stuffed, '94 81
Pork Tenderloin with Apples, Celery, and Potatoes, Grilled, '95 161
Pork Tenderloin with Fruit Stuffing and Shiitake Sauce, '97 218
Pork Tenderloin with Lime and Chipotle, Sweet, '04 184
Pork Tenderloin with Molasses Sauce, Grilled, '97 193
Pork Tenderloin with Orange Marmalade, '91 49
Pork Tenderloin with Parmesan-Pepper Toasts, Herbed, '98 242
Pork Tenderloin with Yogurt and Lime, Grilled, '04 216
Pork with Garlic, Sweet, '04 17
Quesadillas, Breakfast Sausage, '04 183
Potatoes, Breakfast-Stuffed, '00 179
Pot Roast, Marinated, '85 21
Quail with Mushroom Gravy, Baked, '89 273
Quesadillas, Chicken-and-Black Bean, '96 288
Quesadillas, Quick, '89 87
Quesadillas, Shrimp-and-Roasted Pepper, '00 215
Quiche, Crustless Veggie Sausage, '03 175
Quiche, Eggless, '87 220
Quiche, Fiesta, '92 47
Quiches, Individual Spinach, '86 38
Quiche, Spinach, '85 49; '91 204
Quiche, Swiss-Zucchini, '82 49
Ravioli, Mediterranean, '93 301
Red Beans and Couscous, '99 22
Red Snapper, Blackened, '90 27
Red Snapper Rolls, Cucumber-Stuffed, '83 176
Red Snapper Veracruz, '88 149; '92 142
Rice-and-Lentil Pilaf, '88 17
Rice, Dirty, '03 147
Risotto with Vegetables, '98 193
Roast Beef, Deli-Style, '93 15
Roast, Roasted Lime-Cilantro Eye of Round, '04 88
Salmon Burgers, '95 24
Salmon Fillets, Cracked Pepper, '00 140
Salmon Fillets with Red Wine Garlic Sauce, '94 250
Salmon in Parchment, '95 311
Salmon Loaf with Cucumber-Dill Sauce, '86 5
Salmon-Pesto Vermicelli, '92 200
Salmon Steaks with Tarragon Sauce, Grilled, '97 42
Salmon with Ginger Vinaigrette, Sesame-Crusted, '95 162
Salmon with Horseradish Sauce, Poached, '91 183
Salmon with Lemon and Olive Oil, Broiled, '04 46
Salmon with Stir-Fried Vegetables, Glazed, '02 69
Salmon with Yellow Pepper Sauce, Poached, '98 230
Sausage, Dieters' Spicy, '85 49
Scallop Kebabs, Grilled, '83 101
Scallops, Grilled Sweet-and-Sour, '01 92
Scallops in Vegetable Nests, '91 70
Scallops with Cilantro-Lime Vinaigrette, Grilled Orange, '94 77
Scallops with Orange-Ginger Sauce, Sesame-Crusted, '97 125
Scallops with Tomato-Mango Salsa, Seared, '95 122
Scramble, Veggie, '01 288
Shells, Spinach-Stuffed, '99 64
Shrimp and Pasta, Sautéed, '96 288
Shrimp-and-Vegetable Medley Stir-Fry, '99 205

Shrimp, Barbecued, '90 28
Shrimp, Beer-Broiled, '87 142
Shrimp Cancun en Papillote, '91 136
Shrimp Enchiladas in Tomatillo Sauce, '95 310
Shrimp Étouffée, '90 229
Shrimp Fettuccine, '94 84
Shrimp, Grilled Sweet-and-Sour, '97 100
Shrimp Rémoulade, '03 146
Shrimp Risotto, '00 95; '02 124
Shrimp Skillet, Quick, '87 50
Shrimp, Stir-Fry, '96 129
Shrimp, Sweet-and-Sour, '83 278
Shrimp with Citrus Salsa, Grilled, '97 141
Shrimp with Cranberry-Citrus Salsa, Sautéed,
    '97 290
Shrimp with Onion and Red Pepper, Sweet-and-
    Sour, '02 84
Shrimp with Orange Dipping Sauce, Coconut-
    Pecan, '03 212
Shrimp with Orzo, Fire-Roasted, '99 42
Shrimp with Pasta, Asian, '04 128
Shrimp with Peanut Sauce, '93 303
Shrimp with Roasted Red Pepper Cream, '03 97
Shrimp with Yogurt-Cucumber Sauce, '04 216
Sirloin in Vodka Sauce, '03 96
Sirloin, Mustard Marinated, '94 41
Sirloin Steaks with Thyme Pesto, '97 182
Sirloin with Zesty Corn Salsa, Cilantro-Garlic,
    '02 193
Snapper à l'Orange, Baked, '85 181
Snapper, Honey-Curried, '85 181
Snapper, Poached, '83 101
Snapper with Creamy Dill Sauce, Peppered,
    '94 42
Snow Peas and Red Pepper, Sesame, '84 175
Sole Divan, '87 21
Sole Véronique, '85 181
Spaghetti and Meatballs, White, '03 34
Spaghetti, Meaty, '82 19
Spinach-and-Cheese Calzones, '95 310
Steak au Poivre, '88 232
Steak Diane, '92 306
Steak, Fast-and-Easy Stir-Fried, '87 50
Steak in Red Wine Sauce, Skillet, '85 21
Steak, Italian-Stuffed, '88 232
Steak Kebabs, '82 4; '93 95
Steak lo Mein, '90 100
Steak, Marinated, '88 233
Steak, Mexican Marinated, '88 148
Steak, Mock Country-Fried, '87 163
Steak, Pepper-Beef, '85 21
Stew, Burgundy Beef, '88 234
Stir-Fry, Curried Beef, '01 162
Stroganoff, Creamy Beef, '02 124
Swordfish, Mediterranean, '02 237
Swordfish-Shiitake Skewers, '97 168
Swordfish Stir-Fry, '96 128
Swordfish with Avocado-Lime Sauce, Grilled,
    '97 127
Swordfish with Caper Sauce, Grilled, '95 230
Tacoritos, '90 133
Tacos, Jerk Steak, '01 170
Tacos, Loaded Veggie, '00 294
Tacos, Skillet Veggie, '01 170
Tacos with Spicy Cream Sauce, Shrimp, '01 170
Tagine, Vegetable, '96 289
Tenderloins, Honey-Grilled, '92 199; '00 126
Tenderloin, Spinach-Stuffed, '89 311
Tofu, Stroganoff, '84 202
Tomato with Tuna Pasta, Stuffed, '88 54
Trout, Baked, '95 106
Trout Fillets with Capers, '95 252
Trout, Grilled, '95 106
Trout, Poached, '95 106

Tuna Croquettes with Parsley Sauce, '86 108
Tuna Steaks on Mixed Greens with Lemon-Basil
    Vinaigrette, Seared, '94 205
Tuna with Poblano Salsa, Grilled, '91 135
Tuna with Rosemary, Broiled, '93 127
Tuna with Tangy Mustard Sauce, '92 201
Turkey-Asparagus Pilaf, '88 200
Turkey Breast and Gravy, Roast, '88 303
Turkey Breast, Stuffed, '87 270
Turkey Breast with Cranberry Salsa, Grilled,
    '95 252
Turkey Breast with Special Gravy, Roast, '86 282
Turkey Burgers, '98 22
Turkey, Citrus-and-Herb, '01 254
Turkey Cutlets, Oven-Fried, '91 121
Turkey Cutlets with Pepper Salsa, Spicy, '88 26
Turkey Lasagna, '91 130
Turkey, Lazy Day, '93 93
Turkey Piccata, '91 137
Turkey Strips with Roasted Peppers and Beans,
    Herbed, '04 282
Turkey Tenderloins with Lingonberry Sauce,
    '97 289
Veal and Carrots, Company, '85 22
Veal, Lemon, '93 35
Veal Marsala, '91 310
Veal Picante, '87 31
Veal Piccata with Capers, '87 142
Veal Scallopini, '83 8
Vegetables and Chicken, Glazed Stir-Fry, '99 205
Vegetarian Supper, '86 222
Veggie-and-Pork Stir-Fry, Mixed, '99 206
Vermicelli and Sprouts with Red Clam Sauce,
    '86 143
Vermicelli, Scallop-Vegetable, '87 143
Zucchini Frittata, '86 103
Zucchini with Pasta, Stuffed, '97 101
Marinade, Soy-and-Ginger, '96 129
Mayonnaise, Adobo, '02 203
Mayonnaise, Basil, '98 144
Mayonnaise, Dried Tomato, '98 144
Mayonnaise, Lemon, '98 144
Mayonnaise, Mediterranean, '98 144
Mayonnaise, Onion, '98 144
Mayonnaise, Roasted Red Pepper, '98 144
Meatballs, '89 237
Meatballs, Turkey, '89 237
Meat Mixture, Basic, '92 241
Muesli, Bran-and-Fruit, '91 134
Navy Beans, Curried, '00 201
Oatmeal, Applesauce, '89 108
Oatmeal, Fruited, '88 19
Olive Oil, Basil-Infused, '95 231
Olive Oil, Lemon-Infused, '95 231
Pancakes, Honey, '91 139
Pancakes, Oatmeal, '89 107
Pancakes, Shredded Wheat, '84 59
Pancakes, Whole Wheat-Oat, '93 16
Pasta, Asian Pesto, '95 189
Pasta-Basil Toss, '87 33
Pasta, Caesar Salad, '95 230
Pasta, Garden, '82 199
Pasta, Grilled Vegetable, '97 142
Pasta Provençale, '88 90
Pasta, Tomato-Basil, '94 204
Peaches, Spicy Baked, '86 39
Pear Breakfast Treat, '87 72
Pears, Champagne-Poached, '01 289
Pears, Wine-Poached, '98 230
Pickles, Lime, '98 206
Pico de Gallo, '96 227; '04 89
Pizza Crust, Special, '90 139
Pizza Crusts, Skillet, '94 218
Pizza on a Bagel, '93 M94

Pizza, Plum-and-Sweet Onion, '98 193
Polenta, Grilled, '00 126
Potatoes, Breakfast-Stuffed, '00 179
Preserves, Fig, '89 140
Preserves, Peach, '89 140
Relish, Cranberry, '86 283; '91 257
Relish, Green Tomato, '98 124
Relish, Holiday Cranberry, '88 304
Relish, Papaya-Basil, '94 82
Relish, Sweet Onion, '96 206
Relish, White Bean, '93 229
Rice
    Apple-Cinnamon Rice, '86 249
    Black-Eyed Peas, Rice with, '93 66
    Blended Rice, '96 68
    Brown Rice, Calico, '86 33
    Casserole, Colorful Rice, '82 199
    Coconut Rice, '00 201
    Herb Rice, '91 257
    Lime-Flavored Rice, '84 175
    Mexican Rice, Spicy, '88 149
    Mix, Fruited Curry-Rice, '86 326
    Onion Rice, Seasoned, '82 166
    Orange Rice, '82 200
    Peppered Rice, '82 4
    Pilaf, Browned Rice, '87 305
    Pilaf, Brown Rice, '90 136; '91 82
    Pilaf, Onion Rice, '04 236
    Pilaf, Rice-and-Lentil, '88 17
    Risotto, Roasted Garlic-and-Cheese, '04 283
    Shell, Rice-Cheese, '82 49
    Southwestern Rice, '90 121
    Spanish Rice with Tofu, '88 26
    Tex-Mex Rice with Corn, '03 129
    Tomatoes and Basil, Rice with, '95 232
    White Rice, Fluffy, '03 65
    Wild Rice and Mushrooms, '83 278
    Wild Rice Bulgur, '91 83
    Wild Rice, Veggie, '00 141
    Yellow Rice, '91 136
Salad Dressings
    Avocado Sauce, Chunky, '03 128
    Balsamic Dressing, '99 259
    Blue Cheese Dressing, '82 166
    Blue Cheese Dressing, Creamy, '91 307
    Blue Cheese Vinaigrette, '90 280
    Caper Vinaigrette, '91 310
    Cilantro-Lime Vinaigrette, '94 77
    Cilantro Vinaigrette, '97 126
    Coconut Dressing, '87 251
    Creamy Dressing, '93 318
    Creole Dressing, '02 69
    Cucumber-Mint Dressing, '87 153
    Cucumber Salad Dressing, Creamy, '82 79
    Curry Dressing, '82 78
    Dijon Vinaigrette, '03 237
    Dressing, '01 58
    French Dressing, Miracle, '82 79
    Fruit, Salad Dressing for, '86 40
    Gorgonzola Dressing, Creamy, '03 34
    Greek Salad Dressing, '03 290
    Herb-Mustard Vinaigrette, '02 84
    Herb Salad Dressing, '86 40
    Honey-Mustard Dressing, '90 111
    Horseradish Dressing, '87 152; '91 32
    Lemon-Basil Vinaigrette, '94 205
    Lemon-Caper Dressing, '96 69
    Lemon-Molasses Dressing, '97 195
    Lemon-Yogurt Dressing, '93 17
    Lemon-Yogurt Slaw or Salad Dressing, '88 54
    Lime Dressing, '83 120
    Lime-Peanut Dressing, '01 26
    Miso-Ginger Dressing, Creamy, '02 144
    Orange-Poppy Seed Dressing, '87 187

HEALTHY & LIGHT, Salad Dressings
(continued)

Oregano-Feta Dressing, '01 57
Papaya Seed Dressing, '95 204
Pineapple-Poppy Seed Dressing, '85 55
Poppy Seed Dressing, '01 56
Raspberry Dressing, '87 153; '95 202
Roasted Red Pepper-Dill Dressing, '02 144
Soy-Sesame Dressing, '87 153
Spicy Southwestern Dressing, '94 136
Spring Garden Dressing, '85 157
Stay Trim Dressing, '86 40
Sweet-and-Sour Dressing, '87 305
Tangy Dressing, '83 9
Thousand Island Dressing, Special, '82 79
Vinaigrette Dressing, '95 231
Vinaigrette, Spicy Lime, '01 217
Wine Vinegar Dressing, '93 126
Yogurt Dressing, '85 59, 215; '88 27
Yogurt Dressing, Sweet-Hot, '86 40
Yogurt-Herb Dressing, '92 96
Yogurt-Honey Poppy Seed Dressing, '83 177

Salads

Ambrosia, Brunch, '83 57
Apple-Apricot Salad, '88 121
Apple-Bran Salad, Lemony, '86 223
Apple Cider Salad Mold, '85 54
Apple Salad, Spicy, '85 215
Apple Salad, Triple, '88 122
Apple Toss, Sesame-, '88 21
Asparagus, Marinated, '84 67
Asparagus Salad, '88 121; '94 67
Asparagus Vinaigrette, Light, '82 50
Aspic, Light Tomato, '85 83
Aspic, Three-Layer, '88 120
Aspic, Tomato-Crab, '85 287
Aspic with Horseradish Dressing, Crisp
    Vegetable, '87 152
Avocado Citrus Salad, '01 133
Barley-Broccoli Salad, '90 135
Bean-and-Rice Salad, Marinated, '87 152
Bean-and-Veggie Salad, Sweet-and-Hot, '04 184
Bean Salad, Marinated, '85 137, 296
Bean Salad, Supreme, '91 202
Bean Salad with Lime-Mustard Dressing, One-,
    '00 202
Beans with Sprouts, Sweet-and-Sour, '86 32
Beef-and-Broccoli Salad, '87 187
Beef Fajita Salad, '91 70
Beef Salad, Stir-Fry, '96 129
Beet Salad, Fresh, '02 236
Black Bean-and-Barley Salad, '94 174
Black Bean Salad, '89 217
Black-Eyed Pea Salad, '95 203; '99 174
Black-Eyed Pea Salad, Marinated, '93 190
Broccoli-Corn Salad, '87 24
Broccoli Salad, '01 58
Brown Rice-and-Vegetable Salad, '84 202
Brown Rice Confetti Salad, '94 174
Caesar Salad, '92 71
Caesar Salad, Baby Romaine, '97 128
Cantaloupe, Fruit-Filled, '83 120
Carrot-and-Seed Salad, Fruity, '86 223
Carrot-Pineapple Salad, '91 83
Carrot-Raisin Salad, '84 174
Cauliflower-Vegetable Salad, '85 158
Cherry-Apple Salad, '86 31
Cherry Salad, Fresh, '83 120
Cherry Tomato-Caper Salad, '00 140
Chicken and Roasted Red Pepper Salad, '03 291
Chicken-and-Veggie Spaghetti Salad, '04 129
Chicken-and-Walnut Salad, Sunburst, '93 91

Chicken-Blueberry Salad, '02 177
Chicken-Fruit Salad, '82 79
Chicken Noodle Salad, '95 25
Chicken Pasta Salad, '88 89
Chicken-Raspberry Salad, Marinated, '93 190
Chicken Salad, Blue Cheese, '94 81
Chicken Salad, Crunchy, '86 207
Chicken Salad, Grilled Asian, '96 158
Chicken Salad, Moroccan Grilled, '95 231
Chicken Salad, Special, '85 82
Chicken Salad, Tarragon, '90 199
Chicken Salad with Mango Chutney, Grilled,
    '96 182
Chicken Salad with Raspberry Dressing, Grilled,
    '95 202
Chicken Taco Salad, '94 M136
Chile-Tomato Salad, Spicy, '88 121
Citrus Salad, Tangy, '89 34
Coleslaw, Crunchy, '86 295
Coleslaw, Light and Creamy, '93 318
Coleslaw with Garden Vegetables, '01 57
Composé, Salad, '93 126
Corn Salad, '85 236
Corn Salad, Wheat Berry-and-Roasted, '94 175
Cottage Cheese Salad in Tomatoes, '86 208
Couscous Salad, Basil-and-Tomato, '94 175
Couscous Salad with Dried Tomato Vinaigrette,
    '96 244
Crab-and-Asparagus Salad, '92 141
Crab-Wild Rice Salad, '86 207
Cucumber Mousse, '88 121
Cucumber Salad, Creamy, '01 56
Cucumber Salad, Dilled, '92 72
Cucumber-Yogurt Salad, '87 33
Dijon Vinaigrette, Salad with, '03 237
English Pea-and-Apple Salad, '87 24
Fennel and Radicchio with Orange Vinaigrette,
    Grilled, '95 253
Freezer Salad, '94 118
Fruit Cups, Sangría, '89 34
Fruit Cup, Winter, '02 22
Fruit, Dressed-Up, '82 5
Fruit Salad, Chef's, '86 35
Fruit Salad, Curried, '85 107
Fruit with Lime Sauce, Fresh, '02 68
Fruit with Mint-Balsamic Tea, Fresh, '95 232
Garden-Patch Salad Molds, '86 283
Garden Salad, Summer, '87 153
Gazpacho Molded Salad, '92 323
Grapefruit Salad, '88 122
Grape Salad Mold, '83 120
Greek Salad, '03 290
Green Beans with Creamy Tarragon Dressing,
    '93 191
Green Beans with Smoked Almonds, Thyme-
    Scented, '01 57
Green Salad, Mixed, '90 230
Greens, Crimson, '87 153
Greens with Blue Cheese Vinaigrette, Mixed,
    '90 280
Greens with Raspberry Dressing, Peppery,
    '95 254
Hominy-Bean Salad, '88 266
Italian Bread Salad, '99 259
Italian Salad, Cheesy, '84 33
Jicama-Orange Salad, '90 122
Layered Salad, '86 35
Legumes, Marinated, '90 197
Lentils-and-Rice Salad, '90 197
Lettuce, Confetti-Stuffed, '87 24
Lettuces with Mustard Vinaigrette, Baby, '93 67
Lima Bean-Tomato Salad, '85 137
Lime-Potato Salad, '02 22
Macaroni-Cheese Salad, Dilled, '86 208

Macaroni-Chicken Salad, Dilled, '92 142
Macaroni-Tuna Salad, Whole Wheat, '84 193
Mandarin Salad Molds, '85 54
Meal-in-One Salad, '86 43
Melon Ball Bowl with Cucumber-Mint Dressing,
    '87 153
Mixed Greens with Raspberries and Walnuts,
    '98 194
Mushroom-Zucchini Salad, '85 8
New Potato Salad, '84 139
Niçoise, Salad, '86 35
Oriental Salad Bowl, '87 153
Paella Salad, '86 207
Pasta-and-Tomato Salad, Herbed, '92 144
Pasta Salad, '84 139; '89 217
Pasta Salad, Garden, '86 188
Pasta with Apple, Curried, '02 68
Peaches in a Garden Nest, '87 154
Pear Salad with Jicama and Snow Peas, '01 56
Pork Salad, Oriental, '92 140
Pork Salad, Thai, '00 249
Potato Salad, '90 122
Potato Salad, Dill, '99 104
Potato Salad, Hot-and-Light, '93 90
Potato Salad, Layered, '03 183
Potato Salad, Pesto, '90 164
Potato Slices, Marinated, '93 98
Rice-and-Bean Salad, Zesty, '02 84
Rice-and-Vegetable Salad, '86 42
Rice-Shrimp Salad, '92 142
Roasted Tomato-and-Pepper Salad, '01 196
Roasted Vegetable Salad with Dried Peach
    Vinaigrette, '97 265
Romaine with Caper Vinaigrette, Hearts of,
    '91 310
Salmon-and-Wild Rice Salad, Oriental, '94 173
Salmon Salad, Chilled Poached, '96 68
Seafood Salad Sussex Shores, '93 98
Shrimp-and-Couscous Salad, '96 157
Shrimp-and-Rice Salad, '92 307
Shrimp Salad, Fruited, '86 156
Shrimp Salad, Marinated, '85 82
Slaw, Apple-Carrot, '92 243
Slaw, Cabbage-Pineapple, '92 182
Slaw, Chinese Cabbage, '89 312
Slaw, Green Bean, '95 108
Slaw, Healthy, '92 183
Slaw, Red Cabbage-and-Apple, '87 31
Slaw, Tangy Ginger, '01 92
Slaw, Vegetable, '00 42
Spinach-Blue Cheese Salad, '82 166
Spinach-Kiwifruit Salad, '87 305
Spinach Salad, Citrus, '90 59
Spinach Salad, Tangy, '00 24
Spinach Salad, Wilted, '93 125
Spinach Salad with Orange Dressing, '87 187
Sprout Salad, '90 137
Steak Salad Cups, Pepper, '86 206
Steak Salad with Peach Salsa, '97 183
Strawberry-Pretzel Salad, '03 290
Strawberry Salad, Frozen, '94 119
Sweet Potato Salad with Rosemary-Honey
    Vinaigrette, '98 243
Tabbouleh Salad, '91 70; '94 174; '01 57
Tabbouleh Salad, Southwestern, '01 216
Taco Salad, Beefy, '03 128
Tofu Salad, '88 27
Tomato-Cucumber Salad, '92 199
Tomato-Cucumber Salad with Yogurt-Herb
    Dressing, '92 96
Tomatoes Stuffed with Sea Slaw, '89 96
Tortellini Salad, '89 237
Tossed Salad, Grecian, '04 283
Tuna-and-Cannellini Bean Salad, '86 143

Tuna Chef Salad, '82 78
Tuna-Mac in Tomatoes, '87 188
Tuna-Pasta Salad, '92 141
Tuna Salad, Curried, '86 208
Turkey Waldorf Salad with Yogurt Dressing, '88 53
Turnip Salad, '85 235
Vegetable Salad, Crispy Marinated, '84 193
Vegetable Salad, Grilled, '94 203
Vegetable Salad, Italian, '82 19
Vegetable Salad, Marinated, '84 13
Vegetable Salad, Minted, '88 23
Vegetable Salad, Tarragon-, '85 288
Vegetable Salad, Winter, '86 42
Vegetables, Zesty Marinated, '82 272
White Bean-and-Tuna Salad, '01 35
Wild Rice Salad, '93 191
Wild Rice Salad with Spicy Lime Vinaigrette, '01 217
Salt, Dragon, '03 236
Sandwiches
Bagel, Breakfast on a, '94 66
Bean Burgers with Adobo Mayonnaise, '02 202
Breakfast Sandwiches, Open-Faced, '92 140
Cheese Sandwiches with Artichoke-Tomato Salsa, Herbed, '96 182
Chicken Pita, Oriental, '89 216
Chicken Sandwiches, Marinated, '86 M45
Chicken Sandwich with Fresh Salsa, Broiled, '00 59
Crab Sandwiches, Open-Faced, '87 106
Eggplant Parmesan Sandwiches, '03 213
Eggplant Sandwiches, Open-Face, '95 124
Eggplant, Tomato, and Feta Sandwiches, '98 106
Flank Steak Sandwiches with Apple Barbecue Sauce, '99 173
Garden Sandwiches, Open-Faced, '87 105
Ham Sandwiches, Open-Face, '85 8
Heroes, Healthy, '90 177
Lamb Pockets with Dilled Cucumber Topping, '87 104
London Broil Sandwiches with Yogurt-Cucumber Sauce, '01 162
Open-Face Sandwiches, '84 13
Picnic Loaf, Mediterranean, '96 156
Pimiento Cheese Sandwiches, '82 278
Pitas, Acadian Stuffed, '90 177
Pita Sandwiches, '84 139
Pita, Stuffed, '89 87
Pita, Tuna-Veggie Stuffed, '01 216
Pizza Sandwiches, Open-Face, '85 22
Rollup, Hot Ham-and-Cheese, '01 217
Seafood Po'Boy, Grilled, '96 244
Seafood Sandwiches, Caribbean, '98 105
Shrimp Salad Sandwiches, '90 178
Sloppy Toms, '91 51
Tabbouleh Pitas, '98 105
Tofu-Veggie Sandwiches, Open-Face, '86 5
Turkey and Ham Pine-Berry Sandwiches, '00 59
Turkey-in-the-Slaw Sandwich, '90 177
Turkey-Roasted Pepper Sandwiches, Smoked, '94 66
Vegetable Pitas, Garbanzo-, '00 58
Vegetable Pockets, '85 215
Vegetarian Melt, Open-Faced, '87 106
Vegetarian Pita Sandwiches, '84 193
Wraps, Chicken-Cranberry, '01 34
Sauces and Gravies
Alfredo Sauce, '94 84
Avocado Sauce, Chunky, '03 128
Barbecue Sauce, Apple, '99 173
Barbecue Sauce, Easy, '82 178
Barbecue Sauce, LBJ's Texas, '97 42
Barbecue Sauce, Special, '82 177

Barbecue Sauce, Tangy, '99 104
Basil-Brown Butter Sauce, '93 92
Champagne Sauce, '90 29
Cheese Sauce, Guilt-Free, '93 M95
Cream Sauce, '03 237
Creole Sauce, '90 28; '02 284
Cucumber-Dill Sauce, '86 5
Dill Sauce, Creamy, '94 42
Dipping Sauce, Olive Oil-Balsamic, '04 46
Ginger Dipping Sauce, '03 64
Ginger-Soy Sauce, '91 33
Ginger Vinaigrette, '95 162
Gravy, '88 303
Gravy, Sausage, '94 20
Greek Sauce, '91 183
Hollandaise Sauce, Mock, '85 49; '93 68
Honey-Horseradish Dip, '02 309
Horseradish Sauce, '91 183
Jalapeño Sauce, '93 230
Jalapeño Tartar Sauce, '96 69
Lemon-Chive Sauce, '86 249
Lemon-Molasses Dressing, '97 195
Lemon Sauce, '82 290
Mandarin Sauce, '84 60
Mandarin-Teriyaki Sauce, '96 68
Mango-Pineapple Hot Sauce, '04 183
Marinade, Tangy Light, '82 178
Marinara Sauce, '82 178; '89 239; '92 18
Mediterranean Sauce, '94 83
Mushroom Sauce, '83 205; '91 221
Mushroom Sauce, Spicy Sherried, '89 239
Mustard-Hollandaise Sauce, Mock, '87 269
Mustard Sauce, '87 22
Mustard Sauce, Easy, '94 83
Mustard Sauce, Light, '82 178
Mustard Sauce, Tangy, '92 201
Orange Dipping Sauce, '03 M212
Parmesan Sauce, '92 17
Parsley Sauce, '86 108
Peanut Sauce, Spicy, '04 134
Pesto, Dried Tomato, '94 249
Pesto, Sage, '97 22
Picante Sauce, Processed, '91 257
Pizza Sauce, '84 33
Rancheros Sauce, '88 148
Red Chile Sauce, '94 251
Reduction Sauce, Cider-Port Wine, '96 245
Red Wine Garlic Sauce, '94 250
Roasted Red Pepper Sauce, '00 58
Rosemary-Cherry Sauce, '02 193
Rosemary Sauce, '97 127
Salsa, '88 147
Salsa, Artichoke-Tomato, '96 182
Salsa, Black Bean, '93 155
Salsa, Black Bean-and-Corn, '94 80
Salsa, Cranberry-Citrus, '97 290
Salsa Cruda, '88 148
Salsa, Cucumber-Dill, '95 107
Salsa, Dried Chile, '97 265
Salsa, Fiesta Onion, '94 82
Salsa, Fresh, '00 59
Salsa, Fresh Citrus, '03 291
Salsa, Fresh Vegetable, '98 194
Salsa, Hot Kiwifruit, '94 82
Salsa, Mango, '04 59
Salsa, Peach, '97 183
Salsa, Pepper, '88 26
Salsa, Pineapple, '96 226; '03 128
Salsa, Poblano, '91 135
Salsa, Smoky Three-Bean, '02 202
Salsa, Tomato-Avocado, '94 83
Salsa, Vegetable, '96 208
Salsa Verde, Roasted, '96 182
Salsa, Warm Pineapple, '02 144

Salsa, Zesty Corn, '02 193
Sauerbraten Sauce, '93 16
Seafood Sauce, '89 239
Seafood Sauce, Red, '95 107
Spaghetti Sauce, Lentil, '90 198
Swiss Sauce, '83 M195
Tahini Sauce, '03 183
Tarragon Sauce, '83 56; '97 42
Tartar Sauce, '95 107; '99 174
Tomato Sauce, '85 193, 244
Tomato Sauce, Spicy, '88 19
Vegetable-Cheese Potato Topper, '86 6
White Sauce, Low-Calorie Medium, '87 26
Yogurt-Cucumber Sauce, '04 216
Zesty Sauce, '94 82
Zippy Sauce, '86 44
Sausage, Country, '92 242
Sausage, Italian, '92 242
Seasoning, Herb, '99 63
Shells and Cheese, Creamy, '01 216
Soups and Stews
Asparagus Soup, '84 67
Bean-and-Hominy Soup, '95 23
Bean and Pasta Soup, '94 220
Bean-and-Turkey Soup, '93 319
Bean Soup, Leafy, '86 223
Bean Soup, Quick, '99 97
Beef-and-Barley Vegetable Soup, '89 31
Beef-and-Pepperoni Soup, Italian-Style, '00 316
Beef Stew, '90 230
Beef Stew, Quick, '92 71
Black Bean Soup, '88 266; '98 291
Black Bean Soup, Carolina, '92 139
Black Bean Soup, Marge Clyde's, '96 29
Borscht, Ruby Red, '83 176
Bouillon, Court-, '98 229
Bouillon, Tomato, '83 8
Broccoli Soup, Creamy, '91 307
Broccoli Soup, Light Cream of, '93 17
Broccoli Soup, Mock Cream of, '85 288
Broccoli-Swiss Soup, '86 6
Butternut Soup, '02 68
Butternut Squash-Lime Soup, '03 236
Cantaloupe Soup, '83 120
Carrot-and-Butternut Squash Soup with Parslied Croutons, '97 217
Carrot-Leek Soup, '86 34
Carrot Soup, '98 123
Chicken-and-Buttermilk Soup, Country, '02 144
Chicken, Artichoke, and Mushroom Soup, '92 324
Chicken, Kale, and Chickpea Stew, '98 47
Chicken Soup, Curried, '86 34
Chicken-Vegetable Soup, '88 18
Chili, Full-of-Veggies, '00 294
Chili, Spicy 3-Bean, '03 291
Chili Vegetable Soup, '94 120
Chili, Vegetarian, '84 280
Chowder, Basque Fish, '86 36
Chowder, Chicken-and-Roasted Vegetable, '97 21
Chowder, Clam, '86 36; '89 95
Chowder, Corn, '91 132
Chowder, Corn-and-Poblano, '03 193
Chowder, Maryland Crab, '97 23
Chowder, Potato-Corn, '94 66
Chowder, Seafood, '92 122
Chowder with Sage Pesto, White Bean, '97 22
Cilantro Soup, Cream of, '00 249
Corn-and-Crab Soup, Fresh, '92 183
Crab Soup, Cream of, '88 302
Cucumber Soup, Cold Minted, '86 34
Cucumber-Yogurt Soup, '83 205
Fish-and-Vegetable Stew, '87 220
French Market Soup, '92 49

Gazpacho, Chilled, '84 138
Gazpacho, Citrus, '96 70
Gazpacho, Tropical, '95 204
Gumbo, Catfish, '90 278
Gumbo, Chicken-and-Sausage, '94 20
Gumbo, Light Seafood-Okra, '86 155
Gumbo, Seafood, '96 98
Ham-and-Bean Soup, Spicy, '94 322
Hot-and-Sour Soup, '91 50
Mex-Tex Soup, '90 278
Minestrone Soup, '86 144; '91 258
Minestrone Soup Mix, '91 258
Navy Bean Soup, '84 280
New Year's Day Soup, '00 25
Okra-and-Shrimp Soup, '94 323
Peach Soup, '83 120
Pepper-and-Chicken Soup, Roasted, '90 58
Pepper Soup, Spicy, '93 98
Plum Soup, '85 107
Potato Soup, Hearty, '98 292
Roasted Red Pepper Soup, '96 245
Seafood Stew, '84 280
Spinach Egg Drop Soup, '03 65
Spinach Soup, Oriental, '83 151
Split Pea-and-Lentil Soup, Oven-Baked,
   '00 316
Split Pea Soup, '90 198; '94 322
Squash Bisque, '84 280
Sweet Potato-and-Pear Bisque, '00 317
Sweet Potato-and-Sausage Soup, '95 23
Tomato Soup, '89 217
Tomato Soup, Easy, '84 14
Tomato Soup Plus, '88 170
Tortilla Soup, '94 136; '98 291
Turkey-Tomato Stew, '90 279
Vegetable-Beef Stew, '94 323
Vegetable Soup, '86 187; '88 266; '98 291
Vegetable Soup, Light, '84 280
Vegetable Stew, '00 248
Vegetable Stew, Mixed, '84 13
Wild Mushroom Soup, '04 203
Zucchini Soup with Fresh Vegetable Salsa,
   Chilled, '98 194
Sour Cream, Mock, '83 71, 205
Spice Mix, Tex-Mex, '94 135
Spice Rub, Caribbean, '02 144
Spice Rub, Moroccan, '95 231
Spread, Blue Cheese, '95 79
Spread, Cottage Cheese, '87 107
Spread, Hawaiian Ham, '87 106
Spread, Light Strawberry, '85 55
Spread, Low-Calorie Pimiento Cheese, '85 215
Spread, Peachy-Raisin, '86 326
Spread, Raisin-Nut, '95 79
Spread, Strawberry, '95 79
Spread, Sugarless Fruit, '84 60
Spread, Tasty Chicken, '84 193
Spread, Vegetable-Egg, '87 106
Syrup, Maple, '93 16
Topping, Apple, '89 107
Topping, Oat Crunch, '89 108
Topping, Yogurt-Cheese, '88 55
Tortellini with Rosemary-Parmesan Sauce, '92 284
Tortilla Rollups, '89 87
Vegetables
Acorn Squash, Fruited, '85 235; '90 228
Acorn Squash with Nutmeg, '85 267
Acorn Squash with Rosemary, Grilled, '96 266
Artichokes, Shrimp-Stuffed, '84 67
Artichokes, Stuffed, '99 64

Artichokes Stuffed with Shrimp and Scallops,
   '84 174
Asparagus, Company, '85 82
Asparagus, Stir-Fried, '87 52
Asparagus Vinaigrette, '90 138
Asparagus with Ginger, '04 237
Barley and Vegetables, '91 81
Beans, Lemon-Mint, '88 22
Beans, Texas Ranch, '90 198
Beets, Ginger-Marmalade Glazed, '93 35
Beets, Harvard, '83 M195
Beets, Orange, '91 219
Beets, Orange-Glazed, '86 187
Beets, Pickled, '87 163
Black Bean Terrine with Fresh Tomato Coulis and
   Jalapeño Sauce, '93 230
Black-Eyed Peas, '93 180
Black-Eyed Peas, Creole, '98 22
Black-Eyed Peas, Seasoned, '85 138
Black-Eyed Peas, Spicy Hot, '90 135
Bread Bowl, Veggie, '01 132
Broccoli and Cauliflower, Roasted, '01 132
Broccoli and Walnut Sauté, '95 52
Broccoli Casserole, '88 265
Broccoli, Easy Orange, '85 267
Broccoli, Garlic, '93 35; '95 54
Broccoli, Lemon, '95 53
Broccoli, Sesame, '85 8
Broccoli Toss, '86 294
Broccoli with Horseradish Sauce, '84 33
Broccoli with Tangy Chive Sauce, Steamed,
   '83 101
Brussels Sprouts, Casserole of, '86 294
Brussels Sprouts, Glorified, '86 282
Brussels Sprouts in Mustard Sauce, '90 228
Brussels Sprouts, Marinated, '88 265
Brussels Sprouts Medley, '85 267
Bundles, Vegetable, '93 181
Butterbeans, '90 166
Butternut-Orange Bake, '86 295
Cabbage, Skillet, '90 229
Cabbage, Sweet-and-Sour, '86 295
Cabbage with Caraway, '93 181
Carrots and Onions, Herbed, '87 31
Carrots and Pineapple, Curried, '90 228
Carrots, Dilled Baby, '92 145
Carrots, Ginger, '83 9
Carrots, Glazed, '88 304
Carrots, Golden, '85 267
Carrots, Lemon-Dill Steamed, '93 180
Carrots, Light Glazed, '92 227
Carrots, Marinated, '86 108
Carrots Marsala, '83 56
Carrots, Orange-Spiced, '88 18
Carrots Polynesian, Spiced, '88 85
Carrots, Rosemary, '91 219
Carrot Strips, Orangy, '89 312
Carrots, Tropical, '84 34
Carrot-Sweet Potato Puree, '02 M285
Cauliflower Sauté, '94 67
Cauliflower-Snow Pea Medley, '87 305
Celeriac and Carrots, '91 219
Celery-Parmesan Toss, '84 34
Chard with Onion and Apple, Sautéed, '98 48
Corn Casserole, Chili-, '88 266
Corn, Creamy Baked, '90 60
Corn in the Style of Oaxaca, Grilled, '04 134
Corn-on-the-Cob, Grilled, '90 166
Corn Pudding, Fresh, '89 172
Corn, Roasted Red Pepper, '91 122
Corn, Southern-Style Creamed, '92 201
Corn, Spicy Mexican, '93 90
Crêpes, Vegetable-Filled Bran, '86 44
Crunchy Vegetables, '99 43

Curry, Vegetable, '04 217
Eggplant Casserole, Spicy Hot, '93 92
Eggplant, Ratatouille-Bran Stuffed, '86 44
Eggplant, Spicy Oriental, '96 130
English Pea Medley, '85 236
English Peas, Deluxe, '84 68
French Fries, Oven, '91 122
French Fries, Seasoned, '96 245
Fries, Salty Rosemary, '03 213
Fries, Spicy Oven, '02 34
Green Bean Medley, Peppery, '93 181
Green Beans and Potatoes, '91 221
Green Beans, Herbed, '83 177
Green Beans, Indian-Style, '88 265
Green Beans, Italian, '90 164; '92 183
Green Beans Italiano, '86 144
Green Beans, Lemony, '99 259
Green Beans, Seasoned, '88 304
Green Beans with Mushrooms, '93 89
Green Beans with New Potatoes, '87 164
Green Beans with Oregano, '97 218
Green Beans with Tomatoes, '85 137
Green Tomatoes, '89 174
Green Tomatoes, Oven-Fried, '91 122
Grilled Vegetables, '92 124
Grilled Vegetables, Italian-Style, '92 143
Grilled Vegetables, Marinated, '95 162; '00 126
Hash Brown Casserole, Creamy, '03 193
Hominy, Mexican, '91 133
Kale with Tomato and Onion, '92 244
Kebabs, Marinated Vegetable, '83 M195
Kebabs, Vegetable, '01 132
Kidney Bean Casserole, '90 136
Leeks Vinaigrette, Warm, '98 47
Lima Beans Creole, '85 137
Marinated Vegetables, '88 170; '99 105
Marinated Vegetables, Creole-, '02 69
Medley, Chinese Vegetable, '84 33
Mixed Vegetables, '83 M195
Mushrooms, Flavor-Stuffed, '85 288
Mushrooms, Grilled Portabello, '95 123
Mushrooms, Microwave Portabello, '95 M123
Mushrooms, Sautéed Portabello, '95 123
Mushrooms, Savory Fresh, '85 268
New Potatoes, Herbed, '83 9
New Potatoes, Roasted, '90 138
New Potato Medley, '90 279
Okra-and-Tomato Bake, '89 173
Okra and Tomatoes, Grilled, '98 124
Okra, Corn, and Tomatoes, '95 203
Okra, Oven-Fried, '91 121
Onion-Potato Bake, '83 M195
Onion Rings, Crispy Baked, '93 247
Onions and Wine, Stuffed, '85 268
Onions, Citrus, '04 89
Onions, Roasted Sweet, '04 282
Onions, Stuffed Vidalia, '89 172
Onions Stuffed with Peas, '84 68
Parsnips, Glazed, '91 220
Peas-and-Corn Medley, '85 138
Peas and Ham, Southern, '85 138
Peas and Peppers, Stir-Fried, '87 51
Peperonata, '97 291
Pepper Kebabs, Pretty, '90 166
Peppers, Carrot-and-Cabbage Stuffed, '99 63
Peppers, Stuffed, '84 202
Pilaf, Barley-Vegetable, '91 33
Potato Bake, Smoky Mashed, '00 214
Potato-Cheese Dream, '91 307
Potatoes and Turnips, Scalloped, '85 235
Potatoes au Gratin, '93 90
Potatoes, Buttermilk-Basil Mashed, '95 330
Potatoes, Confetti Twice-Baked, '02 35
Potatoes, Cottage, '93 M92

Potatoes, Cream Cheese Mashed, '02 35
Potatoes, Double-Cheese, '86 6
Potatoes, Herbed, '91 220
Potatoes, Light Scalloped, '89 311
Potatoes, Mexican-Stuffed, '91 131
Potatoes, Mushroom-Dill-Topped, '86 41
Potatoes, Rosemary-Roasted, '95 20
Potatoes, Scalloped, '92 48
Potatoes, Stuffed, '89 173
Potatoes, Twice Baked Cottage-Style, '91 135
Potatoes, Vegetable-Topped Stuffed, '85 235
Potato Thins, Roasted, '02 23
Potato, Twice-Baked, '90 M295
Potato Wedges, '94 M119
Potato Wedges, Lemon, '88 21
Ragout, Vegetable, '89 172
Ratatouille, Microwave, '95 M232
Red Cabbage-and-Apple Slaw, '91 309
Rice Toss, Vegetable-, '91 309
Rice, Vegetables and, '93 91
Risotto Primavera, '95 163
Roasted Root Vegetables, Rosemary, '01 255
Roasted Summer Vegetables, '98 213
Rollup, Veggie, '01 109
Rutabaga, Honey, '91 220
Rutabagas, Mashed, '86 295
Sautéed Vegetable Medley, '83 101
Sauté, Tossed Vegetable, '92 138
Snap Beans, Sweet-and-Sour, '89 173
Snow Peas with Red Pepper, '90 102
Spaghetti Squash Sauté, '98 212
Spinach-Gorgonzola Custards, Savory, '02 284
Spinach Quiche, '85 49; '91 204
Spinach Soufflé, '86 108
Spinach with Pine Nuts, Baby, '03 64
Squash Casserole, '87 163
Squash Stuffed with Spinach Pesto, '89 M133
Steamed Garden Vegetables, '93 155
Steamed Herbed Vegetables, '93 M303
Steamed Vegetable Medley, '90 29
Stir-Fried Vegetables, '90 136
Stir-Fried Vegetables with Curry, '87 51
Stir-Fry, Almond-Vegetable, '86 222
Stir-Fry, Mixed Veggie, '99 206
Stir-Fry, Vegetable, '99 204
Stir-Fry, Vegetable Medley, '99 205
Stir-Fry Vegetables, Glazed, '99 205
Sugar Snap Peas with Basil and Lemon, '93 66
Summer Vegetables, '91 136
Summer Vegetables, Cheesy, '94 119
Sweet Potato-Apple Bake, '86 282
Sweet Potato Casserole, '03 M24
Sweet Potatoes-and-Apple Casserole, '90 228
Sweet Potatoes and Onions, Oven-Roasted, '00 24
Sweet Potatoes, Orange-Spice Mashed, '02 34
Sweet Potatoes, Roasted Gingered, '01 92
Sweet Potato Puff, '85 235
Sweet Potato Puree, '92 306
Tomato Coulis, Fresh, '93 230
Tomatoes and Okra, '87 164
Tomatoes, Bean-Stuffed, '84 34
Tomatoes, Cheese Herbed-Topped, '86 108
Tomatoes, Cheesy Puff-Top, '86 187
Tomatoes, Fire-and-Ice, '03 183
Tomatoes, Grilled, '85 158
Tomatoes, Parmesan-Stuffed, '92 182
Tomatoes, Spinach-Topped, '88 265
Tomatoes, Stuffed Scalloped, '90 29
Tomatoes with Basil Vinaigrette, Grilled, '97 168
Tomato Slices, Herbed, '89 173
Torta, Mexican, '88 149
Turnips and Carrots Julienne, '86 295
Turnips, Braised, '91 219
Yellow Squash, Tomato-Stuffed, '00 43

Zucchini-and-Tomato Casserole, '88 265
Zucchini and Tomato with Herbs, '92 182
Zucchini-Basil Delight, '85 267
Zucchini-Basil Scramble, '87 34
Zucchini Dressing, '86 282
Zucchini Fans, '91 33
Zucchini Spears, Oven-Fried, '91 121
Zucchini, Stuffed, '86 187; '89 M133
Zucchini with Feta, Greek Grilled, '95 190
Zucchini with Pecans, '87 31
Vinegar, Raspberry Wine, '93 191
Vinegar, Shallot-Tarragon-Garlic, '93 191
Waffles, Light, '91 139
Waffles, Oat Bran, '92 139
Waffles, Oatmeal, '89 107
Wild Rice-Fennel Pilaf, '97 127
Yogurt Snack, '88 55

HEARTS OF PALM
Chicken Rolls, Hearts of Palm, '89 201
Marinated Asparagus and Hearts of Palm, '90 91
Salad, Different Vegetable, '82 143
Salad, Hearts of Palm, '81 252
Salad, Hearts-of-Palm, '87 138
Salad, Hearts of Palm, '89 276; '96 86
Salad, Italian Tossed, '00 167
Salad with Basil-and-Garlic Dressing, Hearts of
    Palm, '94 55
Salad with Lemon-Dill Vinaigrette, Green, '99 27
Sandwich, Hearts of Palm, '92 191
Spread, Hearts of Palm, '90 293

HOMINY
Bacon, Eggs, and Hominy, '85 143
Bake, Chili Hominy, '81 282; '82 58
Bake, Hominy-Sausage, '88 51
Casserole, Cheesy Hominy, '83 170
Casserole, Chile-Hominy, '81 29
Casserole), Four-Part Hominy (Cheesy Hominy,
    '96 158
Casserole, Hominy-and-Corn, '97 291
Casserole, Hominy-Chili, '86 255
Caviar, Texas, '86 218
Cheese Hominy, Hot, '84 77
Chiles and Cheese, Hominy with, '86 78
Gold Coast Hominy, '83 52
Jalapeño Hominy, '82 51
Mexican Hominy, '86 255; '91 133, 162
Mexihominy, '96 189
Ole, Hominy, '01 17
Salad, Hominy-Bean, '88 266
Skillet, Hominy-Sausage, '81 29
Soup, Bean-and-Hominy, '95 23
Soup, Black, White, and Red All Over, '95 126
Soup, Southwest, '86 255

HONEY
Ambrosia, Honey Bee, '83 267
Apple Quarters, Honey-Baked, '86 93
Apple Rings, Honey, '80 243
Apples and Pear, Honey-Baked, '97 303
Apples, Honey-Baked, '83 234; '84 244
Apples, Honey-Yogurt, '92 46
Apples, Stuffed, '99 247
Bananas, Honey-Baked, '81 268
Breads
    Applesauce-Honey Nut Bread, '87 300
    Banana Bread, Honey-, '91 68
    Biscuits, Honey Angel, '95 138; '03 111
    Buns, Honey-Oat, '98 27
    Buns, Honey Oatmeal, '83 154
    Cinnamon Swirl Bread, Honey-, '88 287
    Curry Bread, Honey-, '89 250
    Graham Bread, Honey, '99 211
    Granola Bread, Honey-, '86 56
    Muffins, Banana-Honey-Nut, '88 62
    Muffins, Honey Bran, '88 171

    Muffins, Honey-Bran, '89 250
    Muffins, Honey-Oatmeal, '84 229
    Muffins, Honey-Wheat, '83 96; '88 263
    Muffins, Oatmeal-Honey, '83 95
    Muffins, Orange-Honey, '88 284
    Muffins, Peanut Butter-Honey, '82 56
    Oat Bread, Honey-, '89 107; '93 232; '98 27
    Oatmeal Bread, Honey, '80 60
    Rolls, Dilled Honey-Wheat, '83 254
    Rolls, Honey Wheat, '83 278
    Rolls, Super Honey, '80 115
    Swirl, Honey-Walnut, '80 21
    Twist, Honey, '79 80
    Wheat Bread, Honey, '85 18, 268
    Wheat Bread, Honey-, '91 223
    Whole Wheat Honey Bread, '82 65; '83 106
    Zucchini-Honey Bread, '89 143
Brie, Honey-Mustard, '91 252
Brownies, Heavenly Honey, '79 83
Butter, Cinnamon-Honey, '89 281
Butter, Honey, '93 309; '94 206; '95 139; '97 307;
    '03 111
Butter, Honey-Lemon, '04 231
Butter, Honey-Orange, '79 36; '85 19
Cake, Honey, '92 250
Cake, Honey-Apple, '99 210
Cake, Honey-Oatmeal, '87 222
Cake, Southern Honey, '89 251
Cake Squares, Honey, '89 250
Carrots, Honey-Glazed, '80 115; '84 121; '85 18;
    '99 63
Carrots, Honey-Kissed, '84 122
Carrots with Honey, '02 59
Chicken, Baked Honey, '99 110
Chicken, Honey, '82 55; '88 67
Chicken, Honey Barbecue, '04 197
Chicken, Honey-Curry, '87 36
Chicken, Honey-Glazed Grilled, '99 213
Chicken, Honey-Lime Grilled, '96 189; '98 332
Chicken, Honey-Pecan, '03 147
Chicken Thighs, Honey-Pecan, '02 127
Chicken Wings, Grilled Honey, '96 111
Chicken Wings, Honey-Glazed, '91 251
Chops, Honey-Glazed, '97 200
Cornbread, Honey, '83 286; '84 17
Crunch, Honey-and-Spice, '94 290
Dip, Coconut-Honey Fruit, '84 171
Dip, Creamy Honey-Herb, '98 135
Dip, Honey-Horseradish, '02 309
Dip, Peanut Butter-Honey, '85 19
Dressings
    Applesauce Salad Dressing, Honey-, '99 210
    Basil-Honey Dressing, '97 30
    Berry Dressing, Orange Salad with Honey-,
        '89 250
    Buttermilk-Honey Dressing, '96 243
    Celery-Honey Dressing, '80 42
    Dijon-Honey Dressing, '89 45; '99 333
    Dijon Salad Dressing, Creamy Honey-, '99 245
    Dijon Vinaigrette, Honey-, '04 321
    French Dressing, Honey, '87 81
    Honey Dressing, '79 242; '83 146; '87 129
    Lemon Dressing, Fruit Salad with Honey-, '93 21
    Lemon Dressing, Honey-, '95 133
    Lime Dressing, Honey-, '83 139; '93 71
    Lime-Honey Dressing, '92 213
    Lime-Honey Fruit Salad Dressing, '87 81
    Mustard Dressing, Honey-, '90 55, 111, 146;
        '00 54; '01 230
    Orange Salad with Honey Dressing, '89 14
    Pecan Dressing, Honey-, '03 28
    Spinach Salad with Honey Dressing, '90 16
    Tomato-Honey French Dressing, '81 105
    Vinaigrette, Honey-Mustard, '94 249

HONEY, Dressings
(continued)

    Vinaigrette, Honey-Orange, '91 255
    Vinaigrette, Lemon-Honey, '96 65
    Walnut Dressing, Honey-, '93 107
    Yogurt Dressing, Honey-, '93 172
Duck with Parsnip Mash, Honey-Orange-Glazed
    Muscovy, '97 262
Filling, Honey, '88 287
Filling, Honey-Walnut, '80 21
Flavored Honey, '97 30
Frosting, Honey Chocolate, '79 83
Glaze, Chocolate-Honey, '82 306
Glaze, Cranberry-Honey, '89 273
Glaze, Honey, '88 287
Glaze, Honey-Nut, '87 15
Grapes, Honeyed, '95 47
Ham, Honey-Orange Glazed, '83 320
Ham Slice, Honey-Glazed, '81 104
Ice Cream, Honey, '99 212
Ice Cream, Honey-Vanilla, '95 178
Jelly, Honey-Lemon, '97 29
Kebabs, Honey Ham, '80 156
Leeks, Honey-Glazed, '86 62
Lemon Honey, '94 16; '96 124
Loaves, Hint o' Honey, '81 104
Marinade, Garlic-Honey, '93 102
Marinade, Honey-Mustard, '93 103
Mousse, Honeyed Chocolate, '87 223
Mustard, Hot Honey, '93 240
Mustard, Peppered Honey, '95 312
Onions, Honey, '81 86
Onions, Honey-Paprika Sweet, '92 52
Pancakes, Honey, '91 139
Peaches, Honey-Sweet, '85 107
Peaches 'n' Cream, Honeyed, '93 134
Pear Honey, '90 159
Pear Honey, Gingered, '97 62
Pears, Honey-Baked, '93 47
Pears, Pineapple-Honey, '86 94
Pecans, Honeycomb, '84 300
Pecans, Sugar-and-Honey, '86 319
Pie, Honey Apple, '00 331
Pie, Honeyed Orzo-Pecan, '04 219
Pork Chops, Honey-Lime, '91 33
Pork Chops, Honey-Pecan, '01 82
Pork, Honey-Roasted, '02 282
Pork Loin, Garlic-Honey Marinated, '99 334
Pork Tenderloin, Honey-Garlic, '01 16
Pork Tenderloin, Honey-Mustard, '95 52
Pork Tenderloins, Honey-Garlic, '01 318
Pork Tenderloins, Pepper-Honey, '98 33
Pork Tenderloin with Avocado-Peach Salsa,
    Honeyed, '02 159
Preserves, Honeyed Peach, '85 130
Puffs, Honey, '96 153
Relish, Cherry-Honey, '97 32
Rice, Honey, '85 83
Rutabaga, Honey, '91 220
Salad, Honey Chicken, '04 51
Salad, Honey Fruit, '80 276
Sauces
    Barbecue Sauce, Honey, '04 197
    Butter Sauce, Honey-, '85 18; '98 45
    Chicken in Honey Sauce, '89 82
    Chicken Strips with Honey Sauce, '03 27
    Chocolate Sauce, Honey-, '89 251
    Cinnamon-Pecan-Honey Pancake Sauce, '88 46
    Honey Sauce, '99 210
    Lemon Mustard Sauce, Honey-, '84 275
    Lime Sauce, Honey-, '82 85
    Mustard Sauce, Honey-, '85 13

    Mustard Sauce, Smoked Ribs with Honey-,
    '92 168
    Orange-Honey Sauce, '97 236
    Orange Sauce, Honey-, '85 108
    Poppy Seed Sauce, Honey-, '93 13
    Sundae Sauce, Honeyscotch, '82 167
    Yogurt Sauce, Honey-, '92 307
Shrimp, Tangy Honeyed, '94 32
Smoothie, Fruited Honey-Yogurt, '88 231; '89 23
Smoothie, Honey-Banana, '89 144
Smoothie, Honey-Yogurt, '97 326
Snack Mix, Honey-Nut, '02 187
Snapper, Honey-Curried, '85 181
Spareribs, Honey-Glazed, '82 163
Spread, Honey, '81 229
Spread, Honey Mustard-Butter, '99 86
Spread, Honey-Nut, '87 157; '03 46
Stir-Fry, Honey-Butternut, '93 184
Syrup, Honey, '96 21
Syrup, Maple-Honey-Cinnamon, '85 19
Tart, Honey-Pecan, '99 212
Tea, Honey, '81 105
Tenderloins, Honey-Grilled, '00 126
Tomatoes, Honey-Baked, '02 166
Topping, Honey, '83 154
Turkey Salad, Honey-Mustard, '92 309; '01 230
Vegetables, Honey-Dijon, '98 311
Vegetables, Honey-Glazed Roasted Fall, '99 244
Vegetables, Honey-Mustard Marinated, '93 236
Vegetables, Honey-Roasted, '97 29
Vinaigrette, Sweet Potato Salad with Rosemary-
    Honey, '98 243
Whip, Peaches with Honey-Lime, '85 108
Yogurt, Orange Slices with Honey, '91 68
HONEYDEW. *See* **MELONS.**
HORS D'OEUVRES. *See* **APPETIZERS.**
HOT DOGS. *See* **FRANKFURTERS.**
HUSH PUPPIES
Acorn Squash Puppies, '94 268
Aunt Jenny's Hush Puppies, '84 88
Bacon Hush Puppies, '91 201
Baked Hush Puppies, '89 53; '95 108
Beer Hush Puppies, Fiery, '86 233
Buttermilk Hush Puppies, '00 172
Corn, Hush Puppies with, '83 286; '84 17
Corn Soufflé Hush Puppies, '98 M328
Cracker Hush Puppies, '80 99
Creole Hush Puppies, '98 43
Easy Hush Puppies, '81 191; '85 14
Golden Hush Puppies, '82 135
Green Onion-Tomato Hush Puppies, '97 84
Hush Puppies, '84 102; '87 15; '92 168; '99 32;
    '01 148, 325
Lela's Hush Puppies, '04 164
Mexican Hush Puppies, '90 214
Mexican Hush Puppies, Cheesy, '91 201
Mississippi Hush Puppies, '97 84
Onion Hush Puppies, '85 14
Peppery Hush Puppies, '80 221; '88 111
Shrimp Puppies, Hot-to-Trot, '97 84
Squash Puppies, '01 179
Tomato-Onion Hush Puppies, '91 201
Topsail Island Hush Puppies, '79 152

ICE CREAMS. *See also* **SHERBETS.**
Alaska, Apple Baked, '80 226
Alaska, Baked, '84 105; '85 295
Alaska, Brownie Baked, '80 66
Alaska, Mint Patty, '80 219
Alaskas, Banana Split, '87 10
Almond-Fudge Ice Cream, '93 205
Almond Ice Cream, '98 221
Amaretto Freeze, '82 182

Apricot Ice Cream, '99 146
Balls, Almond Ice Cream, '86 315
Balls, Cinnamon-Chip Ice Cream, '00 198
Balls, Cinnamon-Chocolate Chip Ice-Cream,
    '02 143
Balls, Easy Ice Cream, '84 106
Balls, Nutty Ice Cream, '89 72
Banana-Coconut Ice Cream, '02 164
Banana-Graham Ice Cream, '91 56
Banana-Nut Ice Cream, '00 143
Bananas Foster, Elegant, '81 59
Banana Split Ice Cream, '80 176
Banana Split Pie, Layered, '83 189
Beverages
    Almond Float, Nutmeg-, '84 106
    Amaretto Breeze, '83 172
    Apple Juice Shrub, Shenandoah, '79 282
    Banana Flip, '83 303
    Banana-Pineapple Milk Shake, '84 59
    Banana Smoothie, '87 160
    Berry Milk Shake, Double-, '00 81
    Berry Smoothie, Four-, '97 173
    Brandy Cream, '84 312; '00 271
    Cappuccino Cooler, Low-Fat, '01 166
    Champagne Delight, '83 304
    Chocoholic Smoothie, '97 173
    Chocolate-Mint Smoothie, '84 166
    Coffee Floats, Maple-, '86 195
    Coffee Punch, Creamy, '81 50
    Coffee Refresher, Velvet, '79 149
    Coffee Soda, '97 272
    Cranberry Float, Sparkling, '86 195
    Cranberry-Orange Soda, '79 148
    Cranberry Shake, '83 171
    Fruit Float, Frosty, '87 159
    Ginger Fizz, Ice Cream, '83 303
    Golden Dream, '82 100
    Kahlúa Velvet Frosty, '82 244
    Lime Cooler, '87 160
    Lime Fizz, '81 172
    Lime-Pineapple Punch, '83 142
    Mocha Melt, Spiced, '01 240
    Mocha Punch, '84 166
    Orange Milk Shake, '84 166
    Orange Shake, Peachy, '81 156
    Peach Frosty, '81 156
    Peanut Butter Milkshakes, '85 198
    Peanut Butter Shake, '82 48
    Pineapple-Buttermilk Shake, '01 173
    Pineapple-Buttermilk Shake, Light, '01 173
    Pineapple Smoothie, Peachy-, '97 173
    Pineapple Soda, '90 179
    Pink Soda, Blushing, '90 104
    Punch, Creamy Nog, '01 240
    Punch, Parsonage, '79 148
    Raisin Shake, Amazin', '86 195
    Raspberry Fizz, Rosy, '90 179
    Rum Coffee Cream, Icy, '83 172
    Shake, Pep, '79 38
    Strawberry-Banana Float, '87 160
    Strawberry-Banana Shake, Double, '01 173
    Strawberry Milkshake, Fresh, '82 113
    Strawberry-Pineapple Shake, '84 166
    Strawberry Punch, Creamy, '86 195
    Strawberry Smoothie, '86 183
    Strawberry Soda, Old-Fashioned, '79 149
    Tahitian Flower, '87 159
    Vanilla Cream, '97 272
    Vanilla Frosty, French, '79 148
    Whispers, '86 317
Black Forest Ice Cream, '88 203
Blueberry Ice Cream, '88 203
Blueberry-Peach Ice Cream, '00 153
Bombe, Amber, '80 255

Bombe, Ice Cream, '82 305; '90 269
Bombe with Raspberry Sauce, Creamy, '89 322
Bourbon Ice Cream, '87 139
Bourbon-Pecan Ice Cream, '00 260
Brownie Dessert, Special-Occasion, '87 139
Brownies, Chocolate Ice Cream, '89 124
Butter Crisp Ice Cream, '92 132
Buttermilk-Lime Ice Cream, '04 103
Butter Pecan Ice Cream, '80 176; '86 129; '88 202
Butter-Pecan Ice Cream, '96 134
Cake for Grown-Ups, Ice Cream, '88 M192
Cake, Fruity Ice Cream, '87 110
Cake, Ice Cream, '86 321; '89 71
Cake, Ice Cream Angel, '83 23
Cake, Praline Ice Cream, '80 84
Candy Crunch Ice Cream, '79 166
Cantaloupe Ice Cream, '79 177
Caramel Ice Cream Dessert, '95 36
Caramel-Vanilla Helado (Caramel-Vanilla Ice
    Cream), '81 67
Cherry Ice Cream, '84 184; '99 156
Cherry-Nut Ice Cream, '86 129
Cherry-Pecan Ice Cream, '88 203
Chocolate-Almond Ice Cream, No-Cook, '04 179
Chocolate Chunk-Peanut Butter Ice Cream, '85 297;
    '86 120
Chocolate Cookie Ice Cream, '95 245
Chocolate-Covered Peanut Ice Cream, '88 203
Chocolate Ice Cream, '80 176; '86 129
Chocolate Ice Cream, Double-, '88 203
Chocolate Ice Cream, Mexican, '91 162
Chocolate Ice Cream, No-Cook, '04 179
Cinnamon Ice Cream, '95 126
Cinnamon Ice Cream Sombreros, '93 276
Coconut Ice Cream, '98 180
Coconut Ice Cream, Fresh, '79 166
Coconut Ice Cream, No-Cook, '04 179
Coconut Ice Cream, Simple, '02 232
Coconut Ice Cream, Toasted, '00 143
Coffee Ice Cream, '88 202
Coffee Ice Cream Crunch, '82 182
Cookies and Cream Ice Cream, '88 203
Crêpes, Coffee Ice Cream, '84 85
Crêpes, Strawberry Ice Cream, '87 290
Delight, Ice Cream, '80 69
Dessert, Decadent Ice Cream, '91 56
Dessert, Ice Cream-Toffee, '00 176; '03 182; '04 82
Dessert, Layered Ice Cream, '83 189; '84 94, 105;
    '86 163
Dessert, Rocky Road Ice Cream, '00 332
Fennel Ice Cream, '95 281
Fig Ice Cream, '87 139
Fig-Mint Ice Cream, No-Cook, '04 179
Frangelica Cream, '89 291
French-Fried Ice Cream, '85 141
Fried Ice Cream, Coconut, '85 141
Fried Ice Cream Puffs, '85 141
Fruit Cream, Frozen, '94 129
Fudge-Peanut Ice Cream Dessert, '88 167
Galore and More, Ice Cream, '91 144
Granitas
    Coffee-Kahlúa Granita, '88 118
    Ginger Tea Granita, '98 334
    Grape Granita, '88 118
    Honeydew Granita, '87 162
    Mint Tea Granita, '88 117
    Orange Granita, '88 118
    Raspberry Liqueur Granita, '88 117
    Watermelon Granita, '96 179; '98 165;
        '04 171
    Wild Raspberry Tea Granita, '99 89
Hawaiian Frappé, '81 178
Honey Ice Cream, '99 212
Honey-Vanilla Ice Cream, '95 178

Ice Milks
    Banana Yogurt Ice Milk, '89 199
    Strawberry Ice Milk, Fresh, '92 94
Ices
    Apricot Yogurt Ice, '81 177
    Avocado Ice, '83 179
    Champagne Ice, '90 315
    Cider Ice, '83 162
    Cranberry-Apple Ice, '82 290
    Cranberry Ice, Tangy, '87 305
    Cranberry-Orange Ice, Tart, '86 317
    Fruit Ice, '86 176
    Fruit Ice, Mixed, '81 178
    Fruit Ice, Three-, '02 51
    Grapefruit Ice, '91 122
    Grape Ice, '83 162
    Kiwi Ice, '84 315
    Lemon Ice, '00 176; '01 330; '02 201
    Merlot Ice, '93 323
    Muscadine Ice, '82 202
    Peach Ice, '81 178
    Peach-Yogurt Ice, '84 83
    Pink Grapefruit Ice, '85 304
    Raspberry Ice, '92 268
    Strawberry Ice, '84 175; '85 108
    Strawberry-Orange Ice, '86 196
    Tropical Ice, '99 105
    Watermelon Ice, '91 173
    Wine Ice, '83 163
Irish Cream Ice Cream, '98 221
Italian-Style Ice Cream, '79 245
Kick-the-Can Ice Cream, '00 171
Layered Ice-Cream Freeze, Two-, '01 197
Lemonade Ice Cream, '88 202
Lemon Ice Cream, '79 142; '83 170; '91 65;
    '97 160; '00 55
Lemon Ice Cream Tarts, '80 152
Lime Ice Cream, Fresh, '97 160
Loaf, Pink Lemonade Ice Cream, '88 202
Log, Ice Cream Yule, '83 253
Making Ice Cream, About, '82 171
Mango Ice Cream, '86 216
Mint-Chocolate Chip Ice Cream, '88 202
Mint-Chocolate Chip Ice Cream Squares, '94 245
Mint Ice-Cream Angel Dessert, Triple, '93 86
Mint Ice Cream Dessert, '88 66
Mocha Ice Cream, '88 202; '97 M145
Oatmeal in a Slow Cooker with Ice Cream, '99 193
Orange Ice Cream, '97 160
Orange Pekoe-Chocolate Ice Cream, '99 90
Orange-Pineapple Ice Cream, '86 117
Parfaits, Chocolate-Crème de Menthe, '85 161
Parfaits, Coffee Crunch, '82 159
Parfait, Strawberry, '79 99
Parfait, Surprise Strawberry, '86 151
Peach-Almond Ice Cream, '89 156
Peach Ice Cream, '81 184; '82 171; '83 159; '86 15;
    '93 135; '98 221
Peach Ice Cream, Creamy, '85 177
Peach Ice Cream, Deluxe, '80 176; '90 314
Peach Ice Cream, Fresh, '95 195
Peach Ice Cream, No-Cook, '04 179
Peach Ice Cream, Summertime, '02 158
Peanut Butter Ice Cream, '81 103; '88 64, 203;
    '00 143
Peanut Ice Cream, '92 132
Pecan-Caramel Crunch Ice Cream, '02 322
Peppermint Ice Cream, '80 176; '86 129
Pies
    Banana Split Pie, Layered, '83 189
    Caramel Ice Cream Pie, '82 181
    Carrot Ice Cream Pie, '86 200
    Chocolate-Ice Cream Pie, '87 224
    Chocolate Ice Cream Pie, '91 56

    Chocolate-Mint Ice Cream Pie, '81 144
    Chocolate-Peanut Butter Ice Cream Pie, '98 244
    Coffee Ice Cream Pie, '79 231
    Divine Ice Cream Pie, Absolutely, '82 181
    Double-Delight Ice Cream Pie, '89 72
    Heavenly Ice Cream Pie, '82 181
    Kona Ice Cream Pie, '83 189
    Lemon Ice Cream Pie, '80 70
    Lemony Ice Cream Pie, '99 207
    Meringue-Pecan Crust, Ice Cream Pie with,
        '88 127
    Mincemeat Ice Cream Pie, '99 285
    Mint Ice Cream Pie, Triple, '98 217
    Nutty Ice Cream Pie, '91 180
    Orange Cream Pie, '03 35
    Peanutty Ice Cream Pie, '82 56
    Peppermint Candy-Ice Cream Pie, '87 260
    Pumpkin Ice Cream Pie, '81 272
    Pumpkin-Ice Cream Pie, '87 243
    Rum-Fruit Sauce, Ice Cream Pie with, '84 312
    Spectacular, Ice-Cream Pie, '90 314
    Sundae Pie, Ice Cream, '94 244
Piña Colada Ice Cream, '91 181
Pineapple-Mint Ice Cream, '84 186
Praline Freeze, '90 48
Praline Ice Cream, '89 318
Pralines and Cream Ice Cream, '82 184; '83 159
Pumpkin, Ice Cream, '96 255
Rainbow Candy Ice Cream, '88 202
Raspberry Ice Cream, '80 176
Raspberry Ice Cream, Fresh, '86 152
Rocky Road Ice Cream Dessert, '00 332
Roll, Chocolate-Frosted Ice Cream, '84 200
Roll, Strawberry Ice Cream, '84 105
Rum-Raisin Ice Cream, '97 145
Salad, Ice Cream, '79 126
Sandwiches, Chocolate Cookie Ice Cream, '87 147
Sandwiches, Chocolate Ice Cream, '89 72
Sandwiches, Chocolate Ice-Cream, '04 329
Sandwiches, Ice Cream, '99 147
Sandwiches, Oatmeal Crispy Ice Cream, '93 199
Sandwiches, Peanut Butter Cookie Ice Cream,
    '93 199
Sandwich Shells, Brownie Ice Cream, '88 195
Scuppernong Ice Cream, '88 216
Snow Ice Cream, '88 10
Sorbets
    Ambrosia Sorbet, '04 317
    Apricot-Almond Sorbet, '98 126
    Avocado Sorbet, '88 117
    Banana-Orange Sorbet, '88 117
    Berry Sorbet, Very, '90 85
    Blackberry-Lemon Sorbet, '02 85
    Blueberry-Kirsch Sorbet, '83 120
    Cantaloupe Sorbet, '03 171
    Cherry Sorbet, '03 171
    Chocolate Sorbet, '97 111
    Cran-Apple Spice Sorbet, '93 153
    Cranberry Juice Sorbet, '85 259
    Cranberry Sorbet, '82 251
    Grapefruit-Mint Sorbet, '93 153
    Grapefruit Sorbet, '03 171
    Lemon Sorbet, '93 153; '03 171
    Mango Sorbet, '86 196
    Merlot Sorbet, '97 111
    Orange Sorbet, '03 171
    Orange Sorbet, Fresh, '92 143
    Peach Sorbet, '93 153; '97 110
    Pear-Lemon Sorbet, '88 116
    Pineapple Sorbet, '03 171
    Pink Grapefruit and Tarragon Sorbet, '95 163
    Raspberry Sorbet, '03 171
    Strawberry-Champagne Sorbet, '83 162; '95 20
    Strawberry Margarita Sorbet, '89 111

ICE CREAMS, Sorbets
(continued)

Strawberry-Passion Fruit Sorbet, '98 180
Strawberry Sorbet, '88 117; '93 153; '03 171
Tropical Sorbet, '97 110
Watermelon Sorbet, '92 190; '99 166; '03 171
South Seas Ice Cream with Sweet Heat Salsa and
Cinnamon Crisps, '04 315
Spiced Ice Cream, '98 259; '99 26
Squares, Ice Cream Party, '91 214
Straw-Ba-Nut Ice Cream, '80 177
Strawberries and Cream, '92 132
Strawberry-Banana-Nut Ice Cream, '88 203
Strawberry Ice Cream, '80 177; '98 221
Strawberry Ice Cream Crêpes, '88 135
Strawberry Ice Cream, Fresh, '89 111
Strawberry Ice Cream, Homemade, '84 184
Strawberry Ice Cream, No-Cook, '04 179
Strawberry Ice Cream, Old-Fashioned, '79 94
Strawberry Ice Cream, Very, '81 155
Sundaes
Apple Ice Cream Sundaes, Spicy, '86 M195
Cocoa-Kahlúa Sundaes, '83 M58
Hot Fudge Sundae Dessert, '84 313
Ice Cream Sundae, '01 64
Mauna Loa Sundaes, '80 126
Peach Sundaes Flambé, '81 88
Pear Sundaes, Quick, '86 71
Strawberry Sundaes, Hot, '81 M5
Tropical Sundae, '04 179
Toffee Ice Cream, '88 202
Toffee Ice Cream Dessert, '87 110
Toffee Ice-Cream Dessert, '97 134
Treats, Crunchy Ice Cream, '86 300; '87 178
Tropical Paradise, Frozen, '89 206
Turtle Ice Cream, No-Cook, '04 M179
Tutti-Frutti Ice Cream, '86 129
Vanilla-Cinnamon Ice Cream, '00 127; '01 195
Vanilla Custard Ice Cream, '92 148; '96 145;
'98 221; '00 143
Vanilla Ice Cream, '80 176; '86 129; '91 174;
'04 275
Vanilla Ice Cream, Basic, '88 202
Vanilla Ice Cream, Country, '82 143
Vanilla Ice Cream, No-Cook, '04 179
Vanilla Ice Cream, Old-Fashioned, '97 166
Vanilla Ice Cream Spectacular, '82 166
ICE CUBES. *See* **BEVERAGES.**
ICINGS. *See* **FROSTINGS.**

JAMBALAYAS
Black-Eyed Pea Jambalaya, '92 70
Cajun Jambalaya, Smoky, '96 62
Chicken-and-Ham Jambalaya with Shrimp,
'04 99
Chicken-and-Sausage Jambalaya, '88 200;
'91 216; '01 278; '02 36; '03 201
Creole Jambalaya, '81 51; '87 210; '03 83
de Covington, Jambalaya, '87 211
Good Luck Jambalaya, '87 11
Jambalaya, '84 282; '98 317; '03 144; '04 288
Mix, Jambalaya, '98 317
1-2-3 Jambalaya, '97 301
Oven Jambalaya, '84 44
Red Rice Jambalaya, '91 18
Sausage Jambalaya, '80 210; '84 249
Seafood Jambalaya, Three-, '82 126
Shrimp Jambalaya, Creole, '92 99
Smoked Sausage Jambalaya, '79 42
Trail Jambalaya, '93 179
Tuna Jambalaya, '83 44

JAMS AND JELLIES
Apple Jelly, '82 149
Apple Jelly, Spiced, '95 251
Apple-Mint Jelly, '87 134
Apricot Jam, Golden, '80 31
Apricot Jam, Quick-Cooked, '99 146
Banana Jam, '82 296
Basil Jelly, '82 301
Basil Jelly, Tart, '03 135
Blackberry Jam, '82 149; '89 138; '99 M131
Blackberry Jelly, '82 149
Blueberry Jam, '79 120; '85 130
Cantaloupe-Peach Jam, '95 143
Champagne Jelly, '90 248
Chile Piquin Jelly, '94 28
Christmas Brunch Jam, '81 286
Christmas Jam, '88 288
Conserves
Apple-Cranberry Conserve, '82 308
Blueberry Conserve, '82 149
Cranberry Conserve, '79 243; '85 266; '03 278
Cranberry Conserve, Caramelized Chicken with,
'98 320
Cranberry-Coriander Conserve, '04 287
Fruit Conserve, Dried, '82 308
Peach Conserve, '79 120
Crabapple Jelly, '79 120; '81 217; '89 139
Cranberry-Wine Jelly, '81 290
Di-Calcium Phosphate Solution, '89 138
Fig Jam, '86 206
Freezer
Blackberry Jam, Freezer, '84 M181
Christmas Freezer Jelly, '86 M288
Garlic Pepper Jelly, '99 221
Grape-Burgundy Freezer Jelly, '85 130
Peach Jam, Freezer, '83 182; '84 M182
Peach-Plum Freezer Jam, '85 130
Plum Jam, Freezer, '89 M156
Raspberry Freezer Jam, '84 M181
Strawberry Freezer Jam, '84 M182
Strawberry Preserves, Freezer, '82 112
Garlic Jelly, '99 283
Grape Jelly, '89 140
Grape Jelly, Quick, '89 M156
Grape Jelly, Thyme-, '89 193
Green Pepper Jelly, Unusual, '82 132
Green Tomato-Blueberry Jam, '01 140
Green Tomato Jam, '79 121
Honey-Lemon Jelly, '97 29
Jalapeño Jelly, '92 230; '96 292
Jalapeño Pepper Jelly, Quick, '96 275
Kudzu Blossom Jelly, '95 198
Lemon Jam, Tri-Berry, '98 214
Lime Jelly, '94 23
Marmalades
Apple Marmalade, '79 120
Blueberry-Citrus Marmalade, Spicy, '03 135
Blueberry Marmalade, '96 145
Carrot-Citrus Marmalade, '81 148
Carrot-Orange Marmalade, '03 134
Citrus Marmalade, '80 101; '97 32
Citrus Marmalade, Combination, '80 50
Citrus Marmalade, Mixed, '81 43
Fruit Marmalade, Delicious, '81 285
Grapefruit Marmalade, '82 308
Green Tomato Marmalade, '01 140
Kumquat Marmalade, '90 48
Muscadine Marmalade, '98 220
Onion Marmalade, Fruited, '97 27
Orange Marmalade, '81 42
Orange Marmalade, Sunny, '02 27
Orange-Pineapple Marmalade, '82 150;
'89 M156
Peach-Orange Marmalade, '82 150

Pear Marmalade, '79 196
Strawberry-Pineapple Marmalade, '85 130
Tomato Marmalade, '00 170
Watermelon-and-Ginger Marmalade, '98 164
Mint Jelly, '79 121; '82 301; '03 135
Muscadine Jelly, Wild, '79 32
Onion Jelly, '93 135
Peach-Banana Jam, Rosy, '80 142
Peach Jam, '93 135
Peach Jam, Spiced, '00 51
Peach-Rosemary Jam, '03 134
Pear Jam, Paradise, '84 300
Pear Jam, Spiced, '98 214
Pepper Jelly, '79 121
Pineapple Jam, '81 147
Pineapple-Orange Mint Jelly, '92 105
Plum Jelly, '82 150
Port Wine Jelly with Whipped Cream, '84 254
Preserves
Custard Preserves, '98 126
Fig Preserves, '79 140; '82 150; '89 140; '96 195;
'00 175
Fruity Preserves, '98 214
Mango-Pineapple Preserves, '79 137
Peach Preserves, '81 147; '89 140
Peach Preserves, Honeyed, '85 130
Peach Preserves, Old-Fashioned, '82 150
Pear Preserves, '82 195
Plum Preserves, '03 161
Strawberry-Fig Preserves, Quick, '96 194
Strawberry Preserves, '79 120; '81 96
Strawberry Preserves Deluxe, '82 150
Tomato Preserves, '98 214
Watermelon Preserves, '79 120
Raspberry Jam, Mock, '96 168
Red Bell Pepper Jam, '95 242
Red Pepper Jelly, '89 M156
Red Zinger Jelly, '99 89
Refrigerator
Berry Refrigerator Jam, '89 139
Blueberry Refrigerator Jam, '89 139
Pepper Jelly, Easiest, '03 135
Plum Refrigerator Jam, '89 139
Rose Geranium Jelly, '82 301
Rosemary Jelly, '82 301
Sage Jelly, '82 301
Sangría Jelly, '93 341
Scuppernong Jelly, '98 220
Southwest Jelly, '03 135
Strawberry Jam, '89 138
Strawberry Jelly, '81 147
Strawberry-Port Jam, '03 134
Thyme Jelly, '82 301
Wine Jelly, '88 243; '98 125
Wine Jelly, Rosy, '85 306
Zucchini Jam, '00 168
JÍCAMA
Compote, Jícama-Fruit, '92 49
French-Fried Jícama, '81 88
Parsleyed Jícama, '81 88
Pico de Gallo, '98 174
Salad, Cranberry-Strawberry-Jícama, '02 300
Salad, Fruit-Jícama, '00 203
Salad, Jícama, '87 123
Salad, Jícama-and-Orange, '88 246
Salad, Jícama-Fruit, '86 83
Salad, Jícama-Orange, '86 83; '90 122
Salad, Pear, Jícama, and Snow Pea, '01 329
Salad with Jícama and Snow Peas, Pear,
'01 56
Soup with Crunchy Jícama, Tomatillo,
'97 143
Tomatillo Soup with Crunchy Jícama, '92 245
Wreath, Tex-Mex, '96 241

KEBABS

Antipasto Kebabs, '94 144
Beef
  Beef Kebabs, '85 110
  Chile-Beef Kebabs, '94 251
  Deluxe Beef Kebabs, '82 182
  Flank Steak Skewers, Lemon, '02 134
  Grilled Kebabs, Spicy, '98 158
  Hot-and-Spicy Kebabs, '87 193
  Marinated Beef Kebabs, '82 105; '85 159
  Marinated Beef Kebabs with Rice, '84 32
  Marinated Beef Kebabs with Vegetables, '99 292
  Meatball Kebabs, '95 192
  Pineapple-Beef Kebabs, '83 212
  Saucy Beef Kebabs, '83 109
  Shish Kebabs, Beef Tenderloin, '00 200
  Shrimp Kebabs, Steak-and-, '00 124
  Sirloin Kebabs, Marinated, '82 162
  Spirited Beef Kebabs, '87 142
  Steak-and-Shrimp Kebabs, '80 184
  Steak-and-Vegetable Kebabs, '04 218
  Steak Kebabs, '82 4; '93 95
  Steak Kebabs, Barbecued, '79 89
  Steak Kebabs, Marinated, '80 184
  Steak on a Stick, '83 109
  Steak with Vegetables, Skewered, '81 124
  Stick, Beef on a, '99 336
  Teriyaki Beef Kebabs, '80 207
  Vegetable Kebabs, Beef-and-, '91 148
  Vegetables, Beef Kebabs with, '90 148
Cantaloupe Wedges, Grilled, '87 162
Cheese Kebabs, Peppered, '91 279
Fish Kebabs, '98 223
Fruit Kebabs, '86 181; '89 85
Fruit Kebabs, Grilled, '97 147
Fruit Kebabs, Winter, '89 34
Fruit Kebabs with Coconut Dressing, '87 251
Fruit Kebabs with Mint Marinade, '82 157
Fruity Mermaid Kebabs, '91 177
Ham Kebabs, Honey, '80 156
Ham Kebabs, Swiss-, '81 124
Lamb Kebabs, '85 159; '86 90; '92 129; '95 192;
  '00 220; '03 136
Lamb Kebabs, Apricot-Grilled, '98 102
Lamb Kebabs, Rosemary Marinated, '93 203
Lamb Kebabs, Saucy, '89 167
Lamb Kebabs, Savory, '80 184
Lamb, Rosemary-Skewered, '97 190
Lamb Shish Kebabs, '79 142; '93 70
Liver Kebabs, '80 185
Mixed Grill with Spicy Peanut Sauce, Saté, '04 134
Oysters Brochette, '80 56
Pepper Kebabs, Pretty, '90 166
Pineapple-Pork Kebabs, '99 144
Pineapple Skewers with Rum Sauce, Grilled, '04 247
Pork Kebabs, Margarita, '98 M223
Pork Kebabs, Spicy, '82 182
Pork Kebabs with Sesame Seeds, '00 337
Pork Tenders, Skewered, '00 200
Poultry
  Chicken-Avocado Kebabs, '82 9; '83 68
  Chicken, Garlic-Grilled, '87 180
  Chicken Kebabs, '87 141; '03 180
  Chicken Kebabs, Good-and-Easy, '85 87
  Chicken Kebabs, Marinated, '84 M144
  Chicken Kebabs, Oriental, '95 193
  Chicken Kebabs, Pineapple-, '86 M328
  Chicken Kebabs, Sesame, '82 165
  Chicken Kebabs, Soy-, '86 156
  Chicken Kebabs Supreme, '81 124
  Chicken Livers en Brochette, '84 222
  Chicken Sate, '99 134
  Chicken, Sesame, '97 256
  Chicken Skewers, Taco-, '99 119
  Chicken Skewers with Peanut Sauce, '02 173;
    '04 324
  Chicken-Vegetable Kebabs, '03 95
  Chicken with Cha-Cha Salsa, Grilled Bahamian,
    '97 160
  Duck Kebabs with Almond Rice, Grilled, '91 291
  Hawaiian Kebabs, '85 157
  Pineapple Kebabs, Chicken-, '00 200
  Rumaki Kebabs, '82 182
  Turkey-and-Fruit Kebabs, '88 140
Salmon Kebabs, '81 182
Scallop-Bacon Kebabs, '81 111
Scallop Kebabs, Grilled, '83 101
Scallop Kebabs, Sea, '82 162
Scallops en Brochette with Vegetables, '80 163
Seafood Brochette, '87 96
Shish Kebabs, '82 182; '85 M112
Shish Kebabs, Overnight, '81 124
Shish Kebabs Teriyaki, '85 37
Shrimp
  Appetizer Shrimp Kebabs, '91 251
  Barbecued Shrimp, '90 28
  Grilled Shrimp with Smoky Sweet Sauce,
    Mexican-, '03 32
  Jerk Shrimp with Creamy Tomatillo Sauce,
    Grilled, '01 332
  Marinated and Grilled Shrimp, '87 141
  Marinated Shrimp, Grilled, '87 173
  Marinated Shrimp Kebabs, '84 276; '85 158
  Scallop Kebabs, Grilled Shrimp-and-, '92 210
  Shrimp Kebabs, '80 150, 184
  Steak-and-Shrimp Kebabs, '80 184; '00 124
  Vegetable Salsa, Shrimp Skewers with,
    '98 32, 223
Squash-and-Pepper Kebabs, Summery, '95 193
Swordfish-Shiitake Skewers, '97 168
Tomatoes with Basil Vinaigrette, Grilled,
  '97 168
Vegetable Kebabs, '01 132
Vegetable Kebabs, Easy, '02 142
Vegetable Kebabs, Fresh, '81 158; '92 101
Vegetable Kebabs, Grilled, '93 170
Vegetable Kebabs, Marinated, '83 M195
Vegetable Kebabs, Tangy Marinated, '88 142
Vegetable Skewers, Grilled, '94 160
Venison Kebabs, '82 215; '88 249
Watermelon, Sherried, '92 117

KIWIFRUIT

Chutney, Kiwifruit-Onion, '93 125
Dessert, Kiwi-and-Orange, '93 295
Glace, Sabayon, '89 306
Ice, Kiwi, '84 315
Jubilee, Kiwi, '83 120
Meringue Cups, Kiwi and Cream in, '81 279
Muffins, Kiwifruit, '87 255
Orange Roughy, Kiwi, '87 193
Parfait, Kiwi, '86 199; '87 55
Pizza, Kiwi-Berry, '86 198; '87 55
Pizza, Kiwifruit, '89 306
Pops, Kiwi Margarita, '99 133
Salad, Peach-and-Kiwi, '90 180
Salad, Spinach-Kiwifruit, '87 305
Salsa, Hot Kiwifruit, '94 82
Slushy, Kiwi-Peach, '00 201
Spritzer, Kiwi-Lemonade, '03 89
Spritzer, Strawberry-Kiwi-Lemonade, '03 89
Tart, Kiwifruit, '89 232
Tart, Kiwifruit-Peach, '88 20

KUGEL

Apricot Noodle Kugel, '92 251
Mushroom Matzo Kugel, '00 83
Noodle Casserole, Sweet, '02 238
Nu Awlins Kugel, '94 229
Sweet Kugel, '90 254
Vegetable-Noodle Kugel, '96 228

LAMB

Barbecued Lamb, '79 58
Burgers, Mesquite-Grilled Lamb, '88 59
Burgers with Cucumber Sauce, Lamb, '98 102
Burgoo, Five-Meat, '87 3
Casserole, Moussaka, '79 179
Chops
  Apples, Lamb Chops with Minted, '00 20
  Baked Lamb Chops, Easy, '02 66
  Barbecued Lamb Chops, '79 89
  Broiled Lamb Chops, '85 22
  Broiled Lamb Chops with Southwestern Butter,
    '01 194
  Dijonaise, Gourmet Lamb Chops, '82 93
  Dijon Lamb Chops, '84 277
  Dijon Lamb Chops, Creamy, '04 108
  Dijon-Rosemary Lamb Chops, '95 285; '99 333
  Fried Lamb Chops, '02 66
  Glazed Lamb Chops, '02 66
  Grilled Lamb Chops, '91 163
  Grilled Lamb Chops, Rosemary, '03 125
  Grilled Lamb Chops with Chipotle and Cilantro
    Oils, '02 96; '03 98
  Grilled Lamb Chops with Rosemary Sauce and
    Wild Rice-Fennel Pilaf, '97 127
  Herbs, Lamb Chops with, '90 164
  Maple-Glazed Lamb Chops with Zesty
    Horseradish Sauce, '04 284
  Mint Aioli, Lamb Chops with, '01 70
  Minted Apples, Lamb Chops with, '99 230
  Orange Lamb Chops, '83 35
  Peppercorn-Crusted Lamb Chops, '92 142
  Rosemary-Cherry Lamb Chops, Smart and Saucy,
    '02 193
  Rosemary Lamb Chops, Joan's, '97 42
  Sage Lamb Chops, '96 M328
  Shrimp, Lamb Chops with, '88 58
  Teriyaki, Lamb Chops, '85 109
  Teriyaki Lamb Chops, '87 60
Curried Lamb with Rice, '82 93
Curried Lamb with Rice Mold, '85 36
Curry, Creamy Lamb, '04 202
Curry with Rice, Lamb, '80 83; '81 10
Fillets of Lamb with Vegetables, '85 36
Grape Leaves, Stuffed, '94 48
Grilled Lamb with Sweet Pepper Relish, '95 104
Kebabs
  Grilled Lamb Kebabs, Apricot-, '98 102
  Lamb Kebabs, '85 159; '86 90; '92 129; '95 192;
    '00 220; '03 136
  Marinated Lamb Kebabs, Rosemary, '93 203
  Rosemary-Skewered Lamb, '97 190
  Saucy Lamb Kebabs, '89 167
  Savory Lamb Kebabs, '80 184
  Shish Kebabs, '82 182; '85 M112
  Shish Kebabs, Lamb, '79 142; '93 70
  Shish Kebabs, Overnight, '81 124
  Shish Kebabs Teriyaki, '85 37
Leg of Lamb
  Cranberry Leg of Lamb, '90 52
  Curried Leg of Lamb with Cucumber-Yogurt
    Sauce, '03 44
  Extraordinaire, Lamb, '99 242
  Glazed Lamb, Honey-Mustard, '90 52
  Glazed Leg of Lamb, '86 90
  Greek-Style Leg of Lamb, '93 170
  Grilled Lamb with Mango Salsa, '95 104
  Grilled Leg of Lamb, '96 88; '98 103
  Half of Leg of Lamb, '86 90
  Hawaii, Lamb, '81 58

LAMB, Leg of Lamb
(continued)

Hunter Sauce, Leg of Lamb with, **'95** 317
Leg of Lamb, **'86** 90; **'95** 285
Mustard Sauce, Leg of Lamb with, **'89** 71
Roasted Lamb Rosemary, **'88** 244
Roasted Leg of Lamb with Port, **'02** 258
Roasted Rosemary Lamb, **'86** 89
Roast, Garlic-Rolled Lamb, **'92** 128; **'93** 113
Roast Leg of Lamb, **'87** 96; **'99** 242; **'00** 275;
   '01 159
Sandwiches, Lamb, **'97** 107
Smoked Leg of Lamb, **'98** 102
Stuffed Leg of Lamb, **'82** 93; **'87** 248
Stuffed Leg of Lamb, Garlic-and-Herb, **'99** 241
Meatballs with Yogurt Sauce, Lamb, **'85** 132
Meat Loaf, Greek, **'96** 251; **'97** 103
Meat Loaf, Minted Lamb, **'93** 248
Meat Loaf with Feta Cheese, Lamb, **'97** 24
Mint-Crusted Lamb, **'99** 163
Moussaka, **'87** 166
Patties, Grilled Lamb, **'02** 167
Pie, Lamb, **'90** 26
Pilaf, Hearty Lamb, **'83** 101
Pockets with Dilled Cucumber Topping, Lamb,
   '87 104
Quenelles, Veal-Vermicelli Soup with, **'94** 14
Rack, Greek Lemon Lamb, **'97** 247
Rack of Lamb, **'89** 270
Rack of Lamb, Dijon, **'02** 276
Rack of Lamb, Marinated, **'94** 55
Rack of Lamb, Mint-Crusted, **'98** 118
Rack of Lamb with Cherry-Wine Sauce, Hazelnut-
   Crusted, **'95** 284
Rack of Lamb with Herb Mustard Glaze, **'81** 260
Rack, Pistachio-Crusted Lamb, **'03** 242
Roasted Lamb with Vegetables, **'98** 266
Roast of Lamb, Crown, **'81** 58
Roast, Rolled Lamb, **'95** 285
Rosemary-Crusted Lamb with Tzatziki Sauce,
   '04 108
Salad, Spinach-Lamb, **'85** 58
Shanks, Barbecued Lamb, **'92** 128; **'93** 113
Shanks, Braised Lamb, **'00** 62
Shanks Braised with Tomatoes, Lamb, **'03** 87
Shanks Milanaise, Lamb, **'82** 93
Soup with Spring Vegetables, Lamb, **'04** 108
Steak, Destin Lamb, **'92** 129; **'93** 113
Steaks with Béarnaise Sauce, Lamb, **'85** 37
Stewed Lamb with Five Spices, **'92** 72
Stew, Emerald Isle, **'95** 71
Stew-in-a-Loaf, Lamb, **'85** 37
Stew, Lamb, **'79** 293; **'88** 58
Stew, Lamb-and-Okra, **'97** 156
Stew with Popovers, Lamb, **'94** 43
Stir-Fry, Indian, **'92** 126
LASAGNA
Beefy Lasagna, **'80** 81
Bun, Lasagna in a, **'90** 176
Cheesy Lasagna, **'82** 224; **'88** 299
Chicken Lasagna, **'87** M302; **'88** 90; **'92** 197;
   '93 25; **'96** 16
Chicken Lasagna Bake, **'95** 55
Chicken Lasagna Florentine, **'95** 158; **'02** 232
Chicken Lasagna, Heavenly, **'00** 310
Chicken Lasagna, Southwestern, **'03** 173
Crabmeat-and-Spinach Lasagna, **'04** 292
Crabmeat Lasagna, **'96** 290
Crawfish Lasagna, **'91** 89
Cups, Lasagna, **'04** 293
Easy Lasagna, **'92** M197; **'93** M24
Egg-Noodle Lasagna, **'04** 219

Ellie's Lasagna, **'02** 186
Extra-Easy Lasagna, **'00** 326
Gourmet White Lasagna, **'96** 225
Green Chile-Chicken Lasagna, **'00** 338
Ground Sirloin Lasagna, **'03** 143
Ham-and-Chicken Lasagna, Creamy, **'95** 88
Italian Sausage Lasagna, **'96** 225
Lasagna, **'82** 119; **'83** M6; **'98** 95
Lean Lasagna, **'86** 37
Light Lasagna, **'95** 212
Maria, Lasagna, **'90** 191
Meatball Lasagna, **'00** 243; **'03** 142
Mexican Lasagna, **'89** 63; **'98** 283; **'01** 282
Mexican Lasagna, Easy, **'03** 22
Microwave Lasagna, **'96** M225
Noodles Lasagna, Lots of, **'91** M127
One-Step Lasagna, **'89** M129
Pizza, Lasagna, **'85** 285
Polenta Lasagna with Cream Sauce, **'03** 237
Quick Lasagna, **'84** 220
Quick 'n Easy Lasagna, **'80** M10
Roasted Vegetable-Meat Lasagna, **'99** M332
Rolls, Pepper-Topped Lasagna, **'89** M36
Rollups, Artichoke-Red Pepper, **'02** 231
Sausage Lasagna, **'83** 288
Sausage-Lasagna Rollups, **'80** 236
Sausage Pinwheels, Lasagna, **'79** 6
Simple Lasagna, **'81** 188
South-of-the-Border Lasagna, **'84** 31
Spinach-Black Bean Lasagna, **'02** 44
Supreme, Lasagna, **'92** 198; **'93** 24
Texas Lasagna, **'98** 52
Tofu Lasagna, **'83** 312
Tuna Lasagna, **'83** 44; **'84** 123
Turkey Lasagna, **'83** 239; **'91** 130
Turkey-Picante Lasagna, **'97** 93
Two, Lasagna for, **'81** 91
Vegetable
Avocado-Vegetable Lasagna, **'01** 310
Casserole, Vegetable Lasagna, **'92** 198; **'93** 25
Cheese-Vegetable Lasagna, Saucy, **'01** 306
Cheesy Vegetable Lasagna, **'79** 84
Colorful Vegetable Lasagna, **'87** 19
Florentine, Creamy Lasagna, **'91** 94
Florentine, Lasagna, **'88** 196
Garden Lasagna, **'83** 119
Spaghetti Squash Lasagna, **'84** 127
Spinach-Bean Lasagna, **'92** 96
Spinach Lasagna, **'79** 25; **'81** 243
Spinach Lasagna, Cheesy, **'80** 32; **'83** 204;
   '01 196
Spinach Lasagna, Won Ton, **'04** 129
Vegetable Lasagna, **'84** 201; **'93** 320; **'95** 211;
   '96 47; **'99** 97
Zucchini Lasagna, **'85** 194
Vintage Lasagna, **'79** 194
Zesty Lasagna, **'87** M188
LEEKS
Bisque, Crab-and-Leek, **'94** 104
Brussels Sprouts and Almonds, Leeks with, **'00** 222
Chicken and Leeks in Parchment, **'97** 290
Creamed Leeks, **'00** 222
Dilled Lemon-Butter, Leeks in, **'90** M98
Dilly Leek Combo, **'82** 26
Dip, Creamy Leek, **'86** 77
Fritters, Leek-and-Potato, **'00** 324
Glazed Leeks, **'82** 26
Glazed Leeks, Honey-, **'86** 62
Linguine, Leeks and Peppers with, **'98** 68
Medley, Carrot-and-Leek, **'88** 102
Orange Sauce, Leeks in, **'88** 86
Potatoes, Creamy Leek Mashed, **'02** 291
Potatoes, Leek Mashed, **'02** 98; **'03** 293
Quiche, Cheddar-Leek, **'88** 198

Roasted Leeks, **'00** 222
Roasted Potatoes, Carrots, and Leeks, **'94** 276
Soup, Carrot-and-Leek, **'02** 260
Soup, Carrot-Leek, **'86** 34
Soup, Cream of Leek, **'99** 276
Soup, Cream of Mushroom-and-Leek, **'01** 312
Soup, Cream of Squash and Leek, **'04** 42
Soup, Leek-and-Potato, **'84** 112
Soup, Leek-Vegetable, **'86** 304
Soup, Watercress-and-Leek, **'86** 161
Tarragon Leeks, **'84** 66
Tart, Leek-Goat Cheese, **'04** 109
Tart, Tomato-Leek-Bacon, **'03** 325
Terrine, Cold Chicken-Leek, **'92** 145
Veal Cutlets with Leeks and Zinfandel Cream,
   '96 237
Vinaigrette, Warm Leeks, **'98** 47
LEMON
Antipasto, Lemon-Vinaigrette Marinated, **'04** 256
Apples, Chilled Poached Lemon, **'86** 182
Artichoke Hearts with Lemon, **'90** 98
Asparagus, Lemon-Marinated, **'03** 119
Asparagus, Lemon-Sesame, **'91** 31
Asparagus with Lemon, **'98** 103
Bagel Chips, Lemon-and-Herb, **'91** 139
Basil, Cream of Tomato Soup with Lemon, **'96** 124
Beans, Lemon-Mint, **'88** 22
Beverages
Apple Lemonade, **'89** 212; **'03** 169
Berry Delicious Lemonade, **'93** 205
Blackberry Lemonade, **'99** 130; **'03** 89
Blueberry Lemonade, **'98** 179
Caribbean Cooler, **'95** 203
Cayenne Lemonade, **'03** 169
Cherry-Berry Lemonade, **'03** 89
Claret Lemonade, **'93** 72
Concentrate, Lemonade, **'89** 110
Cooler, Lemon, **'82** 48
Cooler, Watermelon-Lemonade, **'04** 172
Cranberry Lemonade, Spiced, **'87** 292
Cubes, Lemonade, **'95** 201
Cubes, Lemonade Ice, **'02** 48
Cubes, Lemon-Mint, **'95** 201
Dazzling Lemonade, **'97** 99
Frappé, Lemon, **'92** 44
Fresh Lemonade, **'00** 139
Fresh Squeezed Lemonade, **'81** 172
Fresh-Squeezed Lemonade, **'99** 220
Front Porch Lemonade, **'90** 156
Glass, Lemonade by the, **'96** 161
Homemade Lemonade, **'01** 143
Hot Buttered Lemonade, **'88** 208; **'94** 18
Loaded Lemonade, **'01** 93
Margaritas, Lemon-Lime, **'94** 227
Margaritas, Mock, **'99** 120
Mist, Orange-Lemon, **'79** 288; **'80** 35
Orange-Mint Lemonade, **'88** 82
Piña Coladas, **'95** 203
Pineapple Lemonade, **'93** 194
Pink Lemonade, **'01** 163
Punch, Lemonade-Bourbon, **'95** 287
Punch, Lemon Balm, **'80** 42
Punch, Lemon Champagne, **'94** 176
Punch, Pink, **'96** 190
Punch, Sparkling Lemonade, **'88** 276
Punch, Strawberry-Lemonade, **'85** 116; **'91** 175
Raspberry Lemonade, **'03** 89
Sipper, Sunshine, **'86** 179
Slush, Lemon, **'00** 271
Slush, Lemon-Rum, **'00** 271; **'04** 240
Slush, Pink Lemonade, **'80** 151
Slush, Strawberry-Lemonade, **'03** 169
Southern Breeze, **'02** 185
Spritzer, Kiwi-Lemonade, **'03** 89

Spritzer, Lemon-Mint, '99 175
Spritzer, Strawberry-Kiwi-Lemonade, '03 89
Strawberry Lemonade, '80 160
Sunny Spring Lemonade, '00 70
Sweetened Preserved Lemons, '95 141
Sweet-Tart Lemonade, '96 161; '02 160
Syrup, Cherry-Lemonade, '86 214
Tea, Almond-Lemonade, '86 229; '99 207
Tea Cubes, Lemonade with Frozen, '85 161
Tea, Lemon, '82 156
Tea, Lemon-Mint, '85 162
Tea, Minted Lemon Iced, '00 131
Tea, Sparkling Summer, '96 172
Tea Tingler, Lemon, '95 200
Velvet, Lemon, '90 15
Watermelon Lemonade, '98 165

Breads
Biscuits, Lemon Drop, '97 332
Blueberry-Lemon Bread, '85 190
French Bread, Lemony, '97 147
Knots, Glazed Lemon, '86 290
Lemon Bread, '79 275; '87 256
Muffins, Blueberry-Lemon, '79 7
Muffins, Fresh Lemon, '79 161
Muffins, Lemon, '88 119, M275
Muffins, Lemon-Blueberry, '03 26
Muffins, Lemon-Raspberry, '92 119; '03 306
Muffins, Poppy Seed-Lemon, '96 280
Nut Bread, Lemon-, '79 24
Pancakes, Lemon-Blueberry, '04 148
Pecan Bread, Lemon-, '83 54
Scones, Lemon-Poppy Seed, '97 44
Scones, Lemon-Raisin, '87 69
Spirals, French Lemon, '81 94
Tea Bread, Lemon, '92 268; '93 183; '04 209
Tea Bread, Lemon-Almond, '04 209
Tea Loaf, Lemon-Cream, '84 50
Broccoli Goldenrod, Lemon-, '84 M89
Broccoli, Lemon, '88 119; '95 53
Broccoli, Lemon Pepper Steamed, '02 215
Broccoli, Lemony Herbed, '02 45
Brussels Sprouts with Celery, Lemony, '85 25
Butter, Asparagus in Lemon, '80 M123
Butter, Asparagus with Lemon, '87 M151; '98 168
Butter, Catfish Pecan with Lemon-Thyme-Pecan,
    '04 68
Butter, Citrus, '97 307
Butter, Garlic-Lemon, '04 54
Butter, Green Beans with Lemon-Dill, '99 141
Butter, Honey-Lemon, '04 231
Butter, Lemon, '95 32; '96 124; '02 141
Butter, Lemon-Anchovy, '97 307
Butter, Lemon Pepper, '97 307
Butter, Thyme-Lemon, '96 121
Cabbage, Lemon-Butter, '88 156
Canapés, Lemon-Cheese, '87 93
Carrot Bundles, Lemon-, '91 80
Carrot Marmalemon, '96 107
Carrots and Rutabaga, Lemon-Glazed, '97 46
Carrots, Lemon, '82 300; '83 111
Carrots, Lemon-Dill Steamed, '93 180
Carrots, Lemon-Glazed, '84 16
Cauliflower, Easy Lemon, '83 322
Cheese Party Bites, Lemon-, '95 160
Cheese Patty, Lemon-Pepper, '84 117
Corn on the Cob, Lemony, '89 200
Couscous, Lemon, '96 154; '00 99; '02 237
Couscous with Raisins, Almonds, and Lemon,
    '00 295
Cream, Broccoli with Lemon, '89 245
Cream, Lemon, '03 213
Crêpes with Fruit Filling, Lemon, '82 46
Cucumbers, Lemony, '89 102
Curd, Lemon, '94 315

Desserts
Apples, Chilled Poached Lemon, '86 182
Bars Deluxe, Lemon, '79 35
Bars, Lemon Yogurt Wheat, '79 93
Bars, Luscious Lemon, '01 161
Bars, Tangy Lemon, '86 217
Cake, Coconut-Lemon, '95 319
Cake, Easy Lemon, '83 24
Cake, General Robert E. Lee Orange-Lemon,
    '88 92
Cake, Glazed Lemon, '86 70
Cake, Lemon Angel, '80 147; '97 163
Cake, Lemon-Coconut Cream, '81 179
Cake, Lemon-Coconut Sheet, '85 117
Cake, Lemon Curd Pound, '04 278
Cake, Lemon Geranium Pound, '01 131
Cake, Lemon Gold, '83 301
Cake, Lemon Meringue, '89 296; '99 118
Cake, Lemon-Pineapple, '86 60, 239
Cake, Lemon-Poppy Seed, '93 154
Cake, Lemon Pound, '82 88; '03 94
Cake, Lemon Pudding, '83 106
Cake, Lemon-Raspberry, '91 247
Cake, Lemon-Sour Cream Pound, '87 38
Cake, Lemon Sour Cream Pound, '01 117
Cake, Lemon Tea, '82 169
Cake, Lemony Pound, '96 60
Cake, Lightly Lemon Coffee, '81 14
Cake, Luscious Lemon, '93 81
Cake, Luscious Lemon Layer, '86 61
Cake, Old-Fashioned Lemon Layer, '85 191
Cake Roll, Elegant Lemon, '80 70
Cake Roll, Lemon, '89 312
Cake, Strawberry-Lemon Sheet, '04 137
Cake, Sullivan's Lemon-Almond Pound, '04 278
Cake, Tart Lemon-Cheese, '88 7; '03 317
Cake with Blueberry Sauce, Buttermilk-Lemon
    Pudding, '95 135
Cake with Mint Berries and Cream, Lemon
    Pound, '99 183
Cake, Yogurt-Lemon-Nut, '89 169
Candied Lemon Peel, '94 199
Charlotte Russe, Fresh Lemon, '80 13
Charlotte Russe, Lemon, '84 192
Cheesecake, Lemon, '86 194; '91 308; '92 24
Cheesecake, Lemon Delight, '95 219
Cheesecake, Lemony Passover, '02 51
Cheesecake, Luscious Lemon, '90 M196
Cheesecake, Strawberry-Lemon, '04 237
Cheesecakes with Raspberry Sauce, Mini Lemon,
    '02 123
Cheesecake with Orange-Pineapple Glaze,
    Lemon, '81 60
Chocolate-Lemon Creams, '98 M235
Cookies, Lemon, '03 298
Cookies, Lemonade, '79 51
Cookies, Lemon-Almond, '02 293
Cookies, Lemon-Basil Butter, '01 117
Cookies, Lemon Butter, '01 90
Cookies, Lemon-Coconut, '02 293
Cookies, Lemon Crinkle, '81 287
Cookies, Lemon Ice Box, '02 293
Cookies, Lemon-Iced Chocolate Spice, '97 123
Cookies, Lemon-Pecan, '02 293
Cookies, Lemon-Poppy Seed, '02 293
Cookies, Lemon Thumbprint, '03 298
Cookies, Lemon Thyme, '96 124
Cookies, Lemony Cutout, '85 323
Cookies, Sunshine Lemon, '86 69
Cream Cheese Dessert, Lemon-, '84 95
Cream, Frozen Lemon, '83 118
Cream, Lemon, '82 237; '91 119; '04 300
Cream, Lemon-Blueberry, '92 153
Cream Puffs, Lemon, '93 254

Cream Puffs, Strawberry-Lemon, '87 75
Cream, Strawberries 'n Lemon, '85 120
Cream, Strawberries with Lemon, '90 170
Crisp, Lemon-Blackberry, '98 171
Crisps, Lemon, '95 272
Cupcakes, Lemonade, '04 163
Cupcakes, Lemon-Blueberry Ice-Cream, '01 172
Cupcakes, Lemon Moist, '82 112; '83 153
Cups, Baked Lemon, '87 128
Curd, Fresh Fruit with Lemon, '88 21
Curd, Lemon, '87 139; '89 334; '94 315;
    '04 259, 279
Curd with Berries, Lemon, '90 102
Custard in Meringue Cups, Lemon, '80 295;
    '81 172
Custards, Lemon-Buttermilk, '89 49
Dainties, Lemon Pecan, '80 208
Delight, Lemon, '82 227
Divinity, Lemon, '97 316
Filling, Creamy Lemon, '80 70
Filling, Lemon, '81 172; '84 137; '85 191;
    '86 235; '87 293; '89 312; '90 308; '94 122;
    '95 319; '97 255; '99 118
Filling, Lemon-Apricot, '90 105
Filling, Lemon-Cheese, '79 68; '88 7; '03 317
Filling, Lemon Cream, '84 23; '87 14
Filling, Lemon Icebox Pie, '03 104
Filling, Lemon-Orange, '81 71
Filling, Strawberry-Lemon, '04 137
Frosting, Creamy Lemon, '79 93
Frosting, Lemon, '85 191; '86 217; '93 81
Frosting, Lemon Buttercream, '83 301; '86 61;
    '91 247; '03 105
Frosting, Lemon-Butter Cream, '85 117
Frosting, Lemon-Coconut, '90 253
Frosting, Lemon-Cream Cheese, '81 157
Frosting, Lemony White, '88 7; '03 317
Frosting, Orange-Lemon, '88 92
Fruitcake, Lemon, '83 258
Glaze, Lemon, '79 285; '86 194; '87 41; '92 269;
    '93 154, 183; '97 123; '01 117
Ice Cream, Lemon, '79 142; '83 170; '91 65;
    '97 160; '00 55
Ice Cream, Lemonade, '88 202
Ice, Lemon, '00 176; '01 330; '02 201
Layered Lemon Dessert, '88 134
Logs, Hazelnut-Lemon, '84 117
Mandel Bread, '99 57
Melting Moments, '85 191
Meringue, Chocolate Pudding with Lemon,
    '88 258
Meringue Cream Cups, Lemon, '84 23
Mousse, Lemon Cloud, '90 90
Mousse, Strawberry-Lemon, '82 128
Mousse with Raspberry Sauce, Lemon, '91 96;
    '92 130
Napoleons, Blueberry-Lemon, '94 122
Parfaits, Strawberry-Lemon, '84 198
Pastry Shell, Lemon in, '84 137
Pears, Lemon Poached, '82 74
Pie, Angel, '79 123
Pie, Apple-Lemon Chess, '86 220
Pie, Aunt Kitty's Lemon, '98 275
Pie, Best-Ever Lemon Meringue, '94 208
Pie, Buttermilk Lemon, '81 120; '82 23
Pie, Buttermilk-Lemon, '88 297
Pie, Buttermilk-Lemon Cream, '88 99
Pie, Deluxe Lemon Meringue, '81 172; '90 313
Pie Filling, Lemon Meringue, '04 110
Pie, Frozen Lemonade, '92 101
Pie, Frozen Lemon Cream, '82 86
Pie, Lemonade, '91 42
Pie, Lemon-Blueberry Cream, '02 92
Pie, Lemon-Buttermilk, '91 272

LEMON, Desserts
(continued)

Pie, Lemon Cheese, **'81** 136; **'82** 146
Pie, Lemon Chess, **'79** 32; **'82** 196; **'00** 60; **'02** 107; **'03** 217, 259
Pie, Lemon-Cottage Cheese, **'79** 44
Pie, Lemon Cottage Cheese, **'81** 143
Pie, Lemon Fluff, **'92** 342; **'93** 46
Pie, Lemon Ice Cream, **'80** 70
Pie, Lemon-Lime Chess, **'01** 23
Pie, Lemon Meringue, **'85** M112; **'86** 130; **'04** 110
Pie, Lemon-Orange, **'85** 172
Pie, Lemon Parfait, **'94** 310
Pie, Lemon-Pecan, **'93** 251
Pie, Lemon-Sour Cream, **'82** 169
Pie, Lemon Sponge, **'83** 192
Pie, Lemon-Strawberry, **'88** 127
Pie, Lemon Twirl, **'84** 94
Pie, Lemony Cherry, **'92** 30
Pie, Lemony Ice Cream, **'99** 207
Pie, Slice of Lemon, **'84** 23
Pie, Tart Lemon, **'91** 275
Pie, Tart Lemon-Apple, **'80** 100
Pie, Whipped Lemon, **'79** 124
Pops, Cherry-Berry Lemonade, **'03** 89
Pops, Deep Blue Sea, **'94** 143
Pops, Sangría, **'99** 133
Pudding, Baked Lemon, **'04** 295
Pudding, Layered Lemon, **'82** 128
Pudding, Lemon, **'79** 86; **'81** 99
Pudding, Lemon Cake, **'92** 96; **'98** 35
Pudding, Lemon Fluff, **'85** 304
Pudding, Lemon-Pear, **'96** 283
Pudding, Old-Fashioned Lemon Bread, **'88** 95
Roll, Snow-Capped Lemon, **'79** 68
Rolls with Raspberry Sauce, Lemon Angel, **'94** 294
Sauce, Blueberry-Lemon, **'01** 117
Sauce, Cheesecake with Raspberry-Lemon, **'96** 30
Sauce, Lemon, **'84** 258, 306; **'85** 77, 190; **'91** 240; **'96** 283; **'01** 184; **'04** 98
Sauce, Lemon Cream, **'93** 200
Sauce, Lemon Dessert, **'87** M165
Sauce, Tart Lemon, **'85** 191
Sherbet, Lemon, **'91** 309
Sherbet, Lemon Cream, **'79** 114
Sherbet, Lemon-Pineapple, **'96** 330
Solid, Lemon, **'93** 279
Sorbet, Blackberry-Lemon, **'02** 85
Sorbet, Lemon, **'93** 153; **'03** 171
Sorbet, Pear-Lemon, **'88** 116
Soufflé, Cold Lemon-Lime, **'84** 24
Soufflé, Lemon, **'82** 170, 252; **'94** 199
Soufflés, Quick Lemon Sauce, **'88** 43
Soufflé, Tart Lemon, **'85** 82
Soufflé with Raspberry-Amaretto Sauce, Frozen Lemon, **'88** 130
Sponge Cups, Lemon, **'83** 10
Squares, Golden Carrot-Lemon, **'80** 40
Squares, Lemon, **'81** 197; **'97** 329
Squares, Lemon-Pecan, **'89** 124
Squares, Lemony Cream Cheese, **'82** 159
Strawberry-Lemon Dessert, **'86** 162
Tart) Caky Flaky Tart (Tart Lemon, **'96** 159
Tart, Double-Decker Lemon, **'04** 111
Tart Filling, Tangy Lemon, **'04** 111
Tarts, Berry Good Lemon, **'91** 119
Tarts, Dainty Lemon, **'82** 304
Tarts, Golden Lemon, **'85** 191
Tart Shells, Lemon, **'88** 195

Tarts, Lemon, **'82** 156; **'83** 79
Tarts, Lemon-Cheese, **'79** 2
Tarts, Lemon Ice Cream, **'80** 152
Tarts, Lemon-Sour Cream, **'81** 304
Tart, Strawberry-Lemon, **'89** 111
Tart, Tangy Lemon, **'01** 245; **'04** 111
Topping, Lemon-Pineapple, **'86** 60
Torte with Raspberry Sauce, Lemon Meringue, **'93** 82
Trifle, All Seasons Lemon, **'95** 219
Trifle, Lemon-Blueberry, **'88** 210
Yogurt, Lemon-Chiffon Frozen, **'85** 54
Yummies, Lemon, **'81** 301
Zephers, Lemon, **'81** 172
Dip, Pink Lemonade-Lime, **'04** 133
Dressing
Broccoli with Lemon Dressing, Chilled, **'88** 270
Caper Dressing, Lemon-, **'96** 69
Cream Dressing, Lemon, **'82** 170
Creamy Lemon Dressing, **'88** M193
French Dressing, Green Salad with Lemony, **'85** 67
Herb Dressing, Lemon-, **'97** 92
Herb Dressing, Lemon-and-, **'92** 108
Herb Salad Dressing, Lemon-, **'82** 67
Honey-Lemon Dressing, **'95** 133
Honey-Lemon Dressing, Fruit Salad with, **'93** 21
Lemon Dressing, **'04** 167
Molasses Dressing, Lemon-, **'97** 195
Mustard Dressing, Lemon-, **'02** 52
Pepper Dressing, Lemon-, **'87** 55
Salad Dressing, Lemon, **'79** 8
Tomato Slices with Lemon Dressing, **'87** 167
Vinaigrette, Fresh Lemon, **'04** 30
Vinaigrette, Lemon, **'04** 169
Yogurt Dressing, Lemon-, **'93** 17
Yogurt Slaw or Salad Dressing, Lemon-, **'88** 54
Glaze, Lemon, **'97** 332
Green Beans, Lemon, **'89** 275
Green Beans, Lemon-Dill, **'01** 181
Green Beans, Lemon-Pecan, **'04** 285
Green Beans, Lemon-Walnut, **'93** 304
Green Beans, Lemony, **'85** 190; **'99** 259
Green Beans with Lemon, **'03** 66
Honey, Lemon, **'94** 16; **'96** 124
Jam, Tri-Berry Lemon, **'98** 214
Jelly, Honey-Lemon, **'97** 29
Linguine, Lemon, **'97** 228
Main Dishes
Beef, Spicy Lemon Thai, **'97** 320
Beef, Thai Lemon, **'97** 292
Catfish, Fried Lemon-Rosemary, **'02** 319
Catfish, Lemon Barbecued, **'88** 271; **'89** 202
Chicken and Vegetables, Lemon, **'88** 118
Chicken, Baked Lemon, **'85** 190
Chicken Breasts, Lemon, **'89** 18
Chicken, Clay Oven-Roasted Citrus, **'98** 108
Chicken Cutlets with Lemon, **'85** 8
Chicken, Greek Lemon, **'90** 65
Chicken, Grilled Yogurt-Lemon, **'81** 111
Chicken in Lemon and Wine, **'83** 281
Chicken in Lemon Marinade, **'98** 128
Chicken, Lemon, **'81** M138; **'86** 173; **'96** 49
Chicken, Lemonade, **'82** 163
Chicken, Lemon Barbecued, **'93** 215
Chicken, Lemon-Basil, **'02** 91
Chicken, Lemon-Dill, **'93** 19
Chicken, Lemon-Fried, **'79** 77
Chicken, Lemon Fried, **'82** 275
Chicken, Lemon-Frosted, **'88** 170
Chicken, Lemon-Garlic, **'89** M132; **'90** 35
Chicken, Lemon-Garlic Roasted, **'98** 108
Chicken, Lemon-Herb, **'85** 127; **'00** 90
Chicken, Lemon-Herb Grilled, **'95** 87

Chicken, Lemon-Mustard, **'99** 109
Chicken, Lemon-Pepper, **'89** 104
Chicken, Lemon-Roasted, **'95** 24
Chicken, Lemon-Rosemary, **'94** 201
Chicken, Lemon-Spinach, **'97** 104
Chicken, Lemony Pecan, **'96** 82
Chicken Nuggets, Lemon-, **'86** 337; **'87** 283
Chicken Piccata, Herbed, **'88** 28
Chicken Sauté, Lemon-Dill, **'91** 186
Chicken, Sweet-and-Sour Lemon, **'84** 93
Chicken, Sweet Lemon, **'79** 218
Chicken, Sweet Lemon-, **'84** 69
Chicken Tenders, Lemon, **'03** 184
Chicken with Lemon, Garlic, and Rosemary, Roasted, **'97** 61
Cornish Hens, Lemon Roasted, **'82** 260
Cutlets, Lemon-Flavored, **'79** 105
Fillets, Lemon-Coated, **'80** M53
Flank Steak, Lemon-Lime, **'95** 55
Flounder Thermidor, **'85** 190
Lamb Rack, Greek Lemon, **'97** 247
Linguine with Garlic and Lemon, **'88** 91
Mackerel, Lemon-Baked, **'79** 182
Pork Chops, Lemon-Herb, **'84** 81; **'89** M132
Pork Chops, Lemony, **'88** 118
Pork Chops, Lemony Pan-Fried, **'03** 205
Pork Piccata, **'94** 57; **'99** 332
Ribs, Lemon Baked, **'81** 166
Ribs, Lemon Grilled, **'81** 154
Salmon with Lemon and Olive Oil, Broiled, **'04** 46
Shrimp and Pasta, Lemon, **'96** 124
Shrimp in Lemon Butter, **'84** 163
Shrimp, Lemon-Garlic Broiled, **'82** 29; **'86** 182
Shrimp, Luscious Lemon, **'88** 150
Snapper with Crabmeat Relish, Lemony Pecan-Crusted, **'99** 298
Spareribs, Lemony Sweet, **'80** 73
Steak Skewers, Lemon Flank, **'02** 134
Steak with Brandy Sauce, Lemon-Butter, **'85** 78
Tuna with Lemon and Capers, **'97** 180
Turkey-Basil Piccata, **'96** 49
Turkey Piccata, **'91** 137
Turkey Piccata with Caper Sauce, **'98** 49
Veal, Lemon, **'93** 35
Veal Piccata, **'92** 181
Veal Piccata, Lemon, **'86** 118
Veal with Artichoke Hearts, Lemon, **'87** 219
Marinade, Lemon-Soy, **'91** 194
Marmalade, Citrus, **'80** 101
Mashed Potatoes, Lemon, **'04** 181
Mayonnaise, Gremolata, **'00** 136
Mayonnaise, Lemon, **'95** 32; **'98** 144; **'99** 178; **'04** 56
Mayonnaise, Lemon-Basil, **'03** 208
Mayonnaise, Lemon-Cream, **'85** 264
Mayonnaise, Lemon-Dill, **'99** 267
Mold, Cheesy Lemon, **'79** 241
Mold, Lemon-Cucumber, **'87** 90
New Potatoes, Lemon-Buttered, **'84** 149; **'90** 268; **'98** 159
New Potatoes, Lemony, **'82** 158
Olive Oil, Lemon-Infused, **'95** 231
Olives, Lemon-Garlic, **'94** 118
Pancakes with Strawberry Butter, Lemon, **'99** 44
Pasta, Lemon-Garlic, **'95** 181
Pilaf, Lemon, **'97** 322
Pilaf, Lemon-and-Pine Nut, **'97** 51
Potatoes, Creamy Lemon-Poppy Seed Mashed, **'03** 294
Potatoes, Herbed Lemon Mashed, **'93** 208
Potatoes, Lemon and Nutmeg, **'80** 36
Potatoes, Lemon-Herb Stuffed, **'83** 173
Potatoes, Lemon-Steamed, **'86** 177

Potatoes, Oregano-and-Lemon Skillet, '93 54
Potato Wedges, Lemon, '88 21
Potato Wedges, Lemony, '90 M61
Preserved Lemons, Fresh, '00 17
Relish, Lemon-Date, '96 271
Relish, Lemony Cranberry, '79 243
Rice, Lemon, '89 166
Rice, Lemony, '99 46
Rice Pilaf, Lemon, '01 36; '04 82
Risotto, Lemon-Lime, '97 213
Roses, Lemon, '82 280
Salads
  Apple-Bran Salad, Lemony, '86 223
  Asparagus Salad, Creamy Lemon-, '93 116
  Cauliflower-Lemon Salad, '81 23
  Cheese Salad, Lemon-, '85 240
  Chicken Salad Wraps, Lemon-Basil, '00 216
  Congealed Lemon-Tomato Salad, '89 178
  Congealed Salad, Lemon-Cranberry, '87 311
  Congealed Salad, Lemon-Vegetable, '85 22
  Cream Salad, Lemon-, '88 250
  Freeze, Fruity Lemon, '82 145
  Fruit Salad, Lemonade, '84 24
  Onion Salad, Lemon-, '85 252
  Potato Salad, Lemon-Basil, '97 63; '01 178
  Tossed Salad, Lively Lemon, '00 16
Sauces
  Asparagus with Lemon Sauce, '86 62
  Barbecue Sauce, Herbed Lemon, '94 154;
    '98 334
  Barbecue Sauce, Lemony, '88 M177; '95 31
  Basting Sauce, Lemon, '95 32
  Broccoli with Lemon Sauce, '91 292; '92 256
  Broccoli with Lemon Sauce and Pecans, '86 71
  Brussels Sprouts in Lemon Sauce, '82 269
  Butter Sauce, Lemon-, '84 252; '92 337; '99 198
  Butter Sauce, New Potatoes with Lemon-, '00 103
  Catfish with Lemon Sauce, Pecan, '03 185
  Celery Sauce, Baked Fillets in Lemon-, '84 91
  Cheese Sauce, Lemon-, '91 24
  Cheese Sauce, Lemony, '84 183
  Chicken Scaloppine in Lemon Sauce, '00 166
  Cream Sauce, Braised Chicken Breast in Lemon,
    '94 184
  Cream Sauce, Lemon, '99 53
  Cucumber Sauce, Lemony, '89 245
  Dill Sauce, Potatoes and Green Beans with
    Lemon-, '01 89
  Dipping Sauce, Lemon, '02 134
  Garlic Sauce, Shrimp in Lemon, '83 67
  Honey-Lemon Mustard Sauce, '84 275
  Hot Lemon-Herb Sauce, '91 286
  Lemon Sauce, '82 290
  Meunière Sauce, Lemon, '88 222
  Mustard Sauce, Salmon Steaks with Lemon-,
    '97 124
  New Potatoes with Lemon Sauce, '86 130
  Parsley Sauce, Lemon, '81 106
  Parsley Sauce, Lemon, '93 48
  Red Snapper with Lemon Sauce, '01 83
  Tartar Sauce, Lemony, '95 32
  Tomato-Lemon Sauce, Salmon with Almonds
    and, '04 23
  Vanilla Sauce, Lemon-, '02 231
  Veal Scaloppine in Lemon Sauce, '00 166
  Zesty Lemon Sauce, '97 318
Slices, Fluted Lemon, '82 51
Soup, Egg-Lemon, '96 88
Soup, Lemon-Egg Drop, '93 81
Spinach, Creamy Lemon, '82 302
Spinach with Feta, Lemon, '85 190
Spinach with Lemon and Pepper, '97 105
Spread, Lemon-Raisin, '01 48
Sprouts, Lemon, '85 288

Squeezers, Lemon, '95 32
Sugar, Lemon-Mint, '95 32
Sugar Snap Peas, Lemon-Scented, '02 282
Sugar Snap Peas with Basil and Lemon, '93 66
Sweetened Preserved Lemons, '95 141
Vegetables, Honey-Glazed Roasted Fall, '99 244
Vegetables, Lemon, '93 83
Vermicelli, Lemon, '84 329
Vinaigrette, Lemon, '95 31
Vinaigrette, Lemon-Basil, '94 205
Vinaigrette, Lemon-Dill, '99 27
Vinaigrette, Lemon-Honey, '96 65
Vinaigrette, Peppery Lemon, '01 122
Vinegar, Lemon, '95 31; '96 124
Vinegar, Lemon-Mint, '85 124
Vinegar, Raspberry-Lemon, '87 134
Vinegar, Spicy Oregano-Lemon, '85 124
Wild Rice, Pecan-Lemon, '92 211
Wonton Chips, Lemon-and-Herb, '91 138
Yogurt Coleslaw, Grilled Chicken Breasts with
    Lemon-, '98 148
Zucchini, Lemon-Garlic, '89 226
LENTILS
Baked Lentils with Cheese, '84 113
Bean Pot Lentils, '01 35
Burgers, Lentil, '95 123
Burritos, Lentil, '99 287
Casserole, Lentils-and-Rice, '93 301
Liver, Mock Chopped, '00 281
Marinated Lentils, Tangy, '00 94
Pasta and Lentils, Cheesy, '99 287
Pilaf, Rice-and-Lentil, '88 17
Rice, Lentils and, '99 236
Salad, Lentil-and-Orzo, '03 127
Salad, Lentils-and-Rice, '90 197
Salad, Mediterranean Lentil, '96 239
Salad, Winter, '97 304; '98 19
Samosas, '96 239
Sauce, Lentil Spaghetti, '90 198
Soup, Beefy Lentil, '87 282
Soup, Lentil, '83 292; '86 304; '91 28; '97 304;
    '98 19
Soup, Oven-Baked Split Pea-and-Lentil, '00 316
Soup, Spanish-Style Lentil, '96 239
Spanish-Style Lentils and Rice, '03 201
Spread, Lentil, '99 288
Stew, Lentil-Rice, '82 232
Supper, Lentil-and-Rice, '84 202
Tacos, Lentil, '88 197
Tex-Mex Lentils, '99 288
Vegetables, Savory Lentils and, '98 29
LIGHT & EASY. *See* **HEALTHY & LIGHT.**
LIME
Beverages
  Apple Limeade, Pink, '89 46
  Cooler, Grape-Lime, '94 227
  Cooler, Lime, '87 160
  Daiquiris, Freezer Lime, '79 141
  Fizz, Frosty Lime, '90 104
  Fizz, Lime, '81 172
  Fresh Limeade, '00 139
  Fuzz Buzz, '82 160
  Limeade, '01 143
  Margarita Granita, '02 49
  Margaritas, Frosted, '84 115
  Margaritas, Frosty, '83 172
  Margaritas, Lemon-Lime, '94 227
  Margaritas, Mock, '99 120
  Margaritas, Orange-Lime, '97 140
  Margaritas, Pitcher, '83 175
  Pineapple Limeade, '01 235
  Punch, Brew-Ha-Ha, '98 255
  Punch, Calypso Presbyterian Church Women's
    Lime, '95 141

Punch, Foamy Lime, '82 264
Punch, Lime, '84 58
Punch, Lime-Pineapple, '83 142
Punch, Lime Slush, '90 273
Punch, Orange-Lime, '82 160
Refresher, Cantaloupe-Lime, '01 332
Rio Grande Limeade, '01 186
Swamp Breeze, '01 146
Tea, Lime, '98 198
Tea, Lime-Mint, '97 122
Butter, Cilantro-Lime, '98 156; '01 24; '02 109
Butter, Grilled Corn with Jalapeño-Lime, '01 158;
    '04 178
Candied Lime Strips, '94 137
Crackers, Tortilla-Lime, '99 17
Cream, Cilantro-Lime, '98 129
Cream, Ginger-Lime, '95 227
Desserts
  Cake, Key Lime, '91 214
  Cake, Lime Icebox Pie, '03 104
  Cakes, Creamy Lime, '04 89
  Cheesecake with Raspberry Sauce, Lime, '00 204
  Cheesecake with Strawberry-Butter Sauce, Key
    Lime, '96 87
  Cheesecake with Strawberry Sauce, Key Lime,
    '03 55
  Cream, Lime-Rum, '93 169
  Curd, Key Lime, '96 126
  Filling, Lime Icebox Pie, '03 104
  Frosting, Lime Buttercream, '03 105
  Ice Cream, Buttermilk-Lime, '04 103
  Ice Cream, Fresh Lime, '97 160
  Key Lime Bars with Macadamia Crust, '99 282
  Loaf, Lime Layer, '85 96
  Mousse Freeze, Luscious Lime, '81 173
  Parfaits, Lime, '80 153
  Parfaits, Surf-and-Sand, '93 169
  Pie, Key Lime, '91 42; '96 171; '00 120; '03 179;
    '04 254
  Pie, Lemon-Lime Chess, '01 23
  Pie, Lime Chiffon, '86 130
  Pie, Lime Fluff, '84 43
  Pie, Manny and Isa's Key Lime, '95 118
  Pies, Key Lime, '95 86; '97 162
  Pies, Lime Party, '92 65
  Pie with Gingersnap Crust, Margarita-Key Lime,
    '01 187
  Pie with Minted Tropical Salsa, Key Lime,
    '99 333
  Refresher, Lime-Mint, '82 144
  Sherbet, Creamy Lime, '84 165
  Sherbet, Lime, '82 159; '89 202
  Soufflé, Cold Lemon-Lime, '84 24
  Squares, Lime, '79 2
  Tart in Coconut Crust, Key Lime, '89 160
  Tartlets, Key Lime Curd, '01 250
  Tart, Lime, '98 272
  Tart, Lime-and-Macadamia Nut, '03 295
  Tart, Lime-Pineapple, '88 6
  Tornadoes for Grown-Ups, Texas, '94 143
  Whip, Lime, '89 199
Dip, Lime-Dill, '92 65
Dip, Orange-Lime, '96 248
Dressing, Asparagus with Warm Citrus, '96 M86
Dressing, Creamy Lime, '04 46
Dressing, Honey-Lime, '83 139; '93 71
Dressing, Lime, '79 2; '83 120
Dressing, Lime-Honey, '92 213
Dressing, Lime-Honey Fruit Salad, '87 81
Dressing, Lime-Parsley, '85 131
Dressing, Lime-Peanut, '01 26
Dressing, Lime Sherbet, '80 221
Dressing, One-Bean Salad with Lime-Mustard,
    '00 202

LIME
(continued)

Dressing, Spinach Salad with Chili-Lime, '94 63
Fruit and Veggies with Lime, Spicy, '04 141
Jelly, Lime, '94 23
Main Dishes
Beef Stir-Fry, Lime-Ginger, '92 65
Bow Ties, Black Beans, and Key Limes, '96 291
Catfish, Lime-Orange, '02 22
Chicken Breasts, Lime-Roasted, '97 100
Chicken, Grilled Lime-Jalapeño, '91 87
Chicken, Honey-Lime Grilled, '96 189; '98 332
Chicken, Limeade, '01 257
Chicken, Lime-Grilled, '02 142; '04 320
Chicken with Grilled Pineapple, Lime, '04 88
Chicken with Lime Butter, '84 68
Chicken with Orange, Lime, and Ginger Sauce,
'92 123
Flank Steak, Lemon-Lime, '95 55
Pork Chops, Honey-Lime, '91 33
Pork Tenderloin with Lime and Chipotle, Sweet,
'04 184
Pork Tenderloin with Yogurt and Lime, Grilled,
'04 216
Red Snapper with Lime, Stuffed, '83 246
Roast, Roasted Lime-Cilantro Eye of Round,
'04 88
Swordfish with Avocado-Lime Sauce, Grilled,
'97 127
Turkey Tenderloins, Lime-Buttered, '92 127
Veal, Amaretto-Lime, '93 54
Marinade, Fruit with Lime, '98 92
Marinade, Southwestern, '99 141
Marmalade, Citrus, '80 101
Mayonnaise, Flavored, '97 328
Mayonnaise, Lime-Cayenne, '04 121
Muffins, Key Lime, '95 50
Mustard, Key Lime, '94 278
Oil, Cilantro, '03 98
Onions, Citrus, '04 89
Pesto, Cilantro, '98 145
Pickles, Lime, '96 206
Popcorn, Spicy Nut, '02 287
Rice, Lime-Flavored, '84 175
Risotto, Lemon-Lime, '97 213
Salad, Beef-and-Lime Rice, '03 172
Salad, Emerald, '81 143
Salad, Frosted Lime-Cheese, '79 286
Salad, Lime-Carrot, '92 65
Salad, Lime Congealed, '02 257
Salad, Lime-Potato, '02 22
Salad, Pear-Lime, '84 152
Salad, Pineapple-Lime, '84 320
Salad, Snowy Emerald, '87 311
Salad, Zesty Shredded, '04 324
Sauce, Avocado-Lime, '03 90
Sauce, Creamy Lime, '04 119
Sauce, Fresh Fruit with Lime, '02 68
Sauce, Honey-Lime, '82 85
Sauce, Lime Hollandaise, '93 121
Sauce, Lime-Saffron, '94 71
Sauce, Sour Cream-Lime, '91 286
Slaw, Tangy, '02 215
Sopa de Lima, '79 211
Soup, Butternut Squash-Lime, '03 236
Soup, Lime, '88 31; '02 168
Sour Cream, Lime, '04 324
Sweet Potatoes, Lime, '02 307
Vinaigrette, Cilantro-Lime, '94 77
Vinaigrette, Pistachio-Lime, '97 148
Vinaigrette, Spicy Lime, '01 217
Whip, Peaches with Honey-Lime, '85 108

LINGUINE
Alfredo, Bourbon-Pecan, '96 291
Alfredo, Linguine, '04 96
Artichoke and Shrimp Linguine, '95 210
Artichoke Hearts, Pasta with, '86 209
Baked Linguine with Meat Sauce, '01 41
Basil Pasta, Fresh Tomato Sauce over, '93 176
Bay Scallops, Linguine with, '97 201
Beef Stir-Fry, Italian, '99 35
Broccoli Linguine, '98 30
Cacciatore, Hearty Chicken, '02 269
Carbonara, Linguine, '87 108
Casserole, Linguine with Meat Sauce, '03 22
Chicken-and-Pepper Pasta, '03 199
Chicken-Broccoli Linguine, '98 30
Chicken Linguine, '01 128
Chicken, Sicilian, '97 142
Chicken, Taste-of-Texas Pasta and, '92 78
Clam Linguine, '95 212
Clam Linguine, Quick, '90 233
Clam Sauce, Linguine in, '81 83
Clam Sauce, Linguine with, '84 124; '88 90;
'89 178
Clam Sauce with Linguine, '84 9
Cracked Pepper Linguine, '97 228
Crawfish Pasta, Creamy, '03 277
Creole Sauce, Pasta with Crescent City Grill,
'04 289
Dried Tomato-Basil Pesto Linguine, Flank Steak
and, '04 101
Favorite Pasta, My, '95 213
Garlic and Lemon, Linguine with, '88 91
Green Beans and Walnut Sauce, Linguine with,
'04 128
Greens, Creamy Pasta with, '00 91
Leeks and Peppers with Linguine, '98 68
Lemon Linguine, '97 228
Mussels Linguine, '90 M112
Parmesan, Creamy Pasta with, '98 233
Pasta Verde, '84 201
Peas and Pasta, '99 68
Pepper-Pesto Linguine, Grilled, '04 136
Pepper-Sausage Pasta, Three, '02 122
Pesto and Pasta, '92 98
Pesto Pasta, Asian, '95 189
Pesto Primavera, '96 170
Primavera, Peppery Pasta, '02 161
Red Pepper Sauce, Linguine with, '93 127
Salad, Pasta, '84 139
Salad Pasta, Caesar, '95 230
Salad, Peanutty Spicy Noodle, '04 72
Salad, Sesame Noodle, '02 186
Sausage and Peppers, Linguine with,
'03 170
Seafood Delight, '86 208
Seafood Linguine, '79 227
Seafood Sauce, Linguine with, '83 232
Shrimp and Linguine, Spicy, '92 34
Shrimp and Pasta, Mediterranean, '95 286
Shrimp and Pasta, Sautéed, '96 288
Shrimp Marinara, '84 233
Shrimp Scampi, '00 283
Shrimp, Spicy Pasta and, '97 67
Spinach, Linguine with, '91 30
Tomato-Cream Sauce, Linguine with,
'86 158
Tomato Sauce with Linguine, Fresh, '02 213
Turkey Scaloppine, '04 321
Vegetables, Noodles with Spring, '02 125
Vegetables, Traveling Linguine with Roasted,
'93 178
Verde, Pasta, '84 201
Whole Wheat Linguine, '84 177
Zucchini with Pasta, Stuffed, '97 101

LIVER
Appetizers
Chicken Liver and Bacon Roll-Ups, '80 200;
'81 57
Chicken Livers, Party, '83 242
Chicken Liver Turnovers, '79 141
Pâté, Chicken Liver, '79 153; '81 235; '83 108;
'84 205
Pâté, Country, '86 66
Pâté, Duck Liver, '79 227
Pâté, Liver-Cheese, '85 276
Pâté with Cognac, '86 159
Pâté with Madeira Sauce, Liver, '93 323
Rumaki, '80 M136
Spread, Liver, '89 161
Spread, Sherried Liver, '80 86
Barbecued Liver, '85 219
Beef Liver Patties, '81 277
Beef Liver with Balsamic Vinegar, '98 130
Calf's Liver with Vegetables, '85 219
Chicken
Chopped Chicken Livers, Grandma Rose's,
'96 105
en Brochette, Chicken Livers, '84 222
Fried Chicken Livers, '96 105
Garlic Chicken Livers, '96 105
Italian Sauce, Chicken Livers in, '83 117
Marsala Wine Sauce, Chicken Livers with, '81 76
Mushrooms, Chicken Livers with, '81 133
Omelet, Chicken Liver, '82 44
Orange Sauce, Chicken Livers in, '82 218
Party Chicken Livers, '83 242
Pâté, Chicken Liver, '79 153; '81 235; '83 108;
'84 205
Potatoes, Chicken Livers and, '82 218
Rice, Chicken Livers with, '80 200; '81 58;
'84 292
Rice Dish, Chicken Livers and, '82 218
Risotto, Chicken Livers, '82 218
Roll-Ups, Chicken Liver and Bacon, '80 200;
'81 57
Rumaki Kebabs, '82 182
Sautéed Chicken Livers, '80 200; '81 57
Scrumptious Chicken Livers, '84 230
Stroganoff, Chicken Livers, '80 200; '81 57
Supreme, Chicken Livers, '81 298
Turnovers, Chicken Liver, '79 141
Wine Sauce, Chicken Livers in, '81 104
Creole Liver, '85 219; '86 108; '96 236
Creole Sauce, Liver in, '87 33
French-Style Liver, '80 10
Gravy, Liver and, '80 10
Herbs, Liver with, '81 277
Italiano, Liver, '85 219
Kebabs, Liver, '80 185
Loaf, Skillet Liver, '80 11
Mock Chopped Liver, '00 281
Noodle Dinner, Creamy Liver and, '80 11
Saucy Liver, '81 277
Sauté, Liver, '81 277
Spanish-Style Liver, '80 11
Stroganoff, Liver, '79 54
Sweet-and-Sour Liver, '81 277
LIVING LIGHT. *See* **HEALTHY & LIGHT.**
LOBSTER
Beef Tenderloin, Lobster-Stuffed, '87 248
Beef Tenderloin, Stuffed, '00 124
Beignets, Lobster-and-Roasted Corn, '00 51
Clambake, Backyard, '81 92
Crab-Stuffed Lobster Tails, '95 326
Creamy Lobster, '79 181
How to Cook Lobster, '81 169
Medaillons in Garlic-Chive Butter Sauce, Lobster,
'90 96

Orange Sauce, Lobster Tails with Spiced, '86 155
Salad, Lobster, '89 249; '90 69
Salad, Lobster and Orange, '82 207
Salad with Tarragon Vinaigrette, Lobster, '97 163
Shooters, Lobster Scallion, '00 197
Soup, Spicy Thai Lobster, '94 102
Taco with Yellow Tomato Salsa and Jicama Salad,
    Warm Lobster, '87 122
Thermidor, Lobster, '85 103

MACADAMIA

Apples, Calypso Caramel, '03 M216
Beans, Hawaiian-Style Baked, '86 210
Brownies, Macadamia-Fudge Designer, '94 51
Cake, Macadamia-Fudge, '01 278
Caramels, Coconut-Macadamia, '98 305
Chicken, Macadamia-Mango, '02 162
Chunks of Snow, '02 298
Coffee Cake, Macadamia Ring, '85 326
Cookies, Chunky Macadamia Nut White Chocolate,
    '92 207
Cookies, Coconut-Macadamia, '98 294
Cookies, White Chocolate-Macadamia Nut, '94 315
Crème Brûlée, White Chocolate-Macadamia Nut,
    '95 323
Crust, Chocolate-Macadamia Crumb, '96 254
Crust, Key Lime Bars with Macadamia, '99 282
Crusts, Coconut Cream Tarts with Macadamia Nut,
    '97 62
French Toast, Macadamia, '86 96
French Toast, Macadamia Nut, '95 282
Grouper Macadamia, '85 127
Mahi Mahi, Macadamia, '88 164
Oat Snowball, Macadamia, '92 274
Pie, Coconut-Macadamia Nut, '97 110
Pie, Frozen Chocolate-Macadamia Nut, '96 254
Pie, Hawaiian Banana Cream, '90 105
Pie, Macadamia, '80 238
Pie, Pear-Macadamia, '93 260
Salad, Macadamia Chicken, '80 138
Sauce, Brandy-Macadamia, '82 311
Tart, Lime-and-Macadamia Nut, '03 295
Toffee, Hawaiian, '04 235
Topping, Macadamia-Fudge, '01 278

MACARONI. *See also* **PASTAS.**

Beans, Pasta with, '99 236
Beef and Macaroni, Easy, '02 188
Beef and Macaroni, Skillet, '82 130
Beef-Macaroni Bake, '94 255
Beef-Macaroni Combo, '79 194
Beef 'n' Pasta, Easy Skillet, '02 63
Casserole, Chicken-Macaroni, '85 219
Casserole, Macaroni, '84 220; '87 154
Casserole, Macaroni and Chicken, '80 260
Casserole, Macaroni-Ham, '81 M177; '83 283
Casserole, Mushroom-Macaroni, '95 180
Casserole, Spinach-Beef-Macaroni, '83 313

Cheese

Baked Macaroni and Cheese, '82 199; '00 271;
    '02 26; '03 184
Baked Macaroni with Spinach, '99 244
Bake, Macaroni-and-Cheese, '01 41
Blue Cheese and Walnuts, Macaroni with,
    '02 M208
Blue Cheese, Macaroni and, '93 248; '94 44
Broccoli Macaroni and Cheese, '02 36
Broccoli Mac 'n' Cheese, '00 53
Caramelized Onion Macaroni and Cheese,
    '04 231
Casserole, Macaroni-Cheese-Beef, '95 125
Cheeseburger Macaroni, '02 119
Chicken Macaroni and Cheese, '02 63
Chicken Macaroni and Cheese, Spicy, '02 63
Creamy Macaroni and Cheese, '93 249; '94 45;
    '02 26
Deluxe, Macaroni-and-Cheese, '79 84
Deluxe, Macaroni and Cheese, '80 236
Divine Macaroni and Cheese, '99 314
Double Cheese Macaroni, '82 224
Eleanor's Macaroni and Cheese, '97 253
Extra Cheesy Macaroni, '00 92
Golden Macaroni and Cheese, '04 24
Gorgonzola Macaroni, '97 28
Italian Macaroni and Cheese, '04 327
Jack-in-the-Macaroni Bake, '93 249; '94 45
Macaroni and Cheese, '83 M7; '88 M147, M90;
    '90 30; '00 273
Mexican Macaroni, '96 73
Mousse, Macaroni, '96 73
Mushroom Bake, Cheesy Macaroni-, '81 243
Mushroom Bake, Macaroni-, '97 96
Old-Fashioned Macaroni and Cheese, '92 215
Peppers, Macaroni-and-Cheese-Stuffed, '80 65
Pizza, Maca-, '99 195
Primavera, Macaroni, '96 73
Puff, Macaroni and Cheese, '79 5
Quick-and-Easy Macaroni and Cheese, '00 15
Salad, Macaroni and Cheese, '97 203
Souper Macaroni and Cheese, '00 92
Soup, Macaroni and Cheese, '95 264
Soup, Pimiento "Mac and Cheese," '97 M325
Tasty Macaroni and Cheese, '83 288
Texas Cheeses with Roasted Chiles, Mac and,
    '04 207
Tex-Mex Macaroni and Cheese, '00 92
Thick-and-Rich Macaroni and Cheese, '84 329
Three-Cheese Macaroni, '00 M92
Tomatoes, Macaroni, Cheese, and, '95 213
Tomato Macaroni and Cheese, Spicy, '03 68
Veggie Mac-and-Cheese, '01 111
Wine, Macaroni-and-Cheese with, '86 78
Dinner, Sausage Skillet, '83 29
Glorious Macaroni, '84 76
Ground Beef and Macaroni, '85 218
Mexican Luncheon, '87 192
Oysters with Macaroni, Scalloped, '80 297

Salads

Acini di Pepe Salad, '83 163
Barbecue Macaroni Salad, '82 276
Cheese Salad, Macaroni and, '97 203
Chicken-Pasta Salad, Zesty, '02 186
Chicken Salad, Dilled Macaroni-, '92 142
Chicken Salad, Macaroni-, '85 296; '86 302
Confetti Macaroni Salad, '82 132; '85 297
Crabmeat Salad, Macaroni-, '81 153
Crunchy Macaroni Salad, '82 24
Dilled Macaroni-Cheese Salad, '86 208
Dilled Macaroni Salad, '89 161
Garden Macaroni Salad, '84 290; '92 64
Gourmet Macaroni Salad, '81 253
Ham and Macaroni Salad, '79 220
Ham Salad, Macaroni-, '85 218
Hearty Macaroni Salad, '84 90
Kidney Bean-Salami Pasta Toss, '85 165
Macaroni Salad, '87 92
Olive Clubhouse Salad, '81 114
Overnight Pasta Salad, '82 276
Pineapple Macaroni Salad, '79 220
Refreshing Macaroni Salad, '80 177
Salmon-and-Macaroni Salad, '81 114
Salmon Salad, Macaroni-, '82 232
Shell Macaroni Salad, '92 163
Shell Salad, Macaroni, '87 38
Shrimp Macaroni Salad, '79 220
Shrimp-Macaroni Salad, '85 219
Shrimp Salad, Festive Macaroni-, '85 165
Shrimp Salad, Macaroni-, '85 121
Spiral Macaroni Salad, '82 276
Sweet-and-Sour Macaroni Salad, '85 166
Taco Macaroni Salad, '85 165
Tuna Macaroni Salad, '83 44, 145
Tuna-Macaroni Salad, '84 66
Tuna Salad, Whole Wheat Macaroni-, '84 193
Turkey Macaroni Salad, '83 282
Two, Macaroni Salad for, '81 31
Vegetable Salad, Macaroni-, '86 209
Véronique, Macaroni Salad, '85 164
Supper Supreme, Sunday, '79 76
Tomatoes, Tuna-Mac in, '87 188
Toss, Corkscrew Macaroni, '83 163
Treat, Tuna-Macaroni, '82 131
Whole Wheat Macaroni with Pesto, '89 238

MANGOES

Beef and Rice, Mango-, '88 138
Bread, Mango, '96 205
Cake, Mango, '83 150
Chicken, Macadamia-Mango, '02 162
Chutney, Blue-Ribbon Mango, '96 206
Chutney, Mango, '89 141; '96 182; '03 123
Cooler, Caribbean, '98 333
Crêpes, Mango-Pineapple, '86 216
Dessert Tamales, Mango, '94 190
Frappé, Mango, '86 216
Ice Cream, Mango, '86 216
Margaritas, Mango, '96 126
Orange Smoothie, Mango-, '86 216
Pan Dowdy, Mango, '83 150
Pico de Gallo, Mango, '04 318
Pie, Green Mango, '79 137
Pie, Mango Cream, '03 122
Pie, Mango-Ginger, '88 138
Pork Loin, Tropical, '96 86
Preserves, Mango-Pineapple, '79 137
Relish, Mango, '89 198
Salad, Fresh Mango, '84 126
Salad, Mango, '79 137; '03 122
Salad Sandwiches, Mango-Crab, '99 72
Salad with Mango, Chicken, '86 215
Salsa, Avocado-Mango, '00 328
Salsa, Fresh Mango, '00 122
Salsa, Mango, '91 182; '95 104; '98 232;
    '00 124, 337; '02 163; '04 59
Salsa, Mango-and-Bell Pepper, '00 247
Salsa, Minted Mango, '96 206
Salsa, Seared Scallops with Tomato-Mango, '95 122
Salsa, Tropical, '96 14
Sandwiches, Mango-Chicken Pita, '03 123
Sauce, Mango, '83 120
Sauce, Mango-Pineapple Hot, '04 183
Sauce, Mango-Spiced Rum, '86 215
Slaw, Mango, '93 31; '94 71
Smoothie, Mango, '03 122
Sorbet, Mango, '86 196
Soup, Chilled Mango-Cantaloupe, '96 205
Torta, Mango Chutney, '96 322
Vinegar, Mango-Cilantro, '95 190

MANICOTTI

Cannelloni, '85 60; '92 17
Cheesy Manicotti, '83 216
Chicken Manicotti, Creamy, '85 60
Chili Manicotti, '89 247; '99 239
Chipotle Manicotti, Creamy, '03 96
Ground Beef-and-Tomato Manicotti, '03 257
Make-Ahead Manicotti, '98 68
Quick Manicotti, '79 6
Sausage-and-Tomato Manicotti, Cheesy, '03 257
Seafood Manicotti, '94 195
Shrimp Manicotti, '97 96
Special Manicotti, '88 50
Spinach Manicotti, '82 199
Stuffed Manicotti, '83 M6

MANICOTTI
(continued)

Stuffed Manicotti, Meaty, '00 19
Stuffed Manicotti, Saucy, '83 288
Stuffed Manicotti, Spinach-, '88 255
Zucchini Manicotti, '84 194
MARINADES
Asian Marinade, '99 141
Basic Marinade, '99 141; '02 19
Beef Marinade, Tangy, '86 113
Cheese Marinade, '04 238
Chicken Marinade, Zesty, '03 180
Cinnamon-Soy Marinade, '93 103
Citrus Marinade, '93 103; '04 51
Garlic-Basil Marinade, '94 160
Garlic-Honey Marinade, '93 102
Honey-Mustard Marinade, '93 103
Italian Marinade, '03 180
Lemon Marinade, Chicken in, '98 128
Lemon-Molasses Dressing, '97 195
Lemon-Soy Marinade, '91 194
Light Marinade, Tangy, '82 178
Lime Marinade, Fruit with, '98 92
Marinade, '86 153; '92 283
Mexican Marinade, Flank Steak in, '98 128
Minty Marinade, '92 105
Oriental Marinade, '93 102
Oriental Marinade, Seafood in, '98 128
Raspberry Vinaigrette, '96 275
Southwestern Marinade, '93 102; '99 141; '00 177
Soy-and-Ginger Marinade, '96 129
Sweet-and-Sour Marinade, '86 113
Teriyaki Marinade, '86 114; '93 102
Vegetable Marinade, '92 231
MARMALADES. *See also* **JAMS AND
        JELLIES/Marmalades.**
MARSHMALLOWS
Ambrosia, Carrot-Marshmallow, '80 5
Bars, Broadway Brownie, '97 M35
Bars, Chewy Chocolate Cereal, '97 317
Bird's Nests, '95 102
Birds' Nests, '04 84
Brownies, Chewy Marshmallow, '83 306
Brownies, Chocolate-Marshmallow, '01 246
Brownies, Choco-Mallow, '87 198; '90 309
Brownies, No-Bake, '94 330
Cake, Cola, '00 120
Cake, Mississippi Mud, '04 136
Cake, No-Egg Chocolate Marshmallow, '87 97
Chocolate, Hot Laced Marshmallow, '93 53
Coffee Mallow, '80 109
Cream, Orange-Mallow, '94 295
Dip, Marshmallow Fruit, '84 171
Frosting, Chocolate-Marshmallow, '83 245; '04 210
Fudge, Butterscotch-Peanut, '98 M282
Fudge, Peanut Butter, '02 296
Ice Cream Dessert, Rocky Road, '00 332
Monster Mouths, '95 274
Munchies, Pop Graham, '96 28
Parfaits, Mocha-Mallow, '80 219
Pie, Coffee, '96 148
Piglets, '98 203
Pizza Dessert, Rocky Road, '99 196
Popcorn Balls, Marshmallow, '90 226
Pudding, Banana-Mallow, '86 139
Salad, Waldorf, '97 204
Sauce, Marshmallow, '91 91
S'mores, Grilled Pound Cake, '98 179
S'mores, Indoor, '01 33
Squares, Chocolate-Marshmallow, '92 M50
Sugarplum Fairy Wands, '97 M286
Sushi Bars, '00 50

Sushi Bars, Confetti, '00 50
Sushi, Crisp Rice Cereal, '00 50
Treat, Toasty Marshmallow, '00 200
MAYONNAISE
Adobo Mayonnaise, '02 203
Aioli (Garlic Mayonnaise), '88 221
Aioli, Picante, '99 53
Anchovy Mayonnaise, '86 179
Apricot Mayonnaise, '97 320
Avocado Mayonnaise, '00 335
Avocado Mayonnaise, Spicy Salmon Fillets with,
        '02 327
Basil Mayonnaise, '98 144
Béarnaise Mayonnaise, '00 136
Caramelized Onion Mayonnaise, '00 218
Cilantro Mayonnaise, '98 51
Citrus Mayonnaise, Creamy, '92 107
Curry Mayonnaise, '95 66
Dill-Garlic Mayonnaise, '92 320
Dill Mayonnaise, '96 197
Dip, Artichokes with Herb-Mayonnaise, '84 67
Dip, Seasoned Mayonnaise Artichoke, '80 87
Dressing, Mayonnaise, '86 11; '00 217
Dressing, Southwestern Mayonnaise, '99 245
Dried Tomato Mayonnaise, '98 144
Flavored Mayonnaise, '94 167; '96 123; '97 328
Garlic-Dill Mayonnaise, '00 324
Garlic Mayonnaise, '92 56
Gremolata Mayonnaise, '00 136
Herbed Mayonnaise, '82 85, 192
Homemade Mayonnaise, '80 155; '90 81; '99 180
Homemade Mayonnaise, Easy, '84 12
Italian Herbed Mayonnaise, '92 320
Lemon-Basil Mayonnaise, '03 208
Lemon-Cream Mayonnaise, '85 264
Lemon-Dill Mayonnaise, '99 267
Lemon Mayonnaise, '95 32; '98 144; '99 178;
        '04 56
Lime-Cayenne Mayonnaise, '04 121
Mediterranean Mayonnaise, '98 144
Onion Mayonnaise, '98 144
Parmesan Mayonnaise, '86 79
Raspberry Mayonnaise, '97 107
Roasted Garlic Mayonnaise, '97 47
Roasted Red Pepper Mayonnaise, '98 144
Rosemary-Garlic Mayonnaise, '01 322
Russian Mayonnaise, '80 137
Sauce, Herb-Mayonnaise, '85 73
Sauce, Zesty, '97 312
Spread, Dijon-Mayo, '96 199
Tasty Mayonnaise, '82 192
Tex-Mex Mayonnaise, '01 134
Thai Mayonnaise, Spicy, '02 52
Thyme Mayonnaise, '96 121; '00 333
Tomato-Basil Mayonnaise, '00 136
Watercress Mayonnaise, '93 119
Wine Mayonnaise, Hot, '81 83
MEATBALLS
Appetizers
Baked Meatballs, '02 25
Bourbon Meatballs, '00 252
Brandied Meatballs, '83 78
Chafing Dish Meatballs, '81 260
Chestnut Meatballs, '79 110
Cocktail Meatballs, '79 63, 207
Flavorful Meatballs, '84 206
German Meatballs, Crisp, '92 326
Ham Balls, '86 256
Ham Balls, Appetizer, '82 39
Hawaiian Meatballs, Tangy, '79 129
Polynesian Meatballs, '80 207
Quesadillas, Meatball, '00 242
Red Delicious Meatballs, '85 85
Saucy Party Meatballs, '80 149

Sauerkraut Meatballs, '86 257
Spiced Meatballs, '79 284
Spicy Holiday Meatballs, '01 238
Spicy Party Meatballs, '00 242
Sweet-and-Sour Meatballs, '82 247; '99 325
Sweet-and-Sour Meatballs, Spicy, '03 186
Sweet-and-Sour Party Meatballs, '79 233
Tamale Balls, Tangy, '89 60
Tamale Meatballs, '80 194
Zesty Meatballs, '80 250
Bacon Meatballs, Burgundy-, '80 283
Bacon-Wrapped Meatballs, '79 81
Baked Meatballs, '02 25
Beef Balls Heidelberg, '83 164; '84 39
Charleston Press Club Meatballs, '93 129
Chinese Meatballs, '83 116; '87 194
Creole, Meatball-Okra, '83 156
Creole, Meatballs, '82 233
Espanol, Meatballs, '82 110
Golden Nugget Meatballs, '82 233
Gravy, Meatballs in, '79 136
Ham Balls, '84 91; '86 256
Hawaiian Meatballs, '85 86
Italian Meatball Packets, '04 222
Kebabs, Meatball, '95 192
Lamb Meatballs with Yogurt Sauce, '85 132
Lasagna, Meatball, '00 243; '03 142
Meatballs, '89 237
Minestrone, Meatball, '00 242
Mock Meatballs, '81 243
Oven Barbecued Meatballs, '82 233
Pineapple and Peppers, Meatballs with, '90 145
Pizza Meatballs, '85 86
Processor Meatballs, Quick, '87 111
Royal Meatballs, '87 268; '88 102; '89 67
Sandwiches, Meatball, '04 170
Sandwiches, Open-Faced Meatball, '99 239
Sandwich, Giant Meatball, '92 196
Sauce with Meatballs, Pasta, '01 55
Saucy Meatballs, '85 68; '90 122
Sauerbraten Meatballs, '85 85
Sloppy Joe Meatball Hoagies, '00 242
Soup, Mexican Meatball, '98 315
Spaghetti-and-Herb Meatballs, '84 75
Spaghetti and Meatballs, White, '03 34
Spaghetti, Country-Style, '02 25
Spaghetti with Meatballs, '81 38
Spicy Meatballs and Sausage, '79 163
Stew, Meatball, '79 198; '98 30
Stroganoff, Meatball, '81 297; '02 50
Stroganoff, Mushroom-Meatball, '85 85
Swedish Meatballs, '80 80; '86 256
Sweet-and-Sour Meatballs, '82 233, 247; '86 240
Turkey Meatballs, '89 237
Veal Meatballs, European, '85 30
Venison Sausage Balls, '80 42
MEAT LOAF
Alabama Meat Loaf, '04 188
All-American Meat Loaf, '92 341; '93 46
Barbecued Meat Loaf, '80 60; '81 275; '84 50;
        '87 216
Barbecue Meat Loaf Sandwiches, '04 188
Basic Meat Loaf, '88 M14
Beef Loaf, Glazed, '86 19
Beef Loaves, Individual Barbecued, '95 242
Beef-Vegetable Loaf, '79 164
Blue Cheese Meat Loaf Roll, '93 247
Cheeseburger Loaf, '81 236, 276
Cheeseburger Meat Loaf, '03 204
Cheesy Meat Roll, '82 136
Chili Meat Loaf, '81 275
Corny Meat Loaf, '86 68
Crunchy Meat Loaf Oriental, '79 212
Curried Meat Loaf, '86 43

Easy Meat Loaf, '88 M214; '95 125; '97 24
Elegant Meat Loaf, '89 243
Family-Style Meat Loaf, '93 18
Fennel Meat Loaf, '88 46
German Meat Loaf, '87 216
Gonzales Meat Loaf, '04 206
Greek Meat Loaf, '96 251; '97 103
Ham Loaf, '79 180; '80 272
Ham Loaf, Cranberry-, '82 M77
Ham Loaf, Glazed, '79 187; '90 212
Ham Loaf, Hawaiian, '79 71
Ham Loaf, Pineapple Upside-Down, '79 253
Ham Loaf, Saucy, '86 M328
Ham Loaf, Spicy, '80 110
Ham Loaf, Supreme, '79 242
Ham Loaf, Upside-Down, '82 40
Ham Loaves, '90 235
Ham Loaves, Country, '86 255
Ham Ring, '84 91
Ham Ring, Chili-Sauced, '81 M122
Hurry-Up Meat Loaf, '82 21
Hurry-Up Meat Loaves, '88 15
Individual Meat Loaves, '81 279; '82 24; '83 154;
    '92 229; '00 214
Italian Meat Loaf, '79 187
Ketchup-and-Bacon-Topped Meat Loaf, Sweet,
    '03 203
Lamb Meat Loaf with Feta Cheese, '97 24
Liver Loaf, Skillet, '80 111
Meat Loaf, '81 170; '89 109
Mexicali Meat Loaf, '81 275
Mexican Meat Loaf, '87 217
Mini Alabama Meat Loaves, '04 188
Miniature Meat Loaves, '85 24
Mini Mexican Meat Loaves, '02 90
Mini-Teriyaki Meat Loaf, '90 69
Mozzarella-Layered Meat Loaf, '79 71
My-Ami's Meat Loaf, '94 229
Oriental Meat Loaf, '81 M122; '83 M194
Parsleyed Meat Loaf, '83 35
Parsley Meat Loaf, '87 22
Pineapple Loaves, Individual, '81 M121
Pizza Meat Loaf, Cheesy, '81 M121
Reuben Loaf, '95 338
Roll, Meat Loaf, '79 129
Sandwiches, Grilled Cheese Meat Loaf, '04 188
Sandwich, Meat Loaf, '01 210
Saucy Meat Loaves, '79 186
Savory Meat Loaf, '87 216
Southwestern Meat Loaf, '93 248
Special Meat Loaf, '89 70
Spicy Meat Loaf, '79 71
Sprout Meat Loaf, '85 51
Stuffed Beef Log, '79 71
Stuffed Meat Loaf, '79 187
Stuffed Meat Loaf, Rolled, '80 80
Sun-Dried Tomatoes and Herbs, Meat Loaf with,
    '92 192
Supreme, Meat Loaf, '92 33
Swedish Meat Loaf, '81 M121
Sweet 'n' Saucy Meat Loaf, '01 210
Tasty Meat Loaf, '83 213
Teriyaki Meat Loaf, '03 172
Tex-Mex Meat Loaf for Two, '90 234
Tomato Gravy, Meat Loaf with, '00 330
Triple Meat Loaf, '79 186
Turkey Loaf, '92 33
Turkey Loaf, Cranberry-Glazed, '86 171
Turkey Loaf, Ground, '86 171
Turkey Meat Loaf, Spinach-Stuffed, '97 24
Veal Meat Loaf, '93 292
Vegetable Meat Loaf, '85 M29
Wellington, Meat Loaf, '79 186; '87 284
Wrap, Meat Loaf in a, '89 122

MELONS
Balls and Cherries in Kirsch, Melon, '91 91
Balls, Fiery Sweet Melon, '92 311
Balls, Mellowed-Out Melon, '88 182
Bowl with Cucumber-Mint Dressing, Melon Ball,
    '87 153
Cantaloupe
  Berry-Filled Melon, '86 93
  Chutney, Cantaloupe, '00 108
  Chutney, Fresh Cantaloupe, '97 148
  Compote, Cantaloupe, '81 147
  Compote, Melon Ball, '85 157
  Cream Delight, Cantaloupe, '82 179
  Delight, Cantaloupe, '89 204
  Frozen Cantaloupe Cream, '82 159
  Fruit-Filled Cantaloupe, '83 120
  Fruit Medley, Minted, '80 182
  Grilled Cantaloupe Wedges, '87 162
  Ice Cream, Cantaloupe, '79 177
  Jam, Cantaloupe-Peach, '95 143
  Mold, Double-Grape Cantaloupe, '79 173
  Pickled Cantaloupe, '99 171
  Pickled Cantaloupe, Sweet, '89 197
  Pie, Cantaloupe, '86 163
  Pie, Cantaloupe Cream, '79 177
  Pie, Cantaloupe Meringue, '88 182
  Punch, Cantaloupe, '81 147; '00 140
  Refresher, Cantaloupe-Lime, '01 332
  Salad, Avocado-Melon, '82 164
  Salad, Cantaloupe, '86 182
  Salad, Cantaloupe-Cheese, '88 184
  Salad, Cantaloupe Colada, '97 148
  Salad, Cantaloupe Cooler, '79 176
  Salad, Cantaloupe Green, '91 126
  Salad, Cantaloupe-Pecan, '86 178
  Salad, Melon-Berry, '90 180
  Salad with Dill Dressing, Melon, '88 182
  Salad with Pistachio-Lime Vinaigrette,
      Cantaloupe-Spinach, '97 148
  Sherbet, Cantaloupe, '88 183
  Sherbet-Cantaloupe Surprise, '91 105
  Sherbet, Frosty Cantaloupe, '82 144
  Sorbet, Cantaloupe, '03 171
  Soup, Cantaloupe, '83 120; '88 160
  Soup, Chilled Cantaloupe, '81 156; '97 148
  Soup, Chilled Mango-Cantaloupe, '96 205
  Soup, Fresh Cantaloupe, '84 190
  Soup, Melon, '80 182
  Southern Plantation Cantaloupe, '82 179
  Sundae, Cantaloupe, '89 166
  Sweet-and-Hot Melon, '92 163
  Wedges with Berry Sauce, Melon, '86 178
  Whip, Cantaloupe, '89 198
Citrus Mingle, Melon-, '79 177
Compote, Grilled Chicken Breasts with Fig-and-
    Melon, '00 163
Cooler, Melon, '81 146
Fruit Bowl, Sparkling Fresh, '80 146
Fruit Cup with Mint Dressing, Fresh, '80 183
Fruit Deluxe, Marinated, '81 146
Honeydew
  Boats, Honeydew Fruit, '81 147
  Bowl, Honeydew Fruit, '84 186
  Cooler, Melon Ball, '86 131
  Cups, Honeydew Fruit, '82 179
  Dessert, Honeydew-Berry, '83 120
  Granita, Honeydew, '87 162
  Grapes, Honeydew Melon with, '91 91
  Salad, Fruited Ham, '81 146
  Salad, Melon and Shrimp Curry, '97 129
  Salad, Melon-Berry, '90 180
  Salad with Apricot Cream Dressing, Honeydew,
      '84 191
  Salad with Dill Dressing, Melon, '88 182

  Soup, Melon, '80 182
  Wedges with Berry Sauce, Melon, '86 178
Julep, Melon-Mint, '86 196
Julep, Rainbow Melon, '80 183
Melange, Melon, '84 139
Minted Melon, '96 123
Minted Melon Cocktail, '81 146
Mint Sauce, Melons in, '85 164
Salad, Congealed Melon Ball, '84 125
Salad, Georgia Summer, '92 179
Salad, Melon-and-Prosciutto, '92 191
Salad, Summertime Melon, '82 101
Salad with Orange-Raspberry Vinaigrette, Grilled
    Melon, '95 144
Salsa, Hot Melon, '95 144
Soup, Swirled Melon, '87 162
Watermelon
  Balls, Minted Melon, '87 162
  Basket, Watermelon Fruit, '84 161
  Compote, Watermelon-Cherry, '90 180
  Cookies, Watermelon, '92 179
  Cooler, Melon Ball, '86 131
  Cooler, Watermelon-Lemonade, '04 172
  Cooler, Watermelon-Strawberry, '98 178
  Daiquiri, Watermelon, '95 143; '98 165; '04 172
  Frost, Watermelon, '86 196
  Granita, Watermelon, '96 179; '98 165; '04 171
  Ice, Watermelon, '91 173
  Lemonade, Watermelon, '98 165
  Looks-Like Watermelon, '03 179
  Margaritas, Watermelon, '02 185
  Marmalade, Watermelon-and-Ginger, '98 164
  Mousse, Frozen Watermelon, '91 96; '92 130
  Pickles, Watermelon Rind, '81 174; '98 164
  Pie, Watermelon, '95 144
  Preserves, Watermelon, '79 120
  Prosciutto, Watermelon and, '98 164
  Punch, Watermelon, '89 204; '92 190; '00 140
  Salad, Watermelon-Prosciutto, '04 171
  Salad with Celery-Nut Dressing, Watermelon,
      '80 182
  Salad with Peppered Peanuts in a Zesty Citrus
      Dressing, Grilled Shrimp, Orange, and
      Watermelon, '04 308
  Salsa, Watermelon, '98 164
  Sauce, Melon Balls in Watermelon, '79 177
  Sherbet, Light Watermelon, '81 147
  Sherbet, Watermelon, '79 155; '92 124
  Sherried Watermelon, '92 117
  Slush, Watermelon-Berry, '90 137
  Sorbet, Watermelon, '92 190; '99 166; '03 171
  Soup, Chilled Watermelon, '03 168
  Sparkle, Watermelon, '84 191
MERINGUES
Acorns, Meringue, '93 284
Asparagus Meringue, '88 131
Baked Pear Meringues, '85 232
Bars, Meringue-Chocolate Chip, '84 118
Basket, Summer Berry, '84 158
Baskets with Fresh Fruit and Ice Cream, Meringue,
    '98 179
Cake, Brown Sugar Meringue, '81 70
Cake, Cinderella Fantasy, '98 70
Cake, Orange Meringue, '86 336; '87 84
Cakes, Spanish Wind, '84 157
Coconut Kisses, '90 106
Coffee Kisses, Chocolate-Dipped, '96 313
Coffee Meringues with Butterscotch Mousse,
    '93 254
Cooked Meringue, '86 130
Cooked Meringue, Easy, '82 207; '83 158
Cookies, Forget 'em, '83 256
Cookies, Heavenly Chocolate-Chip Meringue,
    '01 218

MERINGUES
(continued)

Cookies, Meringue, '98 71
Cookies, Meringue Kiss, '86 121
Cookies, Meringue Surprise, '86 320
Cookies, Vanilla Meringue, '01 197
Cran-Apple Mousse Filling, Meringues with,
  '93 254
Cups, Kiwi and Cream in Meringue, '81 279
Cups, Lemon Custard in Meringue, '80 295; '81 172
Cups, Lemon Meringue Cream, '84 23
Dream Drops, '99 328
Fingers, Chocolate-Almond Meringue, '84 158
Flowers, Meringue, '84 156
Frosting, Brown Sugar Meringue, '81 70
Frosting, Italian Meringue, '98 70
Frosting, Meringue, '86 336; '87 84; '99 118
Ghosts, White Meringue, '99 246
Holiday Meringues, '88 280
Meringue, '87 207; '94 208; '97 109
Meringues, '02 62
Mixture, Basic Meringue, '98 70
Mushrooms, Meringue, '96 317
Orange Meringues, '95 318
Parfaits, Strawberry Meringue, '02 62
Pavlova, '92 101
Peach Melba Meringues, '87 76
Peach Melba Meringues with Buttermilk Custard
  Sauce, '96 183
Pears with Meringue, Amaretto, '90 58
Pineapple, Meringue-Topped, '84 178
Piping Meringue, '84 156
Shell, Cinnamon Meringue, '82 263
Shells, Fruited Meringue, '87 32
Shells, Fruit-Filled Meringue, '86 151
Strawberry Meringues, '84 188
Strawberry Meringue Torte, '88 136
Toffee Meringue Torte, '87 118
Tropical Meringues, '98 71
Vacherin Moka, '80 55

MICROWAVE. Includes microwave conversions. *See
  also* **CASSEROLES/Microwave.**

Appetizers
  Bacon-Chestnut Wraps, '84 M216
  Brie-and-Cranberry Chutney Melt, '98 M318
  Brie Appetizer, Bit-of-, '88 M8
  Brie, Chutney-Bacon, '90 M292
  Brie, Tropical Breeze, '94 M18
  Canapés, Green Onion, '84 M216
  Cheese Log, Toasted Pecan, '86 M288
  Cheese Sticks, Peppery, '81 M289
  Crab-Zucchini Bites, '84 M216
  Dip, Apple, '96 M190
  Dip, Bill D's Black-Eyed Pea, '97 M89
  Dip, Black-Eyed Pea, '04 M18
  Dip, Cheddar-Bacon, '89 M119
  Dip, Chili-and-Cheese, '89 M328
  Dip, Chipped Beef, '88 M8
  Dip, Creamy Crab, '80 M135
  Dip, Hot Artichoke Seafood, '85 M212
  Dip, Mexican Artichoke, '90 M292
  Dip, Monterey Shrimp, '99 M65
  Dip, Nacho, '93 M330
  Dip, Quick Fiesta, '95 M237; '99 M197
  Dip, Quick Pizza, '00 M168
  Dip, Shrimp, '88 M261
  Dip, Sweet-and-Spicy Mustard, '96 M274
  Eggs, Double Stuffed Spinach-and-Bacon,
    '00 M333
  Franks, Saucy Appetizer, '84 M12
  Mix, Spicy Party, '81 M138
  Mushrooms, Shrimp-Stuffed, '80 M135

Mushrooms, Spinach-Stuffed, '88 M261; '89 M133
Mushrooms, Tipsy, '84 M216
Nachos, Make-Ahead, '80 M135
Nuts, Sherry-Orange, '86 M289
Nuts, Spiced, '91 M316
Pâté, Chicken Liver, '88 M132
Pecans, Spicy, '81 M289
Pizzas, Appetizer, '89 M118
Plantain Chips, '95 M203
Popcorn, Caramel, '86 M212
Popcorn, Garlic, '83 M315
Potato Shell Appetizers, '89 M119
Potato Skins, Cheese, '84 M239
Rumaki, '80 M136
Rumaki, Scallop, '98 M173
Spread, Artichoke-Parmesan, '92 M95
Spread, Chicken Salad Party, '88 M8
Spread, Hearts of Palm, '90 M293
Spread, Hot Beef, '84 M216
Spread, Seafood, '86 M58
Spread, Spinach-Bacon, '92 M310
Sweet Potato Chips, '95 M203
Tostadas, Party, '98 M33
Wings and Ribs, Thai, '97 M225
Apples, Honey-Glazed, '90 M125
Apples, Rosy Cinnamon, '87 M37
Apples, Spicy Poached, '90 M141

Beverages
  Café Colombian Royal, '80 M290
  Cappuccino, Mocha, '02 M220
  Champions' Cooler, '96 M181
  Chocolate, Flaming Brandied, '80 M290
  Coffee, Fireside, '03 M298
  Coffee, Mocha, '85 M329
  Fizz, Berry Blue, '03 M164
  Hot Chocolate, Creole, '80 M290
  Hot Chocolate Mix, Deluxe, '80 M290
  Mocha, Mexican, '93 M341
  Mocha, Spirited Hot, '91 M260
  Spoons, Dipped Chocolate-Almond, '95 M277
  Tomato Cocktail, '83 M203
Blanching Chart, Microwave, '80 M181

Breads
  Biscuit Bread, Brown Sugar, '02 M224
  Breakfast Ring, Almond-Vanilla, '04 M249
  Buns, Cinnamon-Apple Breakfast, '00 M198
  Caramel Ring, Easy, '85 M89
  Cheese-Herb Bread, '84 M144
  Chocolate Loaf Bread, '88 M188
  Coffee Cake, Cinnamon, '83 M203
  Coffee Cake, Orange, '85 M88
  Coffee Cake Ring, '85 M89
  Coffee Ring, Sugarplum, '83 M37
  Egg Bread, Braided, '03 M234
  English Muffin Bread, '95 M79
  French Toast, Baked Apple, '03 M283
  French Toast, Easy, '82 M172
  Muffins, Apple-Bran, '85 M89
  Muffins, Cheesy Cornbread, '88 M275
  Muffins, Cinnamon-Nut, '85 M88
  Muffins, Corn, '82 M282
  Muffins, Cranberry Streusel Cake, '88 M274
  Muffins, Fudge Brownie, '95 M50
  Muffins, Lemon, '88 M275
  Muffins, Whole Wheat Bran, '88 M274
  Pizza Bread Rollups, '04 M35
  Pumpkin Bread, Harvest, '90 M215
  Rolls, Cherry-Almond, '84 M198
  Rolls, Cinnamon, '99 M284
  Rolls, Dinner, '93 M326
  Rolls, Easy Orange, '89 M131
  Tomato-Cheese Bread, '99 M157
  Waffles, Honey-Buttered Peanut Butter, '94 M206
  Whole Wheat-Rye Bread, '83 M37

Butter, Cinnamon, '01 M309
Butter, Sweet Potato, '95 M290
Chart, Shortcuts, '89 M134
Chutney, Autumn Fruit, '88 M230
Croutons, '86 M288
Croutons, Microwave, '86 M227
Desserts. *See also* **MICROWAVE/Sauces and
  Gravies.**
  Apple-Almond Bake, '02 M209
  Apple Crumble, Whole Wheat-, '90 M213
  Apple Dessert, Honey-Baked, '90 M213
  Apple-Nut Crunch, '82 M238
  Apple Rings, Cinnamon, '82 M237
  Apples and Cream, Brandied, '82 M237
  Apples, Candy, '01 M205
  Apples, Caramel, '89 M231
  Apples, Caramel-Peanut, '93 M244
  Apples, Easy Baked, '82 M238
  Balls, Buckeye, '00 M280; '01 M322
  Bananas Foster, '83 M114
  Banana Splits, French Toast, '96 M164
  Bark, Cherry-Pistachio, '00 M41
  Bars, Blackberry Jam, '82 M185
  Bars, Chewy Peanut, '80 M172
  Bars, Chewy Praline-Chocolate Fudge, '04 M330
  Bars, Chewy Scotch, '98 M291
  Bars, Date-Oat, '80 M172
  Bars, Gooey Turtle, '96 M189
  Bars, Peanut Butter-and-Fudge, '80 M172
  Blueberry Dessert, Easy, '89 M130
  Brie, Almond-Raspberry, '94 M89
  Brownie Bars, Broadway, '97 M35
  Brownies à la Mode, Magnolias Cream Cheese,
    '97 M178
  Brownies, Banana-Split, '03 M43
  Brownies, Basic, '97 M34
  Brownies, Biscuit Mix, '94 M51
  Brownies, Caramel-Pecan Filled, '03 M43
  Brownies, Chocolate-Mint, '85 M294
  Brownies, Cream Cheese, '04 M330
  Brownies, Dark Chocolate, '00 M211
  Brownies, Double Chocolate, '04 M220
  Brownies, Frosted, '97 M87
  Brownies, Frosted Peanut Butter, '00 M155
  Brownies, Layered, '02 M252
  Brownies, Magnolia Cream Cheese, '01 M63
  Brownies, Mississippi Mud, '89 M25
  Brownies, Mississippi Mud Dessert, '01 M314
  Brownies, Nutty Fudge, '80 M171
  Brownies, Passover, '98 M104
  Brownies, Quick, '87 M302
  Brownies with Caramel Frosting, Double
    Chocolate, '04 M220
  Cake Batter, Chocolate Velvet, '03 M286
  Cake, Chocolate-Raspberry, '01 319
  Cake for Grown-Ups, Ice Cream, '88 M192
  Cake, Fruit and Spice, '87 M97
  Cake, Fudge, '94 M293
  Cake, German Chocolate, '83 M233
  Cake, German Chocolate Pound, '97 M254
  Cake, No-Egg Chocolate Marshmallow, '87 M97
  Cake, Old-Fashioned Carrot, '83 M232
  Cake, Peanut Butter, '83 M233
  Cake, Shortbread Fudge, '03 M331
  Cakes, Miniature Chocolate Truffle Tree,
    '97 M285
  Cakes, Spring's Little, '01 M91
  Candies, Turtle, '93 M41
  Candy Bow, '99 M306
  Candy Box, White, '97 M54
  Candy Cups, Rocky Road-Peanut Butter,
    '04 M330
  Caramel Apples, '03 M216
  Caramel Apples, Calypso, '03 M216

Charlotte Russe, '82 M142
Cheesecake, Chocolate-Amaretto, '85 M294
Cheesecake, Chocolate-Wrapped Banana,
   '99 M48
Cheesecake, Fudge, '98 M213
Cheesecake, Luscious Lemon, '90 M196
Cheesecake, Peach-Caramel, '02 M158
Cheesecake, Pear-Berry, '82 M141
Cherries, Chocolate-Covered, '97 M55
Cherries Jubilee, Quick, '82 M100
Chocolate-Coffee Cones, '96 M316
Chocolate Hearts, Crispy, '03 M41
Chocolate-Lemon Creams, '98 M235
Chocolate-Marshmallow Squares, '92 M50
Chocolate-Mint Parfaits, '90 M15
Chocolate Mint Snowballs, '04 M211
Chocolate-Peanut Butter Bites, '92 M317
Chocolate Peanutty Swirls, '94 M330
Chocolate Rudolph Reindeer, '04 M254
Clusters, Toasted Pecan, '00 M14
Cobbler, Apple-Pecan, '84 M198
Cobbler, Sweet Potato, '99 M255
Cobbler, Sweet Potato-Apple, '04 M232
Coconut Joys, Chocolate-Covered, '98 M282
Coconut Robin's Nests, '98 M111
Coffee Cakes, Banana-Toffee, '02 M324
Coffee Cake, Triple-Chocolate, '04 M299
Cookie Bites, Toffee, '03 M273
Cookies, Angel Shortbread, '97 M285
Cookies, Chocolate-Almond Surprise, '88 M45
Cookies, Doubly-Good Chocolate, '82 M185
Cookies, Keyboard, '94 M330
Cookies, Nutty Oatmeal-Chocolate Chip,
   '82 M185
Cookies, Peanut Butter-Toffee Turtle, '02 M325
Cookies, Rudolph, '99 M309
Cookies, Spice, '87 M278
Cookies, Spider, '93 M166
Cookies, Wedding, '82 M185
Cream, Bavarian, '86 M165
Cream, Vanilla, '83 M115
Crème, Orange-Tapioca, '82 M283
Crisp, Pear, '02 M233
Crunch, White Chocolate-Peanut Butter,
   '02 M296
Crust, Chocolate, '90 M15
Crust, Graham Cracker, '88 M45; '91 M234
Crust, Microwaved Graham Cracker, '82 M141
Cupcakes, Cinnamon-Chocolate, '81 M139
Cups, Vanilla Lace, '98 M93
Custard, Chocolate-Topped Amaretto, '87 M37
Divinity, Peanut, '87 M278
Dumplings, Cinnamon Apple, '97 M330
Éclairs, Mini Tiramisù, '03 M41
Filling, Chocolate-Coffee Buttercream, '00 M287
Filling, Chocolate Truffle, '04 M253
Filling, Nutty Cranberry, '00 M306
Fondant, Faux, '98 M154
Frosting, Buttery Cinnamon, '81 M139
Frosting, Caramel, '81 M289
Frosting, Chocolate, '80 M171; '83 M233;
   '87 M97; '89 M25; '97 M87
Frosting, Chocolate Buttercream, '98 M100
Frosting, Coconut-Pecan, '83 M233
Frosting, Cream Cheese, '83 M233
Frosting, Mint Chocolate, '99 M176
Frosting, White Chocolate Buttercream,
   '97 M284
Fudge, Butterscotch-Peanut, '98 M282
Fudge, Double-Good, '79 M263; '91 M92
Fudge, Double Good, '87 M278
Fudge, Double-Good, '95 M50
Fudge, Microwave Chocolate, '92 M50; '02 M31
Fudge, Quick-and-Easy, '88 M190

Fudge Squares, Chocolate-Peanut Butter,
   '97 M54
Ganache, Chocolate, '00 M72; '01 M235;
   '03 M286
Ganache, Mocha, '04 M260
Ganache, Simple Chocolate, '03 M212
Ghosts, Little, '03 M212
Ghosts on a Stick, '00 M235
Glaze, Brownie, '02 M252
Glaze, Chocolate, '91 M296; '97 M35;
   '01 M45, M126
Glaze, French Chocolate, '98 M57
Glaze, Vanilla, '04 M84
Glaze, White Chocolate, '01 M45
Grahams, Caramel-Apple, '04 M183
Grahams, Peanut Butter-Apple, '04 M183
Holly Leaves, '99 M306
Ice Cream, Mocha, '97 M145
Ice Cream, No-Cook Turtle, '04 M179
Jam Squares, '81 M289
Jamwiches, Sweetheart, '03 M41
Jellyrolls, Raspberry, '93 M255
Kahlúa Delight, Make-Ahead, '84 M89
Kahlúa Velvet Dessert, '85 M294
Macaroons, White Chocolate Tropical, '00 M166
Millionaires, '79 M262; '97 M55
Mousse, Chocolate, '02 M277
Mousse, White Chocolate, '98 M57, M111
Napoleons, Caramel-Apple, '01 M313
Nuggets, Golden North Pole, '99 M309
Oatmeal Cherry-Apple Crisp, '90 M16
Oranges, Wine-Poached, '84 M323
Pastries, Chocolate-Chestnut, '02 M273
Pastry, Basic, '81 M268
Pastry, Basic Microwave, '82 M142; '85 M113
Pastry, Double-Crust, '82 M298
Pastry Strips, Decorated, '02 M296
Peaches, Gingersnap, '85 M329
Peach Melba, '83 M114
Peanut Brittle, '79 M263
Peanut Brittle, Chocolate-Dipped, '02 M223
Peanut Brittle, Classic, '02 M223
Peanut Brittle, Popcorn, '02 M223
Peanut Butter Slice-and-Bakes, '82 M185
Peanut Clusters, '98 M282
Peanut-Fudge Bites, '91 M231; '92 M68
Pears with Dark Chocolate Sauce, Poached,
   '90 M141
Pecan Brittle, '91 M272; '02 M223
Pecan Brittle, Microwave, '97 M245
Pecan-Coconut Clusters, '86 M251
Pie, Apple-Cranberry, '99 M255
Pie, Best-Ever Chocolate, '88 M45
Pie, Caramel-Banana, '86 M165
Pie, Cranberry-Apple Holiday, '81 M269
Pie, Double Chocolate, '82 M282
Pie, Easy Cherry, '82 M299
Pie, Festive Pumpkin, '81 M269
Pie, Fluffy Eggnog, '81 M269
Pie, Frosty Pumpkin-Praline, '91 M234
Pie, Glazed Strawberry, '82 M142
Pie, Lemon Meringue, '85 M112
Pie, Microwave Chocolate, '90 M15
Pie, Nutty Cranberry, '82 M298
Pie, Old-Fashioned Apple, '82 M299
Pie, Old-Fashioned Pecan, '81 M269
Pie, Quick Pumpkin, '88 M230
Pixies, Chocolate, '00 M155
Pizza, Banana Split-Brownie, '96 M164
Plums, Poached, '90 M141
Popcorn Delight, '00 M133
Pots de Crème, '84 M145
Pots de Crème, Mocha, '88 M45
Pralines, '86 M288

Pralines, Old-Fashioned, '89 M318
Pralines, Southern, '79 M263
Pudding, Bread, '89 M130
Pudding, Brown Sugar-Pecan, '86 M165
Pudding, Butternut Squash, '89 M313; '90 M19
Pudding, Chocolate-Almond, '82 M142
Pudding, Creamy Banana, '89 M130
Pudding, Mandarin-Almond, '85 M12
Pudding, Pecan-Mocha, '89 M130
Pudding, Pumpkin, '89 M313; '90 M20
Pudding, White Chocolate Bread, '00 M104
Reindeer Food, Magic, '99 M309
Sachertorte, Shortcut, '99 M243
Shortbread, Marble-Topped Hazelnut, '99 M29
Soufflé, Brandy Alexander, '83 M114
Spooky Ghosts, '98 M256
Squares, Crispy Peanut, '01 M161
Stars, White Chocolate, '00 M307
Sticky Fingers, '03 M168
Strawberries, Chocolate-Dipped, '98 M100
Sugarplum Fairy Wands, '97 M286
Sundaes, Chocolate Mint, '03 M120
Sundaes, Cocoa-Kahlúa, '83 M58
Sundaes, Hot Strawberry, '81 M5
Sundaes, Spicy Apple Ice Cream, '86 M195
Tart, Caramel Turtle Truffle, '93 M131
Tart, Cranberry-Apple, '97 M316
Tart, Rustic Apple-Cranberry, '01 M314
Toffee, Microwave, '92 M317
Toffee, Microwave Peanut, '04 M234
Toffee, Nutty, '79 M263
Torte, Bourbon-Chocolate, '98 M84
Torte, Chocolate-Almond, '96 M253
Torte, X-Treme Chocolate Double Nut Caramel
   Ladyfinger, '04 M315
Truffles, Hazelnut, '97 M54
Truffles, Raspberry-Fudge, '00 M41
Truffles, Yule Street, '90 M242
Waffles with Apples and Caramel, Gingerbread,
   '98 M237
Zuppa Inglese, '99 M267
Doughnuts with Strawberry Preserves, Hanukkah,
   '01 M275

Eggs and Omelets
Baked Eggs Florentine, '86 M12
Benedict, Easy Eggs, '80 M268
Benedict, Light Eggs, '93 M68
Casserole, Saucy Scrambled Egg, '89 M213
Casserole, Sausage-Egg, '86 M12
Cheddar Eggs, '94 M141
Creamed Eggs in Patty Shells, '80 M267
Medley, Cheddary Egg, '81 M176
Olé Omelet, '87 M124
Pie, Omelet, '00 M35
Poached Eggs, Microwave, '02 M131
Sausage Omelet, Puffy, '80 M268
Scramble, Bacon-and-Eggs, '80 M267
Scrambled Eggs, Creamy Onion, '83 M203
Vegetable Omelet, Golden, '82 M123
Frosting. *See* **MICROWAVE/Desserts.**
Fruit Bake, Cranberry-Mustard, '90 M287
Fruit Compote, Hot, '90 M124
Fruit Melange, '88 M295
Granola, Superhero, '98 M206
Grits, Quick Cheese, '83 M203
Jam, Blackberry, '99 M131
Jam, Freezer Blackberry, '84 M181
Jam, Freezer Peach, '84 M182
Jam, Freezer Plum, '89 M156
Jam, Raspberry Freezer, '84 M181
Jam, Strawberry Freezer, '84 M182
Jelly, Christmas Freezer, '86 M288
Jelly, Quick Grape, '89 M156
Jelly, Red Pepper, '89 M156

MICROWAVE
(continued)

Macaroni and Cheese, '83 M7; '88 M147, M190
Macaroni with Blue Cheese and Walnuts, '02 M208
Main Dishes
Beans and Franks, Jiffy, '91 M172
Beans-and-Franks, Polynesian, '84 M11
Beef Casserole, Easy, '86 M58
Beef Casserole, Layered, '82 M203
Beef Pie, Sensational, '03 M284
Beef Roast, Easy, '89 M65
Beef with Mashed Potatoes and Chipotle Cream,
　Grilled, '02 M320
Beef with Pea Pods, Oriental, '86 M328
Broccoli-Ham au Gratin, '90 M239
Burgers, Barbara's Big Juicy, '03 M138;
　'04 M178
Burgers, Blue Cheese, '89 M66
Casserole, Mexi, '83 M87
Casserole, Mexican, '92 M22
Casserole, Microwave Mexican, '90 M231
Catfish, Microwave, '89 M52
Catfish, Spicy-Seasoned, '89 M66
Chicken alla Romano, '83 M58
Chicken-and-Broccoli Stroganoff, '89 M248
Chicken and Cashews, Ginger, '85 M11
Chicken-and-Corn Cakes with Avocado Cream,
　Southwestern, '97 M311
Chicken and Dumplings with Vegetables,
　'85 M56
Chicken and Pasta, Pesto, '89 M132
Chicken and Spinach Rollups, '82 M68
Chicken-and-Vegetable Platter, '88 M52
Chicken and Vegetables Vermouth, '87 M37
Chicken-Asparagus Rolls, '86 M211
Chicken, Barbecued, '89 M167
Chicken Breasts, Breaded, '89 M196
Chicken Breasts, Herb-Seasoned, '93 M325
Chicken, Crispy Parmesan, '80 M76
Chicken, Crunchy Spiced, '85 M57
Chicken Delicacy, '99 M23
Chicken Dinner, Hot-and-Spicy, '94 M94
Chicken Divan, '80 M10; '87 M218
Chicken Divan Casserole, '82 M203
Chicken Divan Quiche, '88 M125
Chicken, Easy, '89 M129
Chicken Enchiladas, Creamy, '01 M94
Chicken Enchiladas Verde, '00 M240
Chicken, Ginger-Nut, '90 M33
Chicken in a Bag, '86 M57
Chicken Kebabs, Marinated, '84 M144
Chicken Kebabs, Pineapple-, '86 M328
Chicken Lasagna, '87 M302
Chicken, Lemon, '81 M138
Chicken, Lemon-Garlic, '89 M132
Chicken Mexicana, '91 M127
Chicken, Orange, '86 M140
Chicken, Pineapple, '83 M194
Chicken, Tangy Herbed, '87 M302
Chicken Teriyaki, '80 M76
Chicken Tetrazzini, '80 M75
Chicken Tetrazzini, Cheesy, '83 M87
Chicken Toss, Quick, '87 M124
Chicken, Vegetable-Stuffed, '89 M65
Chicken with Noodles, Sesame, '88 M125
Chicken with Pecan-Rice Dressing, '85 M57
Chicken with Tomato-Basil Pasta, Basil-Stuffed,
　'94 M204
Chicken with White Barbecue Sauce,
　'89 M84
Chicken with Wild Rice, Elegant, '80 M76
Chicken, Zesty Barbecued, '80 M76

Chiles Rellenos with Walnut Cream Sauce,
　Havarti-and-Corn-Stuffed, '93 M275
Chili-Cheese Dogs, '81 M176
Chili, Microwave, '91 M232
Chili, Turkey-Bean, '88 M213
Cornish Hens, Orange-Glazed Stuffed, '84 M89
Crab Imperial, Pineapple-, '84 M286
Crabmeat and Mushrooms on Toast Points,
　'82 M91
Crabmeat Imperial, Speedy, '90 M112
Crab, Shrimp, and Artichoke au Gratin, '90 M240
Crawfish Delicacy, '99 M23
Crêpes, Sherried Beef, '85 M29
Dinner, Easy Steamed, '83 M314
Dogs, Taco, '02 M57
Filet Mignon Patties, Mock, '82 M68
Fillets, Apple-Carrot Stuffed, '88 M192
Fillets, Lemon-Coated, '80 M53
Fillets, Parmesan, '86 M112
Fillets, Spanish-Style, '86 M112
Fish Amandine, Fillet of, '80 M54
Fish-and-Potato Platter, '89 M248
Fish-and-Vegetable Dinner, '91 M196
Fish, Creole, '87 M79
Fish Delight, '86 M212
Fish, Easy Italian, '86 M112
Fish, Herb-Coated, '86 M112
Fish in Creamy Swiss Sauce, Poached, '80 M53
Fish Rolls, Vegetable-Filled, '86 M251
Fish Steaks, Soy, '86 M112
Fish, Sweet-and-Sour, '80 M54
Fish with Greek Sauce, Poached, '91 M183
Flautas, Rancho Ramillete, '96 M125
Flounder Amandine, '89 M196
Flounder, Baked, '90 M316
Frankfurters, Barbecued, '84 M12
Grits, Sausage-Cheese, '90 M238
Grouper Fillets, Breaded, '89 M36
Grouper with Confetti Vegetables, '88 M189
Grouper with Sautéed Vegetables, '90 M233
Haddock Fillets with Zucchini Stuffing, '88 M191
Haddock Italiano, '81 M4
Halibut Steaks Italiano, '88 M191
Halibut with Swiss Sauce, '83 M195
Ham and Apples, Baked, '82 M237
Ham and Apples, Grilled, '96 M303
Ham and Chicken, Creamed, '81 M74
Ham-Asparagus Dinner, '80 M10
Hamburger Patties, '82 M172
Ham Casserole, Macaroni-, '81 M177
Ham Loaf, Cranberry-, '82 M77
Ham Loaf, Saucy, '86 M328
Ham, Marmalade-Glazed, '89 M196
Ham Ring, Chili-Sauced, '81 M122
Ham Roll Casserole, '91 M127
Ham Slice, Fruited, '83 M317
Ham Steak, Glazed, '91 M13
Ham, Sweet-and-Sour Glazed, '88 M15
Ham Tetrazzini, '82 M77
Ham Towers, Cheesy, '82 M77
Ham with Bourbon Glaze, Baked, '98 M271;
　'01 M42
Ham with Raisin Sauce, '82 M76
Kebabs, Shish, '85 M112
Kielbasa and Cabbage, '89 M196
Lamb Chops, Sage, '96 M328
Lasagna, '83 M6
Lasagna, Easy, '92 M197; '93 M24
Lasagna, Lots of Noodles, '91 M127
Lasagna, Microwave, '96 M225
Lasagna, One-Step, '89 M129
Lasagna, Quick 'n Easy, '80 M10
Lasagna, Roasted Vegetable-Meat, '99 M332
Lasagna Rolls, Pepper-Topped, '89 M36

Lasagna, Zesty, '87 M188
Manicotti, Stuffed, '83 M6
Meat Loaf, Basic, '88 M14
Meat Loaf, Cheesy Pizza, '81 M121
Meat Loaf, Easy, '88 M214
Meat Loaf, Oriental, '81 M122; '83 M194
Meat Loaf, Swedish, '81 M121
Meat Loaf, Vegetable, '85 M29
Monkfish, Greek-Style, '87 M79
Mussels Linguine, '90 M112
Orange Roughy with Spinach Pesto, '88 M192
Oysters on the Half Shell, Dressed, '87 M79
Paella, Party, '88 M189
Papillote, Ocean, '84 M287
Patties, Cracked Pepper, '89 M131
Peppers, Beef-Stuffed, '91 M127
Peppers, Hearty Stuffed, '88 M214
Pie, Country Breakfast, '93 M328
Pineapple Loaves, Individual, '81 M121
Pizza Casserole, Microwave, '89 M248
Pizza, Jiffy Jazzed-Up, '83 M314
Pizzas, Muffuletta, '00 M335
Pizza, Taco, '89 M177
Pork Casserole, Cheesy, '81 M74
Pork Chop, Saucy, '86 M140
Pork Chops, Lemon-Herb, '89 M132
Pork Chops, Pineapple, '87 M124
Pork Chops with Apricot Glaze, Stuffed, '89 M36
Pork Enchiladas, '97 M94
Pork Kebabs, Margarita, '98 M223
Pork Loin Roast with Red Currant Sauce,
　'89 M84
Pork Roast, Orange-Glazed, '04 M236
Potatoes, Chili-Topped, '98 M289
Potatoes, Frank-Filled, '84 M11
Pot Roast, Basic, '81 M208
Pot Roast, Company, '88 M14
Pot Roast with Vegetables, '81 M208
Pot Roast with Vegetables, Marinated, '88 M52
Quesadillas, Easy, '98 M205
Quiche, Benedict, '80 M107
Quiche, Crab, '82 M122
Quiche Lorraine, '80 M108; '99 M218
Quiche, Spicy Sausage, '80 M108
Quiche, Spinach-Mushroom, '81 M74
Quiche, Vegetable, '87 M219
Red Beans and Rice, Easy, '99 M219
Ribs, Sweet-and-Sour, '89 M84
Round Steak over Rice, Burgundy, '90 M33
Salmon Patties, Open-Faced, '87 M218
Sausage and Rice Casserole, Oriental, '82 M123
Sausage Casserole, Easy, '87 M189
Sausage Dinner, Beefy, '80 M9
Sausage-Egg Casserole, '86 M12
Sausage Jambalaya Casserole, '82 M203
Shrimp Creole, '90 M220
Shrimp, Garlic-Buttered, '86 M226
Shrimp in Cream Sauce, '84 M286
Shrimp, Quick Curried, '84 M198
Shrimp, Sweet-and-Sour, '90 M112
Sloppy Joes, Pocket, '85 M328
Snapper Provençal, '91 M170
Sole, Saucy, '82 M68
Sole with Cucumber Sauce, '84 M286
Spaghetti, Easy, '83 M317
Spaghetti Pie, '81 M32
Spinach-Tenderloin Pinwheels, '89 M118
Squash with Meat Sauce, Spaghetti, '88 M180
Steak, Onion-Smothered, '87 M189
Taco Pies, Individual, '82 M282
Tacos, Jiffy, '83 M318
Tacos, Microwave, '88 M213
Tortilla Pie, '85 M211
Trout, Sunshine, '84 M286

Trout with Orange Sauce, Pecan-Crusted, '98 M82
Tuna Casserole, Easy, '82 M203
Turkey Breast and Gravy, Savory Seasoned, '89 M309
Turkey Casserole, Crunchy, '89 M282
Turkey Divan, Creamy, '90 M34
Turkey-Noodle-Poppyseed Casserole, '90 M239
Turkey Scaloppine, Easy, '95 M192
Veal and Carrots in Wine Sauce, '86 M139
Veal, Italian Style, '82 M68
Welsh Rarebit with Tomatoes and Bacon, '92 M159
Zucchini, Beef-Stuffed, '86 M139
Marmalade, Orange-Pineapple, '89 M156
Mustard, Coarse-and-Sweet, '86 M288
Noodles, Cheesy Parmesan, '83 M7
Pancakes with Apple-Pear Sauce, Oatmeal Mini-, '97 M272
Party Mix, White Chocolate, '03 M289
Pastry, Microwaved Quiche, '81 M74; '82 M122
Pastry, Quiche, '80 M107
Peaches, Bay Laurel, '90 M124
Peaches with Rum, Ginger, '84 M323
Pears, Gingered, '89 M231
Pears, Marmalade Breakfast, '83 M203
Pears, Spiced Fall, '89 M231
Pickles, Peppery Texas, '04 M161
Pineapple, Scalloped, '84 M323
Pizza on a Bagel, '93 M94
Popcorn, Chili, '00 M223
Popcorn Clusters, Caramel-Nut, '00 M223
Pumpkin, Cooked Fresh, '88 M230
Pumpkin Seeds, Seasoned, '91 M234
Pumpkin Seeds, Toasted, '88 M230
Relish, Cranberry-Orange, '81 M289
Relish, Quick Corn, '90 M13
Relish, Spicy Apple, '84 M323
Relish, Tipsy Cranberry, '92 M310
Rice, Almond, '85 M112
Rice, Basic Long-Grain, '83 M285
Rice, Basic Quick-Cooking, '83 M285
Rice, Chicken-Flavored, '84 M144
Rice, Curry-Spiced, '86 M226
Rice, Herb, '91 M257
Rice, Herbed, '83 M285
Rice, Jiffy Spanish, '90 M176
Rice, Oriental, '85 M12, 146
Rice, Parsleyed, '83 M58
Rice with Almonds, Curried, '83 M285
Risotto, Microwave, '97 M213
Rosemary, Sugared, '04 M279

Salads
Artichokes with Orzo Salad, '88 M193
Beef Salad, Tangy, '87 M218
Chef Salad, Microwave, '90 M146
Chicken Salad, Special, '88 M193
Chicken Taco Salad, '94 M136
Dressing, Raspberry Salad, '03 M28
Fast-and-Easy Salad, '85 M328
Fried Okra Salad, '97 M157
Fruit Salad with Mint Sauce, '88 M96
Green Beans-and-Cheese Salad, '91 M159
Pork-and-Spinach Salad, Mandarin, '88 M126
Potato Salad, Chunky, '81 M138
Potato Salad, German-Style, '88 M194
Spaghetti Squash Salad, '99 M322
Spinach Salad, Sweet-Sour, '85 M112
Spinach Salad, Wilted, '81 M4
Squash Salad, '03 M184
Taco Salad Cups, '85 M29
Tomato-Pasta Salad, '97 M160
Tuna Salad, Cheese-Sauced, '87 M124

Sandwiches
Asparagus-and-Ham Melt Sandwiches, '88 M96
Breakfast Pita Pockets, '89 M21
Breakfast Sandwiches, '82 M123; '89 M230
Brown Bread-Cream Cheese Sandwiches, '87 M6
Burgers, Pizza, '80 M201
Cheese-Steak Wraps, '00 M335
Chicken Tortas, Grilled, '01 M187
Crabmeat Sandwiches, Deluxe, '81 M74
Frankfurter Sandwiches, '84 M11
Fruit-and-Cheese Breakfast Sandwiches, '89 M21
Grilled Cheese Sandwiches, '82 M172
Hot Brown Sandwiches, '80 M202
Pita Sandwiches, Denver, '86 M12
Pita Sandwiches, Hot, '87 M6
Pizza Sandwiches, Open-Face, '84 M198
Pork Sandwiches, Party, '88 M273
Reuben Sandwiches, '80 M201
Sausage-Cheese Muffin Sandwiches, '92 M212
Sausage in a Bun, '89 M22
Tuna Sandwiches, Hot, '86 M194

Sauces and Gravies
Almond-Vanilla Custard Sauce, '88 M177
Amaretto-Strawberry Sauce, '87 M165
Apple Dessert Sauce, '87 M165
Apple-Pear Sauce, '97 M272
Barbecue Sauce, Lemony, '88 M177
Béchamel Sauce, '84 M239
Blueberry Sauce, '89 M130
Cheese Sauce, '79 M156; '82 M123
Cheese Sauce, Guilt-Free, '93 M95
Cheesy Vegetable Sauce, '92 M134
Cherry Sauce, Elegant, '79 M156
Chocolate Cherry Sauce, '87 M165
Chocolate Mint Sauce, Quick, '86 M58
Chocolate-Peanut Butter Sauce, '79 M156
Chocolate-Praline Sauce, '85 M295
Chocolate Sauce, Creamy, '88 M177
Crab Marinara Sauce, Quick, '85 M151
Cranberry Sauce, Holiday, '02 M311
Cream Sauce, Sherried, '85 M152
Curry Sauce, '79 M156; '84 M71
Dill Sauce, '84 M70
Dill Sauce, Creamy, '79 M156
Garlic-Cheese Sauce, '84 M70
Hollandaise Sauce, '80 M107, M268; '88 M177
Horseradish-Mustard Sauce, Creamy, '88 M177
Horseradish Sauce, '88 M273
Jezebel Sauce, Gingered, '04 M138
Lemon Dessert Sauce, '87 M165
Mint Sauce, '88 M96
Mushroom Sauce, '84 M70
Mustard Sauce, '84 M70
Orange Dipping Sauce, '03 M212
Orange Sauce, '84 M286
Orange Sauce, Sweet, '93 M325
Parsley-Garlic Sauce, '84 M70
Peach-Berry Sauce, '87 M165
Peanut Dessert Sauce, '86 M251
Pineapple Ice Cream Sauce, '81 M289
Praline Ice Cream Sauce, Southern, '86 M227
Sour Cream Sauce, '82 M68
Swiss Sauce, '83 M195
Taco Sauce, '82 M283
Tomato Sauce, Herbed Fresh, '85 M151
Tomato Sauce, Italian, '82 M68
Vanilla Sauce, '97 M15
Vegetable-Cheese Sauce, '85 M152
White Sauce, Basic, '79 M156
Shortcuts, '89 M134
Snack Mix, Make-Ahead, '04 M92

Soups and Stews
Bacon-Beer Cheese Soup, '87 M7
Beef Stew with Parsley Dumplings, '85 M246
Broccoli Soup, '86 M194
Broccoli Soup, Cream of, '80 M225
Carrot-Mint Soup, Chilled, '90 M168
Carrot Soup, Creamy, '92 M218
Cauliflower Soup, Cream of, '87 M7
Cheddar-Potato Soup, '03 M283
Cheese Soup, Bacon-Topped, '80 M224
Cheese Soup, Monterey Jack, '85 M211
Chicken-and-Wild Rice Soup, Creamy, '98 M334
Chicken Broth, Easy Microwave, '90 M167
Chicken Soup, Quick, '86 M72
Chili, Basic, '82 M11
Chili, Beefy Sausage, '82 M11
Chili, Cheese-Topped, '82 M11
Chili, Chunky, '82 M11
Chili with Rice, '82 M11
Chowder, Corn, '84 M38
Chowder, Creamy Green Bean, Mushroom, and Ham, '99 M336
Chowder, Creamy Ham, '88 M53
Chowder, Fish, '84 M38
Chowder, New England Clam, '86 M72
Crab Soup, Creamy, '80 M224
Cream Cheese Soup, Austrian, '98 M85
Cucumber Soup, Dilled, '90 M167
Egg-Drop Soup, '85 M12
Garden Harvest Soup, Italian, '90 M167
Mushroom Soup, '86 M73
Mushroom Soup, Curried, '84 M89
Onion Soup, French, '86 M212
Onion Soup, Shortcut French, '85 M328
Oyster-and-Artichoke Soup, Louisiana, '92 M81
Pea Soup, Spring, '88 M96
Potato-Bacon Soup, '84 M38
Potato Soup, Cream of, '80 M224
Potato-Yogurt Soup, '92 M217
Strawberry Soup Supreme, '81 M144
Tomato-Celery Soup, '83 M58
Tomato-Vegetable Soup, '81 M177
Vegetable Soup, Beefy, '84 M38
Vegetable Soup, Chunky, '89 M283
Spoons, Dipped Chocolate-Almond, '95 M277
Spread, Peachy Cream Cheese, '90 M215
Topper, Sticky Bun Toast, '99 M72
Topping, Streusel, '88 M275

Vegetables
Acorn Rings, Easy Glazed, '81 M231
Acorn Squash, Cranberry-Filled, '81 M231
Acorn Squash, Sausage-Stuffed, '81 M231
Artichokes, '92 M107
Artichokes, Quick 'n' Easy Whole Cooked, '96 M132
Artichokes, Stuffed, '91 M117
Artichokes, Whole Cooked, '04 M53
Asparagus-Carrot-Squash Toss, '91 M45
Asparagus in Lemon Butter, '80 M123
Asparagus, Lemon-Sesame, '91 M31
Asparagus-Pea Casserole, '88 M294
Asparagus with Almond Sauce, '91 M117
Asparagus with Lemon Butter, '87 M151
Asparagus with Warm Citrus Dressing, '96 M86
Beans, Marinated Italian, '86 M226
Beets, Harvard, '83 M195
Beets with Sour Cream Dressing, '88 M295
Black-Eyed Peas, '03 M49
Black-Eyed Peas, Fresh, '81 M165
Broccoli au Gratin, '82 M20
Broccoli Casserole, Cheesy, '95 M191
Broccoli Casserole, Easy, '03 M49
Broccoli, Chinese, '85 M12
Broccoli Goldenrod, Lemon-, '84 M89
Broccoli, Marinated Fresh, '81 M139
Broccoli-Swiss Cheese Casserole, '85 M211
Butternut Squash, Apple-Stuffed, '81 M232
Butternut Squash Ring, '81 M232

MICROWAVE, Vegetables
(continued)

Carrots-and-Celery, Scalloped, '84 M112
Carrots, Orange-Fennel, '92 M133
Carrots, Orange-Glazed, '81 M165; '90 M98
Carrots, Peach-Glazed, '90 M13
Carrots, Spice-Glazed, '83 M58
Carrot-Sweet Potato Puree, '00 M32; '02 M285
Corn-and-Bean Casserole, '90 M208
Corn Fix-Up, Quick, '81 M4
Corn, Mexi-, '82 M21
Corn on the Cob, Chili, '03 M185
Corn on the Cob, Fresh Basil, '00 M170
Corn on the Cob, Microwaved, '80 M122
Corn on the Cob, Parmesan, '88 M187
Corn on the Cob, Spicy, '87 M151
Corn, Parslied, '90 M155
Corn, Seasoned Fresh, '83 M147
Corn, Southern-Style Creamed, '81 M165
Eggplant, Easy, '87 M151
Fresh Vegetables, Microwaving, '82 M138
Garden Harvest, '85 M142
Green Bean Gratin, Gourmet, '99 M334
Green Beans, '87 M151
Green Beans Amandine, '82 M20
Green Beans, Bacon-Topped, '80 M123
Green Beans, Baked, '91 M159
Green Beans, French, '90 M208
Green Beans, Garlic, '91 M159
Green Beans, Herbed, '83 M147; '88 M190
Green Beans, Nutty, '88 M187
Green Beans Oriental, '91 M158
Green Beans, Tangy, '85 M142
Green Beans with Marjoram, Fresh, '91 M159
Green Peas, Company, '91 M31
Julienne Vegetables with Walnuts, '86 M251
Kebabs, Marinated Vegetable, '83 M195
Leeks in Dilled Lemon-Butter, '90 M98
Mashed Potatoes, Speedy Garlic, '04 M81
Medley, Garden Vegetable, '91 M45
Medley, Vegetable, '89 M129
Medley, Vegetable-Cheese, '99 M287
Mixed Vegetables, '83 M195
Mushrooms, Microwave Portabello, '95 M123
New Potatoes, Herbed, '83 M148
New Potatoes, Seasoned, '87 M151
New Potato Gratin, Creamy, '01 M320
Okra and Tomatoes, Fresh, '81 M165
Okra, Corn, and Peppers, '87 M151
Okra Medley, '88 M185
Onion-Potato Bake, '83 M195
Onions and Peppers, Sautéed, '83 M148
Onions, Micro-Baked, '82 M32
"Pasta," Garden-Fresh, '94 M134
Peas and Peppers, Minted, '90 M99
Peas in a Potato Nest, '84 M239
Peas with Almonds, Curried, '88 M294
Pepper Cups, Hot Vegetable, '88 M188
Platter, Vegetable, '88 M187
Potato Casserole, Creamy, '84 M113
Potatoes, Basil-Cheese, '90 M316
Potatoes, Blue Cheese Stuffed, '92 M228
Potatoes, Broccoli-Shrimp Stuffed, '92 M228
Potatoes, Cheesy Bacon-Stuffed, '81 M61
Potatoes, Chili-Cheese, '90 M62
Potatoes, Chili-Topped, '98 M289
Potatoes, Cottage, '93 M92
Potatoes, Creamy Cheese, '88 M146
Potatoes, Hearty Stuffed, '89 M282
Potatoes, Italian Mashed, '03 M135
Potatoes, Jalapeño-Ham Stuffed, '81 M61
Potatoes, Micro-Baked, '81 M61

Potatoes, Parmesan, '90 M62; '92 M341;
    '93 M46
Potatoes, Quick Baked, '92 M134
Potatoes, Quick Browned, '82 M172
Potatoes, Seafood-Stuffed, '95 M192
Potatoes, Shrimp-Sauced, '81 M61
Potatoes, Soufflé, '90 M14
Potatoes, Summertime, '86 M195
Potatoes, Taco-Topped, '93 M18
Potatoes, Twice-Baked, '91 M185
Potatoes with Béchamel Sauce, Stuffed, '84 M239
Potatoes with Chives, '81 M61
Potatoes with Hot Bacon Dressing, '88 M294
Potatoes with Tomato Gravy, Mashed, '02 M17
Potatoes, Zesty Stuffed, '94 M46
Potato Fans, Parmesan, '84 M240
Potato Fans, Parmesan-, '88 M190
Potato, Twice-Baked, '90 M295
Potato Wedges, '94 M119
Potato Wedges, Lemony, '90 M61
Ratatouille, Microwave, '95 M232
Snow Peas and Tomatoes, Basil, '88 M185
Spaghetti Squash with Meat Sauce, '88 M180
Spinach Casserole, '91 M31
Spinach Delight, '84 M144
Spuds, Mushroom-Swiss, '96 M238
Squash, Amarillo, '99 M218
Squash-and-Pepper Toss, Crisp, '87 M152
Squash Bake, Cheddar-, '84 M113
Squash Casserole, Jiffy, '81 M144
Squash, Country Club, '88 M16
Squash Medley, Fresh, '81 M165
Squash Mexican, Stuffed, '90 M200
Squash, Stuffed Summer, '02 M181
Squash, Stuffed White, '90 M201
Squash Stuffed with Spinach Pesto, '89 M133
Squash Toss, Simple, '85 M142
Steamed Herbed Vegetables, '93 M303
Stir-Fry, Vegetable, '82 M172
Sweet Potato Casserole, '03 M24
Sweet Potatoes, Applesauce, '91 M292;
    '92 M256
Sweet Potatoes, Cinnamon-Apple, '95 M23
Sweet Potatoes, Orange-Baked, '88 M294
Tomatoes with Walnut-Rice Stuffing, '91 M102
Tomatoes, Zippy Mustard, '86 M226
Zucchini and Carrots, Julienne, '90 M14
Zucchini Boats, '85 M143
Zucchini-Egg Casserole, '84 M113
Zucchini, Italian, '83 M147
Zucchini, Southwestern Stuffed, '03 M127
Zucchini, Stuffed, '89 M133
Vinaigrette Dressing and Croutons, '86 M288

MINCEMEAT
Apples, Baked Mincemeat-Filled, '80 276
Apples, Stuffed, '99 247
Bars, Mincemeat-Spice, '88 231; '89 22
Cake, Mincemeat Spice, '79 246
Cakes, Mini-Mincemeat Nut, '88 257
Cheesecake, Holiday Mincemeat, '00 319
Cookies, Mincemeat, '79 51
Cookies, Mincemeat Drop, '79 246
Cookies, Mincemeat Sweetheart, '87 293
Cookies, Pear Mincemeat, '84 264
Homemade Mincemeat, '79 245
Peaches, Mincemeat, '85 178
Peaches with Mincemeat, Brandied, '81 47
Pear Mincemeat, '79 196; '84 264; '88 226
Pies
Apple-Mincemeat Pie, '85 316
Cheese Pie, Mincemeat-, '80 253
Chiffon Pie, Mincemeat, '79 245
Holiday Mincemeat Pie, '80 282; '87 213
Ice Cream Pie, Mincemeat, '99 285

Kentucky Mincemeat Pie, '95 302
Peach Pie, Mincemeat-, '80 295; '81 188
Pear Mincemeat Pie, '84 264; '88 226
Pear-Mincemeat Pie, '98 258
Pear-Mince Pie, '81 271
Spirited Mince Pie, '92 316
Pudding, Steamed Mincemeat, '80 264
Salad, Holiday Mincemeat, '85 263
Salad, Mincemeat, '94 282
Stuffing, Mincemeat, '00 319
MINTS. *See* **APPETIZERS/Mints.**
MOUSSES
Amaretto Mousse, '86 188
Apricot Mousse, '82 72; '91 297
Asparagus Mousse Salad, '86 252
Avocado Mousse with Shrimp Salad, '98 333
Butter Pecan Mousse, '95 286
Butterscotch Mousse, '93 254
Catfish Mousse, '92 327
Caviar Mousse, '82 71; '85 86; '92 83
Chicken Mousse, Curried, '95 328
Chocolate
Almond Mousse, Chocolate-, '93 316
Amaretto-Chocolate Mousse, '86 50
Amaretto-Chocolate Mousse, Elegant, '86 337
au Grand Marnier, Chocolate Mousse, '91 296
Baked Alaska Chocolate Mousse, '85 195
Blender Chocolate Mousse, '82 71
Blender-Quick Chocolate Mousse, '80 269
Brandy-Chocolate Mousse, '85 102
Cake, Cappuccino Mousse, '99 154
Cake, Chocolate Mousse, '87 264; '98 270;
    '03 320
Cake, Chocolate-Peanut Butter Mousse, '98 71
Cake, Strawberry-Studded White Chocolate
    Mousse, '99 154
Chocolate Mousse, '88 280; '97 282; '02 M277
Creamy Chocolate Mousse, '87 133
Honeyed Chocolate Mousse, '87 223
Kid-Pleasin' Chocolate Mousse, '90 271
Loaf with Raspberry Puree, Chocolate Mousse,
    '97 34
Mint Chocolate Mousse Tarts, '03 283
Mocha Mousse Torte, '04 260
Orange Liqueur, Chocolate Mousse with, '02 315
Orange Mousse, Chocolate-, '81 16, 205
Parfait, Chocolate Mousse, '94 90
Peanut Butter Mousse Parfaits, Chocolate-, '98 71
Pie, Chocolate-Amaretto Mousse, '80 180; '81 30
Pie, Chocolate Mousse, '81 136
Present, Chocolate Mousse, '99 281
Quick-as-a-Wink Mousse, '84 311
Quick Chocolate Mousse, '85 87
Roll, Chocolate Mousse, '88 280
Rum Mousse, Chocolate, '86 189
Truffle Mousse with Raspberry Sauce, Chocolate,
    '95 327
White Chocolate Mousse, '91 247; '93 315;
    '97 282; '98 57, M111; '99 155
White Chocolate Mousse, Quick, '99 155
White Chocolate Mousse Torte, '99 154
Coconut-Pineapple Mousse, '94 198
Coffee Mousse, '84 126
Coffee-Nut Mousse, '86 319
Crabmeat Mousse, '90 190; '91 244; '94 159
Crab Mousse, '79 117; '95 327
Cran-Apple Mousse, '93 255
Crème de Menthe Mousse, '80 109
Cucumber Mousse, '79 11; '88 121
Cucumber Mousse with Dill Sauce, '95 216
Ham Mousse Pitas, '95 328
Horseradish Mousse, '84 126
Lemon Cloud Mousse, '90 90
Lemon Mousse with Raspberry Sauce, '91 96; '92 130

Lime Mousse Freeze, Luscious, '81 173
Macaroni Mousse, '96 73
Margarita Tacos, '97 167
Mustard Mousse, '84 127; '86 184; '95 328
Orange Mousse, '86 69; '94 198
Oyster Mousse, '81 245
Oyster Mousse, Smoked, '84 320; '99 162
Peach Macaroon Mousse, '80 153
Peach Mousse, '85 54
Peppermint Candy Mousse, '82 71; '94 198
Peppermint Mousse, '93 315
Pineapple Mousse, Elegant, '79 230
Pumpkin Mousse, '91 96; '92 130
Raspberry Mousse, '81 34; '04 260
Raspberry Mousse in Chocolate Crinkle Cups,
    '93 270
Rhubarb Mousse, '88 93
Roquefort Mousse, '82 71
Salmon Dill Mousse, '81 21
Salmon Mousse, Irresistible, '79 284
Sherried Mousse, '81 247
Shrimp Mousse, '79 57; '87 196, 251
Strawberry-Lemon Mousse, '82 128
Strawberry Mousse, '81 95
Strawberry Mousse, Fresh, '82 72
Tuna Mousse, '80 275
Watercress Mousse, '88 104
Watermelon Mousse, Frozen, '91 96; '92 130

MUFFINS
Almond Muffins, '90 87
Almond Muffins, Peachy-, '86 301
Apple
    Apple Muffins, '83 96; '84 193; '87 23; '99 234
    Applesauce Muffins, '84 284; '91 141
    Bite-Size Applesauce Muffins, '82 104
    Bran Muffins, Apple-, '85 M89
    Carrot Muffins, Apple-, '91 213
    Cinnamon Oat Bran Muffins, Apple-, '89 106
    Fresh Apple Muffins, '84 264
    Oat Muffins, Spicy Apple-, '86 45
    Pumpkin-Apple Muffins, '96 242
    Spiced Apple Muffins, '79 60
    Spice Muffins, Applesauce, '88 236
Banana
    Banana Muffins, '80 88; '84 75
    Bran Muffins, Banana, '83 48
    Chocolate Chip Muffins, Jumbo Banana-, '93 339
    Chocolate Muffins, Banana-, '94 197
    Honey-Nut Muffins, Banana-, '88 62
    Nut Muffins, Banana-, '93 140
    Oat Bran-Banana Muffins, '91 18
    Oat Bran Muffins, Banana, '89 106
    Oatmeal Muffins, Banana-, '84 20
    Oat Muffins, Banana-, '87 188
    Orange Muffins, Banana-, '84 148
    Poppyseed Muffins, Banana-, '89 205
    Praline Muffins, Banana-, '04 21
    Raisin Muffins, Banana-, '89 218
    Surprise Muffins, Banana, '82 105
Barbecue Muffins, '96 246
Basic Cupcake Muffins, '90 87
Basic Sweet Muffins, '99 234
Biscuit Muffins, '98 136
Blueberry
    Batter, Blueberry Muffin, '04 200
    Blueberry Muffins, '80 143; '91 140, 203;
        '99 234; '04 200, 209
    Bran Muffins, Blueberry-, '89 23
    Buttermilk Muffins, Blueberry, '80 16
    Cinnamon Muffins, Blueberry-, '02 177
    Cream Cheese Muffins, Blueberry-, '86 14
    Easy Blueberry Muffins, '81 197
    Golden Blueberry Muffins, '79 235
    Ice Cream Muffins, Blueberry, '82 143

    Lemon-Blueberry Muffins, '03 26
    Lemon Muffins, Blueberry-, '79 7
    Oat Bran Muffins, Blueberry, '89 106
    Oatmeal Muffins, Blueberry-, '87 24
    Oat Muffins, Blueberry-, '92 119
    Old-Fashioned Blueberry Muffins, '86 161
    Speedy Blueberry Muffins, '95 135
    Streusel Muffins, Blueberry, '80 46
    Streusel Muffins, Blueberry-, '96 146; '01 131
    Streusel Topping, Blueberry Muffins with,
        '88 129
    Sweet Muffins, Blueberry, '00 210
Bran
    All-Bran Oat Bran Muffins, '91 134
    Apple-Bran Muffins, '85 M89
    Apple-Cinnamon Oat Bran Muffins, '89 106
    Banana Bran Muffins, '83 48
    Banana Muffins, Oat Bran-, '91 18
    Banana Oat Bran Muffins, '89 106
    Big Batch Moist Bran Muffins, '95 214
    Blueberry-Bran Muffins, '89 23
    Blueberry Oat Bran Muffins, '89 106
    Bran Muffins, '84 53
    Buttermilk Muffins, Bran-, '85 7
    Cranberry Oat Bran Muffins, '89 107
    Easy Bran Muffins, '83 55
    Ever-Ready Bran Muffins, '81 106
    Fiber Muffins, High-, '85 250
    Freezer Bran Muffins, '91 141
    Fruit-and-Bran Muffins, '04 22
    Honey Bran Muffins, '88 171
    Honey-Bran Muffins, '89 250
    Made of Bran, Muffins, '86 103
    Maple-Bran Muffins, '90 66
    Quick Bran Muffins, '86 85
    Raisin Oat Bran Muffins, '89 106
    Refrigerator Bran Muffins, '79 6
    Sour Cream-Bran Muffins, '87 98
    Spiced Bran Muffins, '84 229
    Two, Bran Muffins for, '84 211
    Whole Wheat Bran Muffins, '88 M274
Breakfast Bites, '86 15
Breakfast Muffins, '04 209
Broccoli-Chicken Muffins, '96 27
Broccoli Cornbread Muffins, '03 81
Butter Muffins, '00 260
Carrot-and-Raisin Muffins, '87 24
Carrot-Date-Nut Muffins, '86 262
Carrot-Pineapple Muffins, '81 6
Carrot-Wheat Muffins, '88 9
Carrot-Zucchini Muffins, '01 200
Cheese
    Bacon-and-Cheese Muffins, '89 205
    Bacon-Cheese Muffins, '96 280
    Caraway-Cheese Muffins, '91 213
    Cheddar Muffins, '89 15
    Cheddar Muffins, Peppered, '99 234
    Cheddar-Raisin Muffins, '91 51
    Cheese Muffins, '96 54; '97 287
    Chive-and-Cheese Muffins, '04 332
    Cornbread Muffins, Cheesy, '88 M275
    Dilly Cheese Muffins, '95 245; '96 55
    English Cheese Muffins, '02 41
    Green Onion-and-Cream Cheese Muffins, '01 289
    Ham-and-Cheddar Muffins, '03 81
    Ham-and-Cheddar Muffins, Reduced-Fat, '03 81
    Ham-and-Cheese Muffins, '92 252; '93 144
    Ham-and-Swiss Muffins, '03 81
    Herb-Cheese Muffins, Buttery, '03 232
    Marvelous Cheese Muffins, '83 96
    Parmesan Cheese Muffins, '04 209
    Pepper-Cheese Muffins, '96 280
    Pepper Muffin Mix, Cheese-and-, '89 330
    Pepper Muffins, Cheese-and-, '84 139

    Sandwiches, Sausage-Cheese Muffin, '92 M212
    Sausage-and-Cheese Muffins, '03 81
    Sausage-Cheese Muffins, '86 213
    Sausage Muffins, Cheesy, '92 252; '93 144
    Sesame-Cheese Muffins, '86 16; '03 81
Cherry Muffins, '82 105
Cherry Muffins, Dried, '94 59
Cherry-Nut Muffins, '90 87
Chicken-and-Green Chile Muffins, '03 81
Chive Muffins, '91 34
Chocolate Chip Muffins, '90 87
Cinnamon-Nut Muffins, '85 M88
Cinnamon-Pecan Muffins, '84 219
Coconut-Molasses Muffins, '82 210
Coconut Muffins, '95 214
Coffee Cake Muffins, '79 7; '98 160
Corn
    Angel Cornbread Muffins, Heavenly, '98 43
    Blue Corn Muffins, '89 145; '92 52
    Cheesy Cornbread Muffins, '88 M275
    Cornmeal Muffins, '80 90; '88 92; '91 19;
        '96 248
    Corn Muffins, '82 M282; '84 16; '98 313
    Jalapeño-Corn Muffins, '93 164
    Miniature Cornmeal Muffins, '93 119
    Oat Muffins, Corn-, '89 108
    Parmesan Corn Muffins, '01 255
    Quick Corn Muffins, '88 15
    Sage-Corn Muffins, '83 207
    Sour Cream Corn Muffins, '95 176
    Southern Cornbread Muffins, '85 201
    Southwestern Corn Muffins, '02 212
    Southwestern Muffins, '91 34
    Spicy Cornbread Muffins, '90 59
    Sunny Corn Muffins, '96 166
    Tex-Mex Corn Muffins, '92 253; '93 144
    Tomato Corn Muffins, '81 137
    Yeast Muffins, Cornmeal, '92 49
Cranberry Muffins, '81 249
Cranberry Muffins, Miniature, '90 294
Cranberry Oat Bran Muffins, '89 107
Cranberry-Orange Muffins, '04 209
Cranberry-Pecan Muffins, '84 269
Cranberry Streusel Cake Muffins, '88 M274
Date Muffins, '79 142; '00 239
Date Muffins, Miniature, '02 171
Date Muffins, Orange-, '92 119; '97 243
Date Muffins, Surprise, '79 216
Date-Nut Muffins, '84 75; '99 234
Dill Mini-Muffins, Dasher's, '04 252
Dino-Mite Muffins, '94 197
Egg Muffins, One-, '83 9
English Muffins, '87 49; '88 76
English Muffins, Raisin, '80 75
Fig Muffins, '86 206
French Breakfast Puffs, '96 67
Fruit-and-Bran Muffins, '04 22
Fudge Brownie Muffins, '95 M50
Gingerbread Bites with Orange-Cream Cheese
    Frosting, '04 258
Gingerbread Muffins, '81 285; '00 15
Gingerbread Muffins, Last-Minute, '82 105
Grain Muffins, Four-, '80 46
Granola Muffins, '95 78
Ham-and-Cheddar Muffins, '03 81
Ham-and-Cheddar Muffins, Reduced-Fat, '03 81
Ham-and-Cheese Muffins, '92 252; '93 144
Ham-and-Swiss Muffins, '03 81
Herb Muffins, '96 280
Honey Bran Muffins, '88 171
Honey-Bran Muffins, '89 250
Honey-Oatmeal Muffins, '84 229
Honey-Wheat Muffins, '83 96; '88 263
Jam Muffins, '79 7

MUFFINS
(continued)

Jelly-Filled Muffins, '80 16
Key Lime Muffins, '95 50
Kiwifruit Muffins, '87 255
Lemon Muffins, '88 119, M275
Lemon Muffins, Fresh, '79 161
Lemon-Raspberry Muffins, '92 119; '03 306
Magic Muffins, '79 244
Mayonnaise Muffins, '83 57; '86 16
Merry Muffins, '82 253
Mix, Quick, '94 167
Mix, Quick Bread, '81 90
Monster Muffins, '94 256
Morning Glory Muffins, '93 327
Muffins, '81 90
Nut Crunch Muffins, Best Ever, '82 65; '83 106
Nut Muffins, Tasty, '79 208
Nutty Muffins, '86 141
Oat
    All-Bran Oat Bran Muffins, '91 134
    Apple-Cinnamon Oat Bran Muffins, '89 106
    Apple-Oat Muffins, Spicy, '86 45
    Banana Muffins, Oat Bran-, '91 18
    Banana Oat Bran Muffins, '89 106
    Banana-Oatmeal Muffins, '84 20
    Banana-Oat Muffins, '87 188
    Batter, Oatmeal Muffin, '04 201
    Best-Ever Oatmeal Muffins, '84 242
    Blueberry Oat Bran Muffins, '89 106
    Blueberry-Oatmeal Muffins, '87 24
    Blueberry-Oat Muffins, '92 119
    Bran Muffins, Oatmeal, '81 236
    Bran Muffins, Oatmeal-, '91 83
    Corn-Oat Muffins, '89 108
    Cranberry Oat Bran Muffins, '89 107
    Honey Muffins, Oatmeal-, '83 95
    Honey-Oatmeal Muffins, '84 229
    Oat Bran Muffins, '89 106
    Oatmeal Muffins, '82 129, 210; '84 72, 140;
      '92 163; '04 201
    Orange-Oatmeal Muffins, '85 202; '00 24
    Raisin Oat Bran Muffins, '89 106
Okra Muffins, Fresh, '93 161
Onion-Dill Muffins, '92 253; '93 144
Orange
    Banana-Orange Muffins, '84 148
    Blossom Muffins, Orange, '96 54
    Cranberry-Orange Muffins, '04 209
    Date Muffins, Orange-, '92 119; '97 243
    Ginger Muffins, Orange-, '89 41
    Honey Muffins, Orange-, '88 284
    Honey Spread, Orange Juice Muffins with,
      '81 229
    Oatmeal Muffins, Orange-, '85 202; '00 24
    Orange Muffins, '79 236; '81 107; '83 54;
      '89 205; '97 271
    Pecan Muffins, Orange-, '83 96; '99 56
    Pecan-Orange Muffins, '97 163
    Raisin Muffins, Orange-, '97 153
    Streusel-Topped Orange Muffins, '84 74
Peach Muffins, Special, '84 74
Peach Streusel Muffins, '03 167
Peanut Butter-Banana Muffins, '03 195
Peanut Butter-Chocolate Chip Muffins, '94 167
Peanut Butter-Honey Muffins, '82 56
Peanut Butter Muffins, '80 86; '87 158; '99 111
Peanut Butter Muffins, Jelly-Topped, '96 279
Peanut Muffins, '91 223
Pear-Ginger Muffins, '91 240
Pecan Muffins, '80 16
Pecan Muffins, Chunky, '88 9

Pecan Muffins, Country, '83 222
Pecan Muffins, Orange-, '83 96; '99 56
Pecan-Orange Muffins, '97 163
Pecan Pie Muffin Batter, '04 200
Pecan-Pie Muffins, '01 206
Pecan Pie Muffins, '04 201
Pineapple Muffins, '81 14, 250
Plum Good Muffins, '83 96
Plum Muffin Batter, Spiced, '04 201
Plum Muffins, Spiced, '04 201
Poppy Seed-Lemon Muffins, '96 280
Poppy Seed Muffins, '81 63; '91 34
Prune Muffins, Miniature, '85 223
Prune Muffins, Spicy, '97 271
Pumpkin-Apple Muffins, '96 242
Pumpkin Muffins, '79 206, 275; '81 272; '04 112
Pumpkin Muffins, Holiday, '03 281
Pumpkin Muffins, Nutty, '86 291
Raisin Muffins, Banana-, '89 218
Raisin Muffins, Breakfast, '84 59
Raisin-Nut Muffins, '92 46
Raisin Oat Bran Muffins, '89 106
Raisin-Pecan Ginger Muffins, '88 9
Raspberry-Streusel Muffins, '96 54
Rum Muffins, Hot Buttered, '96 280
Rum-Nut Muffins, '90 87
Sausage Muffins, '88 52; '95 49
Sour Cream Muffins, '90 283
Sour Cream Muffins, Mini, '88 283
Squash Muffins, '91 69
Strawberry Muffins, '99 234
Sunshine Muffins, '86 9
Sweet Potato Muffins, '81 224; '85 6; '87 280;
    '92 31
Taylor House Muffins, '96 48
Tea Muffins, '82 105
Tropical Muffins, '84 299
Twin Mountain Muffins, '96 280
Wheat Germ-Prune Muffins, '81 106
Wheat Muffins, Fruited, '79 93
Whole Wheat Bran Muffins, '88 M274
Whole Wheat Raisin Muffins, '85 207
Yam Muffins, '79 7
Yeast Muffins, Quick, '84 69
Yellow Squash Muffins, '81 163
Yogurt-Muesli Muffins, '90 215
Yogurt Muffins, '88 55
Zucchini Muffins, '83 121; '86 146
MUSHROOMS
Appetizers, Chicken-Mushroom, '88 210
Artichokes, Ham-Mushroom-Stuffed, '95 228
Aztec Mushrooms, '82 51
Balls, Cheese and Mushroom, '79 63
Canapés, Mushroom, '97 23
Champignons au Vin, '79 47
Cheesecake, Spinach-Mushroom, '92 326
Coquilles St. Jacques, '97 201
Creamed Mushrooms on Toast, '81 190
Curried Mushrooms, '84 214
Dip, Hot Mushroom, '89 48
Drunk Mushrooms, '83 174
Egg Rolls, Chinese, '96 101
Egg Rolls, Scrumptious, '96 101
Elephant Ears, Mushroom-and-Brie Petite, '00 87
English Peas with Mushrooms, '98 286
Filling in a Peel, Mushroom, '84 214
Filling, Mushroom, '81 89; '82 259; '83 51; '88 84
Filling, Spinach-Mushroom, '80 215
Fluted Mushrooms, '82 280
French-Fried Mushrooms, '82 78
French-Fried Mushrooms with Tartar Sauce, '86 233
Garlic and Mushrooms, '95 165
Gravy, Mushroom, '99 34
Gravy, Roast with Onion-and-Mushroom, '00 293

Gravy, Salisbury Steak with Mushroom, '03 202
Gravy, Shallot, '02 239
Logs, Mushroom, '84 206
Main Dishes
    Beef in a Blanket, Bourbon Peppered, '00 109
    Beef, Marinated Stuffed Fillet of, '99 165
    Beef Stroganoff, '03 23
    Beef Tenderloin in Wine Sauce, '02 136
    Beef Tenderloin with Mushrooms, '87 115
    Beef Tenderloin with Mushroom Sauce, '88 3
    Beef Tenderloin with Mushroom-Sherry Sauce,
      '87 306
    Beef Wellingtons, Mini, '01 252
    Bouchées aux Fruits de Mer, '98 267
    Brisket, Saucy, '00 83
    Brunch Egg Nests, '03 246
    Burger, Grilled Portobello, '98 331
    Burgers, Brie-Mushroom, '95 128
    Burgers, Grilled Portobello Pizza, '00 89
    Burgers, Mushroom, '89 164; '97 101; '99 135
    Burgers, Portobello Mushroom, '01 144
    Burgers with Avocado Mayonnaise, Portobello,
      '00 335
    Cacciatore, Hearty Chicken, '02 269
    Casserole, Crab-and-Mushroom, '89 96
    Casserole, Egg-Mushroom, '83 49
    Casserole, Sausage-Mushroom Breakfast, '86 95
    Cassoulet, Easy Chicken, '00 43
    Chicken and Mushrooms in Wine Sauce, '81 109
    Chicken and Pasta, Mediterranean, '03 63
    Chicken-and-Rice Bake, Herbed, '02 215
    Chicken, Asparagus, and Mushrooms with Penne
      Pasta, '98 212
    Chicken Bake, Mushroom-, '89 147
    Chicken Florentine with Mushroom Sauce,
      '87 250
    Chicken Livers with Mushrooms, '81 133
    Chicken Madrid, '97 326
    Chicken-Mushroom Bundles, '80 157
    Chicken-Mushroom Dinner, '81 3
    Chicken Sauté with Artichokes and Mushrooms,
      '03 57
    Chicken with Artichokes and Mushrooms, '90 35
    Chicken with Fennel and Mushrooms, '97 93
    Chicken with Lemon Mashed Potatoes,
      Smothered, '04 180
    Chicken with Mushroom Sauce, '99 22
    Chicken with Sautéed Peppers and Mushrooms,
      Herb-Stuffed, '91 26
    Crabmeat and Mushrooms on Toast Points,
      '82 M91
    Creamed Mushrooms in Wild Rice Ring, '80 270
    Crêpes, Cheese and Mushroom, '81 88
    Crêpes, Coquilles St. Jacques, '83 13
    Crêpes, Mushroom-Cheese, '87 289; '88 135
    Egg Delight, Mushroom-, '83 14
    Eggs, Garden District, '04 66
    Eggs, Saucy Mushrooms and, '79 138
    Eggs, Sherried Mushroom, '83 49
    Filet Mignons with Shiitake Madeira Sauce,
      '95 265
    Filet Mignon with Mushroom Sauce, '94 250
    Filets Mignons, Skillet, '03 258
    Flank Steak and Mushrooms, '87 61
    Flank Steaks with Mushrooms, '00 121
    Fricassee, White Chicken, '98 122
    Grits with Chicken Sausage and Shiitake
      Mushrooms, Cheese, '03 254
    Hamburger Steaks, Mushroom-Stuffed, '99 202
    Hot Browns, '98 287
    Macaroni-Mushroom Bake, Cheesy, '81 243
    Muffin Stacks, Mushroom-Topped, '80 271
    Omelet, Broccoli-Mushroom, '85 45
    Omelet, Golden Cheese-Shiitake, '95 265

Omelet, Rolled Mushroom, '82 70
Patty Shells, Mushrooms and Eggs in, '85 143;
    '88 197
Pizza, Cheese-and-Mushroom, '83 226
Pizza, Portobello, '03 175
Pizzas, Grilled Portobello, '00 89
Pork Chops, Apricot-Mushroom Stuffed, '95 287
Pork Chops, Italian, '02 307
Pork Chops, Weeknight, '97 200
Pork Chops with Mushrooms, Creamy, '01 137
Pork Loin with Apples and Mushrooms, Roast,
    '92 218
Pork Loin with Mushrooms and Garlic, Roasted,
    '92 301
Pork, Moo Shu, '99 237
Pork Tenderloin, Apple-Mushroom, '95 53
Pork Tenderloin with Fruit Stuffing and Shiitake
    Sauce, '97 218
Portabello Mushrooms, Grilled, '95 123
Portobello-Pine Nut Pizza, '99 216
Pot Roast, Mushroom, '79 17; '96 250
Pot Roast with Mushroom Gravy, '02 90
Quail Stroganoff, '99 41
Quail with Mushroom Gravy, Baked, '89 273
Quail with Mushrooms, '85 138
Quail with Mushrooms, Baked, '81 259
Quesadillas, Spinach, Mushroom, and Cilantro,
    '00 148
Quiche, Ham-and-Mushroom, '81 11
Quiche Lorraine, Mushroom-, '86 242
Quiche, Mushroom, '81 244
Quiche, Spinach-Mushroom, '81 M74
Quiche, Zucchini-Mushroom, '79 127
Ragoût of Wild Mushrooms with Creamy Grits,
    '92 238
Ragù with Tortellini, Wild Mushroom, '04 220
Rib-Eyes, Italian, '98 215
Risotto, Redneck, '98 107
Roast, Savory Chuck, '00 18
Roast with Onion-and-Mushroom Gravy, '00 293
Salisbury Steak with Mushroom Gravy, '03 202
Salmon with Mushrooms and Green Onions,
    Fresh, '93 180
Scallop-Mushroom Fettuccine, '96 198
Scallops and Mushrooms, Creamy, '83 144
Shrimp and Mushrooms with Angel Hair Pasta,
    '92 34
Shrimp-Mushroom Italienne, Green Pasta with,
    '79 170
Sirloin in Vodka Sauce, '03 96
Spaghetti with Mushrooms, Spicy, '85 2
Spinach and Mushrooms with Bow Tie Pasta,
    '95 341
Steak with Ham-and-Mushroom Sauce, '83 109
Steak with Mushroom Sauce, '83 212
Stir-Fry, Shiitake-Chicken, '89 61
Stroganoff, Chicken, '99 41
Stroganoff, Creamy Beef, '02 124
Stroganoff, Mushroom, '81 298
Stroganoff, Mushroom-Meatball, '85 85
Stroganoff, Quail, '99 41
Swordfish-Shiitake Skewers, '97 168
Tart, Smoked Portabello Mushroom, '94 163
Turkey Scaloppine with Angel Hair Pasta,
    '02 44
Veal-and-Mushrooms Marsala, '89 44
Veal-Cepe Sauté, '89 62
Veal Scallopini with Shiitakes, '99 232
Venison Loin, Mushroom-Crusted, '94 302
Vermicelli with Mushrooms, '79 195
Marinated
    Caps, Marinated Mushroom, '83 128
    Easy Marinated Mushrooms, '86 217
    Herb Mushrooms, Marinated, '86 327

Marinated Mushrooms, '80 82, 270; '81 69;
    '86 135; '91 306; '92 328
Mexican Marinated Mushrooms, '81 66
Rosemary-Red Wine Vinaigrette, Marinated
    Mushrooms in, '97 63
Salad, Marinated Mushroom, '88 215; '90 181
Special Marinated Mushrooms, '83 13
Meringue Mushrooms, '96 317
Pastry Cups, Mushroom-Almond, '88 210
Pâté de Champignon, '93 171
Pâté in Pastry, Turkey-Mushroom, '92 327
Pâté, Mushroom, '89 157
Patty Shells, Mushrooms and Eggs in, '85 143;
    '88 197
Patty Shells, Mushrooms in, '80 283
Phyllo Bites, Sausage-Mushroom-, '89 284
Piroshki, '92 84
Portabello Mushrooms, Microwave, '95 M123
Portabello Mushrooms, Sautéed, '95 123
Portobello Mushrooms, '03 176
Portobello Mushrooms and Asparagus, Grilled,
    '02 122
Potatoes, Shrimp-and-Mushroom Stuffed, '99 308
Quiche, Mushroom-Spinach-Swiss, '03 59
Quiche, Southwestern, '04 41
Rice, Holiday, '98 289
Rollups, Mushroom, '85 318
Salads
    Cheesy-Mushroom Salad, Quick, '89 128
    Chicken Salad, Asian, '99 124
    Fabulous Mushroom Salad, '81 190
    Fresh Mushroom Salad, '93 65
    Greens, Cucumber Asian, '98 66
    Greens with Walnuts, Mixed, '99 107
    Grilled Mushroom-Asparagus Salad, '02 122
    Marinated Mushroom Salad, '88 215; '90 181
    Marinated Mushrooms in Rosemary-Red Wine
        Vinaigrette, '97 63
    Pepper Salad, Mushroom-and-, '86 68
    Portobello Salad, Grilled, '99 216
    Portobello Salad, Grilled Tomato, Bell Pepper,
        and, '98 211
    Rice Salad with Fresh Mushrooms, '80 231
    Spinach and Mushroom Salad, '80 112
    Spinach-Enoki Salad, '89 62
    Watercress-and-Mushroom Salad, '88 104
    Zucchini Salad, Mushroom-, '85 8
Sandwiches, Toasted Mushroom, '87 281
Sandwiches with Curry-Mustard Sauce, Mushroom
    Bagel, '96 249
Sauces. *See also* **MUSHROOMS/Gravy.**
    Beef Tenderloin with Mushroom Sauce, '88 3
    Chanterelle Brown Sauce, '89 62
    Cheese Sauce, Mushroom-, '83 190; '86 48
    Chicken Florentine with Mushroom Sauce,
        '87 250
    Chicken with Mushroom Sauce, '99 22; '04 255
    Cream Sauce, '03 237
    Creole Sauce, '98 98
    Dill Sauce, Mushroom-, '80 271
    Eggs Baked in Mushroom Sauce, '93 47
    Filet Mignon with Mushroom Sauce, '94 250
    Ham-and-Mushroom Sauce, Steak with, '83 109
    Mole Sauce, Burgundy, '98 174
    Mushroom Sauce, '81 90, 200; '82 46;
        '83 71, 205, 212; '84 M70; '85 40; '86 198;
        '87 36, 186, 284; '91 221; '03 255
    Omelets with Mushroom Sauce, Puffy, '85 40
    Onion-Mushroom Sauce, '85 224; '86 84
    Portobello-Alfredo Sauce, Fettuccine with,
        '04 135
    Savory Mushroom Sauce, '96 236
    Sherried Mushroom Sauce, Green Beans in,
        '93 206

Sherried Mushroom Sauce, Spicy, '89 239
Sherry Sauce, Beef Tenderloin with Mushroom-,
    '87 306
Shiitake Madeira Sauce, Filet Mignons with,
    '95 265
Shiitake Sauce, Pork Tenderloin with Fruit
    Stuffing and, '97 218
Spinach Loaf with Mushroom Sauce, '01 277
Steak with Mushroom Sauce, '83 212
Tomatoes with Mushroom Sauce, Broiled,
    '81 103
Vermicelli, Mushroom Sauce Supreme on,
    '86 158
Wine Sauce, Mushroom-, '84 84; '86 24; '00 125
Zucchini-Mushroom Sauce, '93 71
Shiitakes, Grilled, '95 265
Side Dishes
    Acorn Squash-Mushroom Puree, '93 305
    à la King, Mushrooms, '89 285
    Asparagus and Mushrooms, '85 108
    Asparagus-and-Mushroom Sauté, '93 115
    Asparagus-and-Mushroom Tostadas with Goat
        Cheese, '03 242
    au Gratin, Mushrooms, '81 108
    Baked Mushrooms, Creamy, '87 127
    Bake, Windsor Mushroom, '88 132
    Bread Pudding, Mushroom, '99 58
    Casserole, Mushroom, '95 211; '96 47
    Casserole, Mushroom-Artichoke, '87 241
    Casserole, Mushroom-Cheese, '83 216
    Casserole, Mushroom Deluxe, '96 20
    Casserole, Mushroom-Macaroni, '95 180
    Casserole, Mushroom-Potato, '84 5
    Creamed Oyster Mushrooms, '89 61
    Dressing, Whole Wheat-Mushroom, '84 283
    Eggplant, Mushroom-Stuffed, '83 136
    Fresh Mushrooms, Savory, '85 268
    Green Bean Casserole, '02 197
    Green Beans, Mushroom-Bacon, '91 291;
        '92 255
    Green Beans with Bacon and Mushrooms, '92 13
    Green Beans with Mushrooms, '82 21; '93 89
    Green Beans with Mushrooms and Sage, '02 314
    Green Peas with Mushrooms, '80 101
    Heavenly Mushrooms, '87 281
    Herbed Mushrooms, '84 214; '88 176
    Kugel, Mushroom Matzo, '00 83
    Macaroni-Mushroom Bake, '97 96
    Mixed-Up Mushrooms, '01 213
    Newburg, Mushroom, '88 252
    Noodles and Mushrooms, Cheesy, '79 84
    Panuchos, Mushroom, '83 51
    Pasta 1-2-3, Mushroom, '97 102
    Peas and Mushrooms, '83 141
    Peas and Mushrooms, Buttered, '82 204
    Peas with Mushrooms, Creamy, '84 196
    Pepper-Mushroom Medley, '90 98
    Pie with Mushrooms, Vidalia Onion, '02 183
    Portobello Mushrooms, Sautéed, '96 273
    Potatoes, Buffet, '98 92
    Potatoes, Mushroom-Dill-Topped, '86 41
    Potatoes, Mushroom Scalloped, '87 191
    Quiche, Mushroom, '80 222; '89 285
    Quiches, Wild Rice-and-Mushroom, '93 237
    Rice, Baked Mushroom, '92 170; '95 84
    Rice, Easy Mushroom, '89 286
    Rice, Holiday, '98 289
    Roasted Green Beans with Mushrooms, '04 182
    Sautéed Mushrooms, '84 35
    Sautéed Mushrooms, Easy, '81 131
    Sautéed Mushroom Spectacular, '83 206
    Sauté, Mixed Mushroom, '89 62
    Seasoned Mushrooms, '83 291
    Sherried Mushrooms, '83 13

MUSHROOMS, Side Dishes
(continued)

Soufflés, Mushroom, **'87** 282
Sour Cream-Dill Sauce, Mushrooms in, **'84** 215
Sparkling Mushrooms, **'94** 24
Spinach and Mushrooms with Bow Tie Pasta,
   '95 341
Spinach with Mushrooms, **'80** 19
Stir-Fried Mushrooms with Bacon, **'80** 123
Supreme, Mushrooms, **'84** 214
Tarts, Mushroom, **'88** 161
Tomatoes, Mushroom-Stuffed, **'86** 218; **'96** 106
Turnovers, Tiny Mushroom, **'86** 24
Vermouth, Mushrooms in, **'89** 203
Wild Mushroom-and-Onion Pot Pies, **'98** 296
Wild Rice and Mushrooms, **'83** 278
Wild Rice with Morels, **'89** 62
Wine Sauce, Mushrooms with, **'85** 292
Yellow Squash, Mushroom-Stuffed, **'84** 154
Zesty Mushrooms, **'93** 218
Zucchini with Mushrooms, Sautéed, **'94** 135
Soups
Avocado-Mushroom Soup, Creamy, **'85** 25
Bisque, Brisk Mushroom, **'81** 190
Chicken, Artichoke, and Mushroom Soup,
   '92 324
Chowder, Creamy Green Bean, Mushroom, and
   Ham, **'99** M336
Chowder, Mushroom, **'79** 16
Chowder, Mushroom-Potato, **'92** 331
Chunky Mushroom Soup, **'88** 12
Consommé aux Champignons, **'79** 48
Consommé, Brown Rice, **'98** 288
Corn Soup with Shiitakes and Shrimp, Sweet,
   '99 168
Cream of Mushroom-and-Leek Soup, **'01** 312
Cream of Mushroom Soup, **'84** 5; **'85** 93, 261
Creamy Mushroom Soup, **'79** 243; **'81** 307
Curried Mushroom Soup, **'84** M89
Elegant Mushroom Soup, **'83** 99
Fresh Mushroom Soup, **'81** 109; **'90** 190
Mushroom Soup, **'82** 286; **'86** M73; **'94** 54
Onion Soup, Mushroom-, **'80** 25
Oyster-and-Mushroom Soup, **'87** 39
Rice Soup, Mushroom-, **'90** 32
Rice Soup, Wildest, **'01** 66
Sherried Mushroom Soup, **'96** 104
Shiitake Soup, Cream of, **'95** 265
Wild Mushroom Soup, **'98** 281; **'04** 203
Sour Cream, Mushrooms in, **'00** 106
Spread, Eggplant-Mushroom, **'92** 156
Spread, Hot Mushroom, **'81** 190
Spuds, Mushroom-Swiss, **'96** M238
Stewed Anasazi Beans with Mushrooms, **'95** 226
Strudel, Crab-and-Mushroom, **'98** 28
Stuffed
Appetizers, Stuffed Mushroom, **'88** 210
Artichoke-Stuffed Mushrooms, **'01** 239
Beef-Stuffed Mushrooms, **'00** 278
Black Olive-Stuffed Mushrooms, **'86** 258
Canapés, Mushroom, **'80** 285
Cheese 'n' Bacon-Stuffed Mushrooms, **'86** 258
Cheese-Stuffed Mushrooms, Elegant, **'81** 57
Chicken-Stuffed Mushrooms, **'80** 162
Crab, Mushrooms Stuffed with, **'82** 249
Crab-Stuffed Mushroom Caps, **'84** 160
Crab-Stuffed Mushrooms, **'81** 190; **'97** 102
Crawfish-Stuffed Mushrooms, **'86** 258
Delight, Stuffed Mushroom, **'87** 281
Flavor-Stuffed Mushrooms, **'85** 288
Florentine, Stuffed Mushrooms, **'82** 270
Ham, Mushrooms Stuffed with, **'97** 237

Italian Sausage-Stuffed Mushrooms, **'83** 127
Parmesan Stuffed Mushrooms, **'83** 115
Pâté-Stuffed Mushrooms, **'85** 118
Pecan-Stuffed Mushrooms, **'84** 261
Pesto-Stuffed Mushrooms, **'86** 150
Pistachio-Stuffed Mushrooms, **'86** 141
Ricotta-Stuffed Mushrooms, **'85** 20
Samurai 'shrooms, **'93** 258
Sausage-Stuffed Mushrooms, **'80** 248; **'91** 164
Seasoned Stuffed Mushrooms, **'84** 206
Shiitakes Parmigiana, Stuffed, **'98** 25
Shrimp-Stuffed Mushrooms, **'80** M135; **'99** 324
Spinach-Stuffed Mushrooms, **'86** 81;
   '88 131, M261; **'89** M133
Stems, Mushrooms with, **'86** 258
Stuffed Mushrooms, **'79** 212; **'81** 239;
   '83 13, 66, 126, 136; **'93** 172
Vegetable Mushroom Caps, **'81** 246
Stuffing, Cornish Hens with Barley-Mushroom,
   '97 242
Stuffing, Grilled Rainbow Trout with Mushroom,
   '97 162
Stuffing, Sausage-and-Wild Mushroom, **'96** 267
Tapas, Majorcan Mushroom, **'95** 159
Tarts, Hot Sherried Mushroom, **'83** 78
Tipsy Mushrooms, **'84** M216
Tomatoes, Veracruz, **'97** 169
Tomatoes with Curry Sauce, Stuffed, **'97** 170
Turnovers, Hot Mushroom, **'89** 285; **'97** 102
MUSSELS. *See* **SEAFOOD.**
MUSTARD
Bourbon Mustard, **'93** 240
Bread, Mustard, **'01** 146
Brie, Honey-Mustard, **'91** 252
Brussels Sprouts Dijon, **'96** 91
Brussels Sprouts with Shallots and Mustard, **'85** 258
Butter, Chive-Mustard, **'98** 156
Butter, Jalapeño-Pecan-Mustard, **'03** 205
Chicken, Dijon, **'99** 21
Chicken Dijon, **'04** 196
Chicken, Lemon-Mustard, **'99** 109
Chicken, Mustard, **'93** 239
Coarse-and-Sweet Mustard, **'86** M288
Compote, Baked Mustard Fruit, **'85** 47
Cream, Mustard-Horseradish, **'02** 53
Dip, Sweet-and-Spicy Mustard, **'96** M274
Dressing, Dijon-Honey, **'89** 45; **'99** 333
Dressing, Herbed Mustard, **'00** 145
Dressing, Honey-Mustard, **'90** 55, 111, 146; **'00** 54;
   '01 230
Dressing, Lemon-Mustard, **'02** 52
Dressing, Mustard, **'80** 112
Dressing, One-Bean Salad with Lime-Mustard,
   '00 202
Dressing, Tangy Mustard, **'93** 323
Easy Sweet-Tangy Mustard, **'01** 247
Fish, Spicy Mustard, **'99** 90
Flounder Dijon, **'85** 95
Fruit Bake, Mustard, **'90** 291
Glaze, Apple-Stuffed Tenderloin with Praline-
   Mustard, **'97** 216
Glaze, Game Hens with Chutney-Mustard, **'93** 66
Glaze, Roast Chicken with Pineapple-Mustard, **'89** 83
Herbed Mustard, **'87** 134
Homemade Mustard, **'81** 77
Homemade Mustard, Zesty, **'82** 55
Honey Mustard, Hot, **'93** 240
Honey Mustard, Peppered, **'95** 312
Horseradish Mustard, **'93** 240
Horseradish Mustard, Lower Sodium, **'86** 325
Hot German Mustard, **'82** 298
Hot Mustard, Chinese, **'85** 12
Hot Mustard, Really, **'95** 312
Hot Sweet Mustard, **'85** 12

Jalapeño Mustard, **'93** 240; **'95** 312
Key Lime Mustard, **'94** 278
Lamb Chops, Dijon-Rosemary, **'99** 333
Marinade, Honey-Mustard, **'93** 103
Mousse, Mustard, **'84** 127; **'86** 184; **'95** 328
Orange Roughy Dijon, **'99** 122
Pork Chops, Spicy Brown Mustard, **'03** 205
Pork Loin, Orange-Dijon, **'00** 259
Pork Tenderloin, Honey-Mustard, **'95** 52
Raspberry Mustard, **'95** 313
Sauces
Asparagus in Mustard Sauce, Chilled, **'88** 130
Barbecue Sauce, Mustard, **'84** 173
Chutney-Mustard Sauce, **'89** 242
Cream Sauce, Chicken in Mustard, **'92** 181
Cream Sauce, Mustard, **'88** 61
Creamy Mustard Sauce, **'80** 272; **'86** 257;
   '87 232; **'93** 240
Creamy Mustard Sauce, Champagne-Poached
   Chicken with, **'94** 24
Creole Mustard Sauce, **'99** 142
Curry-Mustard Sauce, **'96** 249
Dijon-Caper Cream Sauce, Broiled Salmon with,
   '98 329
Dijon Horseradish Sauce, **'03** 297
Dijon Mustard Sauce, Creamy, **'04** 198
Dijon Sauce, Orange-, **'00** 259
Easy Mustard Sauce, **'94** 83
Extra-Special Mustard Sauce, **'79** 82
Hamburger Steaks with Mustard Sauce, **'84** 230
Hollandaise Sauce, Mock Mustard-, **'87** 269
Honey-Lemon Mustard Sauce, **'84** 275
Honey-Mustard Sauce, **'85** 13
Honey-Mustard Sauce, Smoked Ribs with,
   '92 168
Horseradish-Mustard Sauce, Creamy, **'88** M177
Hot Mustard Sauce, **'93** 240
Leg of Lamb with Mustard Sauce, **'89** 71
Lemon-Mustard Sauce, Salmon Steaks with,
   '97 124
Light Mustard Sauce, **'82** 178
Mild Mustard Sauce, **'85** 224; **'86** 84
Mustard Sauce, **'80** 222, 283; **'83** 21, 321;
   '84 M70, 289; **'85** 148; **'86** 185; **'87** 22;
   '89 122, 333; **'90** 19, 97; **'92** 302; **'93** 118;
   '99 270; **'00** 32; **'01** 102; **'02** 162, 245
Pork Tenderloin with Mustard Sauce, **'99** 145;
   '03 238
Sausage Sandwiches with Mustard Sauce,
   '84 250
Scallops with Mustard Sauce, **'84** 163
Smoked Sausages with Mustard Sauce, **'81** 56
Sour Cream Sauce, Mustard-, **'81** 68
Special Mustard Sauce, **'01** 159
Stone Crab Mustard Sauce, **'80** 3
Sweet Mustard Sauce, **'85** 12
Tangy Mustard Sauce, **'92** 201
Tarragon-Mustard Sauce, Turkey Cutlets with,
   '93 239
Vinaigrette Sauce, Mustard-, **'84** 174
Vinegar Sauce, Shrimp with Mustard-, **'93** 240
Spread, Chive-Mustard, **'91** 12
Spread, Honey Mustard-Butter, **'99** 86
Spread, Mustard, **'86** 105
Sweet Cider Mustard, **'95** 312
Vegetables, Honey-Dijon, **'98** 311
Vegetables, Honey-Mustard Marinated, **'93** 236
Vinaigrette, Baby Lettuces with Mustard, **'93** 67
Vinaigrette, Dijon, **'00** 222; **'02** 18
Vinaigrette, Greens with Dijon, **'98** 332
Vinaigrette, Herb-Mustard, **'02** 84
Vinaigrette, Honey-Dijon, **'04** 321
Vinaigrette, Honey-Mustard, **'94** 249
Vinaigrette, Mustard, **'96** 184; **'01** 102

NECTARINES

Apple Juice, Nectarines in, '83 183
Butter, Nectarine, '79 175
Cobbler with Blueberry Muffin Crust, Nectarine,
    '04 200
Cocktail, Nectarine, '85 107
Royale, Nectarines, '85 132
Salad, Nectarine Chicken, '79 175
Sherbet, Nectarine, '89 199
Shortcake, Warm Blueberry-Nectarine, '97 205

NOODLES

Caraway Buttered Noodles, '87 230
Casserole, Eggplant and Noodle, '82 230
Casserole, Sweet Noodle, '02 238
Casserole, Vegetable Noodle, '91 30
Egg Foo Yong Noodles, '98 233
Green Noodles, '80 211
Kugel, Apricot Noodle, '92 251
Kugel, Nu Awlins, '94 229
Kugel, Sweet, '90 254
Kugel, Vegetable-Noodle, '96 228
Lo Mein Noodles and Broccoli, '97 18
Main Dishes
  Beef and Noodles, Easy, '83 288
  Beef Bake, Asian Noodle, '98 31
  Beef over Rice Noodles, Shredded, '85 74
  Beefy Noodle Dinner, '81 179
  Cakes with Coconut-Beef Stir-Fry, Noodle,
    '97 18
  Casserole, Beef-and-Noodles, '84 72
  Casserole, Beef, Cheese, and Noodle, '99 58
  Casserole, Chicken and Green Noodle, '80 32
  Casserole, Chicken-Noodle, '94 286
  Casserole, Chicken Noodle, '01 308
  Casserole, Fabulous Tuna-Noodle, '02 63
  Casserole, Ham, '96 302
  Casserole, Ham and Noodle, '80 300
  Casserole, Sausage and Noodle, '82 123
  Casserole, Sausage-and-Noodle, '95 255
  Casserole, Shrimp-and-Noodle, '90 240
  Casserole, Stroganoff, '98 48
  Casserole, Turkey-Noodle-Poppyseed, '90 239
  Cheesy Noodles and Mushrooms, '79 84
  Chicken and Spinach Noodles, '82 19
  Chicken with Noodles, Sesame, '88 M125
  Chicken with Spicy Soba Noodles, Grilled, '00 93
  Chili with Noodles, '81 282; '82 57
  Chow Mein over Crispy Noodles, '85 286
  Fried Noodles with Shrimp, '02 174
  Ham and Swiss on Noodles, '87 108
  Hamburger-Noodle Bake, '81 140
  Ham-Noodle Skillet, '87 78
  Hoisin Noodles with Shrimp, '98 233
  Italian Sauce with Noodles, '84 250
  Lasagna, Egg-Noodle, '04 219
  Lasagna, Lots of Noodles, '91 M127
  Liver and Noodle Dinner, Creamy, '80 11
  Pad Thai, '97 202
  Pork-and-Noodle Bake, '88 98
  Pork-and-Noodles Skillet Dinner, '88 199
  Ring, Noodle, '85 285
  Sausage and Mixed Vegetables, Pasta with,
    '87 249
  Sausage-Noodle Bake, '81 92
  Sausage, Pasta with Broccoli and, '87 109
  Scallops and Pasta, Fresh, '83 164
  Sesame Noodles, '01 188
  Shrimp and Noodles, Creamy, '92 100
  Sour Cream-Noodle Bake, '79 55
  Stew with Noodles, Hungarian, '80 263
  Szechuan Noodles with Spicy Beef Sauce, '97 95
  Taco Beef-Noodle Bake, '81 141
  Tempura Udon, '00 93

Turkey Noodle Bake, '93 243
  Veal Sauce, Noodles with, '80 236
Orange Noodles, '84 177
Pancake, Szechuan Ginger Stir-Fry with Noodle,
    '97 292
Parmesan Noodles, '83 118
Parmesan Noodles, Cheesy, '83 M7
Parslied Noodles, '85 31
Ramen Noodle Satay, '98 233
Salad, Chicken Noodle, '95 25
Salad, Ham-Noodle, '85 249
Salad, Noodle Chicken, '03 143
Salad, Peanut-Noodle, '02 163
Salad, Ramen Noodle, '88 41; '97 18; '02 24
Salad, Sesame Noodle, '02 186
Soup, Chicken Noodle, '80 264; '95 45; '98 30
Soup Mix, Turkey-Noodle, '89 330
Soup, Turkey-Noodle, '91 312
Spinach with Noodles, Creamed, '84 29
Thai Coconut Broth with Noodles, '98 295
Vegetables, Noodles with Spring, '02 125
White Noodles, '80 211

NUTS. *See* **ALMONDS; APPETIZERS/Nuts;**
    MACADAMIA; PEANUTS; PECANS;
    WALNUTS.

OATMEAL

Applesauce Oatmeal, '89 108
Bake, Pear-Oatmeal, '89 208
Bars and Cookies
  Apple-Nut Cookies, '80 228
  Apple-Oatmeal Cookies, '85 215; '90 218
  Apple-Oat Snack Squares, '00 332
  Apricot-Oatmeal Bars, '86 216; '04 331
  Banana Oatmeal Cookies, '79 217
  Breakfast Cookies, '97 52
  Breakfast Cookies, Take-Along, '84 59
  Brownies, Elephant Stomp, '03 43
  Brownies, Oat, '89 59
  Brownies, Oatmeal, '87 199
  Brownies, Oat 'n' Crunch, '91 233
  Cake Mix Oatmeal Cookies, '96 247
  Caramel Bars, Oatmeal-, '85 247
  Carrot Cookies, Oatmeal-, '94 292
  Chocolate Chip Cookies, '00 276
  Chocolate Chip Cookies, Nutty Oatmeal-,
    '82 M185
  Chocolate Chip-Oatmeal Cookies, '84 119
  Chocolate Chippers, Oatmeal-, '90 218
  Chocolate Chunk Cookies, Nutty Oatmeal-,
    '01 19
  Chocolate Morsel Cookies, Oatmeal-, '95 46
  Chocolate-Oatmeal Cookies, '80 105
  Chocolate-Raisin Oatmeal Cookies, '95 136
  Chocolate-Topped Oatmeal Bars, '86 110
  Cinnamon Oatmeal Cookies, '84 72
  Clear-the-Cupboard Cookies, '99 278;
    '02 176
  Coconut Cookies, Oatmeal-, '80 218
  Coconut Crispies, Oatmeal-, '01 19
  Coconut-Macadamia Cookies, '98 294
  Coconut-Oatmeal Cookies, Crispy, '93 80
  Crackers, Oatmeal-Wheat Germ, '84 236
  Cranberry-Caramel Bars, '98 277
  Crispies, Oat, '83 96
  Crispy Oat Cookies, '88 203; '90 311
  Crispy Oatmeal Cookies, '89 328
  Crunchy Oatmeal Cookies, '85 202
  Date Bars, Layered Oatmeal-, '85 10
  Date Cookies, Oatmeal-, '82 109
  Date-Filled Oatmeal Cookies, '86 314
  Date-Oat Bars, '80 M172
  Date Sandwich Cookies, Oatmeal-, '83 257

Double-Chip Oatmeal Cookies, '03 200
Easy Oatmeal Cookies, '80 105
Fibber McGee Cookies, '95 72
Fudge Bars, Yummy, '87 158
Ginger-Oatmeal Sorghum Cookies, '00 230;
    '02 230
Granola Bars, '83 305
Granola Bars, No-Bake, '97 220
Krispies, Oatmeal, '85 115
Lace Cookies, '86 8
Lace Cookies, Crunchy, '01 294
Layered Oatmeal-Date Bars, '85 10
Macadamia-Oat Snowballs, '92 274
Nut Crispies, Oatmeal, '80 208
Nutty Oatmeal Cookies, '81 130
Oatmeal Cookies, '92 82; '99 280
Old-Fashioned Oatmeal Cookies, '80 106;
    '85 250
Olympic Medal Cookies, '96 180
Orange-Glazed Oatmeal Cookies, '80 60
Orange Slice Cookies, '98 324
Peanut Butter Chocolate Chip Cookies, Oatmeal-,
    '92 207
Peanut Butter Cookies, Oatmeal-, '85 171
Peanut Butter-Oatmeal Cookies, '81 218; '84 72
Peanut Cookies, Oats-and-, '89 60
Peanutty Oatmeal Cookies, '80 106; '83 95
Pudding-Oatmeal Cookies, '98 215
Raisin Cookies, Frosted Oatmeal-, '79 290
Raisin Cookies, Oatmeal-, '87 221; '93 127
Raisin-Oatmeal Cookies, '01 19
Red, White, and Blue Cookies, Chewy, '03 163
Slice-and-Bake Oatmeal Cookies, '80 105
Special Oatmeal Cookies, '81 236
Spice Cookies, Giant Oatmeal-, '80 105; '03 59
Spicy Oatmeal Cookies, '81 197; '01 19
Sunshine Cookies, Oatmeal, '89 59
Toasted Oatmeal Cookies, '92 273; '95 136
Toffee Cookies, Oatmeal-, '04 234
Toffee Lizzies, Crispy Oatmeal-, '95 136
White Chocolate Chip-Oatmeal Cookies, '99 127;
    '04 43
Breads
  Biscuits, Oatmeal, '89 108
  Blueberry-Oatmeal Bread, '83 139
  Buns, Honey-Oat, '98 27
  Buns, Honey Oatmeal, '83 154
  Buttermilk-Oatmeal Bread, '97 212
  Caraway-Raisin Oat Bread, '86 44
  Dill-Oat Bread, '91 95
  Herbed Oatmeal Pan Bread, '97 243
  Honey-Oat Bread, '89 107; '98 27
  Honey Oatmeal Bread, '80 60
  Loaf, Banana-Oat Tea, '87 256
  Loaf, Pumpkin-Oatmeal, '81 49
  Molasses Bread, Oatmeal-, '97 194
  Muffin Batter, Oatmeal, '04 201
  Muffins, Banana-Oat, '87 188
  Muffins, Banana-Oatmeal, '84 20
  Muffins, Best-Ever Oatmeal, '84 242
  Muffins, Blueberry-Oat, '92 119
  Muffins, Blueberry-Oatmeal, '87 24
  Muffins, Corn-Oat, '89 108
  Muffins, Honey-Oatmeal, '84 229
  Muffins, Oat Bran, '89 106
  Muffins, Oat Bran-Banana, '91 18
  Muffins, Oatmeal, '82 129, 210; '84 72, 140;
    '92 163; '04 201
  Muffins, Oatmeal Bran, '81 236
  Muffins, Oatmeal-Bran, '91 83
  Muffins, Oatmeal-Honey, '83 95
  Muffins, Orange-Oatmeal, '85 202; '00 24
  Muffins, Spicy Apple-Oat, '86 45
  Oatmeal Bread, '81 236, 300; '92 212; '97 130

OATMEAL, Breads
(continued)

    Oatmeal Raisin Bread, '81 14
    Oatmeal-Raisin Bread, '83 59
    Oat-Molasses Bread, '82 139
    Rolls, Oatmeal-Cinnamon-Pecan, '96 50
    Rolls, Oatmeal Dinner, '01 44
    Round Oatmeal Bread, '84 20
    Whole Wheat-Oatmeal Bread, '87 85
Breakfast Oatmeal Surprise, '93 178
Breakfast Oatmeal, Swiss Style, '81 49
Burgers, Black Bean, '98 144
Burgers, Pinto, '98 51
Burgers, Spicy Bean, '00 84
Cake, Applesauce-Oatmeal, '92 119
Cake, Dutch Oatmeal, '83 95
Cake, Golden Apple-Oatmeal, '86 301
Cake, Honey-Oatmeal, '87 222
Cake, Oatmeal, '01 58
Cake, Saucy Pudding, '98 196
Cereal, Full-of-Fiber Hot, '89 208
Coffee Cake, Oatmeal-Coconut, '83 312
Crisp, Oatmeal Cherry-Apple, '90 M16
Crust, Nutty Oat, '89 251
Fruited Oatmeal, '88 19
Granola, '99 212
Granola, Crunchy, '81 218; '84 144
Granola, Easy, '81 49
Granola, Fruity, '84 148
Granola, Healthful, '97 204
Granola, Homemade, '84 58
Granola, Mixed Fruit, '01 290
Granola, Sunny Orange, '84 212
Granola, Superhero, '98 M206
Hamburgers, Meatless Walnut, '96 243
Ice Cream Sandwiches, Oatmeal Crispy, '93 199
Mix, Rolled Oats, '84 72
Muesli, '89 208
Muesli, Homestyle, '91 315
Pancakes, Oat, '89 227
Pancakes, Oatmeal, '80 44; '89 107
Pancakes, Oatmeal-Brown Sugar, '88 203
Pancakes, Whole Wheat-Oat, '93 16
Pancakes with Apple-Pear Sauce, Oatmeal Mini-,
    '97 M272
Piecrust, Crisp Cereal, '83 100
Piecrust, Oatmeal, '79 79
Slow Cooker with Ice Cream, Oatmeal in a, '99 193
Topping, Oat Crunch, '89 108
Topping, Oatmeal Cookie, '95 291
Waffles, Banana-Oatmeal, '94 206
Waffles, Oatmeal, '89 107
Waffles, Oatmeal-Nut, '83 96
OILS. *See also* **SEASONINGS.**
Basic Recipe, '96 122
Basil-Infused Olive Oil, '95 231
Basil Oil, '96 122
Black Pepper Oil, '96 122
Chile Pepper Oil, '96 122
Chili Oil, '96 234
Chipotle Oil, '02 97; '03 98
Chive Oil, '96 122
Cilantro Oil, '02 97; '03 98
Dill Oil, '96 122
Ginger Oil, '96 122
Lemon-Infused Olive Oil, '95 231
Mint Oil, '96 122
Oregano Oil, '96 122
Parsley Oil, '96 234
Roasted Garlic Oil, '96 122
Rosemary Oil, '96 122; '02 122
Sage Oil, '96 122

Thyme Oil, '96 122
Vanilla Oil, '94 243
OKRA
Bake, Okra-and-Tomato, '89 173
Bake, Okra-Tomato, '80 298; '81 26
Bake, Tomato-and-Okra, '03 158
Bisque, Okra-and-Shrimp, '97 156
Caponata, Okra, '97 157
Casserole, Okra, '79 160
Chowder, Quick Okra, '80 185
Combo, Field Peas, Okra, and Corn, '01 214
Corn, and Peppers, Okra, '87 M151
Corn, and Tomatoes, Okra, '95 203
Cream, Okra and Corn in, '79 160
Creole, Corn-and-Okra, '89 127
Creole, Meatball-Okra, '83 156
Creole Okra, '81 182
Creole, Okra, '02 234
Creole, Okra-Corn, '83 157
Dills, Okra, '97 157
Étouffée, Okra, '98 207
Fresh Okra and Tomatoes, '87 89
Fried
    Cheese, Okra with, '80 185
    Crispy Fried Okra, '86 169
    Croutons, Salad Greens and Veggies with Fried
      Okra, '96 178
    Crunchy Fried Okra, '01 165
    Deep-Fried Okra, '90 154
    Fingers, Okra, '85 196
    French-Fried Okra, '82 126
    Fried Okra, '79 122; '86 211; '87 89; '88 111;
      '00 205; '03 311
    Fritter-Fried Okra, '86 218
    Fritters, Okra, '79 160; '92 133; '98 159
    Green Tomatoes, Fried Okra and, '93 160; '01 325
    Green Tomatoes, Okra and, '79 160
    Nutty Okra, '03 136
    Old-Time Fried Okra, '80 185
    Oven-Fried Okra, '91 121
    Pods, Fried Okra, '00 205
    Potatoes, Fried Okra and, '97 136
    Potato Fry, Okra-, '81 159
    Puffs, Okra, '83 157
    Rellenos, Okra, '97 156
    Salad, Fried Okra, '97 M157; '04 167
Goulash, Okra, '93 160
Grilled Okra and Tomatoes, '98 124
Gumbo, Deep South Okra, '79 48
Gumbo Freezer Mix, Okra, '86 210; '01 165
Gumbo, Light Seafood-Okra, '86 155
Gumbo, Okra, '86 210; '91 206; '01 165
Gumbo, Old-Style Shrimp, '98 97
How to Can Okra, '80 127
Medley, Corn-and-Okra, '99 203
Medley, Okra, '88 M185
Medley, Okra-Corn-Tomato, '81 159
Muffins, Fresh Okra, '93 161
Pickled Okra, '98 177
Pickles, Okra, '81 173
Pilaf, Okra, '80 185; '82 126; '93 160
Pilâu, Okra, '99 184
Plantation Okra, '82 126
Polenta with Cheese and Okra, Baked, '99 232
Salad, Okra, '90 155
Salad, Okra-Walnut, '04 291
Salad with Feta, Marinated Green Bean-and-Okra,
    '00 131
Sautéed Corn and Okra, '84 158
Sauté, Spicy Okra-Tomato-Corn, '04 327
Skillet Okra, '95 179
Soup, Charleston Okra, '87 156
Soup, Okra-and-Shrimp, '94 323
Soup, Sausage and Okra, '80 209

Soup with Fou-Fou, Okra, '96 325
Stewed Okra, Southern, '82 134
Stew, Lamb-and-Okra, '97 156
Stew, Old-Fashioned Okra, '84 158
Stew, Quick Okra, '97 88
Stir-Fried Okra, '96 177
Stir-Fried Okra, Simple, '03 166
Surprise, Okra, '79 160; '84 158
Tomato Combo, Okra-, '83 157
Tomatoes and Okra, '86 170; '87 164; '00 182
Tomatoes, Fresh Okra and, '81 M165
Tomatoes, Okra and, '80 185; '81 139; '92 215;
    '98 286
Tomatoes with Okra, '85 106
Vinaigrette, Okra-Corn-and-Tomato, '90 173
OLIVES
Antipasto, Easy, '85 114
Antipasto, Grandpa's, '98 183
Appetizers, Cheesy Olive, '85 113
Appetizers, Cheesy-Olive, '87 246
Ball, Blue Cheese-Olive, '82 248
Ball, Olive Cheese, '80 258
Balls, Pumpkin Patch Cheese, '99 245
Biscuits with Olive-Parsley Spread, Cream Cheese-
    and-Olive, '04 238
Biscuits with Sun-Dried Tomato Spread and Bacon,
    Cream Cheese-and-Olive, '02 313
Biscuits with Tapenade, Cream Cheese-and-Olive,
    '02 313
Black Olives, Shrimp Spaghetti with, '85 13
Black Olive-Stuffed Mushrooms, '86 258
Bread, Olive, '93 78
Bread, Olive-Dill Casserole, '92 16
Bruschetta, Caper-and-Olive, '00 276
Butter, Mediterranean, '97 307
Butter, Olive, '91 295
Casserole, Turkey-Olive, '87 268
Caviar, Mexican, '98 135
Chalupas, Chicken-Olive, '81 227
Cheesecake, Three-Layer, '99 140
Cheese, Cream Cheese-and-Olive Pimiento, '01 169;
    '03 315
Chicken-and-Rice Valencia, '85 113
Chicken Breasts, Greek, '98 19
Chicken, Spanish, '98 183
Cream Cheese, Bacon-Olive, '04 196
Crostini, Festive, '98 183
Crostini, Olive, '02 205
Dip, Monterey Shrimp, '99 65
Elephant Ears Provençale, Baby, '00 87
Filling, Chicken-Olive, '81 227
Greek Olive Cups, '99 221
Green Olives, Chicken with, '03 87
Lemon-Garlic Olives, '94 118
Marinated Cheese, Olives, and Peppers, '04 238
Marinated Green Beans with Tomatoes, Olives, and
    Feta, '03 163
Marinated Olives, '01 187
Marinated Olives and Peppers, '04 71
Marinated Olives, Balsamic, '02 135
Marinated Olives, Caliente, '95 177
Marinated Olives, Herb-, '92 176
Monster Eyes, '02 222
Muffuletta Loaf, '97 86
Muffulettas, '98 184
Olivata, '04 159
Orzo, Mozzarella-and-Olive, '97 249
Party Olives, Citrus, '03 124
Pesto, Olive-Rosemary, '01 317
Pizzas, Eggplant, '98 183
Pork Chops, Greek-Style Baked, '04 44
Potatoes, Olive, '80 114
Potatoes, Tangy Olive, '04 214
Quiche, Chicken-Olive-Cheddar, '03 58

Relish, Flank Steak with Tomato-Olive, '03 210
Relish with Coriander, Green Olive, '96 323; '97 27
Salad, Doodles Olive, '94 35
Salad, Greek Chicken, '97 92; '98 329
Salad, Greek Pasta, '02 139
Salad, Italian Olive, '94 35
Salad, Mexican Olive, '85 84
Salad Mix, Muffy, '94 34
Salad, Olive, '98 184; '00 335; '04 27
Salad, Olive Clubhouse, '81 114
Salad, Olive-Potato, '85 114
Salad with Sherry Vinaigrette, Shrimp, Orange, and
   Olive, '93 177
Salsa, Olive, '00 277
Sandwich, Deli Stuffed, '98 287
Sandwiches, Bacon-Olive Party, '04 196
Sandwiches, Goat Cheese-Olive, '04 272
Sandwiches, Mini Muffuletta Bacon-Olive Party,
   '04 196
Sandwiches, Olive-Nut Spread, '04 259
Sandwiches, Olive Tea, '02 252
Sandwiches, Rolled Olive, '01 241
Sauce, Roasted Red Pepper, '98 16
Scaciati, Olives, '99 266
Snack, Open-Faced Cheese-and-Olive, '89 97
Spread, Antipasto, '81 25
Spread, Cheese-Olive, '79 82
Spread, Cream Cheese-Olive, '82 35
Spread, Creamy Olive, '81 290
Spread, Feta-and-Apple, '99 106
Spread, Tomatoes with Olive, '85 114
Stuffed Olives, Almond-, '88 95
Tapenade, '92 194; '00 135; '01 70; '04 194
Toss, Cauliflower-Olive, '85 198; '86 147
Toss, Tomato-Olive Pasta, '86 209

OMELETS

Apple Omelet Stack, '94 50
Bacon-and-Potato Omelet, Open-Faced, '02 246
Baked Omelets, '94 50
Broccoli-Mushroom Omelet, '85 45
Cheese Omelet, Herbed, '93 47
Cheese Omelet, Puffed, '89 227
Cheese Omelet, Zippy, '87 287
Cheese-Shiitake Omelet, Golden, '95 265
Cheesy Picante Omelet, '86 95
Chicken Liver Omelet, '82 44
Country Omelets, '91 128
Creole Sauce, Omelets with, '89 228
Dessert Omelet, Puffy, '00 35
Dill-Cheese-Ham Omelet, '95 33
Filling, Greek Omelet, '80 68
Filling, Spanish Omelet, '80 68
Fluffy Omelet, '84 56
Garden Omelet, '99 174
George's Omelets, '80 68
Ham and Cheese Omelet, '79 262; '80 123
Ham-and-Cheese Omelet, '02 246
Indian Omelet, '99 92
Mexican Omelet, '79 128; '81 225
Mushroom Omelet, Rolled, '82 70
Mushroom Sauce, Puffy Omelets with, '85 40
Olé Omelet, '87 M124
Olé, Omelet, '94 31
Oven-Baked Omelet, Farmer's, '03 204
Oyster Omelets, Smoked, '84 96
Pie, Omelet, '00 M35
Potato Omelet, Family-Size, '94 31
Potato-Sprout Omelet, '79 128
Primavera, Omelet, '87 71
Rising Sun Omelet, '82 281; '83 42
Rolled Omelet, '89 228
Sandwich, Omelet, '86 95
Sausage Filling, Omelet with, '81 43
Sausage Omelet, Puffy, '80 M268

Shrimp-and-Cheddar Omelet, '84 57
Shrimp-and-Cheese Omelet, '94 31
Shrimp-and-Vegetable Oven Omelet, '99 286
Sour Cream-Ham Omelet, '79 261
Spanish Omelet, '81 201; '83 243; '84 101; '00 35
Spanish Omelet with Fresh Avocado Salsa, '02 247
Spanish-Style Omelets, '83 188
Spinach, Cheddar, and Bacon Omelet, '03 204
Spinach-Cheese Omelet, '83 119
Strawberry-Sour Cream Omelet, '89 229
Sunrise Omelet, '83 289
Swiss Oven Omelet, '80 189
Tarragon Omelet, '89 144
Tex-Mex Omelet con Carne, '81 209
Vegetable Omelet, Beefy, '83 188
Vegetable Omelet, Cheddar-, '83 205
Vegetable Omelet, Cheesy, '85 49
Vegetable Omelet, Fresh, '84 211
Vegetable Omelet, Golden, '82 M123
Vegetable Omelet, Puffy, '83 188
Vegetable-Pasta Oven Omelet, '99 286
Vegetarian Omelet, '84 114
Veggie Omelet, Creamy, '02 248
White Wine Omelet, '79 103
Yogurt-Avocado Omelet, '81 33
Zucchini Omelet, '81 99

ONIONS

Appetizers, Bacon-Onion, '94 290
Bake, Cheese Onion, '82 32
Baked Onions, Micro-, '82 M32
Baked Onions, Spicy, '84 65
Baked Onions, Sweet-and-Sour, '90 34
Bake, Four Onion, '93 304
Bake, Onion-Potato, '83 M195
Bake, Romano Onion, '90 98
Barbecued Onions, '88 86
Beans, Buzz's Pot of, '03 19
Beans, Hearty Baked, '01 259
Beans, K.C. Baked, '98 244; '03 107
Beef à la Beer, '98 64
Beef à la Mode, '98 122
Beef and Onions, Smothered, '85 293
Beef Stroganoff, '03 23
Black Beans, Cuban, '99 56
Black-Eyed Peas, '03 M49
Black-Eyed Peas, Hearty, '02 107
Black-Eyed Peas, Michelle's, '03 16
Black-Eyed Peas, Pickled, '01 30

Breads

Biscuits, Cheesy Onion, '95 98
Buns, Cheesy Onion, '85 5
Buns, Onion-Cheese, '88 218
Buns, Potato-Caramelized Onion, '03 234
Cheese Bread, Onion-, '79 180; '81 8
Cheese Supper Bread, Onion-, '83 112
Cornbread, Onion, '88 283
Cornbread, Onion-Topped, '84 153
Cornbread, Sweet Onion, '98 252
Dill Bread, Easy Onion-, '85 5
Easy Onion Bread, '81 162
Flatbread, Parmesan-Onion, '98 65
Flatbread, Quick, '00 119
Focaccia, Mustard-and-Onion, '90 321; '92 97
Focaccia, Onion, '93 77
Focaccia, Roquefort-and-Onion, '98 54
French Bread, Onion-Cheese, '89 29
French Onion Bread, '91 90
Herb Bread, Onion-, '90 165
Herb Bread, Toasted Onion-, '83 266
Hush Puppies, Onion, '85 14
Hush Puppies, Tomato-Onion, '91 201
Loaves, Onion Twist, '84 300
Muffins, Onion-Dill, '92 253; '93 144
Parmesan Bread, Onion-, '84 284

Poppy Seed Twist, Onion-, '97 242
Rolls, Onion-and-Sesame, '95 292
Rolls, Onion-Bacon, '99 47
Rolls, Onion Twist, '89 288
Rolls, Poppy Seed Onion, '81 63
Rye Bread, Onion-, '99 55
Burgers, Open-Faced Chicken-Onion, '94 139
Burritos, Potato-and-Egg, '02 72
Butter, Onion, '86 253
Cakes, Black-Eyed Pea, '01 32
Caponata alla Siciliana, '02 269
Caramelized Onion-and-Gorgonzola Mashed
   Potatoes, '01 256
Caramelized Onion-and-Pecan Brussels Sprouts,
   '99 254
Caramelized Onion BLT, '03 90
Caramelized Onion Macaroni and Cheese, '04 231
Caramelized Onion Mayonnaise, '00 218
Caramelized Onions, '03 90, 235
Caramelized Onions, Beef Burgers with, '98 143
Caramelized Onions, Chicken Cobbler with, '00 44
Caramelized Onions, Green Beans with, '95 288;
   '00 33
Caramelized Onions, Mediterranean, '96 273
Caramelized Onions, Pepper Burgers with, '00 218
Caramelized Onions, Potato Casserole with, '03 231
Caramelized Onions, Potato-Horseradish Gratin
   with, '99 314
Carrots, Scalloped, '02 129
Carrots with Bacon and Onion, Glazed, '87 200;
   '02 283
Casserole, Cheesy Onion, '79 101
Chard with Onion and Apple, Sautéed, '98 48
Cheese Onions, Sherried, '82 32
Chicken and Onions, Down-Home, '02 271
Chicken in Coconut Milk, '97 202
Chicken, Onion-Crusted, '88 40
Chicken Sandwich, Jerk, '98 333
Chicken, Slow-Roasted, '98 108
Chicken with Rice, Moorish, '98 127
Chili, White Christmas, '98 266
Chutney, Cranberry, '98 276
Collard Greens, Esau's, '03 17
Confit, Roasted Shallot-Garlic, '94 303
Corn, Skillet Creamed, '02 204
Couscous, Spinach-and-Onion, '98 23
Crème Brûlée, Onion, '95 324
Crunch Sticks, Onion Crescent, '90 206
Curried Onions, '90 34
Custards, Savory Spinach-Gorgonzola, '02 284
Deluxe, Broccoli-Onion, '81 75
Dip, Cheesy Onion, '83 145
Dip, Chunky Onion, '84 257
Dip, Cream Cheese-Onion, '79 236
Dip, Curry-Onion, '93 313
Dip, Swiss-Onion, '95 93
Dressing, Cornbread, '98 269
Dressing, Green Pepper-Onion Salad, '84 12
Dressing, Onion-French, '84 283

Fried

Beer-Battered Onion Rings, '92 52
Buttermilk Batter-Fried Onion Rings, '02 131
Crisp Fried Onion Rings, '84 65
Crispy Fried Onion Rings, '80 108
Crispy Onion Rings, '86 110
Deluxe Fried Onion Rings, '80 108
Easy Onion Rings, '80 108
Favorite Fried Onion Rings, '81 86
French-Fried Onion Rings, '88 111
French-Fried Onion Rings Supreme, '80 109
Green Onions, Fried, '81 106
Leonard's-Style Onion Rings, '90 120
Rings, Fried Onion, '83 85; '85 69
Rings, South-of-the-Border Onion, '96 217

ONIONS
(continued)

Glazed Apple and Onion, Pork Chops with Mustard-, **'01** 47
Glazed Carrots and Onions, **'83** 25; **'87** 128
Glazed Onions, **'84** 104; **'97** 306; **'99** 24
Gourmet Onions, **'81** 86
Gravy, Fried Quail with Onion, **'82** 214
Gravy, Pork Chops in Onion, **'99** 222
Gravy, Roast with Onion-and-Mushroom, **'00** 293
Gravy, Southwestern, **'99** 34
Green Beans, Lorraine's, **'99** 319
Green Beans with Onion and Basil, Italian, **'03** 241
Green Beans with Purple Onion, Spicy, **'98** 286
Green Onions
Biscuits, Cheesy Onion, **'01** 330
Butterbeans with Bacon and Green Onions, **'96** 267
Canapés, Green Onion, **'84** M216
Cheese Ball, Pinecone, **'98** 265
Crostini, Green Onion, **'96** 93
Cukes and Scallions, **'91** 168
Dip, Onion, **'94** 21
Dressing, Green Onion, **'96** 17
Eggs, Creamy Onion Scrambled, **'83** M203
Grilled Green Onions, Chicken with, **'01** 94
Hoecakes, Green Onion, **'88** 112
Hush Puppies, Green Onion-Tomato, **'97** 84
Lima Beans and Scallions, Fresh, **'82** 133
Lobster Scallion Shooters, **'00** 197
Mayonnaise, Mediterranean, **'98** 144
Muffins, Green Onion-and-Cream Cheese, **'01** 289
Pie, Green Onion, **'98** 159
Pie, Tumbleweed, **'98** 205
Pork-and-Onions with Bean Sauce, **'85** 76
Potatoes, Green Onion-and-Bacon Mashed, **'02** 110
Quiche, Cheesy Green Onion, **'83** 194; **'84** 42
Relish, Green Onion, **'84** 65
Salmon with Mushrooms and Green Onions, Fresh, **'93** 180
Sauce, Onion-Mushroom, **'85** 224; **'86** 84
Sautéed Onions and Peppers, **'83** M148
Scallion Hoe Cake Medaillons, Skillet Hoppin' John with, **'02** 326
Soup, Creamed Green Onion, **'83** 82
Soup, Green Onion, **'84** 112
Spread, Chutney-Onion Cheese, **'01** 94
Spread, Green Onion-Cheese, **'92** 24
Teasers, Green Onion, **'82** 42
Tempura-Battered Green Onions, **'96** 93
Grilled Onion Flowers with Pecans, **'96** 217
Grilled Squash and Onion, **'79** 150
Grits with Grilled Chicken and Onions, **'99** 17
Hamburger Steaks, Smothered, **'00** 289
Hash Browns, Smothered-Covered, **'02** 248
Herbed Carrots and Onions, **'87** 31
Herbed Onions, **'84** 149
Honey Onions, **'81** 86
Hush Puppies, Corn Soufflé, **'98** M328
Italian Dressing, Tomato, Onion, and Cucumber in, **'81** 83
Kale with Tomato and Onion, **'92** 244
Kuchen, Onion, **'90** 34
Loaf, Poppy-Onion, **'04** 35
Marinade, Basic, **'99** 141; **'02** 19
Marmalade, Fruited Onion, **'96** 323; **'97** 27
Mayonnaise, Onion, **'98** 144
Meat Loaf, French Market, **'02** 33
Meat Loaf, Moist-and-Saucy, **'99** 270

Medley, Cabbage-Onion-Sweet Pepper, **'96** 252; **'97** 28
Mums, Onion, **'96** 318
Oven-Browned Onions, **'02** 221
Patties, Potato-Onion, **'95** 269
Pearl Onions, Beef Burgundy with, **'81** 108
Pearl Onions, Glazed, **'85** 258
Pearl Onions, Green Beans with Roasted Red Peppers and, **'93** 260
Pearl Onions, Snap Peas and, **'89** 280
Pearl Onions, Sweet-and-Sour, **'96** 216
Peas with Onions, Buttered, **'80** 242
Pickled Cocktail Onions, **'89** 197
Pickled Refrigerator Onion Rings, **'84** 265
Pie, Beef-and-Onion Cornbread, **'01** 298
Pie, Onion, **'82** 191
Pie, Summer Garden, **'02** 182
Pilau, Sausage, **'99** 184
Polenta Triangles, **'98** 181
Potatoes and Onions, Cheesy, **'00** 275
Pot Pie with Cranberry-Pecan Crusts, Turkey, **'02** 198
Pot Roast, Root Beer, **'04** 212
Pot Roast, Sweet-and-Sour, **'99** 291
Pudding, Kathy's Onion, **'95** 318
Quiche, Onion, **'83** 121
Red Onions, Grilled, **'03** 139
Relish, Hot, **'01** 123
Relish, Pepper-Onion, **'84** 180
Rice, Braised, **'98** 45
Rice Pilaf, Greek, **'01** 146
Rice, Red, **'97** 138
Rice, Seasoned Onion, **'82** 166
Risotto, Easy Baked, **'99** 120
Risotto with Saffron, Pistachio, **'98** 272
Roasted Celery Root, Carrots, and Onions, **'98** 293
Roasted Onion Guacamole, **'00** 334
Roasted Onions, Rosemary, **'98** 16
Roasted Sweet Potatoes and Onions, **'01** 234
Roast, Pumpernickel, **'97** 234
Ropa Vieja, **'98** 20
Salad, Classic Broccoli-Raisin, **'02** 24
Salad Dressing, Vinaigrette, **'02** 25
Salad, Lemon-Onion, **'85** 252
Salad, Lettuce-Wedge, **'02** 65
Salad, Roasted Onion, **'95** 65; **'03** 142
Salad, Tomato-Cucumber-Onion, **'81** 239
Salad, Tomato-Red Onion, **'04** 181
Salad with Onion and Celery, Potato, **'02** 138
Salad with Peppered Cheese Crisps, Roasted Onion Pasta, **'98** 107
Salsa Salpicon, **'03** 33
Salsa Verde, **'96** 160
Sandwiches, Steak-and-Onion, **'02** 126
Sauce, Beef Tenderloin with Five-Onion, **'98** 272
Sauce, Brussels Sprouts in Onion, **'81** 308
Sauce, Come Back, **'00** 211
Sauce, Creole, **'02** 32
Sauce, Green Barbecue, **'02** 183
Sauce, Onion, **'82** 72; **'87** 248
Sauce, Onion-Balsamic, **'99** 44
Sauce, Onion Cream, **'87** 232
Sauce, Onion-Parsley, **'85** 148
Sauce, Pepper-Onion, **'84** 125
Sauce, Sweet 'n' Saucy, **'01** 210
Sauerbraten, **'98** 278
Sautéed Apples, Onions, and Pears over Spinach, **'94** 212
Selecting and Storing Onions, **'84** 65
Shallot Salad, Caramelized, **'96** 308
Shells, Cheese and Limas in Onion, **'81** 86
Shrimp Bourbon, **'00** 125
Shrimp, Marinated, **'98** 317

Shrimp with Onion and Red Pepper, Sweet-and-Sour, **'02** 84
Soufflé, Onion, **'79** 247
Soups
Caramelized French Onion Soup, **'00** 218
Caramelized Onion Soup with Goat Cheese-and-Chive Croutons, **'01** 312
Cheese Onion Soup, Double-, **'85** 227
Cheese Soup, Onion-, **'87** 81
Classic Onion Soup, **'84** 65
Creamy Onion Soup, **'90** 211
Double Cheese-Topped Onion Soup, **'79** 49
Easy Onion Soup, **'85** 226
French Onion-Beef Soup, **'87** 54
French Onion Soup, **'79** 49; **'80** 188; **'83** 126; **'85** 226; **'86** M212; **'90** 31; **'93** 246; **'04** 243
French Onion Soup, Shortcut, **'85** M328
French Onion Soup, Toasty, **'81** 306
Green Onion Soup, **'84** 112
Green Onion Soup, Creamed, **'83** 82
Mexican Onion Soup, **'04** 243
Mushroom-Onion Soup, **'80** 25
Onion Soup, **'99** 96
Oven-Browned Onion Soup, **'79** 49
Potato Soup, Creamy Onion-and-, **'92** 51; **'97** 304
Rich Onion Soup, **'85** 226
Superb Onion Soup, **'81** 86
Three-Onion Soup, **'96** 217
Tomato-Onion Soup, **'04** 243
Vichyssoise, **'86** 181
Vidalia Onion Soup, Beefy, **'97** 212
Sour Cream, Cucumber and Onion in, **'81** 69
Spaghetti with Smothered Onions, **'97** 229
Spinach with Crowder Peas, **'00** 159
Spread, Braunschweiger-Onion, **'79** 82
Squares, Creamy Onion, **'79** 48
Squares, Sausage-Onion, **'83** 112
Squash, Basil Summer, **'01** 180
Squash, Creole, **'01** 180
Steak, Onion-Smothered, **'87** M189
Stew, Beef-and-Onion, **'87** 18
Stuffed
Baked Onions, Stuffed, **'82** 32
Baked Stuffed Onions, **'83** 135
Baked Sweet Onions, **'98** 130
Broccoli-Stuffed Onions, **'84** 154
Cheese-Stuffed Onions, **'90** 34
Peas, Onions Stuffed with, **'84** 68
Ratatouille-Stuffed Onions, **'96** 91
Sweet Onions, Stuffed, **'91** 79
Vidalia Onions, Stuffed, **'89** 172
Wine, Stuffed Onions and, **'85** 268
Stuffing, Rice-and-Onion, **'88** 246
Sweet
Applesauce, Sweet Onion, **'02** 319
Baked Sweet Onions, **'91** 79
Blossom, Onion, **'94** 226
Butter, Sweet Onion, **'93** 124
Cabbage, Scalloped, **'01** 43
Cakes, Southwestern Cornbread Dressing, **'01** 233
Caramelized Florida Sweet Onions, Balsamic, **'94** 163
Caramelized Onion, Corn with Bacon and, **'99** 94
Caramelized Onion, Green Beans with, **'00** 33
Caramelized Onions, **'00** 218; **'01** 61; **'03** 90; **'04** 30
Casserole, French Onion, **'95** 26
Casserole, Sweet Onion, **'00** 103
Chutney, Kiwifruit-Onion, **'93** 125
Citrus Onions, **'04** 89
Creole Onions, **'82** 32
Eye of Round, Slow Cooker Spicy Marinated, **'99** 291

Eye of Round, Spicy Marinated, '99 291
Flatbread, Quick, '00 119
Grilled Stuffed Onions, '95 180
Honey-Paprika Sweet Onions, '92 52
Hot Onions, Sweet-, '85 139
Jelly, Onion, '93 135
Marinated Bermuda Onions, '92 194
Oven-Roasted Sweet Potatoes and Onions, '00 24
Parmesan Onions, '93 170
Pickled Onion and Cucumber, '02 126
Pie, Onion, '00 283
Pie, Onion-Cheese, '88 86
Pizza, Chicken-and-Purple Onion, '97 47
Pizza, Plum-and-Sweet Onion, '98 193
Pot Pies, Wild Mushroom-and-Onion, '98 296
Puddings, Onion, '02 126
Pudding, Sweet Onion, '00 260; '02 310
Relish, Onion, '91 79
Relish, Purple Onion, '95 253
Relish, Sweet Onion, '93 124; '96 206; '99 204
Ribs and Onions, Tangy, '99 136
Rice Pilaf, Onion, '04 236
Rings, Crispy Baked Onion, '93 247
Risotto, Onion, '99 94; '02 97; '03 98
Risotto, Sweet Onion, '03 217
Roasted Sweet Onions, '04 282
Salad Bowl, Spinach-and-Onion, '81 157
Salad, Grilled Onion, '99 96
Salad, Marinated Orange-Onion, '91 231; '92 68
Salad, Orange-Onion, '89 41
Salsa, Fiesta Onion, '94 82
Sauce, Spicy, '99 291
Sauce, Vidalia Onion, '99 52
Shortcake, Onion, '92 51
Slaw, Sweet Onion, '98 171
Smoky Sweet Onions, '97 191
Stir-Fry, Sweet Onion-Asparagus, '98 135
Stuffed Sweet Onions, '91 79
Tart, Caramelized Onion, '99 96
Tarts, Sweet Onion, '95 229
Tomatoes and Okra, '00 182
Trout, Sweet Onion-Stuffed, '99 52
Vidalia Deep Dish, '89 120
Vidalia Onion-Balsamic Vinaigrette, '04 317
Vidalia Onion Dip, Baked, '02 88
Vidalia Onion Gravy, Roasted Red Pepper-and-,
    '03 323
Vidalia Onion Pie with Mushrooms, '02 183
Vidalia Onion Sauté, '89 119
Vidalia Onions, Baked, '00 102
Vidalia Onions, Cheesy Baked, '01 145
Vidalia Onion Soufflé, '04 167
Vidalia Onions, Stuffed, '89 172
Vidalia Onions with Pecans and Roasted Carrots,
    Roasted, '92 340
Vidalia Sandwiches on Salt-Rising Bread, '79 145
Vidalias, Marinated, '89 119
Vidalia-Tomato Salad, '84 65
Vinaigrette, Spinach Salad with Apple-Onion,
    '94 276
Vinaigrette, Vidalia Onion, '99 168
Sweet Potatoes with Cumin, Mashed, '99 244
Swordfish, Mediterranean, '02 237
Taters, Buck's, '95 72
Toasties, Onion, '97 225
Turkey, New Year's, '97 255
Turnips and Onions, '83 242
Veal and Onions, Herbed, '79 108
Vinaigrette, Asian, '97 146
Vinegar Sauce, Whole Onions with Warm, '94 172
ON THE LIGHT SIDE. See HEALTHY & LIGHT.
ORANGES. See also AMBROSIA.
Appetizer, Orange-Berry, '85 81
Apples, Orange-Ginger Roasted, '01 184

Apples, Orange-Glazed, '82 51
Baked Fruit, Ginger-Orange, '93 313
Baked Oranges, '79 247; '89 41
Baked Orange Slices, '89 88
Baskets, Orange, '93 286
Beverages
Blend, Orange, '95 276
Blush, Orange, '80 51
Brandy Smash, Orange, '99 30
Breakfast Eye-Opener, '87 199
Champagne with Orange Juice, '91 71
Cider, Apple-Orange, '92 20
Cider, Hot Mulled Apple-Orange, '97 301
Cocktail, Citrus Wine, '99 93
Cocktail, Orange-Champagne, '79 39
Cocktail, Orange-Cranberry, '01 103
Cocktail, Tomato-Orange Juice, '83 169
Coffee, Orange, '96 313
Coffee, Viennese Orange, '84 54
Cooler, Apricot-Orange-Carrot, '96 108
Cooler, Citrus, '82 160
Cruising Drink, '00 167
Cubes, Florida, '95 201
Flip, Orange-Banana, '82 48
Flips, Orange Blossom, '80 51
Frosty, Orange, '86 101
Frosty Sours, '81 156
Jogger's Sunrise, '93 213
Jubilee, Orange, '03 305
Juicy, Orange, '90 178
Lemonade, Orange-Mint, '88 82
Liqueur, Orange, '81 287
Magnolia Blossoms, '87 72
Magnolias, '82 196
Margaritas, Orange-Lime, '97 140
Mimosa, '04 106
Mist, Orange-Lemon, '79 288; '80 35
Nog, Orange Spiced, '82 48
Pick-Me-Up, Orange, '80 232
Pineapple Drink, Orange-, '89 35
Pirate's Painkiller, '99 161
Punch, Champagne, '96 277; '98 310
Punch, Champagne Blossom, '99 290
Punch, Citrus Party, '83 141
Punch, Orange Blossom, '83 142
Punch, Orange-Lime, '82 160
Punch, Orange-Mint, '82 121
Punch, Orange Sherbet Party, '83 142
Punch, Orange Soda, '87 214
Punch, Pineapple-Orange, '85 236
Punch, Refreshing Orange, '81 39
Refresher, Grapefruit-Orange, '82 174
Sangría, '81 67
Sangría, Easy Citrus, '80 218
Sangría, Orange, '81 237
Shake, Orange Milk, '84 166
Shake, Peachy Orange, '81 156
Shake, Pineapple-Orange-Banana, '97 172
Shake, Strawberry-Orange Breakfast, '87 186
Shake, Tropical, '87 200
Slush, Banana-Orange, '80 48; '81 155
Slush, Orange, '82 49
Slush, Strawberry-Orange, '83 172
Slush, Vodka-Orange, '89 92
Smoothie, Mango-Orange, '86 216
Smoothie, Orange-Banana, '97 173
Smoothie, Tropical, '81 50
Soda, Cranberry-Orange, '79 148
Soda, Homemade Orange, '03 141
Sunrise, Bourbon, '01 326
Sunshine Fizz, '92 44
Syrup, Orange, '96 161
Tea, Marmalade, '98 330
Thing, Orange, '04 290

Whip, Orange-Banana, '95 244
Whiskey Sours, Frozen Orange-, '92 67
Breads
Anise-Orange Bread, '83 295
Apricot-Orange Bread, '92 285
Baba au Orange, '86 138
Biscuits, Cranberry-Orange-Glazed, '04 280
Biscuits, Orange, '88 85
Blueberry-Orange Bread, '87 140; '02 21
Breakfast Ring, Orange, '81 229
Coffee Cake, Cranberry-Orange, '82 283
Coffee Cake, Nutty Orange, '95 160
Coffee Cake, Orange, '85 M88
Coffee Cake, Orange Butter, '89 229
Coffee Cake, Orange Marmalade Swirl,
    '81 107
Coffee Cake, Orange-Pecan, '86 86
Coffee Ring, Caramel-Orange, '80 45
Cranberry Bread, Orange-, '85 266
Cranberry-Orange Bread, '87 244
Cream Cheese Bread, Orange-, '82 210
Doughnuts, Orange Spiced, '79 136
French Toast, Orange, '83 292; '84 78; '86 329
French Toast with Orange Sauce, '82 47
Kulich, '01 87
Muffins, Banana-Orange, '84 148
Muffins, Cranberry-Orange, '04 209
Muffins, Orange, '79 236; '81 107; '83 54;
    '89 205; '97 271
Muffins, Orange Blossom, '96 54
Muffins, Orange-Date, '92 119; '97 243
Muffins, Orange-Ginger, '89 41
Muffins, Orange-Honey, '88 284
Muffins, Orange-Oatmeal, '85 202; '00 24
Muffins, Orange-Pecan, '83 96; '99 56
Muffins, Orange-Raisin, '97 153
Muffins, Pecan-Orange, '97 163
Muffins, Streusel-Topped Orange, '84 74
Muffins with Honey Spread, Orange Juice,
    '81 229
Nut Bread, Blueberry-Orange, '84 141
Nut Bread, Cranberry-Orange, '80 288
Nut Bread, Orange-, '82 75
Nut Loaf, Orange, '80 226
Pecan Bread, Glazed Orange-, '81 250
Pecan Bread, Orange-, '79 148
Pecan Loaves, Orange-, '79 215
Poppy Seed Bread, Orange-, '04 300
Puffs, Upside-Down Orange, '83 57
Pumpkin Bread, Orange-, '87 300
Rolls, Apricot-Orange Sweet, '03 235
Rolls, Citrus-Pecan, '03 256
Rolls, Easy Orange, '89 M131
Rolls, Frosted Hot Orange, '80 257
Rolls, Glazed Orange, '90 194
Rolls, Kitchen Express Orange, '98 252
Rolls, Luscious Orange, '86 298
Rolls, Orange, '80 22; '82 17; '88 79; '96 321;
    '01 257
Rolls, Orange Butter, '82 206; '83 33
Rolls, Speedy Orange, '89 287
Rye Bread, Swedish Orange-, '85 111
Scones, Cranberry-Orange, '97 45
Scones, Orange-Pecan, '94 215; '01 72
Scones with Orange Butter, Double-Orange,
    '97 44
Tea Bread, Orange, '79 234
Toast, Orange Praline, '79 36
Toast Topper, Orange, '79 36
Whole Wheat Orange Bread, '85 5
Broiled Orange Halves, '85 288
Broth, Tortellini in Citrus, '99 292
Butter, Citrus, '97 307
Butter, Honey-Orange, '79 36; '85 19

ORANGES
(continued)

Butter, Orange, '81 8, 42; '90 323; '92 319; '94 115;
  '97 44
Butter, Orange-Pecan, '84 75; '97 15
Butter, Prune-Orange, '92 49
Butter, Tomato-Curry-Orange, '93 159
Chutney, Cranberry-Orange, '79 292
Chutney, Orange-Cranberry, '86 266
Couscous, Orange-Ginger, '00 295
Cranberry Oranges, Brandied, '98 309
Cream, Beef Fillets with Orange, '97 66
Cream Cheese, Orange, '91 177
Cream, Orange, '90 126
Desserts
  Alaska, Orange, '83 177
  Ambrosia, Pineapple-Orange, '88 252
  Apples, Orange-Pecan Baked, '85 45
  Apples with Cookie Crumbs, Orange Baked,
    '95 271
  Apples with Orange Sauce, Baked, '84 314
  Baked Orange Elegance, '80 13
  Balls, Orange, '94 331
  Balls, Orange-Nut, '02 297
  Bananas Foster, Orange-Glazed, '91 91
  Bananas with Orange Sauce, Baked, '79 115
  Bars, Pineapple-Orange, '82 129
  Baskets, Orange, '81 308
  Biscochos, Betty's, '00 325
  Biscotti, Orange-Pecan, '01 207
  Cake, Aztec Pound, '96 61
  Cake, Chocolate-Orange Pound, '89 94
  Cake, Fresh Orange, '83 300
  Cake, Fresh Orange Chiffon, '88 179
  Cake, Fresh Orange Italian Cream, '02 294
  Cake, General Robert E. Lee Orange-Lemon,
    '88 92
  Cake, Mandarin Orange, '83 24
  Cake, Mandarin-Rum, '84 150
  Cake, Orange, '86 61; '95 320
  Cake, Orange Angel Food, '96 246
  Cake, Orange Blossom, '96 162
  Cake, Orange Butter, '95 46
  Cake, Orange Chiffon, '91 56
  Cake, Orange-Coconut Angel Food, '94 294
  Cake, Orange-Cranberry, '85 314
  Cake, Orange Cream, '99 118
  Cake, Orange-Date, '94 60
  Cake, Orange Date-Nut, '01 285
  Cake, Orange Liqueur, '87 84
  Cake, Orange Marmalade, '85 53
  Cake, Orange Meringue, '86 336; '87 84
  Cake, Orange Nut, '80 70
  Cake, Orange-Nut Butter, '80 254
  Cake, Orange-Pecan Crunch, '83 10
  Cake, Orange-Pecan Pound, '93 13
  Cake, Orange-Pecan-Spice Pound, '02 295
  Cake, Orange Pound, '87 84, 221; '92 69
  Cake, Orange Rum, '79 2
  Cake, Orange-Slice, '81 264
  Cake, Orange Streusel, '88 10
  Cake, Pig Pickin', '04 112
  Cake, Praline-Filled Carrot, '03 332
  Cake, Rum-Orange Coconut, '88 224
  Cake, Sour Cream-Orange Pecan Pound, '89 207
  Cake Squares, Apple-Orange, '84 150
  Cake Squares, Orange, '81 34
  Cake Squares, Orange-Pumpkin, '83 242
  Cake, Williamsburg Orange, '81 120; '82 23
  Cake with Orange Icebox Pie Filling, Orange
    Chiffon, '03 105
  Candied Orange Peel, '81 286

Candied Orange Rind, '96 162; '97 32
Candied Orange Zest, '95 320
Champagne Oranges, '93 83
Cheesecake, Orange, '81 84; '85 38
Chiffon Dessert, Orange, '93 295
Chocolate-Orange Delights, '93 52
Chocolate-Orange Roll, '87 21
Cookies, Carrot-Orange, '83 149
Cookies, Chocolate-Dipped Orange, '04 299
Cookies, Frosted Orange, '83 114
Cookies, Orange-Chocolate, '83 113
Cookies, Orange-Glazed Oatmeal, '80 60
Cookies, Orange-Pecan, '88 119
Cookies, Orange Refrigerator, '86 230
Cookies, Orange-Slice, '89 294
Cookies, Orange Slice, '98 324
Cookies, Orange Sugar, '89 329
Cookies, White Chocolate-Orange Dream,
  '98 294
Cran-Orange Surprise, '94 143
Cream Dessert, Orange, '80 254; '84 165
Cream, Orange, '81 12; '00 27
Cream, Orange Chantilly, '84 156
Cream, Orange-Coconut, '84 24
Cream, Orange-Mallow, '94 295
Cream, Orange Whipped, '88 83
Crème Brûlée, Orange, '95 323
Crème, Orange-Tapioca, '82 M283
Crêpes, Amaretto-and-Orange, '86 260
Crêpes, Chocolate-Orange, '85 263
Crêpes, Orange Dream, '82 183
Crinkles, Orange, '95 272
Crispies, Grandmom Lucy's Orange, '02 253
Crispies, Orange, '84 205
Crisp, Orange-Apple, '80 295
Cupcakes, Orange, '97 32
Curd, Fresh Orange, '02 294
Dip, Creamy Orange, '84 117
Dip, Orange-Flavored Cream Cheese, '03 93
Dip, Orange Marmalade-Cream Cheese, '03 93
Éclairs, Miniature Orange, '95 92
Filling, Citrus, '02 221
Filling, Lemon-Orange, '81 71
Filling, Orange, '79 229; '86 336; '87 84;
  '88 224; '96 316
Filling, Orange Cream, '99 118
Filling, Orange Curd, '96 120
Filling, Orange Icebox Pie, '03 104
Filling, Orange-Pineapple Fried Pie, '96 109
Fingers, Orange, '87 57
Flambé, Dessert Orange, '85 313
Flan, Almond-Orange, '04 241
Flan, Orange, '84 95
Frosted Oranges, '83 270
Frosting, Citrus Cream Cheese, '99 223
Frosting, Creamy Orange, '83 24, 241
Frosting, Orange, '81 7; '86 61; '88 119
Frosting, Orange Butter, '83 300
Frosting, Orange Buttercream, '80 70; '99 117;
  '03 105
Frosting, Orange Cream, '81 207; '82 14
Frosting, Orange-Cream Cheese, '81 70; '82 16;
  '92 19; '04 258
Frosting, Orange-Lemon, '88 92
Frozen Orange Dessert, '92 44
Fruit Dessert Orange, '84 314
Fudge, Orange-Walnut, '92 288
Glazed Oranges and Pineapple, '86 318
Grand Marnier, Oranges, '92 82
Grand Marnier, Oranges in, '95 142
Grand Oranges and Strawberries, '03 119
Granita, Orange, '88 118
Ice Cream, Orange, '97 160
Ice Cream, Orange-Pineapple, '86 117

Ice, Strawberry-Orange, '86 196
Ice, Tart Cranberry-Orange, '86 317
Juice, Strawberries with Brandied Orange, '82 160
Kiwi-and-Orange Dessert, '93 295
Meringues, Orange, '95 318
Molded Dessert, Orange, '83 302
Mousse, Chocolate-Orange, '81 16, 205
Mousse, Orange, '86 69; '94 198
Mousse with Orange Liqueur, Chocolate, '02 315
Parfaits, Chilled Orange, '80 219
Parfaits, Orange Cream, '94 198
Pastry Cream, Grand Marnier, '01 45
Peanut Brittle, Orange, '80 302
Pears Flambé, Orange-Poached, '85 313
Pears in Orange Sauce, Poached, '82 19
Pears, Orange Poached, '80 218
Pie, Coconut-Orange Chess, '89 169
Pie, Florida Orange, '91 43
Pie, Frosty Orange, '90 296
Pie, Lemon-Orange, '85 172
Pie, Orange Ambrosia, '80 237
Pie, Orange Chess, '88 204; '01 23
Pie, Orange Chiffon, '87 260
Pie, Orange-Coconut, '90 90
Pie, Orange-Coconut Cream, '94 208
Pie, Orange Cream, '03 35
Pie, Orange Dream, '02 93
Pie, Orange Meringue, '81 12, 309
Pie, Orange-Pecan, '79 282; '83 222
Pie, Sweet Potato-Orange, '88 207
Pie, Tangerine Chess, '01 23
Poached Oranges, Wine-, '84 M323
Pops, Hawaiian Orange-Pineapple, '94 143
Pops, Orange-Banana, '82 129
Pops, Orange Float, '99 132
Pops, Strawberry-Orange, '03 179
Pralines, Orange, '92 313; '93 51
Pudding, Mandarin-Almond, '85 M12
Pudding, Orange, '81 85; '82 111; '83 153
Pudding, Orange Custard, '88 174
Pumpkin-Orange Delight, '86 321
Rice Cream with Mandarin Oranges, '85 317
Roulage, Chocolate-Orange, '94 314
Sections with Chocolate and Raspberry Sauce,
  Orange, '97 33
Sherbet Ambrosia Cups, '82 159
Sherbet, Banana-Orange, '83 162
Sherbet, Orange, '79 155
Sherbet, Three-Ingredient Orange, '01 105
Sherbet with Blackberry Sauce, Orange, '94 232
Shortbread Madeleines, Orange, '88 242
Shortbread, Orange, '91 272
Shortcake, Fresh Orange, '80 100
Shortcake, Orange-Strawberry, '95 100
Slices, Burgundy-Spiced Orange, '93 294
Sorbet, Banana-Orange, '88 117
Sorbet, Fresh Orange, '92 143
Sorbet, Orange, '03 171
Soufflé, Chilled Orange, '84 317; '86 189
Soufflé, Frozen Orange, '79 211
Soufflé, Grand Marnier, '79 281
Soufflé, Orange Dessert, '83 206
Special, Orange Blossom, '79 48
Squares, Orange-Crunch, '86 136
Squash Brûlée, Orange-, '94 267
Tapioca Fluff, Orange, '87 31
Tartlets, Creamy Citrus, '02 136
Tarts, Frozen Orange, '80 154
Tarts, Orange, '96 317
Tarts, Orange Curd, '92 193
Topping, Whipped Orange, '80 254
Truffles, Orange-Pecan, '95 92
Turnovers, Orange-Apple, '99 294
Whipped Cream, Orange, '02 315

Dip, Creamy Orange, '87 247
Dip, Marmalade, '99 324
Dip, Orange Fruit, '96 190
Dip, Orange-Lime, '96 248
Dip, Orange Sour Cream, '79 208
Dip, Spicy Orange, '85 230
Dressings
  Blossom Dressing, Orange, '82 266
  Citrus-Cilantro Dressing, '00 160
  Citrus-Herb Dressing, '04 182
  Citrus Ranch Dressing, Fresh, '04 91
  Coconut Dressing, Orange-, '80 158
  Coconut-Orange Dressing, '97 93
  Cranberry-Orange Dressing, '91 287
  Curd Dressing, Orange-, '93 22
  Hot Citrus Dressing, '00 108
  Mandarin Dressing, '89 137
  Marmalade-Fruit Dressing, '84 171
  Nutmeg Dressing, Carrot-Raisin Salad with Orange-, '98 19
  Orange Dressing, '81 141; '97 129
  Poppy Seed Dressing, Orange-, '87 187
  Vinaigrette Dressing, Tangy Orange, '93 46
  Vinaigrette, Grilled Asparagus Salad with Orange, '99 102
  Vinaigrette, Grilled Fennel and Radicchio with Orange, '95 253
  Vinaigrette, Honey-Orange, '91 255
  Vinaigrette, Orange, '96 65; '97 229; '98 288
  Vinaigrette, Orange-Raspberry, '95 144; '96 155; '01 178
  Yogurt Dressing, Orange-, '85 304
Filling, Cheese-and-Orange, '93 159
Filling, Orange, '89 287
Filling, Orange-Cheese, '90 47
French Toast, Orange-Stuffed, '98 54
Fritters, Puffy Orange, '81 169
Glaze. *See* **ORANGES/Sauces and Glazes.**
Grand Oranges, '01 131
Granola, Sunny Orange, '84 212
Gravy, Orange, '81 259; '89 323
Grits, Orange, '81 47
Honey Yogurt, Orange Slices with, '91 68
Jelly, Pineapple-Orange Mint, '92 105
Main Dishes
  Catfish Amandine, Mandarin, '84 183
  Catfish, Lime-Orange, '02 22
  Chicken à l'Orange, '84 277
  Chicken à l'Orange, Stir-Fry, '83 82
  Chicken Breasts with Orange-Ginger Sauce, '97 47
  Chicken Breasts with Orange Sauce, '79 77
  Chicken Breasts with Parslied Rice, Orange, '87 242
  Chicken, Crispy Mandarin, '86 119
  Chicken Drummettes, Orange-Pecan, '93 158
  Chicken, Grilled Ginger-Orange, '91 26
  Chicken in Orange-Almond Sauce, '79 219; '80 13
  Chicken in Orange Sauce, '83 8
  Chicken in Orange Sauce, Skillet, '94 252
  Chicken Livers in Orange Sauce, '82 218
  Chicken, Orange, '83 278; '86 M140
  Chicken, Orange-Avocado, '80 38
  Chicken, Orange Barbecued, '88 123
  Chicken, Skillet-Seared Orange, '96 68
  Chicken Stir-Fry, Kyoto Orange-, '87 96
  Chicken Stir-Fry, Orange-, '84 68
  Chicken with Black Beans and Oranges, '00 94
  Chicken with Broccoli, Spicy Ginger-and-Orange, '02 309
  Chicken with Orange, Lime, and Ginger Sauce, '92 123
  Chicken with Wild Rice, Orange-Glazed Roasted, '02 85

Chuck Roast, Orange Marinated, '85 179
Cornish Hens, à l'Orange, '95 325
Cornish Hens, Orange-Glazed, '83 267; '99 293; '00 292
Cornish Hens, Orange-Glazed Grilled, '86 250
Cornish Hens, Orange-Glazed Stuffed, '84 M89
Cornish Hens with Cranberry-Orange Sauce, '86 119
Cornish Hens with Orange Glaze, '79 244
Duck, Chafing Dish Orange, '79 226
Duck with Orange Sauce, Grilled, '94 305
Duck with Parsnip Mash, Honey-Orange-Glazed Muscovy, '97 262
Fish à l'Orange, Fillet of, '89 180
Halibut with Orange-Curry Sauce, '87 91
Ham, Cranberry-Orange Glazed, '81 295
Ham, Orange-Glazed, '89 324
Ham, Sweet Orange-Glazed, '02 286
Hens with Cranberry Salsa, Orange-Ginger, '98 321
Lamb Chops, Orange, '83 35
Lobster Tails with Spiced Orange Sauce, '86 155
Porc à l'Orange, '80 242
Pork Chops, Orange, '84 81
Pork Chops, Orange-Cranberry, '86 335; '87 84
Pork Chops, Orange-Glazed, '81 234; '82 25; '83 39; '91 84
Pork, Garlic-Orange Roast, '03 277
Pork Loin, Orange-Dijon, '00 259
Pork Loin, Scuppernong-Orange Glazed, '98 220
Pork Roast, Orange-Glazed, '04 M236
Pork Tenderloins, Orange-Cranberry Glazed, '00 314
Pork Tenderloin with Orange Marmalade, '91 49
Pork Tenderloin with Orange Marmalade, Grilled, '03 181
Salmon, Orange-Basil, '97 165
Scallops with Orange-Ginger Sauce, Sesame-Crusted, '97 125
Scampi, Orange, '85 303
Shrimp in Orange Sauce, '99 292; '00 292
Snapper à l'Orange, Baked, '85 181
Snapper, Orangy, '88 23
Spareribs, Orange-Glazed, '84 296
Spareribs with Orange Barbecue Sauce, '83 11
Swordfish Steaks, Orange-Ginger Marinated, '93 271
Turkey Breast with Orange-Raspberry Glaze, '91 253
Turkey-Orange Skillet, Oriental, '86 284
Turkey Slices, Orange-, '90 53
Mandarin Orange Spread Sandwiches, Chicken-, '04 259
Marmalade, Carrot-Orange, '03 134
Marmalade, Orange, '81 42
Marmalade, Orange-Pineapple, '82 150; '89 M156
Marmalade, Peach-Orange, '82 150
Marmalade, Sunny Orange, '02 27
Noodles, Orange, '84 177
Nuts, Sherry-Orange, '86 M289
Pancakes, Orange-Yogurt, '87 225
Pancakes with Sunshine Orange Sauce, Orange, '97 70
Pears and Oranges, Spicy, '89 305
Pears, Marmalade Breakfast, '83 M203
Pears, Orange-Glazed, '79 247
Pecans, Orange, '84 299; '87 292
Pecans, Orange-Glazed, '97 225
Popcorn, Orange, '86 230
Prunes, Orange-Spiced, '85 224
Relish, Cranberry-Orange, '81 M289; '88 254; '99 15
Rice à l'Orange, '90 236
Rice, Miami, '96 86

Rice, Orange, '79 43; '81 175; '82 200
Rice, Orange-Herb, '89 286
Salads
  Almond Salad, Orange-, '99 107
  Ambrosia Supreme, Orange, '79 37
  Aspic, Orange-and-Carrot, '86 199
  Avocado-Orange Salad, '91 44
  Avocado Salad, Orange-, '99 331
  Beet Salad, Orange-and-, '88 43
  Broccoli-Orange Salad, '94 281
  Buttermilk Salad, Orange-, '95 134
  Carrot Salad, Orange-, '80 89; '84 325
  Carrot-Tangerine Salad, '83 316; '84 16
  Cauliflower Salad, Orange-, '82 266
  Cherry-Orange Salad, '79 74; '82 56
  Chicken-and-Orange Salad, Curried, '87 144
  Chicken Salad, '96 67
  Chicken Salad, Persian, '81 12
  Company's Coming Salad, '96 64
  Congealed Salad, Pineapple-Orange, '83 218
  Cottage Cheese Salad, Orange-, '79 44
  Cranberry-Orange Delight, '90 168
  Creamy Orange Salad, '84 124
  Cup, Orange Fruit, '91 277
  Cups, Citrus Salad in Orange, '85 47
  Cups, Orange, '86 92
  Cups, Orange Salad, '85 40
  Fennel Salad, Tuscan, '02 170
  Frosted Orange Salad, '81 154; '83 123
  Grapefruit-Orange Salad, '91 276
  Grapefruit Salad, Orange-, '93 294
  Grilled Shrimp, Orange, and Watermelon Salad with Peppered Peanuts in a Zesty Citrus Dressing, '04 308
  Honey-Berry Dressing, Orange Salad with, '89 250
  Honey Dressing, Orange Salad with, '89 14
  Jeweled Orange Salad, '83 210
  Jicama-and-Orange Salad, '88 246
  Jicama-Orange Salad, '86 83; '90 122
  Lobster and Orange Salad, '82 207
  Mandarin Chicken, Carousel, '79 88
  Mandarin Ham-and-Rice Salad, '87 145
  Mandarin Orange and Pineapple Salad, '82 266
  Mandarin Orange-Lettuce Salad, '92 79
  Mandarin Orange Salad, '81 252; '84 161
  Mandarin Orange Salad, Congealed, '89 327
  Mandarin Orange Tossed Salad, '92 303
  Mandarin Pork-and-Spinach Salad, '88 M126
  Mandarin Rice Salad, '88 271
  Mandarin Salad, Bacon-, '02 87
  Mandarin Salad, Broccoli-, '93 325
  Mandarin Salad Molds, '85 54
  Mandarin Salad Oriental, '02 175
  Mandarin Spinach Salad, '85 163
  Mandarin Tossed Salad, '89 12
  Marinated Orange-Onion Salad, '91 231; '92 68
  Mimosa Salad, '98 310
  Minted Orange Salad, '92 105
  Onion Salad, Orange-, '89 41
  Pear Salad, Orange-, '84 164
  Poppy Seed Salad, Orange-, '98 87; '03 121
  Quick Orange Salad, '87 80
  Red Cabbage Citrus Salad, '94 72
  Romaine Salad, Orange-, '84 325; '87 239
  Scallop Salad, Thai-Rific Orange, '04 317
  Sesame-Citrus Green Salad, '86 33
  Sherbet Salad, Orange, '81 154
  Shrimp-and-Orange Rice Salad, Zesty, '87 155
  Shrimp, Orange, and Olive Salad with Sherry Vinaigrette, '93 177
  Shrimp Salad, Orange-, '84 197
  Slaw, Cabbage-Orange, '79 135

Spinach-and-Orange Salad, '86 15
Spinach, Hot Spiked, '97 195
Spinach-Orange Salad, Warm, '00 112
Spinach Salad, Orange-, '83 316; '84 16
Strawberry Salad with Orange-Curd Dressing, Orange-, '93 22
Sunshine Delight, '86 117
Surprise Salad, Orange, '79 12
Tropical Orange Salad, '92 97
Turkey-in-the-Orange Salad, '93 21
Turkish Salad, '96 137
Walnut Salad, Orange, '80 246
Watercress-Orange Salad with Blue Cheese, '04 45

Sauces and Glazes
Almond Sauce, Grilled Snapper with Orange-, '01 158
Bourbon Glaze, Orange-, '03 249
Butter Glaze, Orange, '90 194
Caramel Sauce, Pears with Orange-, '95 281
Chocolate-Orange Sauce, '86 165; '94 314
Coconut-Orange Sauce, '85 189
Curry Sauce and Coconut Rice, Polynesian Pork Tenderloin with Orange-, '04 309
Dessert Sauce, Orange, '86 337; '87 58
Dijon Sauce, Orange-, '00 259
Dipping Sauce, Orange, '03 M212
Fresh Orange Glaze, '88 179
Fresh Orange Sauce, '85 209
Ginger Sauce, Chicken Breasts with Orange-, '97 47
Ginger Sauce, Sesame-Crusted Scallops with Orange-, '97 125
Hard Sauce, Orange, '88 225
Honey-Orange Sauce, '85 108
Honey Sauce, Orange-, '97 236
Liqueur Sauce, Orange, '86 142
Mandarin Orange Sauce, '89 204
Mandarin Sauce, '84 60
Mandarin-Teriyaki Sauce, '96 68
Maraschino-Orange Sauce, '96 164
Nutty Orange Glaze, '80 45
Orange Glaze, '79 2; '80 257; '81 34, 107; '82 75, 206; '83 33, 114, 140, 267; '84 161; '86 298; '92 263; '95 320; '99 293; '02 221; '03 35, 281, 307
Orange Sauce, '82 47; '83 10, 277; '84 M286; '86 294; '98 83
Pineapple Glaze, Orange-, '81 60
Pineapple-Orange Sauce, '84 14
Raspberry-Orange Sauce, '88 22; '92 154
Salsa, Orange-Black Bean, '98 231
Scuppernong-Orange Glaze, '98 220
Shrimp in Orange Sauce, '99 292; '00 292
Strawberry-Orange Sauce, '96 95
Sunshine Orange Sauce, '97 70
Sweet Orange Sauce, '93 M325
Syrup, Orange, '80 228; '89 254; '96 164; '97 32; '02 295
Syrup, Orange-Ginger, '03 167
Syrup, Orange Marmalade, '96 27
Sauté, Orange-Watercress, '98 83
Slices, Spicy Orange, '81 12
Snack Balls, Orange-Almond, '95 214
Soup, Carrot-Orange, '79 172
Special, Orange Blossom, '88 158
Spread, Date-Orange-Nut, '02 59
Spread, Orange Cheese, '87 292
Spread, Tropical Cheese, '95 46
Stuffing, Cranberry-Orange-Pecan, '01 249

Vegetables
Asparagus with Orange Butter Sauce, '85 43
Asparagus with Orange Sauce, '83 46
Beets, Glazed Orange, '02 138
Beets, Orange, '91 219
Beets, Orange-Ginger, '80 137
Beets, Orange-Glazed, '81 167; '85 289; '86 187; '99 24
Beets, Spicy Orange, '94 280
Broccoli, Easy Orange, '85 267
Broccoli with Orange Sauce, '80 243; '04 285
Brussels Sprouts, Orange, '84 34
Butternut-Orange Bake, '86 295
Cabbage Cooked in Orange Juice, '97 129
Carrots and Turnips, Sunset Orange, '94 213
Carrots in Orange Sauce, '82 107
Carrots, Julienned Orange, '04 297
Carrots, Orange-Fennel, '92 133
Carrots, Orange-Glazed, '79 12; '81 M165; '90 M98
Carrots, Orange-Raisin, '80 24
Carrots, Orange-Spiced, '88 18
Carrot Strips, Orangy, '89 312
Celery in Orange Sauce, '79 70
Green Peas in Orange Sauce, '88 97
Leeks in Orange Sauce, '88 86
Peas, Orange-Ginger, '04 294
Potatoes, Orange Mashed, '96 33
Rutabaga, Glazed, '99 284
Squash à l'Orange, '85 230
Sweet Potatoes, Candied, '01 49
Sweet Potatoes, Coconut-Orange, '84 252
Sweet Potatoes in Orange Cups, '82 272
Sweet Potatoes, Orange, '86 279
Sweet Potatoes, Orange-Baked, '88 M294
Sweet Potatoes, Orange-Glazed, '81 223; '83 280
Sweet Potatoes, Orange-Spice Mashed, '02 34
Sweet Potatoes, Pineapple-Orange, '96 46
Sweet Potato-Orange Bake, '83 226
Sweet Potato-Stuffed Orange Cups, '81 223
Vinegar, Orange, '95 31

ORZO
Chicken, Orzo, and Spinach Casserole, '02 124
Grouper with Orzo, Pesto, '97 321
Marinara on Beds of Spinach and Orzo, '93 320
Mozzarella-and-Olive Orzo, '97 249
Pie, Honeyed Orzo-Pecan, '04 219
Primavera, Orzo, '92 192
Sage Orzo, Chicken Breasts with, '98 169
Salad, Artichokes with Orzo, '88 M193
Salad, Confetti Orzo, '92 173
Salad, Lentil-and-Orzo, '03 127
Salad, Peppers Stuffed with Shrimp-and-Orzo, '91 203
Salad, Shrimp-and-Orzo, '99 182
Salad, Summer Vegetable-and-Orzo, '00 165
Salad with Sesame Dressing, Orzo, '96 137
Shrimp with Orzo, Fire-Roasted, '99 42
Three-Grain Rice, '95 166

OYSTERS
Appetizers
Annapolis, Oysters, '89 195
Artichoke Oysters, '96 154
Bacon, Oysters in, '83 211
Barbecued Oysters, '82 247
Bienville, Baked Oysters, '90 27
Bienville, Oysters, '93 257
Casino, Oysters à la, '80 296
Creamed Oysters, '92 254
Dip, Smoked Oyster, '79 233
Dressed Oysters on the Half Shell, '87 M79
Fried Bacon-Wrapped Oysters, '02 103
Fritters, Oyster, '97 20
Mousse, Oyster, '81 245

Mousse, Smoked Oyster, '84 320
Spread, Smoked Oyster, '91 64
Stuffed Oysters, Crabmeat, '94 328
Baked Oysters, Bacon-, '86 132
Baked Oysters Italiano, '89 97
Baked Oysters on the Half Shell, '93 269
Bake, Oyster-and-Corn, '83 34; '84 44
Bisque, Oyster, '83 252; '96 276; '99 320
Brochette, Oysters, '80 56
Casserole, Oyster-and-Spinach, '83 34; '84 44
Casserole, Oyster-and-Wild Rice, '83 34; '84 44
Chesapeake, Oysters, '92 254
Chowder, Oyster, '83 229
Chowder, Oyster-Corn, '83 211
Dressing, Crabmeat-and-Oyster, '02 243
Dressing, Ma E's Traditional Oyster-Cornbread, '96 35
Dressing, Oyster, '79 250
Dressing, Oyster Bread, '82 251
Eggplant-and-Oyster Louisiane, '95 196
Fresh Oysters, Preparing, '82 127
Fried Bacon-Wrapped Oysters, '02 103
Fried Oysters, '85 104; '99 320
Fried Oysters, Delicious, '83 212
Fried Oysters, Southern, '88 111
Fried Raw Oysters, '81 135; '82 14
Fritters, Oyster, '79 31
Grilled Oysters Mornay, '89 195
Gumbo, Chicken and Oyster, '81 198
Gumbo, Duck, Oyster, and Sausage, '79 226
Gumbo, Seafood, '83 90; '87 210
Johnny Reb, Oysters, '82 42
Loaves, Spinach-Oyster, '84 213
Main Dishes
Baked Oysters over Toast Points, '84 214
Bienville, Oysters, '79 182
Buccaneer, Oysters, '87 40
Casserole, Oyster, '79 228
Casserole, Oyster-and-Chicken, '99 320
Casserole, Wild Rice-Oyster, '86 256
Cornbread, Oysters Casino on, '79 34
Crabmeat, Creamy Oysters and, '83 211
Creamed Oysters in Acorn Squash, '97 20
Creamed Oysters, Pan-Fried Grits with, '93 62
Crêpes, Virginia, '79 264
Fried Oyster Bubbles, '80 296
Fried Oysters, Southwest, '03 45
Fry, Hangtown, '80 297
Gino, Oysters à la, '81 126
Ham, Edwards' Oysters and, '86 253
Landmark, Oyster, '84 88
Loaf, Crusty Oyster, '92 254
Mornay, Seafood, '83 67
Omelets, Smoked Oyster, '84 96
Pie, Turkey-and-Oyster, '82 267
Pilaf, Oyster, '97 20
Poor Boys, Oyster-and-Bacon, '87 40
Rockefeller, Oysters, '98 222; '03 272
Rockefeller, Southern Oysters, '80 212
Sandwich, Oyster Submarine, '80 92
Sautéed Oysters, '86 132
Sautéed Seafood Platter, '83 89
Scalloped Oysters, '79 225; '84 213; '86 132; '90 249; '95 318; '99 321
Scalloped Oysters with Macaroni, '80 297
Shrimp Sauce, Oysters in, '87 40
Smoky Oysters Supreme, '87 60
Stewed in Cream, Oysters, '93 50
St. Jacques, Oysters, '80 103
Stuffing, Roast Turkey with Oyster, '80 251
Mousse, Smoked Oyster, '99 162
Nachos, Texas Oyster, '87 39
Patty Shells, Oysters in, '83 212; '85 257
Pie, Creole Oyster, '84 214

Pierre, Oysters, **'02** 102
Po'boys, Dressed Mini Oyster, **'01** 33
Po'boys, Dressed Oyster, **'02** 184
Scalloped Oysters, **'79** 225; **'84** 213; **'95** 318
Smoked Oysters, Deviled Eggs with, **'84** 161
Soup, Chicken, Ham, and Oyster, **'79** 198
Soup, Louisiana Oyster-and-Artichoke, **'92** 81
Soup, Oyster, **'79** 228; **'83** 211; **'02** 102
Soup, Oyster-and-Artichoke, **'97** 21
Soup, Oyster-and-Mushroom, **'87** 39
Soup, Oyster-Cheese, **'84** 213
Soup, Oyster-Turnip, **'94** 328
Spinach Salad with Oysters and Red Wine
    Vinaigrette, **'94** 327
Stew, Company Oyster, **'80** 297
Stew, Golden Oyster, **'86** 132
Stew, Holiday Oyster, **'85** 264
Stew, Oyster, **'80** 221
Stew, Oyster-Broccoli, **'89** 242
Stew, Oyster-Sausage, **'89** 242
Stew, Potato-Oyster, **'89** 243
Topless Oysters, **'01** 249
Wild Rice and Oysters, **'92** 339

Pancakes

Ambrosia Pancakes with Orange Syrup, **'89** 254
Apple-Filled Pancake, **'86** 96
Apple Pancakes with Caramel Sauce, Baked, **'04** 249
Apple Pancakes with Cider Sauce, Spicy, **'87** 224
Applesauce Pancakes, **'79** 114
Apple-Topped Pancakes, **'93** 339
Apricot Delight, **'81** 42
Baked Pancake, Arkansas German-, **'96** 53
Banana-Nut Pancakes, **'98** 160
Banana Pancakes, **'03** 305
Banana Pancakes with Peanut Butter and Jelly
    Syrups, **'01** 24
Best Pancakes, **'99** 194
Black Bean Pancakes with Gazpacho Butter, **'92** 86
Blueberry Buttermilk Pancakes, **'79** 114
Blueberry Pancakes, **'85** 152; **'89** 138
Blueberry Pancakes, Sour Cream, **'81** 164
Blue Cornmeal-Blueberry Pancakes, **'94** 115
Bran Pancakes with Cinnamon Syrup, **'91** 315
Buttermilk Griddle Cakes, **'81** 120; **'82** 22
Buttermilk Pancakes, **'83** 243; **'84** 101; **'97** 256
Buttermilk Pancakes with Fruit Topping, **'89** 50
Christmas Tree Hotcakes, **'03** 305
Cornmeal Batter Cakes, **'87** 16
Cornmeal Pancakes, Hearty, **'88** 129
Corn Pancakes, **'93** 43
Cottage Cheese Pancakes, **'79** 115
Cracklin' Cakes, Grannie's, **'98** 252
Cream Cheese Pancakes, **'97** 70
Dessert Pancakes, Luau, **'88** 154
Easy Pancakes, **'92** 203
Featherweight Pancakes, **'99** 43
Fluffy Pancakes, **'86** 137
Fruit Topping, Pancakes with, **'81** 42
Gingerbread Pancakes, **'84** 242; **'95** 282; **'96** 27
Ginger Pancakes, Dessert, **'88** 153
Gorditas with Turkey Mole, **'03** 18
Griddle Cakes, Levee Camp, **'03** 29
Ham Griddle Cakes, **'89** 255
Honey Pancakes, **'91** 139
Island Pancakes, **'87** 225
Latkes, **'90** 254
Latkes, Potato, **'97** 252
Latkes, Sweet Potato, **'01** 275
Lemon-Blueberry Pancakes, **'04** 148
Lemon Pancakes with Strawberry Butter, **'99** 44
Maple-Bacon Oven Pancake, **'89** 255
Mix, Quick Bread, **'81** 90

Noodle Pancake, Szechuan Ginger Stir-Fry with,
    '97 292
Oatmeal-Brown Sugar Pancakes, **'88** 203
Oatmeal Mini-Pancakes with Apple-Pear Sauce,
    '97 M272
Oatmeal Pancakes, **'80** 44; **'89** 107
Oat Pancakes, **'89** 227
Orange Pancakes with Sunshine Orange Sauce, **'97** 70
Orange-Yogurt Pancakes, **'87** 225
Oven-Baked Pancake for Two, **'89** 227
Pancakes, **'81** 90
Peach Pancake, Baked, **'97** 71
Peanut Butter Pancakes, **'97** 271
Pecan Pancakes, **'03** 305
Pecan Pancakes, Toasted, **'99** 43
Popover Pancake, Brunch, **'96** 28
Potato-Chive Pancakes, Quick, **'04** 248
Potato-Ham Pancakes, **'96** 138
Potato Pancake, **'85** 20
Potato Pancakes, **'79** 115; **'89** 144
Potato Pancakes, German, **'98** 279
Potato Pancakes, Leftover, **'96** 138
Potato Pancakes, Moist, **'80** 36
Potato Pancakes, Old-Fashioned, **'96** 138
Potato Pancakes, Parsley-, **'96** 251; **'97** 103
Potato-Two Potato Pancakes, One, **'96** 138
Pumpkin Pancakes, **'80** 228
Refrigerator Pancakes, Overnight, **'93** 196
Rice Pancakes, **'85** 147
Sauce, Cinnamon-Pecan-Honey Pancake, **'88** 46
Sauce, Peach-Blueberry Pancake, **'82** 177
Sausage Rollups, Pancake-, **'83** 246; **'84** 42
Sausage Wedges, Pancake-, **'93** 196
Sour Cream Pancakes, **'79** 213
Sour Cream Pancakes, Fluffy, **'79** 209
Sour Cream Pancakes with Fruit Topping, **'90** 142
Squash Pancakes, Granola-, **'94** 267
Strawberry Pancakes, **'84** 219
Supper Pancake, **'86** 242
Suppertime Pancakes, **'03** 278
Sweet Potato-Chive Pancakes, Quick, **'04** 248
Sweet Potato Pancakes, **'87** 280
Sweet Potato Pancakes with Goat Cheese, **'96** 271
Vegetable Pancakes, **'88** 297; **'98** 236
Vegetable-Rice Pancakes, **'93** 43
Veggie Pancakes, **'00** 85
Wheat Germ-Banana Pancakes, **'79** 114
Wheat Germ Pancakes, **'86** 242
Wheat Pancakes, Shredded, **'84** 59
Wheat Quick Pancakes, **'85** 278
Whole Grain Pancakes, **'93** 123
Whole Wheat-Oat Pancakes, **'93** 16
Whole Wheat Pancakes, **'83** 18
Wild Rice Pancakes, **'02** 238
Zucchini Pancakes, **'93** 43

PARSNIPS
Broccoli and Parsnips with Horseradish, **'02** 235
Candied Parsnips, **'86** 224
Fried Parsnips, **'96** 36
Glazed Carrots and Parsnips, **'02** 129
Glazed Parsnips, **'91** 220
Mash, Parsnip, **'97** 263
Medley, Parsnip-Carrot, **'96** 36
Scalloped Root Vegetables, **'98** 310
Soufflé, Golden Parsnip, **'83** 266
Soup, Gingered Carrot-and-Parsnip, **'03** 221
Sugar-Crusted Parsnips, **'88** 229

PASTAS. *See also* **COUSCOUS; FETTUCCINE;**
    LASAGNA; LINGUINE; MACARONI;
    MANICOTTI; NOODLES; ORZO;
    SALADS/Pasta; SPAGHETTI.
Angel Hair, Goat Cheese-Stuffed Chicken Breasts
    over, **'97** 144
Angel Hair Pasta, Scallops and, **'99** 176

Angel Hair Pasta, Shrimp and Mushrooms with,
    '92 34
Angel Hair Pasta, Szechuan Chicken with, **'97** 91
Angel Hair Pasta, Turkey Scaloppine with, **'02** 44
Angel Hair Pasta with Shrimp and Asparagus,
    '92 100
Angel Hair Pasta with Tomato Cream Sauce, **'93** 292
Angel Hair Pasta with Veal and Shrimp, **'04** 223
Antipasto, Pasta, **'85** 286
Asparagus Pasta with Toasted Pecans, **'04** 90
Asparagus, Tomatoes, and Shrimp, Garlicky Pasta
    with, **'95** 82
Bacon Pasta, **'97** 52
Bake, Cheesy Pasta, **'02** 161
Bake, Layered Pasta, **'04** 326
Basil-Cheese Pasta, **'96** 136
Beans and Greens, Pasta with, **'02** 202
Beans and Pasta, **'99** 35
Beans, Pasta with, **'99** 236
Bow Tie Pasta, Spinach and Mushrooms with,
    '95 341
Bow-Tie Pesto, **'94** 231
Bow Ties, Black Beans, and Key Limes, **'96** 291
Bow Ties with Crab and Vegetables, **'98** 233
Bow-Tie with Marinara, **'94** 64
Broccoli Pasta, **'84** 176
Cabbage and Cheese Sauce, Pasta with, **'00** 105
Cannelloni, **'85** 60; **'92** 17
Cannelloni with Roasted Red Bell Pepper Sauce,
    Chicken, **'02** 287
Casserole, Crawfish Pasta, **'97** 106
Casserole, Freezer Eggplant-Sausage-Pasta, **'95** 197
Casseroles, Hot Brown Pasta, **'96** 290
Catfish and Artichokes, Pasta with, **'90** 123
Cherry Tomatoes over Pasta, Herbed, **'95** 229
Chicken-and-Broccoli Pasta, **'87** 286
Chicken and Pasta, Mediterranean, **'03** 63
Chicken, Bird's-Nest, **'88** 152
Chicken Caesar Pasta, **'97** 87
Chicken Pasta, Spicy, **'02** 125
Chicken Picante Pasta, **'01** 164
Clam Sauce, Pasta with, **'84** 291
Collards and Sausage, Pasta with, **'94** 230
Cucumbers and Pasta, Asian, **'96** 177
Curried Pasta with Apple, **'02** 68
Dinner, One-Pot Pasta, **'00** 173
Dressing, Pasta Salad, **'86** 121
Fennel, Pasta with, **'98** 46
Frittata, Firecracker Pasta, **'94** 230
Garden-Fresh dPasta,d, **'94** M134
Garlic Pasta with Marinara Sauce, **'92** 78
Green Pasta with Shrimp-Mushroom Italienne,
    '79 170
Greens, Pasta with, **'96** 47
Herb-and-Tomato Pasta, **'96** 122
Italian Pasta, Weeknight, **'03** 48
Late-Night Pasta Chez Frank, **'95** 228
Lemon Shrimp and Pasta, **'96** 124
Lentils, Cheesy Pasta and, **'99** 287
Mamma Mia Pasta, **'95** 25
Mediterranean Pasta, **'95** 341; **'96** 122
Minestrone, Dixie, **'94** 230
Mostaccioli Alfredo, **'91** 47
Mostaccioli Casserole, **'04** 316
Oregano Pasta, **'84** 176
Pastitsio, **'99** 167
Penne, Cheesy Chicken, **'00** 289
Penne, Garden Sauté with, **'98** 207
Penne Pasta, Chicken, Asparagus, and Mushrooms
    with, **'98** 212
Penne Pasta, Spicy Vegetables with, **'04** 195
Penne, Spicy Cheesy Chicken, **'00** 289
Penne with Pancetta, **'00** 51
Penne with Spinach and Feta, **'03** 170; **'04** 328

PASTAS
(continued)

Peppery Pasta, '94 164
Pesto and Pasta, '92 98
Pesto-Clam Sauce, Pasta with, '98 17
Pie, Broccoli-and-Turkey Pasta, '88 269
Pimiento Pasta, '84 176
Potpourri, Pasta, '94 33
Primavera
  Almost Pasta Primavera, '86 38
  Chicken-Pasta Primavera, '91 72
  Creamy Pasta Primavera, '95 167
  Garden Spiral Primavera, '91 30
  Pasta Primavera, '85 86; '89 105; '93 168;
    '97 228
  Smoked Turkey Pasta Primavera, '90 84
  Tomato-Pasta Primavera, '86 209
Prosciutto, Party Pasta with, '94 176
Provençale, Pasta, '88 90
Pumpkin Pasta, '98 241
Ravioli, Green Bean Alfredo with Cheese, '01 180
Ravioli, Homemade, '87 230
Ravioli, Mediterranean, '93 301
Ravioli Pasta, Homemade, '87 231
Ravioli, St. Louis Toasted, '95 117
Ravioli with Creamy Pesto Sauce, '92 79
Rotelle, Chicken and Tomato with, '87 108
Rotelle, Shrimp, '85 165
Rotini, Baked, '01 185
Rotini Romano, '87 193
Salad Dressing, Herbed Pasta, '96 106
Salads
  Acini di Pepe Salad, '83 163
  Artichoke-Pasta Salad, '94 180
  Asian Peanut-and-Pasta Salad, '03 127
  Bayou Pasta Salad, '00 203
  Bean-Pasta Salad, Marinated, '94 167; '97 328
  Bean Salad, Pasta-, '86 169
  Beef-Pasta Salad, Spicy, '01 311
  Bow Tie Pasta, '01 164
  Broccoli-Cauliflower Pasta Salad, '88 269
  Broccoli-Cheese-Pasta Salad, '96 184
  Chicken-and-Bow Tie Pasta, '01 164
  Chicken-and-Pasta Salad, Hoisin, '99 125
  Chicken Pasta Salad, '88 89
  Chicken-Pasta Salad, Grilled, '94 64
  Chicken-Pasta Salad, Zesty, '02 186
  Chicken Salad, Tarragon Pasta-, '87 155
  Confetti-Pasta Salad, Easy, '92 220
  Crabmeat-Shrimp Pasta Salad, '86 208
  Crunchy Pasta Salad, '85 166
  Fruited Pasta Salad, '92 108
  Garden Pasta Salad, '86 188
  Greek Pasta Salad, '02 139
  Ham-and-Pasta Salad, '90 128
  Ham-and-Pea Pasta Salad, '00 217
  Ham-Dijon Pasta Salad, '92 191
  Ham, Pasta Salad with, '92 108
  Ham-Pecan-Blue Cheese Pasta Salad, '90 62
  Herbed Pasta-and-Tomato Salad, '92 144
  Italian Salad, '87 145
  Luncheon Pasta Salad, '90 191
  Main-Dish Pasta Salad, '82 199
  Oriental Pasta Salad, '90 63
  Overnight Pasta Salad, '82 276
  Pasta Salad, '84 139; '86 120; '87 36; '89 217;
    '90 62, 91; '00 213; '01 127
  Pesto Pasta Salad, Fresh, '01 61
  Pistachio-Pasta Salad, '86 141
  Presto Pasta Salad, '90 63
  Ratatouille Pasta Salad, '90 74
  Ravioli Salad, Caesar, '95 183

Roasted Onion Pasta Salad with Peppered Cheese
  Crisps, '98 107
Rotelle Salad, Crunchy, '86 209
Rotini Salad, '88 42
Salmon-Pasta Salad, '87 9
Salmon Salad Shells, '85 286
Seafood Pasta Salad, '90 62
Seashell Salad, '86 209
Shell Salad, Tossed, '91 256
Shrimp Pasta Salad with Green Goddess
  Dressing, '02 139
Shrimp Salad, Pasta-and-, '83 163
Smoked Mozzarella Pasta Salad, '03 126
Southwestern Pasta Salad, '94 278
Tomato-Pasta Salad, '97 M160
Tortellini Pasta Salad, Cheese, '02 139
Tortellini-Pesto Salad, '92 22
Tortellini Salad, '89 237; '02 186
Tortellini Salad, Chicken, '87 288
Tortellini Salad, Garden, '91 44
Tortellini Salad, Terrific, '96 134
Tuna-Pasta Salad, '91 43; '92 141; '00 247
Tuna Pasta Salad, '92 108
Turkey 'n' Pasta Salad, Ranch-Style, '94 184
Vegetable Pasta Salad, '89 256; '91 143
Vegetable-Pasta Salad, '92 167
Vegetable Salad, Pasta-, '95 238
Veggie Salad, Pasta-, '96 106
Vermicelli Salad, Shrimp, '88 139
Vermicelli Vinaigrette Salad, '82 189
Ziti-Cheddar Salad, '85 165
Sauce, Pasta, '01 53
Sauce, Pecan Pasta, '96 262
Sausage and Bell Peppers, Pasta with, '02 63
Sausage and Kale, Pasta with, '03 279
Sausage and Pasta, Skillet, '97 267
Scallops and Pasta, Fresh, '83 164
Scampi, Speedy, '02 161
Shells
  Bake, Quick Crab, '87 192
  Bites, Pesto-Cheese Pasta, '87 251
  Casserole, Seashell-Provolone, '80 189
  Casserole, Turkey, '96 302
  Cavatini, '94 214
  Cheese, Creamy Shells and, '01 216
  Florentine, Layered Pasta, '00 56
  Florentine Pasta Shells, '00 326
  Garden Pasta Medley, '89 256
  Greens and Bacon, Shelly, '96 290
  Italiano, Pasta, '01 41
  Jumbo Seashells Florentine, '79 6
  Peppers and Broccoli, Pasta with, '91 69
  Seafood and Pasta, '90 234
  Spinach Shells, '97 50
  Stuffed Shells, Cheesy Beef-, '83 217
  Stuffed Shells, Mexican, '91 87
  Stuffed Shells, Sausage-, '96 102
  Stuffed Shells, Southwestern, '93 234; '99 238
  Stuffed Shells, Spinach-, '85 60; '87 20; '99 64
  Stuffed with Five Cheeses, Pasta, '88 197
  Taco Pasta, Easy, '03 124
  Tuna Pasta, Stuffed Tomato with, '88 54
Shrimp-and-Goat Cheese Pasta, Garlic, '00 174
Shrimp and Pasta, '91 207
Shrimp and Pasta, Herbed, '92 329; '97 228
Shrimp and Pasta with Cream Sauce, '98 295
Shrimp and Pasta with Two Cheeses, '98 49
Shrimp-and-Spinach Pasta, '01 258
Shrimp Elégante, '83 48
Shrimp-Pasta Medley, '88 302
Shrimp Scampi, '95 209
Shrimp Scampi, Pasta with, '01 83
Shrimp with Pasta, Asian, '04 128
Smoked Salmon-Caper-and-Dill Pasta, '98 169

Snappy Pasta, '83 164
Soup, Bean and Pasta, '94 220
Spaghettini with Green Beans and Walnut Brown
  Butter, '03 170
Spinach-Mustard Twist, '86 209
Spinach Pesto-Pasta, '91 314
Steak with Pasta and Sesame-Ginger Butter, '99 142
Straw and Hay Pasta, '80 211
Summer Pasta, '04 223
Toasted Rice and Pasta, '95 57
Tomato-Basil Pasta, '94 204
Tomatoes and Basil, Pasta with Fresh, '98 233
Tomato-Garlic Pasta, '94 177
Tomato Pasta, Italian, '93 201
Tomato Pasta, Southwestern, '93 201
Tortellini. *See also* **PASTAS/Salads.**
  Alfredo with Prosciutto and Artichoke Hearts,
    Tortellini, '02 322
  Carbonara, Creamy Tortellini, '99 171
  Carbonara, Tortellini, '91 47
  Citrus Broth, Tortellini in, '99 292
  Creamy Tortellini, '99 171
  Kebabs, Antipasto, '94 144
  Parsley-Caper Sauce, Tortellini with, '93 175
  Ragù with Tortellini, Wild Mushroom, '04 220
  Rosemary-Parmesan Sauce, Tortellini with,
    '92 284
  Shrimp and Tortellini, '92 34
  Soup, Japanese Tortellini, '96 330
  Soup, Sausage-Tortellini, '99 20
  Soup, Seafood-Tortellini, '97 324
  Soup, Spinach-Tortellini, '99 317
  Soup, Tortellini, '98 68; '00 14
  Soup with Tortellini, Italian Sausage, '88 46
  Spinach Tortellini with Tomato Sauce, '88 302
  Tapas with Spicy Ranch Dip, Tortellini, '98 318
  Tomatoes, Quick Pasta and, '92 180
  Tomato Pesto Dip with Tortellini, Creamy,
    '00 196
Toss, Garden Pasta, '00 57
Toss, Pasta-Basil, '87 33
Tricolor Pasta with Clam Sauce, '93 272
Turkey-Basil Pasta, Creamy, '89 216
Vegetable Pasta, Grilled, '97 142
Vegetables and Pasta, Roasted, '93 184
Vegetable Sauce, Pasta with, '83 163
Vegetables, Pasta and, '89 255
Vegetables, Pasta and Garden, '87 192
Vegetable Stir-Fry Pasta, '96 29
Verde, Pasta, '84 201
Vermicelli
  Anchovy-Garlic Sauce over Vermicelli, '86 158
  Casserole, Chicken-and-Pasta, '97 192
  Chicken and Pasta, Quick, '93 14
  Chicken Vermicelli, '01 237
  Clam Sauce, Pasta with, '84 291
  Clam Sauce, Vermicelli with, '85 295
  Frittata, Pasta, '85 286
  Garden Pasta, '82 199
  Lemon Vermicelli, '84 329
  Mushroom Sauce Supreme on Vermicelli, '86 158
  Mushrooms, Vermicelli with, '79 195
  Pie, Spinach-Pasta, '85 286
  Platter, Cold Pasta, '88 42
  Red Clam Sauce, Vermicelli and Sprouts with,
    '86 143
  Rice with Vermicelli, Buttery, '02 258
  Salmon-Pesto Vermicelli, '92 200
  Scallop-Vegetable Vermicelli, '87 143
  Shrimp and Feta Cheese on Vermicelli, '87 108
  Soup with Quenelles, Veal-Vermicelli, '94 14
  Spinach Sauce, Vermicelli with Fresh, '89 256
  Tetrazzini, Chicken, '02 171; '04 221
  Tomato Pasta, Caribbean, '93 201

Tomato Sauce, Vermicelli with, '83 164
Toss, Asparagus-Vermicelli, '00 102
Vegetable Sauce, Vermicelli with Chunky, '04 180
Vinaigrette, Italian Pasta, '92 78
Ziti, Baked, '94 65
Ziti with Sausage and Broccoli, '95 340

PÂTÉS
Black-Eyed Pea Pâté, '91 12; '93 97
Braunschweiger Pâté, '83 251
Champignon, Pâté de, '93 171
Cheese Pâté, Chutney-, '84 152
Cheese Pâté, Chutney-Glazed, '02 279
Cheese Pâté, Four-, '89 284
Cheese Pâté, Layered, '86 105
Cheese Pâté, Sherry, '95 215
Chicken Liver Pâté, '79 153; '81 235; '83 108; '84 205; '88 M132
Chicken Pâté, Curried, '00 106
Chutney-and-Blue Cheese Pâté, '02 279
Cognac, Pâté with, '86 159
Country Pâté, '86 66
Crab Pâté, '79 233
Cream Cheese Pâté, '80 154
Duck Liver Pâté, '79 227
Duck Pâté, '79 226
en Croûte, Pâté, '86 65
Ham Pâté, '85 279
Lentil Pâté, '92 285
Lima Bean-and-Fresh Herb Pâté, '04 70
Liver-Cheese Pâté, '85 276
Liver Pâté with Madeira Sauce, '93 323
Maison, Pâté, '84 222
Mock Pâté, '87 251
Mushroom Pâté, '89 157
Pastry, Pâté, '86 65
Pork Pâté with Spinach and Cream, '83 224
Shrimp Pâté on Crostini, '98 316
Shrimp Pâté with Dill Sauce, '85 39
Spread, Quick Pâté, '84 117
Turkey-Mushroom Pâté in Pastry, '92 327
Vegetable-Chicken Pâté, '86 66
Wine Pâté, '90 36

PEACHES
Alaska, Peachy Melba, '88 266
Ambrosia, Peach, '83 53
Baked Peaches, '92 179
Baked Peaches and Sausage, '82 50
Baked Peaches, Spicy, '86 39
Baked Peaches with Ginger, Oven-, '82 170
Bay Laurel Peaches, '90 124
Beverages
Bellini, '01 89
Bellinis, '88 77
Bellinis, Frosted, '97 122
Bellinis, Mint, '02 136
Bellini Spritzers, '90 110
Christmas Blossom, '99 321
Cooler, Peach, '85 198; '86 6
Cream, Peaches 'n' Almond, '86 229
Daiquiris, Peach, '90 322
Frost, Peach, '89 155
Frosty, Peach, '81 156; '83 318
Fuzz Buzz, '82 160
Petals, Peach, '90 104
Pick-Me-Up, Peach, '89 183
Refresher, Peach, '86 103
Refresher, Peach Yogurt, '03 166
Shake, Get-Up-and-Go, '00 179
Shake, Peach Melba, '02 158
Shake, Peach Melba Sundae, '93 134
Shake, Peachy Orange, '81 156
Shake, Pep, '79 38
Slush, Peach, '04 141

Slushy, Kiwi-Peach, '00 201
Smash, Peach, '88 161
Smoothie, Banana-Peach Buttermilk, '04 22
Smoothie, Peachy-Pineapple, '97 173
Smoothie, Strawberry-Peach, '89 182
Tea, Peach Iced, '02 181
Bombe with Raspberry Sauce, Creamy, '89 322
Brandied Peaches with Mincemeat, '81 47
Brandy Peaches, '85 275
Bread, Georgia Peach, '79 161
Bread, Peach, '82 170
Bread, Tipsy Peach, '02 21
Butter, Golden Peach, '91 178
Cake, Fresh Peach, '85 178
Cake, Peach-Almond Pound, '89 86
Cake, Peaches and Cream, '80 142
Cake, Peaches-and-Cream, '96 118
Cake, Peach Upside-Down, '87 8
Cake, Peachy Almond-Butter, '90 107
Cake, Peachy Picnic, '79 178
Caramel Peaches, '93 134
Cardinale, Peach, '89 155
Champagne, Peaches, '79 146
Charlotte, Peach, '79 68
Cheesecake, Peach-Caramel, '02 M158
Cheesecake, Peaches 'n' Cream, '88 137
Cobblers
Apricot Cobbler, Peach-, '99 255
Blueberry Cobbler, Peachy, '80 143
Blueberry-Peach Cobbler, No-Dough, '86 177
Caramel Cobbler, Peach-, '86 300; '87 178
Cranberry-Peach Cobbler, '92 322
Crinkle, Peach, '91 20
Crisp, Peach, '83 113; '92 13; '93 134
Double Crust Peach Cobbler, '03 310
Easy Peach Cobbler, '97 137; '99 206
Fresh Peach Cobbler, '82 139; '89 154
Grenadine-Peach Cobbler, '85 178
Lattice-Topped Peach Cobbler, '79 154
Old-Fashioned Peach Cobbler, '82 170
Peach Cobbler, '83 175; '84 178; '90 219; '95 264
(Peach Cobbler), I Fall to Peaches, '96 159
Pecan-Peach Cobbler, '04 120
Praline Biscuits, Peach Cobbler with, '92 180
Quick Peach Cobbler, '79 215; '81 142
Spicy Peach Cobbler, '85 178
Supreme, Peach Cobbler, '81 184; '90 313
Too-Easy Peach Cobbler, '04 28
Compote, Berry-Peach, '82 133
Compote, Peach-Berry, '89 112
Crabapple Peaches, Broiled Pork Chops with, '81 83
Cream, Bavarian Peach, '82 171
Cream Cheese, Peachy, '92 289
Cream, Honeyed Peaches 'n', '93 134
Cream, Peach Almond, '82 108
Cream, Peaches and, '95 196
Cream, Peachy-Apricot, '86 163
Crêpes, Fresh Peach, '84 186
Crêpes, Peach, '82 184
Crisp, Gingered Peach, '97 303
Crisp, Peach-and-Raspberry, '02 232
Crumble, Easy Peach, '83 116
Curried Ham and Peaches, '82 60
Custard Dessert, Fresh Peach, '86 162
Dessert, Layered Peach, '95 196
Dessert, Peach-Blueberry, '92 184
Dessert, Peachy Melt-Away, '87 298
Dessert, Quick Peach, '85 178
Dip, Creole Peach, '80 142
Dip, Peachy, '92 179
Dressing, Peach, '90 180
Dumplings, Peach, '80 143; '85 177; '96 172
Filling, Peach, '89 154; '90 107; '96 119

Flambé, Banana-Peach, '85 316
Flambé, Peach Sundaes, '81 88
Flip, Peach, '79 217
Fluff, Peach, '95 176
Foster, Peaches, '86 240
Freeze, Creamy Peach, '82 144
French Toast, Peach-Filled, '98 160
French Toast, Peachy, '98 56
Frost, Peach, '84 164
Ginger Peaches with Rum, '84 M323
Gingersnap Peaches, '85 M329
Grilled Balsamic-Glazed Peaches, '02 159
Honey-Lime Whip, Peaches with, '85 108
Ice Cream, Blueberry-Peach, '00 153
Ice Cream, Creamy Peach, '85 177
Ice Cream, Deluxe Peach, '80 176; '90 314
Ice Cream, Fresh Peach, '95 195
Ice Cream, No-Cook Peach, '04 179
Ice Cream, Peach, '81 184; '82 171; '83 159; '86 15; '93 135; '98 221
Ice Cream, Peach-Almond, '89 156
Ice Cream, Summertime Peach, '02 158
Ice, Peach, '81 178
Ice, Peach-Yogurt, '84 83
Jam, Spiced Peach, '00 51
Ketchup, Peach, '95 306
Ketchup, Spicy Peach, '03 139
Main Dishes
Chicken Breasts, Peach-Stuffed, '79 177
Chicken Peach Dinner, '79 77
Chicken, Peachy, '90 212
Chicken with Peaches, Bourbon-Laced Tipsy, '97 136
Chicken with Peach Sauce, '98 334
Ham, Peach Holiday, '04 251
Ham, Peachy Glazed, '96 189
Ham Roast, Peachy, '86 118
Ham with Cherry-Peach, Chutney, Glazed, '97 315
Pork Chops, Peachy, '89 310
Pork Loin Dijonnaise with Peach Sauce, '97 87
Pork Steaks, Peachy, '79 166
Spareribs, Peach-Glazed, '86 14
Marinated Peaches, '91 91
Melba, Peach, '81 83; '83 M114
Meringues, Peach Melba, '87 76
Meringues with Buttermilk Custard Sauce, Peach Melba, '96 183
Mold, Peachy Berry Cream, '83 130
Mousse, Peach, '85 54
Mousse, Peach Macaroon, '80 153
Muffins, Peach Streusel, '03 167
Muffins, Peachy-Almond, '86 301
Muffins, Special Peach, '84 74
Nest, Peaches in a Garden, '87 154
Pancake, Baked Peach, '97 71
Pancake, Brunch Popover, '96 28
Parfait, Peach, '82 166
Parfaits, Sugar-Free Peachy Cheesecake, '02 326
Pies
Blackberry Pie, Peach-and-, '89 136
Blueberry-Peach Pie, '94 158
Chiffon Pie, Peach, '89 155
Cranberry Pie, Peach-, '83 249
Cream Pie, Peaches-and-, '81 184
Filling, Fresh Peach Pie, '95 195
Fresh Peach Pie, '82 170; '95 195
Fresh Peach Pie, Elizabeth and Phoebe's, '96 119
Fried Peach Pies, '81 272
Fried Pies, Delicious, '83 84
Fried Pies, Easy Peach, '85 178
Fried Pies, Ginger-Peach, '00 212
Georgia Peach-and-Praline Pie, '98 196
Little Peach Pies, '86 303

PEACHES, Pies
(continued)

    Luscious Peach Pie, **'81** 136
    Melba Pie, Peach, **'98** 216
    Mincemeat-Peach Pie, **'80** 295; **'81** 188
    Praline Pie, Peach, **'89** 136
    Quick Peach Pie, **'89** 252
    Rhubarb-Peach Pie, **'86** 140
Pops, Peach, **'04** 141
Preservation
    Butter, Peach, **'82** 308
    Chutney, Peach, **'84** 179; **'96** 207
    Conserve, Peach, **'79** 120
    Honey-Sweet Peaches, **'85** 107
    Jam, Cantaloupe-Peach, **'95** 143
    Jam, Freezer Peach, **'83** 182; **'84** M182
    Jam, Peach, **'93** 135
    Jam, Peach-Plum Freezer, **'85** 130
    Jam, Peach-Rosemary, **'03** 134
    Jam, Rosy Peach-Banana, **'80** 142
    Marmalade, Peach-Orange, **'82** 150
    Mincemeat Peaches, **'85** 178
    Pears, Peaches and, **'85** 106
    Pickled Peaches, Perfect, **'85** 178
    Pickles, Peach, **'85** 177; **'99** 170
    Preserves, Custard, **'98** 126
    Preserves, Honeyed Peach, **'85** 130
    Preserves, Old-Fashioned Peach, **'82** 150
    Preserves, Peach, **'81** 147; **'89** 140
    Relish, Peach, **'85** 136
    Spiced Peaches, Brandy, **'80** 142
Preserves, Cream Cheese and Peach, **'84** 264
Pudding, Peachy Bread, **'88** 175
Puffs, Peach Sweet Potato, **'87** 280
Salads
    Chicken Salad, Peachy, **'97** 193
    Cream Salad, Peaches-and-, **'83** 108
    Easy Peach Salad Supreme, **'79** 177
    Fluff, Peach, **'95** 176
    Frosted Peach Salad, **'82** 145
    Frozen Peach Salad, **'82** 54
    Fruit Salad, Peachy, **'89** 206
    Georgia Peach Salad, **'80** 142
    Indian Chief Salad, **'96** 287
    Kiwi Salad, Peach-and-, **'90** 180
    Party Salad, Peach, **'84** 290
    Pickled Peach Salad, **'80** 104; **'85** 264; **'04** 269
    Pinwheel Salad, Peach, **'79** 11
    Ring, Spicy Peach-Cranberry, **'85** 264
    Slaw, Party Peach, **'86** 250
    Spiced Peach Salad, **'94** 68
    Summer Salad, Georgia, **'92** 179
    Sunny Day Salad, **'96** 90
Sauces
    Berry Sauce, Peach-, **'87** M165
    Blueberry Pancake Sauce, Peach-, **'82** 177
    Blueberry Sauce, Peach-, **'81** 170
    Chicken with Peach Sauce, **'98** 334
    Creamy Peach Sauce, **'85** 189
    Fresh Peach Sauce, **'87** 167
    Fresh Peach Sauce, Creamy, **'79** 177
    Peach Sauce, **'84** 144; **'92** 203
    Praline Sauce, Peach-, **'85** 161
    Rib Sauce, Peach, **'01** 248
    Salsa, Avocado-Peach, **'02** 159
    Salsa, Fresh Peach, **'95** 195
    Salsa, Peach, **'91** 183; **'96** 14; **'97** 183
    Salsa, Peachy Green Tomato, **'99** 143
    Strawberry-Peach Sauce, **'92** 154
    Tangy Peach Sauce, **'96** 89
Sherbet Cooler, Peachy, **'91** 187
Sherbet, Peach, **'90** 179

Sherbet, Three-Ingredient Peach, **'01** 105
Shortcakes, Spicy Peach, **'89** 154
Sorbet, Peach, **'93** 153; **'97** 110
Soup, Chilled Peach, **'97** 159
Soup, Cream of Peach, **'99** 207
Soup, Peach, **'83** 120, 180
Soup, Peach-Plum, **'87** 157
Spiced Peach Dessert, **'83** 9
Spiced Peaches, **'91** 72, 148
Spiced Peaches, Ginger, **'86** 15
Spiced Peaches with Nutty Dumplings, **'87** 164
Split, Peach, **'85** 277
Spread, Peachy Cream Cheese, **'90** M215
Spread, Peachy-Raisin, **'86** 326
Strawberry Sauce, Peaches with, **'85** 8
Stuffed Peaches, Macaroon-, **'79** 178
Stuffed Peach Halves, **'86** 196
Sweet Potatoes and Peaches, **'86** 11
Tart, Cream Cheese-Peach, **'99** 169
Tart, Golden Peach Meringue, **'98** 197
Tart, Kiwifruit-Peach, **'88** 20
Tart, Peach Cream, **'90** 173
Tarts, Peachy Keen, **'91** 118
Tart with Brandy Sauce, Peach, **'98** 119
Topping, Peach, **'94** 22
Topping, Raspberry-Peach, **'87** 126
Torte, Frozen Peach, **'93** 135
Trifle, Georgia Peach, **'04** 169
Trifle, Peach, **'92** 179
Vinaigrette, Roasted Vegetable Salad with Dried
    Peach, **'97** 265
Vinegar, Peach-Mint, **'95** 190
Wine Sauce, Peaches in, **'79** 184
Yogurt, Frozen Fresh Peach, **'90** 139
PEANUT BUTTER
Apple, Piggy, **'94** 194
Bird's Nests, **'95** 102
Birds' Nests, Peanut-Butter, **'04** 84
Bread, Peanut Butter, **'86** 171; **'88** 64; **'99** 111
Cake, Chocolate-Peanut Butter, **'84** 240
Cake, Chocolate-Peanut Butter Mousse, **'98** 71
Cake, Fudgy Peanut Butter, **'85** 91
Cake, Peanut Butter, **'79** 51; **'83** M233
Cake, Peanut Butter-and-Jelly, **'85** 34
Cake, Peanut Butter-Banana, **'80** 87
Cake, Peanut Butter-Fudge, **'96** 254; **'01** 59
Cake, Peanut Butter Swirl, **'86** 109
Candies
    Balls, Buckeye, **'00** M280; **'01** M322
    Balls, Chocolate-Peanut Butter, **'80** 87
    Balls, No-Cook Candy, **'85** 14
    Balls, Peanut Butter-Chocolate, **'80** 269
    Bites, Chocolate-Peanut Butter, **'92** M317
    Bites, Peanut Butter Elf, **'91** 275
    Chocolate Peanutty Swirls, **'94** M330
    Creams, Peanut Butter, **'79** 273
    Crunch, White Chocolate-Peanut Butter,
      '02 M296
    Cups, Rocky Road-Peanut Butter Candy,
      '04 M330
    Drops, Chocolate-Peanut Butter, **'92** 322
    Eggs, Peanut Butter Easter, **'87** 86
    Fudge Bites, Peanut-, **'91** M231; **'92** M68
    Fudge, Chocolate-Peanut Butter, **'87** 257; **'90** 311
    Fudge, Creamy Peanut Butter, **'92** 240
    Fudge, Diamond, **'92** 193
    Fudge, Double-Good, **'79** M263; **'95** M50
    Fudge, Double Peanut, **'85** 91
    Fudge, Four Chips, **'92** 318
    Fudge, Marbled Peanut Butter, **'88** 65
    Fudge, Peanut Butter, **'80** 302; **'89** 307; **'95** 51;
      '02 296
    Fudge-Peanut Butter Chewies, **'98** 215
    Fudge Squares, Chocolate-Peanut Butter, **'97** M54

Peanut Butter Candy, **'93** 166
Pralines, Chocolate-Peanut Butter, **'92** 313;
    '93 51
Pralines, Peanut Butter, **'92** 313; **'93** 51
Squares, Peanut Butter-Chocolate Candy, **'82** 56
Tiger Butter, **'86** 48
Yummies, Peanut Butter, **'83** 223
Cheese Ball, Peanut Butter-, **'86** 136
Cheesecake, Peanut Butter, **'94** 142
Chicken, Maple-Balsamic, **'04** 195
Chicken, Peanut Butter-Marmalade, **'81** 282; **'82** 30
Chicken Strips, Nutty, **'99** 111
"Concrete," All Shook Up, **'94** 114
Cones, Chocolate-Peanut Butter, **'85** 14
Cookies
    Bars, Chewy Chocolate Cereal, **'97** 317
    Bars, Peanut Butter, **'84** 243; **'93** 166
    Bars, Peanut Butter-and-Fudge, **'80** M172
    Bars, Peanut Butter-Jam, **'94** 291
    Bars, Peanut Butter 'n' Jelly, **'83** 305
    Black-Eyed Susans, **'00** 291
    Brownies, Chocolate Chip-Peanut Butter, **'84** 73
    Brownies, Chocolate-Peanut Butter Chip, **'91** 306
    Brownies, Elephant Stomp, **'03** 43
    Brownies, Frosted Peanut Butter, **'92** 272;
      '00 M155
    Brownies, Peanut Butter, **'87** 199
    Chocolate Chip Cookies, Freezer Peanut Butter-,
      '86 230
    Chocolate Chip-Peanut Butter Cookies, **'99** 68
    Chocolate Chunk Cookies, Peanut Butter and,
      '94 169
    Chocolate Chunk-Peanut Cookies, **'04** 125
    Chocolate Chunk-Peanut Cookies, Double,
      '04 125
    Chocolate Kiss Cookies, Peanut Butter-, **'86** 49
    Chocolate-Peanut Bars, **'03** 195
    Chocolate-Peanut Butter Cookies, **'85** 90
    Chocolate-Peanut Butter Cups, **'97** 134
    Chocolate Treats, Crispy Peanut Butter-, **'02** 287
    Choco-Peanut Chip Cookies, **'92** 318
    Choco Surprise Cookies, **'80** 60
    Cinnamon Cookies, Peanut Butter-, **'84** 30
    Coconut Cookies, Peanut Butter-, **'83** 113
    Crisp Peanuttiest Cookies, **'88** 65
    Crisps, Peanut Butter, **'79** 50
    Cup Cookies, Peanut Butter, **'03** 298
    Cups, Chocolate-Peanut Butter, **'85** 14
    Double Chip Cookies, **'81** 301
    Double-Chip Peanut Butter Cookies, **'89** 169
    Double Peanut Butter Cookies, **'80** 209
    Easter Basket and Eggs, **'95** 101
    Easy Peanut Butter Cookies, **'92** 272
    Kiss Cookies, Peanut Butter-, **'03** 42
    Logs, No-Bake Peanut Butter, **'84** 211
    Macaroons, Chewy Peanut Butter, **'95** 214
    Miracle Cookies, **'83** 149
    Monster Cookies, **'84** 36
    No-Bake Peanut Butter Cookies, **'94** 197
    Oatmeal Cookies, Double-Chip, **'03** 200
    Oatmeal Cookies, Peanut Butter-, **'81** 218; **'84** 72
    Oatmeal-Peanut Butter Chocolate Chip Cookies,
      '92 207
    Oatmeal-Peanut Butter Cookies, **'85** 171
    Olympic Medal Cookies, **'96** 180
    Peanut Blossom Cookies, **'95** 245; **'96** 55;
      '97 324
    Peanut Butter Cookies, **'82** 56; **'87** 58
    Quick Peanut Butter Cookies, **'86** 109; **'02** 229;
      '03 131
    Shortbread, Peanut Butter, **'95** 321
    Slice-and-Bakes, Peanut Butter, **'82** M185
    Snaps, Peanut Butter, **'81** 237
    Spooky Eyes, **'95** 273

Spooky Ghosts, '98 M256
Squares, Chocolate Chip-Peanut Butter, '84 118
Squares, Crispy Peanut, '01 M161
Squares, Peanut Butter, '83 116
Temptations, Peanut Butter, '84 29
Treats, Crispy Peanut Butter-Chocolate, '03 271
Truffle Cookies, Peanut, '93 212
Turtle Cookies, Peanut Butter-Toffee, '02 M325
Cooler, Peanut Butter, '84 115
Cracker Bites, Miniature Peanut Butter, '02 298
Cupcakes, Chocolate Surprise, '85 91
Delights, Choco-Peanut, '99 197
Dessert, Crunchy Peanut-Buttery, '92 204
Dessert, Peanut Butter, '92 164
Dessert, Rocky Road Pizza, '99 196
Dip, Indonesian, '96 190
Dip, Peanut Butter, '86 135; '01 109
Dip, Peanut Butter-Honey, '85 19
Dip, Peanut Butter Lovers', '93 162
Dough, Peanut Butter Fun, '00 171
Eclairs, Peanut Butter-Chocolate, '01 45
Filling, Peanut Butter, '96 229
Fingers, Peanut Butter, '79 256
French Toast, Peanut Butter, '93 166
French Toast, Peanut Butter and Jelly, '00 198
Frosting, Chocolate-Peanut Butter, '84 240; '87 222;
    '00 120
Frosting, Creamy Peanut, '80 87
Frosting, Peanut Butter, '83 223; '84 153; '85 34
Frosting, Peanut Butter-Fudge, '87 184
Frosting, Peanut Butter Swirl, '86 109
Frosts, Peanut Butter, '84 153
Frozen Peanut Butter Delight, '88 137
Grahams, Peanut Butter-Apple, '04 M183
Granola, Peanut Butter, '82 296
Hearts, Crispy Chocolate, '03 M41
Ice Cream, Chocolate Chunk-Peanut Butter, '85 297;
    '86 120
Ice Cream, Peanut Butter, '81 103; '88 64, 203;
    '00 143
Ice Cream Sandwiches, Peanut Butter Cookie,
    '93 199
Milkshakes, Peanut Butter, '85 198
Monster Mouths, '95 274
Mousse Parfaits, Chocolate-Peanut Butter, '98 71
Muffins, Jelly-Topped Peanut Butter, '96 279
Muffins, Peanut Butter, '80 86; '87 158; '99 111
Muffins, Peanut Butter-Banana, '03 195
Muffins, Peanut Butter-Chocolate Chip, '94 167
Muffins, Peanut Butter-Honey, '82 56
Napoleons, Peanut Butter-and-Chocolate, '94 121
Nuggets, Golden North Pole, '99 M309
Pancakes, Peanut Butter, '97 271
Parfait, Bodacious Peanut, '95 167
Parfaits, Crunchy Peanut Butter, '79 176; '80 6
Pastry Cream, Peanut Butter, '01 45
Pie, Chocolate-Peanut Butter, '85 91
Pie, Chocolate-Peanut Butter Ice Cream, '98 244
Pie, Chocolate-Peanut Butter Swirl, '87 262
Pie, Fluffy Peanut Butter, '94 246
Pie, Fudgy Peanut Butter Cup, '04 211
Pie, Peanut Butter, '85 275; '86 109; '89 252
Pie, Peanut Butter-Banana, '01 315
Pie, Peanut Butter Cream, '79 50; '88 65
Pie, Peanut Butter Meringue, '84 30
Pie, Tin Roof, '85 91
Pie, "Working for Peanuts," '93 115
Pinecones, Peanut Butter-Suet, '93 286
Pizza, Peanut Butter-Fruit, '94 60
Pudding, Chocolate-Peanut Butter Cookie, '03 183
Pudding, Peanut Butter, '85 95; '88 32; '00 27
Pudding, Peanut Butter-Banana, '93 340
Rollups, Peanut Butter, '99 103
Salad Dressing, Peanut Butter, '03 195

Salad, Thai Green Apple, '99 111
Sandwiches, Peanut Butter-and-Jelly "Fish," '91 177
Sandwiches, Peanut-Cheese-Raisin, '88 140
Sandwiches, Spider, '93 193
Sandwich, Peanut Butter Breakfast, '82 55
Sauce, Chocolate-Peanut Butter, '79 91, M156
Sauce, Hoisin Peanut Dipping, '99 14
Sauce, Pasta with Peanut, '95 252
Sauce, Peanut, '99 134; '02 173; '04 324
Sauce, Peanut Butter, '03 289
Sauce, Peanut Butter Barbecue, '81 233
Sauce, Peanut Butter Ice Cream, '84 30
Sauce, Spicy Peanut, '96 93; '04 134
Shake, PBJ, '93 292
Shake, Peanut Butter, '82 48
Shake, Peanut Butter-Banana, '97 172
Snacks, Chocolate-Peanut Butter, '90 226
Soup, Cream of Curried Peanut, '02 242
Soup, Cream of Peanut, '92 193; '93 288
Soup, Cream of Peanut Butter, '84 29
Soup, Creamy Peanut, '79 50
Soup, Peanut Butter, '89 28
Spread, Peanut Butter, '92 21; '96 90
Syrups, Banana Pancakes with Peanut Butter and
    Jelly, '01 24
Tarts, Chocolate-Peanut Butter, '92 277
Tarts, Peanut Butter, '97 329
Topping, Streusel, '03 195
Torte, Peanut Butter Turtle, '04 316
Trifle, Peanut Butter-Brownie, '03 200
Vinaigrette, Sesame-Soy, '97 180
Waffles, Honey-Buttered Peanut Butter, '94 M206
Wings and Ribs, Thai, '97 M225
PEANUTS
Appetizer, Fiery Cheese-and-Chutney, '04 177
Apples, Caramel-Peanut, '93 M244
Apples, Peanutty Stuffed, '85 25
Balls, Peanut-Date, '81 92
Bananas, Nutty, '79 251
Bars, Chewy Chocolate Cereal, '97 317
Bars, Chewy Peanut, '80 M172
Bars, Fruit and Nut Granola, '81 49
Bars, Peanut, '89 307
Beef Stir-Fry, Peanutty, '95 157
Bread, Peanut, '87 184
Bread, Peanut Lover's, '93 211
Cake, Chocolate-Caramel-Nut, '83 23
Cake, Chocolate-Peanut Cluster, '87 184
Cakes, Nutty, '89 50
Cake, Super Peanutty Layer, '83 222
Candies
Brittle, Chocolate-Dipped Peanut, '02 M223
Brittle, Classic Peanut, '02 M223
Brittle, Cooktop, '02 223
Brittle, Golden Peanut, '83 223
Brittle, Never-Fail Peanut, '79 273
Brittle, Orange Peanut, '80 302
Brittle, Peanut, '79 M263; '80 87; '84 298; '92 240
Brittle, Popcorn Peanut, '02 M223
Brittle with Crushed Peanuts, '87 184
Chocolate Nut Teasers, '91 35
Chocolate-Peanut Crispies, '93 80
Clusters, Chocolate-Peanut, '81 16
Clusters, Nut, '81 254
Clusters, Peanut, '87 184; '92 288; '98 M282
Clusters, Peanutty, '83 143
Divinity, Peanut, '85 233; '87 M278
Filling, Nut, '91 35
Fudge, Butterscotch-Peanut, '98 M282
Fudge, Double Peanut, '85 91
Squares, Caramel-Peanut, '85 247
Toffee, Microwave Peanut, '04 M234
Celery, Nutty Stuffed, '03 184
Chesapeake Nuts, '93 269

Chicken, Ginger-Nut, '90 M33
Chicken, Peanut-Roasted, '01 107
Chicken Strips, Nutty, '99 111
Chicken with Peanuts, Oriental, '82 236
Cookies, Chocolate Chunk-Peanut, '04 125
Cookies, Chocolate-Peanut, '83 223
Cookies, Crisp Peanuttiest, '88 65
Cookies, Double Chocolate Chunk-Peanut, '04 125
Cookies, Fibber McGee, '95 72
Cookies, Oats-and-Peanut, '89 60
Cookies, Peanutty Oatmeal, '80 106; '83 95
Cookies, Salted Peanut, '87 92
Crunchy Munchies, '94 196
Crust, Peanut-Graham, '99 49
Crust, Peanut-Graham Cracker, '79 50
Crust, Sweet Potatoes with Peanut, '93 212
Dessert, Fudge-Peanut Ice Cream, '88 167
Dessert, Peanut-Chocolate, '80 86
Dressing, Lime-Peanut, '01 26
Dressing, Peanut-Ginger, '95 177
Dressing, Roast Turkey with Peanut, '79 283
Filling, Peanut, '93 211
Frosting, Creamy Peanut, '80 87
Fruit Dressing, Nutty, '88 68
Granola, Crunchy Peanut, '90 48
Granola, Superhero, '98 M206
Hearts, Crispy Chocolate, '03 M41
Hot Chili Nuts, '81 254
Hot Peanuts, '00 278
Ice Cream, Chocolate-Covered Peanut, '88 203
Ice Cream, Peanut, '92 132
Mix, Jalapeño Nut, '96 27
Mix, Nutty Snack, '92 22
Mix, Starry Snack, '00 329
Muffins, Peanut, '91 223
Okra, Nutty, '03 136
Pad Thai, '97 202
Pesto and Pasta, Spinach-Peanut, '93 212
Pesto, Thai Peanut, '98 145
Pie, Caramel-Nut Crunch, '94 244
Pie, Caramel-Peanut, '86 259
Pie, Peanut Raisin, '79 85
Pie, Peanutty Ice Cream, '82 56
Pie, "Working for Peanuts," '93 115
Polvorones, '00 123
Popcorn and Peanuts, Candied, '82 295
Popcorn Clusters, Caramel-Nut, '00 M223
Popcorn, Crazy Mixed-Up, '97 245
Popcorn, Oriental, '98 205
Power Munch, '96 180
Puff Nibbles, '84 191
Reindeer Food, Magic, '99 M309
Salad, Asian Peanut-and-Pasta, '03 127
Salad, Broccoli-Peanut, '92 35
Salad, Eight-Layer, '99 107
Salad, Green Bean-Peanut, '86 117
Salad, Nutty Cabbage, '87 42
Salad, Nutty Green, '87 168
Salad, Peanut-Apple, '80 5
Salad, Peanut-Noodle, '02 163
Salad, Peanutty Spicy Noodle, '04 72
Salad, Sweet Peanut-Chicken, '03 54
Sauce, Hot Indonesian Peanut, '93 211
Sauce, Peanut Dessert, '86 M251
Sauce, Peanut Hot, '86 305
Sauce, Pork Chops with Peanut, '83 29
Sauce, Shrimp with Peanut, '93 303
Sauce, Thai Dipping, '97 236
Sauce, Thai-Style Noodles with Peanut Basil,
    '98 133
Shortbread, Peanut-Toffee, '04 329
Slaw, Banana-Nut, '86 250
Slaw, Chinese Peanut, '93 212
Slaw, Nutty Cabbage, '88 218

PEANUTS
(continued)

Slaw, Peanut, '85 139
Slaw, Peanutty-Pear, '86 250
Snack Mix, Sweet 'n' Savory, '03 199
Snack, Toasted Cereal, '85 215
Soup, Chilled Peanut, '79 130
Soup, Creamy Peanut, '79 50
Soup, Peanut, '87 184; '00 325
Spiced Nuts, '91 M316
Spicy Nuts, '82 161
Spread, Cheddar-Swiss, '99 106
Sugar-and-Spice Peanuts, '04 197
Sugared Peanuts, '82 249

PEARS
Amaretto Pears with Meringue, '90 M58
Appetizers, Pear-Pecan, '96 262
Apples 'n' Pears, Saucy, '96 72
Baked Apples and Pear, Honey-, '97 303
Baked in Molasses-Port Sauce, Pears, '97 195
Baked Pears à la Mode, '95 129
Baked Pears Elegant, '91 48
Baked Pears, Honey-, '93 47
Belle Helene, Pears, '86 164
Braised Red Cabbage and Pears, '01 298
Bread, Pear, '80 218
Cake, Caramel-Glazed Pear, '02 196
Cake, Ginger-Pear Upside-Down, '97 205
Cake, Pear Preserve, '85 52
Cake, Pear Preserves, '00 139
Cakes with Praline Sauce, Pear, '96 284
Cake, Upside-Down Sunburst, '87 9
Cake with Caramel Drizzle, Pear, '86 247
Cheesecake, Pear-Berry, '82 141
Cheesecake, Pear-Glazed, '79 67
Chicken and Pears, Glazed, '99 21
Chutney, Sunny Pear, '01 281
Cobbler, Best Ever Pear, '82 194
Cobbler, Ginger-Pear, '03 232
Cobbler, Pear-Ginger, '01 214
Cobbler with Oatmeal Muffin Crust, Caramel Apple-
    Pear, '04 201
Coconut Pears, Spicy, '83 207
Compote, Pear-Cranberry, '02 196
Cookies, Pear Mincemeat, '84 264
Cream, Pears in Orange, '84 245
Crème Chantilly, Holiday Pears with, '91 297
Crème de Menthe Pears, '94 50
Crisp, Cranberry-Pear, '83 207; '97 16
Crisp, Pear, '02 M233
Crisp, Raspberry-Pear, '89 109
Crostini, Pear-and-Gorgonzola, '02 314
Crumble, Pear, '85 221
Dressing, Pear, '83 146
Dumplings, Pear, '97 210
en Croute, Pears, '93 210
Flaming Pears, '84 313
Fritters, Ol' Timey Pear, '86 51
Gingered Pears, '89 M231
Gratin, Pear-Blue Cheese, '93 328
Honey, Gingered Pear, '97 62
Meringues, Baked Pear, '85 232
Muffins, Pear-Ginger, '91 240
Muscadine Sauce, Pears in, '88 216
Orange-Caramel Sauce, Pears with, '95 281
Pan-Roasted Pears, Beef Tenderloin with, '02 197
Pies
    Apple-Pear Pie, '83 249
    Apple-Pear Pull-Up Pie, '98 259
    Apple Pie, Natural Pear-, '88 226
    Backyard Pear Pie, '93 237
    Cheddar-Pear Pie, '02 197

Crumble Pie, Pear, '83 207
Deep-Dish Pear Pie, '80 219
Delicious Pear Pie, '88 226
Double-Crust Pear Pie, '82 194
French Pear Pie, '87 213
Fried Pies, Dried Cherry-and-Pear, '00 213
Ginger-Pear Pie, '93 48
Macadamia Pie, Pear-, '93 260
Mincemeat Pie, Pear, '84 264; '88 226
Mincemeat Pie, Pear, '98 258
Mince Pie, Pear-, '81 271
Praline Pie, Pear-, '97 192
Rhubarb-Raspberry Pear Pie, '95 119
Streusel Pie, Pear, '83 234; '84 244; '97 109
Tennessee Pear Pie, '85 230
Poached
Belle Helene, Pears, '86 164
Blue, Pears, '99 246
Caramel Sauce, Poached Pears with White, '99 28
Champagne-Poached Pears, '01 289
Curried Poached Pears with Coconut-Chicken
    Salad, '97 93
Custard, Poached Pears in, '88 20
Dark Chocolate Sauce, Poached Pears with,
    '90 M141
Honey-Yogurt Sauce, Poached Pears with, '92 306
Lemon Poached Pears, '82 74
Orange Poached Pears, '80 218
Orange-Poached Pears Flambé, '85 313
Orange Sauce, Poached Pears in, '82 19
Raspberry-Orange Sauce, Poached Pear Fans
    with, '88 22
Raspberry Sauce, Poached Pears with, '84 213;
    '87 69; '88 223
Red Wine, Pears in, '82 254
Red Wine, Pears Poached in, '83 302
Stewed Pears, '98 280
Vanilla Poached Pears, '90 57
Wine-Poached Pears, '98 230
Wine, Poached Pears in, '82 194
Wine-Poached Pears with Berry Sauce, '86 144
Pork Chops with Pears, Rosemary-Crusted, '01 316
Preservation
Butter, Pear, '85 130
Butter, Spiced Pear, '80 218
Chutney, Hot-and-Spicy Cranberry-Pear, '00 255
Chutney, Pear, '95 251; '98 243
Chutney, Pear-Apple, '89 141
Honey, Pear, '90 159
Jam, Paradise Pear, '84 300
Jam, Spiced Pear, '98 214
Marmalade, Pear, '79 196
Mincemeat, Pear, '79 196; '84 264; '88 226
Peaches and Pears, '85 106
Pickles, Mustard Pear, '79 196
Preserves, Pear, '82 195
Relish, Aunt Glennie's Pear, '95 305
Relish, Pear, '79 196
Relish, Peppery Pear, '89 141
Pudding, Lemon-Pear, '96 283
Puree, Grapefruit with Pear-Berry, '89 213
Relish, Cranberry-Pear, '85 232
Salads
Blue Cheese-Pear-Apple Salad, '81 224
Bluegrass Salad, '02 255
Celery Salad, Pear-and-, '87 56
Crunchy Pear Salad, '83 234; '84 244
Festive Fruit Salad, '80 16
Fresh Pear Salad with Asian Sesame Dressing,
    '02 196
Golden Pear Salad, '91 58
Harvest Salad with Cider Vinaigrette, '99 322
Jícama, and Snow Pea Salad, Pear, '01 329
Jícama and Snow Peas, Pear Salad with, '01 56

Lime Salad, Pear-, '84 152
Orange-Pear Salad, '84 164
Pineapple-Pear Delight, '82 54
Raspberry Cream, Pear Salad with, '00 311
Royal Pear Salad, '84 265
Sautéed Apples, Onions, and Pears over Spinach,
    '94 212
Slaw, Peanutty-Pear, '86 250
Slaw, "Think Pink," '94 247
Spinach Salad, Festive Pear-and-, '85 131
Spinach Salad with Sautéed Pears, '94 237
Swiss Cheese Salad, Pear-, '91 237
Wild Rice Salad, Pear-and-Cranberry, '03 199
Sauce, Apple-Pear, '97 M272
Sauce, Pear, '92 164
Sautéed Pears, '03 195
Shake, Strawberry-Pear, '92 139
Shortcakes, Ginger-Pear, '03 194
Side Dishes
Baked Pears, Honey-, '93 47
Bake, Pear-Oatmeal, '89 208
Blue Cheese Sauce, Brunch Pears with, '90 142
Breakfast Pears, Marmalade, '83 M203
Breakfast Treat, Pear, '87 72
Casserole, Pear-Sweet Potato, '86 280
Crème de Menthe Pears, '94 50
Filled Pears, Cheese-, '81 268
Glazed Pears, Orange-, '79 247
Oranges, Spicy Pears and, '89 305
Pineapple-Honey Pears, '86 94
Plate, Pretty Pear, '89 225
Ruby Pears, '81 288
Soda Pop Pears, '95 55
Spiced Fall Pears, '89 M231
Spiced Pears, '89 305
Stuffing, Acorn Squash with Pear, '01 293
Sugared Pears, Maple-, '81 232
Wild Rice, Cranberry-Pear, '83 279
Wine, Pears in Red, '82 254
Sorbet, Pear-Lemon, '88 116
Soup, Pumpkin-Pear, '92 234
Spread, Pear-Cream Cheese, '93 80
Strudel, Pear, '98 253
Stuffed Pears, Almond-, '83 207
Stuffed with Cheese, Pears, '82 290
Sundaes, Quick Pear, '86 71
Tart, Almond-Pear, '01 253
Tart, Pear, '82 304; '92 72
Tart with White Caramel Sauce, Pear, '92 195
Whip, Pear, '89 94
PEAS
Baked Peas, Chinese-Style, '86 305
Black-Eyed. *See also* **PEAS/Salads.**
    Best Ever Plain Ole Peas, '88 2
    Black-Eyed Peas, '93 180; '03 M49
    Bread, Black-Eyed Pea, '02 224
    Cajun Black-Eyed Peas, '96 218
    Cajun Peas, '88 3
    Cakes, Black-Eyed Pea, '01 32
    Casserole, Reunion Pea, '87 11
    Caviar, Texas, '86 218; '99 84; '01 160, 257
    Chinese Peas, '88 3
    con Queso, Black-Eyed Pea, '96 274
    Cornbread, Black-Eyed Pea, '98 44
    Cornbread, One-Dish Black-Eyed Pea,
        '03 215
    Creole Black-Eyed Peas, '86 252; '98 22
    Creole Black-Eyes and Rice, '85 6
    Delight, Tomato-Pea, '84 196
    Dinner, Black-Eyed Pea Skillet, '86 6
    Dip, Bill D's Black-Eyed Pea, '97 M89
    Dip, Black-Eyed Pea, '81 8; '04 M18
    Dip, Chili-and-Black-Eyed Pea, '92 155
    Easy Black-Eyed Peas, '99 204

Farmer's Beans and Rice with Rosemary Biscuits,
    '99 16
Flips, Pea, '80 7
Fresh Black-Eyed Peas, '81 M165
Gravy, Black-Eyed Pea, '87 12
Ham Hocks, Black-Eyed Peas with, '79 122;
    '89 16
Hearty Black-Eyed Peas, '85 7; '00 22; '02 107
Hopping Good Peas, '80 7
Hopping John, '80 7; '90 12; '96 272
Hopping John, Skillet, '79 10
Hopping John Stuffing, Pork Roast with, '01 25
Hopping John with Grilled Pork Medaillons,
    '93 229
Hopping John with Ham, '81 7
Hoppin' John, '02 271
Hoppin' John Waffle Stack, '04 19
Hoppin' John with Scallion Hoe Cake
    Medaillons, Skillet, '02 326
Hummus, Black-Eyed Pea, '94 123; '03 60
Jalapeño Black-Eyed Peas, '88 166
Jambalaya, Black-Eyed Pea, '92 70
Jambalaya, Good Luck, '87 11
Marinated Black-Eyed Peas, '82 156; '88 101;
    '01 30
Mexican Black-Eyed Peas, '84 327
Mexicano, Black-Eyed Peas, '79 10
Mexi-Peas, '88 3
Michelle's Black-Eyed Peas, '03 16
Passion Peas, '89 17
Pâté, Black-Eyed Pea, '91 12; '93 97
Pickled Black-Eyed Peas, '79 10; '01 30
Pinwheels, Black-Eyed Pea, '85 300; '86 18
Potatoes, Black-Eyed Pea-Spinach-Stuffed, '95 22
Quick Black-Eyed Peas and Ham, '00 336
Relish, Zesty Black-Eyed Pea, '95 56
Rice, Black-Eyed Peas with, '83 12; '90 208;
    '91 13
Rice with Black-Eyed Peas, '93 66
Salad, Black-Eyed Pea-and-Sweet Potato, '01 198
Salsa, Black-Eyed Pea, '93 164
Salsa, Chunky Black-Eyed Pea, '01 333
Sausage, Black-Eyed Peas with, '86 7
Seasoned Black-Eyed Peas, '85 138
Soup, Beefy Black-Eyed, '85 6
Soup, Black-Eyed Pea, '97 213
Soup, New Year's Day, '00 25
Southern-Style Black-Eyed Peas, '82 107
South-of-the-Border Black-Eyed Peas, '86 7
Spaghetti, Black-Eyed Pea, '81 7
Special, Black-Eyed Pea, '86 7
Spicy Black-Eyed Peas, '92 23
Spicy Black-Eyed Peas, Hot-and-, '84 9; '99 235
Spicy Hot Black-Eyed Peas, '81 8
Spicy-Hot Black-Eyed Peas, '90 135
Spread, Black-Eyed Pea, '86 77
Stew, Collard, '02 17
Stew, Collard 'n' Black-Eyed Pea, '04 24
Stew, Ham-and-Black-Eyed Pea, '93 20
Stew with Rice, Black-Eyed Pea, '04 19
Sweet-and-Sour Black-Eyed Peas, '85 290
Sweet-and-Sour Peas, '88 3
Tasty Black-Eyed Peas, '89 68
Vinaigrette, Black-Eyed Pea, '86 7
Casserole, Curry Pea, '87 154
Couscous with Peas and Feta, '01 158
Crowder Peas, Peppered Tuna with, '00 159
Crowder Peas, Spinach with, '00 159
Dip, Corn-and-Field Pea, '01 177
English. *See also* **PEAS/Salads.**
    Baked Tuna and Peas in Wine Sauce, '83 196
    Braised Belgian Endive and Peas, '93 22
    Braised Rice and Peas, '79 101
    Broil, Tomato-English Pea, '83 192

Buttered Peas and Mushrooms, '82 204
Buttered Peas with Onions, '80 242
Carrots and Peas, Mint-Glazed, '90 291
Casserole, Asparagus-and-English Pea, '86 324
Casserole, Asparagus and Peas, '80 152
Casserole, Asparagus-Pea, '88 M294
Casserole, Cauliflower-Pea, '85 260
Casserole, Cheesy English Pea, '83 216
Casserole, English Pea-Pimiento, '83 207
Casserole, Quick Fresh English Pea, '84 145
Casserole Supreme, Pea, '82 281; '83 32
Cauliflower and Peas with Curried Almonds,
    '79 221; '80 82
Cauliflower, Peas and, '82 288
Celery, Deluxe Peas and, '81 267
Celery, Peas and, '93 289
Company Green Peas, '91 31
Continental, Peas, '84 254
Country-Style Peas, '80 101
Country Style, Peas, '81 101
Creamed Peas and New Potatoes, '79 102
Creole Peas, Quick, '84 123
Curried Peas with Almonds, '88 M294
Deluxe English Peas, '84 68
Deviled Peas in Toast Cups, '86 280
Dumplings, Green Peas and, '80 102
Glazed English Peas, '83 111
Italian Peas, '81 83
Lettuce Peas, French, '86 62
Medley, English Pea, '85 236
Medley, Spring Pea, '83 141
Minted Peas, '83 141; '87 56
Mushrooms, Creamy Peas with, '84 196
Mushrooms, English Peas with, '98 286
Mushrooms, Green Peas with, '80 101
Mushrooms, Peas and, '83 141
Onions Stuffed with Peas, '84 68
Orange-Ginger Peas, '04 294
Orange Sauce, Green Peas in, '88 97
Party Peas, '79 102
Pasta, Peas and, '99 68
Perfection, Peas to, '94 321
Pignoli, Peas, '83 190
Potatoes with Dill, Peas and, '99 67
Potato Nest, Peas in a, '84 M239
Rice, Cashew Fried, '99 171
Rice, Holiday Peas and, '86 328
Rice, Peas and, '88 97
Rice with Green Peas, '87 45
Risotto with Shellfish and Peas, '96 131
Sauce, Green Pea, '83 22
Sautéed Peas and Bacon, '89 331
Scallions, Peas and, '80 101
Sherry, Peas with, '80 102
Soup, Chilled Pea, '84 181
Soup, Cold Curried Pea, '91 120
Soup Elégante, Pea, '79 53
Soup, English Pea, '96 56
Soup, Fresh Pea, '86 181
Soup, Mardi Gras, '96 56
Soup, Pea, '99 67
Soup, Peppery Pea, '82 271
Soup, Potato-Pea, '94 90
Soup, Spring Pea, '88 M96
Special Peas, '88 97; '95 133
Field Pea Patties, '00 158
Field Peas and Spinach, '99 169
Field Peas, Okra, and Corn Combo, '01 214
Green Peas with Crispy Bacon, '04 60
Ham, Southern Peas and, '85 138
Hoppin' John, Esau's, '03 17
Medley, Peas-and-Corn, '85 138
Mess of Peas, A, '00 158
Pasta, Peas and, '93 139

Peppery Peas O' Plenty, '04 34
Pigeon Peas, Rice with, '92 157
Pink-Eyed Pea Salsa, '00 158
Rice and Peas, Caribbean, '02 275
Salads
    Asparagus Salad, Peas-and-, '83 141
    Black-Eyed Pea Salad, '80 112; '86 225;
        '88 92, 221; '90 173; '95 203; '97 305; '98 52;
        '99 174
    Black-Eyed Pea Salad, Black Bean and, '03 54
    Black-Eyed Pea Salad, Fearrington House Goat
        Cheese and, '95 60
    Black-Eyed Pea Salad, Marinated, '93 190
    Black-Eyed Pea Salad, Overnight, '81 280
    Black-Eyed Pea Salad with Benedictine Dressing,
        '98 83
    Black-Eyed Peas, Zesty, '89 147
    Black-Eyed Salad, Hot Bacon and, '85 7
    Cauliflower and Pea Salad, Savory, '81 280
    Cauliflower-Pea Salad, '87 231
    Cheddar-Pea Salad, '84 82
    Chicken-and-Black-Eyed Pea Salad, '97 305
    Chicken-Pea Salad, '83 218
    Chilled Dilly Peas, '90 143
    Corn-and-Pea Salad, '90 181
    Creamy Pea Salad, '80 111
    Crunchy Pea Salad, '90 143; '00 103
    Dilled Pea Salad, '97 305; '98 18
    Dilled Peas-and-Potatoes Vinaigrette, '01 327
    English Pea-and-Apple Salad, '87 24
    English Pea Salad, '81 280; '90 143
    English Pea Salad, Cauliflower-, '95 66
    English Pea Salad, Lettuce-, '91 208
    English Pea Salad, Marinated, '82 54
    Field Pea Salad, Mixed, '00 325
    Green Pea Salad, '96 88
    Hoppin' John Salad, '96 64; '01 250
    Marinated Pea Salad, '81 204
    Mexi-Pea Salad, '81 7
    Minted Pea Salad, '91 119
    Pasta Salad, Ham-and-Pea, '00 217
    Pea Salad, '98 274
    Plentiful P's Salad, '87 12
    Rice-Pea Salad, '85 163
    Snow Pea Salad, Pear, Jícama, and, '01 329
    Snow Peas, Pear Salad with Jícama and, '01 56
    Special Peas, '95 133
    Special Pea Salad, '83 239
    Sugar Snap Pea Salad, '86 115
    Three Pea Salad, '84 290
Snow. *See also* **PEAS/Salads.**
    Basil Snow Peas and Tomatoes, '88 M185
    Beef and Snow Peas, Oriental, '79 105
    Beef with Pea Pods, Oriental, '86 M328
    Cashew Pea Pods, '92 343
    Chicken with Snow Peas, '83 137
    Chinese Peas, Easy, '83 206
    Crunchy Snow Peas and Dip, '86 62
    en Papillote, Fish with Snow Peas, '86 144
    Medley, Cauliflower-Snow Pea, '87 305
    Peas and Snow Peas, '88 67
    Peppers, Minted Peas and, '90 M99
    Pineapple, Snow Peas and, '91 120
    Piquant, Snow Peas, '79 21
    Red Pepper, Snow Peas with, '90 102
    Sesame Snow Peas and Red Pepper, '84 175
    Shrimp Combo, Snow Pea-, '79 57
    Shrimp with Snow Peas, '85 75
    Skillet Snow Peas with Celery, '84 123
    Slaw, Zesty, '97 324
    Stir-Fried Peas and Peppers, '87 51
    Stir-Fry, Beef and Pea, '82 98
    Stir-Fry Beef and Pea Pods, '80 19
    Stir-Fry, Beef and Snow Pea, '82 98

PEAS, Snow
(continued)

    Stir-Fry Beef and Snow Peas, **'83** 22
    Stir-Fry, Chicken and Snow Pea, **'95** 157
    Stir-Fry, Potato-Snow Pea, **'86** 173
    Stuffed Snow Peas, **'84** 80
    Stuffed Snow Peas, Crab-, **'85** 288
    Tomatoes, Snow Peas and, **'83** 111
Soup, Country-Style Pea, **'86** 267
Soup, Cream Pea, **'90** 211
Soup, French Market, **'94** 317
Soup Mix, French Market, **'94** 317
Soup, Oven-Baked Split Pea-and-Lentil, **'00** 316
Soup, Pea-and-Watercress, **'93** 162
Soup, Split Pea, **'88** 235; **'89** 17; **'90** 198; **'94** 322
Soup, Split Pea and Frankfurter, **'79** 64
Sugar Snap
    Appetizers, Sugar Snap Pea, **'86** 115
    Basil and Lemon, Sugar Snap Peas with, **'93** 66
    Bell Peppers, Sugar Snap Peas with, **'03** 255
    Champagne Dressing, Sugar Snap Peas with, **'99** 166
    Creamed Sugar Snaps and Carrots, **'93** 139
    Dilled Peas and Potatoes Vinaigrette, **'00** 102
    Dip, Sugar Peas with, **'86** 170
    Dip, Sugar Snap, **'88** 91
    Goat Cheese, Sugar Snap Peas and, **'01** 112
    Lemon-Scented Sugar Snap Peas, **'02** 282
    Pearl Onions, Snap Peas and, **'89** 280
    Peppers, Sugar Snaps and, **'93** 139
    Pickled Sugar Snap Peas, **'01** 112
    Potato Salad with Sugar Snap Peas, **'91** 120
    Roasted Garlic Dressing, Snap Peas with, **'99** 269
    Steamed Sugar Snap Peas, **'99** 71; **'04** 81
    Vegetable Medley, Spring, **'86** 115
PECANS. *See also* **PRALINE.**
Acorn Squash with Molasses and Pecans, **'85** 205
Appetizers
    Ball, Date-Nut, **'92** 326
    Ball, Deviled Pecan, **'80** 258
    Ball, Party Pecan Cheese, **'81** 235
    Ball, Pecan Cheese, **'83** 127
    Ball, Pinecone Cheese, **'98** 265
    Balls, Date-Nut, **'85** 10
    Ball, Tuna-Pecan, **'87** 94
    Barbecued Pecans, **'83** 222
    Bites, Cheesy Pecan, **'82** 248
    Blue Cheese Logs, **'04** 53
    Brie, Kahlúa-Pecan, **'92** 289
    Brie with Brown Sugar and Nuts, **'03** 282
    Brown Sugar Pecans, **'81** 266
    Candied Nuts, **'81** 261
    Cheese Brick, **'99** 170
    Chesapeake Nuts, **'93** 269
    Chicken Fingers, Buttermilk-Pecan, **'93** 165
    Christmas Eve Pecans, **'91** 276
    Christmas Pecans, **'03** 300
    Citrusy Pecans, **'03** 292; **'04** 146
    Coffee 'n' Spice Pecans, **'88** 256
    Cranberry-Nut Triangles, **'04** 273
    Crisps, Blue Cheese, **'98** 285
    Curried Nuts, Spicy, **'82** 250
    Curried Pecans, **'91** 208
    Deviled Nuts, **'93** 118
    Glazed Pecans, **'81** 254; **'82** 136
    Grapes, Blue Cheese-Pecan, **'95** 48
    Greek Olive Cups, **'99** 221
    Honeycomb Pecans, **'84** 300
    Hot-and-Spicy Pecans, **'89** 161
    Hot Pepper Pecans, **'85** 4
    Hot Smoky Pecans, **'98** 173
    Log, Chicken-Pecan, **'81** 290

    Log, Roquefort Pecan, **'89** 247
    Log, Toasted Pecan Cheese, **'86** M288
    Mexico Nuts, **'01** 27
    Mix, Jalapeño Nut, **'96** 27
    Mushrooms, Pecan-Stuffed, **'84** 261
    Nippy Nuts, **'93** 301
    Orange-Glazed Pecans, **'97** 225
    Orange Nuts, Sherry-, **'86** M289
    Orange Pecans, **'84** 299; **'87** 292
    Pear-Pecan Appetizers, **'96** 262
    Pepper Pecans, **'87** 137; **'93** 79
    Pesto-Spiced Nuts, **'95** 173
    Popcorn Balls, Nutty, **'88** 227
    Quick Party Nuts, **'04** 197
    Roasted Bacon Pecans, **'96** 262
    Roasted Pecans, Creole, **'01** 241
    Rolls, Blue Cheese, **'00** 210
    Salted Pecans, Southern, **'80** 285
    Sandwiches, Olive Tea, **'02** 252
    Savory Southern Pecans, **'95** 240
    Shortbread, Jalapeño-Pecan, **'03** 108
    Smoky Pecans, **'01** 168
    Spiced Nuts, **'91** M316
    Spiced Pecans, **'79** 296; **'80** 31; **'81** 286
    Spicy Pecans, **'81** M289; **'93** 279; **'01** 206
    Spread, Carrot-Pecan, **'96** 108
    Spread, Nutty Carrot, **'94** 123
    Spread Sandwiches, Olive-Nut, **'04** 259
    Sticks, Pecan, **'01** 242
    Sugar and Spice Pecans, **'82** 297
    Sugar-and-Spice Pecans, **'86** 121; **'94** 272
    Sweet-and-Spicy Pecans, **'92** 321; **'00** 334; **'01** 20
    Tarts, Apricot-Pecan-Brie, **'97** 236
    Tarts, Toasty Southern Pecan, **'95** 329
    Toasted Chili Pecans, **'85** 154
    Toasted Pecans, **'84** 321; **'86** 229; **'03** 300
    Toasted Pecans, Buttery, **'88** 77
    Torte, Showstopping Appetizer, **'98** 319
    Wafers, Pecan-Cheese, **'81** 119
    Wafers, Sage-Pecan Cheese, **'93** 12
Apples, Caramel, **'03** M216
Apples, Orange-Pecan Baked, **'85** 45
Apples, Pecan-and-Dried Fruit Baked, **'03** 269
Apples, Taffy Pecan, **'99** 247
Balls, Orange-Nut, **'02** 297
Bars, Creamy No-Bake, **'97** 166
Biscuits, Elf, **'99** 309
Blueberry Yum Yum, **'98** 91
Bourbon Balls, **'02** 30
Bourbon-Pecan Alfredo, **'96** 291
Breads
    Apple-Nut Bread, **'85** 281
    Applesauce Nut Bread, **'81** 305
    Applesauce-Pecan Bread, **'90** 66
    Apricot-Nut Loaf, Tasty, **'82** 10
    Apricot-Pecan Bread, **'97** 266
    Banana-Nut Bread, **'86** 8, 70; **'04** 259
    Banana-Nut-Raisin Bread, **'81** 59
    Biscuit Braid, Apple-Pecan, **'02** 326
    Biscuit Bread, Brown Sugar, **'02** M224
    Biscuits, Nutty Tea, **'89** 210
    Biscuits, Peppered Pork with Pecan, **'01** 33
    Biscuits with Cinnamon Butter, Cinnamon-Pecan, **'01** 309
    Bourbon-Pecan Bread, **'93** 308; **'96** 27
    Buns, Nutty, **'86** 290
    Cheddar-Nut Bread, **'85** 41; **'03** 42
    Cherry Nut Bread, **'81** 306; **'82** 36
    Cherry-Nut Bread, Quick, **'85** 55
    Chocolate Date-Nut Bread, **'81** 284
    Coconut-Pecan Coils, **'90** 196
    Cornbread, Pecan, **'94** 169; **'98** 252
    Crescent Twists, Pecan, **'99** 47; **'03** 36
    Date-Nut Loaf, **'85** 10

French Toast, Caramel-Pecan, **'03** 328
Fritters, Broccoli-Cauliflower, **'02** 45
Kahlúa Fruit-Nut Bread, **'79** 235
Lemon-Pecan Bread, **'83** 54
Maple-Nut Coffee Twist, **'86** 290
Maraschino Cherry Nut Bread, **'79** 234
Mini-Cinnis, Mama's, **'02** 41
Monkey Bread Bites, **'04** 333
Muffin Batter, Pecan Pie, **'04** 200
Muffins, Banana-Nut, **'93** 140
Muffins, Cherry-Nut, **'90** 87
Muffins, Chunky Pecan, **'88** 9
Muffins, Cinnamon-Nut, **'85** M88
Muffins, Cinnamon-Pecan, **'84** 219
Muffins, Coffee Cake, **'98** 160
Muffins, Country Pecan, **'83** 222
Muffins, Cranberry-Pecan, **'84** 269
Muffins, Date, **'00** 239
Muffins, Date-Nut, **'99** 234
Muffins, Nutty Pumpkin, **'86** 291
Muffins, Orange-Pecan, **'83** 96; **'99** 56
Muffins, Pecan, **'80** 16
Muffins, Pecan-Orange, **'97** 163
Muffins, Pecan-Pie, **'01** 206
Muffins, Pecan Pie, **'04** 201
Muffins, Raisin-Nut, **'92** 46
Muffins, Raisin-Pecan Ginger, **'88** 9
Muffins, Rum-Nut, **'90** 87
Orange-Nut Bread, **'82** 75
Orange Nut Loaf, **'80** 226
Orange-Pecan Bread, **'79** 148
Orange-Pecan Bread, Glazed, **'81** 250
Orange-Pecan Loaves, **'79** 215
Persimmon Date-Nut Bread, **'82** 218
Pineapple-Nut Bread, **'79** 215
Pineapple-Pecan Loaf Bread, **'87** 256
Popovers, Giant Pecan, **'83** 208
Prune-Nut Bread, **'87** 255; **'91** 55
Pull-Away Bread, Cinnamon, **'98** 137
Pumpkin Muffins, **'04** 112
Pumpkin-Nut Bread, **'83** 294
Pumpkin-Pecan Bread, **'87** 221; **'02** 224
Roll, Banana-Nut, **'85** 112
Rolls, Buttered Rum-Nut, **'86** 291
Rolls, Caramel-Nut, **'86** 312
Rolls, Cinnamon-Pecan, **'98** 251
Rolls, Citrus-Pecan, **'03** 256
Rolls, Easy Cinnamon-Pecan, **'89** 307
Rolls, Oatmeal-Cinnamon-Pecan, **'96** 50
Rolls, Pecan, **'81** 62
Rolls, Pecan-Golden Raisin Sweet, **'03** 235
Scones, Merry Cranberry-Nut Yeast, **'99** 274
Scones, Mocha-Pecan, **'97** 45
Scones, Orange-Pecan, **'94** 215; **'01** 72
Strawberry-Nut Bread, **'79** 24
Whole Wheat Date-Nut Bread, **'04** 208
Whole Wheat Nut Bread, **'04** 208
Whole Wheat Raisin-Nut Bread, **'04** 208
Wine-Date Nut Bread, **'82** 253
Brittle, Chocolate, **'83** 315
Brittle, Microwave Pecan, **'97** M245
Brittle, Pecan, **'91** 272; **'02** M223
Broccoli with Lemon Sauce and Pecans, **'86** 71
Butter, Beehive, **'00** 68
Buttered Pecans, Green Beans with, **'92** 61
Butter, Jalapeño-Pecan-Mustard, **'03** 205
Butter, Orange-Pecan, **'84** 75; **'97** 15
Butter, Pecan, **'97** 307
Cakes
    Apple-Pecan Cake, **'92** 167
    Banana-Nut Cake, **'92** 120
    Banana Split Cake, **'99** 48
    Bourbon-Pecan Cake, **'84** 25
    Butter Brickle Loaf Cakes, **'98** 137

Butter Pecan Cake, '80 229
Butter Pecan Cake, Caramel-Filled, '88 278
Candy Bar Cake, '98 90
Carrot Cake, Pecan-, '99 223
Carrot Cake, Praline-Filled, '03 332
Cheesecake, Butter Pecan, '86 61
Cheesecake, Chocolate-Caramel-Pecan, '91 197
Cheesecake, Lemony Passover, '02 51
Cheesecake, Pecan, '85 38
Cheesecake, Pecan Pie, '02 318; '03 316
Cheesecake, Pecan Praline, '03 269
Cheesecake, Praline, '83 270; '89 93
Chocolate-Bourbon-Pecan Cake, '03 287
Chocolate-Nut Cake, Rich, '86 8
Chocolate-Praline Pecan Cake, '03 288
Cinnamon Swirl Cake, '01 255
Coffee Cake, Apple-Pecan, '84 242
Coffee Cake, Cinnamon-Pecan, '87 69
Coffee Cake, Nutty Orange, '95 160
Coffee Cake, Orange-Pecan, '86 86
Coffee Cake, Pecan-Topped, '81 41
Coffee Cake, Triple-Chocolate, '04 M299
Cupcakes, Apple-Nut, '82 279
Date Nut Cake, '79 176; '80 5
Dump Cake, Tropical, '02 128
Fruitcake, Sherry-Nut, '00 299
Fruitcake, White, '00 299
Funnel Cakes, Nutty, '91 233
Kentucky Pecan Cake, '84 263
Maple Nut Cake, '96 17
Mississippi Mud Cake, '04 136
Orange Date-Nut Cake, '01 285
Orange-Nut Butter Cake, '80 254
Orange Nut Cake, '80 70
Orange-Pecan Crunch Cake, '83 10
Pear Cake, Caramel-Glazed, '02 196
Pecan Cake, '97 256
Pie Cake, Pecan, '98 254; '03 316
Pineapple-Pecan Upside-Down Cake, '84 25
Pineapple Upside-Down Cake, Spiced, '02 214
Pound Cake, Bourbon-Pecan, '91 270
Pound Cake, Brown Sugar-Rum, '96 60
Pound Cake, Butterscotch-Pecan, '92 153
Pound Cake, Cream Cheese-Bourbon-Pecan,
    '04 280
Pound Cake, Cream Cheese-Coconut-Pecan,
    '04 280
Pound Cake, Eggnog-Pecan, '95 313
Pound Cake, Gentleman's, '00 287
Pound Cake, Marbled Pecan, '93 313
Pound Cake, Orange-Pecan, '93 13
Pound Cake, Orange-Pecan-Spice, '02 295
Pound Cake, Pecan, '01 253
Pound Cake, Praline, '82 88
Pound Cake, Sour Cream-Orange Pecan, '89 207
Praline Glaze, Pecan Cake with, '82 196
Praline Ice Cream Cake, '80 84
Roulade, Pecan, '87 183
Roulage, Toffee-Pecan, '94 312
Shortcake, Banana-Pecan, '93 43
Sweet Potato Cake with Citrus Filling, '02 221
Candy, Chocolate-Nut Log, '86 335
Candy, Cola, '02 298
Candy, Divinity, '01 271
Caramel Corn, Nutty, '92 317
Caramelized Onion-and-Pecan Brussels Sprouts,
    '99 254
Caramel O's, '99 196
Caramel-Pecan Triangles, '99 281
Carrots and Celery with Pecans, '84 254
Cassata, '01 125
Casserole, Carrot-Pecan, '93 44; '98 231; '02 282
Catfish, Crispy, '03 101
Catfish Pecan, '85 53

Catfish, Pecan, '98 329
Catfish Pecan with Lemon-Thyme-Pecan Butter,
    '04 68
Catfish with Lemon Sauce, Pecan, '03 185
Cheese, Pecan Pimiento, '01 169; '03 315
Chicken, Buttermilk-Pecan, '89 166; '97 252
Chicken Drummettes, Orange-Pecan, '93 158
Chicken, Honey-Pecan, '03 147
Chicken, Lemony Pecan, '96 82
Chicken, Nutty Oven-Fried, '85 160
Chicken, Oven-Fried Pecan, '84 288
Chicken, Pecan, '90 54; '99 332
Chicken Thighs, Honey-Pecan, '02 127
Chocolate Date-Nut Delight, '88 168
Clusters, Pecan, '81 266; '98 305
Clusters, Pecan-Coconut, '86 M251
Clusters, Roasted Pecan, '85 233; '90 310; '03 315
Clusters, Toasted Pecan, '00 M14
Coating, Salmon Bake with Pecan-Crunch, '95 209
Cobbler, Apple-Pecan, '84 M198
Cobbler, Apple-Pecan Pie, '04 200
Cobbler, Blueberry-Pecan, '00 154; '03 106
Cobbler, Pecan-Peach, '04 120
Coffee, Praline-Flavored, '87 69
Cookies
    Bars, Butter Pecan Turtle, '90 70
    Bars, Gooey Pecan, '94 133
    Bars, Pecan, '82 209
    Biscotti, Orange-Pecan, '01 207
    Brownie Mix, Blond, '01 247
    Brownies, Caramel-Pecan Filled, '03 M43
    Brownies, Chocolate-Glazed, '01 143
    Brownies, Chocolate-Pecan, '81 64
    Brownies, Coconut-Pecan-Frosted, '97 99
    Brownies, Double-Chocolate, '04 100
    Brownies, Layered, '02 M252
    Brownies, Nutty Blonde, '81 64
    Brownies, Nutty Cocoa, '81 64
    Brownies, Nutty Fudge, '80 M171
    Brownies, Praline, '93 243
    Brown Sugar-Pecan Cookies, '91 236
    Butter Cookies, Pecan-, '83 113
    Butter Pecan Cookies, '82 139
    Butter Pecan Shortbread Cookies, '80 282
    Butterscotch-Pecan Cookies, '84 36
    Cheese Crispies, Pecan-, '87 168
    Cherry Nut Nuggets, '81 286
    Cherry Pecan Cookies, '82 136
    Chocolate Chubbies, '01 144
    Chocolate Cookies, Chewy, '97 166
    Chocolate-Nut Chews, '81 92
    Chocolate-Nut Freezer Cookies, '88 217
    Cinnamon Cookies, GrandLady's, '00 323
    Crescent Cookies, Pecan, '85 324; '97 274
    Crescents, Pecan, '04 284
    Crispies, Pecan, '99 337
    Cupcake Cookies, '04 273
    Date Balls, '01 90
    Easy Pecan Cookies, '80 208
    English Rocks, '01 295
    Fruitcake Cookies, '98 294
    Fudge-Pecan Chewies, Alabama, '95 143
    Graham Cracker Layered Cookies, '98 94
    Icebox Cookies, Cinnamon Chip, '01 308
    Lemon-Pecan Cookies, '02 293
    Lemon Pecan Dainties, '80 208
    Oatmeal-Chocolate Chip Cookies, Nutty, '82 185
    Oatmeal-Chocolate Chunk Cookies, Nutty,
        '01 19
    Oatmeal Cookies, Nutty, '81 130
    Oatmeal Nut Crispies, '80 208
    Orange-Pecan Cookies, '88 119
    Pfeffernïesse, '01 65
    Pie Cookies, Pecan, '92 289; '00 290

Praline-Chocolate Chip Cookies, Crispy, '02 229;
    '03 131
Praline Cookies, '91 271
Praline Cookies, Crispy, '02 229; '03 131
Praline Shortbread Cookies, '88 242
Praline Thumbprint Cookies, '89 328
Sandies, Basil-Pecan, '97 166
Sand Tarts, '00 323
Scotch Bars, Chewy, '98 M291
Shells, Pecan Lace, '97 167
Shortbreads, Pecan-Cornmeal, '04 230
Squares, Butter Pecan Pie, '81 262
Squares, Congo, '96 94
Squares, Easy Pecan, '81 230
Squares, Lemon-Pecan, '89 124
Squares, Pecan, '79 205; '90 69; '98 336; '04 271
Squares, Twice-Baked Pecan, '79 291
Sticks, Crispy Pecan, '00 258
Sugar Pecan Crisps, '86 230
Sugarplum Sticks, '95 321
Wedding Cookies, '00 332
    White Chocolate Chip-Oatmeal Cookies, '04 43
Cornmeal Rounds, Pecan-, '95 99
Crunch, Apple-Nut, '82 M238
Crunchy Munchies, '94 196
Cupcakes, Apple-Nut, '82 279
Dessert, Maple Nut, '81 84
Dessert, Nutty Fudgy Frozen, '94 28
Dessert, Turtle, '04 127
Divinity, Mrs. Floyd's, '00 315
Dressing, Andouille Sausage, Apple, and Pecan,
    '02 249
Dressing, Chicken with Pecan-Rice, '85 M57
Dressing, Cornbread, Sausage, and Pecan, '99 257
Dressing, Crabmeat-and-Oyster, '02 243
Dressing, Fruit-and-Pecan, '84 252
Dressing, Honey-Pecan, '03 28
Dressing, Louise's Cornbread, '03 251
Dressing, Mess o' Greens Salad with Warm Pecan,
    '98 250
Dressing, Pecan, Rice, and Crawfish, '00 252
Dressing, Pecan-Sage, '80 262
Dressing, Watermelon Salad with Celery-Nut,
    '80 182
Dumplings, Spiced Peaches with Nutty, '87 164
Eggs, Pecan-Stuffed, '80 78
Eggs, Pecan-Stuffed Deviled, '04 93
Fettuccine, Chicken-Pecan, '86 52
Filling, Cranberry-Pecan, '04 305
Filling, Fruit-Nut, '80 289
Filling, Nut, '91 35
Filling, Nutty Fruit, '99 306
Filling, Pecan, '04 305
Filling, Pecan Pie, '98 254; '03 316
Fritters, Chocolate-Covered Pecan, '79 205
Frosting, Banana-Nut, '79 115
Frosting, Butter Pecan, '80 229
Frosting, Cherry-Nut Cream Cheese, '96 249
Frosting, Chocolate Nut, '80 140
Frosting, Coconut-Pecan, '81 296; '83 M233;
    '84 43, 322; '97 99; '03 289
Frosting, Cream Cheese-Butter Pecan, '03 288
Frosting, Divinity, '01 270
Frosting, Nutty Coconut, '86 8
Frosting, Nutty Cream Cheese, '85 117; '96 263
Frosting, Pecan, '86 86
Frosting, Pecan-Cream Cheese, '02 294
Fruit Compote, Warm Praline, '85 260
Fudge, Buttermilk, '97 317
Fudge, Cherry Nut, '83 315
Fudge, Creamy Pecan, '84 321
Fudge, Nutty White, '81 253
Fudge-Peanut Butter Chewies, '98 215
Fudge, Quick Nut, '83 316

PECANS

(continued)

Garnish, Pastry, '98 254; '03 317
Glaze, Buttered Rum, '03 94
Glazed Nuts, '88 222
Glazed Pecan Halves, '02 295
Glaze, Honey-Nut, '87 15
Glaze, Praline, '82 196
Goose, Fruit- and Pecan-Stuffed, '83 268
Grahams, Praline, '92 239
Granola, Nutty, '90 95
Granola, Pecan-Coconut, '02 70
Green Beans, '97 263
Green Beans, Lemon-Pecan, '04 285
Green Beans, Nutty, '88 M187
Ham, Praline, '85 302; '96 303
Ice Cream, Banana-Nut, '00 143
Ice Cream, Bourbon-Pecan, '00 260
Ice Cream, Butter Pecan, '80 176; '86 129; '88 202
Ice Cream, Butter-Pecan, '96 134
Ice Cream, Cherry-Nut, '86 129
Ice Cream, Cherry-Pecan, '88 203
Ice Cream, Pecan-Caramel Crunch, '02 322
Ice Cream, Praline, '89 318
Ice Cream, Pralines and Cream, '82 184; '83 159
Ice Cream, Straw-Ba-Nut, '80 177
Ice Cream, Strawberry-Banana-Nut, '88 203
Millionaires, '97 M55
Mousse, Butter Pecan, '95 286
Onion Flowers with Pecans, Grilled, '96 217
Onions with Pecans and Roasted Carrots, Roasted
  Vidalia, '92 340
Orange Pecans, '84 299; '87 292
Pancakes, Pecan, '03 305
Pancakes, Toasted Pecan, '99 43
Penuche, Coffee, '98 305
Pesto, '00 118
Pesto, Cilantro-Pecan, '04 36
Pesto, Garden, '04 186
Pies and Pastries
  Baklava, '96 20
  Bourbon-Chocolate Pecan Pie, '98 258
  Bourbon-Pecan Pie, '85 90
  Bourbon-Pecan Pie, Frozen, '89 251
  Bourbon-Pecan Pumpkin Pie, '87 264
  Caramel-Pecan Apple Pie, '85 247
  Caramel-Pecan Pie, '88 282
  Cherry-Pecan Pie, '92 30
  Chess Pie, Chocolate-Pecan, '00 60; '02 107
  Chocolate-Banana-Pecan Cream Pie, '94 210
  Chocolate Fudge Pie, '98 336
  Chocolate-Pecan Chess Pie, '93 251
  Chocolate Pecan Pie, '80 237; '83 12; '90 184
  Chocolate-Pecan Pie, '91 272; '02 176
  Chocolate-Praline Pie, '86 259
  Choco-Pecan Pie, '82 86
  Cinnamon-Almond-Pecan Pie, '98 89
  Coconut-Pecan Chess Pie, '81 248
  Coconut Pecan Pie, '81 161
  Coffee Pecan Pie, '82 74
  Cranberry-Pecan Crusts, '02 198
  Cranberry-Pecan Pie, '92 316
  Cranberry Pie, Nutty, '82 298
  Crust, Nutty Oat, '89 251
  Crust, Pecan, '86 317; '89 291; '98 180
  Crust, Spiced Nut, '87 295
  Custard Pecan Pie, '87 184
  Date-Pecan Pie, '80 15
  Golden Pecan Pie, '81 266
  Grandmother's Pecan Pie, '86 269
  Holiday Pecan Pie, '81 296
  Honey-Pecan Finger Pies, '90 184

Hot Fudge Sauce, Pecan Pie with, '01 306
Ice Cream Pie, Nutty, '91 180
Individual Pecan Pies, '85 295
Layered Pecan Pie, '83 305
Lemon-Pecan Pie, '93 251
Louisiana Pecan Pie, '92 83
Maple-Pecan Pie, '81 266
Maverick Lunar Pie, '98 111
Mincemeat Ice Cream Pie, '99 285
Miniature Pecan Pies, '79 205; '86 13
Mississippi Pecan Pie, '98 146
Mocha Pecan Mud Pie, '00 245
Molasses-Pecan Pie, '86 259
Mom's Pecan Pie, '02 249
Mystery Pecan Pie, '02 249
Old-Fashioned Pecan Pie, '81 M269
Orange-Pecan Pie, '79 282; '83 222
Orzo-Pecan Pie, Honeyed, '04 219
Peach Praline Pie, '89 136
Pecan Pie, '79 251; '80 57; '85 255; '90 312;
  '92 234; '98 275; '01 244
Praline Pastries, '89 318
Praline-Topped Pumpkin Pie, '00 332
Pumpkin-Pecan Pie, '85 233, 282
Pumpkin Pie, Nutty, '82 67
Raisin-Pecan Pie, '87 213
Shell, Pecan Pastry, '97 275; '98 36
Simmie's Pecan Pie, '00 254
Special, Old Pecan Street, '93 251
Spicy Pecan Pie, '84 240
Strudel, Autumn-Apple, '98 253
Sweet Potato-Pecan Pie, '83 90
Tart, Apricot-Nut, '99 249
Tart, Fudge Truffle-Pecan, '99 315; '02 208
Tart, Honey-Pecan, '99 212
Tartlets, Kentucky Derby, '00 107
Tartlets, Zamaani's Nutty Yam, '02 21
Tarts, Apple-Pecan, '80 282
Tarts, Bourbon-Chocolate-Pecan, '96 264
Tarts, Easy Pecan, '84 313
Tarts, Pecan, '81 266
Tarts, Special Pecan, '87 224
Tart with Caramel Sauce, Chocolate-Pecan,
  '93 296; '94 234
Tart with Praline Cream, Pecan, '90 256
Tassies, Teatime, '84 321
Texas Pecan Pie, '83 159
Texas Star Pecan Pie, '90 184
Tiny Pecan Pies, '79 225
Turtle Pecan Pie, '93 250
Vanilla Custard, Pecan Pie with Chilled, '00 331
Popcorn Balls, Nutty, '88 227
Popcorn, Crazy Mixed-Up, '97 245
Popcorn, Spicy Nut, '02 287
Popcorn, Trick or Treat, '03 210
Popovers, Pecan, '01 206
Pork, Cajun Pecan, '01 27
Pork Chops, Honey-Pecan, '01 82
Pork Chops with Beer Sauce, Pecan-Breaded,
  '95 266
Pork Chops with Pecans and Apples, Commune's
  Maple-Glazed, '04 102
Pork Loin, Apricot-Pecan Stuffed, '94 274
Pork Loin Roast, Festive, '03 255
Praline Freeze, '89 60; '90 48
Praline Pecans, '97 285
Pudding, Brown Sugar-Pecan, '86 M165
Pudding, Pecan-Mocha, '89 M130
Pudding with Hot Rum Sauce, Apple-Nut, '79 86
Quad, Chocolate, '02 272
Quiche, Chicken-Pecan, '91 206
Rice, Island, '98 276
Rice, Nutted, '85 269
Rice, Orphan's, '03 32; '04 218

Rice, Pecan, '85 53; '04 204
Rice, Shrimp-and-Scallop Sauté with Pecan, '90 317
Rice, Speedy Skillet Pecan, '04 328
Roll, Date Nut, '79 249
Rolls, Pecan, '79 285
Roughy with Brown Butter Sauce, Pecan, '91 64
Roulade, Pecan, '87 183
Rugalach, Cranberry-Pecan, '04 305
Salad, Apple-Nut, '80 226
Salad, Beet-Nut, '79 74
Salad, Cantaloupe-Pecan, '86 178
Salad, Creamy Carrot-Nut, '86 331
Salad, Endive, Bacon, and Pecan, '89 12
Salad, Ham-Pecan-Blue Cheese Pasta, '90 62
Salad, Spinach-Pecan, '89 128; '01 284
Salad, Strawberry-Nut, '94 132
Salad, Watercress, '97 249
Sandwiches, Rolled Olive, '01 241
Sauces
  Bourbon Praline Sauce, '81 170
  Butter Pecan Sauce, '91 174
  Butter Sauce, Pecan-, '91 65
  Butterscotch-Pecan Sauce, '82 212
  Chocolate-Praline Sauce, '85 M295
  Cinnamon-Pecan-Honey Pancake Sauce, '88 46
  Date-Nut Sundae Sauce, '82 167
  Éclairs with Pecan Sauce, '83 219
  Pasta Sauce, Pecan, '96 262
  Peach-Praline Sauce, '85 161
  Pecan Sauce, '83 219
  Praline Ice Cream Sauce, '85 189
  Praline Ice Cream Sauce, Southern, '86 M227
  Praline Sauce, '83 25; '84 143; '89 95; '92 282;
    '94 206, 312
  Tartar Sauce, Pecan, '03 101
Shrimp with Orange Dipping Sauce, Coconut-Pecan,
  '03 212
Snack Mix, Honey-Nut, '02 187
Spiced Pecans, '03 332
Spicy Pecans, '01 206; '02 304
Spread, Beet-and-Pecan Sandwich, '99 274
Spread, Honey-Nut, '87 157
Spread, Nutty Cream Cheese, '89 327
Spread, Pimiento Cheese, '99 106, 276
Spread, Raisin-Nut, '95 79
Squash, Apple-and-Pecan-Filled, '88 228
Sticky Bun Toast Topper, '99 M72
Stuffing, Chicken Breasts with Pecan-Sausage,
  '94 212
Stuffing, Cranberry, '04 246
Stuffing, Cranberry-Orange-Pecan, '01 249
Stuffing, Cranberry-Pecan, '96 309
Stuffing, Pecan, '79 292; '80 32
Stuffing, Piglet's, '04 270
Stuffing, Spicy Pecan-Cornbread, '01 207
Stuffing, Wild Duck with Pecan, '85 269
Sugar-and-Honey Pecans, '86 319
Sugared Pecans, '82 167; '01 271
Sugarplums, Pecan Shortbread, '83 298
Sweet-and-Spicy Pecans, '00 81, 334; '03 178
Sweet-and-Spicy Texas Pecans, '02 306
Sweet Potato Cakes, '01 105
Sweet Potato Stacks, Bourbon-, '04 246
Syrup, Chunky Pecan, '85 278
Syrup, Maple-Nut, '80 228
Tarts, Coconut-Pecan Cookie, '04 305
Tarts, Pecan-Raisin, '03 246
Tarts, Pecan-Raisin Mini-, '03 246
Toasted Pecans, Asparagus Pasta with, '04 90
Toast, Orange Praline, '79 36
Toffee, Bourbon-Pecan, '04 235
Toffee, Microwave, '92 M317
Toffee, Mildred's, '04 235
Toffee, Nutty, '79 M263

Toffee, Pecan, '00 42
Topping, Apple-Nut, '93 162
Topping, Butter-Pecan, '95 158
Topping, Cinnamon-Pecan, '85 277
Topping, Coconut-Pecan, '04 41
Topping, Crunchy Cereal, '96 216
Topping, Maple-Pecan Ice Cream, '98 317
Topping, Nutty, '85 256
Topping, Pecan, '94 36
Topping, Streusel, '96 216; '01 214; '04 194
Torte, Apricot, '02 220
Torte, Carob-Pecan, '85 218
Torte, Chocolate-Pecan, '89 42
Torte, Graham Cracker-Nut, '97 275; '98 35
Torte, Ground Pecan, '04 273
Torte, Heavenly Pecan, '81 266
Torte, Mocha-Pecan, '86 26
Torte, X-Treme Chocolate Double Nut Caramel
    Ladyfinger, '04 M315
Trout with Orange Sauce, Pecan-Crusted, '98 M82
Turkey Cutlets, Pecan-Crusted, '94 282
Vinaigrette, Pecan, '00 162
Waffles, Pecan, '87 225
Waffles, Pumpkin-Nut, '86 96
Waffles, Southern Chicken-Pecan, '82 231
Wild Rice, Pecan-Lemon, '92 211
Zucchini with Pecans, '87 31

PEPPERMINT

Bavarian, Peppermint, '80 153
Brownies, Chocolate-Peppermint, '88 262
Brownies, Pistachio-Mint, '94 50
Brownies, Southern Chocolate-Mint, '93 216
Butter Mints, '03 300
Cake, Chocolate-Mint, '03 286
Cake, Peppermint Candy, '89 254
Cake, Red Velvet Peppermint, '98 308
Cheesecake Bites, Mint, '99 282
Cheesecake, Frozen Peppermint, '94 143
Chocolate Mint Freeze, '88 167
Cookies, Chocolate-Chocolate Chip-Peppermint,
    '97 289
Cookies, Peppermint, '95 322
Cookies, Peppermint Candy, '88 286
Cookies, Peppermint Sandwich, '92 277
Crème Brûlée, Peppermint, '95 323
Crescents, Peppermint, '03 273
Cupcakes, Chocolate-Peppermint Candy, '03 M287
Dessert, Peppermint Wafer, '79 176; '80 7
Dessert, Triple Mint Ice-Cream Angel, '93 86
Filling, Mint-Cream, '96 229
Filling, Peppermint, '81 119; '89 254
Flip, Hot Peppermint, '86 329
Fondue, Peppermint, '94 332; '95 35
Frosting, Mint Cream, '93 216
Frosting, Peppermint Cream Cheese, '98 308
Frosting, Pink Peppermint Birthday Cake, '92 269
Frosting, Quick Peppermint, '98 308
Hot Cocoa Mix, Minted, '91 316
Ice Cream, Peppermint, '80 176; '86 129
Mints, Party, '79 273; '81 119
Mousse, Peppermint, '93 315
Mousse, Peppermint Candy, '82 71; '94 198
Parfait, Peppermint, '93 315
Parfaits, Chocolate-Peppermint, '88 65
Patties, Peppermint, '86 278
Peabody Peppermint Patti, The, '99 321
Pie, Brownie-Mint, '97 303
Pie, Fudgy Chocolate Malt-Peppermint, '00 313
Pie, Peppermint Candy-Ice Cream, '87 260
Pie, Triple Mint Ice Cream, '98 217
Pralines, Chocolate-Mint, '92 313; '93 51
Punch, Cupid's Creamy Peppermint, '04 253
Rounds, Peppermint, '94 19
Sauce, Chocolate-Peppermint, '94 205
Shortbread, Butter-Mint, '99 28
Snowball Surprises, '93 315
Soufflé, Chocolate Mint, '81 16
Special Mints, '99 323
Squares, Chocolate-Peppermint, '81 119
Twists, Mint, '86 106
Wreaths, Melt-Away Peppermint, '85 324

PEPPERS

Antipasto, Grandpa's, '98 183
Appetizers, Basil-Pepper, '98 133
Banana Peppers, Stuffed, '02 55
Banana Peppers, Stuffed Hungarian Yellow, '00 132
Bell Peppers, Pasta with Sausage and, '02 63
Burritos, Breakfast, '99 103
Casserole, Southwestern, '99 216
Cherry Pepper Appetizers, Fiery Stuffed, '97 269
Chicken with Angel Hair Pasta, Szechuan, '97 91

Chile

Adobo Mayonnaise, '02 203
Adobo, Puerco en, '88 116
Ancho Base, '95 205
Ancho-Beer Mashers, '98 248
Ancho Chile Butter, '99 93
Ancho Chile Cream, '87 121
Ancho Chile Sauce, '87 122
Ancho Chile Succotash with Serrano Chile
    Polenta, '98 104
Ancho Cream Sauce, Boneless Pork Chops with,
    '95 205
Ancho Mashers, '03 243
Casserole, Chile-Cheese, '82 90
Casserole, Chile 'n' Cheese Breakfast, '88 57
Casserole, Chiles Rellenos, '79 84; '84 31, 234;
    '92 18
Casserole, Chili-Corn, '88 266
Casserole, Chili-Rice, '79 54
Casserole, Mexican Rice, '83 31
Casserole, Sausage-Chile Rellenos, '88 52
Caviar, Mexican, '98 135
Cheesecake, Chicken-Chile, '92 42
Cheese, Chile-Pimiento, '04 325
Cheeses, Mexican Grilled, '97 170
Chicken, Jamaican Jerk, '99 121
Chicken Madrid, '97 326
Chicken with Salsa, Baked Chile, '88 147
Chimichangas (Fried Burritos), '81 196; '85 244
Chipotle Baby Back Ribs, Smoky, '04 87
Chipotle Butter, '01 234
Chipotle Caesar Dressing, '04 119
Chipotle Caesar Salad, '04 119
Chipotle Chicken Wings, Sweet-and-Spicy,
    '04 176
Chipotle Cream, Grilled Beef with Mashed
    Potatoes and, '02 M320
Chipotle 'Cue Sauce, Smoky, '04 87
Chipotle Grilled Pork Ribs, '01 319
Chipotle Hollandaise Sauce, '03 53
Chipotle Manicotti, Creamy, '03 96
Chipotle-Marinated Quail, '04 240
Chipotle-Marinated Quail, Pan-Roasted, '98 201
Chipotle Oil, '02 97; '03 98
Chipotle Pepper Butter, '97 307
Chipotle Pork Chops on Smoked Gouda Grits,
    Grilled Maple, '04 172
Chipotle Pork on Smoked Gouda Grits with Sweet
    Onion Applesauce, Maple-, '02 319
Chipotle Roasted Chicken, '03 44
Chipotle Rub, '04 87
Chipotle Salsa, Chicken-and-Brie Quesadillas
    with, '99 311
Chipotle Tostadas, Chickpea-, '01 54; '03 181
con Queso, Chile, '80 194
con Queso Supreme, Chile, '80 265
Dip, Artichoke-Chile, '98 234
Dip, Cheese-and-Chile, '83 31
Dip, Hot Chile, '82 248
Dip, Hot Chile-Beef, '83 218
Dipsy Devil, '00 132
Dressing, Southwestern Mayonnaise, '99 245
Egg Rolls, Chiles Rellenos, '86 296
Eggs, Chile, '88 80
Enchiladas, Chicken-Chile, '97 313
Enchiladas, New Mexican Flat, '85 245
Green Chile-and-Fish Casserole, '84 32
Green Chile Biscuits, '04 233
Green Chile Casserole, Corn-and-, '89 68
Green Chile-Cheddar Cheese with Avocado-
    Mango Salsa, Smoky, '00 328
Green Chile-Cheese Pie, '84 234
Green Chile-Chicken Lasagna, '00 338
Green Chile-Cornbread Dressing, '93 306
Green Chile Enchiladas, '02 188
Green Chile, Muffins, Chicken-and-, '03 81
Green Chile-Pimiento Cheese, '01 61
Green Chile Quiche, '83 31
Green Chile Quiche, Squash-and-, '88 143
Green Chile Sauce, '82 220
Green Chiles, Cheese Grits with, '95 208
Green Chile-Sour Cream Enchiladas, '84 234
Green Chiles, Potato Chowder with, '00 329
Green Chiles, Rice and, '83 152
Green Chiles, Stuffed, '93 208
Green Chiles, Stuffed Red Peppers with Cheesy
    Polenta and, '04 169
Green Chiles, Stuffed Squash with, '83 148
Grits, Chile-Blue Cheese, '04 240
Grits, Saga Blue-Chile, '98 202
Jelly, Chile Piquin, '94 28
Jus, Chile Corn, '00 197
Kebabs, Chile-Beef, '94 251
Oil, Chile Pepper, '96 122
Okra Dills, '97 157
Pickled Chiles Medley, Fiery, '01 333
Pickles, Peppery Texas, '04 M161
Pico de Gallo, '97 141; '98 87
Poblano-and-Corn Quesadillas, '01 333
Poblano Chicken, Creamy, '98 42
Poblano Chile con Queso, Roasted, '01 186
Poblano Chowder, Corn-and-, '03 193
Poblano-Cilantro Pesto, Central Market's, '04 101
Poblano Salad, Avocado-Corn-, '01 320
Poblanos, Corn-Stuffed, '97 269
Poblano-Shrimp Enchiladas, '00 311
Poblanos Stuffed with Pork and Fruit, '97 269
Poblanos with Mango Salsa, Crab-and-Goat
    Cheese, '04 59
Poblanos with Walnut Cream Sauce, Pork-Stuffed,
    '01 229
Poblano Vinaigrette, '99 71
Pork Chops, Chile Pepper, '02 210
Potatoes, Chile Mashed, '00 161
Pudding, Southwestern Corn, '03 178
Quiche, Chile Pepper, '82 224
Quiche, Chiles Rellenos, '02 321
Quiche, Shrimp, '83 50
Red Chile Enchilada Sauce, '85 245
Red Chile Powder, '85 245
Red Chile Sauce, '85 245; '94 251; '95 17
Rellenos, Cheese Chiles, '96 24
Rellenos, Chiles (Stuffed Chiles), '82 220;
    '83 150; '88 116; '89 226
Rellenos Potatoes, Papa's, '96 238
Rellenos, Roasted Chiles, '95 64
Rellenos, Southern-Style Chiles, '96 24
Rellenos with Tomatillo Sauce, Roasted Chiles,
    '94 203
Rellenos with Walnut Cream Sauce, Havarti-and-
    Corn-Stuffed Chiles, '93 M275

PEPPERS, Chile
(continued)

Rice, Chili-Cheesy, '79 43
Rice, Hot Pepper, '92 310
Roasted Chiles, Mac and Texas Cheeses with,
  '04 211
Rollups, Cream Cheese, '98 134
Salad, Spicy Chile-Tomato, '88 121
Salsa, Double Chile, '91 182
Salsa, Dried Chile, '97 265
Salsa, Pepper, '88 26
Salsa with Homemade Tostados, Hot Chile,
  '88 115
Salsa, Zesty Santa Fe, '03 198
Sauce, Drunken, '03 33
Sauce, Pepper, '01 211; '02 106
Sauce, Racy Pesto, '97 67
Sauce, Tex-Mex Secret, '04 127
Serrano Chile Blue Cornbread, '94 114
Serrano Chile Polenta, '98 104
Serrano Salsa, Roasted, '95 207
Soufflés, Chile-Cheese, '96 219
Spread, Chile-Cheese, '02 205
Squash, Chile, '84 77
Squash, Mexican, '83 31
Steaks, Mexican Pepper-Cheese, '97 190
Tacos, Shrimp-and-Pepper Soft, '95 339
Tamales, Hot, '83 51
Tamales, Sweet, '83 52
Turnovers, Chile-Ham, '88 64
Verde, Chili, '95 14
Verde, Light Chile, '88 148
Verde Sauce, '93 275; '00 241
Vinaigrette, Hot Chile, '98 200
Waffles, Corn-Chile, '94 206
Cornbread, Lynda's Mex-Tex, '01 273
Cornbread, Mexican, '01 247
Dip, Pepperoncini-Cream Cheese, '91 252
Dressing, Jeweled Hot Bacon, '97 196
Eggs, Tex-Mex Deviled, '97 247
Fajitas with Pico de Gallo, '98 87
Fillet, Acapulco, '98 174
Filling, Crêpe, '96 48
Firecrackers, Texas, '95 96
Frittata, Bell Pepper, '96 204
Green
Beans, Frolickers Baked, '03 92
Beef and Green Peppers, '79 104
Beefed-Up Peppers, '82 186
Black Beans, Traditional Cuban, '98 21
Bread, Pepper, '85 156
Casserole, Peppered Pork Chop, '82 25
Casserole, Peppery Potato, '95 182
Chicken Peppers, Devilish, '80 65
Coleslaw, Memphis-Style, '98 104
Coleslaw, Old-Fashioned, '99 235
Coleslaw, Sour Cream, '99 220
Cups, Potato Salad in Pepper, '79 78
Deluxe, Peppers, '81 159
Dressing, Green Pepper-Onion Salad, '84 12
Fried Pepper Strips, '82 208
Gazpacho, White, '97 181
Hamburger Steak, '99 45
Jelly, Pepper, '79 121
Jelly, Unusual Green Pepper, '82 132
Linguine, Leeks and Peppers with, '98 68
Meatballs with Pineapple and Peppers, '90 145
Meat Loaf, French Market, '02 33
Medley, Pepper-Mushroom, '90 98
Mexican Green Peppers, '80 65
Muffins, Cheese-and-Pepper, '84 139
Onions, Baked Sweet, '98 130

Oriental Radishes, '01 101
Pizza Peppers, '83 135
Pork, Sweet-and-Sour, '00 110
Potato Salad 'n' Peppers, '83 135
Ratatouille, '85 92
Relish, Pepper, '83 183
Relish, Pepper-Onion, '84 180
Rice, Charleston, '97 310
Rice, Red, '97 138
Salad, Ruby-and-Emerald, '85 79
Sauce, Green Bell Pepper, '97 261
Sauce, Pepper-Onion, '84 125
Sauce, Red or Green Pepper, '91 85
Sausage and Peppers, Italian, '84 9
Sautéed Onions and Peppers, '83 M148
Sauté, Tomato-Pepper, '84 142
Soup, Green Pepper, '88 250
Soup, Mexican Cheese, '97 268
Spaghetti with Pork and Peppers, '98 131
Spread, Roasted Pepper, '94 123
Squash Oregano, Summer, '97 165
Stacks, Pepper-Cheese, '87 80
Steak and Rice, Pepper, '81 17
Steak, Pepper, '81 273; '85 57; '88 113
Steak, Pepper-Beef, '85 21
Steak, Simple Pepper, '01 82
Stir-Fried Sweet Peppers with Tomatoes, '93 207
Stir-Fry Steak, Pepper, '81 240
Stuffed Green Peppers, '03 62
Stuffed Green Peppers, Beefy, '81 86
Stuffed Green Peppers, Ham-, '80 65
Stuffed Pepper Medley, '82 131
Stuffed Peppers, '81 239; '83 66; '84 202
Stuffed Peppers, Beef-, '84 154; '85 146;
  '91 M127
Stuffed Peppers, Corn-, '84 104
Stuffed Peppers, Curried Chicken-, '87 19
Stuffed Peppers for Two, '80 84
Stuffed Peppers, Ham-and-Corn, '81 87
Stuffed Peppers, Hearty, '88 M214
Stuffed Peppers, Macaroni-and-Cheese-, '80 65
Stuffed Peppers, Rice-, '80 65; '99 241
Stuffed Peppers, Shrimp-, '80 162; '86 131, 197;
  '97 268
Stuffed Peppers, Spinach-, '82 180
Stuffed Peppers with Rice and Ham, '82 131
Stuffed with Beef, Peppers, '84 72
Taco Peppers, '81 86
Turkey with Peppers, '92 182
Veal and Peppers, Spaghetti with, '81 201; '82 14
Grilled Pepper-Pesto Linguine, '04 136
Grill, Three-Pepper, '02 122
Grits, Mexican Cheese, '02 34
Guacamole Crisps, '98 173
Hush Puppies, Mississippi, '97 84
Jalapeño
Afterburners, '03 159
Beans, Texas Pinto, '01 65
Biscuits, Cornmeal-Jalapeño, '94 214
Black-Eyed Peas, Jalapeño, '88 166
Bread, Jalapeño Pepper, '83 121
Brussels Sprouts, Spicy, '02 307
Burgers with Roasted Bell Pepper Ketchup,
  Jalapeño-Stuffed, '97 318
Butter, Grilled Corn with Jalapeño-Lime,
  '01 158; '04 178
Butter, Jalapeño, '97 306
Butter, Jalapeño-Chili, '98 156
Butter, Jalapeño-Pecan-Mustard, '03 205
Casserole, Jalapeño Corn, '83 256
Casserole, Jalapeño Rice, '81 66
Celery, Jalapeño Stuffed, '79 70
Cheese, Jalapeño Pimiento, '98 315; '01 169
Cheese, Shrimp with Herbed Jalapeño, '87 112

Cheesy Jalapeño Peppers, '80 195
Chicken Casserole, Jalapeño, '02 50
Chicken, Grilled Jalapeño, '93 213
Chicken, Grilled Lime-Jalapeño, '91 87
Chicken Jalapeño, Easy, '92 310
Chicken Legs, Jalapeño Oven-Fried, '94 94
Chutney, Jeweled Pepper, '94 316
Chutney, Mango, '03 123
Coleslaw, Jalapeño, '97 26
con Queso, Chili, '80 194; '97 25
Cornbread, Beefy Jalapeño, '82 142
Cornbread, Cheddar-Jalapeño, '85 3
Cornbread, Jalapeño, '85 200; '94 78; '98 178
Cornbread, Southwestern Hot-Water, '01 29
Cups, Hot Vegetable Pepper, '88 M188
Dip, Mexican Fiesta, '98 234
Dressing, Creamy Jalapeño-Cilantro, '04 311
Eggs, Armadillo, '97 270
Eggs, Mexican Deviled, '04 93
Fried Jalapeños, '96 292
Fritters, Corn-Jalapeño, '96 153
Fritters, Squash-Jalapeño, '98 249
Grits, Jalapeño Cheese, '85 43
Grits, Jalapeño-Cheese, '00 239; '01 328
Guacamole, Margarita, '97 167
Heroes, Open-Faced Jalapeño, '90 144
Hominy, Jalapeño, '82 51
Jelly, Easiest Pepper, '03 135
Jelly, Jalapeño, '92 230; '96 292
Jelly, Mint, '03 135
Jelly, Quick Jalapeño Pepper, '96 275
Jelly, Southwest, '03 135
Loaf, Jalapeño-Cheese, '84 76
Muffins, Jalapeño-Corn, '93 164
Mustard, Jalapeño, '93 240; '95 312
Nachos, Smoked, '01 146
Nachos, Tuna, '96 201
New Potatoes, Cheesy Jalapeño, '01 89
Nut Mix, Jalapeño, '96 27
Onion Rings, South-of-the-Border, '96 217
Pickled Jalapeño Peppers, '93 136
Pico de Gallo, '04 32, 89, 311
Pie, Jalapeño Cheese, '96 292
Pimiento Cheese, Jalapeño, '03 315
Pork, Jalapeño Grilled, '99 160
Pork Tenderloin, Jalapeño-Glazed, '03 186
Pork Tenderloins, Pepper-Honey, '98 33
Potatoes, Jalapeño, '84 39
Potatoes, Jalapeño-Ham Stuffed, '81 M61
Puffs, Cajun Hot, '94 277
Quesadillas, Bacon-Jalapeño-Tomato, '95 240
Quesadillas, Western, '97 65
Quiche, Cheesy Jalapeño, '84 31
Quiche, Jalapeño-Corn, '85 122
Quiche Squares, Cheesy Hot, '79 124
Rice, Hot Pepper, '92 310
Rice, Jalapeño, '79 43
Rice, Jalapeño Hot, '80 126
Rollups, Mexican, '98 134
Salad, Jalapeño Potato, '97 64
Salsa, Cranberry-Jalapeño, '01 234
Salsa, Double Chile, '91 182
Salsa, Hot, '98 135
Salsa Picante, '84 108
Salsa Picante, Homemade, '81 67
Salsa Verde, Roasted, '96 182
Salsa, Watermelon, '98 164
Sauce, Fried Green Tomatillos with Jalapeño
  Dipping, '97 143
Sauce, Hot Chile, '92 156
Sauce, Jalapeño, '80 193; '93 230
Sauce, Jalapeño-Cranberry, '92 310
Sauce, Jalapeño Tartar, '96 69; '98 129
Sauce, San Antonio Hot, '84 291

Sausage, Grilled Pork, Cheddar, and Jalapeño, '98 311
Sherbet, Jalapeño-Mint, '98 202
Shortbread, Jalapeño-Pecan, '03 108
Spread, Jalapeño-Cheese, '82 248
Squares, Jalapeño Cheese, '80 195
Stuffed Jalapeño Peppers, '96 215
Stuffed Jalapeño Peppers, Fried, '95 22
Stuffed Jalapeños, '98 234
Stuffed Jalapeños, Fiery Fried, '90 118
Stuffed Jalapeños, Hot, '99 123
Stuffed Jalapeños, Shrimp-, '88 115
Tacos, Shrimp-and-Pepper Soft, '95 339
Vinegar, Southwest, '94 200
Ketchup, Jalapeño-Stuffed Burgers with Roasted
    Bell Pepper, '97 318
Lamb, Rosemary-Skewered, '97 190
Linguine with Sausage and Peppers, '03 170
Marinated Roasted Peppers, '97 123
Meatball Packets, Italian, '04 222
Olives, Marinated, '01 187
Pasta, Chicken-and-Pepper, '03 199
Pasta, Three Pepper-Sausage, '02 122
Pasta with Peppers and Broccoli, '91 69
Peas, A Mess of, '00 158
Pico de Gallo, '04 61
Pizza, Mexican Chicken, '97 321
Pizza, Peppers-and-Cheese, '03 235
Pork Chops with White Rice, '02 312
Red
    Bread, Roasted Red Bell Pepper, '95 241
    Brie en Croûte, Stuffed, '97 162
    Bruschetta, Red-and-Green, '01 62
    Bruschetta, Roasted Red Pepper, '00 278
    Butter, Fillet of Beef with Red Pepper, '96 32
    Butter, Roasted Red Bell Pepper, '95 242
    Carrots, Balsamic Baby, '02 43
    Cheese, Grilled, '97 328
    Crêpes, Goat Cheese-Filled Cornbread, '98 43
    Crostini, Roasted Peppers-Feta Cheese, '96 87
    Crostini, Spinach-Red Pepper, '03 34
    Cucumber-and-Pepper Combo, '88 176
    Cups, Hot Vegetable Pepper, '88 M188
    Curried Corn and Sweet Red Peppers, '95 47
    Dip, Chickpea-and-Red Pepper, '99 138
    Dressing, Roasted Red Pepper-Dill, '02 144
    Focaccia, Rosemary-Red Pepper, '01 307
    Fries, Red Pepper-Polenta, '00 196
    Green Beans with Shallots and Red Bell Pepper,
        '97 251
    Hummus, Red Pepper, '00 132; '02 31
    Jam, Red Bell Pepper, '95 242
    Jelly, Red Pepper, '89 M156
    Marinated Cheese, Olives, and Peppers, '04 238
    Marinated Mirlitons, Artichokes, and Peppers,
        '00 246
    Marinated Olives and Peppers, '04 71
    Mayonnaise, Roasted Red Pepper, '98 144
    Okra, Corn, and Peppers, '87 M151
    Pasta with Greens, Creamy, '00 91
    Peas and Peppers, Minted, '90 M99
    Peas and Peppers, Stir-Fried, '87 51
    Pizza, Red Pepper Hummus, '01 56
    Pizza, Roasted Pepper, '94 218
    Potatoes with Sweet Red Peppers, '87 192
    Puree, Red Pepper, '93 275; '00 241
    Rémoulade Sauce, Red Pepper, '01 145
    Roasted Pepper-Tomato Bruschetta, '02 213
    Roasted Pepper Vinaigrette, '04 142
    Roasted Red Bell Pepper Dressing, '03 28
    Roasted Red Pepper-and-Vidalia Onion Gravy,
        '03 323
    Roasted Red Pepper Cream, Shrimp with, '03 97
    Roasted Red Pepper-Feta Crostini, '04 69

Roasted Red Pepper Rémoulade, '04 144
Roasted Red Pepper Salad, Chicken and, '03 291
Roasted Red Peppers and Pearl Onions, Green
    Beans with, '93 260
Roasted Red Peppers, Potato Salad with, '04 100
Rollups, Artichoke-Red Pepper, '02 231
Rollups, Roasted Red Pepper, '98 285
Roll with Cilantro Hollandaise Sauce,
    Southwestern, '99 16
Round Steak, Red Pepper, '88 214
Salad, Broccoli and Red Pepper, '83 224
Salad, Roasted Red Pepper-and-Green Bean,
    '99 322
Salad, Roasted Red Pepper and Watercress, '90 55
Salad, Tuna-and-Red Pepper, '93 143
Salad with Avocado, Potato, '98 332
Salsa, Roasted Red Pepper, '01 100
Sandwiches, Mozzarella-Pepper Bagel, '98 145
Sandwiches, Smoked Turkey-Roasted Pepper,
    '94 66
Sauce, Linguine with Red Pepper, '93 127
Sauce, Red Bell Pepper, '99 267
Sauce, Red or Green Pepper, '91 85
Sauce, Red Pepper, '98 322; '02 165
Sauce, Red Pepper-Garlic, '98 140
Sauce, Roasted Red Bell Pepper, '02 287
Sauce, Roasted Red Pepper, '98 16; '00 58
Sautéed Peppers and Mushrooms, Herb-Stuffed
    Chicken with, '91 26
Shrimp with Onion and Red Pepper, Sweet-and-
    Sour, '02 84
Slaw, Napa Cabbage, '02 280
Snow Peas and Red Pepper, Sesame, '84 175
Snow Peas with Red Pepper, '90 102
Soup, Chilled Roasted Pepper and Tomato, '01 128
Soup, Chilled Sweet Red Pepper, '93 69
Soup, Cream of Roasted Sweet Red Pepper, '95 65
Soup, Red Bell Pepper, '98 104
Soup, Roasted Red Pepper, '96 245
Soup, Spicy Pepper, '93 98
Spinach with Red Pepper Ribbons, Holiday, '03 260
Spread, Roasted Red Bell Pepper, '97 217
Squash-and-Pepper Toss, Crisp, '87 M152
Stuffed Peppers with Chicken and Corn, '02 147
Stuffed Red Peppers with Cheesy Polenta and
    Green Chiles, '04 169
Sugar Snap Peas with Bell Peppers, '03 255
Tomatoes, Scalloped, '00 183
Vinaigrette, Roasted Bell Pepper, '99 70
Vinaigrette, Roasted Pepper, '00 134
Zucchini, Roasted, '02 89
Relish, Grandma's Pepper, '04 158
Relish, Hot, '01 123
Roasted Pepper Quesadillas, Shrimp-and-, '00 215
Roasted Peppers and Beans, Herbed Turkey Strips
    with, '04 282
Roasted Tomato-and-Pepper Salad, '01 196
Salad, Gazpacho-Chicken, '00 203
Salad, Grilled Tomato, Bell Pepper, and Portobello,
    '98 211
Salad, Pasta, '00 213
Salad, Winter Cabbage, '98 284
Salsa, '01 273
Salsa, Banana, '96 85
Salsa, Caribbean, '96 70
Salsa, Cha-Cha, '97 160
Salsa, Cherry, '99 156
Salsa, Corn, '00 164
Salsa, Fiery, '01 174
Salsa, Fresh Tomatillo, '97 143
Salsa, Mango, '02 163
Salsa, Mango-and-Bell Pepper, '00 247
Salsa, Roasted, '95 130
Sandwich, Giant Ham-and-Pepper, '96 74

Sauce, Creamy Roasted Pepper, '96 183
Sauce, Miss Kitty's Chili, '04 231
Sausage and Peppers with Parmesan Cheese Grits,
    '02 233
Scallops and Angel Hair Pasta, '99 176
Shrimp, Charleston Harbor Pickled, '99 275
Shrimp, Marinated, '98 317
Shrimp Rellenos, '00 174
Skillet, Pork-Pepper, '01 309
Soup, Mardi Gras, '96 56
Soup, Roasted Yellow Bell Pepper, '96 56
Steak and Rice, Skillet Pepper, '04 326
Stuffed Peppers, Barbecued Shrimp and Cornbread-,
    '97 261
Stuffed Peppers, Carrot-and-Cabbage, '99 63
Stuffed Peppers, Spicy, '98 243
Sweet
    Chicken Breasts with Curried Peppers, '90 227
    Chicken Sauté, Sweet Pepper-, '89 104
    Chicken Scaloppine with Peppers, '85 78
    Chicken, Sicilian, '97 142
    Chowder, Bell Pepper-Cheese, '95 240
    Flank Steak with Sweet Peppers, Grilled, '90 138
    Green Beans and Pepper Strips, '86 170
    Kebabs, Pretty Pepper, '90 166
    Kebabs, Summery Squash-and-Pepper, '95 193
    Marinated Roasted Peppers, '92 176
    Medley, Cabbage-Onion-Sweet Pepper, '96 252;
        '97 28
    Medley, Rainbow Pepper, '91 126
    Parmesan Pepper Toss, '93 208
    Pasta, Peppery, '94 164
    Pesto, Pepper, '89 103; '90 97
    Relish, Confetti Pepper, '91 195
    Relish, Sweet Pepper, '95 104
    Roasted Bell Peppers in Olive Oil, '95 242
    Roasted Peppers, Marinated, '87 90
    Roasted Peppers with Balsamic Vinaigrette,
        '94 128
    Salad, Chilled Turkey-and-Pepper Stir-Fry,
        '88 140
    Salad, Mixed Pepper, '89 103
    Salad, Mushroom-and-Pepper, '86 68
    Salad, Three-Pepper, '91 162
    Salsa, Mixed Pepper, '91 181
    Salsa, Yellowfin Tuna with Corn, Pepper, and
        Tomato, '94 164
    Sausage and Peppers, '95 165
    Sausage, Sweet Peppery, '95 69
    Sautéed Sweet Peppers, '89 102
    Sauté, Julienne Pepper, '89 104
    Soup, Bell Pepper, '89 103
    Soup, Roasted Pepper-and-Chicken, '90 58
    Soup, Sweet Pepper, '93 277
    Spread, Roasted Pepper, '94 123
    Stuffed with Shrimp-and-Orzo Salad, Peppers,
        '91 203
    Sugar Snaps and Peppers, '93 139
    Tacos, Grilled Pepper, '95 340
    Topping, Rainbow Pepper, '90 117
Terrine with Tomato-Basil Vinaigrette, Blue Cheese,
    '99 288
Turkey and Peppers in Cornbread Crust, '95 312
Yellow Pepper Sauce, '02 165
Yellow Pepper Sauce, Poached Salmon with, '98 230
PERSIMMONS
Bread, Persimmon, '80 228
Bread, Persimmon Date-Nut, '82 218
Cake, Persimmon, '79 205
Cookies, Persimmon, '96 242
Cookies, Persimmon-Raisin, '85 232
Pie, Persimmon, '79 206
Pudding, Persimmon, '79 206; '00 254
Salad, Persimmon Fruit, '79 206

PESTOS. *See also* **RELISHES, SALSAS, SAUCES, TOPPINGS.**
Basil Pesto, '03 208; '04 101
Basil Pesto Focaccia, '00 195
Bow-Tie Pesto, '94 231
Butter, Pesto, '97 307
Cilantro-Black Walnut Pesto, Littleneck Clams with, '97 164
Cilantro-Pecan Pesto, '04 36
Cilantro Pesto, '98 145; '00 148
Dip, Pesto, '95 93; '97 226
Dip with Tortellini, Creamy Tomato Pesto, '00 196
Dried Tomato-Basil Pesto, '04 101
Fresh Pesto, '86 150
Garden Pesto, '04 186
Garden Pesto, Lucinda's, '01 100
Garlic Pesto, '84 108
Goat Cheese, Pesto, '03 110
Homemade Pesto, '01 22
Nuts, Pesto-Spiced, '95 173
Olive-Rosemary Pesto, '01 317
Pasta, Asian Pesto, '95 189
Pasta, Pesto and, '92 98
Peanut Pesto, Thai, '98 145
Pepper Pesto, '89 103; '90 97
Pesto, '80 242; '96 207; '00 118
Pizza, Nutty Pesto, '97 267
Poblano-Cilantro Pesto, Central Market's, '04 101
Primavera, Pesto, '96 170
Roasted Garlic-Basil Pesto, '98 145
Roasted Garlic-Rosemary Pesto, '97 46
Rosemary Pesto, Grilled Pork Tenderloins with, '04 82
Ruth's Pesto, '96 170
Sage Pesto, '97 22
Sauce, Pasta with Pesto-Clam, '98 17
Sauce, Pesto, '89 280; '91 94; '95 267
Sauce, Racy Pesto, '97 67
Sauce, Walnut-Parmesan Pesto, '96 251; '97 104
Shortbread, Pesto, '03 108
Spinach-Peanut Pesto and Pasta, '93 212
Spinach Pesto-Pasta, '91 314
Spinach Pesto Sauce, '93 59
Tart, Tomato-Pesto, '00 195
Thyme Pesto, Sirloin Steaks with, '97 182
Tomatoes Pesto, '86 150
Tomato Pesto, Dried, '90 204; '94 249; '01 62
Torte, Pesto, '02 278
PETITS FOURS. *See* **CAKES/Petits Fours.**
PHEASANT. *See* **GAME.**
PICANTE SAUCE. *See* **SALSAS, SAUCES.**
PICKLES
Asparagus, Pickled, '83 46; '04 161
Beet Pickles, '81 210
Beets, Easy Pickled, '80 137
Beets, Pickled, '81 216; '97 229; '02 138
Broccoli, Pickled, '81 308
Cantaloupe, Sweet Pickled, '89 197
Carrots, Pickled, '93 12
Chayote Squash Pickles, '89 197
Cucumber Chips, '85 176
Cucumber Pickles, Freezer, '99 87
Cucumber Pickles, Sour, '85 176
Cucumber Rounds, Easy Pickled, '90 143
Cucumber Sandwich Pickles, '81 174
Dill Pickle Rémoulade, '04 311
Dill Pickles, '81 174
Dill Pickles, Fried, '84 206
Dills, Lazy Wife, '87 149
Eggs, Beet Pickled, '84 287
Eggs, Spiced Pickled, '84 288
Figs, Pickled, '79 140
Fire-and-Ice Pickles, '94 316
Green Tomato Pickles, '87 134; '01 141

Hot-and-Sweet Freezer Pickles, '04 160
Icicle Pickles, Sweet, '85 176
Jalapeño Peppers, Pickled, '93 136
Lime Pickles, '96 206
Mixed Pickles, '81 174
No-Cook Sweet-and-Spicy Pickles, '04 176
Okra Dills, '97 157
Okra Pickles, '81 173
Onion Rings, Pickled Refrigerator, '84 265
Onions, Pickled Cocktail, '89 197
Peaches, Perfect Pickled, '85 178
Peach Pickles, '85 177; '99 170
Pear Pickles, Mustard, '79 196
Peppery Texas Pickles, '04 M161
Pineapple, Pickled, '79 24
Problem Chart, Pickle, '85 176
Squash Pickles, '81 174; '87 150; '97 119; '99 170
Sweet Pickles, Quick, '87 149
Tempura Dill Pickles, '04 123
Watermelon Rind Pickles, '81 174; '84 106; '98 164
Yellow Squash, Pickled, '93 136
Zucchini, Dilled Fresh, '81 174
PIES, PUFFS, AND PASTRIES
Almond Pie, Toasted, '86 163
Ambrosia Pie, '79 284
Angel Pie, '79 123; '80 238
Apple. *See also* **PIES, PUFFS, AND PASTRIES/Cobblers, Crisps, and Crumbles; Pastries; Tarts; Turnovers.**
Amandine Pie, Apple-, '89 215
American Apple Pie, '91 197
Applesauce Pie, '98 259; '99 26; '01 213
Autumn Apple Pie, '79 205
Berry-Apple Pie, '88 251
Blackberry-Apple Pie, '87 130
Bourbon Pie, Apple-, '95 302
Brandy-Apple Pie, '86 301
Brandy Raisin-Apple Pie, '83 192
Buttermilk Custard Pie, Warm Apple-, '99 98
Cake, Apple Pie, '82 226
Chess Pie, Apple-Lemon, '86 220
Cider Pie, Apple, '84 227
Cinnamon Crème, Apple Pie with Warm, '99 337
Cinnamon Sauce, Apple Pie with Hot, '88 210
Covered Apple Cake, '89 317
Cran-Apple Pie, '92 304
Cranberry-Apple Holiday Pie, '81 M269
Cranberry-Apple Pie, '79 264
Cranberry-Apple-Raisin Pie, '98 270
Cranberry Pie, Apple-, '97 276; '99 M269
Cream Cheese Pie, Apple-, '81 247
Custard Pie, Apple, '88 236
Dutch Apple Pie, '81 105; '82 273
Easy-Crust Apple Pie, '87 11
Fresh Apple Pie, '84 178
Fried Apple Pies, '81 217; '86 302; '88 112, 225; '94 61
Fried Pies, Honeyed Apple-Cranberry, '02 214
Georgie's Apple Pie, '02 325
Grandmother's Apple Pie, '87 212
Granny Smith Apple Pie, '01 143
Grated Apple Pie, '83 304
Holiday Apple Pie, '87 260
Honey Apple Pie, '00 331
Lemon-Apple Pie, Tart, '80 100
Maple Pie, Apple-, '97 276
Mexican Apple Pie, '94 97
Mincemeat Pie, Apple-, '85 316
No-Crust Apple Pie, '88 204
Old-Fashioned Apple Pie, '82 M299; '88 94
Pear-Apple Pie, Natural, '88 226
Pear Pie, Apple-, '83 249
Pear Pull-Up Pie, Apple-, '98 259
Pineapple Pie, Apple-, '97 276

Praline-Apple Pie, '99 331
Raisin Brandy Pie, Apple-, '89 58
Red Apple Pie, '79 282
Upside-Down Southern Apple Pie, '88 226
Apricot Cream Fried Pies, '00 212
Apricot Fried Pies, '86 269
Apricot Hand Pies, Dried, '98 259
Apricot Pies, Fried, '95 215
Apricot Pies, Special, '94 60
Apricot Pie, Yogurt-, '85 132
Apricot Surprise Pie, '88 99
Banana Cream Pie, '84 48; '87 207
Banana Cream Pie, Hawaiian, '90 105
Banana Pie with Hot Buttered Rum Sauce, '88 204
Bavarian Cream Pie, '79 281
Blackberry Cream Pie, '81 132
Blackberry Pie, '84 141; '86 152
Blackberry Pie, Creamy, '88 179
Blackberry Pie, Fresh, '03 164
Black Walnut Pie, '97 275; '98 35
Blueberry. *See also* **PIES, PUFFS, AND PASTRIES/Cobblers, Crisps, and Crumbles.**
Banana Pie, Blueberry-, '93 115
Chilled Blueberry Pie, '89 136
Cream Cheese Pie, Blueberry-, '88 154
Cream Pie, Blueberry, '84 142
Cream Pie, Fresh Blueberry, '80 144
Fresh Blueberry Pie, '83 183; '85 152
Kuchen, Blueberry, '80 143
Lemon-Blueberry Cream Pie, '02 92
Old-Fashioned Blueberry Pie, '89 136
Peach Pie, Blueberry-, '94 158
Red, White, and Blueberry Pie, '98 162
Sour Cream Pie, Blueberry-, '83 183
Spicy Blueberry Pie, '96 147
Streusel Pie, Fresh Blueberry, '89 137
Boston Cream Pie, '83 220
Bourbon Pie, Kentucky, '84 87
Boysenberry Pie, '82 133
Brownie Pie, Crustless, '82 33
Bumbleberry Pie, '97 163
Buttermilk Chess Pie, '92 214
Buttermilk-Lemon Cream Pie, '88 99
Buttermilk Lemon Pie, '81 120; '82 23
Buttermilk-Lemon Pie, '88 297
Buttermilk Pie, '82 53; '83 158; '88 93; '92 95; '98 290
Buttermilk Pie, Lemon-, '91 272
Buttermilk Pie, Old-Fashioned, '79 72
Buttermilk Pie, Rancher's, '04 208
Butterscotch Cream Pie, '84 48; '87 207
Butterscotch Meringue Pie, '83 158
Butterscotch Pie, '97 212
Cantaloupe Cream Pie, '79 177
Cantaloupe Meringue Pie, '88 182
Cantaloupe Pie, '86 163
Caramel-Banana Pie, '86 M165
Caramel Banana Pie, Luscious, '79 115
Caramel Meringue Pie, '97 109
Caramel-Nut Crunch Pie, '94 244
Caramel-Peanut Pie, '86 259
Caramel Pie, '96 72
Caramel Pie, Burnt, '82 53
Caviar Pie, '79 154
Cheese. *See also* **PIES, PUFFS, AND PASTRIES/Crusts, Pastries, Tarts, Turnovers, Vegetable.**
Apple-Cream Cheese Pie, '81 247
Blueberry-Cream Cheese Pie, '88 154
Chocolate-Cream Cheese Pie, '80 69
Chocolate Cream Cheese Pie, '92 240
Cottage Cheese Pie, '82 85
Cream Puffs with Chicken Salad, Cheesy, '86 260
Fruited Cheese Pie, '92 228

Hors d'Oeuvre Pie, Cheesy, '88 91
Lemon Cheese Pie, '81 136; '82 146
Lemon-Cottage Cheese Pie, '79 44
Lemon Cottage Cheese Pie, '81 143
Make-Ahead Cheesecake Pie, '81 233
Mascarpone Cream Pie with Berry Glaze, '00 312
Mincement-Cheese Pie, '80 253
Phyllo Cheesecakes, Little, '87 275
Tiramisù Toffee Trifle Pie, '00 312
Yogurt-Cheese Pie, '82 121
Cherry-Berry Pie, '92 316
Cherry Confetti Pie, No-Bake, '93 114
Cherry Cream Pie with Almond Pastry, '92 30
Cherry Pie, Coconut Crumb, '92 30
Cherry Pie, Easy, '82 299
Cherry Pie, Fresh, '88 178
Cherry Pie, Lemony, '92 30
Cherry Pie, Prize-Winning, '82 57
Cherry Pie, Red, '83 192
Cherry Pie, Scrumptious, '83 250
Chess Pie, Brown Sugar, '86 220
Chess Pie, Buttermilk, '92 214
Chess Pie, Classic, '00 60; '02 107
Chess Pie, Old-Fashioned, '86 220
Chocolate. *See also* **PIES, PUFFS, AND PASTRIES/Crusts, Ice Cream, Pastries, Tarts.**
Almond Pie, Creamy Chocolate-, '85 102
Amandine, Chocolate Pie, '83 300
Amaretto Mousse Pie, Chocolate-, '80 180; '81 30
Banana-Pecan Cream Pie, Chocolate-, '94 210
Bavarian Pie, Chocolate, '89 326
Berry Pie, Heavenly Chocolate-, '85 102
Best-Ever Chocolate Pie, '88 M45
Black Bottom Pie, '82 53
Black-Bottom Pie, '98 161
Black Bottom Pie, Weidmann's, '95 118
Bourbon Pie, Chocolate, '88 99
Cake, Chocolate Pastry, '91 196
Chess Pie, Chocolate, '81 161; '86 220; '92 13
Chess Pie, Chocolate-Pecan, '00 60; '02 107
Chilled Chocolate Pie, '88 99
Chip Pie, Chocolate, '85 114
Coffee Cream Pie, '94 209
Cream Cheese Pie, Chocolate-, '80 69
Cream Cheese Pie, Chocolate, '92 240
Cream Pie, Chocolate, '83 192; '84 49; '87 208; '94 208
Creamy Chocolate Pie, '85 298; '86 119
Double Chocolate Pie, '82 M282
Easy Chocolate Pie, '83 158
Fox Hunter's Pie, '97 109
French Silk Pie, '80 247
Frozen Chocolate Brownie Pie, '96 57
Frozen Chocolate-Macadamia Nut Pie, '96 254
Frozen Chocolate Pie, '80 154
Frozen Chocolate Pie with Pecan Crust, '89 291; '98 180
Fudge Pie, '87 168; '89 252; '01 129
Fudge Pie, Chocolate, '98 336
Fudge Pie, Sweetheart, '86 316; '90 313
German Chocolate Pie, '93 129
Heaven, Chocolate, '98 323
Heavenly Chocolate Pie, '87 260
Meringue Pie, Chocolate, '80 238; '82 206; '83 158; '92 216
Meringue Pie, Chocolate-Filled, '86 121
Microwave Chocolate Pie, '90 M15
Mint Pie, Brownie-, '97 303
Mocha Crunch Pie, Chocolate-, '81 136
Mocha Pie, '94 168
Mousse Pie, Chocolate, '81 136
Mud Pie, Decadent, '89 252
Mud Pie, Mississippi, '89 26

Mud Pie, Tipsy, '80 255; '97 251
Peanut Butter Pie, Chocolate-, '85 91
Peanut Butter Swirl Pie, Chocolate-, '87 262
Pecan Chess Pie, Chocolate-, '93 251
Pecan Pie, Bourbon-Chocolate, '98 258
Pecan Pie, Choco, '82 86
Pecan Pie, Chocolate, '80 237; '83 12; '90 184
Pecan Pie, Chocolate-, '91 272; '02 176
Pecan Pie, Turtle, '93 250
Peppermint Pie, Fudgy Chocolate Malt-, '00 313
Pizza Dolce (Italian Sweet Pies), '00 283
Praline Pie, Chocolate-, '86 259
Silk Pie, Chocolate, '88 67
Strawberry-Chocolate Truffle Pie, '89 112
Whipped Cream Pie, Chocolate, '79 124
White Chocolate-Banana Cream Pie, '94 314
Christmas Pie, White, '88 281; '93 289
Cobblers, Crisps, and Crumbles
à la Mode, Apple Cobbler, '97 16
Apple Bake, Cinnamon-, '04 29
Apple-Berry Cobbler, '04 330
Apple Cobbler, Country, '99 255
Apple Cobbler, Easy, '83 174
Apple Cobbler for Two, '85 261
Apple Cobbler, New-Fashioned, '91 221
Apple Crisp, '84 122; '98 215
Apple Crisp, Tart, '92 226
Apple Dumpling Cobbler, '04 29
Apple-Gingerbread Cobbler, '03 21; '04 219
Apple-Pear Cobbler with Oatmeal Muffin Crust, Caramel, '04 201
Apple-Pecan Cobbler, '84 M198
Apple-Pecan Pie Cobbler, '04 200
Apple-Vinegar Biscuit Cobbler, '01 215
Apple Walnut Cobbler, '79 154
Apple-Walnut Cobbler, '81 248
Apricot Cobbler with Custard Sauce, '97 16
Apricot Cobble Up, '82 138
Berry-Cherry Cobbler, '83 270
Berry Cobbler, Mixed-, '02 214
Berry Cobbler, Three-, '04 29
Berry Cobbler, Too-Easy, '04 28
Berry Crisp, '83 130
Blackberry-Almond Cobbler, '81 132
Blackberry Cobbler, '82 139; '83 175; '99 131; '02 17
Blackberry Cobbler, Deep-Dish, '80 186
Blackberry Cobbler, Deluxe, '81 132
Blackberry Cobbler, Juicy, '89 137
Blackberry Cobbler, New-Fashioned, '87 164
Blackberry Cobbler, Southern, '81 132
Blueberry Buckle, '85 30
Blueberry Cobbler, '83 175
Blueberry Cobbler, Easy, '83 183
Blueberry Cobbler, Fresh, '80 144
Blueberry Cobbler, Peachy, '80 143
Blueberry Cobbler, Warm, '98 153
Blueberry Crisp, '84 177
Blueberry Crunch, Fresh, '82 143
Blueberry, Huckle-Buckle, '86 151
Blueberry-Peach Cobbler, No-Dough, '86 177
Blueberry-Pecan Cobbler, '00 154; '03 106
Blueberry Pinwheel Cobbler, '87 140
Blueberry Slump, Quick, '91 20
Blueberry Upside-Down Cobbler, '96 146
Boysenberry Cobbler, '82 133
Caramel-Applesauce Cobbler with Bourbon-Pecan Ice Cream, '00 260
Cherry-Apple Bake, '04 29
Cherry Cheesecake Cobbler, Double-, '03 21
Cherry Cobbler, '82 91, 139; '99 156
Cherry Cobbler, Colossal, '89 137
Cherry Cobbler, Fresh, '84 178
Cherry Cobbler, Too-Easy, '04 28

Cherry Crisp, '91 20
Cherry Slump, '83 139
Cranberry-and-Apple Cobbler, '84 306; '90 294
Cranberry-Apple Cobbler with Cinnamon Biscuits, '99 256
Cranberry Cobbler, '81 275
Cranberry Cobbler, Easy, '86 260
Cranberry Cobbler Roll, '80 288; '81 248
Cranberry-Peach Cobbler, '92 322
Cranberry-Pear Crisp, '83 207; '97 16
Cran-Blueberry Cobbler, '04 28
Fig-and-Raspberry Cobbler, '02 160
Fig Cobbler, '79 140
Fig Cobbler, Cajun, '94 196
Fig Cobbler, Super, '86 206
Fruit Cobbler, '99 33
Fruit Cobbler, Quick, '91 20
Ginger-Pear Cobbler, '03 232
Grenadine-Peach Cobbler, '85 178
Lemon-Blackberry Crisp, '98 171
Muscadine Cobbler, '98 221
Nectarine Cobbler with Blueberry Muffin Crust, '04 200
Peach-and-Raspberry Crisp, '02 232
Peach-Apricot Cobbler, '99 255
Peach-Caramel Cobbler, '86 300; '87 178
Peach Cobbler, '83 175; '84 178; '90 219; '95 264
Peach Cobbler, Double Crust, '03 310
Peach Cobbler, Easy, '97 137; '99 206
Peach Cobbler, Fresh, '82 139; '89 154
(Peach Cobbler), I Fall to Peaches, '96 159
Peach Cobbler, Lattice-Topped, '79 154
Peach Cobbler, Old-Fashioned, '82 170
Peach Cobbler, Quick, '79 215; '81 142
Peach Cobbler, Spicy, '85 178
Peach Cobbler Supreme, '81 184; '90 313
Peach Cobbler, Too-Easy, '04 28
Peach Cobbler with Praline Biscuits, '92 180
Peach Crinkle, '91 20
Peach Crisp, '83 113; '92 13; '93 134
Peach Crumble, Easy, '83 116
Pear Cobbler, Best Ever, '82 194
Pear Crisp, '02 M233
Pear Crumble, '85 221
Pear-Ginger Cobbler, '01 214
Pecan-Peach Cobbler, '04 120
Pineapple-Apple Betty, '85 46
Pineapple Crisp, Tropical, '02 232
Plum Brown Betty, Bourbon-, '97 177
Plum Cobbler, '99 254; '03 161
Plum Cobbler, Crunchy, '88 152
Plum Cobbler with Spiced Plum Muffin Crust, '04 201
Raspberry-Cherry Cobbler, '93 230
Strawberry Cobbler, Fresh, '96 84
Strawberry-Rhubarb Cobbler, '88 93
Strawberry-Rhubarb Cobbler, Rosy, '79 154
Strawberry-Rhubarb Crisp, '95 119
Sweet Potato-Apple Cobbler, '04 M232
Sweet Potato Cobbler, '99 255; '01 214
Vegetable Cobbler, Autumn, '01 215
Coconut
Blender Coconut Pie, '84 236
Butter Coconut Pie, '01 244
Buttermilk-Coconut Pie, '94 246
Caramel Pies, Coconut-, '87 260
Cherry Pie, Coconut Crumb, '92 30
Chess Pie, Coconut, '86 220; '00 60; '02 107
Chess Pie, Coconut-Orange, '89 169
Chess Pie, Coconut-Pecan, '81 248
Cloud, Coconut, '80 70
Coconut Pie, '93 115

PIES, PUFFS, AND PASTRIES, Coconut
(continued)

Cream Pie, Coconut, '80 238; '81 136; '82 85;
'84 49; '87 207; '89 236; '90 312; '98 161;
'02 92; '03 106
Cream Pie, Fresh Coconut, '80 289
Cream Pie, Surprise Coconut, '92 43
Creamy Coco-Nana Pie, '00 95
Crunch Pie, Coconut, '90 105
Custard Pie, Coconut, '82 33
French Coconut Pie, '90 162
Macadamia Nut Pie, Coconut-, '97 110
Macaroon Pie, Coconut, '88 204
Magic Coconut Pie, '79 53
Mock Coconut Pie, '86 200
Orange-Coconut Cream Pie, '94 208
Orange-Coconut Pie, '90 90
Pecan Pie, Coconut, '81 161
Pineapple Pie, Coconut-, '84 256
Puffs, Coconut, '87 277
Quick Coconut Pie, '83 115
Toasted Coconut Pie, '90 105
Coffee Cream Pie, '94 209
Coffee Pie, '96 148
Cracker Pie, '79 113
Cranberry-Cherry Pie, Tart, '87 299
Cranberry Freezer Pie, Festive, '84 306
Cranberry Pie, Frosty, '79 249
Cranberry Pie, Nutty, '82 M298
Cranberry Pie, Walnut-, '87 259
Cranberry-Raisin Pie, '80 283; '85 316
Cranberry Streusel Pie, '98 258
Cran-Raspberry Pie, '87 244
Cream Pie, Texas, '81 181
Crème de Menthe Pie, Quick, '88 127
Crusts. *See also* **PIES, PUFFS, AND
PASTRIES/Pastries.**
Black Iron Skillet Piecrust, Universal, '99 33
Brown Sugar Crust, '92 118
Butter Crust, '90 173
Cereal Piecrust, Crisp, '82 209; '83 100
Cheese Crust, '80 286; '86 264
Cheese Grits Crust Batter, '03 21
Chocolate-Coconut Crust, '87 261
Chocolate-Coconut Pie Shell, '82 210; '83 100
Chocolate Crumb Crust, '87 261
Chocolate Crust, '87 264; '90 M15
Chocolate Cups, '80 207
Chocolate-Macadamia Crumb Crust, '96 254
Chocolate Wafer Crust, '89 42, 93
Cinnamon Meringue Shell, '82 263
Coconut Crust, '89 160
Cookie Crust, Spicy, '88 7
Cornbread Crust Batter, '03 20
Cracker Crust, '88 97
Cranberry-Pecan Crusts, '02 198
Crumb Crust, Cheesy, '88 86
Crust, '89 272
Decorating Pie Crusts, '83 248
Deluxe Piecrust, '79 79
Gingersnap Crumb Crust, '96 279
Ginger Snap Crust, '88 138
Gingersnap Crust, '89 93; '90 296; '98 161;
'01 187
Graham Cracker Crust, '79 45; '86 32; '87 139,
243; '88 M45, 55, 67; '89 93, 326; '90 296;
'91 197, M234, 308; '94 310
Graham Cracker Crust, Microwaved, '82 M141
Graham Cracker Crust, Peanut-, '79 50
Graham Cracker Crusts, '97 162
Graham Crust, Peanut-, '99 49
Italian Sweet Crust, Plum Pie with, '79 162

Lattice Crust, '90 294
Macadamia Nut Crusts, Coconut Cream Tarts
with, '97 62
Nut Crust, Spiced, '87 295
Nutty Oat Crust, '89 251
Oatmeal Piecrust, '79 79
Parmesan Crust, '94 304
Pecan Crust, '86 317; '89 291; '98 180
Perfect Piecrust, Making, '82 234
Pizza Crust, '80 233; '83 226; '86 77
Pizza Crust, Crispy, '87 181
Rice-Cheese Shell, '82 49
Rice Crust, Crispy, '84 43
Spice Crust, '82 298
Sugar Cookie Crust, '93 131
Tart Crust, '84 178; '90 58; '97 86
Vanilla Wafer Crust, '98 216
Wafer Crust, '02 209
Whole Wheat Crust, '82 298
Custard Pie, Egg, '99 82
Custard Pie, Old-Fashioned Egg, '82 261
Custard Pie, Perfect, '82 92
Custard Pie, Quick 'n' Easy, '96 28
Daiquiri Pie, '79 68
Daiquiri Pie, Daring, '92 191
Dream Pie, '80 90
Eggnog Chiffon Pie, '86 281
Eggnog Pie, '80 254; '83 205; '86 317; '87 295
Eggnog Pie, Fluffy, '81 M269
Empanadas de Calabaza (Pumpkin Empanadas),
'94 28
Fried Pies, '96 109
Fried Pies, Delicious, '83 84
Fried Pies, Dried Cherry-and-Pear, '00 213
Fried Pies with Fruit Salsa, Lone Star, '97 124
Fried Strawberry Pies, '02 147
Fruitcake Pie, '80 237
Fruit Pie, Crispy-Crust, '88 68
Fruit Pie, Dried, '83 249
Fruit Pie, Japanese, '80 238
Fruit Pies, Baked, '84 7
Grapefruit Chess Pie, '01 23
Grapefruit Meringue Pie, '96 56
Grape Juice Pie, '79 123
Grape Pie, '85 212
Grasshopper Freeze, Creamy, '81 180
Grasshopper Pie, '83 145
Ice Cream
Absolutely Divine Ice Cream Pie, '82 181
Caramel Ice Cream Pie, '82 181
Carrot Ice Cream Pie, '86 200
Chocolate-Ice Cream Pie, '87 224
Chocolate Ice Cream Pie, '91 56
Chocolate-Mint Ice Cream Pie, '81 144
Chocolate-Peanut Butter Ice Cream Pie, '98 244
Coffee Ice Cream Pie, '79 231
Delight, Ice Cream, '80 69
Double-Delight Ice Cream Pie, '89 72
Heavenly Ice Cream Pie, '82 181
Kona Ice Cream Pie, '83 189
Lemon Ice Cream Pie, '80 70
Lemony Ice Cream Pie, '99 207
Meringue-Pecan Crust, Ice Cream Pie with,
'88 127
Mincemeat Ice Cream Pie, '99 285
Mint Ice Cream Pie, Triple, '98 217
Nutty Ice Cream Pie, '91 180
Orange Cream Pie, '03 35
Peanut Butter Cup Pie, Fudgy, '04 211
Peanutty Ice Cream Pie, '82 56
Peppermint Candy-Ice Cream Pie, '87 260
Pumpkin Ice Cream Pie, '81 272
Pumpkin-Ice Cream Pie, '87 243
Rum-Fruit Sauce, Ice Cream Pie with, '84 312

Spectacular, Ice-Cream Pie, '90 314
Sundae Pie, Ice Cream, '94 244
Jamwiches, Sweetheart, '03 M41
Kahlúa Pie, '83 191
Key Lime Pie, '91 42; '96 171; '00 120; '03 179;
'04 254
Key Lime Pie, Manny and Isa's, '95 118
Key Lime Pies, '95 86; '97 162
Key Lime Pie with Gingersnap Crust, Margarita-,
'01 187
Key Lime Pie with Minted Tropical Salsa, '99 333
Lemon
Aunt Kitty's Lemon Pie, '98 275
Blueberry Cream Pie, Lemon-, '02 92
Buttermilk-Lemon Cream Pie, '88 99
Buttermilk Lemon Pie, '81 120; '82 23
Buttermilk-Lemon Pie, '88 297
Buttermilk Pie, Lemon-, '91 272
Cheese Pie, Lemon, '81 136; '82 146
Cherry Pie, Lemony, '92 30
Chess Pie, Apple-Lemon, '86 220
Chess Pie, Lemon, '79 32; '82 196; '00 60;
'02 107; '03 217, 259
Chess Pie, Lemon-Lime, '01 23
Cottage Cheese Pie, Lemon-, '79 44
Cottage Cheese Pie, Lemon, '81 143
Cream Pie, Frozen Lemon, '82 86
Filling, Lemon Icebox Pie, '03 104
Filling, Lemon Meringue Pie, '04 110
Fluff Pie, Lemon, '92 342; '93 46
Frozen Lemonade Pie, '92 101
Heavenly Pie, '83 158
Ice Cream Pie, Lemon, '80 70
Lemonade Pie, '91 42
Magnolia Pie, '94 210
Meringue Pie, Best-Ever Lemon, '94 208
Meringue Pie, Deluxe Lemon, '81 172; '90 313
Meringue Pie, Lemon, '85 M112; '86 130; '04 110
Orange Pie, Lemon-, '85 172
Parfait Pie, Lemon, '94 310
Pastry Shell, Lemon in, '84 137
Pecan Pie, Lemon-, '93 251
Slice of Lemon Pie, '84 23
Sour Cream Pie, Lemon-, '82 169
Sponge Pie, Lemon, '83 192
Strawberry Pie, Lemon-, '88 127
Tart Lemon-Apple Pie, '80 100
Tart Lemon Pie, '91 275
Twirl Pie, Lemon, '84 94
Whipped Lemon Pie, '79 124
Lime Chiffon Pie, '86 130
Lime Fluff Pie, '84 43
Lime Party Pies, '92 65
Macadamia Pie, '80 238
Main Dish. *See also* **PIES, PUFFS, AND
PASTRIES/Tarts, Turnovers.**
Artichoke Pie, '79 25
Barbecue Pot Pie with Cheese Grits Crust, '03 21
Barbecue Pot Pie with Mashed Potato Crust,
'03 21
Beef-and-Onion Cornbread Pie, '01 298
Beef in a Blanket, Bourbon Peppered, '00 109
Beef Pies, Carry-Along, '80 224; '81 56
Beef Pie, Sensational, '03 M284
Beef Pies, Fried, '96 108
Beef Pies, Savory, '01 230
Beef Pot Pie, Oriental, '92 253
Beef Pot Pies with Yorkshire Pudding Topping,
'93 45
Beef Roast Pot Pie, '88 296
Beef Wellingtons, Mini, '01 252
Bouchées aux Fruits de Mer, '98 267
Breakfast Pie, '86 242
Breakfast Pie, Country, '93 M328

Broccoli-and-Turkey Pasta Pie, '88 269
Broccoli-Beef Pie, '83 196
Brunch Egg Nests, '03 246
Brunswick Stew-Cornbread Pie, '02 121
Burrito Pie, Mexican, '87 287
Calzones, All-Star Pizza, '95 308
Calzones, Easy, '99 133
Cheese-Beef Pie, '85 33
Cheeseburger Pie, '89 121
Cheeseburger Pie, Jack-O'-Lantern, '00 234
Cheese Pie, Mexican, '82 9; '83 69
Chicken-and-Egg Pot Pie, '00 98
Chicken Breasts in Phyllo Pastry, '91 105
Chicken Breasts Wellington, '84 22
Chicken Cobbler, Spicy Tex-Mex, '03 324
Chicken Cobbler with Caramelized Onions,
   '00 44
Chicken, Company Creamed, '82 84
Chicken Dumpling Pie, '95 245; '96 55; '00 336
Chicken in Pastry, '86 122
Chicken in Phyllo, '87 286
Chicken in Phyllo, Cheese-Stuffed, '01 251
Chicken in Phyllo, Cheesy, '02 308
Chicken in Puff Pastry, Spinach-Stuffed, '92 125
Chicken Phyllo Pie, Greek, '92 328
Chicken Pie, '81 281; '82 31
Chicken Pie, Biscuit-Topped, '86 157, 264
Chicken Pie, Cheesy Mexican, '82 142
Chicken Pie, Deluxe, '88 298
Chicken Pie, Double-Crust, '87 111
Chicken Pie, Egg-Stra Special, '86 264
Chicken Pie, Nana's, '90 25
Chicken Pie, Savory Southern, '90 24
Chicken Pot Pie, '81 210; '82 114; '84 21; '94 21;
   '95 54, 256; '96 75; '01 282; '03 247
Chicken Pot Pie, Double-Crust, '90 220
Chicken Pot Pie, Easy, '83 156; '89 218
Chicken Pot Pie in Biscuit Bowls, '03 222
Chicken Pot Pie, Old-Fashioned, '92 271
Chicken Pot Pie, Thick 'n' Crusty, '87 267;
   '88 102; '89 67
Chicken Pot Pie with Cheese Crust, '86 264
Chicken Presents, Holiday, '01 251
Chicken Salad in Cream Puff Bowl, '86 232
Chicken-Vegetable Pot Pie, '81 281; '82 30
Chili-Tamale Pie, '82 9; '83 68
Cornbread-Sausage-Apple Pie, '87 171
Cornbread-Tamale Pie, '92 123
Corn Burger Pie, '83 156
Country Pie, '83 155
Enchilada Pie, '83 155
Fish in a Crust, '84 294
Game Pot Pie with Parmesan Crust, '94 304
Green Chile-Cheese Pie, '84 234
Grits-and-Ham Pie, Crustless, '86 103
Grits Fiesta Pie, '92 43
Ham-and-Cheese Pie, '95 256; '96 75
Ham and Eggs Mornay, '02 130
Ham-and-Greens Pot Pie with Cornbread Crust,
   '03 20
Ham-Broccoli Pot Pie, '03 83
Hamburger Pie, '81 92; '84 13
Hamburger Pie, Deep-Dish, '00 334
Ham Pie, Golden, '87 78
Ham Pie with Cheese Crust, '80 286
Ham Pot Pie, '90 25
Ham Towers, Cheesy, '82 77
Hot Dog Deluxe, '97 140
Lamb Pie, '90 26
Meat-and-Potato Pie, '84 23
Meat Loaf in a Wrap, '89 122
Meat Pie, Continental, '95 256; '96 75
Meat Pie, Italian, '89 109; '01 297
Meat Pie, Mexicali, '81 194

Meat Pie, Old-Fashioned, '82 110
Meat Pie, Reuben, '80 189
Meat Pies, Cornish, '84 23
Meat Pies, Natchitoches, '84 21; '91 241
Omelet Pie, '00 M35
Oyster Pie, Creole, '84 214
Pancake, Supper, '86 242
Pea Flips, '80 7
Pineapple-Chicken Salad Pie, '80 138
Pizza Pie, Meaty, '03 145
Pot Pie Filling, '03 247
Sausage-and-Cornbread Pie, '90 25
Sausage Log, Phyllo, '84 294
Sausage Pizza Pie, Link-, '85 33
Seafood Pie, Hot, '80 32
Shepherd Pie, '83 116
Shepherd's Pie, '92 168; '00 55
Shrimp Puffs, Luncheon, '85 72
Sombrero Pie, '81 140
Spaghetti-Ham Pie, '93 19
Spaghetti Pie, '81 32
Spaghetti Pie, Weeknight, '95 312
Spanakopita, '86 58
Spinach-Pasta Pie, '85 286
Taco Pie, '88 256
Taco Pie, Crescent, '80 80
Taco Pie, Double-Crust, '88 272; '89 180
Taco Pies, Individual, '82 M282
Torta Mexican Style, '89 122
Tortilla Pie, '85 M211; '96 135
Tortilla Pie, Montezuma, '83 199
Tumbleweed Pie, '98 205
Tuna Pie with Cheese Roll Crust, '80 286
Tuna-Rice Pie, '84 123
Turkey-and-Dressing Pie, '84 326
Turkey-and-Oyster Pie, '82 267
Turkey-Cheese Pie, '88 264
Turkey Pie, '80 285
Turkey Pie, Crumb-Crust Curried, '86 265
Turkey Pie, Golden, '79 253
Turkey Pie, Lattice-Topped, '81 277; '82 7
Turkey Pie, Potato-Topped, '86 265
Turkey Pot Pie, '86 265; '90 24; '93 45
Turkey Pot Pie with Biscuit Crust, '98 296
Turkey Pot Pie with Cranberry-Pecan Crusts,
   '02 198
Turkey-Sausage Pie, '01 297
Turkey-Vegetable-Sausage Cobbler, '04 325
Vegetable-Beef Pies, '80 286
Zucchini-Ham-Cheese Pie, '80 272
Mango Cream Pie, '03 122
Mango-Ginger Pie, '88 138
Mango Pie, Green, '79 137
Mincemeat Chiffon Pie, '79 245
Mincemeat-Peach Pie, '80 295; '81 188
Mincemeat Pie, Holiday, '80 282; '83 250; '87 213
Mincemeat Pie, Kentucky, '95 302
Mincemeat Pie, Pear, '84 264; '88 226
Mince Pie, Spirited, '92 316
Mint Pie, Candy-Crust, '92 191
Mocha Meringue Pie, '80 242; '88 163
Molasses Pie, '86 20
Muscadine Pie, '82 202
Nesselrode Pie, Fluffy, '87 261
Orange Ambrosia Pie, '80 237
Orange Blossom Special, '79 48
Orange Chess Pie, '88 204; '01 23
Orange Chiffon Pie, '87 260
Orange-Coconut Pie, '90 90
Orange Dream Pie, '02 93
Orange Meringue Pie, '81 12, 309
Orange Pie, Florida, '91 43
Orange Pie, Frosty, '90 296
Papaya Pie, '86 53

Pastries. *See also* **PIES, PUFFS, AND
   PASTRIES/Crusts.**
Almond Combs, '84 136
Almond Pastry, '85 177; '89 317; '92 30
Apple Bundles, Quick, '04 242
Apple Dumplings, Old-Fashioned, '84 226
Apple Flan, '81 309
Apple Foldovers, '84 136
Apple Roll, '82 178
Apple Rolls, Luscious, '88 225
Apple Squares, '92 311
Apple Strudel, '85 259; '89 267; '92 269; '97 238
Apricot-Cream Cheese Pastries, '03 245
Apricot Pastries, '83 297
Apricot Pinwheels, '87 276
Baklava, '96 20
Blackberry Roll, '82 178
Blueberry Kuchen, '80 143
Brie en Croute, Stuffed, '97 162
Briwatts with Fruit, '98 211
Burritos, Hot Phyllo, '98 312
Butter Pastry, Golden, '84 22
Calzones, Spinach-and-Cheese, '95 310
Calzones, Surprise, '00 282
Camembert Bars, '86 58
Cannoli, '80 58
Cheddar Cheese Pastry, '80 219; '82 194
Cheddar Pastry, '86 206
Cheese Danish, '97 31
Cheese Pastries, Date-Filled, '83 259
Cheese Pastry, '88 56
Cheese Puffs, '97 240
Cheese Puffs, Mexican, '87 8
Cheese Rolls, '80 286
Chicken, B'steeya with, '98 210
Chicken Puffs, Appetizer, '85 72
Chipped Beef Spread in Puff Pastry, '98 M335
Chocolate-Chestnut Pastries, '02 M273
Chocolate Pastry Shell, '87 262
Chocolate-Raspberry Bags, '95 97
Cinnamon-Apple Rolls, '02 215
Citrus Pastry, Hint-of-, '93 260
Coconut Puffs, '87 277
Cornmeal Pastry, '81 140
Cornmeal Pastry Cups, '90 69
Cornucopia, Pastry, '95 307
Cream Cheese Danish, '98 325
Cream Cheese Pastries, '80 250
Cream Cheese Pastry, '82 39; '86 24, 78; '89 136;
   '96 228, 264
Cream Cheese Pastry Mini Shells, '99 180
Cream Cheese Pastry Shells, '86 13
Cream Cheese Pastry Shells, Miniature, '87 190
Cream Cheese Patty Shells, '81 266; '82 249
Cream Cheese Shells, '79 2
Cream Horns, '84 137
Cream Puff Pastry, '85 72; '96 191
Cream Puffs, '98 316
Cream Puffs, Captivating, '81 180
Cream Puff Tree, '96 310
Danish Pastry Puffs, '85 311
Double-Crust Pastry, '81 105; '82 85, M298;
   '83 248; '85 191; '87 299; '88 94, 178
Double-Crust Pastry, Flaky, '82 57
Dumplings, Apple-Cranberry, '00 16
Éclairs, Banana-Chocolate, '01 45
Éclairs , Chocolate, '96 191
Éclairs, Mocha, '01 45
Éclairs, Peanut Butter-Chocolate, '01 45
Éclairs, Pistachio-Cream, '91 296
Éclairs, Strawberry Cream, '01 45
Éclairs, Vanilla Cream-Filled, '01 45
Éclairs with Pecan Sauce, '83 219
Elephant Ears, Garlic-and-Herb Baby, '00 87

Elephant Ears, Mushroom-and-Brie Petite, '00 87
Elephant Ears, Parmesan-Pepper Baby, '00 87
Elephant Ears Provençale, Baby, '00 87
Elephant Ears, Southwestern Baby, '00 87
Empanadas, '92 156
Empanadas, Pork Picadillo, '03 60
Empanadas, Pumpkin, '82 223
Feta Squares, '02 59
Fig Snacks, Sliced, '86 206
Firecrackers, Texas, '99 94
Flaky Pastry, '80 224; '81 56, 210; '83 156
Fruit Basket Strudel, '87 276
Fruit Puff, Giant, '85 72
Garnish, Pastry, '98 254; '03 317
German Pastries, '86 78
Gingersnap Crust, '01 187
Greek Olive Cups, '99 221
Guava Puffs, '92 247
Java Cream Puffs, '81 187
Lemon Cream Puffs, '93 254
Light Pastry, '92 95
Make-Ahead Pastry, '82 209; '83 100
Maple Cream Coffee Treat, '90 50
Mexican Fiesta Confection, '82 223
Microwave Pastry, Basic, '82 M142; '85 M113
Mix, Perfect Pastry, '81 142
Mocha Pastry Shell, '81 136
Mushroom-Almond Pastry Cups, '88 210
Napoleon, Giant Apple, '99 282
Napoleons, '84 138
Napoleons, Banana, '00 50
Napoleons, Berry, '94 120
Napoleons, Blueberry, '96 147
Napoleons, Blueberry-Lemon, '94 122
Napoleons, Caramel-Apple, '01 M313
Napoleons, Coffee, '95 276
Napoleons, Peanut Butter-and-Chocolate, '94 121
Napoleons, Strawberry, '81 126
Never Fail Pastry, '79 79
Orange Shortcake, Fresh, '80 100
Palmiers, '87 277
Papaya-Pineapple Roll, '94 18
Paste Pastry, Common, '94 17
Pastry, '82 85, 139, 259; '83 84, 91, 175;
   '84 21, 23; '87 212, 267; '88 103, 198, 225;
   '89 67, 137, 154, 214, 267; '91 23, 241;
   '92 84, 157; '98 272; '99 131; '00 95, 170
Pastry, Basic, '79 282; '81 M268; '82 114;
   '84 48; '89 215; '91 119; '94 210
Pâté Pastry, '86 65
Pear Dumplings, '97 210
Pears en Croute, '93 210
Pecan Pastry Shell, '97 275; '98 36
Phyllo Baskets, Walnut-, '93 210
Phyllo Bowls, '95 58
Phyllo Cheesecakes, Little, '87 275
Phyllo-Cheese Triangles, '87 246
Phyllo, Goat Cheese Wrapped in, '99 43
Phyllo Nests, Nutty, '87 277
Phyllo Tartlet Shells, '95 216
Pineapple Phyllo Bundles, '87 277
Piroshki, '92 84
Pistachio Twists, '02 164
Plum Kuchen, '79 161
Potato-and-Blue Cheese Pastries, '03 258
Potatoes, Phyllo, '02 219
Praline Pastries, '89 318
Preserve-Filled Foldovers, '80 7
Processor Pastry, '87 67
Processor Pie Dough, Quick Food, '84 219

Profiteroles, '84 208
Profiteroles with Warm Cranberry Compote,
   Pumpkin-Spiced, '97 264
Puff Pastry, Basic, '84 135
Puff Pastry Baskets, '93 177
Puff Pastry Baskets, Tropical, '93 177
Puff Pastry Bowls, '95 58
Puff Pastry, Quick, '84 207
Puffs, Blue Cheese, '04 18
Puffs, Blue Cheese-and-Bacon, '01 236
Puffs, Cocktail, '91 106
Puffs, Sweet, '89 91
Quiche Pastry, '80 M107
Quiche Pastry, Microwaved, '81 M74; '82 M122
Raisin Pastry Bites, '90 86
Raspberry-Nut Strudel, '83 304
Raspberry Party Puffs, '90 170
Roquefort Firecrackers, '97 19
Rugalach, Cranberry-Pecan, '04 305
Rugelach, '85 276
Samosas, '89 266
Savory Pastry, '90 24
Seasoned Pastry, '79 253
Sesame Pastry Shell, '82 67
Shell, Pastry, '84 31, 127; '87 262; '89 236;
   '93 289; '94 158
Shell, Perfect Pastry, '81 142
Shells, Pastry, '83 93
Shell, Water-Whipped Baked Pastry, '95 246
Shortcake Pastry, '80 100
Shrimp Bundles with Chive Butter Sauce, Crispy,
   '03 91
Sopaipillas, '89 268
Spanakopita, '96 233
Spinach and Artichokes in Puff Pastry, '00 277
Spinach-and-Cheese Pastries, Greek, '96 76
Spinach-Artichoke-Tomato Puffs, '95 284
Spinach Strudels, '93 249
Sticks, Sugared Piecrust, '02 17
Strawberry Cream Puffs, '81 95
Strawberry-Lemon Cream Puffs, '87 75
Strips, Decorated Pastry, '02 M296
Strudel, Autumn-Apple, '98 253
Strudel, Chicken-Goat Cheese, '98 28
Strudel, Crab-and-Mushroom, '98 28
Strudel, Fig, '98 253
Strudel, Meatless Mexican, '98 29
Strudel, Pear, '98 253
Strudel, Reuben, '98 28
Strudels, Dried Fruit, '01 48
Strudel with White Wine Gravy, Chicken-Herb,
   '04 318
Sugar Cookie Pastry, '91 119
Tart Pastry, '89 232; '90 92; '91 118
Tart Pastry, Heart, '87 14
Tart Shell, '87 77; '88 20
Tart Shell, Chocolate, '99 315; '02 208
Tart Shells, '82 304; '83 279; '85 300;
   '86 18, 105; '88 4; '90 84; '91 13
Tart Shells, Cheese, '88 88
Tart Shells, Cheese Pastry, '85 216
Tart Shells, Tea, '85 120
Timbale Shells, '82 108
Triple-Crust Pastry, '80 186
Turkey-Mushroom Pâté in Pastry, '92 327
Tutti-Frutti Cream Puffs, '79 231
Vegetable Oil Pastry, '91 204
Whole Wheat Pastry, '81 229

Peach. *See also* **PIES, PUFFS, AND
   PASTRIES/Cobblers, Crisps, and
   Crumbles; Tarts.**
Blackberry Pie, Peach-and-, '89 136
Blueberry-Peach Pie, '94 158
Chiffon Pie, Peach, '89 155

Cranberry Pie, Peach-, '83 249
Cream Pie, Dried Peach, '84 146
Cream Pie, Peaches-and-, '81 184
Filling, Fresh Peach Pie, '95 195
Fresh Peach Pie, '82 170; '95 195
Fresh Peach Pie, Elizabeth and Phoebe's, '96 119
Fried Peach Pies, '81 272
Fried Pies, Easy Peach, '85 178
Fried Pies, Ginger-Peach, '00 212
Georgia Peach-and-Praline Pie, '98 196
Little Peach Pies, '86 303
Luscious Peach Pie, '81 136
Melba Pie, Peach, '98 216
Mincemeat-Peach Pie, '80 295; '81 188
Praline Pie, Peach, '89 136
Quick Peach Pie, '89 252
Rhubarb-Peach Pie, '86 140
Peanut Butter-Banana Pie, '01 315
Peanut Butter Cream Pie, '79 50; '88 65
Peanut Butter Cup Pie, Fudgy, '04 211
Peanut Butter Meringue Pie, '84 30
Peanut Butter Pie, '85 275; '86 109; '89 252
Peanut Butter Pie, Fluffy, '94 246
Peanut-Raisin Pie, '79 85
Peanuts" Pie, "Working for, '93 115
Pear
Backyard Pear Pie, '93 237
Cheddar-Pear Pie, '02 197
Crumble Pie, Pear, '83 207
Deep-Dish Pear Pie, '80 219
Delicious Pear Pie, '88 226
Double-Crust Pear Pie, '82 194
French Pear Pie, '87 213
Fried Pies, Dried Cherry-and-Pear, '00 213
Ginger-Pear Pie, '93 48
Macadamia Pie, Pear-, '93 260
Mincemeat Pie, Pear, '84 264; '88 226
Mincemeat Pie, Pear-, '98 258
Mince Pie, Pear-, '81 271
Praline Pie, Pear-, '97 192
Streusel Pie, Pear, '83 234; '84 244; '97 109
Tennessee Pear Pie, '85 230
Pecan. *See also* **PIES, PUFFS, AND
   PASTRIES/Crusts, Pastries, Tarts.**
Bourbon-Chocolate Pecan Pie, '98 258
Bourbon Pecan Pie, '85 90
Bourbon-Pecan Pie, Frozen, '89 251
Bourbon-Pecan Pumpkin Pie, '87 264
Butter Pecan Pie Squares, '81 262
Caramel-Pecan Apple Pie, '85 247
Caramel-Pecan Pie, '88 282
Cherry-Pecan Pie, '92 30
Chess Pie, Chocolate-Pecan, '02 107
Chocolate-Banana-Pecan Cream Pie, '94 210
Chocolate-Pecan Chess Pie, '93 251; '00 60
Chocolate Pecan Pie, '80 237; '83 12; '90 184
Chocolate-Pecan Pie, '91 272; '02 176
Choco-Pecan Pie, '82 86
Cinnamon-Almond-Pecan Pie, '98 89
Coconut-Pecan Chess Pie, '81 248
Coconut Pecan Pie, '81 161
Coffee Pecan Pie, '82 74
Cranberry-Pecan Pie, '92 316
Custard Pecan Pie, '87 184
Date-Pecan Pie, '80 15
Golden Pecan Pie, '81 266
Grandmother's Pecan Pie, '86 269
Holiday Pecan Pie, '81 296
Honey-Pecan Finger Pies, '90 184
Hot Fudge Sauce, Pecan Pie with, '01 306
Individual Pecan Pies, '85 295
Layered Pecan Pie, '83 305
Lemon-Pecan Pie, '93 251
Louisiana Pecan Pie, '92 83

Maple-Pecan Pie, '81 266
Miniature Pecan Pies, '79 205; '86 13
Mississippi Pecan Pie, '98 146
Mocha Pecan Mud Pie, '00 245
Molasses-Pecan Pie, '86 259
Mom's Pecan Pie, '02 249
Mystery Pecan Pie, '02 249
Old-Fashioned Pecan Pie, '81 M269
Orange-Pecan Pie, '79 282; '83 222
Orzo-Pecan Pie, Honeyed, '04 219
Pecan Pie, '79 251; '80 57; '85 255; '90 312;
    '92 234; '98 275; '01 244
Pumpkin-Pecan Pie, '85 233, 282
Pumpkin Pie, Nutty, '82 67
Raisin-Pecan Pie, '87 213
Simmie's Pecan Pie, '00 254
Special, Old Pecan Street, '93 251
Spicy Pecan Pie, '84 240
Sweet Potato-Pecan Pie, '83 90
Texas Pecan Pie, '83 159
Texas Star Pecan Pie, '90 184
Tiny Pecan Pies, '79 225
Turtle Pecan Pie, '93 250
    Vanilla Custard, Pecan Pie with Chilled, '00 331
Persimmon Pie, '79 206
Pineapple-Coconut Chess Pie, '92 214
Pineapple-Grits Pie, '96 236
Pineapple Pie, '80 237; '89 252
Pineapple Pie, Double-Crust, '82 85
Pineapple Pie, Fresh, '91 178
Pistachio Pie, '80 56
Plum Cream Pie, Easy, '86 174
Plum Pie, Streusel-Topped, '88 153
Plum Pie with Italian Sweet Crust, '79 162
Pumpkin
    Autumn Pumpkin Pie, '87 213
    Bourbon-Pecan Pumpkin Pie, '87 264
    Chiffon Pie, Pumpkin, '84 312
    Cracked Caramel-Pumpkin Pie, '99 254
    Festive Pumpkin Pie, '81 M269
    Fluffy Pumpkin Pie, '80 283
    Frosty Pumpkin Pie, '96 279
    Gingersnap Streusel Pumpkin Pie, '01 315
    Ice Cream Pie, Pumpkin, '81 272
    Ice Cream Pie, Pumpkin-, '87 243
    Layered Pie, Elegant Pumpkin-Walnut, '02 244
    Mama's Pumpkin Pie, '96 242
    Meringue, Pumpkin Pie with, '92 268
    New-Fashioned Pumpkin Pie, '90 296
    Nutty Pumpkin Pie, '82 67
    Pecan Pie, Pumpkin-, '85 233, 282
    Praline Pie, Frosty Pumpkin-, '91 M234
    Praline Pie, Pumpkin, '80 244
    Praline-Topped Pumpkin Pie, '00 332
    Quick Pumpkin Pie, '88 M230
    Rich Pumpkin Pie, '86 292
    Sour Cream-Pumpkin Pie, '84 263
    Spiced Nut Crust, Pumpkin Pie in, '87 295
    Spicy Pumpkin Pies, '84 322
    Supreme, Pumpkin Pie, '82 217
    Traditional Pumpkin Pie, '85 256
Raisin Pie, '83 220
Raisin Pie, Spiced, '84 148
Raspberry Baked Alaska Pie, '98 216
Raspberry Cream Pie, '94 209
Rhubarb-Peach Pie, '86 140
Rhubarb-Raisin Pie, '79 112
Rhubarb-Raspberry Pear Pie, '95 119
Rum Bisque Pie, '79 123
Rum Cream Pie, '85 212
Scuppernong Pie, '88 216
Sour Cream Pie, '86 260
Sour Cream Pie, Tropical, '79 176; '80 6
Strawberry Angel Pie, '88 136

Strawberry-Banana Glazed Pie, '81 181
Strawberry Custard Pie, '00 81
Strawberry-Glaze Pie, '81 141
Strawberry Pie, Chilled, '82 112
Strawberry Pie, Easy, '02 146
Strawberry Pie, Glazed, '82 M142
Strawberry-Rhubarb Pie, '98 99
Strawberry Yogurt Pie, '80 232
Strawberry-Yogurt Pie, '85 122; '86 124
Tangerine Chess Pie, '01 23
Tarts
    Almond-Apple Tart, '01 253
    Almond-Pear Tart, '01 253
    Almond Tart, '89 232
    Almond Tassies, Lucky, '91 13
    Almond Tea Tarts, '85 120
    Apple-Cranberry Tart, Rustic, '01 M314
    Apple-Cream Cheese Tart, '96 228
    Apple Cream Tart, '84 207
    Apple-Pecan Tarts, '80 282
    Apple Tart, Creamed, '94 17
    Apple Tart, Deluxe, '84 227
    Apple Tarts, Brandied, '96 284; '99 28
    Apple Tart, Upside-Down, '98 35
    Apple Tart with Cheese Pastry, '88 225
    Apricot-Almond Tart, '97 99
    Apricot-Apple Crumb Tart, '94 60
    Apricot-Nut Tart, '99 249
    Apricot-Pecan-Brie Tarts, '97 236
    Apricot Tarts, '79 282; '88 281
    Bakewell Tart, '97 110
    Berry Tartlets, Fresh, '91 98
    Berry Tart, Pick-a-, '91 118
    Blackberry Pudding Tarts, '93 200; '00 147
    Blackberry Supremes, '99 179
    Black Bottom Mocha-Cream Tart, '92 304
    Blue Cheese Appetizer Tarts, '85 300; '86 18
    Bouilli, Tarte à la, '83 92
    Bourbon-Chocolate-Pecan Tarts, '96 264
    Caramel Tarts, '82 43
    Caramel Tarts, Tiny, '99 179
    Caramel Turtle Truffle Tart, '93 M131
    Cheese Tart, Herb-, '87 98
    Cheese Tartlets, '88 211
    Cherry and Blackberry Tart, '83 225
    Cherry Tarts, Cheery, '80 238
    Chess Tarts, '90 83
    Chicken Salad Tarts, '84 257
    Chicken Tarts, Deviled, '94 14
    Chocolate-Amaretto Heavenly Tarts, '88 4
    Chocolate-Cherry Tart, '97 33
    Chocolate Chess Tarts, '92 214
    Chocolate Custard Tart, '99 27
    Chocolate-Peanut Butter Tarts, '92 277
    Chocolate-Pecan Tart with Caramel Sauce,
        '93 296; '94 234
    Chocolate Tarts, Bluegrass, '90 84
    Citrus Tartlets, Creamy, '02 136
    Coconut Cream Tarts with Macadamia Nut
        Crusts, '97 62
    Coconut-Pecan Cookie Tarts, '04 305
    Coffee Tart, '99 67
    Country Ham-and-Asparagus Tartlets, '98 82
    Cranberry-Apple Tart, '97 M316
    Cranberry-Cream Cheese Tarts, '80 154
    Cranberry Holiday Tarts, '83 279
    Cranberry-Nut Tart, '84 305
    Cranberry Tartlets, Fresh, '87 244
    Cran-Raspberry Meringue Tarts, '92 286
    Cream Cheese-Peach Tart, '99 169
    Cream Cheese Tarts, '84 74; '90 312
    Derby Tarts, Miniature, '90 92
    Eggnog Tarts, Creamy, '79 255
    French Silk Tarts, '79 236

Fruit Tart, Fancy, '82 128; '91 119
Fruit Tart, Fresh, '84 178; '90 58
Fruit Tart, King Cake, '96 57
Fruit Tartlets, Fresh, '93 96
Fruit Tart, Open-Face, '84 207
Fruit Tart, Rainbow, '82 304
Fruit Tarts, Bowl-Me-Over Fresh, '93 200
Fudge Pie, Sweetheart, '03 319
Fudge Truffle-Pecan Tart, '99 315; '02 208
Grapefruit Tart, '04 43
Grape Tart, Green, '87 77
Grasshopper Tarts, '80 220; '89 275
Ham-and-Cheese Tart, '92 332
Ham Tart, Supreme, '84 22
Heart Tarts, '87 14
Honey-Pecan Tart, '99 212
Kentucky Derby Tartlets, '00 107
Kentucky Derby Tarts, '79 102
Key Lime Curd Tartlets, '01 250
Key Lime Tart in Coconut Crust, '89 160
Kiwifruit-Peach Tart, '88 20
Kiwifruit Tart, '89 232
Lady Baltimore Tarts, '88 282
Leek-Goat Cheese Tart, '04 109
Lemon-Cheese Tarts, '79 2
Lemon Ice Cream Tarts, '80 152
Lemon-Sour Cream Tarts, '81 304
Lemon Tart), Caky Flaky Tart (Tart, '96 159
Lemon Tart, Double-Decker, '04 111
Lemon Tart Filling, Tangy, '04 111
Lemon Tarts, '82 156; '83 79
Lemon Tarts, Berry Good, '91 119
Lemon Tarts, Dainty, '82 304
Lemon Tarts, Golden, '85 191
Lemon Tart Shells, '88 195
Lemon Tart, Tangy, '01 245; '04 111
Lime-and-Macadamia Nut Tart, '03 295
Lime-Pineapple Tart, '88 6
Lime Tart, '98 272
Little Bits, '79 196
Midnight Delights, '95 278
Milan, Tart, '87 70
Miniature Tarts, '96 120
Mint Chocolate Mousse Tarts, '03 283
Mushroom Tarts, '88 161
Mushroom Tarts, Hot Sherried, '83 78
Onion Tart, Caramelized, '99 96
Orange Curd Tarts, '92 193
Orange Tarts, '96 317
Orange Tarts, Frozen, '80 154
Party Tarts, '95 90
Peach Cream Tart, '90 173
Peach Meringue Tart, Golden, '98 197
Peach Tart with Brandy Sauce, '98 119
Peachy Keen Tarts, '91 118
Peanut Butter Tarts, '97 329
Pear Tart, '82 304; '92 72
Pear Tart with White Caramel Sauce, '92 195
Pecan-Raisin Mini-Tarts, '03 246
Pecan-Raisin Tarts, '03 246
Pecan Tarts, '81 266
Pecan Tarts, Easy, '84 313
Pecan Tarts, Special, '87 224
Pecan Tarts, Toasty Southern, '95 329
Pecan Tart with Praline Cream, '90 256
Picadillo Tarts, '91 279
Pine Nut Tart, '97 86
Pommes, La Tarte aux, '80 125
Portabello Mushroom Tart, Smoked, '94 163
Potato Tarts, Phyllo, '98 69
Prune Tarts, Brandied, '85 223
Puddin' Pies, President Tyler's, '80 43
Pumpkin Tarts, No-Bake, '86 291
Raspberry-Almond Tarts, '99 280

PIES, PUFFS, AND PASTRIES, Tarts
(continued)

Raspberry-Brie Tartlets, **'04** 287
Raspberry Jelly Tarts, **'00** 208
Rutabaga-Spinach Tart, **'98** 274
Sausage 'n' Cheese Tarts, **'88** 51
Scuppernong Pudding Tarts, **'98** 221
Seafood Tartlets, **'87** 247
Shrimp 'n' Grits Tarts, **'03** 254
Shrimp Tart, **'87** 70
Shrimp Tartlets, **'00** 71
Southwestern Tart, **'04** 109
Spinach Tarts, **'82** 249
Squash Tart, **'96** 83
Strawberry Dream Tart, **'92** 118
Strawberry-Lemon Tart, **'89** 111
Strawberry-Mascarpone Tart, **'02** 146
Strawberry Tart, **'84** 138; **'89** 272; **'00** 82; **'01** 71
Strawberry Tarts, **'80** 70
Sweet Onion Tarts, **'95** 229
Teatime Tassies, **'84** 321
Tomato-Basil Tart, **'98** 132
Tomato-Cheese Tart, Dried, **'90** 203
Tomato-Leek-Bacon Tart, **'03** 325
Tomato-Pesto Tart, **'00** 195; **'02** 108
Tomato-Pesto Tarts, Mini, **'02** 108
Tomato Tart, **'03** 158
Tomato Tart, Fresh, **'95** 170
Tomato Tart, Herbed, **'96** 94
White Chocolate Chess Tart, **'95** 303
Yam Tartlets, Zamaani's Nutty, **'02** 21
Tin Roof Pie, **'85** 91
Tiramisù Toffee Trifle Pie, **'04** 195
Transparent Pie, **'80** 238
Turnovers
Apple Turnovers, Baked, **'93** 338
Apple Turnovers, Delicious, **'86** 25
Apple Turnovers, Fried, **'81** 161
Apple Turnovers, Puffy, **'87** 276
Apricot Turnovers, Fried, **'86** 24
Cheesy Sesame Seed Turnovers, **'91** 252
Chicken Liver Turnovers, **'79** 141
Cranberry Pockets, **'96** 320
Fruit Turnovers, **'79** 150
Ham Turnovers, Party, **'82** 39
Meat Turnovers, **'86** 326
Mushroom Turnovers, Hot, **'89** 285; **'97** 102
Mushroom Turnovers, Tiny, **'86** 24
Orange-Apple Turnovers, **'99** 294
Reuben Turnovers, **'94** 253
Roast Beef Turnovers, **'88** 273; **'89** 180
Salmon-Spinach Turnovers, **'83** 44
Sausage-Cheese Turnovers, **'88** 231
Turkey Turnovers, Home-Style, **'94** 325
Turkey Turnovers, Mexican, **'02** 245
Turnip-Bacon Turnovers, **'04** 213
Turnip Turnovers, **'04** 212
Vegetable Turnovers, **'86** 24
Vanilla Cream Pie, Fruit-Topped, **'84** 49
Vegetable. *See also* **PIES, PUFFS, AND PASTRIES/Tarts, Turnovers.**
Artichoke Flan, **'96** 22
Asparagus Pie, Cheesy, **'01** 103
Asparagus Squares, **'02** 183
Broccoli-Cheese Pie, **'84** 235
Butternut Squash Chiffon Pie, **'83** 296; **'84** 285
Butternut Squash Pie, **'80** 40; **'87** 212
Butternut Squash Pie, Spicy, **'80** 296
Carrot Custard Pie, **'79** 45
Carrot Pie, **'83** 117
Cauliflower-Carrot Pie, **'82** 191
Corn Pie, Quick and Cheesy, **'82** 191

Corn Pie with Fresh Tomato Salsa, Buttercrust, **'95** 181
Florentine Crêpe Pie, **'79** 34
Green Onion Pie, **'98** 159
Green Tomato Pie, **'79** 195; **'01** 141
Green Tomato Pie Filling, **'01** 141
Jalapeño Cheese Pie, **'96** 292
Maque Choux Pies, **'02** 182
Mushrooms in Patty Shells, **'80** 283
Onion-Cheese Pie, **'88** 86
Onion Pie, **'82** 191; **'00** 283
Pinto Bean Pie, **'80** 40
Ratatouille Pie, **'88** 198
Scallopini Pie, **'94** 133
Spaghetti Squash Pie, **'80** 186
Spinach Pie, **'82** 191; **'88** 56; **'00** 26
Spinach Pie, Greek, **'85** 59
Spinach, Pie Pan, **'94** 195
Spinach Pie Parma, **'96** 203
Spinach Pie, Super Special, **'04** 60
Spinach Pie with Muenster Crust, **'95** 48
Squash Pie, Italian, **'02** 183
Squash Pie, Savory, **'00** 170
Squash Pie, Spicy, **'85** 9
Summer Garden Pie, **'02** 182
Summer Pie, Savory, **'99** 159; **'03** 182
Sweet Potato Cream Pie, Southern, **'87** 260
Sweet Potato Meringue Pie, **'81** 126; **'83** 225
Sweet Potato-Orange Pie, **'88** 207
Sweet Potato-Pecan Pie, **'83** 90
Sweet Potato Pie, **'79** 207; **'85** 255, 275; **'86** 269; **'89** 289; **'96** 131, 326; **'00** 232; **'01** 243; **'04** 331
Sweet Potato Pie, Carolina, **'89** 295
Sweet Potato Pie, No-Crust, **'84** 236
Sweet Potato Pie, Old-Fashioned, **'79** 9
Sweet Potato Pie, Speedy, **'90** 219
Sweet Potato Pone Pie, **'80** 288
Tomato Pie, **'88** 198; **'97** 249; **'02** 172
Vidalia Onion Pie with Mushrooms, **'02** 183
Wild Mushroom-and-Onion Pot Pies, **'98** 296
Yam Pie, Louisiana, **'81** 223
Zucchini Pie, **'98** 236
Zucchini Pie, Cheesy, **'82** 191
Zucchini Pie, Italian-Style, **'83** 43
Watermelon Pie, **'95** 144

PIMIENTO
Asparagus with Pimientos, **'98** 286
Ball, Pimiento Cheese, **'80** 258
Bread, Pimiento-Cheese, **'85** 223
Casserole, English Pea-Pimiento, **'83** 207
Corn Sticks, Pimiento-Cheese, **'03** 20
Eggs, Pimiento-Deviled, **'84** 143
Green Beans with Pimiento, Tangy, **'00** 170; **'01** 21
Hoagies, Bacon, Pimiento, and Cheese, **'90** 144
Pasta, Pimiento, **'84** 176
Popovers, Pimiento, **'79** 138
Salsa, Fiery Steak with Pimiento Cheese, **'99** 331
Sandwiches, Pimiento Cheese, **'82** 278
Sandwiches, Pimiento Cheese Finger, **'99** 86
Sauce, Cauliflower with Pimiento, **'87** 232
Sauce, Pimiento Cheese, **'02** 291
Soup, Cream of Pimiento, **'96** 45; **'01** 72
Soup, Pimiento "Mac and Cheese,", **'97** M325
Spreads
Cheddar-Swiss Spread, **'99** 106
Cheese, Cream Cheese-and-Olive Pimiento, **'01** 169; **'03** 315
Cheese, Fabulous Pimiento, **'98** 315
Cheese, Jalapeño Pimiento, **'01** 169; **'03** 315
Cheese, Pecan Pimiento, **'01** 169; **'03** 315
Cheese, Pimiento, **'01** 169; **'03** 139
Chunky Pimiento Cheese, **'86** 295
Creamy Pimiento Cheese, **'86** 296

Creamy Pimiento Cheese Spread, **'92** 159
Feta-and-Apple Spread, **'99** 106
Four-Cheese Spread, **'99** 106
Garlic Pimiento Cheese Spread, **'79** 58
Green Chile-Pimiento Cheese, **'01** 61
Ham and Pimiento Spread, **'80** 285; **'81** 56
Jalapeño Pimiento Cheese, **'98** 315
Low-Calorie Pimiento Cheese Spread, **'85** 215
Peppered Pimiento Cheese, **'01** 137
Pimiento Cheese Spread, **'82** 35; **'83** 93; **'86** 127; **'99** 106, 276
Three Cheeses, Pimiento and, **'86** 296
West Texas Pimiento Cheese, **'84** 9
White Cheddar Pimiento Cheese, **'99** 106
Topping, Pimiento, **'83** 93
Vinaigrette, Pimiento, **'00** 167
PINEAPPLE
Acorn Squash, Pineapple-Stuffed, **'84** 255
Appetizer, Shrimp-Pineapple, **'85** 80
Applesauce, Hot Spiced, **'01** 60
Bacon-Wrapped Pineapple Chunks, **'84** 25
Baked Pineapple, **'83** 261; **'84** 287
Bake, Pineapple, **'79** 251; **'96** 84
Bake, Pineapple-Cheese, **'79** 106
Ball, Pineapple Cheese, **'81** 160
Ball, Pineapple-Cheese, **'84** 26
Beans, Hawaiian-Style Baked, **'86** 210
Beets with Pineapple, **'79** 249; **'82** 204
Betty, Pineapple-Apple, **'85** 46
Beverages
Blue Woo-Woo, **'94** 226
Bole, **'97** 245
Coconut-Pineapple Drink, **'83** 172
Cooler, Pineapple, **'90** 207
Float, Pineapple Sherbet, **'79** 148
Hot Buttered Pineapple Drink, **'91** 260
Lemonade, Pineapple, **'93** 194
Limeade, Pineapple, **'01** 235
Milk Shake, Banana-Pineapple, **'84** 59
Milkshake, Pineapple, **'87** 199
Milk Shake, Pineapple, **'94** 113
Nectar, Hot Pineapple, **'90** 21
Nog, Speedy Breakfast, **'82** 47
Orange-Pineapple Drink, **'89** 35
Piña Coladas, **'95** 203; **'96** 127
Piña Colada Slush, **'95** 90
Punch, Brew-Ha-Ha, **'98** 255
Punch, Champagne, **'99** 30
Punch, Cranberry-Pineapple, **'00** 284
Punch, False-Kick, **'82** 121
Punch, Frosty Pineapple, **'91** 66
Punch, Hot Pineapple, **'82** 264
Punch, Lime-Pineapple, **'83** 142
Punch, Pineapple, **'79** 174; **'80** 128
Punch, Pineapple-Citrus, **'96** 134
Punch, Pineapple Fruit, **'02** 49
Punch, Pineapple-Gin, **'95** 140
Punch, Pineapple-Mint, **'88** 209
Punch, Pineapple-Orange, **'85** 236
Punch, Pineapple Sherbet, **'95** 141
Punch, Spiced Pineapple, **'83** 33; **'92** 66
Sangría, Pineapple, **'91** 176
Shake, Light Pineapple-Buttermilk, **'01** 173
Shake, Pineapple-Banana, **'85** 215
Shake, Pineapple-Buttermilk, **'01** 173
Shake, Pineapple-Orange-Banana, **'97** 172
Shake, Strawberry-Pineapple, **'84** 166
Shake, Tropical, **'00** 179
Slush, Pineapple, **'88** 82
Slush, Pineapple-Banana, **'90** 14
Smoothie, Easy Pineapple, **'00** 199
Smoothie, Peachy-Pineapple, **'97** 173
Smoothie, Pineapple, **'97** 172
Smoothie, Quick Banana-Pineapple, **'93** 195

Soda, Pineapple, '90 179
Spiced Pineapple Sparkle, '92 322
Spritzer, Pineapple-Grapefruit, '04 143
Strawberry Slush, Pineapple-, '94 227
Tea, Pineapple, '93 165
Wassail, Pineapple, '01 240
Wassail, Pineapple-Apricot, '83 275
Yogurt Whirl, Pineapple-, '91 132

Breads
Apricot Bread, Pineapple-, '84 7
Buns, Easy Pineapple, '85 14
Carrot Bread, Pineapple-, '79 106
Carrot-Pineapple Bread, '82 210
Coffee Cake, Pineapple-Coconut, '94 49; '03 198
Doughnuts, Pineapple Drop, '83 95
Hawaiian Loaf, '80 225
Muffins, Carrot-Pineapple, '81 6
Muffins, Morning Glory, '93 327
Muffins, Pineapple, '81 14, 250
Muffins, Sunshine, '86 9
Nut Bread, Pineapple-, '79 215
Pecan Loaf Bread, Pineapple-, '87 256
Pineapple Bread, '83 139
Puffs, Pineapple Breakfast, '98 326
Rolls, Cranberry-Pineapple, '86 275
Rolls, Pineapple Angel, '89 72
Cabbage with Pineapple, Red, '97 215
Carrots and Pineapple, Curried, '90 228
Carrots, Pineapple, '83 198
Citrus, Pineapple and Fresh, '89 206
Curried Pineapple, '03 201

Desserts
Ambrosia, Pineapple-Orange, '88 252
Baked Pineapple with Natillas Sauce, '83 179
Bars, Pineapple-Orange, '82 129
Basket, Summer Berry, '84 158
Boats with Rum Sauce, Pineapple, '97 192
Cake, Banana Split, '99 48
Cake, Cajun, '87 138
Cake, Carrot, '98 275
Cake, Cherry-Pineapple Dump, '02 128
Cake, Coconut-Pineapple, '89 56
Cake, Coconut-Pineapple Layer, '80 140
Cake, Express Pineapple Upside-Down, '03 65
Cake, Fresh Pineapple Upside-Down, '97 204
Cake, Heavenly Pineapple, '83 303
Cake, Hummingbird, '03 315
Cake, Lemon-Pineapple, '86 60, 239
Cake, Lightened Hummingbird, '01 34
Cake, Nanny's Famous Coconut-Pineapple, '97 277
Cake, Pig Pickin', '04 112
Cake, Pineapple-Cherry Dump, '04 91
Cake, Pineapple-Coconut, '00 86
Cake, Pineapple-Pecan Upside-Down, '84 25
Cake, Pineapple Pound, '79 148
Cake, Pineapple Right-Side-Up Snack, '99 28
Cake, Pineapple Upside-Down, '80 102; '88 10
Cake Roll, Coconut-Pineapple, '84 304
Cake Roll, Pineapple Upside-Down, '96 162
Cake, Skillet Pineapple Upside-Down, '85 242;
    '03 65
Cake, Spiced Pineapple Upside-Down, '02 214
Cake, Stacked Pineapple Upside-Down, '86 239
Cake, Tropical Dump, '02 128
Cake, Zucchini-Pineapple, '95 160
Charlotte, Pineapple, '90 288
Cheesecake, Festive Piña Colada, '01 286
Cheesecake, Pineapple, '81 32
Cheesecake, Tropical Tofu, '00 204
Cheesecake, Ultimate Pineapple, '85 38
Chimichangas, Pineapple Dessert, '86 4
Chocolate-Drizzled Pineapple with Raspberry
    Sauce, '90 57
Cookies, Pineapple, '79 216

Cream, Pineapple 'n', '88 202
Crème Brûlée, Piña Colada, '04 246
Crêpes, Mango-Pineapple, '86 216
Crisp, Tropical Pineapple, '02 232
Delight, Fresh Pineapple, '79 111
Delight, Pineapple-Almond, '85 96
Filling, Orange-Pineapple Fried Pie, '96 109
Filling, Pineapple, '80 140; '83 179; '84 153;
    '89 57; '97 277
Flan, Pineapple, '01 85
Frappé, Hawaiian, '81 178
Fritters, Pineapple, '88 112
Frosting, Pineapple-Cream Cheese, '95 160
Frozen Tropical Paradise, '89 206
Glaze, '01 286
Glazed Oranges and Pineapple, '86 318
Glaze, Orange-Pineapple, '81 60
Glaze, Pineapple, '83 143; '85 38; '97 55
Grilled Pineapple with Vanilla-Cinnamon Ice
    Cream, '00 127; '01 195
Ice Cream, Orange-Pineapple, '86 117
Ice Cream, Pineapple-Mint, '84 186
Meringue-Topped Pineapple, '84 178
Mint Dessert, Pineapple-, '96 127
Mousse, Coconut-Pineapple, '94 198
Mousse, Elegant Pineapple, '79 230
Noodle Casserole, Sweet, '02 238
Papaya-Pineapple Roll, '94 18
Parfait, Pineapple, '84 83
Pears, Pineapple-Honey, '86 94
Phyllo Bundles, Pineapple, '87 277
Pie, Apple-Pineapple, '97 276
Pie, Coconut-Pineapple, '84 256
Pie, Double-Crust Pineapple, '82 85
Pie, Fresh Pineapple, '91 178
Pie, Pineapple, '80 237; '89 252
Pie, Pineapple-Chicken Salad, '80 138
Pie, Pineapple-Coconut Chess, '92 214
Pie, Pineapple-Grits, '96 236
Pie, Rancher's Buttermilk, '04 208
Pizza, Apple-Pineapple Dessert, '00 313
Pops, Hawaiian Orange-Pineapple, '94 143
Pops, Pineapple-Yogurt, '91 173
Pudding, Piña Colada Bread, '98 34
Pudding, Pineapple, '80 102
Pudding with Vanilla-Nutmeg Sauce, Pineapple-
    Apple Bread, '02 208
Sauce, Banana-Pineapple, '83 48
Sauce, Pineapple Ice Cream, '81 M289
Sauce, Pineapple-Orange, '84 14
Sauce, Pineapple-Rum, '84 275
Sherbet, Buttermilk, '99 99
Sherbet, Creamy Pineapple, '79 155
Sherbet, Easy Pineapple, '92 199
Sherbet, Lemon-Pineapple, '96 330
Sherbet, Pineapple, '81 177; '84 83; '89 199
Skewers with Rum Sauce, Grilled Pineapple,
    '04 247
Sopaipillas, Pineapple, '83 179
Sorbet, Pineapple, '03 171
Soufflé, Pineapple Dessert, '80 153
Spritz, Pineapple, '86 94
Stuffed Pineapple, '00 160
Sundaes, Mauna Loa, '80 126
Tart, Lime-Pineapple, '88 6
Topping, Cherry-Pineapple, '87 126
Topping, Lemon-Pineapple, '86 60
Topping, Pineapple, '86 239
Trifle, Pineapple Angel Food, '93 86
Tropical Snow, '86 34
Dip, Cheesy Pineapple, '80 249
Dip, Pineapple-Ginger, '86 104
Dressing, Fruit Salad with Pineapple, '85 207
Dressing, Pineapple Cream, '83 81

Dressing, Pineapple-Poppy Seed, '85 55
Fried Pineapple, '81 232
Fritters, Pineapple, '00 238
Gazpacho, Pineapple, '01 85
Glaze, Pineapple, '83 143; '84 26; '85 38
Gratin, Pineapple, '93 328
Ham-Pineapple Nibbles, '95 283
Hawaiian Dream Boats, '86 151
Jam, Pineapple, '81 147
Jelly, Pineapple-Orange Mint, '92 105

Main Dishes
Beans and Franks, Hawaiian Baked, '80 136
Beefburgers Hawaiian, '86 137
Burgers, Pineapple, '82 169
Chicken and Pineapple, '81 281; '82 30
Chicken and Rice, Island, '04 165
Chicken Bake, Pineapple, '82 120
Chicken Breasts, Hawaiian Stuffed, '99 64
Chicken, Hawaiian Sesame, '81 106
Chicken Oriental, '01 36
Chicken, Oriental Pineapple, '84 288
Chicken, Piña Colada, '86 21
Chicken, Pineapple, '83 M194; '85 3
Chicken Stir-Fry, Pineapple-, '89 176
Chicken, Sweet-and-Sour, '97 325
Chicken with Grilled Pineapple, Lime, '04 88
Chicken with Pineapple-Mustard Glaze, Roast,
    '89 83
Chicken with Pineapple, Oriental, '86 42
Chops, Pineapple-Curry Glazed, '82 106
Crab Imperial, Pineapple-, '84 M286
Flank Steak in Mexican Marinade, '98 128
Franks, Hawaiian, '81 202
Fried Rice, Spicy Shrimp-and-Pineapple, '03 285
Ham, Citrus-and-Spice, '88 40
Ham Loaf, Pineapple Upside-Down, '79 253
Ham Patties, Pineapple-, '80 110
Ham, Pineapple-Baked, '86 48
Ham, Pineapple-Flavored, '87 160
Ham, Pineapple-Glazed, '01 288; '03 82
Ham-Potato-Pineapple Bake, '93 302
Ham Sandwich Loaf, Pineapple-, '91 167
Kebabs, Chicken-Pineapple, '00 200
Kebabs, Pineapple-Beef, '83 212
Kebabs, Pineapple-Chicken, '86 M328
Kebabs, Pineapple-Pork, '99 144
Loaves, Individual Pineapple, '81 M121
Loaves, Mini Teriyaki, '98 224
Meatballs, Chinese, '87 194
Meatballs, Polynesian, '80 207
Meatballs with Pineapple and Peppers, '90 145
Meat Loaf, Teriyaki, '98 224
Pizza, Ham-and-Pineapple, '96 169
Pork and Pineapple, Polynesian, '83 102
Pork Chops, Hawaiian, '86 212
Pork Chops, Pineapple, '87 M124
Pork, Pineapple, '82 60
Pork, Pineapple Sweet-and-Sour, '82 120
Pork Roast, Pineapple, '79 41
Pot Roast, Hawaiian, '81 298
Pot Roast, Polynesian, '80 59
Shrimp Oriental, '01 36
Marmalade, Orange-Pineapple, '82 150; '89 M156
Marmalade, Strawberry-Pineapple, '85 130
Melts, Pineapple-Turkey, '03 196
Pears, Pineapple-Honey, '86 94
Pickled Pineapple, '79 24
Preserves, Mango-Pineapple, '79 137
Puro de Piña, '02 82
Relish, Cranberry, '98 310
Relish, Pineapple-Coconut, '96 323; '97 27
Rice with Pineapple, Curried, '79 142
Rollups, Creamy Pineapple-and-Ham, '04 163
Salad Dressing, Pineapple, '81 36

PINEAPPLE
(continued)

Salads
    Boat Aloha, Pineapple, **'80** 102
    Boats Ahoy, Pineapple, **'80** 148
    Buttermilk Salad, Pineapple-, **'82** 80
    Carrot-Pineapple Salad, **'91** 83
    Celery Salad, Pineapple-, **'85** 95
    Chicken Salad, Pineapple-Nut, **'83** 80
    Chicken Salad, South Sea Island, **'97** 88
    Citrus, Pineapple and Fresh, **'89** 206
    Coleslaw, Curried Pineapple, **'88** 172
    Congealed Salad, Lime, **'02** 257
    Congealed Salad, Pineapple-Cucumber, **'83** 118
    Congealed Salad, Pineapple-Orange, **'83** 218
    Cranberry-Pineapple Salad, Frozen, **'91** 237
    Cucumber-Pineapple Salad, **'84** 124
    Daiquiri Salad, Pineapple, **'84** 232
    Delight, Pineapple-Pear, **'82** 54
    Fresh Pineapple Boats, **'83** 153
    Frosted Salad, Heavenly, **'79** 286
    Frosty Pineapple Salad, **'89** 278
    Frozen Salads, Paper Cup, **'00** 176
    Fruit Salad, Icy Pineapple-, **'87** 9
    Lime Salad, Pineapple-, **'84** 320
    Macaroni Salad, Pineapple, **'79** 220
    Mandarin Orange and Pineapple Salad, **'82** 266
    Mold, Minted Pineapple, **'85** 240
    Shrimp Salad, Aloha, **'95** 46
    Slaw, Apple-Pineapple, **'79** 241
    Slaw, Cabbage-Pineapple, **'92** 182
    Slaw, Colorful Pineapple, **'86** 250
    Slaw, Pineapple, **'94** 49; **'99** 26
    Slaw, Pineapple-Almond, **'92** 171
    Slaw Sandwiches, Ham-and-Pineapple, **'96** 199
    Slaw, Zesty, **'97** 324
    Waldorf, Pineapple, **'97** 86
    Waldorf Salad, Pineapple, **'92** 97
 Salsa, Cranberry, **'99** 316
 Salsa, Pineapple, **'96** 226; **'03** 128; **'04** 196
 Salsa, Spicy Pineapple, **'97** 165
 Salsa, Warm Pineapple, **'02** 144
 Sandwich, Pineapple-Turkey, **'01** 85
 Sauce, Banana-Pineapple, **'83** 48
 Sauce, Jezebel, **'81** 29; **'82** 55
 Sauce, Mango-Pineapple Hot, **'04** 183
 Sauce, Maui, **'99** 310
 Sauce, Pineapple, **'84** 236; **'92** 203
 Sauce, Pineapple-Curry, **'79** 252
 Sauce, Pineapple-Rhubarb, **'88** 94
 Sauce, Raisin-Pineapple, **'82** 177
 Sauce, Sweet-and-Sour Pineapple, **'85** 66
 Scalloped Pineapple, **'79** 106; **'82** 254; **'84** M323
 Shells, Pineapple, **'96** 127
 Skewered Pineapple and Strawberries, **'84** 251
 Slicing Pineapples, Instructions for, **'82** 94
 Snow Peas and Pineapple, **'91** 120
 Spiced Pineapple, **'80** 102; **'02** 239
 Spread, Coconut-Pineapple, **'93** 309
 Spread, Hawaiian Cheese, **'87** 158
 Spread, Pineapple-Cheese, **'86** 126; **'91** 167
 Spread, Pineapple-Cream Cheese, **'82** 35
 Spread, Pineapple Sandwich, **'84** 166
 Spritz, Pineapple, **'86** 94
 Sweet Potatoes, Pineapple-Orange, **'96** 46
 Vinaigrette, Black Pepper-Pineapple, **'97** 181
PITA. *See* **APPETIZERS/ Pita; BREADS;**
    SANDWICHES/Pita.
PIZZA
 Appetizers
    Appetizer Pizzas, **'89** M118
    Bites, Pizza, **'95** 244
    Cocktail Pizzas, **'79** 110
    Dip, Pizza, **'99** 65
    Dip, Quick Pizza, **'00** M168
    Horns, Pizza, **'89** 214
    Party Pizzettes, **'80** 192
    Pita Pizzas, **'89** 19
    Shellfish Pizza, **'91** 224
    Shrimp Pizza Wedges, **'89** 158
    Slices, Pizza, **'84** 269
    Snacks, Pizza Party, **'86** 262
    Snacks, Tasty Little Pizza, **'79** 248
    Squares, Pizza, **'87** 168
    Turnovers, Little Pizza, **'85** 327
    Zucchini Pizzas, **'88** 212
 Artichoke and Prosciutto, Pizza with, **'87** 182
 Bagel, Pizza on a, **'93** M94
 Bake, Upside-Down Pizza, **'98** 224
 Barbecue Chicken Pizza, **'03** 49
 Bayou Pizza, The Best of the, **'95** 268
 Beef-and-Sausage Pizza, Double Cheesy, **'86** 77
 Blazing Sunset Pizza, **'95** 267
 Bobolis, Easy Cheesy, **'92** 278
 Bread, Pizza Batter, **'85** 56
 Breakfast Pizza, **'85** 44; **'88** 288; **'90** 140, 178;
    '97 172; **'00** 193
 Broccoli Supreme Pizza, **'02** 312
 Burger, Pizza, **'87** 185
 Burgers, All-American Pizza, **'92** 148
 Burgers, Easy Pizza, **'82** 190
 Burger Snacks, Pizza-, **'84** 30
 Burgers, Pizza, **'80** M201; **'81** 73; **'89** 165
 Calzone, **'85** 94
 Calzones, All-Star Pizza, **'95** 308
 Casserole, Microwave Pizza, **'89** M248
 Casserole, Pizza, **'88** 273; **'89** 181
 Casserole, Quick Pizza, **'83** 266
 Casserole, Upside-Down Pizza, **'03** 284
 Cheese-and-Mushroom Pizza, **'83** 226
 Cheeseburger Pizza, **'97** 318
 Cheese Pizza, Quick 3-, **'00** 94
 Chicken-and-Purple Onion Pizza, **'97** 47
 Chicken-and-Three-Cheese French Bread Pizzas,
    '96 94
 Chicken Barbecue Pizza, Quick 'n' Easy, **'04** 139
 Chicken Fajita Pizza, **'03** 235
 Chicken Parmesan Pizza, **'00** 134
 Chicken Pizza, **'94** 218
 Chicken Pizza, Mexican, **'97** 321
 Chicken Pizza with Mango Pico de Gallo, Fajita,
    '04 318
 Clam Pizza, Baby, **'87** 182
 Crusts
    Crispy Pizza Crust, **'87** 181; **'89** 64
    Parmesan Pizza Crust, **'93** 58
    Pizza Crust, **'80** 233; **'83** 226; **'85** 243; **'86** 77;
     '04 208
    Skillet Pizza Crusts, **'94** 218
    Special Pizza Crust, **'90** 139
    Thick Crust, **'81** 214
    Thin Crust, **'81** 214
    Whole Wheat Crust, **'94** 78
    Whole Wheat Pizza Crust, **'93** 58
 Cups, Pizza, **'81** 215
 Deep-Dish Mediterranean Pizza, **'80** 163
 Deep-Dish Pizza, **'01** 29
 Deep-Dish Pizza Luncheon Pie, **'80** 286
 Deep-Dish Vegetarian Pizza, **'85** 243
 Dessert
    Apple-Pineapple Dessert Pizza, **'00** 313
    Banana Split-Brownie Pizza, **'96** M164
    Blueberry Pizza, **'96** 147
    Chocolate Pizza, **'91** 298
    Cookie, Pizza, **'90** 49
    Cookies, Candy Shop Pizza, **'02** 299
    Cranberry Dessert Pizzas, **'96** 320
    Dolce (Italian Sweet Pies), Pizza, **'00** 283
    Kiwi-Berry Pizza, **'86** 198; **'87** 55
    Kiwifruit Pizza, **'89** 306
    Peanut Butter-Fruit Pizza, **'94** 60
    Rocky Road Pizza Dessert, **'99** 196
    Strawberry Pizza, **'79** 94
 Dogs, Grilled Pizza, **'97** 139
 Dough, Pizza, **'04** 58
 Easy Pizza, **'92** 181
 Eggplant Pizza, **'85** 221
 Eggplant Pizzas, **'98** 183
 Eggplant, Tomato, and Feta Pizza, Greek, **'01** 312
 Fiesta Pizza, **'00** 85
 Five-Ring Pizzas, **'96** 180
 French Bread, Pizza on, **'82** 131
 Garden Pizza, **'89** 108
 Greek Pizza, **'03** 145
 Grilled Pizza, **'97** 190
 Grilled Pizzas, **'93** 178; **'98** 176
 Ground Beef Pizza, Cheesy, **'03** 62
 Gruyère-Chicken Pizza, **'87** 182
 Ham-and-Eggs Crescent Pizza, **'93** 47
 Ham-and-Pineapple Pizza, **'96** 169
 Hamburger Pizza, Quick, **'85** 243
 Herb Pizza, Easy, **'92** 99
 Homemade Pizza, Best Ever, **'80** 233
 Hot Dog Pizzas, **'93** 78
 Hummus Pizza, Red Pepper, **'01** 56
 Individual Pizzas, **'03** 219
 Italian-Style Pizza, Original, **'87** 182
 Jazzed-Up Pizza, Jiffy, **'83** M314
 King Henry Pizza, The, **'95** 267
 Lasagna Pizza, **'85** 285
 Maca-Pizza, **'99** 195
 Meatballs, Pizza, **'85** 86
 Meat Loaf, Cheesy Pizza, **'81** 121
 Meaty Pizza Pie, **'03** 145
 Mexican Pizza, **'94** 218, 327; **'99** 119; **'02** 72
 Mexican Pizza, Cheesy, **'00** 314
 Mozzarella and Basil Pizza, Fresh, **'04** 58
 Muffuletta Pizzas, **'00** M335
 Pan Pizza, Quick, **'86** 160
 Pepperoni Pizza, Thick 'n' Crusty, **'85** 244
 Pepper Pizza, Roasted, **'94** 218
 Peppers-and-Cheese Pizza, **'03** 235
 Peppers, Pizza, **'83** 135
 Pesto Pizza, **'87** 182; **'94** 218
 Pesto Pizza, Nutty, **'97** 267
 Phyllo Pizza, **'94** 91
 Pie, Pizza, **'91** 23
 Pita Pizza Snack, **'94** 193
 Plum-and-Sweet Onion Pizza, **'98** 193
 Pocket Pizzas, Easy, **'90** 168
 Popcorn, Pizza-Flavored, **'85** 236
 Portobello-Pine Nut Pizza, **'99** 216
 Portobello Pizza, **'03** 175
 Portobello Pizza Burgers, Grilled, **'00** 89
 Portobello Pizzas, Grilled, **'00** 89
 Potato Pizzas, Roasted, **'99** 16
 Pumpkins, Pizza, **'98** 255
 Quiche, Pizza, **'86** 53
 Quick Little Pizzas, **'88** 227
 Reuben Pizza, **'03** 69
 Rollups, Pizza, **'99** 197
 Rollups, Pizza Bread, **'04** M35
 Salad Pizza, **'87** 182
 Sandwiches, Open-Face Pizza, **'82** 3; **'83** 85;
    '84 M198; **'85** 22
 Sandwich, Giant Pizza, **'80** 93
 Sauce, Pizza, **'84** 33; **'85** 285; **'00** 314
 Sauce, Traditional Pizza, **'95** 267
 Sausage-Pepperoni Pizza, Spicy, **'83** 226
 Sausage Pizza Pie, Link-, **'85** 33

Sausage-Potato Pizza, '01 199
Scones, Pizza, '03 207
Seafood Alfredo Pizza, '03 236
Shellfish Pizza, '91 224
Shrimp-and-Dried Tomato Pizza, '97 49
Sicilian Pizza, '01 125
Snacks, Pizza, '01 231
Southern Classic Pizza, '95 268
Southwest Deluxe Pizza, '95 268
Southwestern Pizza, '03 146
Speedy Pizza, '81 214
Squares, Easy Pizza, '02 61
Sticks, Pizza, '98 255
Sunburst, Pizza, '94 245
Supreme, Pizza, '81 214
Swiss Steak, Pizza, '02 36
Taco Pizza, '89 M177; '98 176; '00 293
Tacos, Pizza-Flavored Chicken, '95 340
Tostada Pizza, '81 16; '82 13
Turkey-Vegetable Pizza, '90 139
Two-Way Pizza, '79 93
Upside-Down Pizza, '91 185
Vegetable Pizza, '89 64; '94 218
Vegetable Pizza, Grilled, '98 176
Vegetable Pizzas, Grilled, '97 323
Vegetarian Pizza, Deep-Dish, '85 243
Vegetarian Processor Pizza, '89 225
Veggie Pizza, '94 78
Veggie Pizzas, '99 97
Veggie Pizza, Southwestern, '95 126
Veggie Sausage Pizzas, '00 294
Wedges, Toasted Pizza Crust, '03 280
Whole Wheat Pizza, '84 33
Wide-Eyed Pizzas, '90 94
PLANTAINS
Chips, Plantain, '95 M203
Chips), Tostones de Plátano (Plantain, '92 158
Fried Plantains, '99 121
PLUMS
Betty, Bourbon-PlumBrown, '97 177
Brandied Plums, '97 176
Bread Pudding, Refrigerator Plum, '97 177
Bread, Sugar Plum, '80 256
Butter, Plum, '88 152
Cake, Plum, '97 177
Chutney, Plum, '84 179
Cobbler, Crunchy Plum, '88 152
Cobbler, Plum, '99 254; '03 161
Cobbler with Spiced Plum Muffin Crust, Plum,
    '04 201
Coffee Cake, Plum Preserves, '02 211
Crunch, Layered Plum, '86 174
Fajitas, Plum Good, '94 115
Ham, Plum, '80 110
Jam, Freezer Plum, '89 M156
Jam, Peach-Plum Freezer, '85 130
Jam, Plum Refrigerator, '89 139
Jelly, Plum, '82 150
Kuchen, Plum, '79 161
Muffin Batter, Spiced Plum, '04 201
Muffins, Plum Good, '83 96
Muffins, Spiced Plum, '04 201
Pheasant, Gin-Marinated, '02 250
Pie, Easy Plum Cream, '86 174
Pie, Streusel-Topped Plum, '88 153
Pie with Italian Sweet Crust, Plum, '79 162
Pizza, Plum-and-Sweet Onion, '98 193
Poached Plums, '90 M141
Port Wine, Plums in, '97 176
Preserves, Plum, '03 161
Pudding, Flamed Plum, '84 276
Pudding-Gelatin Mold, Plum, '86 300; '87 178
Pudding, Light Plum, '86 318
Pudding, Old-Fashioned Plum, '80 264

Pudding, Plum, '79 281
Salad, Crisp Plum, '03 161
Salsa, Plum, '97 176
Sauce, Chinese Plum, '82 237
Sauce, Crispy Ribs with Plum, '98 182
Sauce, Fresh Plum, '94 129; '97 176
Sauce, Gingered Plum, '87 175
Sauce, Plum, '80 249; '82 40; '88 152
Sauce, Quail with Red Plum, '80 48
Sauce, Spareribs in Plum, '99 136
Sauce, Spicy Plum, '86 11
Slush, Plum, '84 139
Soup, Chilled Plum, '03 161
Soup, Chilled Purple Plum, '79 162
Soup, Peach-Plum, '87 157
Soup, Plum, '85 107
Soup, Plum-and-Wine, '00 144
POLENTA
Baked Polenta with Cheese and Okra, '99 232
Basic Polenta, '95 164
Cheesy Polenta and Green Chiles, Stuffed Red
    Peppers With, '04 169
Chicken with Polenta, '02 87
Crab Polenta, '00 277
Fries, Red Pepper-Polenta, '00 196
Grilled Polenta, '00 126
Grilled Polenta with Black Bean Salsa, '93 155
Lasagna with Cream Sauce, Polenta, '03 237
Sausage, Polenta with, '93 32
Serrano Chile Polenta, '98 104
Triangles, Polenta, '98 181
POMEGRANATE
Salad Dressing, Pomegranate, '96 241
Syrup, Pomegranate, '96 241
Wreath, Tex-Mex, '96 241
POPCORN
Asian Popcorn, Quick-and-Easy, '00 223
Bacon-Cheese Popcorn, '86 74
Balls, Marshmallow Popcorn, '90 226
Balls, Nutty Popcorn, '88 227
Basil, Garlic, and Parmesan Popcorn, '00 223
Cake, Popcorn-Gumdrop, '87 262
Candied Popcorn and Peanuts, '82 295
Caramel
    Baked Caramel Corn, '81 218
    Candy, Caramel Corn, '84 243
    Caramel Corn, '88 64
    Caramel Popcorn, '79 219; '86 M212
    Clusters, Caramel-Nut Popcorn, '00 M223
    Crispy Caramel Corn, '04 112
    Crispy Caramel Popcorn, '85 247
    Crunch, Caramel, '95 165
    Crunch Popcorn, Caramel, '96 255
    Ghoul's Hands, '94 256
    Nutty Caramel Corn, '92 317
    Oven-Made Caramel Corn, '91 233
Cheese Popcorn, '98 205
Cheesy Barbecue Popcorn, '95 239
Chili Popcorn, '91 17; '95 166; '00 M223
Chocolate Popcorn, Delicious, '00 223
Cinnamon-Popcorn Crunch, '86 136
Crazy Mixed-Up Popcorn, '97 245
Delight, Popcorn, '00 M133
Flavored Popcorn, '98 205
Garlic Popcorn, '83 M315
Harvest Popcorn, '84 300
Herb-Seasoned Popcorn, '94 122
Honey-and-Spice Crunch, '94 290
Kettle Corn, '04 187
Mexican Popcorn, '98 205
Mix, Curried Popcorn, '86 326
Mix, Party, '96 306; '97 322; '98 234
Munchies, Pop Graham, '96 28
Nut Popcorn, Spicy, '02 287; '03 272

Nutty Popcorn, '85 208
Orange Popcorn, '86 230
Oriental Popcorn, '86 74; '98 205
Peanut Brittle, Popcorn, '02 M223
Pizza-Flavored Popcorn, '85 236
Pizzazz, Popcorn with, '93 245
Pretzel Popcorn, '84 30
Ranch Popcorn, '98 205
Rosemary Popcorn with Pine Nuts, '00 223
Scramble, Popcorn, '87 185
Sesame-Cheese Popcorn, '79 220
Spiced Popcorn Snack, '87 8
Trick or Treat Popcorn, '03 210
PORK. *See also* **BACON, CASSEROLES, HAM,
    SAUSAGE.**
Apple Cider Pork and Vegetables, '97 210
Backbone and Rice, Pork, '03 252
Backbones, Smoked Country-Style, '82 162
Bake, Pork-and-Noodle, '88 98
Bake, Pork Spaghetti, '81 11
Barbecue
    Bannister's Barbecue, '92 166
    Barbecued Pork, '80 72
    Chops, Barbecued Pork, '81 10
    Chops, Barbecued Stuffed, '87 229
    Chops, Marinated Barbecued Pork, '79 90
    Chops, Oven-Barbecued Pork, '81 234; '82 26;
        '83 40
    Chops with Tangy Barbecue Sauce, Pork, '99 104
    Home-Style Barbecue, '88 145
    Quesadillas, Barbecue, '02 121
    Ribs, Apple Barbecued, '80 111
    Ribs, Barbecue, '99 68
    Ribs, Barbecued, '80 111; '85 159; '91 205
    Ribs, Barbecued Country-Style, '95 237
    Ribs, Country-Style Barbecued, '79 42
    Ribs, Herbed Barbecued, '86 185
    Ribs, Oven-Barbecued Pork, '88 132
    Ribs, Slow-Cooker Barbecue, '03 160
    Ribs, Smoky Barbecued, '80 111
    Ribs, Tangy Barbecued, '83 160
    Ribs with Blender Barbecue Sauce, '90 12
    Roast, Barbecued Pork, '82 11; '03 147
    Roast, Barbecued Pork Loin, '93 34
    Roast, Barbecue Pork, '82 97; '83 104
    Roast, Berry Barbecued Pork, '80 288
    Roast, Oven-Barbecued Pork, '91 50
    Sandwiches, Barbecue Pork, '00 23
    Shoulder, Barbecued Pork, '81 111; '82 11
    Shoulder, Barbecue Pork, '00 274
    Spaghetti, Barbecue, '02 121
    Spareribs, Apple-Barbecue, '90 160
    Spareribs, Barbecued, '81 112; '82 12; '86 232;
        '95 236
    Spareribs, Barbecued Country-Style, '80 73
    Spareribs, Easy Barbecued, '82 97; '83 104
    Spareribs, Saucy Barbecued, '79 14
    Spareribs, Southern Barbecued, '79 90
    Spareribs, Spicy Barbecued, '84 93
    Spareribs, Tangy Barbecued, '82 106
    Spareribs with Orange Barbecue Sauce, '83 11
    Spicy Barbecued Pork, '84 296
    Sundae, Barbecue, '02 121
Bean Sauce, Pork-and-Onions with, '85 76
Brunch Eggs, '85 44
Burgers, Hearty Sauced Pork, '84 125
Burgoo, Five-Meat, '87 3
Burgoo, Harry Young's, '87 3
Burgoo, Kentucky, '97 138
Burritos, '80 196
Burritos, Meat-and-Bean, '81 194
Cabbage Leaves, Stuffed, '00 270
Calabaza Guisada con Puerco (Pumpkin Cooked
    with Pork), '80 193

Casserole, Cheesy Pork, '81 M74
Casserole, Pork, '83 116
Cassoulet, '96 328
Chalupa, Bean, '80 223
Chalupas, Pork, '83 160
Chile Verde, Light, '88 148
Chili, Double-Meat, '79 269; '80 12
Chili Verde, '95 14
Chops. *See also* **PORK/Barbecue.**
  Apple-a-Day Pork Chops, An, '01 35
  Apple and Onion, Pork Chops with Mustard-
    Glazed, '01 47
  Apple-Kraut Pork Chops, '84 50
  Apple Pork Chops, '91 198
  Apple Pork Chops, Spicy, '87 230
  Apples, Pork Chops with Minted, '00 21
  Apricot-Sauced Pork Chops, '85 22
  Arlo, Pork, '87 229
  Baked Pork Chops and Apples, '81 10
  Baked Pork Chops, Greek-Style, '04 44
  Bake, Fiesta Pork, '79 265
  Balsamic Pork Chops, '01 128, 208
  Balsamic Pork Chops with Apples, '03 204
  Barbecue-Battered Pork Chops, '04 139
  Beans, Pork Chops with Baked, '93 18
  Black Bean-and-Corn Salsa Pork Chops, '01 320
  Boneless Pork Chops with Ancho Cream Sauce,
    '95 205
  Bourbon-Braised Pork Chops, '85 89
  Broiled Pork Chops, '89 191
  Broiled Pork Chops with Crabapple Peaches,
    '81 83
  Burritos with Pico de Gallo, Pork, '97 140
  Cajun Pecan Pork, '01 27
  Calypso Loin Chops with Mango Salsa, '98 232
  Carne Adovada, '91 162
  Casserole, Peppered Pork Chop, '81 235; '82 25;
    '83 39
  Casserole, Pork Chop, '94 255
  Casserole, Pork Chop-Vegetable, '90 208
  Cheesy Pork Chops, '83 102
  Chile Pepper Pork Chops, '02 210
  Chili Chops, '87 10
  Chili, Spicy 3-Bean, '03 291
  Chinese Pork Chops, '97 320
  Cider Pork Chops, '02 307; '03 271
  Cider-Sauced Pork Chops, '86 213; '87 81
  Company Pork Chops, '85 109
  Cornbread-Apple Stuffing, Pork Chops with,
    '99 14
  Costillas Rellenos (Stuffed Pork Chops),
    '82 219
  Country Pride Pork Chops, '79 159
  Couscous with Currants, Pine Nuts, and Pork,
    '00 295
  Cranberry Pork, '90 293
  Cranberry Pork Chops, '80 288; '90 53
  Creamy Gravy, Pork Chops and, '81 207
  Creamy Pork Chops, '01 208
  Creole Pork Chops, '83 102
  Creole-Style Pork Chops, '91 49
  Crusted Pork Chops, Flavorful, '04 44
  Curried Apricot Pork Chops, '89 191
  Dill-Cream Gravy, Pork Chops with, '84 81
  Dinner, Pork Chop, '80 84; '81 180; '88 25
  Dumplings, Make-Ahead Pork, '03 64
  Enchiladas, Pork, '97 M94
  Farm-Style Pork Chops, '02 42
  Fiesta, Pork Chops, '86 118
  Fried Pork Chops with Cream Gravy, '03 24

Fried Pork Chops with Roasted Vegetables,
  '98 153
Fruited Pork Chops, '87 194
Fruit-Topped Pork Chops, '94 41
Garlic-Parmesan Pork Chops, '02 61
Garlic Sauce, Pork in, '04 181
Glazed Apple Pork Chops, '86 300
Glazed Chops, Honey-, '97 200
Glazed Chops, Pineapple-Curry, '82 106
Glazed Chops with Vegetables, '98 132
Glazed Pork Chops, '86 185
Glazed Pork Chops, Apple-, '84 212; '87 35
Glazed Pork Chops, Bourbon-, '04 44
Glazed Pork Chops, Orange-, '81 234; '82 25;
  '83 39; '84 234; '91 84
Glazed Pork Chops with Green Mole Sauce,
  Tamarind-, '95 266
Glazed Pork Chops With Pecans and Apples,
  Commune's Maple-, '04 102
Glazed Pork Chops with Rice, Fruit-, '82 73
Glazed Pork Steaks, '83 178
Gourmet Pork Chops, '79 180
Gravy, Pork Chops and, '96 71
Gravy, Pork Chops in, '91 137
Grilled Asian Pork Chops, '02 307; '03 271
Grilled Maple Chipotle Pork Chops on Smoked
  Gouda Grits, '04 172
Grilled Pork Chops, '88 113; '98 246
Grilled Pork Chops, Hawaiian, '85 159
Grilled Pork Chops, Marinated, '81 110
Grilled Pork Chops with Garlic Mashed Potatoes,
  '02 281
Hawaiian Pork Chops, '86 212; '87 82
Herbed Pork Chops, '97 147
Herb-Peppered Pork Chops, '98 60
Honey-Lime Pork Chops, '91 33
Honey-Pecan Pork Chops, '01 82
Italiano, Pork Chops, '80 72
Italian, Pork Chops, '79 47; '98 334
Italian Pork Chops, '02 307; '03 271
Jardiniere, Pork Chops, '81 112; '82 12
Lemon-Herb Pork Chops, '84 81; '89 M132
Lemony Pork Chops, '88 118
Marinated Pork Chops, '89 249
Meal for Two, Pork Chop, '81 273
Mexican Pork Chops, '99 108
Moo Shu Pork, '99 237
Moroccan Spiced Pork Chops, '01 230
Mushrooms, Creamy Pork Chops with, '01 137
Mustard-Apricot Pork Chops, '89 225
Onion Gravy, Pork Chops in, '99 222
Orange-Cranberry Pork Chops, '86 335; '87 84
Orange Pork Chops, '84 81
Oriental Pork Chops, '84 81; '90 212
Pan-Fried Pork Chops, '02 16
Pan-Fried Pork Chops, Lemony, '03 205
Parmesan Pork Chops with Apples, '93 338
Peachy Pork Chops, '89 310
Peanut Sauce, Pork Chops with, '83 29
Pecan-Breaded Pork Chops with Beer Sauce,
  '95 266
Pineapple Pork Chops, '87 M124
Pineapple Salsa, Pork Chops with Warm, '02 144
Pleasing Pork Chops, '79 125
Polynesian Pork and Pineapple, '83 102
Potatoes and Chops, Easy Scalloped, '00 289
Potatoes, Pork Chops and Scalloped, '98 16
Potato Scallop, Pork Chops and, '82 114
Pretzel Pork Chops, '01 208
Rice, Pork Chops and Spanish, '83 103; '85 293
Rice, Pork Chops with White, '02 312
Rice, Savannah Pork Chops and, '00 236
Ripieno, Pork Chops with, '97 245
Risotti, Pork Chops, '81 234; '82 26

Rosemary-Crusted Pork Chops with Pears,
  '01 316
Rosemary Pork Chops, '98 329
Salad, Thai Pork, '00 249
Salsa, Pork Chops with Black-and-White, '97 200
Saucy Company Pork Chops, '83 102
Saucy Pork Chop, '86 M140
Saucy Pork Dinner, '97 26
Sauerkraut, Pork Chops and, '88 98
Savory Pork Chops, '87 194
Sherry-Apple Pork Chops, '88 40
Sherry, Chops in, '79 125
Skillet Dinner, Pork, '98 131; '00 335
Skillet Dinner, Pork Chop, '79 125
Skillet Pork Chops, Easy, '79 255
Skillet, Pork-Pepper, '01 309
Smoked Pork Chops with Jalapeño-Cherry Sauce,
  '01 208
Sour Cream Sauce, Pork Chops with, '83 102
Southwestern Pork Chops, '98 131
Spaghetti with Pork and Peppers, '98 131
Special, Pork Chop, '79 81
Spicy Brown Mustard Pork Chops, '03 205
Stew With Rice, Black-Eyed Pea, '04 19
Stir-Fry, Mixed Veggie-and-Pork, '99 206
Stuffed Baked Pork Chops, '79 222; '80 64
Stuffed Pork Chops, '84 195; '86 89; '02 204
Stuffed Pork Chops, Apple-, '79 125
Stuffed Pork Chops, Apple-Crumb, '81 234;
  '82 26; '83 39
Stuffed Pork Chops, Apple-Sage, '04 250
Stuffed Pork Chops, Apricot-, '86 76; '92 219;
  '03 49
Stuffed Pork Chops, Apricot-Mushroom, '95 287
Stuffed Pork Chops, Braised, '87 249
Stuffed Pork Chops, Cheese-, '84 81
Stuffed Pork Chops, Easy, '81 10
Stuffed Pork Chops, Fruit-, '82 136
Stuffed Pork Chops, Fruited, '86 197
Stuffed Pork Chops, Rice-, '83 102
Stuffed Pork Chops with Apricot Glaze,
  '89 M36
Stuffed with Prunes, Pork Chops, '84 7
Sweet-and-Sour Apple Sauce, Pork Chops with,
  '98 132
Sweet-and-Sour Pork Chops, '83 160
Sweet Potatoes, Pork Chops with, '96 269
Tacos with Pineapple Salsa, Pork, '03 128
Tuscan Pork Chops, '03 205
Vegetable Pork Chops, Skillet, '85 179
Vegetables, Golden Chops with, '89 218
Vegetables, Pork Chops and Garden, '88 297
Weeknight Pork Chops, '97 200
White Bean Puree, Pork Chops with, '96 226
Chorizo, Simple, '04 207
Chow Mein, Pork, '80 208; '90 101
Combo, Vegetable-Pork, '85 113
Curry, Hurry, '79 103
Cutlets, Apple-Glazed Pork, '92 181
Dinner, Pork-and-Noodles Skillet, '88 199
Dumplings, Steamed Sesame, '97 208
Egg Rolls, '86 81
Egg Rolls, Chinese, '96 101
Eggrolls, Shrimp and Pork, '82 240; '83 18
Egg Rolls, Vietnamese, '96 101
Eggs, Tulsa, '87 95
Empanadas, Pork Picadillo, '03 60
Fillets With Dark Cherry Sauce, Pork, '04 221
Hominy, Mexican, '86 255
Hot-and-Spicy Pork, '81 228
Kebabs, Spicy Pork, '82 182
Kebabs with Sesame Seeds, Pork, '00 337
Kung Pao Pork, '96 49
Leg of Pork with Cranberry Glaze, '88 244

Maple-Chipotle Pork on Smoked Gouda Grits with Sweet Onion Applesauce, '02 319
Marinated Pork Strips, '92 219
Meatballs in Gravy, '79 136
Meatballs, Sauerkraut, '86 257
Meatballs, Tangy Hawaiian, '79 129
Meat Loaf
  Alabama Meat Loaf, '04 188
  Family-Style Meat Loaf, '93 18
  Italian Meat Loaf, '79 187
  Mini Alabama Meat Loaves, '04 188
  Mozzarella-Layered Meat Loaf, '79 71
  Savory Meat Loaf, '87 216
  Skillet Liver Loaf, '80 11
  Stuffed Meat Loaf, '79 187
  Swedish Meat Loaf, '81 M121
  Triple Meat Loaf, '79 186
Meat Mixture, Basic, '92 241
Oriental, Pork, '81 212
Paella, Chicken-Pork-Shrimp, '82 245
Pâté, Country, '86 66
Pâté en Croûte, '86 65
Pâté with Spinach and Cream, Pork, '83 224
Picadillo II, '93 72
Picadillo, Taquitos With Pork, '04 206
Pie, Continental Meat, '95 256; '96 75
Pies, Natchitoches Meat, '84 21; '91 241
Pie, Sombrero, '81 140
Pilaf, Fruited Pork, '82 246
Pineapple Pork, '82 60
Poblanos Stuffed with Pork and Fruit, '97 269
Poblanos with Walnut Cream Sauce, Pork-Stuffed, '01 229
Polynesian Pork, '85 78
Posole, '95 226
Pot Pie with Cheese Grits Crust, Barbecue, '03 21
Quesadillas, Barbecued Pork, '04 187
Rack of Pork, Herb-Crusted, '97 262
Ribs. *See also* **PORK/Barbecue.**
  Adams' Ribs, '95 236; '00 177; '03 312
  Baby Back Ribs, '04 86
  Baby Back Ribs, Barbecued, '97 234
  Baby Back Ribs, Smoky Chipotle, '04 87
  Baby Back Ribs, Sweet-and-Sour, '04 87
  Baby Loin Back Ribs, John Wills's, '90 120
  Baked and Grilled Spareribs, '97 211
  Baked Ribs, Easy, '86 20
  Baked Ribs, Lemon, '81 166
  Chinese Spareribs, '81 10
  Chinese-Style Spareribs, '02 93
  Crispy Ribs with Plum Sauce, '98 182
  Ginger Pork Ribs, '96 100
  Glazed Spareribs, '88 98
  Glazed Spareribs, Honey-, '82 163
  Glazed Spareribs, Orange-, '84 296
  Glazed Spareribs, Peach-, '86 14
  Grilled Maple Spareribs, '99 136
  Grilled Pork Ribs, Chipotle, '01 319
  Grilled Ribs, Lemon, '81 154
  Jamaican Jerk Raspberry Ribs, '00 88
  Lemony Sweet Spareribs, '80 73
  Maple Spareribs, '99 136
  McCoy, Ribs, '04 132
  Plantation Ribs, '84 217
  Plum Sauce, Spareribs in, '99 136
  Puerco en Adobo, '88 116
  Saucy Oven Spareribs, '80 207
  Saucy-Sweet Ribs, '81 166
  Smoked Ribs, '88 169
  Smoked Ribs with Honey-Mustard Sauce, '92 168
  Smoky Oven Ribs, '81 166
  Smoky Ribs, '84 172
  Spareribs, Southern, '95 116

Spicy Spareribs, '89 168
Spicy-Sweet Ribs and Beans, '02 299; '03 314
Stuffed Spareribs, Fruit-, '79 14
Sweet-and-Sour Ribs, '89 M84
Sweet-and-Sour Spareribs, '83 21
Tangy Ribs and Onions, '99 136
Thai Wings and Ribs, '97 M225
Rice, Pork Fried, '89 99
Risotto, Pork, '82 60
Roasts. *See also* **PORK/Barbecue.**
  à l'Orange, Porc, '80 242
  Apples and Mushrooms, Roast Pork Loin with, '92 218
  Arista of Pork, '81 260
  Braised Pork, Brown Sugar, '84 36
  Braised Tuscan Pork Loin, '04 202
  Brunswick Stew, Easy, '00 138
  Chinese Roast Pork, '91 308
  Company Pork Roast, '99 276
  Crickhollow Roast Pork, '99 200
  Crown Pork Flambé, Stuffed, '83 263
  Crown Pork Roast, Stuffed, '89 272
  Crown Pork Roast with Cranberry-Pecan Stuffing, '96 309
  Crown Pork Roast With Cranberry Stuffing, Johnston County, '04 245
  Crown Roast of Pork, Royal, '80 252
  Crown Roast of Pork, Stuffed, '86 323
  Crown Roast of Pork with Cranberry-Sausage Stuffing, '88 49
  Dijonnaise with Peach Sauce, Pork Loin, '97 87
  Festive Pork Loin Roast, '03 255
  Festive Pork Roast, '01 276
  Fig-Balsamic Roasted Pork Loin, '03 45
  Garlic-Orange Roast Pork, '03 277
  Glazed Pork Loin, '87 229
  Glazed Pork Loin, Cranberry-, '04 251
  Glazed Pork Loin, Scuppernong-Orange, '98 220
  Glazed Pork Roast, Cherry-, '91 84
  Glazed Pork Roast, Orange-, '04 M236
  Grilled Pork, Honey-and-Herb, '90 148
  Grilled Pork, Jalapeño, '99 160
  Grilled Pork Loin, Grandma Ruth's, '96 250
  Grilled Pork Loin, Honey-, '92 219
  Grilled Pork Roast, '97 323
  Honey-Roasted Pork, '96 251; '02 282
  Indonesian Pork Roast, '81 227
  Italian Pork Roast, '91 238; '92 27
  Jezebel Sauce, Pork Roast with, '02 218
  Loin of Pork, Roast, '84 276
  Loin, Roast Pork, '88 221; '01 222
  Loin Roast with Red Currant Sauce, Pork, '89 M84
  Mandarin Pork Roast, '83 47
  Marinated Pork Loin, '01 331
  Marinated Pork Loin, Garlic-Honey, '99 334
  Marinated Pork Roast, '80 71; '84 260
  Minted Pork Loin, '99 96
  Mix, Mexican Meat, '00 292
  Orange-Dijon Pork Loin, '00 259
  Peppercorn Pork Roast, '97 248
  Pernil (Pork Roast), '92 157
  Pineapple Pork Roast, '79 41
  Pineapple Sweet-and-Sour Pork, '82 120
  Raisin Sauce, Pork Loin with, '02 278
  Rio Grande Pork Roast, '84 35, 296
  Roasted Pork, '01 233, 237
  Roasted Pork Loin, '96 32
  Roasted Pork Loin with Mushrooms and Garlic, '92 301
  Rolled Pork with Rhubarb Sauce, '96 134
  Sandwiches, Easy Spanish Pork Dip, '04 312
  Slow-Roasted Pork, '02 274
  Smoked Boston Butt, '01 129

Smoked Pork, '99 81; '01 233; '03 121
Smoked Pork Loin Mahogany, '91 148
Smoked Pork Shoulder, '82 225; '01 147
Spiced Cherry Sauce, Roast Pork with, '89 324
Stew, Baja Pork, '98 283
Stew, Brunswick, '01 219
Stuffed Pork Loin, Apricot-Pecan, '94 274
Stuffed Pork Loin, Fruitcake-, '95 250
Stuffed Pork Loin Roast, Prune-, '80 29
Stuffed Pork Rib Roast, Sausage-, '94 240
Stuffed Pork Roast, '81 111; '82 12; '85 229
Stuffed Pork Shoulder, '81 11
Stuffed Pork, Spinach-and-Herb, '89 193
Stuffed with Wild Rice, Pork Loin, '84 35
Stuffing, Pork Roast with Hopping John, '01 25
Tomato Sauce, Pork Roast with, '87 249
Tropical Pork Loin, '96 86
Zesty Pork Roast, '85 179
Salad, Mandarin Pork-and-Spinach, '88 M126
Salad, Oriental Pork, '92 140
Salad, "Pig in the Garden," '92 255
Salad, Pork-'n'-Bean, '87 83
Salad, Thai Green Apple, '99 111
Sandwiches, Party Pork, '88 M273
Sandwiches with Rosemary-Garlic Mayonnaise, Adobo Pork, '01 322
Sauce, Italian Meat, '01 160
Sausage, Pork, '81 55; '97 243
Sauté, Plum Delicious Pork, '89 105
Scaloppine, Pork, '04 221
Sesame Pork on Mixed Greens, Hot, '97 19
Sesame Pork Rounds, '89 122
Sloppy Joes, Pork, '86 294
Soup, Guadalajara, '88 30
Soup, Homemade, '79 198
Soup, Pork Rind, '03 33
Spring Rolls with Sweet Chili Sauce, Shanghai, '01 236
Steaks, Herbed Pork, '80 72
Steaks, Peachy Pork, '79 166
Stew, Bama Brunswick, '87 4
Stew, Breeden Liles's Brunswick, '91 14
Stew, Brunswick, '80 264; '97 315; '03 29
Stew, Camp, '02 42
Stew, Dan Dickerson's Brunswick, '91 16
Stew, Easy Brunswick, '92 280; '99 235
Stew, Georgian Brunswick, '92 35
Stew, Pancho Villa, '94 44
Stew, Sonny Frye's Brunswick, '87 4
Stew, Virginia Ramsey's Favorite Brunswick, '91 16
Stir-Fried Pork, '87 51
Stir-Fried Pork in Garlic Sauce, '84 141
Stir-Fry Pork and Cashews, '01 16
Strata, English Muffin Breakfast, '03 100
St. Tammany, Pork, '82 260
Swedish Porkburgers, '79 42
Sweet-and-Pungent Pork, '86 118
Sweet-and-Sour Pork, '79 42; '80 72, 227; '81 26, 104, 111; '82 12; '84 218; '85 34, 194; '86 241; '90 317; '92 219
Tamales, '80 195
Tamales, Hot, '83 51
Tasso Fettuccine, Crawfish and, '96 290
Tasso Gravy, '96 270
Tempting Twosome, '81 240
Tenderloin
  Apple Butter Pork Tenderloin, '99 145
  Apple-Ginger Pork Tenderloin, '86 75
  Apple-Mushroom Pork Tenderloin, '95 53
  Apricot Sauce, Pork Tenderloin with, '99 44
  Asian Pork Tenderloin, '02 33
  Asian Pork Tenderloin with Spicy Sweet Potatoes, '02 207
  Blackberry Sauce, Pork Medaillons with, '02 136

PORK, Tenderloin
(continued)

Blue Cheese, Pork Tenderloin with, '86 76
Cacciatore, Pork, '95 69
Coriander-Pepper Pork Tenderloins, '99 145
Cornmeal Biscuits, Pork Tenderloin on, '04 257
Curried Pork Tenderloin, '86 76
Danish Pork Tenderloin, '82 186
Deep-Fried Whole Pork Tenderloin with Mint Sauce, '04 313
Fruit Stuffing and Shiitake Sauce, Pork Tenderloin with, '97 218
Garlic, Sweet Pork with, '04 17
Glazed Pork Tenderloin, '90 315
Glazed Pork Tenderloin, Jalapeño-, '03 186
Glazed Pork Tenderloins, Orange-Cranberry, '00 314
Grilled Marinated Pork Tenderloin, '91 199
Grilled Pork Medaillons, '93 229
Grilled Pork Tacos with Cucumber-Radish Salsa, Adobo, '01 186
Grilled Pork Tenderloin, '88 98; '91 163; '94 88; '02 187
Grilled Pork Tenderloin, Garlic, '90 172
Grilled Pork Tenderloin, Molasses-, '96 265
Grilled Pork Tenderloins, '94 158
Grilled Pork Tenderloin, Spicy, '04 96
Grilled Pork Tenderloins with Rosemary Pesto, '01 174; '04 82
Grilled Pork Tenderloin, Tropical Spinach Salad with, '04 51
Grilled Pork Tenderloin with Apples, Celery, and Potatoes, '95 161
Grilled Pork Tenderloin with Brown Sauce, '89 32
Grilled Pork Tenderloin with Gingered Jezebel Sauce, '04 138
Grilled Pork Tenderloin with Molasses Sauce, '97 193
Grilled Pork Tenderloin with Orange Marmalade, '03 181
Grilled Pork Tenderloin with Yogurt and Lime, '04 216
Grilled Pork with Salsa, '90 128
Grilled Tenderloins, Honey-, '92 199; '00 126
Herb-Crusted Pork Tenderloin with Horseradish-Roasted New Potatoes, '98 168
Herbed Pork Tenderloin with Parmesan-Pepper Toasts, '98 242
Honeyed Pork Tenderloin with Avocado-Peach Salsa, '02 159
Honey-Garlic Pork Tenderloin, '01 16
Honey-Garlic Pork Tenderloins, '01 318
Honey-Mustard Pork Tenderloin, '95 52
Honey-Mustard Pork Tenderloin with Miniature Buttermilk Biscuits, '02 103
Jamaican Jerk Pork Sandwiches with Apricot Mayonnaise, '97 320
Jamaican Pork Tenderloin with Sauce Caribe, '02 320
Kebabs, Margarita Pork, '98 M223
Kebabs, Pineapple-Pork, '99 144
Lamb Extraordinaire, '99 242
Marinated Pork Tenderloin, '84 175
Marinated Pork Tenderloin, Bourbon-, '04 168
Marinated Pork Tenderloin with Jezebel Sauce, '96 212
Marsala, Pork, '90 35
Medaillons in Mustard Sauce, Pork, '90 96; '00 32
Medaillons of Pork with Vegetables, '88 223
Medaillons with Chutney Sauce, Pork, '87 35

Medaillons with Fresh Fruit, Pork, '97 104
Medaillons with Port Wine and Dried Cranberry Sauce, Pork, '95 330
Molasses Pork Tenderloin with Red Wine Sauce, '02 290
Mustard Sauce, Pork Tenderloin with, '92 302; '99 145; '03 238
Onion-Balsamic Sauce, Pork Tenderloin with, '99 44
Orange Marmalade, Pork Tenderloin with, '91 49
Oven-Roasted Vegetables and Pork, '99 259
Parmigiana, Easy Pork, '94 57
Peking Pork Tenderloin, '93 173
Peppered Bacon-Wrapped Pork Tenderloin, '02 55
Peppered Pork with Pecan Biscuits, '01 33
Pepper-Honey Pork Tenderloins, '98 33
Piccata, Pork, '94 57; '99 332
Piccata, Pork Tenderloin, '86 76
Pinwheels, Herbed Pork, '92 23
Pinwheels, Spinach-Tenderloin, '89 M118
Platter, Tenderloin, '79 42
Polynesian Pork Tenderloin with Orange-Curry Sauce and Coconut Rice, '04 309
Roasted Pork Tenderloins, Herb-, '00 96
Roast Pork Tenderloin, '84 35
Rosemary Pesto, Pork Tenderloin with, '98 16
Salad, Grilled Pork Cosmopolitan, '04 123
Salad with Spicy Tomato Dressing, Pork-and-Rice, '03 143
Sandwiches, Beef and Pork Tenderloin, '80 175
Sandwiches, Pork Tenderloin, '00 333
Sandwiches with Bourbon Sauce, Pork Tenderloin, '02 53
Sandwiches with Cranberry-Coriander Conserve, Pork Tenderloin, '04 286
Scaloppine Marsala, Pork, '94 57
Scaloppine, Olive-Pork, '89 191
Sesame Pork, '01 177
Sesame Pork Tenderloin, '95 53
Skewered Pork Tenders, '00 200
Spiced Pork Tenderloin with Chili-Cranberry Glaze, '98 320
Spiked Pork Tenderloin with Sunny Pear Chutney, '01 280
Stir-Fry, Sweet-and-Sour Pork, '03 92
Stuffed Pork Tenderloin, '00 213
Stuffed Pork Tenderloins, Fruit-, '87 270
Stuffed Pork Tenderloin, Southern-Style, '99 45
Stuffed Pork Tenderloin, Spinach-and-Bacon, '94 81
Stuffed Tenderloin with Praline-Mustard Glaze, Apple-, '97 216
Sunrise Pork Tenderloin, '79 103
Sweet-and-Sour Pork, '00 110
Sweet Pork Tenderloin with Lime and Chipotle, '04 184
Towers, Pork Tenderloin, '86 75
Vegetables, Pork Tenderloin with, '01 122
Terrine, Jeweled Pork, '84 130
Terrine of Pork and Veal, '93 287
Turnip Greens, Simple, '01 211
Wontons, Crispy Fried, '83 21
POTATOES. *See also* **SWEET POTATOES.**
Accordion Potatoes, '98 69
Anna, Potatoes, '97 53
Anna with Rosemary, Potatoes, '84 290
Appetizers, Fiery Stuffed Cherry Pepper, '97 269
Appetizers, Potato Shell, '89 M119
Bacon Dressing, Potatoes with Hot, '88 M294
Bake, Chive-Potato, '82 229
Baked. *See also* **POTATOES/Stuffed.**
Avocado-Topped Potatoes, '83 3

Beef and Chicken-Topped Potatoes, Creamed, '83 210
Broccoli-and-Almond-Topped Potatoes, '83 3
Broccoli-Topped Baked Potatoes, '86 17
Buck's Taters, '95 72
Buffalo Chicken Twice-Baked Potatoes, '04 184
Cheese Sauce, Baked Potatoes with, '83 239
Cheesy Frank-Topped Potatoes, '83 3
Chili Potatoes, Roasted, '97 53
Chili-Topped Potatoes, '83 3; '98 M289
Crabmeat-Topped Potatoes, '83 3; '95 22
Croquettes, Baked Potato, '97 30
Easy Oven-Baked Potatoes, '82 202
Frank-Filled Potatoes, '84 M11
Fries, Baked Potato, '96 90
Garden Potato Cups, '83 76
Garden-Topped Potatoes, '83 4
Gumbo Potatoes, '95 22
Mexican-Topped Potatoes, '83 3
Micro-Baked Potatoes, '81 M61
Million Dollar Potatoes, '83 210
Mushroom-Dill-Topped Potatoes, '86 41
Mushroom Filling in a Peel, '84 214
New Potatoes, Baked, '90 90
Parmesan-Cream Potatoes, '97 54
Pleated Potatoes, Baked, '93 54
Quick Baked Potatoes, '92 M134
Quick Potatoes, '94 283
Rosemary-Baked Potatoes, '95 23
Rosemary-Roasted Potatoes, '95 20
Salad, Baked Potato, '97 319
Salmon-Topped Potatoes, '84 124
Sausage-Vegetable-Topped Potatoes, '98 29
Shrimp-Sauced Potatoes, '81 M61
Skins, Baked Potato, '86 81
Skins, Cheese Potato, '84 M239
Skins, Cheesy Potato, '82 78
Smoked Baked Potatoes, '97 25
Southwestern Potato Boats, '96 33
Sweet-and-Sour-Topped Potatoes, '83 4
Taco-Baked Potatoes, '84 119
Taco-Topped Potatoes, '93 M18
Twice-Baked Potatoes, Confetti, '02 35
Wedges, Potato, '94 M119
Bake, Ham-Potato-Pineapple, '93 302
Bake, Herbed Fish and Potato, '79 287
Bake, Onion-Potato, '83 M195
Bake, Potato, '83 209
Barbecued Potatoes, '91 311; '92 26
Basil-Cheese Potatoes, '90 M316
Basque-Style Potatoes, '79 46
Beans and Potatoes, Down-Home, '85 254
Beans and Potatoes, Snap, '98 177
Beef Hash, '99 62
Beets, Potato-Stuffed, '83 234
Blini with Sour Cream and Caviar, Potato, '01 274
Breads
Biscuits, Potato-Bacon, '94 214
Bowls, Irish Tater Bread, '96 111
Buns, Potato-Caramelized Onion, '03 234
Dough, Potato Sourdough Bread, '94 324; '95 77
Lightbread, Potato, '80 225
Loaves, Potato, '86 162
Old-Fashioned Potato Bread, '86 57
Potato Bread, '85 56
Rolls, Easy Potato, '89 287
Rolls, Feathery Light Potato, '81 305; '82 36
Rolls, Homemade Potato, '82 252
Rolls, Potato, '81 300; '99 290
Rolls, Potato Sourdough, '94 325; '95 77
Rolls, Potato Sourdough Cinnamon, '94 325; '95 77
Rolls, Potato Yeast, '87 53; '98 92
Rolls, Refrigerated Potato, '83 254

Rolls, Refrigerator Potato, '87 15
Rolls, Southern Potato, '86 299
Rolls, Super Potato, '85 145
Rolls, Supreme Potato, '82 130
Rolls, Whole Wheat Potato, '89 50
Sourdough Bread, Potato, '94 325; '95 77
Starter Food, '94 324; '95 77
Starter, Potato Sourdough, '94 324; '95 77
Toast, Potato-Crusted Texas, '94 142
Yeast, Potato, '87 53
Breakfast, Farmer's, '81 44
Breakfast Potatoes, '91 68
Breakfast Potatoes, Mexican, '81 209
Brisket, Aunt Suzi's, '02 321
Broiled Marinated Potatoes, '93 54
Browned Potatoes, Quick, '82 M172
Burgers, Potato-Crusted Crab, '94 139
Burritos, Breakfast, '99 103
Burritos, Potato-and-Egg, '02 72
Candy, Potato, '79 273
Caraway Potatoes, '85 85
Caraway Potatoes, Cheesy, '86 17
Casseroles
   au Gratin, Potatoes, '93 90, 217; '02 197
   au Gratin, Potatoes and Eggs, '79 107
   au Gratin, Potatoes-and-Zucchini, '84 5
   au Gratin, Shredded Potatoes, '89 69
   Beef Casserole, Easy, '00 208
   Beefy Potato Casserole, '03 218
   Breakfast Casserole, Potato, '80 52
   Broccoli-Cheese Bake, Potato-, '80 114
   Brunch for a Bunch, '88 57
   Buffet Potatoes, '98 92
   Campfire Casserole, '00 173
   Caramelized Onions, Potato Casserole with, '03 231
   Cheddar Cheese Potatoes, Double, '00 331
   Cheese Casserole, Potato-, '79 101
   Cheese Dream, Potato-, '91 307
   Cheese Potatoes, Creamy, '88 M146
   Cheese Potatoes, Double-, '86 6
   Cheese Potatoes, Two-, '80 114
   Cheesy Potato Casserole, '80 244; '83 53; '92 229
   Cheesy Potatoes, '82 211
   Cheesy Potatoes and Onions, '00 275
   Chicken Livers and Potatoes, '82 218
   Chive Potatoes, Cheesy, '79 46
   Christmas Potatoes, '88 252
   Cottage Potatoes, '89 69
   Creamy Potato Bake, '82 201
   Creamy Potato Casserole, '84 M113
   Creamy Potatoes with Ham Bits, '87 191
   Deviled Potatoes, Hot, '84 296; '85 196
   Easy Potato Casserole, '80 114
   Egg Casserole, Cheesy Potato-, '84 5
   Eggplant Casserole, Potato-, '87 166
   Escalloped Potatoes, '01 239
   Fish and Potato Bake, Herbed, '80 34
   Fluffy Potato Casserole, '80 268
   Gourmet, Potatoes, '80 114
   Gratin, Potato-and-Rutabaga, '96 237
   Gratin, Potato-Butternut Squash-and-Gruyère, '01 43
   Gratin, Smoky Potato, '00 233
   Gratin with Caramelized Onions, Potato-Horseradish, '99 314
   Gruyère Potatoes, '83 193
   Ham-and-Potato Casserole, '83 M87; '96 103
   Ham-and-Potato Casserole, Cheesy, '84 326
   Hash Brown Breakfast Casserole, '03 306
   Hash Brown Breakfast Casserole, Sausage-, '03 218
   Hash Brown Casserole, Cheesy, '03 218

   Hash Brown Casserole, Creamy, '03 193
   Hash Brown Cheese Bake, '82 50
   Hash Brown-Cheese Bake, '97 323
   Hash Brown-Ham-Cheese Bake, '97 323
   Hash Brown Potato Casserole, '81 40
   Holiday Potato Casserole, '92 302
   Irish Potato Casserole, '81 263
   Italian Casserole, '80 81
   Italian-Style Potatoes, '89 69
   Jalapeño Potatoes, '84 39
   Lemon and Nutmeg Potatoes, '80 36
   Lorraine, Potatoes, '87 190
   Mashed Potato Bake, Smoky, '00 214; '01 21
   Mashed-Potato Bake, Swirled, '03 293
   Mashed Potato Casserole, '85 296; '99 223
   Mashed Potato Casserole, Three-Cheese, '03 72
   Meat and Potatoes, Italian-Style, '03 97
   Missy Potatoes, '85 259
   Moussaka, Potatoes, '93 44
   Mushroom-Potato Casserole, '84 5
   Olive Potatoes, '80 114
   Pepper Jack-Potato Casserole, '03 218
   Peppery Potato Casserole, '95 182
   Potato Casserole, '87 190; '99 274
   Processor Potato Casserole, '86 159
   Rosemary's Potatoes, '98 53
   Russian Potatoes, '03 255
   Saucy Potato Casserole, '81 276
   Saucy Potatoes for Company, '82 202
   Sausage-Potato Casserole, '86 217
   Sausage-Spud Bake, Sunday Night Spicy Cheesy, '03 331
   Scalloped Potatoes, '82 300; '83 211; '92 48
   Scalloped Potatoes and Turnips, '85 235
   Scalloped Potatoes, Cheesy, '83 82; '96 33
   Scalloped Potatoes, Light, '89 311
   Scalloped Potatoes, Mushroom, '87 191
   Scalloped Potatoes, Out-of-This-World, '04 296
   Scalloped Potatoes, Party, '87 191
   Scalloped Potatoes, Pork Chops and, '98 16
   Scalloped Potatoes, Skillet, '79 46
   Scalloped Potatoes, Special, '88 162
   Scalloped Potatoes, Wayside, '79 283
   Scalloped Potatoes, Winter Herb Garden, '99 289
   Scalloped Potatoes with Pimiento, '81 75
   Scalloped Potatoes with Sweet Marjoram and Parmesan Cheese, '91 246
   Scallop, Pork Chops and Potato, '82 114
   Shoestring Potato Tuna Bake, '82 211
   Sour Cream Potatoes, '84 39
   Swirled Mashed-Potato Bake, '02 98
   Thyme-Potato Bake, '96 121
   Tomato Bake, Potato-, '86 17
   Tomato Casserole, Saucy Potato-, '79 46
Caviar Potatoes, '84 80
Charcoal Potatoes, '88 129
Chicken and Potatoes, Roasted, '98 289
Chicken Fajita Spuds With Black Bean Salsa, '04 25
Chicken, Spanish, '98 183
Chili-Cheese Potatoes, '90 M62
Chili, Savory Potato, '83 284
Chowder. *See* **POTATOES/Soups.**
Colcannon, '90 64
Corn Dogs and Taters, '02 57
Cottage Potatoes, '89 69; '93 M92
Creamed Potatoes, '83 25
Cream-Wine Sauce, Potatoes in, '86 18
Creole Potatoes, '87 138
Crisps, Potato, '96 175
Croquettes, Parmesan Potato, '84 210
Croquettes, Potato, '87 116
Doughnuts, Chocolate-Glazed Potato, '85 6
Doughnuts, Old-Fashioned Potato, '84 56
Dumplings, Chicken and Potato, '99 326

Dumplings, Venison Stew with Potato, '87 304
Egg, Eagle Nest, '99 194
Eggs and Meat, Potatoes with, '91 311; '92 25
Fans, Parmesan Potato, '84 M240
Feta Cheese, Potatoes with, '84 295; '85 196
Fish-and-Potato Platter, '89 M248
Fried
   Almond-Fried Potatoes, '82 25
   Bacon-Fried Taters, '02 55
   Baskets, Potato, '86 193; '99 166
   Battered Catfish and Chips, '02 140
   Boxty, '02 67
   Catfish and Chips, Potato-Crusted, '02 140
   Catfish with Warm Pinto Bean-and-Bacon Salsa, Potato-Crusted, '03 331
   Chips, Homemade Potato, '82 25
   Crinkle-Cut Fries, '99 59; '04 122
   French Fries, '99 59; '04 122
   French Fries, Seasoned, '96 245
   Herb French Fries, '82 211
   Herb-Fried Potatoes, '82 25
   Latkes, '84 318; '90 254
   Latkes, Potato, '97 252; '00 281
   Latkes with Lemon-Date Relish, Potato, '96 271
   Nests with Savory Shavings, Potato, '84 209
   Okra and Potatoes, Fried, '97 136
   Okra-Potato Fry, '81 159
   Oven French Fries, '91 122
   Oven-Fried Potatoes, '82 25
   Oven Fries, Cheesy, '91 187
   Oven Fries, Parmesan, '98 235
   Oven Fries, Spicy, '02 34
   Patties, Fried Potato, '82 25; '93 54
   Patties, Potato-Onion, '95 269
   (Plantain Chips), Tostones de Plátano, '92 158
   Puffs, Potato, '80 36
   Rosemary Fries, Salty, '03 213
   Shavings, Savory, '84 209
   Southern-Fried Catfish and Chips, '02 140
   Southern-Fried Potatoes, '82 25; '97 53
   Special Potatoes, '83 169
   Steak Fries, Seasoned, '04 127
   Waffle Chips, '99 59; '04 122
   Wedges, Beer-Batter Potato, '83 211
Frittata, Potato, '89 145
Frittata, Potato-Bacon, '95 269; '98 330
Fritters, Cheese-Stuffed Potato, '96 153
Fritters, Leek-and-Potato, '00 324
Fritters, Potato-Ham, '98 249
Fritters With Lime-Cayenne Mayonnaise, Chicken-and-Mashed Potato, '04 121
Garlic-Parsley Potatoes, '90 290
Garlic Potatoes, '84 296; '85 196
Gnocchi à la Narciso, '97 246
Golden Potatoes, '96 139
Gratin, Dual Potato, '93 328
Gratin Potatoes, '02 276
Green and Gold, '00 91
Green Beans and Potatoes, '91 221
Green Beans with Ham and Potatoes, '01 223
Grilled Herb Potatoes, '84 172
Grilled Irish Potatoes, '97 53
Grilled Potatoes, Italian, '98 171
Hash, Beef, '95 24
Hash Brown Bake, '95 281
Hash Brown Potatoes, '81 48
Hash Browns, Carrot, '96 107
Hash Browns, Cheesy Sweet Potato, '02 248
Hash Browns, Company, '79 268; '80 14
Hash Browns, Convenient, '95 135
Hash Browns, Franks and, '80 166
Hash Brown Skillet Breakfast, '82 5
Hash Browns, Rosemary-Garlic, '02 248
Hash Browns, Smothered-Covered, '02 248

POTATOES
(continued)

Hash Browns, Sweet Potato, '02 248
Hash with Rosemary, Potato, '98 16
Herb Butter, Potatoes with, '81 276
Herbed Potatoes, '91 220
Herbed Potatoes with Ham, '00 318
Herb Potatoes, '88 134
Italiano, Potatoes, '89 174
Mashed
Ancho-Beer Mashers, '98 248
Ancho Mashers, '03 243
Bake, Creamy Potato, '88 41
Bake, Smoky Mashed Potato, '00 214; '01 21
Bake, Swirled Mashed-Potato, '02 98
Basic Mashed Potatoes, '92 330
Beef With Mashed Potatoes and Chipotle Cream, Grilled, '02 M320
Bites, Mashed Potato, '98 249
Blue Cheese Mashed Potatoes, '92 330
Bowls, Mashed Potato, '97 199
Buttermilk-Basil Mashed Potatoes, '95 330
Caramelized Onion-and-Gorgonzola Mashed Potatoes, '01 256
Casserole, Mashed Potato, '85 296; '99 223
Casserole, Three-Cheese Mashed Potato, '03 72
Celery Potatoes, Whipped, '94 305; '99 45; '01 212
Celery Root Mashed Potatoes, '98 293
Cheese Mashed Potatoes, Three-, '00 112
Cheesy Mashed Potatoes, '02 98
Chile Mashed Potatoes, '00 161
Chive-Cream Cheese Mashed Potatoes, '92 330
Chive Mashed Potatoes, '97 308
Chive Potatoes, Creamy, '00 109
Crab Marinière, Mashed Potatoes with, '99 165
Cream Cheese Mashed Potatoes, '97 14; '02 35
Creamy Mashed Potatoes, '00 315
Crust, Barbecue Pot Pie with Mashed Potato, '03 21
Dill-Sour Cream Mashed Potatoes, '92 330
Duchesse, Potatoes, '84 210
Duchess Potatoes, '93 288
Feta Mashed Potatoes, '92 330
Fix-Ahead Mashed Potatoes, '89 70
Flank Steak, Mashed Potato-Stuffed, '01 25
Fluffy Potatoes, '84 296; '85 196
Garlic-Gruyère Mashed Potatoes, '98 322
Garlic Mashed Potatoes, '92 330; '93 328; '97 308; '02 281
Garlic Mashed Potatoes, Speedy, '04 M81
Garlic Smashed Potatoes, Loaded, '01 325
Good Old Mashed Potatoes, '92 215
Green Onion-and-Bacon Mashed Potatoes, '02 110
Harvest Mashed Potatoes, '98 248
Herbed Lemon Mashed Potatoes, '93 208
Horseradish Mashed Potatoes, '98 69, 118
Italian Mashed Potatoes, '03 M135
Jazzy Mashed Potatoes, '87 192
Leek Mashed Potatoes, '02 98; '03 293
Leek Mashed Potatoes, Creamy, '02 291
Lemon Mashed Potatoes, '04 181
Lemon-Poppy Seed Mashed Potatoes, Creamy, '03 294
Mexican Mashed Potatoes, '92 330
Nest, Peas in a Potato, '84 M239
Nests, Mashed Potato, '94 141
Old-Fashioned Mashed Potatoes, '89 234
Orange Mashed Potatoes, '96 33
Parsnip Mash, '97 263
Pesto Mashed Potatoes, '92 330

Quick-and-Easy Mashed Potatoes, '93 41
Roasted Garlic Mashed Potatoes, '95 288
Roasted Garlic-Parmesan Mashed Potatoes, '97 263; '00 146
Seasoned Potatoes, '87 253
Snow-Capped Potatoes, '84 255
Stuffed Mashed Potatoes, '98 328
Sweet-and-Savory Mashed Potatoes, Baked, '02 244
Thunderbolt Potatoes, '94 213
Tomato Gravy, Mashed Potatoes with, '02 M17
Topping, Mashed Potato, '89 243
Turnips and Potatoes, '79 254
Twice-Baked Mashed Potatoes, '04 97
Mexican-Style Potatoes, '91 78
Mustard Greens and Potatoes, '86 224
Mustard Potatoes, '79 32
New Potatoes
Baked New Potatoes, '90 90
Basil Cream Sauce, New Potatoes with, '91 46
Blue Cheese Potatoes, '98 247; '04 214
Browned New Potatoes, '86 244
Caviar Potatoes, Appetizer, '86 223
Chard and Potatoes, Creamy, '98 250
Cheese Potatoes, Double-, '86 6
Cheesy New Potatoes, '85 156
Creamed Peas and New Potatoes, '79 102
Creamy Potatoes and Broccoli, '92 61
Feta Cheese Potatoes, '04 214
Garden New Potatoes, '91 80
Garlic New Potatoes, '92 54
Gratin, Creamy New Potato, '01 M320
Gratin with Lima Beans and Egg, New Potato, '01 71
Green Beans with New Potatoes, '87 164
Ham-Stuffed New Potatoes, '88 211
Herbed New Potatoes, '81 102; '83 9, M148
Herb-Roasted Potatoes, '01 89
Jalapeño New Potatoes, Cheesy, '01 89
Lemon-Buttered New Potatoes, '84 149; '90 268; '98 159
Lemon-Butter Sauce, New Potatoes with, '00 103
Lemon-Dill Sauce, Potatoes and Green Beans with, '01 89
Lemon Sauce, New Potatoes with, '86 130
Lemony New Potatoes, '82 158
Medley, New Potato, '90 279
Medley, Potato, '92 61
Parsley-Chive Sauce, New Potatoes with, '84 212
Parsley New Potatoes, '79 122
Roasted Caraway Potatoes, '96 82
Roasted New Potatoes, '90 138
Roasted New Potatoes, Crispy, '98 166
Roasted New Potatoes, Herb-Crusted Pork Tenderloin with Horseradish-, '98 168
Roasted Potatoes, Jan's, '01 224
Salad, Asparagus-and-New Potato, '86 69
Salad, New Potato, '84 120, 139; '94 162; '01 142
Seasoned New Potatoes, '87 M151
Skillet, Potato-Vegetable, '92 61
Steamed Potatoes, Lemon-, '86 177
Summertime Potatoes, '86 M195
Olive Potatoes, Tangy, '04 214
Omelet, Family-Size Potato, '94 31
Omelet, Open-Faced Bacon-and-Potato, '02 246
Omelet, Potato-Sprout, '79 128
Omelets, Country, '91 128
Oven Potatoes, Crispy, '82 96
Pancake, Potato, '85 20
Pancakes, German Potato, '98 279
Pancakes, Leftover Potato, '96 138
Pancakes, Moist Potato, '80 36
Pancakes, Old-Fashioned Potato, '96 138
Pancakes, One Potato-Two Potato, '96 138

Pancakes, Parsley-Potato, '96 251; '97 103
Pancakes, Potato, '79 115; '89 144
Pancakes, Potato-Ham, '96 138
Pancakes, Quick Potato-Chive, '04 248
Parmesan-Paprika Potatoes, '99 169
Parmesan Potatoes, '82 270; '90 M62; '92 M341; '93 M46
Parmesan-Potato Fans, '88 M190
Parmesan Potato Wedges, '95 181
Parslied Potatoes, '86 18
Pastries, Potato-and-Blue Cheese, '03 258
Patties, Thunderbolt Potato, '94 213
Peas and Potatoes Vinaigrette, Dilled, '00 102
Peas and Potatoes with Dill, '99 67
Peppers, Potatoes with Sweet Red, '87 192
Phyllo Potatoes, '02 219
Pie, Country Breakfast, '93 M328
Pie, Meat-and-Potato, '84 23
Pie, Potato-Topped Turkey, '86 265
Pie, Shepherd's, '00 55
Pizza, Sausage-Potato, '01 199
Pizzas, Roasted Potato, '99 16
Point Clear Potatoes, '02 250
Pork Tenderloin with Apples, Celery, and Potatoes, Grilled, '95 161
Pudding, Carrot-Potato, '94 279
Puff, Potato-Cheese, '95 269
Puffs, Celeried Potato, '89 279
Quiche, Crustless Potato, '83 49
Red Potatoes, Green Beans and, '03 158
Roasted Green Beans, Potatoes, and Fennel, '00 322
Roasted Potatoes, '99 60
Roasted Potatoes, Carrots, and Leeks, '94 276
Roasted Potatoes, Garlic-, '95 87, 342
Roasted Potatoes, Oven-, '98 103
Roasted Potato Thins, '02 23
Roasted Potato Trio, '00 311; '02 310
Rolls. *See* **POTATOES/Breads.**
Rosemary, Potatoes Anna with, '84 209
Roses, Potato, '81 246
Sage Potatoes, '94 320
Salads
Any Day Potato Salad, '81 154
Avocado, Potato Salad with, '98 332
Avocado-Potato Salad with Horseradish Dressing, '96 200
Bacon-Topped Potato Salad, '85 59
Baked Potato Salad, '97 319
Basil Potato Salad, '94 178
Bean Salad, Potato-, '82 301
Blue Cheese-Potato Salad, '91 208
Broccoli-Potato Salad, Hot, '85 23
Charletta's Potato Salad, '98 153
Chunky Potato Salad, '81 M138
Cobb Salad, Potato, '03 140
Colorful Potato Salad, '01 94
Confetti Potato Salad, '80 5; '88 16
Corned Beef-Potato Salad, '85 213
Corned Beef Salad, Potato-, '81 36
Cottage Cheese-Potato Salad, '79 147, 285
Creamy Potato Salad, '80 178; '88 171; '92 241; '98 175; '01 334
Creole Potato Salad, '99 136
Cucumbers and Tomatoes, Potato Salad with, '03 92
Curried Potato Salad, '99 137
Deluxe Potato Salad, '80 155
Dill-and-Sour Cream Potato Salad, '93 105; '94 100
Dill Potato Salad, '85 213; '94 179; '99 104
Dill Potato Salad, Hot, '79 78
Dutch Potato Salad, Hot, '86 297; '87 176
Festive Potato Salad, '89 315
Fipps Family Potato Salad, '02 138

Fish-Potato Salad, Smoked, '84 233
French-Style Potato Salad, '88 171
Fruity Potato Salad, '85 214
Garden Patch Potato Salad, '84 82
German Potato Salad, '82 134, 239; '84 18;
     '92 169; '97 195; '98 175
German Potato Salad, Hot, '79 78; '94 254
German-Style Potato Salad, '83 23; '88 M194
Goat Cheese and Potato Salad, Warm, '96 234
Grecian Potato Salad, '82 55
Greek Potato Salad, '98 276
Green Bean-Potato Salad, '83 80; '01 181; '04 142
Green Bean-Red Potato Salad, '96 175
Green Bean Salad, Potato-and-, '00 162
Ham-and-Egg Potato Salad, '86 84
Ham and Potato Salad, '80 272
Ham-and-Potato Salad, '95 94
Herbed Potato Salad, '87 171; '94 164
Horseradish Potato Salad, '98 175
Hot-and-Light Potato Salad, '93 90
Hot Potato Greens, '97 20
Hot Potato Salad, '79 78; '81 276; '86 10
Hot Potato Salad Supreme, '79 78
Jalapeño Potato Salad, '97 64
Joy's Potato Salad, '99 83
Layered Creamy Potato Salad, '81 23
Layered Potato Salad, '03 183
Lemon-Basil Potato Salad, '97 63; '01 178
Light Potato Salad, '02 138
Lime-Potato Salad, '02 22
Marinated Potato Slices, '93 98
Mediterranean Spring Salad, '80 148
Mustard Potato Salad, '86 302
New Potato Salad, '84 120, 139; '94 162; '01 142
New Potato Salad, Asparagus-and-, '86 69
Niçoise, Salad, '03 35
Olive-Potato Salad, '85 114
Onion and Celery, Potato Salad with, '02 138
Parmesan Potato Salad, Hot, '79 78
Parslied Potato Salad, '85 240
Patio Potato Salad, '90 160
Peas-and-Potatoes Vinaigrette, Dilled, '01 327
Pepper Cups, Potato Salad in, '79 78
Peppers, Potato Salad 'n', '83 135
Pesto Potato Salad, '90 164
Pickle-Potato Salad, Sweet, '85 213
Pickle, Potato Salad with Sweet, '02 138
Pole Bean-Potato Salad, Hot, '79 74
Potato Salad, '90 122; '94 160; '00 195; '01 163;
     '03 163
Red Potato Salad, '93 119; '96 172; '02 138
Roasted New Potato Salad, '04 91
Roasted-Potato Salad, Creamy, '97 161
Roasted Red Peppers, Potato Salad With, '04 100
Salmon-Potato Salad, '87 285
Saucy Potato Salad, '87 123
Savory Potato Salad, '80 30
Shrimp-and-Potato Salad, '96 211
Smoked Salmon Potato Salad, '97 64
Sour Cream Potato Salad, '79 104; '80 79; '99 137
Sour Cream-Potato Salad, '84 149
Southern-Style Potato Salad, '04 199
South-of-the-Border Potato Salad, '94 178
Spicy Potato Salad, '97 305
Steak Salad Niçoise, Grilled, '98 148
Sugar Snap Peas, Potato Salad with, '91 120
Sweet and Sour Potato Salad, '80 152
Sweet-and-Sour Potato Salad, '92 106
Tri Club Potato Salad, '92 166
Tuna-Potato Salad, '84 289
Vegetable Potato Salad, '03 136
Warm Potato-and-Sausage Salad, '96 25
Warm Potato Salad with Smoked Sausage,
     '97 267

Scalloped Potatoes and Chops, Easy, '00 289
Scalloped Potatoes, Barbecue, '04 139
Scalloped Potatoes with Ham, '02 42
Scalloped Root Vegetables, '98 310
Seasoned Potatoes, Simple, '01 259
Skillet Potatoes, Oregano-and-Lemon, '93 54
Skillet Potatoes, Peppy, '86 110
Skins, Baked Potato, '86 81
Skins, Cheesy Potato, '82 78
Skin Snack, Potato, '91 18
Slims, Potato, '81 276
Soufflé, Cheesy Potato, '89 332
Soufflé Potatoes, '84 295; '85 196; '90 14
Soups
     Asparagus-Potato Soup, '85 23
     Asparagus Soup, '98 290
     Bacon Soup, Potato-, '84 M38
     Baked Potato Soup, '91 311; '92 26; '03 29
     Beet Soup, Potato-, '88 156
     Bisque, Spinach-Potato, '86 66
     Bisque, Squash, '98 290
     Carrot Soup, Potato-, '88 297
     Celery-and-Potato Soup, '84 279
     Cheddar-Potato Soup, '03 M283
     Cheesy Potato-and-Wild Rice Soup, '89 16
     Chowder, Mushroom-Potato, '92 331
     Chowder, Potato-Corn, '94 66
     Chowder, Potato-Vegetable, '98 335
     Chowder with Green Chiles, Potato, '00 329
     Chowder with Ham, Potato, '99 141
     Chowder, Yukon Gold-Cheese, '03 296
     Cream of Potato Soup, '80 M224; '82 21
     Cream of Potato Soup, Golden, '86 302
     Creamy Potato Soup, '81 19, 98; '84 112
     Cucumber-Potato Soup, Chilled, '85 93
     Cucumber Soup, Cold Potato-, '88 160
     Easy Potato Soup, '92 17
     Garlic-and-Potato Soup, Golden, '04 214
     Hearty Potato Soup, '98 292
     Holiday Potato Soup, '79 236
     Irish Potato Soup, '99 54
     Kale Soup, Creamy, '96 203
     Leek-and-Potato Soup, '84 112
     Leek Soup, Cream of, '99 276
     Onion-and-Potato Soup, Creamy, '92 51; '97 304
     Pea Soup, Potato-, '94 90
     Potato Soup, '82 278; '83 292; '92 263
     Sausage-Potato Soup, '80 25
     Sausage Soup, Easy Potato-, '98 315
     Special Potato Soup, '82 3
     Subtle Potato Potage, '80 78
     Three-Potato Soup, '86 16
     Vichyssoise, '86 181
     Vichyssoise with Mint Cream, Cucumber, '98 246
     Yogurt Soup, Potato-, '92 217
Spread, Creamy Potato-Garlic, '02 35
Steak 'n Potatoes, Skillet, '81 18
Stew, Frogmore, '00 174, 336
Stew, Meatball, '98 30
Stew, Potato-Oyster, '89 243
Stir-Fry, Potato, '93 240
Stir-Fry, Potato-Snow Pea, '86 173
Stuffed
     Alfredo, Potatoes, '89 204
     Bacon-Stuffed Potatoes, '86 193
     Bacon-Stuffed Potatoes, Cheesy, '81 M61
     Baked Potatoes, Stuffed, '83 322; '00 293
     Baked Stuffed Potatoes, '84 38
     Béchamel Sauce, Stuffed Potatoes with,
          '84 M239
     Black-Eyed Pea-Spinach-Stuffed Potatoes, '95 22
     Blue Cheese Potatoes, Bacon-Topped, '79 46
     Blue Cheese Stuffed Potatoes, '81 276
     Blue Cheese-Stuffed Potatoes, '89 69

     Breakfast-Stuffed Potatoes, '00 179
     Broccoli Bakers, '99 308
     Broccoli-Shrimp Stuffed Potatoes, '92 M228
     Caviar Potatoes, Appetizer, '86 223
     Cheddar, Broccoli, and Ham Stuffed Potatoes,
          '04 26
     Cheese-and-Chive Potatoes, Creamy, '99 308
     Cheese Sauce, Stuffed Potatoes with, '87 192
     Cheesy Stuffed Potatoes, '02 175
     Chicken-Cheese Stuffed Potatoes, '86 55
     Chicken Fajita Spuds, '96 238
     Chive-and-Gorganzola Stuffed Potatoes, Creamy,
          '99 308
     Chives, Potatoes with, '81 M61
     Chive-Stuffed Baked Potatoes, '79 52
     Chive-Stuffed Potatoes, Cheesy, '91 128
     Chive-Stuffed Potatoes, Creamy, '80 268
     Crab-Stuffed Potatoes, '91 311; '92 26; '99 307
     Crab-Stuffed Potatoes, Cheesy, '86 17
     Creamy Stuffed Baked Potatoes, '86 55
     Creamy Stuffed Potatoes, '79 211
     Fish-Stuffed Potatoes, '92 306
     Fluffy Stuffed Potatoes, '86 223
     Franks and Potatoes, Stuffed, '81 202
     Ham-Stuffed Baked Potatoes, '02 52
     Ham Stuffed Potatoes, '79 210
     Hearty Stuffed Potatoes, '89 M282
     Herb Stuffed Potatoes, '79 211
     Jalapeño-Ham Stuffed Potatoes, '81 M61
     Lemon-Herb Stuffed Potatoes, '83 173
     Mexican-Stuffed Potatoes, '91 131
     Mushroom-Swiss Spuds, '96 M238
     Patchwork Potatoes, '86 54
     Rellenos Potatoes, Papa's, '96 238
     Roquefort, Potatoes, '79 211
     Savory Stuffed Potatoes, '81 101
     Seafood-Stuffed Potatoes, '95 M192
     Shrimp-and-Mushroom Stuffed Potatoes, '99 308
     Shrimp Boats, '79 57
     Shrimp-Stuffed Potatoes, Creamy, '80 36
     South-of-the-Border Stuffed Potatoes, '86 54
     Stuffed Potatoes, '89 173; '01 48; '02 283
     Summertime Potatoes, '86 M195
     Tuna Stuffed Potatoes, '79 210
     Twice Baked Cottage-Style Potatoes, '91 135
     Twice-Baked Potato, '90 M295
     Twice-Baked Potatoes, '83 227; '91 185
     Vegetable-Topped Stuffed Potatoes, '85 235
     Yogurt-Stuffed Potatoes, '88 24
     Zesty Stuffed Potatoes, '94 M46
Tacos, Breakfast, '91 316
Tarts, Phyllo Potato, '98 69
Tortilla Campesina, '89 85
Tortilla Espanola, '92 175
Tortilla, Potato, '00 85
Vinaigrette, Potato-Broccoli, '85 84
Wedges, Lemon Potato, '88 21
Wedges, Lemony Potato, '90 M61
POULTRY. See CHICKEN, CORNISH HENS,
     GAME, TURKEY.
PRALINE. See also CANDIES/ Praline.
     Almonds, Praline, '97 285
     Bananas, Praline, '84 313
     Bars, Chewy Praline-Chocolate Fudge, '04 M330
     Brownies, Praline, '93 243
     Buns, Praline, '90 195
     Buttercream, Praline, '95 243
     Cake, Chocolate-Praline, '01 235
     Cake, Chocolate-Praline Pecan, '03 288
     Cake, Praline, '81 162
     Cake, Praline Cream, '01 272
     Cake, Praline-Filled Carrot, '03 332
     Cake, Praline Ice Cream, '80 84
     Cake, Praline Pound, '82 88

PRALINE
(continued)

Cheesecake, Pecan Praline, '03 269
Cheesecake, Praline, '83 270; '89 93
Cheesecake, Praline-Crusted, '99 295
Coffee, Praline, '97 17; '01 291
Coffee, Praline-Flavored, '87 69
Compote, Warm Praline Fruit, '85 260
Cookies, Crispy Praline, '03 131
Cookies, Crispy Praline-Chocolate Chip, '03 131
Cookies, Praline, '91 271
Cookies, Praline Shortbread, '88 242
Cookies, Praline Thumbprint, '89 328
Cream, Praline, '01 272
Filling, Praline, '89 328
Filling, Praline Cream, '03 332
Freeze, Praline, '89 60; '90 48
French Toast, Praline, '98 55
Frosting, Praline, '01 235
Glaze, Apple-Stuffed Tenderloin with Praline-
    Mustard, '97 216
Glaze, Praline, '82 196
Ham, Praline, '85 302; '96 303
Horns, Praline, '96 316
Ice Cream, Praline, '89 318
Ice Cream, Pralines and Cream, '82 184; '83 159
Icing, Praline Fudge, '04 331
Muffins, Banana-Praline, '04 21
Pastries, Praline, '89 318
Pecans, Praline, '97 285
Pie, Chocolate-Praline, '86 259
Pie, Frosty Pumpkin-Praline, '91 M234
Pie, Georgia Peach-and-Praline, '98 196
Pie, Peach Praline, '89 136
Pie, Pear-Praline, '97 192
Pie, Praline-Apple, '99 331
Pie, Praline-Topped Pumpkin, '00 332
Pie, Pumpkin Praline, '80 244
Powder, Praline, '95 243
Sauce, Bourbon Praline, '81 170
Sauce, Chocolate-Praline, '85 M295
Sauce, Peach-Praline, '85 161
Sauce, Praline, '83 25; '84 143; '89 95; '92 282;
    '93 214; '94 206, 312; '96 285
Sauce, Praline Ice Cream, '85 189
Sauce, Southern Praline Ice Cream, '86 M227
Sweet Potatoes and Apples, Praline, '03 260
Sweet Potatoes, Praline-Topped, '98 96
Toast, Orange Praline, '79 36
Torte, Chocolate Praline, '84 165
Torte, Lucy's Apricot Praline, '95 243
Torte, Praline-Pumpkin, '01 285
PRESERVES. *See* **JAMS AND JELLIES.**
PRESSURE COOKER
Carrots Polynesian, '79 45
Chicken Marengo, '92 70
Jambalaya, Black-Eyed Pea, '92 70
Meat Mix, Mexican, '00 292
Pot Roast with Vegetables, '00 18
Roast Beef, Pressure Cooker, '01 86
Roast, Pressure-Cooker, '91 289
Roast with Onion-and-Mushroom Gravy, '00 293
Stew, Quick Beef, '92 71
PRETZELS
Brownies, Saucepan Pretzel, '85 171
Chocolate-Covered Pretzels, '82 295
Dressing, Pretzel, '86 280
Flying Brooms, '98 255
Frosted Pretzels, '92 280
Garlands, Pretzel, '93 286
Herb Pretzels with Lower Sodium Horseradish
    Mustard, '86 325

Homemade Pretzels, '84 159; '91 185
Nuggets, Golden North Pole, '99 M309
Popcorn, Pretzel, '84 30
Reindeer Food, Magic, '99 M309
Salad, Strawberry-Pretzel, '03 290
Soft Pretzels, '83 18
Soft Pretzels, Chewy, '87 159
Whole Wheat Pretzels, '89 20
PRUNES
Bavarian, Prune, '86 223
Bread, Prune-Nut, '87 255; '91 55
Butter, Prune-Orange, '92 49
Cake and Sauce, Prune, '85 118
Cake, Prune, '85 223
Cake, Spicy Prune, '79 136
Chicken with Prunes, Saffron, '97 264
Compote, Baked Prune, '94 50
Merlot, Prunes in, '98 18
Muffins, Miniature Prune, '85 223
Muffins, Spicy Prune, '97 271
Muffins, Wheat Germ-Prune, '81 106
Orange-Spiced Prunes, '85 224
Pork Chops Stuffed with Prunes, '84 7
Pork Loin Roast, Prune-Stuffed, '80 29
Raspberry Prunes, '82 124
Relish, Peppy Prune, '90 227
Stuffed Prunes, '85 47
Tarts, Brandied Prune, '85 223
Tzimmes, '95 102
PUDDINGS. *See also* **CUSTARDS, MOUSSES.**
Almond Cream, '00 27
Apple-Nut Pudding with Hot Rum Sauce, '79 86
Applesauce-Graham Cracker Pudding, '81 34
Banana
    Almost Banana Pudding, '88 174
    Banana Pudding, '82 53; '84 94; '85 255;
        '88 16, 32; '03 24
    Basic Banana Pudding, '81 59
    Best-Ever Banana Pudding, '00 332
    Creamy Banana Pudding, '89 M130
    Cupcakes, Banana Pudding Ice-Cream, '01 173
    Delicious Banana Pudding, '80 9
    Fudge-Banana Pudding, '97 331
    Graham Banana Pudding, '02 62
    Mallow Pudding, Banana-, '86 139
    No-Bake Banana Pudding, '91 172; '99 197
    Old-Fashioned Banana Pudding, '92 94
    Over-the-Moon Banana Pudding, '03 140
    Peanut Butter-Banana Pudding, '93 340
    Pops, Banana Pudding Parfait, '96 180
    Sour Cream Banana Pudding, '98 90
    Sugar Biscuits, Banana Pudding with, '04 72
    Surprise Banana Pudding, '86 7
    Trifle, Banana Pudding, '98 273
Beach, The, '95 168
Black-and-White Pudding, Rich, '01 111
Blackberry Pudding Tarts, '93 200; '00 147
Blueberry-Raspberry Pudding, Russian, '97 128
Bread
    Almond-Cream Cheese Bread Pudding with
        Amaretto Cream Sauce, Layered, '03 330
    Amish Bread Pudding, '80 8
    Apple-Raisin Bread Pudding, '88 175
    Apricot Bread Pudding, '85 24
    Bananas Foster Bread Pudding, '04 235
    Biscuit Pudding, '79 86; '93 51
    Blueberry Bread Pudding, '88 154; '03 119
    Blueberry-Lemon Sauce, Bread Pudding with,
        '01 117
    Bread Pudding, '89 M130; '90 219
    Buttermilk Bread Pudding with Butter-Rum
        Sauce, '95 134
    Cheesy Bread Pudding, '83 68
    Chocolate Biscuit Bread Pudding, '94 215

    Chocolate Bread Pudding, '80 8
    Chocolate Bread Pudding with Custard Sauce,
        '03 244
    Chocolate Bread Pudding with Whiskey Sauce,
        '99 277
    Cinnamon-Raisin Bread Pudding, '01 315
    Cinnamon Toast Pudding with Caramel Sauce,
        '96 284
    Cranberry-Raisin Bread Pudding, Stuffed
        Pumpkin with, '02 231
    Croissant Bread Pudding, '03 66
    Custard Sauce, Bread Pudding with, '97 313
    Durfee's Bread Pudding, '96 48
    Fig-Walnut Pudding, '03 244
    French Bread Pudding, '85 231
    Lemon Bread Pudding, Old-Fashioned, '88 95
    Mushroom Bread Pudding, '99 58
    Old-Fashioned Bread Pudding, '83 213; '88 175;
        '00 105; '01 223
    Old-Fashioned Bread Pudding with Bourbon
        Custard Sauce, '95 271
    Old-Fashioned Bread Pudding with Rum Sauce,
        '88 32
    Peachy Bread Pudding, '88 175
    Piña Colada Bread Pudding, '98 34
    Pineapple-Apple Bread Pudding with Vanilla-
        Nutmeg Sauce, '02 208
    Plum Bread Pudding, Refrigerator, '97 177
    Pumpkin Bread Pudding, '98 240
    Raisin Bread Pudding, '94 215
    Raisin Bread Pudding with Bourbon Sauce,
        '98 336
    Rosemary-Tasso Bread Pudding, '00 104
    Sauce, Bread Pudding, '04 235
    Spiced Bread Pudding, '93 52
    Sweet Potato Bread Pudding, '94 241
    Sweet Roll Pudding, '96 283
    Tennessee Bread Pudding with Bourbon Sauce,
        '93 51
    Vanilla Sauce, Bread Pudding with, '97 M15
    Whiskey Sauce, Bread Pudding with, '80 58;
        '90 230; '92 93
    White Chocolate Bread Pudding, '00 M104
Brownie Pudding, '79 265; '80 295
Brown Sugar-Pecan Pudding, '86 M165
Butternut Squash Pudding, '89 M313; '90 M19
Cake, Apple Pudding, '01 47
Cake, Black Forest Pudding, '02 210
Cake, Carrot Pudding, '83 24
Cake, Danish Pudding, '91 269
Cake, Lemon Pudding, '83 106
Cake Pudding, Chocolate, '81 99
Cake Pudding, Hot Fudge Sundae, '88 167
Cake Pudding, Lemon, '92 96; '98 35
Cake Pudding, Wine, '79 230
Cake, Saucy Pudding, '98 196
Cake with Blueberry Sauce, Buttermilk-Lemon
    Pudding, '95 135
Chocolate-Almond Pudding, '82 M142; '88 24
Chocolate-Almond Silk Pudding, '96 266
Chocolate Cookie Pudding, '03 183
Chocolate-Peanut Butter Cookie Pudding, '03 183
Chocolate Pudding, '02 323
Chocolate Pudding, Creamy, '83 106
Chocolate Pudding, Fudgy, '96 285
Chocolate-Rum Dessert, '81 247
Christmas Pudding, '79 230
Christmas Pudding, Flaming, '85 312
Christmas Pudding with Brandy Sauce, Baked,
    '88 279
Coconut Cream, '00 27
Coffee Cream, '00 27
Cookies, Pudding-Oatmeal, '98 215
Cranberry Pudding, '84 306

Finger Painting Never Tasted So Good, '95 167
French Vanilla Latte Pudding, '03 M282
Frozen Ozark Pudding, '88 127
Fruit Pudding Compote, Fresh, '86 151
Hansel Pudding, '80 9
Holland Rusk Pudding, Yia Yia's, '93 124
Hot Fudge Pudding, '81 208
Kugel, Nu Awlins, '94 229
Lemon Fluff Pudding, '85 304
Lemon-Pear Pudding, '96 283
Lemon Pudding, '79 86; '81 99
Lemon Pudding, Baked, '04 295
Lemon Pudding, Layered, '82 128
Mandarin-Almond Pudding, '85 M12
Mocha-Chocolate Cookie Pudding, '03 183
Orange Cream, '00 27
Orange Custard Pudding, '88 174
Orange Pudding, '81 85; '82 111; '83 153
Orange-Tapioca Crème, '82 M283
Peanut Butter-Banana Pudding, '93 340
Peanut Butter Pudding, '85 95; '88 32; '00 27
Peanut Parfait, Bodacious, '95 167
Pecan-Mocha Pudding, '89 M130
Persimmon Pudding, '00 254
Pineapple Pudding, '80 102
Plum Pudding, '79 281
Plum Pudding, Flamed, '84 276
Plum Pudding-Gelatin Mold, '86 300; '87 178
Plum Pudding, Light, '86 318
Plum Pudding, Old-Fashioned, '80 264
Pumpkin Pudding, '89 M313; '90 M20
Pumpkin Pudding, Baked, '80 244
Raisin-Pumpkin Pudding, '84 315
Raspberry Pudding, '92 92
Rice
  Amaretto Rice Pudding, '86 334
  Apple Rice Pudding, '91 217
  Brown Rice Pudding, '85 77
  Creamy Rice Pudding, '81 51, 205
  English Rice Pudding, '04 98
  Fruited Rice Pudding, '81 205; '86 95
  Fudgy Rice Pudding, '81 205
  Old-Fashioned Rice Pudding, '85 147; '03 285
  Raisin-Rice Pudding, '87 46
  Velvety Rice Pudding, '81 205
Rum Pudding with Raspberry Sauce, '82 288
Savory
  Carrot-Potato Pudding, '94 279
  Cheese Pudding, Baked, '86 78
  Corn-Cheese Pudding, '80 244
  Corn Pudding, '79 276; '81 128; '86 192;
    '90 219; '98 124; '99 71, 270
  Corn Pudding, Baked, '83 314
  Corn Pudding, Creamy, '81 267
  Corn Pudding, Dashiell, '98 274
  Corn Pudding, Easy, '83 280
  Corn Pudding, Fresh, '80 157, 165; '89 172
  Corn Pudding, Southwestern, '01 165; '03 178
  Corn Pudding, Tee's, '95 318; '01 165; '03 178
  Green Tomato-Tomatillo-Corn Pudding, '04 103
  Grits Pudding, '96 28
  Onion Pudding, Kathy's, '95 318
  Onion Puddings, '02 126
  Onion Pudding, Sweet, '02 310
  Persimmon Pudding, '79 206
  Rosemary-Tasso Bread Pudding, '00 104
  Squash Pudding, '82 277; '83 15
  Sweet Onion Pudding, '00 260
  Sweet Potato Pudding, '79 244; '86 52
  Turnip Pudding, '94 213
  Yorkshire Pudding, '80 252; '98 86
  Yorkshire Puddings, Mini Prime Ribs and,
    '01 283
Scuppernong Pudding Tarts, '98 221

Snowflake Pudding, '85 30
Snow White Pudding, '85 77
Steamed Date Pudding, '79 86
Steamed Ginger Pudding, '96 283
Steamed Holiday Pudding, '84 275
Steamed Mincemeat Pudding, '80 264
Summer Pudding, '98 217; '04 159
Tipsy Pudding, Parson's, '80 156
Vanilla Cream, '00 27
Vanilla Pudding, '88 32
Vanilla Pudding, Creamy, '83 227
Woodford Pudding, '79 86
PUMPKIN
Baked Pumpkin, '82 217
Bars and Cookies
  Cake Bars, Pumpkin, '80 245
  Chocolate Chip Cookies, Pumpkin-, '93 235
  Drop Cookies, Pumpkin, '79 206
  Great Pumpkin Cookies, '91 234
  Jack-o'-Lantern Cookies, '87 214
  Nut Bars, Pumpkin, '82 217
  Peppy Pumpkin Cookies, '89 253
  Pumpkin Bars, '80 40
  Walnut Cookies, Frosted Pumpkin-, '82 217
Bisque, Spicy Pumpkin, '86 67
Breads
  Brother Boniface's Pumpkin Bread, '98 26
  Coconut Bread, Pumpkin-, '87 255
  Cream Cheese and Preserves, Pumpkin Bread
    with, '84 264
  Empanadas, '02 82
  Gingerbread with Caramel Sauce, Pumpkin,
    '93 235
  Harvest Pumpkin Bread, '90 M215
  Harvest Pumpkin Loaf, '85 232
  Holiday Pumpkin Bread, '03 281
  Moist Pumpkin Bread, '80 245
  Muffins, Holiday Pumpkin, '03 281
  Muffins, Monster, '94 256
  Muffins, Nutty Pumpkin, '86 291
  Muffins, Pumpkin, '79 206, 275; '81 272;
    '04 112
  Muffins, Pumpkin-Apple, '96 242
  Nut Bread, Pumpkin-, '83 294
  Oatmeal Loaf, Pumpkin-, '81 49
  Orange-Pumpkin Bread, '87 300
  Pancakes, Pumpkin, '80 228
  Pecan Bread, Pumpkin-, '87 221; '02 224
  Pumpkin Bread, '81 8
  Rolls, Pumpkin, '87 254
  Spiced Pumpkin Bread, '91 233
Cake Bars, Pumpkin, '80 245
Cake, Pumpkin, '81 272; '93 303; '98 241
Cake, Pumpkin Date, '79 251
Cake, Pumpkin Kahlúa, '86 292
Cake, Pumpkin Layer, '80 245
Cake, Pumpkin Pound, '92 235
Cake Squares, Orange-Pumpkin, '83 242
Cake with Little Ghosts, Pumpkin, '03 212
Calabaza Guisada con Puerco (Pumpkin Cooked
  with Pork), '80 193
Cheese Ball, Pumpkin, '02 222
Cheesecake, Pumpkin, '80 254; '85 280; '96 268
Chiffon, Pumpkin, '82 216; '86 283; '88 260
Chips, Pumpkin, '98 241
Chocolate Pumpkin, '96 254
Chowder, Pumpkin-Corn, '97 219
Cooked Fresh Pumpkin, '88 M230
Cookies. *See* **PUMPKIN/Bars and Cookies.**
Cupcakes, Pumpkin, '85 121
Custard, Pumpkin, '88 279
Delight, Pumpkin-Orange, '86 321
Dessert, Frozen Pumpkin, '88 167
Dessert, Pumpkin Chiffon, '88 128

Dip, Pumpkin Pie, '01 242
Doughnut Drops, Pumpkin, '90 323
Empanadas de Calabaza (Pumpkin Empanadas),
  '94 28
Empanadas, Pumpkin, '82 223
Flan, Pumpkin, '82 217; '97 219
Ice Cream Pumpkin, '96 255
Mold, Pumpkin, '82 311
Mousse, Pumpkin, '91 96; '92 130
Pasta, Pumpkin, '98 241
Pies
  Autumn Pumpkin Pie, '87 213
  Bourbon-Pecan Pumpkin Pie, '87 264
  Chiffon Pie, Pumpkin, '84 312
  Cracked Caramel-Pumpkin Pie, '99 254
  Festive Pumpkin Pie, '81 M269
  Fluffy Pumpkin Pie, '80 283
  Frosty Pumpkin Pie, '96 279
  Gingersnap Streusel Pumpkin Pie, '01 315
  Ice Cream Pie, Pumpkin, '81 272
  Ice Cream Pie, Pumpkin-, '87 243
  Layered Pie, Elegant Pumpkin-Walnut,
    '02 244
  Mama's Pumpkin Pie, '96 242
  Meringue, Pumpkin Pie with, '92 268
  New-Fashioned Pumpkin Pie, '90 296
  Nutty Pumpkin Pie, '82 67
  Pecan Pie, Pumpkin-, '85 233, 282
  Praline Pie, Frosty Pumpkin-, '91 M234
  Praline Pie, Pumpkin, '80 244
  Praline-Topped Pumpkin Pie, '00 332
  Quick Pumpkin Pie, '88 M230
  Rich Pumpkin Pie, '86 292
  Sour Cream-Pumpkin Pie, '84 263
  Spiced Nut Crust, Pumpkin Pie in, '87 295
  Spicy Pumpkin Pies, '84 322
  Supreme, Pumpkin Pie, '82 217
  Traditional Pumpkin Pie, '85 256
Pizza Pumpkins, '98 255
Profiteroles with Warm Cranberry Compote,
  Pumpkin-Spiced, '97 264
Pudding, Baked Pumpkin, '80 244
Pudding, Pumpkin, '89 M313; '90 M20
Pudding, Pumpkin Bread, '98 240
Pudding, Raisin-Pumpkin, '84 315
Puree, Pumpkin, '00 296
Risotto with Shrimp, Pumpkin, '98 240
Roll, Pumpkin, '79 206; '91 297; '04 297
Sauce, Beurre Blanc, '98 240
Sauce, Pumpkin Seed, '88 246
Seeds, Roasted Pumpkin, '03 211
Seeds, Santa Fe, '02 145
Seeds, Seasoned Pumpkin, '91 234
Seeds, Toasted Pumpkin, '88 M230; '98 241
Soup, Cream of Pumpkin, '93 234
Soup, Creamy Southwestern Pumpkin, '03 221
Soup, Curried Pumpkin, '96 242
Soup, Pumpkin, '79 48
Soup, Pumpkin-Pear, '92 234
Soup, Pumpkin-Tomato, '86 291
Soup Stock, Pumpkin, '00 296
Soup with Ginger-Lime Cream, Pumpkin-Corn,
  '95 227
Soup with Sweet Croutons, Pumpkin, '00 296
Stuffed Pumpkin with Cranberry-Raisin Bread
  Pudding, '02 231
Swirl, Easy Pumpkin, '93 234
Tarts, No-Bake Pumpkin, '86 291
Torte, Praline-Pumpkin, '01 285
Waffles, Pumpkin, '95 282
Waffles, Pumpkin-Nut, '86 96
Waffles with Mandarin Orange Sauce, Dessert
  Pumpkin, '89 204
PUNCH. *See* **BEVERAGES/Alcoholic, Punch.**

QUAIL. *See* GAME/Quail.

QUESADILLAS
Apple Pie 'n' Cheddar Quesadillas, '03 61
Apple Quesadillas, '99 248
Bacon-Jalapeño-Tomato Quesadillas, '95 240
Barbecue Quesadillas, '02 121
Chicken-and-Black Bean Quesadillas, '96 288
Chicken-and-Brie Quesadillas with Chipotle Salsa, '99 311
Chicken Quesadillas, Grilled, '04 36
Chicken Quesadillas, Sesame-Ginger, '00 147
Chicken Quesadillas, Spicy, '95 42
Chorizo, Black Bean, and Corn Quesadillas, '00 148
Corn-and-Squash Quesadillas, Grilled, '02 123
Crab Quesadillas with Mango Salsa, Beefy, '00 124
Dessert Quesadillas, '02 54
Easy Quesadillas, '98 M205
Greek Quesadillas, '03 61
Green Chile Quesadillas, '90 121
Meatball Quesadillas, '00 242
Poblano-and-Corn Quesadillas, '01 333
Pork Quesadillas, Barbecued, '04 187
Quick Fiesta Quesadillas, '02 246
Quick Quesadillas, '89 87; '02 143
Roasted Vegetable Quesadillas, '04 322
Salmon Quesadilla with Cucumber Salsa, Grilled, '95 131
Sausage Quesadillas, '90 118
Sausage Quesadillas, Breakfast, '04 183
Shrimp-and-Roasted Pepper Quesadillas, '00 215
Spinach, Mushroom, and Cilantro Quesadillas, '00 148
Torta, Quesadilla, '97 325
Vegetable Quesadillas, '97 65
Vegetable Quesadilla with Roasted Salsa, Northern New Mexican, '95 130
Western Quesadillas, '97 65

QUICHES
Artichoke Quiche, '91 71
Asparagus-Tomato Quiche, '88 198
Broccoli Quiche, Easy, '82 34
Broccoli Quiche, Italian, '85 45
Broccoli-Rice Quiche, '81 228
Casserole, Quiche, '95 33
Cauliflower Quiche, '83 86
Cheese
  Bacon-Cheese Quiches, Miniature, '83 93
  Blue Cheese Quiche, '84 52
  Canadian Bacon-and-Brie Quiche, '04 248
  Cheddar-Leek Quiche, '88 198
  Chiles Rellenos Quiche, '02 321
  Cream Cheese Quiche, '96 203
  Green Onion Quiche, Cheesy, '83 194; '84 42
  Ham-and-Cheese Quiches, Individual, '98 24
  Ham-Cheese Quiche, '79 26
  Ham Quiche, Cheesy, '79 127
  Jalapeño Quiche, Cheesy, '84 31
  Mexican Cheese Pie, '83 69
  Miniature Cheese Quiches, '80 150
  Sausage-Cheddar Quiche, '79 26
  Sealed with a Quiche, '95 135
  Spinach Quiche, Cheesy, '81 228
  Spinach Quiches, Triple-Cheese, '00 220
  Squares, Cheesy Hot Quiche, '79 124
  Squares, Quiche, '84 222
  Swiss Alpine Quiche, '90 18
  Swiss-Zucchini Quiche, '82 49
  Tarragon Cocktail Quiches, '84 127
  Vegetable Quiche, Cheese-, '81 228
  Zucchini Quiche, Cheesy, '83 312
Chicken Divan Quiche, '88 M125
Chicken-Olive-Cheddar Quiche, '03 58
Chicken-Pecan Quiche, '91 206
Chile Pepper Quiche, '82 224
Clam Quiche, '83 215
Crabmeat-Parmesan Quiche, '03 59
Crab Quiche, '82 M122, 243
Crab Quiche, Almond-Topped, '79 127
Crab Quiche, Quick, '84 96
Crab Quiche, Sherried, '83 180
Crab Quiche, Simple, '85 207
Eggless Quiche, '87 220
Fiesta Quiche, '92 47
Green Chile Quiche, '83 31
Individual Quiches, '98 101
Jalapeño-Corn Quiche, '85 122
Lorraine, Classic Quiche, '81 131
Lorraine, Mushroom-Quiche, '86 242
Lorraine, Peppery Quiche, '81 228
Lorraine, Perfect Quiche, '79 127
Lorraine, Quiche, '79 40; '80 M108; '99 M218; '01 88
Meat
  Bacon-Cheese Quiches, Miniature, '83 93
  Bacon Quiche, '85 60
  Bacon Quiche, Spinach-and-, '00 240
  Benedict Quiche, '80 M107
  Canadian Bacon-and-Brie Quiche, '04 248
  Ham-and-Cheese Quiches, Individual, '98 24
  Ham-and-Grits Crustless Quiche, '94 89
  Ham-and-Mushroom Quiche, '81 11
  Ham-and-Vegetable Quiche, '84 326
  Ham-Cheese Quiche, '79 26
  Ham Quiche, '80 110
  Ham Quiche, Cheesy, '79 127
  Ham Quiche, Country, '87 287
  Ham Quiche, Crustless, '84 235
  Mexican Quiche Cups, '02 72
  Sausage-Apple Quiche, Crustless, '87 70
  Sausage-Cheddar Quiche, '79 26
  Sausage Quiche, Easy, '79 261
  Sausage Quiche, Italian, '81 200
  Sausage Quiche, Spicy, '80 M108
  Sausage Quiche, Zucchini-, '83 122
Mexicali Quiche with Avocado Topping, '93 309; '94 96
Miniature
  Bacon-Cheese Quiches, Miniature, '83 93
  Cheese Quiches, Miniature, '80 150
  Individual Ham-and-Cheese Quiches, '98 24
  Individual Spinach Quiches, '86 38
  Olive Quiche Appetizers, '86 159
  Shrimp Miniquiches, '87 146
  Spinach Quichelets, '87 67
  Spinach Quiches, '01 241
  Spinach Quiches, Miniature, '82 38
  Squares, Quiche, '84 222
  Tarragon Cocktail Quiches, '84 127
  Wild Rice-and-Mushroom Quiches, '93 237
Mushroom Quiche, '80 222; '81 244; '89 285
Noël, Quiche, '82 310
Onion Quiche, '83 121
Pastry, Microwaved Quiche, '81 M74; '82 M123
Pastry, Quiche, '80 M107
Pizza Quiche, '86 53
Potato Quiche, Crustless, '83 49
Salmon-and-Dill Quiche, '03 58
Salmon Quiche, '82 87; '87 38
Shrimp-and-Artichoke Quiche, '03 196
Shrimp Quiche, '83 50
South-of-the-Border Quiche, '93 321
Southwestern Quiche, '04 41
Spinach
  Bacon Quiche, Spinach-and-, '00 240
  Cheese Spinach Quiches, Triple-, '00 220
  Cheesy Spinach Quiche, '81 228
  Crustless Spinach Quiche, '84 235
  Greek Spinach Quiche, '86 10
  Individual Spinach Quiches, '86 38
  Miniature Spinach Quiches, '82 38
  Mushroom Quiche, Spinach-, '81 M74
  Mushroom-Spinach-Swiss Quiche, '03 59
  No-Crust Spinach Quiche, '90 142
  Spinach Quiche, '81 44; '85 49; '91 204
  Spinach Quichelets, '87 67
  Spinach Quiches, '01 241
  Tomato Florentine Quiche, '04 332
Springtime Quiche, '83 122
Squash-and-Green Chile Quiche, '88 143
Tasty Quiche, '82 264
Vegetable Quiche, '87 M219
Vegetable Quiche, Light, '97 332
Veggie Sausage Quiche, Crustless, '03 175
Zucchini Frittata, '86 103
Zucchini-Mushroom Quiche, '79 127
Zucchini Pie, Italian-Style, '83 43
Zucchini-Sausage Quiche, '83 122

QUICK & EASY
Appetizers
  Bacon-Cheese Fingers, '00 133
  Brie, Chutney-Bacon, '90 M292
  Brie in Rye, Raspberry, '93 252
  Bruschetta, Roasted Pepper-Tomato, '02 213
  Cashews, Caribbean, '04 196
  Caviar, Homemade Cowboy, '94 64
  Caviar, Texas, '01 257
  Cereal Bites, Buttery, '89 97
  Cheese-and-Olive Snack, Open-Faced, '89 97
  Cheese Ball, '91 200
  Cheese Ball, Apple, '98 250
  Cheese Ball, Peppered, '94 118
  Cheese Fondue, Party, '92 20
  Cheese Loaf, Four-Layer, '99 222
  Cheese Snack, '89 98
  Chicken-Cheese Ball, '93 216
  Chicken Strips, Sesame, '98 250
  Cinnamon Sticks, '95 244
  Cocktail Smoky Links, '90 168
  Crackers, Snack, '00 133
  Crackers, Tomato-Blue Cheese, '02 213
  Cream Cheese, Bacon-Olive, '04 196
  Dip and Vegetable Platter, Curry, '89 327
  Dip, Bean, '89 97
  Dip, Cheese-Crab, '91 200
  Dip, Chili-and-Cheese, '89 M328
  Dip, Corn-and-Field Pea, '01 177
  Dip, Fiesta, '92 263
  Dip, Meaty Cheese, '92 160
  Dip, Mexican Artichoke, '90 M292
  Dip, Quick Nacho, '90 168
  Dip, Super Seafood, '90 292
  Dip, Sweet Fruit, '89 328
  Dip with Tortellini, Creamy Tomato Pesto, '00 196
  Guacamole, '96 160
  Ham Appetillas, '93 63
  Jelly, Garlic Pepper, '99 221
  Kielbasa, Sweet-and-Sour, '89 327
  Meatballs, Spicy Party, '00 242
  Mushrooms, Marinated, '91 306
  Nachos, Tex-Mex, '89 97
  Nuts, Quick Party, '04 197
  Olive Cups, Greek, '99 221
  Olives, Lemon-Garlic, '94 118
  Parmesan Cheese Bites, '99 221; '02 108
  Peanuts, Sugar-and-Spice, '04 197
  Pepperoni Pie Hors d'Oeuvres, '98 251
  Pistachios, Spicy, '04 197
  Pizza Bites, '95 244
  Quesadillas, Quick, '02 143
  Rollups, Spinach, '98 251

Sandwiches, Bacon-Olive Party, '04 196
Sandwiches, Mini Muffuletta Bacon-Olive Party, '04 196
Spread, Buttery Boursin Cheese, '94 301
Spread, Cheese, '99 24
Spread, Chunky Artichoke, '89 98
Spread, Crabmeat-Horseradish, '90 292
Spread, Creamy Clam, '91 274
Spread, Fruited Cream Cheese, '91 306
Spread, Garlic Boursin Cheese, '94 301
Spread, Hearts of Palm, '90 M293
Spread, Nutty Cream Cheese, '89 327
Spread, Shrimp, '96 104
Spread, Tuna, '91 305
Apples, Curried, '93 252
Beans, Baked, '01 127, 334
Beans, Refried, '96 160
Beans, Skillet Barbecued, '93 217
Beverages
Cider, Apple-Orange, '92 20
Cocktail, Orange-Cranberry, '01 103
Margaritas, Blue, '02 143
Orange-Banana Whip, '95 244
Punch, Percolator, '91 306
Punch, Pink, '96 190
Tea, Easy Mint, '91 187
Black Beans and Rice, '89 178
Black Beans and Yellow Rice, '95 126
Breads
Biscuit Bowls, '03 222
Biscuits, Cheese Garlic, '03 185
Biscuits, Deluxe Omelet, '98 101
Biscuits, Easy Cheddar, '01 103
Biscuits, Easy Herb, '90 283
Biscuits, Green Chile, '04 233
Biscuits, Lightnin' Cheese, '90 283
Biscuits, Quick, '89 30
Breadsticks, Italian Cheese, '95 126
Breadsticks, Sesame-Cheese, '97 31
Cinnamon Loaves, '99 260
Cinnamon Loaves, Miniature, '99 260
Croissants, Cream Cheese, '92 159
Crostini, Feta-Tomato, '92 159
Danish, Cheese, '97 31
Focaccia, Basil Pesto, '00 195
Focaccia, Herb, '97 31
French Bread, Chive-Garlic, '89 29
French Bread, Lemony, '97 147
French Bread, Onion-Cheese, '89 29
Garlic Bread, '04 288
Garlic Bread, Buttery, '02 25
Garlic Bread, Quick, '90 283
Greek Bread, '89 200
Mayonnaise Bread, '89 29
Mini-Cinnis, Mama's, '02 41
Muffins, Barbecue, '96 246
Muffins, English Cheese, '02 41
Muffins, Orange-Pecan, '99 56
Muffins, Sour Cream, '90 283
Parmesan-Wine Bread, '97 31
Pizza Crust Wedges, Toasted, '03 280
Rolls, Almond Crescent, '90 283
Rolls, Cinnamon Tea, '92 263
Rolls, Mayonnaise, '90 283
Rolls, Orange, '01 257
Rolls, Spoon, '91 275
Scones, Classic Cream, '02 41
Sesame Knots, '89 29
Waffles with Cilantro-Lime Butter, Corn, '02 109
Butter, Cilantro, '98 182
Butter, Cilantro-Lime, '01 24; '02 109
Butter, Cinnamon, '92 319
Butter, Garlic, '00 90
Butter, Green Peppercorn, '90 117

Butter, Orange, '92 319
Butter, Southwestern, '92 320
Coffee Cake, Cowboy, '95 84
Desserts
Apple Dessert, Creamy Dutch, '91 19
Apples and Pear, Honey-Baked, '97 303
Apples 'n' Pears, Saucy, '96 72
Apricot-Almond Squares, '95 272
Bars, Gooey Turtle, '96 M189
Bars, Peanut Butter, '93 166
Blueberry Slump, Quick, '91 20
Brownies, Chocolate-Peanut Butter Chip, '91 306
Brownies, Gooey, '97 133
Brownies, No-Bake, '94 330
Brownies, Rich, '95 84
Cake, Carrot-Raisin, '01 58
Cake Dessert Sandwich, Grilled Pound, '94 171
Cake, Éclair, '93 42
Cake, Ice Cream, '89 71
Cake, Oatmeal, '01 58
Cake, Peanut Butter-Fudge, '01 59
Cake, Texas, '01 59
Cake with Strawberry-Banana Topping, Pound, '89 200
Candies, Turtle, '93 M41
Candy, Peanut Butter, '93 166
Cherry Crisp, '91 20
Chocolate Crunchies, '92 50
Chocolate Dip, '92 50
Chocolate-Marshmallow Squares, '92 M50
Chocolate-Peanut Butter Cups, '97 134
Chocolate Peanutty Swirls, '94 M330
Cobbler, Quick Fruit, '91 20
Cookies, Cake Mix, '97 133
Cookies, Cake Mix Oatmeal, '96 247
Cookies, Double-Chocolate, '95 272
Cookies, Easy, '00 133
Cookies, Keyboard, '94 M330
Cookies, Spider, '93 166
Cranberry-Orange Delight, '90 168
Cream Dessert, Triple, '94 244
Cupcakes, Chewy Chocolate, '01 334
Cupcake Surprises, '01 299
Frosting, Fudge, '01 59
Fruit Kebabs, Grilled, '97 147
Fudge, Creamy Peanut Butter, '92 240
Fudge, Microwave Chocolate, '92 M50
Ice-Cream Balls, Cinnamon-Chocolate Chip, '02 143
Ice Cream Balls, Nutty, '89 72
Ice Cream, Chocolate Cookie, '95 245
Ice Cream, Cinnamon, '95 126
Ice-Cream Dessert, Toffee, '97 134
Ice Cream Sandwiches, Chocolate, '89 72
Ice Cream-Toffee Dessert, '00 176
Ice, Lemon, '00 176
Ice, Mimosa, '94 24
Lemon Crisps, '95 272
Omelet, Puffy Dessert, '00 35
Orange Balls, '94 331
Orange Crinkles, '95 272
Peach Crinkle, '91 20
Peach Crisp, Gingered, '97 303
Pie, Blueberry-Banana, '93 115
Pie, Brownie-Mint, '97 303
Pie, Caramel, '96 72
Pie, Caramel-Nut Crunch, '94 244
Pie, Chocolate Cream Cheese, '92 240
Pie, Coconut, '93 115
Pie, Decadent Mud, '89 252
Pie, Double-Delight Ice Cream, '89 72
Pie, Fudge, '89 252
Pie, Ice Cream Sundae, '94 244
Pie, No-Bake Cherry Confetti, '93 114

Pie, Peanut Butter, '89 252
Pie, Pineapple, '89 252
Pie, Quick Peach, '89 252
Pie, Tart Lemon, '91 275
Pie, "Working for Peanuts," '93 115
Polka Dots, '95 272
Praline Grahams, '92 239
Pudding, No-Bake Banana, '91 172
Sauce, Toffee, '94 72
Sherbet Cooler, Peachy, '91 187
Sherbet, Lemon-Pineapple, '96 330
Strawberries, Christmas, '94 331
Sundae, Hot Apple Spice, '92 239
Topping, Hot Fudge Ice Cream, '98 317
Topping, Hot Fudge Ice-Cream, '02 109
Topping, Maple-Pecan Ice Cream, '98 317
Trifles, Easy Individual, '92 239
Truffles, Bittersweet, '94 330
White Chocolate Salties, '92 50
Dressing, Sweet Cornbread, '97 303
Egg Roll-Ups, Spicy, '90 140
Eggs, Chicken-Stuffed, '98 102
Eggs, Deviled, '01 299
Eggs, Scotch, '98 101
Fettuccine and Vegetables, '97 178
Fettuccine, Spinach Alfredo, '01 164
Fettuccine with Poppy Seeds, '91 48
French Toast, Peanut Butter, '93 166
Glaze, Orange, '92 263
Linguine, Fresh Tomato Sauce with, '02 213
Macaroni and Cheese, Baked, '03 184
Main Dishes
Antipasto Kebabs, '94 144
Barbecue, Chuck Roast, '96 71
Beans and Franks, Jiffy, '91 M172
Beef and Broccoli, Quick, '91 123
Beef Burgundy, '95 69
Beef Roll-Ups, Mexican, '90 176
Bow-Tie with Marinara, '94 64
Burgers, Garlic Turkey, '99 135
Burgers, Mushroom, '99 135
Burgers, Spinach-Feta, '99 135
Burritos, Tex-Mex, '95 34
Burritos, Vegetarian, '93 319
Casserole, Beef, '01 199
Casserole, Chicken, '96 103; '96 302
Casserole, Chicken-and-Pasta, '97 192
Casserole, Chicken-and-Wild Rice, '97 192
Casserole, Chili, '90 176
Casserole, Creamy Chicken-Green Bean, '97 158
Casserole, Easy Enchilada, '02 143
Casserole, Ham, '96 302
Casserole, Ham-and-Potato, '96 103
Casserole, Ham Roll, '91 M127
Casserole, Holiday Leftovers, '04 232
Casserole, Macaroni-Cheese-Beef, '95 125
Casserole, Quiche, '95 33
Casserole, Tuna, '96 103
Casserole, Turkey, '96 302
Casserole, Vegetarian, '96 302
Chicken à la King, '93 14
Chicken and Artichokes, Italian, '95 68; '00 219
Chicken and Dumplings, Quick, '95 125
Chicken and Pasta, Quick, '93 14
Chicken and Potato Dumplings, '99 326
Chicken and Potatoes, Roasted, '98 289
Chicken and Rice, Creole, '92 262
Chicken and Tortilla Dumplings, '99 327
Chicken, Biscuit Dumplings and, '99 326
Chicken Breasts, Lemon, '89 18
Chicken Breasts, Salsa-Topped, '94 144
Chicken Breast Tarragon, Broiled, '89 310
Chicken, Cajun Fried, '01 334
Chicken Caruso and Rice, '89 177

QUICK & EASY, Main Dishes
(continued)

Chicken, Cheesy Mexican, '01 199; '02 91
Chicken, Corn Flake, '91 172
Chicken Delicacy, '99 M23
Chicken, Grilled, '89 200
Chicken, Honey-Lime Grilled, '96 189
Chicken in Biscuit Bowls, Creamed, '03 222
Chicken in Mustard Cream Sauce, '92 181
Chicken in Pita, Peppery, '93 62
Chicken-Italian Dressing Bake, '91 199
Chicken, Lemon, '96 49
Chicken, Lemon-Basil, '02 91
Chicken, Lemon-Garlic, '90 35
Chicken, Lemon-Herb, '00 90
Chicken, Lemon-Pepper, '89 104
Chicken, Limeade, '01 257
Chicken, Mediterranean, '94 72
Chicken Mexicana, '91 M127
Chicken Nuggets, Baked, '89 18
Chicken Nuggets, Sweet-and-Sour, '90 168
Chicken, Oregano, '95 84
Chicken Packets, '96 104
Chicken, Paprika, '95 125
Chicken Parmesan, '00 219
Chicken Picante Pasta, '01 164
Chicken Pot Pie, Easy, '89 218
Chicken Pot Pie in Biscuit Bowls, '03 222
Chicken, Quick, '90 117
Chicken, Quick Curried, '89 219
Chicken, Roast, '93 14
Chicken Sauté, Lemon-Dill, '91 186
Chicken Sauté, Sweet Pepper-, '89 104
Chicken, Sesame-Ginger, '00 219
Chicken Skillet Dinner, Curried, '95 47
Chicken Stir-Fry, Thai, '00 23
Chicken, Szechuan, '98 155
Chicken Tostadas, '93 204
Chicken with Artichokes and Mushrooms, '90 35
Chicken with Creamy Mustard Sauce,
    Champagne-Poached, '94 24
Chicken with Fennel and Mushrooms, '97 93
Chicken with Fresh Herbs and Vegetables, '02 91
Chicken with Sweet Soy Slaw and Dipping Sauce,
    Grilled, '04 123
Chili and Enchiladas, '00 55
Chili, Easy Texas, '90 201
Chili, Quick-and-Easy, '92 20
Chili, Vegetable, '97 179
Chili with Beans, Easy, '92 262
Chimichangas, Oven-Fried Chicken, '90 M175
Chops with Vegetables, Golden, '89 218
Cornish Hens, Jelly-Glazed, '93 251
Crab Bake, Easy, '95 209
Crab Imperial, Easy, '93 128
Crabmeat Brunch Scramble, '95 32
Crab Tostadas, '93 203
Crawfish Delicacy, '99 M23
Eggplant Sauté, '96 135
Eggs, Cheese-Chive Scrambled, '95 34
Enchiladas, Cheese, '95 311
Enchiladas, Pork, '97 M94
Enchiladas, Quicker, '96 103
Enchiladas, Weeknight, '93 63
Fettuccine, Ranch House, '03 123
Fettuccine with Chicken-and-Creamy Herb Sauce,
    '01 257
Fettuccine with Shrimp-and-Creamy Herb Sauce,
    '01 257
Filet Mignon with Horseradish Gravy, '92 262
Fish, Caesar's, '90 76
Fish in Caper Sauce, '95 209

Fish, Mexi-Style Oven-Fried, '90 76
Fish, Oven-Fried, '91 172
Flank Steak, Cheese-Stuffed, '98 182
Flautas, '00 293
Flounder, Broiled, '89 310
Flounder, Quick Crunchy, '90 76
Frittata, Ham-and-Broccoli, '98 101
Grouper, Guadalajara, '98 17
Grouper with Sautéed Vegetables, '90 M233
Haddock Fillets in White Wine, '90 76
Ham-and-Cheese Bundles, '93 63
Hamburgers Mexicali, '93 217
Hamburgers Teriyaki, '89 309
Ham, Peachy Glazed, '96 189
Ham Slice, Apricot-Glazed, '93 252
Jambalaya, '98 317
Kielbasa-Vegetable Dinner, '91 274
Lasagna, Ellie's, '02 186
Lasagna, Lots of Noodles, '91 M127
Lasagna, Meatball, '00 243
Lasagna, Turkey-Picante, '97 93
Lasagna, Vegetable, '93 320
Linguine, Leeks and Peppers with, '98 68
Linguine, Quick Clam, '90 233
Linguine with Clam Sauce, '89 178
Mahimahi Grape Sauce, '91 218
Manicotti, Make-Ahead, '98 68
Marinara on Beds of Spinach and Orzo, '93 320
Meatballs, Baked, '02 25
Meat Loaf, Easy, '95 125
Meat Loaf, Teriyaki, '03 172
Mexican Stack-Up, '95 69
Mexicorn Main Dish, '96 189
Omelet, Dill-Cheese-Ham, '95 33
Omelet, Family-Size Potato, '94 31
Omelet Olé, '94 31
Omelet, Shrimp-and-Cheese, '94 31
Omelet, Spanish, '00 35
Pancakes, Apple, '01 24
Pancakes with Peanut Butter and Jelly Syrups,
    Banana, '01 24
Pasta, Basil-Cheese, '96 136
Pasta, Easy Taco, '03 124
Pasta Florentine, Layered, '00 56
Pasta Primavera, Peppery, '02 161
Pasta with Cabbage and Cheese Sauce, '00 105
Pasta with Pesto-Clam Sauce, '98 17
Pasta with Sausage and Kale, '03 279
Pasta with Shrimp, '01 164
Pasta with Tomato Cream Sauce, Angel Hair,
    '93 292
Peppers, Beef-Stuffed, '91 M127
Pie, Omelet, '00 M35
Pie, Shepherd's, '00 55
Pizza, Chicken Fajita, '03 235
Pizza, Peppers-and-Cheese, '03 235
Pizza, Sausage-Potato, '01 199
Pizza, Seafood Alfredo, '03 236
Pizza Squares, Easy, '02 61
Pizza, Taco, '89 177; '00 293
Pork Cacciatore, '95 69
Pork Chops and Gravy, '96 71
Pork Chops and Scalloped Potatoes, '98 16
Pork Chops, Balsamic, '01 208
Pork Chops, Creamy, '01 208
Pork Chops, Garlic-Parmesan, '02 61
Pork Chops, Herbed, '97 147
Pork Chops, Lemony Pan-Fried, '03 205
Pork Chops, Peachy, '89 310
Pork Chops, Pretzel, '01 208
Pork Chops, Spicy Brown Mustard, '03 205
Pork Chops, Tuscan, '03 205
Pork Chops with Jalapeño-Cherry Sauce,
    Smoked, '01 208

Pork Cutlets, Apple-Glazed, '92 181
Pork, Kung Pao, '96 49
Pork Marsala, '90 35
Pork Sauté, Plum Delicious, '89 105
Pork, Sesame, '01 177
Pork Tenderloin, Grilled Marinated, '91 199
Potatoes, Chili-Topped, '98 M289
Potatoes, Stuffed Baked, '00 293
Potatoes with Ham, Herbed, '00 318
Quesadillas, Meatball, '00 242
Quesadillas, Western, '97 65
Rib-Eye Steaks with Roquefort Glaze, '89 310
Rice-and-Black Bean Tostadas, '97 65
Roast, Easy Rump, '93 217
Roast with Onion-and-Mushroom Gravy, '00 293
Salmon Bake with Pecan-Crunch Coating,
    '95 209
Salmon with Sweet Soy Slaw and Dipping Sauce,
    Grilled, '04 123
Sausage Dinner, Italian, '91 218
Sausage, Sweet Peppery, '95 69
Scallops in Vermouth-Cream Sauce, '96 49
Scampi, Speedy, '02 161
Seafood and Pasta, '90 234
Shrimp-and-Black Bean Tostadas, '93 204
Shrimp and Cabbage, Asian, '00 105
Shrimp and Grits, Garlic-Chili, '00 23
Shrimp and Wine Sauce, '98 50
Shrimp, Boiled, '04 147
Shrimp Creole, Easy, '95 68
Shrimp, Fiery Cajun, '91 218
Shrimp Scampi, '95 209
Shrimp Stir-Fry, Cajun, '92 127
Shrimp Versailles, '90 233
Shrimp with Green Peppercorn Tartar Sauce,
    Boiled, '94 144
Sloppy Joes, '91 172
Snapper, Oven-Fried, '90 75
Snapper with Rosemary, Glazed, '98 51
Sole Royale, '89 104
Spaghetti and Meat Sauce, Quick, '94 64
Spaghetti Carbonara, '03 123
Spaghetti, Country-Style, '02 25
Spaghetti Pie, Weeknight, '95 312
Spaghetti with Fresh Tomato Sauce, '96 135
Steak and Gravy, Zippy, '90 35
Steak in Pepper Cream, '94 117
Steak Parmesan, '93 41
Stir-Fry Beef and Asparagus, '91 124
Stir-Fry, Chicken and Snow Pea, '95 157
Stir-Fry, Easy Chicken, '91 124
Stir-Fry, Hurry-Up Chicken, '91 124
Stir-Fry, Indian, '92 126
Stir-Fry, Italian, '92 126
Stir-Fry, Mexican, '92 126
Stir-Fry, Orange Roughy, '98 50
Stir-Fry, Peanutty Beef, '95 157
Stir-Fry, Sausage, '98 156
Stroganoff, Beef, '92 20
Swiss Steak, Easy, '00 90
Swiss Steak Monterey, '99 23
Tacos, Chicken-and-Bean, '93 293
Tacos, Easy, '96 159
Tacos Wrapidos, '03 172
Tortilla Pie, '96 135
Tuna, Grilled Florida, '93 128
Turkey à la King, '04 232
Turkey and Peppers in Cornbread Crust, '95 312
Turkey-Basil Piccata, '96 49
Turkey Cutlets, Parmesan, '01 81
Turkey Divan, Quick, '89 178
Turkey Mignons, Sesame-Crusted, '01 81
Turkey Mignons with Creamy Wine Sauce,
    Sesame-Crusted, '02 109

Turkey Sauté, '89 105
Turkey Scaloppine, Easy, '95 M192
Turkey Tenders, Baked, '01 81
Turkey Tenders, Sautéed, '01 81
Turkey Tetrazzini, '00 318
Turkey with Peppers, '92 182
Veal Marsala, '91 218
Veal Piccata, '92 181
Vegetarian Sauté, '95 69
Ziti, Baked, '94 65
Mayonnaise, Dill-Garlic, '92 320
Mayonnaise, Italian Herbed, '92 320
Meat Mix, Mexican, '00 292
Mix, Fish Herb, '98 51
Mix, Jambalaya, '98 317
Mostaccioli Alfredo, '91 47
Pancakes, Easy, '92 203
Pasta Bake, Cheesy, '02 161
Pizza, Breakfast, '90 140
Pizza, Southwestern Veggie, '95 126
Popcorn Delight, '00 M133
Quiches, Individual, '98 101
Relish, Quick Corn, '90 M13
Rice, Baked Mushroom, '95 84
Rice, Cajun Dirty, '04 288
Rice, Curried, '98 237
Rice, Jiffy Spanish, '90 M176
Rice, Picadillo, '98 237
Rice Primavera, '98 237

Salads and Salad Dressings
Apple Salad, '00 176
Asparagus and Tomatoes with Herb Vinaigrette, '99 56
Bacon-Lettuce-Mozzarella-and-Tomato Salad, '98 209
Banana Split Salad, '91 58
Bean Salad, Quick, '89 128
Bean Salad, Sweet, '01 46
Beef-and-Lime Rice Salad, '03 172
Bing Cherry Salad, '01 46
Broccoli-Cauliflower Salad, '00 90
Carrot Salad, Harvest, '89 128
Chef's Salad, '98 209
Chicken-and-Bow Tie Pasta, '01 164
Chicken-Pasta Salad, Grilled, '94 64
Chicken-Pasta Salad, Zesty, '02 186
Chicken-Rice Salad, '97 93
Chicken Salad Italian, '89 18
Chicken Salad, Peachy, '97 193
Chicken Salad, Roasted, '93 14
Chicken Salad, Vegetable Patch, '04 92
Citrus and Greens, Holiday, '03 280
Coleslaw, Old-Fashioned Sweet, '93 128
Corn Salad, Festive, '92 263
Cucumber-and-Tomato Salad, '01 127
Cucumber Salad with Roasted Red Bell Pepper Dressing, '03 28
Dressing, '01 127
Frozen Salads, Paper Cup, '00 176
Fruit Bowl, Colorful, '91 58
Fruit Medley, Yogurt-Granola, '91 58
Fruit Salad, Frozen, '97 158
Fruit Salad, Layered, '91 58
Fruit Salad, Sunny, '91 58
Fruit Salad with Honey-Pecan Dressing, '03 28
Fruit Salad, Yogurt, '96 247
Greek Salad, '94 202
Green-and-Gold Salad with Fresh Citrus Ranch Dressing, '04 91
Green Salad, Garlic-Tarragon, '92 79
Honey-Pecan Dressing, '03 28
Leaf Lettuce Salad with Sweet-and-Sour Dressing, Red, '03 28
Lettuce Salad, Blue Cheese-Stuffed, '94 202

Mandarin Orange-Lettuce Salad, '92 79
Marinara Vinaigrette, '94 64
Marinated Salad, '91 186
Mexican Salad, '94 202
Mushroom Salad, Quick Cheesy-, '89 128
Pasta, Bow Tie, '01 164
Pasta Salad, '90 62; '01 127
Pasta Salad Dressing, '01 164
Pasta Salad, Ham-Pecan-Blue Cheese, '90 62
Pasta Salad, Oriental, '90 63
Pasta Salad, Presto, '90 63
Pasta Salad, Seafood, '90 62
Pear Salad, Golden, '91 58
Pork Cosmopolitan Salad, Grilled, '04 123
Potato Salad, Creamy, '01 334
Raspberry Salad Dressing, '03 M28
Red Cabbage Citrus Salad, '94 72
Roasted New Potato Salad, '04 91
Roasted Red Bell Pepper Dressing, '03 28
Romaine Salad with Raspberry Dressing, '03 28
Roquefort Dressing, '93 128
Sesame Noodle Salad, '02 186
Shrimp Salad, '04 147
Shrimp Salad, Aloha, '95 46
Slaw, Freezer, '99 260
Slaw, German Cabbage, '00 105
Spinach-Pecan Salad, '89 128
Squash Salad, '03 M184
Summer Italian Salad, Quick, '92 79
Sweet-and-Sour Dressing, '03 28
Tomato-Asparagus Salad, '92 79
Tomato Flower Salad, '89 128
Tomato-Gruyère-Basil Salad, '99 172
Tortellini Salad, '02 186
Tuna-and-White Bean Salad, '98 209
Vegetable Potato Salad, '03 136
Vinaigrette Dressing, '93 41
Vinaigrette Salad Dressing, '02 25
Wild Rice-and-Shrimp Salad, '02 109
Wild Rice-Chicken Salad, '99 55
Wild Rice-Shrimp Salad, '99 55
Zucchini Salad, '89 128

Sandwiches
Avocado Deluxe Sandwiches, '99 72
BLT Breakfast Sandwiches, '04 171
BLT Croissants, '93 158
BLT in Pita Pockets, '93 158
BLT Sandwiches, Curried, '93 158
Breakfast Sandwiches, Cheesy, '90 140
Cheddar Cheese Sandwiches, Hot, '97 179
Chicken 'n' Cheese Sandwiches, Grilled, '99 240
Chicken Parmigiana Sandwich, '94 65
Chicken Toppers, Creamed, '99 240
Cream Cheese Croissants, '92 159
Ham-and-Cheese Sandwiches, '01 299
Ham-and-Pineapple Slaw Sandwiches, '96 199
Hamwiches, '96 246
Hoagies, Sloppy Joe Meatball, '00 242
Lettuce Sandwich, Date-Nut, '94 202
Mango-Crab Salad Sandwiches, '99 72
Meatball Sandwiches, Open-Faced, '99 239
Pepperoni Pinwheels, '96 247
Pesto-Sandwich, Grilled Italian, '94 170
Pitas, Fajita, '99 239
Pizzas, Easy Pocket, '90 168
Pork Sandwiches, Barbecue, '00 23
Reuben Sandwiches, Open-Face, '91 199
Reubens, Spicy Coleslaw, '04 63
Rollups, Parmesan-Turkey-Ranch, '01 177
Spinach Fondue Sandwich, Grilled, '94 171
Tomato-Cheese-Bacon Melts, '99 72
Tuna Melts, Curried, '95 46
Tuna Roll Sandwiches, '96 199
Turkey Sandwich, Waffle-Grilled, '94 170

Vegetable Pita Sandwiches, '96 199
Welsh Rarebit with Tomatoes and Bacon, '92 M159
Wraps, Spicy Chicken Salad with Cabbage, '04 62
Wraps, Turkey, '00 318

Sauces
Basil and Cream Sauce, '90 117
Chervil-and-Savory Sauce, '90 117
Chicken Curry Sauce, '90 117
Country Ham Sauce, '90 117
Cranberry-Apple Sauce, '92 203
Marinara Sauce, '94 64
Peach Sauce, '92 203
Picante-Bean Sauce, '96 220
Pineapple Sauce, '92 203
Salsa, Texas, '96 160
Salsa, Vegetable, '96 220
Salsa Verde, '96 160
Shrimp Sauce, '04 147
Spaghetti Sauce, Slow-Simmered, '96 72
Tomato-Basil Sauce, '96 220
Tomato Sauce, Dried, '96 220; '99 135
Tomato Sauce, Spicy Gingered, '96 220
Wine Sauce, Creamy, '01 81; '02 109
Seasoning Blend, Taco, '96 159
Snack Mix, Make-Ahead, '04 M92

Soups and Stews
Asparagus Soup, Creamy, '94 225
Black-Eyed Pea Soup, '97 213
Black, White, and Red All Over Soup, '95 126
Broccoli-and-Chicken Soup, '90 202
Cheese-Vegetable Chowder, '02 305
Chicken-and-Wild Rice Soup, '04 26
Chicken Corn Chowder, '02 305
Chicken-Corn Soup, Cheesy, '97 158
Chicken Stew, Santa Fe, '97 193
Chili Bean Soup, '96 71
Clam Chowder, '90 202
Clam Chowder, New England, '98 289
Clam Chowder, Shopping Day, '02 305
Corn Chowder, '90 202
Fiesta Chowder, '02 305
French Soup Maigre, '98 125
Garlic-and-Potato Soup, Golden, '04 214
Gazpacho, Classic Tomato, '99 172
Gumbo, Chicken-Sausage, '04 288
Hot Brown Soup, '00 318
Jambalaya, '04 288
Minestrone, Meatball, '00 242
Mushroom Soup, Sherried, '96 104
Potato Soup, '92 263
Shrimp Chowder, '89 218
Shrimp Chowder, Quick, '04 27
Steak Soup, '99 260
Sweet Potato Chowder, Asian, '97 213
Taco Soup, '94 225; '99 36
Tortellini Soup, '98 68
Tortellini Soup, Japanese, '96 330
Tortilla Soup, '90 201; '04 26
Turkey Soup with Green Chile Biscuits, Fiesta, '04 233
Vegetable-Beef Stew, Shortcut, '89 218
Vegetable Soup, Spicy, '93 293
Veggie Soup, Quick, '91 31
Vidalia Onion Soup, Beefy, '97 212
White Bean Soup, '90 201
White Bean Soup, Spicy, '94 225
Spaghetti with Tomatoes and Garlic, '91 47
Spread, Creamy Pimiento Cheese, '92 159
Spread, Cucumber, '93 158
Spread, Curry, '93 159
Spread, Dijon-Mayo, '96 199
Spread, Garlic-Butter, '96 199

QUICK & EASY
(continued)

Tart, Tomato-Pesto, '00 195
Toast Topper, Sticky Bun, '99 M72
Topping, Rainbow Pepper, '90 117
Tortellini Carbonara, '91 47
Vegetables
Asparagus, Chilled Sesame, '03 67
Asparagus, Lemon-Sesame, '91 M31
Asparagus Pie, Cheesy, '01 103
Beets, Winter, '02 283
Black-Eyed Peas, Easy, '99 204
Broccoli Casserole, Cheesy, '95 M191
Broccoli Parmesan, '97 302
Broccoli, Sesame, '03 67
Brussels Sprouts and Baby Carrots, Glazed,
'97 302
Cabbage, Creole, '00 105
Cabbage Stir-Fry, '04 62
Cabbage Stir-Fry, Spicy, '04 62
Cabbage with Garlic, '04 62
Cajun Vegetable Sauté, '92 62
Carrot Relish, '03 67
Carrots, Peach-Glazed, '90 M13
Carrots with Bacon and Onion, Glazed, '02 283
Corn-and-Okra Medley, '99 203
Corn and Sweet Red Peppers, Curried, '95 47
Corn, Creamy Baked, '02 234
Corn on the Cob, Chili, '03 M185
Corn on the Cob, Lemony, '89 200
Corn Pudding, '98 124
Corn-Rice Casserole, '01 46
Cucumbers, Creamy, '92 62
Eggplant, Heavenly, '93 293
Eggplant Parmesan, '95 84
Eggplant Sauté, '96 135
Green Bean-and-Corn Casserole, '99 36
Green Beans, Chinese, '96 330
Green Beans, Gingered, '02 283
Green Beans, Pesto, '03 185
Green Beans with Buttered Pecans, '92 61
Green Beans with Garlic-Herb Butter, '02 61
Green Beans with Lemon, '03 66
Green Peas, Company, '91 M31
Grilled Vegetables with Cilantro Butter, '98 182
Marinated Vegetables, '99 36
Marinated Veggies, '01 127
'Maters, Zippy, '99 172
exicorn, '96 189
Mexicorn, Black Bean, '96 189
Mexihominy, '96 189
Mushrooms, Sparkling, '94 24
Okra Creole, '02 234
Okra, Nutty, '03 136
Parmesan Vegetables, '97 147
Potatoes au Gratin, '93 217
Potatoes, Blue Cheese, '04 214
Potatoes, Blue Cheese Stuffed, '92 M228
Potatoes, Broccoli-Shrimp Stuffed, '92 M228
Potatoes, Feta Cheese, '04 214
Potatoes, Italian Mashed, '03 M135
Potatoes, Quick-and-Easy Mashed, '93 41
Potatoes, Seafood-Stuffed, '95 M192
Potatoes, Soufflé, '90 M14
Potatoes, Tangy Olive, '04 214
Quesadillas, Vegetable, '97 65
Spinach Casserole, '91 M31
Spinach, Easy Italian, '02 235
Squash Fritters, '99 203
Squash, Skillet, '92 62
Stir-Fry, Convenient Vegetable, '95 157
Stir-Fry, Fresh, '97 179

Stir-Fry, Vegetable, '98 156
Succotash, Quick, '97 302
Sweet Onion Relish, '99 204
Tomatoes, Baked Ranch, '94 72
Tomatoes, Cold Italian, '99 173
Tomatoes, Cornbread-Stuffed, '02 213
Tomatoes, Grilled, '99 173
Tomato-Pesto Tart, '02 108
Tomato-Pesto Tarts, Mini, '02 108
Zucchini and Carrots, Julienne, '90 M14
Zucchini and Carrots, Sautéed, '92 62
Zucchini Fans, Grilled, '89 200
Vinaigrette, Asian, '00 105
Waffles, '01 24
Waffles, Corn, '01 24
Waffles, Rice, '98 124
QUINCE
Compote, Baked Quince, '96 241

Ragoûts

Bean Ragoût with Cilantro-Cornmeal Dumplings,
'97 209
Chicken Ragoût with Cheddar Dumplings, '94 44
Salmon-and-Vegetable Ragoût, '96 45
Veal-and-Artichoke Ragoût, '94 43
Vegetable Ragoût, '89 172; '98 181
Vegetables, Ragoût of Summer, '98 119
White Bean Ragoût, '96 232
RAISINS
Bars, Raisin, '94 228
Breads
Banana-Nut-Raisin Bread, '81 59
Biscuits, Buttermilk-Raisin, '92 338
Biscuits, Cinnamon-Raisin Breakfast, '93 159
Biscuits, Glazed Raisin, '89 210
Boule, Walnut-Raisin Pumpernickel, '02 259
Buns, Hot Cross, '01 88
Buns, Rum-Raisin, '80 22
Butternut-Raisin Bread, '79 25
Caraway-Raisin Oat Bread, '86 44
Chicken Salad on Raisin Bread, Curried, '85 96
Cinnamon Pull-Aparts, Raisin, '82 205; '83 32
Cinnamon Raisin Bread, '80 22
Cranberry Bread, Raisin-, '81 305; '82 36
Homemade Raisin Bread, '87 300
Irish Bread, '02 67
Muffins, Banana-Raisin, '89 218
Muffins, Breakfast Raisin, '84 59
Muffins, Carrot-and-Raisin, '87 24
Muffins, Cheddar-Raisin, '91 51
Muffins, Orange-Raisin, '97 153
Muffins, Raisin English, '80 75
Muffins, Raisin-Nut, '92 46
Muffins, Raisin-Pecan Ginger, '88 9
Muffins, Whole Wheat Raisin, '85 207
Oatmeal Raisin Bread, '81 14
Oatmeal-Raisin Bread, '83 59
Pastry Bites, Raisin, '90 86
Pumpkin Bread, Holiday, '03 281
Rolls, Pecan-Golden Raisin Sweet, '03 235
Rolls, Raisin Cinnamon, '81 107
Rolls, Raisin-Cinnamon, '91 240
Rollups, Sweet Raisin, '86 290
Round Raisin Bread, '89 230
Saffron Bread, '96 50
Salt-Free Raisin Batter Bread, '86 33
Scones, Currant, '84 117; '92 332
Scones, Lemon-Raisin, '87 69
Teacakes, Currant, '80 88
Whole Wheat Bread, Raisin-, '93 77
Whole Wheat Raisin-Nut Bread, '04 208
Bugs in a Rug, '95 178
Butter, Almond-Raisin, '02 258

Butter, Raisin, '81 272
Cake, Carrot-Raisin, '01 58
Cake, Saucy Pudding, '98 196
Cake, Spicy Raisin Layer, '79 230
Cake, Winter Squash-Spice Bundt, '99 248
Candy, Mixed Raisin, '84 111
Carrots, Orange-Raisin, '80 24
Chocolate-Bran Raisin Jumbos, '91 142
Chutney, Cranberry, '98 318
Chutney, Pear, '98 243
Coffee Cake, Cinnamon-Raisin, '93 180
Coffee Cake, Spicy Raisin, '88 63
Conserve, Cranberry, '03 278
Cookies, Alltime Favorite Raisin, '80 24
Cookies, Chocolate-Raisin Oatmeal, '95 136
Cookies, Frosted Oatmeal-Raisin, '79 290
Cookies, Fruitcake, '98 294
Cookies, Nugget, '79 291
Cookies, Oatmeal, '99 280
Cookies, Oatmeal-Raisin, '87 221; '93 127
Cookies, Persimmon-Raisin, '85 232
Cookies, Pudding Oatmeal, '98 215
Cookies, Raisin-Oatmeal, '01 19
Cookies, Spice, '03 307
Cookies, Spicy Oatmeal, '01 19
Couscous with Raisins, Almonds, and Lemon,
'00 295
Currants, Pine Nuts, and Pork, Couscous with,
'00 295
Filling, Raisin, '90 86
Gingersnaps, Raisin, '85 324
Granola Gorp, '89 59
Granola, Healthful, '97 204
Granola, Superhero, '98 206
Granola Treats, Raisin-, '92 22
Gravy, Currant, '83 276
Ham, Raisin, '80 124
Ice Cream, Rum-Raisin, '97 145
Mix, Raisin-Nut Party, '83 60
Mix, Starry Snack, '00 329
Onions, Glazed, '97 306
Pie, Apple-Raisin Brandy, '89 58
Pie, Brandy Raisin-Apple, '83 192
Pie, Cranberry-Apple-Raisin, '98 270
Pie, Cranberry-Raisin, '80 283; '85 316
Pie, Peanut-Raisin, '79 85
Pie, Raisin, '83 220
Pie, Raisin-Pecan, '87 213
Pie, Rhubarb-Raisin, '79 112
Pie, Spiced Raisin, '84 148
Pork Chops, An Apple-a-Day, '01 35
Preserves, Plum, '03 161
Pudding, Apple-Raisin Bread, '88 175
Pudding, Cinnamon-Raisin Bread, '01 315
Pudding, Raisin Bread, '94 215
Pudding, Raisin-Pumpkin, '84 315
Pudding, Raisin-Rice, '87 46
Pudding, Stuffed Pumpkin with Cranberry-Raisin
Bread, '02 231
Pudding with Bourbon Sauce, Raisin Bread, '98 336
Relish, Apple-Raisin, '03 83
Relish, Raisin, '92 310
Rice, Curried, '98 237
Rice, Island, '98 276
Rice Pilaf, Persian, '02 167
Rice with Curry, Raisin, '85 83
Salad, Carrot-Raisin, '83 117; '84 174; '87 10
Salad, Classic Broccoli-Raisin, '02 24
Salad, Creamy Broccoli-Raisin, '92 106
Salad, Curried Apple-Raisin, '80 24
Salad with Orange-Nutmeg Dressing, Carrot-Raisin,
'97 305; '98 19
Sandwiches, Peanut-Cheese-Raisin, '88 140
Sandwich, Raisin Country, '91 168

Sauce, Baked Ham with Cranberry-Raisin, '88 244
Sauce, Caramel-Raisin, '88 127
Sauce, Ham with Raisin, '82 M76
Sauce, Raisin, '83 59, 215; '84 91, 275; '87 127;
   '89 58; '99 19; '02 278
Sauce, Raisin-Pineapple, '82 177
Sauce, Rum-Raisin, '84 7; '94 295
Shake, Amazin' Raisin, '86 195
Shortbread, Rum-Currant, '98 277
Slaw, Sweet Potato-Currant, '93 246
Spread, Creamy Raisin, '90 36
Spread, Lemon-Raisin, '01 48
Spread, Peachy-Raisin, '86 326
Spread, Raisin-Nut, '95 79
Tarts, Pecan-Raisin, '03 246
Tarts, Pecan-Raisin Mini-, '03 246

RASPBERRIES
Appetizer, Orange-Berry, '85 81
Bars, Raspberry, '82 209; '84 212
Bavarian, Raspberry-Strawberry, '89 15
Beverages
  "Concrete," Foxtreat, '94 113
  Cooler, Raspberry, '89 171
  Cranberry-Raspberry Drink, '97 154
  Cubes, Berry-Good, '95 201
  Fizz, Rosy Raspberry, '90 179
  Kir, Raspberry, '86 183
  Lemonade, Dazzling, '97 99
  Lemonade, Raspberry, '03 89
  Punch, Raspberry-Rosé, '87 242
  Punch, Raspberry Sherbet, '95 141
  Punch, Raspberry Sparkle, '84 57
  Punch, Sunset, '96 278
  Shake, Peach Melba Sundae, '93 134
  Shake, Raspberry-and-Banana, '89 183
  Shakes, Raspberry Milk, '95 238
  Shrub, Berry, '95 29
  Shrub, Red Raspberry, '97 132
  Slush, Watermelon-Berry, '90 137
  Smoothie, Four-Berry, '97 173
  Southern Breeze, '02 185
  Spritzers, Raspberry, '99 207
  Syrup, Berry, '96 161
  Tea, Rasp-Berry Good, '95 200
  Tea, Sangría, '94 131
Biscuits, Raspberry-Almond, '93 160
Bisque, Banana-Raspberry, '93 161
Bordeaux, Beauberries, '98 18
Brie, Almond-Raspberry, '94 M89
Brie in Rye, Raspberry, '93 252
Brownies, Raspberry, '92 274; '97 M35
Cake, Blackberry-Raspberry Truffle, '03 245
Cake, Chocolate-Raspberry, '92 173; '01 M319
Cake, Lemon-Raspberry, '91 247
Cake Loaf, Pretty and Pink Pound, '96 60
Cake, Raspberry-Fudge, '97 34
Cake, White Chocolate-Raspberry, '98 323
Candied Flowers and Raspberries, '98 155
Cheesecake, Chocolate-Raspberry Truffle, '91 270
Chicken, Jamaican Jerk Raspberry, '00 88
Chicken, Raspberry, '97 66
Chocolate Cups, Miniature, '87 132
Chocolate-Raspberry Bags, '95 97
Chocolates, Raspberry Cream, '91 36
Cobbler, Berry-Cherry, '83 270
Cobbler, Fig-and-Raspberry, '02 160
Cobbler, Raspberry-Cherry, '93 230
Coffee Cake, Raspberry, '83 112
Coffee Cake, Raspberry-Cheese, '97 231
Compote, Berry, '81 275
Compote, Berry-Peach, '82 133
Compote, Spicy Grapefruit-Berry, '91 19
Cookies, Raspberry Swirl, '90 111
Cream, Pear Salad with Raspberry, '00 311

Crème Brûlée, Berry, '95 323
Crème Brûlée, Double Raspberry, '95 323
Crêpes, Raspberry, '87 126
Crêpes Suzette, Raspberry, '84 84
Crêpes with Yogurt Filling, Fresh Raspberry, '93 123
Crisp, Peach-and-Raspberry, '02 232
Crisp, Raspberry-Pear, '89 109
Custard with Raspberries, Almond Crème, '88 174
Custard with Raspberries, Amaretto, '86 152
Dessert, Frozen Raspberry, '84 192
Dessert, Raspberry-Jellyroll, '85 95
Dessert, Raspberry Sauce, '80 147
Dream, Raspberry, '83 108
Filling, Raspberry, '90 111
Fluff, Raspberry, '89 198
Gazpacho, Berry, '97 181
Glaze, Raspberry, '00 88
Glaze, Turkey Breast with Orange-Raspberry, '91 253
Granita, Raspberry Liqueur, '88 117
Granita, Wild Raspberry Tea, '99 89
Ice Cream, Fresh Raspberry, '86 152
Ice Cream, Raspberry, '80 176
Ice, Raspberry, '92 268
Jam, Berry Refrigerator, '89 139
Jam, Mock Raspberry, '96 168
Jam, Raspberry Freezer, '84 M181
Jellyrolls, Raspberry, '93 M255
Lemon Curd with Berries, '90 102
Mayonnaise, Raspberry, '97 107
Mousse in Chocolate Crinkle Cups, Raspberry,
  '93 270
Mousse, Raspberry, '81 34; '04 260
Muffins, Lemon-Raspberry, '92 119; '03 306
Muffins, Raspberry-Streusel, '96 54
Mustard, Raspberry, '95 313
Napoleons, Berry, '94 120
Parfait, White Chocolate-Raspberry Swirl, '93 315
Pie, Bumbleberry, '97 163
Pie, Cherry-Berry, '92 316
Pie, Cran-Raspberry, '87 244
Pie, Raspberry Baked Alaska, '98 216
Pie, Raspberry Cream, '94 209
Pie, Rhubarb-Raspberry Pear, '95 119
Prunes, Raspberry, '82 124
Pudding, Raspberry, '92 92
Pudding, Russian Blueberry-Raspberry, '97 128
Puffs, Raspberry Party, '90 170
Puree, Chocolate Mousse Loaf with Raspberry,
  '97 34
Puree, Fruit Compote with Raspberry, '88 81
Ribs, Jamaican Jerk Raspberry, '00 88
Salads and Salad Dressings
  Chicken-Raspberry Salad, Marinated, '93 190
  Frozen Raspberry Salad, '79 287; '80 35
  Fruit Mounds, Raspberry, '79 35
  Greens with Raspberries and Walnuts, Mixed,
    '98 194
  Maple Dressing, Bibb Salad with Raspberry-,
    '91 246
  Mixed Greens with Raspberry Dressing, '97 50
  Mold, Raspberry Holiday, '84 253
  Peppery Greens with Raspberry Dressing,
    '95 254
  Raspberry Dressing, '87 153; '95 202
  Raspberry Salad, '86 286
  Raspberry Salad Dressing, '94 158; '03 M28
  Ribbon Salad, Raspberry, '87 236
  Vinaigrette, Gourmet Greens with Raspberry,
    '00 163
  Vinaigrette, Orange-Raspberry, '95 144; '96 155
  Vinaigrette, Raspberry, '94 249; '96 275;
    '97 146; '98 184
  Walnut Salad, Raspberry-, '94 158
  Wine Salad, Raspberry-, '91 256

Sauces
  Amaretto Sauce, Raspberry-, '88 130
  Berry Sauce, '94 130
  Chocolate and Raspberry Sauce, Orange Sections
    with, '97 33
  Crimson Raspberry Sauce, '79 91; '85 30
  Custard Sauce, Fresh Berries with Raspberry,
    '88 163
  Duck Breasts with Raspberry Sauce, '87 240
  Flambé, Raspberry Sauce, '84 142
  Fresh Raspberry Sauce, '93 120
  Lemon Sauce, Cheesecake with Raspberry-,
    '96 30
  Lime Cheesecake with Raspberry Sauce,
    '00 204
  Melba Sauce, '87 77
  Mimosa Sauce, Berry, '90 315
  Orange Sauce, Raspberry-, '88 22; '92 154
  Peach-Berry Sauce, '87 M165
  Poached Pears with Raspberry Sauce, '87 69;
    '88 223
  Raspberry Sauce, '82 289; '83 108; '84 73, 213;
    '87 69, 117, 183; '88 267; '89 183, 322;
    '91 96, 180, 270; '92 130; '93 82, 99, 315;
    '94 295; '95 327; '96 183, 310; '98 157, 216;
    '99 167, 259; '02 123; '03 319; '04 33
  Tea-Berry Sauce, '94 130; '99 334
Sherbet, Raspberry, '83 162
Shortbread, Raspberry, '99 29; '02 33
Shortcake, Chocolate-Raspberry, '95 99
Sorbet, Raspberry, '03 171
Soufflé, Raspberry, '86 188
Soufflé, Raspberry-Topped, '85 317
Soup, Chilled Raspberry, '81 130
Soup, Raspberry, '00 144
Soup, Sherry-Berry Dessert, '91 180
Spirited Raspberries, '95 142
Strudel, Raspberry-Nut, '83 304
Sweet Potatoes, Raspberry, '87 280
Tart, Bakewell, '97 110
Tartlets, Fresh Berry, '91 98
Tartlets, Raspberry-Brie, '04 287
Tart, Pick-a-Berry, '91 118
Tarts, Berry Good Lemon, '91 119
Tarts, Cran-Raspberry Meringue, '92 286
Tarts, Raspberry-Almond, '99 280
Tarts, Raspberry Jelly, '00 208
Tea Cake, Raspberry, '91 271
Tea Cakes, Royal Raspberry, '02 253
Topping, Raspberry, '85 317
Topping, Raspberry-Peach, '87 126
Trifle, Raspberry, '88 259
Trifles, Individual Raspberry, '99 112
Truffles, Raspberry-Fudge, '00 M41
Vinaigrette, Raspberry, '04 50
Vinegar, Raspberry, '97 146
Vinegar, Raspberry-Lemon, '87 134
Vinegar, Raspberry-Thyme, '95 190
Vinegar, Raspberry Wine, '93 191

RELISHES. *See also* **CHUTNEYS, PESTOS,
    SALSAS, SAUCES, TOPPINGS.**
Antipasto Relish, '86 327
Apple-Celery Relish, '89 141
Apple-Raisin Relish, '03 83
Apple Relish, '96 323; '97 27
Apple Relish, Spicy, '84 M323
Avocado Relish, '87 120
Beet Relish, '84 179
Beet Relish, Colorful, '85 136
Black Bean-Tomatillo Relish, '87 121
Black-Eyed Pea Relish, Zesty, '95 56
Cabbage Relish, '83 260
Cabbage Relish, Spanish, '95 270
Carrot Relish, '03 67

RELISHES
(continued)

Cherry-Honey Relish, '97 32
Chow Chow, '82 196
Chowchow, '87 150; '00 158
Chowchow, Nannie's, '95 250
Confit, Roasted Shallot-Garlic, '94 303
Corn-and-Tomato Relish, Sweet White, '00 130
Corn Relish, '81 129, 175; '83 189; '84 107;
    '85 136; '87 120, 245; '92 241
Corn Relish, Easy, '83 260
Corn Relish, Quick, '90 13
Corn Relish, Summer, '89 127
Corn Relish, Sweet, '93 119
Corn Relish, Virginia, '79 283
Crabmeat Relish, '99 198
Cran-Apple Relish, '84 300
Cranberry-Black Bean Relish, '03 243
Cranberry-Nut Relish, '86 275
Cranberry-Orange Relish, '81 M289; '88 254;
    '99 15
Cranberry-Pear Relish, '85 232
Cranberry Relish, '81 275; '83 144; '85 258, 264;
    '86 283; '87 245; '91 257; '92 341; '95 318;
    '98 310; '02 276
Cranberry Relish, Frozen, '95 302
Cranberry Relish, Holiday, '88 304
Cranberry Relish, Lemony, '79 243
Cranberry Relish, Old-Fashioned, '82 297
Cranberry Relish, Tipsy, '92 M310
Cucumber Relish, '85 176; '96 23
Eggplant Relish, '95 342
Fruit Relish, Fresh, '95 158
Garden Relish, '83 259
Garden Relish, End-of-the-, '80 179
Green Olive Relish with Coriander, '96 323; '97 27
Green Onion Relish, '84 65
Green Tomato Relish, '96 168; '98 124
Green Tomato Sweet Relish, '93 136
Horseradish Relish, '01 60
Hot Relish, '01 123
India Relish, '84 179
Jerusalem Artichoke Relish, '89 197
Kraut Relish, '91 232
Lemon-Date Relish, '96 271
Mango Relish, '89 198
Onion Relish, '91 79
Onion Relish, Sweet, '93 124; '96 206; '99 204
Orange Slices, Spicy, '81 12
Papaya-Basil Relish, '94 82
Peach Relish, '85 136
Pear Relish, '79 196
Pear Relish, Aunt Glennie's, '95 305
Pear Relish, Peppery, '89 141
Pepper-Onion Relish, '84 180
Pepper Relish, '83 183
Pepper Relish, Confetti, '91 195
Pepper Relish, Grandma's, '04 158
Pepper Relish, Sweet, '95 104
Pineapple-Coconut Relish, '96 323; '97 27
Plums, Brandied, '97 176
Prune Relish, Peppy, '90 227
Purple Onion Relish, '95 253
Raisin Relish, '92 310
Salad, Relish, '84 121
Sauerkraut Relish, '85 136
Summer Squash Relish, Pollock with, '92 200
Tomato-Olive Relish, Flank Steak with, '03 210
Tomato Relish, '85 188
Tomato Relish, Easy, '80 126
Vegetable Relish, '90 147
Vegetable Relish, Eight-, '84 179

White Bean Relish, '93 229
Zucchini Relish, '87 200
Zucchini Relish, Sweet, '95 159
RHUBARB
Ambrosia, Rhubarb, '88 93
Bavarian, Rhubarb-Strawberry, '86 140
Cake, Rhubarb Upside-Down, '00 87
Chutney, Rhubarb, '87 245
Cobbler, Rosy Strawberry-Rhubarb, '79 154
Cobbler, Strawberry-Rhubarb, '88 93
Crisp, Rhubarb, '91 146; '92 130
Crisp, Strawberry-Rhubarb, '95 119
Mousse, Rhubarb, '88 93
Pie, Bumbleberry, '97 163
Pie, Rhubarb-Peach, '86 140
Pie, Rhubarb-Raisin, '79 112
Pie, Rhubarb-Raspberry Pear, '95 119
Pie, Strawberry-Rhubarb, '98 99
Salad, Rhubarb, '91 146; '92 129
Salad, Rhubarb Congealed, '86 140
Salad, Tart Rhubarb, '91 146; '92 129
Sauce, Chilled Rhubarb, '88 94
Sauce, Pineapple-Rhubarb, '88 94
Sauce, Rolled Pork with Rhubarb, '96 134
Squares, Rhubarb, '91 146; '92 129
Squares, Rosy Rhubarb, '79 111
Whip, Rhubarb, '79 112
RICE
Almond Rice, '81 195; '85 M112; '89 100; '91 291
à l'Orange, Rice, '90 236
Apple-Cinnamon Rice, '86 249
Arabic Rice, '94 200
Asparagus, Rice and, '93 324
Bacon-Chive Rice, '83 129
Balls, Rice, '81 51
Basic Long-Grain Rice, '83 M285
Basic Molding Rice, '86 221
Basic Quick-Cooking Rice, '83 M285
Basic Rice, '79 64
Beans and Rice. *See also* **RICE/Salads.**
    Black Beans and Rice, '80 222; '89 178; '91 82;
        '95 309
    Black Beans and Yellow Rice, '95 126
    Black Beans and Yellow Rice, Easy, '92 308
    Black Beans with Yellow Rice, '82 2
    Cajun Peas, '88 3
    Cajun Red Beans and Rice, '83 26
    Caribbean Beans and Rice, '99 121
    Creole Beans and Rice, '80 223
    Farmer's Beans and Rice with Rosemary Biscuits,
        '99 16
    Kidney Beans and Rice, Smoky, '03 290
    New Orleans Red Beans and Rice, '97 235
    Red Beans and Rice, '80 58; '83 89; '84 37;
        '87 45; '90 27; '96 218; '02 35
    Red Beans and Rice, Delta, '98 146
    Red Beans and Rice, Easy, '90 220; '99 M219
    Red Beans and Rice, Spicy, '02 56
    Sausage, Beans, and Rice, Texas, '84 296
    South Texas Beans and Rice, '85 252
Beans with Coconut Milk, Spicy, '03 175
Black-Eyed Peas, Rice with, '93 66
Black-Eyed Peas with Rice, '83 12; '90 208; '91 13
Black-Eyes and Rice, Creole, '85 6
Blended Rice, '96 68
Braised Rice, '98 45
Braised Rice and Peas, '79 101
Brown Rice
    Brown Rice, '82 275
    Calico Brown Rice, '86 33
    Casserole, Brown Rice, '87 118
    Chicken and Brown Rice, Roast, '83 268
    Chicken-Brown Rice Bake, '91 314
    Confetti Rice, '89 146

Consommé, Brown Rice, '98 288
Cornish Hens with Brown Rice, '82 275
Garden Rice, '92 12
Mix, Fruited Curry-Rice, '86 326
Mix, Fruited Rice, '97 317
Pancakes, Vegetable-Rice, '93 43
Parmesan, Brown Rice, '84 196
Pecan Rice, '85 53
Pilaf, Brown Rice, '90 136; '91 82
Pudding, Brown Rice, '85 77
Rolls, Crunchy Cabbage-Rice, '85 32
Salad, Brown Rice-and-Vegetable, '84 202
Salad, Brown Rice Confetti, '94 174
Salad, Orange Vinaigrette Rice, '98 288
Salad, Zesty Rice-and-Bean, '02 84
Spanish Brown Rice, '84 196
Stew, Lentil-Rice, '82 232
Stuffing, Tomatoes with Walnut-Rice, '91 102
Vegetables and Rice, '93 91
Brussels Sprouts and Rice, '79 288; '80 26
Buttery Rice with Vermicelli, '02 258
Cabbage Leaves, Stuffed, '00 270
Calas, Easy, '92 89
Calas, Quick, '96 64
Calico Rice, '85 83
Casseroles. *See also* **RICE/Brown Rice, Wild
    Rice.**
    Almond Rice, '91 291
    au Gratin, Rice, '83 129
    au Gratin Supreme, Rice, '86 78
    Baked Rice, '94 270
    Baked Spicy Rice, '96 125
    Beef and Rice, Spiced, '84 285
    Black-Eyed Peas with Rice, '83 12
    Broccoli-Rice Casserole, '81 101
    Broccoli with Rice, Holiday, '87 252
    Chantilly, Rice, '86 82
    Cheese-Parslied Rice, '89 99
    Chicken and Rice, '95 54
    Chicken and Rice Casserole, '80 260
    Chicken-and-Rice Casserole, Creamy, '02 309
    Chicken-and-Rice Casserole, Crispy, '03 203
    Chicken-and-Rice Casseroles, '01 52
    Chicken Casserole, '96 302
    Chicken Casserole, Rice-and-, '87 154
    Chicken-Rice Casserole, '86 52; '99 215
    Chicken-Rice Casserole, Creamy, '99 21
    Chiles, Rice-and-Cheese con, '89 99
    Chiles, Rice and Green, '83 152
    Chili-Cheesy Rice, '79 43
    Chili-Rice Casserole, '79 54
    Colorful Rice Casserole, '82 199
    Cornish Hens-and-Rice Casserole, '92 267
    Corn-Rice Casserole, '01 46
    Fiesta Rice, '84 76
    French Rice, '83 24
    Golden Rice, '79 270
    Green Rice Bake, '79 43
    Green Rice Casserole, '95 181
    Ham-and-Rice Casserole, '84 75
    Ham Casserole, '98 314
    Ham-Rice-Tomato Bake, '87 78
    Jalapeño Rice Casserole, '81 66
    Lentils-and-Rice Casserole, '93 301
    Lentils and Rice, Spanish-Style, '03 201
    Mexican Rice Casserole, '83 31
    Mushroom Rice, Baked, '92 170; '95 84
    Mushroom Rice, Easy, '89 286
    Pepper Rice, Hot, '92 310
    Red Rice, Savannah, '95 27
    Rice Casserole, '87 45
    Sausage-and-Rice Bake, Creole, '88 58
    Sausage and Rice Casserole, Oriental, '82 M123
    Sausage Casserole, Skillet, '99 123

Sausage-Rice Casserole, '82 50; '83 75
Shrimp and Rice Casserole, '79 228
Shrimp-and-Rice Casserole, '94 328
Shrimp Casserole, Spicy, '96 62
Spanish Rice Casserole, '79 192
Spinach Rice, '85 146
Squash Casserole, Creamy Rice and, '95 26
Strata, Cheese-Rice, '81 176
Vegetarian Casserole, '96 302
Zucchini-Rice Casserole Italiano, '89 146
Charleston Rice, '97 310
Chicken-Flavored Rice, '84 M144
Coconut Rice, '00 201
Coconut Rice, Polynesian Pork Tenderloin with
Orange-Curry Sauce and, '04 309
Consommé Rice, '80 246
Cooler, Rice-and-Cinnamon, '00 139
Cream with Mandarin Oranges, Rice, '85 317
Creole Rice, '90 183
Cumin Rice, '85 83
Curried Rice, '90 183; '97 51; '98 237; '04 21
Curried Rice, Quick, '86 81
Curried Rice with Almonds, '83 M285
Curried Rice with Pineapple, '79 142
Curry-Spiced Rice, '86 M226
Custard, Baked Rice, '92 308
(Date-Nut Rice), Basted Dates and Basted Rice,
'96 158
Dirty Rice, '86 142
Dirty Rice, Cajun, '04 288
Dressing, Crabmeat-and-Oyster, '02 243
Dressing, Pecan, Rice, and Crawfish, '00 252
Dressing, Rice, '91 217; '01 222
Dressing, Roast Turkey with Rice, '82 286
Dressing, Southern Rice, '99 256
Empanadas, Easy Turkey, '96 63

Fried Rice
Bacon Fried Rice, '80 115
Calas, Easy, '92 89
Calas, Quick, '96 64
Cashew Fried Rice, '99 171
Chicken-Cashew Fried Rice, '99 171
Easy Fried Rice, '84 76
Egg Fried Rice, '79 252; '80 19
Fried Rice, '83 129; '84 197; '88 67; '00 273
Ham Fried Rice, '04 125
Pork Fried Rice, '89 99
Refried Rice, Shrimp and, '89 176
Sausage, Fried Rice with, '83 12
Shrimp-and-Pineapple Fried Rice, Spicy, '03 285
Special, Fried Rice, '80 56
Turkey Fried Rice, '83 282
Turkey "Fried" Rice, '00 97
Two, Fried Rice for, '81 31
Ginger Rice, Fluffy, '83 102
Glorified Rice, '83 129
Grape Leaves, Stuffed, '94 48
Green Peas, Rice with, '87 45
Green Rice, Celebrity, '81 207
Herbed Rice, '83 M285; '93 278
Herb Rice, '91 257
Holiday Rice, '98 289
Honey Rice, '85 83
Hopping John, Skillet, '79 10
Hoppin' John, Esau's, '03 17
Indian Rice, '96 202
Island Rice, '98 276
Jardin, Rice, '01 106
Journey Cakes, '04 99
Journey Cakes, Rosemary-Garlic, '04 99
Journey Cakes, Tomato, Parmesan, and Kalamata
Olive, '04 99
Lemon Rice, '89 166
Lemony Rice, '99 46

Lentils and Rice, '99 236
Lime-Flavored Rice, '84 175
Lyonnaise, Rice, '83 151

Main Dishes. *See also* **RICE/Beans and Rice,
Brown Rice, Casseroles, Pilaf, Risotto, Wild
Rice.**
Arroz con Pollo, '01 279
Beef and Cauliflower over Rice, '93 94
Beef and Rice, Curried, '88 164
Beef-and-Rice Dinner, Mexican, '88 199
Beef and Rice, Mango-, '88 138
Beef and Rice, Spicy, '83 231
Beef over Rice Noodles, Shredded, '85 74
Beef Rollups with Rice, Royal, '79 105
Beef Tips on Rice, '85 87
Black-Eyed Peas with Rice, '90 208
Boudin, Old-Fashioned, '85 250
Cabbage Rolls, Stuffed, '88 18
Chicken-and-Rice Bake, Herbed, '02 215
Chicken-and-Rice Cacciatore, Quick, '88 38
Chicken and Rice, Creole, '92 262
Chicken and Rice Dressing, '79 288
Chicken and Rice, Island, '04 165
Chicken and Rice, One-Dish, '01 279
Chicken and Rice, Shortcut, '90 220
Chicken-and-Rice Skillet Dinner, '98 127
Chicken and Rice, Spicy, '88 200
Chicken and Rice, Sweet-and-Sour, '03 97
Chicken-and-Rice Valencia, '85 113
Chicken Breasts, Celebrity, '95 60
Chicken Caruso and Rice, '89 177
Chicken Livers and Rice Dish, '82 218
Chicken Livers with Rice, '80 200; '81 58;
'84 292
Chicken over Confetti Rice Squares, Creamed,
'81 282; '82 31
Chicken over Rice, Cajun, '88 102; '89 67
Chicken-Rice Medaillons in Pepper Pesto, '90 97
Chicken, Rice-Stuffed, '81 4
Chicken, Rice-Stuffed Roasted, '88 38
Chicken, Roasted Stuffed, '98 109
Chicken, Salsa Rice and, '99 109
Chicken, Sanibel Island, '97 66
Chicken with Curried Rice, '98 127
Chicken with Pecan-Rice Dressing, '85 M57
Chicken with Rice, Moorish, '98 127
Chicken with Rice, Roast, '95 261
Chicken with Rice, Sherry, '81 97
Chili with Rice, '82 11
Cornish Hens, Rice-Stuffed, '82 302
Curried Rice, '97 51
Dirty Rice, '03 147
Dirty Rice, Hot, '93 219
Egg and Rice Bake, '83 119
Fruited Rice, Far East, '81 175
Ham Rolls, Rice-Stuffed, '83 190
Ham with Rice, Curried, '80 111
Hoppin' John with Scallion Hoe Cake
Medaillons, Skillet, '02 326
Indian Rice, '79 64
Jollof Rice Dinner, '91 230; '92 325
Lamb Curry with Rice, '80 83; '81 10
Lentil-and-Rice Supper, '84 202
Meatballs Paprikash with Rice, '85 31
Mexican Dinner, Quick, '98 224
Oriental Rice, '85 146
Paella, Chicken-Pork-Shrimp, '82 245
Paella, Seafood, '82 245
Paella, Spanish, '85 26
Paella Valenciana, '82 246
Pancakes, Rice, '85 147
Peppers, Beef-Stuffed, '85 146
Peppers, Rice-Stuffed, '80 65; '99 241
Pepper Steak and Rice, '81 17

Peppers with Rice and Ham, Stuffed, '82 131
Pork Chops and Rice, Savannah, '00 236
Pork Chops and Spanish Rice, '83 103; '85 293
Pork Chops, Rice-Stuffed, '83 102
Pork Chops with White Rice, '02 312
Pork Roast with Hopping John Stuffing, '01 25
Red Rice, '92 235
Red Rice Jambalaya, '91 18
Sausage and Rice, Italian, '86 53
Shrimp and Refried Rice, '89 176
Shrimp and Rice, Oriental, '90 183
Shrimp and Sausage Rice, '79 64
Shrimp-and-Scallop Sauté with Pecan Rice,
'90 317
Shrimp Creole in a Rice Ring, '86 222
Shrimp, Curried Rice and, '83 231
Shrimp Sauté, Confetti, '97 104
Skillet Dinner, Antipasto, '97 327
Skillet, Hamburger-Rice, '00 236
Strudel, Meatless Mexican, '98 29
Tostadas, Rice-and-Black Bean, '97 65
Tuna-Rice Pie, '84 123
Turkey and Rice, Herbed, '97 327
Turkey with Rice Dressing, Roast, '82 286
Medley, Rice, '79 270
Mélange, Rice, '87 240

Mexican Rice
Dinner, Quick Mexican, '98 224
Dressing, Mexican Rice, '87 253
Jalapeño Hot Rice, '80 126
Jalapeño Rice, '79 43
Mexican Rice, '83 85; '85 147; '91 217; '01 273
Mold, Chile-Rice, '86 221
Orphan's Rice, '03 32
Spanish Rice, '81 51; '83 209; '90 183; '94 27
Spanish Rice, Chicken Wings with, '00 202
Spanish Rice, Jiffy, '90 176
Spanish Rice, Pork Chops and, '83 103; '85 293
Spanish Rice with Tofu, '88 26
Spanish-Style Rice, '83 152
Spicy Mexican Rice, '88 149
Tex-Mex Rice with Corn, '03 129
Miami Rice, '96 86
Mix, Fruited Rice, '90 267
Mix, Herb-Rice, '91 257
Mix, Seasoned Rice, '01 248
Mold, Curried Rice, '85 36
Mold, Saffron Rice, '86 221
Mushroom Rice, Baked, '92 170; '95 84
Nutted Rice, '85 269
Orange-Herb Rice, '89 286
Orange Rice, '79 43; '81 175; '82 200
Oriental Rice, '85 M12, 146
Orphan's Rice, '04 218
Oven Rice, '83 89
Paella, Garden, '82 245
Paella Rice Mix, '94 168
Paella, Roasted-Vegetable, '04 89
Pancakes, Rice, '85 147
Parsleyed Rice, '83 M58
Parsley Rice, '84 197; '85 95
Parslied Rice, '87 167, 243
Parslied Rice, Creamy, '88 255
Peas and Rice, '88 97
Peas and Rice, Holiday, '86 328
Peas, Caribbean Rice and, '02 275
Pecan Rice, '04 204
Pecan Rice, Speedy Skillet, '04 328
Peppered Rice, '82 4
Picadillo Rice, '98 237
Pigeon Peas, Rice with, '92 157

Pilaf
Apricot Rice Pilaf, '99 146
Browned Rice Pilaf, '87 305

RICE, Pilaf
(continued)

    Brown Rice Pilaf, '90 136; '91 82
    Chicken-and-Smoked Sausage Pilau, '04 204
    Chicken Pilaf, '82 246
    Chicken Pilau, '99 184
    Chicken-Vegetable Pilaf, '97 51
    Cinnamon Rice Pilaf, '01 229
    Fruit-and-Vegetable Rice Pilaf, '84 196
    Fruited Pork Pilaf, '82 246
    Fruited Rice Pilaf, '04 271
    Fruited Rice Pilaf, Chicken Breasts with, '92 307
    Greek Rice Pilaf, '01 146
    Ham Pilaf Mold, '86 222
    Lemon-and-Pine Nut Pilaf, '97 51
    Lemon Pilaf, '97 322
    Lemon Rice Pilaf, '01 36; '04 82
    Lentil Pilaf, Rice-and-, '88 17
    Near-Eastern Pilaf, '82 246
    Okra Pilaf, '80 185; '82 126; '93 160
    Okra Pilau, '99 184
    Onion Rice Pilaf, '04 236
    Oyster Pilaf, '97 20
    Persian Rice Pilaf, '02 167
    Rice Pilaf, '86 82; '87 229; '88 42; '89 286
    Saffron Rice Pilaf, '04 204
    Sausage Pilâu, '99 184
    Savory Pilaf, '83 93
    Shrimp Pilaf, '82 246
    Shrimp Pilau, '99 184
    Turkey-Asparagus Pilaf, '88 200
    Turkey-Rice Pilaf, '86 284
    Turkish Pilaf, '79 184
    White Rice Pilaf, '97 238
    Wild Rice-Fennel Pilaf, '97 127
  Pork Backbone and Rice, '03 252
  Primavera, Rice, '98 237
  Pudding, Amaretto Rice, '86 334
  Pudding, Apple Rice, '91 217
  Pudding, Creamy Rice, '81 51, 205
  Pudding, English Rice, '04 98
  Pudding, Fruited Rice, '81 205; '86 95
  Pudding, Fudgy Rice, '81 205
  Pudding, Old-Fashioned Rice, '85 147; '03 285
  Pudding, Raisin-Rice, '87 46
  Pudding, Velvety Rice, '81 205
  Quiche, Broccoli-Rice, '81 228
  Raisin Rice with Curry, '85 83
  Red Rice, '97 138; '00 289; '02 119
  Red Rice and Ham, '00 289
  Red Rice, Savannah, '80 119; '89 286
  Ring, Oregano Rice, '86 222
  Ring, Rice-Carrot, '79 246
  Ring with Beets, Rice, '79 225
  Risotto
    alla Milanese, Risotto, '85 228
    Asparagus Risotto, '03 68
    Baked Risotto, Easy, '99 120
    Broccoli Risotto with Parmesan, '99 120
    Chicken-and-Roasted Shallot Risotto, Smoked,
      '00 30
    Collard Green Risotto and Pot Liquor, '01 121
    Collards, Risotto with, '96 203
    Crawfish Risotto, '99 120
    Creamy Risotto, '03 285
    Green Bean Risotto, '03 68
    Greens, Risotto with, '96 132
    Lemon-Lime Risotto, '97 213
    Microwave Risotto, '97 M213
    Onion Risotto, '99 94; '02 97; '03 98
    Pinot Noir Risotto with Rosemary Chicken,
      '97 214

    Pistachio Risotto with Saffron, '98 272
    Primavera, Risotto, '95 163; '00 138
    Pumpkin Risotto with Shrimp, '98 240
    Risotto, '95 280
    Roasted Garlic-and-Cheese Risotto, '04 283
    Seafood Risotto, '95 280
    Shellfish and Peas, Risotto with, '96 131
    Shrimp and Asparagus, Risotto with, '03 86
    Shrimp Risotto, '00 95; '02 124
    Southwestern Risotto, '92 211
    Sweet Onion Risotto, '03 217
    Tomato-Basil Risotto, '95 269
    Vegetables, Risotto with, '98 193
  Rolls, Shrimp-and-Romaine, '97 197
  Saffron Rice, '79 43; '93 282; '97 51
  Saffron Rice Mold, '86 221
  Salads
    Artichoke-Chicken-Rice Salad, '94 132
    Artichoke-Chicken-Rice Salad, Mediterranean,
      '97 321
    Artichoke Hearts, Rice Salad with, '80 232
    Artichoke-Rice Salad, '80 178; '81 41; '85 81;
      '01 144
    Avocado Salad, Rice-and-, '89 146
    Bacon, Rice Salad with, '79 52
    Bean-and-Rice Salad, Marinated, '87 152
    Bean Salad, Rice-and-, '85 22
    Beans-and-Rice Salad, '91 44
    Beef-and-Lime Rice Salad, '03 172
    Black Bean-and-Rice Salad, '00 327
    Cabbage Salad with Honey-Dijon Vinaigrette,
      Rice-, '04 321
    Chicken-and-Rice Salad, '97 92
    Chicken-and-Rice Salad, Hot, '83 22
    Chicken-Rice Salad, '81 203; '97 93
    Chicken-Rice Salad, Grilled, '98 148
    Chicken-Rice Salad, Nutty, '83 157
    Chutneyed Rice Salad, '88 100
    Colorful Rice Salad, '81 253
    Confetti Rice Salad, '80 232
    Crunchy Rice Salad, '82 302
    Curried Chicken-Rice Salad, '92 190
    Curried Rice Salad, '80 84; '85 147, 220; '96 240
    Curry Rice Salad, '89 146
    Egg-Rice Salad, '84 18; '86 169
    Ham-and-Rice Salad, Colorful, '90 319
    Ham-and-Rice Salad, Mandarin, '87 145
    Ham-Rice Toss, '82 40
    Hearty Rice Salad, '82 233
    Herbed Rice Salad, '96 123
    Hoppin' John Salad, '96 64
    Lentils-and-Rice Salad, '90 197
    Mandarin Rice Salad, '88 271
    Mardi Gras Rice, '91 217
    Molded Gazpacho-Rice Salad, '86 221
    Mushrooms, Rice Salad with Fresh, '80 231
    Paella Salad, '86 207
    Pea Salad, Rice-, '85 163
    Pebble Salad, '91 27
    Pine Nut, Rice, and Feta Salad, '96 26; '98 331
    Pork-and-Rice Salad with Spicy Tomato
      Dressing, '03 143
    Primavera Salad, Rice, '00 131
    Red Rice Salad, Charleston, '79 146
    Rice Salad, '79 74; '81 51
    Salmon-Rice Salad, '84 289
    Shrimp-and-Orange Rice Salad, Zesty, '87 155
    Shrimp and Rice Salad, '80 231; '82 207
    Shrimp-and-Rice Salad, '92 307
    Shrimp-Rice Salad, Baked, '83 22
    Shrimp-Rice Salad, Tangy, '84 66
    Shrimp Salad, Rice-, '79 270; '92 142
    Shrimp Salad, Rice-and-, '83 82
    Spinach-Rice Salad, '94 63

    Tomatoes and Basil, Rice with, '95 232
    Tuna-Rice Salad, '87 202
    Vegetable-Rice Salad, '80 148; '83 198; '85 87
    Vegetable Salad, Rice-and-, '86 42
    Zesty Rice Salad, '81 23
  Savory Rice, '89 201
  Seasoned Onion Rice, '82 166
  Seasoned Rice, '79 244; '83 212
  Seasoned Rice, Pork Sausage-, '00 236
  Shell, Rice-Cheese, '82 49
  Shrimp Over Rice, Texas Pesto, '03 327
  Shrimp with Rice, '03 219
  Soufflé, Rice-Cheese, '79 270
  Soup, Chicken-and-Rice, '88 236
  Soup, Mushroom-Rice, '90 32
  Soup, Tomato-and-Rice, '85 24
  Soup, Turkey-Rice, '90 89
  Southern Rice, '90 250
  Southwestern Rice, '90 121
  Spanish Rice. *See* **RICE/Mexican Rice.**
  Spicy Rice, '83 215; '85 256; '99 214
  Steak and Rice, Skillet Pepper, '04 326
  Steamed Rice, Oven-, '89 226
  Stew with Rice, Black-Eyed Pea, '04 19
  Strata, Cheese-Rice, '81 176
  Stuffing, Pork Roast, with Hopping John, '01 25
  Stuffing, Rice, '95 290
  Stuffing, Rice-and-Onion, '88 246
  Succotash, Savory, '96 63
  Sweet Jamaican Rice, '96 71
  Three-Grain Rice, '95 166
  Timbales, Green Rice, '97 62
  Timbales, Rice, '94 32
  Timbales, Spinach-Rice, '88 271
  Toasted Herb Rice, '04 295
  Toasted Rice and Pasta, '95 57
  Tomatoes and Basil, Rice with, '95 232
  Tomatoes, Italian-Style, '97 169
  Tomato Rice, '02 169
  Tortilla Bites with Sesame-Soy Dipping Sauce,
    '02 145
  Vegetable-Rice Toss, '91 309
  Vegetables, Rice with, '79 64; '85 83
  Vegetables, Rice with Spring, '96 132
  Waffles, Rice, '98 124
  Waldorf Rice, '84 281
  White Rice, Fluffy, '03 65
  Wild Rice. *See also* **RICE/Pilaf.**
    Almond Wild Rice, '86 50
    Belvedere, Wild Rice, '86 82
    Bulgur, Wild Rice, '91 83
    Casserole, Chicken-and-Wild Rice, '97 192;
      '00 257
    Casserole, Chicken-Wild Rice, '84 241; '85 65
    Casserole, Duck and Wild Rice, '79 224
    Casserole, Leslie's Favorite Chicken-and-Wild
      Rice, '00 209; '03 107
    Casserole, Oyster-and-Wild Rice, '83 34; '84 44
    Casserole, Sausage and Wild Rice, '83 196
    Casserole, Sausage-Wild Rice, '84 250
    Casserole, Turkey-and-Sausage Wild Rice,
      '03 239
    Casserole, Veal and Wild Rice, '79 180
    Casserole, Wild Rice, '82 199; '95 176
    Casserole, Wild Rice-Oyster, '86 256
    Chicken and Wild Rice, '79 248; '01 279
    Chicken-Fried Wild Rice, '89 24; '91 132
    Chicken Rollups, '88 38
    Chicken, Wild Rice-Stuffed, '79 219
    Chicken-Wild Rice Supreme, '79 77
    Chicken with Wild Rice, Elegant, '80 M76
    Chicken with Wild Rice, Orange-Glazed Roasted,
      '02 85
    Cranberry-Almond Wild Rice, '04 204

Cranberry-Pear Wild Rice, '83 279
Creole, Wild Rice-and-Shrimp, '84 292
Dressed-Up Wild Rice, '92 60
Eggs with Wild Rice, Scrambled, '80 42
Gourmet Wild Rice, '89 271
Grapes, Wild Rice with, '95 48
Morels, Wild Rice with, '89 62
Mushrooms, Wild Rice and, '83 278
Oysters, Wild Rice and, '92 339
Pancakes, Wild Rice, '02 238
Pear-and-Cranberry Wild Rice Salad, '03 199
Pecan-Lemon Wild Rice, '92 211
Popped Wild Rice, '85 65
Pork Loin Stuffed with Wild Rice, '84 35
Quiches, Wild Rice-and-Mushroom, '93 237
Ring, Creamed Mushrooms in Wild Rice, '80 270
Ring, Wild Rice, '83 253
Salad, Crab and Wild Rice, '79 116
Salad, Crab-Wild Rice, '86 207
Salad, Orange Vinaigrette Rice, '98 288
Salad, Oriental Salmon-and-Wild Rice, '94 173
Salad, Springtime Wild Rice, '88 100
Salad, Wild Rice, '85 65; '89 147; '93 191;
    '01 247
Salad, Wild Rice-and-Chicken, '02 52
Salad, Wild Rice-and-Corn, '98 288
Salad, Wild Rice-and-Cranberry, '99 272
Salad, Wild Rice-and-Kidney Bean, '01 175
Salad, Wild Rice-and-Roasted Vegetable, '99 316
Salad, Wild Rice-and-Shrimp, '02 109
Salad, Wild Rice-Chicken, '83 146; '99 55;
    '01 72
Salad, Wild Rice-Green Apple, '92 90
Salad, Wild Rice-Shrimp, '99 55
Salad, Wild Tuna, '95 243
Salad with Spicy Lime Vinaigrette, Wild Rice,
    '01 217
Sausage and Wild Rice, '85 65
Sausage, Wild Rice and, '86 268
Scallops and Wild Rice, '90 129
Soup, Cheesy Potato-and-Wild Rice, '89 16
Soup, Chicken-and-Wild Rice, '04 26
Soup, Creamy Chicken-and-Wild Rice, '98 M334
Soup, Tomato-Beef-Wild Rice, '04 42
Soup, Wildest Rice, '01 66
Stuffing, Cornish Hens with Wild Rice, '79 222;
    '80 64; '82 136
Turkey Breast, Wild Rice-Stuffed, '97 281
Veggie Wild Rice, '00 141
Yellow Rice, '91 136
Yellow Rice, Black Beans with, '82 2
Yellow Rice, Easy Black Beans and, '92 308
Yellow Rice with Water Chestnuts, '85 24
RISOTTO. *See* **RICE/Risotto.**
ROLLS AND BUNS. *See also* **BREADS.**
Angel's Wing Rolls, '95 329
Apple Pinwheel, Quick, '85 42
Beer-Parmesan Rolls, '03 259
Blueberry Pinwheels, '82 205
Broccoli-Cheddar Rolls, '91 21
Buttered Rum-Nut Rolls, '86 291
Butterscotch Pinwheels, '90 49
Cajun Bread Knots, '03 63
Caramel-Chocolate Sticky Buns, Easy, '95 36
Caramel Rolls, Easy, '90 195
Caramel Sticky Buns, '00 52
Centerpiece Rolls, '94 276
Cheese-Apricot Sweet Rolls, '90 195
Cherry-Almond Rolls, '84 M198
Cinnamon
    Breakfast Buns, Cinnamon-Apple, '00 M198
    Breakfast Rolls, Cinnamon, '00 243
    Chocolate-Cinnamon Buns, '85 5
    Cinnamon Buns, '91 68

Cinnamon Rolls, '79 80; '88 290; '92 270;
    '96 321; '98 325; '99 M284; '01 44, 242;
    '03 247
Cream Cheese-Filled Cinnamon Rolls, '02 327
Crisps, Cinnamon, '81 113
Dough, Cinnamon Roll, '03 247
Easy Cinnamon Rolls, '85 290
Filling, Cinnamon Roll, '03 247
Glazed Cinnamon Rolls, '86 312
Icing, Cinnamon Roll, '03 247
Mini-Cinnis, Mama's, '02 41
Old-Fashioned Cinnamon Rolls, '86 298;
    '90 196; '92 226
Pecan Rolls, Cinnamon-, '98 251
Pecan Rolls, Easy Cinnamon-, '89 307
Potato Sourdough Cinnamon Rolls, '94 325;
    '95 77
Raisin Cinnamon Pull-Aparts, '82 205; '83 32
Raisin Cinnamon Rolls, '81 107
Raisin-Cinnamon Rolls, '91 240
Rollups, Cinnamon Toast, '99 194
Spiral Cinnamon Rolls, '82 205; '83 32
Sticky Buns, Cinnamon, '83 244
Tea Rolls, Cinnamon, '92 263
Tiny Cinnamon Rolls, '97 271; '98 330
Twists, Cinnamon, '83 53
Cornmeal Rolls, '79 60; '89 184
Crescent
Almond Crescent Rolls, '90 283
Apricot-Cheese Crescents, '99 284
Apricot Crescents, '90 181
Butter Crescent Rolls, '95 292
Butter-Rich Crescent Rolls, '81 211
Buttery Crescent Rolls, '83 180
Chocolate Crescents, '03 283
Crescent Rolls, '84 267; '89 235
Deep South Crescent Rolls, '82 309; '83 16
Easy Crescent Rolls, '79 60
Festive Crescents, '80 281
French-Style Crescent Rolls, '82 288
Hurry-Up Crescent Rolls, '97 50
Pecan Crescent Twists, '03 36
Yogurt Crescent Rolls, '91 123
Croissants, Cream Cheese, '92 159
Crunchy Rolls, '97 160
Dinner
Dinner Rolls, '79 251; '89 312; '93 M326
Fancy Dinner Rolls, '86 299
Freezer Dinner Rolls, '90 251
How to Shape Dinner Rolls, '83 323
Italian Dinner Rolls, '83 254
Italiano Dinner Rolls, '85 32
Oatmeal Dinner Rolls, '01 44
Refrigerator Dinner Rolls, '81 78
Sour Cream Dinner Rolls, '97 253
Whole Wheat Dinner Rolls, '91 53
Dried Cherry-Walnut Sweet Rolls, '03 235
Garlic Rolls, Easy, '86 234
Italian Bread Knots, '03 63
Jam Teasers, '81 8
Lemon Knots, Glazed, '86 290
Mayonnaise Rolls, '90 283
Nutty Buns, '86 290
Onion-and-Sesame Rolls, '95 292
Onion-Bacon Rolls, '99 47
Onion Buns, Cheesy, '85 5
Onion-Cheese Buns, '88 218
Onion Rolls, Poppy Seed, '81 63
Onion Twist Rolls, '89 288
Orange
Apricot-Orange Sweet Rolls, '03 235
Butter Rolls, Orange, '82 206; '83 33
Easy Orange Rolls, '89 M131
Frosted Hot Orange Rolls, '80 257

Glazed Orange Rolls, '90 194
Kitchen Express Orange Rolls, '98 252
Luscious Orange Rolls, '86 298
Orange Rolls, '80 22; '82 17; '88 79; '96 321;
    '01 257
Speedy Orange Rolls, '89 287
Parker House Rolls, Italian, '99 47
Parmesan Rolls, '79 181
Parsley-Garlic Rolls, '93 319
Pecan-Golden Raisin Sweet Rolls, '03 235
Pineapple Buns, Easy, '85 14
Potato
Caramelized Onion Buns, Potato-, '03 234
Easy Potato Rolls, '89 287
Feathery Light Potato Rolls, '81 305; '82 36
Homemade Potato Rolls, '82 252
Potato Rolls, '81 300; '99 290
Refrigerated Potato Rolls, '83 254
Refrigerator Potato Rolls, '87 15
Sourdough Cinnamon Rolls, Potato, '94 325;
    '95 77
Sourdough Rolls, Potato, '94 325; '95 77
Southern Potato Rolls, '86 299
Super Potato Rolls, '85 145
Supreme Potato Rolls, '82 130
Whole Wheat Potato Rolls, '89 50
Yeast Rolls, Potato, '87 53
Pull-Apart Buns, Easy, '83 100
Pumpkin Rolls, '87 254
Quick Rolls, '95 245; '96 54
Raisin Rollups, Sweet, '86 290
Refrigerator
Big-Batch Rolls, '88 289
Bran Rolls, '85 145
Brioche, Morrison House, '96 53
Buttermilk Refrigerator Rolls, '81 120; '82 22
Butter Rolls, Homemade, '00 137
Caramel Breakfast Rolls, '79 193
Caramel-Nut Rolls, '86 312
Caramel Sticky Buns, Overnight, '00 52
Cloverleaf Refrigerator Rolls, '80 256
Croissants, '83 54
Herb Rolls, '98 325
Icebox Rolls, '80 242
Lemon Spirals, French, '81 94
Low-Sodium Refrigerator Rolls, '82 67
Overnight Rolls, '86 233
Parker House Refrigerator Rolls, '82 310;
    '83 17
Party Refrigerator Rolls, '79 248
Party Rolls, '98 251
Potato Rolls, Refrigerated, '83 254
Potato Rolls, Refrigerator, '87 15
Refrigerator Rolls, '82 287; '91 53
Reuben Buns, '88 298
Sour Cream Rolls, '80 71
Sour Cream Yeast Rolls, '85 259; '90 17; '93 232;
    '00 33
Spoon Rolls, '87 15; '91 275
Sweet Rolls, Yummy, '80 281
Three-Day Refrigerator Rolls, '86 306
Twists, Austrian, '80 45
Wixie's Refrigerator Rolls, '99 82
Yeast Rolls, Refrigerator, '81 296, 307; '82 309;
    '83 17, 118; '91 80; '98 109, 325
Reuben Rolls, Snappy, '02 58
Romano Sesame Rolls, '87 144
Rum Rolls, Easy, '79 287; '80 35
Sesame Knots, '89 29
Snack Buns, '87 279
Southwestern Knots, '03 63
Sticky Buns, Christmas Morning, '97 245
Sweet Rolls, Quick Breakfast, '90 195
Toasted Rolls with Herb Butter, '89 70

ROLLS AND BUNS
(continued)

Wheat
Dinner Rolls, Whole Wheat, **'91** 53
Easy Whole Wheat Rolls, **'86** 286; **'87** 74
Feather Rolls, Shredded Wheat, **'82** 309; **'83** 16
Hearty Whole Wheat Bread and Rolls, **'79** 92
Honey Wheat Rolls, **'83** 278
Honey-Wheat Rolls, Dilled, **'83** 254
Light Wheat Rolls, **'87** 254
Pan Rolls, Whole Grain, **'89** 256
Petite Whole Wheat Rolls, **'85** 146
Potato Rolls, Whole Wheat, **'89** 50
Wholesome Whole Wheat Rolls, **'92** 31
Whole Wheat Buns, **'86** 236
Whole Wheat Rolls, **'79** 275; **'90** 111; **'96** 50
Yeast. *See also* **ROLLS AND BUNS/Cinnamon,**
Crescent, Dinner, Potato, Refrigerator,
Wheat.
Anise Rolls, **'89** 91
Baguettes and Rolls, **'98** 168
Basic Angel Rolls, **'89** 72
Best-Ever Yeast Rolls, **'90** 46
Blueberry Buns, Deluxe, **'81** 164
Bolillos, **'88** 247; **'02** 81
Bow Ties, **'96** 321
Bran Yeast Rolls, **'87** 116
Butter-and-Herb Rolls, **'86** 306
Butterhorn Rolls, **'89** 288
Butterhorns, **'84** 267
Buttermilk Rolls, Quick, **'83** 155
Buttermilk Yeast Rolls, **'79** 59
Butter Rolls, **'00** 257
Butter Rolls, Homemade, **'01** 21
Caraway Puffs, **'82** 174
Cheese Buns, Hurry-Up, **'81** 300
Cheese Crescents, **'82** 18
Chocolate Sticky Buns, **'81** 300; **'82** 124
Citrus-Pecan Rolls, **'03** 256
Cloverleaf Rolls, **'82** 18; **'96** 321
Cloverleaf Rolls, Light, **'83** 290
Coconut-Pecan Coils, **'90** 196
Cornmeal Yeast Rolls, **'86** 177
Cottage Cheese Rolls, **'81** 78
Cranberry-Pineapple Rolls, **'86** 275
Cranberry Rolls, **'00** 244
Cream Cheese Pinches, **'87** 85
Crescent Rolls, **'97** 199
Dough, Basic Roll, **'82** 17
Dough, Sweet Roll, **'79** 80
Easy Yeast Rolls, **'81** 78; **'86** 16; **'03** 256
Fantan Rolls, French, **'80** 276
Finger Rolls, **'83** 254
Hard Rolls, **'86** 85, 306
Herb Rolls, **'01** 44
Holiday Sparkle Rolls, **'83** 296
Honey-Oat Buns, **'98** 27
Honey Oatmeal Buns, **'83** 154
Honey Rolls, Super, **'80** 115
Hot Cross Buns, **'81** 77; **'95** 100; **'01** 88
Hot Rolls, Best, **'00** 97
Hurry-Up Yeast Rolls, **'90** 90
Icebox Rolls, **'04** 70
Jam Kolaches, **'85** 290
Low-Sodium Yeast Rolls, **'84** 228
Make-Ahead Yeast Rolls, **'95** 307
Molletes, **'02** 83
Molletes, Chocolate, **'02** 83
Molletes, Pink, **'02** 83
Molletes, Red, **'02** 83
Molletes, Yellow, **'02** 83
Moravian Feast Buns, **'83** 295

Oatmeal-Cinnamon-Pecan Rolls, **'96** 50
Onion Buns, Cheesy, **'85** 5
Onion Twist Rolls, **'89** 288
Overnight Yeast Rolls, **'96** 321
Pan Rolls, **'88** 76
Pan Rolls, Brown-and-Serve, **'91** 52
Parkerhouse Rolls, Super, **'81** 78
Pecan Rolls, **'81** 62
Pepperoni Rolls, Ground-, **'83** 244
Pineapple Angel Rolls, **'89** 72
Pinwheel Rolls, Sweet, **'90** 46
Potato Yeast Rolls, **'98** 92
Praline Buns, **'90** 195
Pumpernickel Rolls, German-Style, **'02** 259
Pumpernickel Rolls with Caraway, German-Style,
'02 259
Puro de Piña, **'02** 82
Quick Yeast Rolls, **'84** 267; **'95** 45
Refrigerator Yeast Rolls, **'81** 296, 307; **'82** 309;
'83 17, 118; **'91** 80; **'98** 109, 325
Rounds, Individual Bread, **'83** 159
Rum Buns, **'81** 299
Rum-Raisin Buns, **'80** 22
Saffron Rolls, **'83** 296
Semitas, **'02** 81
Sesame Buns, **'82** 17
60-Minute Rolls, **'96** 321
Slow-Rise Yeast Rolls, **'97** 131
Sourdough Hot Rolls, **'82** 201
Special Rolls, Extra-, **'88** 257
Speedy Yeast Rolls, **'82** 309; **'83** 17
Spoon Rolls, **'04** 47
S Rolls, **'96** 321
Sticky Buns, **'80** 23
Sweet Potato Rolls, **'93** 172; **'97** 107
Sweet Rolls, Mexican, **'81** 285
Tasty Rolls, **'90** 85
Wixie's Yeast Rolls, **'03** 121
Yam Rolls, Golden, **'86** 299
RUTABAGAS
au Gratin, Rutabaga, **'79** 254
Bacon, Rutabaga with, **'83** 243
Boiled Rutabagas, **'86** 224
Buttered Rutabagas, **'81** 274
Creamy Rutabaga, **'79** 254
Fried Rutabaga, **'99** 285
Glazed Carrots and Rutabaga, Lemon-, **'97** 46
Glazed Rutabaga, **'88** 229; **'99** 284
Gratin, Potato-and-Rutabaga, **'96** 237
Honey Rutabaga, **'91** 220
Mashed Rutabagas, **'86** 295
Mash, Rutabaga-Carrot, **'02** 275
Roasted Rutabaga, Greek-, **'99** 285
Simple Rutabaga, **'83** 243
Skillet, Rutabaga-Cabbage, **'99** 285
Soufflé, Rutabaga, **'01** 213
Steamed Rutabagas, **'81** 274
Tart, Rutabaga-Spinach, **'98** 274
Whip, Rutabaga, **'95** 179

SALAD DRESSINGS. *See also* **MAYONNAISE.**
Almond Salad Dressing, **'81** 37
Apple Dressing, **'83** 181; **'92** 216
Apricot Dressing, **'99** 245
Artichoke Dressing, **'84** 126
Asian Dressing, **'00** 93
Asian Salad Dressing, **'96** 327
Avocado Cream, **'92** 158
Avocado Dressing, **'80** 15; **'92** 321; **'96** 138
Avocado Sauce, Chunky, **'03** 128
Bacon Dressing, Hot, **'84** 12
Bacon Dressing, Jeweled Hot, **'97** 196
Balsamic Dressing, **'95** 281; **'96** 137; **'99** 259

Banana-Poppy Seed Dressing, **'98** 184
Barbecue Dressing, **'99** 124
Barbecue Salad Dressing, **'80** 74
Basil-and-Garlic Dressing, **'94** 55
Basil Dressing, **'88** 24
Basil-Honey Dressing, **'97** 30
B. B.'s Salad Dressing, **'91** 65
Benedictine Dressing, **'98** 83
Blender Dressing, **'80** 78
Buttermilk-Chive Dressing, **'04** 105
Buttermilk Dressing, Down-Home, **'84** 114
Buttermilk-Honey Dressing, **'96** 243
Buttermilk Salad Dressing, **'79** 69
Caesar Dressing, Chipotle, **'04** 119
Caesar Salad Dressing, **'82** 94
Caesar Salad Dressing, Creamy, **'96** 326
Celery-Honey Dressing, **'80** 42
Celery Seed Dressing, **'82** 265
Celery Seed Salad Dressing, **'82** 94
Cheese
Barbecue Salad Dressing, Cheesy-, **'92** 255
Blue Cheese-Buttermilk Dressing, **'01** 112
Blue Cheese Dressing, **'79** 69; **'82** 166; **'86** 233;
'90 286; **'97** 98; **'98** 248; **'99** 244 ; **'00** 217;
'03 72
Blue Cheese Dressing, Creamy, **'81** 150;
'91 307
Blue Cheese Dressing, Low-Fat, **'00** 337
Blue Cheese Dressing, Special, **'80** 30
Blue Cheese Dressing, Tangy, **'87** 81
Blue Cheese Dressing, Zesty, **'79** 104
Blue Cheese Salad Dressing, **'82** 94
Blue Cheese Salad Dressing, Creamy, **'86** 123
Dairy Land Salad Dressing, **'86** 85
Fluff Dressing, Cheese, **'91** 256
Gorgonzola Dressing, Creamy, **'03** 34
Oregano-Feta Dressing, **'01** 57
Parmesan Dressing, **'86** 192; **'97** 326;
'01 96, 101
Romano Dressing, **'80** 174
Roquefort Cheese Dressing, Thick, **'97** 63
Roquefort Dressing, **'79** 85; **'80** 74; **'93** 128
Roquefort Dressing, Creamy, **'84** 12
Chutney Dressing, **'00** 53
Chutney Dressing, Warm, **'02** 242
Citrus-Cilantro·Dressing, **'93** 310; **'94** 97; **'00** 160
Citrus Dressing, **'85** 92
Citrus Dressing, Black Bean Salsa with, **'01** 60
Citrus Ranch Dressing, Fresh, **'04** 91
Coconut Dressing, **'87** 251
Coconut-Orange Dressing, **'97** 93
Cooked Dressing, **'99** 82
Cooked Salad Dressing, **'90** 231
Cranberry-Orange Dressing, **'91** 287
Creamy Dressing, **'79** 159; **'83** 81; **'85** 26;
'92 45, 241; **'93** 318; **'95** 66
Creamy Salad Dressing, **'83** 181
Creole Dressing, **'02** 69
Cucumber-Curry Dressing, **'89** 179
Cucumber Dressing, **'80** 74; **'90** 144
Cucumber-Mint Dressing, **'87** 153
Cucumber-Radish Dressing, **'00** 99
Cucumber Salad Dressing, Creamy, **'82** 79
Curried Dressing, **'84** 115; **'00** 217
Curry Dressing, **'80** 242; **'82** 78; **'97** 63
Curry Salad Dressing, **'96** 326
Date Dressing, **'87** 57
Delightful Salad Dressing, **'83** 181
Dijon Dressing, **'94** 282; **'96** 176
Dijon-Honey Dressing, **'89** 45; **'99** 333
Dill Dressing, **'88** 182
Dill Dressing, Creamy, **'91** 213
Dilly Dressing, **'80** 74
Egg Dressing, **'86** 79

French
Creamy French Dressing, '81 60; '90 286
French Dressing, '89 46
Grapefruit French Dressing, '80 101
Honey French Dressing, '87 81
Miracle French Dressing, '82 79
Onion-French Dressing, '84 283
Piquant French Dressing, '87 202; '88 43
Sassy French Dressing, '99 245
Spicy French Dressing, '81 150; '86 123
Sweet French Dressing, '82 94
Tangy French Dressing, '84 12
Tomato-Honey French Dressing, '81 105
Fruit
Avocado Fruit Salad Dressing, '82 93
Coconut-Fruit Dressing, Tangy, '84 171
Creamy Fruit Salad Dressing, '82 94
Dressing for Fruit Salad, '87 81
Fluffy Fruit Dressing, '79 69
Fresh Fruit Dressing, '87 134
Fruit Salad Dressing, '79 69; '93 184
Lime-Honey Fruit Salad Dressing, '87 81
Marmalade-Fruit Dressing, '84 171
Red Fruit Salad Dressing, '83 231
Salad Dressing for Fruit, '86 40
Sweet-and-Sour Fruit Dressing, '84 125
Whipped Cream Fruit Dressing, '79 270
Garden Dew Dressing, '86 50
Garlic-Herb Salad Dressing, Creamy, '84 66
Garlic Salad Dressing, '86 123
Garlic Salad Dressing, Creamy, '03 211
Ginger Dressing, '82 194; '88 61; '90 160; '93 290;
'96 127
Grandpa Jim's Salad Dressing, '01 182
Grapefruit Salad Dressing, '84 262
Greek Dressing, '02 139
Greek Goddess Dressing, '81 150
Greek Salad Dressing, '90 286; '03 290
Green Goddess Dressing, '02 139
Green Pepper-Onion Salad Dressing, '84 12
Guacamole Dressing, '92 64
Herb Dressing, '80 122; '03 35
Herb Dressing, Lite, '02 18
Herbed Salad Dressing, '88 29; '99 245
Herb-Mayonnaise Sauce, '85 73
Herb Salad Dressing, '86 40
Honey-Applesauce Salad Dressing, '99 210
Honey-Dijon Salad Dressing, Creamy, '99 245
Honey Dressing, '79 242; '83 146; '87 129
Honey-Lemon Dressing, '95 133
Honey-Lime Dressing, '83 139; '93 71
Honey-Mustard Dressing, '90 55, 111, 146; '00 54;
'01 230
Honey-Pecan Dressing, '03 28
Honey-Walnut Dressing, '93 107
Horseradish Dressing, '96 200
Italian
Cream Dressing, Italian, '89 83
Creamy Italian-American Salad Dressing, '79 69
Grapefruit Salad Dressing, '84 262
Italian Dressing, '79 52; '85 261; '89 166
Italian Salad Dressing, '80 82; '84 12
Sour Cream Italian Dressing, '89 45
Special Italian Dressing, '79 190
Lemon-and-Herb Dressing, '92 108
Lemon-Caper Dressing, '96 69
Lemon Cream Dressing, '82 170
Lemon Dressing, '04 167
Lemon Dressing, Creamy, '88 M193
Lemon-Herb Dressing, '97 92
Lemon-Herb Salad Dressing, '82 67
Lemon-Molasses Dressing, '97 195
Lemon-Mustard Dressing, '02 52
Lemon-Pepper Dressing, '87 55

Lemon Salad Dressing, '79 8
Lime Dressing, '79 2; '83 120
Lime Dressing, Creamy, '04 46
Lime-Honey Dressing, '92 213
Lime-Parsley Dressing, '85 131
Lime-Peanut Dressing, '01 26
Lime Sherbet Dressing, '80 221
Magnificent Seven Salad Dressing, '89 45
Margarita Dressing, '94 107
Mayonnaise Dressing, '86 11; '00 217
Mayonnaise Dressing, Herbed-, '86 119
Mayonnaise Dressing, Southwestern, '99 245
Mint Dressing, '80 183
Mint Dressing, Fresh, '84 126
Miso-Ginger Dressing, Creamy, '02 144
Mix, Salad Dressing, '99 245
Mustard Dressing, '80 112
Mustard Dressing, Herbed, '00 145
Mustard Dressing, Tangy, '93 323
Olive Oil Dressing, '84 266
Olive Oil, Flavored, '89 193
Orange Blossom Dressing, '82 266
Orange-Coconut Dressing, '80 158
Orange Cream, '90 126
Orange-Curd Dressing, '93 22
Orange Dressing, '81 141
Orange-Poppy Seed Dressing, '87 187
Oregano Dressing, '86 141
Oriental Dressing, '91 277
Oriental Salad Dressing, '96 93
Papaya Seed Dressing, '95 204
Paprika Dressing, '86 191
Pasta Salad Dressing, '86 121; '01 164
Pasta Salad Dressing, Herbed, '96 106
Peach Dressing, '90 180
Peanut Butter Salad Dressing, '03 195
Peanut-Ginger Dressing, '95 177
Pear Dressing, '83 146
Pepper Dressing, '80 174
Peppery Salad Dressing, '79 69
Pesto Salad Dressing, '86 150
Pineapple Cream Dressing, '83 81
Pineapple-Poppy Seed Dressing, '85 55
Pineapple Salad Dressing, '81 36
Pomegranate Salad Dressing, '96 241
Poppy Seed Dressing, '80 152; '81 63, 252;
'83 153, 316; '84 16; '86 123, 305; '88 78;
'91 169; '92 191; '93 65, 168; '96 240; '01 56
Poppy Seed Dressing, Blender, '79 176
Poppy Seed Dressing, Tart, '03 241
Purple Parrot Sensation Dressing, '04 289
Raspberry Dressing, '87 153; '95 202
Raspberry Salad Dressing, '94 158; '03 M28
Red Wine Dressing, '98 246
Rémoulade Dressing, '86 123
Rémoulade Sauce, '99 164
Roasted Red Bell Pepper Dressing, '03 28
Roasted Red Pepper-Dill Dressing, '02 144
Rosemary Dressing, '81 131
Rum Dressing, '80 139
Russian Dressing, '80 4
Russian Sour Cream Dressing, '79 55
Russian-Style Dressing, '83 181
Russian-Style Salad Dressing, '86 305
Salad Dressing, '90 161; '04 317
Sesame Dressing, '96 137
Sesame Seed Dressing, '87 81
Sesame-Soy Dressing, '93 106
Slaw Dressing, Sweet, '98 184
Sour Cream Dressing, '82 165; '86 331
Sour Cream-Horseradish Dressing, '00 17
Sour Cream Sauce, '87 233; '02 169
Southwestern Dressing, Spicy, '94 136
Southwestern Salad Dressing, Creamy, '94 278

Soy Dressing, '86 191
Soy-Ginger Salad Dressing, '96 123
Soy-Sesame Dressing, '87 153
Spicy Dressing, '80 55
Spinach Salad Dressing, '83 181; '93 250
Stay Trim Dressing, '86 40
Strawberry Dressing, Creamy, '84 161
Sugar-and-Vinegar Dressing, '04 174
Sweet-and-Sour Dressing, '80 247; '84 70, 161;
'85 163; '87 305; '89 62; '91 126; '94 281;
'03 28
Sweet-and-Sour Dressing, Citrus Salad with,
'01 104
Sweet-Sour Dressing, '80 246
Tangy Dressing, '83 9
Tangy Red Dressing, '86 191
Tangy Salad Dressing, '80 146; '84 115
Tarragon Dressing, '90 55
Thousand Island Dressing, '80 74; '81 104; '83 135;
'86 123
Thousand Island Dressing, Special, '82 79
Tomato Dressing, Fresh, '00 182
Tomato Dressing, Spicy, '03 143
Tomato Salad Dressing, Fresh, '83 193
Tossed Salad Dressing, '84 115
Touchdown Salad Dressing, '81 197
Vanilla Oil, '94 243
Vinaigrette
Apple Cider Vinaigrette, '98 284; '01 306
Apricot Vinaigrette, '02 120
Asian Vinaigrette, '97 146; '98 142; '00 105
Balsamic Vinaigrette, '99 230; '00 81; '01 20;
'03 178
Balsamic Vinaigrette, Tangy, '03 101
Basic Vinaigrette, '94 249
Basil-Red Wine Vinaigrette, '96 65
Basil Vinaigrette, '93 106; '97 146; '02 275
Basil Vinaigrette, Fresh, '04 51
Beet Vinaigrette, '97 229
Blackberry-Basil Vinaigrette, '04 97
Black Pepper-Pineapple Vinaigrette, '97 181
Black Pepper Vinaigrette, '98 284
Blueberry Vinaigrette, '00 154
Blue Cheese Vinaigrette, '89 45; '90 55, 280
Caper Vinaigrette, '91 310
Cider Vinaigrette, '99 322
Cilantro-Lime Vinaigrette, '94 77
Cilantro Vinaigrette, '97 126
Citrus Dressing, Hot, '00 108
Cranberry Vinaigrette, '98 321
Creamy Vinaigrette, '98 130
Croutons, Vinaigrette Dressing and, '86 M288
Curry Vinaigrette, Warm, '93 107
Dijon Vinaigrette, '95 301; '00 222; '02 18;
'03 237
Garlic-Blue Cheese Vinaigrette, '92 57
Garlic-Chive Vinaigrette, '91 44
Garlic Dressing, '79 269; '80 14
Garlic-Ginger Vinaigrette Dressing, '92 195
Garlic Vinaigrette, '95 65; '03 142
Ginger-Curry Vinaigrette, '97 146
Greens and Vinaigrette, '98 168
Greens, Vinaigrette with, '98 184
Herbed Vinaigrette, '93 120
Herb-Mustard Vinaigrette, '02 84
Herb Vinaigrette, Fresh, '99 183
Honey-Dijon Vinaigrette, '04 321
Honey-Mustard Vinaigrette, '94 249
Honey-Orange Vinaigrette, '91 255
Hot Chile Vinaigrette, '98 200
Italian Vinaigrette, Red, '97 46
Lemon-Basil Vinaigrette, '94 205
Lemon-Dill Vinaigrette, '99 27
Lemon-Honey Vinaigrette, '96 65

SALAD DRESSINGS, Vinaigrette
(continued)

Lemon Vinaigrette, '95 31; '04 169
Lemon Vinaigrette, Fresh, '04 30
Lemon Vinaigrette, Peppery, '01 122
Lime Vinaigrette, Spicy, '01 217
Maple-Walnut Vinaigrette, '04 45
Marinara Vinaigrette, '94 64
Mint Vinaigrette, '02 65
Mustard Vinaigrette, '96 184; '01 102
Orange-Raspberry Vinaigrette, '95 144; '96 155;
    '01 178
Orange Vinaigrette, '96 65; '97 229; '98 288
Orange Vinaigrette Dressing, Tangy, '92 341;
    '93 46
Oregano Vinaigrette, '00 331
Oregano-Vinaigrette Dressing, '79 113
Papaya Vinaigrette Dressing, '95 206
Parsley Dressing, Sweet, '02 120
Peach Vinaigrette, Roasted Vegetable Salad with
    Dried, '97 265
Pecan Vinaigrette, '00 162
Pimiento Vinaigrette, '00 167
Pistachio-Lime Vinaigrette, '97 148
Poppy Seed Vinaigrette, '94 249
Raspberry Vinaigrette, '94 249; '96 275; '97 146;
    '98 184; '04 50
Red Wine Vinaigrette, '94 327
Roasted Bell Pepper Vinaigrette, '99 70
Roasted Garlic Vinaigrette, '97 47
Roasted Pepper Vinaigrette, '00 134
Rose Vinaigrette, '01 121
Sesame Dressing, Asian, '02 196
Sesame-Soy Vinaigrette, '97 180; '01 195
Soy Vinaigrette, '97 18
Sweet-and-Sour Balsamic Vinaigrette, '97 146
Sweet-and-Sour Dressing, '02 24
Sweet-Hot Vinaigrette, '04 105
Tarragon Vinaigrette, '94 201
Tomato-Basil Vinaigrette, '99 288
Tomato Vinaigrette, Dried, '93 272
Vanilla Vinaigrette, '94 242
Versatile Vinaigrette, '93 140
Vidalia Onion-Balsamic Vinaigrette, '04 317
Vidalia Onion Vinaigrette, '99 168
Vinaigrette, '94 179; '95 61; '99 107; '01 329
Vinaigrette Dressing, '79 171; '87 138;
    '89 12, 220, 256; '90 173; '92 303; '93 41;
    '95 231; '97 250
Vinaigrette Salad Dressing, '02 25
White Wine Vinaigrette, '89 46
Wine Vinegar Dressing, '92 91; '93 126
Walnut Dressing, '99 125
Whipped Cream Salad Dressing, '82 145
Wine Dressing, Creamy, '85 20
Yogurt
Coconut Dressing, '87 251
Creamy Dressing, '93 318
Cucumber-Mint Dressing, '87 153
Dill Dressing, '88 182
Garden Dressing, Spring, '85 157
Ginger-Yogurt Dressing, '81 302
Herb Dressing, Yogurt-, '92 96
Honey-Lime Dressing, '93 71
Honey-Mustard Dressing, '90 111
Honey Poppy Seed Dressing, Yogurt-, '83 177
Honey-Yogurt Dressing, '93 172
Horseradish Dressing, '87 152; '91 32
Lemon-Yogurt Dressing, '93 17
Lemon-Yogurt Slaw or Salad Dressing, '88 54
Orange-Yogurt Dressing, '85 304
Strawberry Dressing, Creamy, '84 161

Sweet-Hot Yogurt Dressing, '86 40
Tangy Yogurt, '02 258
Yogurt Dressing, '85 59, 215; '88 27
Yogurt Salad Dressing, '79 69
Zesty Salad Dressing, '92 60
SALADS. *See also* **AMBROSIA, ASPIC, SLAWS.**
Acini di Pepe Salad, '83 163
Alfalfa-Celery Salad, Overnight, '82 97
Almond-Citrus Salad, '01 42
Antipasto, Easy, '85 114
Antipasto, Pasta, '85 286
Antipasto Salad, '84 66; '89 145
Antipasto, Salad, '96 161
Antipasto Salad, Layered, '92 220
Apple. *See also* **SALADS/Congealed, Waldorf.**
Apple Salad, '87 233; '00 176
Avocado-Apple Salad with Maple-Walnut
    Vinaigrette, '04 45
Beet Salad, Apple-, '91 237
Blue Cheese Dressing, Apple Salad with, '87 103
Blue Cheese-Pear-Apple Salad, '81 224
Bran Salad, Lemony Apple-, '86 223
Carrot Salad, Apple-, '85 22
Cheesy Apple Salad, '86 301
Chicken-Apple Salad, '90 216
Cranberry-Apple Salad, '02 255
Crunchy Apple Salad, '80 138
Double Apple Salad, '84 227
English Pea-and-Apple Salad, '87 24
Fennel-and-Apple Salad, '00 321
Fresh Apple Salad, '81 207
Frozen Apple-Cream Salad, '82 80
Grapefruit-Apple Salad, '89 41
Nut Salad, Apple-, '80 226
Peanut-Apple Salad, '80 5
Raisin Salad, Curried Apple-, '80 24
Rudolph's Apple Salad, '02 277
Sesame-Apple Toss, '88 21
Snow Salad, Apple, '81 224
Spicy Apple Salad, '85 215
Spinach Salad, Apple-, '99 222; '02 230
Stuffed Apple Ring Salad, '91 198
Stuffed Apple Salad, '92 266
Summer Apple Salad, '80 149
Swiss-Apple Salad, '84 81
Thai Green Apple Salad, '99 111
Turkey-Apple Salad, '88 123; '90 181
Wedges with Poppyseed Dressing, Apple, '86 131
Zucchini Salad, Apple-and-, '97 216
Apricot Salad, Frosted, '80 248
Artichoke-Goat Cheese Salad, '98 118
Artichoke-Pasta Salad, '94 180
Artichoke-Rice Salad, '80 178; '81 41; '85 81;
    '01 144
Artichoke Salad, '86 333
Artichoke Salad, Marinated, '83 241; '95 66
Artichokes Vinaigrette, '88 101
Artichokes with Orzo Salad, '88 M193
Artichoke-Tomato Salad, '82 239
Asian Salad Gift, '96 327
Asparagus
Artichoke Salad, Asparagus-, '85 162
Asparagus Salad, '94 67
Avocado-Asparagus Salad, '00 331
Chicken Salad, Asparagus-, '89 83
Chicken Salad with Asparagus, Curried, '81 36
Crab-and-Asparagus Salad, '92 141
Cups, Asparagus Salad, '83 47
Easy Asparagus Salad, '88 131
Egg Salad, Asparagus-and-, '86 305
Fresh Asparagus Salad, '01 159
Ginger Asparagus, Chilled, '02 64
Grilled Asparagus Salad with Orange Vinaigrette,
    '01 110

Grilled Mushroom-Asparagus Salad, '02 122
Horseradish Salad, Asparagus-, '87 80
Marinated Asparagus, '83 46; '86 92
Marinated Asparagus Medley, '91 105
Marinated Asparagus Salad, '79 20
Papaya Salsa, Asparagus Salad with, '97 144
Peas-and-Asparagus Salad, '83 141
Roasted-Beet, and Goat Cheese Salad, Asparagus,
    '02 96
Roasted Beet, and Goat Cheese Salad, Asparagus,
    '03 98
Tarragon Marinade, Asparagus with, '83 47
Tomatoes with Herb Vinaigrette, Asparagus and,
    '99 56
Vinaigrette, Asparagus, '80 77; '90 138
Vinaigrette, Asparagus Salad, '88 56
Vinaigrette, Light Asparagus, '82 50
Yogurt Dressing, Asparagus with, '79 66
Australian Outback Salad, '92 45
Avocado Acapulco, '83 2
Avocado and Zucchini Salad, Creamy, '79 208
Avocado-Apple Salad with Maple-Walnut
    Vinaigrette, '04 45
Avocado-Bread Salad, '02 210
Avocado Citrus Salad, '01 133
Avocado-Corn-Poblano Salad, '01 320
Avocado Garbanzo Salad, '81 33
Avocado-Grapefruit Salad, '85 26; '93 282
Avocado-Melon Salad, '82 164
Avocado-Orange Salad, '91 44
Avocado Salad, '81 195; '82 9; '83 69; '92 246;
    '97 250; '02 99
Avocado Salad, Citrus-, '82 265
Avocado Salad, Spanish, '87 41
Avocados, Salmon-Stuffed, '86 74
Avocados, Shrimp-Filled, '83 2
Avocado with Crabmeat, '86 119
Baby Blue Salad, '00 81; '01 20; '03 178
Bacon-Lettuce-Mozzarella-and-Tomato Salad,
    '98 209
Bacon-Mandarin Salad, '02 87
Banana Salad, '87 80
Banana Salad, Frozen, '82 80, 132
Bananas, Nutty, '79 251
Barley-Broccoli Salad, '90 135
Barley Salad, '92 212
Bean
Black Bean-and-Barley Salad, '94 174
Black Bean and Black-Eyed Pea Salad, '03 54
Black Bean-and-Cheese Salad, '92 217
Black Bean-and-Rice Salad, '00 327
Black Bean Salad, '89 217; '97 196; '98 208;
    '01 198
Chicken-Black Bean Salad, '99 124
Chickpea Salad, '01 55
Chilled Bean Salad, '80 178
Confetti Bean Salad, '01 198
Cucumber-Bean Salad, '83 81
Fennel-Salad, Bean-and-, '01 198
Five-Bean Salad, Hot, '81 149
Four-Bean Salad, '79 20; '84 82
Full o' Beans Salad, '81 38
Garbanzo Salad, '82 2
Garbanzo Salad, Avocado-, '81 33
Garbanzo Salad, Couscous-and-, '02 65
Green Bean-and-Okra Salad with Feta, Marinated,
    '00 131
Green Bean-and-Tomato Salad, '86 180
Green Bean-Peanut Salad, '86 117
Green Bean-Potato Salad, '83 80; '01 181
Green Bean-Red Potato Salad, '96 175
Green Bean Salad, '87 90
Green Bean Salad, Cold, '84 106
Green Bean Salad, Crispy, '82 239

Green Bean Salad, German, **'92** 169
Green Bean Salad, Hot, **'86** 298; **'87** 176
Green Bean Salad in Tomatoes, **'01** 181
Green Bean Salad, Lettuce and, **'80** 79
Green Bean Salad, Molded, **'85** 252
Green Bean Salad, Paprika-, **'86** 191
Green Bean Salad, Pickled, **'82** 239
Green Bean Salad, Roasted Red Pepper-and-, **'99** 322
Green Bean Salad, Speedy, **'84** 283
Green Bean Salad, Tomato-and-, **'97** 162
Green Bean Salad with Feta, **'04** 169
Green Beans-and-Cheese Salad, **'91** 159
Green Beans, Dill-Icious, **'98** 53
Green Beans, Marinated, **'83** 145
Green Beans Vinaigrette, **'83** 25
Green Beans Vinaigrette, Kentucky Wonder, **'94** 158
Green Bean, Walnut, and Feta Salad, **'96** 273; **'00** 321
Hacienda Salad, **'81** 67
Hominy-Bean Salad, **'88** 266
Hot German-Style Bean Salad, **'91** 314
Kidney Bean Salad, Wild Rice-and-, **'01** 175
Kidney Bean-Salami Pasta Toss, **'85** 165
Layered Southwestern Salad, **'01** 97
Lima Beans, Chilly, **'81** 206
Lima Bean-Tomato Salad, **'85** 137
Lima Salad), You Lima My Life (Paprika, **'96** 159
Marinated Bean-and-Rice Salad, **'87** 152
Marinated Bean-Pasta Salad, **'94** 167; **'97** 328
Marinated Bean Salad, **'85** 137, 296; **'89** 314; **'93** 312; **'94** 167; **'98** 331
Marinated Bean Salad, Crunchy, **'84** 197
Marinated Corn-Bean Salad, **'87** 9
Mexican Salad, **'81** 113; **'94** 202
Mexican-Style Salad, **'83** 240
Mexican Tossed Salad, **'81** 280
Mixed Bean Salad, **'83** 217
Niçoise, Salad, **'86** 35
Overnight Fiesta Salad, **'83** 80
Pasta-Bean Salad, **'86** 169
Pinto Salad, **'86** 169
Pole Bean-Potato Salad, Hot, **'79** 74
Pork-'n'-Bean Salad, **'87** 83
Potato-Bean Salad, **'82** 301
Quick Bean Salad, **'89** 128
Rice-and-Bean Salad, **'85** 22
Rice-and-Bean Salad, Zesty, **'02** 84
Rice Salad, Beans-and-, **'91** 44
Sandwiches, Bean Salad, **'81** 243
Saucy Bean Salad, **'84** 18
Sausage Salad, Bean-and-, **'91** 313
Six-Bean Salad, Colorful, **'87** 82
Southwest Salad, **'81** 113; **'03** 280
Spicy Bean Salad, **'96** 46
Sprout Salad, Bean, **'82** 113
Supreme Bean Salad, **'91** 202
Sweet-and-Hot Bean-and-Veggie Salad, **'04** 184
Sweet-and-Sour Bean Salad, **'85** 198; **'86** 147
Sweet Bean Salad, **'01** 46
Tabbouleh Salad, Southwestern, **'01** 216
White Bean-and-Tuna Salad, **'01** 35
White Bean-and-Tuna Salad Sandwiches, **'02** 31
White Bean Salad, Tuna-and-, **'98** 209
White Beans, Caesar Salad with, **'93** 30
White Bean-Tuna Salad, **'98** 208
Beet-and-Sugared Walnut Salad with Orange Vinaigrette, Roasted, **'97** 229
Beet, Apple, and Walnut Salad, **'98** 269
Beet Salad, Fresh, **'02** 236
Beet Salad, Marinated, **'83** 216
Beets and Cauliflower, Chilled, **'80** 137
Berry Grapefruit Cup, **'79** 242

Black Cherry Salad, Frozen, **'89** 163
Blue Cheese-Pear-Apple Salad, **'81** 224
Blue Cheese Salad, **'88** 48
Blue Cheese Salad with Spicy Pecans, **'02** 300
Bluegrass Salad, **'02** 255
Boats, Salad, **'80** 93
Bok Choy Salad, **'01** 129
Bread Salad, Italian, **'03** 54
Bread Salad, Italian BLT, **'03** 90
Broccoli. *See also* **SALADS/Cauliflower.**
  Broccoli Salad, **'82** 24; **'85** 249; **'90** 292; **'95** 95; **'99** 84; **'00** 213; **'01** 58
  Carrot-Broccoli Salad, **'99** 26
  Cauliflower, and Carrot Salad, Broccoli, **'04** 140
  Cauliflower Pasta Salad, Broccoli-, **'88** 269
  Cauliflower Salad, Broccoli-, **'92** 97; **'00** 90
  Cauliflower Salad, Broccoli and, **'81** 280
  Cauliflower Salad, Broccoli 'n', **'90** 32
  Cauliflower Salad, Creamy Broccoli and, **'81** 23
  Cauliflower Toss, Crunchy Broccoli and, **'83** 25
  Cheese-Pasta Salad, Broccoli-, **'96** 184
  Chilled Broccoli with Lemon Dressing, **'88** 270
  Corn Salad, Broccoli-, **'87** 24
  Creamy Broccoli Salad, **'79** 143
  Crunchy Broccoli Salad, **'83** 39
  Curried Broccoli Salad, **'86** 225
  Fresh Broccoli Salad, **'82** 34; **'87** 103
  Grape Salad, Broccoli-, **'01** 163
  Mandarin Salad, Broccoli-, **'93** 325
  Marinated Broccoli, **'81** 40
  Marinated Broccoli Salad, **'83** 240
  Medley, Broccoli, **'81** 206
  Orange Salad, Broccoli-, **'94** 281
  Peanut Salad, Broccoli-, **'92** 35
  Raisin Salad, Classic Broccoli-, **'02** 24
  Raisin Salad, Creamy Broccoli-, **'92** 106
  Ramen Noodle Salad, **'02** 24
  Red Pepper Salad, Broccoli and, **'83** 224
  Supreme, Broccoli Salad, **'83** 260
  Warm Broccoli Salad, **'92** 35
Brussels Sprouts Salad, **'87** 233
Cabbage and Fruit Salad, **'79** 286
Cabbage Salad, **'87** 120, 233
Cabbage Salad, Austrian Hash with, **'95** 262
Cabbage Salad, Chinese, **'81** 271
Cabbage Salad, Garden, **'81** 210
Cabbage Salad, Nutty, **'87** 42
Cabbage Salad, Overnight, **'79** 83
Cabbage Salad, Tangy, **'82** 55
Cabbage Salad, Wilted, **'94** 281
Cabbage Salad, Winter, **'98** 284
Cabbage, Sweet-Sour Red, **'79** 5
Caesar
  Caesar Salad, **'80** 112; **'86** 80; **'92** 71; **'99** 265; **'00** 19; **'02** 269
  Chicken Caesar Salad, **'96** 26
  Chipotle Caesar Salad, **'04** 119
  Easy Caesar Salad, **'87** 116
  Flippo Caesar Salad, **'87** 61
  Gift, Caesar Salad, **'96** 326
  Greek Caesar Salad, **'96** 64
  Margarita Salad, Caesar, **'94** 107
  Maui Caesar Salad, **'94** 107
  Mock Caesar Salad, **'92** 283
  Oriental Caesar Salad, **'94** 107
  Romaine Caesar Salad, Baby, **'97** 128
  Southern Caesar Salad, **'94** 106
  Turkey Caesar Salad, **'93** 320
  White Beans, Caesar Salad with, **'93** 30
Cantaloupe-Cheese Salad, **'88** 184
Cantaloupe Colada Salad, **'97** 148
Cantaloupe Cooler Salad, **'79** 176
Cantaloupe-Pecan Salad, **'86** 178
Cantaloupe Salad, **'86** 182

Cantaloupe-Spinach Salad with Pistachio-Lime Vinaigrette, **'97** 148
Caponata, Sicilian-Style, **'01** 124
Carrot
  Apple-Carrot Salad, **'85** 22
  Broccoli Salad, Carrot-, **'99** 26
  Caraway Salad, Carrot-, **'89** 105
  Dill Salad, Carrot-and-, **'02** 129; **'03** 99
  Favorite Carrot Salad, **'80** 33
  Fruit Toss, Carrot-, **'82** 235
  Harvest Carrot Salad, **'89** 128
  Honey-Sweet Carrot Salad, **'89** 161
  Marinated Carrots, Creamy, **'87** 200
  Orange-Carrot Salad, **'80** 89; **'84** 325
  Raisin Salad, Carrot-, **'83** 117; **'84** 174; **'87** 10
  Raisin Salad with Orange-Nutmeg Dressing, Carrot-, **'97** 305; **'98** 19
  Ring, Festive Carrot, **'82** 16
  Seed Salad, Fruity Carrot-and-, **'86** 223
  Shredded Carrot Salad, **'80** 178
  Simple Carrot Salad, **'82** 101; **'84** 152
  Sunshine Carrot Salad, **'82** 132
  Sweet-and-Sour Carrot Salad, **'98** 211
  Tangerine Salad, Carrot-, **'83** 316; **'84** 16
  Turkey-Carrot Salad, **'86** 283
  Turnip-and-Carrot Salad, **'91** 212
  Zucchini Salad, Carrot-and-, **'83** 240
Cauliflower. *See also* **SALADS/Broccoli.**
  Beets and Cauliflower, Chilled, **'80** 137
  Broccoli, Cauliflower, and Carrot Salad, **'04** 140
  Broccoli-Cauliflower Salad, **'00** 90
  Broccoli Crunch, Cauliflower-, **'88** 216
  Broccoli Salad, Cauliflower-, **'79** 20
  Broccoli Toss, Cauliflower-, **'82** 54
  Broccoli Toss, Italian Cauliflower-, **'88** 269
  Brussels Sprouts Salad, Cauliflower-, **'83** 240
  Cauliflower Salad, **'79** 221; **'80** 83; **'81** 225; **'84** 291; **'85** 240, 279; **'92** 36
  Celery-and-Cauliflower Salad, **'83** 39
  Corned Beef-Cauliflower Salad, **'83** 16
  Creamy Cauliflower Salad, **'82** 102; **'04** 36
  Crunchy Cauliflower Salad, **'80** 4; **'82** 75
  English Pea Salad, Cauliflower-, **'95** 66
  Layered Cauliflower Salad, **'83** 240
  Marinated Cauliflower Salad, **'82** 303; **'84** 232
  Olive Toss, Cauliflower-, **'85** 198; **'86** 147
  Orange-Cauliflower Salad, **'82** 266
  Parmesan and Bacon, Cauliflower with, **'96** 137
  Pea Salad, Cauliflower-, **'87** 231
  Pea Salad, Savory Cauliflower and, **'81** 280
  Sweet-and-Sour Cauliflower Salad, **'81** 2
  Vegetable Salad, Cauliflower-, **'85** 158
Celery Salad, **'79** 70
Cheese Salad, Warm, **'97** 246
Cheesy Italian Salad, **'84** 33
Chef's
  Bowl, Chef's Salad, **'84** 66
  Chef's Salad, **'86** 186; **'98** 209
  Combination Chef's Salad, **'86** 47
  Fruited Chef Salad, **'85** 222
  Fruit Salad, Chef's, **'86** 35
  Garden Salad, Chef's, **'83** 146
  Mexican Chef Salad, **'85** 84; **'92** 64
  Microwave Chef Salad, **'90** M146
  Vinaigrette Chef's Salad, **'81** 9
  Zucchini Chef's Salad, **'83** 143
Cherry-Orange Salad, **'79** 74; **'82** 56
Cherry Salad, Delicious Frozen, **'81** 252
Cherry Salad, Fresh, **'83** 120
Cherry Salad, Frozen, **'79** 126
Cherry Salad with Honey-Lime Dressing, **'83** 139
Cherry Salad with Sherry Dressing, **'79** 165

SALADS
(continued)

Chicken. *See also* **SALADS/Congealed.**
Almond-Chicken Salad Shanghai, '90 160
Almond Salad, Chicken-, '81 133
Aloha Chicken Salad, '80 297
Amandine, Chicken Salad, '81 37
Ambrosia, Chicken Salad, '85 216
Apple Salad, Chicken-, '90 216
Apricot-Chicken Salad, '99 163
Apricot Salsa, Chicken with, '98 126
Artichoke-Chicken-Rice Salad, '94 132
Artichoke-Chicken-Rice Salad, Mediterranean, '97 321
Artichokes, Chicken Salad with, '86 186
Asian Chicken Salad, '99 124
Asparagus-Chicken Salad, '89 83
Aspic-Topped Chicken Salad, '88 88
Autumn Chicken Salad, '01 312
Avocado-Chicken Salad, '87 107
Avocado Salad, Chicken-, '80 139
Avocado Salad, Fruited Chicken, '82 101
Avocado Salad Platter, Chicken-, '83 2
Avocado Salad, Tossed Chicken-, '80 4
Avocados, Chicken Salad in, '85 216
Baked Chicken Salad, '86 297; '87 176
Barbecue Chicken Salad, Warm, '99 124
Basil-Chicken-Vegetable Salad, '92 162
Black-and-Blue Salad, '00 337
Black Bean Salad, Chicken-, '99 124
Black-Eyed Pea Salad, Chicken-and-, '97 305
BLT Chicken Salad, '87 144
Blueberry Salad, Chicken-, '02 177
Blue Cheese Chicken Salad, '94 81
Blue Cheese, Chicken Salad with, '97 97
Bow Tie Pasta, Chicken-and-, '01 164
Broccoli-Chicken Salad, '90 129; '00 53
Buffalo Tenders Salad, '03 184
Caesar Salad, Chicken, '96 26
Celery Salad, Chicken-, '81 187
Chicken Salad, '86 232, 261; '96 67
Chop Suey Salad, '81 37
Chutney-Chicken Salad, '87 74
Chutney Salad, Chicken, '82 108
Cobb Salad, Southern-Style, '01 112
Coconut-Chicken Salad, Curried Poached Pears with, '97 93
Coleslaw, Chicken, '84 2
Cream Puff Bowl, Chicken Salad in, '86 232
Crisp Salad, Crunchy, '95 28
Crunchy Chicken Salad, '86 157, 207
Curried Chicken-and-Orange Salad, '87 144
Curried Chicken-Rice Salad, '92 190
Curried Chicken Salad, '79 219; '84 66; '85 96; '86 131; '89 176
Curried Chicken Salad on Raisin Bread, '85 96
Curried Chicken Salad, Royal, '96 200
Curried Chicken Salad with Asparagus, '81 36
Dilled Chicken Salad, '91 212
Fancy Chicken Salad, '79 55
Filling, Chicken Salad, '87 106
Fried Chicken Ginger Salad, '93 290
Fried Chicken Salad, Fiesta, '03 120
Fruit, Chicken Salad with, '82 171
Fruit-Chicken Salad with Blueberry Vinaigrette, Summer, '00 154
Fruited Chicken Salad, '84 25, 290; '88 88; '90 318
Fruited Chicken Salad in Avocados, '87 41
Fruit Salad, Chicken-, '82 79; '90 234
Fruit Salad, Chicken-and-, '01 178
Fruity Chicken Salad, '83 157

Gazpacho-Chicken Salad, '00 203
Grapes, Chicken Salad with, '86 117
Greek Chicken Salad, '97 92; '98 329
Green Salad with Chicken, Mixed, '80 54
Grilled Asian Chicken Salad, '96 158
Grilled Chicken-and-Fruit Salad, '96 155
Grilled Chicken on Greens, '99 201
Grilled Chicken-Rice Salad, '98 148
Grilled Chicken Salad, Moroccan, '95 231
Grilled Chicken Salad with Mango Chutney, '96 182
Hoisin Chicken-and-Pasta Salad, '99 125
Honey Chicken Salad, '04 51
Horseradish Salad, Chicken-, '02 235
Hot Chicken Salad, '81 201; '83 196; '98 290
Hot Chicken Salad, Country Club-Style, '86 10
Hot Chicken Salad, Crunchy, '80 138
Hot Chicken Salad Pinwheel, '80 139
Italian, Chicken Salad, '89 18
Layered Chicken Salad, '89 162
Lemon-Chicken Salad, Lively, '00 16
Macadamia Chicken Salad, '80 138
Macaroni-Chicken Salad, '85 296; '86 302
Macaroni-Chicken Salad, Dilled, '92 142
Mama Hudson's Chicken Salad, '93 238
Mandarin Chicken, Carousel, '79 88
Mango, Chicken Salad with, '86 215
Marinated Chicken-Grape Salad, '85 74
Marinated Chicken-Raspberry Salad, '93 190
Marinated Chicken Strips and Vegetables, '00 54
Melts, Open-Faced Cheesy Chicken Salad, '00 134
Mexican Chicken Salad, '85 84; '88 272
Mexican Chicken Tortilla Salads, '95 129
Minted Chicken Salad, '92 104
Nectarine Chicken Salad, '79 175
Noodle Chicken Salad, '03 143
Noodle Salad, Chicken, '95 25
Old-Fashioned Chicken Salad, '83 79
Oriental Chicken Salad, '85 216; '88 271; '91 43; '96 92
Oriental, Chicken Salad, '90 146
Overnight Salad, '97 305; '98 18
Parmesan-Chicken Salad, '98 234
Pasta-Chicken Salad, Tarragon, '87 155
Pasta Salad, Chicken, '88 89
Pasta Salad, Grilled Chicken-, '94 64
Pasta Salad, Zesty Chicken-, '02 186
Peachy Chicken Salad, '97 193
Peanut-Chicken Salad, Sweet, '03 54
Pea Salad, Chicken-, '83 218
Persian Chicken Salad, '81 12
Pineapple-Chicken Salad Pie, '80 138
Pineapple-Nut Chicken Salad, '83 80
Pocket, Chicken Salad in a, '84 139
Polynesian Chicken Salad, '88 272
Poulet Rémoulade, '87 144
Rice Salad, Chicken-, '81 203; '97 93
Rice Salad, Chicken-and-, '97 92
Rice Salad, Curried Chicken-, '92 190
Rice Salad, Grilled Chicken-, '98 148
Rice Salad, Hot Chicken-and-, '83 22
Rice Salad, Nutty Chicken-, '83 157
Roasted Chicken Salad, '93 14
Roasted Red Pepper Salad, Chicken and, '03 291
Sandwiches, Asian Chicken Salad, '98 223
Sandwiches, Chicken-Salad Finger, '85 119
Sandwiches, Grilled Chicken Salad, '00 164
Sandwiches, Hot Chicken Salad, '96 74
Sherried Chicken-and-Grape Salad, '01 61
South Sea Island Chicken Salad, '97 88
Southwestern Chicken Salad, '88 88
Southwestern Chicken Salad Spirals, '02 58
Spaghetti Salad, Chicken-, '90 146

Spaghetti Salad, Chicken-and-Veggie, '04 129
Special Chicken Salad, '85 82; '87 183; '88 M193
Spicy Chicken Salad with Cabbage Wraps, '04 62
Spicy Chicken Salad with Veggies, '04 177
Spinach-Strawberry Salad, Chicken-, '97 92
Spinach Tossed Salad, Chicken-and-, '83 157
Spread, Chicken Salad Party, '88 M8
Spread, Curried Chicken Salad, '00 68
Stack-Up Salad, Chicken, '83 80
Strawberry-Chicken Salad, '04 50
Summer Chicken Salad, '83 145
Summery Chicken Salad, '95 138
Super Chicken Salad, '82 174
Supreme, Chicken Salad, '79 107, 152; '89 176
Taco Chicken Salad, Ranch, '97 315
Taco Salad, Chicken, '94 M136
Tahitian Chicken Salad, '84 120
Tarragon Chicken Salad, '90 199
Tarts, Chicken Salad, '84 257
Thai Chicken Salad, '95 177
Thai Lettuce Folds, '94 47
Tortellini Salad, Chicken, '87 288
Tortilla Salads, Mexican Chicken, '95 129
Tropical Chicken Boats for Two, '82 186
Tropical Chicken Salad, '85 216; '96 127
Twist, Chicken Salad with a, '84 221
Vegetable-Chicken Salad, '91 287
Vegetable Patch Chicken Salad, '04 92
Walnut-Chicken Salad, '89 14; '96 243
Walnut Salad, Sunburst Chicken-and-, '93 91
Wild Rice-and-Chicken Salad, '02 52
Wild Rice-Chicken Salad, '83 146; '99 55; '01 72
Wraps, Lemon-Basil Chicken Salad, '00 216
Citrus and Greens, Holiday, '03 280
Citrus-Blue Cheese Salad, '92 220
Citrus Salad, '87 103
Citrus Salad Bowl, '86 335; '87 83
Citrus Salad in Orange Cups, '85 47
Citrus Salad, Southern-Style, '84 262
Citrus Salad, Tangy, '89 34
Citrus Vinaigrette Salad, '86 192
Congealed
Apple-Apricot Salad, '88 121
Apple Cider Salad, '83 123
Apple Cider Salad Mold, '85 54
Apple Crunch Salad, '84 232; '86 331
Apple Salad, Congealed, '85 252
Apple Salad, Triple, '88 122
Apricot Congealed Salad, '02 256
Apricot Fruit Salad, '82 132
Apricot Nectar Salad, '83 218; '87 236
Apricot Salad, '81 251; '83 123
Apricot Salad, Creamy, '85 263
Asheville Salad, '86 199
Asparagus-Cucumber Mold, '85 252
Asparagus Mold, '80 104
Asparagus Mousse Salad, '86 252
Asparagus Salad, '88 121
Asparagus Salad, Congealed, '83 260
Asparagus Salad, Creamy Lemon-, '93 116
Asparagus Salad, Tart, '81 203
Avocado Crunch Salad, Congealed, '85 26
Avocado Salad, Congealed, '84 266
Avocado Salads, Congealed, '87 42
Beet-Nut Salad, '79 74
Beet Salad Mold, '82 267
Beet Salad, Pickled, '83 234
Beet Salad, Tangy, '86 199
Berry Salad, Layered, '79 173
Bing Cherry-and-Cranberry Salad, '04 297
Bing Cherry-Grapefruit Salad, '00 285
Bing Cherry Salad, '01 46
Broccoli Salad, Congealed, '84 124
Cantaloupe, Southern Plantation, '82 179

Carrot-Nut Salad, Creamy, '86 331
Carrot-Pineapple Salad, '91 83
Carrot Salad, '82 137
Cauliflower-Lemon Salad, '81 23
Cheese Molds, Snowcap, '79 242
Cherry-Apple Salad, '86 31
Cherry Cola Salad, '80 104
Cherry-Cola Salad, '91 224; '95 94
Cherry Fruit Salad, '87 236
Cherry-Salad, Best, '82 302
Cherry Salad, Congealed, '89 278
Cherry Salad, Festive, '84 265
Cherry Salad, Port Wine-, '86 11
Cherry Salad, Sweet, '89 326
Cherry-Wine Salad, Elegant, '82 56
Chicken-Cucumber Mold, '80 175
Chicken Jewel Ring Salad, '83 282
Chicken-Pea Salad, '83 218
Chicken Salad Mold, '83 80; '84 163
Chicken Salad Ring, '90 123
Chile-Tomato Salad, Spicy, '88 121
Christmas Salad, '88 249
Christmas Snow Salad, '82 266
Citrus Mold, Sparkling, '86 331
Citrus Salad Mold, Golden, '85 303
Corned Beef Salad, '80 104
Corned Beef Salad, Molded, '82 86
Crabmeat-and-Asparagus, Congealed Salad with,
    '84 86
Cranberry-Apple Mold, '89 277
Cranberry Congealed Salad, '91 296; '02 292
Cranberry Congealed Salad Parfaits, Frosted,
    '02 292
Cranberry Gelatin Mold, '92 271
Cranberry Mold, '79 250
Cranberry-Orange Delight, '90 168
Cranberry Ring, '90 291
Cranberry Salad, '99 290
Cranberry Salad, Congealed, '90 124
Cranberry Salad, Festive, '81 264, 296
Cranberry Salad, Frosted, '90 288
Cranberry Salad, Holiday, '82 266, 288; '95 301
Cranberry Salad, Jellied, '83 279; '85 281
Cranberry Salad, Layered, '84 322; '86 325
Cranberry Salad Ring, '80 247
Crème de Menthe Salad, '82 122
Creole Salad, '79 147
Cucumber Mold, Creamy, '84 164
Cucumber Mousse, '88 121
Cucumber-Pineapple Salad, '84 124
Cucumber Salad, Creamy, '86 147; '92 97
Cucumber Salad Mold, '82 111; '83 81, 253
Eggnog Christmas Salad, '86 281
Egg Salad, Deviled, '83 124
Emerald Salad, '81 143
Emerald Salad, Snowy, '87 311
Fall Salad with Ginger Dressing, '82 194
Frosted Salad, Heavenly, '79 286
Fruit, Jeweled Congealed Fresh, '95 89
Fruit Mold, Sherried, '90 124
Fruit Salad, Cherry, '87 236
Fruit Salad, Sparkling, '82 266
Fruit Salad, Spiced Autumn, '87 228
Garden-Patch Salad Molds, '86 283
Garden Salad, Molded, '86 199
Gazpacho Molded Salad, '92 323
Gazpacho Salad Mold, '87 311
Gazpacho Salad, Molded, '79 159
Gazpacho Salad with Avocado Cream, Congealed,
    '92 158
Grape-Cantaloupe Mold, Double, '79 173
Grapefruit Congealed Salad, '83 190
Grapefruit-Orange Salad, '91 276
Grapefruit Salad, '83 124; '84 325; '88 122

Grapefruit Salad, Congealed, '84 325; '85 279
Grape Salad Mold, '83 120
Green Bean Salad, Molded, '85 252
Green Spring Salad, '83 124
Ham Salad, Congealed, '81 36
Holiday Jewel Salad, '81 252
Horseradish Salad, '85 66
Layered Congealed Salad, '81 143
Layered Holiday Salad, '81 252
Layered Salad, Make Ahead, '81 296
Layer Mold, Three-, '82 54
Lemon-Cheese Salad, '85 240
Lemon-Cranberry Congealed Salad, '87 311
Lemon-Cream Salad, '88 250
Lemon-Cucumber Mold, '87 90
Lemon Mold, Cheesy, '79 241
Lemon-Onion Salad, '85 252
Lemon-Tomato Salad, Congealed, '89 178
Lemon-Vegetable Congealed Salad, '85 22
Lime-Carrot Salad, '92 65
Lime-Cheese Salad, Frosted, '79 286
Lime Congealed Salad, '02 257
Lime Sherbet Salad, '80 104
Mandarin Orange Salad, Congealed, '89 327
Mandarin Salad Molds, '85 54
Melon Ball Salad, Congealed, '84 125
Mimosa Salad, '98 310
Mincemeat Salad, '94 282
Mincemeat Salad, Holiday, '85 263
Molds, Perfection, '81 153
Mosaic Salad, '89 313
Orange-Buttermilk Salad, '95 134
Orange-Pear Salad, '84 164
Orange Salad, Creamy, '84 124
Orange Salad, Frosted, '81 154; '83 123
Orange Salad, Jeweled, '83 210
Orange Sherbet Salad, '81 154
Orange Surprise Salad, '79 12
Peach-Cranberry Ring, Spicy, '85 264
Peaches-and-Cream Salad, '83 108
Peach Fluff, '95 176
Peach Frost, '84 164
Peach Party Salad, '84 290
Peach Pinwheel Salad, '79 11
Peach Salad, Pickled, '80 104; '85 264
Peach Salad, Spiced, '94 68
Peachy Berry Cream Mold, '83 130
Pear-Lime Salad, '84 152
Pear Salad, Royal, '84 265
Pickled Peach Salad, '04 269
Pimiento Salad, Sunshine, '84 124
Pineapple-Buttermilk Salad, '82 80
Pineapple-Cucumber Congealed Salad, '83 118
Pineapple Daiquiri Salad, '84 232
Pineapple-Lime Salad, '84 320
Pineapple Mold, Minted, '85 240
Pineapple-Orange Congealed Salad, '83 218
Pineapple-Pear Delight, '82 54
Raspberry Fruit Mounds, '79 35
Raspberry Holiday Mold, '84 253
Raspberry Ribbon Salad, '87 236
Raspberry Salad, '86 286
Raspberry-Wine Salad, '91 256
Rhubarb Congealed Salad, '86 140
Rhubarb Salad, '91 146; '92 129
Rhubarb Salad, Tart, '91 146; '92 129
Ribbon Salad, Christmas, '02 257
Roquefort Salad, Creamy, '79 73
Ruby-and-Emerald Salad, '85 79
Salmon Salad, Chilly, '80 104
Sangría Salad, '86 331
Shrimp Salad, '84 221
Strawberry-Nut Salad, '94 132
Strawberry-Pretzel Salad, '03 290

Strawberry Salad, Hidden Treasure, '79 11
Strawberry-Wine Salad Mold, '83 261
Sunshine Delight, '86 117
Tomato Mold, Tangy, '79 74
Tomato Ring, Tangy, '84 164
Tomato Salad, Frozen, '84 52
Tomato-Vegetable Ring, '81 302
Tuna-Cheese Mold, Creamy, '81 135
Tuna Ring, Creamy, '80 275
Tuna Salad, Congealed, '84 163
Tuna Salad, Creamy, '82 87, 208
Tuna Salad, Luncheon, '81 135
Vegetable Congealed Salad, Cheesy-, '86 199
Vegetable Congealed Salad, Fresh, '91 229
Vegetable Relish Salad, '82 267
Vegetable Salad, Congealed, '79 276
Vegetable Salad, Congealed Fresh, '82 240
Waldorf Salad, Congealed, '82 80
Waldorf Salad, Molded, '84 326
Corn-and-Pea Salad, '90 181
Cornbread Salad, '87 172
Cornbread Salad, Dianne's Southwestern, '04 133
Cornbread Salad, Mexican, '95 210
Corn-in-the-Shuck Salad, '93 236
Corn Salad, '80 247; '81 139; '85 236; '91 27;
    '95 214; '02 234
Corn Salad, Chilled, '79 20
Corn Salad, Colorful, '00 139
Corn Salad, Confetti, '96 168
Corn Salad, Festive, '92 263
Corn Salad, Fresh, '91 126; '94 162
Corn Salad, Marinated, '89 126
Corn Salad, Roasted, '97 196
Corn Salad, Shoepeg, '81 23
Corn Salad, Tangy, '88 176
Corn Salad, Tasty, '84 289
Cottage Cheese-Banana Splits, '87 56
Cottage Cheese Salad, Different, '85 328; '86 22
Cottage Cheese Salad in Tomatoes, '86 208
Cottage Cheese Salad, Out-of-This-World, '79 44
Cottage-Tomato Salad, '85 163
Couscous Salad, Curried, '91 44
Couscous Salad, Mediterranean, '03 127
Couscous Salad with Dried Tomato Vinaigrette,
    '96 244
Couscous Salad with Fennel and Goat Cheese,
    Israeli, '00 312
Cranberry. See also SALADS/Congealed.
    Apple Salad, Cranberry-, '02 255
    Cheese Ribbon Salad, Cranberry-, '79 241
    Christmas Salad, Cranberry, '79 243
    Cloud, Cranberry, '90 287
    Cranberry Salad, '88 250
    Frozen Cranberry-Pineapple Salad, '91 237
    Holiday Salad, Cranberry, '89 277
    Oriental, Cranberry, '79 126
    Spinach-and-Cranberry Salad with Warm
        Chutney Dressing, '02 242
    Strawberry-Jícama Salad, Cranberry-, '02 300
    Tart Cranberry Salad, '79 286
    Whipped Cream Salad, Cranberry-, '83 261
    Wild Rice-and-Cranberry Salad, '99 272
Crunchy-Creamy Salad, '88 100
Cucumber-Almond Salad, '86 147
Cucumber and Tomato Salad, Dilled, '81 153
Cucumber Cooler, Simple, '86 147
Cucumber Mousse, '79 11
Cucumber Mousse with Dill Sauce, '95 216
Cucumber Salad, Cool, '03 165
Cucumber Salad, Creamy, '01 56; '02 258
Cucumber Salad, Dilled, '82 229; '92 72; '93 65
Cucumber Salad, Marinated, '82 111
Cucumber Salad with Roasted Red Bell Pepper
    Dressing, '03 28

SALADS
(continued)

Cucumbers and Artichokes, Marinated, **'82** 111
Cucumbers, Cool, **'84** 152
Cucumbers in Sour Cream, **'79** 52; **'80** 178
Cucumber-Tomato Salad, **'90** 144
Cucumber-Tomato Salad, Marinated, **'02** 167
Cucumber-Vinaigrette Oriental, **'85** 198; **'86** 147
Cucumber-Yogurt Salad, **'87** 33
Cukes and Scallions, **'91** 168
Curried Salad Gift, **'96** 326
Curry Salad, Hot Indian, **'83** 23
Eggplant Salad, **'90** 99
Egg-Rice Salad, **'84** 18; **'86** 169
Egg Salad, Bacon-Horseradish, **'94** 181
Egg Salad Club Sandwiches, **'02** 203
Egg Salad Club, Sweet-Pickle, **'02** 203
Egg Salad, Green Vegetable and, **'79** 191
Egg Salad Sandwiches, **'03** 179
Egg Salad Spread, Cottage-, **'82** 146
Egg Salad Tacos, Mexican, **'94** 181
Egg Salad, Yolkless, **'94** 181
Endive, Bacon, and Pecan Salad, **'89** 12
Endive-Tomato Starburst Salad, **'93** 323
Endive with Arugula Tabbouleh, **'98** 67
Escarole-and-Bacon Salad, **'84** 85
Fennel and Radicchio with Orange Vinaigrette,
    Grilled, **'95** 253
Fennel Salad, Marinated, **'93** 56
Fennel Salad, Tuscan, **'02** 170
Fish. *See also* **SALADS/Seafood.**
  Confetti Salad, **'80** 4
  Crawfish Salad, Dilled, **'83** 126
  Meal-in-One Salad, **'82** 232
  Salmon-and-Egg Salad, Smoked, **'02** 203
  Salmon-and-Macaroni Salad, **'81** 114
  Salmon-and-Wild Rice Salad, Oriental, **'94** 173
  Salmon on Mixed Greens with Creamy Dill
      Dressing, **'93** 143
  Salmon-Pasta Salad, **'87** 9
  Salmon-Rice Salad, **'84** 289
  Salmon Salad, **'89** 99
  Salmon Salad, Broiled, **'92** 108
  Salmon Salad, Chilled Poached, **'96** 68
  Salmon Salad, Crunchy, **'81** 148
  Salmon Salad, Scandinavian, **'98** 208
  Salmon Salad Shells, **'85** 286
  Salmon Salad, Simple, **'91** 23
  Salmon Salad, Summertime, **'82** 207
  Salmon-Spinach Salad, **'87** 145
  Salmon-Stuffed Avocados, **'86** 74
  Swordfish Salad, **'00** 18
  Trout-and-Tomato Salad with Black Pepper
      Vinaigrette, **'98** 284
  Tuna-and-Almond Salad, Crunchy, **'04** 72
  Tuna-and-Cannellini Bean Salad, **'86** 143
  Tuna-and-Red Pepper Salad, **'93** 143
  Tuna-and-White Bean Salad, **'98** 209
  Tuna Chef Salad, **'82** 78
  Tuna-Egg Salad, **'81** 135
  Tuna Macaroni Salad, **'83** 44
  Tuna-Macaroni Salad, **'83** 145; **'84** 66
  Tuna-Mac in Tomatoes, **'87** 188
  Tuna-Pasta Salad, **'91** 43; **'92** 141; **'00** 247
  Tuna Pasta Salad, **'92** 108
  Tuna-Potato Salad, **'84** 289
  Tuna-Rice Salad, **'87** 202
  Tuna Salad, Cheese-Sauced, **'87** M124
  Tuna Salad, Company, **'87** 201
  Tuna Salad, Crunchy, **'87** 201
  Tuna Salad, Curried, **'86** 208
  Tuna Salad, Favorite, **'82** 208

Tuna Salad, Flavorful, **'81** 37
Tuna Salad, Fresh Greens and, **'80** 55
Tuna Salad, Layered, **'84** 221
Tuna Salad Rolls, Hot, **'84** 281
Tuna Salad Sandwiches, White Bean-and-, **'02** 31
Tuna Salad, Swiss, **'86** 186
Tuna Salad, White Bean-, **'98** 208
Tuna Salad, White Bean-and-, **'01** 35
Tuna Salad, Whole Wheat Macaroni-, **'84** 193
Tuna Salad, Wild, **'95** 243
Tuna Salad with Grapes, Curried, **'87** 201
Tuna-Taco Salad, **'87** 145
Freezer Salad, **'94** 118
Fruit. *See also* **SALADS/Congealed.**
  Almond-Citrus Salad, **'96** 274
  Ambrosia, Mixed Fruit, **'83** 10
  Avocado Citrus Salad, **'01** 133
  Avocado Fruit Salad, **'87** 41
  Avocado-Fruit Salad with Honey-Yogurt
      Dressing, **'93** 172
  Banana Split Salad, **'91** 58
  Berry-Citrus Twist, **'95** 100
  Blackberry-Basil Vinaigrette, Fruit Salad with,
      '04 97
  Cabbage and Fruit Salad, **'79** 286
  Chef Salad, Fruited, **'85** 222
  Chef's Fruit Salad, **'86** 35
  Chicken-and-Fruit Salad, **'01** 178
  Chicken-and-Fruit Salad, Grilled, **'96** 155
  Chicken-Fruit Salad, **'82** 79; **'90** 234
  Chicken Salad, Fruited, **'84** 25, 290; **'88** 88;
      '90 318
  Chicken Salad, Fruity, **'83** 157
  Chicken Salad in Avocados, Fruited, **'87** 41
  Chicken Salad with Fruit, **'82** 171
  Chilled Fruit with Dressing, **'85** 222
  Citrus-and-Avocado Salad, **'99** 26
  Citrus and Greens with Orange-Ginger Dressing,
      '96 240
  Citrus-Cilantro Dressing, Fruit Salad with,
      '93 310; **'94** 97; **'00** 160
  Citrus Dressing, Fruit Salad with, **'88** 6
  Citrus Salad with Sweet-and-Sour Dressing,
      '01 104
  Citrus-Strawberry Salad, **'04** 249
  Coconut Fruit Bowl, **'83** 111
  Coconut Salad, Chunky Fruit-and-, **'84** 24
  Colorful Fruit Salad, **'82** 113
  Cottage Cheese-and-Fruit Salad, **'86** 16
  Cottage-Fruit Split, **'86** 169
  Cracked Wheat-Fruit Salad, **'96** 240
  Cream Dressing, Fruit Salad with, **'89** 277
  Creamy Fruit Salad, **'84** 265; **'04** 333
  Creamy Holiday Fruit Salad, **'90** 251
  Cups, Royal Fruit, **'81** 146
  Cups, Sangría Fruit, **'89** 34
  Cups with Pineapple Cream Dressing, Fruit,
      '83 81
  Curried Fruit Salad, **'85** 107
  Date Dressing, Fruit Salad with, **'87** 57
  Delight, Fruit, **'86** 131
  Dressed-Up Fruit, **'82** 5
  Easy Fruit Salad, **'80** 221
  Easy Patio Fruit Salad, **'88** 184
  Favorite Fruit Salad, **'99** 220
  Festive Fruit Salad, **'80** 16
  Fresh Fruit Bowl, Sparkling, **'80** 146
  Fresh Fruit Cup with Mint Dressing, **'80** 183
  Fresh Fruit Salad, **'82** 165; **'97** 122
  Fresh Fruit Salad Pita, **'02** 99
  Fresh Fruit Salad with Celery-Honey Dressing,
      '80 42
  Fresh Fruit Salad with Celery Seed Dressing,
      '00 68

Fresh Fruit Salad with Orange-Ginger Syrup,
    '03 167
Fresh Fruit Salad with Poppy-Seed Dressing,
    '80 137
Fresh Fruit Salad with Poppy Seed Dressing,
    '91 168
Fresh Fruit with Lemon Sauce, **'82** 290
Fresh Fruit with Lime Sauce, **'02** 68
Frisky Fruit Salad, **'85** 46
Frozen Fruit Salad, **'83** 110; **'97** 158; **'00** 160
Frozen Fruit Salad, Dreamy, **'79** 126
Frozen Fruit Salad, Luscious, **'81** 204
Frozen Fruit Salad, Summertime, **'89** 111
Frozen Salad, Christmas Wreath, **'79** 241
Frozen Salads, Paper Cup, **'00** 176
Fruit Salad, **'83** 209; **'89** 277; **'03** 42
Gingered Fruit Salad, **'95** 95
Glazed Fruit Salad, **'83** 48; **'84** 290
Green-and-Gold Salad with Fresh Citrus Ranch
    Dressing, **'04** 91
Green Fruit Salad with Honey-Lime Dressing,
    '93 71
Hawaiian Fruit Dish, **'82** 112
Heavenly Salad, **'81** 252
Holiday Fruit Salad, **'87** 236
Honeydew Fruit Boats, **'81** 147
Honeydew Fruit Bowl, **'84** 186
Honey Dressing, Fruit Salad with, **'87** 129
Honey Fruit Salad, **'80** 276
Honey-Lemon Dressing, Fruit Salad with, **'93** 21
Honey-Pecan Dressing, Fruit Salad with, **'03** 28
Hurry-Up Fruit Salad, **'87** 236
Jícama-Fruit Salad, **'86** 83
Jícama Salad, Fruit-, **'00** 203
Layered Fruit Salad, **'84** 290; **'89** 277; **'91** 58
Lemonade Fruit Salad, **'84** 24
Lemon Freeze, Fruity, **'82** 145
Lettuce and Fruit Salad with Poppy Seed
    Dressing, **'80** 152
Main Dish Fruit Salad, **'83** 119
Marinated Fruit Bowl, **'80** 297
Marinated Fruit Deluxe, **'81** 146
Medley, Chilled Fruit, **'84** 60
Medley, Fruit Cup, **'85** 47
Mélange Delight, Fruit, **'81** 302
Melon Balls in Watermelon Sauce, **'79** 177
Melon-Citrus Mingle, **'79** 177
Melon Cocktail, Minted, **'81** 146
Melon Cooler, **'81** 146
Melon Melange, **'84** 139
Melon Salad, Summertime, **'82** 101
Melon Salad with Orange-Raspberry Vinaigrette,
    Grilled, **'95** 144
Minted Fruit Medley, **'80** 182
Minted Fruit Toss, **'99** 160
Mint-Gin Fruit Salad, **'92** 92
Mint Sauce, Fruit Salad with, **'88** M96
Mixed Fruit Cup, **'87** 233
Mixed Fruit Salad, Banana-, **'79** 270
Mixed Fruit with Sour Cream Sauce, **'02** 169
Multi-Fruit Salad, **'93** 184
Nut Salad, Cheesy Fruit-'n'-, **'87** 56
Old-Fashioned Fruit Salad, **'82** 80
Orange Cream, Fresh Fruit Salad with, **'90** 126
Orange Fruit Cup, **'91** 277
Oriental Dressing, Fruit Salad with, **'91** 277
Party Freeze Salad, **'82** 145
Pasta Salad, Fruited, **'92** 108
Peachy Fruit Salad, **'89** 206
Persimmon Fruit Salad, **'79** 206
Picks, Fruit on, **'80** 159
Pineapple Dressing, Fruit Salad with, **'85** 207
Pineapple-Fruit Salad, Icy, **'87** 9
Platter, Fresh Fruit Salad, **'92** 213

Platter, Fruit Salad, '83 261
Poppy Seed Dressing, Fruit Salad with, '88 78
Quick-and-Easy Fruit Salad, '81 99
Refreshing Fruit Salad, '85 92
Rhapsody, Fruit, '80 158
Rum, Fruit Cup with, '83 55
Sherried Fruit Mélange, '80 158
Shrimp Salad, Fruited, '86 156
Sour Cream Fruit Salad, '80 138
Spiced Fruit Salad, '98 54
Spring Mix Salad, Fruity, '04 105
Springtime Fruit Salad, '81 96
Summer Fruit-Chicken Salad with Blueberry
    Vinaigrette, '00 154
Summer Fruit Salad, '82 164; '92 171
Summer Fruit Salad with Blueberry Vinaigrette,
    '00 154
Summer Salad, '93 179
Summer Salad, Favorite, '80 158
Summer Salad, Georgia, '92 179
Sunny Day Salad, '96 90
Sunny Fruit Salad, '91 58
Sunny Salad, '80 138
Sweet-and-Sour Fruit Salad, '80 13; '84 125
Sweet Potato Fruit Salad, '00 325
Tossed Fruit Salad, '92 106
Tropical Fruit Salad, '89 306; '02 163
Tropical Fruit Salad with Fresh Mint Dressing,
    '84 126
Turkey Salad, Fruit-and-, '89 176
Turkey Salad, Fruit-and-Spice, '94 325
Twenty-Four-Hour Fruit Salad, '96 279
Vanilla Fruit Cup, '80 183
Watermelon Fruit Basket, '84 161
White Wine, Fruit in, '81 48
Winter Fruit-and-Cucumber Salad, '02 274
Winter Fruit Cup, '02 22
Winter Fruit Delight, '80 243
Winter Fruit Salad, '80 248; '82 23
Winter Fruit with Poppy Seed Dressing, '95 317
Wreath, Della Robbia Fruit, '87 294
Wreath, Tex-Mex, '96 241
Yogurt Fruit Salad, '81 114; '96 247
Yogurt-Granola Fruit Medley, '91 58
Gazpacho Salad, '91 313
Goat Cheese Salad, Warm, '01 179
Gorgonzola-Walnut Salad, '96 170
Grapefruit-Apple Salad, '89 41
Grapefruit-Avocado Salad, '83 316; '84 16; '89 41
Grapefruit-Banana Salad with Celery Seed Dressing,
    '91 237
Grapefruit Combo Salad, '80 50
Grapefruit-Cucumber Salad, '80 100
Grapefruit Winter Salad, '84 24
Greek Salad, '87 103; '93 208; '94 160, 202;
    '03 290
Greek Salad, Dawn's World-Famous, '98 276
Greek-Style Salad, '91 27
Green. *See also* **SALADS/Caesar, Spinach.**
    Apple and Brie, Salad Greens with, '93 241
    Baby Lettuces with Vidalia Onion Vinaigrette,
        Salad of, '99 168
    Balsamico, Insalata, '94 46
    Balsamic-Pesto Salad, '96 274
    B.B.'s Salad Dressing, Green Salad with, '91 65
    Bibb Salad, Tossed, '87 128
    Bibb Salad with Fried Green Tomatoes, Kentucky,
        '01 121
    Bibb Salad with Raspberry-Maple Dressing,
        '91 246
    BLT Salad, Layered, '01 96
    Boston Lettuce and Watercress Salad, '93 65
    Bouquet, A Salad, '91 44
    California Green Salad, '81 84

Cantaloupe Green Salad, '91 126
Chinese Green Salad, '88 48
Citrus Green Salad, '85 304
Citrus Salad, Southern-Style, '84 262
Collard Greens Salad, '96 325
Combination Salad Bowl, '85 132
Combo Salad Bowl, '81 9
Company's Coming Salad, '79 113; '96 64
Cranberry-Topped Green Salad, '87 311
Crimson Greens, '87 153
Crunchy Green Salad, '89 321
Cucumber Asian Greens, '98 66
Dijon Vinaigrette, Greens with, '98 332
Dijon Vinaigrette, Salad with, '03 237
Endive Salad, Avocado-, '94 88
Endive-Watercress Salad, '93 22
Fast-and-Easy Salad, '85 M328
Fenron Salad, '79 85
Garden Salad, '85 92; '89 166; '92 60
Garden Salad Centerpiece, '83 171
Garden Salad, Herbed, '85 328; '86 22
Garden Salad, Summer, '87 153
Garden Salad Toss, '81 9
Garden Salad with Buttermilk Dressing, '96 94
Garden Salad with Rosemary Dressing, Fresh,
    '81 131
Garlic-Tarragon Green Salad, '92 79
Goat Cheese and Greens, '90 54
Goat Cheese Salad, Baked, '96 26
Gourmet Greens with Raspberry Vinaigrette,
    '00 163
Grapefruit Salad, Greens and, '95 301
Grecian Green Salad, '84 266
Grecian Tossed Salad, '79 174
Herbed Earl Grey Vinaigrette, Salad Greens with,
    '99 89
Hill Country Salad, '81 9
Hot Chile Vinaigrette, Greens with, '98 200
Lemon-Dill Vinaigrette, Green Salad with, '99 27
Lemony French Dressing, Green Salad with,
    '85 67
Lettuce, Cheesy Stuffed, '79 175
Lettuce, Confetti-Stuffed, '87 24
Lettuce, Delicate Garden, '87 62
Lettuce-English Pea Salad, '91 208
Lettuce, Garden-Stuffed, '83 135
Lettuce Salad, Blue Cheese Stuffed, '94 202
Lettuce Salad, French, '84 187
Lettuce Salad, Tennessee-Killed, '88 86
Lettuce Salad, Wilted, '82 302
Lettuce Salad, Wilted Bacon-and-, '85 69
Lettuces with Mustard Vinaigrette, Baby, '93 67
Lettuce-Wedge Salad, '02 65
Lettuce Wedges with Blue Cheese Dressing,
    Iceberg, '00 217; '03 72
Lettuce Wedges with Pimiento Dressing, '84 212
Lettuce, Wilted, '86 269
Lettuce with Sour Cream Dressing Deluxe, '88 48
Marinated Cheese Dressing, Green Salad with,
    '93 206
Mediterranean Salad, '90 99
Mesclun with Tarragon Dressing, '90 55
Mess o' Greens Salad with Warm Pecan Dressing,
    '98 250
Mint-Fresh Green Salad, '92 105
Mixed Green Salad, '90 230
Mixed Green Salad, Wilted, '85 69
Mixed Green Salad with Chicken, '80 54
Mixed Greens, Hot Sesame Pork on, '97 19
Mixed Greens Salad, '87 62
Mixed Greens with Blue Cheese Vinaigrette,
    '89 274; '90 280
Mixed Greens with Creamy Garlic Dressing,
    '04 322

Mixed Greens with Parmesan Walnuts, '95 301
Mixed Greens with Raspberries and Walnuts,
    '98 194
Mixed Greens with Raspberry Dressing, '97 50
Mixed Greens with Roquefort Firecrackers,
    '97 19
Mixed Greens with Seasoned Almonds and Tangy
    Balsamic Vinaigrette, '03 101
Mixed Greens with Tarragon Vinaigrette, '95 326
Mixed Greens with Walnuts, '99 107
Nutty Green Salad, '87 168
Orange-Poppy Seed Salad, '98 87
Oriental, Green Salad, '85 92
Peppery Greens with Raspberry Dressing,
    '95 254
Purple Parrot Sensation Salad, '04 289
Ranch House Salad with Pecan Vinaigrette,
    '00 162
Red-and-Green Salad, '90 55
Red Leaf Lettuce Salad with Sweet-and-Sour
    Dressing, '03 28
Rich Green Salad, '99 203
Robust Salad, '90 181
Romaine Salad, Tangy, '80 155
Romaine Salad with Buttermilk-Chive Dressing,
    Grilled, '04 105
Romaine Salad with Raspberry Dressing, '03 28
Romaine-Spinach Salad, '89 123
Romaine Toss, Crunchy, '00 30
Romaine Toss, Easy, '00 97
Romaine with Caper Vinaigrette, Hearts of,
    '91 310
Salmagundi Salad, '83 146
Savory Green Salad, '82 74
Sensational Salad, '84 320
Sesame-Citrus Green Salad, '86 33
Shredded Salad, Zesty, '04 324
Shrimp, Green Salad with, '88 49
Simply Good Salad, '85 131
Southwest Salad, Easy, '03 47
Soy Dressing, Green Salad with, '86 191
Spring Salad, '87 62
Spring Salad, Mediterranean, '80 148
Spring Salad Wedges, '87 62
Summer Salad, Crisp, '85 92
Summertime Salad, '79 143; '84 195
Sweet-and-Sour Green Salad, '94 281
Tangy Wilted Salad, '85 69
Tarragon Salad, '97 165
Tossed Mixed Green Salad, '84 126
Tossed Salad, Blue Cheese, '84 195
Tossed Salad, Boston, '84 85
Tossed Salad, Colorful, '90 55
Tossed Salad, Radish-Dressed, '79 104
Veggies with Fried Okra Croutons, Salad Greens
    and, '96 178
Vinaigrette, Greens and, '98 168
Vinaigrette with Greens, '98 184
Watercress-and-Mushroom Salad, '88 104
Watercress Salad, '97 249
Watercress Salad, Roasted Red Pepper and, '90 55
Winter Green Holiday Salad with Cranberry
    Vinaigrette, '98 321
Winter Salad, '95 280
Greens, Grilled Catfish Over Mixed, '04 326
Guacamole Salad, '80 14; '87 181
Guacamole-Tomato Salad, '81 302
Harvest Salad with Cider Vinaigrette, '99 322
Hearts of Palm Salad, '81 252; '89 276; '96 86
Hearts-of-Palm Salad, '87 138
Herb Salad, '87 90
Honeydew Salad with Apricot Cream Dressing,
    '84 191
Hoppin' John Salad, '96 64

SALADS
(continued)

Ice Cream Salad, '79 126
Indian Chief Salad, '96 287
Italian Bread Salad, '99 259
Italian House Salad, '02 300
Italian Salad, '87 145
Jícama-and-Orange Salad, '88 246
Jícama-Orange Salad, '86 83; '90 122
Jícama Salad, '87 123
Layered Overnight Salad, '90 319
Layered Salad, '86 35, 79
Layered Salad, Cheesy, '81 37
Layered Salad Deluxe, '81 153
Layered Salad, Hearty, '86 79
Layered Salad, Majestic, '86 79
Layered Salad, Make-Ahead, '81 296
Layered Salad, Mexican, '02 65
Layered Salad, Old-Fashioned, '01 96
Layered Salad, Overnight, '81 188
Layered Salad, Tex-Mex, '03 201
Layer Salad, Eight-, '99 107
Legumes, Marinated, '90 197
Lentil-and-Orzo Salad, '03 127
Lentil Salad, Mediterranean, '96 239
Lentils-and-Rice Salad, '90 197
Macaroni. See **SALADS/Pasta.**
Magnolia Blossom Salad, '89 123
Main-Dish Salad, '86 191
Mandarin, Salad, '84 231
Mandarin Spinach Salad, '85 163
Mandarin Tossed Salad, '89 12
Mango Salad, '79 137; '03 122
Mango Salad, Fresh, '84 126
Meal in a Bowl, '96 138
Meal-in-One Salad, '86 43
Meat
  Beef-and-Broccoli Salad, '87 187
  Beef-and-Lime Rice Salad, '03 172
  Beef Fajita Salad, '91 70
  Beef-Pasta Salad, Spicy, '01 311
  Beef Salad, Gingered, '88 61
  Beef Salad Niçoise, '99 159
  Beef Salad, Peking, '88 60
  Beef Salad, Spicy, '02 174
  Beef Salad, Stir-Fry, '96 129
  Beef Salad, Tangy, '87 M218
  Beef Salad, Western-Style, '93 321
  Beef Salad with Cilantro, '97 202
  Beef Salad, Zesty, '79 56
  Beef Vinaigrette Salad, '95 177
  Chili-Corn Chip Stack-Up Salad, '04 242
  Chili Salad, Spicy, '86 71
  Committee, Salad by, '87 288
  Corned Beef-Cauliflower Salad, '83 16
  Corned Beef-Potato Salad, '85 213
  Corned Beef Salad, '80 104
  Corned Beef Salad, Molded, '82 86
  Corned Beef Salad, Potato-, '81 36
  Corned Beef Salad, Vegetable-, '80 148
  Dude Ranch Salad, '80 15
  Ham-and-Apple Salad, '88 139
  Ham-and-Cheese Salad, '88 138
  Ham and Cheese Toss, '79 55
  Ham and Macaroni Salad, '79 220
  Ham-and-Pasta Salad, '90 128
  Ham-and-Rice Salad, Colorful, '90 319
  Ham-and-Rice Salad, Mandarin, '87 145
  Ham-Dijon Pasta Salad, '92 191
  Ham 'n Egg Salad, '81 36
  Ham-Noodle Salad, '85 249
  Ham-Rice Toss, '82 40

Ham Salad, Congealed, '81 36
Ham Salad, Crunchy Baked, '83 23
Ham Salad, Fruited, '81 36, 146
Ham Salad, Hearty, '82 40
Ham Salad Sandwich, Tangy, '80 272
Ham Salad, Spicy Italian, '85 74
Ham Salad Spread, '87 92
Ham Salad, Tropical, '89 175
Ham-Sweet Potato Salad, Hawaiian, '82 232
Mexican Dinner Salad, '98 330
Mexican Salad in a Shell, '86 4
Mexican Salad Supper, '82 9; '83 68
Paella Salad, '86 207
"Pig in the Garden" Salad, '92 255
Pork-and-Rice Salad with Spicy Tomato
  Dressing, '03 143
Pork-and-Spinach Salad, Mandarin, '88 M126
Pork Cosmopolitan Salad, Grilled, '04 123
Pork Salad, Oriental, '92 140
Pork Salad, Thai, '00 249
Roast Beef Salad, '80 223; '81 56; '90 318
Roast Beef Salad, Cucumber-, '89 162
Rolls, Hearty Salad, '81 206
Sirloin Salad, Grilled, '94 129
Steak Salad Cups, Pepper, '86 206
Steak Salad, Greek, '92 107
Steak Salad Niçoise, Grilled, '98 148
Steak Salad with Peach Salsa, '97 183
Taco Salad, '79 56; '83 145; '84 221; '85 84;
  '89 332; '90 20; '02 188
Taco Salad, Beefy, '03 128
Taco Salad Cups, '85 M29
Taco Salad, Party, '97 19
Taco Salad, Spicy, '87 287
Melon-and-Prosciutto Salad, '92 191
Melon Balls, Minted, '87 162
Melon-Berry Salad, '90 180
Melon Salad with Dill Dressing, '88 182
Mexican Salad with Avocado Dressing, '92 321
Mexicorn-Bean Salad, '96 184
Middle Eastern Salad, '87 107
Minestrone Salad, '79 220
Mix, Muffy Salad, '94 34
Mozzarella-Tomato-Basil Salad, Fresh, '93 131
Mozzarella-Tomato Basil Salad, Fresh, '02 110
Mushroom-and-Pepper Salad, '86 68
Mushroom-Asparagus Salad, Grilled, '02 122
Mushroom Salad, Fabulous, '81 190
Mushroom Salad, Fresh, '93 65
Mushroom Salad, Marinated, '88 215; '90 181
Mushroom Salad, Quick Cheesy-, '89 128
Mushrooms in Rosemary-Red Wine Vinaigrette,
  Marinated, '97 63
Mushroom-Zucchini Salad, '85 8
Niçoise, Salad, '03 35
Okra-Corn-and-Tomato Vinaigrette, '90 173
Okra Salad, '90 155
Okra Salad, Fried, '97 M157; '04 167
Okra-Walnut Salad, '04 291
Olive Clubhouse Salad, '81 114
Olive Salad, '98 184; '00 335; '04 27
Olive Salad, Doodles, '94 35
Olive Salad, Italian, '94 35
Olive Salad, Mexican, '85 84
Onion Salad, Grilled, '99 96
Onion Salad, Roasted, '95 65; '03 142
Orange
  Almond Salad, Orange-, '99 107
  Avocado Salad, Orange-, '99 331
  Beet Salad, Orange-and-, '88 43
  Carrot Salad, Orange-, '80 89; '84 325
  Cauliflower Salad, Orange-., '82 266
  Cottage Cheese Salad, Orange-, '79 44
  Cups, Orange, '86 92

  Cups, Orange Salad, '85 40
  Grapefruit Salad, Orange-, '93 294
  Honey-Berry Dressing, Orange Salad with,
    '89 250
  Honey Dressing, Orange Salad with, '89 14
  Mandarin Orange and Pineapple Salad, '82 266
  Mandarin Orange-Lettuce Salad, '92 79
  Mandarin Orange Salad, '81 252; '84 161
  Mandarin Orange Tossed Salad, '92 303
  Mandarin, Salad, '84 231
  Mandarin Salad Oriental, '02 175
  Mandarin Spinach Salad, '85 163
  Mandarin Tossed Salad, '89 12
  Marinated Orange-Onion Salad, '91 231; '92 68
  Onion Salad, Orange-, '89 41
  Poppy Seed Salad, Orange-, '03 121
  Quick Orange Salad, '87 80
  Romaine Salad, Orange-, '84 325; '87 239
  Shrimp Salad, Orange-, '84 197
  Spinach Salad, Orange-, '83 316; '84 16
  Strawberry Salad with Orange-Curd Dressing,
    Orange-, '93 22
  Tropical Orange Salad, '92 97
  Walnut Salad, Orange, '80 246
  Watercress-Orange Salad with Blue Cheese,
    '04 45
Oriental Salad Bowl, '87 153
Orzo Salad, Confetti, '92 173
Orzo Salad with Sesame Dressing, '96 137
Paella Salad, '86 207
Pasta
  Artichoke-Pasta Salad, '94 180
  Asian Peanut-and-Pasta Salad, '03 127
  Bayou Pasta Salad, '00 203
  Bean-Pasta Salad, Marinated, '94 167
  Bean Salad, Pasta-, '86 169
  Beef-Pasta Salad, Spicy, '01 311
  Bow Tie Pasta, '01 164
  Bow Tie Pasta, Chicken-and-, '01 164
  Broccoli-Cauliflower Pasta Salad, '88 269
  Caesar Salad Pasta, '95 230
  Chicken Pasta Salad, '88 89
  Chicken-Pasta Salad, Grilled, '94 64
  Chicken-Pasta Salad, Zesty, '02 186
  Chicken Salad, Tarragon Pasta-, '87 155
  Cold Pasta Platter, '88 42
  Crabmeat-Shrimp Pasta Salad, '86 208
  Crunchy Pasta Salad, '85 166
  Easy Confetti-Pasta Salad, '92 220
  Fruited Pasta Salad, '92 108
  Garden Pasta Salad, '86 188
  Greek Pasta Salad, '02 139
  Ham-and-Pasta Salad, '90 128
  Ham-and-Pea Pasta Salad, '00 217
  Ham, Pasta Salad with, '92 108
  Ham-Pecan-Blue Cheese Pasta Salad, '90 62
  Herbed Pasta-and-Tomato Salad, '92 144
  Hoisin Chicken-and-Pasta Salad, '99 125
  Luncheon Pasta Salad, '90 191
  Macaroni and Cheese Salad, '97 203
  Macaroni-Cheese Salad, Dilled, '86 208
  Macaroni-Chicken Salad, '85 296; '86 302
  Macaroni-Chicken Salad, Dilled, '92 142
  Macaroni-Crabmeat Salad, '81 153
  Macaroni-Ham Salad, '85 218
  Macaroni Salad, '87 92
  Macaroni Salad, Barbecue, '82 276
  Macaroni Salad, Confetti, '82 132; '85 297
  Macaroni Salad, Crunchy, '82 24
  Macaroni Salad, Dilled, '89 161
  Macaroni Salad for Two, '81 31
  Macaroni Salad, Garden, '84 290; '92 64
  Macaroni Salad, Gourmet, '81 253
  Macaroni Salad, Ham and, '79 220

Macaroni Salad, Hearty, '84 90
Macaroni Salad, Pineapple, '79 220
Macaroni Salad, Refreshing, '80 177
Macaroni Salad, Shell, '92 163
Macaroni Salad, Spiral, '82 276
Macaroni Salad, Sweet-and-Sour, '85 166
Macaroni Salad, Taco, '85 165
Macaroni Salad, Turkey, '83 282
Macaroni Salad Véronique, '85 164
Macaroni-Salmon Salad, '82 232
Macaroni Shell Salad, '87 38
Macaroni-Shrimp Salad, '85 121
Macaroni-Shrimp Salad, Festive, '85 165
Macaroni Toss, Corkscrew, '83 163
Macaroni-Tuna Salad, Whole Wheat, '84 193
Macaroni-Vegetable Salad, '86 209
Main-Dish Pasta Salad, '82 199
Marinated Bean-Pasta Salad, '97 328
Mediterranean Salad, '95 132
Medley, Garden Pasta, '89 256
Noodle Salad, Peanutty Spicy, '04 72
Noodle Salad, Sesame, '02 186
Oriental Pasta Salad, '90 63
Overnight Pasta Salad, '82 276
Pasta Salad, '84 139; '86 120; '87 36; '90 62, 91;
    '00 213; '01 127
Pesto Pasta Salad, Fresh, '01 61
Pistachio-Pasta Salad, '86 141
Plentiful P's Salad, '87 12
Presto Pasta Salad, '90 63
Ramen Noodle Salad, '88 41
Ratatouille Pasta Salad, '90 74
Ravioli Salad, Caesar, '95 183
Roasted Onion Pasta Salad with Peppered Cheese
    Crisps, '98 107
Rotelle Salad, Crunchy, '86 209
Rotini Salad, '88 42
Seafood Pasta Salad, '90 62
Seashell Salad, '86 209
Shell Salad, Tossed, '91 256
Shrimp Pasta Salad with Green Goddess
    Dressing, '02 139
Shrimp Salad, Pasta-and-, '83 163
Smoked Mozzarella Pasta Salad, '03 126
Snappy Pasta, '83 164
Southwestern Pasta Salad, '94 278
Spaghetti Salad, '82 277; '84 205
Spaghetti Salad, Chicken-, '90 146
Spinach-Mustard Twist, '86 209
Tomato-Pasta Salad, '97 M160
Tortellini Pasta Salad, Cheese, '02 139
Tortellini-Pesto Salad, '92 22
Tortellini Salad, '89 237; '02 186
Tortellini Salad, Chicken, '87 288
Tortellini Salad, Garden, '91 44
Tortellini Salad, Terrific, '96 134
Turkey 'n' Pasta Salad, Ranch-Style, '94 184
Vegetable Salad, Pasta-, '95 238
Veggie Salad, Pasta-, '96 106
Vermicelli Vinaigrette Salad, '82 189
Vinaigrette, Italian Pasta, '92 78
Ziti-Cheddar Salad, '85 165
Pea
Asparagus Salad, Peas-and-, '83 141
Black-Eyed Pea Salad, '80 112; '86 225;
    '88 92, 221; '90 173; '95 203; '97 305; '98 52;
    '99 174
Black-Eyed Pea Salad, Chicken-and-, '97 305
Black-Eyed Pea Salad, Fearrington House Goat
    Cheese and, '95 60
Black-Eyed Pea Salad, Marinated, '93 190
Black-Eyed Pea Salad, Overnight, '81 280
Black-Eyed Pea Salad with Benedictine Dressing,
    '98 83

Black-Eyed Peas, Marinated, '82 156
Black-Eyed Peas, Zesty, '89 147
Black-Eyed Pea Vinaigrette, '86 7
Black-Eyed Salad, Hot Bacon and, '85 7
Cauliflower and Pea Salad, Savory, '81 280
Cauliflower-Pea Salad, '87 231
Cheddar-Pea Salad, '84 82
Chicken-Pea Salad, '83 218
Corn-and-Pea Salad, '90 181
Creamy Pea Salad, '80 111
Crunchy Pea Salad, '90 143; '00 103
Dilled Pea Salad, '97 305; '98 18
English Pea-and-Apple Salad, '87 24
English Pea Salad, '81 280; '90 143
English Pea Salad, Cauliflower-, '95 66
English Pea Salad, Marinated, '82 54
Field Pea Salad, Mixed, '00 325
Green Pea Salad, '96 88
Hoppin' John Salad, '01 250
Marinated Pea Salad, '81 204
Mexi-Pea Salad, '81 7
Minted Pea Salad, '91 119
Pea Salad, '98 274
Plentiful P's Salad, '87 12
Special Peas, '95 133
Special Pea Salad, '83 239
Sugar Snap Pea Salad, '86 115
Three Pea Salad, '84 290
Peach-and-Kiwi Salad, '90 180
Peaches in a Garden Nest, '87 154
Peach Salad, Frosted, '82 145
Peach Salad, Frozen, '82 54
Peach Salad, Georgia, '80 142
Peach Salad Supreme, Easy, '79 177
Peanut-Apple Salad, '80 5
Peanut-Noodle Salad, '02 163
Pear-and-Celery Salad, '87 56
Pear-and-Cranberry Wild Rice Salad, '03 199
Pear-and-Spinach Salad, Festive, '85 131
Pear, Jícama, and Snow Pea Salad, '01 329
Pear Plate, Pretty, '89 225
Pear Salad, Crunchy, '83 234; '84 244
Pear Salad, Golden, '91 58
Pear Salad with Asian Sesame Dressing, Fresh,
    '02 196
Pear Salad with Jícama and Snow Peas, '01 56
Pear Salad with Raspberry Cream, '00 311
Pear-Swiss Cheese Salad, '91 237
Pepper-Cheese Stacks, '87 80
Pepperoni-and-Broccoli Salad, '83 216
Pepper Salad, Mixed, '89 103
Pepper Salad, Roasted Tomato-and-, '01 196
Pepper Salad, Three-, '91 162
Pineapple Boat Aloha, '80 102
Pineapple Boats Ahoy, '80 148
Pineapple Boats, Fresh, '83 153
Pineapple-Celery Salad, '85 95
Pineapple Salad, Frosty, '89 278
Pineapple Waldorf, '97 86
Pineapple Waldorf Salad, '92 97
Pita Salad Sandwiches, '83 134
Pizza, Salad, '87 182
Plum Salad, Crisp, '03 161
Portobello Salad, Grilled, '99 216
Potato Salads, Cold
Any Day Potato Salad, '81 154
Asparagus-and-New Potato Salad, '86 69
Avocado, Potato Salad with, '98 332
Avocado-Potato Salad with Horseradish Dressing,
    '96 200
Bacon-Topped Potato Salad, '85 59
Baked Potato Salad, '97 319
Basil Potato Salad, '94 178
Bean Salad, Potato-, '82 301

Blue Cheese-Potato Salad, '91 208
Charletta's Potato Salad, '98 153
Chunky Potato Salad, '81 M138
Cobb Salad, Potato, '03 140
Confetti Potato Salad, '80 5; '88 16
Corned Beef-Potato Salad, '85 213
Corned Beef Salad, Potato-, '81 36
Cottage Cheese-Potato Salad, '79 147, 285
Creamy Potato Salad, '80 178; '88 171; '92 241;
    '98 175; '01 334
Creole Potato Salad, '99 136
Cucumbers and Tomatoes, Potato Salad with,
    '03 92
Curried Potato Salad, '99 137
Deluxe Potato Salad, '80 155
Dill-and-Sour Cream Potato Salad, '93 105;
    '94 100
Dill Potato Salad, '85 213; '94 179; '99 104
Festive Potato Salad, '89 315
Fipps Family Potato Salad, '02 138
Fish-Potato Salad, Smoked, '84 233
French-Style Potato Salad, '88 171
Fruity Potato Salad, '85 214
Garden Patch Potato Salad, '84 82
Grecian Potato Salad, '82 55
Greek Potato Salad, '98 276
Green Bean-Potato Salad, '83 80; '01 181;
    '04 142
Green Bean-Red Potato Salad, '96 175
Green Bean Salad, Potato-and-, '00 162
Ham-and-Egg Potato Salad, '86 84
Ham and Potato Salad, '80 272
Ham-and-Potato Salad, '95 94
Herbed Potato Salad, '87 171; '94 164
Horseradish Potato Salad, '98 175
Jalapeño Potato Salad, '97 64
Joy's Potato Salad, '99 83
Layered Creamy Potato Salad, '81 23
Layered Potato Salad, '03 183
Light Potato Salad, '02 138
Lime-Potato Salad, '02 22
Marinated Potato Slices, '93 98
Mustard Potato Salad, '86 302
New Potato Salad, '84 120, 139; '94 162; '01 142
Olive-Potato Salad, '85 114
Onion and Celery, Potato Salad with, '02 138
Parslied Potato Salad, '85 240
Patio Potato Salad, '90 160
Peas-and-Potatoes Vinaigrette, Dilled, '01 327
Peppers, Potato Salad 'n', '83 135
Pickle-Potato Salad, Sweet, '85 213
Pickle, Potato Salad with Sweet, '02 138
Potato Salad, '90 122; '94 160; '00 195; '01 163;
    '03 163
Red Potato Salad, '93 119; '96 172; '02 138
Roasted New Potato Salad, '04 91
Roasted-Potato Salad, Creamy, '97 161
Roasted Red Peppers, Potato Salad with,
    '04 100
Salmon-Potato Salad, '87 285
Salmon Potato Salad, Smoked, '97 64
Saucy Potato Salad, '87 123
Savory Potato Salad, '80 30
Shrimp-and-Potato Salad, '96 211
Sour Cream Potato Salad, '79 104; '80 79;
    '99 137
Sour Cream-Potato Salad, '84 149
Southern-Style Potato Salad, '04 199
South-of-the-Border Potato Salad, '94 178
Spicy Potato Salad, '97 305
Spring Salad, Mediterranean, '80 148
Sweet and Sour Potato Salad, '80 152
Sweet Potato-Apple Salad, '96 240
Sweet Potato Fruit Salad, '00 325

SALADS, Potato Salads, Cold
(continued)

Sweet Potato Salad, Black-Eyed Pea-and-, '01 198
Sweet Potato Salad, Fresh, '86 226
Tri Club Potato Salad, '92 166
Tuna-Potato Salad, '84 289
Potato Salads, Hot or Warm
Baked Potato Salad, '97 319
Broccoli-Potato Salad, Hot, '85 23
Colorful Potato Salad, '01 94
Dill Potato Salad, Hot, '79 78
Dutch Potato Salad, Hot, '86 297; '87 176
Fipps Family Potato Salad, '02 138
German Potato Salad, '82 134, 239; '84 18; '92 169; '97 195; '98 175
German Potato Salad, Hot, '79 78; '94 254
German-Style Potato Salad, '83 23; '88 M194
Goat Cheese and Potato Salad, Warm, '96 234
Greens, Hot Potato, '97 20
Lemon-Basil Potato Salad, '97 63; '01 178
Light Potato Salad, '02 138
Light Potato Salad, Hot-and-, '93 90
Onion and Celery, Potato Salad with, '02 138
Parmesan Potato Salad, Hot, '79 78
Pepper Cups, Potato Salad in, '79 78
Pesto Potato Salad, '90 164
Pickle, Potato Salad with Sweet, '02 138
Pole Bean-Potato Salad, Hot, '79 74
Potato Salad, Hot, '79 78; '81 276; '86 10
Red Potato Salad, '02 138
Sausage Salad, Warm Potato-and-, '96 25
Savory Potato Salad, '80 30
Smoked Sausage, Warm Potato Salad with, '97 267
Sugar Snap Peas, Potato Salad with, '91 120
Supreme, Hot Potato Salad, '79 78
Sweet-and-Sour Potato Salad, '92 106
Sweet Potato Salad with Rosemary-Honey Vinaigrette, '98 243
Vegetable Potato Salad, '03 136
Radish Toss, Chilled, '01 101
Ramen Noodle Salad, '97 18
Raspberry Salad, Frozen, '79 287; '80 35
Raspberry-Walnut Salad, '94 158
Red Cabbage Citrus Salad, '94 72
Relish Salad, '84 121
Rémoulade, Dill Pickle, '04 311
Rice. *See also* **SALADS/Vegatable.**
Artichoke-Chicken-Rice Salad, Mediterranean, '97 321
Artichoke Hearts, Rice Salad with, '80 232
Artichoke-Rice Salad, '80 178; '81 41; '85 81; '01 144
Avocado Salad, Rice-and-, '89 146
Bacon, Rice Salad with, '79 52
Bean-and-Rice Salad, Marinated, '87 152
Bean Salad, Rice-and-, '85 22
Bean Salad, Zesty Rice-and-, '02 84
Beans-and-Rice Salad, '91 44
Beef-and-Lime Rice Salad, '03 172
Brown Rice-and-Vegetable Salad, '84 202
Brown Rice Confetti Salad, '94 174
Cabbage Salad with Honey-Dijon Vinaigrette, Rice-, '04 321
Chicken-and-Rice Salad, '97 92
Chicken-and-Rice Salad, Hot, '83 22
Chicken-Rice Salad, '81 203; '97 93
Chicken-Rice Salad, Curried, '92 190
Chicken-Rice Salad, Grilled, '98 148
Chicken-Rice Salad, Nutty, '83 157
Chutneyed Rice Salad, '88 100

Colorful Rice Salad, '81 253
Confetti Rice Salad, '80 232
Crunchy Rice Salad, '82 302
Curried Rice Salad, '80 84; '85 147, 220; '96 240
Curry Rice Salad, '89 146
Egg-Rice Salad, '84 18; '86 169
Ham-and-Rice Salad, Colorful, '90 319
Ham-and-Rice Salad, Mandarin, '87 145
Ham-Rice Toss, '82 40
Hearty Rice Salad, '82 233
Herbed Rice Salad, '96 123
Madras Salad, '86 82
Mandarin Rice Salad, '88 271
Mardi Gras Rice, '91 217
Meal-in-One Salad, '86 43
Molded Gazpacho-Rice Salad, '86 221
Mushrooms, Rice Salad with Fresh, '80 231
Orange Vinaigrette Rice Salad, '98 288
Paella Salad, '86 207
Pea Salad, Rice-, '85 163
Pebble Salad, '91 27
Pine Nut, Rice, and Feta Salad, '96 26; '98 331
Pork-and-Rice Salad with Spicy Tomato Dressing, '03 143
Primavera Salad, Rice, '00 131
Red Rice Salad, Charleston, '79 146
Rice Salad, '79 74; '81 51
Ring, Rice-Carrot, '79 246
Shrimp and Rice Salad, '80 231; '82 207
Shrimp-and-Rice Salad, '92 307
Shrimp-Rice Salad, Tangy, '84 66
Shrimp Salad, Rice-, '79 270; '92 142
Shrimp Salad, Rice-and-, '83 82
Spinach-Rice Salad, '94 63
Tomatoes and Basil, Rice with, '95 232
Tuna Salad, Wild, '95 243
Vegetable-Rice Salad, '80 148; '83 198; '85 87
Wild Rice-and-Chicken Salad, '02 52
Wild Rice-and-Corn Salad, '98 288
Wild Rice-and-Cranberry Salad, '99 272
Wild Rice-and-Kidney Bean Salad, '01 175
Wild Rice-and-Roasted Vegetable Salad, '99 316
Wild Rice-and-Shrimp Salad, '02 109
Wild Rice-Chicken Salad, '83 146; '99 55
Wild Rice-Green Apple Salad, '92 90
Wild Rice Salad, '85 65; '89 147; '93 191; '01 247
Wild Rice Salad, Crab-, '86 207
Wild Rice Salad, Crab and, '79 116
Wild Rice Salad, Oriental Salmon-and-, '94 173
Wild Rice Salad, Springtime, '88 100
Wild Rice Salad with Spicy Lime Vinaigrette, '01 217
Wild Rice-Shrimp Salad, '99 55
Zesty Rice Salad, '81 23
Roasted Red Pepper-and-Green Bean Salad, '99 322
Sandwich, Tuscan Feta Salad, '99 289
Sauerkraut Salad, '80 178; '97 195
Sauerkraut Salad, Crunchy, '87 9
Seafood. *See also* **SALADS/Fish, Shrimp.**
Baked Seafood Salad, '86 10
Blue Crab Salad with Asian Vinaigrette, '98 142
Crab-and-Asparagus Salad, '92 141
Crab-and-Endive Salad, Marinated, '93 22
Crab and Wild Rice Salad, '79 116
Crab-Avocado Salad, '81 114
Crab Cakes with Greens and Dijon Dressing, '96 176
Crab Louis, '95 94
Crab Luncheon Salad, '00 17
Crabmeat, Avocado with, '86 119
Crabmeat Luncheon Salad, '82 207
Crabmeat Salad, '91 169

Crabmeat Salad with Creamy Gingered Dressing, Caribbean, '97 263
Crabmeat-Shrimp Pasta Salad, '86 208
Crab Mousse, '79 117
Crab Salad, Chesapeake, '89 195
Crab Salad, Cucumber-and-, '98 208
Crab Salad, Delightful, '87 145
Crab Salad Sandwiches, Mango-, '99 72
Crab-Wild Rice Salad, '86 207
Fleur-de-lis Salad, '99 164
Hot Seafood Salad, '79 117; '80 164
Lobster and Orange Salad, '82 207
Lobster Salad, '89 249; '90 69
Lobster Salad with Tarragon Vinaigrette, '97 163
Paella Salad, '86 207
Polynesian Seafood Salad, '79 57
Scallop Salad, Thai-Rific Orange, '04 317
Seafood Salad, '90 88
Smoky Seafood Salad, '84 46
Sussex Shores, Seafood Salad, '93 98
Tropical Salad, '85 91
Sesame-Almond Salad, '89 123
Shallot Salad, Caramelized, '96 308
Shrimp
Aloha Shrimp Salad, '95 46
Artichoke Salad, Shrimp-and-, '04 50
Avocado Salad, Shrimp and, '80 266
Avocados, Shrimp-Filled, '83 2
Avocado Stuffed with Shrimp Salad, '82 207
Baked Shrimp-Rice Salad, '83 22
Bowl, Mediterranean Shrimp, '80 174
Caribbean Shrimp-and-Black Bean Salad, '93 143
Coastal Shrimp Salad, '00 17
Couscous Salad, Shrimp-and-, '96 157
Creamy Shrimp Salad, '79 56
Croissants, Shrimp Salad on, '96 175
Curried Shrimp Salad, '00 217
Curry Salad, Melon and Shrimp, '97 129
Egg Salad Club, Shrimp-, '02 203
Egg Salad, Tossed Shrimp-, '80 4
Endive Salad, Shrimp-, '85 73
Filling, Shrimp Salad, '87 106
Fruited Shrimp Salad, '86 156
Grapefruit-and-Shrimp Salad, '88 5
Green Salad with Shrimp, '88 49
Grilled Shrimp, Orange, and Watermelon Salad with Peppered Peanuts in a Zesty Citrus Dressing, '04 308
Half Shell, Shrimp Salad on the, '86 73
Individual Shrimp Salads, '83 146
Layered Shrimp Salad, '88 100
Macaroni Salad, Shrimp, '79 220
Macaroni Salad, Shrimp-, '85 219
Marinated Shrimp Salad, '85 82; '93 321; '99 169
Mousse, Shrimp, '79 57
Orange, and Olive Salad with Sherry Vinaigrette, Shrimp, '93 177
Orange-Shrimp Salad, '84 197
Oriental Shrimp Salad, '91 313
Orzo Salad, Peppers Stuffed with Shrimp-and-, '91 203
Orzo Salad, Shrimp-and-, '99 182
Pasta Salad with Green Goddess Dressing, Shrimp, '02 139
Pastry, Shrimp Salad in, '86 105
Picnic Shrimp Salad, '95 182
Potato Salad, Shrimp-and-, '96 211
Rémoulade, Shrimp, '90 255
Rice-and-Shrimp Salad, '83 82
Rice Salad, Shrimp and, '80 231; '82 207
Rice Salad, Shrimp-and-, '92 307
Rotelle, Shrimp, '85 165
Salad, Shrimp, '04 147
Sandwiches, Shrimp-and-Egg Salad, '94 182

Sandwiches, Shrimp Salad, '90 178
Shrimp Salad, '81 94; '86 186; '93 238; '98 333
Super Shrimp Salad, '81 37
Tangy Shrimp-Rice Salad, '84 66
Vegetable-Shrimp Salad, '79 190
Vermicelli Salad, Shrimp, '88 139
Wild Rice-and-Shrimp Salad, '02 109
Wild Rice-Shrimp Salad, '99 55
Zesty Shrimp-and-Orange Rice Salad, '87 155
Southwestern Spiral Salad, '98 66
Spaghetti Squash Salad, '99 M322
Spaghetti Squash Salad, Marinated, '94 134
Spinach
Apple-Onion Vinaigrette, Spinach Salad with, '94 276
Apple Salad, Spinach-, '90 89; '92 13; '97 308
Apple-Spinach Salad, '97 14; '99 222; '02 230
Apricot Salad, Spinach-, '94 63
Apricot Vinaigrette, Spinach Salad with, '02 120
Arranged Spinach Salad, '91 210; '92 160
Bacon Salad, Spinach and, '81 143
Beet Salad, Spinach-, '83 227
Blue Cheese Dressing, Spinach Salad with Zesty, '02 121
Blue Cheese Salad, Spinach-, '82 166
Blues, Spinach Salad with the, '95 66
Chili-Lime Dressing, Spinach Salad with, '94 63
Citrus Dressing, Spinach Salad with, '88 133
Citrus Spinach Salad, '90 59
Combination Spinach Salad, '85 327; '86 22
Cranberry Salad with Warm Chutney Dressing, Spinach-and-, '02 242
Creamy Dressing, Crisp Spinach Salad with, '83 81
Creamy Spinach Salad, '83 60
Crunchy Spinach Salad, '80 147; '81 225
Curry Spinach Salad, '80 242
Dijon Spinach Salad, '89 282
Dried Tomato Vinaigrette, Spinach Salad with, '93 272
Easy Spinach Salad, '91 249
Enoki Salad, Spinach-, '89 62
Festive Spinach Salad, '80 247
French Spinach Salad, '79 8
Fresh Spinach Salad, '82 73; '83 240; '84 15, 77; '86 130
Fresh Spinach Salad Delight, '80 146
Garlic-Ginger Vinaigrette Dressing, Spinach Salad with, '92 195
Green Spinach Salad, '79 142
Grits-Spinach Salad, Stacked, '98 66
Honey Dressing, Spinach Salad with, '90 16
Hot Bacon Dressing, Spinach Salad with, '82 211
Hot Citrus Dressing, Spinach Salad with, '00 108
Hot Spiked Spinach, '97 195
Kiwifruit Salad, Spinach-, '87 305
Lamb Salad, Spinach-, '85 58
Layered Spinach Salad, '80 5; '89 163
Lettuce Salad, Layered Spinach-, '84 266
Mandarin Spinach Salad, '85 163
Minted Spinach Salad, '94 63
Mushroom Salad, Spinach and, '80 112
Mustard Twist, Spinach-, '86 209
Onion Salad Bowl, Spinach-and-, '81 157
Orange Dressing, Spinach Salad with, '87 187
Orange Salad, Spinach-and-, '86 15
Orange Salad, Warm Spinach-, '00 112
Orange-Spinach Salad, '83 316; '84 16
Oriental Spinach Salad, '82 23
Oysters and Red Wine Vinaigrette, Spinach Salad with, '94 327
Parsley Dressing, Spinach Salad with Sweet, '02 120
Pear-and-Spinach Salad, Festive, '85 131

Pecan Salad, Spinach-, '89 128; '01 284
Pickled Spinach, '81 69
Poppy Seed Dressing, Spinach Salad with, '91 210; '92 160
Pork-and-Spinach Salad, Mandarin, '88 M126
Raspberry Cream Dressing, Spinach Salad with, '94 321
Rice Salad, Spinach-, '94 63
Russian Dressing, Spinach Salad with, '79 144
Salmon-Spinach Salad, '87 145
Sesame Salad, Spinach-, '91 211; '92 160
Sesame Spinach Salad, '90 292
Southern Spinach Salad, '80 55
Southern Spinach Salad with Cheese Grits Croutons and Vidalia Onion-Balsamic Vinaigrette, '04 316
Special Spinach Salad, '80 78
Spicy Dressing, Fresh Spinach with, '80 55
Spinach Salad, '82 102; '86 302; '87 62; '88 299; '92 281, 341; '93 46, 65; '03 246
Springtime Spinach Salad, '81 114
Sprout Salad, Fresh Spinach-, '82 281; '83 42
Strawberry Salad with Tart Poppy Seed Dressing, Spinach-and-, '03 241
Strawberry-Spinach Salad, '91 169; '93 168
Sun-Dried Tomato Salad, Spinach and, '93 250
Supreme, Spinach Salad, '79 243
Sweet-Sour Spinach Salad, '85 M112
Tangy Spinach Salad, '00 24
Tossed Spinach Salad, '01 159
Tropical Spinach Salad, '90 231
Tropical Spinach Salad with Grilled Chicken, '04 51
Tropical Spinach Salad with Grilled Pork Tenderloin, '04 51
Tropical Spinach Salad with Grilled Shrimp, '04 51
Wilted, Spinach Salad, '81 M4; '89 123; '91 210; '92 160; '93 125
Zesty Spinach Salad, '79 88
Sprout Salad, '90 137
Sprout Salad, Crunchy, '98 52
Sprout Salad, Spanish, '85 327; '86 22
Squash Salad, '03 M184
Strawberry Salad, Frozen, '94 119
Strawberry Yogurt Salad, '80 232
Suzie or Steven Salad, '98 204
Tabbouleh, '85 148; '93 70; '99 175
Tabbouleh Salad, '91 70; '92 212; '94 174; '01 57
(Tabbouleh Salad), Boot Scoot Tabbouli, '96 159
Taco Salad, '79 56; '83 145; '84 221; '85 84; '89 332; '90 20
Taco Salad Cups, '85 M29
Taco Salad, Meatless, '81 204
Taco Salad, Party, '97 19
Taco Salad, Spicy, '87 287
Tart Cranberry Salad, '79 286
Tofu Salad, '88 27
Tomato. *See also* **SALADS/Congealed.**
Artichoke-Tomato Salad, '82 239
Asparagus and Tomatoes with Herb Vinaigrette, '99 56
Asparagus Salad, Tomato-, '92 79
Avocado Salad, Tomato-, '86 74
Basil-and-Tomato Couscous Salad, '94 175
Basil-Mozzarella Salad, Tomato-, '95 171
Bibb Salad with Fried Green Tomatoes, Kentucky, '01 121
Charred Tomato Salad, '01 158
Cherry Tomato-Caper Salad, '00 140; '02 32
Cherry Tomato Salad, '87 156
Cottage Cheese Salad in Tomatoes, '86 208
Cottage-Tomato Salad, '85 163
Cucumber-and-Tomato Salad, '01 127

Cucumber and Tomato Salad, Dilled, '81 153
Cucumber-Onion Salad, Tomato-, '81 239
Cucumber Salad, Tomato-, '86 218; '92 199
Cucumber Salad with Yogurt-Herb Dressing, Tomato-, '92 96
Cucumber Summer Salad, Tomato-and-, '93 141
Cucumber-Tomato Salad, '90 144
Endive-Tomato Starburst Salad, '93 323
Feta Salad, Tomato-, '81 246; '91 168
Flower Salad, Tomato, '89 128
Grape Tomatoes with Capers, '01 329
Green Bean Salad, Tomato-and-, '97 162
Gruyère-Basil Salad, Tomato-, '99 172
Guacamole-Tomato Salad, '81 302
Herbed Tomatoes, '83 173
Herb Salad, Tomato-, '89 220
Italian BLT Bread Salad, '03 90
Italian Tomato Salad, '01 124
Lima Bean-Tomato Salad, '85 137
Marinated Cucumber-Tomato Salad, '02 167
Marinated Salsa Tomatoes, '82 164
Marinated Tomato and Brie Salad, '95 95
Marinated Tomato-and-Cucumber Salad, '92 216
Marinated Tomatoes, '85 156, 163; '89 174, 202
Marinated Tomato Slices, '83 193
Mozzarella Salad, Tomato-, '89 220
Mozzarella-Tomato-Basil Salad, Fresh, '93 131
Napoleon, Tomato, '00 182
Okra-Corn-and-Tomato Vinaigrette, '90 173
Onion, and Cucumber in Italian Dressing, Tomato, '81 83
Oregano, Tomatoes, '83 145
Pasta Salad, Tomato-, '97 M160
Petal Salad, Tomato, '79 88
Red Onion Salad, Tomato-, '04 181
Refresher, Tomato, '81 94
Relish Salad, Tomato, '83 111
Roasted Tomato-and-Pepper Salad, '01 196
Slices with Lemon Dressing, Tomato, '87 167
Stuffed Tomatoes, Avocado-, '82 101
Stuffed Tomatoes, Cold, '80 100
Stuffed Tomato Salad, Artichoke-, '82 101
Stuffed Tomato Salad, Crab-, '80 148
Stuffed Tomato Salad, Oriental-, '82 101
Stuffed with Sea Slaw, Tomatoes, '89 96
Summer Tomato Salad, '94 201
Summer Tomato Treat, '79 143
Trout-and-Tomato Salad with Black Pepper Vinaigrette, '98 284
Tuna with Warm Tomato Salad, '97 179
Vidalia-Tomato Salad, '84 65
Vinaigrette, Tomato-Basil, '87 89
Vinaigrette, Tomatoes, '84 106
Watercress-Tomato Salad, '85 132
Tossed Salad, Grecian, '04 283
Tossed Salad, Italian, '00 167
Tossed Salad with Parmesan Dressing, '86 192
Turkey
Bacon Dressing, Turkey Salad with Hot, '87 285
Bake, Turkey Salad, '79 253
Carrot Salad, Turkey-, '86 283
Curried Turkey Salad, '88 140
Curried Turkey Salad, Chutney, '98 314
Fruit-and-Spice Turkey Salad, '94 325
Fruitful Turkey Salad, '84 197
Fruit Salad, Turkey-, '79 56
Fruit Salad, Turkey, '83 233; '84 244
Holiday Turkey Salad, '84 320
Honey-Mustard Turkey Salad, '92 309; '01 230
Hot Turkey Salad, '86 10, 297; '87 176
Layered Cornbread-and-Turkey Salad, '02 141
Layered Turkey Salad, '86 332; '92 220
Macaroni Salad, Turkey, '83 282
Orange Salad, Turkey-in-the-, '93 21

SALADS, Turkey
(continued)

Polynesian Turkey Salad, **'87** 285
Ranch-Style Turkey 'n' Pasta Salad, **'94** 184
Sandwiches, Turkey Salad Pita, **'87** 202; **'88** 43
Smoked, Turkey Salad, **'96** 184
Southwestern, Turkey Salad, **'91** 313
Stir-Fry Salad, Chilled Turkey-and-Pepper, **'88** 140
Straw Salad, Turkey-in-the-, **'96** 286
Taco Salad, Turkey, **'95** 25
Turkey Salad, **'90** 318
Waldorf Salad with Yogurt Dressing, Turkey, **'88** 53
Walnut Salad, Turkey-, **'03** 239
Walnuts, Turkey Salad with Sautéed, **'86** 117
Zucchini Salad, Turkey-, **'85** 74
Turkish Salad, **'96** 137
Turnip-and-Carrot Salad, **'91** 212
Turnip Salad, **'85** 235
Turnip Salad, Irish, **'94** 178
Vegetable. *See also* **SALADS/Congealed, Pasta.**
Antipasto, Vegetable, **'85** 263
Basil-Chicken-Vegetable Salad, **'92** 162
Bean Salad, Veggie-, **'04** 328
Boats, Salad, **'80** 93
Calico Salad, **'82** 35
Cauliflower-Vegetable Salad, **'85** 158
Chicken Salad, Vegetable-, **'91** 287
Chilled Vegetable Salad, **'00** 285
Chinese Salad, **'80** 4
Colorful Vegetable Salad, **'04** 34
Composée, Salad, **'79** 171
Composé, Salad, **'93** 126
Corned Beef Salad, Vegetable-, **'80** 148
Creamy Vegetable Salad, **'79** 47
Creole Salad, **'79** 147
Crunchy Vegetable Salad, **'79** 11; **'80** 217; **'83** 216
Different Vegetable Salad, **'82** 143
Easy Vegetable Salad, **'83** 316; **'84** 16
Extravaganza, Salad, **'87** 233
Garden Marinade, **'81** 23
Garden Medley Salad, **'80** 122
Garden Salad, **'85** 92; **'87** 62; **'89** 166; **'92** 60
Garden Salad Bowl, **'82** 239
Garden Salad with Tomato-Cream Cheese Dressing, **'79** 173
Greek Salad, Garden, **'86** 173
Greek Salad, Quick, **'02** 24
Greek Vegetable Salad, **'99** 202
Green-and-White Vegetable Salad, **'79** 286
Green Vegetable and Egg Salad, **'79** 191
Green Vegetable Salad, Overnight, **'80** 5
Grilled Marinated Vegetable Salad, **'01** 143
Grilled Vegetable Salad, **'94** 203; **'00** 146
Healthy Salad, **'95** 133
Horseradish Dressing, Vegetable Salad with, **'92** 85
Italian Garden Salad, **'99** 203
Italian Vegetable Salad, **'81** 253; **'82** 19
Layered Vegetable Salad with Parmesan Dressing, **'01** 96
Loaded Veggie Salad, **'03** 58
Luncheon Salad, **'84** 232
Marinade, Fresh Vegetable, **'83** 209
Marinade, Garden, **'81** 23
Marinade, Medley, **'79** 20
Marinade, Tossed Vegetable, **'84** 266
Marinated Combo Salad, **'82** 267
Marinated Garden Salad, **'00** 178
Marinated Garden Vegetables, **'87** 252

Marinated Mixed Vegetables, **'89** 276; **'92** 106
Marinated Salad, **'83** 170; **'91** 186
Marinated Salad, Eight-Vegetable, **'80** 218
Marinated Salad, Zesty, **'90** 90
Marinated Summer Salad, **'81** 153
Marinated Tex-Mex Salad, **'93** 106
Marinated Vegetable-Bacon Bowl, **'79** 191
Marinated Vegetable Patch Salad, **'84** 232
Marinated Vegetables, **'79** 146; **'81** 239; **'85** 67; **'88** 4, 170
Marinated Vegetable Salad, **'79** 106, 143; **'81** 280; **'82** 163; **'83** 260; **'84** 13; **'87** 243; **'92** 64, 91; **'97** 219; **'02** 211
Marinated Vegetable Salad, Crispy, **'84** 193
Marinated Vegetable Salad, Fresh, **'86** 173
Marinated Vegetables, Creole-, **'02** 69
Marinated Vegetables, Sweet-and-Sour, **'83** 266
Marinated Vegetables, Zesty, **'82** 272
Marinated Veggies, **'01** 127
Marinate, Fresh Vegetable, **'80** 33; **'81** 230
Meal-in-One Salad, **'82** 232
Medley Salad, Vegetable, **'88** 86
Mexican Salad, **'81** 36, 113
Minted Vegetable Salad, **'88** 23; **'98** 158
Mixed Vegetable Salad, **'80** 115; **'81** 302; **'82** 239; **'83** 317; **'84** 16; **'86** 136
Next-Day Vegetable Salad, **'83** 81
Oriental Salad, Make-Ahead, **'82** 163
Oriental Vegetable Salad, **'84** 290
Overnight Vegetable Salad, **'90** 33
Panzanella, **'00** 62
Party Vegetable Salad, **'86** 79
Pasta and Vegetables, **'89** 255
Pasta Salad, Vegetable, **'89** 256; **'91** 143
Pasta Salad, Vegetable-, **'92** 167
Pebble Salad, **'91** 27
Pita Bread Salad, **'95** 86
Primavera Salad, **'93** 140
Primavera Salad, Rice, **'00** 131
Quick Summer Italian Salad, **'92** 79
Radish-Vegetable Salad with Parmesan Dressing, **'01** 101
Rainbow Salad, **'02** 18
Rainbow Vegetable Salad, **'83** 111
Red, White, and Green Salad, **'90** 18
Refrigerated Vegetable Salad, **'84** 120
Rice-and-Vegetable Salad, **'86** 42
Riviera, Salade, **'89** 12
Roasted Vegetable Salad, Wild Rice-and-, **'99** 316
Rolls, Picnic Salad, **'79** 127
Rolls, Vegetable Salad, **'82** 278
Senator's Salad, **'79** 191
Seven-Layer Vegetable Salad, **'79** 88
Spaghetti-Vegetable Salad, **'97** 196
Spring Vegetable Salad, **'88** 48
Sprout Salad, Crunchy, **'96** 45
Summer Salad with Citrus Marinade, **'92** 133
Summer Vegetable-and-Orzo Salad, **'00** 165
Swedish Vegetable Salad, **'82** 23
Sweet-and-Sour Vegetable Salad, **'81** 25
Tangy Vegetable Toss, **'79** 144
Tarragon-Vegetable Salad, **'85** 288
Tomato, Bell Pepper, and Portobello Salad, Grilled, **'98** 211
Tossed Salad, Lively Lemon, **'00** 16
Variety Salad, **'79** 113
Vegetable Salad, **'98** 92; **'00** 136
Vinaigrette Salad, Vegetable-Chicken, **'86** 135
Vinaigrette, Vegetables, **'82** 225, 290
Walnuts, Vegetable Salad with, **'86** 118
Warm Vegetable Salad, **'95** 174
Winter Salad, **'97** 304
Winter Vegetable Salad, **'86** 42
Winter Vegetable Salad, Baked, **'04** 45

Waldorf. *See also* **SALADS/Congealed.**
Creamy Waldorf Salad, **'87** 311
Deluxe Waldorf Salad, **'83** 81
Frozen Waldorf Salad, **'79** 126; **'82** 145
Jiffy Waldorf Salad, **'88** 100
New Wave Waldorf Salad, **'92** 36
Old-Fashioned Waldorf Salad, **'81** 295
Overnight Waldorf Salad, **'81** 309
Pineapple Waldorf, **'97** 86
Pineapple Waldorf Salad, **'92** 97
Southern Classic Waldorf Salad, **'92** 36
Tropical Waldorf Salad, **'89** 12
Turkey Waldorf Salad with Yogurt Dressing, **'88** 53
Waldorf Salad, **'89** 278; **'97** 204
Winter Waldorf Salad, **'04** 245
Watercress Orange Salad, **'04** 45
Watercress Salad, **'79** 144
Watercress-Tomato Salad, **'85** 132
Watermelon-Prosciutto Salad, **'04** 171
Watermelon Salad with Celery-Nut Dressing, **'80** 182
Watermelon Sparkle, **'84** 191
Wheat Berry-and-Roasted Corn Salad, **'94** 175
Wheat Salad with Citrus and Mint, **'99** 163
Winter Salad, **'98** 19
Yogurt-Cucumber Salad, **'82** 122
Yogurt Salad, Frozen, **'92** 303
Zucchini-Artichoke Salad, **'91** 229
Zucchini Chef's Salad, **'83** 143
Zucchini-Corn Marinated Salad, **'98** 236
Zucchini, Marinated, **'80** 33
Zucchini Salad, **'82** 104; **'87** 103; **'89** 128
Zucchini Salad, Marinated, **'82** 164; **'90** 32
Zucchini Salad, Summer, **'95** 229
SALMON
Almonds and Tomato-Lemon Sauce, Salmon with, **'04** 23
Baked Salmon with Caribbean Fruit Salsa, Blitzen's, **'04** 252
Bake with Pecan-Crunch Coating, Salmon, **'95** 209
Ball, Salmon, **'80** 149; **'86** 262
Ball, Smoky Salmon Cheese, **'82** 247
Barbecued Salmon, **'81** 181
Bisque, Smoked Salmon-Whiskey, **'00** 65
Blackened Salmon with Mango Salsa, **'00** 337
Broiled Salmon with Dijon-Caper Cream Sauce, **'98** 329
Broiled Salmon with Lemon and Olive Oil, **'04** 46
Burgers, Salmon, **'89** 98; **'95** 24; **'98** 144
Canapés, Smoked Salmon, **'99** 140
Carbonara, Salmon, **'83** 43
Casserole, Salmon, **'81** 22
Cheesecake, Smoked Salmon, **'99** 92
Chili-Rubbed Salmon, **'97** 124
Chilled Salmon with Dill Sauce, **'84** 285
Chowder, Salmon, **'97** 125
Cracked Pepper Salmon Fillets, **'00** 140
Croquettes, Baked Salmon, **'81** 22
Dip, Extra-Creamy Smoked Salmon, **'03** 240
Fettuccine, Salmon, **'90** 123
Fillets with Avocado Mayonnaise, Spicy Salmon, **'02** 327
Fillets with Red Wine Garlic Sauce, Salmon, **'94** 250
Fillets with Sweet Corn Relish, Salmon, **'93** 119
Florentine, Salmon, **'83** 43
Glazed Salmon, Caramelized Maple-and-Garlic-, **'01** 275
Glazed Salmon with Stir-Fried Vegetables, **'02** 69
Grilled Salmon with Mustard-Molasses Glaze, **'01** 209
Grilled Salmon with Sweet Soy Slaw and Dipping Sauce, **'04** 123
Grilled Salmon with Tangy Dill Sauce, **'04** 320

Herb-Rubbed Salmon Fillets, Fresh, '03 207
Kebabs, Salmon, '81 182
Loaf, Easy Salmon, '80 4
Loaf, Savory Salmon, '92 33
Loaf with Cucumber-Dill Sauce, Salmon, '86 5
Log, Salmon, '81 22
Log, Salmon Party, '98 154
Mousse, Irresistible Salmon, '79 284
Mousse, Salmon, '83 79
Mousse, Salmon Dill, '81 21
Mushrooms and Green Onions, Fresh Salmon with,
    '93 180
Orange-Basil Salmon, '97 165
Pan-Grilled Salmon, '00 295
Parchment, Salmon in, '95 311
Pasta, Smoked Salmon-Caper-and-Dill, '98 169
Patties, Cheesy Salmon, '89 99
Patties, Open-Faced Salmon, '87 M218
Patties, Salmon, '92 215
Patties with Lemon-Cheese Sauce, Salmon, '91 24
Patties with Sauce, Salmon, '88 164
Poached Salmon, '83 35
Poached Salmon with Emerald Sauce, '90 63
Poached Salmon with Horseradish Sauce, '91 183
Poached Salmon with Yellow Pepper Sauce, '98 230
Potatoes, Salmon-Topped, '84 124
Quesadilla with Cucumber Salsa, Grilled Salmon,
    '95 131
Quiche, Salmon, '82 87; '87 38
Quiche, Salmon-and-Dill, '03 58
Ragout, Salmon-and-Vegetable, '96 45
Roll, Salmon Party, '83 127
Salads
    Avocados, Salmon-Stuffed, '86 74
    Broiled Salmon Salad, '92 108
    Chilly Salmon Salad, '80 104
    Crunchy Salmon Salad, '81 148
    Greens with Creamy Dill Dressing, Salmon on
        Mixed, '93 143
    Macaroni Salad, Salmon-and-, '81 114
    Macaroni-Salmon Salad, '82 232
    Pasta Salad, Salmon-, '87 9
    Poached Salmon Salad, Chilled, '96 68
    Potato Salad, Salmon-, '87 285
    Potato Salad, Smoked Salmon, '97 64
    Rice Salad, Salmon-, '84 289
    Salmon Salad, '89 99
    Scandinavian Salmon Salad, '98 208
    Shells, Salmon Salad, '85 286
    Simple Salmon Salad, '91 23
    Smoked Salmon-and-Egg Salad, '02 203
    Spinach Salad, Salmon-, '87 145
    Summertime Salmon Salad, '82 207
    Wild Rice Salad, Oriental Salmon-and-, '94 173
Salsa, Smoked Salmon, '96 272
Sandwiches, Cucumber-Salmon-Watercress, '03 111
Sandwiches with Dill, Cucumber-Salmon, '02 131
Scalloped Salmon, '81 273
Scalloped Salmon for Two, '89 98
Scaloppine with Vegetable Confetti and Pernod
    Sauce, Salmon, '94 172
Sesame-Crusted Salmon with Ginger Vinaigrette,
    '95 162
Smoked Salmon, '95 114
Smoked Salmon and Cucumber Tartlets, '95 216
Smoked Salmon, Beggar's Purses with, '04 244
Smoked Salmon, Drizzled, '88 91
Smoked Salmon or Mackerel, '84 46
Soufflé, Fresh Salmon, '81 182
Spread, Salmon, '81 149
Spread, Salmon-and-Horseradish, '87 146
Spread, Smoked Salmon, '84 324; '98 285
Spread with Capers, Smoked Salmon, '98 49
Steaks, Baked Salmon, '85 54

Steaks, Glazed Salmon, '86 256
Steaks, Grilled Herbed Salmon, '93 176
Steaks, Grilled Salmon, '94 278
Steaks, Marinated Salmon, '87 6
Steaks, Mint-Marinated Salmon, '96 175
Steaks, Oven-Fried Salmon, '81 181
Steaks with Dill Sauce, Salmon, '85 164
Steaks with Lemon-Mustard Sauce, Salmon, '97 124
Steaks with Tarragon Butter, Salmon, '87 155
Steaks with Tarragon Sauce, Grilled Salmon, '97 42
Teriyaki Salmon, Glazed, '97 124
Terrine, Layered Salmon-and-Spinach, '84 132
Turnovers, Salmon-Spinach, '83 44
Vermicelli, Salmon-Pesto, '92 200
SALSAS. *See also* **CHUTNEYS, PESTOS,
    RELISHES, SAUCES, TOPPINGS.**
Apricot Salsa, '98 126
Artichoke-Tomato Salsa, '96 182
Avocado-Corn Salsa, '94 201; '99 335
Avocado-Feta Salsa, '96 15
Avocado-Mango Salsa, '00 328
Avocado-Peach Salsa, '02 159
Avocado Salsa, '91 182
Avocado Salsa, Fresh, '02 247
Banana Salsa, '96 85
Bean Salsa, Smoky Three-, '02 202
Black-and-White Salsa, Pork Chops with, '97 200
Black Bean-and-Corn Salsa, '94 80
Black Bean-and-Corn Salsa Pork Chops, '01 320
Black Bean-Corn Salsa, '96 126; '04 322
Black Bean Salsa, '93 155; '94 161; '97 226;
    '00 122; '03 146, 323; '04 25
Black Bean Salsa, Chunky, '03 25
Black Bean Salsa with Citrus Dressing, '01 60
Black-Eyed Pea Salsa, '93 164
Black-Eyed Pea Salsa, Chunky, '01 333
Broiled Salsa Parmesan, '98 33
Caribbean Salsa, '96 70
Cha-Cha Salsa, '97 160; '98 333
Cheesecake, Salsa, '98 33
Cherry Salsa, '99 156
Chile Salsa, Double, '91 182
Chile Salsa with Homemade Tostados, Hot, '88 115
Chipotle Salsa, Chicken-and-Brie Quesadillas with,
    '99 311
Chunky Salsa, '86 130; '90 206
Citrus Salsa, Fresh, '03 291
Citrus Salsa, Grilled Shrimp with, '97 141
Colorful Salsa, '99 119
Corn-Black Bean Salsa, '96 15
Corn, Pepper, and Tomato Salsa, Yellowfin Tuna
    with, '94 164
Corn Salsa, '00 164
Corn Salsa, Grilled, '99 162
Corn Salsa, Spicy, '93 322
Corn Salsa, Sweet, '95 156
Corn Salsa, Zesty, '02 193
Crab-and-Ginger Salsa with Sesame Wontons, Spicy,
    '01 283
Cranberry-Citrus Salsa, '97 290
Cranberry-Jalapeño Salsa, '01 234
Cranberry Salsa, '98 321; '99 316; '00 269; '01 254
Cruda, Salsa, '87 180; '88 148
Cucumber-Dill Salsa, '95 107
Cucumber-Radish Salsa, '01 187
Cucumber Salsa, '95 131
Dried Chile Salsa, '97 265
Fiery Salsa, '01 174
Fresh Salsa, '95 42; '00 59; '04 274
Fresh Summer Salsa, '87 89
Fruit Salsa, '97 124; '02 54; '04 168
Fruit Salsa, Caribbean, '04 252
Fruit Salsa with Cinnamon Crisps, '01 108
Garden Salsa, '91 182

Green Salsa, Creamy, '91 162
Green Tomato Salsa, Peachy, '99 143
Hill Country Salsa, '97 123
Hot Mexican Salsa, '85 136
Hot Salsa, '98 135
Kale with Salsa, Southwest, '94 246
Kiwifruit Salsa, Hot, '94 82
Mango-and-Bell Pepper Salsa, '00 247
Mango Salsa, '91 182; '95 104; '98 232;
    '00 124, 337; '02 163; '04 59
Mango Salsa, Fresh, '00 122
Mango Salsa, Minted, '96 206
Melon Salsa, Hot, '95 144
Mexi-Corn Salsa, '91 182
Olive Salsa, '00 277
One-Minute Salsa, '95 93
Onion Salsa, Fiesta, '94 82
Orange-Black Bean Salsa, '98 231
Papaya Salsa, '94 173
Papaya Salsa, Asparagus Salad with, '97 144
Party Salsa, Quick, '03 292
Peach Salsa, '91 183; '96 14; '97 183
Peach Salsa, Fresh, '95 195
Pepper Salsa, '88 26
Pepper Salsa, Mixed, '91 181
Picante, Homemade Salsa, '81 67
Picante, Salsa, '04 41
Picante with Shrimp, Salsa, '92 210
Pimiento Cheese Salsa, Fiery Steak with, '99 331
Pineapple Salsa, '96 226; '03 128; '04 196
Pineapple Salsa, Spicy, '97 165
Pineapple Salsa, Warm, '02 144
Pink-Eyed Pea Salsa, '00 158
Pinto Bean-and-Bacon Salsa, Warm, '03 331
Plum Salsa, '97 176
Poblano Salsa, '91 135
Quick Party Salsa, '04 146
Radish-Cucumber Salsa, '04 119
Red Bean Salsa, '97 227
Red Salsa, '90 172
Roasted Red Pepper Salsa, '01 100
Roasted Salsa, '95 130
Roasted Salsa Verde, '96 182
Salpicon, Salsa, '03 33
Salsa, '80 196; '87 217; '88 147; '97 171; '01 273;
    '03 95
Santa Fe Salsa, Zesty, '03 198
Serrano Salsa, Roasted, '95 207
Simple Salsa, '01 60
Smoked Salmon Salsa, '96 272
Southwestern Salsa with Black Beans and Corn, '96 275
Spaghetti, Salsa, '00 58
Strawberry Salsa, Balsamic, '02 86
Summer Salsa, '98 172
Summer Salsa, Spicy, '03 186
Sweet Heat Salsa and Cinnamon Crisps, South Seas
    Ice Cream with, '04 315
Sweet Salsa, '98 174
Texas Salsa, '96 160
Tomatillo Salsa, '92 245; '02 123
Tomatillo Salsa, Fresh, '97 143
Tomatillo Salsa, Grilled Chicken with, '02 123
Tomatillo Salsa, Roasted, '95 64
Tomato-Avocado Salsa, '94 83
Tomato-Basil Salsa, Pan-Fried Roughy with, '99 123
Tomato-Mango Salsa, Seared Scallops with, '95 122
Tomato Salsa, '87 120; '96 15; '02 118
Tomato Salsa, Fresh, '91 182; '95 181; '01 249
Tomato Salsa, Roasted, '95 64
Tomato Salsa, Three, '93 138
Tropical Rainbow Salsa, '94 161
Tropical Salsa, '96 14; '01 60
Tropical Salsa, Key Lime Pie with Minted, '99 333
Vegetable Salsa, '96 208, 220

SALSAS
(continued)

Vegetable Salsa, Fresh, **'98** 194
Vegetable Salsa, Greek, **'98** 32
Vegetable Salsa, Shrimp Skewers with, **'98** 32, 223
Verde, Salsa, **'91** 182; **'96** 160
Warm-and-Spicy Salsa, **'99** 279
Watermelon Salsa, **'98** 164
Yellow Tomato Salsa, **'87** 122

SANDWICHES
Apple Breakfast Sandwiches, **'92** 332
Apple-Cinnamon Breakfast Sandwiches, **'85** 298
Apple Party Sandwiches, **'92** 234
Apple Pockets, Toasted Cream Cheese-and-,
   '01 200
Apple Sandwiches, **'79** 164; **'80** 130
Asparagus Grill Sandwiches, **'79** 164; **'80** 130
Asparagus Sandwich, Warm, **'99** 102
Asparagus Spear Sandwiches, **'84** 165
Avocado, Bacon, and Cheese Sandwiches, **'87** 279
Avocado Deluxe Sandwiches, **'99** 72
Bacon, Cheese, and Tomato Sandwiches, **'84** 14
Bacon, Cheese, and Tomato Sandwiches, Grilled,
   '97 170
Bacon-Cheese Sandwiches, Grilled, **'83** 242
Bacon 'n' Egg Breakfast Empanadas, **'02** 324
Bacon, Pimiento, and Cheese Hoagies, **'90** 144
Bacon Sandwiches, Open-Faced Cheesy, **'80** 78
Bagel, Breakfast on a, **'94** 66
Bagels, Meal-in-One, **'88** 159
Bar, Super Summer Sandwich, **'91** 143
Basket of Sandwiches, Bread, **'86** 126
Bat Sandwiches, **'00** 234
Bean Burgers with Adobo Mayonnaise, **'02** 202
Beef. *See also* **SANDWICHES/Pita.**
   Bacon, and Blue Cheese Sandwiches, Beef,
      '96 23
   Barbecue Beef Sandwiches, **'99** 327; **'01** 136
   Barbecued Beef Sandwiches, **'81** 25; **'82** 31;
      '83 34
   Barbecue Sandwiches, Debate, **'97** 234
   Barbecue, Slow-Cooker Beef, **'02** 299
   Beef-Eater Sandwiches, **'86** 72
   Calzones, Beef-and-Pepperoni, **'03** 202
   Calzones, Ground Beef, **'97** 95
   Cheeseburger Biscuits, **'79** 194
   Cheesesteaks, Chimichurri, **'04** 312
   Corned Beef and Cheese Sandwich, **'79** 214
   Corned Beef Sandwiches, **'83** 291; **'85** 242;
      '92 234
   Corned Beef Sandwiches, Barbecued, **'83** 130
   Corned Beef Sandwiches, Grilled, **'87** 54
   Dilly Beef Sandwiches, **'98** 288
   Flank Steak Sandwiches with Apple Barbecue
      Sauce, **'99** 173
   French Beef Slice, **'79** 125
   French Dip Sandwiches, **'97** 211
   Grilled Cheese Meat Loaf Sandwiches, **'04** 188
   Grilled Roast Beef-and-Brie Sandwiches, **'03** 296
   Gumbo Joes, **'88** 158
   Hot Beef Sandwiches, **'00** 98
   Jalapeño Heroes, Open-Faced, **'90** 144
   Kraut Sandwich, Beef-and-, **'91** 167
   Loaf, Big Wheel, **'84** 281
   London Broil Sandwiches with Yogurt-Cucumber
      Sauce, **'01** 162
   Meatball Sandwiches, **'04** 170
   Meatball Sandwich, Giant, **'92** 196
   Meat Loaf Sandwich, **'01** 210
   Meat Loaf Sandwiches, Barbecue, **'04** 188
   Open-Faced Italian Sandwich, Beef-and-
      Artichoke, **'98** 22

Pizza Sandwiches, Open-Face, **'82** 3; **'83** 85;
   '84 M198; **'85** 22
Pork Tenderloin Sandwiches, Beef and, **'80** 175
Reuben Puffs, **'98** 231
Reuben Sandwiches, **'80** M201
Reuben Sandwiches, Broiled, **'81** 240; **'83** 69
Reuben Sandwiches, Crispy, **'85** 299
Reuben Sandwiches, Grilled, **'81** 206
Reuben Sandwiches, Open-Face, **'91** 199
Reuben Sandwich, Rolled, **'99** 219
Reubens, Golden-Baked Mini, **'01** 62
Reubens, Open-Faced Coleslaw, **'03** 169
Reubens, Oven-Grilled, **'97** 304
Reubens, Party, **'90** 61
Reubens, Spicy Coleslaw, **'04** 63
Reubens, Summer, **'00** 134
Reuben Turnovers, **'94** 253
Roast Beef Hero Sandwich, **'91** 167
Roast Beef Slices, **'02** 246
Rolls with Mustard-Horseradish Cream, Beef,
   '02 53
Roll-Ups, Savory Beef and Cheese, **'96** 235
Sloppy Joes, **'91** 172
Steak-and-Onion Sandwiches, **'02** 126
Steak Bagel Sandwiches, **'96** 249
Steak Sandwiches, **'96** 136
Steak Stroganoff Sandwiches, **'85** 110
Taco Joes, **'91** 167
Tenderloin Picnic Sandwiches, Beef, **'90** 91
Wake-Up Sandwiches, **'84** 58
Wraps, Cheese-Steak, **'00** M335
BLT Breakfast Sandwiches, **'04** 171
BLT, Caramelized Onion, **'03** 90
BLT Croissants, **'93** 158
BLT Sandwiches, Curried, **'93** 158
BLT Sandwiches, Italian, **'02** 230
BLT's, Cheesy, **'85** 92
Breakfast Sandwiches, **'80** 52; **'82** M123;
   '89 M230
Breakfast Sandwiches, Cheesy, **'90** 140
Breakfast Sandwiches, Open-Faced, **'92** 140
Brown Bread-Cream Cheese Sandwiches, **'87** M6
Bunwiches, **'80** 92
Burgers, Chicken-Cheese, **'04** 56
Calla Lily Sandwiches, **'91** 106
Calzone, **'85** 94
Calzones, Surprise, **'00** 282
Calzones with Italian Tomato Sauce, **'03** 202
Calzones with Pasta Sauce, **'01** 54
Cheddar Cheese Sandwiches, Hot, **'97** 179
Cheese Sandwiches, Hot French, **'82** 3
Cheese Sandwiches, Leafy, **'90** 56
Cheese Sandwiches with Artichoke-Tomato Salsa,
   Herbed, **'96** 182
Cheese Tea Sandwiches, **'92** 276
Chicken. *See also* **SANDWICHES/Pita.**
   Bagel Sandwiches, Chicken-Benedict, **'96** 250
   Baked Chicken Sandwiches, **'79** 164; **'80** 130;
      '84 165
   Broiled Chicken Sandwiches with Fresh Salsa,
      '00 59
   Cheese Chicken Sandwich, Ham 'n', **'95** 153
   Cheese Sandwiches, Toasted Chicken-and-,
      '85 242
   Cheesy Chicken Sandwiches, **'82** 190
   Chutney-Chicken Croissants, **'92** 22
   Club Sandwiches, Chicken, **'86** 160
   Creamed Chicken Toppers, **'99** 240
   Crispy Chicken Sandwich, **'81** 114
   Curried Chicken Salad on Raisin Bread, **'85** 96
   Curried Chicken Tea Sandwiches, **'97** 23
   Dagwoods, Chicken-Avocado, **'96** 200; **'99** 337
   English Muffin Delight, **'82** 45
   Finger Sandwiches, Chicken-Salad, **'85** 119

   Focaccia with Roasted Pepper Vinaigrette,
      Stuffed, **'00** 134
   Gouda Lover's Chicken Sandwiches, **'99** 195
   Grilled Chicken-and-Pesto Clubs, **'01** 22
   Grilled Chicken 'n' Cheese Sandwiches, **'99** 240
   Hot Chicken Sandwiches, **'83** 291
   Jamaican Chicken Sandwich, **'95** 153
   Jerk Chicken Sandwich, **'98** 333
   Mandarin Orange Spread Sandwiches, Chicken-,
      '04 259
   Marinated Chicken in a Sandwich, **'86** 185
   Marinated Chicken Sandwiches, **'86** M45
   Mozzarella Melt, Italian Chicken-, **'95** 153
   Open-Faced Mexican Sandwiches, **'98** 230
   Open-Faced Sandwiches, Summer, **'99** 201
   Panini, Chicken Florentine, **'02** 236
   Parmigiana Sandwich, Chicken, **'94** 65
   Puffed Chicken Sandwiches, **'82** 35
   Salad Melts, Open-Faced Cheesy Chicken,
      '00 134
   Salad Sandwiches, Asian Chicken, **'98** 223
   Salad Sandwiches, Grilled Chicken, **'00** 164
   Salad Sandwiches, Hot Chicken, **'96** 74
   Salad with Artichokes, Chicken, **'86** 186
   Salad Wraps, Lemon-Basil Chicken, **'00** 216
   Saucy Chick-Wiches, **'81** 25; **'82** 31; **'83** 34
   Southwestern Chicken Sandwiches, **'96** 23
   Spread, Tasty Chicken, **'84** 193
   Sprout Sandwiches, Polynesian, **'85** 51
   Sub, Chicken, **'98** 287
   Tortas, Grilled Chicken, **'01** M187
   Wraps, Chicken-Cranberry, **'01** 34
   Wraps, Thai Chicken-Avocado, **'02** 206
Chili con Queso Sandwiches, Grilled, **'96** 139
Christmas Tree Sandwiches, **'92** 279
Club Sandwich Bar, Easy, **'91** 279
Club Sandwiches, Double-Decker, **'91** 231; **'92** 68
Club Sandwiches, Egg Salad, **'02** 203
Club Sandwiches, Tangy, **'80** 93
Club Sandwich, Italian, **'01** 22
Clubs, Cobb, **'01** 22
Club, Shrimp-Egg Salad, **'02** 203
Club, Sweet-Pickle Egg Salad, **'02** 203
Confetti Sandwiches, **'79** 236
Crab Burgers, Potato-Crusted, **'94** 139
Cream Cheese Party Sandwiches, Nutty, **'00** 119
Crostini, Feta-Tomato, **'92** 159
Cucumber Pinwheel Sandwiches, **'85** 120
Cucumber-Salmon-Watercress Sandwiches, **'03** 111
Cucumber Sandwiches, **'88** 159; **'90** 81; **'94** 14;
   '97 99; **'00** 208
Cucumber Sandwiches, Dainty, **'81** 119
Curried Tea Sandwiches, **'91** 314
Date-Nut Lettuce Sandwich, **'94** 202
Deli Stuffed Sandwich, **'98** 287
Dried Tomato-and-Basil Sandwiches, **'99** 274
Eggplant Sandwiches, **'99** 240
Eggplant Sandwiches, Baked, **'82** 230
Eggplant Sandwiches, Open-Face, **'95** 124
Eggplant, Tomato, and Feta Sandwiches, **'98** 106
Egg Salad Sandwiches, **'03** 179
Egg Sandwiches, Open-Face, **'83** 292; **'84** 78;
   '86 160
Egg Sandwiches, Open-Faced Cheesy, **'86** 67
Egg Sandwiches, Saucy, **'91** 160
Eggsclusive Sandwiches, **'79** 164; **'80** 130
Eggs-Tra Special Sandwiches, **'81** 240; **'83** 69
Eggwiches, Croissant, **'91** 160
Feta Salad Sandwich, Tuscan, **'99** 289
Fish. *See also* **SANDWICHES/Pita.**
   Amberjack Sandwiches, Grilled, **'91** 195
   Catfish Sandwiches, Fried, **'02** 60
   Grouper Sandwiches, Batter-Fried, **'96** 197
   Heroes, Neptune, **'84** 281

Po'boys, Zesty Fish, '03 120
Salmon Sandwiches with Dill, Cucumber-,
    '02 131
Tuna-Apple Sandwiches, Curried, '00 247
Tuna Burgers, Zippy, '81 135
Tuna Cheesies, '82 191
Tuna Club Sandwiches, '83 134
Tuna Melts, '02 60
Tuna Melts, Curried, '95 46
Tuna Melts, Hot, '95 126; '96 201
Tuna Melt, Southwestern, '96 201
Tuna Melts, Southwestern, '95 127
Tuna Melts, Tempting, '88 158
Tuna Salad Rolls, Hot, '84 281
Tuna Salad Sandwiches, White Bean-and-, '02 31
Tuna Salad, Swiss, '86 186
Tuna Sandwich Boats, '91 166
Tuna Sandwiches, French Toasted, '80 275
Tuna Sandwiches, Grilled-, '02 173
Tuna Sandwiches, Hot, '85 299; '86 M194
Tuna Waffle-Wich, Hot, '88 272; '89 181
Focaccia Sandwiches, '98 53
Focaccia with Roasted Pepper Vinaigrette, Stuffed,
    '04 142
Frankfurter Sandwiches, '84 M11
French Toast Sandwiches, Strawberry-, '91 160
Fruit-and-Cheese Breakfast Sandwiches, '89 M21
Fruit Sandwiches, Glazed Breakfast, '93 178
Garden Sandwiches, Grilled, '98 315
Garden Sandwiches, Open-Faced, '87 105
Garden, The, '83 134
Goat Cheese-Olive Sandwiches, '04 272
Good-Start Sandwiches, '99 134
Grilled Bacon, Cheese, and Tomato Sandwiches,
    '97 170
Grilled Cheese, '97 328
Grilled Cheese Sandwiches, '82 M172; '94 167
Grilled Cheese Sandwich, Mexican, '92 63
Grilled Cheeses, Mexican, '97 170
Grilled Four-Cheese Sandwich with Tomato,
    Avocado, and Bacon, '00 199
Grilled Sandwiches, Tasty, '84 30
Grilled Vegetable Sandwiches, '01 310
Grills, Double Cheese, '97 170
Grills, Triple Cheese, '97 170
Guacamole Sandwiches, '82 9; '83 68
Guacamole Subs, '84 293
Ham. *See also* **SANDWICHES/Pita.**
    Asparagus-and-Ham Melt Sandwiches, '88 M96
    Asparagus Sandwiches, Ham-and-, '01 307
    Baked Ham Sandwiches, '81 29
    Basket of Sandwiches, Bread, '86 126
    Blue Cheese-Ham Sandwiches, Creamy, '87 279
    Cheese-and-Ham Striped Tea Sandwiches,
        Cheshire Claret, '94 16
    Cheese Chicken Sandwich, Ham 'n', '95 153
    Cheese Rolls, Ham-and-, '82 3
    Cheese Sandwiches, Ham-and-, '01 299
    Cheese Sandwiches, Hot Ham-and-, '85 299
    Cheese Sandwiches, Tiny Ham-and-, '99 87
    Cheese Sandwich Round, Ham-and-, '94 326
    Cheese Sandwich, Tex-Mex Ham-and-, '86 4
    Country Ham Loaves, '86 255
    Croissant Sandwiches, '89 161
    Deviled Delight, '83 130
    French Market Sandwiches, '98 230
    Giant Ham-and-Pepper Sandwich, '96 74
    Grinder Sandwich, '85 299
    Hamwiches, '96 246
    Hideaways, Ham, '81 29
    Holiday Ham Sandwiches, '02 286
    Hot Ham Sandwiches, '79 214
    Hot Rods, Ham, '86 136
    Loaf, Big Wheel, '84 281

Muffuletta, '04 27
Omelet Sandwich, '86 95
Open-Face Ham Sandwiches, '82 40; '85 8
Open-Face Sandwiches, '84 13
Panhandle Sandwiches, '01 56
Party Ham Sandwiches, '97 240
Pineapple-Ham Sandwich Loaf, '91 167
Pineapple Slaw Sandwiches, Ham-and-, '96 199
Po-Boy, Pain-Perdu, '93 291
Po'Boys, Guacamole-Topped Ham, '04 170
Quesadillas, Quick Fiesta, '02 246
Reuben Melts, Southern, '03 69
Rollups, Creamy Pineapple-and-Ham, '04 163
Salad Boats, '80 93
Salad Sandwich, Tangy Ham, '80 272
Sebastian, The, '94 184
Swiss-and-Asparagus Sandwiches, Ham-, '01 52
Swiss, Ham and Eggs à la, '88 158
Swiss Sandwiches, Ham-and-, '98 287
Swiss Sandwiches, Tangy Ham-and-, '85 164
Turkey and Ham Pine-Berry Sandwiches, '00 59
Turkey Specials, Cheesy Ham-and-, '84 14
Virginia Ham Sandwiches, '80 155
Yummy Sandwiches, '81 229
Hamburgers, Meatless Walnut, '96 243
Hearts of Palm Sandwich, '92 191
Heroes, Healthy, '90 177
Hero, E-Z, '92 63
Hot Browns, '98 287
Hot Brown Sandwiches, '80 M202
Hot Browns, Baby, '00 107; '03 238
Hot Browns, Biscuit, '02 94
Hot Browns, Kentucky, '02 94
Hot Browns, Southwestern, '02 94
Hot Browns with Fried Cheese Grits, '02 94
Italian Pesto Sandwich, Grilled, '94 170
Lamb Sandwiches, '97 107
Loaf, Mediterranean Picnic, '96 156
Mayflower Sandwiches, '96 287
Meal-in-One Sandwiches, '80 218
Meatball Sandwiches, Open-Faced, '99 239
Melts, Bacon-and-Cheese, '04 324
Monte Cristo Sandwiches, '83 134; '97 319
Monte Cristo Sandwiches, Open-Faced, '01 171
Mozzarella-Pepper Bagel Sandwiches, '98 145
Muffaletta-Style Po-Boys, '83 230
Muffin Stacks, Mushroom-Topped, '80 271
Muffuletta Bacon-Olive Party Sandwiches, Mini,
    '04 196
Muffuletta, Doodles, '94 35
Muffuletta Loaf, '97 86
Muffuletta, Napoleon House, '94 35
Muffulettas, '98 184
"Muffy" Sandwich, Fertitta's, '94 34
Mushroom Bagel Sandwiches with Curry-Mustard
    Sauce, '96 249
Mushroom Sandwiches, Toasted, '87 281
Olive-Nut Spread Sandwiches, '04 259
Olive Sandwiches, Rolled, '01 241
Olive Tea Sandwiches, '02 252
Open-Faced Sandwiches, '79 214
Open-Faced Sandwiches, Super, '97 52
Open-Faced Summer Sandwiches, '01 171
Orange Blossom Special, '88 158
Party Sandwiches, Bacon-Olive, '04 196
Party Sandwiches, Double-Filled, '93 159
Party Sandwiches, Duck, '02 48
Party Sandwiches, Easter Bunny, '02 48
Party Sandwiches, Easter Egg, '02 48
Party Sandwiches, Flower, '02 48
Peanut Butter-and-Jelly "Fish" Sandwiches, '91 177
Peanut Butter-and-Jelly Sandwiches, Christmas
    Tree, '85 319
Peanut Butter Breakfast Sandwich, '82 55

Peanut-Cheese-Raisin Sandwiches, '88 140
Philly Firecrackers, '01 142
Pigs in a Blanket, '03 167
Pimiento Cheese Finger Sandwiches, '99 86
Pimiento Cheese Sandwiches, '82 278
Pineapple-Turkey Melts, '03 196
Pita
    Alfalfa Pocket Bread Sandwiches, '82 282;
        '83 41
    Avocado Salad-Hummus Pita, '02 99
    Bavarian Pita Sandwiches, '83 31
    Bean Salad Sandwiches, '81 243
    Beef Pitas, Curried, '85 220
    Beef Pocket Sandwich, Saucy, '80 92
    Beef Salad Pocket Sandwiches, '83 267
    BLT in Pita Pockets, '93 158
    Breakfast Pita Pockets, '89 M21
    Chef's Salad, '86 186
    Chicken-Almond Pocket Sandwiches, '81 240;
        '83 69
    Chicken Pita, Oriental, '89 216
    Chicken Salad in a Pocket, '88 139
    Chicken-Spinach Pita Pockets, '01 66
    Denver Pita Sandwiches, '86 M12
    Dried Beef Pita Sandwiches, '86 160
    Fajita Pitas, '99 239
    Falafel Sandwiches, '96 23
    Fruit Salad Pita, Fresh, '02 99
    Garbanzo-Vegetable Pitas, '00 58
    Ham-and-Cheese Pita Pockets, '90 271
    Ham-and-Cheese Pita Sandwiches, '87 202;
        '88 44
    Ham and Swiss in the Pocket, '83 31
    Hearty Pocket Sandwiches, '80 93
    Hot Pita Sandwiches, '83 217; '87 M6
    Lamb Pockets with Dilled Cucumber Topping,
        '87 104
    Mango-Chicken Pita Sandwiches, '03 123
    Oriental Stuffed Pockets, '79 14
    Pita Sandwiches, '84 139
    Salad Sandwiches, Pita, '83 134
    Sloppy Joe Pocket Sandwiches, '81 200
    Spinach-Walnut Pitas, '87 202; '88 43
    Steaks, Greek Pocket, '81 262
    Stuffed Pita, '89 87
    Stuffed Pitas, Acadian, '90 177
    Tabbouleh Pitas, '98 105
    Taco Pitas, '83 31
    Tuna-in-a-Pita Pocket, '87 202
    Tuna Pockets, '88 139
    Tuna Roll Sandwiches, '96 199
    Turkey-Mozzarella Rounds, '82 3
    Turkey Salad Pita Sandwiches, '87 202; '88 43
    Vegetable Pita Sandwiches, '96 199
    Vegetable Pockets, '85 215
    Vegetarian Pita Sandwiches, '84 193
Pizza Sandwiches, Open-Face, '82 3; '83 85;
    '84 M198; '85 22
Pizza Sandwich, Giant, '80 93
Pork Dip Sandwiches, Easy Spanish, '04 312
Pork Sandwiches, Barbecue, '00 23
Pork Sandwiches, Party, '88 M273
Pork Sandwiches with Apricot Mayonnaise,
    Jamaican Jerk, '97 320
Pork Sandwiches with Rosemary-Garlic
    Mayonnaise, Adobo, '01 322
Pork Tenderloin Sandwiches, '00 333
Pork Tenderloin Sandwiches with Bourbon Sauce,
    '02 53
Pork Tenderloin Sandwiches with Cranberry-
    Coriander Conserve, '04 286
Pork with Pecan Biscuits, Peppered, '01 33
Portobello Mushroom Burgers, '01 144
Portobello Pizza Burgers, Grilled, '00 89

SANDWICHES
(continued)

Pound Cake Dessert Sandwich, Grilled, '94 171
Raisin Country Sandwich, '91 168
Rarebit, Tangy Welsh, '88 159
Rarebit, Uptown Welsh, '87 279
Rarebit, Welsh, '00 239
Rarebit with Tomatoes and Bacon, Welsh, '92 M159
Rollups, Parmesan-Turkey-Ranch, '01 177
Salad Rolls, Hearty, '81 206
Salami Sandwiches, Open-Faced, '87 279
Sausage and Pepper Loaves, Italian, '83 11
Sausage Burgers, '96 102
Sausage-Cheese Loaves, '88 235
Sausage-Cheese Muffin Sandwiches, '92 M212
Sausage in a Sleeping Bag, '98 206
Sausage Sandwiches with Mustard Sauce, '84 250
Sausage Sandwich, Italian, '80 92
Sausage Sloppy Joes, Italian, '86 160
Sausage-Stuffed French Loaf, '90 19
Seafood. *See also* **SANDWICHES/Pita.**
Caribbean Seafood Sandwiches, '98 105
Club Sandwich, South Seas, '84 282
Crab-and-Cheese Sandwiches, Hot, '87 279
Crab Burgers, '00 58
Crab Cake Sandwiches, '02 60
Crab Cake Sandwiches, Miniature, '96 306
Crabmeat Sandwiches, '84 285
Crabmeat Sandwiches, Avocado-, '83 2
Crabmeat Sandwiches, Deluxe, '81 M74
Crab Melts, Open-Faced, '01 171
Crab Salad Sandwiches, Mango-, '99 72
Crab Sandwiches, Open-Faced, '87 106
Crab Sandwiches, Puffy, '83 291
Crab Tomato Sandwiches, Open-Face, '81 29
English Muffin Delight, '82 45
Hot Brown, Seafood, '88 158
Oyster-and-Bacon Poor Boys, '87 40
Oyster Loaves, Spinach-, '84 213
Oyster Po'boys, Dressed, '02 184
Oyster Po'boys, Dressed Mini, '01 33
Oyster Submarine Sandwich, '80 92
Po'Boy, Grilled Seafood, '96 244
Shrimp-and-Egg Salad Sandwiches, '94 182
Shrimp Burgers, '03 110
Shrimp-Cheese Sandwiches, '85 242
Shrimp-Cornbread Sandwiches, Open-Faced, '02 141
Shrimp Destin, '82 29
Shrimp Gyros with Herbed Yogurt Spread, Grilled-, '02 169
Shrimp Po' Boys, '97 312
Shrimp Po'boys, '02 184
Shrimp Rolls, '03 162
Shrimp Salad, '86 186
Shrimp Salad on Croissants, '96 175
Shrimp Salad Sandwiches, '90 178
Sloppy Joe Meatball Hoagies, '00 242
Sloppy Toms, '91 51
Snack Buns, '87 279
Snackwiches, '88 172
Spider Sandwiches, '93 193
Spinach Fondue Sandwiches, Grilled, '99 337
Spinach Fondue Sandwich, Grilled, '94 171
Spinach Sandwiches, Fresh, '85 59
Squash Sandwiches, Skillet, '98 144
Stacking Sandwiches, '86 127
Sticky Fingers, '03 M168
Stromboli, '88 272
Stuffed Sandwich, Italian, '99 15
Stuffin' Muffin, '99 193
Submarine Sandwiches, Superb, '84 250

Sweet Smoky Sandwiches, '97 219
Tea Sandwiches, Gingered, '84 116
Tempting Twosome, '81 240; '83 69
Tofu-Veggie Sandwiches, Open-Face, '86 5
Tomatillo Sandwiches, Open-Faced, '92 246
Tomato-Cheese-Bacon Melts, '99 72
Tomatoes with Cheese Sauce over Toast, '88 159
Tomato Sandwiches, Fried Green, '04 145
Tomato Sandwiches, Miniature, '00 130
Tomato Sandwich, Floyd's Favorite, '95 172; '00 182
Tomato, Swiss, and Bacon Sandwiches, '04 140
Torta, Mediterranean, '98 23
Tortilla Stack-Ups, '92 196
Tuna. *See also* **SANDWICHES/Fish, Pita.**
Turkey and Ham Pine-Berry Sandwiches, '00 59
Turkey-Asparagus Sandwiches, '96 74
Turkey-Cheese Dogs, '97 203
Turkey-Cheese Puffs, '87 301
Turkey-Cranberry Croissant, '96 320
Turkey Hero Sandwiches, '92 196
Turkey Hero with Garlic Sauce, '90 145
Turkey-in-the-Slaw Sandwich, '90 177
Turkey, Mozzarella, and Blackberry Sandwiches, Smoked, '99 220
Turkey Open-Facers, '82 190
Turkey-Roasted Pepper Sandwiches, Smoked, '94 66
Turkey Sandwiches with Cranberry Salsa, '00 269
Turkey Sandwich, Hot, '93 306
Turkey Sandwich, Pineapple-, '01 85
Turkey Sandwich, Waffle-Grilled, '94 170
Turkey Schoolwich Sandwiches, '00 198
Turkey Tea Sandwiches, '99 86
Turkey Turnovers, Mexican, '02 245
Turkey Wraps, Smoked, '01 61
Vegetable Garden Heroes, '84 14
Vegetable Puff Sandwich, '85 51
Vegetable Salad Rolls, '82 278
Vegetable Sandwiches, Creamy, '97 122
Vegetarian Melt, Open-Faced, '87 106
Vegewiches, '99 86
Veggie Sandwich, Big, '92 196
Victoria Sandwiches, '94 16
Vidalia Sandwiches on Salt-Rising Bread, '79 145
Watercress-Cucumber Sandwiches, '97 108
Watercress Sandwiches, '90 82
Wrap, Garden, '03 168
Wrapidos, Tacos, '03 172
Wrap, Mediterranean, '03 168
Wrap, BLT, '04 298
Wraps, Black Bean, '00 211
Wraps, Chicken-and-Bean Slaw, '04 163
Wraps, Club, '01 23
Wrap, Southwest BLT, '03 90
Wraps, Smoked Turkey, '01 61
Wraps, Spicy Chicken Salad with Cabbage, '04 62
Wraps, Thai Chicken-Avocado, '02 206
Wraps, Turkey, '00 318
Wrap, Turkey, '03 168
Wreath, Festive Sandwich, '86 333
Zucchini Sandwiches, Open-Faced, '88 159
SAUCES. *See also* **CHOCOLATE/Sauces;**
CHUTNEYS; DESSERTS/Sauces;
GRAVIES; MARINADES;
MUSTARD/Sauces; PESTOS; RELISHES;
SALSAS; SYRUPS; TOPPINGS.
Aioli, Mint, '01 71
Aioli, Picante, '99 53
Alfredo Sauce, '94 84
Almond Sauce, Asparagus with, '91 117
Ancho Chile Cream, '87 121
Ancho Chile Sauce, '87 122
Anchovy-Garlic Sauce over Vermicelli, '86 158
Avgolemono Sauce, '94 48

Avocado Sauce, Chunky, '03 128
Balsamic Sauce, '98 319
Barbecue
Apple Barbecue Sauce, '99 173
Bannister's Barbecue Sauce, '92 166
Barbecue Sauce, '84 172; '86 153; '88 218; '91 16, 205; '93 129; '94 27
Basting Sauce, '90 120
Basting Sauce, Grill, '00 177
Beer Barbecue Sauce, '84 173
Bourbon Barbecue Sauce, '85 90
Chipotle 'Cue Sauce, Smoky, '04 87
Cider Vinegar Barbecue Sauce, '01 148
Cola Barbecue Sauce, '03 130; '04 104
Crickhollow Barbecue Sauce, '99 200
Dressed-Up Barbecue Sauce, '84 173
Eastern-Style Barbecue Sauce, '88 145
Easy Barbecue Sauce, '79 90; '82 178
Green Barbecue Sauce, '02 183
Handcrafted Barbecue Sauce, '98 45
Honey Barbecue Sauce, '04 197
John Wills's Barbecue Sauce, '92 255
Lemon Barbecue Sauce, Herbed, '94 154; '98 334
Lemony Barbecue Sauce, '95 31
Maple Syrup Barbecue Sauce, '94 154
Mustard Barbecue Sauce, '84 173
Oven Barbecue Sauce, '82 233
Paprika Barbecue Sauce, '79 90
Peanut Butter Barbecue Sauce, '81 233
Peppery Barbecue Sauce, '00 255
Piquant Barbecue Sauce, '79 159
Savory Barbecue Sauce, '86 153
Southwest Barbecue Sauce, Spicy, '94 154
Special Barbecue Sauce, '82 177
Sweet-and-Sour 'Cue Sauce, '04 87
Sweet-and-Tangy Barbecue Sauce, '00 119
Sweet Sauce, '90 120
Tangy Barbecue Sauce, '97 323; '99 104; '00 230
Texas Barbecue Sauce, '99 210
The Sauce, '00 177
Thick and Robust Barbecue Sauce, '94 95
Thick and Sweet Barbecue Sauce, '94 95
Thin and Tasty Barbecue Sauce, '94 95
Tomato Barbecue Sauce, Fresh, '84 172
Vinegar Sauce, Peppery, '01 148
Western-Style Barbecue Sauce, '88 145
White Barbecue Sauce, '94 95
White Barbecue Sauce, Chicken with, '89 M84; '97 322; '01 168
Zippy Barbecue Sauce, '92 166
Basil and Cream Sauce, '90 118
Basil-Brown Butter Sauce, '93 92
Basil Cream, '89 159
Basil Cream Sauce, New Potatoes with, '91 46
Basil Sauce, '90 85
Basil Sauce, Asparagus with, '86 33
Basting Sauce, '01 106
Basting Sauce, Grilled Chicken with, '01 146
Bean Sauce, Pork-and-Onions with, '85 76
Béarnaise Sauce, '83 138; '85 37; '86 193; '89 201; '96 133, 174
Béarnaise Sauce, Blender, '81 90
Béarnaise Sauce, Classic, '86 244
Béarnaise Sauce, Quick, '82 84
Béchamel Sauce, '80 190; '83 277; '84 M239; '87 286; '91 94; '96 239
Beef-and-Pasta Sauce Dip, Creamy, '01 108
Beef Sauce, Szechuan Noodles with Spicy, '97 95
Beer Sauce, '95 266
Beurre Blanc Sauce, '98 240
Black Bean Sauce, '93 59; '98 46
Black Bean Sauce, Spicy Beef Fillets with, '97 184
Bordelaise Sauce, '83 138, 262
Bouillon Sauce, '80 8

Bourbon Sauce, '02 53
Brandy-Butter Sauce, '79 230
Brandy Sauce, Carrots in, '83 86
Brandy Sauce, Lemony-Butter Steak with, '85 78
Brisket Mopping Sauce, '03 188
Brisket Red Sauce, '03 188
Broccoli Sauce, '91 85
Brown Butter Sauce, '91 65
Brown Sauce, '89 32; '94 15, 240
Buttermilk Sauce, '84 6
Butter Sauce, '86 268
Butter Sauce, Vegetable, '86 174
Caramel-Brandy Sauce, Steaks with, '03 56
Caramel Sauce, '04 249
Caribe, Jamaican Pork Tenderloin with Sauce,
    '02 320
Catsup Sauce, '81 228
Catsup Topping, '81 170
Champagne-Saffron Sauce, Scallops with, '93 177
Champagne Sauce, '90 29
Champagne Sauce, Chicken Breasts with, '86 49
Chanterelle Brown Sauce, '89 62
Cheese
    Blue Cheese Sauce, '90 142; '94 320
    Blue Cheese Sauce, Fettuccine with, '98 247
    Brussels Sprouts with Cheese Sauce, '79 246
    Cheddar Cheese Sauce, '91 286
    Cheddar-Cider Sauce, '98 242
    Cheese Sauce, '79 M156; '81 43, 44, 225;
        '82 M123; '83 49, 138, 188; '84 57; '85 92;
        '86 241; '88 78, 272; '89 181, 229; '90 235;
        '93 48; '02 94; '04 281
    Cottage Cheese Sauce, '87 232
    Cream Sauce, Cheesy, '82 79
    Easy Cheese Sauce, '79 22
    Garlic-Cheese Sauce, '84 M70
    Goat Cheese Sauce, Asparagus with, '93 116
    Guilt-Free Cheese Sauce, '93 M95
    Heather Sauce, '84 182
    Lemon-Cheese Sauce, '91 24
    Lemony Cheese Sauce, '84 183
    Monterey Jack Sauce, '84 293
    Mornay Sauce, '80 120; '81 90; '83 138; '84 295;
        '89 195
    Mushroom-Cheese Sauce, '83 190; '86 48
    Parmesan Cheese Sauce, '79 165; '80 162;
        '85 143
    Parmesan Sauce, '92 17
    Parmesan-Sour Cream Sauce, Baked Fish with,
        '01 209
    Pimiento Cheese Sauce, '02 291
    Rich Cheese Sauce, '81 89
    Roquefort Sauce, '89 321
    Rosemary-Parmesan Sauce, Tortellini with,
        '92 284
    Seafood Cheese Sauce, '89 240
    Stilton-Portobello Sauce, Beef Filets with,
        '00 309
    Swiss Cheese Sauce, '79 35; '87 289; '88 135;
        '03 52
    Swiss Sauce, '83 M195
    Swiss Sauce, Creamy, '80 M53
    Topper, Vegetable-Cheese Potato, '86 6
    Turnips in Cheese Sauce, '84 229
    Vegetable-Cheese Sauce, '85 M152
    Vegetable Sauce, Cheesy, '92 M134
    Walnut-Parmesan Pesto Sauce, '97 104
    Wine-Cheese Sauce, '00 310
Chervil-and-Savory Sauce, '90 117
Chervil Sauce, '83 128
Chicken-and-Creamy Herb Sauce, Fettuccine with,
    '01 257
Chicken Curry Sauce, '90 117
Chicken Sauce, Creamy, '81 91

Chile Corn Jus, '00 197
Chile Sauce, Hot, '92 156
Chili Meat Sauce, '83 4
Chili Sauce, '81 175; '94 287
Chili Sauce, Chunky, '85 188
Chili Sauce, Miss Kitty's, '04 231
Chili Sauce, Spicy, '87 127
Chili Sauce, Sweet, '01 237
Chive Butter Sauce, '03 91
Chive Sauce, Steamed Broccoli with Tangy, '83 101
Cider-Port Wine Reduction Sauce, '96 245
Cider Sauce, '87 224
Cilantro Cream, '87 121
Cilantro Vinaigrette, '97 126
Clam Sauce, Tricolor Pasta with, '93 272
Cocktail Sauce, '87 128; '90 242
Cocktail Sauce, Boiled Shrimp with, '79 151
Cocktail Sauce, Coastal, '92 254
Cocktail Sauce, Delta, '91 147
Cocktail Sauce, French Fried Zucchini with, '86 146
Cocktail Sauce, Southwestern, '98 46
Cocktail Sauce, Spicy, '83 258
Come Back Sauce, '00 211
Corn Sauce, Fresh, '98 43
Cream Sauce, '85 291; '93 157; '01 43; '03 237
Cream Sauce, Brandied, '82 70
Cream Sauce, Peppery, '88 206
Cream Sauce, Sherried, '84 210; '85 M152
Cream Sauce, Shrimp in, '84 M286
Cream Sauce, Spicy, '82 45
Cream-Wine Sauce, Potatoes in, '86 18
Creamy Sauce, '79 41
Creamy Sauce, Grilled Chicken, with, '01 318
Creolaise Sauce, '83 91, 262
Creole Sauce, '89 228; '90 28; '92 87; '98 98, 142;
    '02 32, 284
Creole Sauce, Crescent City Grill, '04 289
Cress Sauce, '96 176
Cucumber-and-Yogurt Dipping Sauce, '02 172
Cucumber Cream Sauce, '92 33
Cucumber-Dill Sauce, '86 5; '91 62; '92 51
Cucumber Dipping Sauce, '94 47
Cucumber Sauce, '82 111; '84 M286; '92 41
Cucumber Sauce, Lamb Burgers with, '98 102
Cucumber Sauce, Lemony, '89 245
Cucumber Sauce, Tuna Steaks with, '97 180
Cucumber Sauce, White Bean Spread with Creamy,
    '00 178
Cucumber-Yogurt Sauce, '03 44
Cumberland Sauce, '92 309; '00 256
Currant Jelly Sauce, Quail with, '86 94
Currant Sauce, '87 240
Curried Cream Sauce, Turkey Slices with, '91 60
Curried Rum Sauce, '91 164
Curried Sour Cream Sauce, '90 174
Curry-Mustard Sauce, '96 249
Curry Sauce, '79 M156; '83 138; '84 M71; '94 54;
    '95 18; '97 170; '99 92
Curry Sauce, Asparagus with, '90 17
Curry Sauce, Chicken, '90 117
Custard Sauce, '89 291
Custard Sauce, Bourbon, '95 271
Dijon-Caper Cream Sauce, Broiled Salmon with,
    '98 329
Dijon Horseradish Sauce, '03 297
Dijon Mustard Sauce, Creamy, '04 198
Dijon Sauce, '03 93
Dijon Vinaigrette, '00 222
Dill Sauce, '84 M70, 107; '85 39; '88 162; '95 216;
    '98 157
Dill Sauce, Chilled Salmon with, '84 285
Dill Sauce, Creamy, '79 M156; '94 42
Dill Sauce, Salmon Steaks with, '85 164
Dill Sauce, Tangy, '04 320

Dipper's Delight, '98 93
Dipping Sauce, Citrus, '97 208
Dipping Sauce, "Come Back," '96 213
Dipping Sauce, Creamy Cilantro, '03 327
Dipping Sauce, Fried Green Tomatillos with
    Jalapeño, '97 143
Dipping Sauce, Ginger, '03 64
Dipping Sauce, Grilled Chicken with Sweet Soy
    Slaw and, '04 123
Dipping Sauce, Grilled Salmon with Sweet Soy Slaw
    and, '04 123
Dipping Sauce, Hoisin Peanut, '99 14
Dipping Sauce, Olive Oil-Balsamic, '04 46
Dipping Sauce, Orange, '03 M212
Dipping Sauce, Sesame-Soy, '02 145
Dipping Sauce, Thai, '97 236
Drunken Sauce, '03 33
Dunk Sauce, John's, '97 129
Egg Foo Yong Sauce, '86 232
Emerald Sauce, '90 63
Enchilada Sauce, '81 194
Enchilada Sauce, Red Chile, '85 245
Florentine Sauce, '93 48
Foo Yong Sauce, '80 223
French Sauce, Broccoli with, '81 295
Fruit
    Apple-Bourbon Sauce, '99 142
    Apple-Horseradish Sauce, '82 229
    Apple-Pear Sauce, '97 M272
    Apple Sauce, Pork Chops with Sweet-and-Sour,
        '98 132
    Apricot Sauce, '87 172
    Apricot-Sauced Pork Chops, '85 22
    Apricot Sauce, Pork Tenderloin with, '99 44
    Avocado Béarnaise Sauce, '01 317
    Avocado-Lime Sauce, '03 90
    Avocado-Lime Sauce, Grilled Swordfish with,
        '97 127
    Avocado Sauce, '80 198; '83 200
    Avocado-Tomatillo Sauce, '95 206
    Blackberry Sauce, Pork Medaillons with, '02 136
    Blueberry Sauce, '80 144; '86 248
    Cherry-Merlot Sauce and Gorgonzola, Peppered
        Sirloin with, '02 320
    Cherry Sauce, '83 276; '84 91; '91 67
    Cherry Sauce, Elegant, '79 M156
    Cherry Sauce, Pork Fillets with Dark, '04 221
    Cherry Sauce, Roast Ducklings with, '86 312
    Cherry Sauce, Roast Pork with Spiced, '89 324
    Cherry Sauce, Royal, '85 224; '86 83
    Cherry Sauce, Spicy, '83 244
    Cherry-Wine Sauce, '95 285
    Citrus Sauce, Stuffed Flounder Rolls with,
        '85 180
    Cranberry-Apple Sauce, '92 203
    Cranberry-Apple Sauce, Double, '03 231
    Cranberry-Apricot Sauce, Fresh, '87 243
    Cranberry Jezebel Sauce, '03 250
    Cranberry Juice Sauce, '85 224; '86 83
    Cranberry-Raisin Sauce, Baked Ham with,
        '88 244
    Cranberry Sauce, '92 269
    Cranberry Sauce, Baked, '88 257
    Cranberry Sauce, Cornish Hens with, '79 180
    Cranberry Sauce, Fresh, '79 283; '84 275;
        '04 271
    Cranberry Sauce, Holiday, '02 M311
    Cranberry Sauce, Spiced, '96 267
    Cranberry Sauce, Tart, '83 261
    Cranberry Wine Sauce, '83 276
    Devonshire Cream, Mock, '81 288
    Devonshire Sauce, Processor, '86 337; '87 58
    Dipping Sauce, Citrus, '97 208
    Fruit Sauce, '81 177

SAUCES, Fruit
(continued)

Grand Marnier Fruit Sauce, '90 93
Grape Sauce, Mahimahi in, '91 218
Honey-Lime Sauce, '82 85
Jezebel Sauce, '81 29; '82 55; '93 331; '96 212;
    '02 219
Jezebel Sauce, Gingered, '04 M138
Lemon Basting Sauce, '95 32
Lemon-Butter Sauce, '84 252; '92 337
Lemon-Butter Sauce, New Potatoes with, '00 103
Lemon-Celery Sauce, Baked Fillets in, '84 91
Lemon-Cheese Sauce, '91 24
Lemon Cream Sauce, '99 53
Lemon Cream Sauce, Braised Chicken Breast in,
    '94 184
Lemon-Dill Sauce, Potatoes and Green Beans
    with, '01 89
Lemon Dipping Sauce, '02 134
Lemon Garlic Sauce, Shrimp in, '83 67
Lemon-Herb Sauce, Hot, '91 286
Lemon Meunière Sauce, '88 222
Lemon-Mustard Sauce, Salmon Steaks with, '97 124
Lemon Parsley Sauce, '81 106
Lemon-Parsley Sauce, '93 48
Lemon Sauce, '82 290
Lemon Sauce, Asparagus with, '86 62
Lemon Sauce, Chicken Scallopini with, '86 156
Lemon Sauce, Pecan Catfish with, '03 185
Lemon Sauce, Red Snapper with, '01 83
Lemon Sauce, Zesty, '97 318
Lime-Saffron Sauce, '94 71
Lime Sauce, Creamy, '04 119
Lime Sauce, Fresh Fruit with, '02 68
Lime Sauce, Sour Cream-, '91 286
Mandarin-Almond Cream Sauce, '84 183
Mandarin Sauce, '84 60
Mandarin-Teriyaki Sauce, '96 68
Mango-Pineapple Hot Sauce, '04 183
Maraschino-Orange Sauce, '96 164
Mimosa, Sauce, '88 288
Muscadine Sauce, '04 231
Orange-Almond Sauce, Chicken in, '79 219;
    '80 13
Orange-Almond Sauce, Grilled Snapper with,
    '01 158
Orange Butter Sauce, Asparagus with, '85 43
Orange-Curry Sauce and Coconut Rice,
    Polynesian Pork Tenderloin with, '04 309
Orange-Dijon Sauce, '00 259
Orange-Ginger Sauce, Chicken Breasts with,
    '97 47
Orange-Ginger Sauce, Sesame-Crusted Scallops
    with, '97 125
Orange-Honey Sauce, '97 236
Orange, Lime, and Ginger Sauce, Chicken with,
    '92 123
Orange Liqueur Sauce, '86 142
Orange Sauce, '82 47; '83 10, 277; '84 M286;
    '98 83
Orange Sauce, Asparagus with, '83 46
Orange Sauce, Broccoli with, '04 285
Orange Sauce, Brussels Sprouts in, '86 55
Orange Sauce, Celery in, '79 70
Orange Sauce, Chicken Breasts with, '79 77
Orange Sauce, Grilled Duck with, '94 305
Orange Sauce, Lobster Tails with Spiced, '86 155
Orange Sauce, Shrimp in, '99 292
Orange Sauce, Sunshine, '97 70
Orange Sauce, Sweet, '93 M325
Peach-Blueberry Pancake Sauce, '82 177
Peach-Blueberry Sauce, '81 170

Peach Sauce, '92 203
Peach Sauce, Creamy Fresh, '79 177
Peach Sauce, Pork Loin Dijonnaise with,
    '97 87
Peach Sauce, Tangy, '96 89
Pineapple-Curry Sauce, '79 252
Pineapple-Rhubarb Sauce, '88 94
Pineapple Sauce, '84 236; '92 203
Pineapple Sauce, Raisin-, '82 177
Plum Sauce, '80 249; '82 40; '88 152
Plum Sauce, Chinese, '82 237
Plum Sauce, Crispy Ribs with, '98 182
Plum Sauce, Fresh, '97 176
Plum Sauce, Gingered, '87 175
Plum Sauce, Red, '80 49
Plum Sauce, Spareribs in, '99 136
Plum Sauce, Spicy, '86 11
Rosemary-Cherry Sauce, '02 193
Strawberry-Banana Sauce, '81 41
Strawberry Sauce, Make-Ahead French Toast
    with, '02 131
Tangy Sauce for Fruit, '90 161
Tomatillo Sauce, '94 231; '95 206; '97 25
Tomatillo Sauce, Grilled Jerk Shrimp with
    Creamy, '01 332
Tomatillo Sauce, Roasted Chiles Rellenos with,
    '94 203
Tropical Fruit Sauce, Grilled Shrimp with,
    '01 195
White Grape Sauce, '80 38
Garlic Buerre Blanc Sauce, '88 222
Garlic-Butter Sauce, '95 327
Garlic-Chive Butter Sauce, '90 96
Garlic-Ginger Butter Sauce, '94 89
Garlic Sauce, '92 56
Garlic Sauce, Chicken with, '00 270
Garlic Sauce, Pork in, '04 181
Garlic Sauce, Roasted, '95 268; '98 176
Garlic Sauce, Stir-Fried Pork in, '84 141
Garlic Sauce, Turkey Hero with, '90 145
Ginger-Soy Sauce, '91 33
Ginger Vinaigrette, '95 162
Greek Sauce, '91 183
Green Bell Pepper Sauce, '97 261
Green Chile Sauce, '82 220
Green Mole Sauce, '95 267
Green Pea Sauce, '83 22
Green Peppercorn Sauce, Beef Fillets with, '02 285
Green Peppercorn Sauce, Beef Tenderloin Filets
    with, '00 309
Green Sauce, Herbed, '86 244
Grill Basting Sauce, '95 236; '03 312
Guacamole, '89 226
Ham-and-Mushroom Sauce, Steak with, '83 109
Ham Sauce, Country, '90 117; '96 24
Henry Bain Sauce, Beef Tenderloin with, '00 107;
    '01 20; '04 52
Herb Butter Sauce, Corn with, '79 150
Herb-Mayonnaise Sauce, '85 73
Herb Sauce, '91 29
Herb Sauce, Green, '83 36
Herb Sauce, Spicy, '03 281
Hollandaise Sauce, '80 M107, M268; '81 90;
    '83 137; '85 295; '86 94; '87 195;
    '88 58, M177, 222; '89 24; '92 93; '95 86;
    '98 55; '03 52
Hollandaise Sauce, Blender, '79 39; '82 84, 234
Hollandaise Sauce, Broccoli with, '79 244, 276
Hollandaise Sauce, Broccoli with Mock, '82 272
Hollandaise Sauce, Chipotle, '03 53
Hollandaise Sauce, Classic, '88 53
Hollandaise Sauce, Easy Dilled, '92 107
Hollandaise Sauce, Lime, '93 121
Hollandaise Sauce, Mock, '85 49; '93 68

Hollandaise Sauce, Zesty, '04 284
Hollandaise-Shrimp Sauce, Flounder with, '86 234
Hollandaise, Tangy, '85 148
Hollandaise, Tasso, '04 67
Hollandaise, Three-Pepper, '96 52
Honey-Butter Sauce, '85 18; '98 45
Honey-Lemon Mustard Sauce, '84 275
Honey-Mustard Sauce, '85 13
Honey-Mustard Sauce, Smoked Ribs with, '92 168
Honey-Poppy Seed Sauce, '93 13
Honey Sauce, '99 210
Honey Sauce, Chicken in, '89 82
Honey Sauce, Chicken Strips with, '03 27
Horseradish Cream Sauce, Pepper-Seared Beef
    Tenderloin with, '01 280
Horseradish-Mustard Sauce, Creamy, '88 M177
Horseradish Sauce, '84 190; '85 224; '86 83;
    '87 127; '88 207, M273; '91 183; '93 215;
    '02 19
Horseradish Sauce and Curried Bananas, Fillets
    with, '85 230
Horseradish Sauce, Broccoli with, '81 2; '83 206;
    '84 33
Horseradish Sauce, Carrots and Broccoli with,
    '91 246
Horseradish Sauce, Spicy, '02 235
Horseradish Sauce, Zesty, '04 284
Horseradish Sour Cream, '86 244
Hot Diggity Dog Sauce, '93 198
Hot Sauce, '79 185; '83 74
Hot Sauce, San Antonio, '84 291
Hunter Sauce, '95 317
Italian Sauce, '80 63; '90 67
Italian Sauce, Quick, '82 230
Italian-Style Sauce, '83 250
Jalapeño-Cherry Sauce, Smoked Pork Chops with,
    '01 208
Jalapeño-Cranberry Sauce, '92 310
Jalapeño Dipping Sauce, Fried Green Tomatillos
    with, '97 143
Jalapeño Sauce, '80 193
Jalapeño Tartar Sauce, '96 69; '98 129
Jezebel Sauce, '81 29; '82 55; '93 331; '96 212;
    '02 219
Juniper Sauce, '93 278
Lingonberry Sauce, Turkey Tenderloins with, '97 289
Louis Sauce, '03 66
Mahogany Sauce, '91 148
Maple Brown Sauce, '96 232
Maple-Cider Sauce, '95 288
Marinara Sauce, '82 178; '89 239; '92 18
Maui Sauce, '99 310
Meat Sauce for Spaghetti, '00 256
Meat Sauce, Italian, '01 160
Meat Sauce, Spaghetti with, '02 188
Mediterranean Sauce, '94 83
Meunière Sauce, '80 57
Mexican Sauce, '80 198
Microwaving Sauces, '84 M70
Mint Sauce, '84 107; '88 M96
Mint Sauce over Vegetables, '92 104
Molasses Sauce, Grilled Pork Tenderloin with,
    '97 193
Mole Sauce, Burgundy, '98 174
Mushroom-Dill Sauce, '80 271
Mushroom Sauce, '81 90, 200; '82 46;
    '83 71, 205, 212; '84 M70; '85 40; '86 198;
    '87 36, 186, 284; '91 221; '03 255
Mushroom Sauce, Chicken with, '99 22; '04 255
Mushroom Sauce, Eggs Baked in, '93 47
Mushroom Sauce, Filet Mignon with, '94 250
Mushroom Sauce, Savory, '96 236
Mushroom Sauce, Spicy Sherried, '89 239
Mushroom Sauce, Spinach Loaf with, '01 277

Mushroom Sauce Supreme on Vermicelli, '86 158
Mushroom-Wine Sauce, '84 84; '86 24; '00 125
Mustard Sauce, '01 102; '02 162, 245
Mustard Sauce, Special, '01 159
Natillas Sauce, '83 179
Niçoise, Sauce, '96 190
Not-So-Secret Sauce, '03 139
Olive-Butter Sauce, Broccoli with, '83 118
Onion-Balsamic Sauce, '99 44
Onion Cream Sauce, '87 232
Onion-Mushroom Sauce, '85 224; '86 84
Onion-Parsley Sauce, '85 148
Onion Sauce, '82 72; '87 248
Onion Sauce, Brussels Sprouts in, '81 308
Pancake Sauce, Cinnamon-Pecan-Honey, '88 46
Parsley-Caper Sauce, Tortellini with, '93 175
Parsley-Chive Sauce, '84 212
Parsley-Garlic Sauce, '83 138; '84 M70
Parsley Sauce, '82 248; '86 108
Peanut Basil Sauce, Thai-Style Noodles with, '98 133
Peanut Dipping Sauce, Hoisin, '99 14
Peanut Hot Sauce, '86 305
Peanut Sauce, '99 134; '02 173; '04 324
Peanut Sauce, Hot Indonesian, '93 211
Peanut Sauce, Shrimp with, '93 303
Peanut Sauce, Spicy, '96 93; '04 134
Pecan-Butter Sauce, '91 65
Pecan Pasta Sauce, '96 262
Pepper-Onion Sauce, '84 125
Pepper Sauce, '01 211; '02 106
Pesto-Clam Sauce, Pasta with, '98 17
Pesto Sauce, '89 280; '91 94; '95 267
Pesto Sauce, Racy, '97 67
Picante-Bean Sauce, '96 220
Pico de Gallo, '98 174
Pig Sauce, '98 203
Pintos, Texas Souper, '98 51
Pizza Sauce, '00 314
Pizza Sauce, Traditional, '95 267
Portobello-Alfredo Sauce, Fettuccine with, '04 135
Port Wine Sauce, '84 252
Pumpkin Seed Sauce, '88 246
Raisin Sauce, '83 59, 215; '84 91, 275; '87 127;
    '89 58; '99 19; '02 278
Raisin Sauce, Ham with, '82 M76
Red Bell Pepper Sauce, '99 267
Red Chile Sauce, '94 251; '95 17
Red Chili Sauce, '85 245
Red Hot Sauce, '93 158
Red or Green Pepper Sauce, '91 85
Red Pepper-Garlic Sauce, '98 140
Red Pepper Sauce, '98 322; '02 165
Red Sauce, Zippy, '91 147
Red Wine-Butter Sauce, '96 173
Red Wine Garlic Sauce, '94 250
Red Wine Sauce, '02 290
Rémoulade, Braised Shrimp with Garlic, '98 133
Rémoulade, Criolla, '97 227
Rémoulade, Roasted Red Pepper, '04 144
Rémoulade Sauce, '80 58; '81 89; '82 178;
    '91 147; '93 280; '94 139; '99 164; '00 44;
    '02 134, 184; '04 66
Rémoulade Sauce, Red Pepper, '01 145
Rémoulade Sauce, Shrimp with, '91 29
Rémoulade, Watercress, '01 326
Rhubarb Sauce, Chilled, '88 94
Rib Sauce, Peach, '01 248
Roasted Pepper Sauce, Creamy, '96 183
Roasted Red Bell Pepper Sauce, '02 287
Roasted Red Pepper Sauce, '98 16; '00 58
Rosemary Sauce, '97 127
Rum Sauce, Mango-Spiced, '86 215
Sauerbraten Sauce, '93 16
Savory Sauce, '84 196

Seafood
    Cheese Sauce, Seafood, '89 240
    Clam Sauce, Linguine with, '84 124; '88 90;
        '89 178
    Clam Sauce, Pasta with, '84 291
    Clam Sauce, Vermicelli and Sprouts with Red,
        '86 143
    Clam Sauce, Vermicelli with, '85 295
    Clam Sauce with Linguine, '84 9
    Crab and Shrimp Sauce Piquante, '83 92
    Crab Marinara Sauce, Quick, '85 M151
    Delight, Seafood Sauce, '82 91
    Linguine with Seafood Sauce, '83 232
    Red Seafood Sauce, '95 107
    Seafood Sauce, '79 3; '82 84; '83 36; '86 304;
        '89 239
    Shrimp-and-Almond Sauce, '87 282
    Shrimp-and-Creamy Herb Sauce, Fettuccine with,
        '01 257
    Shrimp Cocktail Sauce, '01 182
    Shrimp Sauce, '87 138, 232; '01 182; '04 147
    Shrimp Sauce, Broccoli and Cauliflower with,
        '84 248
    Shrimp Sauce, Creamy, '03 53
    Shrimp Sauce, Flounder Fillets in, '83 227
    Shrimp Sauce, Flounder with Hollandaise-,
        '86 234
    Shrimp Sauce, Grandpa Jim's, '01 182
    Shrimp Sauce, Oysters in, '87 40
    Stone Crab Mustard Sauce, '80 3
    Stone Crab Sauce, Tangy, '80 3
    Tartar Sauce, Pecan, '03 101
Seasoning Sauce, '00 110
Sesame-Ginger Sauce, '00 148
Sesame Sauce, Vegetables with, '83 112
Sesame-Soy Dipping Sauce, '02 145
Shallot-Thyme Sauce, '96 121
Sherry Sauce, '87 96
Shiitake Madeira Sauce, Filet Mignons with, '95 265
Shiitake Sauce, Pork Tenderloin with Fruit Stuffing
    and, '97 218
Smoky Sweet Sauce, '03 32
Sofrito, '92 158
Sour Cream-Dill Sauce, Mushrooms in, '84 215
Sour Cream-Horseradish Sauce, '88 4
Sour Cream, Mock, '83 71, 205
Sour Cream Sauce, '82 68; '84 132; '87 233;
    '93 162; '00 194; '02 169
Sour Cream Sauce, Broccoli with, '87 127
Soy Sauce, Grilled Trout with Ginger and, '85 228
Soy Sauce, Sweet, '03 248
Spaghetti Sauce, Grisanti, '94 194
Special Sauce, Morton's, '01 331
Spicy Sauce, '99 291
Spinach Pasta Sauce, '93 71
Spinach Sauce, Fettuccine with, '84 329
Spinach Sauce, Vermicelli with Fresh, '89 256
Stilton-Portobello Sauce, Beef Fillets with, '02 310
Sunshine Sauce, '87 96
Sweet-and-Sour Apple Sauce, Pork Chops with,
    '98 132
Sweet-and-Sour Sauce, '80 20; '85 12, 34; '86 240
Sweet 'n' Saucy Sauce, '01 210
Sweet Sauce, '01 106
Taco Sauce, '82 M283; '93 69
Tahini Sauce, '96 23; '03 183
Tarragon-Mustard Sauce, Turkey Cutlets with,
    '93 239
Tarragon Sauce, '83 56; '84 190; '87 229; '97 42
Tartar Sauce, '79 184; '81 134; '82 135; '86 233;
    '91 147; '95 107, 155; '99 174; '01 316;
    '02 60
Tartar Sauce, Boiled Shrimp with Green Peppercorn,
    '94 144

Tartar Sauce, Bold-and-Spicy, '86 180
Tartar Sauce, Creamy, '80 164
Tartar Sauce, Lemony, '95 32
Tartar Sauce, Quick, '87 128
Tartar Sauce, Shrimp with, '00 178
Tartar Sauce, Spicy, '04 313
Tempura Sauce, Basic, '81 68
Teriyaki Sauce, '93 258
Tex-Mex Secret Sauce, '04 127
The Sauce, '95 237; '03 312
Tomatillo Sauce, '94 231; '95 206; '97 25; '04 119
Tomatillo Sauce, Grilled Jerk Shrimp with Creamy,
    '01 332
Tomatillo Sauce, Roasted Chiles Rellenos with,
    '94 203
Tomato
    Basic Tomato Sauce, '04 145
    Basil Cream, Tomato-, '99 240
    Basil Sauce, Tomato, '91 85
    Basil Sauce, Tomato-, '92 180; '96 220; '97 144;
        '02 182
    Basil-Tomato Sauce, '92 198; '93 25, 48, 65
    Caper Sauce, Turkey Cutlets with Tomato-, '91 61
    Chunky Tomato Sauce, '95 264
    Cream Sauce, Angel Hair Pasta with Tomato,
        '93 292
    Cream Sauce, Linguine with Tomato-, '86 158
    Cream, Tomato, '94 70
    Creamy Tomato Sauce, '93 71
    Cucumber Sauce, Tomato-, '98 45
    Dried Tomato Sauce, '96 220; '99 135
    Fish in Tomato Sauce, '85 75
    Fresh Tomato Sauce, '83 224; '87 171
    Fresh Tomato Sauce over Basil Pasta, '93 176
    Gingered Tomato Sauce, Spicy, '96 220
    Green Beans in Tomato Sauce, '01 84
    Green Chiles, Tomato Sauce with, '81 196
    Herbed Fresh Tomato Sauce, '85 M151
    Herbed Tomato Sauce, '86 277
    Herb Sauce, Tomato-and-, '00 125
    Hot Sauce, Kleberg, '94 28
    Italian-Style Tomato Sauce, '87 182
    Italian Tomato Sauce, '82 M68; '92 57; '03 202
    Italian Tomato Sauce for Spaghetti, '81 134
    Lemon Sauce, Salmon with Almonds and
        Tomato-, '04 23
    Light Tomato Sauce, '97 246
    Marinara Sauce, '89 239; '92 18; '94 64; '99 266
    Meat Sauce, Italian, '83 193
    Pasta Sauce, '01 53
    Pasta Sauce with Meatballs, '01 55
    Picante Sauce, '94 116
    Picante Sauce, Homemade, '90 205
    Picante Sauce, Processed, '91 257
    Pico de Gallo, '79 185; '86 19; '97 141;
        '02 168, 306
    Pizza Sauce, '80 163; '84 33; '85 285
    Ranchero Sauce, '96 168
    Rancheros Sauce, '88 148
    Red Pepper-Tomato Sauce, '93 59
    Red Sauce and Meatballs, '04 17
    Refrigerator Tomato Sauce, '85 188
    Roasted Garlic-Tomato Sauce, '97 46
    Seasoned Tomato Sauce, '83 150
    Spaghetti Meat Sauce for 4, Easy, '92 244
    Spaghetti Meat Sauce for 25, Easy, '92 245
    Spaghetti Sauce, Beer, '85 13
    Spaghetti Sauce, Dried Tomato, '90 202
    Spaghetti Sauce, Herbed, '85 13
    Spaghetti Sauce, Lentil, '90 198
    Spaghetti Sauce, Meat Loaves with, '03 204
    Spaghetti Sauce, Sicilian, '03 62
    Spaghetti Sauce, Slow-Simmered, '96 72
    Spaghetti Sauce, Thick, '84 118

SAUCES, Tomato
(continued)

Spaghetti Sauce, Turkey, '85 13
Spicy Sauce, '84 77
Spicy Tomato Sauce, '84 294; '88 19
Sweet-and-Sour Tomato Sauce, Stuffed Chicken
    Breasts with, '01 120
Taco Sauce, '94 30
Tarragon-Tomato Sauce, '84 131
Tomato Sauce, '85 193, 244; '87 249; '88 116;
    '97 96, 269; '99 270; '04 43
Vermicelli with Tomato Sauce, '83 164
Zesty Tomato Sauce, '98 176
Turkey Mole, '03 18
Tzatziki Sauce, '04 108
Vanilla Wine Sauce, Pan-Fried Grouper with,
    '94 241
Vegetable Sauce, '89 98
Vegetable Sauce, Greek Fish with, '82 72
Vegetable Sauce, Pasta with, '83 163
Vegetable Sauce, Tangy, '89 280
Vegetable Sauce, Vermicelli with Chunky,
    '04 180
Velouté Sauce, '84 22
Venison Reduction Sauce, '94 303
Verde Sauce, '93 275; '00 241
Vermouth-Cream Sauce, Scallops in, '96 49
Vidalia Onion Sauce, '99 52
Vinaigrette, Versatile, '93 141
Vinegar Basting Sauce, '91 205
Walnut Cream Sauce, '93 275; '01 229
Walnut-Parmesan Pesto Sauce, '96 251
Walnut Sauce, Linguine with Green Beans and,
    '04 128
Walnut Sauce, Spaghetti with Parsley and, '80 30
Watercress Sauce, '91 85
Whiskey Sauce, '80 58
White Butter Sauce, '92 107
White Dipping Sauce, '00 167
White Sauce, '82 269; '83 138, 245; '87 166
White Sauce, Asparagus, '80 147
White Sauce, Basic, '79 M156; '81 89
White Sauce, Low-Calorie, Medium, '87 26
White Sauce, Medium, '93 48
White Sauce, Thick, '82 42
Wine Reduction Sauce, '94 270; '00 321
Wine Sauce, Beef Cubes in, '79 264
Wine Sauce, Beef Tenderloin in, '02 136
Wine Sauce, Broccoli with, '84 187
Wine Sauce, Chicken in, '80 8
Wine Sauce, Creamy, '01 81; '02 109
Wine Sauce, Marsala, '81 77
Wine Sauce, Mushrooms with, '85 292
Wine Sauce, Red Snapper in, '85 138
Wine Sauce, Shrimp and, '98 50
Wine Sauce, Skillet Steak in Red, '85 21
Wine Sauce, Veal and Carrots in, '86 M139
Wine Sauce, White, '84 132; '89 24; '92 41; '93 49
Yellow Pepper Sauce, '02 165
Yellow Pepper Sauce, Poached Salmon with,
    '98 230
Yogurt-Cucumber Sauce, '04 216
Yogurt-Cucumber Sauce, London Broil Sandwiches
    with, '01 162
Yogurt-Horseradish Sauce, '85 66
Yogurt Sauce, '89 283
Yogurt Sauce, Creamy, '91 238; '92 28
Yogurt Sauce, Lamb Meatballs with, '85 132
Zesty Sauce, '94 82; '97 312
Zippy Sauce, '86 44
Zucchini-Mushroom Sauce, '93 71
Zucchini Sauce, Spaghetti with, '81 38

SAUERKRAUT
Bratwurst and Sauerkraut, '84 250
Bratwurst Dinner, Krause's Café, '87 238
Cake, Sauerkraut, '94 254
Franks, Beany Kraut and, '79 64
Homemade Sauerkraut, '81 216
Meatballs, Sauerkraut, '86 257
Pork Chops and Sauerkraut, '88 98
Relish, Kraut, '91 232
Relish, Sauerkraut, '85 136
Reuben Casserole, Chicken, '03 69
Reuben Pizza, '03 69
Reuben Puffs, '98 231
Reuben Rolls, Snappy, '02 58
Reuben Sandwiches, '80 M201
Reuben Sandwiches, Broiled, '81 240; '83 69
Reuben Sandwiches, Cripsy, '85 299
Reuben Sandwiches, Grilled, '81 206
Reuben Sandwiches, Open-Face, '91 199
Reuben Sandwich, Rolled, '99 219
Reubens, Oven-Grilled, '97 304
Reubens, Party, '90 61
Reuben Turnovers, '94 253
Salad, Crunchy Sauerkraut, '87 9
Salad, Sauerkraut, '80 178; '97 195
Sandwich, Beef-and-Kraut, '91 167
Sausage and Kraut, '83 11
Sausage-Apple Kraut Dinner, '02 234
SAUSAGE
Acorn Squash, Sausage-Stuffed, '81 231; '83 296;
    '84 285
Acorn Squash with Sausage, '85 9
Andouille, '92 242
Andouille Grits, Grilled, '04 165
Andouille Gumbo, Chicken-, '98 14
Andouille Sausage, Apple, and Pecan Dressing,
    '02 249
Appetizers
    Balls in Cheese Pastry, Sausage, '80 248
    Balls, Sausage, '98 93
    Balls, Sausage-Apple, '90 85
    Balls, Venison Sausage, '80 42
    Basil-Pepper Appetizers, '98 133
    Cheese Queso, Chunky, '99 279
    Chile con Queso Supreme, '80 265
    Cocktail Sausages, Saucy, '87 173
    Cocktail Smoky Links, '90 168
    Dip, Braunschweiger-and-Beer, '85 69
    Dip, Chili con Queso, '86 81
    Dumplings, Make-Ahead Pork, '03 64
    Egg Rolls, Golden Sausage, '03 284
    Kielbasa, Sweet-and-Sour, '89 327
    Meatballs, Chestnut, '79 110
    Meatballs, Crisp German, '92 326
    Meatballs, Sweet-and-Sour, '82 247
    Monster Eyes, '02 222
    Mushrooms, Italian Sausage-Stuffed., '83 127
    Mushrooms, Sausage-Stuffed, '80 248; '91 164
    Pepperoni Pie hors d'Oeuvres, '98 251
    Phyllo Bites, Sausage-Mushroom-, '89 284
    Pizza Snacks, '01 231
    Pizza Snacks, Tasty Little, '79 248
    Puffs, Cajun Hot, '94 277
    Quesadillas, Sausage, '90 118
    Rolls with Sweet-and-Sour Sauce, Sausage,
        '83 74
    Rye Appetizers, Party, '86 262
    Ryes, Sausage Party, '89 315
    Salami Rollups, '90 226
    Smoked Sausages with Mustard Sauce, '81 56
    Squares, Chile-Sausage, '86 297
    Sticks, Beef, '93 331
    Sweet-and-Sour Sausage, '88 296
    Turkey Sausage Turnovers, '95 239

Baked Peaches and Sausage, '82 50
Baked Sausage Patties, '90 82
Bake, Sausage Egg, '81 225
Barbecued Sausage, '86 153
Basic Sausage, '88 104
Beans, and Rice, Texas Sausage, '84 296
Beans, Spicy-Hot, '89 17
Bean Supper, Sausage-and-, '02 233
Black-Eyed Peas, Creole, '98 22
Black-Eyed Peas, Easy, '99 204
Black-Eyed Peas Mexicano, '79 10
Black-Eyed Peas with Sausage, '86 7
Boudin, Old-Fashioned, '85 250
Bourbon Sausage Dogs, '02 57
Bratwurst and Sauerkraut, '84 250
Bratwurst Dinner, Krause's Café, '87 238
Bratwurst, Grilled, '94 253; '01 159
Breads
    Biscuit Bites, Sausage, '84 95
    Biscuits, Cheesy Sausage, '80 78
    Biscuits, Ham, '99 233
    Biscuits, Pepperoni, '84 95
    Biscuits, Southern Sausage and, '82 43
    Biscuits with Sausage, Angel Heart, '87 156
    Biscuits with Sausage, Best, '99 103
    Black-Eyed Pea Bread, '02 224
    Muffins, Cheesy Sausage, '92 252; '93 144
    Muffins, Sausage, '88 52; '95 49
    Muffins, Sausage-Cheese, '86 213
    Pig-in-a-Blanket Bread, '99 134
    Rolls, Ground-Pepperoni, '83 244
    Waffles, Sausage, '83 50
Breakfast Delight, '93 195
Burritos, Breakfast, '84 57; '90 192
Cabbage, Italian Stuffed, '84 294
Cabbage Rolls, Hot-and-Spicy, '84 249
Cabbage, Sausage-Sauced, '81 271
Cabbage, Stuffed, '84 282
Cabbage with Polish Sausage, '83 104
Calzones with Pasta Sauce, '01 54
Casseroles
    Beefy Sausage Dinner, '80 M9
    Breakfast Casserole, '91 285; '99 273;
        '01 130, 243
    Breakfast Casserole, Brie-and-Sausage, '00 284;
        '03 36
    Breakfast Casserole, Sausage, '81 270
    Breakfast Casserole, Sausage-Ham, '01 54;
        '04 332
    Breakfast Casserole, Sausage-Hash Brown,
        '03 218
    Breakfast Casserole, Sausage-Mushroom, '86 95
    Breakfast Dish, Sausage-Apricot, '82 10
    Breakfast, Mexican, '00 194
    Broccoli Casserole, Sausage and, '80 33
    Brunch Casserole, '82 124
    Brunch Casserole, Italian, '03 29
    Brunch for a Bunch, '88 57
    Cajun Casserole, Ragin', '02 199
    Cheese Bake, Sausage-, '88 58
    Cheesy Sausage Casserole, '82 124
    Chicken Sausage and Shiitake Mushrooms,
        Cheese Grits with, '03 254
    Chile Rellenos Casserole, Sausage-, '88 52
    Chiles Rellenos Casserole, '98 48
    Country Sausage Casserole, '79 192
    Creole Sausage-and-Rice Bake, '88 58
    Crunchy Sausage Casserole, '81 288
    Easy Sausage Casserole, '87 M189
    Egg Casserole, Sausage-, '86 M12
    Egg Casserole, Sausage-and-, '94 284
    Eggplant Main Dish, Sausage-, '80 211
    Eggplant Parmesan, '86 53
    Eggplant-Sausage Bake, '85 221

Eggplant-Sausage Casserole, '84 215
Eggplant-Sausage-Pasta Casserole, Freezer,
    '95 197
Enchiladas, Breakfast, '04 281
Grits-Sausage Casserole, '84 75; '86 241
Ground Beef and Sausage Casserole, '80 260
Hawaiian Sausage Casserole, '85 42
Hominy-Sausage Bake, '88 51
Italian Casserole, '90 238
Italian Sausage Brunch, '88 57
Jambalaya Casserole, Sausage, '82 M203
Lasagna Florentine, Creamy, '91 94
Lasagna, Gourmet White, '96 225
Lasagna, Italian Sausage, '96 225
Lasagna Maria, '90 191
Lasagna, Mexican, '01 282
Lasagna Rollups, Sausage-, '80 236
Lasagna, Sausage, '83 288
Lasagna Sausage Pinwheels, '79 6
Macaroni and Cheese, Tex-Mex, '00 92
Manicotti, Cheesy Sausage-and-Tomato, '03 257
Manicotti, Meaty Stuffed, '00 19
Manicotti, Saucy Stuffed, '83 288
Mostaccioli Casserole, '04 316
Noodle Bake, Sausage-, '81 92
Noodle Casserole, Sausage and, '82 123
Noodle Casserole, Sausage-and-, '95 255
Paella Casserole, '95 254
Pizza Casserole, Upside-Down, '03 284
Potato Casserole, Sausage-, '86 217
Rice Casserole, Oriental Sausage and, '82 M123
Rice Casserole, Sausage-, '82 50; '83 75
Salami-Corn Casserole, '80 209
Sausage Casserole, '81 112; '82 12
Shells, Sausage-Stuffed, '96 102
Skillet Sausage Casserole, '99 123
Smoked Sausage-Egg Bake, '85 248
Spanish Rice Casserole, '79 192
Spud Bake, Sunday Night Spicy Cheesy Sausage-,
    '03 331
Strata, Christmas Morning, '95 282
Swiss Sausage Casserole, '80 209
Turkey-and-Sausage Wild Rice Casserole,
    '03 239
Venison-Vegetable Bake, '87 304
Wild Rice and Sausage, '86 268
Wild Rice Casserole, Sausage-, '84 250
Wild Rice Casserole, Sausage and, '83 196
Zucchini and Sausages, Baked, '80 300
Cassoulet, '96 328
Cassoulet, Easy Herb Crust, '01 311
Chicken Rolls Elégante, '80 210
Chicken Sausage with Fennel, '98 312
Chicken, Stuffed Alfredo, '04 56
Chicken with Tomatoes and Sausage, '97 266
Chili, Beefy Sausage, '82 11
Chili, Company, '82 311
Chili con Carne, Beef and Sausage, '83 284
Chili Goes Southwest, Basic, '93 326
Chili, Hearty Kielbasa, '91 28
Chili, Hotto Lotto, '89 316
Chili-I-Cious, '89 315
Chili, Lolly's Pop, '89 316
Chili, Now, Thatsa, '95 16
Chili, Sausage-Beef, '86 232
Chili, Texas-Style, '82 311; '83 30
Chorizo, '92 241
Chorizo and Egg Tortillas, '81 193
Chorizo, Black Bean, and Corn Quesadillas,
    '00 148
Chorizo, Breakfast, '91 77
Chorizo Carbonara, '94 230
Chorizo Grits with Red Bean Salsa, Shrimp-
    Manchego-, '97 227

Chorizo (Spicy Spanish Sausage), '81 193
Chorizo, Spoonbread with Simple, '04 207
Chorizo Substitute, '87 238
Chowder, Clam-and-Sausage, '94 104
Chowder, Sausage-Bean, '83 20
Cobbler, Turkey-Vegetable-Sausage, '04 325
Corn Boil, Monroe County, '96 167
Corn Maque Choux, Cajun, '01 284
Country Sausage, '88 104; '92 242
Country Sausage, Spiced, '88 104
Crêpes, Apple Breakfast, '97 331
Crêpes, Cheesy Sausage, '82 240; '83 71
Crêpes, Sausage, '88 295
Crêpes, Sausage-Filled, '79 39; '98 266; '99 25
Dinner, Sausage-and-Bean, '95 108
Dinner, Sausage-Vegetable, '84 250
Dressing, Cajun, '82 307
Dressing, Cornbread-and-Sausage, '83 213
Dressing, Cornbread-Sausage, '82 307; '85 280
Dressing, Cornbread, Sausage, and Pecan, '99 257
Dressing, Fruited Turkey, '99 257
Dressing, Harvest Sausage, '88 254
Dressing, Louise's Cornbread, '03 251
Dressing, Rice, '01 222
Dressing, Sausage, '86 280
Dressing, Sausage-Apple, '93 305; '94 296
Dressing, Sausage-Cornbread, '95 289
Dressing, Southern Rice, '99 256
Dressing, Turkey with Sausage-Cornbread, '83 287
Eggplant, Sausage Stuffed, '81 204
Eggplant, Sausage-Stuffed, '91 211
Egg Rolls with Creamy Cilantro Dipping Sauce,
    Tex-Mex, '03 327
Eggs, Armadillo, '97 270
Eggs Creole, '92 86
Eggs, Scotch, '79 261; '83 289; '98 101
Filling, Omelet with Sausage, '81 43
Fondue, Beer-and-Cheddar, '03 223
Garlic Sausage, '88 104
Gravy, Sausage, '92 271; '94 20; '97 243; '03 67
Gravy, Sawmill, '03 67
Grilled Pork, Cheddar, and Jalapeño Sausage,
    '98 311
Grits and Sausage, Country, '83 54
Grits Italiano, '92 43
Grits, Nassau, '99 214
Grits, Sausage, '86 92
Grits, Sausage-Cheese, '90 238
Grits with Sausage, '99 233
Gumbo, Chicken-and-Sausage, '89 275; '90 256;
    '94 20; '00 221; '01 324; '03 313; '04 213
Gumbo, Dove and Sausage, '81 199
Gumbo, Duck, Oyster, and Sausage, '79 226
Gumbo, The Gullah House, '92 237
Gumbo with Smoked Sausage, Chicken, '81 199
Gumbo Ya Ya, '87 210
Gumbo z'Herbes, '94 239
Homemade Sausage, Spicy, '84 320
Hominy-Sausage Skillet, '81 29
Italian Meat Sauce, '83 193
Italian Sauce with Noodles, '84 250
Italian Sausage, '88 104; '92 242
Italian Sausage and Peppers, '84 9
Italian Sausage and Rice, '86 53
Italian Sausage Dinner, '91 218
Italian Sausage Quiche, '81 200
Italian Sausage Soup, '84 235
Italian Sausage Soup with Tortellini, '88 46
Italian Sausage Supper, '88 164
Italian Sausage-Zucchini Soup, '84 4
Italian Turkey Sausage, Marinara Sauce with,
    '89 239
Jalapeños, Hot Stuffed, '99 123
Jambalaya, '03 144; '04 288

Jambalaya, Chicken-and-Sausage, '88 200; '91 216;
    '01 278; '02 36; '03 201
Jambalaya, Creole, '81 51; '03 83
Jambalaya de Covington, '87 211
Jambalaya, Northshore, '87 45
Jambalaya, 1-2-3, '97 301
Jambalaya, Oven, '84 44
Jambalaya, Sausage, '80 210; '84 249
Jambalaya, Smoked Sausage, '79 42
Jambalaya, Smoky Cajun, '96 62
Jambalaya, Trail, '93 179
Kielbasa, '92 242
Kielbasa and Cabbage, '85 67; '89 M196
Kielbasa, Cabbage, '87 42
Kielbasa-Vegetable Dinner, '91 274
Kielbasa with Beans, Easy Cheesy, '01 28
Kraut Dinner, Sausage-Apple, '02 234
Kraut, Sausage and, '83 11
Linguine with Sausage and Peppers, '03 170
Loaf, Hawaiian Ham, '79 71
Loaf, Skillet Liver, '80 11
Log, Phyllo Sausage, '84 294
Log, Stuffed Beef, '79 71
Meatballs and Sausage, Spicy, '79 163
Meat Loaf, French Market, '02 33
Meat Loaf, Mozzarella-Layered, '79 71
Meat Loaf, Sweet 'n' Saucy, '01 210
Mexican Luncheon, '87 192
Minestrone, Cheesy, '99 17
Muffins, Breakfast, '04 209
Muffins, Sausage-and-Cheese, '03 81
Omelet, Puffy Sausage, '80 M268
Omelet with Fresh Avocado Salsa, Spanish, '02 247
Onions, Baked Stuffed, '83 135
Paella, '97 328
Paella, Shortcut, '01 309
Pancake-Sausage Wedges, '93 196
Pasta, Three Pepper-Sausage, '02 122
Pasta with Broccoli and Sausage, '87 109; '97 266
Pasta with Collards and Sausage, '94 230
Pasta with Sausage and Bell Peppers, '02 63
Pasta with Sausage and Kale, '03 279
Pasta with Sausage and Mixed Vegetables, '84 249
Patties, Apples on Sausage, '82 120
Pepperoni-and-Broccoli Salad, '83 216
Pepperoni Pasta, '83 105
Pepperoni Pinwheels, '96 247
Pepperoni Soup, Italian-Style Beef-and-, '00 316
Pepperoni-Squash Toss, '84 127
Peppers, Sausage and, '95 165
Peppers with Parmesan Cheese Grits, Sausage and,
    '02 233
Pie, Breakfast, '86 242
Pie, Cornbread-Sausage-Apple, '87 171
Pie, Sausage-and-Cornbread, '90 25
Pie, Tumbleweed, '98 205
Pie, Turkey-Sausage, '01 297
Pigs in a Blanket, '03 167
Pilau, Sausage, '99 184
Pintos and Sausage, Hearty, '88 296
Pinwheels, Sausage, '80 209; '93 238
Pizza, Breakfast, '85 44; '88 288
Pizza, Deep-Dish, '01 29
Pizza, Double Cheesy Beef-and-Sausage, '86 77
Pizza Luncheon Pie, Deep-Dish, '80 286
Pizza, Mexican, '02 72
Pizza Peppers, '83 135
Pizza Pie, Link-Sausage, '85 33
Pizza, Sausage-Potato, '01 199
Pizza, Speedy, '81 214
Pizza, Spicy Sausage-Pepperoni, '83 226
Pizza, The King Henry, '95 267
Pizza, Thick 'n' Crusty Pepperoni, '85 244
Polenta with Sausage, '93 32

SAUSAGE

(continued)

Polish Sausage, Cabbage with, '83 104
Pork Rib Roast, Sausage Stuffed, '94 240
Pork Sausage, '81 55; '97 243
Pork Sausage Ring, '80 49
Pork Tenderloin, Stuffed, '00 213
Potato-and-Sausage Salad, Warm, '96 25
Potatoes, Mexican-Topped, '83 3
Potatoes, Sausage-Vegetable-Topped, '98 29
Potatoes with Eggs and Meat, '91 311; '92 25
Potato Salad with Smoked Sausage, Warm, '97 267
Quesadillas, Breakfast Sausage, '04 183
Quiche, Crustless Sausage-Apple, '87 70
Quiche, Crustless Veggie Sausage, '03 175
Quiche Cups, Mexican, '02 72
Quiche, Easy Sausage, '79 261
Quiche, Pizza, '86 53
Quiche, Sausage-Cheddar, '79 26
Quiche, South-of-the-Border, '93 321
Quiche, Spicy Sausage, '80 M108
Quiche with Avocado Topping, Mexicali, '93 309;
  '94 96
Quiche, Zucchini-Sausage, '83 122
Ratatouille, Sausage, '89 248
Red Beans and Rice, '02 35
Red Beans and Rice, Delta, '98 146
Red Beans and Rice, New Orleans, '97 235
Red Beans and Rice, Spicy, '02 56
Red Rice, '00 289
Rice, Cajun Dirty, '04 288
Rice, Pork Sausage-Seasoned, '00 236
Rice, Shrimp and Sausage, '79 64
Rice with Sausage, Fried, '83 12
Risotto, Redneck, '98 107
Rollups, Pancake-Sausage, '83 246; '84 42
Rollups, Sausage-Bacon, '88 51
Roll-Ups, Spicy Egg, '90 140
Salad, Bean-and-Sausage, '91 313
Salad, Warm Potato-and-Sausage, '96 25
Sandwiches
  Breakfast Pita Pockets, '89 M21
  Breakfast Sandwiches, '80 52
  Bun, Sausage in a, '89 M22
  Burgers, All-American Pizza, '92 148
  Burgers, Sausage, '83 212; '96 102
  Calzone, '85 94
  Calzones, Beef-and-Pepperoni, '03 202
  Cheese Muffin Sandwiches, Sausage-, '92 M212
  Italian Sausage and Pepper Loaves, '83 11
  Italian Sausage Sandwich, '80 92
  Italian Sausage Sloppy Joes, '86 160
  Loaf, Sausage-Stuffed French, '90 19
  Loaves, Sausage-Cheese, '88 235
  Muffuletta Loaf, '97 86
  Mustard Sauce, Sausage Sandwiches with,
    '84 250
  Pepperoni and Cheese Loaf, '82 32
  Pizza Sandwich, Giant, '80 93
  Salami Sandwiches, Open-Faced, '87 279
  Sleeping Bag, Sausage in a, '98 206
Sauce, Sicilian Spaghetti, '03 62
Shrimp and Sausage over Creamy Grits with Tasso
  Gravy, Spicy, '92 236
Shrimp Sausage, '97 164
Skillet Dinner, Sausage, '83 29
Skillet Express, Sausage, '83 117
Skillet, Mexican-Style, '83 12
Skillet Sausage and Cabbage, '01 28
Skillet Sausage and Pasta, '97 267
Skillet Supper, Chicken-and-Sausage, '03 49
Skillet Supper, Sausage, '85 293

Smoked Sausage, '86 154
Smoked Sausage, Chicken Gumbo with, '81 199
Smoked Sausage Jambalaya, '79 42
Smoked Sausage Pilau, Chicken-and-, '04 204
Smoked Sausage Stew, '82 231
Soup, Easy Potato-Sausage, '98 315
Soup, Peasant, '01 54
Soup, Polish Sausage, '99 317
Soup, Sausage and Okra, '80 209
Soup, Sausage-Bean, '85 88
Soup, Sausage-Potato, '80 25
Soup, Sausage, Spinach, and Bean, '99 311
Soup, Sausage-Tortellini, '99 20
Soup, Spicy Sausage-Bean, '83 229
Soup, Sweet Potato-and-Sausage, '95 23
Spaghetti Dinner, Sausage, '79 194
Spaghetti, Italian, '81 38
Spaghetti, Italian Zucchini, '85 2
Spaghetti, Real Italian, '81 233
Spaghetti, Sausage, '83 160
Spicy Sausage, Dieters', '85 49
Squares, Chile-Sausage, '86 297
Squares, Sausage-Onion, '83 112
Squash, Harvest, '80 214
Squash, Sausage-Stuffed, '81 183
Stew, Frogmore, '92 236; '00 174, 336; '03 181
Stew, Mirliton, '02 57
Stew, Oyster-Sausage, '89 242
Stew, Venison Sausage, '87 238
Stir-Fry, Sausage, '82 236; '98 156
Stir-Fry Sausage and Vegetables, '86 213; '87 82
Strata, Sausage, '83 243; '84 101
Stuffing, Chicken Breasts with Pecan-Sausage,
  '94 212
Stuffing, Crown Roast of Pork with Cranberry-
  Sausage, '88 49
Stuffing, Sausage, '99 293; '00 292; '03 255
Stuffing, Sausage-and-Wild Mushroom, '96 267
Summer Sausage, '99 85
Supper, Cabbage, '89 314
Supper, Sausage, '01 28
Supper, Sausage-Bean, '86 52
Surprise, Sausage, '83 245; '84 42
Sweet Peppery Sausage, '95 69
Tacos, Breakfast, '80 43; '95 340
Tamales, Breakfast, '00 122
Taquitos, Breakfast, '87 237
Tarts, Sausage 'n' Cheese, '88 51
Tasso Bread Pudding, Rosemary-, '00 104
Tomatoes, Italian-Style, '97 169
Tomatoes, Sausage-Stuffed, '80 47
Tortilla Campesina, '89 85
Tortillas, Egg-and-Sausage, '83 246; '84 42
Turban Squash, Sausage-Stuffed, '80 214
Turnovers, Sausage-Cheese, '88 231; '89 22
Vegetables and Sausage, Spicy, '80 82
Vegetable Skillet, Sausage-, '96 102
Veggie Sausage Pizzas, '00 294
Waffle Stack, Hoppin' John, '04 19
Wild Rice, Sausage and, '85 65
Ziti with Sausage and Broccoli, '95 340
Zucchini and Sausage, Sautéed, '83 289
SCALLOPS
Angel Hair Pasta, Scallops and, '99 176
Appetizer, Scallop, '86 155
Appetizers, Flaky Scallop, '86 327
Artichokes Stuffed with Shrimp and Scallops,
  '84 174
Bacon-Wrapped Scallops, '87 94
Bacon-Wrapped Scallops with Orange-Honey
  Sauce, '97 236
Baked Gruyère Scallops, '92 57
Bay Scallops, Linguine with, '97 201
Broiled Scallops, '91 170

Broiled Scallops with Tartar Sauce, '80 164
Broth with Black Beans and Cilantro, Southwestern
  Scallop, '87 123
Cakes, Crab-and-Scallop, '02 165
Casserole, Creamy Shrimp-and-Scallops, '01 256
Casserole, Scallop, '79 228
Ceviche (Marinated Raw Fish), '82 220
Champagne-Saffron Sauce, Scallops with, '93 177
Cheese Scallops, Chip and, '80 301
Coquilles Saint Cyrano, '86 90
Coquilles St. Jacques, '97 201
Creamy Scallops and Mushrooms, '83 144
Crêpes, Coquilles St. Jacques, '83 13
en Brochette with Vegetables, Scallops, '80 163
Fettuccine, Scallop-Mushroom, '96 198
Ginger Scallops, '99 177
Grilled Orange Scallops with Cilantro-Lime
  Vinaigrette, '94 77
Grilled Scallops, Marinated, '84 171
Grilled Sweet-and-Sour Scallops, '01 92
Kebabs, Grilled Scallop, '83 101
Kebabs, Grilled Shrimp-and-Scallop, '92 210
Kebabs, Scallop-Bacon, '81 111
Kebabs, Sea Scallop, '82 162
Maple Scallops, '99 176
Mornay, Scallops, '80 164
Mornay, Shrimp and Scallops, '97 238
Mustard Sauce, Scallops with, '84 163
Pasta, Fresh Scallops and, '83 164
Provençal, Scallops, '85 66
Rumaki, Scallop, '98 M173
Salad, Thai-Rific Orange Scallop, '04 317
Sautéed Scallops with Cranberry Relish, '83 144
Sauté, Scallop, '88 28
Sauté, Shrimp-and-Scallop, '85 103
Sauté with Pecan Rice, Shrimp-and-Scallop, '90 317
Savannah, Scallops, '79 145
Seared Scallops with Tomato-Mango Salsa, '95 122
Seared Sea Scallops with Tomato Puree, '97 201
Sesame-Crusted Scallops with Orange-Ginger
  Sauce, '97 125
Sherried Scallops, '83 281
Stir-Fry, Scallop, '94 32
Supreme, Seafood, '82 284
Tostada, Grilled Scallops, '87 120
Vegetable Nests, Scallops in, '91 70
Vegetables, Bay Scallops with, '84 233
Vermicelli, Scallop-Vegetable, '87 143
Vermouth-Cream Sauce, Scallops in, '96 49
Véronique, Scallops, '83 144
Wild Rice, Scallops and, '90 129
Wine, Scallops in, '91 48
SCONES. *See* **BREADS.**
SEAFOOD. *See also* **CASSEROLES, CLAMS,
  CRAB, CRAWFISH, FISH, LOBSTER,
  OYSTERS, SALMON, SCALLOPS,
  SHRIMP, TUNA.**
Appetizer, Layered Seafood, '88 2
Bisque, Seafood, '86 66
Boil, Low Country Seafood, '80 119
Boil, Southern Shellfish, '93 258
Bouchees aux Fruits de Mer, '98 267
Bouillabaisse, Florida, '79 158
Brochette, Seafood, '87 96
Broiled Shellfish, Quick, '79 228
Butter, Seafood, '97 306
Cakes with Jalapeño Tartar Sauce, Seafood, '98 129
Calamari, Fried, '00 283
Casserole, Seafood, '87 109; '89 63
Chowder, Curried Seafood, '94 103
Chowder, Seafood, '85 9; '92 122
Chowder, So-Quick Seafood, '01 18
Chowder, Southern Seafood, '83 20
Cioppino, Gulf Coast, '94 102

Crêpes in Wine-Cheese Sauce, Shellfish, '00 310
Delight, Seafood, '86 208
Dip, Hot Artichoke-Seafood, '80 241
Dip, Hot Artichoke Seafood, '85 M212
Dip, Hot Cheesy Seafood, '84 221
Dip, Seafood, '79 3
Dip, Super Seafood, '90 292
Eggplant, Seafood Stuffed, '79 187
Gumbos
Cajun Seafood Gumbo, '94 238
Champion Seafood Gumbo, '86 293
Chicken-Ham-Seafood Gumbo, '81 6
Creole Gumbo, '86 228
Creole Gumbo, Quick, '82 87
Creole Seafood Gumbo, '82 278
Ham and Seafood Gumbo, '81 199
Okra Gumbo, Light Seafood-, '86 155
Seafood Gumbo, '79 198, 286; '80 34; '81 5;
'83 90; '84 87, 92; '87 210; '90 154; '96 98
Spicy Seafood Gumbo, '91 207
Whole Crabs, Seafood Gumbo with, '85 2
Hot Brown, Seafood, '88 158
Imperials, Individual Seafood, '84 162
Jambalaya, Three-Seafood, '82 126
Linguine, Seafood, '79 227
Manicotti, Seafood, '94 195
Mayonnaise, Seafood with Dill, '86 234
Mold, Chilled Seafood, '86 70
Mornay, Seafood, '83 67
Mussels Linguine, '90 M112
Mussels Marinara, '00 283
Mussel Soup, '93 259
Oriental Marinade, Seafood in, '98 128
Paella, Chicken-Seafood, '88 68
Paella, Party, '88 M189
Paella, Seafood, '82 245
Papillote, Ocean, '84 M287
Parmesan, Savannah Seafood, '99 312
Pasta, Herbed Seafood, '04 255
Pasta, Seafood and, '90 234
Pie, Hot Seafood, '80 32
Pizza, Seafood Alfredo, '03 236
Po' Boy, Grilled Seafood, '96 244
Potatoes, Seafood-Stuffed, '95 M192
Prawns with Winter Cabbage Salad, '98 284
Risotto, Seafood, '95 280
Risotto with Shellfish and Peas, '96 131
Robert, Seafood, '97 106
Salads
Baked Seafood Salad, '86 10
Hot Seafood Salad, '79 117; '80 164
Paella Salad, '86 207
Pasta Salad, Seafood, '90 62
Polynesian Seafood Salad, '79 57
Seafood Salad, '90 88
Seaside Salad, '86 183
Slaw, Seafood, '79 56
Smoky Seafood Salad, '84 46
Sussex Shores, Seafood Salad, '93 98
Sandwiches, Caribbean Seafood, '98 105
Sauce Delight, Seafood, '82 91
Sauce, Linguine with Seafood, '83 232
Sauce, Red Seafood, '95 107
Sauce, Seafood, '79 3; '82 48; '86 304; '89 239
Sauce, Seafood Cheese, '89 240
Sautéed Seafood Platter, '83 89
Seasoning Blend, Bay Seafood, '92 121
Seasoning Blend, Fish-and-Seafood, '88 28
Seasoning Rub, Seafood, '93 101
Soup, Seafood-Tortellini, '97 324
Spread, Grandma Reed's Seafood, '98 268
Spread, Seafood, '86 M58; '87 146
Spread, Seafood Sandwich, '82 87
Stew, Seafood, '84 280

Stir-Fry with Noodle Pancake, Szechuan Ginger,
'97 292
Stock, Seafood, '94 238
Supreme, Seafood, '82 284
Tartlets, Seafood, '87 247
Tempura, Basic, '81 68
Tempura, Cornmeal, '81 68
Terrine with Dill Sauce, Asparagus-Seafood,
'98 157
SEASONINGS. *See also* **MARINADES, OILS,
SPICE.**
Adobo, '92 158
Barbecue Rub, '03 130; '04 104
Barbecue Rub, All-Purpose, '03 130; '04 104
Barbecue Rub, Master Class, '98 244
Basil Puree, '03 208
Bay Seafood Seasoning Blend, '92 121
Better-Than-Potpourri Brew, '95 271
Blend, Seasoning, '82 296
Chipotle Rub, '04 87
Court-Bouillon, '98 229
Creole Rub, '93 101
Creole Seasoning Blend, '92 121
Creole Seasoning, Crescent City Grill, '04 289
Dry Rub, Biltmore, '99 231; '00 20
Essence, Emeril's, '99 198
Fish-and-Seafood Seasoning Blend, '88 28
Fish Herb Mix, '98 51
Five-Spice Powder Blend, '92 121
Garlic, Herbed Roasted, '94 177
Garlic Puree, Roasted, '92 55
Garlic, Roasted, '94 177; '96 304
Ginger Rub, '04 87
Greek Seasoning Blend, '92 121
Gremolata, '95 280
Gremolata, Citrus-Mint, '04 108
Ground Seasoning Blend, '92 121
Herb Rub, '93 102
Herb Seasoning, '99 63
Herbs Seasoning Blend, '92 121
Hoisin Mixture, '99 125
Italian Breadcrumb Mix, '99 265
Jamaican Jerk Rub, '00 88
Jerk Rub, '93 101
Lemon-Mint Sugar, '95 32
Lemon Squeezers, '95 32
Marinade, Italian, '03 180
Marinade, Zesty Chicken, '03 180
Meat Seasoning, '98 62
Meat Seasoning Blend, '88 29
Mexican Rub, '93 102
Mix, GOPPS Seasoning, '92 305
Mix, Melvyn's Seasoning, '04 132
Mix, Seasoning, '91 64; '00 322
Mix, Weaver D's Seasoning, '96 248
Moroccan Spice Rub, '95 231
Olive Oil, Basil-Infused, '95 231
Olive Oil, Lemon-Infused, '95 231
Poultry Seasoning Blend, '88 28
Roux, '03 111
Rub, Brisket, '03 188
Rub, Caribbean Spice, '02 144
Rub, Mediterranean, '03 180
Salt, Dragon, '03 236
Salt, Gourmet Seasoning, '82 297; '97 254
Sauce, Seasoning, '00 110
Sazon, '92 157
Seafood Seasoning Rub, '93 101
Southwest Seasoning, '95 266
Spice Blend, Southwestern, '03 180
Taco Seasoning Blend, '96 159
Vanilla Extract, '94 243; '97 288
Vanilla Sugar, '94 243
Vegetable Seasoning Blend, '88 29

SHERBETS. *See also* **ICE CREAMS.**
Ambrosia Cups, Sherbet, '82 159
Apricot Sherbet, '81 177; '92 164
Avocado Sherbet, '83 162
Banana-Orange Sherbet, '83 162
Beverages
Float, Pineapple Sherbet, '79 148
Punch, Double Sherbet, '79 232
Punch, Orange Sherbet Party, '83 142
Punch, Pineapple Sherbet, '95 141
Punch, Raspberry Sherbet, '95 141
Smoothie, Citrus, '99 196
Smoothie, Orange-Banana, '97 173
Smoothie, Pineapple, '97 172
Blackberry Sherbet, 1-2-3, '99 130; '00 21
Blackberry Sherbet, Three-Ingredient, '01 105
Blueberry Sherbet, '04 283
Buttermilk Sherbet, '84 184; '99 99
Cantaloupe Sherbet, '88 183
Cantaloupe Sherbet, Frosty, '82 144
Cranberry Sherbet, '88 280
Dessert, Layered Sherbet, '87 109
Dessert, Macaroon-Sherbet Frozen, '79 212
Fruit Punch Sherbet, '86 129
Fruit Sherbet, Freezer, '86 334
Fruit Sherbet, Frozen, '79 155
Fruit Sherbet, Instant, '85 158
Jalapeño-Mint Sherbet, '98 202
Lemon Cream Sherbet, '79 114
Lemon-Pineapple Sherbet, '96 330
Lemon Sherbet, '91 309
Lime Sherbet, '82 159; '89 202
Lime Sherbet, Creamy, '84 165
Mexican Sherbet, '79 155
Mint Sherbet, Fresh, '88 23
Nectarine Sherbet, '89 199
Orange Sherbet, '79 155
Orange Sherbet Salad, '81 154
Orange Sherbet, Three-Ingredient, '01 105
Orange Sherbet with Blackberry Sauce, '94 232
Peach Sherbet, '90 179
Peach Sherbet, Three-Ingredient, '01 105
Pineapple Sherbet, '81 177; '84 83; '89 199
Pineapple Sherbet, Creamy, '79 155
Pineapple Sherbet, Easy, '92 199
Raspberry Sherbet, '83 162
Strawberry Sherbet, '82 112, 160
Strawberry Sherbet, Three-Ingredient, '01 105
Watermelon Sherbet, '79 155; '92 124
Watermelon Sherbet, Light, '81 147
SHRIMP
Appetizers
Afterburners, '03 159
Artichoke-and-Shrimp Appetizer, '93 271
Bacon-Shrimp Bites, '98 234; '99 213
Bacon, Shrimp 'n', '98 222
Ball, Curried Shrimp Cheese, '86 135
Balls, Curried Shrimp, '94 180
Ball, Shrimp-Cheese, '85 208
Barbecue Shrimp, '96 210; '97 58; '00 30
Bayou, Shrimp, '88 261
Biscuits, Shrimp-and-Grits, '02 313
Boiled Shrimp, '79 3
Boiled Shrimp, Spicy, '83 320; '84 289
Boiled Shrimp with Cocktail Sauce, '79 151
Boil, Southern Shellfish, '93 258
Braised Shrimp with Garlic Rémoulade, '98 133
Bundles with Chive Butter Sauce, Crispy Shrimp,
'03 91
Butter on Crostini, Shrimp, '04 259
Butter, Shrimp, '92 91
Cajun Shrimp, '89 283
Canapés, Shrimp, '84 116
Canapés, Shrimp-and-Cucumber, '93 164

SHRIMP, Appetizers
(continued)

Cheese Appetizer, Shrimp-and-, '01 134
Cheesecake, Shrimp-and-Gruyère, '92 57
Cheese, Shrimp with Herbed Jalapeño, '87 112
Chilled Shrimp with Rémoulade Sauce, '02 134
Cocktail, Mexican Shrimp, '00 249
Cocktail, Shrimp, '87 173; '96 174
Coconut-Beer Shrimp, '85 230; '89 23
Coconut Shrimp with Mustard Sauce, '02 245
Croustades, Shrimp, '97 23
Dilled Shrimp, '88 150
Dip, Chunky Shrimp, '96 214
Dip, Hot Shrimp, '87 190
Dip, Monterey Shrimp, '99 65
Dippers, Shrimp, '84 324
Dip, Quick Shrimp, '79 153
Dip, Shrimp, '86 84; '88 M261; '98 67; '01 194
Dip, Zesty Shrimp, '80 150
Double-Dip Shrimp, '99 112
Egg Rolls, '86 81
Eggrolls, Shrimp and Pork, '82 240; '83 18
Filling, Shrimp, '89 320
Fried Marinated Shrimp with Mango Slaw, '93 31
Garlic-and-Rosemary Shrimp, '01 101; '04 52
Grilled Jerk Shrimp with Creamy Tomatillo
    Sauce, '01 332
Grilled Zucchini-Wrapped Shrimp, '98 200
Jalapeños, Shrimp-Stuffed, '88 115
Kebabs, Appetizer Shrimp, '91 251
Kebabs, Shrimp, '80 150
Key West Shrimp, '94 278
Lemon Shrimp, Luscious, '88 150
Manale, Shrimp, '86 268
Marinated Shrimp and Artichokes, '97 89;
    '98 335
Marinated Shrimp and Cucumber, '91 166
Marinated Shrimp, Icy, '84 215
Miniquiches, Shrimp, '87 146
Mold, Shrimp, '87 94
Mold with Asparagus, Shrimp, '93 214
Mousse, Shrimp, '79 57; '87 196, 251
Mushrooms, Shrimp-Stuffed, '80 M135; '99 324
Oven-Fried Shrimp with Marmalade Dip, '99 324
Pâté on Crostini, Shrimp, '98 316
Pâté with Dill Sauce, Shrimp, '85 39
Pickled Shrimp, '94 182
Pickled Shrimp, Charleston Harbor, '99 275
Pickled Shrimp, New Orleans, '79 145
Pickle, Shrimp-in-a-, '86 326
Pineapple Appetizer, Shrimp-, '85 80
Pizza Wedges, Shrimp, '89 158
Puffs, Gouda-Shrimp, '79 234
Puffs, Shrimp, '96 211; '98 316
Rémoulade, Galatoire's Shrimp, '04 103
Rémoulade, Shrimp, '83 173; '90 255; '03 146
Rock Shrimp Conga, '80 2
Rolls with Sweet Soy Sauce, Jumbo Shrimp,
    '03 248
Rounds, Shrimp, '98 167
Salsa Picante with Shrimp, '92 210
Sesame Shrimp, '95 92
Sherried Garlic Shrimp, '92 175
Skewers with Vegetable Salsa, Shrimp, '98 32
Smoked Shrimp, Stove-Top, '01 168
Soufflé Roll, Shrimp, '89 320
Spread, Chunky Shrimp, '85 300; '86 18
Spread, Curried Shrimp, '87 158
Spread, Shrimp, '81 306; '85 135; '87 111;
    '93 205; '96 104
Spread, Shrimp-Cucumber, '79 81
Spread, Tempting Shrimp, '79 57

Spread, Zippy Shrimp, '90 36
Spring Rolls with Sweet Chili Sauce, Shanghai,
    '01 236
Steamed Shrimp, '03 206
Tangy Shrimp, '04 18
Tartlets, Shrimp, '00 71
Toast, Shrimp, '86 91; '00 109
Tree, Shrimp, '83 320; '84 288; '85 318
Vegetable Appetizer, Shrimp-and-, '97 161
Zucchini-Shrimp Appetizers, '89 311
Ariosto, Shrimp and Chicken, '79 31
Artichokes, Shrimp-Stuffed, '84 67; '87 55
Artichokes, Shrimp Stuffed, '94 62
Artichokes Stuffed with Shrimp and Scallops, '84 174
au Gratin, Crab, Shrimp, and Artichoke, '90 240
au Gratin, Shrimp, '85 79
Avocados, Shrimp-Filled, '83 2
Baked Shrimp, '87 35
Baked Shrimp, Spicy, '97 324
Barbecued Shrimp, '82 74; '84 93; '90 28
Barbecued Shrimp and Cornbread-Stuffed Peppers,
    '97 261
Barbecued Shrimp, Cajun, '87 95
Barbecue Shrimp, Hickory-Smoked, '00 89
Barbecue Shrimp, New Orleans, '02 201
Boats, Shrimp, '79 57
Boiled Shrimp, '79 3; '04 147
Boiled Shrimp, Ray Kidd's, '84 87
Boiled Shrimp, Special, '83 36
Boiled Shrimp Supper, '94 200
Boiled Shrimp with Green Peppercorn Tartar Sauce,
    '94 144
Bourbon, Shrimp, '00 125
Breakfast Shrimp, Classic Charleston, '93 60
Broiled Shrimp, Beer-, '87 142
Broiled Shrimp, Garlic-, '83 193
Broiled Shrimp, Lemon-Garlic, '82 29; '86 182
Broiled Shrimp Supreme, '79 3
Burgers, Shrimp, '03 110
Cabbage, Asian Shrimp and, '00 105
Cajun Shrimp, Fiery, '91 218
Cakes with Watercress Rémoulade, Shrimp, '01 326
Cashew Shrimp Supreme, '83 29
Casserole, Chayotes and Shrimp, '80 230
Casserole, Cheesy Shrimp-and-Grits, '03 28
Casserole, Crab-and-Shrimp, '84 71
Casserole, Creamy Shrimp-and-Scallops, '01 256
Casserole, Miss Hannah's, '92 236
Casserole, Shrimp, '85 240
Casserole, Shrimp-and-Chicken, '91 102
Casserole, Shrimp-and-Noodle, '90 240
Casserole, Shrimp and Rice, '79 228
Casserole, Shrimp-and-Rice, '94 328
Casserole, Spicy Shrimp, '96 62
Casserole, Turkey-and-Shrimp Florentine, '92 122
Catfish, Crown Room's Shrimp-Stuffed, '84 182
C'est Bon, Shrimp, '94 195
Chicken Breasts, Stuffed, '88 50
Chowder, Quick Shrimp, '04 27
Chow Mein, Shrimp, '82 30
Coconut-Pecan Shrimp with Orange Dipping Sauce,
    '03 212
Coconut Shrimp, '00 175
Creamed Shrimp on Pecan-Cornmeal Rounds,
    '95 99
Cream Sauce, Shrimp in, '84 M286
Creole, Easy Shrimp, '95 68
Creole in a Rice Ring, Shrimp, '86 222
Creole, Shrimp, '86 256; '87 18; '90 M220; '93 282;
    '96 210; '03 109
Creole, Special Shrimp, '87 172
Creole, Spicy Shrimp, '79 181
Creole, Wild Rice-and-Shrimp, '84 292
Croquettes, Nannie's Shrimp, '98 316

Curry

Charleston-Style Shrimp Curry, '84 109
Creamy Shrimp Curry, '90 145
Curried Shrimp, '84 110
Eggs, Saucy Shrimp-Curried, '84 143
Ginger Shrimp, Curry-, '00 316
Hot Red Curry Shrimp, '02 125
Polynesian Shrimp Curry, '89 23
Quick Curried Shrimp, '84 M198
Rice and Shrimp, Curried, '83 231
Salad, Curried Shrimp, '00 217
Sauce, Hawaiian Shrimp with Curry, '94 54
Shrimp Curry, '99 91
Shrimp Malai Curry, '84 110
Sour Cream and Shrimp Curry, '81 10
Sour Cream Shrimp Curry, '80 83
West Indian Curried Shrimp, '79 227
Daufuskie Shrimp, '00 174
Dee-Lish, Shrimp, '90 216
de Jonghe, Shrimp, '79 228
Delight, English Muffin, '82 45
Delight, Shrimp, '79 192
Destin, Shrimp, '82 29; '03 314
Dijonnaise, Shrimp, '87 91
Dilled Sauced Shrimp, '86 88
Dinner, Jollof Rice, '91 230; '92 325
di Santo, Shrimp, '99 265
Egg Foo Yong, '80 19; '86 232
Egg Foo Yong, Shrimp, '83 22
Eggplant à la Creole, '96 177
Eggplant-Shrimp Medley, '79 188
Eggplant, Shrimp-Stuffed, '92 99
Eggrolls, Shrimp and Pork, '82 240; '83 18
Egg Rolls, Vietnamese, '96 101
Eggs Benedict, Shrimp-and-Grits, '03 53
Eggs, Shrimp and Crab Scrambled, '79 261
Eggs, Shrimp-Stuffed, '00 70
Élégante, Shrimp, '83 48
Enchiladas in Tomatillo Sauce, Shrimp, '95 310
Enchiladas, Poblano-Shrimp, '00 311
Enchiladas, Shrimp, '01 104
en Papillote, Shrimp Cancun, '91 136
en Papillote, Shrimp with Asparagus, '86 145
Étouffée, Crab-and-Shrimp, '89 96
Étouffée, Shrimp, '79 4; '90 229
Feta Cheese, Shrimp with, '00 221
Filling, Shrimp and Dill, '97 171
Firecracker Shrimp, '03 144
Fire-Roasted Shrimp with Orzo, '99 42
Fish with Shrimp, Veracruz, '86 130
Flambé, Prawns, '89 24
Florentine, Chicken-and-Shrimp, '89 64
Flounder Stuffed with Shrimp, '88 51
Fondue, Shrimp, '86 244
French-Fried Shrimp, '79 4
French Shrimp, '80 85
Fresh Shrimp, Preparing, '82 127
Fried Marinated Shrimp with Mango Slaw, '93 31
Fried Noodles with Shrimp, '02 174
Fried Rice, Spicy Shrimp-and-Pineapple, '03 285
Fried Shrimp, '03 109
Fried Shrimp, Coconut, '96 248
Fried Shrimp, Cracker-Breaded, '04 122
Fried Shrimp, Golden, '82 29
Fried Shrimp, Gulf Coast, '91 29
Fried Shrimp, Puffy, '79 4
Fried Shrimp with Apricot Sauce, '87 172
Fritters, Shrimp, '00 238
Garlic-Buttered Shrimp, '86 M226
Garlic-Chili Shrimp and Grits, '00 23
Garlic Shrimp, '79 268; '80 14
Garlic Shrimp and Grits, '03 246
Gin and Ginger, Shrimp with, '95 205
Grilled Garlic Shrimp, '99 178

Grilled Margarita-Marinated Shrimp, '97 167
Grilled Parsleyed Shrimp and Vegetables, '04 256
Grilled Shrimp, '85 103
Grilled Shrimp with Citrus Salsa, '97 141
Grilled Shrimp with Smoky Sweet Sauce, Mexican-, '03 32
Grilled Shrimp with Tropical Fruit Sauce, '01 195
Grilled Sweet-and-Sour Shrimp, '97 100
Grits, Crook's Corner Shrimp and, '04 102
Grits, Shrimp and, '01 258
Grits with Red Bean Salsa, Shrimp-Manchego-Chorizo, '97 227
Gumbo, Shrimp-Crab, '03 111
Gyros with Herbed Yogurt Spread, Grilled-Shrimp, '02 169
Hoisin Shrimp, '99 237
Honeyed Shrimp, Tangy, '94 32
Jambalaya with Shrimp, Chicken-and-Ham, '04 99
Kebabs, Grilled Shrimp-and-Scallop, '92 210
Kebabs, Marinated Shrimp, '84 276; '85 158
Kebabs, Shrimp, '80 150, 184
Kebabs, Steak-and-Shrimp, '80 184; '00 124
Lamb Chops with Shrimp, '88 58
Lemon Butter, Shrimp in, '84 163
Lemon Garlic Sauce, Shrimp in, '83 67
Lemon Shrimp, Luscious, '88 150
Marinara, Shrimp, '84 233
Marinated and Grilled Shrimp, '87 141
Marinated Shrimp, '98 317; '02 254
Marinated Shrimp, Grilled, '87 173
Marinated Shrimp, Grilled Margarita-, '97 167
Marinated Shrimp with Capers, '00 279
Marinated Shrimp with Louis Sauce, Citrus-, '03 66
Marinated Shrimp, Zesty, '87 173
Martinis with Napa Cabbage Slaw, Shrimp, '02 280
Mediterranean Shrimp Bowl, '80 174
Melba, Shrimp, '84 86
Mirlitons, Shrimp-and-Ham Stuffed, '03 251
Mirlitons, Stuffed, '97 263; '00 246
Mornay, Shrimp and Scallops, '97 238
Mustard-Vinegar Sauce, Shrimp with, '93 240
Noodles, Sesame, '01 188
Omelet, Shrimp-and-Cheddar, '84 57
Omelet, Shrimp-and-Cheese, '94 31
Omelet, Shrimp-and-Vegetable Oven, '99 286
Orange Sauce, Shrimp in, '99 292; '00 292
Oriental, Shrimp, '01 36
Oven Shrimp, Vic's, '95 215
Pad Thai, '97 202
Paella, '97 328
Paella Casserole, '95 254
Paella, Chicken-Pork-Shrimp, '82 245
Paella, Party, '88 M189
Paella, Shortcut, '01 309
Paella, Shrimp-and-Chicken, '94 168
Paella, Spanish, '85 26
Paella Valenciana, '82 246
Palermo, Shrimp, '04 241
Pasta. *See also* **SHRIMP/Salads.**
Angel Hair Pasta, Shrimp and Mushrooms with, '92 34
Angel Hair Pasta with Shrimp and Asparagus, '92 100
Angel Hair Pasta with Veal and Shrimp, '04 223
Asian Shrimp with Pasta, '04 128
Asparagus, Tomatoes, and Shrimp, Garlicky Pasta with, '95 82
Cheeses, Shrimp and Pasta with Two, '98 49
Cream Sauce, Shrimp and Pasta with, '98 295
Fettuccine and Shrimp with Dried Tomato Pesto, '94 249
Fettuccine, Dilled Shrimp with, '99 141
Fettuccine, Shrimp, '94 84; '96 210
Fettuccine, Shrimp-Herb, '01 308

Fettuccine with Shrimp-and-Creamy Herb Sauce, '01 257
Fettuccine with Shrimp and Tomatoes, '96 198
Garlic-and-Rosemary Shrimp, '01 101
Garlic Shrimp-and-Goat Cheese Pasta, '00 174
Green Pasta with Shrimp-Mushroom Italienne, '79 170
Herbed Shrimp and Pasta, '92 329; '97 228
Lemon Shrimp and Pasta, '96 124
Linguine, Artichoke and Shrimp, '95 210
Linguine, Spicy Shrimp and, '92 34
Manicotti, Shrimp, '97 96
Mediterranean Shrimp and Pasta, '95 286
Medley, Shrimp-Pasta, '88 302
Noodles, Creamy Shrimp and, '92 100
Noodles with Shrimp, Hoisin, '98 233
Pasta with Shrimp, '01 164
Primavera, Shrimp with Pasta, '93 168
Roasted Red Pepper Cream, Shrimp with, '03 97
Rotelle, Shrimp, '85 165
Salad, Pasta-and-Shrimp, '83 163
Sautéed Shrimp and Pasta, '96 288
Scampi, Pasta with Shrimp, '01 83
Scampi, Shrimp, '95 209
Shrimp and Pasta, '91 207
Spaghetti, Shrimp-and-Vegetable, '91 170
Spaghetti with Black Olives, Shrimp, '85 13
Spicy Pasta and Shrimp, '97 67
Spinach Pasta, Shrimp-and-, '01 258
Tomato Pasta, Shrimp-, '98 172
Tortellini, Shrimp and, '92 34
Vermicelli Salad, Shrimp, '88 139
Vermicelli, Shrimp and Feta Cheese on, '87 108
Patties, Shrimp, '92 128
Peanut Sauce, Shrimp with, '93 303
Peppers, Shrimp-Stuffed, '80 162; '86 131, 197; '97 268
Peppers, Spicy Stuffed, '98 243
Pesto Shrimp Over Rice, Texas, '03 327
Pilaf, Shrimp, '82 246
Pilau, Shrimp, '99 184
Pilau, Shrimp-and-Dried Tomato, '97 49
Pizza, The Best of the Bayou, '95 268
Platter with Béarnaise Sauce, Artichoke and Shrimp, '96 132
Po' Boys, Shrimp, '97 312
Po'boys, Shrimp, '02 184
Polynesian Shrimp, '79 3
Potatoes, Broccoli-Shrimp Stuffed, '92 M228
Potatoes, Creamy Shrimp-Stuffed, '80 36
Potatoes, Shrimp-and-Mushroom Stuffed, '99 308
Potatoes, Shrimp-Sauced, '81 M61
Puff, Shrimp-Crab, '79 57
Puffs, Luncheon Shrimp, '85 72
Puppies, Hot-to-Trot Shrimp, '97 84
Quesadillas, Shrimp-and-Roasted Pepper, '00 215
Quesadillas with Shrimp and Brie, '94 173
Quiche, Shrimp, '83 50
Quiche, Shrimp-and-Artichoke, '03 196
Redfish with Shrimp and Crab, Coastal Bend, '01 281
Rellenos, Shrimp, '00 174
Rémoulade Sauce, Shrimp with, '91 29
Rice, Oriental Shrimp and, '90 183
Rice, Shrimp and Refried, '89 176
Rice, Shrimp and Sausage, '79 64
Rice, Shrimp with, '03 219
Risotto, Shrimp, '00 95; '02 124
Risotto with Shrimp and Asparagus, '03 86
Risotto with Shrimp, Pumpkin, '98 240
Rock Shrimp Tails, Batter-Fried, '80 2
Rock Shrimp Tails, Broiled, '80 3
Rock Shrimp Tails, Sweet-and-Sour, '80 3
Rolls, Shrimp, '03 162

Rolls, Shrimp-and-Romaine, '97 197
Rollups, Shrimp-Stuffed, '82 234
Sailor Shrimp for Two, '82 276
Salads
Aloha Shrimp Salad, '95 46
Artichoke Salad, Shrimp-and-, '04 50
Aspic, Shrimp-Coleslaw, '79 88
Aspic, Shrimp-Cucumber, '83 108
Aspic with Shrimp, Tomato, '79 241
Avocado Salad, Shrimp and, '80 266
Avocado Stuffed with Shrimp Salad, '82 207
Black Bean Salad, Caribbean Shrimp-and-, '93 143
Coastal Shrimp Salad, '00 17
Couscous Salad, Shrimp-and-, '96 157
Crabmeat-Shrimp Pasta Salad, '86 208
Creamy Shrimp Salad, '79 56
Croissants, Shrimp Salad on, '96 175
Curried Shrimp Salad, '00 217
Egg Salad Club, Shrimp-, '02 203
Egg Salad Sandwiches, Shrimp-and-, '94 182
Endive Salad, Shrimp-, '85 73
Filling, Shrimp Salad, '87 106
Fleur-de-lis Salad, '99 164
Fruited Shrimp Salad, '86 156
Grapefruit-and-Shrimp Salad, '88 5
Greek Salad, Dawn's World-Famous, '98 276
Green Salad with Shrimp, '88 49
Grilled Shrimp, Orange, and Watermelon Salad with Peppered Peanuts in a Zesty Citrus Dressing, '04 308
Half Shell, Shrimp Salad on the, '86 73
Individual Shrimp Salads, '83 146
Layered Shrimp Salad, '88 100
Macaroni Salad, Shrimp, '79 220
Macaroni Salad, Shrimp-, '85 219
Macaroni-Shrimp Salad, '85 121
Macaroni-Shrimp Salad, Festive, '85 165
Marinated Shrimp Salad, '85 82; '93 321; '99 169
Melon and Shrimp Curry Salad, '97 129
Orange, and Olive Salad with Sherry Vinaigrette, Shrimp, '93 177
Orange Rice Salad, Zesty Shrimp-and-, '87 155
Orange-Shrimp Salad, '84 197
Oriental Shrimp Salad, '91 313
Orzo Salad, Peppers Stuffed with Shrimp-and-, '91 203
Orzo Salad, Shrimp-and-, '99 182
Pasta-and-Shrimp Salad, '83 163
Pasta Salad with Green Goddess Dressing, Shrimp, '02 139
Pastry, Shrimp Salad in, '86 105
Picnic Shrimp Salad, '95 182
Potato Salad, Shrimp-and-, '96 211
Rice-and-Shrimp Salad, '83 82
Rice Salad, Baked Shrimp-, '83 22
Rice Salad, Shrimp and, '80 231; '82 207
Rice Salad, Shrimp-and-, '92 307
Rice Salad, Tangy Shrimp-, '84 66
Rice-Shrimp Salad, '79 270; '92 142
Sandwiches, Shrimp Salad, '90 178
Sea Slaw, Tomatoes Stuffed with, '89 96
Shrimp Salad, '81 94; '84 221; '86 186; '93 238; '98 333; '04 147
Spinach Salad with Grilled Shrimp, Tropical, '04 51
Super Shrimp Salad, '81 37
Tossed Shrimp-Egg Salad, '80 4
Vegetable-Shrimp Salad, '79 190
Vermicelli Salad, Shrimp, '88 139
Walnut Salad, Shrimp-, '86 182
Wild Rice-and-Shrimp Salad, '02 109
Wild Rice-Shrimp Salad, '99 55

SHRIMP
(continued)

Sandwiches, Open-Faced Shrimp-Cornbread, **'02** 141
Sandwiches, Shrimp-Cheese, **'85** 242
Sauce, Broccoli and Cauliflower with Shrimp, **'84** 248
Sauce, Creamy Shrimp, **'03** 53
Sauce, Flounder Fillets in Shrimp, **'83** 227
Sauce, Flounder with Hollandaise-Shrimp, **'86** 234
Sauce, Grandpa Jim's Shrimp, **'01** 182
Sauce, Oysters in Shrimp, **'87** 40
Sauce Piquante, Crab and Shrimp, **'83** 92
Sauce, Shrimp, **'87** 138, 232; **'01** 182; **'04** 147
Sauce, Shrimp-and-Almond, **'87** 282
Sauce, Shrimp Cocktail, **'01** 182
Sausage over Creamy Grits with Tasso Gravy, Spicy Shrimp and, **'92** 236
Sausage, Shrimp, **'97** 164
Sauté, Confetti Shrimp, **'97** 104
Sautéed Shrimp, **'79** 3
Sautéed Shrimp and Thai Coconut Broth with Noodles, **'98** 295
Sautéed Shrimp with Country Ham and Capers, **'04** 241
Sautéed Shrimp with Cranberry-Citrus Salsa, **'97** 290
Sauté, Shrimp-and-Grouper, **'87** 91
Sauté, Shrimp-and-Scallop, **'85** 103
Sauté with Pecan Rice, Shrimp-and-Scallop, **'90** 317
Scampi, Easy, **'84** 291
Scampi, Orange, **'85** 303
Scampi, Quick, **'88** 301
Scampi, Shrimp, **'84** 230; **'92** 117; **'93** 70; **'00** 283
Scampi, Speedy, **'02** 161
Shells, Creamy Shrimp, **'79** 4
Sirloin Supreme, Shrimp and, **'81** 131
Skewers with Vegetable Salsa, Shrimp, **'98** 32, 223
Skillet, Quick Shrimp, **'87** 50
Smoked Shrimp, Citrus-Marinated, **'95** 114
Snow Pea-Shrimp Combo, **'79** 57
Snow Peas, Shrimp with, **'85** 75
Soups
  Bisque, Curried Butternut-Shrimp, **'01** 248
  Bisque, Okra-and-Shrimp, **'97** 156
  Bisque, Seafarer's, **'97** 67
  Bisque, Shrimp, **'95** 19
  Bisque, Shrimp-Chile, **'94** 272
  Bisque, Shrimp-Cucumber, **'79** 172
  Bisque, Shrimp-Vegetable, **'82** 313; **'83** 66
  Bisque, Tomato-Shrimp, **'86** 66
  Bouillabaisse, Marcelle's, **'99** 200
  Cheese Soup, Shrimp-, **'01** 145
  Chowder, Artichoke-Shrimp, **'03** 91
  Chowder, Shrimp, **'89** 218
  Chowder, Shrimp and Corn, **'79** 199
  Corn Soup, Shrimp-and-, **'84** 88
  Corn Soup with Shiitakes and Shrimp, Sweet, **'99** 168
  Enchilada Soup, Shrimp, **'94** 103
  Gazpacho, Shrimp-Cream Cheese, **'94** 137
  Gumbo, **'01** 160
  Gumbo, Crab and Shrimp, **'81** 200
  Gumbo, Old-Style Shrimp, **'98** 97
  Gumbo, Quick Shrimp, **'86** 71
  Gumbo, Shrimp, **'81** 199
  Gumbo, Shrimp-Crab, **'98** 15
  Jambalaya, Creole Shrimp, **'92** 99
  Mushroom Soup, Shrimp-, **'85** 87
  Okra-and-Shrimp Soup, **'94** 323
  Stock, Shrimp, **'93** 60
Spicy Shrimp and Grits, **'04** 176

Spread, Shrimp, **'81** 306; **'85** 135; **'87** 111; **'93** 205; **'96** 104
Spread, Shrimp-Cucumber, **'79** 81
Squash, Stuffed, **'01** 223
Steak and Shrimp, **'88** 123
Stew and Grits, Shrimp, **'80** 118
Stewed Shrimp with Dumplings, **'79** 31
Stew, Frogmore, **'92** 236; **'00** 174, 336; **'03** 181
Stew over Grits, Shrimp, **'88** 126; **'89** 47
Stew, Shrimp, **'83** 4
Stir-Fry, Beef-and-Shrimp, **'93** 32
Stir-Fry, Cajun Shrimp, **'92** 127
Stir-Fry Shrimp, **'96** 129; **'01** 95
Stir-Fry, Shrimp, **'01** 258
Stir-Fry, Shrimp-and-Vegetable Medley, **'99** 205
Stir-Fry Shrimp and Vegetables, **'87** 91
Stroganoff, Oven-Baked Shrimp, **'81** 297
Stroganoff, Shrimp, **'79** 81
Stroganoff, Strolling-Through-the-Holidays, **'01** 282
Stuffed Shrimp Bundles, Crab-, **'81** 176
Stuffed Shrimp, Crab-, **'84** 259
Stuffed Shrimp, Parmesan-, **'85** 103
Stuffed Shrimp with Hollandaise Sauce, **'95** 86
Sweet-and-Sour Shrimp, **'83** 278; **'90** M112
Sweet-and-Sour Shrimp and Chicken, **'87** 267; **'88** 103; **'89** 66
Sweet-and-Sour Shrimp with Onion and Red Pepper, **'02** 84
Szechuan Shrimp, **'86** 173
Tacos, Shrimp-and-Pepper Soft, **'95** 339
Tacos with Spicy Cream Sauce, Shrimp, **'01** 170
Tartar Sauce, Shrimp with, **'00** 178
Tart, Shrimp, **'87** 70
Tarts, Shrimp 'n' Grits, **'03** 254
Tempura "Shrimps," French-Fried, **'97** 128
Tempura Udon, **'00** 93
Topping, Shrimp, **'93** 291
Tostadas, Shrimp-and-Black Bean, **'93** 204
Vegetables, Shrimp and, **'82** 6
Versailles, Shrimp, **'90** 233
Wine Sauce, Shrimp and, **'98** 50
Yellow Squash, Shrimp-Stuffed, **'84** 194
Yogurt-Cucumber Sauce, Shrimp with, **'04** 216
SLAWS
Apple-Bacon Coleslaw, **'04** 181
Apple-Carrot Slaw, **'92** 243
Apple Coleslaw, **'89** 315
Apple-Pineapple Slaw, **'79** 241
Apple Slaw, Fresh, **'81** 63
Apple Slaw, Nutty, **'88** 216
Asian Slaw, **'99** 108
Asian Slaw, Crispy, **'97** 180; **'01** 195
Aspic, Shrimp-Coleslaw, **'79** 88
Bacon Coleslaw, **'83** 58
Banana-Nut Slaw, **'86** 250
Barbecue Coleslaw, **'97** 139
Barbecue Coleslaw, Best, **'97** 214; **'04** 100
Blue Cheese Coleslaw, **'89** 13; **'95** 270
Broccoli Slaw, **'01** 49
Broccoli Slaw, Sweet, **'96** 20; **'98** 332
Broccoli Slaw, Zesty, **'93** 246
Buttermilk Dressing Coleslaw, **'04** 24
Cabbage-Orange Slaw, **'79** 135
Cabbage-Pineapple Slaw, **'92** 182
Cabbage Slaw, Chinese, **'89** 312; **'01** 36
Cabbage Slaw, Crunchy, **'02** 95
Cabbage Slaw, Fresh, **'85** 139
Cabbage Slaw, Nutty, **'88** 218
Cabbage Slaw, Sweet, **'79** 76
Cauliflower Slaw, **'92** 167
Celery Root-and-Carrot Slaw, Shredded, **'98** 293
Chicken Coleslaw, **'84** 2
Chili Coleslaw, **'80** 178
Coleslaw, **'79** 152; **'82** 135; **'02** 57; **'03** 252

Colorful Coleslaw, **'88** 166
Confetti Slaw, **'89** 48
Cooked Dressing, Aunt Beulah's Coleslaw with, **'99** 82
Corn and Cabbage Slaw, **'79** 135
Cottage Coleslaw, **'80** 64
Country-Style Coleslaw, **'83** 59
Creamy Coleslaw, **'83** 170; **'98** 244; **'02** 167
Creamy Sweet Coleslaw, **'01** 148; **'03** 105
Crunchy Coleslaw, **'86** 295
Cucumber Slaw, Creamy, **'89** 49
Cumin-Celery-Scented Coleslaw, **'02** 51
Curried Coleslaw, **'85** 139
Danny's Slaw, **'00** 275
Dill Slaw, Creamy, **'01** 143
Dressing, Sweet Slaw, **'98** 184
Fiesta Coleslaw, **'04** 275
Freezer Coleslaw, **'89** 49
Freezer Slaw, **'81** 279; **'82** 24; **'83** 154; **'99** 260; **'03** 106
Frozen Coleslaw, **'82** 102
Fruit Coleslaw, Three-, **'86** 250
Fruited Coleslaw, **'83** 209; **'85** 139
German Cabbage Slaw, **'00** 105
Ginger Slaw, Tangy, **'01** 92
Grape-Poppy Seed Slaw, **'86** 225
Grapes and Almonds, Coleslaw with, **'83** 59
Green Bean Slaw, **'95** 108
Guacamole Mexican Coleslaw, **'82** 302
Ham Coleslaw, **'84** 195
Healthy Slaw, **'92** 183
Hot-and-Creamy Dutch Slaw, **'87** 127
Hot-and-Sour Chinese Slaw, **'85** 139
Hot Slaw, **'89** 49
Jalapeño Coleslaw, **'97** 26
Jose Falcón's Slaw, **'04** 207
Kentucky Coleslaw, **'81** 216
Layered Coleslaw, **'86** 180
Layered Slaw, **'93** 214
Lemon-Yogurt Coleslaw, Grilled Chicken Breasts with, **'98** 148
Light and Creamy Coleslaw, **'93** 318
Make-Ahead Coleslaw, **'81** 155
Mango Slaw, **'93** 31; **'94** 71
Marinated Coleslaw, **'79** 135
Marinated Slaw, **'91** 229
Memphis Slaw, **'91** 28
Memphis-Style Coleslaw, **'98** 104
Mexicali Coleslaw, **'84** 18
Mexican Coleslaw, **'89** 48
Mustard Slaw, Texas, **'88** 172
Napa Cabbage Slaw, **'02** 280
Old-Fashioned Coleslaw, **'80** 120; **'82** 225; **'99** 235
Old-Fashioned Slaw, **'84** 149
Old-Fashioned Sweet Coleslaw, **'93** 128
Overnight Cabbage Slaw, **'81** 88; **'82** 7
Overnight Coleslaw, **'79** 135
Overnight Slaw, **'79** 5; **'92** 280
Peach Slaw, Party, **'86** 250
Peanut Slaw, **'85** 139
Peanut Slaw, Chinese, **'93** 212
Pear Slaw, Peanutty-, **'86** 250
Peppery Hot Coleslaw, **'98** 159
Pineapple-Almond Slaw, **'92** 171
Pineapple Coleslaw, Curried, **'88** 172
Pineapple Slaw, **'94** 49; **'99** 26
Pineapple Slaw, Colorful, **'86** 250
Polka Dot Slaw, **'83** 59
Rainbow Slaw, **'01** 259
Red Bean Slaw, **'79** 247
Red Cabbage-and-Apple Slaw, **'87** 31; **'91** 309
Red Cabbage Slaw, **'95** 153
Seafood Slaw, **'79** 56
Sea Slaw, Tomatoes Stuffed with, **'89** 96

Sesame Slaw, **'02** 206
Silks, Slaw, **'93** 236
Sour Cream Coleslaw, **'99** 220
Sour Cream Slaw, **'87** 10
Soy Slaw and Dipping Sauce, Grilled Chicken with Sweet, **'04** 123
Soy Slaw and Dipping Sauce, Grilled Salmon with Sweet, **'04** 123
Swedish Slaw, **'79** 135
Sweet and Crunchy Slaw, **'79** 104
Sweet-and-Sour Hot Slaw, **'92** 63
Sweet-and-Sour Slaw, **'81** 237
Sweet-and-Sour Slaw, Confetti, **'98** 89
Sweet-and-Tangy Slaw, **'04** 199
Sweet Onion Slaw, **'98** 171
Sweet Potato-Currant Slaw, **'93** 246
Sweet Slaw, Creamy, **'00** 172; **'01** 322
Tangy Coleslaw, **'83** 59
Tangy Slaw, **'02** 215
"Think Pink" Slaw, **'94** 247
Tomatoes, Coleslaw with, **'80** 34
Turnip Slaw, **'89** 245
Vegetables, Coleslaw with Garden, **'01** 57
Vegetable Slaw, **'81** 280; **'00** 42
Wraps, Chicken-and-Bean Slaw, **'04** 163
Zesty Slaw, **'82** 127; **'97** 324
Zucchini Coleslaw, Fiesta, **'91** 168

SLOW COOKER
Bean Bake, Slow Cooker Three-, **'99** 88
Beans, Hearty Baked, **'01** 259
Black-Eyed Peas, Hot-and-Spicy, **'99** 235
Butter, Slow Cooker Apple, **'97** 235
Cheese Queso, Chunky, **'99** 279
Desserts
Apples 'n' Pears, Saucy, **'96** 72
Pie, Caramel, **'96** 72
Main Dishes
Barbecue, Chuck Roast, **'96** 71
Beef Barbecue, Slow-Cooker, **'02** 299
Burritos, Easy, **'04** 32
Eye of Round, Slow Cooker Spicy Marinated, **'99** 291
Fajitas, Slow Cooker, **'02** 43
Fajitas, Turkey, **'01** 108
Ham, Pinto Beans with, **'97** 210
Kielbasa with Beans, Easy Cheesy, **'01** 28
Pork and Vegetables, Apple Cider, **'97** 210
Pork Chops and Gravy, **'96** 71
Pork Chops, Farm-Style, **'02** 42
Potatoes with Ham, Scalloped, **'02** 42
Red Beans and Rice, New Orleans, **'97** 235
Ribs and Beans, Spicy Sweet, **'02** 299
Ribs and Beans, Spicy-Sweet, **'03** 314
Ribs, Barbecued Baby Back, **'97** 234
Ribs, Slow-Cooker Barbecue, **'03** 160
Roast Beef, Slow Cooker, **'01** 86
Roast, Pumpernickel, **'97** 234
Roast, Savory Chuck, **'00** 18
Roast, Slow Cooker Chuck, **'98** 32
Oatmeal in a Slow Cooker with Ice Cream, **'99** 193
Onions, Caramelized, **'00** 218
Sandwiches
Adobo Pork Sandwiches with Rosemary-Garlic Mayonnaise, **'01** 322
Barbecue Sandwiches, Debate, **'97** 234
French Dip Sandwiches, **'97** 211
Pork Dip Sandwiches, Easy Spanish, **'04** 312
Sauce, Slow-Simmered Spaghetti, **'96** 72
Soups and Stews
Black Bean Soup, **'98** 291
Brunswick Stew, Easy, **'99** 235
Camp Stew, **'02** 42
Chicken Brunswick Stew, **'97** 234
Chili Bean Soup, **'96** 71

Chili, Big-Batch, **'04** 242
Chili, Easy, **'02** 299
Chili, Slow Cooker Cincinnati-Style, **'00** 34
Chili, Slow-Cooker Red Bean, **'02** 20
French Onion Soup, Caramelized, **'00** 218
Peasant Soup, **'01** 54
Potato Soup, Hearty, **'98** 292
Steak Soup, **'99** 260
Texas Stew, **'97** 211
Tortilla Soup, **'98** 291
Vegetable Soup, **'98** 32, 291

SOUFFLÉS
Blue Cheese Soufflé, **'91** 244
Cheddar Cheese Soufflé, **'98** 24
Cheese Soufflé, **'79** 72, 261; **'94** 116
Cheese Soufflé for Two, **'81** 226
Cheese Soufflé, Rolled, **'89** 13
Cheese Soufflés, Three-, **'96** 219
Cheese Soufflé, Three-Egg, **'87** 234
Chicken-Chestnut Soufflé, **'79** 107
Chile-Cheese Soufflés, **'96** 219
Cornbread, Soufflé, **'96** 34
Crab Soufflé Spread, **'85** 4
Cups, Hot Soufflé, **'85** 284
Dessert
Apricot Soufflé, Baked, **'88** 267
au Chocolat Cointreau, Soufflé, **'94** 56
Banana Daiquiri Soufflé, **'84** 317
Blintz Soufflé, **'88** 155
Brandy Alexander Soufflé, **'82** 173; **'83** M114
Bread Pudding Soufflé, Creole, **'92** 87
Chocolate Mint Soufflé, **'81** 16
Chocolate Soufflé, **'84** 317; **'94** 46
Chocolate Soufflé, Light, **'83** 278
Chocolate Soufflé with White Chocolate Mousse, **'98** 57
Coconut Soufflé, **'79** 73; **'85** 212
Cranberry-Topped Holiday Soufflé, **'84** 306
Cream Cheese Soufflé, **'88** 11
Daiquiri Soufflé, Elegant, **'80** 69
Devonshire Soufflé, Chilled, **'88** 279
Gingerbread Soufflés with Lemon Cream, **'04** 300
Grand Marnier Soufflé, **'79** 281
Grand Marnier Soufflés, **'89** 290; **'03** 318
Grasshopper Soufflé, **'81** 248; **'86** 188
Kahlúa Soufflé, **'82** 173
Lemon-Lime Soufflé, Cold, **'84** 24
Lemon Sauce Soufflés, Quick, **'88** 43
Lemon Soufflé, **'82** 170, 252; **'94** 199
Lemon Soufflé, Tart, **'85** 82
Lemon Soufflé with Raspberry-Amaretto Sauce, Frozen, **'88** 130
Orange Dessert Soufflé, **'83** 206
Orange Soufflé, Chilled, **'84** 317; **'86** 189
Orange Soufflé, Frozen, **'79** 211
Pineapple Dessert Soufflé, **'80** 153
Raspberry Soufflé, **'86** 188
Raspberry-Topped Soufflé, **'85** 317
Vanilla Soufflé, Frozen, **'79** 230; **'82** 173
Vanilla Soufflés with Vanilla Crème Sauce, **'94** 242; **'96** 155
Egg Soufflé Casserole, **'83** 55
Egg Soufflés, Little, **'83** 57
Frozen Soufflés, Individual, **'80** 52
Grits Soufflé, **'80** 30
Grits Soufflé, Garlic-Cheese, **'99** 18
Grits Soufflé, Mexican, **'79** 55
Ham Breakfast Soufflé, Virginia, **'93** 121
Ham Soufflé with Cucumber Sauce, **'92** 41
Individual Soufflés, **'80** 190
Parmesan Soufflés, **'97** 280
Pizzaola Soufflé, Italian, **'98** 232
Pizzaola Soufflé, Mexican, **'98** 232
Rice-Cheese Soufflé, **'79** 270

Roll, Shrimp Soufflé, **'89** 320
Roll, Southwestern Soufflé, **'97** 171
Salmon Soufflé, Fresh, **'81** 182
Sour Cream Soufflé, **'80** 43
Turkey Soufflé, **'80** 271
Vegetable
Asparagus Soufflé, **'79** 66; **'83** 265; **'89** 89
Broccoli Soufflé, **'81** 24
Broccoli Soufflé, Golden, **'84** 283
Broccoli Soufflés, **'96** 218
Butternut Soufflé, **'83** 266
Butternut Squash Soufflé, **'97** 270
Carrot Puff, **'89** 89
Carrot Soufflé, **'79** 73; **'83** 265; **'98** 231; **'99** 25; **'01** 84, 284
Carrot Soufflés, **'96** 309
Cauliflower Soufflé, **'82** 76; **'89** 279; **'90** 17
Corn-and-Cheese Soufflé, **'88** 122
Mushroom Soufflés, **'87** 282
Onion Soufflé, **'79** 247
Parsnip Soufflé, Golden, **'83** 266
Potatoes, Soufflé, **'84** 295; **'85** 196; **'90** 14
Potato Soufflé, Cheesy, **'89** 332
Rutabaga Soufflé, **'01** 213
Spinach Soufflé, **'79** 73; **'81** 304; **'84** 78; **'85** 248; **'86** 108
Spinach Soufflé, Cheese-and-, **'98** 235
Spinach Soufflé, Cheesy, **'81** 53
Spinach Soufflé Deluxe, **'79** 8
Spinach Soufflé Roll, **'80** 215
Squash Soufflé, **'95** 215
Squash Soufflé, Cheesy, **'82** 146
Sweet Potato Soufflé, **'82** 286; **'86** 121; **'93** 325; **'96** 247; **'00** 273
Turnip Soufflé, **'79** 254
Vidalia Onion Soufflé, **'04** 167
Yellow Squash Soufflé, **'89** 89
Zucchini-and-Corn Soufflé, **'83** 265
Zucchini-Corn Soufflés, **'97** 203
Zucchini Soufflé, **'79** 157

SOUPS. *See also* **BEANS/Soups; CHILI; CHOWDERS; GUMBOS; JAMBALAYAS; RAGOÛTS; STEWS.**
Acorn-Butternut Soup, Creamy, **'96** 216
Acorn Squash-and-Apple Soup, Curried, **'03** 221
Acorn Squash Soup, **'91** 294
Acorn Squash Soup, Cream of, **'94** 268
Acorn Squash-Thyme Soup, **'99** 252
Almond Soup, **'79** 48
Artichoke Cream Soup, **'94** 62
Artichoke Soup, **'89** 269
Artichoke Soup, Cream of, **'82** 232
Asparagus Soup, **'84** 67; **'98** 290; **'00** 84
Asparagus Soup, Cream of, **'84** 111
Asparagus Soup, Creamy, **'94** 225
Avocado-Banana-Yogurt Soup, **'80** 78
Avocado-Mushroom Soup, Creamy, **'85** 25
Avocado Soup, **'88** 160
Avocado Soup, Chilled, **'81** 34; **'87** 37; **'93** 108
Avocado Soup, Creamy, **'79** 107; **'01** 176
Avocado Soup, Sherried, **'84** 181
Bacon, Lettuce, and Tomato Soup, **'91** 207
Bean
Bacon Soup, Bean and, **'83** 26
Barley Soup, Hearty Bean-and-, **'86** 304
"Bean Counter" Soup, **'92** 80
Beanolla Soup, **'94** 248
Bean Soup, **'80** 25
Black Beans and Cilantro, Southwestern Scallop Broth with, **'87** 123
Black Bean Soup, **'88** 30, 266; **'89** 28; **'93** 231; **'98** 291; **'02** 121; **'03** 219
Black Bean Soup, Carolina, **'92** 139
Black Bean Soup, Marge Clyde's, **'96** 29

SOUPS, Bean
(continued)

Cabbage-Bean Soup, '97 301
Capitol Hill Bean Soup, '80 222
Chicken Soup, Bean-, '99 283
Chili Bean Soup, '96 71
Chill-Chaser Soup, '87 282
Drunken Bean Soup, '87 283
French Market Soup, '85 277; '92 49; '94 317
Green Bean Soup, Cream of, '84 111
Ham-and-Bean Soup, '84 4
Ham-and-Bean Soup, Spicy, '94 322
Ham Soup, Bean-and-, '04 325
Hominy Soup, Bean-and-, '95 23
Leafy Bean Soup, '86 223
Minestra, '97 246
Mix, Bean Soup, '99 283
Mix, French Market Soup, '85 277; '94 317
Navy Bean Soup, '84 280; '96 19
Navy Bean Soup, Chunky, '83 291
Navy Bean Soup, Savory, '87 282
Pasta Soup, Bean and, '94 220
Quick Bean Soup, '99 97
Red Bean Soup with Walnuts, '96 243
Refried Bean Soup, '96 136
Sausage-Bean Soup, '85 88
Sausage-Bean Soup, Spicy, '83 229
Three-Bean Soup, '89 17
Three-Bean Soup, Spicy, '91 28
Turkey Soup, Bean-and-, '93 319
White Bean Pot, '86 194
White Bean Soup, '83 229; '90 201
White Bean Soup, Spicy, '94 225
Beef-and-Pepperoni Soup, Italian-Style, '00 316
Bell Pepper Soup, '89 103
Bisques
Banana-Raspberry Bisque, '93 161
Butternut-Shrimp Bisque, Curried, '01 248
Butternut Squash Bisque, Roasted, '03 230
Chicken Bisque, Curried, '00 144
Clam Bisque, '86 228
Crab-and-Corn Bisque, '87 137
Crab-and-Leek Bisque, '94 104
Crab-and-Spinach Bisque, '97 241
Crab Bisque, '88 251
Mushroom Bisque, Brisk, '81 190
Okra-and-Shrimp Bisque, '97 156
Oyster Bisque, '83 252; '96 276; '99 320
Pumpkin Bisque, Spicy, '86 67
Seafarer's Bisque, '97 67
Seafood Bisque, '86 66
Shrimp Bisque, '95 19
Shrimp-Chile Bisque, '94 272
Shrimp-Cucumber Bisque, '79 172
Shrimp-Vegetable Bisque, '82 313; '83 66
Smoked Salmon-Whiskey Bisque, '00 65
Spinach-Potato Bisque, '86 66
Squash Bisque, '84 280; '98 290
Stone Crab Bisque, '96 86
Sweet Potato-and-Pear Bisque, '00 317
Tomato-Basil Bisque, '00 49; '02 230
Tomato-Basil Bisque, Make-Ahead, '93 322
Tomato-Shrimp Bisque, '86 66
Tuna Bisque, '79 76
Black-Eyed Pea Soup, '97 213
Black-Eyed Soup, Beefy, '85 6
Black, White, and Red All Over Soup, '95 126
Borscht, Crawfish, '92 84
Borscht, Ruby Red, '83 176
Bouillabaisse, Florida, '79 158
Bouillon, Court-, '98 229
Bouillon, Redfish Court, '83 290; '84 93

Bouillon, Tomato, '83 8
Bourbon with Molasses Sauce, Burned, '95 17
Bread Bowls, Italian, '98 292
Broccoli
Broccoli Soup, '86 161, M194; '87 288
Cheese-and-Broccoli Soup, '89 276
Cheesy-Broccoli Soup, '86 258
Chicken Soup, Broccoli-and-, '90 202
Creamed Broccoli Soup, '85 24
Cream of Broccoli Soup, '79 130; '80 188, M225; '82 314; '83 66; '86 259
Cream-of-Broccoli Soup, '88 56
Cream of Broccoli Soup, Light, '93 17
Cream of Broccoli Soup, Mock, '85 288
Creamy Broccoli Soup, '81 75; '82 13; '83 99; '91 307
Easy Broccoli Soup, '81 307
Fresh Broccoli Soup, '91 86
Hot Broccoli Soup, '81 235; '83 44
Swiss Soup, Broccoli-, '86 6
Butternut-and-Apple Soup, Creamed, '88 228
Butternut Soup, '02 68
Butternut Soup, Creamy, '96 216
Butternut Squash-Lime Soup, '03 236
Butternut Squash Soup, '95 62; '03 276
Butternut Squash Soup, Saffron, '04 187
Cabbage Soup, '83 291; '85 88
Cabbage Soup, Sweet-and-Sour, '89 314
Carrot
Butternut Squash Soup with Parslied Croutons, Carrot-and-, '97 217
Carrot Soup, '80 88; '89 146; '98 123
Cheesy Carrot Soup, '81 262
Chilled Carrot-Mint Soup, '90 M168
Cream of Carrot Soup, '81 307; '88 46; '91 69
Cream Soup, Carrot, '90 210
Creamy Carrot Soup, '92 218
Curried Carrot Soup, '82 157
Leek Soup, Carrot-, '86 34
Leek Soup, Carrot-and-, '02 260
Orange Soup, Carrot-, '79 172
Parsnip Soup, Gingered Carrot-and-, '03 221
Savory Carrot Soup, '84 107
Tomato Soup, Cream of Carrot-and-, '94 176
Cauliflower and Caraway Soup, '82 264
Cauliflower and Watercress Soup, Cream of, '83 126
Cauliflower Soup, '90 211; '99 318
Cauliflower Soup, Cream of, '87 M7; '88 12; '96 277
Cauliflower Soup, Creamy, '82 76
Cauliflower Soup, Fresh, '84 279
Celery Soup, Burnet-, '84 107
Celery Soup, Cream of, '79 71; '90 210
Celery Soup, Light Cream-of-, '82 279
Cheese. *See also* **SOUPS/Onion, Vegetable.**
Anytime Soup, Cheesy, '81 307; '82 314; '83 66
Bacon-Beer Cheese Soup, '87 M7
Bacon-Topped Cheese Soup, '80 M224
Beer-Cheese Soup, '84 246
Blue Satin Soup, '98 248
Broccoli Soup, Cheese-and-, '89 276
Cheddar-Potato Soup, '03 M283
Chunky Cheese Soup, '98 31
Cream Cheese Soup, Austrian, '98 M85
Cream of Cheese Soup, '83 99
Favorite Cheese Soup, Uncle Ed's, '94 228
Gazebo Cheese Soup, '90 158
Hearty Cheese Soup, '84 4
Herbed Cheese Soup, '96 219
Hot Brown Soup, '00 318
Macaroni and Cheese Soup, '95 264
Mexican Cheese Soup, '97 268
Minestrone, Cheesy, '99 17
Monterey Jack Cheese Soup, '81 112; '85 M211

Pimiento "Mac and Cheese" Soup, '97 M325
Rice Soup, Wildest, '01 66
Shrimp-Cheese Soup, '01 145
Velvet Soup, Cheese, '80 74; '92 193
Vichyssoise, Velvety Roquefort, '83 223
Cheeseburger Soup, '04 298
Chocolate Soup, Mexican, '96 277
Chicken. *See* **SOUPS/Poultry.**
Cilantro Soup, Cream of, '00 249
Cilantro Soup with Black Bean Salsa, Cream of, '97 226
Citrus Soup, Fiesta, '01 176
Collard Greens Soup, '00 293
Consommé aux Champignons, '79 48
Consommé, Brown Rice, '98 288
Corn-and-Bourbon Soup, '92 194
Corned Beef Soup, '83 16
Corn Soup, '80 56; '85 243; '87 156
Corn Soup, Cream of, '90 210
Corn Soup, Favorite, '85 155
Corn Soup, Grilled, '87 121
Corn Soup, Pimiento-, '89 126
Corn Soup with Crab, Sweet, '02 159
Corn Soup with Shiitakes and Shrimp, Sweet, '99 168
Cucumber-Buttermilk Soup, Chilled, '95 134
Cucumber-Dill Soup, '01 176
Cucumber Soup, Chilled, '79 144
Cucumber Soup, Cold, '79 130; '81 130
Cucumber Soup, Cold Minted, '86 34
Cucumber Soup, Cream of, '81 98
Cucumber Soup, Creamy, '80 171
Cucumber Soup, Dilled, '90 M167
Cucumber Soup with Dill Cream, '00 130
Cucumber-Yogurt Soup, '82 157; '83 205
Curried Soup, '81 130
Dill Soup, Cold, '84 107
Egg Drop Soup, '83 21; '86 16
Egg-Drop Soup, '85 M12
Egg Drop Soup, Lemon-, '93 81
Egg Drop Soup, Spinach, '03 65
Egg Flower Soup, '81 307; '82 313; '83 65
Egg-Lemon Soup, '96 88
Eggplant Soup, Herbed, '90 173
Eggplant Supper Soup, '85 221
English Pea Soup, '96 56
Fish Soup with Garlic Mayonnaise, Rich, '92 56
French Soup Maigre, '98 125
Fruit. *See also* **SOUPS/Gazpacho.**
Apple Soup, Creamed Butternut-and-, '88 228
Avocado-Banana-Yogurt Soup, '80 78
Cantaloupe Soup, '83 120; '88 160
Cantaloupe Soup, Chilled, '81 156; '97 148
Cantaloupe Soup, Fresh, '84 190
Chestnut Soup, '02 272
Chilled Fresh Fruit Soup, '88 160
Cold Fresh Fruit Soup, '87 157
Dessert, Fruit Soup, '79 172
Dried Fruit Soup, '79 23
Egg-Lemon Soup, '96 88
Fruit Soup, '87 98
Fruit Soup, Fresh, '98 196
Lemon-Egg Drop Soup, '93 81
Lemon Soup, '85 94
Lime Soup, '88 31; '02 168
Mango-Cantaloupe Soup, Chilled, '96 205
Melon Soup, '80 182
Melon Soup, Swirled, '87 162
Orange Soup, Carrot-, '79 172
Peach-Plum Soup, '87 157
Peach Soup, '83 120, 180
Peach Soup, Chilled, '97 159
Peach Soup, Cream of, '99 207
Pear Soup, Pumpkin-, '92 234

Plum-and-Wine Soup, '00 144
Plum Soup, '85 107
Plum Soup, Chilled, '03 161
Plum Soup, Chilled Purple, '79 162
Raspberry Soup, '00 144
Raspberry Soup, Chilled, '81 130
Sherry-Berry Dessert Soup, '91 180
Strawberry-Banana Soup, '86 181
Strawberry Soup, '88 160
Strawberry Soup, Cold, '82 157
Strawberry Soup Supreme, '81 M144
Swedish Fruit Soup, '82 313; '83 65
Watermelon Soup, Chilled, '03 168
Yogurt Fruit Soup, '86 176
Gazpacho
Berry Gazpacho, '97 181
Blanco, Gazpacho, '01 177
Blender Gazpacho, '85 93
Chilled Gazpacho, '84 138
Citrus Gazpacho, '96 70
Classy Gazpacho, '89 220
Cool Gazpacho, '83 140
Crab Gazpacho, '97 181
Gazpacho, '79 172; '80 266; '81 98; '82 73;
  '84 112; '85 164; '91 94; '92 64; '93 215;
  '00 118; '01 157; '02 130
Grilled Gazpacho, Southwestern, '00 84
Herbed Gazpacho, '95 175
Instant Gazpacho, '00 144
Pineapple Gazpacho, '01 85
Saucy Gazpacho, '82 157
Secret Gazpacho, '93 161
Shrimp-Cream Cheese Gazpacho, '94 137
Spring Gazpacho, '81 112
Summer Gazpacho, '84 181
Tomato-Avocado-Corn Gazpacho, '97 182
Tomato Gazpacho, Classic, '99 172
Tropical Gazpacho, '95 204
Vegetable Gazpacho, Grilled, '97 181
Vegetable Gazpacho, Smoked, '93 156
White Gazpacho, '97 181
Yellow Tomato Gazpacho, '04 158
Green Pepper Soup, '88 250
Green Soup, '98 23
Greens Soup, Cream with, '94 277
Guadalajara Soup, '88 30
Ham-and-Bean Soup, Spicy, '94 322
Hamburger Soup, '80 263
Ham Soup, Hearty, '82 4
Harvest Soup, '79 101
Homemade Soup, '79 198
Hot-and-Sour Soup, '83 68; '91 50
Italian Soup, Chunky, '99 20
Kale Soup, Creamy, '96 203
Lamb Soup with Spring Vegetables, '04 108
Leek Soup, Cream of, '99 276
Lentil Soup, '83 292; '86 304; '91 28; '97 304;
  '98 19
Lentil Soup, Beefy, '87 282
Lentil Soup, Spanish-Style, '96 239
Mardi Gras Soup, '96 56
Meatball Soup, Mexican, '98 315
Minestrone, '82 4
Minestrone, Dixie, '94 230
Minestrone, Meatball, '00 242
Minestrone Soup, '84 202; '86 144; '91 258
Minestrone Soup Mix, '91 258
Mushroom-and-Leek Soup, Cream of, '01 312
Mushroom-Onion Soup, '80 25
Mushroom-Rice Soup, '90 32
Mushroom Soup, '82 286; '86 M73; '94 54
Mushroom Soup, Chunky, '88 12
Mushroom Soup, Cream of, '84 5; '85 93, 261
Mushroom Soup, Creamy, '79 243; '81 307

Mushroom Soup, Curried, '84 M89
Mushroom Soup, Elegant, '83 99
Mushroom Soup, Fresh, '81 109; '90 190
Mushroom Soup, Sherried, '96 104
Mushroom Soup, Shrimp-, '85 87
Mushroom Soup, Wild, '98 281; '04 203
Mustard Green Soup, Cream of, '93 280
New Year's Day Soup, '00 25
Okra Soup, Charleston, '87 156
Okra Soup with Fou-Fou, '96 325
Onion
Beefy Vidalia Onion Soup, '97 212
Caramelized French Onion Soup, '00 218
Caramelized Onion Soup with Goat Cheese-and-
  Chive Croutons, '01 312
Cheese Soup, Onion-, '87 81
Classic Onion Soup, '84 65
Creamy Onion Soup, '90 211
Double-Cheese Onion Soup, '85 227
Double Cheese-Topped Onion Soup, '79 49
Easy Onion Soup, '85 226
French Onion-Beef Soup, '87 54
French Onion Soup, '79 49; '80 188; '83 126;
  '85 226; '86 M212; '90 31; '93 246; '04 243
French Onion Soup, Shortcut, '85 M328
French Onion Soup, Toasty, '81 306
Green Onion Soup, '84 112
Green Onion Soup, Creamed, '83 82
Mexican Onion Soup, '04 243
Mushroom-Onion Soup, '80 25
Onion Soup, '99 96
Oven-Browned Onion Soup, '79 49
Potato Soup, Creamy Onion-and-, '92 51; '97 304
Rich Onion Soup, '85 226
Superb Onion Soup, '81 86
Three-Onion Soup, '96 217
Tomato-Onion Soup, '04 243
Oyster Soup, '02 102
Pea-and-Watercress Soup, '93 162
Peanut Butter Soup, '89 28
Peanut Butter Soup, Cream of, '84 29
Peanut Soup, '87 184; '00 325
Peanut Soup, Chilled, '79 130
Peanut Soup, Cream of, '92 193; '93 288
Peanut Soup, Cream of Curried, '02 242
Peanut Soup, Creamy, '79 50
Peasant Soup, '01 54
Pea Soup, '99 67
Pea Soup, Chilled, '84 181
Pea Soup, Cold Curried, '91 120
Pea Soup, Country-Style, '86 267
Pea Soup, Cream, '90 211
Pea Soup Elégante, '79 53
Pea Soup, Fresh, '86 181
Pea Soup, Peppery, '82 271
Pea Soup, Potato-, '94 90
Pea Soup, Spring, '88 M96
Pepper Soup, Spicy, '93 98
Pepper Soup, Sweet, '93 277
Pimiento Soup, Cream of, '96 45; '01 72
Pork Rind Soup, '03 33
Potato
Asparagus-Potato Soup, '85 23
Bacon Soup, Potato-, '84 M38
Baked Potato Soup, '91 311; '92 26; '03 29
Beet Soup, Potato-, '88 156
Carrot Soup, Potato-, '88 297
Celery-and-Potato Soup, '84 279
Chilled Cucumber-Potato Soup, '85 93
Cold Potato-Cucumber Soup, '88 160
Cream of Potato Soup, '80 M224; '82 21
Cream of Potato Soup, Golden, '86 302
Creamy Potato Soup, '81 19, 98; '84 112
Easy Potato Soup, '92 17

Garlic-and-Potato Soup, Golden, '04 214
Hearty Potato Soup, '98 292
Holiday Potato Soup, '79 236
Irish Potato Soup, '99 54
Leek-and-Potato Soup, '84 112
Onion-and-Potato Soup, Creamy, '97 304
Pea Soup, Potato-, '94 90
Potato Soup, '82 278; '83 292; '92 263
Sausage-Potato Soup, '80 25
Sausage Soup, Easy Potato-, '98 315
Special Potato Soup, '82 3
Subtle Potato Potage, '80 78
Sweet Potato-and-Sausage Soup, '95 23
Sweet Potato Soup, '88 250; '02 221
Sweet Potato Soup, Southern, '00 233
Sweet Potato Soup with Rum Cream, '98 271
Sweet Potato Velouté, '94 238
Three-Potato Soup, '86 16
Wild Rice Soup, Cheesy Potato-and-, '89 16
Yogurt Soup, Potato-, '92 217
Pot-of-Gold Soup, '86 259
Poultry
Chicken-Almond Cream Soup, '92 21
Chicken-and-Buttermilk Soup, Country, '02 144
Chicken-and-Rice Soup, '88 236
Chicken-and-Wild Rice Soup, '04 26
Chicken-and-Wild Rice Soup, Creamy, '98 M334
Chicken, Artichoke, and Mushroom Soup,
  '92 324
Chicken Broth, Easy Microwave, '90 M167
Chicken-Corn Soup, Cheesy, '97 158
Chicken Enchilada Soup, '86 22
Chicken, Ham, and Oyster Soup, '79 198
Chicken Noodle Soup, '80 264; '95 45; '98 30
Chicken-Noodle Soup, Chunky, '88 12
Chicken Noodle Soup, Creamy, '99 20
Chicken Soup, '81 98
Chicken Soup, Bean-, '99 283
Chicken Soup, Cream of, '85 243
Chicken Soup, Creamy Asparagus-and-, '95 82
Chicken Soup, Curried, '86 34
Chicken Soup, Fiesta, '04 323
Chicken Soup, Homemade, '82 34
Chicken Soup, Mexican, '84 234; '00 336; '03 63
Chicken Soup, Quick, '86 M72
Chicken Soup, Roasted Pepper-and-, '90 58
Chicken Soup, Spicy, '97 268
Chicken Soup, Witches' Brew, '01 205
Chicken Stock, '95 18
Chicken-Vegetable Soup, '88 18; '99 60
Chicken-Vegetable Soup, Spicy, '02 168
Stock, Light Poultry, '90 31
Tortilla Soup, '00 98, 110
Tortilla Soup, Supereasy, '00 199
Turkey-Barley Soup, '91 312
Turkey Carcass Soup, '86 284
Turkey-Noodle Soup, '91 312
Turkey-Noodle Soup Mix, '89 330
Turkey-Rice Soup, '90 89
Turkey Soup, Curried, '86 332
Turkey Soup, Tempting, '98 314
Turkey Soup, Williamsburg, '90 287
Turkey Soup with Cornbread Dressing
  Dumplings, '03 239
Turkey Soup with Green Chile Biscuits, Fiesta,
  '04 233
Turkey-Vegetable Soup, '84 4; '88 264; '91 312
Pumpkin-Corn Soup with Ginger-Lime Cream,
  '95 227
Pumpkin-Pear Soup, '92 234
Pumpkin Soup, '79 48
Pumpkin Soup, Cream of, '93 234
Pumpkin Soup, Creamy Southwestern, '03 221
Pumpkin Soup, Curried, '96 242

SOUPS

(continued)

Pumpkin Soup with Sweet Croutons, '00 296
Red Bell Pepper Soup, '98 104
Red Pepper Soup, Chilled Sweet, '93 69
Reuben Soup, Cream of, '97 26
Roasted Red Pepper Soup, '96 245
Roasted Yellow Bell Pepper Soup, '96 56
Sausage and Okra Soup, '80 209
Sausage Soup, Italian, '84 235
Sausage Soup, Polish, '99 317
Sausage Soup with Tortellini, Italian, '88 46
Sausage, Spinach, and Bean Soup, '99 311
Sausage-Tortellini Soup, '99 20
Sausage-Zucchini Soup, Italian, '84 4
Seafood
Bouillabaisse, Marcelle's, '99 200
Cioppino, Gulf Coast, '94 102
Clam Florentine Soup, '85 23
Crabmeat Soup, '84 123
Crab Soup, Beaufort, '92 238
Crab Soup, Cream of, '88 302
Crab Soup, Creamy, '80 M224
Crab Soup, Elegant, '80 188
Crab Soup, Fresh Corn-and-, '92 183
Crab Soup, Old-Fashioned, '90 71
Crab Soup, Plantation, '92 237
Crab Soup, Quick, '84 279
Crab Soup, Steamboat's Cream of, '81 127
Crab, Sweet Corn Soup with, '02 159
Lobster Soup, Spicy Thai, '94 102
Mussel Soup, '93 259
Oyster-and-Artichoke Soup, '97 21
Oyster-and-Artichoke Soup, Louisiana, '92 81
Oyster-and-Mushroom Soup, '87 39
Oyster-Cheese Soup, '84 213
Oyster Soup, '79 228; '83 211
Oyster-Turnip Soup, '94 328
Scallop Broth with Black Beans and Cilantro,
    Southwestern, '87 123
She-Crab Soup, '03 137
She-Crab Soup with Marigold, '79 32
Shrimp-and-Corn Soup, '84 88
Shrimp-Cheese Soup, '01 145
Shrimp Enchilada Soup, '94 103
Shrimp Soup, Okra-and-, '94 323
Shrimp, Sweet Corn Soup with Shiitakes and,
    '99 168
Stock, Seafood, '94 238
Tortellini Soup, Seafood-, '97 324
Shiitake Soup, Cream of, '95 265
Sopa de Lima, '79 211
Southwest Soup, '86 255
Spinach Soup, Cream of, '82 38; '90 211
Spinach Soup, Hot Cream of, '84 29
Spinach Soup, Oriental, '83 151
Spinach Soup with Meatballs, Italian, '92 331
Spinach-Tortellini Soup, '99 317
Split Pea and Frankfurter Soup, '79 64
Split Pea-and-Lentil Soup, Oven-Baked, '00 316
Split Pea Soup, '88 235; '89 17; '94 322
Squash and Leek Soup, Cream of, '04 42
Squash Soup, '94 134
Squash Soup, Chilled, '92 173
Squash Soup, Cold Cream of, '81 130
Squash Soup, Cream of, '81 246
Squash Soup, Perky, '85 20
Steak Soup, '99 260
Stock, Beef, '95 17
Stock, Brown Meat, '90 31
Stock, Chicken, '95 18
Stock, Fish, '95 19; '00 65

Stock, Homemade Fish, '92 237
Stock, Light Poultry, '90 31
Stock, Pumpkin Soup, '00 296
Stock, Quick Full-Bodied, '95 17
Stock, Seafood, '94 238
Stock, Vegetable, '90 31
Stock, Venison, '94 302
Summer Soup, Dilled, '99 182
Summer Squash Soup, '83 99; '84 193; '85 136
Sweet Red Pepper Soup, Cream of Roasted, '95 65
Taco Soup, '94 225; '99 36
Tamale Soup, '95 213
Tomatillo Soup with Crunchy Jicama, '92 245;
    '97 143
Tomato
Appetizer Tomato Soup, '86 258
Celery Soup, Tomato-, '83 M58
Chilled Roasted Pepper and Tomato Soup,
    '01 128
Chilled Tomato Soup, '82 155
Cioppino, Gulf Coast, '94 102
Cold Tomato Soup, '88 160
Consommé, Tomato, '88 250
Cream of Tomato Soup with Lemon Basil,
    '96 124
Cream of Tomato Soup with Parmesan Cheese,
    '86 161
Cream Soup, Refreshing Tomato, '79 172
Cream Soup, Tomato-Basil, '97 198
Creamy Tomato Soup, '83 267; '86 258
Dried Tomato-Cream Soup, '90 203
Easy Tomato Soup, '84 14
Fire Water, '80 188
Fresh Tomato Soup, '83 140
Herbed Yogurt and Parmesan Toasts, Tomato
    Soup with, '96 66
Hot Tomato Juice Soup, '86 302
Iced Tomato Soup, '79 170
Mexican Tomato Soup, Icy-Spicy, '90 155
Onion Soup, Tomato-, '04 243
Plus, Tomato Soup, '88 170
Pumpkin-Tomato Soup, '86 291
Rice Soup, Tomato-and-, '85 24
Roasted Garlic-and-Basil Tomato Soup, '01 17
Savory Tomato Soup, '94 91
Sour Cream-Topped Tomato Soup, '80 246
Summer Tomato Soup, '79 130
Tomato Potage, '79 250
Tomato Soup, '81 236; '83 44; '89 217
Tortilla Soup, '00 110
Vegetable Soup, Tomato-, '81 M177; '86 9
Tomato-Beef-Wild Rice Soup, '04 42
Tortellini Soup, '98 68; '00 14
Tortellini Soup, Japanese, '96 330
Tortilla Soup, '88 31, 245; '90 201; '93 197, 274;
    '94 136; '98 291; '99 310; '00 98, 110; '04 26
Tortilla Soup, Spicy, '90 32; '93 108
Turkey. *See* **SOUPS/Poultry.**
Turnip Soup, '92 217
Turnip Soup, Creamy, '84 279
Turtle Soup, '92 92
Turtle Soup au Sherry, '80 56
Veal-Vermicelli Soup with Quenelles, '94 14
Vegetable
Bean Soup, Vegetable-, '83 317
Beef-and-Barley Vegetable Soup, '89 31
Beef and Vegetable Soup, Quick Italian, '96 235
Beef Soup, Hearty Vegetable-, '84 102
Beef Soup, Spicy Vegetable-, '88 11
Beef Soup, Vegetable-, '88 296; '99 219
Beefy Vegetable Soup, '79 113; '84 M38
Beefy Vegetable Soup, Quick, '80 25
Broth, Savory Vegetable, '81 230
Burger Soup, Vegetable-, '82 6

Cheese Soup, Creamy Vegetable-, '81 244
Cheese Soup, Creamy Vegetable, '83 230
Cheese Soup, Vegetable-, '89 15
Cheesy Vegetable Soup, '80 73; '97 241
Chicken-Vegetable Soup, '99 60
Chicken-Vegetable Soup, Spicy, '02 168
Chili Vegetable Soup, '94 120
Chunky Vegetable Soup, '89 M283
Clear Vegetable Soup, '79 130
Cold Garden Vegetable Soup, '84 197
Down-Home Vegetable Soup, '90 32
Garden Harvest Soup, Italian, '90 M167
Garden Soup, '85 241
Garden Vegetable Soup, '83 140; '86 160
Hearty Vegetable Soup, '80 26
Leek-Vegetable Soup, '86 304
Lemongrass-and-Petits Pois Soup, '01 328
Light Vegetable Soup, '84 280
Marvelous Vegetable Soup, '82 3
Mix, Vegetable Soup, '84 148
Old-Fashioned Vegetable Soup, '86 304
Peasant Soup, '01 54
Pot Liquor Soup, '98 273; '01 290
Quick Vegetable Soup, '79 190; '85 24, 32
Quick Veggie Soup, '91 31
Southwestern Vegetable Soup, '97 268
Spanish Fiesta Soup, '01 66
Spicy Vegetable Soup, '79 198; '93 293; '99 337
Stock, Vegetable, '90 31
Vegetable Soup, '80 128; '84 148; '85 106;
    '86 187; '87 83, 123; '88 266; '93 157;
    '98 32, 291
Winter Vegetable Soup, Puree of, '00 322
Venison Soup, '82 216
Vichyssoise, '86 181
Vichyssoise, Cucumber, '94 90
Vichyssoise, Velvety Roquefort, '83 223
Vichyssoise with Mint Cream, Cucumber, '98 246
Watercress-and-Leek Soup, '86 161
Watercress Soup, '79 82; '88 104; '01 176
Watercress Soup, Cream of, '96 66
Zucchini Soup, '82 104; '84 181; '86 181; '89 14
Zucchini Soup, Chilled, '87 90
Zucchini Soup, Cold, '85 265; '92 64; '99 164
Zucchini Soup, Cream of, '83 99
Zucchini Soup, Creamy, '83 140
Zucchini Soup, Dilled, '90 88
Zucchini Soup, Watercress-, '91 72
Zucchini Soup with Cilantro, '93 130
Zucchini Soup with Fresh Vegetable Salsa, Chilled,
    '98 194
SPAETZLE
Spaetzle, '99 242
SPAGHETTI
All-in-One Spaghetti, '98 295
Bacon Spaghetti, '86 213; '87 82
Barbecue Spaghetti, '02 121
Black Bean Spaghetti, '92 217
Black-Eyed Pea Spaghetti, '81 7
Carbonara, Chorizo, '94 230
Carbonara, Salmon, '83 43
Carbonara, Spaghetti, '85 34; '87 167; '03 123
Carbonara, Spaghetti alla, '81 38
Casseroles
Asparagus-Spaghetti Casserole, '80 77
Beef Casserole, Spaghetti and, '79 129
Casserole Spaghetti, '95 132
Chicken-Spaghetti Casserole, '84 15
Chicken Spaghetti, Spicy, '02 327
Florentine Bake, Cheesy, '95 131
Ham-and-Turkey Spaghetti, '95 19
Italian Casserole, '90 238
Low-Fat Spaghetti Casserole, '99 215
Pork Spaghetti Bake, '81 11

Spaghetti Casserole, **'84** 241
Spinach Casserole, Spaghetti-and-, **'02** 199
Tetrazzini, Chicken, **'79** 268; **'80** 75; **'83** 288;
　'99 61
Tetrazzini, Ham, **'82** 77; **'84** 241; **'03** 174
Tetrazzini, Herbed Turkey, **'86** 47
Tetrazzini, Turkey, **'03** 257
Cheese Spaghetti, Three-, **'83** 105
Chicken Spaghetti, **'83** 105; **'87** 221; **'98** 329
Chicken-Vegetable Spaghetti, **'92** 281; **'98** 296
Chili, Cincinnati, **'96** 18
Chili-Spaghetti, Herbed, **'84** 222
Clam Sauce, Pasta with, **'84** 291
Country-Style Spaghetti, **'02** 25
Crawfish Spaghetti, **'85** 104
Easy Spaghetti, **'83** M317; **'84** 72; **'92** 66
Etcetera, Spaghetti, **'83** 105
Ham Spaghetti Skillet, **'83** 283
Herbal Dressing, Spaghetti with, **'86** 158
Hot Dog and Spaghetti Skillet, **'83** 144
Italian Spaghetti, **'81** 38
Italian Spaghetti, Real, **'81** 233
Lemon-Garlic Pasta, **'95** 181
Marzetti's Spaghetti, **'99** 85
Meatballs, Spaghetti-and-Herb, **'84** 75
Meatballs, Spaghetti with, **'81** 38
Meaty Spaghetti, **'82** 19
Mushroom Pasta 1-2-3, **'97** 102
Mushrooms, Spicy Spaghetti with, **'85** 2
One-Pot Spaghetti, **'00** 58
Onions, Spaghetti with Smothered, **'97** 229
Parmesan Noodles, Cheesy, **'83** M7
Parsley and Walnut Sauce, Spaghetti with, **'80** 30
Parsley, Spaghetti with, **'80** 236
Peanut Sauce, Pasta with, **'95** 252
Pepperoni Pasta, **'83** 105
Pepperoni Spaghetti, Quick, **'88** 40
Pie, Spaghetti, **'81** M32
Pie, Spaghetti-Ham, **'93** 19
Pie, Weeknight Spaghetti, **'95** 312
Pizzazz, Spaghetti with, **'80** 85
Pork and Peppers, Spaghetti with, **'98** 131
Pot Roast with Spaghetti, **'80** 59
Salad, Asian Peanut-and-Pasta, **'03** 127
Salad, Chicken-and-Veggie Spaghetti, **'04** 129
Salad, Chicken-Spaghetti, **'90** 146
Salad, Mediterranean, **'95** 132
Salad, Spaghetti, **'82** 277; **'84** 205
Salad, Spaghetti-Vegetable, **'97** 196
Salsa Spaghetti, **'00** 58

Sauces
Beer Spaghetti Sauce, **'85** 13
Grisanti Spaghetti Sauce, **'94** 194
Herbed Spaghetti Sauce, **'85** 13
Italian Tomato Sauce for Spaghetti, **'81** 134
Meat Sauce for Spaghetti, **'00** 256
Meat Sauce, Quick Spaghetti and, **'94** 64
Meat Sauce, Spaghetti with, **'02** 188
Sicilian Spaghetti Sauce, **'03** 62
Slow-Simmered Spaghetti Sauce, **'96** 72
Thick Spaghetti Sauce, **'84** 118
Tomato Sauce, Spaghetti with Fresh, **'96** 135
Turkey Spaghetti Sauce, **'85** 13
Vegetable Sauce, Pasta with, **'83** 163
Zucchini Sauce, Spaghetti with, **'81** 38
Sausage Spaghetti, **'83** 160
Sausage Spaghetti Dinner, **'79** 194
Shrimp and Pasta, **'91** 207
Shrimp-and-Vegetable Spaghetti, **'91** 170
Shrimp, Pasta with, **'01** 164
Shrimp Spaghetti with Black Olives, **'85** 13
Soup, Creamy Chicken Noodle, **'99** 20
Szechuan Noodle Toss, **'91** 30
Thick-and-Spicy Spaghetti, **'83** 287

Tomatoes and Garlic, Spaghetti with, **'91** 47
Tomato Pasta, Italian, **'93** 201
Veal and Peppers, Spaghetti with, **'81** 201; **'82** 14
Veal Spaghetti, **'84** 276
Vegetable Sauce, Pasta with, **'83** 163
Vegetables, Spaghetti with, **'85** 67
Vegetables with Spaghetti, Fresh, **'86** 257
Vegetables with Spaghetti, Sautéed, **'81** 89
White Spaghetti and Meatballs, **'03** 34
Zucchini Spaghetti, **'83** 160
Zucchini Spaghetti, Italian, **'85** 2
SPICE. *See also* **SEASONINGS.**
Balls, Decorative Ribbon-Spice, **'84** 325
Blend, Five-Spice Powder, **'92** 121
Dry Spices, **'90** 120; **'01** 106
Mix, Mulled Wine Spice, **'85** 266
Mix, Tex-Mex Spice, **'94** 135; **'01** 247
Mixture, Moroccan Spice, **'01** 230
Rub, Moroccan Spice, **'95** 231
SPINACH

Appetizers
Bread, Spinach, **'83** 121
Cheese Bites, Spinach-, **'94** 23
Cheesecake, Savory Spinach Appetizer,
　'02 M207
Cheesecake, Spinach-Herb, **'99** 139
Cheesecake, Spinach-Mushroom, **'92** 326
Cheesecake, Spinach Pesto, **'90** 175
con Queso, Easy Spinach, **'88** 101
Crostini, Spinach, **'01** 283
Crostini, Spinach-Red Pepper, **'03** 34
Cups, Cottage Cheese-Spinach, **'87** 190
Dip, Beef-and-Spinach, **'99** 65
Dip, Cheesy Spinach, **'82** 59
Dip, Clam, **'01** 194
Dip, Creamy Spinach, **'88** 132
Dip, Florentine Artichoke, **'96** 274
Dip, Hot Spinach, **'80** 249
Dip, Hot Spinach-Cheese, **'89** 48
Dip in Cabbage, Spinach, **'82** 155
Dip in Sourdough Round, Spinach, **'98** 173
Dip, Pine Nut-Spinach, **'99** 138
Dip, Spinach, **'80** 86; **'86** 159; **'87** 25, 214;
　'93 324
Dip, Spinach-Artichoke, **'00** 26
Eggs, Double Stuffed Spinach-and-Bacon,
　'00 M333
Filling, Spinach, **'95** 316
Loaf, Four-Layer Cheese, **'99** 222
Madeleine in Chafing Dish, Spinach, **'85** 319
Mushrooms, Spinach-Stuffed, **'86** 81;
　'88 131, M261; **'89** M133
Pastries, Greek Spinach-and-Cheese, **'96** 76
Pâté with Spinach and Cream, Pork, **'83** 224
Phyllo-Spinach Triangles, **'87** 53
Phyllo Triangles, Spinach-Filled, **'84** 52
Phyllo Triangles, Spinach-Ricotta, **'88** 212
Pinwheels, Spinach-Tenderloin, **'89** M118
Puff Pastry, Spinach and Artichokes in, **'00** 277
Puffs, Cheese-and-Spinach, **'87** 246
Puffs, Spinach, **'95** 316
Puffs, Spinach-Artichoke-Tomato, **'95** 284
Quichelets, Spinach, **'87** 67
Quiche, No-Crust Spinach, **'90** 142
Quiches, Miniature Spinach, **'82** 38
Quiches, Spinach, **'01** 241
Rollups, Southwestern, **'01** 135
Rollups, Spinach, **'98** 251
Sauce, Herbed Green, **'86** 244
Spanakopita, **'96** 233
Spread, Parmesan-Spinach, **'93** 55
Spread, Savory Spinach, **'82** 180
Spread, Spinach, **'88** 132
Spread, Spinach-Bacon, **'92** M310

Squares, Spinach, **'88** 131
Squash, Spinach-Stuffed, **'02** 165
Strudels, Spinach, **'93** 249
Supreme, Layered Spinach, **'82** 38
Tarts, Spinach, **'82** 249
Terrine, Layered Salmon-and-Spinach, **'84** 132
Wontons, Spinach, **'83** 74
Apples, Onions, and Pears over Spinach, Sautéed,
　'94 212
Baby Spinach with Pine Nuts, **'03** 64
Baked Spinach, Gourmet, **'82** 180
Biscuits and Ham, Green Elf, **'02** 277
Bisque, Crab-and-Spinach, **'97** 241
Bisque, Spinach-Potato, **'86** 66
Bread, Spinach, **'83** 121; **'87** 144
Burgers, Spinach, **'00** 26
Burgers, Spinach-Feta, **'99** 135
Calzones, Spinach-and-Cheese, **'95** 310
Calzones with Italian Tomato Sauce, **'03** 202

Casseroles
Artichoke Bake, Spinach-, **'95** 48
Artichoke Casserole, Spicy Spinach-, **'01** 49
Artichoke Casserole, Spinach-, **'88** 252; **'93** 44;
　'00 254; **'01** 49
Artichoke Casserole, Spinach and, **'81** 103
Beef Casserole, Spinach and, **'79** 192
Beef-Macaroni Casserole, Spinach-, **'83** 313
Cannelloni, **'85** 60; **'92** 17
Celery Casserole, Spinach-and-, **'84** 294
Cheese Bake, Spinach-, **'88** 10
Cheese Casserole, Spinach-, **'83** 216; **'89** 64
Cheesy Florentine Bake, **'95** 131
Cheesy Spinach Casserole, **'81** 263
Chicken, Orzo, and Spinach Casserole, **'02** 124
Company Spinach, **'89** 280
Cottage Cheese-and-Spinach Casserole, **'84** 77
Crab and Spinach Casserole, Creamy, **'80** 3
Creamy Spinach Bake, **'89** 68
Creamy Spinach Casserole, **'86** 111
Delight, Spinach, **'84** M144
Egg Casserole, Spinach and, **'82** 270
Eggplant-Spinach Casserole, **'99** 217
Enchiladas, Chicken-and-Spinach, **'91** 222
Enchiladas, Spinach, **'83** 60; **'84** 14
Florentine Casserole, Turkey-and-Shrimp,
　'92 122
Florentine, Chicken-and-Shrimp, **'89** 64
Florentine, Chicken Lasagna, **'95** 158; **'02** 232
Florentine, Jumbo Seashells, **'79** 6
Florentine Lasagna, **'88** 196
Florentine, Layered Pasta, **'00** 56
Florentine, Pasta Shells, **'00** 326
Florentine, Salmon, **'83** 43
Florentine, Turkey, **'88** 264
Lasagna, Cheesy Spinach, **'80** 32; **'83** 204;
　'01 196
Lasagna Florentine, Chicken, **'95** 158; **'02** 232
Lasagna Florentine, Creamy, **'91** 94
Lasagna, Spinach, **'79** 25; **'81** 243
Lasagna, Spinach-Bean, **'92** 96
Lasagna, Spinach-Black Bean, **'02** 44
Manicotti, Spinach, **'82** 199
Manicotti, Spinach-Stuffed, **'88** 255
Oyster-and-Spinach Casserole, **'83** 34; **'84** 44
Parmesan Casserole, Spinach-, **'82** 281; **'83** 32
Parmesan, Spinach, **'93** 72
Puff, Spinach-Cheese, **'84** 96
Rice Bake, Green, **'79** 43
Rice, Spinach, **'85** 146
Ricotta Bake, Spinach-, **'88** 97
Roll-Ups, Ham and Spinach, **'81** 143
Scalloped Spinach with Cheese, **'79** 8
Shells, Spinach-Stuffed, **'85** 60
Spaghetti-and-Spinach Casserole, **'02** 199

SPINACH, Casseroles
(continued)

    Spinach Casserole, '79 265; '91 31; '99 271
    Supreme, Spinach, '84 77
    Surprise, Spinach, '82 42
    Turkey-Spinach Casserole, '84 71
Cheesy Topped Spinach, '84 85
Chicken Breasts, Fried Spinach-Stuffed, '88 206
Chicken, Garlic-Spinach, '92 56
Chicken in Puff Pastry, Spinach-Stuffed, '92 125
Chicken, Lemon-Spinach, '97 104
Chicken Rolls, Spinach-Stuffed, '86 248
Chinese Spinach, '79 179; '82 39
Chinese Spinach Sauté, '83 208
Cornbread, Spinach, '95 49
Couscous, Spinach-and-Onion, '98 23
Creamed Spinach, '81 54; '86 110; '96 252; '97 28
Creamed Spinach in Pastry Shells, '89 280
Creamed Spinach with Noodles, '84 29
Creamy Spinach, '85 289
Crêpe Cups, Florentine, '89 44
Crêpe Pie, Florentine, '79 34
Crêpes Florentine, '80 190
Crêpes, Spinach-Ricotta, '81 52
Crowder Peas, Spinach with, '00 159
Custards, Savory Spinach-Gorgonzola, '99 313;
    '02 284
Dumplings, Spinach and, '00 85
Eggplant, Spinach-and-Basil Stuffed, '02 147
Eggs Oso Grande, '98 279
Eggs Sardou, '92 93
Enchiladas, Spinach, '83 60; '84 14
Field Peas and Spinach, '99 169
Filling, Spinach, '79 34
Filling, Spinach and Feta, '97 171
Filling, Spinach-Mushroom, '80 215
Filling, Spinach-Ricotta, '81 53
Fish in a Wrap, '97 64
Florentine, Baked Eggs, '86 M12
Florentine, Cheesy Trout, '85 53
Florentine, Chicken, '93 107
Florentine Crêpe Cups, '89 44
Florentine Crêpe Pie, '79 34
Florentine, Crêpes, '80 190
Florentine, Eggs, '79 39; '83 56
Florentine, Fish, '86 35
Florentine in Parchment, Fish, '87 22
Florentine Panini, Chicken, '02 236
Florentine Quiche, Tomato, '04 332
Florentine Sauce, '93 48
Florentine, Stuffed Mushrooms, '82 270
Florentine-Style Eggs, '82 38
Florentine with Mushroom Sauce, Chicken, '87 250
Frittata, Spinach, '81 53
Garden, The, '83 134
Greek Sunburst, '94 245
Grits, Garlicky Ham-and-Spinach, '94 177
Holiday Spinach with Red Pepper Ribbons, '03 260
Italian Spinach, Easy, '02 235
Lemon and Pepper, Spinach with, '97 105
Lemon Spinach, Creamy, '82 302
Lemon Spinach with Feta, '85 190
Loaf with Mushroom Sauce, Spinach, '01 277
Loaves, Spinach-Oyster, '84 213
Marinara on Beds of Spinach and Orzo, '93 320
Meat Loaf, Spinach, '96 131
Meat Loaf, Spinach-Stuffed Turkey, '97 24
Mushrooms, Spinach with, '80 19
Nests, Baked Eggs in Spinach, '82 70
Noodles, Chicken and Spinach, '82 19
Omelet, Spinach, Cheddar, and Bacon, '03 204
Omelet, Spinach-Cheese, '83 119

Oysters Rockefeller, '98 222
Parmesan Spinach, Savory, '85 68
Pastas
    Bow Tie Pasta, Spinach and Mushrooms with,
      '95 341
    Cannelloni with Roasted Red Bell Pepper Sauce,
      Chicken, '02 287
    Fantastic, Spinach, '93 173
    Fettuccine and Spinach, '88 90
    Fettuccine, Creamy Basil Chicken with Spinach,
      '97 328
    Fettuccine, Easy Chicken with Spinach, '88 89
    Fettuccine, Fresh Spinach, '83 60
    Fettuccine, Spinach, '82 179
    Fettuccine, Spinach Alfredo, '01 164
    Fettuccine with Mustard Greens, Spinach, '94 247
    Fettuccine with Spinach Sauce, '84 329
    Green Pasta with Shrimp-Mushroom Italienne,
      '79 170
    Lasagna, Crabmeat-and-Spinach, '04 292
    Lasagna, Won Ton Spinach, '04 129
    Linguine with Spinach, '91 30
    Macaroni with Spinach, Baked, '99 244
    Penne with Spinach and Feta, '03 170; '04 328
    Pesto and Pasta, Spinach-Peanut, '93 212
    Pesto-Pasta, Spinach, '91 314
    Pie, Spinach-Pasta, '85 286
    Sauce, Spinach Pasta, '93 71
    Shells Florentine, Pasta, '00 326
    Shells, Spinach, '97 50
    Shells, Spinach-Stuffed, '87 20; '99 64
    Shrimp-and-Spinach Pasta, '01 258
    Tortellini with Tomato Sauce, Spinach, '88 302
    Verde, Pasta, '84 201
    Vermicelli with Fresh Spinach Sauce, '89 256
Peppers, Spinach-Stuffed, '82 180
Pesto, Orange Roughy with Spinach, '88 M192
Pesto, Squash Stuffed with Spinach, '89 M133
Pie, Greek Spinach, '85 59
Pie Pan Spinach, '94 195
Pie Parma, Spinach, '96 203
Pie, Spinach, '82 191; '88 56; '00 26
Pie, Spinach-Pasta, '85 286
Pie, Super Special Spinach, '04 60
Pie with Cranberry-Pecan Crusts, Turkey Pot,
    '02 198
Pie with Muenster Crust, Spinach, '95 48
Pinwheels, Flank Steak-and-Spinach, '95 56
Pita Pockets, Chicken-Spinach, '01 66
Pitas, Spinach-Walnut, '87 202; '88 43
Pork, Spinach-and-Herb Stuffed, '89 193
Pork Tenderloin, Spinach-and-Bacon Stuffed, '94 81
Potatoes, Black-Eyed Pea-Spinach-Stuffed, '95 22
Quesadillas, Greek, '03 61
Quesadillas, Spinach, Mushroom, and Cilantro,
    '00 148
Quiche, Cheesy Spinach, '81 228
Quiche, Crustless Spinach, '84 235
Quiche, Greek Spinach, '86 10
Quiche, Mushroom-Spinach-Swiss, '03 59
Quiche, No-Crust Spinach, '90 142
Quiches, Individual Spinach, '86 38
Quiche, Spinach, '81 44; '85 49; '91 204
Quiche, Spinach-and-Bacon, '00 240
Quiche, Spinach-Mushroom, '81 M74
Quiches, Triple-Cheese Spinach, '00 220
Ring au Fromage, Spinach, '79 8
Roll, Feta Cheese-Spinach, '91 22
Rolls, Spinach-Ham, '88 78
Rollups, Chicken and Spinach, '80 90; '82 M68
Roll-Ups, Ham and Spinach, '81 143
Rollups, Spinach-and-Ham, '86 84
Rollups, Turkey-Spinach, '00 178
Salad Dressing, Spinach, '83 181; '93 250

Salads
    Apple-Onion Vinaigrette, Spinach Salad with,
      '94 276
    Apple Salad, Spinach-, '90 89; '92 13; '97 308;
      '02 230
    Apple-Spinach Salad, '97 14; '99 222
    Apricot Salad, Spinach-, '94 63
    Apricot Vinaigrette, Spinach Salad with, '02 120
    Arranged Spinach Salad, '91 210; '92 160
    Bacon Dressing, Spinach Salad with Hot, '82 211
    Bacon Salad, Spinach and, '81 143
    Beet Salad, Spinach-, '83 227
    Blue Cheese Dressing, Spinach Salad with Zesty,
      '02 121
    Blue Cheese Salad, Spinach-, '82 166
    Blues, Spinach Salad with the, '95 66
    Cantaloupe-Spinach Salad with Pistachio-Lime
      Vinaigrette, '97 148
    Chicken-and-Spinach Tossed Salad, '83 157
    Chicken-Spinach-Strawberry Salad, '97 92
    Chili-Lime Dressing, Spinach Salad with, '94 63
    Citrus Dressing, Spinach Salad with, '88 133
    Citrus Spinach Salad, '90 59
    Combination Spinach Salad, '85 327; '86 22
    Cranberry Salad with Warm Chutney Dressing,
      Spinach-and-, '02 242
    Creamy Spinach Salad, '83 60
    Crisp Spinach Salad with Creamy Dressing,
      '83 81
    Crunchy Spinach Salad, '80 147; '81 225
    Curry Spinach Salad, '80 242
    Dijon Spinach Salad, '89 282
    Dried Tomato Vinaigrette, Spinach Salad with,
      '93 272
    Easy Spinach Salad, '91 249
    Enoki Salad, Spinach-, '89 62
    Festive Spinach Salad, '80 247
    French Spinach Salad, '79 8
    Fresh Spinach Salad, '82 73; '83 240; '84 15, 77;
      '86 130
    Fresh Spinach Salad Delight, '80 146
    Fresh Spinach-Sprout Salad, '82 281; '83 42
    Fresh Spinach with Spicy Dressing, '80 55
    Garlic-Ginger Vinaigrette Dressing, Spinach
      Salad with, '92 195
    Green Spinach Salad, '79 142
    Grits-Spinach Salad, Stacked, '98 66
    Honey Dressing, Spinach Salad with, '90 16
    Hot Citrus Dressing, Spinach Salad with, '00 108
    Hot Spiked Spinach, '97 195
    Kiwifruit Salad, Spinach-, '87 305
    Lamb Salad, Spinach-, '85 58
    Layered Salad, Make-Ahead, '81 296
    Layered Spinach-Lettuce Salad, '84 266
    Layered Spinach Salad, '80 5; '89 163
    Mandarin Spinach Salad, '85 163
    Minted Spinach Salad, '94 63
    Mushroom Salad, Spinach and, '80 112
    Onion Salad Bowl, Spinach-and-, '81 157
    Orange Dressing, Spinach Salad with, '87 187
    Orange Salad, Spinach-and-, '86 15
    Orange Salad, Warm Spinach-, '00 112
    Orange-Spinach Salad, '83 316; '84 16
    Oriental Spinach Salad, '82 23
    Oysters and Red Wine Vinaigrette, Spinach Salad
      with, '94 327
    Parsley Dressing, Spinach Salad with Sweet,
      '02 120
    Pears, Spinach Salad with Sautéed, '94 237
    Pecan Salad, Spinach-, '89 128; '01 284
    Pickled Spinach, '81 69
    Poppy Seed Dressing, Spinach Salad with,
      '91 210; '92 160
    Pork-and-Spinach Salad, Mandarin, '88 M126

Raspberry Cream Dressing, Spinach Salad with, '94 321
Rice Salad, Spinach-, '94 63
Romaine-Spinach Salad, '89 123
Russian Dressing, Spinach Salad with, '79 144
Salmon-Spinach Salad, '87 145
Sesame Salad, Spinach-, '91 211; '92 160
Sesame Spinach Salad, '90 292
Southern Spinach Salad, '80 55
Southern Spinach Salad with Cheese Grits Croutons and Vidalia Onion-Balsamic Vinaigrette, '04 316
Special Spinach Salad, '80 78
Spinach Salad, '82 102; '86 302; '87 62; '88 299; '92 281, 341; '93 46, 65; '03 246
Springtime Spinach Salad, '81 114
Strawberry Salad with Tart Poppy Seed Dressing, Spinach-and-, '03 241
Strawberry-Spinach Salad, '91 169; '93 168
Sun-Dried Tomato Salad, Spinach and, '93 250
Supreme, Spinach Salad, '79 243
Sweet-Sour Spinach Salad, '85 M112
Tangy Spinach Salad, '00 24
Tossed Spinach Salad, '01 159
Tropical Spinach Salad, '90 231
Tropical Spinach Salad with Grilled Chicken, '04 51
Tropical Spinach Salad with Grilled Pork Tenderloin, '04 51
Tropical Spinach Salad with Grilled Shrimp, '04 51
Turkish Salad, '96 137
Twist, Spinach-Mustard, '86 209
Vinaigrette Spinach, '79 8
Wilted Spinach Salad, '81 M4; '89 123; '91 210; '92 160; '93 125
Zesty Spinach Salad, '79 88
Sandwiches, Fresh Spinach, '85 59
Sandwiches, Grilled Spinach Fondue, '99 337
Sandwich, Grilled Spinach Fondue, '94 171
Sauce, Emerald, '90 63
Sauce, Fettuccine with Spinach, '84 329
Sauce, Herbed Green, '86 244
Sauce, Spinach Pesto, '93 59
Sautéed Spinach, '93 250
Sauté, Fresh Spinach, '93 55; '04 285
Sauté, Tomato-Spinach, '04 23
Sesame Spinach, '98 24
Skillet Spinach, '96 19
Soufflé, Cheese-and-Spinach, '98 235
Soufflé, Cheesy Spinach, '81 53
Soufflé Deluxe, Spinach, '79 8
Soufflé Roll, Spinach, '80 215
Soufflé, Spinach, '79 73; '81 304; '84 78; '85 248; '86 108
Soup, Cream of Spinach, '82 38; '90 211
Soup, Cream with Greens, '94 277
Soup, Green, '98 23
Soup, Hot Cream of Spinach, '84 29
Soup, Oriental Spinach, '83 151
Soup, Sausage, Spinach, and Bean, '99 311
Soup, Spinach Egg Drop, '03 65
Soup, Spinach-Tortellini, '99 317
Soup with Meatballs, Italian Spinach, '92 331
Spanakopita, '86 58; '96 233
Squares, Spinach, '95 49
Squash, Spinach-Stuffed, '82 4; '91 14; '97 119
Stir-Fry Spinach, '81 182
Strudels, Spinach, '93 249
Supreme, Layered Spinach, '82 38
Tart Milan, '87 70
Tart, Rutabaga-Spinach, '98 274
Tenderloin, Spinach-Stuffed, '89 311
Tenderloin, Stuffed Tuscany, '99 269

Terrine, Layered Salmon-and-Spinach, '84 132
Timbales, Green Rice, '97 62
Timbales, Spinach, '84 29
Timbales, Spinach-Rice, '88 271
Tomatoes, Baked Spinach, '90 92
Tomatoes, Spinach-Feta Stuffed, '04 285
Tomatoes, Spinach-Stuffed, '89 203; '93 281
Tomatoes, Spinach-Stuffed Baked, '86 14
Tomatoes, Spinach-Topped, '88 265; '94 321
Tomatoes, Veracruz, '97 169
Turnovers, Salmon-Spinach, '83 44
Wrap, Mediterranean, '03 168
Zucchini Boats with Spinach, '82 252
SPREADS. *See also* **APPETIZERS/Spreads.**
Aioli, Shortcut, '93 157
Ambrosia Spread, '92 50
Apple-Date Spread, '91 231; '92 67
Beef Spread, Hot, '83 50
Beet-and-Pecan Sandwich Spread, '99 274
Braunschweiger-Onion Spread, '79 82
Bread Spread, Party, '82 161
Caraway Spread, '85 276
Caviar Spread, Creamy, '92 58
Cheese
Almond Cheese Spread, '87 292
Aloha Spread, '83 93
Avocado-Cheese Spread, Herbed, '98 335
Bacon-Cheese Spread, '83 241
Bacon-Olive Cream Cheese, '04 196
Basil-Cheese Spread, Fresh, '97 108
Beer Cheese Spread, '81 69; '94 123
Beer-Cheese Spread, '85 69
Beer Spread, Cheesy, '87 196
Blue Cheese Spread, '95 79; '97 240
Boursin Cheese Spread, Buttery, '94 301
Boursin Cheese Spread, Garlic, '94 301
Brie Spread, Apricot, '86 275
Cheddar-Swiss Spread, '99 106
Cheese Spread, '86 135; '96 122; '99 24
Chicken-Artichoke-Cheese Spread Gift Box, '00 328
Chile-Cheese Spread, '86 297; '99 336; '02 205
Chili Cheese Spread, '93 242
Chocolate Cheese Spread, '87 292
Chocolate Chip Cheese Loaves, '91 299; '92 264
Coconut-Cranberry Cheese Spread, '92 328
Confetti Cheese Spread, '84 256
Cottage Cheese Spread, '87 107
Cream Cheese-and-Olive Pimiento Cheese, '01 169; '03 315
Cream Cheese-Olive Spread, '82 35
Cream Cheese Spread, Apricot-, '82 161; '87 158
Cream Cheese Spread, Caviar-, '84 256
Cream Cheese Spread, Cucumber and, '82 140
Cream Cheese Spread, Deviled, '81 235
Cream Cheese Spread, Herb-, '83 24
Cream Cheese Spread, Nutty, '89 327
Cream Cheese Spread, Peachy, '90 M215
Cream Cheese Spread, Pear-, '93 80
Cream Cheese Spread, Pineapple-, '82 35
Cream Cheese Spread, Tri-Flavored, '98 134
Curry-Almond Cheese Spread, '01 238
Edam-Sherry Spread, '84 257
Feta-and-Apple Spread, '99 106
Feta Spread, Herbed, '00 135
Four-Cheese Spread, '99 106
Fruit and Cheese Spread, '81 245
Fruit-and-Cheese Spread, Nutty, '87 246
Garlic-and-Dill Feta Cheese Spread, '04 238
German Cheese Spread, '79 82
Goat Cheese Spread, '02 198
Goat Cheese Torta, '04 186
Gouda Cheese Spread, '90 36
Green Onion-Cheese Spread, '92 24

Gruyère-Apple Spread, '81 160
Hawaiian Cheese Spread, '87 158
Herb-Cheese Spread, '91 124
Herbed Cheese, '88 152
Herbed Cheese Spread, '87 247
Herbed Goat Cheese, '01 310
Horseradish Spread, '03 139
Horseradish Spread, Cheese-, '84 222
Italian Spread, '85 135
Jalapeño-Cheese Spread, '82 248
Jalapeño Pimiento Cheese, '01 169
Make-Ahead Cheese Spread, '93 324
Mexican Cheese Spread, '90 119
Olive Spread, Cheese-, '79 82
Orange Cheese Spread, '87 292
Pesto Goat Cheese, '03 110
Pesto-Goat Cheese Spread, '03 208
Pimiento Cheese, '01 169; '03 139, 315
Pimiento Cheese, Baked, '04 291
Pimiento Cheese, Chile-, '04 325
Pimiento Cheese, Jalapeño, '03 315
Pimiento Cheese, Pecan, '01 169; '03 315
Pimiento Cheese, Peppered, '01 137
Pimiento Cheese Spread, '82 35; '83 93; '86 127; '99 106, 276
Pimiento Cheese Spread, Creamy, '92 159
Pimiento Cheese Spread, Garlic, '79 58
Pimiento Cheese Spread, Low-Calorie, '85 215
Pineapple-Cheese Spread, '86 126; '91 167
Raisin-Nut Spread, '95 79
Rosemary Cheese with Fig Preserves, '02 256
Sandwich Spread, Benedictine, '80 299
Sandwich Spread, Chunky, '82 140
Sombrero Spread, '87 111
Strawberry Spread, '95 79
Sweet Cheese Spread, Creamy, '79 264
Sweet 'n' Sour Spread, '86 184
Swiss Cheese Spread, '90 60
Tipsy Cheese Spread, '80 150
Tomato-Cheddar Spread, '01 321
Tomato-Cheese Spread, '81 157
Tomato-Cheese Spread, Dried, '90 204
Tomato-Cheese Spread, Fiery, '87 196
White Cheddar Pimiento Cheese, '99 106
Zesty Cheese Spread, '82 140
Zippy Cheese Spread, '85 4
Cherry Spread, '93 309
Chicken-Artichoke-Cheese Spread Gift Box, '00 328
Chicken Salad Party Spread, '88 M8
Chicken Spread, Festive, '87 158
Chicken Spread, Low-Fat, '82 290
Chicken Spread, Tasty, '84 193
Chickpea Spread, Creamy, '04 146
Chive-Mustard Spread, '91 12
Chutney Spread, Curried, '89 283
Coconut-Pineapple Spread, '93 309
Corn-and-Walnut Spread, '96 26
Corned Beef Spread, '87 196
Cranberry-Butter Spread, '99 86
Cucumber-Yogurt Spread, '00 135
Curry Spread, '93 159
Date-Orange-Nut Spread, '02 59
Date Spread, Breakfast, '84 7
Date-Walnut Spread, '87 292
Deviled Delight, '83 130
Dijon-Mayo Spread, '96 199
Egg Salad Spread, '86 127
Egg Salad Spread, Cottage-, '82 146
Egg, Sour Cream, and Caviar Spread, '85 279
Fish Spread, Smoked, '92 305
Fruit Spread, '85 135
Fruit Spread, Sugarless, '84 60
Garbanzo Bean Spread, Herbed, '99 160

SPREADS

(continued)

Garlic-Butter Spread, **'96** 199
Garlic Canapés, Roasted, **'96** 95
Garlic Puree, Roasted, **'92** 55
Garlic Spread, **'85** 111
"Guacamole" with Cumin Crisps, Green Goddess,
   '02 205
Ham-and-Egg Spread, **'79** 59
Ham and Pimiento Spread, **'80** 285; **'81** 56
Ham Spread, **'86** 126
Ham Spread, Buttery, **'95** 93; **'97** 98
Ham Spread, Cold, **'82** 248
Ham Spread, Country, **'87** 8
Ham Spread, Deviled, **'79** 81
Ham Spread, Hawaiian, **'87** 106
Honey Mustard-Butter Spread, **'99** 86
Honey-Nut Spread, **'87** 157; **'03** 46
Honey Spread, **'81** 229
Horseradish-Chive Cream, **'02** 313
Horseradish-Ham Spread, **'91** 167
Horseradish, Homemade, **'92** 25
Horseradish Spread, **'90** 243; **'02** 53
Hummus, **'96** 158
Lemon-Raisin Spread, **'01** 48
Lentil Spread, **'99** 288
Lime Dressing, Creamy, **'04** 46
Liver Spread, **'89** 161
Liver Spread, Sherried, **'80** 86
Mustard-Horseradish Cream, **'02** 53
Mustard Spread, **'86** 105
Not-So-Secret Sauce, **'03** 139
Olivata, **'04** 159
Olive-Parsley Spread, Cream Cheese-and-Olive
   Biscuits with, **'04** 238
Olive Spread, Creamy, **'81** 290
Olive Spread, Tomatoes with, **'85** 114
Orange Toast Topper, **'79** 36
Party Spread, Spicy, **'97** 240
Peanut Butter Spread, **'92** 21; **'96** 90
Pineapple Sandwich Spread, **'84** 166
Raisin Spread, Creamy, **'90** 36
Raisin Spread, Peachy-, **'86** 326
Relish Spread, Creamy, **'93** 217
Salad Dressing Spread, **'82** 140
Seafood. *See also* **SPREADS/Trout, Tuna,**
   Whitefish.
   Clam Spread, Creamy, **'91** 274
   Crabmeat-Horseradish Spread, **'90** 292
   Crabmeat Spread, **'79** 81
   Crabmeat Spread, Layered, **'83** 127
   Crab Soufflé Spread, **'85** 4
   Crab Spread, **'93** 167
   Crab Spread, Baked, **'80** 86
   Crab Spread, Hot Artichoke-, **'85** 81
   Crab Spread, Superb, **'81** 255
   Oyster Spread, Smoked, **'91** 64
   Salmon-and-Horseradish Spread, **'87** 146
   Salmon Spread, **'81** 149
   Salmon Spread, Smoked, **'84** 324
   Salmon Spread with Capers, Smoked, **'98** 49
   Sandwich Spread, Seafood, **'82** 87
   Seafood Spread, **'86** M58; **'87** 146
   Shrimp-Cucumber Spread, **'79** 81
   Shrimp Spread, **'81** 306; **'85** 135; **'87** 111;
      '93 205; **'96** 104
   Shrimp Spread, Chunky, **'85** 300
   Shrimp Spread, Curried, **'87** 158
   Shrimp Spread, Tempting, **'79** 57
   Shrimp Spread, Zippy, **'90** 36
   Tuna Tapenade, **'95** 127
Spinach-Bacon Spread, **'92** M310

Spinach Spread, **'88** 132
Spinach Spread, Savory, **'82** 180
Strawberry Spread, Light, **'85** 55
Sun-Dried Tomato Spread and Bacon, Cream
   Cheese-and-Olive Biscuits with, **'02** 313
Sweet 'n' Sour Spread, **'86** 184
Tapenade, **'00** 135; **'04** 194
Trout Spread, Smoked, **'84** 47
Tuna Spread, **'83** 174; **'91** 305
Tuna Spread, Chunky, **'89** 147
Turkey Party Spread, **'83** 282
Turkey Spread, Curried, **'92** 16
Vegetable
   Antipasto Spread, **'81** 25
   Artichoke-Crab Spread, Hot, **'85** 81
   Artichoke Hearts with Caviar, **'79** 142
   Artichoke Spread, Hot, **'79** 110
   Broccamoli Curry Spread, **'88** 55
   Carrot Spread, Nutty, **'94** 123
   Cucumber Spread, **'79** 295; **'80** 31; **'93** 158
   Eggplant Spread, **'86** 278
   Egg Spread, Vegetable-, **'87** 106
   Garden Spread, **'86** 135
   Green Onion-Cheese Spread, **'92** 24
   Green Tomato Sandwich Spread, **'95** 172
   Guacamole Spread, **'90** 119
   Hearts of Palm Spread, **'90** 293
   Mushroom Spread, Hot, **'81** 190
   Party Spread, Vegetable, **'84** 166
   Potato-Garlic Spread, Creamy, **'02** 35
   Radish Spread, Fresh, **'84** 166
   Roasted Pepper Spread, **'94** 123
   Roasted Red Bell Pepper Spread, **'97** 217
   Sandwich Spread, Benedictine, **'80** 299
   Sandwich Spread, Home-Style, **'80** 179
   Sandwich Spread, Vegetable, **'83** 174; **'85** 135
   Tomato Spread, **'94** 123
   Vegetable Spread, **'90** 144
   Watercress Spread, **'88** 103
   White Bean Spread, **'93** 30; **'95** 279; **'96** 122
   White Bean Spread with Creamy Cucumber Sauce,
      '00 178
   Whitefish Spread, Smoked, **'92** 58
   Yogurt Spread, Herbed, **'02** 169
SPROUTS
   Asparagus and Bean Sprouts, **'96** 95
   Beans with Sprouts, Sweet-and-Sour, **'86** 32
   Beef and Bean Sprouts, **'82** 281; **'83** 42
   Meat Loaf, Sprout, **'85** 51
   Omelet, Potato-Sprout, **'79** 128
   Omelet, Rising Sun, **'82** 281
   Patties, Ham-Sprout, **'85** 51
   Rolls with Thai Dipping Sauce, Summer, **'97** 236
   Salad, Bean Sprout, **'82** 113
   Salad, Crunchy Sprout, **'96** 45
   Salad, Fresh Spinach-Sprout, **'82** 281; **'83** 42
   Salad, Spanish Sprout, **'85** 327; **'86** 22
   Salad, Sprout, **'90** 137
   Sandwiches, Alfalfa Pocket Bread, **'82** 282; **'83** 41
   Sandwiches, Polynesian Sprout, **'85** 51
SQUASH. *See also* **CHAYOTES, ZUCCHINI.**
   Acorn. *See also* **SQUASH/Stuffed.**
      Bake, Acorn Squash, **'83** 280
      Baked Sweet Dumpling Squash, **'94** 266
      Bake, Squash, **'82** 107
      Bowls, Acorn Squash, **'96** 216
      Bread, Squash, **'79** 210
      Butter, Acorn Squash-and-Bourbon, **'94** 266
      Cake, Acorn Squash, **'96** 216
      Cake, Winter Squash-Spice Bundt, **'99** 248
      Delight, Acorn Squash, **'81** 267
      Grilled Acorn Squash with Rosemary, **'96** 266
      Orange Squash Brûlée, **'94** 267
      Oysters in Acorn Squash, Creamed, **'97** 20

   Pancakes, Granola-Squash, **'94** 267
   Pear Stuffing, Acorn Squash with, **'01** 293
   Puppies, Acorn Squash, **'94** 268
   Puree, Basic Acorn Squash, **'94** 267
   Rings, Easy Glazed Acorn, **'81** M231
   Rings, Glazed Acorn, **'80** 214
   Sherried Acorn Squash, **'85** 9
   Soup, Acorn Squash, **'91** 294
   Soup, Acorn Squash-Thyme, **'99** 252
   Soup, Cream of Acorn Squash, **'94** 268
   Soup, Creamy Acorn-Butternut, **'96** 216
   Soup, Curried Acorn Squash-and-Apple, **'03** 221
   Sugar-and-Spice Acorn Squash, **'03** 241
Baby Squash, **'93** 118
Basil Butter, Squash and Cherry Tomatoes in,
   '98 328
Basil Summer Squash, **'01** 180
Butternut. *See also* **SQUASH/Stuffed.**
   Bake, Butternut-Orange, **'86** 295
   Baked Butternut Squash, **'85** 205
   Bake, Squash and Apple, **'79** 210
   Bisque, Curried Butternut-Shrimp, **'01** 248
   Bisque, Roasted Butternut Squash, **'03** 230
   Bisque, Squash, **'84** 280
   Bread, Butternut-Raisin, **'79** 25
   Bread, Squash, **'79** 210
   Casserole, Butternut, **'83** 280
   Casserole, Butternut Squash, **'79** 210; **'96** 216;
      '01 293
   Casserole, Squash and Apple, **'79** 209
   Casserole, Sweet Butternut, **'83** 256
   Gratin, Potato-Butternut Squash-and-Gruyère,
      '01 43
   Pie, Butternut Squash, **'80** 40; **'87** 212
   Pie, Butternut Squash Chiffon, **'83** 296; **'84** 285
   Pie, Spicy Butternut Squash, **'80** 296
   Pie, Spicy Squash, **'85** 9
   Pudding, Butternut Squash, **'89** M313; **'90** M19
   Pudding, Squash, **'82** 277; **'83** 15
   Puff, Butternut Squash, **'85** 205
   Puff, Squash, **'01** 293
   Ring, Butternut Squash, **'81** M232
   Sauté, Savory Butternut, **'85** 205
   Skillet Butternut and Bacon, **'85** 9
   Soufflé, Butternut, **'83** 266
   Soufflé, Butternut Squash, **'97** 270
   Soup, Butternut, **'02** 68
   Soup, Butternut Squash, **'95** 62; **'03** 276
   Soup, Butternut Squash-Lime, **'03** 236
   Soup, Creamed Butternut-and-Apple, **'88** 228
   Soup, Cream of Squash and Leek, **'04** 42
   Soup, Creamy Acorn-Butternut, **'96** 216
   Soup, Creamy Butternut, **'96** 216
   Soup, Saffron Butternut Squash, **'04** 187
   Soup with Parslied Croutons, Carrot-and-
      Butternut Squash, **'97** 217
   Stir-Fry, Honey-Butternut, **'93** 184
   Sunshine Squash, **'85** 205
   Whipped Butternut Squash, **'94** 302
   Whipped Squash, Tasty, **'82** 277; **'83** 15
Cajun Squash, **'88** 142
Calabacitas, **'95** 130
Casserole, Broccoli-and-Squash, **'01** 175
Casserole, Calico Squash, **'90** 290
Casserole, Squash, **'87** 163; **'89** 159; **'90** 161;
   '92 342; **'96** 247, 252; **'97** 29
Casserole, Two-Squash, **'79** 101
Chile Squash, **'84** 77
con Crema, Squash, **'89** 148
Creole Squash, **'01** 180
Delight, Squash, **'90** 236
Dilled Summer Squash, **'96** 148
Dressing, Squash, **'83** 315; **'86** 280; **'95** 290;
   '01 160

Dressing, Turkey with Squash, '87 248
Greek-Style Squash, '92 26
Greek-Style Squashes, '96 88
Hubbard Squash, Tart, '80 214
Kebabs, Summery Squash-and-Pepper, '95 193
Marinated Grilled Squash, '02 110
Marinated Squash Medley, '94 126
Medley, Carrot-Lima-Squash, '80 123
Medley, Fresh Squash, '81 M165
Medley, Sautéed Vegetable, '83 101
Medley, Squash, '81 139; '84 128
Mirliton Balls, '90 217
Mirlitons, Shrimp-and-Ham Stuffed, '03 251
Muffins, Squash, '91 69
Oregano, Summer Squash, '97 165
"Pasta," Garden-Fresh, '94 M134
Pattypan-Zucchini Skillet, '82 103
Pickles, Squash, '81 174; '87 150; '97 119; '99 170
Pie, Mock Coconut, '86 200
Pie, Savory Squash, '00 170
Pie, Scallopini, '94 133
Puff, Golden Squash, '82 288
Relish, Pollock with Summer Squash, '92 200
Rosemary, Summer Squash with, '88 143
Salad, Squash, '03 M184
Sandwiches, Skillet Squash, '98 144
Sauté, Squash, '82 67
Scallop, Green-and-Gold, '81 159
Skillet Squash, '82 195
Soup, Dilled Summer, '99 182
South-of-the-Border Squash, '00 137
Spaghetti Squash, '92 340
Spaghetti Squash and Chicken Skillet Casserole, '94 134
Spaghetti Squash, Asian, '94 268
Spaghetti Squash Lasagna, '84 127
Spaghetti Squash Pie, '80 186
Spaghetti Squash Salad, '99 M322
Spaghetti Squash Salad, Marinated, '94 134
Spaghetti Squash Sauté, '98 212
Spaghetti Squash, Sautéed Vegetables with, '84 128
Spaghetti Squash with Meat Sauce, '88 M180
Spaghetti Squash with Sesame Eggplant, '92 252
Stir-Fried Squash Medley, '80 123
Stir-Fry, Squash, '80 184
Stir-Fry, Two-Squash, '86 174
Stuffed
    Acorn Squash, Apple-Stuffed, '83 296; '84 285
    Acorn Squash, Baked, '81 24
    Acorn Squash, Cranberry-Filled, '81 M231
    Acorn Squash, Custard-Filled, '86 334
    Acorn Squash, Deluxe, '80 215
    Acorn Squash, Fruited, '85 235; '90 228
    Acorn Squash, Fruit-Stuffed, '81 295
    Acorn Squash, Ham-Stuffed, '81 239; '83 66
    Acorn Squash-Mushroom Puree, '93 305
    Acorn Squash, Pineapple-Stuffed, '84 255
    Acorn Squash, Sausage-Stuffed, '81 M231; '83 296; '84 285
    Acorn Squash, Stuffed, '82 277; '83 15
    Acorn Squash with Molasses and Pecans, '85 205
    Acorn Squash with Nutmeg, '85 267
    Acorn Squash with Sausage, '85 9
    Acorn Squash with Spiced Cranberry Sauce, Gingered, '96 267
    Apple-and-Pecan-Filled Squash, '88 228
    Apple-Stuffed Squash, '85 206
    Baked Squash, Stuffed, '85 206
    Beef-Stuffed Squash, '83 134
    Butternut Squash, Apple-Stuffed, '81 232
    Chayote, Stuffed, '92 247
    Cheesy Stuffed Squash, '82 134
    Crumb-Stuffed Squash, '89 148
    Green Chiles, Stuffed Squash with, '83 148

Harvest Squash, '80 214
Maple-Flavored Stuffed Squash, '85 205
Mexican, Stuffed Squash, '90 200
Mirlitons, Stuffed, '90 217; '93 278
Parmesan-Stuffed Squash Boats, '79 156
Pattypan Squash, Stuffed, '82 103; '85 136; '88 142
Plantation Squash, '79 225
Sausage-Stuffed Squash, '81 183
Spinach Pesto, Squash Stuffed with, '89 M133
Spinach-Stuffed Squash, '82 4; '91 14; '97 119; '02 165
Stuffed Squash, '98 177
Summer Squash, Stuffed, '02 M181
Turban Chicken Curry, '94 266
Turban Squash, Sausage-Stuffed, '80 214
Turban Squash, Stuffed Turks, '88 228
Vegetable-Stuffed Squash, '84 104
White Squash, Stuffed, '90 M201
Yellow Squash, Garden-Stuffed, '84 106
Yellow Squash, Italian Stuffed, '86 111
Yellow Squash, Mushroom-Stuffed, '84 154
Yellow Squash, Shrimp-Stuffed, '84 194
Yellow Squash with Cheese Sauce, Stuffed, '80 162
Summer Squash, Southern, '98 207
Tart, Squash, '96 83
Tomatoes, Squash-Stuffed, '82 102
Tomato Squash, '86 111
Toss, Pepperoni-Squash, '84 127
Turban Squash, Glazed, '81 24
Yellow. *See also* **SQUASH/Stuffed.**
    à l'Orange, Squash, '85 230
    Amarillo Squash, '99 M218
    Bacon-Flavored Squash, '82 158
    Bake, Cheddar-Squash, '84 M113, 128
    Bake, Cheesy Squash, '80 183
    Bake, Squash and Tomato, '95 180
    Beans, and Tomatoes, Squash, '83 148
    Bisque, Squash, '98 290
    Bread, Spicy Squash, '83 121
    Bread, Yellow Squash, '84 140
    Buttered Summer Squash, '81 84
    Cake, Squash, '86 200
    Casserole, Baked Squash, '83 149
    Casserole, Blender Squash, '81 212
    Casserole, Cheesy Squash, '79 123; '82 M21
    Casserole, Chicken-Squash, '95 121
    Casserole, Company Squash, '81 183
    Casserole, Creamy Rice and Squash, '95 26
    Casserole, Crunchy Squash, '84 293
    Casserole, Fresh Squash, '82 204
    Casserole, Hearty Tex-Mex Squash-Chicken, '99 312; '03 107
    Casserole, Jiffy Squash, '81 M144
    Casserole, Squash, '87 163; '89 159; '90 161; '92 342; '96 247, 252; '97 29; '04 126
    Casserole, Squash and Egg, '80 146
    Casserole, Squash-Carrot, '81 157
    Casserole, Summer Squash, '81 102, 184
    Casserole, Two-Cheese Squash, '04 126
    Casserole, Yellow Squash, '79 179; '85 135; '88 166
    Casserole, Zippy Squash, '80 183
    Corn Casserole, Easy Squash-and-, '03 69
    Country Club Squash, '79 158; '88 M16
    Croquettes, Squash, '79 157; '83 148; '88 142; '97 118
    Dip, Yellow Squash-Zucchini, '89 48
    Dressing, Squash, '83 315; '86 280; '95 290; '01 160
    Fiesta Squash, '82 102
    Fried Yellow Squash, '86 211
    Fritters, Squash, '89 68; '99 203

Fritters, Squash-Jalapeño, '98 249
Greek-Style Squash, '91 285
Grilled Corn and Squash, '02 122
Grilled Corn-and-Squash Quesadillas, '02 123
Grilled Squash and Onion, '79 150
Grilled Squash Fans, '97 118
Grilled Summer Squash and Tomatoes, '99 144
Grilled Vegetables, '84 172
Grilled Yellow Squash and Tomatoes, '00 102
Grilled Yellow Squash Halves, '04 138
Marinated Cucumbers and Squash, '86 146
Medley, Summer Garden, '84 158
Mexican Squash, '82 103
Muffins, Yellow Squash, '81 163
Nicholas, Squash, '94 236
Nosh, Squash, '90 147
Pats, Squash, '80 298; '81 25
Patties, Squash, '79 158
Patties, Summer Squash, '81 184
Pickled Yellow Squash, '93 136
Pickles, Squash, '81 174; '87 150; '97 119; '99 170
Pie, Italian Squash, '02 183
Posh Squash, '81 159
Puffs, Yellow Squash, '82 103
Puppies, Squash, '83 170; '01 179
Quiche, Squash-and-Green Chile, '88 143
Rings, Asparagus in Squash, '87 68
Savory Squash, '99 111
Skillet Squash, '92 62
Skillet Summer Squash, '82 96
Soufflé, Cheesy Squash, '82 146
Soufflé, Squash, '95 215
Soufflé, Yellow Squash, '89 89
Soup, Chilled Squash, '92 173
Soup, Cold Cream of Squash, '81 130
Soup, Cream of Squash, '81 246
Soup, Perky Squash, '85 20
Soup, Squash, '94 134
Soup, Summer Squash, '83 99; '85 136
South-of-the-Border Squash, '89 148; '96 178
Stir-Fried Squash, '97 118
Stir-Fried Squash Medley, '80 123
Stuffed Squash, '01 223
Stuffed Yellow Squash, Tomato-, '00 42
Summer Squash, '80 127; '85 105
Toss, Asparagus-Carrot-Squash, '91 45
Toss, Crisp Squash-and-Pepper, '87 M152
Toss, Simple Squash, '85 M142
Vegetable-Herb Trio, '83 172
STEWS. *See also* **CHILI, CHOWDERS, GUMBOS, JAMBALAYAS, RAGOÛTS, SOUPS.**
    Bean Pot, White, '86 194
    Beef-and-Celery Root Stew, '98 292
    Beef-and-Onion Stew, '87 18
    Beef and Vegetable Stew, Sweet-and-Sour, '85 87
    Beef Stew, '86 51; '90 230; '96 16
    Beef Stew, Burgundy, '88 234
    Beef Stew, Company, '83 85; '97 198
    Beef Stew, Hungarian, '03 35
    Beef Stew, Oven, '79 222; '80 64
    Beef Stew, Quick, '86 302; '92 71
    Beef Stew, Spicy, '86 228
    Beef Stew with Dumplings, '84 3
    Beef Stew with Parsley Dumplings, '81 76; '82 13; '85 M246
    Black-Eyed Pea Stew with Rice, '04 19
    Brown Stew, '85 239
    Brunswick
        Aunt Willette's Brunswick Stew, '85 320
        Bama Brunswick Stew, '87 4
        Blakely Brunswick Stew, '87 4
        Breeden Liles's Brunswick Stew, '91 14

STEWS, Brunswick
(continued)

Brunswick Stew, '80 264; '97 138, 315;
'01 148, 219; '03 29
Chicken Brunswick Stew, '97 234
Chicken Stew, Brunswick, '87 4
Dan Dickerson's Brunswick Stew, '91 16
Easy Brunswick Stew, '92 280; '99 235; '00 138
Family-Size Brunswick Stew, Van Doyle's, '91 14
Favorite Brunswick Stew, Virginia Ramsey's,
'91 16
Gay Neale's Brunswick Stew, '91 17
Georgian Brunswick Stew, '92 35
Jeff Daniel's Brunswick Stew, '91 16
Pie, Brunswick Stew-Cornbread, '02 121
Sonny Frye's Brunswick Stew, '87 4
Virginian Brunswick Stew, '92 34
Burgoo, Five-Meat, '87 3
Burgoo, Harry Young's, '87 3
Burgoo, Kentucky, '88 235; '97 138
Burgoo, Old-Fashioned, '87 3
Burgundy Stew with Drop Dumplings, '83 125
Caldo de Rez (Mexican Beef Stew), '89 276
Camp Stew, '02 42
Catfish Stew, Cajun-Style, '88 12
Chicken, Kale, and Chickpea Stew, '98 47
Chicken Stew, '97 26
Chicken Stew and Dumplings, '84 4
Chicken Stew, Chili-, '90 319
Chicken Stew, Greek-Style, '03 219
Chicken Stew, Santa Fe, '97 193
Chicken Stew, Speedy, '03 42
Chicken Stew, Zesty, '02 127
Chili Stew, Red, '95 226
Collard 'n' Black-Eyed Pea Stew, '04 24
Collard Stew, '02 17
Emerald Isle Stew, '95 71
Étouffée, Crawfish, '02 85
Étouffée, Okra, '98 207
Étouffée, Roasted Quail, '96 34
Fish-and-Vegetable Stew, '87 220
Fisherman's Stew, '81 98
Fricassee, White Chicken, '98 122
Frogmore Stew, '92 236; '00 174, 336; '03 181
Game Pot Pie with Parmesan Crust, '94 304
Garbanzo Stew, Greek, '02 43
Ham-and-Black-Eyed Pea Stew, '93 20
Hamburger Oven Stew, '84 4
Hungarian Stew with Noodles, '80 263
Hunter's Stew, '85 270
Irish Stew, '90 64
Lamb-and-Okra Stew, '97 156
Lamb Stew, '79 293; '88 58
Lamb Stew-in-a-Loaf, '85 37
Lamb Stew with Popovers, '94 43
Lentil-Rice Stew, '82 232
Meatball Stew, '79 198; '98 30
Mexican Stew, '82 231
Mexican Stew Ole, '86 296
Minestrone Stew, '93 184
Mirliton Stew, '02 57
Okra Stew, Old-Fashioned, '84 158
Okra Stew, Quick, '97 88
Oyster-Broccoli Stew, '89 242
Oyster-Sausage Stew, '89 242
Oyster Stew, '80 221
Oyster Stew, Company, '80 297
Oyster Stew, Golden, '86 132
Oyster Stew, Holiday, '85 264
Oyster Stew, Potato-, '89 243
Pancho Villa Stew, '94 44
Pollo en Pipián, Mexican, '88 31

Pork Stew, Baja, '98 283
Reggae Rundown, '96 71
Rib-Tickling Stew, Campeche Bay, '89 317
Sausage Stew, Smoked, '82 231
Seafood Stew, '84 280
Shrimp Creole, '93 282; '96 210
Shrimp Creole, Spicy, '79 181
Shrimp Creole, Wild Rice-and-, '84 292
Shrimp Stew, '83 4
Shrimp Stew and Grits, '80 118
Shrimp Stew over Grits, '88 126; '89 47
Strader Stew, '89 28
Succotash with Serrano Chile Polenta, Ancho Chile,
'98 104
Texas Stew, '97 211
Turkey Stew, Hearty, '79 252
Turkey-Tomato Stew, '90 279
Turnip Greens Stew, '02 17; '04 24
Tzimmes with Brisket, Mixed Fruit, '93 114
Vegetable-Beef Stew, '94 323
Vegetable-Beef Stew, Shortcut, '89 218
Vegetable Stew, '00 248
Vegetable Stew, Mixed, '84 13
Vegetable Tagine, '96 289
Venison Sausage Stew, '87 238
Venison Stew, '86 294
Venison Stew with Potato Dumplings, '87 304
White Wine Stew, '82 228

STRAWBERRIES
Almond Cream Dip with Strawberries, '92 164
Arnaud, Strawberries, '93 50
Balsamic Strawberries, '02 170
Banana-Berry Flip, '88 215; '89 20
Bars, Strawberry, '81 301
Bavarian, Raspberry-Strawberry, '89 15
Bavarian, Rhubarb-Strawberry, '86 140
Beets, Strawberry-Glazed, '83 234
Best-Dressed Berries, '96 317
Beverages
Brandied Orange Juice, Strawberries with,
'82 160
Calypso, Coco-Berry, '89 171
Coolers, Strawberry, '92 67
Cooler, Strawberry, '83 56; '84 51
Cooler, Strawberry-Mint, '84 57
Cooler, Watermelon-Strawberry, '98 178
Cubes, Berry-Good, '95 201
Daiquiris, Creamy Strawberry, '91 66
Daiquiris, Strawberry, '90 125; '98 99
Daiquiri, Strawberry, '81 156
Float, Strawberry-Banana, '87 160
Frost, Banana-Strawberry, '87 199
Frozen Strawberry Refresher, '93 213
Ice Mold, Strawberry, '91 278
Ice Ring, Strawberry, '94 176
Lemonade, Berry Delicious, '93 205
Lemonade, Strawberry, '80 160
Margarita, Strawberry, '04 107
Milkshake, Fresh Strawberry, '82 113
Mimosa, Sparkling Strawberry, '88 169
Pineapple-Strawberry Slush, '94 227
Punch, Berry, '92 67
Punch, Berry-Colada, '96 277
Punch, Champagne, '98 310
Punch, Creamy Strawberry, '86 195
Punch, Strawberry, '90 273
Punch, Strawberry Champagne, '90 315
Punch, Strawberry-Lemonade, '85 116; '91 175
Sangría, Teaberry, '87 147
Shake, Double-Berry Milk, '00 81
Shake, Double Strawberry, '00 179
Shake, Double Strawberry-Banana, '01 173
Shake, Light Double Strawberry-Banana, '01 173
Shake, Strawberry, '97 172

Shake, Strawberry-Banana, '89 35; '97 172
Shake, Strawberry-Cheesecake, '92 44
Shake, Strawberry Milk, '94 113
Shake, Strawberry-Orange Breakfast, '87 186
Shake, Strawberry-Pear, '92 139
Shake, Strawberry-Pineapple, '84 166
Shake, Strawberry-Yogurt, '87 199
Shrub, Berry, '95 29
Slurp, Strawberry, '81 96
Slush, Strawberry, '98 178; '02 185
Slush, Strawberry-Lemonade, '03 169
Slush, Strawberry-Orange, '83 172
Slush, Strawberry Tea, '04 63
Smoothie, Berry-Banana Buttermilk, '00 49
Smoothie, Four-Berry, '97 173
Smoothie, Strawberry, '86 183; '97 173
Smoothie, Strawberry-Banana, '81 59
Smoothie, Strawberry-Peach, '89 182
Smoothie, Tropical, '81 50
Soda, Old-Fashioned Strawberry, '79 149
Soda, Strawberry, '84 115
Sparkler, Strawberry, '99 49
Spritzer, Strawberry, '90 14; '97 272
Spritzer, Strawberry-Kiwi-Lemonade, '03 89
Syrup, Berry, '96 161
Tea, Berry-Mint Iced, '98 332
Tea, Sparkling Strawberry, '94 131
Tea, Strawberry, '88 248
Bordeaux, Beauberries, '98 18
Bread, Strawberry, '81 250; '83 140; '84 49
Bread, Strawberry Jam, '79 216
Bread, Strawberry-Nut, '79 24
Butter, Strawberry, '79 36; '81 286; '91 71;
'99 44, 234
Cake, Chocolate-Strawberry Basket, '98 100
Cake, Layered Strawberry, '00 82
Cake Roll, Strawberries 'n Cream Sponge, '81 95
Cake Roll, Strawberry, '79 49; '83 129; '84 305;
'85 172
Cake, Strawberry Cream, '86 61
Cake, Strawberry Crunch, '79 288; '80 35
Cake, Strawberry Delight, '85 30
Cake, Strawberry-Lemon Sheet, '04 137
Cake, Strawberry Meringue, '86 240
Cake, Strawberry-Studded White Chocolate
Mousse, '99 154
Cake, Strawberry Yogurt Layer, '94 85
Cake, Triple-Decker Strawberry, '04 55
Cake with Strawberries and Chocolate Glaze, White,
'87 76
Cake with Strawberries and Cream, Cream Cheese
Pound, '02 104
Carousel, Strawberry, '91 247
Cheesecake, Almost Strawberry, '86 32
Cheesecake, Strawberry-Lemon, '04 237
Cheesecake, Pear-Berry, '82 M141
Cheesecake, Strawberry, '02 176, 209
Cheese Horseshoe, Strawberry-, '00 106
Cheese Ring, Strawberry-, '86 14
Cherry-Berry on a Cloud, '79 94
Chocolate Combo, Strawberry-, '85 96
Christmas Strawberries, '87 293; '94 331
Citrus Twist, Berry-, '95 100
Cobbler, Fresh Strawberry, '96 84
Cobbler, Rosy Strawberry-Rhubarb, '79 154
Cobbler, Strawberry-Rhubarb, '88 93
Coffee Cake, Strawberry, '85 46
Compote, Peach-Berry, '89 112
Cookie Tarts, Strawberry, '89 112
Cream, Chocolate Baskets with Berry, '92 118
Cream Dip, Fresh Strawberries with, '90 86
Cream in Vanilla Lace Cups, Strawberry, '98 93
Cream Puffs, Strawberry, '81 95
Cream Puffs, Strawberry-Lemon, '87 75

Cream, Strawberries and, '82 100; '92 132
Cream, Strawberries in, '89 88
Cream, Strawberries 'n', '90 30
Cream, Strawberries 'n Lemon, '85 120
Cream, Strawberries with Chocolate, '85 81
Cream, Strawberries with French, '83 191
Cream, Strawberries with Lemon, '90 170
Cream, Strawberries with Strawberry, '84 108
Cream, Strawberry, '88 153
Cream with Fresh Strawberries, Almond, '87 93
Crêpes, Nutritious Brunch, '80 44
Crêpes, Strawberry Dessert, '83 122
Crisp, Strawberry-Rhubarb, '95 119
Croissants, Strawberry or Apricot, '96 303
Deep-Fried Strawberries, '84 109
Delight, Frozen Strawberry, '82 112, 174
Delight, Strawberry, '81 85
Delight, Strawberry Cheese, '79 50
Delight, Strawberry Yogurt, '85 77
Dessert, Chilled Strawberry, '84 164
Dessert, Glazed Strawberry, '84 33
Dessert, Honeydew-Berry, '83 120
Dessert, Strawberry, '83 123
Dessert, Strawberry-Cream Cheese, '83 123
Dessert, Strawberry-Lemon, '86 162
Dessert, Strawberry-Yogurt, '90 295
Dessert, Summer Strawberry, '92 143
Dessert, Sweet-and-Sour Strawberry, '92 54
Dip, Apple-Berry, '01 109
Dipped in White Chocolate, Strawberries, '90 83
Dipped Strawberries, '94 17
Dipped Strawberries, Chocolate-, '98 M100
Dip, Strawberries with Brown Sugar-and-Sour
    Cream, '03 93
Dip, Strawberries with Fluffy Cream Cheese, '03 93
Dip, Strawberries with Mint Yogurt, '03 93
Dip, Strawberries with Vanilla Pudding, '03 93
Dip, Strawberry, '01 109
Divinity, Strawberry, '91 272
Dressing, Creamy Strawberry, '84 161
Éclairs, Strawberry Cream, '01 45
Filling, Strawberry-Lemon, '04 137
Freeze, Strawberry, '04 141
French Toast Sandwiches, Strawberry-, '91 160
Frosting, Strawberry, '89 184
Frosting, Strawberry Buttercream, '04 55
Frost, Strawberry, '81 279; '82 24; '83 154
Frozen Strawberry Cups, '91 173
Fudge Balls, Strawberry, '93 80
Gazpacho, Berry, '97 181
Glaze, Strawberry, '80 35; '83 142
Ham, Strawberry-Glazed, '91 84
Ice Cream Crêpes, Strawberry, '87 290; '88 135
Ice Cream, Fresh Strawberry, '89 111
Ice Cream, Homemade Strawberry, '84 184
Ice Cream, No-Cook Strawberry, '04 179
Ice Cream, Old-Fashioned Strawberry, '79 94
Ice Cream Roll, Strawberry, '84 105
Ice Cream, Straw-Ba-Nut, '80 177
Ice Cream, Strawberry, '80 177; '98 221
Ice Cream, Strawberry-Banana-Nut, '88 203
Ice Cream Torte, Chocolate-Strawberry, '79 7
Ice Cream, Very Strawberry, '81 155
Ice Milk, Fresh Strawberry, '92 94
Ice, Strawberry, '84 175; '85 108
Ice, Strawberry-Orange, '86 196
Jamaica, Strawberries, '85 161; '93 239
Jam, Christmas, '88 288
Jam, Strawberry, '89 138
Jam, Strawberry Freezer, '84 M182
Jam, Strawberry-Port, '03 134
Jellyroll, Easy, '82 176
Jelly, Strawberry, '81 147
Juliet, Strawberries, '84 82

Marinated Strawberries with Balsamic-Strawberry
    Syrup, '02 146
Marmalade, Strawberry-Pineapple, '85 130
Marsala, Strawberries, '88 171
Melon, Berry-Filled, '86 93
Meringues, Strawberry, '84 188
Mousse, Fresh Strawberry, '82 72
Mousse, Strawberry, '81 95
Mousse, Strawberry-Lemon, '82 128
Muffins, Strawberry, '99 234
Napoleons, Strawberry, '81 126
Nests, Strawberry Coconut, '88 136
Omelet, Puffy Dessert, '00 35
Omelet, Strawberry-Sour Cream, '89 229
Oranges and Strawberries, Grand, '03 119
Pancakes, Strawberry, '84 219
Parfait, Crunchy Strawberry-Yogurt, '79 124
Parfaits, Frosty Strawberry, '85 213
Parfaits, Strawberry-Lemon, '84 198
Parfaits, Strawberry Meringue, '02 62
Parfait, Strawberry, '79 99
Parfait, Surprise Strawberry, '86 151
Pies
    Angel Pie, Strawberry, '88 136
    Banana Glazed Pie, Strawberry-, '81 181
    Bumbleberry Pie, '97 163
    Chilled Strawberry Pie, '82 112
    Chocolate-Berry Pie, Heavenly, '85 102
    Chocolate Truffle Pie, Strawberry-, '89 112
    Custard Pie, Strawberry, '00 81
    Easy Strawberry Pie, '02 146
    Fried Strawberry Pies, '02 147
    Glazed Strawberry Pie, '82 M142
    Glaze Pie, Strawberry-, '81 141
    Lemon-Strawberry Pie, '88 127
    Red, White, and Blueberry Pie, '98 162
    Rhubarb Pie, Strawberry-, '98 99
    Yogurt Pie, Strawberry, '80 232
    Yogurt Pie, Strawberry-, '85 122; '86 124
Pizza, Kiwi-Berry, '86 198; '87 55
Pizza, Strawberry, '79 94
Popsicles, Smoothie Strawberry, '82 112
Pops, Strawberry, '04 141
Pops, Strawberry-Cinnamon, '99 132
Pops, Strawberry-Orange, '03 179
Pound Cake with Mint Berries and Cream, Lemon,
    '99 183
Preserves Deluxe, Strawberry, '82 150
Preserves, Freezer Strawberry, '82 112
Preserves, Hanukkah Doughnuts with Strawberry,
    '01 M275
Preserves, Quick Strawberry-Fig, '96 194
Preserves, Strawberry, '79 120; '81 96
Pudding, Summer, '98 217
Puff, Strawberry, '82 5
Raspberry Custard Sauce, Fresh Berries with,
    '88 163
Rock Cream with Strawberries, Old-Fashioned,
    '90 125
Roll, Heavenly Strawberry, '82 176
Roll, Strawberry, '82 120
Romanoff, Strawberries, '84 108; '88 95; '91 126;
    '94 68
Romanoff, Strawberry-Almond, '98 99
Ruby Strawberries, '82 100
Sabayon, Strawberries, '79 94
Salad, Baby Blue, '00 81
Salad, Chicken-Spinach-Strawberry, '97 92
Salad, Citrus-Strawberry, '04 249
Salad, Cranberry-Strawberry-Jícama, '02 300
Salad, Frozen Strawberry, '94 119
Salad, Hidden Treasure Strawberry, '79 11
Salad, Mimosa, '98 310
Salad Mold, Strawberry-Wine, '83 261

Salad, Strawberry-Chicken, '04 50
Salad, Strawberry-Nut, '94 132
Salad, Strawberry-Pretzel, '03 290
Salad, Strawberry-Spinach, '91 169; '93 168
Salad, Strawberry Yogurt, '80 232
Salad with Orange-Curd Dressing, Orange-
    Strawberry, '93 22
Salad with Tart Poppy Seed Dressing, Spinach-and-
    Strawberry, '03 241
Sauces
    Amaretto-Strawberry Sauce, '87 M165
    Arnaud Sauce, Strawberries, '93 50
    Banana Sauce, Strawberry-, '81 41
    Berry Sauce, '87 290; '88 135; '95 103
    Brandied Strawberry Sauce, '88 196
    Butter Sauce, Strawberry-, '96 87
    Crunchy Topping, Strawberry Sauce with,
        '81 170
    Dumplings, Strawberry Sauce with, '84 314
    French Toast with Strawberry Sauce, Make-
        Ahead, '02 131
    Fresh Strawberry Sauce, '82 177
    Melon Wedges with Berry Sauce, '86 178
    Mimosa Sauce, Berry, '90 315
    Old-Fashioned Strawberry Sauce, '94 130
    Orange Sauce, Strawberry-, '96 95
    Peaches with Strawberry Sauce, '85 8
    Peach Sauce, Strawberry-, '92 154
    Salsa, Balsamic Strawberry, '02 86
    Strawberry Sauce, '84 144; '87 93, 198; '92 85;
        '94 121; '03 55
Sherbet, Strawberry, '82 112, 160
Sherbet, Three-Ingredient Strawberry, '01 105
Shortcake, A Favorite Strawberry, '88 136
Shortcake, Chocolate-Strawberry, '89 216
Shortcake, Elegant Strawberry, '88 37
Shortcake Jubilee, Strawberry, '88 209
Shortcake, Orange-Strawberry, '95 100
Shortcake Shells, Strawberry, '88 196
Shortcake Shortcut, '02 105
Shortcakes, Party-Perfect Strawberry, '02 105
Shortcake Squares, Strawberry, '85 122; '86 124
Shortcakes, Round, '02 105
Shortcakes, Strawberry Crispy, '93 42
Shortcake, Strawberry, '81 96; '83 122; '92 184;
    '94 162
Shortcake, Strawberry-Brown Sugar, '00 82
Shortcake, Strawberry Pinwheel, '89 112
Shortcakes with Mint Cream, Strawberry, '97 144
Skewered Pineapple and Strawberries, '84 251
Sorbet, Strawberry, '88 117; '93 153; '03 171
Sorbet, Strawberry-Champagne, '83 162; '95 20
Sorbet, Strawberry Margarita, '89 111
Sorbet, Strawberry-Passion Fruit, '98 180
Sorbet, Very Berry, '90 85
Soup, Cold Strawberry, '82 157
Soup, Sherry-Berry Dessert, '91 180
Soup, Strawberry, '88 160
Soup, Strawberry-Banana, '86 181
Soup Supreme, Strawberry, '81 M144
Spiked Strawberries, '97 58
Spread, Light Strawberry, '85 55
Spread, Strawberry, '95 79
Spumoni and Berries, '91 204
Stuffed Strawberries, '98 155
Stuffed Strawberries with Walnuts, '85 122; '86 124
Sundaes, Hot Strawberry, '81 M5
Supreme, Banana-Berry, '81 205
Swirl, Strawberry, '84 108
Syrup, Strawberry, '02 104
Tartlets, Fresh Berry, '91 98
Tarts, Berry Good Lemon, '91 119
Tarts, Strawberry, '80 70
Tart, Strawberry, '84 138; '89 272; '00 82; '01 71

STRAWBERRIES
(continued)

Tart, Strawberry Dream, '92 118
Tart, Strawberry-Lemon, '89 111
Tart, Strawberry-Mascarpone, '02 146
Tea Cakes and Fresh Strawberries, Telia's, '98 110
Topping, Pound Cake with Strawberry-Banana,
  '89 200
Topping, Strawberry, '86 32; '90 142
Topping, Strawberry-Banana, '87 125
Torte, Spring, '91 57
Torte, Strawberry Meringue, '88 136
Treasure, Berried, '89 124
Trifle, Easy Strawberry, '88 201
Trifle, Strawberry-Sugar Biscuit, '03 84
Whip, Strawberry, '89 198
Zabaglione, Strawberries, '81 95
STROGANOFF
Beef Burgundy Stroganoff, '85 31
Beef Stroganoff, '79 163; '81 179; '91 134; '93 18;
  '03 23
Beef Stroganoff, Creamy, '02 124
Beef Stroganoff, Ground, '84 71
Beef Stroganoff, Light, '86 36
Beef Stroganoff, Quick, '92 20; '99 327
Casserole, Stroganoff, '98 48
Chicken Livers Stroganoff, '80 200; '81 57
Chicken Livers Supreme, '81 298
Chicken Stroganoff, '99 41
Crab Stroganoff, '79 116
Crawfish Stroganoff, '91 89
Hamburger Stroganoff, '82 108, 110
Hamburger Stroganoff, Easy, '79 208
Ham Stroganoff, '82 40
Ham Stroganoff on Cheesy Onion Biscuits, '95 98
Liver Stroganoff, '79 54
Meatballs, European Veal, '85 30
Meatballs Paprikash with Rice, '85 31
Meatball Stroganoff, '81 297; '02 50
Mushroom-Meatball Stroganoff, '85 85
Mushroom Stroganoff, '81 298
Quail Stroganoff, '99 41
Quickie Stroganoff, '81 200
Shrimp Stroganoff, '79 81
Shrimp Stroganoff, Oven-Baked, '81 297
Sirloin Stroganoff, '81 297
Steak Stroganoff Sandwiches, '85 110
Steak Stroganoff with Parslied Noodles, '85 31
Strolling-Through-the-Holidays Stroganoff,
  '01 282
Tofu, Stroganoff, '84 202
Turkey Stroganoff, '91 61
Veal Stroganoff, '79 108
STUFFINGS. *See also* **DRESSINGS.**
Apple-Almond Stuffing, '01 184
Apple-Crumb Stuffing, '81 234; '82 26; '83 39
Apple-Walnut Stuffing, '95 289
Barley-Mushroom Stuffing, Cornish Hens with,
  '97 242
Cornbread-Apple Stuffing, Pork Chops with, '99 14
Cornbread Stuffing, '94 305
Crabmeat Stuffing, '94 68
Crabmeat Stuffing, Chicken Breasts with, '85 302
Crab Stuffing, Tropical Orange Roughy with,
  '99 122
Cranberry-Orange-Pecan Stuffing, '01 249
Cranberry-Pecan Stuffing, '96 309
Cranberry-Sausage Stuffing, Crown Roast of Pork
  with, '88 49
Cranberry Stuffing, '04 246
Fruited Stuffing, Cornish Hens with, '90 191
Fruited Stuffing Mix, '89 331

Fruit Stuffing and Shiitake Sauce, Pork Tenderloin
  with, '97 218
Grits Stuffing, '96 270
Hopping John Stuffing, Pork Roast with, '01 25
Low-Sodium Stuffing, '82 66
Mincemeat Stuffing, '00 319
Mushroom Stuffing, Grilled Rainbow Trout with,
  '97 162
Oyster Stuffing, Roast Turkey with, '80 251
Pear Stuffing, Acorn Squash with, '01 293
Pecan-Cornbread Stuffing, Spicy, '01 207
Pecan-Sausage Stuffing, Chicken Breasts with,
  '94 212
Pecan Stuffing, '79 292; '80 32
Pecan Stuffing, Wild Duck with, '85 269
Piglet's Stuffing, '04 270
Rice-and-Onion Stuffing, '88 246
Rice Stuffing, '95 290
Sausage-and-Wild Mushroom Stuffing, '96 267
Sausage Stuffing, '99 293; '00 292; '03 255
Tangerine Stuffing, '90 16
Vegetable Stuffing, '01 84
Walnut-Rice Stuffing, Tomatoes with, '91 102
Wild Rice Stuffing, Cornish Hens with, '79 222;
  '80 64; '82 136
SWEET-AND-SOUR
Beets, Sweet-and-Sour, '81 167; '82 22; '89 314
Black-Eyed Peas, Sweet-and-Sour, '85 290
Burgers, Sweet-and-Sour, '90 128
Cabbage, Sweet-and-Sour, '86 295; '87 189
Cabbage, Sweet-Sour Red, '79 5
Carrots, Sweet-and-Sour, '82 137
Chicken and Rice, Sweet-and-Sour, '03 97
Chicken Nuggets, Sweet-and-Sour, '90 168
Chicken Stir-Fry, Sweet-and-Sour, '98 204
Chicken, Sweet-and-Sour, '79 106; '86 217, 240;
  '90 161; '91 202; '97 325
Chicken, Sweet-and-Sour Lemon, '84 93
Chicken, Sweet 'n' Sour, '04 311
Chicken Wings, Sweet-and-Sour, '90 206; '96 110
Dessert, Sweet-and-Sour Strawberry, '92 54
Dressing, Citrus Salad with Sweet-and-Sour,
  '01 104
Dressing, Sweet-and-Sour, '80 247; '84 70, 161;
  '85 163; '87 305; '89 62; '91 126; '94 281;
  '02 24; '03 28
Dressing, Sweet-and-Sour Fruit, '84 125
Dressing, Sweet-Sour, '80 246
Fish, Sweet-and-Sour, '80 M54
Green Beans and Carrots, Sweet-and-Sour, '83 6
Green Beans, Sweet-and-Sour, '79 184; '81 158;
  '82 90; '91 250
Ham, Sweet-and-Sour Glazed, '88 M15
Ham, Sweet-Sour Glazed, '83 311
Kale, Sweet-and-Sour, '80 298
Kielbasa, Sweet-and-Sour, '89 327
Liver, Sweet-and-Sour, '81 277
Marinade, Sweet-and-Sour, '86 113; '87 115
Meatballs, Spicy Sweet-and-Sour, '03 186
Meatballs, Sweet-and-Sour, '82 233, 247; '86 240;
  '99 325
Meatballs, Sweet-and-Sour Party, '79 233
Onions, Sweet-and-Sour Baked, '90 34
Pearl Onions, Sweet-and-Sour, '96 216
Peas, Sweet-and-Sour, '88 3
Pork Chops, Sweet-and-Sour, '83 160
Pork, Pineapple Sweet-and-Sour, '82 120
Pork Stir-Fry, Sweet-and-Sour, '03 92
Pork, Sweet-and-Sour, '79 42; '80 72, 227;
  '81 26, 104, 111; '82 12; '84 218; '85 34, 194;
  '86 241; '90 317; '92 219; '00 110
Potatoes, Sweet-and-Sour-Topped, '83 4
Pot Roast, Sweet-and-Sour, '83 8; '99 291
Red Cabbage and Apples, Sweet-and-Sour, '00 62

Riblets, Sweet-and-Sour, '85 276
Ribs, Sweet-and-Sour, '89 M84
Ribs, Sweet-and-Sour Baby Back, '04 87
Ribs, Sweet-and-Sour Grilled, '98 331
Salads
Asparagus, Sweet-and-Sour, '89 159
Bean Salad, Sweet-and-Sour, '85 198; '86 147
Beans, Sweet-and-Sour, '87 197
Beans with Sprouts, Sweet-and-Sour, '86 32
Carrot Salad, Sweet-and-Sour, '98 211
Cauliflower Salad, Sweet-and-Sour, '81 2
Fruit Salad, Sweet-and-Sour, '80 13; '84 125
Green Salad, Sweet-and-Sour, '94 281
Macaroni Salad, Sweet-and-Sour, '85 166
Potato Salad, Sweet and Sour, '80 152
Potato Salad, Sweet-and-Sour, '92 106
Slaw, Confetti Sweet-and-Sour, '98 89
Slaw, Sweet-and-Sour, '81 237
Slaw, Sweet-and-Sour Hot, '92 63
Spinach Salad, Sweet-Sour, '85 M112
Vegetable Salad, Sweet-and-Sour, '81 25
Sauce, Pork Chops with Sweet-and-Sour Apple,
  '98 132
Sauce, Sausage Rolls with Sweet-and-Sour, '83 74
Sauce, Stuffed Chicken Breasts with Sweet-and-
  Sour Tomato, '01 120
Sauce, Sweet-and-Sour, '80 20; '85 12, 34;
  '86 240
Sauce, Sweet-and-Sour 'Cue, '04 87
Sauce, Sweet-and-Sour Pineapple, '85 66
Sausage, Sweet-and-Sour, '88 296
Scallops, Grilled Sweet-and-Sour, '01 92
Shrimp and Chicken, Sweet-and-Sour, '87 267;
  '88 103; '89 66
Shrimp, Grilled Sweet-and-Sour, '97 100
Shrimp, Sweet-and-Sour, '83 278; '90 M112
Shrimp Tails, Sweet-and-Sour Rock, '80 3
Shrimp with Onion and Red Pepper, Sweet-and-
  Sour, '02 84
Snap Beans, Sweet-and-Sour, '89 173
Soup, Sweet-and-Sour Cabbage, '89 314
Spareribs, Sweet-and-Sour, '83 21
Spread, Sweet 'n' Sour, '86 184
Steaks, Sweet-and-Sour Marinated, '83 110
Stew, Sweet-and-Sour Beef and Vegetable, '85 87
Turkey, Sweet-and-Sour, '79 252
Turnips, Sweet-and-Sour, '81 274
Vegetables, Sweet-and-Sour Marinated, '83 266
Vinaigrette, Sweet-and-Sour Balsamic, '97 146
SWEET POTATOES
Apple Shells, Sweet Potatoes in, '85 206
Apples, Sweet Potato-Stuffed, '97 216; '00 232
Apple-Stuffed Sweet Potatoes, '88 207
Bake, Southern Sweet Potato, '85 229
Bake, Sweet Potato-Apricot, '85 206
Balls, Sweet Potato, '86 312
Bisque, Sweet Potato-and-Pear, '00 317
Boats, Sweet Potato, '80 287
Bourbon-Sweet Potato Stacks, '04 246
Brandied Sweet Potatoes, '97 248
Breads
Biscuits, Sweet Potato, '80 287; '84 140; '89 210;
  '98 222; '00 232; '01 250
Biscuits, Sweet Potato Angel, '93 312; '01 42
Muffins, Sweet Potato, '81 224; '85 6; '87 280;
  '92 31
Muffins, Yam, '79 7
Rolls, Golden Yams, '86 299
Rolls, Sweet Potato, '93 172; '97 107
Broiled Sweet Potatoes, Coconut-, '84 231
Butter, Sweet Potato, '95 M290
Candied Sweet Potatoes, '79 9, 251; '86 111;
  '88 207; '97 312; '01 49
Candied Sweet Potatoes, Nannie's, '95 306

Casseroles

Apple Bake, Sweet Potato-, '83 25; '86 282
Apple Casserole, Sweet Potato-and-, '94 280
Apple Casserole, Sweet Potatoes-and-, '90 228
Applesauce Sweet Potatoes, '91 292; '92 256
Apples, Sweet Potatoes and, '97 249
Apricot Sweet Potatoes, '82 228
Bake, Sweet Potato, '80 287
Banana Casserole, Sweet Potato-, '86 276
Bell's Sweet Potato Casserole, '04 271
Berries Casserole, Sweet Potatoes-and-, '84 231
Bourbon Sweet Potatoes, '86 324; '87 280
Candied Sweet Potatoes, '88 207
Coconut-Orange Sweet Potatoes, '84 252
Delight, Sweet Potato, '86 335; '87 83
Eggnog Casserole, Sweet Potato-, '95 291
Festive Sweet Potatoes, '80 244
Glazed Sweet Potato Casserole, '90 250
Glazed Sweet Potatoes, Tropical, '83 226
Gratin, Smoky Potato, '00 233
Holiday Sweet Potato Bake, '90 291
Mashed Sweet Potatoes, '98 269
Mashed Sweet Potatoes, Orange-Spice, '02 34
Orange Bake, Sweet Potato-, '83 226
Peaches, Sweet Potatoes and, '86 11
Pear-Sweet Potato Casserole, '86 280
Pineapple-Orange Sweet Potatoes, '96 46
Pones, Sweet Potato, '96 270
Praline-Topped Sweet Potatoes, '98 96
Puree, Carrot-and-Sweet Potato, '94 56
Royale, Sweet Potatoes, '91 250
Rum Casserole, Sweet Potato-, '84 231
Scallop, Yam-and-Apple, '91 199
Sherry and Walnuts, Sweet Potatoes with,
'86 286
Surprise, Holiday Sweet Potato, '84 254
Surprise, Sweet Potato, '81 267; '97 139
Sweet Potato Casserole, '79 289; '80 26; '85 256;
'89 279; '02 292; '03 M24
Swirled Mashed-Potato Bake, '02 98
Yams, Cornwallis, '79 276
Chips, Boniato, '92 247
Chips, Sweet Potato, '91 138; '93 332; '95 M203;
'97 63
Chips with Blue Cheese, Sweet Potato, '93 290
Chowder, Asian Sweet Potato, '97 213
Chutney, Sweet Potato, '99 45
Cinnamon-Apple Sweet Potatoes, '95 M23
Croquettes, Sweet Potato, '81 223; '96 238
Cups, Sunshine Sweet Potato, '82 195

Desserts

Cakes, Sweet Potato, '01 105
Cake, Sweet Potato, '79 207; '89 295
Cake, Sweet Potato Loaf, '81 224
Cake, Sweet Potato Pound, '83 85
Cake, Sweet Potato Surprise, '80 287
Cake with Citrus Filling, Sweet Potato, '02 221
Cake with Coconut Filling and Caramel Frosting,
Sweet Potato, '03 329
Cheesecake, Sweet Potato, '80 287; '96 312
Cheesecake, Yam, '81 224
Cobbler, Sweet Potato, '99 255; '01 214
Cobbler, Sweet Potato-Apple, '04 M232
Crème Brûlée, Sweet Potato, '02 275
Flan, Sweet Potato, '95 291
Pie, Carolina Sweet Potato, '89 295
Pie, Louisiana Yam, '81 223
Pie, No-Crust Sweet Potato, '84 236
Pie, Old-Fashioned Sweet Potato, '79 9
Pie, Southern Sweet Potato Cream, '87 260
Pie, Speedy Sweet Potato, '90 219
Pie, Sweet Potato, '79 207; '85 255, 275; '86 269;
'89 289; '96 131, 326; '00 232; '01 243;
'04 331

Pie, Sweet Potato Meringue, '81 126;
'83 225
Pie, Sweet Potato-Orange, '88 207
Pie, Sweet Potato-Pecan, '83 90
Pie, Sweet Potato Pone, '80 288
Pudding, Sweet Potato, '80 228; '86 52
Pudding, Sweet Potato Bread, '94 241
Roll, Sweet Potato Log, '82 227
Torte, Caramel-Sweet Potato, '96 312
French-Fried Sweet Potatoes, '81 223
Fried Sweet Potatoes, '83 226
Fried Sweet Potato Strips, '94 238
Fritters, Golden Sweet Potato, '79 9
Fritters, Sweet Potato, '88 44
Glazed Sweet Potatoes, '85 206; '89 274
Glazed Sweet Potatoes, Apple-, '82 303
Glazed Sweet Potatoes, Apricot-, '81 295
Glazed Sweet Potatoes, Orange-, '81 223;
'83 280
Glaze, Sweet Potatoes with Apricot, '89 331
Gravy, Roast Duck with Sweet Potato-Eggplant,
'83 90
Grilled Sweet Potatoes, '93 213
Hash Browns, Cheesy Sweet Potato, '02 248
Hash Browns, Rosemary-Garlic, '02 248
Hash Browns, Sweet Potato, '02 248
Hash, Sweet Potato, '92 337
Latkes, Sweet Potato, '01 275
Lime Sweet Potatoes, '02 307
Maple-Ginger Cream, Sweet Potatoes with,
'97 27
Mashed-Potato Bake, Swirled, '03 293
Mashed Sweet Potatoes, '85 25
Mashed Sweet Potatoes with Cumin, '99 244
Orange-Baked Sweet Potatoes, '88 M294
Orange Cups, Sweet Potatoes in, '82 272
Orange Cups, Sweet Potato-Stuffed, '81 223
Orange Sweet Potatoes, '86 279
Oven-Fried Sweet Potatoes with Chutney, '93 241
Oven-Roasted Sweet Potatoes and Onions, '00 24
Pancakes, Quick Sweet Potato-Chive, '04 248
Pancakes, Sweet Potato, '87 280
Pancakes with Goat Cheese, Sweet Potato, '96 271
Peaks, Sweet Potato, '95 291
Peanut Crust, Sweet Potatoes with, '93 212
Pones, Sweet Potato, '96 270
Pork Chops with Sweet Potatoes, '96 269
Pork Dinner, Saucy, '97 26
Praline Sweet Potatoes and Apples, '03 260
Pudding, Sweet Potato, '79 244; '80 228; '86 52
Puffs, Peach Sweet Potato, '87 280
Puffs, Sweet Potato, '87 253
Puff, Sweet Potato, '85 235
Puree, Carrot-Sweet Potato, '92 90; '00 M32;
'02 M285
Puree, Sweet Potato, '92 306
Raspberry Sweet Potatoes, '87 280
Roasted Gingered Sweet Potatoes, '01 92
Roasted Potato Trio, '00 311; '02 310
Roasted Sweet Potatoes and Onions, '01 234
Sage Vinaigrette, Sweet Potatoes with, '97 270
Salad, Black-Eyed Pea-and-Sweet Potato,
'01 198
Salad, Fresh Sweet Potato, '86 226
Salad, Hawaiian Ham-Sweet Potato, '82 232
Salad, Sweet Potato-Apple, '96 240
Salad, Sweet Potato Fruit, '00 325
Salad with Rosemary-Honey Vinaigrette, Sweet
Potato, '98 243
Scalloped Root Vegetables, '98 310
Scalloped Sweet Potatoes with Apples, '00 253
Slaw, Sweet Potato-Currant, '93 246
Soufflé, Sweet Potato, '82 286; '86 121; '93 325;
'96 247; '00 273

Soup, Southern Sweet Potato, '00 233
Soup, Sweet Potato, '88 250; '02 221
Soup, Sweet Potato-and-Sausage, '95 23
Soup with Rum Cream, Sweet Potato, '98 271
Spicy Island Sweet Potatoes, Caribbean Catfish with,
'04 310
Spicy Sweet Potatoes, '02 207
Stacked Sweet Potato Blues, '95 290
Stuffed Baked Sweet Potatoes, '79 207; '84 231
Stuffed Sweet Potatoes, '86 224
Stuffed Sweet Potatoes, Bacon-, '86 224
Stuffed Sweet Potatoes, Coconut-, '82 204
Stuffed Sweet Potatoes, Fluffy, '79 9
Stuffed with Apples, Sweet Potatoes, '82 228
Supreme, Sweet Potato, '94 196
Tzimmes, '95 102
Tzimmes, Sweet Potato-Beef, '92 234
Velouté, Sweet Potato, '94 238
Waffles, Sweet Potato, '88 208
Waffles with Orange Butter, Sweet Potato, '90 323
Yams, Bourbon, '90 232
Yams, Brandied, '94 273
Yams Cointreau, '92 192
Yams, Rosemary-Garlic, '93 174
Yam Tartlets, Zamaani's Nutty, '02 21

SWISS CHARD

Bundles, Swiss Chard, '94 48
Buttered Chard, '83 36
Creamy Chard and Potatoes, '98 250
Green and Gold, '00 91
Sautéed Chard with Onion and Apple, '98 48
Tomatoes, Swiss Chard with, '83 36

SYRUPS

Almond Syrup, '82 47
Anise Sugar Syrup, '86 248
Apple Syrup, Spiced, '79 114
Apricot Fruit Syrup, '82 10
Barbecue Sauce, Maple Syrup, '94 154
Berry Syrup, '96 161
Blackberry Syrup, '99 131
Bourbon Syrup, '98 277; '03 233
Caramel Syrup, '82 43
Caramel Syrup, Citrus Compote with, '98 313
Cherry-Lemonade Syrup, '86 214
Cinnamon Syrup, '91 315
Citrus Syrup, Sweet, '86 270
Coffee Syrup, '01 64
Fruit Syrup, '86 176
Ginger Syrup, '96 161
Honey Syrup, '96 21
Kirsch Syrup, '80 280
Madeira Syrup, '98 247
Maple-Banana Syrup, '03 47
Maple-Honey-Cinnamon Syrup, '85 19
Maple-Nut Syrup, '80 228
Maple Syrup, '81 120; '82 23; '93 16
Maple Syrup, Homemade, '79 114
Mint Simple Syrup, '03 129
Mint Sugar Syrup, Fresh, '03 89
Mint Syrup, '90 89; '96 161; '97 120
Mocha Latte Syrup, '03 46
Orange-Ginger Syrup, '03 167
Orange Marmalade Syrup, '96 27
Orange Syrup, '80 228; '89 254; '96 161, 164;
'97 32; '02 295
Peanut Butter and Jelly Syrups, Banana Pancakes
with, '01 24
Pecan Syrup, Chunky, '85 278
Pomegranate Syrup, '96 241
Rum Syrup, '95 313
Simple Syrup, '99 161
Strawberry Syrup, '02 104
Sugar Syrup, '93 29; '96 161; '02 161;
'03 224

T

TABBOULEH
Appetizers, Endive with Arugula Tabbouleh, '98 67
Couscous, Tabbouleh, '96 251; '02 200
Endive with Arugula Tabbouleh, '98 67
Pitas, Tabbouleh, '98 105
Salad), Boot Scoot Tabbouli (Tabbouleh, '96 159
Salad, Southwestern Tabbouleh, '01 216
Salad, Tabbouleh, '92 212; '94 174
Tabbouleh, '93 70; '99 175

TACOS
al Carbón, Tacos, '86 19
al Carbón, Tailgate Tacos, '79 185
Appetizer, Layered Taco, '84 206
Bake, Taco, '97 326
Bake, Taco Beef-Noodle, '81 141
Basic Tacos, '83 199
Beef Tacos, Soft, '91 88
Biscuit Bites, Taco, '91 89
Breakfast Tacos, '80 43; '91 316; '95 340
Burgers, Taco, '98 224
Casserole, Taco, '80 33
Catfish Tacos, Baja-Style Fried, '04 311
Cheesecake, Taco, '00 56
Chicken-and-Bean Tacos, '93 293
Chicken Skewers, Taco-, '99 119
Chicken Tacos, Pizza-Flavored, '95 340
Corn Chip Tacos, '81 67
Deep-Dish Taco Squares, '91 88
Dessert Tacos, '97 141
Dip, Hot Taco, '93 238
Dogs, Taco, '02 M57
Easy Tacos, '96 159
Egg Salad Tacos, Mexican, '94 181
Fish Taco Appetizers, '04 324
Fish Tacos, Barbecued, '95 339
Jiffy Tacos, '83 M318
Joes, Taco, '91 167
Lentil Tacos, '88 197
Lobster Taco with Yellow Tomato Salsa and Jicama
    Salad, Warm, '87 122
Margarita Tacos, '97 167
Microwave Tacos, '88 M213
Navajo Tacos, '84 246
Pasta, Easy Taco, '03 124
Peppers, Taco, '81 86
Pepper Tacos, Grilled, '95 340
Pie, Crescent Taco, '80 80
Pie, Double-Crust Taco, '88 272; '89 180
Pies, Individual Taco, '82 M282
Pie, Taco, '88 256
Pitas, Taco, '83 31
Pizza, Taco, '89 M177; '98 176; '00 293
Pork Tacos with Cucumber-Radish Salsa, Adobo
    Grilled, '01 186
Pork Tacos with Pineapple Salsa, '03 128
Potatoes, Taco-Topped, '93 M18
Rolls, Chinese Taco, '95 339
Salad, Beefy Taco, '03 128
Salad, Chicken Taco, '94 M136
Salad Cups, Taco, '85 M29
Salad, Meatless Taco, '81 204
Salad, Party Taco, '97 19
Salad, Spicy Taco, '87 287
Salad, Taco, '79 56; '83 145; '85 84; '89 332;
    '90 20; '02 188
Salad, Taco Macaroni, '85 165
Salad, Tuna-Taco, '87 145
Sauce, Taco, '82 M283; '93 69; '94 30
Seasoning Blend, Taco, '96 159
Shrimp-and-Pepper Soft Tacos, '95 339
Shrimp Tacos with Spicy Cream Sauce, '01 170
Skillet Tacos, Easy, '04 180
Soup, Taco, '94 225; '99 36

Stacks, Soft Taco, '02 54
Steak Tacos, Jerk, '01 170
Tacos, '80 196
Tassies, Taco, '95 339
Teasers, Taco, '01 134
Veggie Tacos, Loaded, '00 294
Veggie Tacos, Skillet, '01 170
Wrapidos, Tacos, '03 172

TAMALES
Bake, Cornbread Tamale, '79 163
Breakfast Tamales, '00 122
Casserole, Quick Tamale, '94 255
Chicken Tamales, '88 151
Dessert Tamales, Mango, '94 190
Dressing, Corny Cornbread, '99 258
Hot Tamales, '83 51
Meatballs, Tamale, '80 194
Miniature Tamales, '85 154
Mozzarella Tamale, '95 70
Pie, Chili-Tamale, '82 9; '83 68
Pie, Cornbread-Tamale, '92 123
Soup, Tamale, '95 213
Sweet Tamales, '83 52
Tamales, '80 195

TASTE OF THE SOUTH
Ambrosia, '04 233
Ambrosia, Kitchen Express, '04 233
Applesauce, Sweet Onion, '02 319
Beverages
Eggnog, Aunt Kat's Creamy, '01 287
Lemonade, Sweet-Tart, '02 160
Mint Julep, Classic, '03 129
Syrup, Mint Simple, '03 129
Tea, Southern Sweet, '02 107
Tea, Southern Sweetened, '00 70
Breads
Beignets, '01 59
Cornbread, Bacon-Cheddar Hot-Water, '01 29;
    '02 107
Cornbread, Baked Hot-Water, '01 29; '02 107
Cornbread, Country Ham Hot-Water, '01 29;
    '02 107
Cornbread, Hot-Water, '01 29; '02 107
Cornbread, Skillet, '00 22
Cornbread, Southwestern Hot-Water, '01 29;
    '02 107
Rolls, Icebox, '04 70
Sally Lunn Bread, '03 27
Spoonbread, '04 58
Spoonbread, Memmie's, '04 57
Brisket Rub, '03 188
Butter, Blackberry, '03 27
Butter, Oven Apple, '00 237
Butter, Spiced Oven Apple, '00 237
Cheese, Cream Cheese-and-Olive Pimiento, '01 169
Cheese, Jalapeño Pimiento, '01 169
Cheese, Pecan Pimiento, '01 169
Cheese, Pimiento, '01 169
Desserts
Brittle, Cooktop, '02 223
Cake, Coca-Cola, '02 181
Cake, Express Pineapple Upside-Down, '03 65
Cake, Skillet Pineapple Upside-Down, '03 65
Cake, Two-Step Pound, '00 36
Cheesecake, Pecan Pie, '02 318
Divinity, Mrs. Floyd's, '00 315
Frosting, Coca-Cola, '02 181
Peanut Brittle, Chocolate-Dipped, '02 M223
Peanut Brittle, Classic, '02 M223
Peanut Brittle, Popcorn, '02 M223
Pecan Brittle, '02 M223
Pie, Chocolate-Pecan Chess, '00 60; '02 107
Pie, Classic Chess, '00 60; '02 107
Pie, Coconut Chess, '00 60; '02 107

Pie, Key Lime, '00 120
Pie, Lemon Chess, '00 60; '02 107
Pralines, '01 201
Tea Cakes, '02 161
Dressing, Andouille Sausage, Apple, and Pecan,
    '02 249
Dressing, Cornbread, '02 249
Eggs, Basic Deviled, '03 88
Gravy, Tomato, '00 216
Grits, Creamy, '00 215
Grits, Garlic-Cheese, '00 215
Grits, Smoked Gouda, '02 319
Macaroni and Cheese, Baked, '02 26
Macaroni and Cheese, Creamy, '02 26
Main Dishes
Brisket, Traditional, '03 188
Catfish, Classic Fried, '01 135
Catfish, Fried Lemon-Rosemary, '02 319
Chicken and Dumplings, '01 231
Chicken, Our Best Southern Fried, '00 142
Country Ham, '00 298
Country Ham with Redeye Gravy, '00 216
Crab Cakes, Faidley's, '01 97
Fried Chicken, Our Best Southern, '02 106
Oysters Rockefeller, '03 272
Oysters, Southwest Fried, '03 45
Pork on Smoked Gouda Grits with Sweet Onion
    Applesauce, Maple-Chipotle, '02 319
Red Beans and Rice, Spicy, '02 56
Ribs, Baby Loin Back, '01 106
Shrimp, New Orleans Barbecue, '02 201
Steak, Chicken-Fried, '01 47
Preserves, Fig, '00 175
Salads
Olive Salad, '04 27
Potato Salad, Fipps Family, '02 138
Potato Salad, Light, '02 138
Potato Salad, Red, '02 138
Potato Salad with Onion and Celery, '02 138
Potato Salad with Sweet Pickle, '02 138
Sandwiches
Hot Browns, Biscuit, '02 94
Hot Browns, Kentucky, '02 94
Hot Browns, Southwestern, '02 94
Hot Browns with Fried Cheese Grits, '02 94
Muffuletta, '04 27
Sauces
Basting Sauce, '01 106
Brisket Mopping Sauce, '03 188
Brisket Red Sauce, '03 188
Cheese Sauce, '02 94
Pepper Sauce, '02 106
Sweet Sauce, '01 106
Soups and Stews
Brunswick Stew, '01 219
Frogmore Stew, '03 181
Gumbo, Chicken-and-Sausage, '04 213
She-Crab Soup, '03 137
Spices, Dry, '01 106
Syrup, Sugar, '02 161
Vegetables
Black-Eyed Peas, Hearty, '00 22; '02 107
Corn Pudding, Southwestern, '01 165
Corn Pudding, Tee's, '01 165
Okra, Fried, '00 205
Okra Pods, Fried, '00 205
Onion Rings, Buttermilk Batter-Fried, '02 131
Squash Casserole, '04 126
Squash Casserole, Two-Cheese, '04 126
Sweet Potato Casserole, '02 309
Tomatoes, Fried Green, '03 173
Turnip Greens and Ham Hocks, Southern,
    '03 220
Turnip Greens, Simple, '02 106

TEA
Cake, Tea Pound, '99 90
Granita, Ginger Tea, '98 334
Granita, Mint Tea, '88 117
Granita, Wild Raspberry Tea, '99 89
Hot
Almond Tea, '85 43; '86 329
Apple-Cinnamon Tea, Hot, '87 57
Apricot Tea, Hot Spiced, '88 248
Brew, Quilter's, '85 43
Cider Tea, '98 241; '99 335
Citrus Tea, Hot, '83 275
Cranberry Tea, Mulled, '01 240
Fruit Tea, Christmas, '83 275
Fruit Tea, Hot Spiced, '87 242
Grape Tea, Spiced, '79 174
Hawaiian Tea, '87 57
Honey Tea, '81 105
Johnny Appleseed Tea, '85 23
Marmalade Tea, '98 330
Minted Tea, '86 101
Mint Tea, Moroccan, '98 211
Mix, Deluxe Spiced Tea, '88 257
Mix, Friendship Tea, '83 283
Mix, Spiced Tea, '86 32
Mix, Sugar-Free Spiced Tea, '91 258
Punch, Cran-Grape-Tea, '92 209
Punch, Spiked Tea, '86 101
Russian Tea, Hot, '97 274
Spiced Tea, Hot, '83 244
Strawberry Tea, '88 248
Yaupon Tea, '79 31
Ice Cream, Orange Pekoe-Chocolate, '99 90
Iced
Almond-Lemonade Tea, '86 229; '99 207
Almond Tea, '89 212; '97 226; '01 93
Apple Tea, Iced, '98 84
Berry-Mint Iced Tea, '98 332
Blackberry Iced Tea, '04 158
Bubbly Iced Tea, '81 168
Cider Tea, '98 241
Citrus Iced Tea, '00 139
Citrus-Mint Tea Cooler, '92 105
Citrus Tea, Iced, '85 162
Cranberry-Apple Tea, '88 169
Cranberry Tea, '94 131; '97 121, 160; '04 63
Cranberry Tea Cooler, '01 322
Cranberry Tea, Holiday, '03 233
Cranberry Tea, Mulled, '01 240
Cubes, Frozen Tea, '85 161
Fruit-and-Mint Iced Tea, '98 84
Fruited Tea Cooler, '94 131
Fruit Tea, Christmas, '01 240
Fruit Tea, Refreshing, '97 122
Ginger-Almond Tea, '94 131
Ginger Tea, '81 100; '96 100
Grapefruit Tea, '92 67
Grape Tea, Spiced, '79 174
Hawaiian Tea, '87 57
Hibiscus Tea, Iced, '04 72
Juleps, Tea, '99 90
Lemon Iced Tea, Minted, '00 131
Lemon-Mint Tea, '85 162
Lemon Tea, '82 156
Lemon Tea Tingler, '95 200
Lime-Mint Tea, '97 122
Lime Tea, '98 198
Long Island Iced Tea, Southern, '90 207
Minted Tea, '88 163; '92 54
Mint Tea, '87 107; '90 89
Mint Tea, Easy, '91 187
Mint Tea, Fresh, '95 88
Mint Tea, Frosted, '84 161
Mint Tea, Fruited, '88 79; '91 81

Mint Tea, Fruity, '04 143
Mint Tea, Iced, '83 170
Mint Tea, Moroccan, '98 211
Passion Tea, '04 63
Peach Iced Tea, '02 181
Pineapple Tea, '93 165
Punch, Apple-Tea, '85 82
Punch, Bourbon-Tea, '87 57
Punch, Citrus-Tea, '85 116
Punch, Cran-Grape-Tea, '92 209
Punch, Minted Tea, '00 164
Punch, Mint Tea, '04 63
Punch, Southern Fresh Fruit, '99 70
Punch, Tea, '90 143, 207
Rasp-Berry Good Tea, '95 200
Red Tea, Iced, '04 143
Sangría, Mock Tea, '99 336
Sangría Tea, '94 131
Sangría , Teaberry, '87 147
Sangría Tea, Pink, '95 200
Sparkling Summer Tea, '96 172
Spiced Iced Tea, '91 209; '97 121
Spiced Tea Cooler, '83 55
Strawberry Tea Slush, '04 63
Strawberry Tea, Sparkling, '94 131
Summer Tea, '85 162
Summertime Tea, '81 167
Sun Tea, Southern, '81 168
Sweetened Tea, Southern, '00 70
Sweet Tea, '98 84
Sweet Tea, Southern, '02 107; '04 107
Thai Iced Tea, '02 174
Tropical Tea-Ser, '95 200
White Grape Iced Tea, '98 84
White Grape Juice Tea, '87 57
Yaupon Tea, '79 31
Jelly, Red Zinger, '99 89
Sauce, Tea-Berry, '94 130; '99 334
Vinaigrette, Salad Greens with Herbed Earl Grey, '99 89

TEMPURA
Basic Tempura, '81 68
Chicken Tempura Delight, '85 66
Cornmeal Tempura, '81 68
Green Onions, Tempura-Battered, '96 93
Sauce, Basic Tempura, '81 68
Sauce, Mustard-Sour Cream, '81 68
"Shrimps," French-Fried Tempura, '97 128
Vegetable Tempura, '79 112

TERRINES
Asparagus-Seafood Terrine with Dill Sauce, '98 157
Banana Split Terrine, '96 164
Black Bean Terrine with Fresh Tomato Coulis and Jalapeño Sauce, '93 230
Black Bean Terrine with Goat Cheese, '87 120
Blue Cheese Terrine with Tomato-Basil Vinaigrette, '99 288
Cheese Terrine, Basil-, '96 322
Cheese Terrine, Italian, '93 64
Chicken-Leek Terrine, Cold, '92 145
Chicken Terrine Ring, '84 132
Chicken-Vegetable Terrine, '84 131
Fruit Terrine with Raspberry Sauce, '98 157
Pork and Veal, Terrine of, '93 287
Pork Terrine, Jeweled, '84 130
Salmon-and-Spinach Terrine, Layered, '84 132
Veal Terrine with Mustard Sauce, '93 118
Vegetable-Chicken Terrine, '83 224

TIMBALES
Cheesy Mexicali Appetizer, '82 108
Chicken Chutney Salad, '82 108
Corn-and-Zucchini Timbales, '92 100
Green Rice Timbales, '97 62
Grits Timbales, '88 223

Grits Timbales, Chives-, '90 172
Hamburger Stroganoff, '82 108
Peach Almond Cream, '82 108
Rice Timbales, '94 32
Shells, Timbale, '82 108
Shrimp Sauté, Confetti, '97 104
Spinach-Rice Timbales, '88 271
Spinach Timbales, '84 29

TOFU
Cheesecake, Tropical Tofu, '00 204
Dip, Tofu, '86 109
Drink, Tofruitti Breakfast, '88 26
Lasagna, Tofu, '83 312
Rice with Tofu, Spanish, '88 26
Salad, Tofu, '88 27
Sandwiches, Open-Face Tofu-Veggie, '86 5
Stroganoff Tofu, '84 202

TOMATILLOS
Beef Saltillo (Beef with Tomatillos), '82 219
Enchiladas Verde, Chicken, '00 M240
Fillets Tomatillo, '94 135
Green Tomatillos with Jalapeño Dipping Sauce, Fried, '97 143
Pudding, Green Tomato-Tomatillo-Corn, '04 103
Relish, Black Bean-Tomatillo, '87 121
Salsa, Fresh Tomatillo, '97 143
Salsa, Grilled Chicken with Tomatillo, '02 123
Salsa, Roasted Tomatillo, '95 64
Salsa, Tomatillo, '92 245; '02 123
Salsa Verde, '96 160
Sandwiches, Open-Faced Tomatillo, '92 246
Sauce, Avocado-Tomatillo, '95 206
Sauce, Drunken, '03 33
Sauce, Green Barbecue, '02 183
Sauce, Grilled Jerk Shrimp with Creamy Tomatillo, '01 332
Sauce, Roasted Chiles Rellenos with Tomatillo, '94 203
Sauce, Shrimp Enchiladas in Tomatillo, '95 310
Sauce, Tomatillo, '94 231; '95 206; '97 25; '04 119
Sauce, Verde, '00 241
Soup with Crunchy Jicama, Tomatillo, '92 245; '97 143
Stacks, Fried Green Tomato, '02 184
Vinaigrette, Poblano, '99 71
Zucchini, Southwestern Stuffed, '03 M127

TOMATOES
Appetizers, Oven-Baked Tomato, '95 172
au Gratin, Zucchini and Tomato, '82 208
Bake, Chicken-Tomato, '83 35
Baked Cheddar Tomatoes, '85 43
Baked Ranch Tomatoes, '94 72
Baked Tomatoes, '83 53; '87 197
Baked Tomatoes, Honey-, '02 166
Baked Tomato Halves, Zippy, '81 182
Bake, Ham-Rice-Tomato, '87 78
Bake, Okra-and-Tomato, '89 173
Bake, Okra-Tomato, '80 298; '81 26
Bake, Potato-Tomato, '86 17
Bake, Tomato-and-Artichoke Heart, '85 81
Bake, Tomato-and-Okra, '03 158
Bake, Zucchini and Tomato, '82 158
Basil, and Cheese, Tomato, '95 165
Basil, Zucchini and Tomatoes, '89 147
Bean-and-Tomato Skillet, '90 316
Beans and Tomatoes, Basil, '83 172
Beans, Texas, '97 139
Beef with Tomatoes and Artichokes, '92 282
Biscuit Bites, Savory Tomato-Bacon, '03 196
Biscuit Cakes, Tomato-Eggplant, '95 170
Biscuits, Fresh Tomato, '04 138
Biscuits, Tomato, '86 72
Biscuits, Tomato-Herb, '94 215
BLT, Caramelized Onion, '03 90

TOMATOES
(continued)

Bowl, Tomato, '81 69
Braised with Tomatoes, Lamb Shanks, '03 87
Breaded Tomatoes, '95 180
Bread, Grilled, '00 88
Bread, Herbed Tomato-Cheese, '88 143
Bread, Tomato-Cheese, '98 172; '99 M157
Broiled Parmesan Tomatoes, '04 322
Broiled Tomatoes, '80 152
Broiled Tomatoes, Quick, '79 153
Broiled Tomatoes, Romano, '80 42
Broiled Tomatoes with Dill Sauce, '80 161
Broiled Tomatoes with Mushroom Sauce, '81 103
Broil, Tomato-English Pea, '83 192
Bruschetta, Caper-and-Olive, '00 276
Bruschetta, Roasted Pepper-Tomato, '02 213
Burgers, Stuffed Southwestern-Style, '99 201
Butterbeans, Bacon, and Tomatoes, '96 36; '00 184
Butter, Tomato, '86 128
Butter, Tomato-Curry-Orange, '93 159
Cabbage and Tomatoes, '83 104
Cabbage and Tomatoes, Tasty, '86 72
Cabbage, Creole, '00 105
Cacciatore, Chicken, '86 42
Cacciatore, Hearty Chicken, '02 269
Canned Flavored Tomatoes, '95 217
Canning Tomatoes, '80 128; '85 106
Caponata, '98 50
Caponata alla Siciliana, '02 269
Casserole, Corn and Tomato, '81 127
Casserole, Corn-and-Tomato, '84 145
Casserole, Eggplant-and-Tomato, '83 187
Casserole, Light Italian, '03 198
Casserole, Saucy Potato-Tomato, '79 46
Casserole, Scalloped Tomato, '88 144
Casserole, Zucchini-and-Tomato, '88 265
Catsup, Spicy Tomato, '83 182
Cauliflower au Gratin, '99 59
Cheese Herbed-Topped Tomatoes, '86 108
Cheese Sauce over Toast, Tomatoes with, '88 159
Cheese-Topped Tomatoes, '81 160
Cheesy Puff-Top Tomatoes, '86 187
Cherry. *See also* **TOMATOES/Dried.**
   Basil Butter, Squash and Cherry Tomatoes in, '98 328
   Bites, Tomato, '84 80
   Brown Butter Sauce, Cherry Tomatoes in, '81 168
   Caviar Tomatoes, '91 12
   Cheesy Cherry Tomatoes, '83 135
   Green Beans with Cherry Tomatoes, '86 177
   Herbed Cherry Tomatoes, '82 128
   Pasta, Herbed Cherry Tomatoes over, '95 229
   Rockefeller, Tomatoes, '97 169
   Rum, Cherry Tomatoes with, '83 192
   Salad, Cherry Tomato, '87 156
   Salad, Cherry Tomato-Caper, '00 140; '02 32
   Sautéed Roma Tomatoes, '92 338
   Stuffed Cherry Tomatoes, '84 160; '88 95, 212; '92 25
   Stuffed Cherry Tomatoes, Crab-, '82 289; '88 78
   Stuffed Cherry Tomatoes, Cucumber-, '88 262
   Stuffed Cherry Tomatoes, Tuna-, '89 214
Chicken, Creamy Tomato-Stuffed, '04 16
Chicken Mediterranean, '01 17
Chicken, Tomato-Baked, '81 281; '82 30
Chicken with Tomatoes and Sausage, '97 266
Chili, Chilly Night, '99 317
Chili in a Biscuit Bowl, '98 224
Chutney, Chicken Bites with Sweet-Hot Tomato, '00 309
Chutney, Tomato, '99 143

Chutney, Tomato-Apple, '84 180
Cocktail, Tomato, '83 M203
Cocktail, Tomato-Clam, '87 252
Cocktail, Tomato Juice, '79 212; '83 230; '90 12
Cocktail, Tomato-Orange Juice, '83 169
Cocktail, Zesty Tomato Juice, '83 289
Couscous, Tabbouleh, '97 103; '02 200
Crackers, Tomato-Blue Cheese, '02 213
Cream, Tomato, '94 70
Creole, Okra, '02 234
Creole-Style Tomatoes-and-Corn, '84 142
Crêpes, Southwestern Cornbread, '98 42
Croissants, BLT, '93 158
Crostini, Festive, '99 M325
Crostini, Feta-Tomato, '92 159
Crostini, Tomato, '99 230
Crostini, Tomato-and-Goat Cheese, '04 168
Delight, Tomato-Pea, '84 196
Dip, Bacon-and-Tomato, '90 147
Dip, Fiesta, '96 212
Dip, Steamed Asparagus with Tomato-Basil, '00 69; '04 53
Dressing, Fresh Tomato, '00 182
Dressing, Fresh Tomato Salad, '83 193
Dressing, Garden Salad with Tomato-Cream Cheese, '79 173
Dressing, Spicy Tomato, '03 143
Dressing, Tomato-Honey French, '81 105
Dried
   Cheese Balls with Sun-Dried Tomatoes, '94 317
   Cheesecake, Sun-Dried Tomato, '03 118
   Cherry Tomatoes, Marinated Dried, '93 23
   Chicken, Undercover, '97 64
   Dip, Cottage Cheese Sun-Dried Tomato, '93 13
   Elephant Ears Provençale, Baby, '00 87
   Fettuccine, Chicken and Dried Tomatoes over, '98 233
   Focaccia, Dried Tomato, '94 65
   Focaccia, Fast Rosemary-Dried Tomato, '98 53
   Goat Cheese, Dried Tomato Mock, '97 105
   Goat Cheese with Sun-Dried Tomatoes and Rosemary, '93 175
   Hummus, Creamy Dried Tomato, '95 284
   Mayonnaise, Dried Tomato, '98 144
   Meat Loaf with Sun-Dried Tomatoes and Herbs, '92 192
   Pesto, Dried Tomato, '90 204; '94 249; '01 62
   Pesto, Dried Tomato-Basil, '04 101
   Pizza, Shrimp-and-Dried Tomato, '97 49
   Salad, Spinach and Sun-Dried Tomato, '93 250
   Sandwiches, Dried Tomato-and-Basil, '99 274
   Sauce, Dried Tomato, '99 135
   Sauce, Dried Tomato Spaghetti, '90 202
   Soup, Dried Tomato-Cream, '90 203
   Spread and Bacon, Cream Cheese-and-Olive Biscuits with Sun-Dried Tomato, '02 313
   Spread, Dried Tomato-Cheese, '90 204
   Spread, Tri-Flavored Cream Cheese, '98 134
   Tart, Dried Tomato-Cheese, '90 203
   Torte, Tomato-Cheese, '97 49; '00 72
   Vinaigrette, Couscous Salad with Dried Tomato, '96 244
   Vinaigrette, Dried Tomato, '93 272
Dumplings, Tomato, '88 144; '97 209
Eggplant Parmigiana, '01 310
Eggs Benedict, Bacon-and-Tomato, '87 195
Eggs, Layered, '96 97
Eggs Oso Grande, '98 279
Enchiladas, Enticing, '99 57
Enchiladas, Healthy Chicken, '02 19
Fettuccine with Shrimp and Tomatoes, '96 198
Fire-and-Ice Tomatoes, '87 92; '03 183
Flank Steak, Tomato-Stuffed, '97 49
Fried Herb Tomatoes, '88 144

Fried Red Tomatoes, '81 102
Fried Ripe Tomatoes, '81 168
Fried Ripe Tomatoes with Gravy, '82 180
Fried Tomatoes, Pan-, '02 67
Fried Tomatoes with Bacon, Saucy, '81 210
Fried Tomatoes with Gravy, '86 211
Gazpacho-Stuffed Endive, '95 287
Gnocchi with Olive Oil, Tomato, and Parmesan, '04 47
Grape Tomatoes, Green Beans with, '03 231
Gratin, Tomato-Zucchini, '95 171
Gravy, Southwestern, '99 34
Gravy, Spicy Tomato, '95 172
Gravy, Tomato, '93 18; '99 35; '00 216, 330; '02 17, 33
Gravy, Tomato-and-Crabmeat Cream, '04 165
Greek Tomatoes, '98 173
Green
   Baked Green Tomatoes, Herb-, '85 214
   Chutney, Green Tomato-Cranberry, '00 140
   Curried Green Tomatoes, '93 138
   Fried Green Tomato Casserole, Stuffed, '04 145
   Fried Green Tomato Cheeseburgers, '94 138
   Fried Green Tomatoes, '79 123; '80 178; '81 210; '85 214
   "Fried" Green Tomatoes, '89 174
   Fried Green Tomatoes, '95 171; '98 172; '03 173
   Fried Green Tomatoes, Blue Willow, '99 143
   Fried Green Tomatoes, Kentucky Bibb Salad with, '01 121
   Fried Green Tomatoes with Roasted Red Pepper Rémoulade and Goat Cheese, '04 144
   Fried Green Tomato Napoleons, '99 230
   Fried Green Tomato Sandwiches, '04 145
   Fried Green Tomato Stacks, '02 184
   Fried Okra and Green Tomatoes, '93 160; '01 325
   Grilled Summer Squash and Tomatoes, '99 144
   Gumbo, Green Tomato, '04 314
   Hot Tomatoes, '93 138
   Italian-Sauced Green Tomatoes, '85 214
   Jam, Green Tomato, '79 121
   Jam, Green Tomato-Blueberry, '01 140
   Marinated Green Tomatoes, '03 139
   Marmalade, Green Tomato, '01 140
   Okra and Green Tomatoes, '79 160
   Oven-Fried Green Tomatoes, '82 107; '91 122
   Pickled Green Tomatoes, '99 143
   Pickles, Green Tomato, '87 134; '01 141
   Pie Filling, Green Tomato, '01 141
   Pie, Green Tomato, '79 195; '01 141
   Pudding, Green Tomato-Tomatillo-Corn, '04 103
   Relish, Green Tomato, '96 168; '98 124
   Relish, Green Tomato Sweet, '93 136
   Salsa, Peachy Green Tomato, '99 143
   Spread, Green Tomato Sandwich, '95 172
Green Beans, Tomato-Feta, '99 59
Green Beans with Tomatoes, '85 137
Grilled Okra and Tomatoes, '98 124
Grilled Tomatoes, '85 158; '99 173
Grilled Tomatoes, Cheesy, '79 150
Grilled Tomatoes with Basil Vinaigrette, '97 168
Grilled Yellow Squash and Tomatoes, '00 102
Grits, Hot Tomato, '95 171; '01 131
Grits, Tomato, '03 199
Grits Wedges, Southwestern, '04 332
Grouper, Guadalajara, '98 17
Guacamole, Margarita, '97 167
"Guacamole" with Cumin Crisps, Green Goddess, '02 205
Herbed Tomatoes, '81 102; '82 49; '83 173
Herbed Tomato Slices, '89 173
Hoppin' John Waffle Stack, '04 19
Hush Puppies, Creole, '98 43
Hush Puppies, Green Onion-Tomato, '97 84

Hush Puppies, Tomato-Onion, '91 201
Italian Tomatoes, Cold, '99 173
Journey Cakes, Tomato, Parmesan, and Kalamata
    Olive, '04 99
Juice, Homemade Tomato, '81 50
Juice, Spicy Tomato, '85 189
Kale with Tomato and Onion, '92 244
Kale with Tomatoes, Spicy, '99 243
Lentils, Tex-Mex, '99 288
Lima and Tomato Combo, Hot, '83 219
Macaroni and Cheese, Spicy Tomato, '03 68
Mahimahi, Middle Eastern, '96 92
Marinade, Bright Tomato, '88 176
Marinara Vinaigrette, '94 64
Marinated Green Beans with Tomatoes, Olives, and
    Feta, '03 163
Marinated Tomatoes with Basil and Balsamic
    Vinegar, '04 140
Marmalade, Tomato, '00 170
Mayonnaise, Tomato-Basil, '00 136
Medley, Okra-Corn-Tomato, '81 159
Medley, Tomato, '81 159
Melts, Tomato-Cheese-Bacon, '99 72
Mexicorn, '96 189
Muffins, Tomato Corn, '81 137
Mussels Marinara, '00 283
Mustard, Green Beans and Tomatoes with, '87 83
Mustard Tomatoes, Zippy, '86 M226
Okra and Tomatoes, '80 185; '81 139; '92 215;
    '98 286
Okra and Tomatoes, Fresh, '81 M165; '87 89
Okra Caponata, '97 157
Okra, Corn, and Tomatoes, '95 203
Okra-Tomato Combo, '83 157
Okra, Tomatoes and, '86 170; '87 164; '00 182
Okra, Tomatoes with, '85 106
Omelet, Farmer's Oven-Baked, '03 204
Onions, Baked Sweet, '98 130
Paella, Shortcut, '01 309
Parmesan Tomatoes, '80 161
Pastas. *See also* **TOMATOES/Sauces.**
    Asparagus, Tomatoes, and Shrimp, Garlicky Pasta
        with, '95 82
    Basil Pasta, Tomato-, '94 204
    Caribbean Tomato Pasta, '93 201
    Fettuccine, Chicken-and-Tomatoes over, '90 204
    Fresh Tomatoes and Basil, Pasta with, '98 233
    Garlic Pasta, Tomato-, '94 177
    Herb-and-Tomato Pasta, '96 122
    Italian Pasta, Weeknight, '03 48
    Italian Tomato Pasta, '93 201
    Late-Night Pasta Chez Frank, '95 228
    Macaroni, Cheese, and Tomatoes, '95 213
    Manicotti, Cheesy Sausage-and-Tomato, '03 257
    Manicotti, Ground Beef-and-Tomato, '03 257
    Penne with Pancetta, '00 51
    Primavera, Tomato-Pasta, '86 209
    Quick Pasta and Tomatoes, '92 180
    Rotelle, Chicken and Tomato with, '87 108
    Shrimp-Tomato Pasta, '98 172
    Southwestern Tomato Pasta, '93 201
    Spaghetti, All-in-One, '98 295
    Spaghetti with Tomatoes and Garlic, '91 47
    Summer Pasta, '04 223
    Tortellini, Creamy Tomato Pesto Dip with,
        '00 196
    Toss, Tomato-Olive Pasta, '86 209
Pesto, Bow-Tie, '94 231
Pesto, Tomatoes, '86 150
Pie, Tomato, '88 198; '97 249; '02 172
Pita Pockets, BLT in, '93 158
Pizza, Breakfast, '00 193
Pizza, Greek Eggplant, Tomato, and Feta, '01 312
Pizza, Nutty Pesto, '97 267

Pizza, Sicilian, '01 125
Pizzas, Roasted Potato, '99 16
Pork Chops and Rice, Savannah, '00 236
Pork Loin, Marinated, '01 331
Potato Boats, Southwestern, '96 33
Preserves, Tomato, '98 214
Provençal, Tomatoes, '82 181
Puffs, Spinach-Artichoke-Tomato, '95 284
Puree, Seared Sea Scallops with Tomato, '97 201
Puree, Seasoned Tomato, '83 182
Quesadillas, Bacon-Jalapeño-Tomato, '95 240
Quesadillas with Chipotle Salsa, Chicken-and-Brie,
    '99 311
Quiche, Asparagus-Tomato, '88 198
Quiche, Tomato Florentine, '04 332
Red Beans and Couscous, '99 22
Red Rice, '00 289
Red Rice and Ham, '00 289
Refresher, Tomato, '81 94; '83 318
Refried Beans, Easy, '99 57
Relish, Easy Tomato, '80 126
Relish, End-of-the-Garden, '80 179
Relish, Flank Steak with Tomato-Olive, '03 210
Relish, Hot, '01 123
Relish, Sweet White Corn-and-Tomato, '00 130
Relish, Tomato, '85 188
Rice, Blended, '96 68
Rice, Charleston, '97 310
Rice, Red, '92 235; '97 138
Rice, Tomato, '02 169
Rice with Tomatoes and Basil, '95 232
Risotto, Tomato-Basil, '95 269
Rollups, Mediterranean, '00 277
Roma Tomatoes, Sautéed, '92 338
Ropa Vieja, '98 20
Rose, Tomato, '82 51; '85 338
Salads
    Artichoke-Stuffed Tomato Salad, '82 101
    Artichoke-Tomato Salad, '82 239
    Asparagus and Tomatoes, Fresh, '94 162
    Asparagus and Tomatoes with Herb Vinaigrette,
        '99 56
    Asparagus Salad, Tomato-, '92 79
    Aspic, Bloody Mary-Tomato, '81 77
    Aspic, Chicken in Tomato, '84 190
    Aspic, Chili Sauce Tomato, '85 252
    Aspic, Classic Tomato, '91 229
    Aspic, Gazpacho, '96 65
    Aspic, Herbed Tomato, '81 73
    Aspic, Layered Tomato, '90 99
    Aspic, Light Tomato, '85 83
    Aspic, Ranch Tomato, '83 218
    Aspic, Spicy Tomato, '81 40; '89 288
    Aspic, Tangy Tomato, '83 124
    Aspic, Tomato-Artichoke, '84 320; '86 92
    Aspic, Tomato-Crab, '85 287
    Aspic with Shrimp, Tomato, '79 241
    Avocado Salad, Tomato-, '86 74
    Bacon-Lettuce-Mozzarella-and-Tomato Salad,
        '98 209
    Basil-and-Tomato Couscous Salad, '94 175
    Basil-Mozzarella Salad, Tomato-, '95 171
    BLT Salad, Layered, '01 96
    Bread Salad, Italian BLT, '03 90
    Charred Tomato Salad, '01 158
    Chile-Tomato Salad, Spicy, '88 121
    Citrus Marinade, Summer Salad with, '92 133
    Coleslaw with Tomatoes, '80 34
    Congealed Lemon-Tomato Salad, '89 178
    Cottage Cheese Salad in Tomatoes, '86 208
    Cottage-Tomato Salad, '85 163
    Crab-Stuffed Tomato Salad, '80 148
    Cucumber-and-Tomato Salad, '01 127
    Cucumber and Tomato Salad, Dilled, '81 153

Cucumber-Onion Salad, Tomato-, '81 239
Cucumber on Tomatoes, Dilled, '84 142
Cucumber Salad, Tomato-, '86 218; '92 199
Cucumber Salad with Yogurt-Herb Dressing,
    Tomato-, '92 96
Cucumber Summer Salad, Tomato-and-,
    '93 141
Cucumber-Tomato Salad, '90 144
Endive-Tomato Starburst Salad, '93 323
Feta Salad, Tomato-, '81 246; '91 168
Flower Salad, Tomato, '89 128
Frozen Tomato Salad, '84 52
Grape Tomatoes with Capers, '01 329
Green Bean Salad, Tomato-and-, '97 162
Grilled Tomato, Bell Pepper, and Portobello
    Salad, '98 211
Gruyère-Basil Salad, Tomato-, '99 172
Guacamole-Tomato Salad, '81 302
Herbed Pasta-and-Tomato Salad, '92 144
Herbed Tomatoes, '83 173
Herb Salad, Tomato-, '89 220
Italian Dressing, Tomato, Onion, and Cucumber
    in, '81 83
Italiano, Tomatoes, '88 29
Italian Tomato Salad, '01 124
Layered Salad, Tex-Mex, '03 201
Lemon Dressing, Tomato Slices with, '87 167
Lima Bean-Tomato Salad, '85 137
Marinated Cucumber-Tomato Salad, '02 167
Marinated Salad, '83 170
Marinated Salsa Tomatoes, '82 164
Marinated Sliced Tomatoes, '92 173
Marinated Tomato and Brie Salad, '95 95
Marinated Tomato-and-Cucumber Salad, '92 216
Marinated Tomatoes, '85 156, 163; '89 174, 202
Marinated Tomato Slices, '82 134; '83 193
Mexican Dinner Salad, '98 330
Mold, Tangy Tomato, '79 74
Mozzarella Salad, Tomato-, '89 220
Mozzarella-Tomato-Basil Salad, Fresh, '93 131
Mozzarella-Tomato Basil Salad, Fresh, '02 110
Napoleon, Tomato, '00 182
Olive Spread, Tomatoes with, '85 114
Oregano Tomatoes, '83 145
Pasta Salad, Tomato-, '97 M160
Petal Salad, Tomato, '79 88
Potato Salad with Cucumbers and Tomatoes,
    '03 92
Red Onion Salad, Tomato-, '04 181
Red, White, and Green Salad, '90 18
Relish Salad, Tomato, '83 111
Ring, Tangy Tomato, '84 164
Ring, Tomato-Vegetable, '81 302
Roasted Tomato-and-Pepper Salad, '01 196
Ruby-and-Emerald Salad, '85 79
Stuffed Tomato Salad, Oriental-, '82 101
Summer Tomato Salad, '94 201
Summer Tomato Treat, '79 143
Trout-and-Tomato Salad with Black Pepper
    Vinaigrette, '98 284
Tuna with Warm Tomato Salad, '97 179
Vidalia-Tomato Salad, '84 65
Vinaigrette, Marinara, '94 64
Vinaigrette, Okra-Corn-and-Tomato, '90 173
Vinaigrette, Tomato-Basil, '87 89
Vinaigrette, Tomatoes, '84 106
Watercress-Tomato Salad, '85 132
Salsas
    Artichoke-Tomato Salsa, '96 182
    Avocado Salsa, Tomato-, '94 83
    Basil Salsa, Pan-Fried Roughy with Tomato-,
        '99 123
    Black Bean Salsa, Chunky, '03 25
    Chunky Salsa, '86 130; '90 206

TOMATOES, Salsas
(continued)

Corn, Pepper, and Tomato Salsa, Yellowfin Tuna with, '94 164
Fresh Salsa, '95 42; '00 59; '04 274
Fresh Tomato Salsa, '91 182; '95 181; '01 249
Hot Salsa, '98 135
Mango Salsa, '98 232
Mango Salsa, Seared Scallops with Tomato-, '95 122
One-Minute Salsa, '95 93
Party Salsa, Quick, '03 292
Peachy Green Tomato Salsa, '99 143
Picante, Salsa, '04 41
Quick Party Salsa, '04 146
Red Salsa, '90 172
Roasted Tomato Salsa, '95 64
Salsa, '88 147; '97 171; '01 273; '03 95
Santa Fe Salsa, Zesty, '03 198
Simple Salsa, '01 60
Strawberry Salsa, Balsamic, '02 86
Summer Salsa, '98 172
Texas Salsa, '96 160
Three Tomato Salsa, '93 138
Tomato Salsa, '87 120; '96 15; '02 118
Warm-and-Spicy Salsa, '99 279
Yellow Tomato Salsa, '87 122
Sandwiches, Bacon, Cheese, and Tomato, '84 14
Sandwiches, Curried BLT, '93 158
Sandwiches, Eggplant, Tomato, and Feta, '98 106
Sandwiches, Grilled Bacon, Cheese, and Tomato, '97 170
Sandwiches, Italian BLT, '02 230
Sandwiches, Miniature Tomato, '00 130
Sandwiches, Open-Face Crab Tomato, '81 29
Sandwiches, Super Open-Faced, '97 52
Sandwiches, Tomato, Swiss, and Bacon, '04 140
Sandwich, Floyd's Favorite Tomato, '95 172; '00 182
Sandwich with Tomato, Avocado, and Bacon, Grilled Four-Cheese, '00 199
Sauces
Asparagus with Tomato Sauce, '83 46
Barbecue Sauce, Green, '02 183
Basic Tomato Sauce, '04 145
Basil Cream, Tomato-, '99 240
Basil Sauce, Tomato, '91 85
Basil Sauce, Tomato-, '92 180; '96 220; '97 144; '02 182
Basil-Tomato Sauce, '92 198; '93 25, 48, 65
Caper Sauce, Turkey Cutlets with Tomato-, '91 61
Chili Sauce, '94 287
Chunky Tomato Sauce, '95 264
Cocktail Sauce, Southwestern, '98 46
Coulis, Fresh Tomato, '93 230
Cream Sauce, Angel Hair Pasta with Tomato, '93 292
Cream Sauce, Linguine with Tomato-, '86 158
Cream, Tomato, '94 70
Creamy Tomato Sauce, '93 71
Creole Sauce, '98 98
Cucumber Sauce, Tomato-, '98 45
Dried Tomato Sauce, '96 220
Fish in Tomato Sauce, '85 75
Fresh Tomato Sauce, '83 224; '87 171
Fresh Tomato Sauce over Basil Pasta, '93 176
Fresh Tomato Sauce, Spaghetti with, '96 135
Fresh Tomato Sauce with Linguine, '02 213
Gingered Tomato Sauce, Spicy, '96 220
Green Beans in Tomato Sauce, '01 84
Green Chiles, Tomato Sauce with, '81 196
Hamburgers with Tomato Sauce, '81 73

Herbed Fresh Tomato Sauce, '85 M151
Herb Sauce, Tomato-and-, '00 125
Hot Sauce, Kleberg, '94 28
Italian-Style Tomato Sauce, '87 182
Italian Tomato Sauce, '82 M68; '92 57; '03 202
Italian Tomato Sauce for Spaghetti, '81 134
Lemon Sauce, Salmon with Almonds and Tomato-, '04 23
Light Tomato Sauce, '97 246
Marinara Sauce, '94 64; '99 266
Meat Sauce, Italian, '01 160
Pesto, Bow-Tie, '94 231
Pesto, Tomatoes, '86 150
Pico de Gallo, '96 227; '97 141; '98 87; '02 168, 306; '04 32, 61, 89, 311
Pintos, Texas Souper, '98 51
Pizza Sauce, Traditional, '95 267
Ranchero Sauce, '96 168
Red Pepper-Tomato Sauce, '93 59
Red Sauce and Meatballs, '04 17
Refrigerator Tomato Sauce, '85 188
Roasted Garlic-Tomato Sauce, '97 46
Seasoned Tomato Sauce, '83 150
Spicy Tomato Sauce, '84 294; '88 19
Spinach Tortellini with Tomato Sauce, '88 302
Sweet-and-Sour Tomato Sauce, Stuffed Chicken Breasts with, '01 120
Tarragon-Tomato Sauce, '84 131
Tomato Sauce, '85 193, 244; '87 249; '88 116; '97 96, 269; '99 270; '04 43
Vegetable-Tomato Sauce, Turkey Patties in, '87 18
Vermicelli with Tomato Sauce, '83 164
Zesty Tomato Sauce, '98 176
Sautéed Tomato with Fresh Mozzarella, '00 163
Sauté, Spicy Okra-Tomato-Corn, '04 327
Sauté, Tomato-Pepper, '84 142
Sauté, Tomato-Spinach, '04 23
Scalloped Tomatoes, '84 142; '00 183
Scalloped Tomato Slices, '81 168
Scallops, Ginger, '99 177
Sesame Tomatoes, '84 142
Shrimp Creole, '03 109
Shrimp, Daufuskie, '00 174
Shrimp with Feta Cheese, '00 221
Sipper, Peppy Tomato, '94 227
Sipper, Spicy Tomato, '86 229
Skillet, Cabbage-and-Tomato, '86 110
Skillet Tomatoes, '81 108
Skillet, Zucchini-Tomato, '93 206
Sloppy Joe Cups, '98 204
Snow Peas and Tomatoes, '83 111
Snow Peas and Tomatoes, Basil, '88 M185
Soufflé, Italian Pizzaola, '98 232
Soups
Appetizer Tomato Soup, '86 258
Bacon, Lettuce, and Tomato Soup, '91 207
Beef-Wild Rice Soup, Tomato-, '04 42
Bisque, Make-Ahead Tomato-Basil, '93 322
Bisque, Tomato-Basil, '00 49; '02 230
Bisque, Tomato-Shrimp, '86 66
Black, White, and Red All Over Soup, '95 126
Bouillon, New Year's Tomato, '94 24
Bouillon, Tomato, '83 8
Carrot-and-Tomato Soup, Cream of, '94 176
Celery Soup, Tomato-, '83 M58
Chilled Roasted Pepper and Tomato Soup, '01 128
Chilled Tomato Soup, '82 155
Chowder, Tomato-Clam, '84 251
Cioppino, Gulf Coast, '94 102
Cold Tomato Soup, '88 160
Consommé, Tomato, '88 250

Cream of Tomato Soup with Lemon Basil, '96 124
Cream of Tomato Soup with Parmesan Cheese, '86 161
Cream Soup, Refreshing Tomato, '79 172
Cream Soup, Tomato-Basil, '97 198
Creamy Tomato Soup, '83 267; '86 258
Easy Tomato Soup, '84 14
French Market Soup, '94 317
Fresh Tomato Soup, '83 140
Gazpacho, '00 118; '01 157; '02 130
Gazpacho, Classic Tomato, '99 172
Gazpacho, Tomato-Avocado-Corn, '97 182
Gazpacho, Yellow Tomato, '04 158
Herbed Yogurt and Parmesan Toasts, Tomato Soup with, '96 66
Hot Tomato Juice Soup, '86 302
Iced Tomato Soup, '79 170
Italian Soup, Chunky, '99 20
Mexican Tomato Soup, Icy-Spicy, '90 155
New Year's Day Soup, '00 25
Onion Soup, Tomato-, '04 243
Plus, Tomato Soup, '88 170
Pork Rind Soup, '03 33
Potage, Tomato, '79 250
Pumpkin-Tomato Soup, '86 291
Rice Soup, Tomato-and-, '85 24
Roasted Garlic-and-Basil Tomato Soup, '01 17
Sausage-Tortellini Soup, '99 20
Savory Tomato Soup, '94 91
Sour Cream-Topped Tomato Soup, '80 246
Summer Tomato Soup, '79 130
Tomato Soup, '81 236; '83 44; '89 217
Tortellini Soup, '98 68; '00 14
Tortilla Soup, '98 291; '00 98, 110
Vegetable Soup, Tomato-, '81 M177; '86 9
Spaghetti, Country-Style, '02 25
Spicy Tomato Warm-Up, '95 328
Spinach-Topped Tomatoes, '88 265; '94 321
Spread, Fiery Tomato-Cheese, '87 196
Spread, Home-Style Sandwich, '80 179
Spread, Peppered Cheese, '01 123
Spread, Tomato, '94 123
Spread, Tomato-Cheddar, '01 321
Spread, Tomato-Cheese, '81 157
Squash and Tomato Bake, '95 180
Squash, Beans, and Tomatoes, '83 148
Squash, Tomato, '86 111
Stack-Ups, Jiffy Tomato, '80 161
Stewed Tomatoes, '83 182; '00 183
Stewed Tomatoes and Greens, '95 234
Stew, Greek Garbanzo, '02 43
Stew, Turkey-Tomato, '90 279
Stir-Fried Sweet Peppers with Tomatoes, '93 207
Stir-Fry, Italian, '92 126
Stir-Fry, Tomato-Zucchini, '80 158
Stir-Fry, Zucchini-and-Tomato, '85 108
Strata, Tomato-Bacon, '03 100
Strata, Tomato-Cheese, '81 209
Stuffed
Avocado-Stuffed Tomatoes, '82 101
Bacon-and-Egg-Stuffed Tomatoes, '80 162
Baked Spinach Tomatoes, '90 92
Baked Stuffed Tomatoes, '88 162
Baked Tangy Tomatoes, '81 168
Baked Tomatoes with Corn, '80 161
Bean-Stuffed Tomatoes, '84 34
Broccoli-Stuffed Tomatoes, '83 136; '93 216
Buffet Tomatoes, '82 180
Cheese-Stuffed Tomatoes, '91 69
Cheesy Stuffed Tomatoes, '80 161
Chile-Cheese Stuffed Tomatoes, '94 141
Cold Stuffed Tomatoes, '80 100
Cornbread-Stuffed Tomatoes, '97 169

Corn-Stuffed Tomatoes, '82 270
Crab-and-Avocado Stuffed Tomatoes, '94 141
Cups, Turkey-Tomato, '84 119
Curry Sauce, Stuffed Tomatoes with, '97 170
Delights, Tomato, '81 140
Easy Stuffed Tomatoes, '82 264
Eggs-and-Tomato Slices, Stuffed, '84 152
Green Bean Salad in Tomatoes, '01 181
Herbed Tomatoes, '82 49
Homestead Tomatoes, Stuffed, '96 87
Hot Tomatoes, '93 138
Italian-Style Tomatoes, '97 169
Maque Chou Stuffed Tomatoes, '87 89
Mushroom-Stuffed Tomatoes, '86 218; '96 106
Parmesan-Stuffed Tomatoes, '92 182
Provençal Tomatoes, '98 267
Puffs, Tomato Cheese, '81 48
Sausage-Stuffed Tomatoes, '80 47
Scalloped Tomatoes, Stuffed, '90 29
Sea Slaw, Tomatoes Stuffed with, '89 96
Spinach-Feta Stuffed Tomatoes, '04 285
Spinach-Stuffed Baked Tomatoes, '86 14
Spinach-Stuffed Tomatoes, '89 203; '93 281
Squash-Stuffed Tomatoes, '82 102
Stuffed Tomatoes, '83 252; '96 82
Tuna-Mac in Tomatoes, '87 188
Tuna Pasta, Stuffed Tomato with, '88 54
Turkey Stuffed Tomatoes, '94 140
Vegetable Stuffed Tomatoes, '94 141
Veracruz Tomatoes, '97 169
Walnut-Rice Stuffing, Tomatoes with, '91 102
Swiss Chard with Tomatoes, '83 36
Swiss Steak Monterey, '99 23
Tabbouleh, '99 175
Tapas, Two-Tomato, '00 308
Tart, Fresh Tomato, '95 170
Tart, Herbed Tomato, '96 94
Tarts, Mini Tomato-Pesto, '02 108
Tart, Tomato, '03 158
Tart, Tomato-Basil, '98 132
Tart, Tomato-Leek-Bacon, '03 325
Tart, Tomato-Pesto, '00 195; '02 108
Tenderloin, Stuffed Tuscany, '99 269
Toasts, Tomato-Basil, '01 254
Topping, Tomato-Basil, '04 327
Venison and Tomatoes, '85 270
Vinaigrette, Tomato-Basil, '99 288
Vinegar, Tomato-Herb, '94 200
Welsh Rarebit with Tomatoes and Bacon, '92 M159
Yellow Squash, Tomato-Stuffed, '00 42
Zippy 'Maters, '99 172
Zucchini and Tomato with Herbs, '92 182
TOPPINGS. *See also* **FROSTINGS, GLAZES,**
    PESTOS, RELISHES, SALSAS, SAUCES,
    SYRUPS.
  Savory
    Almond-Garlic Streusel, '95 159
    Almonds, Sweet-and-Spicy, '96 274; '01 42
    Asian Dressing, '00 93
    Avocado Topping, '93 309; '94 96
    Biscuit Topping, '86 157, 265
    Black Pepper-Pineapple Vinaigrette, '97 181
    Blue Cheese Burger Topping, '93 218
    Breadcrumb Topping, '02 233
    Butter-Pecan Topping, '95 158
    Catsup Topping, '81 170
    Cereal Topping, Crunchy, '96 216
    Cheese Topping, '86 233
    Chestnuts, Braised, '02 272
    Chili Topping, '94 22
    Cilantro-Lime Cream, '98 129
    Citrus-Herb Dressing, '04 182
    Cornbread Topping, '01 215. 298
    Crabmeat Topping, '91 64

Crumble Mix, Asian, '96 327
Eggs and Cheese, '95 165
Garlic Cream, Asparagus with, '00 71
Ginger-Lime Cream, '95 227
Grecian Skillet Rib Eyes, '96 234
Guacamole, '96 170
Guacamole Aïoli, '04 314
Guac, Baine's, '98 88
Horseradish Cream, '90 96; '00 277
Jalapeño-Cilantro Dressing, Creamy, '04 311
Ketchup, Christmas, '97 254
Ketchup, Hoisin, '94 138
Ketchup, Sweet-Hot, '03 139; '04 178
Lemon Cream, '03 213
Lime Sour Cream, '04 324
Marmalade Cream, '03 230
Miso-Ginger Dressing, Creamy, '02 144
Mushrooms, Garlic and, '95 165
Nutty Topping, '86 16
Olive Salad, '00 335
Olive Salad, Doodles, '94 35
Olive Salad, Italian, '94 35
Orange Dressing, '97 129
Parmesan Crisps, '03 142
Peach Ketchup, '95 306
Peach Ketchup, Spicy, '03 139
Peach Topping, '94 22
Pecans, Smoky, '01 168
Pecans, Spicy, '02 304
Pecans, Sweet-and-Spicy, '00 81; '03 178
Pecan Topping, '94 36
Pepper Topping, Rainbow, '90 117
Pico de Gallo, '96 227; '97 141; '98 87;
    '04 32, 61, 89, 311
Pico de Gallo, Mango, '04 318
Pimiento Topping, '83 93
Potato Topping, Mashed, '89 243
Red Curry-Coconut Cream, '00 197
Red Pepper Puree, '93 275; '00 241
Roasted Pepper Vinaigrette, '04 142
Roasted Red Bell Pepper Spread, '97 217
Roquefort Firecrackers, '97 19
Rum Cream, '98 271
Salad Mix, Muffy, '94 34
Salad Topping, Curry, '96 326
Sausage and Peppers, '95 165
Shrimp Topping, '93 291
Sour Cream Topping, Spicy, '95 15
Southwestern Dressing, '91 195
Sweet Potato Chips, '97 63
Tomato, Basil, and Cheese, '95 165
Tomato-Basil Topping, '04 327
Tomatoes, Marinated Green, '03 139
Top-Notch Toppings, '03 139
Tortilla Strips, '04 243
Turkey Mole, '03 18
Turkey-Vegetable Topping, '94 22
Vegetable Dip, Quick Creamy, '00 34
Vegetable Topping, '79 79
Vinaigrette, Warm Garlic, '00 324
Yogurt-Cheese Topping, '88 55
Sweet
  Almond Topping, '85 152; '86 200
  Apple-Nut Topping, '93 162
  Apples 'n' Pears, Saucy, '96 72
  Apple Topping, '89 107
  Apricot Flambé Topping, '98 127
  Bananas Hawaiian, '89 94
  Blackberries Chantilly, '99 130
  Blackberry Syrup, '99 131
  Bourbon Whipped Cream, '04 232
  Brown Sugar Topping, '81 162
  Candied Cream, '04 300
  Caramel Drizzle, '86 247

Chantilly Cream, '83 91
Chocolate Cream, '94 57
Chocolate Ganache, '97 282; '00 M72;
    '03 M286
Chocolate Ganache, Simple, '03 M212
Chocolate-Peanut Topping, '79 222
Cinnamon Crème, Apple Pie with Warm, '99 337
Cinnamon-Pecan Topping, '85 277
Coconut-Pecan Topping, '04 41
Cream Topping, Spicy, '85 177
Crème Chantilly, '91 297
Crème Chantilly, Gingered, '96 163
Crème Patissière, '83 225
Crumb Topping, '83 183; '88 216
Devonshire Cream, Mock, '81 288; '99 275
Firewater Cream, '00 161
Fruit Dressing, Nutty, '88 68
Fruit Fluff, Tropical, '88 68
Fruit Topping, '81 42; '87 225; '89 50; '03 145
Fruity Dessert Topping, '82 167
Ginger-Almond Topping, '01 215
Ginger Cream Topping, '84 312
Ginger-Molasses Whipped Cream, '03 297
Hazelnut Whipped Cream, '94 16
Honey Topping, '83 154
Hot Fudge Ice Cream Topping, '98 317
Hot Fudge Ice-Cream Topping, '02 109
Kahlúa Cream, '91 197
Key Lime Curd, '96 126
Lemon-Blueberry Cream, '92 153
Lemon Cream, '82 237; '04 300
Lemon Curd, '87 139; '94 315
Lemon-Pineapple Topping, '86 60
Lime-Rum Cream, '93 169
Macadamia-Fudge Topping, '01 278
Maple-Mint Cream, '04 33
Maple-Pecan Ice Cream Topping, '98 317
Mocha Cream, '94 47
Mocha Ganache, '04 M260
Nutty Topping, '85 256
Oat Crunch Topping, '89 108
Oatmeal Cookie Topping, '95 291
Orange-Mallow Cream, '94 295
Oranges in Grand Marnier, '95 142
Orange Topping, Whipped, '80 254
Orange Whipped Cream, '02 315
Paint, Egg Yolk, '86 322
Papaya Topping, '86 181
Pears, Sautéed, '03 195
Pear Whip, '89 94
Pecan Halves, Glazed, '02 295
Pineapple Topping, '86 239
Powdered Sugar Paints, '97 286
Praline Cream, '01 272
Raspberries, Spirited, '95 142
Raspberry Topping, '85 317
Rum Cream, '88 154
Rum Cream Topping, '80 255
Rumtopf, '95 142
Sour Cream Topping, '85 298; '86 120
Sticky Bun Toast Topper, '99 M72
Strawberry Cream, '88 153
Strawberry Topping, '86 32; '90 142
Streusel, '85 326
Streusel Topping, '88 154, M275; '94 280;
    '96 216; '01 214; '02 324; '03 195; '04 194
Sugar, Colored, '99 179
Sugared Almonds, '04 105
Sugars, Colored, '90 21; '00 61
Vanilla Cream, '81 248
Vanilla Cream Topping, '02 252
Whipped Cream Topping, '87 264; '89 154;
    '01 285; '03 320
Whipped Topping, Reduced-Calorie, '85 55

TOP-RATED MENU RECIPES
  Appetizers
      Almonds, Sweet-and-Spicy, '01 42
      Asparagus with Garlic Cream, '00 71
      Blue Cheese Logs, '04 53
      Cranberry-Cheese Box, '03 238
      Hot Browns, Baby, '03 238
      Parmesan Cheese Bites, '00 20
      Pecans, Sweet-and-Spicy, '01 20
      Pork Tenderloin with Mustard Sauce, '03 238
      Shrimp, Garlic-and-Rosemary, '04 52
      Shrimp Tartlets, '00 71
      Tomato-Cheese Torte, '00 72
  Apples, Minted, '00 21
  Apples, Spiced, '03 36
  Beverages
      Coffee, Maple, '01 130
      Cranberry Drink, Mulled, '03 36
      Hot Chocolate Deluxe, '00 33
      Slush, Lemon-Rum, '04 240
  Breads
      Biscuits, Quick Whipping Cream, '03 238
      Biscuits, Sweet Potato Angel, '01 42
      Crescent Twists, Pecan, '03 36
      Focaccia with Roasted Pepper Vinaigrette,
          Stuffed, '04 142
      Muffins, Blueberry-Streusel, '01 131
      Parmesan Bread, '00 54
      Rolls, Homemade Butter, '01 21
      Rolls, Sour Cream Yeast, '00 33
      Scones, Orange-Pecan, '01 72
      Waffles, Cornbread, '03 205
  Butter, Jalapeño-Pecan-Mustard, '03 205
  Desserts
      Brownies, Amaretto-Walnut, '04 142
      Cake, Best Carrot Sheet, '03 55
      Cake, Ginger Pound, '02 97
      Cheesecake with Strawberry Sauce, Key Lime,
          '03 55
      Cobbler, Apple-Gingerbread, '04 218
      Cookies, Ginger-Oatmeal Sorghum, '02 230
      Flan, Almond-Orange, '04 241
      Freeze, Grapefruit, '00 241
      Frosting, Cream Cheese, '03 55
      Ganache, Chocolate, '00 M72
      Glaze, Buttermilk, '03 55
      Ice Cream, Lemon, '00 55
      Ice Cream-Toffee Dessert, '04 82
      Ice Cream, Vanilla-Cinnamon, '01 195
      Petits Fours, Chocolate-Almond, '00 72
      Pie, Applesauce, '01 213
      Pie, Lemon Chess, '03 217
      Pie, Tiramisù Toffee Trifle, '04 195
      Pineapple with Vanilla-Cinnamon Ice Cream,
          Grilled, '01 195
      Pudding, Rich Black-and-White, '01 111
      Sauce, Strawberry, '03 55
      Sherbet, 1-2-3 Blackberry, '00 21
      Shortbread, Mocha-Chocolate, '04 173
      Shortbread, Raspberry, '02 33
      Tarts, Blackberry Pudding, '00 147
  Dressing, Honey-Mustard, '00 54
  Grits, Chile-Blue Cheese, '04 240
  Grits, Hot Tomato, '01 131
  Grits, Margaret's Creamy, '00 21
  Grits, Smoked Gouda, '04 173
  Grits, Stackable, '02 204
  Main Dishes
      Beef Fillets with Stilton-Portobello Sauce,
          '02 310
      Beef Tenderloin, Chutneyed, '00 320
      Beef Tenderloin with Henry Bain Sauce, '01 20;
          '04 52
      Burgers, Barbara's Big Juicy, '04 M178
      Casserole, Breakfast, '01 130
      Casserole, Brie-and-Sausage Breakfast, '03 36
      Chicken and Dumplings, '00 111
      Chicken, Buttermilk Baked, '01 212
      Chicken Cakes with Creole Sauce, '02 32
      Chicken, Glazed Roasted, '03 217
      Chicken Strips and Vegetables, Marinated, '00 54
      Enchiladas Verde, Chicken, '00 M240
      Ham with Bourbon Glaze, Baked, '01 M42
      Lamb Chops with Chipotle and Cilantro Oils,
          Grilled, '02 96
      Lamb Chops with Minted Apples, '00 20
      Lasagna, Ground Sirloin, '03 143
      Lasagna, Meatball, '03 142
      Omelet, Farmer's Oven-Baked, '03 204
      Omelet, Spinach, Cheddar, and Bacon, '03 204
      Pork Chops on Smoked Gouda Grits, Grilled
          Maple Chipotle, '04 172
      Pork Chops, Stuffed, '02 204
      Pork Chops with Apples, Balsamic, '03 204
      Pork Chops with Minted Apples, '00 21
      Pork, Honey-Roasted, '02 282
      Pork Medaillons in Mustard Sauce, '00 32
      Pork Tenderloins with Rosemary Pesto, Grilled,
          '04 82
      Quail, Chipotle-Marinated, '04 240
      Shrimp with Tropical Fruit Sauce, Grilled,
          '01 195
      Steak-and-Vegetable Kebabs, '04 218
      Steak, Chicken-Fried, '03 72
      Steaks, Peppered Rib-Eye, '00 146
      Trout Amandine, Classic, '01 110
      Vegetables with Penne Pasta, Spicy, '04 195
  Oil, Chipotle, '02 97
  Oil, Cilantro, '02 97
  Oranges, Grand, '01 131
  Parmesan Crisps, '03 142
  Pinto Beans, Mexican, '00 241
  Rice, Orphan's, '04 218
  Rice Pilaf, Lemon, '04 82
  Risotto, Onion, '02 97
  Risotto, Sweet Onion, '03 217
  Rub, Biltmore Dry, '00 20
  Salads and Salad Dressings
      Almond-Citrus Salad, '01 42
      Apple-Spinach Salad, '02 230
      Asparagus, Roasted-Beet, and Goat Cheese Salad,
          '02 96
      Asparagus Salad with Orange Vinaigrette,
          Grilled, '01 110
      Baby Blue Salad, '01 20
      Blue Cheese Dressing, '03 72
      Cherry Tomato-Caper Salad, '02 32
      Chicken-and-Fruit Salad, '01 178
      Goat Cheese Salad, Warm, '01 179
      Green Bean-Potato Salad, '04 142
      Green Bean, Walnut, and Feta Salad, '00 321
      Lettuce Wedges with Blue Cheese Dressing,
          Iceberg, '03 72
      Potato Salad, Lemon-Basil, '01 178
      Roasted Onion Salad, '03 142
      Slaw, Crispy Asian, '01 195
      Vegetable Salad, Grilled, '00 146
      Vinaigrette, Balsamic, '01 20
      Vinaigrette, Garlic, '03 142
      Vinaigrette, Orange-Raspberry, '01 178
      Vinaigrette, Sesame-Soy, '01 195
      Wild Rice-Chicken Salad, '01 72
  Sandwiches, Italian BLT, '02 230
  Sauces
      Creole Sauce, '02 32
      Mustard Sauce, '00 32
      Verde Sauce, '00 241
      Wine Reduction Sauce, '00 321
  Soups and Stews
      Cream of Pimiento Soup, '01 72
      Tomato-Basil Bisque, '02 230
      Tortilla Soup, '00 110
  Tapenade, '04 194
  Vegetables
      Asparagus with Tomato-Basil Dip, Steamed,
          '04 53
      Butterbeans, Bacon, and Tomatoes, '00 184
      Carrot-Pecan Casserole, '02 282
      Carrots, Apricot-Glazed, '01 212
      Carrot-Sweet Potato Puree, '00 32
      Corn, Buttermilk Fried, '00 184
      Corn, Skillet Creamed, '02 204
      Corn with Jalapeño-Lime Butter, Grilled, '04 178
      Green Beans with Caramelized Onion, '00 33
      Green Beans with Pimiento, Tangy, '01 21
      Greens, Edna's, '00 184
      Onion Pudding, Sweet, '02 310
      Potato Bake, Smoky Mashed, '01 21
      Potato Casserole, Three-Cheese Mashed, '03 72
      Potatoes, Roasted Garlic-Parmesan Mashed,
          '00 146
      Potatoes, Whipped Celery, '01 212
      Potato Trio, Roasted, '02 310
      Red Pepper Puree, '00 241
      Roasted Vegetables, '00 321
      Sugar Snap Peas, Lemon-Scented, '02 282
      Tomatoes, Grilled, '04 178
  Vinaigrette, Roasted Pepper, '04 142
TORTES. *See* **CAKES/Tortes.**
TORTILLAS. *See also* **BURRITOS,
      ENCHILADAS, FAJITAS,
      QUESADILLAS, TAMALES.**
  Appetizers, Tex-Mex Tortilla, '86 297
  Bake, Chicken Tortilla, '82 89
  Bake, Texas Tortilla, '94 285
  Baskets, Tortilla, '94 97
  Bites, Tortilla, '95 42
  Bites with Sesame-Soy Dipping Sauce, Tortilla,
      '02 145
  Buñuelos, '80 199
  Buñuelos, King-Size, '86 5
  Burgers, Tortilla, '94 138
  Campesina, Tortilla, '89 85
  Casserole, Cabin Mexican, '97 95
  Casserole, Chicken Tortilla, '81 166
  Casserole, El Dorado, '81 140
  Casserole, Hearty Tex-Mex Squash-Chicken,
      '03 107
  Casserole, King Ranch Chicken, '00 280
  Casserole, Light King Ranch Chicken, '04 57
  Casserole, Mexican, '00 280
  Casserole, Mexican Chicken, '82 143
  Chalupas, Bean, '83 313
  Chalupas, Chicken, '79 185
  Chalupas, Chicken-Olive, '81 227
  Chalupas, Texas Turkey, '80 196
  Cheese Tortilla Snack, Two-, '90 119
  Cheesy Tortillas, '81 62
  Chicken Acapulco, '84 32
  Chicken, King Ranch, '99 330
  Chicken-Tortilla Stack, Cheesy, '86 3
  Chicken Tostadas, '93 204
  Chilaquiles, '82 220
  Chilaquiles con Pollo, '81 66
  Chimichangas, '86 114
  Chimichangas, Apple, '95 43
  Chimichangas, Baked Spicy Beef, '97 319
  Chimichangas, Bean-and-Cheese, '01 16
  Chimichangas, Chicken, '98 95
  Chimichangas, Oven-Fried Beef, '92 124
  Chimichangas, Pineapple Dessert, '86 4
  Chimichangas, Traditional Spicy Beef, '97 319

Chips, Corn Tortilla, '91 17
Chips, Light Tortilla, '90 278; '91 257
Chips, Tortilla, '91 137
Chorizo and Egg Tortillas, '81 193
Cinnamon Crisps, South Seas Ice Cream with Sweet
    Heat Salsa and, '04 315
Crackers, Bone, '01 204
Crackers, Tortilla-Lime, '99 17
Crisps, Fruit Salsa with Cinnamon, '01 108
Dinner, Quick Mexican, '98 224
Dippers, Rolled Tortilla, '86 4
Dumplings, Chicken and Tortilla, '99 327
Egg-and-Sausage Tortillas, '83 246; '84 42
Eggs Benedict, Southwest, '03 53
Eggs Sonora, '80 196
Espanola, Tortilla, '92 175
Fillet, Acapulco, '98 174
Flautas, '83 199; '00 293
Flautas, Rancho Ramillete, '96 M125
Flautas with Guacamole, Chicken, '89 226
Flour Tortillas, '81 303; '95 44
Flour Tortillas, Never-Fail, '80 198
Franks, Mexican, '93 78
Garlic Crisps, '99 60
Ham Appetillas, '93 63
Huevos con Queso, '00 123
Huevos Rancheros, '82 197; '91 77; '02 72
Jumpin' Jack Tortillas, '02 54
Lasagna, Mexican, '98 283
Lasagna, Southwestern Chicken, '03 173
Lasagna, Texas, '98 52
Migas, '94 26; '98 312
Philly Firecrackers, '01 142
Picadillo, '84 118
Pie, Mexican Cheese, '82 9; '83 69
Pie, Montezuma Tortilla, '83 199
Pie, Tortilla, '85 M211; '96 135
Pigs in a Blanket, Mexican, '00 199
Pizza, Mexican, '99 119
Pizza, Southwestern, '03 146
Potato Tortilla, '00 85
Rollups, Cream Cheese, '98 134
Rollups, Mediterranean, '00 277
Rollups, Mexican, '98 134
Roll-Ups, Mexican Beef, '90 176
Rollups, Parmesan-Turkey-Ranch, '01 177
Rollups, Pizza, '99 197
Rollups, Roasted Red Pepper, '98 285
Rollups, Southwestern, '01 135
Rollups, Spinach, '98 251
Rollups, Tortilla, '89 87
Rollups, Vegetable, '98 134
Rollup, Veggie, '01 109
Salad in a Shell, Mexican, '86 4
Salads, Mexican Chicken Tortilla, '95 129
Salad, Southwestern Spiral, '98 66
Sandwiches, Caribbean Seafood, '98 105
Sandwiches, Guacamole, '82 9; '83 68
Sandwiches, Tuna Roll, '96 199
Sandwich, Tex-Mex Ham-and-Cheese, '86 4
Savory Triangles, '02 54
Snacks, Pesto Tortilla, '89 19
Soft Taco Stacks, '02 54
Soup, Spicy Tortilla, '90 32; '93 108
Soup, Supereasy Tortilla, '00 199
Soup, Tortilla, '88 31, 245; '90 201; '93 197, 274;
    '94 136; '98 291; '99 310; '00 98, 110;
    '04 26
Spinach and Dumplings, '00 85
Spirals, Southwestern Chicken Salad, '02 58
Stack-Ups, Tortilla, '92 196
Steak, Matt's Chicken-Fried, '97 25
Stew, Baja Pork, '98 283
Strips, Tortilla, '04 243

Sweet Tortilla Triangles with Fruit Salsa, '02 54
Tacoritos, '90 133
Taquitos with Pork Picadillo, '04 206
Tostada Compuestas, '81 194
Tostadas, Chicken, '95 122
Tostadas, Chickpea-Chipotle, '01 54; '03 181
Tostadas, Crab, '93 203
Tostadas, Crispy, '83 2
Tostadas, Party, '98 M33
Tostadas, Quick Chicken, '99 159
Tostadas, Rice-and-Black Bean, '97 65
Tostadas, Shrimp-and-Black Bean, '93 204
Tostadas, Super, '83 199
Triangles, Tortilla, '94 107
Wrap, BLT, '04 298
Wrapidos, Tacos, '03 172
Wrap, Mediterranean, '03 168
Wraps, Black Bean, '00 211
Wraps, Cheese-Steak, '00 M335
Wraps, Chicken-and-Bean Slaw, '04 163
Wraps, Chicken-Cranberry, '01 34
Wraps, Club, '01 23
Wraps, Lemon-Basil Chicken Salad, '00 216
Wrap, Southwest BLT, '03 90
Wraps, Smoked Turkey, '01 61
Wraps, Thai Chicken-Avocado, '02 206
Wraps, Turkey, '00 318
Wraps, Western, '99 194
TRUFFLES. *See also* **CANDIES/Truffles.**
TUNA
Amandine, Tuna, '02 165
Appetizers
    Ball, Tuna-Pecan, '87 94
    Cherry Tomatoes, Tuna-Stuffed, '89 214
    Dip, Low-Cal Tuna, '87 25
    Dip, Tasty Tuna, '96 190
    Dip, Tuna-Curry, '84 31
    Mold, Creamy Tuna-Cheese, '81 135
    Mound, Tuna, '80 276
    Mousse, Tuna, '80 275
    Nachos, Tuna, '96 201
    Spread, Chunky Tuna, '89 147
    Spread, Tuna, '83 174; '91 305
Baked Tuna and Peas in Wine Sauce, '83 196
Bake, Shoestring Potato Tuna, '82 211
Barbecued Tuna, '80 275
Bisque, Tuna, '79 76
Broiled Tuna with Rosemary, '93 127
Burgers, Tuna, '95 128; '96 139
Burgers, Zippy Tuna, '81 135
Casserole, Biscuit-Topped Tuna, '79 113
Casserole, Easy Tuna, '82 M203
Casserole, Fabulous Tuna-Noodle, '02 63
Casserole, Nippy Tuna, '84 241
Casserole, Tangy Tuna-Broccoli, '83 75
Casserole, Tuna, '82 119; '96 103
Casserole, Tuna Vegetable, '81 135
Casserole with Cheese Swirls, Tuna, '88 256
Cheesies, Tuna, '82 191
Chopsticks, Tuna, '94 255
Creamed Chipped Tuna, '95 127
Croquettes, Tuna-Egg, '80 275
Croquettes with Parsley Sauce, Tuna, '86 108
Grilled Florida Tuna, '93 128
Grilled Tuna, Inland, '96 197
Grilled Tuna with Poblano Salsa, '91 135
Jambalaya, Tuna, '83 44
Lasagna, Tuna, '83 44; '84 123
Lemon and Capers, Tuna with, '97 180
Loaf, Mediterranean Picnic, '96 156
Macaroni Treat, Tuna-, '82 131
Melts, Curried Tuna, '95 46
Melts, Hot Tuna, '95 126; '96 201
Melt, Southwestern Tuna, '96 201

Melts, Tempting Tuna, '88 158
Melts, Tuna, '02 60
Mustard Sauce, Tuna with Tangy, '92 201
Nachos, Tuna, '95 127
Patties, Tuna, '00 247
Peppered Tuna with Crowder Peas, '00 159
Pie, Tuna-Rice, '84 123
Pie with Cheese Roll Crust, Tuna, '80 286
Pita Pocket, Tuna-in-a-, '87 202
Pita, Tuna-Veggie Stuffed, '01 216
Pockets, Tuna, '88 139
Potatoes, Tuna-Stuffed, '79 210
Salads
    Almond Salad, Crunchy Tuna-and-, '04 72
    Cannellini Bean Salad, Tuna-and-, '86 143
    Cheese-Sauced Tuna Salad, '87 M124
    Chef Salad, Tuna, '82 78
    Company Tuna Salad, '87 201
    Confetti Salad, '80 4
    Congealed Tuna Salad, '84 163
    Creamy Tuna Salad, '82 87, 208
    Crunchy Tuna Salad, '87 201
    Cucumber Tuna Boats, '83 136
    Curried Tuna Salad, '86 208
    Curried Tuna Salad with Grapes, '87 201
    Egg Salad, Tuna-, '81 135
    Eggs, Tuna-Stuffed, '83 83
    Favorite Tuna Salad, '82 208
    Flavorful Tuna Salad, '81 37
    Greens and Tuna Salad, Fresh, '80 55
    Hot Tuna Salad Rolls, '84 281
    Layered Tuna Salad, '84 221
    Luncheon Tuna Salad, '81 135
    Macaroni Salad, Tuna, '83 44, 145
    Macaroni Salad, Tuna-, '84 66
    Macaroni-Tuna Salad, Whole Wheat, '84 193
    Meal-in-One Salad, '82 232
    Niçoise, Salad, '03 35
    Pasta Salad, Tuna-, '91 43; '92 141; '00 247
    Pasta Salad, Tuna, '92 108
    Pasta, Stuffed Tomato with Tuna, '88 54
    Potato Salad, Tuna-, '84 289
    Red Pepper Salad, Tuna-and-, '93 143
    Rice Salad, Tuna-, '87 202
    Ring, Creamy Tuna, '80 275
    Sandwiches, White Bean-and-Tuna Salad,
        '02 31
    Swiss Tuna Salad, '86 186
    Taco Salad, Tuna-, '87 145
    Tomatoes, Tuna-Mac in, '87 188
    Tomato Salad, Tuna with Warm, '97 179
    White Bean-and-Tuna Salad, '01 35
    White Bean Salad, Tuna-and-, '98 209
    White Bean-Tuna Salad, '98 208
    Wild Tuna Salad, '95 243
Sandwich Boats, Tuna, '91 166
Sandwiches, Curried Tuna-Apple, '00 247
Sandwiches, French Toasted Tuna, '80 275
Sandwiches, Grilled-Tuna, '02 173
Sandwiches, Hot Tuna, '85 299; '86 M194
Sandwiches, Tuna Club, '83 134
Sandwiches, Tuna Roll, '96 199
Seared Tuna with Olive-Rosemary Pesto, '01 317
Southwestern Tuna Melts, '95 127
Steaks, Grilled Tuna, '90 129
Steaks on Mixed Greens with Lemon-Basil
    Vinaigrette, Seared Tuna, '94 205
Steaks with Cucumber Sauce, Tuna, '97 180
Steaks with Tarragon Butter, Tuna, '92 328
Tapenade, Tuna, '95 127; '96 201
Vegetables, Tuna with Sautéed, '98 222
Waffle-Wich, Hot Tuna, '88 272; '89 181
Yellowfin Tuna with Corn, Pepper, and Tomato
    Salsa, '94 164

TURKEY

à la King, Turkey, '04 232
Appetizers, Turkey, '91 314
Apple Brandy Turkey, '03 230
Baked Turkey, Cider, '83 263
Baked Turkey Tenders, '01 81
Bake, Layered Ham and Turkey, '79 252
Barbecue, Turkey, '90 158
Black-Eyed Peas, Creole, '98 22
Bourbon Turkey, Hickory-Smoked, '02 270
Bread Rollups, Pizza, '04 M35
Breast and Gravy, Savory Seasoned Turkey, '89 M309
Breast, Apple-Rosemary Turkey, '99 253
Breast, Braised Turkey, '84 260
Breast, Citrus-Marinated Turkey, '94 272
Breast, Citrus-Rosemary Turkey, '02 270
Breast, Herb Butter-Basted Turkey, '86 285
Breast, Herbed Turkey, '92 266
Breast, Maple-Plum Glazed Turkey, '00 285
Breast, Smoky Turkey, '89 323
Breast, Spicy-Sweet Smoked Turkey, '03 250
Breast with Orange-Raspberry Glaze, Turkey, '91 253
Buffet Turkey, '80 29
Cabbage Rolls, Stuffed, '88 18
Casserole, Crunchy Turkey, '89 M282
Casserole, Day-After-the-Holiday, '96 276
Casserole, Golden Turkey, '80 271
Casserole, Stuffed Turkey, '88 246
Casserole, Turkey, '84 327; '96 302
Casserole, Turkey-and-Broccoli, '86 332
Casserole, Turkey-and-Sausage Wild Rice, '03 239
Casserole, Turkey-and-Shrimp Florentine, '92 122
Casserole, Turkey-Asparagus, '86 284
Casserole, Turkey-Olive, '87 268
Casserole, Turkey-Spinach, '84 71
Casserole, Turkey-Swiss, '86 283
Chalupas, Texas Turkey, '80 196
Chili, Southwestern, '91 284
Chili Topping, '84 246
Chili, Turkey-Bean, '88 M213
Chowder, Turkey, '85 10; '91 312
Chowder, Turkey-Corn, '81 98; '96 279
Citrus-and-Herb Turkey, '01 254
Cobbler, Turkey-Vegetable-Sausage, '04 325
Cornbread Crust, Turkey and Peppers in, '95 312
Creamed Turkey, Southern, '80 272
Crêpes, Elegant Turkey, '83 282
Crêpes, Turkey, '92 41
Cups, Turkey-Tomato, '84 119
Curried Cream Sauce, Turkey Slices with, '91 60
Cutlets, Oven-Fried Turkey, '91 121
Cutlets, Parmesan Turkey, '01 81
Cutlets, Pecan-Crusted Turkey, '94 282
Cutlets with Pepper Salsa, Spicy Turkey, '88 26
Cutlets with Sage Gravy, Turkey, '96 268
Cutlets with Tarragon-Mustard Sauce, Turkey, '93 239
Cutlets with Tomato-Caper Sauce, Turkey, '91 61
Deep-Fried Turkey, '92 339; '00 252
Dijon with Garden Vegetables, Turkey, '01 102
Divan, Creamy Turkey, '90 M34
Divan, Quick Turkey, '89 178
Divan, Turkey, '82 268
Dressing, Easy Turkey and, '79 296
Dressing, Fruited Turkey, '99 257
Dressing, Turkey, '85 298
Drumsticks, Grilled Turkey, '89 168
Empanadas, Easy Turkey, '96 63
Fajitas, Turkey, '01 108
Fast-and-Savory Turkey, '87 306
Florentine, Turkey, '88 264
"Fried" Rice, Turkey, '00 97

Galantine of Turkey, '85 150
Giblet Dressing and Turkey Gravy, Turkey with, '91 254
Glazed Turkey Breast, Molasses-Coffee, '03 119
Gravy, Savory Turkey and, '94 326
Gravy, Turkey, '91 255; '94 306
Grilled Turkey Breast with Cranberry Salsa, '95 252
Gumbo, Turkey, '82 268; '85 258
Hash, Turkey, '95 262
Herbed Turkey-in-a-Bag, '91 253
Herbed Turkey Strips with Roasted Peppers and Beans, '04 282
Indian Turkey, '85 302
Italiano, Turkey, '91 62
Jambalaya de Covington, '87 211
Kebabs, Turkey-and-Fruit, '88 140
Lazy Day Turkey, '93 93
Loaf, Cranberry-Glazed Turkey, '86 171
Loaf, Ground Turkey, '86 171
Loaf, Turkey, '92 33
Marinated Turkey, Benny Sauce, '98 306
Marinated Turkey with Peppery Milk Gravy, Buttermilk-, '98 311
Meatballs, Turkey, '89 237
Meat Loaf, Spinach-Stuffed Turkey, '97 24
Meat Mixture, Basic, '92 241
Mignons, Sesame-Crusted Turkey, '01 81
Mignons with Creamy Wine Sauce, Sesame-Crusted Turkey, '02 109
Mix, Ground Meat, '89 143
Mole, Turkey, '03 18
Nachos, Turkey, '90 118
New Year's Turkey, '97 255
Oriental Turkey, '82 268
Parmesan, Turkey, '82 268
Parmigiana, Turkey, '87 193
Pasta
Basil Pasta, Creamy Turkey-, '89 216
Lasagna, Easy, '92 M197; '93 24
Lasagna, Lean, '86 37
Lasagna, Turkey, '83 239; '91 130
Lasagna, Turkey-Picante, '97 93
Noodle Bake, Turkey, '93 243
Noodle-Poppyseed Casserole, Turkey-, '90 239
Noodle Soup Mix, Turkey-, '89 330
Noodle Soup, Turkey-, '91 312
Pie, Broccoli-and-Turkey Pasta, '88 269
Primavera, Smoked Turkey Pasta, '90 84
Salad, Ranch-Style Turkey 'n' Pasta, '94 184
Scaloppine, Turkey, '04 321
Spaghetti, Ham-and-Turkey, '95 19
Spaghetti Sauce, Turkey, '85 13
Stroganoff, Turkey, '91 61
Tetrazzini, Herbed Turkey, '86 47
Tetrazzini, Smoked Turkey, '02 286
Tetrazzini, Turkey, '00 318; '03 257
Pâté in Pastry, Turkey-Mushroom, '92 327
Patties in Vegetable-Tomato Sauce, Turkey, '87 18
Patties, Stuffed Ground Turkey, '86 171
Peppers, Turkey with, '92 182
Piccata, Turkey, '91 137
Piccata, Turkey-Basil, '96 49
Piccata with Caper Sauce, Turkey, '98 49
Pie, Crumb-Crust Curried Turkey, '86 265
Pie, Golden Turkey, '79 253
Pie, Italian Meat, '89 109
Pie, Lattice-Topped Turkey, '81 277; '82 7
Pie, Potato-Topped Turkey, '86 265
Pie, Turkey, '80 285
Pie, Turkey-and-Dressing, '84 326
Pie, Turkey-and-Oyster, '82 267
Pie, Turkey-Cheese, '88 264
Pie, Turkey Pot, '86 265; '90 24; '93 45
Pie, Turkey-Sausage, '01 297

Pie with Biscuit Crust, Turkey Pot, '98 296
Pie with Cranberry-Pecan Crusts, Turkey Pot, '02 198
Pilaf, Turkey-Asparagus, '88 200
Pilaf, Turkey-Rice, '86 284
Pizza, Turkey-Vegetable, '90 139
Puffs, Turkey-Cheese, '87 301
Rice, Herbed Turkey and, '97 327
Rice, Turkey Fried, '83 282
Roasted Turkey, Apple-Rosemary, '99 252
Roasted Turkey Breasts, Jackie's, '98 269
Roasted Turkey, Rosemary, '99 312
Roasted Turkey with Gravy, Old-Fashioned, '04 270
Roasted Turkey with Sausage-and-Wild Mushroom Stuffing, '96 266
Roast Turkey, '79 250; '80 262; '86 47; '88 253; '90 321
Roast Turkey and Cornbread Dressing, '89 324
Roast Turkey and Giblet Gravy, '94 308
Roast Turkey Breast and Gravy, '88 303
Roast Turkey Breast with Special Gravy, '86 282
Roast Turkey, How to, '83 286
Roast Turkey with Grandmother's Dressing, Madeira, '91 254
Roast Turkey with Herbs, '95 305
Roast Turkey with Oyster Stuffing, '80 251
Roast Turkey with Peanut Dressing, '79 283
Roast Turkey with Rice Dressing, '82 286
Roast Turkey with Sage and Thyme, '04 230
Rollups, Turkey, '86 198
Rollups, Turkey-Spinach, '00 178
Salads
Apple Salad, Turkey-, '88 123; '90 181
Bake, Turkey Salad, '79 253
Caesar Salad, Turkey, '93 320
Carrot Salad, Turkey-, '86 283
Curried Turkey Salad, '88 140
Curried Turkey Salad, Chutney, '98 314
Fruit-and-Spice Turkey Salad, '94 325
Fruit-and-Turkey Salad, '89 176
Fruitful Turkey Salad, '84 197
Fruit Salad, Turkey-, '79 56
Fruit Salad, Turkey, '83 233; '84 244
Holiday Turkey Salad, '84 320
Honey-Mustard Turkey Salad, '92 309; '01 230
Hot Bacon Dressing, Turkey Salad with, '87 285
Hot Turkey Salad, '86 10, 297; '87 176
Layered Cornbread-and-Turkey Salad, '02 141
Layered Salad, Old-Fashioned, '01 96
Layered Turkey Salad, '86 332; '92 220
Macaroni Salad, Turkey, '83 282
Meal-in-One Salad, '86 43
Orange Salad, Turkey-in-the-, '93 21
Pasta Salad, Ranch-Style Turkey 'n', '94 184
Polynesian Turkey Salad, '87 285
Sandwiches, Turkey Salad Pita, '87 202; '88 43
Sautéed Walnuts, Turkey Salad with, '86 117
Smoked Turkey Salad, '96 184
Southwestern Turkey Salad, '91 313
Stir-Fry Salad, Chilled Turkey-and-Pepper, '88 140
Straw Salad, Turkey-in-the-, '96 286
Taco Salad, Turkey, '95 25
Turkey Salad, '90 318
Waldorf Salad with Yogurt Dressing, Turkey, '88 53
Walnut Salad, Turkey-, '03 239
Zucchini Salad, Turkey-, '85 74
Sandwiches
Asparagus Sandwiches, Turkey-, '96 74
Burgers, All-American Pizza, '92 148
Burgers, Garlic Turkey, '99 135
Burgers, Grilled Turkey, '91 61
Burgers, Pizza, '89 165

Burgers, Turkey, '98 22
Cheese Dogs, Turkey-, '97 203
Club Sandwiches, Double-Decker, '91 231;
    '92 68
Clubs, Cobb, '01 22
Cranberry Salsa, Turkey Sandwiches with,
    '00 269
Croissant, Turkey-Cranberry, '96 320
Ham-and-Turkey Specials, Cheesy, '84 14
Ham Pine-Berry Sandwiches, Turkey and, '00 59
Hero Sandwiches, Turkey, '92 196
Hero with Garlic Sauce, Turkey, '90 145
Hot Browns, '98 287
Hot Brown Sandwiches, '80 M202
Hot Browns, Baby, '00 107; '03 238
Hot Browns, Biscuit, '02 94
Hot Browns, Kentucky, '02 94
Hot Browns, Southwestern, '02 94
Hot Browns with Fried Cheese Grits, '02 94
Hot Turkey Sandwich, '93 306
Mayflower Sandwiches, '96 287
Meal-in-One Sandwiches, '80 218
Melts, Pineapple-Turkey, '03 196
Monte Cristo Sandwiches, '83 134; '97 319
Monte Cristo Sandwiches, Open-Faced, '01 171
Mozzarella Rounds, Turkey-, '82 3
Open-Faced Sandwiches, '79 214
Open-Facers, Turkey, '82 190
Pineapple-Turkey Sandwich, '01 85
Rollups, Parmesan-Turkey-Ranch, '01 177
Schoolwich Sandwiches, Turkey, '00 198
Slaw Sandwich, Turkey-in-the-, '90 177
Sloppy Toms, '91 51
Smoked Turkey, Mozzarella, and Blackberry
    Sandwiches, '99 220
Smoked Turkey-Roasted Pepper Sandwiches,
    '94 66
Stuffed Sandwich, Deli, '98 287
Sweet Smoky Sandwiches, '97 219
Tea Sandwiches, Turkey, '99 86
Turnovers, Mexican Turkey, '02 245
Waffle-Grilled Turkey Sandwich, '94 170
Wraps, Club, '01 23
Wraps, Smoked Turkey, '01 61
Wraps, Turkey, '00 318
Wrap, Turkey, '03 168
Sausage-Cornbread Dressing, Turkey with, '83 287
Sausage, Marinara Sauce with Italian Turkey,
    '89 239
Sauté, Creamy Turkey, '93 19
Sautéed Turkey Tenders, '01 81
Sauté, Turkey, '89 105
Scaloppine, Easy Turkey, '95 M192
Scaloppine with Angel Hair Pasta, Turkey, '02 44
Schnitzel, Turkey, '84 230
Skillet, Oriental Turkey-Orange, '86 284
Skillet Turkey Dinner, '91 61
Slices, Orange-Turkey, '90 53
Smoked Turkey, '79 293; '84 160; '85 258; '90 249
Smoked Turkey Breast, '88 169; '01 129
Smoked Turkey Medley, '90 128
Smoked Turkey, Seasoned, '97 85
Soufflé, Turkey, '80 271
Soup, Bean-and-Turkey, '93 319
Soup, Curried Turkey, '86 332
Soup, Hot Brown, '00 318
Soup Mix, Turkey-Noodle, '89 330
Soup, Tempting Turkey, '98 314
Soup, Tortilla, '00 98
Soup, Turkey-Barley, '91 312
Soup, Turkey Carcass, '86 284
Soup, Turkey-Noodle, '91 312
Soup, Turkey-Rice, '90 89
Soup, Turkey-Vegetable, '84 4; '88 264; '91 312

Soup, Williamsburg Turkey, '90 287
Soup with Cornbread Dressing Dumplings, Turkey,
    '03 239
Soup with Green Chile Biscuits, Fiesta Turkey,
    '04 233
Spread, Curried Turkey, '92 16
Spread, Turkey Party, '83 282
Squash Dressing, Turkey with, '87 248
Steaks, Grilled Marinated Turkey, '93 170
Stew, Hearty Turkey, '79 252
Stew, Turkey-Tomato, '90 279
Stir-Fry, Italian, '92 126
Stir-Fry, Turkey-Broccoli, '91 62
Stock, Light Poultry, '90 31
Strata, Turkey-Cheddar-Broccoli, '03 100
Stuffed Turkey Breast, '87 270; '89 322
Stuffed Turkey Breast, Wild Rice-, '97 281
Stuffed Turkey Breast with Seasoned Dressing,
    '83 320; '84 128
Sugar-and-Spice Cured Turkey, '02 243
Sweet-and-Sour Turkey, '79 252
Tarragon Cream, Turkey with, '91 60
Tenderloin Scaloppine, Turkey, '02 137
Tenderloins, Lime-Buttered Turkey, '92 127
Tenderloins, Maple-Plum Glazed Turkey, '00 285
Tenderloins with Lingonberry Sauce, Turkey,
    '97 289
Tomatoes, Turkey Stuffed, '94 140
Topping, Turkey-Vegetable, '94 22
Treats, Turkey, '93 256
Turnovers, Home-Style Turkey, '94 325
Turnovers, Turkey Sausage, '95 239
Wild Turkey, Country-Fried, '94 306
TURNIP GREENS. *See* **GREENS.**
TURNIPS
    au Gratin, Turnip, '79 289
    au Gratin, Turnips, '84 229; '88 229; '89 244
    Boiled Turnips, '83 242
    Braised Turnips, '91 219
    Casserole, Baked Turnip, '82 274
    Casserole, Turnip, '83 242; '84 229; '04 213
    Cheese Sauce, Turnips in, '84 229
    Creamy Cooked Turnips, '86 224
    Dip, Turnip Green, '91 13
    Fried Turnips, Shoestring, '81 274
    Gingered Turnips, '82 274
    Glazed Turnips, '81 274
    Greens and Ham Hock, Southern Turnip, '80 119
    Greens, Fresh Turnip, '92 339
    Greens, Old-Fashioned Turnip, '85 255
    Greens Stew, Turnip, '02 17
    Greens, Turnip, '90 13, 232; '95 306
    Greens, Turnip-and-Collard, '92 215
    Greens with Turnips, Turnip, '84 230; '01 211
    Hash Brown Turnips, '79 254
    Julienne, Turnips and Carrots, '86 295
    Onions, Turnips and, '83 242
    Orange Carrots and Turnips, Sunset, '94 213
    Parsleyed Turnips and Carrots, '79 253
    Party Turnips, '84 230
    Potatoes, Turnips and, '79 254
    Pudding, Turnip, '94 213
    Salad, Irish Turnip, '94 178
    Salad, Turnip, '85 235
    Salad, Turnip-and-Carrot, '91 212
    Saucy Turnips, '85 289
    Sauté, Carrot-Turnip, '93 241
    Scalloped Potatoes and Turnips, '85 235
    Scalloped Turnips, '79 254
    Skillet Turnips, Sweet, '04 212
    Slaw, Turnip, '89 245
    Soufflé, Turnip, '79 254
    Soup, Creamy Turnip, '84 279
    Soup, Oyster-Turnip, '94 328

Soup, Turnip, '92 217
Southern Turnips, '87 190
Stir-Fry, Turnip-and-Carrot, '96 36
Supreme, Turnip, '79 254
Sweet-and-Sour Turnips, '81 274
Turnovers, Turnip, '04 212
Turnovers, Turnip-Bacon, '04 213
Whipped Turnip Puff, '00 254
TURTLE
    Fried Cooter (Soft-Shell Turtle), '80 99
    Soup au Sherry, Turtle, '80 56
    Soup, Turtle, '92 92
TZIMMES
    Fruit Tzimmes with Brisket, Mixed, '93 114
    Sweet Potato-Beef Tzimmes, '92 234
    Tzimmes, '95 102

V

VANILLA
Almond Crunch, Vanilla, '93 243
Beach, The, '95 168
Breakfast Ring, Almond-Vanilla, '04 M249
Cakes, Spring's Little, '01 M91
Cake, Vanilla Chiffon, '79 266
Cheesecake, Creamy Vanilla, '89 93
Cookies 'n' Cream Dessert, Gold-Dusted, '94 271
Cookies, Vanilla Meringue, '01 197
Cookies, Vanilla Slice-and-Bake, '85 171
Cream, Vanilla, '81 248; '83 M115; '97 272; '00 27
Crescents, Vanilla, '82 307
Cupcakes, Golden Vanilla, '85 121
Cupcakes, Vanilla, '92 14
Cups, Vanilla Lace, '98 M93
Custard, Baked Vanilla, '82 129
Custard, Pecan Pie with Chilled Vanilla, '00 331
Custard, Vanilla, '99 27
Dessert, Glorified Vanilla Sherry, '81 85
Dip, Strawberries with Vanilla Pudding, '03 93
Éclairs, Vanilla Cream-Filled, '01 45
Extract, Home-Brewed Vanilla, '83 228
Extract, Homemade Vanilla, '83 228
Extract, Vanilla, '94 243; '97 288
Finger Painting Never Tasted So Good, '95 167
Fondant, Faux, '98 M154
Frosting, Vanilla, '84 36; '85 236; '92 14, 274
Frosting, Vanilla Buttercream, '92 239; '94 99;
    '96 229; '97 111; '99 117; '03 286
Frosting, Vanilla-Rum, '85 324
Frosty, French Vanilla, '79 148
Fruit Cup, Vanilla, '80 183
Glaze, Vanilla, '85 M89; '89 211; '04 M84
Ice Cream, Basic Vanilla, '88 202
Ice Cream, Country Vanilla, '82 143
Ice Cream) Helado, Caramel-Vanilla (Caramel-
    Vanilla, '81 67
Ice Cream, Honey-Vanilla, '95 178
Ice Cream, Kick-the-Can, '00 171
Ice Cream, No-Cook Vanilla, '04 179
Ice Cream, Old-Fashioned Vanilla, '97 166
Ice Cream Pumpkin, '96 255
Ice Cream Spectacular, Vanilla, '82 166
Ice Cream, Vanilla, '80 176; '86 129; '91 174;
    '04 275
Ice Cream, Vanilla-Cinnamon, '00 127; '01 195
Ice Cream, Vanilla Custard, '92 148; '96 145;
    '98 221; '00 143
Oil, Vanilla, '94 243
Parfait, Bodacious Peanut, '95 167
Parfaits, Hooray, '96 229
Pastry Cream, Vanilla, '01 45
Pears, Vanilla Poached, '90 57
Pie, Fruit-Topped Vanilla Cream, '84 49
Pralines, Vanilla, '92 313; '93 51
Pudding, Creamy Vanilla, '83 227

VANILLA
(continued)

Pudding, French Vanilla Latte, '03 M282
Pudding, Vanilla, '88 32
Punch, Vanilla-Nut Coffee, '03 282
Sauce, Almond-Vanilla Custard, '88 M177
Sauce, Lemon-Vanilla, '02 231
Sauce, Pan-Fried Grouper with Vanilla Wine,
  '94 241
Sauce, Vanilla, '97 M15
Sauce, Vanilla Crème, '94 243; '96 155
Sauce, Vanilla Custard, '99 27
Sauce, Vanilla-Nutmeg, '02 208
Shortbread, Scottish, '94 242
S'mores, Indoor, '01 33
Soufflé, Frozen Vanilla, '79 230; '82 173
Soufflés with Vanilla Crème Sauce, Vanilla, '94 242;
  '96 155
Spooky Ghosts, '98 M256
Sugar, Vanilla, '94 243
Topping, Vanilla Cream, '02 252
Torte, Chocolate-Vanilla Holiday, '01 252
Vinaigrette, Vanilla, '94 242
Zabaglione with Fruit, Champagne Vanilla, '00 31

VEAL

Amaretto-Lime Veal, '93 54
Amelio, Veal, '86 142
au Madeira, Veal, '81 131
Birds, Veal, '84 260
Burgoo, Five-Meat, '87 3
Casserole, Veal and Wild Rice, '79 180
Casserole, Veal Cutlet, '79 109
Chops, Apple Veal, '87 220
Chops, Herb-Peppered Veal, '98 60
Chops Mediterranean, Veal, '79 108
Company Veal and Carrots, '85 22
Cordon Bleu, Veal, '87 219
Cutlets, Stuffed Veal, '92 329
Cutlets with Leeks and Zinfandel Cream, Veal,
  '96 237
Delight, Veal, '79 109
Grilled Pork Chops, '98 246
Herbed Veal and Onions, '79 108
Herbed Veal with Wine, '86 193
Italian Style, Veal, '82 M68
Lemon Veal, '93 35
Lemon Veal with Artichoke Hearts, '87 219
Marsala, Veal, '91 218, 310
Marsala, Veal-and-Mushrooms, '89 44
Meatballs, European Veal, '85 30
Meat Loaf, Italian, '79 187
Meat Loaf, Savory, '87 216
Meat Loaf, Triple, '79 186
Meat Loaf, Veal, '93 292
New Orleans Veal with Crabmeat, '86 94
Osso Buco, '98 260
Paprika, Veal, '88 113
Parmigiana, Veal, '81 227
Pasta with Veal and Shrimp, Angel Hair, '04 223
Peppercorns, Veal with Green, '87 220
Picante, Veal, '87 31
Piccata, Lemon Veal, '86 118
Piccata, Veal, '92 181
Piccata with Capers, Veal, '87 142
Ragoût, Veal-and-Artichoke, '94 43
Roast, Best Baked Veal, '87 219
Roast with Vegetables, Veal, '89 71
Sauce, Noodles with Veal, '80 236
Sauté, Veal-Cepe, '89 62
Savory Veal, '83 281
Scallopini à la Marsala, Veal, '79 109
Scallopini Marsala, Veal, '85 295

Scallopini of Veal al Sorriso, '79 85
Scallopini, Veal, '83 8, 125
Scallopini with Shiitakes, Veal, '99 232
Scaloppine in Lemon Sauce, Veal, '00 166
Schnitzel, Swiss, '80 189
Skillet Veal, '83 200
Soup with Quenelles, Veal-Vermicelli, '94 14
Spaghetti, Veal, '84 276
Spaghetti with Veal and Peppers, '81 201; '82 14
Steak, Veal, '82 276
Stock, Brown Meat, '90 31
Stroganoff, Veal, '79 108
Supreme, Veal, '85 109
Sweetbreads, Creamed, '90 82
Swirls, Veal-and-Smithfield Ham, '86 253
Terrine of Pork and Veal, '93 287
Terrine with Mustard Sauce, Veal, '93 118
Turkey, New Year's, '97 255
Wine Sauce, Veal and Carrots in, '81 31;
  '86 M139

VEGETABLES. *See also* specific types and
  CASSEROLES.

à la Grill, Vegetables, '88 130
Antipasto Skillet Dinner, '97 327

Appetizers

Antipasto, Easy, '92 24
Antipasto, Grandpa's, '98 183
Antipasto, Lemon-Vinaigrette Marinated, '04 256
Antipasto, Vegetable, '85 263
Bites, Veggie, '91 171
Canapés, Vegetable, '91 252
Caviar, Texas, '99 84; '01 160, 257
Cheesecake, Roasted Vegetable, '99 140
Cheesecake, Vegetable, '96 110
Cocktail, Fresh Vegetable, '82 165
Cream Cheese-Vegetable Squares, '04 293
Dip and Vegetable Platter, Curry, '89 327
Dip, Creamy Vegetable, '83 180; '03 25
Dip, Cucumber-Cheese Vegetable, '83 128
Dip, Fresh Vegetable, '80 249
Dip, Herb Vegetable, '89 269
Dip, Quick Creamy Vegetable, '00 34
Dip, Starburst Vegetable, '82 248
Dip, Tangy Vegetable, '87 196
Dip, Vegetable, '79 52; '82 161; '02 18
Dip, Vegetable Garden, '85 215
Dip, Zippy Vegetable, '84 256
Egg Rolls, Tex-Mex, '01 328
Egg Rolls, Vegetarian, '86 148
Fresh Vegetables, Parsley-Dill Dip with, '85 79
Fried Veggies, '96 19
Hot Vegetable Juice Appetizer, '93 324
Marinated Vegetable Medley, '85 319; '95 91
Marinated Vegetables, '94 183; '96 213
Marinated Vegetables Italian, '90 242
Mushroom Caps, Vegetable, '81 246
Nachos, Vegetable, '91 17
Pâté, Vegetable-Chicken, '86 66
Platter with Creamy Honey-Herb Dip, Vegetable,
  '98 135
Relish Tree, Christmas, '84 257
Rice with Spring Vegetables, '96 132
Rollups, Vegetable, '98 134
Rollup, Veggie, '01 109
Salsa, Greek Vegetable, '98 32
Salsa, Shrimp Skewers with Vegetable, '98 32
Shrimp-and-Vegetable Appetizer, '97 161
Spread, Garden, '86 135
Spread, Garden Vegetable, '93 184
Spread, Vegetable, '90 144
Spread, Vegetable Party, '84 166
Tarragon Vegetable Appetizer, '83 277
Terrine, Chicken-Vegetable, '84 131
Terrine, Vegetable-Chicken, '83 224

Tortilla Bites with Sesame-Soy Dipping Sauce,
  '02 145
Tray, Fresh Vegetable Party, '82 122
Apple Cider Pork and Vegetables, '97 210
Bake, Winter, '99 273
Bake with Sweet Bacon Dressing, Vegetable-
  Chicken, '93 108
Barbecue Hobo Supper, '99 108
Barley and Vegetables, '91 81
Beef and Vegetables, '01 86
Beef and Vegetables, Company, '88 234
Beef and Vegetables, Savory, '79 163
Beef Brisket with Fall Vegetables, '02 237
Benne Veggies, '01 327
Black-Eyed Peas, Marinated, '01 30
Blanching Chart, Microwave, '80 M181
Bolognese, Vegetable, '00 326
Bratwurst, Grilled, '01 159
Bread Bowl, Veggie, '01 132
Bread, Breakaway Vegetable, '82 74
Bread, Herb-Vegetable-Cheese, '88 172
Broth, Vegetables with Arugula, '02 281
Brunswick Stew, Easy, '00 138
Bundles, Vegetable, '93 181
Buñuelos, '93 29
Burgers, Beef-and-Vegetable, '84 125
Burgers, Beefy Vegetable, '98 143
Burgers, Vegetable, '89 164
Burgoo, Kentucky, '97 138
Burritos, Tony's Veggie, '96 289
Burritos, Vegetable, '80 197; '90 134; '92 138
Burritos, Vegetarian, '93 319
Burritos with Avocado Sauce, Vegetable, '83 200
Buttermilk Sauce, Vegetables with, '84 6
Cabbage Rolls, Vegetarian, '91 86
Calabacitas, '95 130

Casseroles

Beef and Vegetable Chow Mein Casserole,
  '83 313
Beefy Vegetable Casserole, '79 248
Brunch Casserole, Italian, '03 29
Cajun Casserole, Ragin', '02 199
Cashew Casserole, '95 166
Cheesy Vegetable Casserole, '81 103
Creamy Vegetable Casserole, '98 96
Curry Casserole, Vegetable-, '91 286; '92 27
Enchiladas, Meatless, '93 106
Fresh Vegetable Casserole, '82 225
Garden Casserole, '82 168; '88 122
Garden Medley, '98 236
Gratin, Summer Vegetable, '03 159
Ham Casserole, Vegetable-and-, '84 91
King Ranch Casserole, '02 210
Lasagna, Avocado-Vegetable, '01 310
Lasagna Casserole, Vegetable, '92 198; '93 25
Lasagna, Cheesy Vegetable, '79 84
Lasagna, Colorful Vegetable, '87 19
Lasagna, Garden, '83 119
Lasagna, Roasted Vegetable-Meat, '99 M332
Lasagna, Saucy Cheese-Vegetable, '01 306
Lasagna, Vegetable, '84 201; '93 320; '95 211;
  '96 47; '99 97
Layered Vegetable Casserole, '91 286; '92 27
Macaroni Primavera, '96 73
Medley Bake, Vegetable, '81 268
Medley, Green Vegetable, '79 287; '80 34
Medley, Vegetable-Cheese, '99 M287
Mexican Vegetarian Casserole, '96 276
Mixed Vegetable Casserole, '83 208, 256; '86 327
Mixed-Vegetable Casserole, '87 154
Noodle Casserole, Vegetable, '91 30
Pork Combo, Vegetable-, '85 113
Rotini, Baked, '01 185
Scalloped Mixed Vegetables, '83 5

Squares, Checkerboard Vegetable, '96 178
Strata, Vegetable-Cheese, '98 98
Swiss Steak, Pizza, '02 36
Swiss Vegetable Medley, '95 26
Tuna Vegetable Casserole, '81 135
Vegetarian Casserole, '96 302
Veggies Casserole, '88 123
Wine Sauce Casserole, Vegetables in, '95 133
Winter Root Vegetable Casserole, '98 265
Cassoulet, Vegetarian, '96 329
Catfish with Vegetables and Basil Cream, Spicy, '03 56
Cheesecake, Layered Vegetable, '91 62; '92 51
Chicken and Dumplings with Vegetables, '85 M56
Chicken-and-Vegetable Platter, '88 M52
Chicken and Vegetables, '88 165
Chicken and Vegetables, Creamed, '91 90
Chicken and Vegetables, Ginger-Poached, '98 229
Chicken and Vegetables, Grilled, '99 200
Chicken and Vegetables, Jim's, '99 237
Chicken and Vegetables, Roast, '81 3
Chicken and Vegetables Vermouth, '87 M37
Chicken and Vegetables with Ginger-Soy Sauce, '91 32
Chicken, Beer-Smothered, '01 107
Chicken Breast with Turned Vegetables and Chive Sauce, Poached, '94 309
Chicken Cacciatore, '99 213
Chicken Chow Mein, '98 283
Chicken, Foil-Wrapped, '99 108
Chicken, Roasted Stuffed, '98 109
Chicken Sausage with Fennel, '98 312
Chicken Skillet, Confetti, '97 327
Chicken Strips and Vegetables, Marinated, '90 110
Chicken, Vegetable-Stuffed, '89 M65
Chicken, Whole Poached, '98 229
Chicken with Fresh Herbs and Vegetables, '02 91
Chicken with Vegetables, Roasted, '98 108
Chicken with Vegetables Vinaigrette, Grilled, '91 26
Chicken with Wine-Soaked Vegetables, Baked, '84 277
Chili, Bodacious, '95 14
Chili, Full-of-Veggies, '00 294
Chili, Mom's, '93 292
Chili, Vegetable, '91 28; '97 179
Chili, Vegetarian, '84 280, 327; '91 284
Chops with Vegetables, Glazed, '98 132
Chops with Vegetables, Golden, '89 218
Chowchow, '00 158
Chowchow, Nannie's, '95 250
Clubs, Cobb, '01 22
Cobbler, Autumn Vegetable, '01 215
Cobbler, Turkey-Vegetable-Sausage, '04 325
con Queso, Chile, '97 25
Cornbread-Vegetable Supper, '97 319
Cornish Hens with Vegetables, Tarragon Roasted, '94 79
Couscous, Vegetables and, '96 136
Crabs, Fried Stuffed Soft-Shell, '98 140
Crackers, Vegetable, '96 105
Crawfish Delicacy, '99 M23
Creamed Spring Vegetables, '87 127
Crêpes, Chicken-Vegetable, '83 70
Crêpes, Vegetable-Filled Bran, '86 44
Croutons, Vegetable-Flavored, '84 148
Crunchy Vegetables, '99 43
Curried Vegetables with Couscous, '04 328
Curry, Vegetable, '99 91; '04 217
Dilled Vegetable Sticks, '88 179
Dinner, Jollof Rice, '91 230; '92 325
Dinner, Pork Skillet, '00 335
Egg Rolls, Vegetarian, '86 148
Enchiladas, Meatless, '93 106
Enchiladas, Vegetable-Cheese, '94 42

en Papillote, Chicken and Vegetables, '86 145
Étouffée, Roasted Quail, '96 34
Fajitas, Slow Cooker, '02 43
Fajitas, Tex-Mex, '01 188
Fall Vegetables, '03 260
Fennel, Braised, '88 46
Fennel, Italian-Style Braised, '93 56
Fennel with Garlic Butter, Steamed, '93 56
Fish-and-Vegetable Dinner, '91 196
Fish and Vegetables, Cheesy, '94 254
Fish and Vegetables, Grilled, '89 179
Fish Rolls, Vegetable-Filled, '86 M251
Fish with Vegetables, Poached, '89 332; '90 18
Flounder Rolls, Vegetable-Stuffed, '87 6
Flounder-Vegetable Medley, '85 217
Freezing Chart, Vegetable, '85 185
Fresh Vegetable Potpourri, '79 208
Fries, Mixed Vegetable, '96 140
Frittata, Fresh Vegetable, '93 140
Frittata, Vegetable, '92 48; '93 183
Garbanzo-Black Bean Medley, '99 236
Garden Combo, '86 172
Garden Harvest, '85 M142
Garden Surprise, '83 112
Garnishes, '82 280; '85 338, 339
Glazed Fall Vegetables, '00 230
Glazed Vegetables, '97 105
Greens, Super-Charged, '01 211
Grilled Marinated Vegetables, '00 137; '04 133
Grilled Parsleyed Shrimp and Vegetables, '04 256
Grilled Vegetable Medley, '98 158
Grilled Vegetables, '84 172; '92 124, 231; '96 123, 173
Grilled Vegetables, Italian-Style, '92 143
Grilled Vegetable Skewers, '94 160
Grilled Vegetables, Marinated, '95 162; '00 126
Grilled Vegetables with Cilantro Butter, '98 182
Grilled Vegetables with Herbs, '00 220
Grouper with Confetti Vegetables, '88 M189
Ham-and-Vegetables, Skillet, '84 90
Hash, Vegetable, '95 262
Herbed-Smoked Vegetables, '85 145
Heroes, Vegetable Garden, '84 14
Honey-Dijon Vegetables, '98 311
Juice Delight, Vegetable, '84 58
Julienne Vegetables, '93 31
Julienne Vegetables with Walnuts, '86 M251
Kebabs, Beef-and-Vegetable, '91 148
Kebabs, Beef Tenderloin Shish, '00 200
Kebabs, Chicken-Vegetable, '03 95
Kebabs, Easy Vegetable, '02 142
Kebabs, Fresh Vegetable, '81 158; '92 101
Kebabs, Grilled Vegetable, '93 170
Kebabs, Marinated Vegetable, '83 M195
Kebabs, Tangy Marinated Vegetable, '88 142
Kebabs, Vegetable, '87 116; '01 132
Kebabs with Vegetables, Beef, '90 148
Kebabs with Vegetables, Marinated Beef, '99 292
Kebabs, Steak-and-Vegetable, '04 218
Kielbasa-Vegetable Dinner, '91 274
Kugel, Vegetable-Noodle, '96 228
Lamb Chops, Easy Baked, '02 66
Lamb with Vegetables, Fillets of, '85 36
Lamb with Vegetables, Roasted, '98 266
Lemon Vegetables, '93 83
Lentils and Vegetables, Savory, '98 29
Limping Susan, '90 155
Liver with Vegetables, Calf's, '85 219
Loaf, Beef-Vegetable, '79 164
Loaf, Pureed Vegetable-Cheese, '85 297
Loaf, Vegetable Meat, '85 M29
Lo Mein, Sesame-Vegetable, '03 91
Marinade, Fresh Vegetable, '83 209
Marinade, Vegetable, '92 231

Marinated Vegetable Medley, '85 319; '89 14; '95 91
Marinated Vegetables, '79 146; '81 239; '85 67; '86 286; '88 4, 170; '96 176; '98 178; '99 36, 105
Marinated Vegetables, Honey-Mustard, '93 236
Marinated Vegetables, Sweet-and-Sour, '83 266
Meatballs and Vegetables with Horseradish Dressing, '91 32
Meat Loaf, Summer, '01 162
Medley, Baked Vegetable, '81 75
Medley, Crunchy Vegetable, '84 254
Medley, Day-by-Day Vegetable, '03 219
Medley, Fresh Vegetable, '85 155
Medley, Garden Vegetable, '91 45
Medley, Herbed Vegetable, '99 46; '00 138
Medley, Italian Vegetable, '88 143
Medley, Masala Vegetable, '94 56
Medley, Mixed Vegetable, '82 126
Medley, Root Vegetable, '03 260
Medley, Sautéed Vegetable, '83 101
Medley, Skillet Vegetable, '81 134
Medley, Spring Vegetable, '86 115
Medley, Summer Garden, '84 158
Medley, Summer Vegetable, '83 208
Medley, Vegetable, '79 102; '83 112; '86 327; '89 M129
Microwaving Fresh Vegetables, '82 M138
Migas, '98 312
Mint Sauce over Vegetables, '92 104
Mirlitons, Stuffed, '97 263
Mixed Vegetables, '83 M195
Mixed Vegetables, Tangy, '96 273
Mosaic of Vegetables, '98 280
Mushroom Caps, Vegetable, '81 246
Nests, Scallops in Vegetable, '91 70
Olive Butter, Vegetables Tossed in, '91 295
Omelet, Beefy Vegetable, '83 188
Omelet, Cheddar-Vegetable, '83 205
Omelet, Cheesy Vegetable, '85 49
Omelet, Creamy Veggie, '02 248
Omelet, Fresh Vegetable, '84 211
Omelet, Garden, '99 174
Omelet, Golden Vegetable, '82 123
Omelet Primavera, '87 71
Omelet, Puffy Vegetable, '83 188
Omelet, Shrimp-and-Vegetable Oven, '99 286
Omelet, Spanish, '00 35
Omelet, Vegetable-Pasta Oven, '99 286
Omelet, Vegetarian, '84 114
Open-Faced Vegetarian Melt, '87 106
Orange Roughy, Vegetable-Topped, '93 67
Orange Roughy with Vegetables, Basil-, '92 98
Osso Buco, '98 260
Packets, Vegetable, '97 64
Paella, '97 328
Paella, Garden, '82 245
Paella, Spanish, '85 26
Pancakes, Vegetable, '88 297; '98 236
Pancakes, Vegetable-Rice, '93 43
Pancakes, Veggie, '00 85
Parmesan Vegetables, '97 147
Pasta. *See also* **VEGETABLES/Casseroles.**
    Beans and Pasta, '99 35
    Bow Ties with Crab and Vegetables, '98 233
    Fennel, Pasta with, '98 46
    Fettuccine and Vegetables, '97 178
    Fettuccine Primavera, '89 238; '94 85
    Fettuccine, Ranch House, '03 123
    Fettuccine, Vegetable, '83 312
    Fettuccini Primavera, '04 64
    Garden Pasta, '82 199
    Garden Vegetables, Pasta and, '87 192
    Grilled Vegetable Pasta, '97 142

VEGETABLES, Pasta
(continued)

Italiano, Pasta, '01 41
Linguine with Roasted Vegetables, Traveling,
    '93 178
Lo Mein, Sesame-Vegetable, '03 91
Mac-and-Cheese, Veggie, '01 111
Mediterranean Pasta, '95 341
Mixed Vegetables, Pasta with Sausage and,
    '84 249
Noodle Ring, Beef and Vegetables in a, '85 285
Noodles with Spring Vegetables, '02 125
Orzo Primavera, '92 192
Penne, Garden Sauté with, '98 207
Penne Pasta, Spicy Vegetables with, '04 195
Potpourri, Pasta, '94 33
Primavera, Almost Pasta, '86 38
Primavera, Chicken-Pasta, '91 72
Primavera, Creamy Pasta, '95 167
Primavera, Garden Spiral, '91 30
Primavera, Pasta, '85 86; '89 105; '93 168;
    '97 228
Primavera, Peppery Pasta, '02 161
Primavera, Smoked Turkey Pasta, '90 84
Roasted Vegetables and Pasta, '93 184
Sauce, Pasta with Vegetable, '83 163
Spaghetti, Chicken-Vegetable, '92 281; '98 296
Spaghetti, Fresh Vegetables with, '86 257
Spaghetti, Sautéed Vegetables with, '81 89
Spaghetti, Shrimp-and-Vegetable, '91 170
Spaghetti with Vegetables, '85 67
Stir-Fry Pasta, Vegetable, '96 29
Toss, Garden Pasta, '00 57
Vermicelli, Chicken, '01 237
Vermicelli, Scallop-Vegetable, '87 143
Vermicelli with Chunky Vegetable Sauce,
    '04 180
Peperonata, '97 291
Pepper Cups, Hot Vegetable, '88 M188
Peppers, Spicy Stuffed, '98 243
Pesto Primavera, '96 170
Picadillo, Lettuce-Wrapped, '03 193
Pickled Confetti Vegetables, '00 133
Pie, Chicken-Vegetable Pot, '81 281; '82 30
Pie Filling, Pot, '03 247
Pie, Savory Summer, '99 159; '03 182
Pies, Maque Choux, '02 182
Pies, Vegetable-Beef, '80 286
Pie with Biscuit Crust, Turkey Pot, '98 296
Pilaf, Barley-Vegetable, '91 33
Pilaf, Chicken-Vegetable, '97 51
Pilaf, Fruit-and-Vegetable Rice, '84 196
Pilau, Chicken, '99 184
Pilau, Shrimp, '99 184
Pitas, Garbanzo-Vegetable, '00 58
Pizza, Blazing Sunset, '95 267
Pizza, Deep-Dish Vegetarian, '85 243
Pizza, Garden, '89 108
Pizza, Grilled Vegetable, '98 176
Pizza, Quick 3-Cheese, '00 94
Pizzas, Grilled Vegetable, '97 323
Pizzas, Individual, '03 219
Pizza, Southwestern Veggie, '95 126
Pizzas, Veggie, '99 97
Pizzas, Veggie Sausage, '00 294
Pizza, Turkey-Vegetable, '90 139
Pizza, Vegetable, '89 64; '94 218
Pizza, Vegetarian Processor, '89 225
Pizza, Veggie, '94 78
Platter, Fresh Vegetable, '92 60
Platter, Vegetable, '88 M187
Pockets, Vegetable, '85 215

Pork Chops and Garden Vegetables, '88 297
Pork Chops, Skillet Vegetable, '85 179
Pork Skillet Dinner, '98 131
Pork Tenderloin with Vegetables, '01 122
Pork with Vegetables, Medallions of, '88 223
Potatoes, Sausage-Vegetable-Topped, '98 29
Potatoes, Vegetable-Topped Stuffed, '85 235
Pot Roast, '00 65
Pot Roast, Italian, '02 88
Pot Roast Medley, Vegetable-, '83 319
Pot Roast of Beef with Vegetables, '98 65
Pot Roast with Vegetables, '80 59; '81 M208;
    '00 18
Pot Roast with Vegetables, Marinated, '88 M52
Primavera, Rice, '98 237
Punch, Hot Vegetable, '93 12
Puree, Smoked Vegetable, '93 156
Quesadillas, Vegetable, '97 65
Quesadilla with Roasted Salsa, Northern New
    Mexican Vegetable, '95 130
Quiche, Cheese-Vegetable, '81 228
Quiche, Ham-and-Vegetable, '84 326
Quiche, Light Vegetable, '97 332
Quiche, Vegetable, '87 M219
Ragoût of Summer Vegetables, '98 119
Ragoût, Salmon-and-Vegetable, '96 45
Ragoût, Vegetable, '89 172; '98 181
Ratatouille, '84 105, 243; '85 92; '89 174
Ratatouille-Bran Stuffed Eggplant, '86 44
Ratatouille, Eggplant-Zucchini, '81 205
Ratatouille, Microwave, '95 M232
Ratatouille Niçoise, '81 22
Ratatouille Pie, '88 198
Ratatouille, Quick-and-Easy, '80 212
Ratatouille, Sausage, '89 248
Ratatouille-Stuffed Eggplant, '83 187
Ratatouille-Stuffed Onions, '96 91
Ratatouille Supreme, '86 172
Reggae Rundown, '96 71
Relish, Eight-Vegetable, '84 179
Relish, Garden, '83 259
Relish, Vegetable, '90 147
Rib-Eyes, Italian, '98 215
Ribs, Braised Short, '98 44
Rice, Garden, '92 12
Rice Jardin, '01 106
Rice, Picadillo, '98 237
Rice Pilaf, White, '97 238
Rice, Spicy, '99 214
Rice Toss, Vegetable-, '91 309
Rice, Vegetables and, '93 91
Rice with Spring Vegetables, '96 132
Rice with Vegetables, '79 64; '85 83
Risotto, Microwave, '97 M213
Risotto Primavera, '95 163; '00 138
Risotto with Vegetables, '98 193
Roast, Easy Banquet, '99 291
Roasted Baby Vegetables, '98 61
Roasted Fall Vegetables, Honey-Glazed, '99 244
Roasted Glazed Vegetables, '01 277
Roasted Root Vegetables, '00 259; '03 243
Roasted Root Vegetables, Rosemary, '01 255
Roasted Summer Vegetables, '98 213
Roasted Vegetable Medley, '01 298, 331
Roasted-Vegetable Paella, '04 89
Roasted Vegetable Quesadillas, '04 322
Roasted Vegetables, '95 64; '99 143; '00 321; '04 47
Roasted Vegetables and Pork, Oven-, '99 259
Roasted Vegetables, Bill's, '00 276
Roasted Vegetables, Fried Pork Chops with, '98 153
Roasted Vegetables, Honey-, '97 29
Roasted Vegetables with Fresh Sage, '00 125
Roasted Winter Vegetables, '97 281
Rolls with Thai Dipping Sauce, Summer, '97 236

Salads
Antipasto, Salad, '96 161
Aspic, Cheesy Vegetable, '81 73
Aspic with Horseradish Dressing, Crisp
    Vegetable, '87 152
Bean-and-Veggie Salad, Sweet-and-Hot, '04 184
Bean Salad, Veggie-, '04 328
Boats, Salad, '80 93
Brown Rice-and-Vegetable Salad, '84 202
Calico Salad, '82 35
Cauliflower-Vegetable Salad, '85 158
Chef's Salad, '98 209
Chicken-and-Veggie Spaghetti Salad, '04 129
Chicken Salad, Lively Lemon-, '00 16
Chicken Salad, Vegetable-, '91 287
Chicken Salad, Vegetable Patch, '04 92
Chicken Salad with Veggies, Spicy, '04 177
Chicken Strips and Vegetables, Marinated, '00 54
Chicken-Vegetable Salad, Basil-, '92 162
Chicken Vinaigrette Salad, Vegetable-, '86 135
Chilled Vegetable Salad, '00 285
Chinese Salad, '80 4
Coleslaw with Garden Vegetables, '01 57
Colorful Vegetable Salad, '04 34
Composée, Salad, '79 171
Composé, Salad, '93 126
Congealed Fresh Vegetable Salad, '82 240
Congealed Salad, Cheesy-Vegetable, '86 199
Congealed Salad, Fresh Vegetable, '91 229
Congealed Salad, Lemon-Vegetable, '85 22
Congealed Vegetable Salad, '79 276
Corned Beef Salad, Vegetable-, '80 148
Corn Salad, Colorful, '00 139
Creamy Vegetable Salad, '79 47
Creole Salad, '79 147
Crunchy Vegetable Salad, '79 11; '80 217;
    '83 216
Different Vegetable Salad, '82 143
Easy Vegetable Salad, '83 316; '84 16
Eight-Layer Salad, '99 107
Fennel Salad, Marinated, '93 56
Freezer Salad, '94 118
Garden Medley Salad, '80 122
Garden Salad, '87 62
Garden Salad Bowl, '82 239
Greek Salad, '93 208
Greek Salad, Dawn's World-Famous, '98 276
Greek Salad, Garden, '86 173
Greek Salad, Quick, '02 24
Greek Vegetable Salad, '99 202
Green-and-White Vegetable Salad, '79 286
Green Salad, Rich, '99 203
Greens and Veggies with Fried Okra Croutons,
    Salad, '96 178
Green Vegetable and Egg Salad, '79 191
Green Vegetable Salad, Overnight, '80 5
Grilled Marinated Vegetable Salad, '01 143
Grilled Vegetable Salad, '94 203; '00 146
Healthy Salad, '95 133
Hoppin' John Salad, '01 250
Horseradish Dressing, Vegetable Salad with,
    '92 85
Italian Garden Salad, '99 203
Italian Vegetable Salad, '81 253; '82 19
Layered Salad, Mexican, '02 65
Layered Vegetable Salad with Parmesan Dressing,
    '01 96
Loaded Veggie Salad, '03 58
Luncheon Salad, '84 232
Macaroni-Vegetable Salad, '86 209
Marinade, Garden, '81 23
Marinade, Medley, '79 20
Marinade, Tossed Vegetable, '84 266
Marinated Combo Salad, '82 267

Marinated Garden Salad, '00 178
Marinated Garden Vegetables, '87 252
Marinated Mixed Vegetables, '89 276; '92 106
Marinated Salad, '91 186
Marinated Salad, Eight-Vegetable, '80 218
Marinated Summer Salad, '81 153
Marinated Vegetable-Bacon Bowl, '79 191
Marinated Vegetable Medley, '95 91
Marinated Vegetable Patch Salad, '84 232
Marinated Vegetables, '85 67; '86 286; '88 4, 170
Marinated Vegetable Salad, '79 106, 143;
    '81 280; '82 163; '83 260; '84 13; '87 243;
    '92 64, 91; '97 219; '02 211
Marinated Vegetable Salad, Crispy, '84 193
Marinated Vegetable Salad, Fresh, '86 173
Marinated Vegetables, Creole-, '02 69
Marinated Vegetables, Honey-Mustard, '93 236
Marinated Vegetables, Zesty, '82 272
Marinated Vegetable Toss, '82 113
Marinated Veggies, '91 46; '01 127
Marinate, Fresh Vegetable, '80 33; '81 230
Meal in a Bowl, '96 138
Meal-in-One Salad, '82 232
Mediterranean Salad, '95 132
Medley Salad, Vegetable, '88 86
Mexican Salad, '81 113
Minted Vegetable Salad, '88 23; '98 158
Mixed Vegetable Salad, '80 115; '81 302;
    '82 239; '83 317; '84 16; '86 136
Next-Day Vegetable Salad, '83 81
Niçoise, Beef Salad, '99 159
Olive Salad, '98 184
Oriental Salad, Make-Ahead, '82 163
Oriental Vegetable Salad, '84 290
Overnight Salad, '98 18
Overnight Vegetable Salad, '90 33
Panzanella, '00 62
Pasta and Vegetables, '89 255
Pasta Salad, Ratatouille, '90 74
Pasta Salad, Vegetable, '89 256; '91 143
Pasta Salad, Vegetable-, '92 167
Pasta Salad with Peppered Cheese Crisps,
    Roasted Onion, '98 107
Pasta-Vegetable Salad, '95 238
Pasta-Veggie Salad, '96 106
Pebble Salad, '91 27
Pita Bread Salad, '95 86
Potato Salad, Vegetable, '03 136
Primavera Salad, '93 140
Quick Summer Italian Salad, '92 79
Radish-Vegetable Salad with Parmesan Dressing,
    '01 101
Rainbow Salad, '02 18
Rainbow Vegetable Salad, '83 111
Refrigerated Vegetable Salad, '84 120
Relish Salad, Vegetable, '82 267
Rice-and-Vegetable Salad, '86 42
Rice Primavera Salad, '00 131
Rice Salad, Vegetable-, '80 148; '83 198; '85 87
Ring, Tomato-Vegetable, '81 302
Riviera, Salade, '89 12
Roasted Vegetable Salad with Dried Peach
    Vinaigrette, '97 265
Rolls, Vegetable Salad, '82 278
Senator's Salad, '79 191
Seven-Layer Vegetable Salad, '79 88
Shrimp Salad, Vegetable-, '79 190
Slaw, Confetti Sweet-and-Sour, '98 89
Slaw, Layered, '93 214
Slaw, Rainbow, '01 259
Slaw, Vegetable, '81 280; '00 42
Spaghetti-Vegetable Salad, '97 196
Spinach Salad with Apricot Vinaigrette, '02 120
Spring Vegetable Salad, '88 48

Sprout Salad, Crunchy, '98 52
Summertime Salad, '79 143
Summer Vegetable-and-Orzo Salad, '00 165
Suzie or Steven Salad, '98 204
Swedish Vegetable Salad, '82 23
Sweet-and-Sour Vegetable Salad, '81 25
Tangy Vegetable Toss, '79 144
Tarragon-Vegetable Salad, '85 288
Tortellini Salad, Garden, '91 44
Tortellini Salad, Terrific, '96 134
Tossed Salad, Lively Lemon, '00 16
Variety Salad, '79 113
Vegetable Salad, '98 92; '00 136
Vinaigrette, Vegetables, '82 225, 290
Walnuts, Vegetable Salad with, '86 118
Warm Vegetable Salad, '95 174
Wild Rice-and-Roasted Vegetable Salad, '99 316
Winter Salad, '97 304
Winter Vegetable Salad, '86 42
Winter Vegetable Salad, Baked, '04 45
Salmon Scaloppine with Vegetable Confetti and
    Pernod Sauce, '94 172
Salsa, Cha-Cha, '97 160; '98 333
Salsa, Colorful, '99 119
Salsa, Fresh Vegetable, '98 194
Salsa, Garden, '91 182
Salsa, Greek Vegetable, '98 32
Salsa, Hill Country, '97 123
Salsa, Shrimp Skewers with Vegetable, '98 32, 223
Salsa, Tropical, '96 14
Salsa, Vegetable, '96 208, 220
Salsa with Citrus Dressing, Black Bean, '01 60
Sandwich, Big Veggie, '92 196
Sandwiches, Creamy Vegetable, '97 122
Sandwiches, Focaccia, '98 53
Sandwiches, Grilled Garden, '98 315
Sandwiches, Grilled Vegetable, '01 310
Sandwiches, Open-Faced Summer, '01 171
Sandwiches, Open-Face Tofu-Veggie, '86 5
Sandwiches, Summer Open-Faced, '99 201
Sandwiches, Vegetable Pita, '96 199
Sandwiches, Vegetarian Pita, '84 193
Sandwich, Vegetable Puff, '85 51
Sauce, Cheesy Vegetable, '92 M134
Sauce, Creole, '98 98
Sauce, Crescent City Grill Creole, '04 289
Sauce, Greek Fish with Vegetable, '82 72
Sauce, Tangy Vegetable, '89 280
Sauce, Turkey Patties in Vegetable-Tomato, '87 18
Sauce, Vegetable, '89 98
Sauce, Vegetable Butter, '86 174
Sauce, Vegetable-Cheese, '85 M152
Sausage, Spicy Vegetables and, '80 82
Sausage Supper, '01 28
Sausage Vegetable Dinner, '84 250
Sausage-Vegetable Skillet, '96 102
Sauté, Cajun Vegetable, '92 62
Sautéed Vegetables, Grouper with, '90 M233
Sautéed Vegetables, Tuna with, '98 222
Sautéed Vegetables with Spaghetti Squash, '84 128
Sauté, Garden, '87 90
Sautéing Fresh Vegetables, '82 138
Sauté, Tossed Vegetable, '92 138
Sauté, Vegetable-Egg, '96 204
Sauté, Vegetarian, '95 69
Scalloped Root Vegetables, '98 310
Scallops en Brochette with Vegetables, '80 163
Scallops with Vegetables, Bay, '84 233
Scramble, Veggie, '01 288
Seafood Robert, '97 106
Seasoning Blend, Vegetable, '88 29
Sesame Sauce, Vegetables with, '83 112
Shrimp and Vegetables, '82 6
Shrimp with Rice, '03 219

Skillet Dinner, Fresh Vegetable, '95 229
Skillet, Potato-Vegetable, '92 61
Skillet, Summer Vegetable, '00 138
Skillet, Vegetable-Beef, '86 172
Skillet Zucchini Combo, '96 178
Soufflé Roll, Southwestern, '97 171
Soups
  Bean Soup, Vegetable-, '83 317
  Beef-and-Barley Vegetable Soup, '89 31
  Beef and Vegetable Soup, Quick Italian, '96 235
  Beef Soup, Hearty Vegetable-, '84 102
  Beef Soup, Spicy Vegetable-, '88 11
  Beef Soup, Vegetable-, '88 296; '99 219
  Beefy Vegetable Soup, '79 113; '84 M38
  Beefy Vegetable Soup, Quick, '80 25
  Bisque, Shrimp-Vegetable, '82 313; '83 66
  Black Bean Soup, '03 219
  Bouillabaisse, Marcelle's, '99 200
  Broth, Savory Vegetable, '81 230
  Burger Soup, Vegetable-, '82 6
  Cheese Soup, Creamy Vegetable-, '81 244
  Cheese Soup, Creamy Vegetable, '83 230
  Cheese Soup, Vegetable-, '89 15
  Cheesy Vegetable Soup, '80 73; '97 241
  Chicken-Vegetable Soup, '88 18; '99 60
  Chicken-Vegetable Soup, Spicy, '02 168
  Chili Vegetable Soup, '94 120
  Chocolate Soup, Mexican, '96 277
  Chowder, Cheese-Vegetable, '02 305
  Chowder, Cheesy Vegetable, '80 25; '83 20;
    '00 272; '01 18
  Chowder, Chicken-and-Roasted Vegetable, '97 21
  Chowder, Chicken-Vegetable, '04 326
  Chowder, Creamy Chicken-Vegetable, '92 20
  Chowder, Easy Vegetable, '97 304
  Chowder, Fiesta, '02 305
  Chowder, Harvest, '83 317
  Chowder, Hearty Vegetable, '88 56
  Chowder, Mixed Greens, '97 262
  Chowder, Oven-Roasted Vegetable, '95 229
  Chowder, Potato-Vegetable, '98 335
  Chunky Vegetable Soup, '89 M283
  Clear Vegetable Soup, '79 130
  Down-Home Vegetable Soup, '90 32
  French Soup Maigre, '98 125
  Garden Soup, '85 241
  Garden Vegetable Soup, '83 140; '86 160
  Garden Vegetable Soup, Cold, '84 197
  Gazpacho, '84 112; '85 164; '01 157
  Gazpacho, Chilled, '84 138
  Gazpacho, Cool, '83 140
  Gazpacho, Grilled Vegetable, '97 181
  Gazpacho, Instant, '00 144
  Gazpacho, Smoked Vegetable, '93 156
  Gazpacho, Southwestern Grilled, '00 84
  Gazpacho, Spring, '81 112
  Gazpacho, Summer, '84 181
  Harvest Soup, '79 101
  Hearty Vegetable Soup, '80 26
  Homemade Soup, '79 198
  Leek-Vegetable Soup, '86 304
  Lemongrass-and-Petits Pois Soup, '01 328
  Light Vegetable Soup, '84 280
  Marvelous Vegetable Soup, '82 3
  Meatball Soup, Mexican, '98 315
  Minestrone, Cheesy, '99 17
  Mix, Vegetable Soup, '84 148
  Old-Fashioned Vegetable Soup, '86 304
  Pot Liquor Soup, '98 273; '01 290
  Quick Vegetable Soup, '79 190; '85 24, 32
  Quick Veggie Soup, '91 31
  Southwestern Vegetable Soup, '97 268
  Spanish Fiesta Soup, '01 66
  Spicy Vegetable Soup, '79 198; '93 293; '99 337

VEGETABLES, Soups
(continued)

Spring Vegetables, Lamb Soup with, '04 108
Stock, Pumpkin Soup, '00 296
Stock, Vegetable, '90 31
Tomato-Vegetable Soup, '81 177; '86 9
Turkey Soup, Tempting, '98 314
Turkey-Vegetable Soup, '84 4; '88 264; '91 312
Vegetable Soup, '80 128; '84 148; '85 106;
    '86 187; '87 83, 123; '88 266; '93 157;
    '98 32, 291
Watercress Soup, '01 176
Winter Vegetable Soup, Puree of, '00 322
Spicy Fruit and Veggies with Lime, '04 141
Spread, Vegetable-Egg, '87 106
Spread, Vegetable Sandwich, '83 174; '85 135
Spring Rolls, '99 238
Squash, Stuffed, '98 177
Squash, Vegetable-Stuffed, '84 104
Steak, Festive Cajun Pepper, '03 23
Steak with Pasta and Sesame-Ginger Butter, '99 142
Steak with Vegetables, Skewered, '81 124
Steak with Vegetables, Swiss, '81 273
Steamed and Minted Garden Toss, '83 173
Steamed Dinner, Easy, '83 M314
Steamed Fish and Vegetables, '91 32
Steamed Garden Vegetables, '93 155
Steamed Herbed Vegetables, '93 M303
Steamed Vegetable Medley, '86 50; '90 29
Steamed Vegetables with Garlic-Ginger Butter
    Sauce, '94 89
Steamed Vegetables with Mustard Sauce, '83 208
Steaming Fresh Vegetables, '82 138, 183
Stew, Brunswick, '01 148, 219; '03 29
Stew, Camp, '02 42
Stew, Easy Brunswick, '99 235
Stew, Fish-and-Vegetable, '87 220
Stew, Frogmore, '00 174, 336; '03 181
Stew, Greek-Style Chicken, '03 219
Stew, Hungarian Beef, '03 35
Stew, Minestrone, '93 184
Stew, Mixed Vegetable, '84 13
Stew, Shortcut Vegetable-Beef, '89 218
Stew, Sweet-and-Sour Beef and Vegetable, '85 87
Stew, Texas, '97 211
Stew, Vegetable, '00 248
Stew, Vegetable-Beef, '94 323
Stew, Zesty Chicken, '02 127
Stir-Fry
Almond-Vegetable Stir-Fry, '86 222
Beef and Vegetables, Stir-Fried, '88 301
Beef-and-Vegetables, Stir-Fry, '84 141
Beef-and-Vegetable Stir-Fry, '81 211; '87 22;
    '99 204
Beef with Chinese Vegetables, '81 211
Beef with Oriental Vegetables, '84 140
Chicken and Vegetables, Almond, '86 21
Chicken and Vegetables, Chinese, '81 212
Chicken and Vegetables, Lemon, '88 118
Chicken-and-Vegetables, Stir-Fry, '86 68
Chicken and Vegetables, Stir-Fry, '86 249
Chicken and Vegetable Stir-Fry, '82 237
Chicken-and-Vegetable Stir-Fry, '96 19
Chicken and Vegetables, Walnut, '85 194
Chicken Stir-Fry, Sweet-and-Sour, '98 204
Chicken, Stir-Fry Vegetables with, '84 195
Chicken-Vegetable Stir-Fry, '83 151; '84 13, 141;
    '01 175
Chicken Vegetable Stir-Fry, '00 245
Chicken with Vegetables, Stir-Fry, '96 128
Chinese Vegetable Pouches, '94 34
Convenient Vegetable Stir-Fry, '95 157

Curried Vegetables, '89 219
Curry, Stir-Fried Vegetables with, '87 51
Fresh Stir-Fry, '97 179
Glazed Stir-Fry Vegetables, '99 205
Glazed Stir-Fry Vegetables and Chicken, '99 205
Lo Mein, Vegetable, '97 321
Medley, Chinese Vegetable, '84 33
Medley, Stir-Fry, '88 156
Medley Stir-Fry, Vegetable, '85 109; '99 205
Mixed Vegetable Stir-Fry, '79 268; '80 14
Mixed Veggie-and-Pork Stir-Fry, '99 206
Mixed Veggie Stir-Fry, '99 206
Orange Roughy-and-Vegetable Stir-Fry, '91 50
Orange Roughy Stir-Fry, '98 50
Oriental Vegetables, '84 26; '85 108
Salmon with Stir-Fried Vegetables, Glazed, '02 69
Sausage and Vegetables, Stir-Fry, '86 213; '87 82
Sausage Stir-Fry, '98 156
Shrimp-and-Vegetable Medley Stir-Fry, '99 205
Shrimp and Vegetables, Stir-Fry, '87 91
Shrimp Stir-Fry, '01 258
Skillet-Fried Vegetables, '88 156
Steak-and-Vegetable Stir-Fry, '84 8
Stir-Fried Vegetables, '79 217; '83 193; '90 136
Stir-Frying Fresh Vegetables, '82 138
Three-Vegetable Stir-Fry, '86 174
Vegetable Stir-Fry, '79 214; '82 M172, 208;
    '84 104; '98 156; '99 204
Stuffing, Piglet's, '04 270
Stuffing, Vegetable, '01 84
Succotash, '85 106; '98 177
Succotash, Easy, '80 165
Succotash, Garden, '04 160
Succotash, Quick, '97 302
Succotash, Summer, '86 170
Succotash with Serrano Chile Polenta, Ancho Chile,
    '98 104
Summer Vegetables, '91 136
Supper, Beef-and-Vegetable, '03 219
Supper, Vegetarian, '86 222
Tacos, Loaded Veggie, '00 294
Tacos, Skillet Veggie, '01 170
Tagine, Vegetable, '96 289
Tangy Vegetable Toss, '97 306
Tempura, Basic, '81 68
Tempura, Cornmeal, '81 68
Tempura Udon, '00 93
Tempura, Vegetable, '79 112
Tempura Vegetables, '00 15
Terrine, Chicken-Vegetable, '84 131
Terrine, Vegetable-Chicken, '83 224
Tomatoes, Vegetable Stuffed, '94 141
Topper, Vegetable-Cheese Potato, '86 6
Topping, Turkey-Vegetable, '94 22
Topping, Vegetable, '79 79
Torta, Mediterranean, '98 23
Torte, Layered Vegetable, '84 52
Trio, Vegetable-Herb, '83 172
Trout, Cornmeal-Crusted, '99 52
Turkey Breasts, Jackie's Roasted, '98 269
Turkey Dijon with Garden Vegetables, '01 102
Turnovers, Vegetable, '86 24
Tzimmes, '95 102
Veal Roast with Vegetables, '89 71
Vegewiches, '99 86
Venison-Vegetable Bake, '87 304
Wild Rice, Veggie, '00 141
Wrap, Garden, '03 168
Yataklete Kilkil, '95 71
Yuca Con Mojo, '93 29
VENISON. *See* **GAME.**
VINEGARS
Basil Vinegar, '93 218
Cranberry Vinegar, '91 288

Dill-and-Chive Vinegar, '84 300
Garlic-Basil Vinegar, '85 124
Herb Vinegar, Five-, '85 124
Herb Vinegar, Homemade, '79 100
Herb Vinegar, Mixed, '84 107
Lemon-Mint Vinegar, '85 124
Lemon Vinegar, '95 31; '96 124
Mango-Cilantro Vinegar, '95 190
Mint Vinegar, '92 104
Orange Vinegar, '95 31
Oregano-Lemon Vinegar, Spicy, '85 124
Peach-Mint Vinegar, '95 190
Raspberry-Lemon Vinegar, '87 134
Raspberry-Thyme Vinegar, '95 190
Raspberry Vinegar, '97 146
Rosemary-Red Wine Vinegar, '97 62
Shallot-Tarragon-Garlic Vinegar, '93 191
Southwest Vinegar, '94 200
Tarragon-Dill Vinegar, '85 124
Tarragon Vinegar, '84 107; '89 194; '94 201;
    '97 165
Tomato-Herb Vinegar, '94 200

WAFFLES

Banana-Ginger Waffles, '86 96
Banana-Oatmeal Waffles, '94 206
Banana Split Waffles, '89 205
Belgian Waffles, '94 206
Brunch Waffles, Crunchy, '81 41
Chocolate Waffles with Strawberry Cream,
    '88 153
Club Soda Waffles, '94 206
Cornbread Waffles, '03 205
Cornmeal Waffles, '85 201; '94 22
Corn Waffles, '01 24
Corn Waffles with Cilantro-Lime Butter, '02 109
Crispy Waffles, '00 243
French Toast, Waffled, '82 47
French Waffles, '86 138
Fudge Waffles, '94 205
Gingerbread Waffles, '91 68
Gingerbread Waffles with Apples and Caramel,
    '98 M237
Light Waffles, '91 139
Oat Bran Waffles, '92 139
Oatmeal-Nut Waffles, '83 96
Oatmeal Waffles, '89 107
Peanut Butter Waffles, Honey-Buttered, '94 M206
Pecan Waffles, '87 225
Pumpkin-Nut Waffles, '86 96
Pumpkin Waffles, '95 282
Pumpkin Waffles with Mandarin Orange Sauce,
    Dessert, '89 204
Quick Bread Mix, '81 90
Quick Mix Waffles, '86 9
Refrigerator Waffles, Best Ever, '87 225
Savory
Chicken-Pecan Waffles, Southern, '82 231
Cornbread Waffles, '79 265; '91 90; '98 42
Corn-Chile Waffles, '94 206
Ham Waffles, '80 44
Rice Waffles, '98 124
Sausage Waffles, '83 50
Tuna Waffle-Wich, Hot, '88 272; '89 181
Sorghum-Ginger Waffles, '85 239
Southern Waffles, '87 225
Stack, Hoppin' John Waffle, '04 19
Sundae, Breakfast, '98 206
Sweet Potato Waffles, '88 208
Sweet Potato Waffles with Orange Butter, '90 323
Wacky Waffles, '93 195
Waffles, '81 90; '01 24
Walnut Waffles, Crunchy, '85 48

Whole Wheat Dessert Waffle, '79 92
Whole Wheat Waffles, '84 228
WALNUTS
Apple-Date-Nut Ring, '90 212
Bars, Magic Cookie, '02 253
Bars, Walnut-Date, '02 287; '03 272
Bonbons, Coconut-Black Walnut, '82 307
Breads
  Apple-Nut Bread, '79 12
  Apple-Nut Bread, Fresh, '87 256
  Applesauce-Honey Nut Bread, '87 300
  Apricot-Nut Bread, '79 24
  Banana-Nut Bread, '01 239
  Boule, Walnut-Raisin Pumpernickel, '02 259
  Carrot-Walnut Bread, '88 284
  Cherry Nut Bread, '81 306; '82 36
  Chocolate Date-Nut Bread, '81 284
  Cinnamon-Nut Bubble Bread, '80 22
  Cranberry-Orange Nut Bread, '80 288
  Date-Nut Bread, '85 306
  Honey-Walnut Swirl, '80 21
  Loaf, Apricot-Nut, '81 8
  Loaf, Blue Ribbon Date-Walnut, '80 15
  Loaf, Nutty Wheat, '90 65
  Muffins, Carrot-Date-Nut, '86 262
  Muffins, Holiday Pumpkin, '03 281
  Muffins, Nutty Pumpkin, '86 291
  Nut Bread, '04 281
  Pumpkin Bread, Holiday, '03 281
  Rolls, Dried Cherry-Walnut Sweet, '03 235
  Scones, Merry Cranberry-Nut Yeast, '99 274
  Twists, Fruit-Nut, '82 253
  Walnut Bread, '93 77
  Wine-Date Nut Bread, '82 253
Brie, Walnut-Baked, '93 241
Brie, Walnut-Fried, '86 244
Broccoli and Walnut Sauté, '95 52
Broccoli, English Walnut, '89 68
Brownies, Amaretto-Walnut, '99 311; '04 142
Brownies, Chocolate, '02 M207
Brownies, Chocolate-Walnut, '89 325
Brownies Deluxe, '03 330
Brownies for Passover, '99 56
Brownies, Walnut-Cream Cheese, '84 240
Burgers, Nutty, '87 185
Burgers, Walnut, '89 163
Butter, Spaghettini with Green Beans and Walnut
  Brown, '03 170
Cake, Apple-Nut, '87 76; '96 268
Cake, Apple-Walnut, '94 242
Cake, Black Walnut, '80 253; '84 316; '90 308
Cake, Black Walnut Pound, '92 16
Cake, Orange Nut, '80 70
Cake, Orange-Nut Butter, '80 254
Cake Roll, Date-Nut, '89 94
Cake, Saucy Pudding, '98 196
Cakes, Mini-Mincemeat Nut, '88 257
Cake, Yogurt-Lemon-Nut, '89 169
Candied Nuts, '81 261
Carrots with Walnuts, Julienne, '84 188
Cheese, Crostini with Walnut-Blue, '01 321
Cheese Logs, Port Wine, '02 279
Cheese Logs, Spicy Monterey Jack, '02 279
Cheese, Nutty Date Dessert, '87 299
Chicken and Vegetables, Walnut, '85 194
Chicken Breasts, Walnut-Stuffed, '85 293
Chicken, Crispy Walnut, '90 89
Chicken, Deep-Fried Walnut, '87 175
Chicken, Walnut, '85 126
Chocolate Chubbies, '01 144
Chocolate-Nut Chews, '81 92
Chutney, Cranberry-Ginger, '00 253
Citrus and Greens, Holiday, '03 280
Cobbler, Apple-Walnut, '79 154; '81 248

Coffee Cake, Cranberry-Nut, '81 250
Coffee Cake, Sour Cream-Walnut, '79 209
Coffee Cake, Walnut, '93 124
Cookies, Apple-Nut, '80 228
Cookies, Cran-bear-y Bread, '02 254
Cookies, Date Pinwheel, '02 93
Cookies, Frosted Pumpkin-Walnut, '82 217
Cookies, Ginger-Oatmeal Sorghum, '02 230
Cookies, Nutty Oatmeal, '81 130
Cookies, Rich Date-Nut Chocolate Chip, '92 207
Cookies, Simply Walnut, '91 236
Cookies, Walnut, '81 301; '97 275; '98 35
Crunch, Apple-Blueberry, '02 128
Cupcakes, Apple-Nut, '82 279
Cups, Chocolate-Walnut, '85 213
Dainties, Choco-Nut, '04 M124
Date Drops, Stuffed, '97 247
Date Moons, '01 295
Dressing, Green Beans with Walnut, '94 279
Dressing, Honey-Walnut, '93 107
Dressing, Walnut, '99 125
Eggplant with Walnuts, Georgian, '01 87
Figs with Prosciutto, Walnuts, and Cream, '96 194
Fillets, Blue Cheese-Walnut Stuffed, '95 327
Filling, Honey-Walnut, '80 21
Finikia, '96 21
Fried Walnuts, Chinese, '81 254
Frosting, Chocolate, '99 271
Frosting, Nutty Coconut, '86 8
Fruit, Cheese, and Nuts, '93 324
Fudge, Buttermilk, '97 317
Fudge, Nutty White, '81 253
Fudge, Orange-Walnut, '92 288
Green Beans, Lemon-Walnut, '93 304
Green Beans with Roquefort Cheese and Walnuts,
  '02 255
Greens with Raspberries and Walnuts, Mixed,
  '98 194
Greens with Walnuts, Mixed, '99 107
Hamburgers, Meatless Walnut, '96 243
Ice Cream Balls, Nutty, '89 72
Macaroni with Blue Cheese and Walnuts, '02 M208
Mandel Bread, '99 57
Meatballs, Mock, '81 243
Mousse, Coffee-Nut, '86 319
Panzanella, '00 62
Parmesan Walnuts, Mixed Greens with, '95 301
Pears Blue, '99 246
Pesto, Littleneck Clams with Cilantro-Black Walnut,
  '97 164
Phyllo Baskets, Walnut-, '93 210
Pie, Black-and-White Fudge, '99 249
Pie, Black Walnut, '97 275; '98 35
Pie, Elegant Pumpkin-Walnut Layered, '02 244
Pie, Sweetheart Fudge, '03 319
Pie, Walnut-Cranberry, '87 259
Pitas, Spinach-Walnut, '87 202; '88 43
Pudding, Fig-Walnut, '03 244
Romaine Toss, Crunchy, '00 30
Salad, Asian Chicken, '99 124
Salad, Beet, Apple, and Walnut, '98 269
Salad, Bluegrass, '02 255
Salad, Gorgonzola-Walnut, '96 170
Salad, Green Bean, Walnut, and Feta, '96 273;
  '00 321
Salad, Okra-Walnut, '04 291
Salad, Orange Walnut, '80 246
Salad, Ramen Noodle, '02 24
Salad, Raspberry-Walnut, '94 158
Salad, Shrimp-Walnut, '86 182
Salad, Sunburst Chicken-and-Walnut, '93 91
Salad, Turkey-Walnut, '03 239
Salad, Tuscan Fennel, '02 170
Salad, Walnut-Chicken, '89 14; '96 243

Salad with Orange Vinaigrette, Roasted Beet-and-
  Sugared Walnut, '97 229
Salad with Sautéed Walnuts, Turkey, '86 117
Salad with Walnuts, Vegetable, '86 118
Sandwich, Date-Nut Lettuce, '94 202
Sandwiches, Nutty Cream Cheese Party, '00 119
Sauce, Apricot-Walnut Hard, '88 153
Sauce, Linguine with Green Beans and Walnut,
  '04 128
Sauce, Spaghetti with Parsley and Walnut, '80 30
Sauce, Walnut Cream, '93 275; '01 229
Sauce, Walnut-Parmesan Pesto, '96 251; '97 104
Sherry-Orange Nuts, '86 M289
Shortbread, Blue Cheese-Walnut, '03 108
Slaw, Nutty Apple, '88 216
Snowcaps, Smoky Mountain, '00 288
Soup with Walnuts, Red Bean, '96 243
Spice Kisses, Walnut, '89 295
Spread, Corn-and-Walnut, '96 26
Spread, Date-Orange-Nut, '02 59
Spread, Date-Walnut, '87 292
Spread, Date-Walnut-Cheese, '96 322
Spread, Honey-Nut, '03 46
Spread, Nutty Fruit-and-Cheese, '87 246; '02 164
Spread with Walnuts, Buttery Blue Cheese, '00 329
Strawberries with Walnuts, Stuffed, '85 122;
  '86 124
Stuffing, Apple-Walnut, '95 289
Stuffing, Sausage, '00 292
Stuffing, Tomatoes with Walnut-Rice, '91 102
Sweet Potatoes with Sherry and Walnuts, '86 286
Swirls, Cranberry-Walnut, '00 290
Syrup, Maple-Nut, '80 228
Tart, Apricot-Nut, '99 249
Toffee, '01 218
Topping, Nutty, '86 16
Vegetables with Walnuts, Julienne, '86 M251
Vinaigrette, Maple-Walnut, '04 45
Wafers, Blue Cheese-Walnut, '00 56
Wafers, Spicy Cheese-Walnut, '03 61
Waffles, Crunchy Walnut, '85 48
Zucchini with Walnuts, '84 213
WATERMELON. *See* **MELONS.**
WHAT'S FOR SUPPER?
Appetizers
  Cherry Pepper Appetizers, Fiery Stuffed,
    '97 269
  Dip, Quick Creamy Vegetable, '00 34
Beans, Hearty Baked, '01 259
Breads
  Biscuits, Fresh Tomato, '04 138
  Breadsticks, Parmesan-Garlic, '99 46
  Cheddar-Nut Bread, '03 42
  Cornbread, Buttermilk, '99 235
  Knots, Cajun Bread, '03 63
  Knots, Italian Bread, '03 63
  Knots, Southwestern, '03 63
  Rolls, Hurry-Up Crescent, '97 50
Cheese Crisps, Peppered, '98 107
Chutney, Cranberry-and-Apricot, '02 286
Couscous, Lemon, '00 99
Desserts
  Apple Bundles, Quick, '04 242
  Cobbler, Warm Blueberry, '98 153
  Cookies, Candy Wrap, '04 139
  Cookies, Peanut Butter-Kiss, '03 42
  Pizza, Apple-Pineapple Dessert, '00 313
  Sundaes, Chocolate Mint, '03 M120
  Turtle Dessert, '04 127
Fried Rice, Cashew, '99 171
Grits, Chili-Cheese, '01 86
Grits, Parmesan Cheese, '02 233
Grits Squares, Chili-Cheese, '01 86
Lemonade, Pink, '01 163

WHAT'S FOR SUPPER?
(continued)

Mac-and-Cheese, Veggie, '01 111
Macaroni-Mushroom Bake, '97 96
Main Dishes
Barbecue Hobo Supper, '99 108
Beef à la Beer, '98 64
Beef à la Mode, '98 122
Beef and Macaroni, Easy, '02 188
Beef and Vegetables, '01 86
Beef-and-Vegetable Supper, '03 219
Beef Barbecue, Slow-Cooker, '02 299
Beef Filets, Spicy, '00 121
Beef Patties, Marmalade-Glazed, '01 136
Beef Stroganoff, '03 23
Beef Stroganoff, Quick, '99 327
Brisket, Oven Barbecue, '01 259
Brisket, Smoky Barbecue, '03 160
Buffalo Hot Wings, '03 184
Buffalo Tenders, '03 184
Burgers, Stuffed Border, '04 127
Burgers, Taco, '98 224
Burgers with Caramelized Onions, Pepper,
 '00 218
Casserole, Beef, Cheese, and Noodle, '99 58
Casserole, Chiles Rellenos, '98 48
Casserole, Creamy Chicken-Rice, '99 21
Casserole, Fajita, '97 96
Casserole, Ham, '98 314
Casserole, Stroganoff, '98 48
Catfish Parmesan, '99 91
Chicken and Pasta, Mediterranean, '03 63
Chicken and Pears, Glazed, '99 21
Chicken-and-Rice Bake, Herbed, '02 215
Chicken and Vegetables, Grilled, '99 200
Chicken Bundles, Southwestern, '02 215
Chicken, Cashew, '01 188
Chicken-Cashew Fried Rice, '99 171
Chicken Casserole D'Iberville, '04 182
Chicken Curry, Indian-Style, '97 119
Chicken Cutlets, Oven-Fried, '04 81
Chicken, Dijon, '99 21
Chicken Fettuccine Alfredo, '00 57
Chicken, Foil-Wrapped, '99 108
Chicken in Foil, Barbecued, '04 222
Chicken, Lime-Grilled, '02 142
Chicken, Marmalade Baked, '99 286
Chicken, Mom's Fried, '01 163
Chicken Olé Foil Supper, '04 222
Chicken Oriental, '01 36
Chicken, Oven-Baked Barbecue, '03 160
Chicken Parmigiana, Zesty, '00 19
Chicken Penne, Cheesy, '00 289
Chicken Penne, Spicy Cheesy, '00 289
Chicken, Pinot Noir Risotto with Rosemary,
 '97 214
Chicken Quarters, Marinated, '02 142
Chicken Tenders, Lemon, '03 184
Chicken Thighs, Herb-Roasted, '02 127
Chicken Thighs, Honey-Pecan, '02 127
Chicken, Undercover, '97 64
Chops, Easy Scalloped Potatoes and, '00 289
Corn Puppies, '97 140
Dinner, Quick Mexican, '98 224
Drumsticks, Tangy, '97 120
Eggs, Armadillo, '97 270
Enchiladas, Enticing, '99 57
Enchiladas, Green Chile, '02 188
Fajitas, Tex-Mex, '01 188
Fillets, Crispy Baked, '99 90
Fish, Baked, '98 122
Fish, Caribbean, '99 109

Fish in a Wrap, '97 64
Flank Steak, Soy-Ginger, '02 90
Flank Steaks with Mushrooms, '00 121
Flounder with Lemon Couscous, Creole, '00 99
Hamburger-Corn Bake, '99 58
Hamburger-Rice Skillet, '00 236
Hamburger Steaks, Smothered, '00 289
Ham, Sweet Orange-Glazed, '02 286
Hot Dog Deluxe, '97 140
Kebabs, Pineapple-Pork, '99 144
Kielbasa with Beans, Easy Cheesy, '01 28
Loaves, Mini Teriyaki, '98 224
Manicotti, Cheesy Sausage-and-Tomato, '03 257
Manicotti, Meaty Stuffed, '00 19
Meatball Packets, Italian, '04 222
Meatballs, Marmalade-Glazed, '01 136
Meat Loaf, Alabama, '04 188
Meat Loaf, Cheeseburger, '03 204
Meat Loaf, Easy, '97 24
Meat Loaf, Spinach-Stuffed Turkey, '97 24
Meat Loaf, Sweet Ketchup-and-Bacon-Topped,
 '03 203
Meat Loaf, Sweet 'n' Saucy, '01 210
Meat Loaf, Teriyaki, '98 224
Meat Loaf with Feta Cheese, Lamb, '97 24
Meat Loaves, Mini Alabama, '04 188
Meat Loaves, Mini Mexican, '02 90
Meat Loaves with Spaghetti Sauce, '03 204
Noodles, Sesame, '01 188
Omelet, Shrimp-and-Vegetable Oven, '99 286
Omelet, Vegetable-Pasta Oven, '99 286
Pasta Toss, Garden, '00 57
Peppers, Shrimp-Stuffed, '97 268
Pie, Beef-and-Onion Cornbread, '01 298
Pie, Italian Meat, '01 297
Pie, Turkey-Sausage, '01 297
Pizza Bake, Upside-Down, '98 224
Pizza, Cheesy Mexican, '00 314
Pizza, Chicken Parmesan, '00 134
Pizza, Deep-Dish, '01 29
Pizza Dogs, Grilled, '97 139
Pizzas, Individual, '03 219
Poblanos, Corn-Stuffed, '97 269
Poblanos Stuffed with Pork and Fruit, '97 269
Pork Chops and Rice, Savannah, '00 236
Pork Chops, Bourbon-Glazed, '04 44
Pork Chops, Flavorful Crusted, '04 44
Pork Chops, Greek-Style Baked, '04 44
Pork Chops in Onion Gravy, '99 222
Pork Chops, Mexican, '99 108
Pork Chops with Roasted Vegetables, Fried,
 '98 153
Pork Loin, Marinated, '01 331
Pork Sausage-Seasoned Rice, '00 236
Pork Stir-Fry, Sweet-and-Sour, '03 92
Pork Tenderloin, Apple Butter, '99 145
Pork Tenderloins, Coriander-Pepper, '99 145
Pork Tenderloin with Gingered Jezebel Sauce,
 Grilled, '04 138
Pork Tenderloin with Mustard Sauce, '99 145
Potatoes, Cheddar, Broccoli, and Ham Stuffed,
 '04 26
Pot Roast, Mexican, '98 64
Pot Roast of Beef with Vegetables, '98 65
Pot Roast, Old-Fashioned, '98 64
Pot Roast with Dumplings, '98 245
Pot Roast with Mushroom Gravy, '02 90
Red Rice, '00 289
Red Rice and Ham, '00 289
Ribs and Beans, Spicy-Sweet, '02 299
Ribs, Slow-Cooker Barbecue, '03 160
Risotto, Redneck, '98 107
Roast, Barbecue, '98 245
Roast Beef, Mary's, '01 86

Roast Beef, Pressure Cooker, '01 86
Roast Beef, Slow Cooker, '01 86
Roast Beef, Sunday, '99 327
Sausage-and-Bean Supper, '02 233
Sausage and Cabbage, Skillet, '01 28
Sausage and Peppers with Parmesan Cheese
 Grits, '02 233
Sausage-Apple Kraut Dinner, '02 234
Sausage Supper, '01 28
Shrimp and Pasta with Cream Sauce, '98 295
Shrimp Manicotti, '97 96
Shrimp Oriental, '01 36
Shrimp with Rice, '03 219
Shrimp with Tartar Sauce, '00 178
Spaghetti, All-in-One, '98 295
Spaghetti, Chicken-Vegetable, '98 296
Spaghetti, One-Pot, '00 58
Spaghetti, Salsa, '00 58
Spaghetti with Meat Sauce, '02 188
Spinach Shells, '97 50
Spuds with Black Bean Salsa, Chicken Fajita,
 '04 25
Steak, Festive Cajun Pepper, '03 23
Steak, Hamburger, '99 45
Steaks, Italian Sirloin, '04 61
Steaks, Stately, '00 121
Tetrazzini, Turkey, '03 257
Thighs, Grilled Tarragon-Dijon, '97 120
Tuna Steaks with Cucumber Sauce, '97 180
Tuna with Lemon and Capers, '97 180
Tuna with Warm Tomato Salad, '97 179
Turkey-Spinach Rollups, '00 178
Vegetable Lo Mein, Sesame-, '03 91
Mayonnaise, Caramelized Onion, '00 218
Meat Base, Savory, '02 188
Penne, Garden Sauté with, '98 207
Pico de Gallo, '04 61
Refried Beans, Easy, '99 57
Rice Pilaf, Lemon, '01 36
Risotto, Lemon-Lime, '97 213
Risotto, Microwave, '97 M213
Salads and Salad Dressings
Apple-Spinach Salad, '99 222
Bacon Dressing, Jeweled Hot, '97 196
Black Bean Salad, '97 196; '98 208
Broccoli-Grape Salad, '01 163
Buffalo Tenders Salad, '03 184
Caesar Salad, '00 19
Chicken on Greens, Grilled, '99 201
Chicken Salad, Gazpacho-, '00 203
Chili-Corn Chip Stack-Up Salad, '04 242
Coleslaw, Old-Fashioned, '99 235
Corn Salad, '02 234
Corn Salad, Roasted, '97 196
Cucumber-Radish Dressing, '00 99
Fried Chicken Salad, Fiesta, '03 120
Fruit-Jícama Salad, '00 203
Fruit Salad, '03 42
Garden Salad, Marinated, '00 178
Greens with Raspberry Dressing, Mixed, '97 50
Noodle Chicken Salad, '03 143
Pasta Salad, Bayou, '00 203
Pasta Salad with Peppered Cheese Crisps,
 Roasted Onion, '98 107
Pork-and-Rice Salad with Spicy Tomato
 Dressing, '03 143
Potato Salad, '01 163
Potato Salad, Charletta's, '98 153
Potato Salad, German, '97 195
Slaw, Chinese Cabbage, '01 36
Slaw, Rainbow, '01 259
Slaw, Tangy, '02 215
Spaghetti-Vegetable Salad, '97 196
Taco Salad, '02 188

Tomato Dressing, Spicy, '03 143
Turkey Salad, Chutney Curried, '98 314
Sandwiches
Barbecue Beef Sandwiches, '99 327; '01 136
Beef-and-Artichoke Open-Faced Italian Sandwich, '98 22
Burgers, Garden Herb, '01 136
Chicken Salad Melts, Open-Faced Cheesy, '00 134
Crab Melts, Open-Faced, '01 171
Fish Po'boys, Zesty, '03 120
Focaccia with Roasted Pepper Vinaigrette, Stuffed, '00 134
Grilled Cheese Meat Loaf Sandwiches, '04 188
Ham Sandwiches, Holiday, '02 286
Meat Loaf Sandwich, '01 210
Meat Loaf Sandwiches, Barbecue, '04 188
Monte Cristo Sandwiches, Open-Faced, '01 171
Open-Faced Sandwiches, Summer, '99 201
Open-Faced Summer Sandwiches, '01 171
Reubens, Summer, '00 134
Sloppy Joes, '02 188
Spread with Creamy Cucumber Sauce, White Bean, '00 178
Torta, Mediterranean, '98 23
Sauces
Black Bean Salsa, '04 25
Jezebel Sauce, Gingered, '04 M138
Pizza Sauce, '00 314
Special Sauce, Morton's, '01 331
Sweet 'n' Saucy Sauce, '01 210
Tex-Mex Secret Sauce, '04 127
Tomato Sauce, '97 96, 269
Soups and Stews
Black Bean Soup, '03 219
Chicken Soup, Mexican, '03 63
Chicken Stew, Greek-Style, '03 219
Chicken Stew, Speedy, '03 42
Chicken Stew, Zesty, '02 127
Chili, Big-Batch, '04 242
Chili, Cincinnati-Style, '00 34
Chili, Easy, '02 299
Chili in a Biscuit Bowl, '98 224
Chili, Slow Cooker Cincinnati-Style, '00 34
Chili, Three-Bean, '00 34
Étouffée, Okra, '98 207
French Onion Soup, Caramelized, '00 218
Fricassee, White Chicken, '98 122
Stew, Easy Brunswick, '99 235
Turkey Soup, Tempting, '98 314
Topping, Breadcrumb, '02 233
Topping, Cornbread, '01 298
Tortellini, Creamy, '99 171
Vegetables
Black-Eyed Peas, Hot-and-Spicy, '99 235
Broccoli, Garlic, '99 46
Broccoli, Lemon Pepper Steamed, '02 215
Broccoli, Stir-Fried, '00 99
Carrots and Green Beans, Dilled, '99 223
Celery, Nutty Stuffed, '03 184
Corn Fritters, '98 207
Corn on the Cob with Garlic-Chive Butter, '01 331
Eggplant Italian Style, '01 111
Fries, Seasoned Steak, '04 127
Green Beans, Garlic, '01 111
Kebabs, Easy Vegetable, '02 142
Mashed Potatoes, Speedy Garlic, '04 M81
Medley, Day-by-Day Vegetable, '03 219
Medley, Vegetable-Cheese, '99 M287
Onions, Caramelized, '00 218
Packets, Vegetable, '97 64
Potato Casserole, Mashed, '99 223
Potatoes, Simple Seasoned, '01 259

Potatoes, Whipped Celery, '99 45
Roasted Vegetable Medley, '01 331
Spinach, Hot Spiked, '97 195
Squash, Southern Summer, '98 207
Vinaigrette, Roasted Pepper, '00 134
WHEAT GERM
Biscuits, Wheat Germ, '86 261
Bread, Banana Wheat, '81 14
Cookies, Breakfast, '97 52
Crackers, Oatmeal-Wheat Germ, '84 236
Crisps, Sesame Wheat, '81 106
Muffins, Carrot-Wheat, '88 9
Muffins, Wheat Germ-Prune, '81 106
Pancakes, Wheat Germ, '86 242
Pancakes, Wheat Germ-Banana, '79 114
Squares , Spicy Wheat Germ, '80 44
WILD RICE. *See* **RICE/Wild Rice.**
WOK COOKING
Beef
Asparagus, Stir-Fry Beef and, '91 124
Broccoli and Beef, Stir-Fry, '83 110
Broccoli, Quick Beef and, '91 123
Broccoli, Stir-Fry Beef and, '79 47
Broccoli Stir-Fry, Beef-and-, '91 46
Carrot Stir-Fry, Beef-and-, '98 335
Chinese Beef Stir-Fry, '83 151
Chinese-Style Beef, '87 50
Chinese Vegetables, Beef with, '81 211
Coconut-Beef Stir-Fry, '97 18
Curried Beef Stir-Fry, '01 162
Hungarian Stir-Fry, '93 64
Indian Stir-Fry, '92 126
Italian Beef Stir-Fry, '99 35
Lime-Ginger Beef Stir-Fry, '92 65
Meatballs, Sweet-and-Sour, '86 240
Mongolian Beef, '85 2, 75; '01 94
Mongolian Beef Stir-Fry, '89 25
Oriental Beef, '85 20
Oriental Vegetables, Beef with, '84 140
Peanutty Beef Stir-Fry, '95 157
Pea Pods, Stir-Fry Beef and, '80 19
Shredded Beef over Rice Noodles, '85 74
Shrimp Stir-Fry, Beef-and-, '93 32
Snow Peas, Oriental Beef and, '79 105
Snow Peas, Stir-Fry Beef and, '83 22
Snow Pea Stir-Fry, Beef and, '82 98
Steak, Chinese Pepper, '82 236
Steak, Fast-and-Easy Stir-Fried, '87 50
Steak, Pepper Stir-Fry, '81 240
Steak Sukiyaki, Flank, '88 233
Stew, Beef, '86 51
Stir-Fried Beef, '84 26
Teriyaki Stir-Fry, '83 110
Thai Lemon Beef, '97 292
Vegetables, Stir-Fried Beef and, '88 301
Vegetables, Stir-Fry Beef-and-, '84 141
Vegetable Stir-Fry, Beef-and-, '81 211; '87 22; '99 204
Wontons, Tex-Mex, '87 196
Broccoli with Sesame Seeds, '02 45
Catfish Stir, '84 184
Cheese Wontons with Hot Sauce, '83 74
Chicken
Almond Chicken and Vegetables, '86 21
à l'Orange, Stir-Fry Chicken, '83 82
Braised Bourbon Chicken, '86 51
Broccoli Stir-Fry, Chicken-, '82 33
Cashew Chicken, '79 255; '83 21; '01 188
Cashews, Chicken with, '79 207
Cashews, Szechwan Chicken with, '81 212
Chinese, Chicken, '94 33
Chinese Chicken and Vegetables, '81 212
Chinese Chicken Stir-Fry, '90 100
Chinese-Style Dinner, '84 26

Curry, Stir-Fried Chicken, '87 51
Easy Chicken Stir-Fry, '91 124
Garden, Chicken-in-a-, '80 18
Herb-Chicken Stir-Fry, '89 177
Hurry-Up Chicken Stir-Fry, '91 124
Italian Stir-Fry, '92 126
Lemon Chicken, '86 173
Mexican Stir-Fry, '92 126
Orange-Chicken Stir-Fry, '84 68
Orange-Chicken Stir-Fry, Kyoto, '87 96
Oriental, Chicken, '01 36
Oriental Chicken with Peanuts, '82 236
Oriental Chicken with Pineapple, '86 42
Pineapple-Chicken Stir-Fry, '89 176
Plum Sauce, Chicken with, '82 236
Princess Chicken, '86 122
Shiitake-Chicken Stir-Fry, '89 61
Snow Pea Stir-Fry, Chicken and, '95 157
Soy and Wine, Chicken in, '84 26
Sweet-and-Sour Chicken, '86 240
Szechuan Chicken, '98 155
Szechwan Chicken, '83 85
Tempura Delight, Chicken, '85 66
Thai Chicken Stir-Fry, '00 23
Vegetables and Chicken, Glazed Stir-Fry, '99 205
Vegetables, Jim's, Chicken and, '99 237
Vegetables, Stir-Fry Chicken with, '96 128
Vegetable Stir-Fry, Chicken-, '83 151; '84 13, 141
Vegetable Stir-Fry, Chicken, '00 245
Vegetable Stir-Fry, Chicken-and-, '82 237; '86 68; '96 19
Vegetables with Chicken, Stir-Fry, '84 195
Walnut Chicken, '85 126
Walnut Chicken and Vegetables, '85 194
Zesty Stir-Fried Chicken, '83 82
Zucchini Stir-Fry, Chicken-, '84 50
Egg Rolls, '86 81
Egg Rolls, Scrumptious, '96 101
Indian Stir-Fry, '92 126
Orange Roughy-and-Vegetable Stir-Fry, '91 50
Orange Roughy Stir-Fry, '98 50
Pasta Potpourri, '94 33
Pear Fritters, Ol' Timey, '86 51
Pork
Cashews, Stir-Fry Pork and, '01 16
Curried Pork Tenderloin, '86 76
Eggrolls, Shrimp and Pork, '82 240; '83 18
Garlic Sauce, Stir-Fried Pork in, '84 141
Ham and Zucchini Stir-Fry, '79 47
Ham Stir-Fry, Easy, '86 332
Hot-and-Spicy Pork, '81 228
Kung Pao Pork, '96 49
Mixed Veggie-and-Pork Stir-Fry, '99 206
Moo Shu Pork, '99 237
Onions with Bean Sauce, Pork-and-, '85 76
Oriental, Pork, '81 212
Sausage, Fried Rice with, '83 12
Sausage Rolls with Sweet-and-Sour Sauce, '83 74
Sausage Stir-Fry, '82 236; '98 156
Stir-Fried Pork, '87 51
Sweet-and-Sour Pork, '79 42; '80 227; '81 26; '85 34, 194
Sweet-and-Sour Pork Stir-Fry, '03 92
Rice, Easy Fried, '84 76
Rice, Egg Fried, '80 19
Rice, Fried, '00 273
Rice Special, Fried, '80 56
Rice with Sausage, Fried, '83 12
Scallop Stir-Fry, '94 32
Shrimp and Refried Rice, '89 176
Shrimp and Sirloin Supreme, '81 131
Shrimp-and-Vegetable Medley Stir-Fry, '99 205
Shrimp and Vegetables, Stir-Fry, '87 91
Shrimp, Hoisin, '99 237

WOK COOKING
(continued)

Shrimp Oriental, '01 36
Shrimp Skillet, Quick, '87 50
Shrimp, Stir-Fry, '96 129; '01 95
Shrimp Stir-Fry, Cajun, '92 127
Shrimp, Szechuan, '86 173
Shrimp, Tangy Honeyed, '94 32
Shrimp with Snow Peas, '85 75
Sugar Flips, '83 74
Swordfish Stir-Fry, '96 128
Szechuan Ginger Stir-Fry with Noodle Pancake, '97 292
Turkey
Broccoli Stir-Fry, Turkey-, '91 62
Rice, Turkey , '00 97
Spring Rolls, '99 238
Vegetables
Asparagus and Mushrooms, '85 108
Asparagus, Stir-Fried, '87 52
Bok Choy-Broccoli Stir-Fry, '84 2
Bok Choy, Stir-Fried, '97 105
Broccoli, Jade-Green, '80 12
Broccoli, Stir-Fried, '83 227
Broccoli, Stir-Fry, '80 19
Broccoli with Sesame, '80 13
Broccoli with Sesame Seeds, '82 34
Brussels Sprouts Stir-Fry, '81 308
Cabbage, Lemon-Butter, '88 156
Cabbage, Stir-Fried, '81 75, 271; '85 109
Chinese Vegetable Medley, '84 33
Chinese Vegetable Pouches, '94 34
Convenient Vegetable Stir-Fry, '95 157
Curry, Stir-Fried Vegetables with, '87 51
Egg Rolls, Vegetarian, '86 148
Fresh Stir-Fry, '97 179
Glazed Stir-Fry Vegetables, '99 205
Green Bean Medley, '85 108
Green Beans, Stir-Fried, '85 148
Greens, Stir-Fried, '94 33; '97 270
Lo Mein, Sesame-Vegetable, '03 91
Medley, Stir-Fry, '88 156
Medley Stir-Fry, Vegetable, '85 109; '99 205
Mixed Vegetable Stir-Fry, '79 268; '80 14
Mixed Veggie Stir-Fry, '99 206
Mushrooms with Bacon, Stir-Fried, '80 123
Onion-Asparagus Stir-Fry, Sweet, '98 135
Oriental Vegetables, '84 26; '85 108
Pasta Potpourri, '94 33
Pasta, Vegetable Stir-Fry, '96 29
Peas and Peppers, Stir-Fried, '87 51
Potato-Snow Pea Stir-Fry, '86 173
Skillet-Fried Vegetables, '88 156
Spinach, Chinese, '79 179
Spinach, Stir-Fry, '81 182
Spinach with Mushrooms, '80 19
Spinach Wontons, '83 74
Squash Medley, '84 128
Squash Medley, Stir-Fried, '80 123
Squash, Stir-Fried, '97 118
Squash Stir-Fry, '80 184
Squash Stir-Fry, Two-, '86 174
Sweet Potato Pudding, '86 52
Three-Vegetable Stir-Fry, '86 174
Tomato-Zucchini Stir-Fry, '80 158
Turnip-and-Carrot Stir-Fry, '96 36
Vegetables, Stir-Fried, '79 217; '83 193; '90 136
Vegetable Stir-Fry, '82 208; '84 104; '99 204
Zucchini-and-Tomato Stir-Fry, '85 108
Zucchini, Italian-Style, '80 123
Zucchini Pesto, '84 194
Zucchini Toss, Stir-Fry, '88 156

WONTONS
Bowls, Wonton Wrapper, '95 58
Cheese Wontons with Hot Sauce, '83 74
Chicken Wontons, '92 284
Chicken Wontons with Hoisin Peanut Dipping Sauce, '99 14
Chips, Baked Wonton, '91 138
Chips, Cinnamon-and-Sugar Wonton, '91 138
Chips, Garlic Wonton, '91 138
Chips, Lemon-and-Herb Wonton, '91 138
Chips, Parmesan Cheese Wonton, '91 138
Fried Wonton Envelopes, '95 96
Fried Wontons, Crispy, '83 21
Fruit-Filled Wontons, '85 287
Lasagna, Won Ton Spinach, '04 129
Lobster Scallion Shooters, '00 197
Moroccan Triangles, Crispy, '03 60
Nibbles, Wonton, '85 287
Pork on Mixed Greens, Hot Sesame, '97 19
Preparation Techniques, '83 74
Sausage Rolls with Sweet-and-Sour Sauce, '83 74
Sesame Dumplings, Steamed, '97 208
Sesame Wontons, Spicy Crab-and-Ginger Salsa with, '01 283
Spinach Wontons, '83 74
Sugar Flips, '83 74
Taco Teasers, '01 134
Tex-Mex Wontons, '87 196

Y OGURT
Apples, Honey-Yogurt, '92 46
Bread, Yogurt, '97 130
Breakfast-in-a-Bowl, '89 87
Carambola-Yogurt Calypso, '90 169
Cheese Appetizer, Yogurt, '04 217
Cheese, Yogurt, '04 217
Chicken, Grilled Yogurt-Lemon, '81 111
Chicken, Savory Yogurt, '91 238; '92 28
Chicken, Yogurt-Sesame, '90 216
Coffee Freeze, Amaretto-, '99 161
Coleslaw, Grilled Chicken Breasts with Lemon-Yogurt, '98 148
Desserts
Bars, Lemon Yogurt Wheat, '79 93
Cake, Strawberry Yogurt Layer, '94 85
Cake, Yogurt-Lemon-Nut, '89 169
Cake, Yogurt Pound, '84 10
Chocolate Yogurt, Mocha Sauce with, '92 243
Dip, Strawberries with Mint Yogurt, '03 93
Ice, Apricot Yogurt, '81 177
Ice Milk, Banana Yogurt, '89 199
Ice, Peach-Yogurt, '84 83
Lemon-Chiffon Frozen Yogurt, '85 54
Nectarines Royale, '85 132
Parfait, Crunchy Strawberry-Yogurt, '79 124
Peach Yogurt, Frozen Fresh, '90 139
Pie, Strawberry Yogurt, '80 232
Pie, Strawberry-Yogurt, '85 122; '86 124
Pie, Yogurt-Apricot, '85 132
Pie, Yogurt-Cheese, '82 121
Pops, Pineapple-Yogurt, '91 173
Sauce, Honey-Yogurt, '92 307
Strawberry Yogurt Delight, '85 77
Strawberry-Yogurt Dessert, '90 295
Tortoni, Apricot-Yogurt, '95 124
Vanilla Frozen Yogurt, '87 125
Dip, Cucumber-Yogurt, '99 93
Dip, Curry, '85 132
Dip, Fruited Yogurt, '84 171
Dip, Yogurt, '94 21
Dip, Yogurt Herring, '80 232
Dressing, Asparagus with Yogurt, '79 66
Dressing, Ginger-Yogurt, '81 302

Dressing, Honey-Yogurt, '93 172
Dressing, Lemon-Yogurt, '93 17
Dressing, Orange-Yogurt, '85 304
Dressing, Sweet-Hot Yogurt, '86 40
Dressing, Turkey Waldorf Salad with Yogurt, '88 53
Dressing, Yogurt, '85 59, 215; '88 27
Dressing, Yogurt-Herb, '92 96
Dressing, Yogurt-Honey Poppy Seed, '83 177
Dressing, Yogurt Salad, '79 69
Filling, Fresh Raspberry Crêpes with Yogurt, '93 123
Fruit Medley, Yogurt-Granola, '91 58
Herbed Yogurt, '96 66
Honey Yogurt, Orange Slices with, '91 68
Lima Beans, Minted, '98 86
Malt, Chocolate-Yogurt, '01 173
Muffins, Yogurt, '88 55
Muffins, Yogurt-Muesli, '90 215
Omelet, Yogurt-Avocado, '81 33
Pancakes, Orange-Yogurt, '87 225
Peach Yogurt Refresher, '03 166
Pineapple-Yogurt Whirl, '91 132
Pork Tenderloin with Yogurt and Lime, Grilled, '04 216
Potatoes, Yogurt-Stuffed, '88 24
Rolls, Yogurt Crescent, '91 123
Salad, Crème de Menthe, '82 122
Salad, Cucumber-Yogurt, '87 33
Salad, Frozen Yogurt, '92 303
Salad, Strawberry Yogurt, '80 232
Salad, Yogurt-Cucumber, '82 122
Salad, Yogurt Fruit, '81 114; '96 247
Sauce, Creamy Yogurt, '91 238; '92 28
Sauce, Cucumber-and-Yogurt Dipping, '02 172
Sauce, Cucumber-Yogurt, '03 44
Sauce, Lamb Meatballs with Yogurt, '85 132
Sauce, London Broil Sandwiches with Yogurt-Cucumber, '01 162
Sauce, Yogurt, '89 283
Sauce, Yogurt-Cucumber, '04 216
Sauce, Yogurt-Horseradish, '85 66
Shake, Light Double Strawberry-Banana, '01 173
Shake, Strawberry-Yogurt, '87 199
Shake, Three-Fruit Yogurt, '01 173
Slaw or Salad Dressing, Lemon-Yogurt, '88 54
Smoothie, Fruited Honey-Yogurt, '88 231; '89 23
Smoothie, Honey-Yogurt, '97 326
Smoothie, Strawberry, '97 173
Smoothie, Yogurt-Fruit, '03 25
Snack, Yogurt, '88 55
Soup, Avocado-Banana-Yogurt, '80 78
Soup, Cucumber-Yogurt, '82 157; '83 205
Soup, Potato-Yogurt, '92 217
Soup, Yogurt Fruit, '86 176
Spread, Cucumber-Yogurt, '00 135
Spread, Herbed Yogurt, '02 169
Sundae, Breakfast, '98 206
Tangy Yogurt, '02 258
Topping, Yogurt-Cheese, '88 55

Z UCCHINI
Appetizers
Caviar, Zucchini, '88 212
Crab-Zucchini Bites, '84 M216
Dip, Yellow Squash-Zucchini, '89 48
French Fried Zucchini with Cocktail Sauce, '86 146
French Fries, Zucchini, '82 78
Fries, Zucchini, '90 147
Hors d'Oeuvres, Zucchini, '80 151
Pizzas, Zucchini, '88 212
Scalloped Zucchini Bites, '91 165
Shrimp Appetizers, Zucchini-, '89 311

Baked Zucchini, '83 209
Baked Zucchini Fans, '87 243
Bars, Zucchini, '85 77
Basil, Zucchini and Tomatoes, '89 147
Boats with Spinach, Zucchini, '82 252
Boats, Zucchini, '85 M143
Breads
  Apple Bread, Zucchini-, '87 255
  Banana-Zucchini Bread, '85 326
  Carrot Bread, Zucchini-, '83 190
  Chocolate-Zucchini Bread, '93 308
  Fritters, Cheesy Zucchini, '88 44
  Fritters, Zucchini, '81 163
  Honey Bread, Zucchini-, '89 143
  Loaves, Zucchini, '96 130
  Muffins, Carrot-Zucchini, '01 200
  Muffins, Zucchini, '83 121; '86 146
  Spiced Zucchini Bread, '79 161; '86 162
  Spicy Zucchini Bread, '81 305; '82 36
  Squares, Zucchini, '82 103
  Zucchini Bread, '85 111; '86 93
Broiled Zucchini, Quick-and-Easy, '86 169
Buttered Zucchini and Carrots, '83 252
Cajun Squash, '88 142
Cake, Chocolate-Zucchini, '85 156; '02 181
Cake, Zucchini, '79 24
Cake, Zucchini-Carrot, '93 20
Cake, Zucchini-Pineapple, '95 160
Calabaza Guisada con Puerco (Pumpkin Cooked
    with Pork), '80 193
Carrots and Zucchini, '84 262
Carrots, Zucchini with Baby, '88 24
Casseroles
  au Gratin, Potatoes-and-Zucchini, '84 5
  au Gratin, Zucchini and Tomato, '82 208
  Bacon, Zucchini, and Cornbread Bake, '99 123
  Beef Bake, Zucchini-, '86 146
  Calabaza Mexicana (Mexican Squash), '81 196
  Carrot and Zucchini Casserole, '83 256
  Carrot Casserole, Zucchini-, '99 61
  Cheese-Egg-Zucchini Casserole, '84 114
  Cheesy Zucchini Casserole, '82 168; '84 145
  Corn-Zucchini Bake, '79 178
  Egg Casserole, Zucchini-, '84 M113
  Eggplant and Zucchini, Italian-Style, '79 289;
    '80 26
  Italian Squash, '79 158
  Italian Zucchini Casserole, '85 59
  Jack Casserole, Zucchini-, '85 296
  Lasagna, Garden, '83 119
  Lasagna, Zucchini, '85 194
  Manicotti, Zucchini, '84 194
  Mexican Squash, '83 31
  Parmesan, Zucchini, '81 108
  Parmesan Zucchini, '81 234
  Rice Casserole Italiano, Zucchini-, '89 146
  Sausages Baked Zucchini and, '80 300
  Scallop, Green-and-Gold, '81 159
  Squash Bake, '82 107
  Squash Casserole, '96 252
  Stuffed Zucchini with Pasta, '97 101
  Tomato Bake, Zucchini and, '82 158
  Tomato Casserole, Zucchini-and-, '88 265
  Zucchini Casserole, '79 157; '87 154
Chicken, Moroccan Garlic, '99 15
Citrus-Herb Dressing, Zucchini with, '04 182
Coleslaw, Fiesta Zucchini, '91 168
Cookies, Spicy Zucchini, '97 273
Corn and Zucchini, '83 190
Corn Combo, Zucchini-, '86 218
Corn, Zucchini and, '86 177
Crab Cakes, Mock, '95 159
Crêpes, Zucchini, '79 157
Crispies, Zucchini, '95 179

Delight, Zucchini-Basil, '85 267
Dilled Fresh Zucchini, '81 174
Dilled Summer Squash, '96 148
Dilled Zucchini and Corn, '83 173
Dressing, Zucchini, '86 282
Easy Zucchini, '87 167
Eggplant and Squash, '83 187
Eggplant and Zucchini, Sautéed, '82 96
Fans, Baked Zucchini, '88 246
Fans, Herb Butter Zucchini, '90 201
Fans, Zucchini, '91 33
Fried Zucchini Strips, '81 184
Fries, Parmesan-Zucchini, '95 129
Frittata, Corn-and-Squash, '89 144
Frittata, Zucchini, '86 103
Fruitcake, Zucchini, '88 284
Fry, Zucchini, '81 102
Gratin, Tomato-Zucchini, '95 171
Green Beans with Zucchini, '84 128; '02 251
Grilled Zucchini Fans, '89 200
Grilled Zucchini with Feta, Greek, '95 190
Herbed Zucchini, '84 104
Italiano, Zucchini, '81 183
Italian Squash, '79 158
Italian-Style Zucchini, '80 123
Italian Zucchini, '83 M147
Jam, Zucchini, '00 168
Julienne Zucchini and Carrots, '90 M14
Lemon-Garlic Zucchini, '89 226
Marinated Squash Medley, '94 126
Marinated Zucchini, '80 33; '89 102
Medley, Zucchini-and-Corn, '80 298; '81 25
Mexican Style, Zucchini, '80 184
Omelet, Zucchini, '81 99
Oven-Fried Zucchini, '86 211
Oven-Fried Zucchini Spears, '91 121
Pancakes, Zucchini, '93 43
Parmesan, Zucchini, '81 108; '82 103
Pecans, Zucchini with, '87 31
Pesto, Zucchini, '84 194
Pie, Cheesy Zucchini, '82 103
Pie, Italian-Style Zucchini, '83 43
Pie, Zucchini, '98 236
Pie, Zucchini-Ham-Cheese, '80 272
Pollo con Calabacita (Mexican Chicken with
    Zucchini), '82 219
Provençal, Zucchini, '86 146
Quiche, Cheesy Zucchini, '83 312
Quiche, Swiss-Zucchini, '82 49
Quiche, Zucchini-Mushroom, '79 127
Quiche, Zucchini-Sausage, '83 122
Ratatouille, Eggplant-Zucchini, '81 205
Relish, Pollock with Summer Squash, '92 200
Relish, Sweet Zucchini, '95 159
Relish, Zucchini, '87 200
Roasted Zucchini, '02 89
Rosemary, Summer Squash with, '88 143
Salad, Apple-and-Zucchini, '97 216
Salad, Carrot-and-Zucchini, '83 240
Salad, Creamy Avocado and Zucchini, '79 208
Salad, Marinated Zucchini, '82 164; '90 32
Salad, Mushroom-Zucchini, '85 8
Salad, Summer Zucchini, '95 229
Salad, Turkey-Zucchini, '85 74
Salad, Zucchini, '82 104; '87 103; '89 128
Salad, Zucchini-Artichoke, '91 229
Salad, Zucchini Chef's, '83 143
Salad, Zucchini-Corn Marinated, '98 236
Sandwiches, Open-Faced Zucchini, '88 159
Sandwiches, Skillet Squash, '98 144
Sauce, Spaghetti with Zucchini, '81 38
Sauce, Zucchini-Mushroom, '93 71
Sautéed with Fresh Mint, Zucchini, '03 87
Sautéed Zucchini, '83 86; '92 60

Sautéed Zucchini and Carrots, '92 62, 99
Sautéed Zucchini and Sausage, '83 289
Sautéed Zucchini with Mushrooms, '94 135
Sauté, Zucchini, '81 183; '84 35
Scramble, Zucchini-Basil, '87 34
Shrimp, Grilled Zucchini-Wrapped, '98 200
Skillet, Pattypan-Zucchini, '82 103
Skillet, Squash, '82 195
Skillet, Zippy Zucchini, '82 158
Skillet, Zucchini-and-Corn, '01 137
Skillet Zucchini Combo, '96 178
Skillet, Zucchini-Tomato, '93 206
Soufflés, Zucchini-Corn, '97 203
Soufflé, Zucchini, '79 157
Soufflé, Zucchini-and-Corn, '83 265
Soups
  Chilled Zucchini Soup, '87 90
  Chilled Zucchini Soup with Fresh Vegetable
    Salsa, '98 194
  Cilantro, Zucchini Soup with, '93 130
  Cold Zucchini Soup, '85 265; '92 64; '99 164
  Cream of Zucchini Soup, '83 99
  Creamy Zucchini Soup, '83 140
  Dilled Summer Soup, '99 182
  Dilled Zucchini Soup, '90 88
  Green Soup, '98 23
  Italian Sausage-Zucchini Soup, '84 4
  Summer Squash Soup, '84 193
  Watercress-Zucchini Soup, '91 72
  Zucchini Soup, '82 104; '84 181; '86 181; '89 14
South-of-the-Border Zucchini, '85 135
Spaghetti, Italian Zucchini, '85 2
Spaghetti, Zucchini, '83 160
Stir-Fried Squash Medley, '80 123
Stir-Fry, Chicken-Zucchini, '84 50
Stir-Fry, Ham and Zucchini, '79 47
Stir-Fry, Squash, '80 184
Stir-Fry, Tomato-Zucchini, '80 158
Stir-Fry, Two-Squash, '86 174
Stir-Fry, Zucchini-and-Tomato, '85 108
Stir-Fry Zucchini Toss, '88 156
Stuffed Zucchini, '86 54, 187; '89 M133
Stuffed Zucchini, Beef-, '86 M139
Stuffed Zucchini, Ham and Cheese, '79 157
Stuffed Zucchini, Italian, '84 119
Stuffed Zucchini Main Dish, '79 215
Stuffed Zucchini, Savory, '80 161
Stuffed Zucchini, Southwestern, '03 M127
Stuffed Zucchini Supreme, '83 136
Stuffing, Haddock Fillets with Zucchini, '88 M191
Timbales, Corn-and-Zucchini, '92 100
Tomatoes with Herbs, Zucchini and, '92 182
Toss, Zucchini, '91 292

Favorite Recipes Journal

Jot down your family's and your favorite recipes for quick and handy reference. And don't forget to include the dishes that drew rave reviews when company came for dinner.

RECIPE	SOURCE/PAGE	REMARKS
Appetizers & Beverages		
Breads		
Desserts		

RECIPE	SOURCE/PAGE	REMARKS

Main Dishes

Side Dishes

Soups & Salads

Southern Living®